MANAGING
PEOPLE AND
ORGANIZATIONS

The Practice of Management Series
HARVARD BUSINESS SCHOOL PUBLICATIONS

The Craft of General Management
Readings selected by Joseph L. Bower

The Entrepreneurial Venture
Readings selected by William A. Sahlman and Howard H. Stevenson

Managing People and Organizations
Readings selected by John J. Gabarro

Strategic Marketing Management
Readings selected by Robert J. Dolan

MANAGING PEOPLE AND ORGANIZATIONS

READINGS SELECTED BY

John J. Gabarro

Harvard Business School

HARVARD BUSINESS SCHOOL PUBLICATIONS
Boston, Massachusetts

Library of Congress Cataloging-in-Publication Data

Managing people and organizations / edited by John J. Gabarro.
   p. cm.—(The Practice of management series)
  Includes index.
  ISBN 0-87584-311-5
  1. Management. I. Gabarro, John J. II. Series.
  HD31.M293918 1991
  658.4--dc20   91-30314
                                                      CIP

The Harvard Business School Publications Practice of Management Series is distributed in the college market by McGraw-Hill Book Company. The readings in each book are available individually through PRIMIS, the McGraw-Hill custom publishing service. Instructors and bookstores should contact their local McGraw-Hill representative for information and ordering.

Printed in the United States of America.

01 00 99 98   5 6 7 8 9 10

JOHN J. GABARRO

John J. Gabarro is UPS Foundation Professor of Human Resource Management at Harvard Business School, where he has taught in the MBA, Advanced Management, International Senior Management, and the Owner-President Management programs. The author or co-author of four books, he is the recipient of a McKinsey Foundation–*Harvard Business Review* Prize and the Johnson Smith Knisely Foundation Award for research on leadership. At Harvard he has served as Area Chair for Organizational Behavior and Human Resource Management and as Faculty Chairman of Harvard's International Senior Management Program.

CONTENTS

Series Preface   xv

Introduction   John J. Gabarro   1

PART ONE
MANAGING AND LEADING IN ORGANIZATIONS

SECTION A
MANAGING PEOPLE

1   The Manager's Job: Folklore and Fact   13
Henry Mintzberg

Contrasting the myths and the facts of managerial life can help answer the basic question, What do managers do?

2   Power, Dependence, and Effective Management   33
John P. Kotter

Managers, who are dependent on others, must generate and use power successfully.

3   Management Time: Who's Got the Monkey?   **50**

William Oncken, Jr., and Donald L. Wass

Effective time management can be achieved through the proper balance of responsibilities in the manager-subordinate relationship.

4   The New Managerial Work   **57**

Rosabeth Moss Kanter

Changes are occurring in two important aspects of managerial work—sources of power and motivation, as illustrated in the profiles of three managers whose jobs are changing.

5   Managing Without Managers   **70**

Ricardo Semler

Three key principles of management—work-force democracy, profit sharing, and free access to information—are applied to a thriving company.

SECTION B
LEADING AN ORGANIZATION

6   Managers and Leaders: Are They Different?   **85**

Abraham Zaleznik

Organizations can foster the development of leaders, whose temperament differs significantly from that of managers.

7   What Leaders Really Do   **102**

John P. Kotter

Leadership—coping with change—is compared with management—coping with complexity. Organizations can create a culture that promotes leadership.

8   Ways Women Lead   **115**

Judy B. Rosener

Women's leadership styles differ from those of men in several important elements.

9   How to Choose a Leadership Pattern   **126**

Robert Tannenbaum and Warren H. Schmidt

Managers must know their own strengths and weaknesses as well as the abilities of their subordinates so that they can choose an appropriate form of leadership.

10   In Praise of Followers   **143**
Robert E. Kelley

Followers have a specific role, and effective and ineffective followers possess certain traits. An organization can cultivate effective followers using a four-step procedure.

PART TWO
MANAGING INDIVIDUALS AND GROUPS

SECTION A
MOTIVATING AND MANAGING INDIVIDUALS

**11   One More Time: How Do You
       Motivate Employees?**   **159**
Frederick Herzberg

There is a difference between inducements, such as fringe benefits, and genuine motivators, such as greater responsibility. Job enrichment is vital to effective motivation.

12   Pygmalion in Management   **179**
J. Sterling Livingston

A framework can be used to draw superior performance from employees through the power of expectation. Managers must be sensitive to their own behavior and its impact on subordinates.

13   Making Performance Appraisal Work   **195**
Michael Beer

Managers and subordinates sometimes have trouble with performance appraisal, but there are several ways to handle these difficulties.

14   Managing Interpersonal Conflict   **213**
James Ware and Louis B. Barnes

Interpersonal conflict can be managed in three ways. Several relevant action questions can help resolve or control conflict.

15   Managing Your Boss   **227**
John J. Gabarro and John P. Kotter

For greater effectiveness at work, subordinates must manage their relationship with their boss. This crucial relationship can be developed and maintained in several ways.

SECTION B
MANAGING GROUP EFFECTIVENESS

16   A Framework for Analyzing Work Groups   241
Michael B. McCaskey

The factors that influence a work group's behavior and performance are group context, design factors, and group culture.

**17   Problem Solving and Conflict Resolution
in Groups   263**
James Ware

Several characteristics of managerial groups enhance and detract from their problem-solving effectiveness. Managers can use basic strategies to influence group behavior.

18   Understanding and Influencing Group Process   279
John J. Gabarro and Anne Harlan

There are seven indicators of the effectiveness of a group in accomplishing its formal tasks.

19   How to Run a Meeting   289
James Ware

Managers must know how to prepare for and run a meeting effectively.

20   Managing a Task Force   298
James Ware

Certain insights can help a manager organize and manage a task force from project conception through completion.

PART THREE
MANAGING ORGANIZATIONAL EFFECTIVENESS

SECTION A
DESIGNING ORGANIZATIONS FOR EFFECTIVENESS

21   Organization Design   313
Jay W. Lorsch

Managers face design issues at two organizational levels: the functional unit and the single-business organization.

22   Organization Design: Fashion or Fit?   332

Henry Mintzberg

An organization's structure can be arranged in five configurations, which serve as an effective tool in diagnosing organizational problems. A misfit results when an organization's design is no longer suited to its task.

23   Functional Integration: Getting All the Troops to Work Together   353

Benson P. Shapiro

Six approaches can be taken to achieve functional integration.

24   Matrix Management: Not a Structure, a Frame of Mind   370

Christopher A. Bartlett and Sumantra Ghoshal

A company can be strategically agile while coordinating complex activities by building a matrix of corporate values and priorities in managers' minds.

25   In Praise of Hierarchy   382

Elliott Jaques

Hierarchy is praiseworthy when it is a design based on accountability and skill, but it can be misused. There are ways to more properly apply hierarchy to an organization's structure.

SECTION B
MANAGING ORGANIZATIONAL CHANGE

26   Choosing Strategies for Change   395

John P. Kotter and Leonard A. Schlesinger

People resist change for several reasons. A change strategy should be selected and implemented systematically.

27   Evolution and Revolution as Organizations Grow   410

Larry E. Greiner

An organization's future is determined less by outside forces than by the organization's own history.

28   Leading Change   424

Michael Beer

Management can channel change when an organization has a vision that it is working toward. Managers must understand the process, cost, and fears of change.

**29 Speed, Simplicity, Self-Confidence: An Interview
with Jack Welch**   **432**
Noel Tichy and Ram Charan

*General Electric is changing its corporate culture and the way its employees think through the
innovative tool called Work-Out and through the company's own Value Statement.*

PART FOUR
MANAGING THE HUMAN RESOURCE

30 Planning with People in Mind   **449**
D. Quinn Mills

*A company must incorporate human resource goals into its long-term business planning. A
model process can be used to enhance the company's business goals and marketplace success.*

31 Career Systems and Strategic Staffing   **464**
Jeffrey A. Sonnenfeld and Maury A. Peiperl

*Managers should be familiar with career systems and their basic elements. A four-cell configura-
tion of career systems can be used to link staffing policy with business strategy.*

32 Reward Systems and the Role of Compensation   **474**
Michael Beer and Richard E. Walton

Reward systems, which have various designs, affect employee satisfaction and motivation.

33 From Control to Commitment in the Workplace   **487**
Richard E. Walton

*A manager must understand the two different strategies for managing a work force—the tradi-
tional control model and the newer commitment approach—as well as the transition between
the two.*

34 From Affirmative Action to Affirming Diversity   **499**
R. Roosevelt Thomas, Jr.

*The demographics of the American work force are changing. Ten guidelines can ensure that this
new diversity is managed successfully.*

35 Management Women and the New Facts of Life   **516**
Felice N. Schwartz

*Women cost more to employ than men. Companies can adapt policies and practices to retain
talented women and eliminate the extra cost of employing them.*

36   Business and the Facts of Family Life   **529**

Fran Sussner Rodgers and Charles Rodgers

Businesses will have to make adjustments to accommodate the new realities of family life. There are a number of ways to lessen the conflict between work and family.

37   Beyond Testing: Coping with Drugs at Work   **543**

James T. Wrich

One approach has proven effective in dealing with the problem of drugs in the workplace.

Index   **555**

SERIES PREFACE

The Harvard Business School has a long and distinguished publishing history. For decades, the School has furnished original educational materials to academic classrooms and executive education programs worldwide. Many of these publications have been used by individual managers to update their knowledge and skills. The Practice of Management Series, developed by Harvard Business School Publications, continues this tradition.

The series addresses major areas of the business curriculum and major topics within those areas. Each of the books strikes a balance between broad coverage of the area and depth of treatment; each has been designed for flexibility of use to accommodate the varying needs of instructors and programs in different academic settings.

These books also will serve as authoritative references for practicing managers. They can provide a refresher on business basics and enduring concepts, and they also offer cutting-edge ideas and techniques.

The main objective of the Practice of Management Series is to make Harvard Business School's continuing explorations into management's best practices more widely and easily available. The books draw on two primary sources of material produced at the School.

Harvard Business School is probably best known for its field research and cases. Faculty members prepare other material for their classrooms, however, including essays that define and explain key business concepts and practices. Like other classroom materials produced at Harvard Business School, these "notes," as they are called at the School, have a consistent point of view—that of the general manager. They have a common purpose—to inform the actual practice of management as opposed to providing a theoretical foundation. The notes are an important source of selections for the books in this series.

The Harvard Business Review has long been recognized by professors and managers as the premier management magazine. Its mix of authors—academics, practicing executives and managers, and consultants—brings to bear a blend of research knowledge and practical intelligence on a wide variety of business topics. Harvard Business Review articles challenge conventional wisdom with fresh approaches and often become a part of enlightened conventional wisdom. The magazine speaks primarily to the practice of management at the level of the general manager. *Harvard Business Review* articles are another essential source of selections for this series.

Finally, this series includes selections published by other distinguished institutions and organizations. In instances where there were gaps in coverage or viewpoint, we have taken the opportunity to tap books and other journals besides the *Harvard Business Review*.

────── ACKNOWLEDGMENTS

The books in this series are the products of a collaborative effort. John J. Gabarro, the Harvard Business School faculty member who wrote the introduction to *Managing People and Organizations*, worked closely with a Harvard Business School Publications editor, John J. Pippa, to select and arrange the best available materials. Professor Gabarro's content expertise, teaching experience, and diligence, together with Mr. Pippa's editorial skill and commitment, have been crucial to the development of the book.

The Harvard Business School faculty whose work is represented in the books have generously taken the time to review their selections. Their cooperation is much appreciated.

Each of the books has been evaluated by practitioners or by professors at other institutions. We would like to thank the following individuals for their careful readings of the manuscript for the collection on organizational behavior and human resource management: Taylor Cox, Jr., School of Business Administration, The University of Michigan; Richard B. Higgins, College of Business Administration, Northeastern University; Robert Drazin, School of Business Administration, Emory University; and Alan L. Wilkins, Graduate School of Management, Brigham Young University. Their evaluations and many useful suggestions have helped us develop and shape this book into a more effective teaching instrument.

We would like to thank Maria Arteta, former Director of Product Management for Harvard Business School Publications; Bill Ellet, Editorial Director of Harvard Business School Publications; and Benson P. Shapiro, Malcolm P. McNair Professor of Marketing and former faculty adviser to Harvard Business School Publications. The Practice of Management Series would not have materialized without their support, guidance, and insight.

INTRODUCTION

This book is about managing people and organizations. The intended audience is practicing managers and MBA students who face the challenges of managing, leading, motivating, and organizing people. The readings have been selected to provide a set of basic concepts and tools for dealing with a range of multifaceted issues that managers must handle to be effective. As such, the book is intended for use not only in MBA and executive education programs—either alone or with an assigned textbook, cases, or other materials—but also as a basic reference for practicing managers.

There have been significant advances in the fields of organizational behavior and management in the last decade. The manager's role, that is, what effective managers really do compared with what theorists have said they should do, is much better understood. Our knowledge of the factors that influence the effectiveness of groups also has expanded, along with our understanding of their potential for self-direction, commitment, and creativity. Similarly, our understanding of organizational design and alternative forms of organization has grown along with our understanding of the management of change. Moreover, developments in human resource management, such as high-commitment work systems and employee involvement, have gone substantially beyond the classic personnel issues of selection, development, and compensation.

The state of both knowledge and practice has grown substantially. So have the challenges, however. If managers have better tools at their disposal today than a decade ago, they also face challenges that are far more demanding.

Much more is expected of managers now than 10 years ago. Being an effective manager requires a deeper level of sophistication and a broader and more versatile set of skills. In most industries the pace of change that organizations (and their people) must cope with is relentless. To be competitive, corporations have had to restructure, downsize, de-layer, and increase spans of control. The simple principles and formulas once found in management texts have become manifestly irrelevant. Companies spawn new organizational forms, such as hybrid organizations, "adhocracies," vendor partnerships, and other kinds of alliances, at a dizzying pace as they scramble for speed and competitive advantage. In addition, the challenges of managing an increasingly diverse work force, the changing role of women in business, and the impact of technology on the nature of work pose human resource issues that simply did not exist to the same extent 10 years ago.

Despite all of this change, some aspects of managing people are fundamental. Certain truths about motivation, group behavior, and organization are as valid today as they were 20 years ago. If anything, the increasing pressures of today's more competitive environment make these basics even more necessary to master. Effective management requires not only dealing with state-of-the-art issues but also handling the essential daily realities of motivating people, solving performance problems, and managing groups efficiently.

The readings in this book were chosen to address both sets of needs: the need for fundamental concepts as well as the newer concepts that address today's emerging imperatives. An important purpose of this book is to bring together a selective set of practice-oriented readings that represent some of the best thinking currently available on both basic and contemporary issues. For this reason, the readings span a broad set of substantive topics and problems in organizational behavior. These include the important question of what constitutes effective management and leadership and whether these two processes are different from each other. At an operational level, the book also addresses the specific aspects of how to manage individuals and groups effectively. Finally, the book examines the broader questions of organizational effectiveness through organizational design choices, organizational change, and the accurate use of human resources.

The readings are distinctly managerial in orientation; they tend to be more problem oriented than theoretical, and they are written for managers from a manager's perspective. In this respect, they are meant to provide frameworks and concepts that ground and supplement existing theory by focusing on practical issues and problems. For this reason, one of the criteria used in choosing these readings is their relevance and usability for managers and MBAs. Many readings were chosen based on the critical reviews and suggestions of business school professors teaching in a variety of programs across the country. Most of the readings that have been included from the *Harvard Business Review* are best-sellers. The background and tool-oriented readings, written by Harvard Business School faculty members, are largely best-selling essays used individually in many classrooms. In this regard, even the most recent readings have passed the tests of user utility and applicability.

OVERVIEW OF THE BOOK

The book is organized into four parts, each of which focuses on a different area of management. Each part contains a mix of readings that cover basic issues as well as readings dealing with emergent or controversial issues. The readings have been chosen so that each part contains a mix of concept-oriented and action-oriented readings. Generally, the more conceptual readings provide a framework or way of thinking about problems, while the action-oriented readings tend to offer guidelines for handling specific problems or issues. Readings in each section are arranged so that they begin with basic descriptive frameworks or concepts and then move to issues that are more applied, normative, and contemporary.

MANAGING AND LEADING IN ORGANIZATIONS

Part One focuses on the manager as an instrument of action and is divided into two sections: one focusing on managerial behavior and the other on leadership. Section A, Managing People, begins with "The Manager's Job: Folklore and Fact" by Mintzberg. This reading challenges much of the mythology of what managers "should do" by succinctly describing what Mintzberg's path-breaking research shows they actually do, the different roles they perform, and their inherent dilemmas. "Power, Dependence, and Effective Management" by Kotter takes these roles one step farther by describing the manager's dependent relationships and discussing several ways of establishing power in them. He also discusses several methods of face-to-face and indirect influence. "Management Time: Who's Got the Monkey?" by Oncken and Wass is a widely reproduced reading on time management and delegation, two problems that always have plagued managers.

The last two readings in Part One present provocative ideas on the transformations occurring in the manager's job. Kanter's "The New Managerial Work" builds on the prior readings but details the structural, career, and competitive pressures that are altering the very nature of managerial work, the quandaries these changes create, and what this means in terms of managing for greater innovation and flexibility. This reading also spells out the implications of these changes for the manager's role, the development of a power base, and the motivation of people when traditional rewards and punishments are no longer available. Section A concludes with Semler's "Managing Without Managers." The author, a highly successful entrepreneur, draws on his experience to argue that the manager's role should become more that of coordinator and counselor and that managers should empower employees through real involvement, access to relevant information, and profit sharing.

Section B, Leading an Organization, goes beyond the manager's job to focus explicitly on leadership. This section begins with a controversial reading entitled "Managers and Leaders: Are They Different?" Zaleznik concludes that the answer is emphatically "yes" and that much of what is considered good management stifles true leadership. "What Leaders Really Do" by Kotter continues the theme by explaining how managers and leaders differ. Unlike Zaleznik, however, Kotter concludes that both are needed. The reading describes what organizations (and some individuals) can do to develop the talents and skills of both managers and leaders. The theme of differences is further pursued in "Ways Women Lead" by Rosener. She argues that, based on her research, women lead differently than men. Women's "interactive" style of leadership has several advantages over the "command-and-control" leadership that characterizes the men in her sample, especially in managing professionals and a more diverse work force.

The last reading on leadership, "How to Choose a Leadership Pattern" by Tannenbaum and Schmidt, outlines several factors that managers should consider about themselves, their subordinates, and their context when determining how participative or directive to be. The section concludes with an article by Kelley, "In Praise of Followers." This provides a useful balance to the prior readings by demonstrating the importance of strong, effective followers and what developing them entails.

MANAGING INDIVIDUALS AND GROUPS

In Part Two, the emphasis shifts from the roles of manager and leader to focus more sharply on managing in face-to-face settings. The first group of readings addresses Motivating and Managing Individuals and opens with two readings on motivation and expectations: Herzberg's "One More Time: How Do You Motivate Employees?" and Livingston's "Pygmalion in Management." Both cover basic motivational issues and complement pieces on motivation-and-expectancy theory.

The next three readings are more tactical. Beer's "Making Performance Appraisal Work" examines the reasons why performance appraisals are difficult to conduct and provides several useful and specific guidelines for conducting them more effectively. In the same vein, Ware and Barnes's "Managing Interpersonal Conflict" describes a framework for diagnosing conflict and describes three alternative approaches and diagnostic criteria to use in deciding how to intervene. This section concludes with a widely reprinted reading on "Managing Your Boss" by Gabarro and Kotter, which argues that managing one's boss is as important as managing one's subordinates. This reading provides basic ideas and suggestions on how to do this effectively, even when the boss proves difficult.

The section on Managing Group Effectiveness begins with a popular reading by McCaskey that offers "A Framework for Analyzing Work Groups." This reading presents the basic contextual, situational, and organizational factors that affect a group's informal social structure, culture, and effectiveness. "Problem Solving and Conflict Resolution in Groups" by Ware reviews several aspects of managerial groups that influence their problem-solving effectiveness, the modes that management groups use for resolving conflict, some criteria to use in deciding whether to use a group to solve a problem, and the implications of this for developing effective groups.

The last three readings in this section are distinctly tactical and action oriented. "Understanding and Influencing Group Process" by Gabarro and Harlan provides guidelines for observing the real-time behavior of a group as well as suggestions for when and how to intervene to improve group effectiveness. The section concludes with two readings by Ware that look at how to manage groups. "How to Run a Meeting" describes the mechanics of planning a meeting, creating an agenda, and effectively managing the meeting. The reading includes the pitfalls to avoid and how to identify the work that is needed beforehand. "Managing a Task Force" focuses on the challenges of managing a temporary group (including cross-functional committees) and provides guidance on how to sharpen the group's mandate, create standards to measure progress, achieve coordination, and (very important) how to avoid predictable difficulties.

MANAGING ORGANIZATIONAL EFFECTIVENESS

In Part Three, the emphasis shifts from face-to-face settings to managing effectiveness at the organizational level. The readings are organized into related sections: Designing Organizations for Effectiveness and Managing Organizational Change.

Section A begins with a basic background reading on "Organization Design" by Lorsch that provides a brief historical perspective and then introduces several fundamental concepts, including contingency theory, the notion of "fit," differentiation, and integration. The reading then describes the essentials of organizing basic functional and single-business units. "Organization Design: Fashion or Fit?" by Mintzberg offers more of an overview by describing five basic configurations of organization, their key elements, and the types of situations for which each configuration is best suited. "Functional Integration: Getting All the Troops to Work Together" by Shapiro builds on the Lorsch reading but pays particular attention to the problem of achieving integration across different functions. Shapiro presents six sets of organizational and cultural variables that managers can use to attain cross-functional integration.

The last two readings in this section tend to be more normative. "Matrix Management: Not a Structure, a Frame of Mind" by Bartlett and Ghoshal argues that under many circumstances (such as those faced by transnational, multi-product corporations) traditional structures are insufficient and matrix organizations are too cumbersome. Instead, the authors believe, what is needed are hybrid forms of organization in which matrix is a mind-set, not a formal structure. They propose several nonstructural variables such as vision, staffing, systems, and culture to achieve this. The final reading, "In Praise of Hierarchy" by Jaques, provides a controversial counterpoint to several other readings in this section (as well as earlier parts of the book). The author argues that hierarchy, having survived for 3,000 years, is still the most effective and basic form of organization. Jaques adds that hierarchy can be highly effective if it is not overlayered and is structured according to accountability, skill, and responsibility.

The section on Managing Organizational Change goes beyond organizational design to focus specifically on the dynamics of change and its implementation. In "Choosing Strategies for Change," Kotter and Schlesinger first examine various sources of resistance to change and methods for overcoming them. Then they establish a framework for developing a change strategy and present the key situational variables to consider. "Evolution and Revolution as Organizations Grow" by Greiner argues that as organizations grow, they pass through five predictable phases of change. Each phase includes a unique set of issues; being aware of these issues and taking appropriate actions at each stage can minimize the problems of transition.

The two final readings in this section have a more tactical orientation. "Leading Change" by Beer presents a simple but multifaceted model of critical dimensions that managers should consider when deciding which factors will enhance or impede change. Specific guidelines for implementing change are offered. In "Speed, Simplicity, Self-Confidence: An Interview with Jack Welch" by Tichy and Charan, one of America's most effective CEOs shares his thoughts on the organizational and cultural changes that General Electric is implementing. The motivations behind these changes also are discussed.

MANAGING THE HUMAN RESOURCE

The readings in Part Four focus on the firm's human resource. The first four readings address basic aspects of human resource management that can influence an organization's effectiveness. The last four readings examine current and emerging human resource issues.

"Planning with People in Mind" by Mills argues for incorporating human resource goals into long-term business planning and, drawing on survey and field data, presents a comprehensive analysis of current practices. "Career Systems and Strategic Staffing" by Sonnenfeld and Peiperl looks at career systems as key aspects of organizational effectiveness. The authors present a model of different types of career systems in terms of supply and assignment flow and the types of organizations in which these systems are likely to be found. "Reward Systems and the Role of Compensation" by Beer and Walton provides a basic primer on different types of reward and compensation systems, their strengths and weaknesses, and guidelines for managers to consider in making reward and compensation decisions. "From Control to Commitment in the Workplace" by Walton describes the differences between control and commitment strategies in work-force management, articulating many of the premises underlying effective work restructuring, job design, and self-directed work teams.

The next three readings consider the challenges of managing a more diverse work force. In "From Affirmative Action to Affirming Diversity," Thomas states that today's demographic realities require going beyond affirmative action to affirming diversity. A company accomplishes this by creating an environment that develops qualified, upwardly mobile women and minorities. The reading then discusses 10 guidelines for effectively managing diversity. The next reading is perhaps one of the most controversial on the topic of women in management. "Management Women and the New Facts of Life" by Schwartz suggests that alternative as well as mainstream career tracks should be available to women, once again raising the famous "Mommy track" debate. A related set of issues is addressed in "Business and the Facts of Family Life" by Rodgers and Rodgers. The authors argue that the increasing prevalence of dual-career couples in the work force requires radical changes in workplace rules and conditions, particularly in the areas of flexible work schedules and child care. The final article, "Beyond Testing: Coping with Drugs at Work" by Wrich, realistically assesses the seriousness of substance abuse in the workplace and discusses the advantages of employee assistance programs as an alternative to drug testing.

As this overview demonstrates, the readings in this book span a broad range of topics, issues, and problems. Although it is impossible for any collection of this size to cover every topic exhaustively, an effort has been made to provide broad coverage of major topics as well as depth within each section. In some areas, such as job design, the interested reader may wish to go beyond the scope of the book. For the most part, however, the collection offers as broad a selection of management-oriented readings as is currently available on organizational behavior.

JOHN J. GABARRO

PART ONE

MANAGING AND LEADING IN ORGANIZATIONS

SECTION A

MANAGING PEOPLE

The Manager's Job: Folklore and Fact   1

HENRY MINTZBERG

In this reading, the author answers the basic question, What do managers do? Contrasting the myths with the facts, he examines the various interpersonal, informational, and decisional roles of managers. He also provides prescriptions for more effective management, along with a list of questions for self-study. He then discusses the importance of training managers to manage.

The author has included a retrospective commentary in which he discusses the diverse reactions to the reading since it was first published, his current perspective, and the important issues that still need to be faced.

If you ask managers what they do, they will most likely tell you that they plan, organize, coordinate, and control. Then watch what they do. Don't be surprised if you can't relate what you see to these words.

When a manager is told that a factory has just burned down and then advises the caller to see whether temporary arrangements can be made to supply customers through a foreign subsidiary, is that manager planning, organizing, coordinating, or controlling? How about when he or she presents a gold watch to a retiring employee? Or attends a conference to meet people in the trade and returns with an interesting new product idea for employees to consider?

These four words, which have dominated management vocabulary since the French industrialist Henri Fayol first introduced them in 1916, tell us little about what managers actually do. At best, they indicate some vague objectives managers have when they work.

The field of management, so devoted to progress and change, has for more than a half a century not seriously addressed the basic question: What do managers do? Without a proper answer, how can we teach management? How can we design planning or information systems for managers? How can we improve the practice of management at all?

Our ignorance of the nature of managerial work shows up in various ways in the modern organization—in boasts by successful managers who never spent a single day in a management training program; in the turnover of corporate planners who never quite understood what it was the manager wanted; in the computer consoles gathering dust in the back room because the managers never used the fancy on-line MIS some analyst thought they needed.

Perhaps most important, our ignorance shows up in the inability of our large public organizations to come to grips with some of their most serious policy problems.

Somehow, in the rush to automate production, to use management science in the functional areas of marketing and finance, and to apply the skills of the behavioral scientist to the problem of worker motivation, the manager—the person in charge of the organization or one of its subunits—has been forgotten.

I intend to break the reader away from Fayol's words and introduce a more supportable and useful description of managerial work. This description derives from my review and synthesis of research on how various managers have spent their time.

In some studies, managers were observed intensively; in a number of others, they kept detailed diaries; in a few studies, their records were analyzed. All kinds of managers were studied—foremen, factory supervisors, staff managers, field sales managers, hospital administrators, presidents of companies and nations, and even street gang leaders. These "managers" worked in the United States, Canada, Sweden, and Great Britain.

A synthesis of these findings paints an interesting picture, one as different from Fayol's classical view as a cubist abstract is from a Renaissance painting. In a sense, this picture will be obvious to anyone who has ever spent a day in a manager's office, either in front of the desk or behind it. Yet, at the same time, this picture throws into doubt much of the folklore that has been accepted about the manager's work.

───── FOLKLORE AND FACTS ABOUT MANAGERIAL WORK

There are four myths about the manager's job that do not bear up under careful scrutiny of the facts.

Folklore: The manager is a reflective, systematic planner. The evidence on this issue is overwhelming, but not a shred of it supports this statement.

Fact: Study after study has shown that managers work at an unrelenting pace, that their activities are characterized by brevity, variety, and discontinuity, and that they are strongly oriented to action and dislike reflective activities. Consider this evidence: Half the activities engaged in by the five chief executives of my study lasted less than nine minutes, and only 10% exceeded one hour.[1] A study of 56 U.S. foremen found that they averaged 583 activities per eight-hour shift, an average of 1 every 48 seconds.[2] The work pace for both chief executives and

---

1. All the data from my study can be found in Henry Mintzberg, *The Nature of Managerial Work* (New York: Harper & Row, 1973).

2. Robert H. Guest, "Of Time and the Foreman," *Personnel* (May 1956): 478.

foremen was unrelenting. The chief executives met a steady stream of callers and mail from the moment they arrived in the morning until they left in the evening. Coffee breaks and lunches were inevitably work related, and ever-present subordinates seemed to usurp any free moment.

A diary study of 160 British middle and top managers found that they worked without interruption for a half hour or more only about once every two days.[3]

Of the verbal contacts the chief executives in my study engaged in, 93% were arranged on an ad hoc basis. Only 1% of the executives' time was spent in open-ended observational tours. Only 1 out of 368 verbal contacts was unrelated to a specific issue and could therefore be called general planning. Another researcher found that "in *not one single case* did a manager report obtaining important external information from a general conversation or other undirected personal communication."[4]

Is this the planner that the classical view describes? Hardly. The manager is simply responding to the pressures of the job. I found that my chief executives terminated many of their own activities, often leaving meetings before the end, and interrupted their desk work to call in subordinates. One president not only placed his desk so that he could look down a long hallway but also left his door open when he was alone—an invitation for subordinates to come in and interrupt him.

Clearly, these managers wanted to encourage the flow of current information. But more significantly, they seemed to be conditioned by their own work loads. They appreciated the opportunity cost of their own time, and they were continually aware of their ever-present obligations—mail to be answered, callers to attend to, and so on. It seems that a manager is always plagued by the possibilities of what might be done and what must be done.

When managers must plan, they seem to do so implicitly in the context of daily actions, not in some abstract process reserved for two weeks in the organization's mountain retreat. The plans of the chief executives I studied seemed to exist only in their heads—as flexible, but often specific, intentions. The traditional literature notwithstanding, the job of managing does not breed reflective planners. Managers respond to stimuli and are conditioned by their jobs to prefer live to delayed action.

Folklore: The effective manager has no regular duties to perform. Managers are constantly being told to spend more time planning and delegating and less time seeing customers and engaging in negotiations. These are not, after all, the true tasks of the manager. To use the popular analogy, the good manager, like the good conductor, carefully orchestrates everything in advance, then sits back,

3. Rosemary Stewart, *Managers and Their Jobs* (London: Macmillan, 1967); *see also* Sune Carlson, *Executive Behaviour* (Stockholm: Strombergs, 1951).

4. Francis J. Aguilar, *Scanning the Business Environment* (New York: Macmillan, 1967), p. 102.

responding occasionally to an unforeseeable exception. But here again the pleasant abstraction just does not seem to hold up.

Fact: Managerial work involves performing a number of regular duties, includ-ing ritual and ceremony, negotiations, and processing of soft information that links the organization with its environment. Consider some evidence from the research:

A study of the work of the presidents of small companies found that they engaged in routine activities because their companies could not afford staff specialists and were so thin on operating personnel that a single absence often required the president to substitute.[5]

One study of field sales managers and another of chief executives suggest that it is a natural part of both jobs to see important customers, assuming the managers wish to keep those customers.[6]

Someone, only half in jest, once described the manager as the person who sees visitors so that other people can get their work done. In my study, I found that certain ceremonial duties—meeting visiting dignitaries, giving out gold watches, presiding at Christmas dinners—were an intrinsic part of the chief executive's job.

Studies of managers' information flow suggest that managers play a key role in securing "soft" external information (much of it available only to them because of their status) and in passing it along to their subordinates.

Folklore: The senior manager needs aggregated information, which a formal management information system best provides. Not too long ago, the words *total information system* were everywhere in the management literature. In keeping with the classical view of the manager as that individual perched on the apex of a regulated, hierarchical system, the literature's manager was to receive all important information from a giant, comprehensive MIS.

But lately, these giant MIS systems are not working—managers are simply not using them. The enthusiasm has waned. A look at how managers actually process information makes it clear why.

Fact: Managers strongly favor verbal media, telephone calls and meetings, over documents. Consider the following:

In two British studies, managers spent an average of 66% and 80% of their time in verbal (oral) communication.[7] In my study of five American chief executives, the figure was 78%.

These five chief executives treated mail processing as a burden to be dispensed with. One came in Saturday morning to process 142 pieces of mail in just over three hours, to "get rid of all the stuff." This same manager looked at

---

5. Unpublished study by Irving Choran, reported in Mintzberg, *The Nature of Managerial Work.*

6. Robert T. Davis, *Performance and Development of Field Sales Managers* (Boston: Division of Research, Harvard Business School, 1957); George H. Copeman, *The Role of the Managing Director* (London: Business Publications, 1963).

7. Stewart, *Managers and Their Jobs;* Tom Burns, "The Directions of Activity and Communica-tion in a Departmental Executive Group," *Human Relations* 7, no. 1 (1954): 73.

the first piece of "hard" mail he had received all week, a standard cost report, and put it aside with the comment, "I never look at this."

These same five chief executives responded immediately to 2 of the 40 routine reports they received during the five weeks of my study and to 4 items in the 104 periodicals. They skimmed most of these periodicals in seconds, almost ritualistically. In all, these chief executives of good-sized organizations initiated on their own—that is, not in response to something else—a grand total of 25 pieces of mail during the 25 days I observed them.

An analysis of the mail the executives received reveals an interesting picture—only 13% was of specific and immediate use. So now we have another piece in the puzzle: not much of the mail provides live, current information—the action of a competitor, the mood of a government legislator, or the rating of last night's television show. Yet this is the information that drove the managers, interrupting their meetings and rescheduling their workdays.

Consider another interesting finding. Managers seem to cherish "soft" information, especially gossip, hearsay, and speculation. Why? The reason is its timeliness; today's gossip may be tomorrow's fact. The manager who misses the telephone call revealing that the company's biggest customer was seen golfing with a main competitor may read about a dramatic drop in sales in the next quarterly report. But then it's too late.

To assess the value of historical, aggregated, "hard" MIS information, consider two of the manager's prime uses for information—to identify problems and opportunities[8] and to build mental models (e.g., how the organization's budget system works, how customers buy products, how changes in the economy affect the organization). The evidence suggests that the manager identifies decision situations and builds models not with the aggregated abstractions an MIS provides but with specific tidbits of data.

Consider the words of Richard Neustadt, who studied the information-collecting habits of Presidents Roosevelt, Truman, and Eisenhower: "It is not information of a general sort that helps a President see personal stakes; not summaries, not surveys, not the *bland amalgams*. Rather . . . it is the odds and ends of *tangible detail* that pieced together in his mind illuminate the underside of issues put before him. To help himself he must reach out as widely as he can for every scrap of fact, opinion, gossip, bearing on his interests and relationships as President. He must become his own director of his own central intelligence."[9]

The manager's emphasis on this verbal media raises two important points. First, verbal information is stored in the brains of people. Only when people write this information down can it be stored in the files of the organization—whether in metal cabinets or on magnetic tape—and managers appar-

---

8. H. Edward Wrapp, "Good Managers Don't Make Policy Decisions," *Harvard Business Review* (September–October 1967): 91. Wrapp refers to this as spotting opportunities and relationships in the stream of operating problems and decisions; in his article, Wrapp raises a number of excellent points related to this analysis.

9. Richard E. Neustadt, *Presidential Power* (New York: John Wiley, 1960), pp. 153–154; italics added.

ently do not write down much of what they hear. Thus the strategic data bank of the organization is not in the memory of its computers but in the minds of its managers.

Second, managers' extensive use of verbal media helps to explain why they are reluctant to delegate tasks. It is not as if they can hand a dossier over to subordinates; they must take the time to dump memory—to tell subordinates all about the subject. But this could take so long that managers may find it easier to do the task themselves. Thus they are damned by their own information system to a dilemma of delegation—to do too much or to delegate to subordinates with inadequate briefing.

Folklore: Management is, or at least is quickly becoming, a science and a profession. By almost any definition of *science* and *profession*, this statement is false. Brief observation of any manager will quickly lay to rest the notion that managers practice a science. A science involves the enaction of systematic, analytically determined procedures or programs. If we do not even know what procedures managers use, how can we prescribe them by scientific analysis? And how can we call management a profession if we cannot specify what managers are to learn? For after all, a profession involves "knowledge of some department of learning or science" (*Random House Dictionary*).[10]

Fact: The managers' programs—to schedule time, process information, make decisions, and so on—remain locked deep inside their brains. Thus, to describe these programs, we rely on words like *judgment* and *intuition*, seldom stopping to realize that they are merely labels for our ignorance.

I was struck during my study by the fact that the executives I was observing—all very competent—are fundamentally indistinguishable from their counterparts of a hundred years ago (or a thousand years ago). The information they need differs, but they seek it in the same way—by word of mouth. Their decisions concern modern technology, but the procedures they use to make those decisions are the same as the procedures used by nineteenth-century managers. Even the computer, so important for the specialized work of the organization, has apparently had no influence on the work procedures of general managers. In fact, the manager is in a kind of loop, with increasingly heavy work pressures but no aid forthcoming from management science.

Considering the facts about managerial work, we can see that the manager's job is enormously complicated and difficult. Managers are overburdened with obligations yet cannot easily delegate their tasks. As a result, they are driven to overwork and forced to do many tasks superficially. Brevity, fragmentation, and verbal communication characterize their work. Yet these are the very characteristics of managerial work that have impeded scientific attempts to improve it. As a result, management scientists have concentrated on

---

10. For a more thorough, though rather different, discussion of this issue, *see* Kenneth R. Andrews, "Toward Professionalism in Business Management," *Harvard Business Review* (March–April 1969): 49.

the specialized functions of the organization, where it is easier to analyze the procedures and quantify the relevant information.[11]

But the pressures of a manager's job are becoming worse. Whereas managers once needed to respond only to owners and directors, they now find that subordinates with democratic norms continually reduce their freedom to issue unexplained orders and that a growing number of outside influences (consumer groups, government agencies, and so on) demand attention. Managers have had nowhere to turn for help. The first step in providing such help is to find out what the manager's job really is.

BACK TO A BASIC DESCRIPTION OF MANAGERIAL WORK

Earlier, I defined the manager as that person in charge of an organization or subunit. Besides CEOs, this definition would include vice presidents, bishops, foremen, hockey coaches, and prime ministers. All these "managers" are vested with formal authority over an organizational unit. From formal authority comes status, which leads to various interpersonal relations, and from these comes access to information. Information, in turn, enables the manager to make decisions and strategies for the unit.

The manager's job can be described in terms of various roles, or organized sets of behaviors identified with a position. My description, shown in *Exhibit 1*, comprises ten roles. As we shall see, formal authority gives rise to the three interpersonal roles, which in turn give rise to the three informational roles; these two sets of roles enable the manager to play the four decisional roles.

INTERPERSONAL ROLES

Three of the manager's roles arise directly from formal authority and involve basic interpersonal relationships. First is the *figurehead* role. As the head of an organizational unit, every manager must perform some ceremonial duties. The president greets the touring dignitaries. The foreman attends the wedding of a lathe operator. The sales manager takes an important customer to lunch.

The chief executives of my study spent 12% of their contact time on ceremonial duties; 17% of their incoming mail dealt with acknowledgments and requests related to their status. For example, a letter to a company president requested free merchandise for a crippled schoolchild; diplomas that needed to be signed were put on the desk of the school superintendent.

Duties that involve interpersonal roles may sometimes be routine, involving little serious communication and no important decision making.

---

11. C. Jackson Grayson, Jr., in "Management Science and Business Practice," *Harvard Business Review* (July–August 1973): 41, explains in similar terms why, as chairman of the Price Commission, he did not use those very techniques that he himself promoted in his earlier career as a management scientist.

EXHIBIT 1
The Manager's Roles

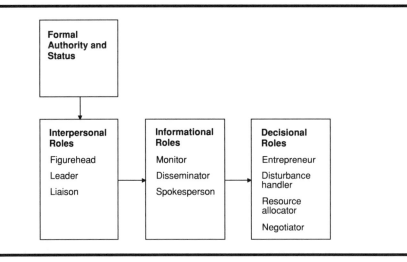

Nevertheless, they are important to the smooth functioning of an organization and cannot be ignored.

Managers are responsible for the work of the people of their unit. Their actions in this regard constitute the *leader* role. Some of these actions involve leadership directly—for example, in most organizations the managers are normally responsible for hiring and training their own staff.

In addition, there is the indirect exercise of the leader role. For example, every manager must motivate and encourage employees, somehow reconciling their individual needs with the goals of the organization. In virtually every contact with the manager, subordinates seeking leadership clues ask, "Does she approve?" "How would she like the report to turn out?" "Is she more interested in market share than in high profits?"

The influence of managers is most clearly seen in the leader role. Formal authority vests them with great potential power; leadership determines in large part how much of it they will realize.

The literature of management has always recognized the leader role, particularly those aspects of it related to motivation. In contrast, until recently it has hardly mentioned the *liaison* role, in which the manager makes contacts outside the vertical chain of command. This is remarkable in light of the finding of virtually every study of managerial work that managers spend as much time with peers and other people outside their units as they do with their own subordinates—and, surprisingly, very little time with their own superiors.

In Rosemary Stewart's diary study, the 160 British middle and top managers spent 47% of their time with peers, 41% of their time with people inside their unit, and only 12% of their time with their superiors. For Robert H. Guest's study of U.S. foremen, the figures were 44%, 46%, and 10%. The chief

EXHIBIT 2
The Chief Executive's Contacts

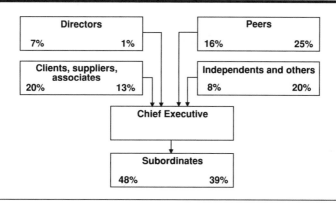

Note: The first figure indicates the proportion of total contact time spent with each group; the second figure indicates the proportion of mail from each group.

executives of my study averaged 44% of their contact time with people outside their organizations, 48% with subordinates, and 7% with directors and trustees.

The contacts the five CEOs made were with an incredibly wide range of people: subordinates; clients, business associates, and suppliers; and peers—managers of similar organizations, government and trade organization officials, fellow directors on outside boards, and independents with no relevant organizational affiliations. The chief executives' time with and mail from these groups is shown in *Exhibit 2*. Guest's study of foremen shows, likewise, that their contacts were numerous and wide-ranging, seldom involving fewer than 25 individuals and often more than 50.

▬▬ INFORMATIONAL ROLES

By virtue of interpersonal contacts, both with subordinates and with a network of contacts, the manager emerges as the nerve center of the organizational unit. The manager may not know everything but typically knows more than subordinates do.

Studies have shown this relationship to hold for all managers, from street gang leaders to U.S. presidents. In *The Human Group*, George C. Homans explains how, because they were at the center of the information flow in their own gangs and were also in close touch with other gang leaders, street gang leaders were better informed than any of their followers.[12] As for presidents,

---

12. George C. Homans, *The Human Group* (New York: Harcourt, Brace & World, 1950), based on the study by William F. Whyte entitled *Street Corner Society,* rev. ed. (Chicago: University of Chicago Press, 1955).

Richard Neustadt observes: "The essence of [Franklin] Roosevelt's technique for information-gathering was competition. 'He would call you in,' one of his aides once told me, 'and he'd ask you to get the story on some complicated business, and you'd come back after a couple of days of hard labor and present the juicy morsel you'd uncovered under a stone somewhere, and *then* you'd find out he knew all about it, along with something else you *didn't* know. Where he got this information from he wouldn't mention, usually, but after he had done this to you once or twice you got damn careful about *your* information.'"[13]

We can see where Roosevelt "got this information" when we consider the relationship between the interpersonal and informational roles. As leader, the manager has formal and easy access to every staff member. In addition, liaison contacts expose the manager to external information to which subordinates often lack access. Many of these contacts are with other managers of equal status, who are themselves nerve centers in their own organization. In this way, the manager develops a powerful database of information.

Processing information is a key part of the manager's job. In my study, the CEOs spent 40% of their contact time on activities devoted exclusively to the transmission of information; 70% of their incoming mail was purely informational (as opposed to requests for action). Managers don't leave meetings or hang up the telephone to get back to work. In large part, communication *is* their work. Three roles describe these informational aspects of managerial work.

As *monitor*, the manager is perpetually scanning the environment for information, interrogating liaison contacts and subordinates, and receiving unsolicited information, much of it as a result of the network of personal contacts. Remember that a good part of the information the manager collects in the monitor role arrives in verbal form, often as gossip, hearsay, and speculation.

In the *disseminator* role, the manager passes some privileged information directly to subordinates, who would otherwise have no access to it. When subordinates lack easy contact with one another, the manager may pass information from one to another.

In the *spokesperson* role, the manager sends some information to people outside the unit—a president makes a speech to lobby for an organization cause, or a foreman suggests a product modification to a supplier. In addition, as a spokesperson, every manager must inform and satisfy the influential people who control the organizational unit. For the foreman, this may simply involve keeping the plant manager informed about the flow of work through the shop.

The president of a large corporation, however, may spend a great amount of time dealing with a host of influences. Directors and shareholders must be advised about finances; consumer groups must be assured that the organization is fulfilling its social responsibilities; and government officials must be satisfied that the organization is abiding by the law.

---

13. Neustadt, *Presidential Power*, p. 157.

——— DECISIONAL ROLES

Information is not, of course, an end in itself; it is the basic input to decision making. One thing is clear in the study of managerial work: the manager plays the major role in the unit's decision-making system. As its formal authority, only the manager can commit the unit to important new courses of action; and as its nerve center, only the manager has full and current information to make the set of decisions that determines the unit's strategy. Four roles describe the manager as decision maker.

As *entrepreneurs,* managers seek to improve the unit, to adapt it to changing conditions in the environment. In the monitor role, presidents are constantly on the lookout for new ideas. When good ones appear, they initiate development projects that they may supervise or delegate to employees (perhaps with the stipulation that they must approve final proposals).

There are two interesting features about these development projects at the CEO level. First, these projects do not involve single decisions or even unified clusters of decisions. Rather, they emerge as a series of small decisions and actions sequenced over time. Apparently, chief executives prolong each project both to fit it into a busy, disjointed schedule, and so that they can comprehend complex issues gradually.

Second, the chief executives I studied supervised as many as 50 of these projects at the same time. Some projects entailed new products or processes; others involved public relations campaigns, improvement of the cash position, reorganization of a weak department, resolution of a morale problem in a foreign division, integration of computer operations, various acquisitions at different stages of development, and so on.

Chief executives appear to maintain a kind of inventory of the development projects in various stages of development. Like jugglers, they keep a number of projects in the air; periodically, one comes down, is given a new burst of energy, and sent back into orbit. At various intervals, they put new projects on-stream and discard old ones.

While the entrepreneur role describes the manager as the voluntary initiator of change, the *disturbance handler* role depicts the manager involuntarily responding to pressures. Here change is beyond the manager's control. The pressures of a situation are too severe to be ignored—a strike looms, a major customer has gone bankrupt, or a supplier reneges on a contract—so the manager must act.

Leonard R. Sayles, who has carried out appropriate research on the manager's job, likens the manager to a symphony orchestra conductor who must "maintain a melodious performance,"[14] while handling musicians' problems and other external disturbances. Indeed, every manager must spend a considerable amount of time responding to high-pressure disturbances. No

---

14. Leonard R. Sayles, *Managerial Behavior* (New York: McGraw-Hill, 1964), p. 162.

organization can be so well run, so standardized, that it has considered every contingency in the uncertain environment in advance. Disturbances arise not only because poor managers ignore situations until they reach crisis proportions but also because good managers cannot possibly anticipate all the consequences of the actions they take.

The third decisional role is that of *resource allocator*. The manager is responsible for deciding who will get what. Perhaps the most important resource the manager allocates is his or her own time. Access to the manager constitutes exposure to the unit's nerve center and decision maker. The manager is also charged with designing the unit's structure, that pattern of formal relationships that determines how work is to be divided and coordinated.

Also, as resource allocator, the manager authorizes the important decisions of the unit before they are implemented. By retaining this power, the manager can ensure that decisions are interrelated. To fragment this power encourages discontinuous decision making and a disjointed strategy.

There are a number of interesting features about the manager's authorization of others' decisions. First, despite the widespread use of capital budgeting procedures—a means of authorizing various capital expenditures at one time—executives in my study made a great many authorization decisions on an ad hoc basis. Apparently, many projects cannot wait or simply do not have the quantifiable costs and benefits that capital budgeting requires.

Second, I found that the chief executives faced incredibly complex choices. They had to consider the impact of each decision on other decisions and on the organization's strategy. They had to ensure that the decision would be acceptable to those who influence the organization, as well as ensure that resources would not be overextended. They had to understand the various costs and benefits as well as the feasibility of the proposal. They also had to consider questions of timing. All this was necessary for the simple approval of someone else's proposal. At the same time, however, the delay could lose time, while quick approval could be ill-considered and quick rejection might discourage the subordinate who had spent months developing a pet project.

One common solution to approving projects is to pick the person instead of the proposal. That is, the manager authorizes those projects presented by people whose judgment he or she trusts. But the manager cannot always use this simple dodge.

The final decisional role is that of *negotiator*. Managers spend considerable time in negotiations: the president of the football team works out a contract with the holdout superstar; the corporation president leads the company's contingent to negotiate a new strike issue; the foreman argues a grievance problem to its conclusion with the shop steward.

These negotiations are an integral part of the manager's job, for only he or she has the authority to commit organizational resources in "real time" and the nerve-center information that important negotiations require.

——— THE INTEGRATED JOB

It should be clear by now that these ten roles are not easily separable. In the terminology of the psychologist, they form a gestalt, an integrated whole. No role can be pulled out of the framework and the job be left intact. For example, a manager without liaison contacts lacks external information. As a result, that manager can neither disseminate the information that employees need nor make decisions that adequately reflect external conditions. (This is a problem for the new person in a managerial position, since he or she has to build up a network of contacts before making effective decisions.)

Here lies a clue to the problems of team management.[15] Two or three people cannot share a single managerial position unless they can act as one entity. This means that they cannot divide up the ten roles unless they can very carefully reintegrate them. The real difficulty lies with the informational roles. Unless there can be full sharing of managerial information—and, as I pointed out earlier, it is primarily verbal—team management breaks down. A single managerial job cannot be arbitrarily split, for example, into internal and external roles, for information from both sources must be brought to bear on the same decisions.

To say that the ten roles form a gestalt is not to say that all managers give equal attention to each role. In fact, I found in my review of the various research studies that sales managers seem to spend relatively more of their time in the interpersonal roles, presumably a reflection of the extrovert nature of the marketing activity. Production managers, on the other hand, give relatively more attention to the decisional roles, presumably a reflection of their concern with efficient work flow. And staff managers spend the most time in the informational roles, since they are experts who manage departments that advise other parts of the organization. Nevertheless, in all cases, the interpersonal, informational, and decisional roles remain inseparable.

——— TOWARD MORE EFFECTIVE MANAGEMENT

This description of managerial work should prove more important to managers than any prescription they might derive from it. That is to say, *the managers' effectiveness is significantly influenced by their insight into their own work.* Performance depends on how well a manager understands and responds to the pressures and dilemmas of the job. Thus managers who can be introspective about their work are likely to be effective at their jobs. The questions in *Exhibit 3* may sound rhetorical; none is meant to be. Even though the questions cannot be answered simply, the manager should address them.

---

15. *See* Richard C. Hodgson, Daniel J. Levinson, and Abraham Zaleznik, *The Executive Role Constellation* (Boston: Division of Research, Harvard Business School, 1965), for a discussion of the sharing of roles.

EXHIBIT 3
Self-Study Questions for Managers

1. Where do I get my information, and how? Can I make greater use of my contacts? Can other people do some of my scanning? In what areas is my knowledge weakest, and how can I get others to provide me with the information I need? Do I have sufficiently powerful mental models of those things I must understand within the organization and in its environment?

2. What information do I disseminate? How important is that information to my subordinates? Do I keep too much information to myself because disseminating it is time-consuming or inconvenient? How can I get more information to others so they can make better decisions?

3. Do I tend to act before information is in? Or do I wait so long for all the information that opportunities pass me by?

4. What pace of change am I asking my organization to tolerate? Is this change balanced so that our operations are neither excessively static nor overly disrupted? Have we sufficiently analyzed the impact of this change on the future of our organization?

5. Am I sufficiently well-informed to pass judgment on subordinates' proposals? Can I leave final authorization for more of the proposals with subordinates? Do we have problems of co-ordination because subordinates already make too many decisions independently?

6. What is my vision for this organization? Are these plans primarily in my own mind in loose form? Should I make them explicit to guide the decisions of others better? Or do I need flexibility to change them at will?

7. How do my subordinates react to my managerial style? Am I sufficiently sensitive to the powerful influence of my actions? Do I fully understand their reactions to my actions? Do I find an appropriate balance between encouragement and pressure? Do I stifle their initiative?

Let us take a look at three specific areas of concern. For the most part, the managerial logjams—the dilemma of delegation, the database centralized in one brain, the problems of working with the management scientist—revolve around the verbal nature of the manager's information. There are great dangers in centralizing the organization's data bank in the minds of its managers. When they leave, they take their memory with them. And when subordinates are out of convenient verbal reach of the manager, they are at an informational disadvantage.

The manager is challenged to find systematic ways to share privileged information. A regular debriefing session with key subordinates, a weekly memory dump on the dictating machine, maintaining a diary for limited circulation, or other similar methods may ease the logjam of work considerably. The time spent disseminating this information will be more than regained when decisions must be made. Of course, some will undoubtedly raise the question of confidentiality.

EXHIBIT 3
Self-Study Questions for Managers (Continued)

8. What kind of external relationships do I maintain, and how? Do I spend too much of my time maintaining them? Are there certain people whom I should get to know better?

9. Is here any system to my time scheduling, or am I just reacting to the pressures of the moment? Do I find the appropriate mix of activities or concentrate on one particular function or problem just because I find it interesting? Am I more efficient with particular kinds of work, at special times of the day or week? Does my schedule reflect this? Can someone else schedule my times (besides my secretary)?

10. Do I overwork? What effect does my work load have on my efficiency? Should I force myself to take breaks or to reduce the pace of my activity?

11. Am I too superficial in what I do? Can I really shift moods as quickly and frequently as my work requires? Should I decrease the amount of fragmentation and interruption in my work?

12. Do I spend too much time on current, tangible activities? Am I a slave to the action and excitement of my work, so that I am no longer able to concentrate on issues? Do key problems receive the attention they deserve? Should I spend more time reading and probing deeply into certain issues? Could I be more reflective? Should I be?

13. Do I use the different media appropriately? Do I know how to make the most of written communication? Do I rely excessively on face-to-face communication, thereby putting all but a few of my subordinates at an informational disadvantage? Do I schedule enough of my meetings on a regular basis? Do I spend enough time observing activities firsthand, or am I detached from the heart of my organization's activities?

14. How do I blend my personal rights and duties? Do my obligations consume all my time? How can I free myself from obligations to ensure that I am taking this organization where I want it to go? How can I turn my obligations to my advantage?

But managers would be well advised to weigh the risks of exposing privileged information against having subordinates who can make effective decisions.

If there is a single theme that runs through this reading, it is that the pressures of the job drive the manager to take on too much work, encourage interruption, respond quickly to every stimulus, seek the tangible and avoid the abstract, make decisions in small increments, and do everything abruptly.

Here again, the manager is challenged to deal consciously with the pressures of superficiality by giving serious attention to the issues that require it, by stepping back in order to see a broad picture, and by making use of analytical inputs. Although effective managers have to be adept at responding quickly to numerous and varying problems, the danger in managerial work is that they will respond to every issue equally (and that means abruptly) and that they will never work the tangible bits and pieces of information into a comprehensive picture of their world.

To create this comprehensive picture, managers can supplement their own models with those of specialists. Economists describe the functioning of markets, operations researchers simulate financial flow processes, and behavioral scientists explain the needs and goals of people. The best of these models can be searched out and learned.

In dealing with complex issues, the senior manager has much to gain from a close relationship with the organization's own management scientists. They have something important that the manager lacks—time to probe complex issues. An effective working relationship hinges on the resolution of what a colleague and I have called "the planning dilemma."[16] Managers have the information and the authority; analysts have the time and the technology. A successful working relationship between the two will be effected when the manager learns to share information and the analyst learns to adapt to the manager's needs. For the analyst, adaptation means worrying less about the elegance of the method and more about its speed and flexibility.

Analysts can help the top manager schedule time, feed in analytical information, monitor projects, develop models to aid in making choices, design contingency plans for disturbances that can be anticipated, and conduct "quick and dirty" analyses for those that cannot. But there can be no cooperation if the analysts are out of the mainstream of the manager's information flow.

The manager is challenged to gain control of his or her own time by turning obligations into advantages and by turning those things he or she wishes to do into obligations. The chief executives of my study initiated only 32% of their own contacts (and another 5% by mutual agreement). And yet to a considerable extent they seemed to control their time. There were two key factors that enabled them to do so.

First, managers have to spend so much time discharging obligations that if they were to view them as just that, they would leave no mark on the organization. Unsuccessful managers blame failure on the obligations. Effective managers turn obligations to advantages. A speech is a chance to lobby for a cause; a meeting is a chance to reorganize a weak department; a visit to an important customer is a chance to extract trade information.

Second, the manager frees some time to do the things that he or she—perhaps no one else—considers important by turning them into obligations. Free time is made, not found. Hoping to leave some time open for contemplation or general planning is tantamount to hoping that the pressures of the job will go away. Managers who want to innovate initiate projects and obligate others to report back to them. Managers who need certain environmental information establish channels that will automatically keep them informed. Managers who have to tour facilities commit themselves publicly.

---

16. James S. Hekimian and Henry Mintzberg, "The Planning Dilemma," *The Management Review* (May 1968): 4.

THE EDUCATOR'S JOB

Finally, a word about the training of managers. Our management schools have done an admirable job of training the organization's specialists— management scientists, marketing researchers, accountants, and organizational-development specialists. But for the most part, they have not trained managers.[17]

Management schools will begin the serious training of managers when skill training takes a serious place next to cognitive learning. Cognitive learning is detached and informational, like reading a book or listening to a lecture. No doubt much important cognitive material must be assimilated by the manager-to-be. But cognitive learning no more makes a manager than it does a swimmer. The latter will drown the first time she jumps into the water if her coach never takes her out of the lecture hall, gets her wet, and gives her feedback on her performance.

In other words, we are taught a skill through practice plus feedback, whether in a real or a simulated situation. Our management schools need to identify the skills managers use, select students who show potential in these skills, put the students into situations where these skills can be practiced and developed, and then give them systematic feedback on their performance.

My description of managerial work suggests a number of important managerial skills—developing peer relationships, carrying out negotiations, motivating subordinates, resolving conflicts, establishing information networks and subsequently disseminating information, making decisions in conditions of extreme ambiguity, and allocating resources. Above all, the manager needs to be introspective in order to continue to learn on the job.

No job is more vital to our society than that of the manager. The manager determines whether our social institutions will serve us well or whether they will squander our talents and resources. It is time to strip away the folklore about managerial work and study it realistically so that we can begin the difficult task of making significant improvements in its performance.

* * *

Fifteen years after this reading was published, the author wrote the following commentary.

RETROSPECTIVE COMMENTARY

Over the years, one reaction has dominated the comments I have received from managers who read "The Manager's Job: Folklore and Fact":

---

17. *See* J. Sterling Livingston, "Myth of the Well-Educated Manager," *Harvard Business Review* (January–February 1971): 79.

"You make me feel so good. I thought all those other managers were planning, organizing, coordinating, and controlling, while I was busy being interrupted, jumping from one issue to another, and trying to keep the lid on the chaos." Yet everything in this reading must have been patently obvious to these people. Why such a reaction to reading what they already knew?

Conversely, how to explain the very different reaction of two media people who called to line up interviews after an article based on this one appeared in the *New York Times*. "Are we glad someone finally let managers have it," both said in passing, a comment that still takes me aback. True, they had read only the account in the *Times*, but that no more let managers have it than did this reading. Why that reaction?

One explanation grows out of the way I now see this reading—as proposing not so much another view of management as another face of it. I like to call it the insightful face, in contrast to the long-dominant professional or cerebral face. One stresses commitment, the other calculation; one sees the world with integrated perspective, the other figures it as the components of a portfolio. The cerebral face operates with the words and numbers of rationality; the insightful face is rooted in the images and feel of a manager's integrity.

Each of these faces implies a different kind of knowing, and that, I believe, explains many managers' reaction to this article. Rationally, they "knew" what managers did—planned, organized, coordinated, and controlled. But deep down that did not feel quite right. The description in this article may have come closer to what they really knew. As for those media people, they weren't railing against management as such but against the cerebral form of management, so pervasive, that they saw impersonalizing the world around them.

In practice, management has to be two-faced—there has to be a balance between the cerebral and the insightful. So, for example, I realized originally that managerial communication was largely oral and that the advent of the computer had not changed anything fundamental in the executive suite—a conclusion I continue to hold. (The greatest threat the personal computer poses is that managers will take it seriously and come to believe that they can manage by remaining in their offices and looking at displays of digital characters.) But I also thought that the dilemma of delegating could be dealt with by periodic debriefings—disseminating words. Now, however, I believe that managers need more ways to convey the images and impressions they carry inside of them. This explains the renewed interest in strategic vision, in culture, and in the roles of intuition and insight in management.

The ten roles I used to describe the manager's job also reflect management's cerebral face, in that they decompose the job more than capture the integration. Indeed, my effort to show a sequence among these roles now seems more consistent with the traditional face of management work than an insightful one. Might we not just as well say that people throughout the organization take actions that inform managers who, by making sense of those actions, develop images and visions that inspire people to subsequent efforts?

Perhaps my greatest disappointment about the research reported here is that it did not stimulate new efforts. In a world so concerned with management, much of the popular literature is superficial and the academic research pedestrian. Certainly, many studies have been carried out over the last 15 years, but the vast majority sought to replicate earlier research. In particular, we remain grossly ignorant about the fundamental content of the manager's job and have barely addressed the major issues and dilemmas in its practice.

But superficiality is not only a problem of the literature. It is also an occupational hazard of the manager's job. Originally I believed this problem could be dealt with; now I see it as inherent in the job. This is because managing insightfully depends on the direct experience and personal knowledge that come from intimate contact. But in organizations grown larger and more diversified, that becomes difficult to achieve. And so managers turn increasingly to the cerebral face, and the delicate balance between the two faces is lost.

Certainly, some organizations manage to sustain their humanity despite their large size—as Tom Peters and Robert Waterman show in their book *In Search of Excellence*. But that book attained its outstanding success precisely because it is about the exceptions, about the organizations so many of us long to be a part of—not the organizations in which we actually work.

Fifteen years ago, I stated that "No job is more vital to our society than that of the manager. It is the manager who determines whether our social institutions serve us well or whether they squander our talents and resources." Now, more than ever, we must strip away the folklore of the manager's job and begin to face its difficult facts.

_____

—— DISCUSSION QUESTIONS

1. The author gives four instances of folklore and fact in managerial work. Give examples that illustrate this folklore/fact dichotomy from your own work experience.
2. The author discusses the ten roles of a manager and the need to establish an integrated whole. He then points out the weaknesses of team management. Do you agree or disagree with this critique of team management?
3. In his description of more effective management, the author presents the challenges a manager must accept and turn to his or her advantage. Give examples from your own life experience in which you have turned challenges to your advantage.
4. Philosophers have admonished us to "Know thyself." Looking at the list of *Self-Study Questions for Managers*, honestly take an inventory of your strengths and weaknesses. (Share them with a classmate and ask for honest feedback. Remember, it's information.)

What are your key strengths? What are weaknesses that you might want to work on?

5. In his retrospective, Mintzberg states, "In practice, management has to be two-faced—there has to be a balance between the cerebral and the insightful." What does the author mean by this assertion?

Power, Dependence, and Effective Management

2

JOHN P. KOTTER

People in general and Americans in particular have always been suspicious of power—the United States was born out of a rebellion, and our political processes were designed to guard against the abuse of power. However, asserts the author of this reading, the negative aspects of power have blinded people to its benefits and uses. Without power, people cannot accomplish very much. This is especially true in management.

As organizations have grown, the author maintains, the number of people that managers need to get their jobs done has increased. As a result, it has become more difficult, if not impossible, for managers to achieve their goals through persuasion or through formal authority alone. They need power. The author describes four different types of power that managers can use, along with persuasion, to influence others. Skillful managers, he concludes, exercise their power with maturity, skill, and sensitivity to the obligations and risks involved.

$\mathbf{A}$mericans, as a rule, are not very comfortable with power or with its dynamics. We often distrust and question the motives of people who we think actively seek power. We have a certain fear of being manipulated. Even those people who think the dynamics of power are inevitable and needed often feel somewhat guilty when they themselves mobilize and use power. Simply put, the overall attitude and feeling toward power, which can easily be traced to the nation's very birth, is negative.

One of the many consequences of this attitude is that power as a topic for rational study and dialogue has not received much attention, even in managerial circles. If the reader doubts this, all he or she need do is flip through some textbooks, journals, or advanced management course descriptions. The word *power* rarely appears.

Note: This reading is based on data from a clinical study of a highly diverse group of 26 organizations including large and small, public and private, manufacturing and service organizations. The study was funded by the Division of Research at the Harvard Business School. As part of the study process, the author interviewed about 250 managers.

This lack of attention to the subject of power merely adds to the already enormous confusion and misunderstanding surrounding the topic of power and management. And this misunderstanding is becoming increasingly burdensome because in today's large and complex organizations the effective performance of most managerial jobs requires one to be skilled at the acquisition and use of power.

From my own observations, I suspect that a large number of managers—especially the young, well-educated ones—perform significantly below their potential because they do not understand the dynamics of power and because they have not nurtured and developed the instincts needed to effectively acquire and use power.

In this reading I hope to clear up some of the confusion regarding power and managerial work by providing tentative answers to three questions:

1. Why are the dynamics of power necessarily an important part of managerial processes?
2. How do effective managers acquire power?
3. How and for what purposes do effective managers use power?

I will not address questions related to the misuse of power, but not because I think they are unimportant. The fact that some managers, some of the time, acquire and use power mostly for their own aggrandizement is obviously a very important issue that deserves attention and careful study. But that is a complex topic unto itself and one that has already received more attention than the subject of this reading.

——— RECOGNIZING DEPENDENCE IN THE MANAGER'S JOB

One of the distinguishing characteristics of typical managers is how dependent they are on the activities of a variety of other people to perform their jobs effectively.[1] Unlike doctors and mathematicians, whose performance is more directly dependent on their own talents and efforts, a manager can be dependent in varying degrees on superiors, subordinates, peers in other parts of the organization, the subordinates of peers, outside suppliers, customers, competitors, unions, regulating agencies, and many others.

These dependency relationships are an inherent part of managerial jobs because of two organizational facts of life: division of labor and limited resources. Because the work in organizations is divided into specialized divisions, departments, and jobs, managers are made directly or indirectly dependent on many others for information, staff services, and cooperation in general. Because

---

1. *See* Leonard R. Sayles, *Managerial Behavior: Administration in Complex Organization* (New York: McGraw-Hill, 1964) as well as Rosemary Stewart, *Managers and Their Jobs* (London: Macmillan, 1967) and *Contrasts in Management* (London: McGraw-Hill, 1976).

of their organizations' limited resources, managers are also dependent on their external environments for support. Without some minimal cooperation from suppliers, competitors, unions, regulatory agencies, and customers, managers cannot help their organizations survive and achieve their objectives.

Dealing with these dependencies and the manager's subsequent vulnerability is an important and difficult part of a manager's job because, while it is theoretically possible that all of these people and organizations would automatically act in just the manner that a manager wants and needs, such is almost never the case in reality. All the people on whom a manager is dependent have limited time, energy, and talent, for which there are competing demands.

Some people may be uncooperative because they are too busy elsewhere, and some because they are not really capable of helping. Others may well have goals, values, and beliefs that are quite different and in conflict with the manager's and may therefore have no desire whatsoever to help or cooperate. This is obviously true of a competing company and sometimes of a union, but it can also apply to a boss who is feeling threatened by a manager's career progress or to a peer whose objectives clash with the manager's.

Indeed, managers often find themselves dependent on many people (and things) whom they do not directly control and who are not cooperating. This is the key to one of the biggest frustrations managers feel in their jobs, even in the top ones, which the following example illustrates:

> After nearly a year of rumors, it was finally announced that the president of ABC Corporation had been elected chairman of the board and that Jim Franklin, the vice president of finance, would replace him as president. While everyone at ABC was aware that a shift would take place soon, it was not at all clear before the announcement who would be the next president. Most people had guessed it would be Phil Cook, the marketing vice president.
>
> Nine months into his job as chief executive officer, Franklin found that Phil Cook (still the marketing vice president) seemed to be fighting him in small and subtle ways. There was never anything blatant, but Cook just did not cooperate with Franklin as the other vice presidents did. Shortly after being elected, Franklin had tried to bypass what he saw as a potential conflict with Cook by telling him that he would understand if Cook would prefer to move somewhere else where he could be a CEO also. Franklin said that it would be a big loss to the company but that he would be willing to help Cook in a number of ways if he wanted to look for a presidential opportunity elsewhere. Cook had thanked him but had said that family and community commitments would prevent him from relocating and all CEO opportunities were bound to be in a different city.
>
> Since the situation did not improve after the tenth and eleventh months, Franklin seriously considered forcing Cook out. When he thought about the consequences of such a move, Franklin became more and more aware of just how dependent he was on Cook. Marketing and sales were generally the keys to success in their industry,

and the company's sales force was one of the best, if not the best, in the industry. Cook had been with the company for 25 years. He had built a strong personal relationship with many of the people in the sales force and was universally popular. A mass exodus just might occur if Cook were fired. The loss of a large number of salespeople, or even a lot of turmoil in the department, could have a serious effect on the company's performance.

After one year as chief executive officer, Franklin found that the situation between Cook and himself had not improved and had become a constant source of frustration.

As a person gains more formal authority in an organization, the areas in which he or she is vulnerable increase and become more complex rather than the reverse. As the previous example suggests, it is not at all unusual for the president of an organization to be in a highly dependent position, a fact often not apparent to either the outsider or to the lower-level manager who covets the president's job.

A considerable amount of the behavior of highly successful managers that seems inexplicable in light of what management texts usually tell us managers do becomes understandable when one considers a manager's need for, and efforts at, managing his or her relationships with others.[2] To be able to plan, organize, budget, staff, control, and evaluate, managers need some control over the many people on whom they are dependent. Trying to control others solely by directing them and on the basis of the power associated with one's position simply will not work—first, because managers are always dependent on some people over whom they have no formal authority, and second, because virtually no one in modern organizations will passively accept and completely obey a constant stream of orders from someone just because he or she is the "boss."

Trying to influence others by means of persuasion alone will not work either. Although it is very powerful and possibly the single most important method of influence, persuasion has some serious drawbacks too. To make it work requires time (often lots of it), skill, and information on the part of the persuader. And persuasion can fail simply because the other person chooses not to listen or does not listen carefully.

This is not to say that directing people on the basis of the formal power of one's position and persuasion are not important means by which successful managers cope. They obviously are. But, even taken together, they are not usually enough.

Successful managers cope with their dependence on others by being sensitive to it, by eliminating or avoiding unnecessary dependence and by establishing power over those others. Good managers then use that power to

---

2. I am talking about the type of inexplicable differences that Henry Mintzberg has found; *see* his article "The Manager's Job: Folklore and Fact," *Harvard Business Review* (March–April 1990): 163.

help them plan, organize, staff, budget, evaluate, and so on. *In other words, it is primarily because of the dependence inherent in managerial jobs that the dynamics of power necessarily form an important part of a manager's processes.*

An argument that took place during a middle-management training seminar I participated in a few years ago helps illustrate further this important relationship between a manager's need for power and the degree of his or her dependence on others:

> Two participants, both managers in their thirties, got into a heated disagreement regarding the acquisition and use of power by managers. One took the position that power was absolutely central to managerial work, while the other argued that it was virtually irrelevant. In support of their positions, each described a very "successful" manager with whom he worked. In one of these examples, the manager seemed to be constantly developing and using power, while in the other, such behavior was rare. Subsequently, both seminar participants were asked to describe their successful managers' jobs in terms of the dependence *inherent* in those jobs.
>
> The young manager who felt power was unimportant described a staff vice president in a small company who was dependent only on his immediate subordinates, his peers, and his boss. This person, Joe Phillips, had to depend on his subordinates to do their jobs appropriately, but, if necessary, he could fill in for any of them or secure replacement for them rather easily. He also had considerable formal authority over them; that is, he could give them raises and new assignments, recommend promotions, and fire them. He was moderately dependent on the other four vice presidents in the company for information and cooperation. They were likewise dependent on him. The president had considerable formal authority over Phillips but was also moderately dependent on him for help, expert advice, the service his staff performed, other information, and general cooperation.
>
> The second young manager—the one who felt power was very important—described a service department manager, Sam Weller, in a large, complex, and growing company who was in quite a different position. Weller was dependent not only on his boss for rewards and information, but also on 30 other individuals who made up the divisional and corporate top management. And while his boss, like Phillips's, was moderately dependent on him too, most of the top managers were not. Because Weller's subordinates, unlike Phillips's, had people reporting to them, Weller was dependent not only on his subordinates but also on his subordinates' subordinates. Because he could not himself easily replace or do most of their technical jobs, unlike Phillips, he was very dependent on all these people.
>
> In addition, for critical supplies, Weller was dependent on two other department managers in the division. Without their timely help, it was impossible for his department to do its job. These departments, however, did not have similar needs for Weller's help and cooperation. Weller was also dependent on local labor union officials and on a

federal agency that regulated the division's industry. Both could shut his division down if they wanted.

Finally, Weller was dependent on two outside suppliers of key materials. Because of the volume of his department's purchase relative to the size of these two companies, he had little power over them.

Under these circumstances, it is hardly surprising that Sam Weller had to spend considerable time and effort acquiring and using power to manage his many dependencies, while Joe Phillips did not.

As this example also illustrates, not all management jobs require an incumbent to be able to provide the same amount of successful power-oriented behavior. But most management jobs today are more like Weller's than Phillips's. And, perhaps more important, the trend over the past two or three decades is away from jobs like Phillips's and toward jobs like Weller's. So long as our technologies continue to become more complex, the average organization continues to grow larger, and the average industry continues to become more competitive and regulated, that trend will continue; as it does so, the effective acquisition and use of power by managers will become even more important.

───── ESTABLISHING POWER IN RELATIONSHIPS

To help cope with the dependency relationships inherent in their jobs, effective managers create, increase, or maintain four different types of power over others.[3] Having power based in these areas puts the manager in a position both to influence those people on whom he or she is dependent when necessary and to avoid being hurt by any of them.

SENSE OF OBLIGATION

One of the ways that successful managers generate power in their relationships with others is to create a sense of obligation in those others. When the manager is successful, the others feel that they should—rightly—allow the manager to influence them within certain limits.

Successful managers often go out of their way to do favors for people who they expect will feel an obligation to return those favors. As can be seen in the following description of a manager by one of his subordinates, some people are very skilled at identifying opportunities for doing favors that cost them very little but that others appreciate very much:

---

3. These categories closely resemble the five developed by John R. P. French and Bertram Raven; see "The Base of Social Power," *Group Dynamics: Research and Theory*, Dorwin Cartwright and Alvin Zandler, eds. (New York: Harper & Row, 1968), Chapter 20. Three of the categories are similar to the types of "authority"-based power described by Max Weber in *The Theory of Social and Economic Organization* (New York: Free Press, 1947).

Most of the people here would walk over hot coals in their bare feet if my boss asked them to. He has an incredible capacity to do little things that mean a lot to people. Today, for example, in his junk mail he came across an advertisement for something that one of my subordinates had in passing once mentioned that he was shopping for. So my boss routed it to him. That probably took 15 seconds of his time, and yet my subordinate really appreciated it. To give you another example, two weeks ago he somehow learned that the purchasing manager's mother had died. On his way home that night, he stopped off at the funeral parlor. Our purchasing manager was, of course, there at the time. I bet he'll remember that brief visit for quite a while.

Recognizing that most people believe that friendship carries with it certain obligations ("A friend in need . . ."), successful managers often try to develop true friendships with those on whom they are dependent. They will also make formal and informal deals in which they give something up in exchange for certain future obligations.

BELIEF IN A MANAGER'S EXPERTISE

A second way successful managers gain power is by building reputations as experts in certain matters. Believing in the manager's expertise, others will often defer to the manager on those matters. Managers usually establish this type of power through visible achievement. The larger the achievement and the more visible it is, the more power the manager tends to develop.

One of the reasons that managers display concern about their professional reputations and their track records is that these have an impact on others' beliefs about their expertise. These factors become particularly important in large settings, where most people have only secondhand information about most other people's professional competence, as the following shows:

Herb Randley and Bert Kline were both 35-year-old vice presidents in a large research and development organization. According to their closest associates, they were equally bright and competent in their technical fields and as managers. Yet Randley had a much stronger professional reputation in most parts of the company, and his ideas generally carried much more weight. Close friends and associates claim the reason that Randley is so much more powerful is related to a number of tactics that he has used more than Kline has.

Randley has published more scientific papers and managerial articles than Kline. Randley has been more selective in the assignments he has worked on, choosing those that are visible and that require his strong suits. He has given more speeches and presentations on projects that are his own achievements. And in meetings in general, he is allegedly forceful in areas where he has expertise and silent in those where he does not.

IDENTIFICATION WITH A MANAGER

A third method by which managers gain power is by fostering others' unconscious identification with them or with ideas they stand for. Sigmund Freud was the first to describe this phenomenon, which is most clearly seen in the way people look up to charismatic leaders. Generally, the more a person finds a manager both consciously and (more important) unconsciously an ideal person, the more he or she will defer to that manager.

Managers develop power based on others' idealized views of them in a number of ways. They try to look and behave in ways that others respect. They go out of their way to be visible to their employees and to give speeches about their organizational goals, values, and ideals. They even consider, while making hiring and promotion decisions, whether they will be able to develop this type of power over the candidates:

> One vice president of sales in a moderate-sized manufacturing company was reputed to be so much in control of his sales force that he could get them to respond to new and different marketing programs in a third of the time taken by the company's best competitors. His power over his employees was based primarily on their strong identification with him and what he stood for. Emigrating to the United States at age 17, this person worked his way up "from nothing." When made a sales manager in 1965, he began recruiting other young immigrants and sons of immigrants from his former country. When made vice president of sales in 1970, he continued to do so. In 1975, 85% of his sales force was made up of people whom he hired directly or who were hired by others he brought in.

PERCEIVED DEPENDENCE ON A MANAGER

The final way that an effective manager often gains power is by feeding others' beliefs that they are dependent on the manager either for help or for not being hurt. The more they perceive they are dependent, the more most people will be inclined to cooperate with such a manager.

There are two methods that successful managers often use to create perceived dependence.

Finding and Acquiring Resources   In the first, the manager identifies and secures (if necessary) resources that another person requires to perform the job, resources that he or she does not possess, and that are not readily available elsewhere. These resources include such things as authority to make certain decisions; control of money, equipment, and office space; access to important people; information and control of information channels; and subordinates. Then the manager takes action so that the other person correctly perceives that the manager has such resources and is willing and ready to use them to help (or hinder) the other person. Consider the following extreme—but true—example.

> When young Tim Babcock was put in charge of a division of a large manufacturing company and told to "turn it around," he spent the first few weeks studying it from afar. He decided that the division was in disastrous shape and that he would need to take many large steps quickly to save it. To be able to do that, he realized he needed to develop considerable power fast over most of the division's management and staff. He did the following:
>
> 1. He gave the division's management two hours' notice of his arrival.
> 2. He arrived in a limousine with six assistants.
> 3. He immediately called a meeting of the 40 top managers.
> 4. He outlined briefly his assessment of the situation, his commitment to turn things around, and the basic direction he wanted things to move in.
> 5. He then fired the four top managers in the room and told them that they had to be out of the building in two hours.
> 6. He then said he would personally dedicate himself to sabotaging the career of anyone who tried to block his efforts to save the division.
> 7. He ended the 60-minute meeting by announcing that his assistants would set up appointments for him with each of them starting at 7:00 the next morning.
>
> Throughout the critical six-month period that followed, those who remained at the division generally cooperated energetically with Mr. Babcock.

Affecting Perceptions of Resources   A second way effective managers gain these types of power is by influencing other persons' perceptions of the manager's resources.[4] In settings where many people are involved and where the manager does not interact continuously with those he or she is dependent on, those people will seldom possess hard facts regarding what relevant resources the manager commands directly or indirectly (through others), what resources he or she will command in the future, or how prepared he or she is to use those resources to help or hinder them. They will be forced to make their own judgments.

Insofar as managers can influence people's judgments, they can generate much more power than one would generally ascribe to them in light of the reality of their resources.

In trying to influence people's judgments, managers pay considerable attention to the "trappings" of power and to their own reputations and images. Among other actions, they sometimes carefully select, decorate, and arrange their offices in ways that give signs of power. They associate with

---

4. For an excellent discussion of this method, *see* Richard E. Neustadt, *Presidential Power* (New York: John Wiley, 1960).

people or organizations that are known to be powerful or that others perceive as powerful. Managers selectively foster rumors concerning their own power. Indeed, those who are particularly skilled at creating power in this way tend to be very sensitive to the impressions that all their actions might have on others.

FORMAL AUTHORITY

Before discussing how managers use their power to influence others, it is useful to see how formal authority relates to power. By *formal authority*, I mean those elements that automatically come with a managerial job—perhaps a title, an office, a budget, the right to make certain decisions, a set of subordinates, a reporting relationship, and so on.

Effective managers use the elements of formal authority as resources to help them develop any or all of the four types of power previously discussed, just as they use other resources (such as their education). Two managers with the same formal authority can have very different amounts of power entirely because of the way they have used that authority. For example:

> By sitting down with employees who are new or with people who are starting new projects and clearly specifying who has the formal authority to do what, one manager creates a strong sense of obligation in others to defer to her authority later.
>
> By selectively withholding or giving the high-quality service his department can provide other departments, one manager makes other managers clearly perceive that they are dependent on him.

On its own, then, formal authority does not guarantee a certain amount of power; it is only a resource that managers can use to generate power in their relationships.

——— EXERCISING POWER TO INFLUENCE OTHERS

Successful managers use the power they develop in their relationships, along with persuasion, to influence people on whom they are dependent to behave in ways that make it possible for the managers to get their jobs done effectively. They use their power to influence others directly, face to face, and in more indirect ways. (See the *Exhibit* on the next page.)

FACE-TO-FACE INFLUENCE

The chief advantage of influencing others directly by exercising any of the types of power is speed. If the power exists and the manager correctly

EXHIBIT
Methods of Influence

FACE-TO-FACE METHODS	WHAT THEY CAN INFLUENCE	ADVANTAGES	DRAWBACKS
Exercise power based on obligation.	Behavior within zone that the other perceives as legitimate in light of the obligation.	Quick. Requires no outlay of tangible resources.	If the request is outside the acceptable zone, it will fail; if it is too far outside, others might see it as illegitimate.
Exercise power based on perceived expertise.	Attitudes and behavior within the zone of perceived expertise.	Quick. Requires no outlay of tangible resources.	If the request is outside the acceptable zone, it will fail; if it is too far outside, others might see it as illegitimate.
Exercise power based on identification with a manager.	Attitudes and behavior that are not in conflict with the ideals that underlie the identification.	Quick. Requires no expenditure of limited resources.	Restricted to influence attempts that are not in conflict with the ideals that underlie the identification.
Exercise power based on perceived dependence.	Wide range of behavior that can be monitored.	Quick. Can often succeed when other methods fail.	Repeated influence attempts encourage the other to gain power over the influencer.
Coercively exercise power based on perceived dependence.	Wide range of behavior that can be easily monitored.	Quick. Can often succeed when other methods fail.	Invites retaliation. Very risky.
Use persuasion.	Very wide range of attitudes and behavior.	Can produce internalized motivation that does not require monitoring. Requires no power or outlay of scarce material resources.	Can be very time-consuming. Requires other person to listen.
Combine these methods.	Depends on the exact combination.	Can be more potent and less risky than using a single method.	More costly than using a single method.

INDIRECT METHODS	WHAT THEY CAN INFLUENCE	ADVANTAGES	DRAWBACKS
Manipulate the other's environment by using any or all of the face-to-face methods.	Wide range of behavior and attitudes.	Can succeed when face-to-face methods fail.	Can be time-consuming. Is complex to implement. Is very risky, especially if used frequently.
Change the forces that continuously act on the individual: Formal organizational arrangements. Informal social arrangements. Technology. Resources available. Statement of organizational goals.	Wide range of behavior and attitudes on a continuous basis.	Has continuous influence, not just a one-shot effect. Can have a very powerful impact.	Often requires a considerable power outlay to achieve.

understands the nature and strength of it, he or she can influence the other person with nothing more than a brief request or command:

> Jones thinks Smith feels obliged to him for past favors. Furthermore, Jones thinks that his request to speed up a project by two days probably falls within a zone that Smith would consider legitimate in light of his own definition of his obligation to Jones. So Jones simply calls Smith and makes his request. Smith pauses for only a second and says yes, he'll do it.

> Manager Johnson has some power based on perceived dependence over manager Baker. When Johnson tells Baker that he wants a report done in 24 hours, Baker grudgingly considers the costs of compliance, of noncompliance, and of complaining to higher authorities. He decides that doing the report is the least costly action and tells Johnson he will do it.

> Porter identifies strongly with Marquette, an older manager who is not her boss. Porter thinks Marquette is the epitome of a great manager and tries to model herself after her. When Marquette asks Porter to work on a special project "that could be very valuable in improving the company's ability to meet new competitive products," Porter agrees without hesitation and works 15 hours per week above and beyond her normal hours to get the project done and done well.

When used to influence others, each of the four types of power has different advantages and drawbacks. For example, power based on perceived expertise or on identification with a manager can often be used to influence attitudes as well as someone's immediate behavior and thus can have a lasting impact. It is very difficult to influence attitudes by using power based on perceived dependence, but if it can be done, it usually has the advantage of being able to influence a much broader range of behavior than the other methods do. When exercising power based on perceived expertise, for example, one can only influence attitudes and behavior within that narrow zone defined by the expertise.

The drawbacks associated with the use of power based on perceived dependence are particularly important to recognize. A person who feels dependent on a manager for rewards (or lack of punishments) might quickly agree to a request from the manager but then not follow through—especially if the manager cannot easily find out if the person has obeyed or not. Repeated influence attempts based on perceived dependence also seem to encourage the other person to try to gain some power to balance the manager's. And perhaps most important, using power based on perceived dependence in a coercive way is very risky. Coercion invites retaliation.

For instance, in the example in which Tim Babcock took such extreme steps to save the division he was assigned to "turn around," his development and use of power based on perceived dependence could have led to mass resignation and the collapse of the division. Babcock fully recognized this risk, however, and behaved as he did because he felt there was simply *no other way* that he could gain the very large amount of quick cooperation needed to save the division.

Effective managers will often draw on more than one form of power to influence someone, or they will combine power with persuasion. In general, they do so because a combination can be more potent and less risky than any single method, as the following description shows:

> One of the best managers we have in the company has lots of power based on one thing or another over most people. But he seldom if ever just tells or asks someone to do something. He almost always takes a few minutes to try to persuade them. The power he has over people generally induces them to listen carefully and certainly disposes them to be influenced. That, of course, makes the persuasion process go quickly and easily. And he never risks getting the other person mad or upset by making what that person thinks is an unfair request or command.

It is also common for managers not to coercively exercise power based on perceived dependence by itself, but to combine it with other methods to reduce the risk of retaliation. In this way, managers are able to have a large impact without leaving the bitter aftertaste of punishment alone.

INDIRECT INFLUENCE METHODS

Effective managers also rely on two types of less direct methods to influence those on whom they are dependent. In the first way, they use any or all of the face-to-face methods to influence other people, who in turn have some specific impact on a desired person.

Product manager Stein needed plant manager Billings to "sign off" on a new product idea (Product X) which Billings thought was terrible. Stein decided that there was no way he could logically persuade Billings because Billings just would not listen to him. With time, Stein felt, he could have broken through that barrier. But he did not have that time. Stein also realized that Billings would never, just because of some deal or favor, sign off on a product he did not believe in. Stein also felt it not worth the risk of trying to force Billings to sign off, so here is what he did:

> On Monday, Stein got Reynolds, a person Billings respected, to send Billings two market research studies that were very favorable to Product X, with a note attached saying, "Have you seen this? I found them rather surprising. I am not sure if I entirely believe them, but still . . ."

> On Tuesday, Stein got a representative of one of the company's biggest customers to mention casually to Billings on the phone that he had

heard a rumor about Product X being introduced soon and was "glad to see you guys are on your toes as usual."

On Wednesday, Stein had two industrial engineers stand about three feet away from Billings as they were waiting for a meeting to begin and talk about the favorable test results on Product X.

On Thursday, Stein set up a meeting to talk about Product X with Billings and invited only people whom Billings liked or respected and who also felt favorably about Product X.

On Friday, Stein went to see Billings and asked him if he was willing to sign off on Product X. He was.

This type of manipulation of the environments of others can influence both behavior and attitudes and can often succeed when other influence methods fail. But it has a number of serious drawbacks. It takes considerable time and energy, and it is quite risky. Many people think it is wrong to try to influence others in this way, even people who, without consciously recognizing it, use this technique themselves. If they think someone is trying, or has tried, to manipulate them, they may retaliate. Furthermore, people who gain the reputation of being manipulators seriously undermine their own capacities for developing power and for influencing others. Almost no one, for example, will want to identify with a manipulator. And virtually no one accepts, at face value, a manipulator's sincere attempts at persuasion. In extreme cases, a reputation as a manipulator can completely ruin a manager's career.

A second way in which managers indirectly influence others is by making permanent changes in an individual's or a group's environment. They change job descriptions, the formal systems that measure performance, the extrinsic incentives available, the tools, people, and other resources that the people or groups work with, the architecture, the norms or values of work groups, and so on. If the manager is successful in making the changes, and the changes have the desired effect on the individual or group, that effect will be sustained over time.

Effective managers recognize that changes in the forces that surround a person can have great impact on that person's behavior. Unlike many of the other influence methods, this one doesn't require a large expenditure of limited resources or effort on the part of the manager on an ongoing basis. Once such a change has been successfully made, it works independently of the manager.

This method of influence is used by all managers to some degree. Many, however, use it sparingly simply because they do not have the power to change the forces acting on the person they wish to influence. In many organizations, only the top managers have the power to change the formal measurement systems, the extrinsic incentives available, the architecture, and so on.

———— GENERATING AND USING POWER SUCCESSFULLY

Managers who are successful at acquiring considerable power and using it to manage their dependence on others tend to share a number of common characteristics:

1. They are sensitive to what others consider to be legitimate behavior in acquiring and using power. They recognize that the four types of power carry with them certain "obligations" regarding their acquisition and use. A person who gains a considerable amount of power based on his perceived expertise is generally expected to be an expert in certain areas. If it ever becomes publicly known that the person is clearly not an expert in those areas, such a person will probably be labeled a "fraud" and will not only lose his power but will suffer other reprimands too.

   A person with whom a number of people identify is expected to act like an ideal leader. If he clearly lets people down, he will not only lose that power, he will also suffer the righteous anger of his ex-followers. Many managers who have created or used power based on perceived dependence in ways that their employees have felt unfair, such as in requesting overtime work, have ended up with unions.

2. They have good intuitive understanding of the various types of power and methods of influence. They are sensitive to what types of power are easiest to develop with different types of people. They recognize, for example, that professionals tend to be more influenced by perceived expertise than by other forms of power. They also have a grasp of all the various methods of influence and what each can accomplish, at what costs, and with what risks. (See the *Exhibit*.) They are good at recognizing the specific conditions in any situation and then at selecting an influence method that is compatible with those conditions.

3. They tend to develop all the types of power, to some degree, and they use all the influence methods mentioned in the *Exhibit*. Unlike managers who are not very good at influencing people, effective managers usually do not think that only some of the methods are useful or that only some of the methods are moral. They recognize that any of the methods, used under the right circumstances, can help contribute to organizational effectiveness with few dysfunctional consequences. At the same time, they generally try to avoid those methods that are more risky than others and those that may have dysfunctional consequences. For example, they manipulate the environment of others only when absolutely necessary.

4. They establish career goals and seek out managerial positions that allow them to successfully develop and use power. They look for jobs, for example, that use their backgrounds and skills to control or manage some critically important problem or environmental contingency that an organization faces. They recognize that success

in that type of job makes others dependent on them and increases their own perceived expertise. They also seek jobs that do not demand a type or a volume of power that is inconsistent with their own skills.

5. They use all of their resources, formal authority, and power to develop still more power. To borrow Edward Banfield's metaphor, they actually look for ways to "invest" their power where they might secure a high positive return.[5] For example, by asking a person to do him two important favors, a manager might be able to finish his construction program one day ahead of schedule. That request may cost him most of the obligation-based power he has over that person, but in return he may significantly increase his perceived expertise as a manager of construction projects in the eyes of everyone in his organization.

   Just as in investing money, there is always some risk involved in using power this way; it is possible to get a zero return for a sizable investment, even for the most powerful manager. Effective managers do not try to avoid risks. Instead, they look for prudent risks, just as they do when investing capital.

6. Effective managers engage in power-oriented behavior in ways that are tempered by maturity and self-control.[6] They seldom, if ever, develop and use power in impulsive ways or for their own aggrandizement.

7. Finally, they also recognize and accept as legitimate that, in using these methods, they clearly influence other people's behavior and lives. Unlike many less effective managers, they are reasonably comfortable in using power to influence people. They recognize, often only intuitively, what this article is all about—that their attempts to establish power and use it are an absolutely necessary part of the successful fulfillment of their difficult managerial role.

Copyright © 1977; revised 1991.

---

5. *See* Edward C. Banfield, *Political Influence* (New York: Free Press, 1965), Chapter 11.

6. *See* David C. McClelland and David H. Burnham, "Power Is the Great Motivator," *Harvard Business Review* (March–April 1976): 100.

———— DISCUSSION QUESTIONS

1. The author claims that the manager's need for power arises out of dependency. Do you agree or disagree with this statement?
2. Is acquiring power an art or a skill? Can anyone do it? If so, elaborate.
3. Kotter mentions that there are four different types of power over others. Are there any others that an effective manager could use?
4. The goal of power is to get others to behave in a desired way. There are direct and indirect ways of achieving this. Give an example of how you've used power recently to get someone else to do what you've wanted them to do. How has another person used power recently to get you to do something that they wanted you to do?

3 Management Time: Who's Got the Monkey?

WILLIAM ONCKEN, JR., AND DONALD L. WASS

In any organization, bosses, peers, and subordinates make demands on a manager's scarce time. Because successful leadership hinges on the effective use of time, managers must gain as much control over their time as they can. By cultivating the ability to assign tasks, delegate responsibility, and foster initiative, managers can minimize or do away with subordinates' demands on their time; they are then free to devote their attention to more critical activities. The analogy of a monkey on the back demonstrates the authors' points.

Why is it that managers are typically running out of time while their subordinates are typically running out of work? In this reading, we shall explore the meaning of management time as it relates to the interaction between managers and their bosses, their own peers, and their subordinates.

Specifically, we shall deal with three different kinds of management time:

Boss-imposed time—to accomplish those activities that the boss requires and that the manager cannot disregard without direct and swift penalty.

System-imposed time—to accommodate those requests to the manager for active support from his or her peers. This assistance must also be provided lest there be penalties, though not always direct or swift ones.

Self-imposed time—to do those things that the manager originates or agrees to do. A certain portion of this kind of time, however, will be taken by subordinates and is called *subordinate-imposed time*. The remaining portion will be his or her own and is called *discretionary time*. Self-imposed time is not subject to penalty since neither the boss nor the system can discipline the manager for not doing what they did not know the manager had intended to do in the first place.

The management of time necessitates that managers get control over the timing and content of what they do. Since what their bosses and the system impose on them are backed up by penalty, managers cannot tamper with those requirements. Thus their self-imposed time becomes their major area of concern.

The managers' strategy is therefore to increase the discretionary component of their self-imposed time by minimizing or doing away with the subordinate component. They will then use the added increment to get better control over their boss-imposed and system-imposed activities. Most managers spend much more subordinate-imposed time than they even faintly realize. Hence we shall use a monkey-on-the-back analogy to examine how subordinate-imposed time comes into being and what the superior can do about it.

——— WHERE IS THE MONKEY?

Let us imagine that a manager is walking down the hall and that he notices one of his subordinates, Jones, coming up the hallway. When the two are abreast of one another, Jones greets the manager with, "Good morning. By the way, we've got a problem. You see . . ." As Jones continues, the manager recognizes in this problem the same two characteristics common to all the problems his subordinates gratuitously bring to his attention. Namely, the manager knows (a) enough to get involved, but (b) not enough to make the on-the-spot decision expected of him. Eventually, the manager says, "So glad you brought this up. I'm in a rush right now. Meanwhile, let me think about it and I'll let you know." Then he and Jones part company.

Let us analyze what has just happened. Before the two of them met, on whose back was the "monkey"? The subordinate's. After they parted, on whose back was it? The manager's. Subordinate-imposed time begins the moment a monkey successfully executes a leap from the back of a subordinate to the back of his or her superior and does not end until the monkey is returned to its proper owner for care and feeding.

In accepting the monkey, the manager has voluntarily assumed a position subordinate to his subordinate. That is, he has allowed Jones to make him her subordinate by doing two things a subordinate is generally expected to do for a boss—the manager has accepted a responsibility from his subordinate, and the manager has promised her a progress report.

The subordinate, to make sure the manager does not miss this point, will later stick her head in the manager's office and cheerily query, "How's it coming?" (This is called supervision.)

Or let us imagine again, in concluding a working conference with another subordinate, Johnson, the manager's parting words are, "Fine. Send me a memo on that."

Let us analyze this one. The monkey is now on the subordinate's back because the next move is his, but it is poised for a leap. Watch that monkey. Johnson dutifully writes the requested memo and drops it in his outbasket. Shortly thereafter, the manager plucks it from his inbasket and reads it. Whose move is it now? The manager's. If he does not make that move soon, he will get a follow-up memo from the subordinate (this is another form of supervision). The longer the manager delays, the more frustrated the subordinate will become (he'll be "spinning his wheels") and the more guilty the manager will feel (his backlog of subordinate-imposed time will be mounting).

Or suppose once again that at a meeting with a third subordinate, Smith, the manager agrees to provide all the necessary backing for a public relations proposal he has just asked Smith to develop. The manager's parting words to her are, "Just let me know how I can help."

Now let us analyze this. Here the monkey is initially on the subordinate's back. But for how long? Smith realizes that she cannot let the manager "know" until her proposal has the manager's approval. And from experience, she also realizes that her proposal will likely be sitting in the manager's briefcase for weeks waiting for him to eventually get to it. Who's really got the monkey? Who will be checking up on whom? Wheelspinning and bottlenecking are on their way again.

A fourth subordinate, Reed, has just been transferred from another part of the company in order to launch and eventually manage a newly created business venture. The manager has said that they should get together soon to hammer out a set of objectives for the new job, and that "I will draw up an initial draft for discussion with you."

Let us analyze this one, too. The subordinate has the new job (by formal assignment) and the full responsibility (by formal delegation), but the manager has the next move. Until he makes it, he will have the monkey and the subordinate will be immobilized.

Why does it all happen? Because in each instance the manager and the subordinate assume at the outset, wittingly or unwittingly, that the matter under consideration is a joint problem. The monkey in each case begins its career astride both their backs. All it has to do now is move the wrong leg, and—presto—the subordinate deftly disappears. The manager is thus left with another acquisition to his menagerie. Of course, monkeys can be trained not to move the wrong leg. But it is easier to prevent them from straddling backs in the first place.

WHO IS WORKING FOR WHOM?

To make what follows more credible, let us suppose that these same four subordinates are so thoughtful and considerate of the superior's time that they are at pains to allow no more than three monkeys to leap from each of their backs to his in any one day. In a five-day week, the manager will have picked up 60 screaming monkeys—far too many to do anything about individually. So he spends the subordinate-imposed time juggling his priorities.

Late Friday afternoon, the manager is in his office with the door closed for privacy in order to contemplate the situation, while his subordinates are waiting outside to get a last chance before the weekend to remind him that he will have to "fish or cut bait." Imagine what they are saying to each other about the manager as they wait: "What a bottleneck. He just can't make up his mind. How anyone ever got that high up in our company without being able to make a decision we'll never know."

Worst of all, the reason the manager cannot make any of these "next moves" is that his time is almost entirely eaten up in meeting his own boss-imposed and system-imposed requirements. To get control of these, he needs discretionary time that is in turn denied him when he is preoccupied with all these monkeys. The manager is caught in a vicious circle.

But time is a-wasting (an understatement). The manager calls his secretary on the intercom and instructs her to tell his subordinates that he will be unavailable to see them until Monday morning. At 7:00 P.M., he drives home, intending with firm resolve to return to the office tomorrow to get caught up over the weekend. He returns bright and early the next day only to see, on the nearest green of the golf course across from his office window, a foursome. Guess who?

That does it. He now knows who is really working for whom. Moreover, he now sees that if he actually accomplishes during this weekend what he came to accomplish, his subordinates' morale will go up so sharply that they will each raise the limit on the number of monkeys they will let jump from their backs to his. In short, he now sees, with the clarity of a revelation on a mountaintop, that the more he gets caught up, the more he will fall behind.

He leaves the office with the speed of a person running away from a plague. His plan? To get caught up on something else he hasn't had time for in years: a weekend with his family. (This is one of the many varieties of discretionary time.)

Sunday night he enjoys ten hours of sweet, untroubled slumber, because he has clear-cut plans for Monday. He is going to get rid of his subordinate-imposed time. In exchange, he will get an equal amount of discretionary time, part of which he will spend with his subordinates to see that they learn the difficult but rewarding managerial art called, "The Care and Feeding of Monkeys."

The manager will also have plenty of discretionary time left over for getting control of the timing and content not only of his boss-imposed time but of his system-imposed time as well. All of this may take months, but compared with the way things have been, the rewards will be enormous. His ultimate objective is to manage his management time.

——— GETTING RID OF THE MONKEYS

The manager returns to the office Monday morning just late enough to permit his four subordinates to collect in his outer office waiting to see him about their monkeys. He calls them in, one by one. The purpose of each interview is to take a monkey, place it on the desk between them, and figure out together how the next move might conceivably be the subordinate's. For certain monkeys, this will take some doing. The subordinate's next move may be so elusive that the manager may decide—just for now—merely to let the monkey sleep on the subordinate's back overnight and have him or her return with it at an appointed time the next morning to continue the joint quest for a more substantive move by the subordinate. (Monkeys sleep just as soundly overnight on subordinates' backs as on superiors'.)

As each subordinate leaves the office, the manager is rewarded by the sight of a monkey leaving his office on the subordinate's back. For the next 24 hours, the subordinate will not be waiting for the manager; instead, the manager will be waiting for the subordinate.

Later, as if to remind himself that there is no law against his engaging in a constructive exercise in the interim, the manager strolls by the subordinate's office, sticks his head in the door, and cheerily asks, "How's it coming?" (The time consumed in doing this is discretionary for the manager and boss-imposed for the subordinate.)

When the subordinate (with the monkey on his or her back) and the manager meet at the appointed hour the next day, the manager explains the ground rules in words to this effect:

"At no time while I am helping you with this or any other problem will your problem become my problem. The instant your problem becomes mine, you will no longer have a problem. I cannot help a person who hasn't got a problem.

"When this meeting is over, the problem will leave this office exactly the way it came in—on your back. You may ask my help at any appointed time, and we will make a joint determination of what the next move will be and which of us will make it.

"In those rare instances where the next move turns out to be mine, you and I will determine it together. I will not make any move alone."

The manager follows this same line of thought with each subordinate until at about 11:00 A.M. he realizes that he has no need to shut his door. His monkeys are gone. They will return—but by appointment only. His appointment calendar will assure this.

TRANSFERRING THE INITIATIVE

What we have been driving at in this monkey-on-the-back analogy is to transfer initiative from superior to subordinate and keep it there. We have tried to highlight a truism as obvious as it is subtle. Namely, before developing initiative in subordinates, the manager must see to it that they *have* the initiative. Once the manager takes it back, they will no longer have it and the discretionary time can be kissed good-bye. It will all revert to subordinate-imposed time.

Nor can both manager and subordinate effectively have the same initiative at the same time. The opener, "Boss, we've got a problem," implies this duality and represents, as noted earlier, a monkey astride two backs, which is a very bad way to start a monkey on its career. Let us, therefore, take a few moments to examine what we prefer to call "The Anatomy of Managerial Initiative."

There are five degrees of initiative that the manager can exercise in relation to the boss and to the system: (1) *wait* until told (lowest initiative); (2) *ask* what to do; (3) *recommend*, then take resulting action; (4) *act*, but advise at once, and (5) *act* on own, then routinely report (highest initiative).

Clearly, the manager should be professional enough not to indulge in initiatives 1 and 2 in relation either to the boss or to the system. A manager who uses initiative 1 has no control over either the timing or content of boss-imposed or system-imposed time, and thereby forfeits any right to complain about what he or she is told to do or when. The manager who uses initiative 2 has control over the timing but not over the content. Initiatives 3, 4, and 5 leave the manager in control of both, with the greatest control being at level 5.

The manager's job, in relation to subordinates' initiatives, is twofold; first, to outlaw the use of initiatives 1 and 2, thus giving subordinates no choice but to learn and master "Completed Staff Work"; then, to see that for each problem leaving the office there is an agreed-upon level of initiative assigned to it, in addition to the agreed-upon time and place of the next manager-subordinate conference. The latter should be duly noted on the manager's appointment calendar.

——— CARE AND FEEDING OF MONKEYS

In order to further clarify our analogy between the monkey-on-the-back and the well-known processes of assigning and controlling, we shall refer briefly to the manager's appointment schedule, which calls for five hard-and-fast rules governing the "Care and Feeding of Monkeys" (violations of these rules will cost discretionary time):

Rule 1   Monkeys should be fed or shot. Otherwise, they will starve to death and the manager will waste valuable time on postmortems or attempted resurrections.

Rule 2   The monkey population should be kept below the maximum number the manager has time to feed. Subordinates will find time to work as many monkeys as he or she finds time to feed, but no more. It shouldn't take more than 5 to 15 minutes to feed a properly prepared monkey.

Rule 3   Monkeys should be fed by appointment only. The manager should not have to be hunting down starving monkeys and feeding them on a catch-as-catch-can basis.

Rule 4   Monkeys should be fed face-to-face or by telephone, but never by mail. (If by mail, the next move will be the manager's—remember?) Documentation may add to the feeding process, but it cannot take the place of feeding.

Rule 5   Every monkey should have an assigned next feeding time and degree of initiative. These may be revised at any time by mutual consent, but never allowed to become vague or indefinite. Otherwise, the monkey will either starve to death or wind up on the manager's back.

CONCLUDING NOTE

"Get control over the timing and content of what you do" is appropriate advice for managing management time. The first order of business is for the manager to enlarge his or her discretionary time by eliminating subordinate-imposed time. The second is for the manager to use a portion of this new-found discretionary time to see to it that each subordinate possesses the initiative without which he or she cannot exercise initiative, and then to see to it that this initiative is in fact taken. The third is for the manager to use another portion of the increased discretionary time to get and keep control of the timing and content of both boss-imposed and system-imposed time.

The result of all this is that the manager's leverage will increase, in turn enabling the value of each hour spent in managing management time to multiply, without theoretical limit.

Copyright © 1974; revised 1991.

DISCUSSION QUESTIONS

1. "Management Time" is one of the most widely read human resource management essays ever published. Can you account for its popularity?
2. Share an instance when you have allowed someone else's "monkey" to jump onto your back. Give an example when you succeeded in passing your monkey on to someone else.
3. Initiative in subordinates is fundamental to managerial time management. What might some stumbling blocks be that would prevent subordinates from having a higher degree of initiative?

The New Managerial Work   4

ROSABETH MOSS KANTER

Downsizing, restructuring, and other organizational changes intended to foster innovation and flexibility have changed the roles and tasks of managers. Collaborative work is increasing, hierarchy fading. To manage effectively in the new organizations, managers need to master change in two critical areas: power and motivation. Rather than exerting direct control over others, managers now and in the future must learn to build relationships, find new sources of ideas and opportunities, and broker deals. Effective managers are no longer watchdogs but integrators and facilitators. Three case histories illuminate the opportunities and dilemmas inherent in these changes.

Managerial work is undergoing such enormous and rapid change that many managers are reinventing their profession as they go. With little precedent to guide them, they are watching hierarchy fade away and the clear distinctions of title, task, department, even corporation, blur. Faced with extraordinary levels of complexity and interdependency, they watch traditional sources of power erode and the old motivational tools lose their magic.

The cause is obvious. Competitive pressures are forcing corporations to adopt new flexible strategies and structures. Many of these are familiar: acquisitions and divestitures aimed at more focused combinations of business activities, reductions in management staff and levels of hierarchy, increased use of performance-based rewards. Other strategies are less common but have an even more profound effect. In a growing number of companies, for example, horizontal ties between peers are replacing vertical ties as channels of activity and communication. Companies are asking corporate staffs and functional departments to play a more strategic role with greater cross-departmental collaboration. Some organizations are turning themselves nearly inside out—buying formerly internal services from outside suppliers, forming strategic alliances and supplier-customer partnerships that bring external relationships inside where they can influence company policy and practice. I call these emerging practices *postentrepreneurial* because they involve the application of entrepreneurial creativity and flexibility to established businesses.

Such changes come highly recommended by the experts who urge organizations to become leaner, less bureaucratic, more entrepreneurial. But so far, theorists have given scant attention to the dramatically altered realities of managerial work in these transformed corporations (see the *Exhibit*). We don't

EXHIBIT
The New Managerial Quandaries

- At American Express, the CEO instituted a program called One Enterprise to encourage collaboration between different lines of business. One Enterprise has led to a range of projects where peers from different divisions work together on such synergistic ventures as cross-marketing, joint purchasing, and cooperative product and market innovation. Employees' rewards are tied to their One Enterprise efforts. Executives set goals and can earn bonuses for their contributions to results in other divisions.

  But how do department managers control their people when they're working on cross-departmental teams? And who determines the size of the rewards when the interests of more than one area are involved?

- At Security Pacific National Bank, internal departments have become forces in the external marketplace. For example, the bank is involved in a joint venture with local auto dealers to sell fast financing for car purchases. And the MIS department is now a profit center selling its services inside and outside the bank.

  But what is the role of bank managers accountable for the success of such entrepreneurial ventures? And how do they shift their orientation from the role of boss in a chain of command to the role of customer?

- At Digital Equipment Corporation, emphasis on supplier partnerships to improve quality and innovation has multiplied the need for cross-functional as well as cross-company collaboration. Key suppliers are included on product-planning teams with engineering, manufacturing, and purchasing staff. Digital uses its human resources staff to train and do performance appraisals of its suppliers, as if they were part of the company. In cases where suppliers are also customers, purchasing and marketing departments also need to work collaboratively.

  But how do managers learn enough about other functions to be credible, let alone influential, members of such teams? How do they maintain adequate communication externally while staying on top of what their own departments are doing? And how do they handle the extra work of responding to projects initiated by other areas?

- At Banc One, a growing reliance on project teams spanning more than 70 affiliated banks has led the CEO to propose eliminating officer titles because of the lack of correlation between status as measured by title and status within the collaborative team.

---

even have good words to describe the new relationships. "Superiors" and "subordinates" hardly seem accurate, and even "bosses" and "their people" imply more control and ownership than managers today actually possess. On top of it all, career paths are no longer straightforward and predictable but have become idiosyncratic and confusing.

Some managers experience the new managerial work as a loss of power because much of their authority used to come from hierarchical position. Now that everything seems negotiable by everyone, they are confused about how to mobilize and motivate staff. For other managers, the shift in roles and tasks

EXHIBIT
The New Managerial Quandaries (Continued)

But then what do rank and hierarchy mean anymore, especially for people whose careers consist of a sequence of projects rather than a sequence of promotions? What does "career" mean? Does it have a shape? Is there a ladder?

· At Alcan, which is trying to find new uses and applications for its core product, aluminum, managers and professionals from line divisions form screening teams to consider and refine new-venture proposals. A venture manager, chosen from the screening team, takes charge of concepts that pass muster, drawing on Alcan's worldwide resources to build the new business. In one case of global synergy, Alcan created a new product for the Japanese market using Swedish and American technology and Canadian manufacturing capacity.

But why should senior managers release staff to serve on screening and project teams for new businesses when their own businesses are making do with fewer and fewer people? How do functionally oriented managers learn enough about worldwide developments to know when they might have something of value to offer someplace else?

And how do the managers of these new ventures ever go back to the conventional line organization as middle managers once their venture has been folded into an established division?

· At IBM, an emphasis on customer partnerships to rebuild market share is leading to practices quite new to the company. In some cases, IBM has formed joint development teams with customers, where engineers from both companies share proprietary data. In others, the company has gone beyond selling equipment to actually managing a customer's management information system. Eastman Kodak has handed its U.S. data center operations to IBM to consolidate and manage, which means lower fixed costs for Kodak and a greater ability to focus on its core businesses rather than on ancillary services. Some 300 former Kodak people still fill Kodak's needs as IBM employees, while two committees of IBM and Kodak managers oversee the partnership.

But who exactly do the data center people work for? Who is in charge? And how do traditional notions of managerial authority square with such a complicated set of relationships?

offers greater personal power. The following case histories illustrate the responses of three managers in three different industries to the opportunities and dilemmas of structural change.

> *Hank is vice president and chief engineer for a leading heavy equipment manufacturer* that is moving aggressively against foreign competition. One of the company's top priorities has been to increase the speed, quality, and cost-effectiveness of product development. So Hank worked with consultants to improve collaboration between manufacturing and other functions and to create closer alliances

between the company and its outside suppliers. Gradually, a highly segmented operation became an integrated process involving project teams drawn from component divisions, functional departments, and external suppliers. But along the way, there were several unusual side effects. Different areas of responsibility overlapped. Some technical and manufacturing people were co-located. Liaisons from functional areas joined the larger development teams. Most unusual of all, project teams had a lot of direct contact with higher levels of the company.

Many of the managers reporting to Hank felt these changes as a loss of power. They didn't always know what their people were doing, but they still believed they ought to know. They no longer had sole input into performance appraisals; other people from other functions had a voice as well, and some of them knew more about employees' project performance. New career paths made it less important to please direct superiors in order to move up the functional line.

Moreover, employees often bypassed Hank's managers and inter-acted directly with decision makers inside and outside the company. Some of these so-called subordinates had contact with division exec-utives and senior corporate staff, and sometimes they sat in on high-level strategy meetings to which their managers were not invited.

At first Hank thought his managers' resistance to the new process was just the normal noise associated with any change. Then he began to realize that something more profound was going on. The reorgani-zation was challenging traditional notions about the role and power of managers and shaking traditional hierarchy to its roots. And no one could see what was taking its place.

When George became head of a major corporate department in a large bank holding company, he thought he had arrived. His title and rank were unmistakable, and his department was responsible for de-termining product-line policy for hundreds of bank branches and the virtual clerks—in George's eyes—who managed them. George staffed his department with MBAs and promised them rapid promotion.

Then the sand seemed to shift beneath him. Losing market position for the first time in recent memory, the bank decided to emphasize direct customer service at the branches. The people George considered clerks began to depart from George's standard policies and to tailor their services to local market conditions. In many cases, they actually demanded services and responses from George's staff, and the results of their requests began to figure in performance reviews of George's department. George's people were spending more and more time in the field with branch managers, and the corporate personnel depart-ment was even trying to assign some of George's MBAs to branch and regional posts.

To complicate matters, the bank's strategy included a growing role for technology. George felt that because he had no direct control over the information systems department, he should not be held fully accountable for every facet of product design and implementation. But fully accountable he was. He had to deploy people to learn the new technology and figure out how to work with it. Furthermore, the bank was asking product departments like George's to find ways to link existing products or develop new ones that crossed traditional categories. So George's people were often away on cross-departmental teams just when he wanted them for some internal assignment.

Instead of presiding over a tidy empire the way his predecessor had, George presided over what looked to him like chaos. The bank said senior executives should be "leaders, not managers," but George didn't know what that meant, especially since he seemed to have lost control over his subordinates' assignments, activities, rewards, and careers. He resented his perceived loss of status.

The CEO tried to show him that good results achieved the new way would bring great monetary rewards, thanks to a performance-based bonus program that was gradually replacing more modest yearly raises. But the pressures on George were also greater, unlike anything he'd ever experienced.

For Sally, purchasing manager at an innovative computer company, a new organizational strategy was a gain rather than a loss, although it changed her relationship with the people reporting to her. Less than ten years out of college, she was hired as an analyst—a semiprofessional, semiclerical job—then promoted to a purchasing manager's job in a sleepy staff department. She didn't expect to go much further in what was then a well-established hierarchy. But after a shocking downturn, top management encouraged employees to rethink traditional ways of doing things. Sally's boss, the head of purchasing, suggested that partnerships with key suppliers might improve quality, speed innovation, and reduce costs.

Soon Sally's backwater was at the center of policymaking, and Sally began to help shape strategy. She organized meetings between her company's senior executives and supplier CEOs. She sent her staff to contribute supplier intelligence at company seminars on technical innovation, and she spent more of her own time with product designers and manufacturing planners. She led senior executives on a tour of supplier facilities, traveling with them in the corporate jet.

Because some suppliers were also important customers, Sally's staff began meeting frequently with marketing managers to share information and address joint problems. Sally and her group were now also acting as internal advocates for major suppliers. Furthermore, many of these external companies now contributed performance appraisals of Sally and her team, and their opinions weighed almost as heavily as those of her superiors.

As a result of the company's new direction, Sally felt more personal power and influence, and her ties to peers in other areas and to top management were stronger. But she no longer felt like a manager directing subordinates. Her staff had become a pool of resources deployed by many others besides Sally. She was exhilarated by her personal opportunities but not quite sure the people she managed should have the same freedom to choose their own assignments. After all, wasn't that a manager's prerogative?

Hank's, George's, and Sally's very different stories say much about the changing nature of managerial work. However hard it is for managers at the very top to remake strategy and structure, they themselves will probably retain their identity, status, and control. For the managers below them, structural change is often much harder. As work units become more participative and team oriented, and as professionals and knowledge workers become more prominent, the distinction between manager and nonmanager begins to erode.

To understand what managers must do to achieve results in the postentrepreneurial corporation, we need to look at the changing picture of how such companies operate. The picture has five elements:

1. There are a greater number and variety of channels for taking action and exerting influence.
2. Relationships of influence are shifting from the vertical to the horizontal, from chain of command to peer networks.
3. The distinction between managers and those managed is diminishing, especially in terms of information, control over assignments, and access to external relationships.
4. External relationships are increasingly important as sources of internal power and influence, even of career development.
5. As a result of the first four changes, career development has become less intelligible but also less circumscribed. There are fewer assured routes to success, which produces anxiety. At the same time, career paths are more open to innovation, which produces opportunity.

To help companies implement their competitive organizational strategies, managers must learn new ways to manage, confronting changes in their own bases of power and recognizing the need for new ways to motivate people.

———— THE BASES OF POWER

The changes I've talked about can be scary for people like George and the managers reporting to Hank, who were trained to know their place, to follow orders, to let the company take care of their careers, to do things by the book. The book is gone. In the new corporation, managers have only themselves to count on for success. They must learn to operate without the crutch of hierarchy. Position, title, and authority are no longer adequate tools, not in a world where subordinates are encouraged to think for themselves and where managers have to work synergistically with other departments and even other companies. Success depends increasingly on tapping into sources of good ideas, on figuring out whose collaboration is needed to act on those ideas, on working with both to produce results. In short, the new managerial work implies very different ways of obtaining and using power.

The postentrepreneurial corporation is not only leaner and flatter, it also has many more channels for action. Cross-functional projects, business-unit joint ventures, labor-management forums, innovation funds that spawn activities outside mainstream budgets and reporting lines, strategic partnerships with suppliers or customers—these are all overlays on the traditional organization chart, strategic pathways that ignore the chain of command.

Their existence has several important implications. For one thing, they create more potential centers of power. As the ways to combine resources increase, the ability to command diminishes. Alternative paths of communication, resource access, and execution erode the authority of those in the nominal chain of command. In other words, the opportunity for greater speed and flexibility undermines hierarchy. As more and more strategic action takes place in these channels, the jobs that focus inward on particular departments decline in power.

As a result, the ability of managers to get things done depends more on the number of networks in which they're centrally involved than on their height in a hierarchy. Of course, power in any organization always has a network component, but rank and formal structure used to be more limiting. For example, access to information and the ability to get informal backing were often confined to the few officially sanctioned contact points between departments or between the company and its vendors or customers. Today these official barriers are disappearing, while so-called informal networks grow in importance.

In the emerging organization, managers add value by deal making, by brokering at interfaces, rather than by presiding over their individual empires. It was traditionally the job of top executives or specialists to scan the business environment for new ideas, opportunities, and resources. This kind of environmental scanning is now an important part of a manager's job at every level and in every function. And the environment to be scanned includes various company divisions, many potential outside partners, and large parts of the world. At the same time, people are encouraged to think about what they know that might have value elsewhere. An engineer designing windshield wipers, for example, might discover properties of rubber adhesion to glass that could be useful in other manufacturing areas.

Every manager must think cross-functionally because every department has to play a strategic role, understanding and contributing to other facets of the business. In Hank's company, the technical managers and staff working on design engineering used to concentrate only on their own areas of expertise. Under the new system, they have to keep in mind what manufacturing does and how it does it. They need to visit plants and build relationships so they can ask informed questions.

One multinational corporation, eager to extend the uses of its core product, put its R&D staff and laboratory personnel in direct contact with marketing experts to discuss lines of research. Similarly, the superior economic track record of Raytheon's New Products Center—dozens of new products and patents yielding profits many times their development costs—derives from the connections it builds between its inventors and the engineering and marketing staffs of the business units it serves.

This strategic and collaborative role is particularly important for the managers and professionals on corporate staffs. They need to serve as integrators and facilitators, not as watchdogs and interventionists. They need to sell their services, justify themselves to the business units they serve, literally compete with outside suppliers. General Foods recently put overhead charges for corporate staff services on a pay-as-you-use basis. Formerly, these charges were either assigned uniformly to users and nonusers alike, or the services were mandatory. Product managers sometimes had to work through as many as eight layers of management and corporate staff to get business plans approved. Now these staffs must prove to the satisfaction of their internal customers that their services add value.

By contrast, some banks still have corporate training departments that do very little except get in the way. They do no actual training, for example, yet they still exercise veto power over urgent divisional training decisions and consultant contracts.

As managers and professionals spend more time working across boundaries with peers and partners over whom they have no direct control, their negotiating skills become essential assets. Alliances and partnerships transform impersonal, arm's-length contracts into relationships involving joint planning and joint decision making. Internal competitors and adversaries become allies on whom managers depend for their own success. At the same time, more managers at more levels are active in the kind of external diplomacy that only the CEO or selected staffs used to conduct.

In the collaborative forums that result, managers are more personally exposed. It is trust that makes partnerships work. Since collaborative ventures often bring together groups with different methods, cultures, symbols, even languages, good deal making depends on empathy—the ability to step into other people's shoes and appreciate their goals. This applies not only to intricate global joint ventures but also to the efforts of engineering and manufacturing to work together more effectively. Effective communication in a cooperative effort rests on more than a simple exchange of information; people must be adept at anticipating the responses of other groups. "Before I get too excited about our department's design ideas," an engineering manager told me, "I'm learning to ask myself, 'What's the marketing position on this? What will manufacturing say?' That sometimes forces me to make changes before I even talk to these groups."

An increase in the number of channels for strategic contact within the postentrepreneurial organization means more opportunities for people with ideas or information to trigger action: salespeople encouraging account managers to build strategic partnerships with customers, for example, or technicians searching for ways to tap new-venture funds to develop software. Moreover, top executives who have to spend more time on cross-boundary relationships are forced to delegate more responsibility to lower-level managers. Delegation is one more blow to hierarchy, of course, since subordinates with greater responsibility are bolder about speaking up, challenging authority, and charting their own course.

For example, it is common for new-venture teams to complain publicly about corporate support departments and to reject their use in favor of external service providers, often to the consternation of more orthodox superiors. A more startling example occurred in a health care company where members of a task force charged with finding synergies among three lines of business shocked corporate executives by criticizing upper-management behavior in their report. Service on the task force had created collective awareness of a shared problem and had given people the courage to confront it.

The search for internal synergies, the development of strategic alliances, and the push for new ventures all emphasize the political side of a leader's work. Executives must be able to juggle a set of constituencies rather than control a set of subordinates. They have to bargain, negotiate, and sell instead of making unilateral decisions and issuing commands. The leader's task, as Chester Barnard recognized long ago, is to develop a network of cooperative relationships among all the people, groups, and organizations that have something to contribute to an economic enterprise. Postentrepreneurial strategies magnify the complexity of this task. After leading Teknowledge, a producer of expert systems software, through development alliances with six corporations including General Motors and Procter & Gamble, company chairman Lee Hecht said he felt like the mayor of a small city. "I have a constituency that won't quit. It takes a hell of a lot of balancing." The kind of power achieved through a network of stakeholders is very different from the kind of power managers wield in a traditional bureaucracy. The new way gets more done, but it also takes more time. And it creates an illusion about freedom and security.

The absence of day-to-day constraints, the admonition to assume responsibility, the pretense of equality, the elimination of visible status markers, the prevalence of candid dialogues across hierarchical levels—these can give employees a false sense that all hierarchy is a thing of the past. Yet at the same time, employees still count on hierarchy to shield them when things go wrong. This combination would create the perfect marriage of freedom and support—freedom when people want to take risks, support when the risks do not work out.

In reality, less-benevolent combinations are also possible, combinations not of freedom and support but of insecurity and loss of control. There is often a pretense in postentrepreneurial companies that status differences have nothing to do with power, that the deference paid to top executives derives from their superior qualifications rather than from the power they have over the fates of others. But the people at the top of the organization chart still wield power— and sometimes in ways that managers below them experience as arbitrary. Unprecedented individual freedom also applies to top managers, who are now free to make previously unimaginable deals, order unimaginable cuts, or launch unimaginable takeovers. The reorganizations that companies undertake in their search for new synergies can uncover the potential unpredictability and cap-riciousness of corporate careers. A man whose company was undergoing drastic restructuring told me, "For all of my ownership share and strategic centrality and voice in decisions, I can still be faced with a shift in direction not of my own making. I can still be reorganized into a corner. I can still be relocated into oblivion. I can still be reviewed out of my special-projects budget."

These realities of power, change, and job security are important because they affect the way people view their leaders. When the illusion of simultaneous freedom and protection fades, the result can be a loss of motivation.

—— SOURCES OF MOTIVATION

One of the essential, unchanging tasks of leaders is to motivate and guide performance. But motivational tools are changing fast. More and more businesses are doing away with the old bureaucratic incentives and using entrepreneurial opportunity to attract the best talent. Managers must exercise more leadership even as they watch their bureaucratic power slip away. Lead-ership, in short, is more difficult yet more critical than ever.

Because of the unpredictability of even the most benign restructuring, managers are less able to guarantee a particular job—or any job at all—no matter what a subordinate's performance level. The reduction in hierarchical levels curtails a manager's ability to promise promotion. New compensation systems that make bonuses and raises dependent on objective performance measures and on team appraisals deprive managers of their role as the sole arbiter of higher pay. Cross-functional and cross-company teams can rob managers of their right to direct or even understand the work their so-called subordinates do. In any case, the shift from routine work, which was amenable to oversight, to "knowledge" work, which often is not, erodes a manager's claim to superior expertise. And partnerships and ventures that put lower-level people in direct contact with each other across departmental and company boundaries cut heavily into the managerial monopoly on information. At a consumer pack-aged-goods manufacturer that replaced several levels of hierarchy with teams, plant team members in direct contact with the sales force often had data on product ordering trends before the higher-level brand managers who set prod-uct policy.

As if the loss of carrots and sticks was not enough, many managers can no longer even give their people clear job standards and easily mastered procedural rules. Postentrepreneurial corporations seek problem-solving, initiative-taking employees who will go the unexpected extra mile for the customer. To complicate the situation further still, the complexities of work in the new organization—projects and relationships clamoring for attention in every direction—exacerbate the feeling of overload.

With the old motivational tool kit depleted, leaders need new and more effective incentives to encourage high performance and build commitment. There are five new tools:

Mission Helping people believe in the importance of their work is essential, especially when other forms of certainty and security have disappeared. Good leaders can inspire others with the power and excitement of their vision and give people a sense of purpose and pride in their work. Pride is often a better source of motivation than the traditional corporate career ladder and the promotion-based reward system. Technical professionals, for example, are often motivated most effectively by the desire to see their work contribute to an excellent final product.

Agenda Control As career paths lose their certainty and companies' futures grow less predictable, people can at least be in charge of their own professional lives. More and more professionals are passing up jobs with glamour and prestige in favor of jobs that give them greater control over their own activities and direction. Leaders give their subordinates this opportunity when they give them release time to work on pet projects, when they emphasize results instead of procedures, and when they delegate work and the decisions about how to do it. Choice of their next project is a potent reward for people who perform well.

Share of Value Creation Entrepreneurial incentives that give teams a piece of the action are highly appropriate in collaborative companies. Because extra rewards are based only on measurable results, this approach also conserves resources. Innovative companies are experimenting with incentives like phantom stock for development of new ventures and other strategic achievements, equity participation in project returns, and bonuses pegged to key performance targets. Given the cross-functional nature of many projects today, rewards of this kind must sometimes be systemwide, but individual managers can also ask for a bonus pool for their own areas, contingent, of course, on meeting performance goals. And everyone can share the kinds of rewards that are abundant and free—awards and recognition.

Learning The chance to learn new skills or apply them in new arenas is an important motivator in a turbulent environment because it is oriented toward securing the future. "The learning organization" promises to become a 1990s business buzzword as companies seek to learn more systematically from their experience and to encourage continuous learning for their people. In the world of high technology, where people understand uncertainty, the attractiveness of any company often lies in its capacity to provide learning and experience. By this calculus, access to training, mentors, and challenging projects is more important than pay or benefits. Some prominent companies—General Electric, for example—have always been able to attract top talent, even when they could not promise upward mobility, because people see them as a training ground, a good place to learn, and a valuable addition to a résumé.

Reputation   Reputation is a key resource in professional careers, and the chance to enhance it can be an outstanding motivator. The professional's reliance on reputation stands in marked contrast to the bureaucrat's anonymity. Professionals have to make a name for themselves, while traditional corporate managers and employees stay behind the scenes. Indeed, the accumulation of reputational capital provides not only an immediate ego boost but also the kind of publicity that can bring other rewards, even other job offers. Managers can enhance reputation—and improve motivation—by creating stars, by providing abundant public recognition and visible awards, by crediting the authors of innovation, by publicizing people outside their own departments, and by plugging people into organizational and professional networks.

The new, collaborative organization is predicated on a logic of flexible work assignments, not of fixed job responsibilities. To promote innovation and responsiveness, two of today's competitive imperatives, managers need to see this new organization as a cluster of activity sets, not as a rigid structure. The work of leadership in this new corporation will be to organize both sequential and synchronous projects of varying length and breadth, through which varying combinations of people will move, depending on the tasks, challenges, and opportunities facing the area and its partners at any given moment.

Leaders need to carve out projects with tangible accomplishments, milestones, and completion dates and then delegate responsibility for these projects to the people who flesh them out. Clearly delimited projects can counter overload by focusing effort and can provide short-term motivation when the fate of the long-term mission is uncertain. Project responsibility leads to ownership of the results and sometimes substitutes for other forms of reward. In companies where product development teams define and run their own projects, members commonly say that the greatest compensation they get is seeing the advertisements for their products. "Hey, that's mine! I did that!" one engineer told me he trumpeted to his family the first time he saw a commercial for his group's innovation.

This sense of ownership, along with a definite time frame, can spur higher levels of effort. Whenever people are engaged in creative or problem-solving projects that will have tangible results by deadline dates, they tend to come in at all hours, to think about the project in their spare time, to invest in it vast sums of physical and emotional energy. Knowing that the project will end and that completion will be an occasion for reward and recognition makes it possible to work much harder.

Leaders in the new organization do not lack motivational tools, but the tools are different from those of traditional corporate bureaucrats. The new rewards are based not on status but on contribution, and they consist not of regular promotion and automatic pay raises but of excitement about mission and a share of the glory and the gains of success. The new security is not employment security (a guaranteed job no matter what) but *employability* security—increased value in the internal and external labor markets. Commitment to the organization still matters, but today managers build commitment by offering project opportunities. The new loyalty is not to the boss or to the company but to projects that actualize a mission and offer challenge, growth, and credit for results.

The old bases of managerial authority are eroding, and new tools of leadership are taking their place. Managers whose power derived from hierarchy and who were accustomed to a limited area of personal control are learning to shift their perspectives and widen their horizons. The new managerial work consists of looking outside a defined area of responsibility to sense opportunities and of forming project teams drawn from any relevant sphere to address them. It involves communication and collaboration across functions, across divisions, and across companies whose activities and resources overlap. Thus rank, title, or official charter will be less important factors in success at the new managerial work than having the knowledge, skills, and sensitivity to mobilize people and motivate them to do their best.

DISCUSSION QUESTIONS

1. This reading is about change and transition. The author lists five elements that characterize the changing picture of postentrepreneurial corporations. Discuss the advantages and disadvantages of change and transition in the workplace. How do people respond? How do you respond?
2. Are the changes discussed in this reading limited to business or are they a reflection of changes elsewhere? Explain.
3. The author advocates a new style of managerial behavior. How easy would you find it to manage in this style? Are there obstacles or problems in managing through influence and collaboration?

5   Managing Without Managers

RICARDO SEMLER

Facing catastrophe, the author, head of a manufacturing company in Brazil, had to make drastic changes in the way the company was managed. The company now operates from three key principles: work-force democracy, profit sharing, and free access to information. Democracy lets employees set their own working conditions; profit sharing rewards them for doing well; access to information tells them how they are doing. The company's management philosophy is antihierarchical and highly unorthodox, but profits are handsome. In this reading, the author explains the obstacles that were overcome to implement these values and the positive results that they caused.

In Brazil, where paternalism and the family business fiefdom still flourish, I am president of a manufacturing company that treats its 800 employees like responsible adults. Most of them—including factory workers—set their own working hours. All have access to the company books. The vast majority vote on many important corporate decisions. Everyone gets paid by the month, regardless of job description, and more than 150 of our management people set their own salaries and bonuses.

This may sound like an unconventional way to run a business, but it seems to work. Close to financial disaster in 1980, Semco is now one of Brazil's fastest-growing companies, with a profit margin in 1988 of 10% on sales of $37 million. Our five factories produce a range of sophisticated products, including marine pumps, digital scanners, commercial dishwashers, truck filters, and mixing equipment for everything from bubble gum to rocket fuel. Our customers include Alcoa, Saab, and General Motors. We've built a number of cookie factories for Nabisco, Nestlé, and United Biscuits. Our multinational competitors include AMF, Worthington Industries, Mitsubishi Heavy Industries, and Carrier.

Management associations, labor unions, and the press have repeatedly named us the best company in Brazil to work for. In fact, we no longer advertise jobs. Word of mouth generates up to 300 applications for every available position. The top five managers—we call them counselors—include a former human resources director of Ford Brazil, a 15-year veteran Chrysler executive, and a man who left his job as president of a larger company to come to Semco.

When I joined the company in 1980, 27 years after my father founded it, Semco had about 100 employees, manufactured hydraulic pumps for ships, generated about $4 million in revenues, and teetered on the brink of catastrophe.

All through 1981 and 1982, we ran from bank to bank looking for loans, and we fought persistent, well-founded rumors that the company was in danger of going under. We often stayed through the night reading files and searching the desk drawers of veteran executives for clues about contracts long since privately made and privately forgotten.

Most managers and outside board members agreed on two immediate needs: to professionalize and to diversify. In fact, both of these measures had been discussed for years but had never progressed beyond wishful thinking.

For two years, holding on by our fingertips, we sought licenses to manufacture other companies' products in Brazil. We traveled constantly. I remember one day being in Oslo for breakfast, New York for lunch, Cincinnati for dinner, and San Francisco for the night. The obstacles were great. Our company lacked an international reputation—and so did our country. Brazil's political eccentricities and draconian business regulations scared away many companies.

Still, good luck and a relentless program of beating the corporate bushes on four continents finally paid off. By 1982, we had signed seven license agreements. Our marine division—once the entire company—was now down to 60% of total sales. Moreover, the managers and directors were all professionals with no connection to the family.

With Semco back on its feet, we entered an acquisitions phase that cost millions of dollars in expenditures and millions more in losses over the next two or three years. All this growth was financed by banks at interest rates that were generally 30% above the rate of inflation, which ranged from 40% to 900% annually. There was no long-term money in Brazil at that time, so all those loans had maximum terms of 90 days. We didn't get one cent from the government or from incentive agencies either, and we never paid out a dime in graft or bribes.

How did we do it and survive? Hard work, of course. And good luck—fundamental to all business success. But most important, I think, were the drastic changes we made in our concept of management. Without those changes, not even hard work and good luck could have pulled us through.

Semco has three fundamental values on which we base some 30 management programs. These values—democracy, profit sharing, and information—work in a complicated circle, with each dependent on the other two. If we eliminated one, the others would be meaningless. Our corporate structure, employee freedoms, union relations, factory size limitations—all are products of our commitment to these principles.

It's never easy to transplant management programs from one company to another. In South America, it's axiomatic that our structure and style cannot be duplicated. Semco is either too small, too big, too far away, too young, too old, or too obnoxious.

We may also be too specialized. We do cellular manufacturing of technologically sophisticated products, and we work at the high end on quality and price. So our critics may be right. Perhaps nothing we've done can be a blueprint for anyone else. Still, in an industrial world whose methods show obvious signs of exhaustion, the merit of sharing experience is to encourage experiment and to plant the seeds of conceptual change. So, what the hell.

━━━ PARTICIPATORY HOT AIR

The first of Semco's three values is democracy, or employee involvement. Clearly, workers who control their working conditions are going to be happier than workers who don't. Just as clearly, there is no contest between the company that buys the grudging compliance of its work force and the company that enjoys the enterprising participation of its employees.

But about 90% of the time, participatory management is just hot air. Not that intentions aren't good. It's just that implementing employee involvement is so complex, so difficult, and, not uncommonly, so frustrating that it is easier to talk about than to do.

We found four big obstacles to effective participatory management: size, hierarchy, lack of motivation, and ignorance. In an immense production unit, people feel tiny, nameless, and incapable of exerting influence on the way work is done or on the final profit made. This sense of helplessness is underlined by managers who, jealous of their power and prerogatives, refuse to let subordinates make any decisions for themselves—sometimes even about going to the bathroom. But even if size and hierarchy can be overcome, why should workers *care* about productivity and company profits? Moreover, even if you can get them to care, how can they tell when they're doing the right thing?

As Antony Jay pointed out back in the 1950s in *Corporation Man,* human beings weren't designed to work in big groups. Until recently, our ancestors were hunters and gatherers. For more than five million years, they refined their ability to work in groups of no more than about a dozen people. Then along comes the industrial revolution, and suddenly workers are trying to function efficiently in factories that employ hundreds and even thousands. Organizing those hundreds into teams of about ten members each may help some, but there's still a limit to how many small teams can work well together. At Semco, we've found the most effective production unit consists of about 150 people. The exact number is open to argument, but it's clear that several thousand people in one facility makes individual involvement an illusion.

When we made the decision to keep our units small, we immediately focused on one facility that had more than 300 people. The unit manufactured commercial food-service equipment—slicers, scales, meat grinders, mixers— and used an MRP II system hooked up to an IBM mainframe with dozens of terminals all over the plant. Paperwork often took two days to make its way from one end of the factory to the other. Excess inventories, late delivery, and quality problems were common. We had tried various worker participation programs, quality circles, kanban systems, and motivation schemes, all of which got off to great starts but lost their momentum within months. The whole thing was just too damn big and complex; there were too many managers in too many layers holding too many meetings. So we decided to break up the facility into three separate plants.

To begin with, we kept all three in the same building but separated everything we could—entrances, receiving docks, inventories, telephones, as well as certain auxiliary functions like personnel, management information systems, and internal controls. We also scrapped the mainframe in favor of three independent, PC-based systems.

The first effect of the breakup was a rise in costs due to duplication of effort and a loss in economies of scale. Unfortunately, balance sheets chalk up items like these as liabilities, all with dollar figures attached, and there's nothing at first to list on the asset side but airy stuff like "heightened involvement" and "a sense of belonging." Yet the longer-term results exceeded our expectations.

Within a year, sales doubled; inventories fell from 136 days to 46; we unveiled eight new products that had been stalled in R&D for two years; and overall quality improved to the point that a one-third rejection rate on federally inspected scales dropped to less than 1%. Increased productivity let us reduce the work force by 32% through attrition and retirement incentives.

I don't claim that size reduction alone accomplished all this, just that size reduction is essential for putting employees in touch with one another so they can coordinate their work. The kind of distance we want to eliminate comes from having too many people in one place, but it also comes from having a pyramidal hierarchy.

—— PYRAMIDS AND CIRCLES

The organizational pyramid is the cause of much corporate evil because the tip is too far from the base. Pyramids emphasize power, promote insecurity, distort communications, hobble interaction, and make it very difficult for the people who plan and the people who execute to move in the same direction. So Semco designed an organizational *circle*. Its greatest advantage is to reduce management levels to three—one corporate level and two operating levels at the manufacturing units.

It consists of three concentric circles. One tiny, central circle contains the five people who integrate the company's movements. These are the counselors I mentioned before. I'm one of them, and except for a couple of legal documents that call me president, counselor is the only title I use. A second, larger circle contains the heads of the eight divisions—we call them partners. Finally, a third, huge circle holds all the other employees. Most of them are the people we call associates; they do the research, design, sales, and manufacturing work and have no one reporting to them on a regular basis. But some of them are the permanent and temporary team and task leaders we call coordinators. We have counselors, partners, coordinators, and associates. That's four titles and three management layers.

The linchpins of the system are the coordinators, a group that includes everyone formerly called foreman, supervisor, manager, head, or chief. The only people who report to coordinators are associates. No coordinator reports to another coordinator—that feature of the system is what ensures the reduction in management layers.

Like anyone else, we value leadership, but it's not the only thing we value. In marine pumps, for example, we have an applications engineer who can look at the layout of a ship and then focus on one particular pump and say, "That pump will fail if you take this thing north of the Arctic Circle." He makes a lot more money than the person who manages his unit. We can change the manager, but this guy knows what kind of pump will work in the Arctic, and that's worth more. Associates often make higher salaries than coordinators and partners, and they can increase their status and compensation without entering the "management" line.

Managers and the status and money they enjoy—in a word, hierarchy—are the single biggest obstacle to participatory management. We had to get the managers out of the way of democratic decision making, and our circular system does that pretty well.

But we go further. We don't hire or promote people until they've been interviewed and accepted by all their future subordinates. Twice a year, subordinates evaluate managers. Also twice a year, everyone in the company anonymously fills out a questionnaire about company credibility and top management competence. Among other things, we ask our employees what it would take to make them quit or go on strike.

We insist on making important decisions collegially, and certain decisions are made by a companywide vote. Several years ago, for example, we needed a bigger plant for our marine division, which makes pumps, compressors, and ship propellers. Real estate agents looked for months and found nothing. So we asked the employees themselves to help, and over the first weekend they found three factories for sale, all of them nearby. We closed up shop for a day, piled everyone into buses, and drove out to inspect the three buildings. Then the workers voted—and they chose a plant the counselors didn't really want. It was an interesting situation—one that tested our commitment to participatory management.

The building stands across the street from a Caterpillar plant that's one of the most frequently struck factories in Brazil. With two tough unions of our own, we weren't looking forward to front-row seats for every labor dispute that came along. But we accepted the employees' decision because we believe that in the long run, letting people participate in the decisions that affect their lives will have a positive effect on employee motivation and morale.

We bought the building and moved in. The workers designed the layout for a flexible manufacturing system, and they hired one of Brazil's foremost artists to paint the whole thing, inside and out, including the machinery. That plant really belongs to its employees. I feel like a guest every time I walk in.

I don't mind. The division's productivity, in dollars per year per employee, has jumped from $14,200 in 1984—the year we moved—to $37,500 in 1988, and for 1989 the goal is $50,000. Over the same period, market share went from 54% to 62%.

Employees also outvoted me on the acquisition of a company that I'm still sure we should have bought. But they felt we weren't ready to digest it, and I lost the vote. In a case like that, the credibility of our management system is at stake. Employee involvement must be real, even when it makes management uneasy. Anyway, what is the future of an acquisition if the people who have to operate it don't believe it's workable?

⸺ HIRING ADULTS

We have other ways of combating hierarchy too. Most of our programs are based on the notion of giving employees control over their own lives. In a word, we hire adults, and then we treat them like adults.

Think about that. Outside the factory, workers are men and women who elect governments, serve in the army, lead community projects, raise and educate families, and make decisions every day about the future. Friends solicit their advice. Salespeople court them. Children and grandchildren look up to them for their wisdom and experience. But the moment they walk into the factory, the company transforms them into adolescents. They have to wear badges and name tags, arrive at a certain time, stand in line to punch the clock or eat their lunch, get permission to go to the bathroom, give lengthy explanations every time they're five minutes late, and follow instructions without asking a lot of questions.

One of my first moves when I took control of Semco was to abolish norms, manuals, rules, and regulations. Everyone knows you can't run a large organization without regulations, but everyone also knows that most regulations are poppycock. They rarely solve problems. On the contrary, there is usually some obscure corner of the rule book that justifies the worst silliness people can think up. Common sense is a riskier tactic because it requires personal responsibility.

It's also true that common sense requires just a touch of civil disobedience every time someone calls attention to something that's not working. We had to free the Thoreaus and the Tom Paines in the factory and recognize that civil disobedience was not an early sign of revolution but a clear indication of common sense at work.

So we replaced all the nitpicking regulations with the rule of common sense and put our employees in the demanding position of using their own judgment.

We have no dress code, for example. The idea that personal appearance is important in a job—any job—is baloney. We've all heard that salespeople, receptionists, and service reps are the company's calling cards, but in fact how utterly silly that is. A company that needs business suits to prove its seriousness probably lacks more meaningful proof. And what customer has ever canceled an order because the receptionist was wearing jeans instead of a dress? Women and men look best when they feel good. IBM is not a great company because its salespeople dress to the special standard that Thomas Watson set. It's a great company that also happens to have this quirk.

We also scrapped the complex company rules about travel expenses— what sorts of accommodations people were entitled to, whether we'd pay for a theater ticket, whether a free call home meant five minutes or ten. We used to spend a lot of time discussing stuff like that. Now we base everything on common sense. Some people stay in four-star hotels and some live like spartans. Some people spend $200 a day while others get by on $125. Or so I suppose. No one checks expenses, so there is no way of knowing. The point is, we don't care. If we can't trust people with our money and their judgment, we sure as hell shouldn't be sending them overseas to do business in our name.

We have done away with security searches, storeroom padlocks, and audits of the petty-cash accounts of veteran employees. Not that we wouldn't prosecute a genuinely criminal violation of our trust. We just refuse to humiliate 97% of the work force to get our hands on the occasional thief or two-bit embezzler.

We encourage—we practically insist on—job rotation every two to five years to prevent boredom. We try hard to provide job security, and for people over 50 or who've been with the company for more than three years, dismissal procedures are extra complicated.

On the more experimental side, we have a program for entry-level management trainees called Lost in Space, whereby we hire a couple of people every year who have no job description at all. A "godfather" looks after them, and for one year they can do anything they like, as long as they try at least 12 different areas or units.

By the same logic that governs our other employee programs, we also have eliminated time clocks. People come and go according to their own schedules—even on the factory floor. I admit this idea is hard to swallow; most manufacturers are not ready for factory-floor flextime. But our reasoning was simple.

First, we use cellular manufacturing systems. At our food-processing equipment plant, for example, one cell makes only slicers, another makes scales, another makes mixers, and so forth. Each cell is self-contained, so products— and their problems—are segregated from each other.

Second, we assumed that all our employees were trustworthy adults. We couldn't believe they would come to work day after day and sit on their hands because no one else was there. Pretty soon, we figured, they would start coordinating their work hours with their coworkers.

And that's exactly what happened, only more so. For example, one man wanted to start at 7 A.M., but because the forklift operator didn't come until 8, he couldn't get his parts. So a general discussion arose, and the upshot was that now everyone knows how to operate a forklift. In fact, most people now can do several jobs. The union has never objected because the initiative came from the workers themselves. It was their idea.

Moreover, the people on the factory floor set the schedule, and if they say that this month they will build 48 commercial dishwashers, then we can go play tennis, because 48 is what they'll build.

In one case, one group decided to make 220 meat slicers. By the end of the month, it had finished the slicers as scheduled—except that even after repeated phone calls, the supplier still hadn't produced the motors. So two employees drove over and talked to the supplier and managed to get delivery at the end of that day, the 31st. Then they stayed all night, the whole work force, and finished the lot at 4:45 the next morning.

When we introduced flexible hours, we decided to hold regular follow-up meetings to track problems and decide how to deal with abuses and production interruptions. That was years ago, and we haven't yet held the first meeting.

━━━ HUNTING THE WOOLLY MAMMOTH

What makes our people behave this way? As Antony Jay points out, corporate man is a very recent animal. At Semco, we try to respect the hunter that dominated the first 99.9% of the history of our species. If you had to kill a mammoth or do without supper, there was no time to draw up an organization chart, assign tasks, or delegate authority. Basically, the person who saw the mammoth from farthest away was the Official Sighter, the one who ran fastest was the Head Runner, whoever threw the most accurate spear was the Grand Marksman, and the person all others respected most and listened to was the Chief. That's all there was to it. Distributing little charts to produce an appearance of order would have been a waste of time. It still is.

What I'm saying is, put ten people together, don't appoint a leader, and you can be sure that one will emerge. So will a sighter, a runner, and whatever else the group needs. We form the groups, but they find their own leaders. That's not a lack of structure, that's just a lack of structure imposed from above.

But getting back to that mammoth, why was it that all the members of the group were so eager to do their share of the work—sighting, running, spearing, chiefing—and to stand aside when someone else could do it better? Because they all got to eat the thing once it was killed and cooked. What mattered was results, not status.

Corporate profit is today's mammoth meat. And though there is a widespread view that profit sharing is some kind of socialist infection, it seems to me that few motivational tools are more capitalist. Everyone agrees that profits should belong to those who risk their capital, that entrepreneurial behavior deserves reward, that the creation of wealth should enrich the creator.

Well, depending on how you define capital and risk, all these truisms can apply as much to workers as to shareholders.

Still, many profit-sharing programs are failures, and we think we know why. Profit sharing won't motivate employees if they see it as just another management gimmick, if the company makes it difficult for them to see how their own work is related to profits and to understand how those profits are divided.

In Semco's case, each division has a separate profit-sharing program. Twice a year, we calculate 23% of after-tax profit on each division income statement and give a check to three employees who've been elected by the workers in their division. These three invest the money until the unit can meet and decide—by simple majority vote—what they want to do with it. In most units, that's turned out to be an equal distribution. If a unit has 150 workers, the total is divided by 150 and handed out. It's that simple. The guy who sweeps the floor gets just as much as the division partner.

One division chose to use the money as a fund to lend out for housing construction. It was a pretty close vote, and the workers may change their minds next year. In the meantime, some of them have already received loans and have begun to build themselves houses. In any case, the employees do what they want with the money. The counselors stay out of it.

Semco's experience has convinced me that profit sharing has an excellent chance of working when it crowns a broad program of employee participation, when the profit-sharing criteria are so clear and simple that the least-gifted employee can understand them, and perhaps most important, when employees have monthly access to the company's vital statistics—costs, overhead, sales, payroll, taxes, profits.

——— TRANSPARENCY

Lots of things contribute to a successful profit-sharing program: low employee turnover, competitive pay, absence of paternalism, refusal to give consolation prizes when profits are down, frequent (quarterly or semiannual) profit distribution, and plenty of opportunity for employees to question the management decisions that affect future profits. But nothing matters more than those vital statistics—short, frank, frequent reports on how the company is doing. Complete transparency. No hocus-pocus, no hanky-panky, no simplifications.

On the contrary, all Semco employees attend classes to learn how to read and understand the numbers, and it's one of their unions that teaches the course. Every month, each employee gets a balance sheet, a profit-and-loss analysis, and a cash-flow statement for his or her division. The reports contain about 70 line items (more, incidentally, than we use to run the company, but we don't want anyone to think we're withholding information).

Many of our executives were alarmed by the decision to share monthly financial results with all employees. They were afraid workers would want to know everything, like how much we pay executives. When we held the first large meeting to discuss these financial reports with the factory committees and the leaders of the metalworkers' union, the first question we got was, "How much do division managers make?" We told them. They gasped. Ever since, the factory workers have called them "maharaja."

But so what? If executives are embarrassed by their salaries, that probably means they aren't earning them. Confidential payrolls are for those who cannot look themselves in the mirror and say with conviction, "I live in a capitalist system that remunerates on a geometric scale. I spent years in school, I have years of experience, I am capable and dedicated and intelligent. I deserve what I get."

I believe that the courage to show the real numbers will always have positive consequences over the long term. On the other hand, we can show only the numbers we bother to put together, and there aren't as many as there used to be. In my view, only the big numbers matter. But Semco's accounting people keep telling me that since the only way to get the big numbers is to add up the small ones, producing a budget or report that includes every tiny detail would require no extra effort. This is an expensive fallacy and a difficult one to eradicate.

A few years ago, the U.S. president of Allis-Chalmers paid Semco a visit. At the end of his factory tour, he leafed through our monthly reports and budgets. At that time, we had our numbers ready on the fifth working day of every month in super-organized folders, and were those numbers comprehensive! On page 67, chart 112.6, for example, you could see how much coffee the workers in Light Manufacturing III had consumed the month before. The man said he was surprised to find such efficiency in a Brazilian company. In fact, he was so impressed that he asked his Brazilian subsidiary, an organization many times our size, to install a similar system there.

For months, we strolled around like peacocks, telling anyone who cared to listen that our budget system was state-of-the-art and that the president of a Big American Company had ordered his people to copy it. But soon we began to realize two things. First, our expenses were always too high, and they never came down because the accounting department was full of overpaid clerks who did nothing but compile them. Second, there were so damn many numbers inside the folder that almost none of our managers read them. In fact, we knew less about the company then, with all that information, than we do now without it.

Today we have a simple accounting system providing limited but relevant information that we can grasp and act on quickly. We pared 400 cost centers down to 50. We beheaded hundreds of classifications and dozens of accounting lines. Finally, we can see the company through the haze.

(As for Allis-Chalmers, I don't know whether it ever adopted our old system in all its terrible completeness, but I hope not. A few years later, it began to suffer severe financial difficulties and eventually lost so much market share and money that it was broken up and sold. I'd hate to think it was our fault.)

In preparing budgets, we believe that the flexibility to change the budget continually is much more important than the detailed consistency of the initial numbers. We also believe in the importance of comparing expectations with results. Naturally, we compare monthly reports with the budget. But we go one step further. At month's end, the coordinators in each area make guesses about unit receipts, profit margins, and expenses. When the official numbers come out a few days later, top managers compare them with the guesses to judge how well the coordinators understand their areas.

What matters in budgets as well as in reports is that the numbers be few and important and that people treat them with something approaching passion. The three monthly reports, with their 70 line items, tell us how to run the company, tell our managers how well they know their units, and tell our employees if there's going to be a profit. Everyone works on the basis of the same information, and everyone looks forward to its appearance with what I'd call fervent curiosity.

And that's all there is to it. Participation gives people control of their work, profit sharing gives them a reason to do it better, information tells them what's working and what isn't.

—— LETTING THEM DO WHATEVER THE HELL THEY WANT

So we don't have systems or staff functions or analysts or anything like that. What we have are people who either sell or make, and there's nothing in between. Is there a marketing department? Not on your life. Marketing is everybody's problem. Everybody knows the price of the products. Everybody knows the cost. Everybody has the monthly statement that says exactly what each of them makes, how much bronze is costing us, how much overtime we paid, all of it. And the employees know that 23% of the after-tax profit is theirs.

We are very, very rigorous about the numbers. We want them in on the fourth day of the month so we can get them back out on the fifth. And because we're so strict with the financial controls, we can be extremely lax about everything else. Employees can paint the walls any color they like. They can come to work whenever they decide. They can wear whatever clothing makes them comfortable. They can do whatever the hell they want. It's up to them to see the connection between productivity and profit and to act on it.

—— DISCUSSION QUESTIONS

1. The author acknowledges the importance of leadership, but he also points out the value of specialized knowledge and the higher compensation that those who possess this knowledge receive from their companies. Do you agree with this compensation system? Explain. What improvements would you make?

2. The reading mentions several innovative practices such as renaming job descriptions, subordinates hiring and evaluating managers as well as having an important voice in the company's decisions, and abolishing rules, regulations, norms, and manuals. As the author states, "It's never easy to transplant management programs from one company to another." Would this be true for companies you've worked for in the past? Would this program work better in a manufacturing company than in a services company?

3. This reading addresses many of the tensions that exist between labor and management such as salaries. Do you think these tensions are adequately addressed? Explain. Are there other tensions that the author has neglected to mention?

4. There are various theories of leadership (group and exchange theories, contingency, path-goal leadership, and so on). Which, if any, of these theories apply to Semco's style? Support your answer with examples from the reading.

LEADING AN ORGANIZATION

Managers and Leaders: Are They Different?

6

ABRAHAM ZALEZNIK

Most societies, including business organizations, are caught between two conflicting needs: for managers to maintain day-to-day operations and for leaders to create new approaches and envision new areas to explore. Why is there a conflict? Can't both managers and leaders exist in the same society? Even better, can't one person be both a manager and a leader?

The author of this reading suggests that because leaders and managers are basically different types of people, the conditions favoring the growth of one may thwart the growth of the other. Using a variety of individual examples, the author shows how managers and leaders have different attitudes toward their goals, careers, relations with others, and themselves. Bureaucratic organizations, in which managers flourish, may be inimical to the growth of leaders. Organizations that encourage close mentoring relationships between junior and senior executives are more likely to foster leaders.

What is the ideal way to develop leadership? Every society provides its own answer to this question, and each, in groping for answers, defines its deepest concerns about the purposes, distributions, and uses of power. Business has contributed its answer to the leadership question by evolving a new breed called the manager. Simultaneously, business has established a new power ethic that favors collective over individual leadership, the cult of the group over that of personality. While ensuring the competence, control, and the balance of power among groups with the potential for rivalry, managerial leadership unfortunately does not necessarily ensure imagination, creativity, or ethical behavior in guiding the destinies of corporate enterprises.

Leadership inevitably requires using power to influence the thoughts and actions of other people. Power in the hands of an individual entails human risks: first, the risk of equating power with the ability to get immediate results; second, the risk of ignoring the many different ways people can legitimately accumulate power; and third, the risk of losing self-control in the desire for power. The need to hedge these risks accounts in part for the development of collective leadership and the managerial ethic. Consequently, an inherent conservatism dominates the culture of large organizations. In *The Second American Revolution*, John D. Rockefeller 3rd describes the conservatism of organizations:

> An organization is a system, with a logic of its own, and all the weight of tradition and inertia. The deck is stacked in favor of the tried and proven way of doing things and against the taking of risks and striking out in new directions.[1]

Out of this conservatism and inertia organizations provide succession to power through the development of managers rather than individual leaders. And the irony of the managerial ethic is that it fosters a bureaucratic culture in business, supposedly the last bastion protecting us from the encroachments and controls of bureaucracy in government and education. Perhaps the risks associated with power in the hands of an individual may be necessary ones for business to take if organizations are to break free of their inertia and bureaucratic conservatism.

MANAGER VERSUS LEADER PERSONALITY

Theodore Levitt has described the essential features of a managerial culture with its emphasis on rationality and control:

> Management consists of the rational assessment of a situation and the systematic selection of goals and purposes (what is to be done?); the systematic development of strategies to achieve these goals; the marshalling of the required resources; the rational design, organization, direction, and control of the activities required to attain the selected purposes; and, finally, the motivating and rewarding of people to do the work.[2]

In other words, whether his or her energies are directed toward goals, resources, organization structures, or people, a manager is a problem solver. The manager asks: "What problems have to be solved, and what are the best ways to achieve results so that people will continue to contribute to this organization?" In this conception, leadership is a practical effort to direct affairs; and to fulfill their tasks, managers require that many people operate at different levels of status and responsibility. Our democratic society is, in fact, unique in having solved the problem of providing well-trained managers for business. The same solution stands ready to be applied to government, education, health care, and other institutions. It takes neither genius nor heroism to be a manager, but rather persistence, tough-mindedness, hard work, intelligence, analytical ability and, perhaps most important, tolerance and good will.

---

1. John D. Rockefeller 3rd, *The Second American Revolution* (New York: Harper & Row, 1973), p. 72.
2. Theodore Levitt, "Management and the 'Post-Industrial' Society," *The Public Interest*, (Summer 1976): 73.

Another conception, however, attaches almost mystical beliefs to what leadership is and assumes that only great people are worthy of the drama of power and politics. Here, leadership is a psychodrama in which, as a precondition for control of a political structure, a lonely person must gain control of him- or herself. Such an expectation of leadership contrasts sharply with the mundane, practical, and yet important conception that leadership is really managing work that other people do.

Two questions come to mind. Is this mystique of leadership merely a holdover from our collective childhood of dependency and our longing for good and heroic parents? Or, is there a basic truth lurking behind the need for leaders that no matter how competent managers are, their leadership stagnates because of their limitations in visualizing purposes and generating value in work? Without this imaginative capacity and the ability to communicate, managers, driven by their narrow purposes, perpetuate group conflicts instead of reforming them into broader desires and goals.

If indeed problems demand greatness, then, judging by past performance, the selection and development of leaders leave a great deal to chance. There are no known ways to train "great" leaders. Furthermore, beyond what we leave to chance, there is a deeper issue in the relationship between the need for competent managers and the longing for great leaders.

What it takes to ensure the supply of people who will assume practical responsibility may inhibit the development of great leaders. Conversely, the presence of great leaders may undermine the development of managers who become very anxious in the relative disorder that leaders seem to generate. The antagonism in aim—to have many competent managers as well as great leaders—often remains obscure in stable and well-developed societies. But the antagonism surfaces during periods of stress and change, as it did in the Western countries during both the Great Depression and World War II. The tension also appears in the struggle for power between theorists and professional managers in revolutionary societies.

It is easy enough to dismiss the dilemma I pose—of training managers while we may need new leaders, or leaders at the expense of managers—by saying that the need is for people who can be *both* managers and leaders. The truth of the matter as I see it, however, is that just as a managerial culture is different from the entrepreneurial culture that develops when leaders appear in organizations, managers and leaders are very different kinds of people. They differ in motivation, personal history, and in how they think and act.

A technologically oriented and economically successful society tends to depreciate the need for great leaders. Such societies hold a deep and abiding faith in rational methods of solving problems, including problems of value, economics, and justice. Once rational methods of solving problems are broken down into elements, organized, and taught as skills, then society's faith in technique over personal qualities in leadership remains the guiding conception for a democratic society contemplating its leadership requirements. But there are times when tinkering and trial and error prove inadequate to the emerging problems of selecting goals, allocating resources, and distributing wealth and opportunity. During such times, the democratic society needs to find leaders who use themselves as the instruments of learning and acting, instead of managers who use their accumulation of collective experience to get where they are going.

The most impressive spokesperson, as well as exemplar of the managerial viewpoint, was Alfred P. Sloan, Jr. who, along with Pierre du Pont, designed the modern corporate structure. Reflecting on what makes one management successful while another fails, Sloan suggested that "good management rests on a reconciliation of centralization and decentralization, or 'decentralization with coordinated control.'"[3]

Sloan's conception of management, as well as his practice, developed by trial and error, and by the accumulation of experience. Sloan wrote:

> There is no hard-and-fast rule for sorting out the various responsibilities and the best way to assign them. The balance which is struck . . . varies according to what is being decided, the circumstances of the time, past experience, and the temperaments and skills of the executive involved.[4]

In other words, in much the same way that the inventors of the late nineteenth century tried, failed, and fitted until they hit on a product or method, managers who innovate in developing organizations are "tinkerers." They do not have a grand design or experience the intuitive flash of insight that, borrowing from modern science, we have come to call the "breakthrough."

Managers and leaders differ fundamentally in their world views. The dimensions for assessing these differences include managers' and leaders' orientations toward their goals, their work, their human relations, and their selves.

ATTITUDES TOWARD GOALS

Managers tend to adopt impersonal, if not passive, attitudes toward goals. Managerial goals arise out of necessities rather than desires, and, therefore, are deeply embedded in the history and culture of the organization.

Frederic G. Donner, chairman and chief executive officer of General Motors from 1958 to 1967, expressed this impersonal and passive attitude toward goals in defining GM's position on product development:

---

3. Alfred P. Sloan, Jr., *My Years with General Motors* (New York: Doubleday & Co. 1964), p. 429.
4. Ibid., p. 429.

To meet the challenge of the marketplace, we must recognize changes in customer needs and desires far enough ahead to have the right products in the right places at the right time and in the right quantity.

We must balance trends in preference against the many compromises that are necessary to make a final product that is both reliable and good looking, that performs well and that sells at a competitive price in the necessary volume. We must design, not just the cars we would like to build, but more importantly, the cars that our customers want to buy.[5]

Nowhere in this formulation of how a product comes into being is there a notion that consumer tastes and preferences arise in part as a result of what manufacturers do. In reality, through product design, advertising, and promotion, consumers learn to like what they then say they need. Few would argue that people who enjoy taking snapshots *need* a camera that also develops pictures. But in response to novelty, convenience, a shorter interval between acting (taking the snap) and gaining pleasure (seeing the shot), the Polaroid camera succeeded in the marketplace. But it is inconceivable that Edwin Land responded to impressions of consumer need. Instead, he translated a technology (polarization of light) into a product, which proliferated and stimulated consumers' desires.

The example of Polaroid and Land suggests how leaders think about goals. They are active instead of reactive, shaping ideas instead of responding to them. Leaders adopt a personal and active attitude toward goals. The influence a leader exerts in altering moods, evoking images and expectations, and in establishing specific desires and objectives determines the direction a business takes. The net result of this influence is to change the way people think about what is desirable, possible, and necessary.

CONCEPTIONS OF WORK

What do managers and leaders do? What is the nature of their respective work?

Leaders and managers differ in their conceptions. Managers tend to view work as an enabling process involving some combination of people and ideas interacting to establish strategies and make decisions. Managers help the process along by a range of skills, including calculating the interests in opposition, staging and timing the surfacing of controversial issues, and reducing tensions. In this enabling process, managers appear flexible in the use of tactics. They negotiate and bargain, on the one hand, and use rewards and

---

5. Ibid., p. 440.

punishments, and other forms of coercion, on the other. Machiavelli wrote for managers and not necessarily for leaders.

Alfred Sloan illustrated how this enabling process works in situations of conflict. The time was the early 1920s when the Ford Motor Co. still dominated the automobile industry using, as did General Motors, the conventional water-cooled engine. With the full backing of Pierre du Pont, Charles Kettering dedicated himself to the design of an air-cooled engine, which, if successful, would have been a great technical and market coup for GM. Kettering believed in his product, but the manufacturing division heads at GM remained skeptical and later opposed the new design on two grounds: first, that it was technically unreliable, and second, that the corporation was putting all its eggs in one basket by investing in a new product instead of attending to the current marketing situation.

In the summer of 1923 after a series of false starts and after its decision to recall the copper-cooled Chevrolets from dealers and customers, GM management reorganized and finally scrapped the project. When it dawned on Kettering that the company had rejected the engine, he was deeply discouraged and wrote to Sloan that without the "organized resistance" against the project it would succeed and that unless the project were saved, he would leave the company.

Alfred Sloan was all too aware of the fact that Kettering was unhappy and indeed intended to leave General Motors. Sloan was also aware of the fact that, while the manufacturing divisions strongly opposed the new engine, Pierre du Pont supported Kettering. Furthermore, Sloan had himself gone on record in a letter to Kettering less than two years earlier expressing full confidence in him. The problem Sloan now had was to make his decision stick, keep Kettering in the organization (he was much too valuable to lose), avoid alienating du Pont, and encourage the division heads to move speedily in developing product lines using conventional water-cooled engines.

The actions that Sloan took in the face of this conflict reveal much about how managers work. First, he tried to reassure Kettering by presenting the problem in a very ambiguous fashion, suggesting that he and the executive committee sided with Kettering, but that it would not be practical to force the divisions to do what they were opposed to. He presented the problem as being a question of the people, not the product. Second, he proposed to reorganize around the problem by consolidating all functions in a new division that would be responsible for the design, production, and marketing of the new car. This solution, however, appeared as ambiguous as his efforts to placate and keep Kettering in General Motors. Sloan wrote: "My plan was to create an independent pilot operation under the sole jurisdiction of Mr. Kettering, a kind of copper-cooled-car division. Mr. Kettering would designate his own chief engineer and his production staff to solve the technical problems of manufacture."[6]

While Sloan did not discuss the practical value of this solution, which included saddling an inventor with management responsibility, he in effect used this plan to limit his conflict with Pierre du Pont.

---

6. Ibid., p. 91.

In effect, the managerial solution that Sloan arranged and pressed for adoption limited the options available to others. The structural solution narrowed choices, even limiting emotional reactions to the point where the key people could do nothing but go along, and even allowed Sloan to say in his memorandum to du Pont, "We have discussed the matter with Mr. Kettering at some length this morning and he agrees with us absolutely on every point we made. He appears to receive the suggestion enthusiastically and has every confidence that it can be put across along these lines."[7]

Having placated people who opposed his views by developing a structural solution that appeared to give something but in reality only limited options, Sloan could then authorize the car division's general manager, with whom he basically agreed, to move quickly in designing water-cooled cars for the immediate market demand.

Years later, Sloan wrote, evidently with tongue in cheek, "The copper-cooled car never came up again in a big way. It just died out, I don't know why."[8]

In order to get people to accept solutions to problems, managers need to coordinate and balance continually. Interestingly enough, this managerial work has much in common with what diplomats and mediators do. The manager aims at shifting balances of power toward solutions acceptable as a compromise among conflicting values.

What about leaders, what do they do? Where managers act to limit choices, leaders work in the opposite direction, to develop fresh approaches to long-standing problems and to open issues for new options. Stanley and Inge Hoffmann, the political scientists, liken the leader's work to that of the artist. But unlike most artists, the leader is an integral part of the aesthetic product. One cannot look at a leader's art without looking at the artist. On Charles de Gaulle as a political artist, they wrote: "And each of his major political acts, however tortuous the means or the details, has been whole, indivisible and unmistakably his own, like an artistic act."[9]

The closest one can get to a product apart from the artist is the ideas that occupy, indeed at times obsess, the leader's mental life. To be effective, however, leaders need to project their ideas into images that excite people, and only then develop choices that give the projected images substance. Consequently, leaders create excitement in work.

John F. Kennedy's brief presidency shows both the strengths and weaknesses connected with the excitement leaders generate in their work. In his inaugural address he said, "Let every nation know, whether it wishes us well or ill, that we shall pay any price, bear any burden, meet any hardship, support any friend, oppose any foe, in order to assure the survival and the success of liberty."

---

7. Ibid., p. 91.
8. Ibid., p. 93.
9. Stanley and Inge Hoffmann, "The Will for Grandeur: de Gaulle as Political Artist," *Daedalus* Summer 1968, p. 849.

This much-quoted statement forced people to react beyond immediate concerns and to identify with Kennedy and with important shared ideals. But upon closer scrutiny the statement must be seen as absurd because it promises a position which if in fact adopted, as in the Vietnam War, could produce disastrous results. Yet unless expectations are aroused and mobilized, with all the dangers of frustration inherent in heightened desire, new thinking and new choice can never come to light.

Leaders work from high-risk positions, indeed often are temperamentally disposed to seek out risk and danger, especially where opportunity and reward appear high. From my observations, why one individual seeks risks while another approaches problems conservatively depends more on his or her personality and less on conscious choice. For some, especially those who become managers, the instinct for survival dominates their need for risk, and their ability to tolerate mundane, practical work assists their survival. The same cannot be said for leaders who sometimes react to mundane work as to an affliction.

RELATIONS WITH OTHERS

Managers prefer to work with people; they avoid solitary activity because it makes them anxious. Several years ago, I directed studies on the psychological aspects of career. The need to seek out others with whom to work and collaborate seemed to stand out as important characteristics of managers. When asked, for example, to write imaginative stories in response to a picture showing a single figure (a boy contemplating a violin, or a man silhouetted in a state of reflection), managers populated their stories with people. The following is an example of a manager's imaginative story about the young boy contemplating a violin:

> Mom and Dad insisted that Junior take music lessons so that someday he can become a concert musician. His instrument was ordered and had just arrived. Junior is weighing the alternatives of playing football with the other kids or playing with the squeak box. He can't understand how his parents could think a violin is better than a touchdown.
>
> After four months of practicing the violin, Junior has had more than enough, Daddy is going out of his mind, and Mommy is willing to give in reluctantly to the men's wishes. Football season is now over, but a good third baseman will take the field next spring.[10]

This story illustrates two themes that clarify managerial attitudes toward human relations. The first, as I have suggested, is to seek out activity with other people, that is, the football team, and the second, is to maintain a low level

---

10. Abraham Zaleznik, Gene W. Dalton, and Louis B. Barnes, *Orientation and Conflict in Career* (Boston: Division of Research, Harvard Business School, 1970), p. 316.

of emotional involvement in these relationships. The low emotional involvement appears in the writer's use of conventional metaphors, even clichés, and in the depiction of the ready transformation of potential conflict into harmonious decisions. In this case, Junior, Mommy, and Daddy agree to give up the violin for manly sports.

These two themes may seem paradoxical, but their coexistence supports what a manager does, including reconciling differences, seeking compromises, and establishing a balance of power. A further idea demonstrated by how the manager wrote the story is that managers may lack empathy, or the capacity to sense intuitively the thoughts and feelings of others. To illustrate attempts to be empathic, here is another story written to the same stimulus picture by someone considered by peers to be a leader:

> This little boy has the appearance of being a sincere artist, one who is deeply affected by the violin, and has an intense desire to master the instrument.
>
> He seems to have just completed his normal practice session and appears to be somewhat crestfallen at his inability to produce the sounds which he is sure lie within the violin.
>
> He appears to be in the process of making a vow to himself to expend the necessary time and effort to play this instrument until he satisfies himself that he is able to bring forth the qualities of music which he feels within himself.
>
> With this type of determination and carry through, this boy became one of the great violinists of his day.[11]

Empathy is not simply a matter of paying attention to other people. It is also the capacity to take in emotional signals and to make them mean something in a relationship with an individual. People who describe another person as "deeply affected" with "intense desire," as capable of feeling "crestfallen" and as one who can "vow to himself," would seem to have an inner perceptiveness that they can use in their relationships with others.

Managers relate to people according to the role they play in a sequence of events or in a decision-making *process*, while leaders, who are concerned with ideas, relate in more intuitive and empathetic ways. The manager's orientation to people, as actors in a sequence of events, deflects his or her attention away from the substance of people's concerns and toward their roles in a process. The distinction is simply between a manager's attention to *how* things get done and a leader's to *what* the events and decisions mean to participants.

In recent years, managers have taken over from game theory the notion that decision-making events can be one of two types: the win-lose situation (or zero-sum game) or the win-win situation in which everybody in the action comes out ahead. As part of the process of reconciling differences among people

---

11. Ibid., p. 294.

and maintaining balances of power, managers strive to convert win-lose into win-win situations.

As an illustration, take the decision of how to allocate capital resources among operating divisions in a large, decentralized organization. On the face of it, the dollars available for distribution are limited at any given time. Presumably, therefore, the more one division gets, the less is available for other divisions.

Managers tend to view this situation (as it affects human relations) as a conversion issue: how to make what seems like a win-lose problem into a win-win problem. Several solutions to this situation come to mind. First, the manager focuses others' attention on procedure and not on substance. Here the actors become engrossed in the bigger problem of how to make decisions, not what decisions to make. Once committed to the bigger problem, the actors have to support the outcome since they were involved in formulating decision rules. Because the actors believe in the rules they formulated, they will accept present losses in the expectation that next time they will win.

Second, the manager communicates to the subordinates indirectly, using *signals* instead of *messages*. A signal has a number of possible implicit positions in it while a message clearly states a position. Signals are inconclusive and subject to reinterpretation should people become upset and angry, while messages involve the direct consequence that some people will indeed not like what they hear. The nature of messages heightens emotional response, and as I have indicated, emotionality makes managers anxious. With signals, the question of who wins and who loses often becomes obscured.

Third, the manager plays for time. Managers seem to recognize that with the passage of time and the delay of major decisions, compromises emerge that take the sting out of win-lose situations; and the original "game" will be superseded by additional ones. Therefore, compromises may mean that one wins and loses simultaneously, depending on which of the games one evaluates.

There are undoubtedly many other tactical moves managers use to change human situations from win-lose to win-win. But the point to be made is that such tactics focus on the decision-making process itself and interest managers rather than leaders. The interest in tactics involves costs as well as benefits, including making organizations fatter in bureaucratic and political intrigue and leaner in direct, hard activity and warm human relationships. Consequently, one often hears subordinates characterize managers as inscrutable, detached, and manipulative. These adjectives arise from the subordinates' perception that they are linked together in a process whose purpose, beyond simply making decisions, is to maintain a controlled as well as rational and equitable structure. These adjectives suggest that managers need order in the face of the potential chaos that many fear in human relationships.

In contrast, one often hears leaders referred to in adjectives rich in emotional content. Leaders attract strong feelings of identity and difference, or of love and hate. Human relations in leader-dominated structures often appear turbulent, intense, and at times even disorganized. Such an atmosphere intensifies individual motivation and often produces unanticipated outcomes. Does this intense motivation lead to innovation and high performance, or does it represent wasted energy?

SENSES OF SELF

In *The Varieties of Religious Experience*, William James describes two basic personality types, "once-born" and "twice-born."[12] People of the former personality type are those for whom adjustments to life have been straightforward and whose lives have been more or less a peaceful flow from the moment of their births. The twice-borns, on the other hand, have not had an easy time of it. Their lives are marked by a continual struggle to attain some sense of order. Unlike the once-borns they cannot take things for granted. According to James, these personalities have equally different world views. For a once-born personality, the sense of self, as a guide to conduct and attitude, derives from a feeling of being at home and in harmony with one's environment. For a twice-born, the sense of self derives from a feeling of profound separateness.

A sense of belonging or of being separate has a practical significance for the kinds of investments managers and leaders make in their careers. Managers see themselves as conservators and regulators of an existing order of affairs with which they personally identify and from which they gain rewards. Perpetuating and strengthening existing institutions enhances a manager's sense of self-worth: he or she is performing in a role that harmonizes with the ideals of duty and responsibility. William James had this harmony in mind—this sense of self as flowing easily to and from the outer world—in defining a once-born personality. If one feels oneself as a member of institutions, contributing to their well-being, then one fulfills a mission in life and feels rewarded for having measured up to ideals. This reward transcends material gains and answers the more fundamental desire for personal integrity which is achieved by identifying with existing institutions.

Leaders tend to be twice-born personalities, people who feel separate from their environment, including other people. They may work in organizations, but they never belong to them. Their sense of who they are does not depend upon memberships, work roles, or other social indicators of identity.

---

12. William James, *The Varieties of Religious Experience* (New York: Mentor Books, 1958).

What seems to follow from this idea about separateness is some theoretical basis for explaining why certain individuals search out opportunities for change. The methods to bring about change may be technological, political, or ideological, but the object is the same: to profoundly alter human, economic, and political relationships.

Sociologists refer to the preparation individuals undergo to perform in roles as the socialization process. Where individuals experience themselves as an integral part of the social structure (their self-esteem gains strength through participation and conformity), social standards exert powerful effects in maintaining the individual's personal sense of continuity, even beyond the early years in the family. The line of development from the family to schools, then to career is cumulative and reinforcing. When the line of development is not reinforcing because of significant disruptions in relationships or other problems experienced in the family or other social institutions, the individual turns inward and struggles to establish self-esteem, identity, and order. Here the psychological dynamics center on the experience with loss and the efforts at recovery.

In considering the development of leadership, we have to examine two different courses of life history: (1) development through socialization, which prepares the individual to guide institutions and to maintain the existing balance of social relations; and (2) development through personal mastery, which impels an individual to struggle for psychological and social change. Society produces its managerial talent through the first line of development, while through the second leaders emerge.

——— DEVELOPMENT OF LEADERSHIP

The development of every person begins in the family. Each person experiences the traumas associated with separating from his or her parents, as well as the pain that follows such frustration. In the same vein, all individuals face the difficulties of achieving self-regulation and self-control. But for some, perhaps a majority, the fortunes of childhood provide adequate gratifications and sufficient opportunities to find substitutes for rewards no longer available. Such individuals, the "once-borns," make moderate identifications with parents and find a harmony between what they expect and what they are able to realize from life.

But suppose the pains of separation are amplified by a combination of parental demands and the individual's needs to the degree that a sense of isolation, of being special, and of wariness disrupts the bonds that attach children to parents and other authority figures? Under such conditions, and given a special aptitude, the origins of which remain mysterious, the person becomes deeply involved in his or her inner world at the expense of interest in the outer world. For such a person, self-esteem no longer depends solely upon positive attachments and real rewards. A form of self-reliance takes hold along with expectations of performance and achievement, and perhaps even the desire to do great works.

Such self-perceptions can come to nothing if the individual's talents are negligible. Even with strong talents, there are no guarantees that achievement will follow, let alone that the end result will be for good rather than evil. Other factors enter into development. For one thing, leaders are like artists and other gifted people who often struggle with neuroses; their ability to function varies considerably even over the short run, and some potential leaders may lose the struggle altogether. Also, beyond early childhood, the patterns of development that affect managers and leaders involve the selective influence of particular people. Just as they appear flexible and evenly distributed in the types of talents available for development, managers form moderate and widely distributed attachments. Leaders, on the other hand, establish, and also break off, intensive one-to-one relationships.

It is a common observation that people with great talents are often only indifferent students. No one, for example, could have predicted Einstein's great achievements on the basis of his mediocre record in school. The reason for mediocrity is obviously not the absence of ability. It may result, instead, from self-absorption and the inability to pay attention to the ordinary tasks at hand. The only sure way an individual can interrupt reverie-like preoccupation and self-absorption is to form a deep attachment to a great teacher or other benevolent person who understands and has the ability to communicate with the gifted individual.

Whether gifted individuals find what they need in one-to-one relationships depends on the availability of sensitive and intuitive mentors who have a vocation in cultivating talent. Fortunately, when the generations do meet and the self-selections occur, we learn more about how to develop leaders and how talented people of different generations influence each other.

While apparently destined for a mediocre career, people who form important one-to-one relationships are able to accelerate and intensify their development through an apprenticeship. The background for such apprenticeships, or the psychological readiness of an individual to benefit from an intensive relationship, depends upon some experience in life that forces the individual to turn inward. A case example will make this point clearer. This example comes from the life of Dwight David Eisenhower, and illustrates the transformation of a career from competent to outstanding.[13]

Dwight Eisenhower's early career in the Army foreshadowed very little about his future development. During World War I, while some of his West

---

13. This example is included in Abraham Zaleznik and Manfred F.R. Kets de Vries, *Power and the Corporate Mind* (Boston: Houghton Mifflin, 1975).

Point classmates were already experiencing the war firsthand in France, Eisenhower felt "embedded in the monotony and unsought safety of the Zone of the Interior . . . that was intolerable punishment."[14]

Shortly after World War I, Eisenhower, then a young officer somewhat pessimistic about his career chances, asked for a transfer to Panama to work under General Fox Connor, a senior officer whom Eisenhower admired. The army turned down Eisenhower's request. This setback was very much on Eisenhower's mind when Ikey, his first-born son, succumbed to influenza. By some sense of responsibility for its own, the army transferred Eisenhower to Panama, where he took up his duties under General Connor with the shadow of his lost son very much upon him.

In a relationship with the kind of father he would have wanted to be, Eisenhower reverted to being the son he lost. In this highly charged situation, Eisenhower began to learn from his mentor. General Connor offered, and Eisenhower gladly took, a magnificent tutorial on the military. The effects of this relationship on Eisenhower cannot be measured quantitatively, but, in Eisenhower's own reflections and the unfolding of his career, one cannot overestimate its significance in the reintegration of a person shattered by grief.

As Eisenhower wrote later about Connor, "Life with General Connor was a sort of graduate school in military affairs and the humanities, leavened by a man who was experienced in his knowledge of men and their conduct. I can never adequately express my gratitude to this one gentleman. . . . In a lifetime of association with great and good men, he is the one more or less invisible figure to whom I owe an incalculable debt."[15]

Some time after his tour of duty with General Connor, Eisenhower's breakthrough occurred. He received orders to attend the Command and General Staff School at Fort Leavenworth, one of the most competitive schools in the army. It was a coveted appointment, and Eisenhower took advantage of the opportunity. Unlike his performance in high school and West Point, his work at the Command School was excellent; he was graduated first in his class.

Psychological biographies of gifted people repeatedly demonstrate the important part a mentor plays in developing an individual. Andrew Carnegie owed much to his senior, Thomas A. Scott. As head of the Western Division of the Pennsylvania Railroad, Scott recognized talent and the desire to learn in the young telegrapher assigned to him. By giving Carnegie increasing responsibility and by providing him with the opportunity to learn through close personal observation, Scott added to Carnegie's self-confidence and sense of achievement. Because of his own personal strength and achievement, Scott did not fear Carnegie's aggressiveness. Rather, he gave it full play in encouraging Carnegie's initiative.

---

14. Dwight D. Eisenhower, *At Ease: Stories I Tell to Friends* (New York: Doubleday, 1967), p. 136.

15. Ibid., p. 187.

Mentors take risks with people. They bet initially on talent they perceive in younger people. Mentors also risk emotional involvement in working closely with their juniors. The risks do not always pay off, but the willingness to take them appears crucial in developing leaders.

——— CAN ORGANIZATIONS DEVELOP LEADERS?

The examples I have given of how leaders develop suggest the importance of personal influence and the one-to-one relationship. For organizations to encourage consciously the development of leaders as compared with managers would mean developing one-to-one relationships between junior and senior executives and, more important, fostering a culture of individualism and possibly elitism. The elitism arises out of the desire to identify talent and other qualities suggestive of the ability to lead and not simply to manage.

A myth about how people learn and develop that seems to have taken hold in the American culture also dominates thinking in business. The myth is that people learn best from their peers. Supposedly, the threat of evaluation and even humiliation recedes in peer relations because of the tendency for mutual identification and the social restraints on authoritarian behavior among equals. Peer training in organizations occurs in various forms. The use, for example, of task forces made up of peers from several interested occupational groups (sales, production, research, and finance) supposedly removes the restraints of authority on the individual's willingness to assert and exchange ideas. As a result, so the theory goes, people interact more freely, listen more objectively to criticism and other points of view and, finally, learn from this healthy interchange.

Another application of peer training exists in some large corporations, such as Philips, N.V. in Holland, where organization structure is built on the principle of joint responsibility of two peers, one representing the commercial end of the business and the other the technical. Formally, both hold equal responsibility for geographic operations or product groups, as the case may be. As a practical matter, it may turn out that one or the other of the peers dominates the management. Nevertheless, the main interaction is between two or more equals.

The principal question I would raise about such arrangements is whether they perpetuate the managerial orientation, and preclude the formation of one-to-one relationships between senior people and potential leaders.

Aware of the possible stifling effects of peer relationships on aggressiveness and individual initiative, another company, much smaller than Philips, utilizes joint responsibility of peers for operating units, with one important difference. The chief executive of this company encourages competition and rivalry among peers, ultimately appointing the one who comes out on top for increased responsibility. These hybrid arrangements produce some unintended consequences that can be disastrous. There is no easy way to limit rivalry.

Instead, it permeates all levels of the operation and opens the way for the formation of cliques in an atmosphere of intrigue.

A large, integrated oil company has accepted the importance of developing leaders through the direct influence of senior on junior executives. One chairman and chief executive officer regularly selected one talented university graduate whom he appointed his special assistant, and with whom he would work closely for a year. At the end of the year, the junior executive would become available for assignment to one of the operating divisions, there assigned to a responsible post rather than a training position. The mentor relationship had acquainted the junior executive firsthand with the use of power, and with the important antidotes to the power disease called *hubris*—performance and integrity.

Working in one-to-one relationships, where there is a formal and recognized difference in the power of the actors, takes a great deal of tolerance for emotional interchange. This interchange, inevitable in close working arrangements, probably accounts for the reluctance of many executives to become involved in such relationships. I wonder whether a greater capacity on the part of senior officers to tolerate competitive impulses and challenging behavior of their subordinates might not be healthy for corporations. At least a greater tolerance for interchange would not favor the managerial team player at the expense of the individual who might become a leader.

I am constantly surprised at the frequency with which chief executives feel threatened by open challenges to their ideas, as though the source of their authority, rather than their specific ideas, were at issue. In one case a chief executive officer, who was troubled by the aggressiveness and sometimes outright rudeness of one of his talented vice presidents, used various indirect methods such as group meetings and hints from outside directors to avoid dealing with his subordinate. I advised the executive to deal head-on with what irritated him. I suggested that by direct, face-to-face confrontation, both he and his subordinate would learn to validate the distinction between the authority to be preserved and the issues to be debated.

To confront is also to tolerate aggressive interchange, and has the net effect of stripping away the veils of ambiguity and signaling so characteristic of managerial cultures, as well as encouraging the emotional relationship leaders need if they are to survive.

──── DISCUSSION QUESTIONS

1. Does the author favor either managers or leaders?
2. Does Zaleznik distinguish too sharply between managers and leaders? Is his description of them realistic?
3. Can managers benefit from mentoring relationships? Can they mentor leaders?
4. Are both managers and leaders essential to an organization? Do their roles ever overlap?

7   What Leaders Really Do

JOHN P. KOTTER

Good leadership, asserts the author, is not an accident—it is a talent that can be developed and refined. In this reading, he delineates the differences between management and leadership, explaining the strengths and weaknesses of each and providing examples of leadership tasks such as setting direction and motivating people. The reading closes with suggestions on how to create a corporate culture in which leadership thrives.

Leadership is different from management, but not for the reasons most people think. Leadership isn't mystical and mysterious. It has nothing to do with having charisma or other exotic personality traits. It is not the province of a chosen few. Nor is leadership necessarily better than management or a replacement for it.

Rather, leadership and management are two distinctive and complementary systems of action. Each has its own function and characteristic activities. Both are necessary for success in an increasingly complex and volatile business environment.

Most U.S. corporations today are overmanaged and underled. They need to develop their capacity to exercise leadership. Successful corporations don't wait for leaders to come along. They actively seek out people with leadership potential and expose them to career experiences designed to develop that potential. Indeed, with careful selection, nurturing, and encouragement, dozens of people can play important leadership roles in a business organization.

But while improving their ability to lead, companies should remember that strong leadership with weak management is no better, and is sometimes actually worse, than the reverse. The real challenge is to combine strong leadership and strong management and use each to balance the other.

Of course, not everyone can be good at both leading and managing. Some people have the capacity to become excellent managers but not strong leaders. Others have great leadership potential but, for a variety of reasons, have great difficulty becoming strong managers. Smart companies value both kinds of people and work hard to make them a part of the team.

But when it comes to preparing people for executive jobs, such companies rightly ignore the recent literature that says people cannot manage *and* lead. They try to develop leader-managers. Once companies understand the fundamental difference between leadership and management, they can begin to groom their top people to provide both.

——— THE DIFFERENCE BETWEEN MANAGEMENT AND LEADERSHIP

Management is about coping with complexity. Its practices and procedures are largely a response to one of the most significant developments of the twentieth century: the emergence of large organizations. Without good management, complex enterprises tend to become chaotic in ways that threaten their very existence. Good management brings a degree of order and consistency to key dimensions such as the quality and profitability of products.

Leadership, by contrast, is about coping with change. Part of the reason it has become so important in recent years is that the business world has become more competitive and more volatile. Faster technological change, greater international competition, the deregulation of markets, overcapacity in capital-intensive industries, an unstable oil cartel, raiders with junk bonds, and the changing demographics of the work force are among the many factors that have contributed to this shift. The net result is that doing what was done yesterday, or doing it 5% better, is no longer a formula for success. Major changes are more and more necessary to survive and compete effectively in this new environment. More change always demands more leadership.

Consider a simple military analogy: a peacetime army usually can survive with good administration and management up and down the hierarchy, coupled with good leadership concentrated at the very top. A wartime army, however, needs competent leadership at all levels. No one yet has figured out how to manage people effectively into battle; they must be led.

These different functions—coping with complexity and coping with change—shape the characteristic activities of management and leadership. Each system of action involves deciding what needs to be done, creating networks of people and relationships that can accomplish an agenda, and then trying to ensure that those people actually do the job. But each accomplishes these three tasks in different ways.

Companies manage complexity first by *planning and budgeting*—setting targets or goals for the future (typically for the next month or year), establishing detailed steps for achieving those targets, and then allocating resources to accomplish those plans. By contrast, leading an organization to constructive change begins by *setting a direction*—developing a vision of the future (often the distant future) along with strategies for producing the changes needed to achieve that vision.

Management develops the capacity to achieve its plan by *organizing and staffing*—creating an organizational structure and set of jobs for accomplishing plan requirements, staffing the jobs with qualified individuals, communicating the plan to those people, delegating responsibility for carrying out the plan, and devising systems to monitor implementation. The equivalent leadership activity, however, is *aligning people.* This means communicating the new direction to those who can create coalitions that understand the vision and are committed to its achievement.

Finally, management ensures plan accomplishment by *controlling and problem solving*—formally and informally comparing results to the plan in some detail by means of reports, meetings, and other tools; identifying deviations; and then planning and organizing to solve the problems. But for leadership, achieving a vision requires *motivating and inspiring*—keeping people moving in the right direction, despite major obstacles to change, by appealing to basic but often untapped human needs, values, and emotions.

A closer examination of each of these activities will help clarify the skills leaders need.

─── SETTING A DIRECTION VERSUS PLANNING AND BUDGETING

Since the function of leadership is to produce change, setting the direction of that change is fundamental to leadership.

Setting direction is never the same as planning or even long-term planning, although people often confuse the two. Planning is a management process, deductive in nature and designed to produce orderly results, not change. Setting a direction is more inductive. Leaders gather a broad range of data and look for patterns, relationships, and linkages that help explain things. What's more, the direction-setting aspect of leadership does not produce plans; it creates vision and strategies. These describe a business, technology, or corporate culture in terms of what it should become over the long term and articulate a feasible way of achieving this goal.

Most discussions of vision have a tendency to degenerate into the mystical. The implication is that a vision is something mysterious that mere mortals, even talented ones, could never hope to have. But developing good business direction isn't magic. It is a tough, sometimes exhausting process of gathering and analyzing information. People who articulate such visions aren't magicians but broad-based strategic thinkers who are willing to take risks.

Nor do visions and strategies have to be brilliantly innovative; in fact, some of the best are not. Effective business visions regularly have an almost mundane quality, usually consisting of ideas that are already well known. The particular combination or patterning of the ideas may be new, but sometimes even that is not the case.

For example, when CEO Jan Carlzon articulated his vision to make Scandinavian Airline Systems (SAS) the best airline in the world for the frequent business traveler, he was not saying anything that everyone in the airline industry didn't already know. Business travelers fly more consistently than other market segments and are generally willing to pay higher fares. Thus focusing on business customers offers an airline the possibility of high margins, steady business, and considerable growth. But in an industry known more for bureaucracy than vision, no company had ever put these simple ideas together and dedicated itself to implementing them. SAS did, and it worked.

What's crucial about a vision is not its originality but how well it serves the interests of important constituencies—customers, stockholders, employees—and how easily it can be translated into a realistic competitive strategy. Bad visions tend to ignore the legitimate needs and rights of important constituencies—favoring, say, employees over customers or stockholders. Or they are strategically unsound. When a company that has never been better than a weak competitor in an industry suddenly starts talking about becoming number one, that is a pipe dream, not a vision.

One of the most frequent mistakes that overmanaged and underled corporations make is to embrace long-term planning as a panacea for their lack of direction and inability to adapt to an increasingly competitive and dynamic business environment. Such an approach misinterprets the nature of direction setting and can never work.

Long-term planning is always time-consuming. Whenever something unexpected happens, plans have to be redone. In a dynamic business environment, the unexpected often becomes the norm, and long-term planning can become an extraordinarily burdensome activity. This is why most successful corporations limit the time frame of their planning activities. Indeed, some even consider long-term planning a contradiction in terms.

In a company without direction, even short-term planning can become a black hole capable of absorbing an infinite amount of time and energy. With no vision and strategy to provide constraints around the planning process or to guide it, every eventuality deserves a plan. Under these circumstances, contingency planning can go on forever, draining time and attention from far more essential activities, yet without ever providing the clear sense of direction that a company desperately needs. After a while, managers inevitably become cynical about all this, and the planning process can degenerate into a highly politicized game.

Planning works best not as a substitute for direction setting but as a complement to it. A competent planning process serves as a useful reality check on direction-setting activities. Likewise, a competent direction-setting process provides a focus in which planning then can be realistically carried out. It helps clarify what kind of planning is essential and what kind is irrelevant (see *Exhibit 1*).

—— ALIGNING PEOPLE VERSUS ORGANIZING AND STAFFING

A central feature of modern organizations is interdependence, where no one has complete autonomy, where most employees are tied to many others by their work, technology, management systems, and hierarchy. These linkages

EXHIBIT 1
Setting Direction: Lou Gerstner at American Express

When Lou Gerstner became president of the Travel Related Services (TRS) arm at American Express in 1979, the unit was facing one of its biggest challenges in AmEx's 130-year history. Hundreds of banks were offering or planning to introduce credit cards through Visa and MasterCard that would compete with the American Express card. And more than two dozen financial service firms were coming into the traveler's checks business. In a mature marketplace, this increase in competition usually reduces margins and prohibits growth.

But that was not how Gerstner saw the business. Before joining American Express, he had spent five years as a consultant to TRS, analyzing the money-losing travel division and the increasingly competitive card operation. Gerstner and his team asked fundamental questions about the economics, market, and competition and developed a deep understanding of the business. In the process, he began to craft a vision of TRS that looked nothing like a 130-year-old company in a mature industry.

Gerstner thought TRS had the potential to become a dynamic and growing enterprise, despite the onslaught of Visa and MasterCard competition from thousands of banks. The key was to focus on the global marketplace and, specifically, on the relatively affluent customer American Express had been traditionally serving with top-of-the-line products. By further segmenting this market, aggressively developing a broad range of new products and services, and investing to increase productivity and to lower costs, TRS could provide the best service possible to customers who had enough discretionary income to buy many more services from TRS than they had in the past.

Within a week of his appointment, Gerstner brought together the people running the card organization and questioned all the principles by which they conducted their business. In particular, he challenged two widely shared beliefs—that the division should have only one product, the green card, and that this product was limited in potential for growth and innovation.

---

present a special challenge when organizations attempt to change. Unless many individuals line up and move together in the same direction, people will tend to fall all over one another. To executives who are overeducated in management and undereducated in leadership, the idea of getting people moving in the same direction appears to be an organizational problem. What executives need to do, however, is not organize people but align them.

Managers organize to create human systems that can implement plans as precisely and efficiently as possible. Typically, this requires a number of potentially complex decisions. A company must choose a structure of jobs and reporting relationships, staff it with individuals suited to the jobs, provide training for those who need it, communicate plans to the work force, and decide how much authority to delegate and to whom. Economic incentives also need to be constructed to accomplish the plan, as well as systems to monitor its implementation. These organizational judgments are much like architectural decisions. It's a question of fit within a particular context.

EXHIBIT 1
Setting Direction: Lou Gerstner at American Express (Continued)

Gerstner also moved quickly to develop a more entrepreneurial culture, to hire and train people who would thrive in it, and to clearly communicate to them the overall direction. He and other top managers rewarded intelligent risk taking. To make entrepreneurship easier, they discouraged unnecessary bureaucracy. They also upgraded hiring standards and created the TRS Graduate Management Program, which offered high-potential young people special training, an enriched set of experiences, and an unusual degree of exposure to people in top management. To encourage risk taking among all TRS employees, Gerstner also established something called the Great Performers program to recognize and reward truly exceptional customer service, a central tenet in the organization's vision.

These initiatives quickly led to new markets, products, and services. TRS expanded its overseas presence dramatically. By 1988, AmEx cards were issued in 29 currencies (as opposed to only 11 a decade earlier). The unit also focused aggressively on two market segments that had historically received little attention: college students and women. In 1981, TRS combined its card and travel-service capabilities to offer corporate clients a unified system to monitor and control travel expenses. And by 1988, AmEx had grown to become the fifth-largest direct-mail merchant in the United States.

Other new products and services included 90-day insurance on all purchases made with the AmEx card, a Platinum American Express card, and a revolving credit card known as Optima. In 1988, the company also switched to image-processing technology for billing, producing a more convenient monthly statement for customers and reducing billing costs by 25%.

As a result of these innovations, TRS's net income increased a phenomenal 500% between 1978 and 1987—a compounded annual rate of about 18%. The business outperformed many so-called high-tech/high-growth companies. With a 1988 return on equity of 28%, it also outperformed most low-growth but high-profit businesses.

Aligning is different. It is more of a communications challenge than a design problem. First, aligning invariably involves talking to many more individuals than organizing does. The target population can involve not only a manager's subordinates but also bosses, peers, staff in other parts of the organization, as well as suppliers, governmental officials, or even customers. Anyone who can help implement the vision and strategies or who can block implementation is relevant.

Trying to get people to comprehend a vision of an alternative future is also a communications challenge of a completely different magnitude from organizing them to fulfill a short-term plan. It's much like the difference between a football quarterback attempting to describe to his team the next two or three plays versus his trying to explain to them a totally new approach to the game to be used in the second half of the season.

Whether delivered with many words or a few carefully chosen symbols, such messages are not necessarily accepted just because they are understood.

EXHIBIT 2
Aligning People: Chuck Trowbridge and Bob Crandall at Eastman Kodak

Eastman Kodak entered the copy business in the early 1970s, concentrating on technically sophisticated machines that sold, on average, for about $60,000 each. Over the next decade, this business grew to nearly $1 billion in revenues. But costs were high, profits were hard to find, and problems were nearly everywhere. In 1984, Kodak had to write off $40 million in inventory.

Most people at the company knew there were problems, but they couldn't agree on how to solve them. So, in his first two months as general manager of the new copy products group, established in 1984, Chuck Trowbridge met with nearly every key person inside his group, as well as with people elsewhere at Kodak who could be important to the copier business. An especially crucial area was the engineering and manufacturing organization, headed by Bob Crandall.

Trowbridge and Crandall's vision for engineering and manufacturing was simple: to become a world-class manufacturing operation and to create a less bureaucratic and more decentralized organization. Still, this message was difficult to convey because it was such a radical departure from previous communications, not only in the copy products group but throughout most of Kodak. So Crandall set up dozens of vehicles to emphasize the new direction and align people to it: weekly meetings with his own 12 direct reports; monthly Copy Product Forums in which a different employee from each of his departments would meet with him as a group; quarterly meetings with all 100 of his supervisors to discuss recent improvements and new projects to achieve still better results; and quarterly State of the Department meetings, where his managers met with everybody in their own departments.

Once a month, Crandall and all those who reported to him would also meet with 80 to 100 people from some area of his organization to discuss anything they

Another big challenge in leadership efforts is credibility—getting people to believe the message. Many things contribute to credibility: the track record of the person delivering the message, the content of the message itself, the communicator's reputation for integrity and trustworthiness, and the consistency between words and deeds.

Finally, aligning leads to empowerment in a way that organizing rarely does. One of the reasons some organizations have difficulty adjusting to rapid changes in markets or technology is that so many people in those companies feel relatively powerless. They have learned from experience that even if they correctly perceive important external changes and then initiate appropriate actions, they are vulnerable to someone higher up who does not like what they have done. Reprimands can take many different forms: "That's against policy" or "We can't afford it" or "Shut up and do as you're told."

Alignment helps overcome this problem by empowering people in at least two ways. First, when a clear sense of direction has been communicated throughout an organization, lower-level employees can initiate actions without the same degree of vulnerability. As long as their behavior is consistent with

EXHIBIT 2
Aligning People: Chuck Trowbridge and Bob Crandall at Eastman Kodak (Continued)

wanted. To align his biggest supplier—the Kodak Apparatus Division, which supplied one-third of the parts used in design and manufacturing—he and his managers met with the top management of that group over lunch every Thursday. More recently, he has created a format called "business meetings," where his managers meet with 12 to 20 people on a specific topic, such as inventory or master scheduling. The goal is to get all of his 1,500 employees in at least one of these focused business meetings each year.

Trowbridge and Crandall also enlisted written communication in their cause. A four- to eight-page *Copy Products Journal* was sent to employees once a month. A program called Dialog Letters gave employees the opportunity to anonymously ask questions of Crandall and his top managers and be guaranteed a reply. But the most visible, and powerful, form of written communication was the chart. In a main hallway near the cafeteria, huge charts vividly reported the quality, cost,

and delivery results for each product, measured against difficult targets. A hundred smaller versions of these charts were scattered throughout the manufacturing area, reporting quality levels and costs for specific work groups.

Results of this intensive alignment process began to appear within six months and still more after a year. These successes made the message more credible and helped get more people on board. Between 1984 and 1988, quality on one of the main product lines increased nearly a hundredfold. Defects per unit went from 30 to 0.3. Over a three-year period, costs on another product line went down nearly 24%. Deliveries on schedule increased from 82% in 1985 to 95% in 1987. Inventory levels dropped by more than 50% between 1984 and 1988, even though the volume of products was increasing. And productivity, measured in units per manufacturing employee, more than doubled between 1985 and 1988.

---

the vision, superiors will have more difficulty reprimanding them. Second, because everyone is aiming at the same target, the probability is less that one person's initiative will be stalled when it comes into conflict with someone else's (see *Exhibit 2*).

——— MOTIVATING PEOPLE VERSUS CONTROLLING AND PROBLEM SOLVING

Since change is the function of leadership, being able to generate highly energized behavior is important for coping with the inevitable barriers to change. Just as direction setting identifies an appropriate path for movement and just as effective alignment gets people moving down that path, successful motivation ensures that they will have the energy to overcome obstacles.

According to the logic of management, control mechanisms compare system behavior with the plan and take action when a deviation is detected. In a well-managed factory, for example, this means the planning process establishes sensible quality targets, the organizing process builds an organization that can achieve those targets, and a control process makes sure that quality lapses are spotted immediately, not in 30 or 60 days, and corrected.

For some of the same reasons that control is so central to management, highly motivated or inspired behavior is almost irrelevant. Managerial processes must be as close as possible to fail-safe and risk-free. That means they cannot be dependent on the unusual or hard to obtain. The whole purpose of systems and structures is to help normal people who behave in normal ways to complete routine jobs successfully, day after day. It's not exciting or glamorous. But that's management.

Leadership is different. Achieving grand visions always requires an occasional burst of energy. Motivation and inspiration energize people, not by pushing them in the right direction as control mechanisms do but by satisfying basic human needs for achievement, a sense of belonging, recognition, self-esteem, a feeling of control over one's life, and the ability to live up to one's ideals. Such feelings touch us deeply and elicit a powerful response.

Good leaders motivate people in a variety of ways. First, they always articulate the organization's vision in a manner that stresses the values of the audience they are addressing. This makes the work important to those individuals. Leaders also regularly involve people in deciding how to achieve the organization's vision (or the part most relevant to a particular individual). This gives people a sense of control. Another important motivational technique is to support employee efforts to realize the vision by providing coaching, feedback, and role modeling, thereby helping people grow professionally and enhancing their self-esteem. Finally, good leaders recognize and reward success, which not only gives people a sense of accomplishment but also makes them feel like they belong to an organization that cares about them. When all this is done, the work itself becomes intrinsically motivating.

The more that change characterizes the business environment, the more that leaders must motivate people to provide leadership as well. When this works, it tends to reproduce leadership across the entire organization, with people occupying multiple leadership roles throughout the hierarchy. This is highly valuable, because coping with change in any complex business demands initiatives from a multitude of people. Nothing less will work.

Of course, leadership from many sources does not necessarily converge. To the contrary, it can easily conflict. For multiple leadership roles to work together, people's actions must be carefully coordinated by mechanisms that differ from those coordinating traditional management roles.

Strong networks of informal relationships—the kind found in companies with healthy cultures—help coordinate leadership activities in much the same way that formal structure coordinates managerial activities. The key difference is that informal networks can deal with the greater demands for coordination associated with nonroutine activities and change. The multitude of communication channels and the trust among the individuals connected by those channels allow for an ongoing process of accommodation and adaptation. When conflicts arise among roles, those same relationships help resolve the conflicts. Perhaps most important, this process of dialogue and accommodation can produce visions that are linked and compatible instead of remote and competitive. All this requires a great deal more communication than is needed to coordinate managerial roles, but unlike formal structure, strong informal networks can handle it.

Of course, informal relations of some sort exist in all corporations. But too often these networks are either very weak—some people are well connected but most are not—or they are highly fragmented—a strong network exists inside the marketing group and inside R&D but not across the two departments. Such networks do not support multiple leadership initiatives well. In fact, extensive informal networks are so important that if they do not exist, creating them has to be the focus of activity early in a major leadership initiative (see *Exhibit 3*).

——— CREATING A CULTURE OF LEADERSHIP

Despite the increasing importance of leadership to business success, the on-the-job experiences of most people actually seem to undermine the development of attributes needed for leadership. Nevertheless, some companies have consistently demonstrated an ability to develop people into outstanding leader-managers. Recruiting people with leadership potential is only the first step. Equally important is managing their career patterns. Individuals who are effective in large leadership roles often share a number of career experiences.

Perhaps the most typical and most important is significant challenge early in a career. Leaders almost always have had opportunities during their twenties and thirties to actually try to lead, to take a risk, and to learn from both triumphs and failures. Such learning seems essential in developing a wide range of leadership skills and perspectives. It also teaches people something about both the difficulty of leadership and its potential for producing change.

Later in their careers, something equally important happens that has to do with broadening. People who provide effective leadership in important jobs always have a chance, before they get into those jobs, to grow beyond the narrow base that characterizes most managerial careers. This is usually the result of lateral career moves or of early promotions to unusually broad job assignments. Sometimes other vehicles help, like special task-force assignments or a lengthy general management course. Whatever the case, the breadth of knowledge developed in this way seems to be helpful in all aspects of leadership. So does the network of relationships that is often acquired both inside and outside the company. When enough people get opportunities like this, the relationships that are built also help create the strong informal networks needed to support multiple leadership initiatives.

EXHIBIT 3
Motivating People: Richard Nicolosi at Procter & Gamble

For about 20 years after its founding in 1956, Procter & Gamble's paper products division experienced little competition for its high-quality, reasonably priced, and well-marketed consumer goods. By the late 1970s, however, the market position of the division had changed. New competitive thrusts hurt P&G badly. For example, industry analysts estimate that the company's market share for disposable diapers fell from 75% in the mid-1970s to 52% in 1984.

That year, Richard Nicolosi came to paper products as the associate general manager, after three years in P&G's smaller and faster-moving soft-drink business. He found a heavily bureaucratic and centralized organization that was overly preoccupied with internal functional goals and projects. Almost all information about customers came through highly quantitative market research. The technical people were rewarded for cost savings, the commercial people focused on volume and share, and the two groups were nearly at war with each other.

During the late summer of 1984, top management announced that Nicolosi would become the head of paper products in October, and by August he was unofficially running the division. Immediately he began to stress the need for the division to become more creative and market driven, instead of just trying to be a low-cost producer. "I had to make it very clear," Nicolosi later reported, "that the rules of the game had changed."

The new direction included a much greater stress on teamwork and multiple leadership roles. Nicolosi pushed a strategy of using groups to manage the division and its specific products. In October, he and his team designated themselves as the paper division "board" and began meeting first monthly and then weekly. In November, they established Category Teams to manage their major brand groups (such as diapers, tissues, towels) and started pushing responsibility down to these teams. "Shun the incremental," Nicolosi stressed, "and go for the leap."

In December, Nicolosi selectively involved himself in more detail in certain activities. He met with the advertising agency and got to know key creative people.

Corporations that do a better-than-average job of developing leaders put an emphasis on creating challenging opportunities for relatively young employees. In many businesses, decentralization is the key. By definition, it pushes responsibility lower in an organization and in the process creates more challenging jobs at lower levels. Johnson & Johnson, 3M, Hewlett-Packard, General Electric, and many other well-known companies have used that approach quite successfully. Some of those same companies also create as many small units as possible so there are a lot of challenging lower-level general management jobs available.

Sometimes these businesses develop additional challenging opportunities by stressing growth through new products or services. Over the years, 3M has had a policy that at least 25% of its revenue should come from products introduced within the last five years. That encourages small new ventures,

EXHIBIT 3
Motivating People: Richard Nicolosi at Procter & Gamble (Continued)

He asked the marketing manager of diapers to report directly to him, eliminating a layer in the hierarchy. He talked more to the people who were working on new product-development projects.

In January 1985, the board announced a new organizational structure that included not only category teams but also new-brand business teams. By the spring, the board was ready to plan an important motivational event to communicate the new paper products vision to as many people as possible. On June 4, 1985, all the Cincinnati-based personnel in paper plus sales district managers and paper plant managers—several thousand people in all—met in the local Masonic Temple. Nicolosi and other board members described their vision of an organization where "each of us is a leader." The event was videotaped, and an edited version was sent to all sales offices and plants for everyone to see.

All these activities helped create an entrepreneurial environment where large numbers of people were motivated to realize the new vision. Most innovations came from people dealing with new prod-ucts. Ultra Pampers, first introduced in February 1985, took the market share of the entire Pampers product line from 40% to 58% and profitability from break-even to positive. And within only a few months of the introduction of Luvs Delux in May 1987, market share for the overall brand grew by 150%.

Other employee initiatives were oriented more toward a functional area, and some came from the bottom of the hierarchy. In the spring of 1986, a few of the division's secretaries, feeling empowered by the new culture, developed a Secretaries Network. This association established subcommittees on training, on rewards and recognition, and on the "secretary of the future." Echoing the sentiments of many of her peers, one paper products secretary said: "I don't see why we too can't contribute to the division's new direction."

By the end of 1988, revenues at the paper products division were up 40% over a four-year period. Profits were up 66%. And this happened despite the fact that the competition continued to get tougher.

---

which in turn offer hundreds of opportunities to test and stretch young people with leadership potential.

Such practices can, almost by themselves, prepare people for small- and medium-sized leadership jobs. But developing people for important leadership positions requires more work on the part of senior executives, often over a long period of time. That work begins with efforts to spot people with great leadership potential early in their careers and to identify what will be needed to stretch and develop them.

Again, there is nothing magic about this process. The methods successful companies use are surprisingly straightforward. They go out of their way to make young employees and people at lower levels in their organizations visible to senior management. Senior managers then judge for themselves who has potential and what the development needs of those people are. Executives also discuss their tentative conclusions among themselves to draw more accurate judgments.

Armed with a clear sense of who has considerable leadership potential and what skills they need to develop, executives in these companies then spend time planning for that development. Sometimes that is done as part of a formal succession planning or high-potential development process; often it is more informal. In either case, the key ingredient appears to be an intelligent assessment of what feasible development opportunities fit each candidate's needs.

To encourage managers to participate in these activities, well-led businesses tend to recognize and award people who successfully develop leaders. This is rarely done as part of a formal compensation or bonus formula, simply because it is so difficult to measure such achievements with precision. But it does become a factor in decisions about promotion, especially to the most senior levels, and that seems to make a big difference. When told that future promotions will depend to some degree on their ability to nurture leaders, even people who say that leadership cannot be developed somehow find ways to do it.

Such strategies help create a corporate culture where people value strong leadership and strive to create it. Just as we need more people to provide leadership in the complex organizations that dominate our world today, we also need more people to develop the cultures that will create that leadership. Institutionalizing a leadership-centered culture is the ultimate act of leadership.

■■■ DISCUSSION QUESTIONS

1. Kotter points out that setting direction is fundamental to leadership, and strategies spring from setting direction. Devise a vision with strategies that would give direction to a business that you would like to lead.
2. Give examples from your life in which you have had a vision and had to align people who could either help implement your vision or block your vision's implementation. How well did you succeed with both types of people? In retrospect, is there anything that you could have done better?
3. Give instances from your own experience in which you have demonstrated leadership qualities and ability. Also give instances in which your leadership potential was nurtured by others and when you have nurtured the leadership potential of others.

Ways Women Lead 8

JUDY B. ROSENER

Women managers are succeeding today, but they are not adopting the command-and-control style of leadership traditionally practiced by men. Instead, they are drawing on the skills and attitudes that they have developed from their experience as women.

Because women have historically been expected to play a supportive and cooperative role, they have learned to manage effectively without relying on power and resource control to motivate others. Women managers, for example, are more likely to practice "interactive leadership"—trying to make every interaction with coworkers positive for all involved by encouraging participation, sharing power and information, and making people feel important. The changes occurring in the workplace today may favor this new type of leadership style.

Women managers who have broken the glass ceiling in medium-sized, nontraditional organizations have proven that effective leaders don't come from one mold. They have demonstrated that using the command-and-control style of managing others, a style generally associated with men in large, traditional organizations, is not the only way to succeed.

The first female executives, because they were breaking new ground, adhered to many of the "rules of conduct" that spelled success for men. Now a second wave of women is making its way into top management, not by adopting the style and habits that have proved successful for men but by drawing on the skills and attitudes they developed from their shared experience as women. These second-generation managerial women are drawing on what is unique to their socialization as women and creating a different path to the top. They are seeking and finding opportunities in fast-changing and growing organizations to show that they can achieve results—in a different way. They are succeeding because of—not in spite of—certain characteristics generally considered to be feminine and inappropriate in leaders.

The women's success shows that a nontraditional leadership style is well-suited to the conditions of some work environments and can increase an organization's chances of surviving in an uncertain world. It supports the belief that there is strength in a diversity of leadership styles.

In a recent survey sponsored by the International Women's Forum, I found a number of unexpected similarities between men and women leaders

115

EXHIBIT
The IWF Survey of Men and Women Leaders

The International Women's Forum was founded in 1982 to give prominent women leaders in diverse professions around the world a way to share their knowledge with each other and with their communities and countries. The organization now has some 37 forums in North America, Europe, Asia, Latin America, and the Middle East. To help other women advance and to educate the public about the contributions women can and are making in government, business, and other fields, the IWF created the Leadership Foundation. The Foundation commissioned me to perform the study of men and women leaders on which this article is based. I conducted the study with the help of Daniel McAllister and Gregory Stephens (Ph.D. students at the Graduate School of Management at the University of California, Irvine) in the spring of 1989.

The survey consisted of an eight-page questionnaire sent to all the IWF members. Each respondent was asked to supply the name of a man in a similar organization with similar responsibilities. The men received the same questionnaire as the IWF members. The respondents were similar in age, occupation, and educational level, which suggests that the matching effort was successful. The response rate was 31%.

The respondents were asked questions about their leadership styles, their organizations, work-family issues, and personal characteristics. The following are among the more intriguing findings, some of which contradict data reported in academic journals and the popular press:

- The women earn the same amount of money as their male counterparts. The average yearly income for men is $136,510; for women it is $140,573. (Most other studies have shown a wage gap between men and women.)

- The men's household income (their own and their spouse's) is much lower than that of the women—$166,454 versus

along with some important differences. (For more on the study and its findings, see the *Exhibit*.) Among these similarities are characteristics related to money and children. I found that the men and women respondents earned the same amount of money (and the household income of the women is twice that of the men). This finding is contrary to most studies, which find a considerable wage gap between men and women, even at the executive level. I also found that just as many men as women experience work-family conflict (although when there are children at home, the women experience slightly more conflict than men).

But the similarities end when men and women describe their leadership performance and how they usually influence those with whom they work. The men are more likely than the women to describe themselves in ways that characterize what some management experts call "transactional" leadership.[1] That is, they view job performance as a series of transactions with subordinates—

---

1. Transactional and transformational leadership were first conceptualized by James McGregor Burns in *Leadership* (New York: Harper & Row, 1978) and later developed by Bernard Bass in *Leadership and Performance Beyond Expectations* (New York: Free Press, 1985).

$300,892. (Only 39% of the men have full-time employed spouses, as opposed to 71% of the women.)

- Both men and women leaders pay their female subordinates roughly $12,000 less than their male subordinates with similar positions and titles.
- Women are more likely than men to use transformational leadership—motivating others by transforming their self-interest into the goals of the organization.
- Women are much more likely than men to use power based on charisma, work record, and contacts (personal power) as opposed to power based on organizational position, title, and the ability to reward and punish (structural power).
- Most men and women describe themselves as having an equal mix of traits that are considered feminine (being excitable, gentle, emotional, submissive, sentimental, understanding, compassionate, sensitive, dependent), mascu-

line (dominant, aggressive, tough, assertive, autocratic, analytical, competitive, independent), and gender-neutral (adaptive, tactful, sincere, conscientious, conventional, reliable, predictable, systematic, efficient).

- Women who describe themselves as predominately feminine or gender-neutral report a higher level of followership among their female subordinates than women who describe themselves as masculine.
- Approximately 67% of the women respondents are married. (Other studies report that only 40% to 50% of women executives are married.)
- Both married men and married women experience moderate levels of conflict between work and family domains. When there are children at home, women experience only slightly higher levels of conflict than men, even though they shoulder a much greater proportion of the child care—61% of the care versus 25% for the men.

exchanging rewards for services rendered or punishment for inadequate performance. The men are also more likely to use power that comes from their organizational position and formal authority.

The women respondents, on the other hand, described themselves in ways that characterize "transformational" leadership—getting subordinates to transform their own self-interest into the interest of the group through concern for a broader goal. Moreover, they ascribe their power to personal characteristics like charisma, interpersonal skills, hard work, or personal contacts rather than to organizational stature.

Intrigued by these differences, I interviewed some of the women respondents who described themselves as transformational. These discussions gave me a better picture of how these women view themselves as leaders and a greater understanding of the important ways in which their leadership style differs from the traditional command-and-control style. I call their leadership style "interactive leadership" because these women actively work to make their interactions with subordinates positive for everyone involved. More specifically, the women encourage participation, share power and information, enhance other people's self-worth, and get others excited about their work. All these things reflect their belief that allowing employees to contribute and to feel powerful and important is a win-win situation—good for the employees and the organization.

—— INTERACTIVE LEADERSHIP

From my discussions with the women interviewees, several patterns emerged. The women leaders made frequent reference to their efforts to encourage participation and share power and information—two things that are often associated with participative management. But their self-description went beyond the usual definitions of participation. Much of what they described were attempts to enhance other people's sense of self-worth and to energize followers. In general, these leaders believe that people perform best when they feel good about themselves and their work, and they try to create situations that contribute to that feeling. In general, they do the following:

Encourage Participation   Inclusion is at the core of interactive leadership. In describing nearly every aspect of management, the women interviewees made reference to trying to make people feel part of the organization. They try to instill this group identity in a variety of ways, including encouraging others to have a say in almost every aspect of work, from setting performance goals to determining strategy. To facilitate inclusion, they create mechanisms that get people to participate, and they use a conversational style that sends signals inviting people to get involved.

One example of the kinds of mechanisms that encourage participation is the "bridge club" that one interviewee, a group executive in charge of mergers and acquisitions at a large East Coast financial firm, created. The club is an informal gathering of people who have information she needs but over whom she has no direct control. The word *bridge* describes the effort to bring together these "members" from different functions. The word *club* captures the relaxed atmosphere.

Despite the fact that attendance at club meetings is voluntary and over and above the usual work demands, the interviewee said that those whose help she needs make the time to come. "They know their contributions are valued, and they appreciate the chance to exchange information across functional boundaries in an informal setting that's fun." She finds participation in the club more effective than memos.

Whether or not the women create special forums for people to interact, they try to make people feel included as a matter of course, often by trying to draw them into the conversation or soliciting their opinions. Frieda Caplan, founder and CEO of Frieda's Finest, a California-based marketer and distributor of unusual fruits and vegetables, described an approach she uses that is typical of the other women interviewed: "When I face a tough decision, I always ask my employees, 'What would you do if you were me?' This approach generates good ideas and introduces my employees to the complexity of management decisions."

Of course, saying that you include others doesn't mean others necessarily feel included. The women acknowledge the possibility that their efforts to draw people in may be seen as symbolic, so they try to avoid that perception by acting on the input they receive. They ask for suggestions before they reach their own conclusions, and they test—and sometimes change—particular decisions before they implement them. These women use participation to clarify their own views by thinking things through out loud and to ensure that they haven't overlooked an important consideration.

The fact that many of the interviewees described their participatory style as coming naturally suggests that these leaders do not consciously adopt it for its business value. Yet they realize that encouraging participation has benefits. For one thing, making it easy for people to express their ideas helps ensure that decisions reflect as much information as possible. To some of the women, this point is just common sense. Susan S. Elliott, president and founder of Systems Service Enterprises, a St. Louis computer consulting company, expressed this view: "I can't come up with a plan and then ask those who manage the accounts to give me their reactions. They're the ones who really know the accounts. They have information I don't have. Without their input I'd be operating in an ivory tower."

Participation also increases support for decisions ultimately reached and reduces the risk that ideas will be undermined by unexpected opposition. Claire Rothman, general manager of the Great Western Forum, a large sports and entertainment arena in Los Angeles, spoke about the value of open disagreement: "When I know ahead of time that someone disagrees with a decision, I can work especially closely with that person to try to get his or her support."

Getting people involved also reduces the risk associated with having only one person handle a client, project, or investment. For Patricia M. Cloherty, senior vice president and general partner of Alan Patricof Associates, a New York venture capital firm, including people in decision making and planning gives investments longevity. If something happens to one person, others will be familiar enough with the situation to adopt the investment. That way, there are no orphans in the portfolio, and a knowledgeable second opinion is always available.

Like most who are familiar with participatory management, these women are aware that being inclusive also has its disadvantages. Soliciting ideas and information from others takes time, often requires giving up some control, opens the door to criticism, and exposes personal and turf conflicts. In addition, asking for ideas and information can be interpreted as not having answers.

Further, it cannot be assumed that everyone wants to participate. Some people prefer being told what to do. When Mary Jane Rynd was a partner in a

Big Eight accounting firm in Arizona (she recently left to start her own company—Rynd, Carneal & Associates), she encountered such a person: "We hired this person from an out-of-state CPA firm because he was experienced and smart—and because it's always fun to hire someone away from another firm. But he was just too cynical to participate. He was suspicious of everybody. I tried everything to get him involved—including him in discussions and giving him pep talks about how we all work together. Nothing worked. He just didn't want to participate."

Like all those who responded to the survey, these women are comfortable using a variety of leadership styles. So when participation doesn't work, they act unilaterally. "I prefer participation," said Elliott, "but there are situations where time is short and I have to take the bull by the horns."

Share Power and Information   Soliciting input from other people suggests a flow of information from employees to the boss. But part of making people feel included is knowing that open communication flows in two directions. These women say they willingly share power and information rather than guard it and they make apparent their reasoning behind decisions. While many leaders see information as power and power as a limited commodity to be coveted, the interviewees seem to be comfortable letting power and information change hands. As Adrienne Hall, vice chairman of Eisaman, Johns & Laws, a large West Coast advertising firm, said, "I know territories shift, so I'm not preoccupied with turf."

One example of power and information sharing is the open strategy sessions held by Debi Coleman, vice president of information systems and technology at Apple Computer. Rather than closeting a small group of key executives in her office to develop a strategy based on her own agenda, she holds a series of meetings over several days and allows a larger group to develop and help choose alternatives.

The interviewees believe that sharing power and information accomplishes several things. It creates loyalty by signaling to coworkers and subordinates that they are trusted and their ideas respected. It also sets an example for other people and therefore can enhance the general communication flow. And it increases the odds that leaders will hear about problems before they explode. Sharing power and information also gives employees and coworkers the wherewithal to reach conclusions, solve problems, and see the justification for decisions.

On a more pragmatic level, many employees have come to expect their bosses to be open and frank. They no longer accept being dictated to but want to be treated as individuals with minds of their own. As Elliott said, "I work with lots of people who are bright and intelligent, so I have to deal with them at an intellectual level. They're very logical, and they want to know the reasons for things. They'll buy in only if it makes sense."

In some cases, sharing information means simply being candid about work-related issues. In early 1990, when Elliott hired as employees many of the people she had been using as independent contractors, she knew the transition would be difficult for everyone. The number of employees nearly doubled overnight, and the nature of working relationships changed. "I warned everyone that we were in for some rough times and reminded them that we would be experiencing them together. I admitted that it would also be hard for me, and I made it clear that I wanted them to feel free to talk to me. I was completely candid and encouraged them to be honest with me. I lost some employees who didn't like the new relationships, but I'm convinced that being open helped me understand my employees better, and it gave them a feeling of support."

Like encouraging participation, sharing power and information has its risks. It allows for the possibility that people will reject, criticize, or otherwise challenge what the leader has to say or, more broadly, her authority. Also, employees get frustrated when leaders listen to—but ultimately reject—their ideas. Because information is a source of power, leaders who share it can be seen as naive or needing to be liked. The interviewees have experienced some of these downsides but find the positives overwhelming.

Enhance the Self-worth of Others   One of the by-products of sharing information and encouraging participation is that employees feel important. During the interviews, the women leaders discussed other ways they build a feeling of self-worth in coworkers and subordinates. They talked about giving others credit and praise and sending small signals of recognition. Most important, they expressed how they refrain from asserting their own superiority, which asserts the inferiority of others. All those I interviewed expressed clear aversion to behavior that sets them apart from others in the company—reserved parking places, separate dining facilities, pulling rank.

Examples of sharing and giving credit to others abound. Caplan, who has been the subject of scores of media reports hailing her innovation of labeling vegetables so consumers know what they are and how to cook them, originally got the idea from a farmer. She said that whenever someone raises the subject, she credits the farmer and downplays her role. Rothman is among the many note-writers: when someone does something out of the ordinary, she writes them a personal note to tell them she noticed. Like many of the women I interviewed, she said she also makes a point of acknowledging good work by talking about it in front of others.

Bolstering coworkers and subordinates is especially important in businesses and jobs that tend to be hard on a person's ego. Investment banking is one example because of the long hours, high pressures, intense competition, and inevitability that some deals will fail. One interviewee in investment banking hosts dinners for her division, gives out gag gifts as party favors, passes out M&Ms at meetings, and throws parties "to celebrate ourselves." These things, she said, balance the anxiety that permeates the environment.

Rynd compensates for the negativity inherent in preparing tax returns: "In my business we have something called a query sheet, where the person who reviews the tax return writes down everything that needs to be corrected. Criticism is built into the system. But at the end of every review, I always include a positive comment—your work paper technique looked good, I appreciate the fact that you got this done on time, or something like that. It seems trivial, but it's one way to remind people that I recognize their good work and not just their shortcomings."

Energize Others   The women leaders spoke of their enthusiasm for work and how they spread their enthusiasm around to make work a challenge that is exhilarating and fun. The women leaders talked about it in those terms and claimed to use their enthusiasm to get others excited. As Rothman said, "There is rarely a person I can't motivate."

Enthusiasm was a dominant theme throughout the interviews. In computer consulting: "Because this business is on the forefront of technology, I'm sort of evangelistic about it, and I want other people to be as excited as I am." In venture capital: "You have to have a head of steam." In executive search: "Getting people excited is an important way to influence those you have no control over." Or in managing sports arenas: "My enthusiasm gets others excited. I infuse them with energy and make them see that even boring jobs contribute to the fun of working in a celebrity business."

Enthusiasm can sometimes be misunderstood. In conservative professions like investment banking, such an upbeat leadership style can be interpreted as cheerleading and can undermine credibility. In many cases, the women said they won and preserved their credibility by achieving results that could be measured easily. One of the women acknowledged that her colleagues don't understand or like her leadership style and have called it cheerleading. "But," she added, "in this business you get credibility from what you produce, and they love the profits I generate." While energy and enthusiasm can inspire some, it doesn't work for everyone. Even Rothman conceded, "Not everyone has a flame that can be lit."

—— PATHS OF LEAST RESISTANCE

Many of the women I interviewed said the behaviors and beliefs that underlie their leadership style come naturally to them. I attribute this to two things: their socialization and the career paths they have chosen. Although socialization patterns and career paths are changing, the average age of the men and women who responded to the survey is 51—old enough to have had experiences that differed *because* of gender.

Until the 1960s, men and women received different signals about what was expected of them. To summarize a subject that many experts have explored in depth, women have been expected to be wives, mothers, community volunteers, teachers, and nurses. In all these roles, they are supposed to be cooperative, supportive, understanding, gentle, and to provide service to others. They are to derive satisfaction and a sense of self-esteem from helping others, including their spouses. While men have had to appear to be competitive, strong, tough, decisive, and in control, women have been allowed to be cooperative, emotional, supportive, and vulnerable. This may explain why women today are more likely than men to be interactive leaders.

Men and women have also had different career opportunities. Women were not expected to have careers, or at least not the same kinds of careers as men, so they either pursued different jobs or were simply denied opportunities men had. Women's career tracks have usually not included long series of organizational positions with formal authority and control of resources. Many women had their first work experiences outside the home as volunteers. While some of the challenges they faced as managers in volunteer organizations are the same as those in any business, in many ways, leading volunteers is different because of the absence of concrete rewards like pay and promotion.

As women entered the business world, they tended to find themselves in positions consistent with the roles they played at home: in staff positions rather than in line positions, supporting the work of others, and in functions like communications or human resources where they had relatively small budgets and few people reporting directly to them.

The fact that most women have lacked formal authority over others and control over resources means that by default they have had to find other ways to accomplish their work. As it turns out, the behaviors that were natural and/or socially acceptable for them have been highly successful in at least some managerial settings.

What came easily to women turned out to be a survival tactic. Although leaders often begin their careers doing what comes naturally and what fits within the constraints of the job, they also develop their skills and styles over time. The women's use of interactive leadership has its roots in socialization, and the women interviewees firmly believe that it benefits their organizations. Through the course of their careers, they have gained conviction that their style is effective. In fact, for some, it was their own success that caused them to formulate their philosophies about what motivates people, how to make good decisions, and what it takes to maximize business performance.

They now have formal authority and control over vast resources, but still they see sharing power and information as an asset rather than a liability. They believe that although pay and promotion are necessary tools of management, what people really want is to feel that they are contributing to a higher purpose and that they have the opportunity as individuals to learn and grow. The women believe that employees and peers perform better when they feel they are part of an organization and can share in its success. Allowing them to get involved and to work to their potential is a way of maximizing their contributions and using human resources most efficiently.

ANOTHER KIND OF DIVERSITY

The IWF survey shows that a nontraditional leadership style can be effective in organizations that accept it. This lesson comes especially hard to those who think of the corporate world as a game of survival of the fittest, where the fittest is always the strongest, toughest, most decisive, and powerful. Such a workplace seems to favor leaders who control people by controlling resources, and by controlling people, gain control of more resources. Asking for information and sharing decision-making power can be seen as serious disadvantages, but what is a disadvantage under one set of circumstances is an advantage under another. The "best" leadership style depends on the organizational context.

Only one of the women interviewees is in a traditional, large-scale company. More typically, the women's organizations are medium-sized and tend to have experienced fast growth and fast change. They demand performance and/or have a high proportion of professional workers. These organizations seem to create opportunities for women and are hospitable to those who use a nontraditional management style.

The degree of growth or change in an organization is an important factor in creating opportunities for women. When change is rampant, everything is up for grabs, and crises are frequent. Crises are generally not desirable, but they do create opportunities for people to prove themselves. Many of the women interviewees said they got their first break because their organizations were in turmoil.

Fast-changing environments also play havoc with tradition. Coming up through the ranks and being part of an established network is no longer important. What is important is how you perform. Also, managers in such environments are open to new solutions, new structures, and new ways of leading.

The fact that many of the women respondents are in organizations that have clear performance standards suggest that they have gained credibility and legitimacy by achieving results. In investment banking, venture capital, accounting, and executive placement, for instance, individual performance is easy to measure.

A high proportion of young professional workers—increasingly typical of organizations—is also a factor in some women's success. Young, educated professionals impose special requirements on their organizations. They demand to participate and contribute. In some cases, they have knowledge or talents their bosses don't have. If they are good performers, they have many employment options. It is easy to imagine that these professionals will respond to leaders who are inclusive and open, who enhance the self-worth of others, and who create a fun work environment. Interactive leaders are likely to win the cooperation needed to achieve their goals.

Interactive leadership has proved to be effective, perhaps even advantageous, in organizations in which the women I interviewed have succeeded.

As the work force increasingly demands participation and the economic environment increasingly requires rapid change, interactive leadership may emerge as the management style of choice for many organizations. For interactive leadership to take root more broadly, however, organizations must be willing to question the notion that the traditional command-and-control leadership style that has brought success in earlier decades is the only way to get results. This may be hard in some organizations, especially those with long histories of male-oriented, command-and-control leadership. Changing these organizations will not be easy. The fact that women are more likely than men to be interactive leaders raises the risk that these companies will perceive interactive leadership as "feminine" and automatically resist it.

Linking interactive leadership directly to being female is a mistake. We know that women are capable of making their way through corporations by adhering to the traditional corporate model and that they can wield power in ways similar to men. Indeed, some women may prefer that style. We also know from the survey findings that some men use the transformational leadership style.

Large, established organizations should expand their definition of effective leadership. If they were to do that, several things might happen, including the disappearance of the glass ceiling and the creation of a wider path for all sorts of executives—men and women—to attain positions of leadership. Widening the path will free potential leaders to lead in ways that play to their individual strengths. Then the newly recognized interactive leadership style can be valued and rewarded as highly as the command-and-control style has been for decades. By valuing a diversity of leadership styles, organizations will find the strength and flexibility to survive in a highly competitive, increasingly diverse economic environment.

——— DISCUSSION QUESTIONS

1. Think of male and female managers you have known or worked with. Did they conform to the leadership styles described by the author? If not, how did they differ?
2. Based on the author's descriptions of the differences between the leadership styles of men and women, do you feel that this reinforces stereotypes or smashes them?
3. The author asserts that socialization and available career paths associated with gender differences have created women's interactive leadership style. What is the future of this effective leadership style as the differences between the socialization and career potential of men and women lessen?

9 How to Choose a Leadership Pattern

ROBERT TANNENBAUM AND WARREN H. SCHMIDT

The authors of this reading explore the dilemma that today's emphasis on participative decision making creates for modern managers. In relating to subordinates, managers may choose a pattern of leadership that ranges from making all the decisions themselves to allowing their subordinates to make decisions within prescribed limits.

In deciding how to lead, managers must consider their values, their confidence in their subordinates, their leadership inclinations, and their tolerance for ambiguity. They must also determine whether their subordinates have the independence, maturity, interest, and knowledge to share in decision making. Other issues to weigh include the ability of subordinates to work together, the complexity of the task, and the pressures of time. Successful managers are aware of all these factors and are able to act in the organization's best interests. In the retrospective commentary, the authors discuss the changes in organizations and in the world that have affected leadership patterns.

- I put most problems into my group's hands and leave it to them to carry the ball from there. I serve merely as a catalyst, mirroring back the people's thoughts and feelings so that they can better understand them."
- "It's foolish to make decisions oneself on matters that affect people. I always talk things over with my subordinates, but I make it clear to them that I'm the one who has to have the final say."
- "Once I have decided on a course of action, I do my best to sell my ideas to my employees."
- "I'm being paid to lead. If I let a lot of other people make the decisions I should be making, then I'm not worth my salt."
- "I believe in getting things done. I can't waste time calling meetings. Someone has to call the shots around here, and I think it should be me."

Each of these statements represents a point of view about good leadership. Considerable experience, factual data, and theoretical principles could be cited to support each statement, even though they seem to be inconsistent when placed together. Such contradictions point up the dilemma in which modern managers frequently find themselves.

———— DEMOCRACY VERSUS AUTHORITY

The problem of how modern managers can be democratic in their relations with subordinates and at the same time maintain the necessary authority and control in the organizations for which they are responsible has come into focus increasingly in recent years.

Earlier in the century this problem was not so acutely felt. The successful executive was generally pictured as possessing intelligence, imagination, initiative, the capacity to make rapid (and generally wise) decisions, and the ability to inspire subordinates. People tended to think of the world as being divided into leaders and followers.

Gradually, however, from the social sciences emerged the concept of group dynamics with its focus on *members* of the group rather than solely on the leader. Research efforts of social scientists underscored the importance of employee involvement and participation in decision making. Evidence began to challenge the efficiency of highly directive leadership, and increasing attention was paid to problems of motivation and human relations.

Through training laboratories in group development that sprang up across the country, many of the newer notions of leadership began to exert an impact. These training laboratories were carefully designed to give people firsthand experience in full participation and decision making. The designated leaders deliberately attempted to reduce their own power and to make group members as responsible as possible for setting their own goals and methods within the laboratory experience.

It was perhaps inevitable that some of the people who attended the training laboratories regarded this kind of leadership as being truly democratic and went home with the determination to build fully participative decision making into their own organizations. Whenever their bosses made a decision without convening a staff meeting, they tended to perceive this as authoritarian behavior. The true symbol of democratic leadership to some was the meeting— and the less directed from the top, the more democratic it was.

Some of the more enthusiastic alumni of these training laboratories began to get the habit of categorizing leader behavior as democratic or authoritarian. Bosses who made too many decisions themselves were thought of as authoritarian, and their directive behavior was often attributed solely to their personalities.

The net result of the research findings and of the human relations training based upon them has been to call into question the stereotype of an effective leader. Consequently, modern managers often find themselves in an uncomfortable state of mind.

Often they are not quite sure how to behave; there are times when they are torn between exerting strong leadership and permissive leadership. Sometimes new knowledge pushes them in one direction ("I should really get the group to help make this decision"), but at the same time their experience pushes them in another direction ("I really understand the problem better than the group and therefore I should make the decision."). They are not sure when a group decision is really appropriate or when holding a staff meeting serves merely as a device for avoiding their own decision-making responsibility.

The purpose of our reading is to suggest a framework that managers may find useful in grappling with this dilemma. First, we shall look at the different patterns of leadership behavior that managers can choose from in relating to their subordinates. Then, we shall turn to some of the questions suggested by this range of patterns. For instance, how important is it for managers' subordinates to know what type of leadership they are using in a situation? What factors should they consider in deciding on a leadership pattern? What difference do their long-run objectives make as compared to their immediate objectives?

———— RANGE OF BEHAVIOR

Exhibit 1 presents the continuum or range of possible leadership behavior available to managers. Each type of action is related to the degree of authority used by the boss and to the amount of freedom available to subordinates in reaching decisions. The actions seen on the extreme left characterize managers

EXHIBIT 1
Continuum of Leadership Behavior

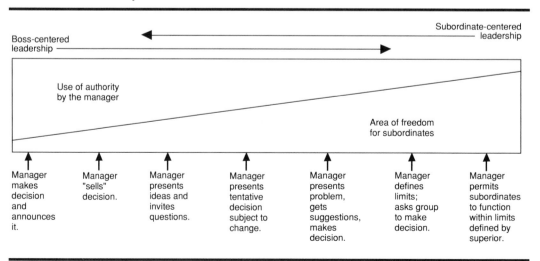

who maintain a high degree of control while those seen on the extreme right characterize managers who release a high degree of control. Neither extreme is absolute; authority and freedom are never without their limitations.

Now let us look more closely at each of the behavior points occurring along this continuum.

The Manager Makes the Decision and Announces It   In this case the boss identifies a problem, considers alternative solutions, chooses one of them, and then reports this decision to the subordinates for implementation. The boss may or may not give consideration to what he or she believes the subordinates will think or feel about the decision; in any case, no opportunity is provided for them to participate directly in the decision-making process. Coercion may or may not be used or implied.

The Manager "Sells" the Decision   Here the manager, as before, takes responsibility for identifying the problem and arriving at a decision. However, rather than simply announcing it, he or she takes the additional step of persuading the subordinates to accept it. In doing so, the boss recognizes the possibility of some resistance among those who will be faced with the decision and seeks to reduce this resistance by indicating, for example, what the employees have to gain from the decision.

The Manager Presents Ideas, Invites Questions   Here the boss who has arrived at a decision and who seeks acceptance of his or her ideas provides an opportunity for subordinates to get a fuller explanation of his or her thinking and intentions. After presenting the ideas, the manager invites questions so that the associates can better understand what he or she is trying to accomplish. This give-and-take also enables the manager and the subordinates to explore more fully the implications of the decision.

The Manager Presents a Tentative Decision Subject to Change   This kind of behavior permits subordinates to exert some influence on the decision. The initiative for identifying and diagnosing the problem remains with the boss. Before meeting with the staff, the manager has thought the problem through and arrived at a decision—but only a tentative one. Before finalizing it, he or she presents the proposed solution for the reaction of those who will be affected by it. He or she says in effect, "I'd like to hear what you have to say about this plan that I have developed. I'll appreciate your frank reactions but will reserve for myself the final decision."

The Manager Presents the Problem, Gets Suggestions, and Then Makes the Decision   Up to this point the boss has come before the group with a solution of his or her own. Not so in this case. The subordinates now get the first chance to suggest solutions. The manager's initial role involves identifying the problem. He or she might, for example, say something of this sort:

"We are faced with a number of complaints from newspapers and the general public on our service policy. What is wrong here? What ideas do you have for coming to grips with this problem?"

The function of the group becomes one of increasing the manager's repertoire of possible solutions to the problem. The purpose is to capitalize on the knowledge and experience of those who are on the firing line. From the expanded list of alternatives developed by the manager and the subordinates, the manager then selects the solution that he or she regards as most promising.[1]

The Manager Defines the Limits and Requests the Group to Make a Decision

At this point the manager passes to the group (possibly taking part as a member) the right to make decisions. Before doing so, however, he or she defines the problem to be solved and the boundaries within which the decision must be made.

An example might be the handling of a parking problem at a plant. The boss decides that this is something that should be worked on by the people involved, so they are called together. Pointing up the existence of the problem, the boss tells them:

"There is the open field just north of the main plant which has been designated for additional employee parking. We can build underground or surface multilevel facilities as long as the cost does not exceed $100,000. Within these limits we are free to work out whatever solution makes sense to us. After we decide on a specific plan, the company will spend the available money in whatever way we indicate."

The Manager Permits the Group to Make Decisions within Prescribed Limits

This represents an extreme degree of group freedom only occasionally encountered in formal organizations as, for instance, in many research groups. Here the team of managers or engineers undertakes the identification and diagnosis of the problem, develops alternative procedures for solving it, and decides on one or more of these alternative solutions. The only limits directly imposed on the group by the organization are those specified by the superior of the team's boss. If the boss participates in the decision-making process, deciding in advance to assist in implementing whatever decision the group makes, he or she attempts to do so with no more authority than any other member of the group.

KEY QUESTIONS

As the continuum in *Exhibit 1* demonstrates, there are a number of ways in which managers can relate to the group or individuals they are supervising.

---

1. For a fuller explanation of this approach, *see* Leo Moore, "Too Much Management, Too Little Change," *Harvard Business Review* (January–February 1956): 41.

At the extreme left of the range, the emphasis is on the manager—on what he or she is interested in, how he or she sees things, how he or she feels about them. As we move toward the subordinate-centered end of the continuum, however, the focus is increasingly on the subordinates—on what they are interested in, how they look at things, how they feel about them.

When business leadership is regarded in this way, a number of questions arise. Let us take four of special importance:

Can bosses ever relinquish their responsibility by delegating it to others?

Our view is that managers must expect to be held responsible by their superiors for the quality of the decisions made, even though operationally these decisions may have been made on a group basis. They should, therefore, be ready to accept whatever risk is involved whenever they delegate decision-making power to subordinates. Delegation is not a way of passing the buck. Also, it should be emphasized that the amount of freedom bosses give to subordinates cannot be greater than the freedom that they themselves have been given by their own superiors.

Should the manager participate with subordinates once he or she has delegated responsibility to them?

Managers should carefully think over this question and decide on their role prior to involving the subordinate group. They should ask if their presence will inhibit or facilitate the problem-solving process. There may be some instances when they should leave the group to let it solve the problem for itself. Typically, however, the boss has useful ideas to contribute and should function as an additional member of the group. In the latter instance, it is important that he or she indicate clearly to the group that he or she is in a *member* role rather than an authority role.

How important is it for the group to recognize what kind of leadership behavior the boss is using?

It makes a great deal of difference. Many relationship problems between bosses and subordinates occur because the bosses fail to make clear how they plan to use their authority. If, for example, the boss actually intends to make a certain decision, but the subordinate group gets the impression that he or she has delegated this authority, considerable confusion and resentment are likely to follow. Problems may also occur when the boss uses a democratic facade to conceal the fact that he or she has already made a decision that he or she hopes the group will accept as its own. The attempt to make them think it was their idea in the first place is a risky one. We believe that it is highly important for managers to be honest and clear in describing what authority they are keeping and what role they are asking their subordinates to assume in solving a particular problem.

Can you tell how democratic a manager is by the number of decisions the subordinates make?

The sheer *number* of decisions is not an accurate index of the amount of freedom that a subordinate group enjoys. More important is the *significance* of the decisions that the boss entrusts to subordinates. Obviously a decision on how to arrange desks is of an entirely different order from a decision involving the introduction of new electronic data-processing equipment. Even though the widest possible limits are given in dealing with the first issue, the group will sense no particular degree of responsibility. For a boss to permit the group to decide equipment policy, even within rather narrow limits, would reflect a greater degree of confidence in them on his or her part.

DECIDING HOW TO LEAD

Now let us turn from the types of leadership which are possible in a company situation to the question of what types are *practical* and *desirable*. What factors or forces should a manager consider in deciding how to manage? Three are of particular importance:

- Forces in the manager
- Forces in the subordinates
- Forces in the situation

We should like briefly to describe these elements and indicate how they might influence a manager's action in a decision-making situation.[2] The strength of each of them will, of course, vary from instance to instance, but managers who are sensitive to them can better assess the problems that face them and determine which mode of leadership behavior is most appropriate for them.

Forces in the Manager   The manager's behavior in any given instance will be influenced greatly by the many forces operating within his or her own personality. Managers will, of course, perceive their leadership problems in a unique way on the basis of their background, knowledge, and experience. Among the important internal forces affecting them will be the following:

1. *Their value system.* How strongly do they feel that individuals should have a share in making the decisions that affect them? Or, how convinced are they that the official who is paid to assume responsibility should personally carry the burden of decision making? The strength of their convictions on questions like these will tend to move managers to one end or the other of the continuum

---

2. *See also* Robert Tannenbaum and Fred Massarik, "Participation by Subordinates in the Managerial Decision-Making Process," *Canadian Journal of Economics and Political Science* (August 1950): 413.

shown in *Exhibit 1*. Their behavior will also be influenced by the relative importance that they attach to organizational efficiency, personal growth of subordinates, and company profits.[3]

2. *Their confidence in subordinates.* Managers differ greatly in the amount of trust they have in other people generally, and this carries over to the particular employees they supervise at a given time. In viewing his or her particular group of subordinates, the manager is likely to consider their knowledge and competence with respect to the problem. A central question managers might ask themselves is "Who is best qualified to deal with this problem?" Often they may, justifiably or not, have more confidence in their own capabilities than in those of subordinates.

3. *Their own leadership inclinations.* There are some managers who seem to function more comfortably and naturally as highly directive leaders. Resolving problems and issuing orders come easily to them. Other managers seem to operate more comfortably in a team role, where they are continually sharing many of their functions with their subordinates.

4. *Their feelings of security in an uncertain situation.* Managers who release control over the decision-making process thereby reduce the predictability of the outcome. Some managers have a greater need than others for predictability and stability in their environment. This tolerance for ambiguity is being viewed increasingly by psychologists as a key variable in a person's manner of dealing with problems.

Managers bring these and other highly personal variables to each situation they face. If they can see them as forces that consciously or unconsciously influence their behavior, they can better understand what makes them prefer to act in a given way. And understanding this, they can often make themselves more effective.

Forces in the Subordinate   Before deciding how to lead a certain group, managers will also want to consider a number of forces affecting their subordinates' behavior. They will want to remember that each employee, like themselves, is influenced by many personality variables. In addition, each subordinate has a set of expectations about how the boss should act in relation to him or her (the phrase "expected behavior" is one we hear more and more often these days at discussions of leadership and teaching). The better managers understand these factors, the more accurately they can determine what kind of behavior on their part will enable subordinates to act most effectively.

Generally speaking, managers can permit subordinates greater freedom if the following essential conditions exist:

---

3. *See* Chris Argyris, "Top Management Dilemma: Company Needs vs. Individual Development," *Personnel* (September 1955): 123–134.

- If the subordinates have relatively high needs for independence. (As we all know, people differ greatly in the amount of direction that they desire.)
- If the subordinates have a readiness to assume responsibility for decision making. (Some see additional responsibility as a tribute to their ability; others see it as passing the buck.)
- If they have a relatively high tolerance for ambiguity. (Some employees prefer to have clear-cut directives given to them; others prefer a wider area of freedom.)
- If they are interested in the problem and feel that it is important.
- If they understand and identify with the goals of the organization.
- If they have the necessary knowledge and experience to deal with the problem.
- If they have learned to expect to share in decision making. (Persons who have come to expect strong leadership and are then suddenly confronted with the request to share more fully in decision making are often upset by this new experience. On the other hand, persons who have enjoyed a considerable amount of freedom resent bosses who begin to make all the decisions themselves.)

Managers will probably tend to make fuller use of their own authority if the above conditions do not exist; at times there may be no realistic alternative to running a "one-man show."

The restrictive effect of many of the forces will, of course, be greatly modified by the general feeling of confidence which subordinates have in the boss. Where they have learned to respect and trust the boss, he or she is free to vary his or her own behavior. The boss will feel certain that he or she will not be perceived as an authoritarian boss on those occasions when he or she makes decisions alone. Similarly, the boss will not be seen as using staff meetings to avoid decision-making responsibility. In a climate of mutual confidence and respect, people tend to feel less threatened by deviations from normal practice, which in turn makes possible a higher degree of flexibility in the whole relationship.

Forces in the Situation   In addition to the forces that exist in managers themselves and in the subordinates, certain characteristics of the general situation will also affect managers' behavior. Among the more critical environmental pressures that surround them are those that stem from the organization, the work group, the nature of the problem, and the pressures of time.

The *type of organization* is one element to consider. Like individuals, organizations have values and traditions that inevitably influence the behavior of the people who work in them. Managers who are newcomers to a company quickly discover that certain kinds of behavior are approved while others are not. They also discover that to deviate radically from what is generally accepted is likely to create problems for them.

These values and traditions are communicated in numerous ways— through job descriptions, policy pronouncements, and public statements by top executives. Some organizations, for example, hold to the notion that the desirable executive is one who is dynamic, imaginative, decisive, and persuasive. Other organizations put more emphasis upon the importance of the executive's ability to work effectively with people—human relations skills. The fact that the person's superiors have a defined concept of what the good executive should be will very likely push the manager toward one end or the other of the behavioral range.

In addition, the amount of employee participation is influenced by such variables as the size of the working units, their geographical distribution, and the degree of inter- and intra-organizational security required to attain company goals. For example, the wide geographical dispersion of an organization may preclude a practical system of participative decision making, even through this would otherwise be desirable. Similarly, the size of the working units or the need for keeping plans confidential may make it necessary for the boss to exercise more control than would otherwise be the case. Factors like these may considerably limit the manager's ability to function flexibly on the continuum.

Before turning decision-making responsibility over to a subordinate group, the boss should consider *group effectiveness*, that is, how effectively its members work together as a unit.

One of the relevant factors here is the experience the group has had in working together. It can generally be expected that a group that has functioned for some time will have developed habits of cooperation and thus be able to tackle a problem more effectively than a new group. It can also be expected that a group of people with similar backgrounds and interests will work more quickly and easily than people with dissimilar backgrounds, because the communication problems are likely to be less complex.

The degree of confidence that the members have in their ability to solve problems as a group is also a key consideration. Finally, such group variables as cohesiveness, permissiveness, mutual acceptance, and commonality of purpose will exert subtle but powerful influence on the group's functioning.

The *nature of the problem* may determine what degree of authority should be delegated by managers to their subordinates. Obviously, managers will ask themselves whether subordinates have the kind of knowledge that is needed. It is possible to do them a real disservice by assigning a problem that their experience does not equip them to handle.

Because the problems faced in large or growing industries increasingly require knowledge of specialists from many different fields, it might be inferred that the more complex a problem, the more anxious a manager will be to get some assistance in solving it. However, this is not always the case. There will be times when the very complexity of the problem calls for one person to work it out. For example, if the manager has most of the background and factual data relevant to a given issue, it may be easier for him or her to think it through than to take the time to fill in the staff on all the pertinent background information.

The key question to ask, of course, is "Have I heard the ideas of everyone who has the necessary knowledge to make a significant contribution to the solution of this problem?"

The *pressure of time* is perhaps the most clearly felt pressure on managers (in spite of the fact that it may sometimes be imagined). The more that they feel the need for an immediate decision, the more difficult it is to involve other people. In organizations that are in a constant state of crisis and crash programming, one is likely to find managers personally using a high degree of authority with relatively little delegation to subordinates. When the time pressure is less intense, however, it becomes much more possible to bring subordinates in on the decision-making process.

These, then, are the principal forces that impinge on managers in any given instance and that tend to determine their tactical behavior in relation to subordinates. In each case their behavior ideally will be that which makes possible the most effective attainment of their immediate goals within the limits facing them.

LONG-RUN STRATEGY

As managers work with their organizations on the problems that come up day to day, their choice of a leadership pattern is usually limited. They must take account of the forces just described and, within the restrictions those factors impose on them, do the best that they can. But as they look ahead months or even years, they can shift their thinking from tactics to large-scale strategy. No longer need they be fettered by all of the forces mentioned, for they can view many of them as variables over which they have some control. They can, for example, gain new insights or skills for themselves, supply training for individual subordinates, and provide participative experiences for their employee group.

In trying to bring about a change in these variables, however, they are faced with a challenging question: At which point along the continuum *should* they act?

Attaining Objectives   The answer depends largely on what they want to accomplish. Let us suppose that they are interested in the same objectives that most modern managers seek to attain when they can shift their attention from the pressure of immediate assignments:

1. To raise the level of employee motivation
2. To increase the readiness of subordinates to accept change
3. To improve the quality of all managerial decisions
4. To develop teamwork and morale
5. To further the individual development of employees

In recent years managers have been deluged with a flow of advice on how best to achieve these longer-run objectives. It is little wonder that they are often both bewildered and annoyed. However, there are some guidelines which they can usefully follow in making a decision.

Most research and much of the experience of recent years give a strong factual basis to the theory that a fairly high degree of subordinate-center behavior is associated with the accomplishment of the five purposes mentioned.[4] This does not mean that managers should always leave all decisions to their assistants. To provide the individual or the group with greater freedom than they are ready for at any given time may very well tend to generate anxieties and therefore inhibit rather than facilitate the attainment of desired objectives. But this should not keep managers from making a continuing effort to confront subordinates with the challenge of freedom.

CONCLUSION

In summary, there are two implications in the basic thesis that we have been developing. The first is that successful leaders are those who are keenly aware of the forces which are most relevant to their behavior at any given time. They accurately understand themselves, the individuals and groups they are dealing with, and the company and broader social environment in which they operate. And certainly they are able to assess the present readiness for growth of their subordinates.

But this sensitivity or understanding is not enough, which brings us to the second implication. Successful leaders are those who are able to behave appropriately in the light of these perceptions. If direction is in order, they are able to direct; if considerable participative freedom is called for, they are able to provide such freedom.

Thus, successful managers of people can be primarily characterized neither as strong leaders nor as permissive ones. Rather, they are people who maintain a high batting average in accurately assessing the forces that determine what their most appropriate behavior at any given time should be and in actually being able to behave accordingly. Being both insightful and flexible, they are less likely to see the problems of leadership as a dilemma.

* * *

The authors wrote the following commentary fifteen years after this reading was first published.

---

4. For example, *see* Warren H. Schmidt and Paul C. Buchanan, *Techniques that Produce Teamwork* (New London, Conn.: Arthur C. Croft Publications, 1954); and Morris S. Viteles, *Motivation and Morale in Industry* (New York: W. W. Norton & Company, Inc., 1953).

——— RETROSPECTIVE COMMENTARY

Since this reading was first published in 1958, there have been many changes in organizations and in the world that have affected leadership patterns. While the article's continued popularity attests to its essential validity, we believe it can be reconsidered and updated to reflect subsequent societal changes and new management concepts.

The reasons for the article's continued relevance can be summarized briefly:

- The article contains insights and perspectives that mesh well with, and help clarify, the experiences of managers, other leaders, and students of leadership. Thus it is useful to individuals in a wide variety of organizations—industrial, governmental, educational, religious, and community.
- The concept of leadership the article defines is reflected in a continuum of leadership behavior (*see Exhibit 1* in original article). Rather than offering a choice between two styles of leadership, democratic or authoritarian, it sanctions a range of behavior.
- The concept does not dictate to managers but helps them to analyze their own behavior. The continuum permits them to review their behavior within a context of other alternatives, without any style being labeled right or wrong.

(We have sometimes wondered if we have, perhaps, made it too easy for anyone to justify his or her style of leadership. It may be a small step between being nonjudgmental and giving the impression that all behavior is equally valid and useful. The latter was not our intention. Indeed, the thrust of our endorsement was for managers who are insightful in assessing relevant forces within themselves, others, and situations, and who can be flexible in responding to these forces.)

In recognizing that our article can be updated, we are acknowledging that organizations do not exist in a vacuum but are affected by changes that occur in society. Consider, for example, the implications for organizations of these recent social developments:

- The youth revolution that expresses distrust and even contempt for organizations identified with the establishment.
- The civil rights movement that demands all minority groups be given a greater opportunity for participation and influence in the organizational processes.
- The ecology and consumer movements that challenge the right of managers to make decisions without considering the interest of people outside the organization.
- The increasing national concern with the quality of working life and its relationship to worker productivity, participation, and satisfaction.

These and other societal changes make effective leadership in this decade a more challenging task, requiring even greater sensitivity and flexibility than was needed in the 1950s. Today's manager is more likely to deal with employees who resent being treated as subordinates, who may be highly critical of any organizational system, who expect to be consulted and to exert influence, and who often stand on the edge of alienation from the institution that needs their loyalty and commitment. In addition, the manager is frequently confronted by a highly turbulent, unpredictable environment.

In response to these social pressures, new concepts of management have emerged in organizations. Open-system theory, with its emphasis on subsystems' interdependency *and* on the interaction of an organization with its environment, has made a powerful impact on managers' approach to problems. Organization development has emerged as a new behavioral science approach to the improvement of individual, group, organizational, and interorganizational performance. New research has added to our understanding of motivation in the work situation. More and more executives have become concerned with social responsibility and have explored the feasibility of social audits. And a growing number of organizations, in Europe and in the United States, have conducted experiments in industrial democracy.

In light of these developments, we submit the following thoughts on how we would rewrite certain points in our original article.

The article described forces in the manager, subordinates, and the situation as givens, with the leadership pattern a result of these forces. We would now give more attention to the *interdependency* of these forces. For example, such interdependency occurs in (a) the interplay between the manager's confidence in subordinates, their readiness to assume responsibility, and the level of group effectiveness; and (b) the impact of the behavior of the manager on that of subordinates, and vice versa.

In discussing the forces in the situation, we primarily identified organizational phenomena. We would now include forces lying outside the organization and would explore the relevant interdependencies between the organization and its environment.

In the original article, we presented the size of the rectangle in *Exhibit 1* as a given, with its boundaries already determined by external forces—in effect, a closed system. We would now recognize the possibility of the manager and/or the subordinates taking the initiative to change those boundaries through interaction with relevant external forces—both within their own organization and in the larger society.

The article portrayed the manager as the principal and almost unilateral actor. He or she initiated and determined group functions, assumed responsibility, and exercised control. Subordinates made inputs and assumed power only at the will of the manager. Although the manager might have taken outside forces into account, it was he or she who decided where to operate on the continuum; that is, whether to announce a decision instead of trying to sell the idea to subordinates, whether to invite questions, to let subordinates decide an issue, and so on. While the manager has retained this clear prerogative in many organizations, it has been challenged in others. Even in situations where managers have retained it, however, the balance in the relationship between managers and subordinates at any given time is arrived at by interaction—direct or indirect—between the two parties.

Although power and its use by managers played a role in our article, we now realize that our concern with cooperation and collaboration, common goals, commitment, trust, and mutual caring limited our vision with respect to the realities of power. We did not attempt to deal with unions, other forms of joint worker action, or with individual workers' expressions of resistance. Today, we would recognize much more clearly the power available to *all* parties and the factors that underlie the interrelated decisions on whether to use it.

In the original article, we used the terms "manager" and "subordinate." We are now uncomfortable with "subordinate" because of its demeaning, dependency-laden connotations and prefer "nonmanager." The titles "manager" and "nonmanager" make the terminological difference functional rather than hierarchical.

We assumed fairly traditional organizational structures in our original article. Now we would alter our formulation to reflect newer organizational modes that are slowly emerging such as industrial democracy, intentional communities, and "phenomenarchy."[5] These new modes are based on observations such as the following:

- Both manager and nonmanagers may be governing forces in their group environment, contributing to the definition of the total area of freedom.
- A group can function without a manager, with managerial functions being shared by group members.
- A group, as a unit, can be delegated authority and can assume responsibility within a larger organizational context.

Our thoughts on the question of leadership have prompted us to design a new behavior continuum (see *Exhibit 2*) in which the total area of freedom shared by manager and nonmanagers is constantly redefined by interactions between them and the forces in the environment.

The arrows in the exhibit indicate the continual flow of interdependent influence among systems and people. The points on the continuum designate the types of manager and nonmanager behavior that become possible with any given amount of freedom available to each. The new continuum is both more

---

5. For a description of phenomenarchy, *see* Will McWhinney, "Phenomenarchy: A Suggestion for Social Redesign," *Journal of Applied Behavioral Science* (May 1973).

EXHIBIT 2
Continuum of Manager-Nonmanager Behavior

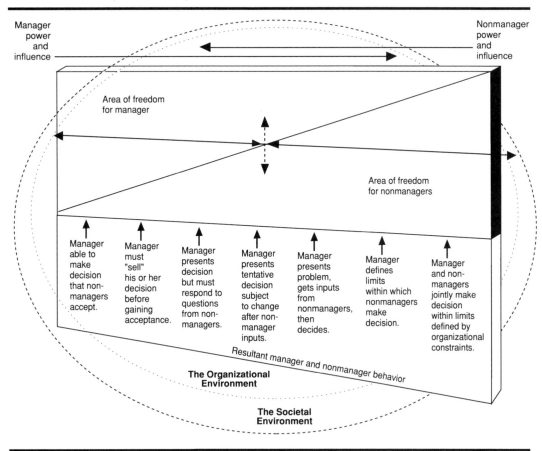

complex and more dynamic than the 1958 version, reflecting the organizational and societal realities of today.

──── DISCUSSION QUESTIONS

1. The authors offer a range of patterns that a leader can choose to employ. Choose two or three of these patterns and give an example of each pattern's effective use. When is it appropriate to be autocratic? Democratic?

2. Society has an effect on an organization and therefore on leadership patterns. The reading lists some of the social developments that

have had implications for organizations, such as the civil rights movement. What current societal developments may influence the organization and its leadership patterns?

3. As a leader, which leadership style do you prefer? Why? As a subordinate, which leadership pattern do you prefer? Why?

4. The authors provide several factors beyond the manager's control that affect leadership style. Can you name other factors that limit the range of leadership behavior that a manager can employ?

5. The demographics of the American workforce are changing at both the managerial and subordinate levels. What are some of these demographic trends? How might these changes affect the choice of leadership style?

In Praise of Followers 10

ROBERT E. KELLEY

Without good followers to back them up, leaders are irrelevant. This reading examines the role of the follower, comparing the traits of effective and ineffective followers. The best followers manage themselves well; are committed to the organization and to a purpose, principle, or person outside themselves; build their competence for maximum impact; and are courageous and honest.

Although companies often nurture leadership skills, they neglect the importance of "followership" skills. The author describes four steps that organizations can take to cultivate effective followers: 1) redefine the roles of leaders and followers as equal but different, 2) hone followership skills, 3) evaluate follower performance and provide feedback, and 4) build organizational structures that encourage followership.

We are convinced that corporations succeed or fail, compete or crumble, on the basis of how well they are led. So we study great leaders of the past and present and spend vast quantities of time and money looking for leaders to hire and trying to cultivate leadership in the employees we already have.[1]

I have no argument with this enthusiasm. Leaders matter greatly. But in searching so zealously for better leaders we tend to lose sight of the people these leaders will lead. Without his armies, after all, Napoleon was just a man with grandiose ambitions. Organizations stand or fall partly on the basis of how well their leaders lead, but partly also on the basis of how well their followers follow.

For example, declining profitability and intensified competition for corporate clients forced a large commercial bank on the East Coast to reorganize its operations and cut its work force. Its most seasoned managers had to spend most of their time in the field working with corporate customers. Time and energies were stretched so thin that one department head decided he had no choice but to delegate the responsibility for reorganization to his staff people, who had recently had training in self-management.

---

1. Author's note: I am indebted to Pat Chew for her contributions to this article. I also want to thank Janet Nordin, Howard Seckler, Paul Brophy, Stuart Mechlin, Ellen Mechlin, and Syed Shariq for their critical input.

Despite grave doubts, the department head set them up as a unit without a leader, responsible to one another and to the bank as a whole for writing their own job descriptions, designing a training program, determining criteria for performance evaluations, planning for operational needs, and helping to achieve overall organizational objectives.

They pulled it off. The bank's officers were delighted and frankly amazed that rank-and-file employees could assume so much responsibility so successfully. In fact, the department's capacity to control and direct itself virtually without leadership saved the organization months of turmoil, and as the bank struggled to remain a major player in its region, valuable management time was freed up to put out other fires.

What was it these singular employees did? Given a goal and parameters, they went where most departments could only have gone under the hands-on guidance of an effective leader. But these employees accepted the delegation of authority and went there alone. They thought for themselves, sharpened their skills, focused their efforts, put on a fine display of grit and spunk and self-control. They followed effectively.

To encourage this kind of effective following in other organizations, we need to understand the nature of the follower's role. To cultivate good followers, we need to understand the human qualities that allow effective "followership" to occur.

——— THE ROLE OF FOLLOWER

Bosses are not necessarily good leaders; subordinates are not necessarily effective followers. Many bosses couldn't lead a horse to water. Many subordinates couldn't follow a parade. Some people avoid either role. Others accept the role thrust upon them and perform it badly.

At different points in their careers, even at different times of the working day, most managers play both roles, though seldom equally well. After all, the leadership role has the glamour and attention. We take courses to learn it, and when we play it well we get applause and recognition. But the reality is that most of us are more often followers than leaders. Even when we have subordinates, we still have bosses. For every committee we chair, we sit as a member on several others.

So followership dominates our lives and organizations, but not our thinking, because our preoccupation with leadership keeps us from considering the nature and the importance of the follower.

What distinguishes an effective from an ineffective follower is enthusiastic, intelligent, and self-reliant participation—without star billing—in the pursuit of an organizational goal. Effective followers differ in their motivations for following and in their perceptions of the role. Some choose followership as their primary role at work and serve as team players who take satisfaction in helping to further a cause, an idea, a product, a service, or more rarely, a person.

Others are leaders in some situations but choose the follower role in a particular context. Both these groups view the role of follower as legitimate, inherently valuable, even virtuous.

Some potentially effective followers derive motivation from ambition. By proving themselves in the follower's role, they hope to win the confidence of peers and superiors and move up the corporate ladder. These people do not see followership as attractive in itself. All the same, they can become good followers if they accept the value of learning the role, studying leaders from a subordinate's perspective, and polishing the followership skills that will always stand them in good stead.

Understanding motivations and perceptions is not enough, however. Since followers with different motivations can perform equally well, I examined the behavior that leads to effective and less effective following among people committed to the organization and came up with two underlying behavioral dimensions that help to explain the difference.

One dimension measures to what degree followers exercise independent, critical thinking. The other ranks them on a passive/active scale. The *Exhibit* identifies five followership patterns.

Sheep are passive and uncritical, lacking in initiative and sense of responsibility. They perform the tasks given them and stop. Yes People are a livelier but equally unenterprising group. Dependent on a leader for inspiration, they can be aggressively deferential, even servile. Bosses weak in judgment and self-confidence tend to like them and to form alliances with them that can stultify the organization.

Alienated Followers are critical and independent in their thinking but passive in carrying out their role. Somehow, sometime, something turned them off. Often cynical, they tend to sink gradually into disgruntled acquiescence, seldom openly opposing a leader's efforts. In the very center of the diagram we have Survivors, who perpetually sample the wind and live by the slogan "better safe than sorry." They are adept at surviving change.

In the upper right-hand corner, finally, we have Effective Followers, who think for themselves and carry out their duties and assignments with energy and assertiveness. Because they are risk takers, self-starters, and independent problem solvers, they get consistently high ratings from peers and many superiors. Followership of this kind can be a positive and acceptable choice for parts or all of our lives—a source of pride and fulfillment.

Effective followers are well-balanced and responsible adults who can succeed without strong leadership. Many followers believe they offer as much value to the organization as leaders do, especially in project or task-force situations. In an organization of effective followers, a leader tends to be more an overseer of change and progress than a hero. As organizational structures flatten, the quality of those who follow will become more and more important. As Chester I. Barnard wrote 50 years ago in *The Functions of the Executive*, "The decision as to whether an order has authority or not lies with the person to whom it is addressed, and does not reside in 'persons of authority' or those who issue orders."

EXHIBIT
Some Followers Are More Effective

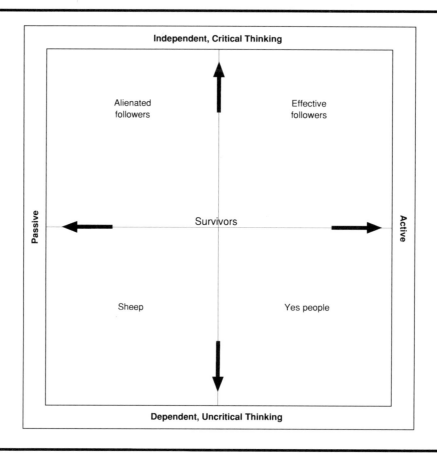

THE QUALITIES OF FOLLOWERS

Effective followers share a number of essential qualities:

1. They manage themselves well.
2. They are committed to the organization and to a purpose, principle, or person outside themselves.
3. They build their competence and focus their efforts for maximum impact.
4. They are courageous, honest, and credible.

Self-management   Paradoxically, the key to being an effective follower is the ability to think for oneself—to exercise control and independence and to work without close supervision. Good followers are people to whom a leader can safely delegate responsibility, people who anticipate needs at their own level of competence and authority.

Another aspect of this paradox is that effective followers see themselves—except in terms of line responsibility—as the equals of the leaders they follow. They are more apt to openly and unapologetically disagree with leadership and less likely to be intimidated by hierarchy and organizational structure. At the same time, they can see that the people they follow are, in turn, following the lead of others, and they try to appreciate the goals and needs of the team and the organization. Ineffective followers, on the other hand, buy into the hierarchy and, seeing themselves as subservient, vacillate between despair over their seeming powerlessness and attempts to manipulate leaders for their own purposes. Either their fear of powerlessness becomes a self-fulfilling prophecy—for themselves and often for their work units as well—or their resentment leads them to undermine the team's goals.

Self-managed followers give their organizations a significant cost advantage because they eliminate much of the need for elaborate supervisory control systems that, in any case, often lower morale. For example, a large midwestern bank redesigned its personnel selection system to attract self-managed workers. Those conducting interviews began to look for particular types of experience and capacities—initiative, teamwork, independent thinking of all kinds—and the bank revamped its orientation program to emphasize self-management. At the executive level, role playing was introduced into the interview process: how you disagree with your boss, how you prioritize your in-basket after a vacation. In the three years since, employee turnover has dropped dramatically, the need for supervisors has decreased, and administrative costs have gone down.

Of course not all leaders and managers like having self-managing subordinates. Some would rather have sheep or yes people. The best that good followers can do in this situation is to protect themselves with a little career self-management; that is, to stay attractive in the marketplace. The qualities that make a good follower are too much in demand to go begging for long.

Commitment   Effective followers are committed to something—a cause, a product, an organization, an idea—in addition to the care of their own lives and careers. Some leaders misinterpret this commitment. Seeing their authority acknowledged, they mistake loyalty to a goal for loyalty to themselves. But the fact is that many effective followers see leaders merely as coadventurers on a worthy crusade, and if they suspect their leader of flagging commitment or conflicting motives they may just withdraw their support, either by changing jobs or by contriving to change leaders.

The opportunities and the dangers posed by this kind of commitment are not hard to see. On the one hand, commitment is contagious. Most people like working with colleagues whose hearts are in their work. Morale stays high. Workers who begin to wander from their purpose are jostled back into line. Projects stay on track and on time. In addition, an appreciation of commitment and the way it works can give managers an extra tool with which to understand and channel the energies and loyalties of their subordinates.

On the other hand, followers who are strongly committed to goals not consistent with the goals of their companies can produce destructive results. Leaders having such followers can even lose control of their organizations.

A scientist at a computer company cared deeply about making computer technology available to the masses, and her work was outstanding. Since her goal was in line with the company's goals, she had few problems with top management. Yet she saw her department leaders essentially as facilitators of her dream, and when managers worked at cross-purposes to that vision, she exercised all of her considerable political skills to their detriment. Her immediate supervisors saw her as a thorn in the side, but she was quite effective in furthering her cause because she saw eye to eye with company leaders. But what if her vision and the company's vision had differed?

Effective followers temper their loyalties to satisfy organizational needs— or they find new organizations. Effective leaders know how to channel the energies of strong commitment in ways that will satisfy corporate goals as well as a follower's personal needs.

Competence and Focus   On the grounds that committed incompetence is still incompetence, effective followers master skills that will be useful to their organizations. They generally hold higher performance standards than the work environment requires, and continuing education is second nature to them, a staple in their professional development.

Less effective followers expect training and development to come to them. The only education they acquire is force-fed. If not sent to a seminar, they don't go. Their competence deteriorates unless some leader gives them parental care and attention.

Good followers take on extra work gladly, but first they do a superb job on their core responsibilities. They are good judges of their own strengths and weaknesses, and they contribute well to teams. Asked to perform in areas where they are poorly qualified, they speak up. Like athletes stretching their capacities, they don't mind chancing failure if they know they can succeed, but they are careful to spare the company wasted energy, lost time, and poor performance by accepting challenges that coworkers are better prepared to meet. Good followers see coworkers as colleagues rather than competitors.

At the same time, effective followers often search for overlooked problems. A woman on a new-product development team discovered that no one was responsible for coordinating engineering, marketing, and manufacturing. She worked out an interdepartmental review schedule that identified the people who should be involved at each stage of development. Instead of burdening her boss with yet another problem, this woman took the initiative to present the issue along with a solution.

Another woman I interviewed described her efforts to fill a dangerous void in the company she cared about. Young managerial talent in this manufacturing corporation had traditionally made careers in production. Convinced that foreign competition would alter the shape of the industry, she realized that marketing was a neglected area. She took classes, attended seminars, and read widely. More important, she visited customers to get feedback about her company's and competitors' products, and she soon knew more about the product's customer appeal and market position than any of her peers. The extra competence did wonders for her own career, but it also helped her company weather a storm it had not seen coming.

Courage   Effective followers are credible, honest, and courageous. They establish themselves as independent, critical thinkers whose knowledge and judgment can be trusted. They give credit where credit is due, admitting mistakes and sharing successes. They form their own views and ethical standards and stand up for what they believe in.

Insightful, candid, and fearless, they can keep leaders and colleagues honest and informed. The other side of the coin of course is that they can also cause great trouble for a leader with questionable ethics.

Jerome LiCari, the former R&D director at Beech-Nut, suspected for several years that the apple concentrate Beech-Nut was buying from a new supplier at 20% below market price was adulterated. His department suggested switching suppliers, but top management at the financially strapped company put the burden of proof on R&D.

By 1981, LiCari had accumulated strong evidence of adulteration and issued a memo recommending a change of supplier. When he got no response, he went to see his boss, the head of operations. According to LiCari, he was threatened with dismissal for lack of team spirit. LiCari then went to the president of Beech-Nut, and when that, too, produced no results, he gave up his three-year good-soldier effort, followed his conscience, and resigned. His last performance evaluation praised his expertise and loyalty, but said his judgment was "colored by naiveté and impractical ideals."

In 1986, Beech-Nut and LiCari's two bosses were indicted on several hundred counts of conspiracy to commit fraud by distributing adulterated apple juice. In November 1987, the company pleaded guilty and agreed to a fine of $2 million. In February 1988, the two executives were found guilty on a majority of the charges. The episode cost Beech-Nut an estimated $25 million and a 20% loss of market share. Asked during the trial if he had been naive, LiCari said, "I guess I was. I thought apple juice should be made from apples."

Is LiCari a good follower? Well, no, not to his dishonest bosses. But yes, he is almost certainly the kind of employee most companies want to have: loyal, honest, candid with his superiors, and thoroughly credible. In an ethical company involved unintentionally in questionable practices, this kind of follower can head off embarrassment, expense, and litigation.

━━━ CULTIVATING EFFECTIVE FOLLOWERS

You may have noticed by now that the qualities that make effective followers are, confusingly enough, pretty much the same qualities found in some effective leaders. This is no mere coincidence, of course. But the confusion underscores an important point. If a person has initiative, self-control, commitment, talent, honesty, credibility, and courage, we say, "Here is a leader!" By definition, a follower cannot exhibit the qualities of leadership. It violates our stereotype.

But our stereotype is ungenerous and wrong. Followership is not a person but a role, and what distinguishes followers from leaders is not intelligence or character but the role they play. As I pointed out at the beginning of this reading, effective followers and effective leaders are often the same people playing different parts at different hours of the day.

In many companies, the leadership track is the only road to career success. In almost all companies, leadership is taught and encouraged while followership is not. Yet effective followership is a prerequisite for organizational success. Your organization can take four steps to cultivate effective followers in your work force.

1. Redefine Followership and Leadership   Our stereotyped but unarticulated definitions of leadership and followership shape our expectations when we occupy either position. If a leader is defined as responsible for motivating followers, he or she will likely act toward followers as if they needed motivation. If we agree that a leader's job is to transform followers, then it must be a follower's job to provide the clay. If followers fail to need transformation, the leader looks ineffective. The way we define the roles clearly influences the outcome of the interaction.

Instead of seeing the leadership role as superior to and more active than the role of the follower, we can think of them as equal but different activities. The operative definitions are roughly these: people who are effective in the leader role have the vision to set corporate goals and strategies, the interpersonal skills to achieve consensus, the verbal capacity to communicate enthusiasm to large and diverse groups of individuals, the organizational talent to coordinate disparate efforts, and, above all, the desire to lead.

People who are effective in the follower role have the vision to see both the forest and the trees, the social capacity to work well with others, the strength of character to flourish without heroic status, the moral and psychological balance to pursue personal and corporate goals at no cost to either, and above all, the desire to participate in a team effort for the accomplishment of some greater common purpose.

This view of leadership and followership can be conveyed to employees directly and indirectly—in training and by example. The qualities that make good followers and the value the company places on effective followership can be articulated in explicit follower training. Perhaps the best way to convey this message, however, is by example. Since each of us plays a follower's part at least from time to time, it is essential that we play it well, that we contribute our competence to the achievement of team goals, that we support the team leader with candor and self-control, that we do our best to appreciate and enjoy the role of quiet contribution to a larger, common cause.

2. Honing Followership Skills   Most organizations assume that leadership has to be taught but that everyone knows how to follow. This assumption is based on three faulty premises: 1) that leaders are more important than followers, 2) that following is simply doing what you are told to do, and 3) that followers inevitably draw their energy and aims, even their talent, from the leader. A program of follower training can correct this misapprehension by focusing on topics such as improving independent, critical thinking and self-management, which includes:

- Disagreeing agreeably
- Building credibility
- Aligning personal and organizational goals and commitments
- Acting responsibly toward the organization, the leader, coworkers, and oneself
- Similarities and differences between leadership and followership roles
- Moving between the two roles with ease

3. Performance Evaluation and Feedback   Most performance evaluations include a section on leadership skills. Followership evaluation would include items like the ones I have discussed. Instead of rating employees on leadership qualities such as self-management, independent thinking, originality, courage, competence, and credibility, we can rate them on these same qualities in both the leadership and followership roles and then evaluate each individual's ability to shift easily from the one role to the other. A variety of performance perspectives will help most people understand better how well they play their various organizational roles.

Moreover, evaluations can come from peers, subordinates, and self as well as from supervisors. The process is simple enough: peers and subordinates who come into regular or significant contact with another employee fill in brief, periodic questionnaires where they rate the individual on followership qualities. Findings are then summarized and given to the employee being rated.

4. Organizational Structures That Encourage Followership   Unless the value of good following is somehow built into the fabric of the organization, it is likely to remain a pleasant conceit to which everyone pays occasional lip service but no dues. Here are four good ways to incorporate the concept into your corporate culture:

- In leaderless groups, all members assume equal responsibility for achieving goals. These are usually small task forces of people who can work together under their own supervision. However hard it is to imagine a group with more than one leader, groups with none at all can be highly productive if their members have the qualities of effective followers.
- Groups with temporary and rotating leadership are another possibility. Again, such groups are probably best kept small and the rotation fairly frequent, although the notion might certainly be extended to include the administration of a small department for, say, six-month terms. Some of these temporary leaders will be less effective than others, of course, and some may be weak indeed, which is why critics maintain that this structure is inefficient. Why not let the best leader lead? Why suffer through the tenure of less effective leaders? There are two reasons. First, experience of the leadership role is essential to the education of effective followers. Second, followers learn that they must compensate for ineffective leadership by exercising their skill as good followers. Rotating leader or not, they are bound to be faced with ineffective leadership more than once in their careers.
- Delegation to the lowest level is a third technique for cultivating good followers. Nordstrom's, the Seattle-based department store chain, gives each sales clerk responsibility for servicing and satisfying the customer, including the authority to make refunds without supervisory approval. This kind of delegation makes even people at the lowest levels responsible for their own decisions and for thinking independently about their work.
- Finally, companies can use rewards to underline the importance of good followership. This is not as easy as it sounds. Managers dependent on yes people and sheep for ego gratification will not leap at the idea of extra rewards for the people who make them most uncomfortable. In my research, I have found that effective followers get mixed treatment. About half the time, their contributions lead to substantial rewards. The other half of the time they are punished by their superiors for exercising judgment, taking risks, and failing to conform. Many managers insist that they want independent subordinates who can think for themselves. In practice, followers who challenge their bosses run the risk of getting fired.

In today's flatter, leaner organization, companies will not succeed without the kind of people who take pride and satisfaction in the role of supporting player, doing the less glorious work without fanfare. Organizations that want the benefits of effective followers must find ways of rewarding them, ways of bringing them into full partnership in the enterprise. Think of the thousands of companies that achieve adequate performance and lackluster profits with employees they treat like second-class citizens. Then imagine for a moment the power of an organization blessed with fully engaged, fully energized, fully appreciated followers.

──── DISCUSSION QUESTIONS

1. Leaders must be followers, and followers often are leaders as illustrated by Jerome LiCari's courage. Provide an instance from your personal experience when you were a follower who led.
2. Articulate a larger common cause that you are committed to as a follower.
3. In a work group of effective and competent followers, is there any real need for a leader? Should one goal of an organization be to make leaders obsolete?
4. This reading makes an important point about stereotypes and their detrimental effects. How have you allowed stereotypes to control your behavior? How have you overcome them?

PART TWO

MANAGING INDIVIDUALS AND GROUPS

SECTION A

MOTIVATING
AND MANAGING
INDIVIDUALS

One More Time: 11
How Do You Motivate Employees?

FREDERICK HERZBERG

According to conventional wisdom, managers don't motivate employees by (figuratively) kicking them; they motivate them by offering them induce-ments—more money, fringe benefits, shorter hours, comfortable surroundings.

In this reading, the author distinguishes between these inducements, which create dissatisfaction if they're absent but do little to inspire employees when they're present, and genuine motivators: recognition of achievement, greater responsibility, and opportunity for advancement. The secret to motivation, the author says, is job enrichment. Among the ways management can produce job enrichment are to remove some controls (while retaining accountability), increase employees' accountability for their own work, give people complete natural work units, and assign individuals specialized tasks so they can become experts in them. The author updates these concepts in the retrospective commentary.

How many articles, books, speeches, and workshops have pleaded plaintively, "How do I get an employee to do what I want?"

The psychology of motivation is tremendously complex, and what has been unraveled with any degree of assurance is small indeed. But the dismal ratio of knowledge to speculation has not dampened the enthusiasm for new forms of snake oil that are constantly coming on the market, many of them with academic testimonials. Doubtless this reading will have no depressing impact on the market for snake oil, but since the ideas expressed in it have been tested in many corporations and other organizations, it will help—I hope—to redress the imbalance in the aforementioned ratio.

—— "MOTIVATING" WITH KITA

In lectures to industry on the problem, I have found that the audiences are anxious for quick and practical answers, so I will begin with a straight-forward, practical formula for moving people.

What is the simplest, surest, and most direct way of getting someone to do something? Ask? But if the person responds that he or she does not want to do it, then that calls for psychological consultation to determine the reason for such obstinacy. Tell the person? The response shows that he or she does not understand you, and now an expert in communication methods has to be brought in to show you how to get through. Give the person a monetary incentive? I do not need to remind the reader of the complexity and difficulty involved in setting up and administering an incentive system. Show the person? This means a costly training program. We need a simple way.

Every audience contains the "direct action" manager who shouts, "Kick the person!" And this type of manager is right. The surest and least circumlocuted way of getting someone to do something is to administer a kick in the rear—to give what might be called the KITA.

There are various forms of KITA, and here are some of them:

Negative Physical KITA   This is a literal application of the term and was frequently used in the past. It has, however, three major drawbacks: 1) it is inelegant; 2) it contradicts the precious image of benevolence that most organizations cherish; and 3) since it is a physical attack, it directly stimulates the autonomic nervous system, and this often results in negative feedback—the employee may just kick you in return. These factors give rise to certain taboos against negative physical KITA.

In uncovering infinite sources of psychological vulnerabilities and the appropriate methods to play tunes on them, psychologists have come to the rescue of those who are no longer permitted to use negative physical KITA. "He took my rug away"; "I wonder what she meant by that"; "The boss is always going around me"—these symptomatic expressions of ego sores that have been rubbed raw are the result of application of:

Negative Psychological KITA   This has several advantages over negative physical KITA. First, the cruelty is not visible; the bleeding is internal and comes much later. Second, since it affects the higher cortical centers of the brain with its inhibitory powers, it reduces the possibility of physical backlash. Third, since the number of psychological pains that a person can feel is almost infinite, the direction and site possibilities of the KITA are increased many times. Fourth, the person administering the kick can manage to be above it all and let the system accomplish the dirty work. Fifth, those who practice it receive some ego satisfaction (one-upmanship), whereas they would find drawing blood abhorrent. Finally, if the employee does complain, he or she can always be accused of being paranoid; there is no tangible evidence of an actual attack.

Now, what does negative KITA accomplish? If I kick you in the rear (physically or psychologically), who is motivated? *I* am motivated; *you* move! Negative KITA does not lead to motivation, but to movement. So:

Positive KITA   Let us consider motivation. If I say to you, "Do this for me or the company, and in return I will give you a reward, an incentive, more status, a promotion, all the quid pro quos that exist in the industrial organization," am I motivating you? The overwhelming opinion I receive from management people is, "Yes, this is motivation."

I have a year-old Schnauzer. When it was a small puppy and I wanted it to move, I kicked it in the rear and it moved. Now that I have finished its obedience training, I hold up a dog biscuit when I want the Schnauzer to move. In this instance, who is motivated—I or the dog? The dog wants the biscuit, but it is I who want it to move. Again, I am the one who is motivated, and the dog is the one who moves. In this instance all I did was apply KITA frontally; I exerted a pull instead of a push. When industry wishes to use such positive KITAs, it has available an incredible number and variety of dog biscuits (jelly beans for humans) to wave in front of employees to get them to jump.

Why is it that managerial audiences are quick to see that negative KITA is *not* motivation, while they are almost unanimous in their judgment that positive KITA *is* motivation? It is because negative KITA is coercion, and positive KITA is co-option. But in fact, it is worse to be co-opted than to be coerced because coercion is externally imposed while co-option means that you gave your compliance. This is why positive KITA is so popular: it is a tradition; it is the American way. The organization does not have to kick you; you kick yourself.

——— MYTHS ABOUT MOTIVATION

Why is KITA not motivation? If I kick my dog (from the front or the back), he will move. And when I want him to move again, what must I do? I must kick him again. Similarly, I can charge a person's battery, and then recharge it, and recharge it again. But it is only when one has a generator of one's own that we can talk about motivation. One then needs no outside stimulation. One *wants* to do it.

With this in mind, we can review some positive KITA personnel practices that were developed as attempts to instill "motivation":

1. Reducing Time Spent at Work   This represents a marvelous way of motivating people to work—getting them off the job! We have reduced (formally and informally) the time spent on the job over the last 50 or 60 years until we are finally on the way to the "6½-day weekend." An interesting variant of this approach is the development of off-hour recreation programs. The philosophy here seems to be that those who play together, work together. The fact is that motivated people seek more hours of work, not fewer.

2. Spiraling Wages   Have these motivated people? Yes, to seek the next wage increase. Some medievalists still can be heard to say that a good depression will get employees moving. They feel that if rising wages don't or won't do the job, reducing them will.

3. Fringe Benefits   Industry has outdone the most welfare-minded of welfare states in dispensing cradle-to-the-grave succor. One company I know of had an informal "fringe benefit of the month club" going for a while. The cost of fringe benefits in this country has reached approximately 25% of the wage dollar, and we still cry for motivation.

People spend less time working for more money and more security than ever before, and the trend cannot be reversed. These benefits are no longer rewards; they are rights. A 6-day week is inhuman, a 10-hour day is exploitation, extended medical coverage is a basic decency, and stock options are the salvation of American initiative. Unless the ante is continuously raised, the psychological reaction of employees is that the company is turning back the clock.

When industry began to realize that both the economic nerve and the lazy nerve of their employees had insatiable appetites, it started to listen to the behavioral scientists who, more out of a humanist tradition than from scientific study, criticized management for not knowing how to deal with people. The next KITA easily followed.

4. Human Relations Training   More than 30 years of teaching and, in many instances, of practicing psychological approaches to handling people have resulted in costly human relations programs and, in the end, the same question: How do you motivate workers? Here, too, escalations have taken place. Thirty years ago it was necessary to request, "Please don't spit on the floor." Today the same admonition requires three "pleases" before the employee feels that a superior has demonstrated the psychologically proper attitude.

The failure of human relations training to produce motivation led to the conclusion that supervisors or managers themselves were not psychologically true to themselves in their practice of interpersonal decency. So an advanced form of human relations KITA, sensitivity training, was unfolded.

5. Sensitivity Training   Do you really, really understand yourself? Do you really, really, really trust other people? Do you really, really, really, really cooperate? The failure of sensitivity training is now being explained, by those who have become opportunistic exploiters of the technique, as a failure to really (five times) conduct proper sensitivity-training courses.

With the realization that there are only temporary gains from comfort and economic and interpersonal KITA, personnel managers concluded that the fault lay not in what they were doing, but in the employee's failure to appreciate what they were doing. This opened up the field of communications, a whole new area of "scientifically" sanctioned KITA.

6. Communications   The professor of communications was invited to join the faculty of management training programs and help in making employees understand what management was doing for them. House organs, briefing sessions, supervisory instruction on the importance of communication, and all sorts of propaganda have proliferated until today there is even an International Council of Industrial Editors. But no motivation resulted, and the obvious thought occurred that perhaps management was not hearing what the employees were saying. That led to the next KITA.

7. Two-way Communication   Management ordered morale surveys, suggestion plans, and group participation programs. Then both employees and management were communicating and listening to each other more than ever, but without much improvement in motivation.

The behavioral scientists began to take another look at their conceptions and their data, and they took human relations one step further. A glimmer of truth was beginning to show through in the writings of the so-called higher-order-need psychologists. People, so they said, want to actualize themselves. Unfortunately, the "actualizing" psychologists got mixed up with the human relations psychologists, and a new KITA emerged.

8. Job Participation   Though it may not have been the theoretical intention, job participation often became a "give-them-the-big-picture" approach. For example, if a man is tightening 10,000 nuts a day on an assembly line with a torque wrench, tell him he is building a Chevrolet. Another approach had the goal of giving employees a "feeling" that they are determining, in some measure, what they do on the job. The goal was to provide a *sense* of achievement rather than a substantive achievement in the task. Real achievement, of course, requires a task that makes it possible.

But still there was no motivation. This led to the inevitable conclusion that the employees must be sick, and therefore to the next KITA.

9. Employee Counseling   The initial use of this form of KITA in a systematic fashion can be credited to the Hawthorne experiment of the Western Electric Company during the 1930s. At that time, it was found that the employees harbored irrational feelings that were interfering with the rational operation of the factory. Counseling in this instance was a means of letting the employees unburden themselves by talking to someone about their problems. Although the counseling techniques were primitive, the program was large indeed.

The counseling approach suffered as a result of experiences during World War II, when the programs themselves were found to be interfering with the operation of the organizations; the counselors had forgotten their role of benevolent listeners and were attempting to do something about the problems that they heard about. Psychological counseling, however, has managed to survive the negative impact of World War II experiences and today is beginning to flourish with renewed sophistication. But, alas, many of these programs, like all the others, do not seem to have lessened the pressure of demands to find out how to motivate workers.

Because KITA results only in short-term movement, it is safe to predict that the cost of these programs will increase steadily and new varieties will be developed as old positive KITAs reach their satiation points.

────── HYGIENE VERSUS MOTIVATORS

Let me rephrase the perennial question this way: How do you install a generator in an employee? A brief review of my motivation-hygiene theory of job attitudes is required before theoretical and practical suggestions can be offered. The theory was first drawn from an examination of events in the lives of engineers and accountants. At least 16 other investigations, using a wide variety of populations, have since been completed, making the original research one of the most replicated studies in the field of job attitudes.

The findings of these studies, along with corroboration from many other investigations using different procedures, suggest that the factors involved in producing job satisfaction (and motivation) are separate and distinct from the factors that lead to job dissatisfaction. Because separate factors need to be considered, depending on whether job satisfaction or job dissatisfaction is being examined, it follows that these two feelings are not opposites of each other. The opposite of job satisfaction is not job dissatisfaction but, rather, *no* job satisfaction; and similarly, the opposite of job dissatisfaction is not job satisfaction, but *no* job dissatisfaction.

Stating the concept presents a problem in semantics, for we normally think of satisfaction and dissatisfaction as opposites—therefore, what is not satisfying must be dissatisfying, and vice versa. But when it comes to understanding the behavior of people in their jobs, more than a play on words is involved.

Two different needs of human beings are involved here. One set of needs can be thought of as stemming from humankind's animal nature—the built-in drive to avoid pain from the environment, plus all the learned drives that become conditioned to the basic biological needs. For example, hunger, a basic biological drive, makes it necessary to earn money, and then money becomes a specific drive. The other set of needs relates to that unique human characteristic, the ability to achieve and, through achievement, to experience psychological growth. The stimuli for the growth needs are tasks that induce growth; in the industrial setting, they are the job content. *Contrariwise*, the stimuli inducing pain-avoidance behavior are found in the job environment.

The growth or *motivator* factors that are intrinsic to the job are: achievement, recognition for achievement, the work itself, responsibility, and growth or advancement. The dissatisfaction-avoidance or *hygiene* (KITA) factors that are extrinsic to the job include: company policy and administration, supervision, interpersonal relationships, working conditions, salary, status, and security.

A composite of the factors that are involved in causing job satisfaction and job dissatisfaction, drawn from samples of 1,685 employees, is shown in

EXHIBIT 1
Factors Affecting Job Attitudes as Reported in 12 Investigations

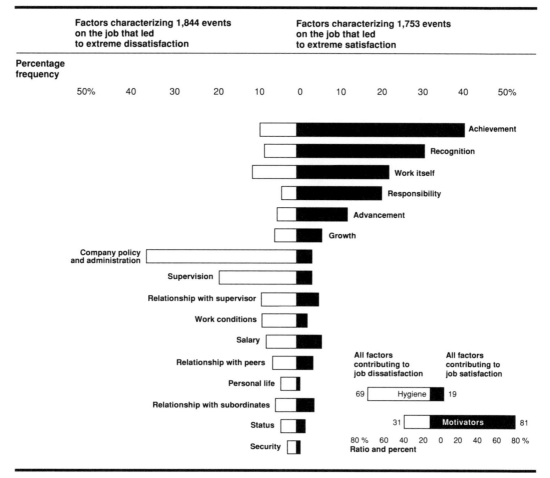

Exhibit 1. The results indicate that motivators were the primary cause of satisfaction, and hygiene factors the primary cause of unhappiness on the job. The employees, studied in 12 different investigations, included lower-level supervisors, professional women, agricultural administrators, men about to retire from management positions, hospital maintenance personnel, manufacturing supervisors, nurses, food handlers, military officers, engineers, scientists, housekeepers, teachers, technicians, female assemblers, accountants, Finnish foreman, and Hungarian engineers.

They were asked what job events had occurred in their work that had led to extreme satisfaction or extreme dissatisfaction on their part. Their responses are broken down in *Exhibit 1* into percentages of total positive job events and of total negative job events. (The figures total more than 100% on both the "hygiene" and "motivators" sides because often at least two factors can be attributed to a single event; advancement, for instance, often accompanies assumption of responsibility.)

To illustrate, a typical response involving achievement that had a negative effect for the employee was, "I was unhappy because I didn't do the job successfully." A typical response in the small number of positive job events in the company policy and administration grouping was, "I was happy because the company reorganized the section so that I didn't report any longer to the guy I didn't get along with."

As the lower right-hand part of *Exhibit 1* shows, of all the factors contributing to job satisfaction, 81% were motivators. And of all the factors contributing to the employees' dissatisfaction over their work, 69% involved hygiene elements.

ETERNAL TRIANGLE

There are three general philosophies of personnel management. The first is based on organizational theory, the second on industrial engineering, and the third on behavioral science.

Organizational theorists believe that human needs are either so irrational or so varied and adjustable to specific situations that the major function of personnel management is to be as pragmatic as the occasion demands. If jobs are organized in a proper manner, they reason, the result will be the most efficient job structure, and the most favorable job attitudes will follow as a matter of course.

Industrial engineers hold that humankind is mechanistically oriented and economically motivated and that human needs are best met by attuning the individual to the most efficient work process. The goal of personnel management therefore should be to concoct the most appropriate incentive system and to design the specific working conditions in a way that facilitates the most efficient use of the human machine. By structuring jobs in a manner that leads to the most efficient operation, engineers believe that they can obtain the optimal organization of work and the proper work attitudes.

Behavioral scientists focus on group sentiments, attitudes of individual employees, and the organization's social and psychological climate. This persuasion emphasizes one or more of the various hygiene and motivator needs. Its approach to personnel management is generally to emphasize some form of human relations education, in the hope of instilling healthy employee attitudes and an organizational climate that is considered to be felicitous to human values. The belief is that proper attitudes will lead to efficient job and organizational structure.

There is always a lively debate about the overall effectiveness of the approaches of organizational theorists and industrial engineers. Manifestly both have achieved much. But the nagging question for behavioral scientists has been: What is the cost in human problems that eventually cause more expense to the

EXHIBIT 2
'Triangle' of Philosophies of Personnel Management

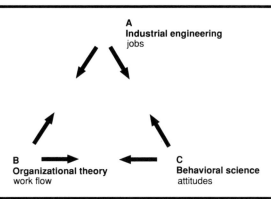

A
Industrial engineering
jobs

B　　　　　　　　　　　　　　　　　C
Organizational theory　　　　　　**Behavioral science**
work flow　　　　　　　　　　　　attitudes

organization—for instance, turnover, absenteeism, errors, violation of safety rules, strikes, restriction of output, higher wages, and greater fringe benefits? On the other hand, behavioral scientists are hard put to document much manifest improvement in personnel management, using their approach.

The three philosophies can be depicted as a triangle, as is done in *Exhibit 2*, with each persuasion claiming the apex angle. The motivation-hygiene theory claims the same angle as industrial engineering, but for opposite goals. Rather than rationalizing the work to increase efficiency, the theory suggests that work be *enriched* to bring about effective utilization of personnel. Such a systematic attempt to motivate employees by manipulating the motivator factors is just beginning.

The term job enrichment describes this embryonic movement. An older term, job enlargement, should be avoided because it is associated with past failures stemming from a misunderstanding of the problem. Job enrichment provides the opportunity for the employee's psychological growth, while job enlargement merely makes a job structurally bigger. Since scientific job enrichment is very new, this reading only suggests the principles and practical steps that have recently emerged from several successful experiments in industry.

JOB LOADING

In attempting to enrich certain jobs, management often reduces the personal contribution of employees rather than giving them opportunities for growth in their accustomed jobs. Such endeavors, which I shall call horizontal job loading (as opposed to vertical loading, or providing motivator factors), have been the problem of earlier job-enlargement programs. Job loading merely enlarges the meaninglessness of the job. Some examples of this approach, and their effect, are:

- Challenging the employee by increasing the amount of production expected. If each tightens 10,000 bolts a day, see if each can tighten 20,000 bolts a day. The arithmetic involved shows that multiplying zero by zero still equals zero.
- Adding another meaningless task to the existing one, usually some routine clerical activity. The arithmetic here is adding zero to zero.
- Rotating the assignments of a number of jobs that need to be enriched. This means washing dishes for a while, then washing silverware. The arithmetic is substituting one zero for another zero.
- Removing the most difficult parts of the assignment in order to free the worker to accomplish more of the less challenging assignments. This traditional engineering approach amounts to subtraction in the hope of accomplishing addition.

These are common forms of horizontal loading that frequently come up in preliminary brainstorming sessions of job enrichment. The principles of vertical loading have not all been worked out as yet, and they remain rather general, but I have furnished seven useful starting points for consideration in *Exhibit 3*.

A SUCCESSFUL APPLICATION

An example from a highly successful job-enrichment experiment can illustrate the distinction between horizontal and vertical loading of a job. The subjects of this study were the stockholder correspondents employed by a very large corporation. Seemingly, the task required of these carefully selected and highly trained correspondents was quite complex and challeng-

EXHIBIT 3
Principles of Vertical Job Loading

PRINCIPLE	MOTIVATORS INVOLVED
A Removing some controls while retaining accountability	Responsibility and personal achievement
B Increasing the accountability of individuals for own work	Responsibility and recognition
C Giving a person a complete natural unit of work (module, division, area, and so on)	Responsibility, achievement, and recognition
D Granting additional authority to employees in their activity; job freedom	Responsibility, achievement, and recognition
E Making periodic reports directly available to the workers themselves rather than to supervisors	Internal recognition
F Introducing new and more difficult tasks not previously handled	Growth and learning
G Assigning individuals specific or specialized tasks, enabling them to become experts	Responsibility, growth, and advancement

ing. But almost all indexes of performance and job attitudes were low, and exit interviewing confirmed that the challenge of the job existed merely as words.

A job-enrichment project was initiated in the form of an experiment with one group, designated as an achieving unit, having its job enriched by the principles described in *Exhibit 3*. A control group continued to do its job in the traditional way. (There were also two "uncommitted" groups of correspondents formed to measure the so-called Hawthorne Effect—that is, to gauge whether productivity and attitudes toward the job changed artificially merely because employees sensed that the company was paying more attention to them in doing something different or novel. The results for these groups were substantially the same as for the control group, and for the sake of simplicity I do not deal with them in this summary.) No changes in hygiene were introduced for either group other than those that would have been made anyway, such as normal pay increases.

The changes for the achieving unit were introduced in the first two months, averaging one per week of the seven motivators listed in *Exhibit 3*. At the end of six months the members of the achieving unit were found to be outperforming their counterparts in the control group, and in addition indicated a marked increase in their liking for their jobs. Other results showed that the achieving group had lower absenteeism and, subsequently, a much higher rate of promotion.

Exhibit 4 illustrates the changes in performance, measured in February and March, before the study period began, and at the end of each month of the study period. The shareholder service index represents quality of letters, including accuracy of information, and speed of response to stockholders' letters of inquiry. The index of a current month was averaged into the average of the two prior months, which means that improvement was harder to obtain if the indexes of the previous months were low. The achievers were performing less well before the six-month period started, and their performance service index continued to decline after the introduction of the motivators, evidently because of uncertainty after their newly granted responsibilities. In the third month, however, performance improved, and soon the members of this group had reached a high level of accomplishment.

Exhibit 5 shows the two groups' attitudes toward their job, measured at the end of March, just before the first motivator was introduced, and again at the end of September. The correspondents were asked 16 questions, all involving motivation. A typical one was, "As you see it, how many opportunities do you feel that you have in your job for making worthwhile contributions?" The answers were scaled from 1 to 5, with 80 as the maximum possible score. The achievers became much more positive about their job, while the attitude of the control unit remained about the same (the drop is not statistically significant).

How was the job of these correspondents restructured? *Exhibit 6* lists the suggestions made that were deemed to be horizontal loading, and the actual vertical loading changes that were incorporated in the job of the achieving unit. The capital letters under "Principle" after "Vertical loading" refer to the

EXHIBIT 4
Shareholder Service Index in Company Experiment

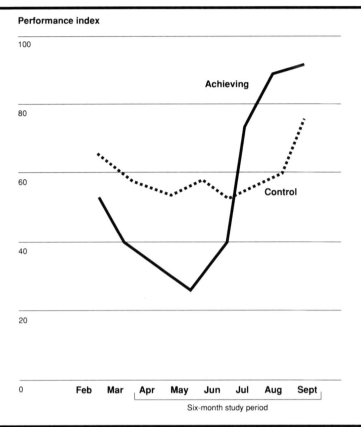

STEPS FOR JOB ENRICHMENT

corresponding letters in *Exhibit 3*. The reader will note that the rejected forms of horizontal loading correspond closely to the list of common manifestations I mentioned earlier.

━━━ STEPS FOR JOB ENRICHMENT

Now that the motivator idea has been described in practice, here are the steps that managers should take in instituting the principle with their employees:

1. Select those jobs in which a) the investment in industrial engineering does not make changes too costly, b) attitudes are poor, c) hygiene is becoming very costly, and d) motivation will make a difference in performance.
2. Approach these jobs with the conviction that they can be changed. Years of tradition have led managers to believe that the content of

the jobs is sacrosanct and the only scope of action that they have is in ways of stimulating people.

3. Brainstorm a list of changes that may enrich the jobs, without concern for their practicality.

4. Screen the list to eliminate suggestions that involve hygiene, rather than actual motivation.

5. Screen the list for generalities, such as "give them more responsibility," that are rarely followed in practice. This might seem obvious, but the motivator words have never left industry; the substance has just been rationalized and organized out. Words like *responsibility*, *growth*, *achievement*, and *challenge*, for example, have been elevated to the lyrics of the patriotic anthem for all organizations. It is the old problem typified by the pledge of allegiance to the flag being more important than contributions to the country—of following the form, rather than the substance.

6. Screen the list to eliminate any *horizontal* loading suggestions.

7. Avoid direct participation by the employees whose jobs are to be enriched. Ideas they have expressed previously certainly constitute a valuable source for recommended changes, but their direct involvement contaminates the process with human-relations *hygiene* and, more specifically, gives them only a *sense* of making a

EXHIBIT 5
Changes in Attitudes Toward Tasks in Company Experiment

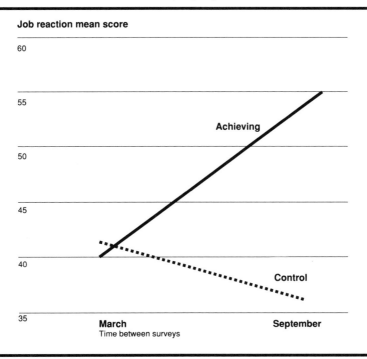

EXHIBIT 6
Enlargement versus Enrichment of Correspondents' Tasks in Company Experiment

HORIZONTAL LOADING SUGGESTIONS *rejected*	VERTICAL LOADING SUGGESTIONS *adopted*	PRINCIPLE
Firm quotas could be set for letters to be answered each day, using a rate which would be hard to reach.	Subject matter experts were appointed within each unit for other members of the unit to consult with before seeking supervisory help. (The supervisor had been answering all specialized and difficult questions.)	G
The secretaries could type the letters themselves, as well as compose them, or take on any other clerical functions.	Correspondents signed their own names on letters. (The supervisor had been signing all letters.)	B
All difficult or complex inquires could be channeled to a few secretaries so that the remainder could achieve high rates of output. These jobs could be exchanged from time to time.	The work of the more experienced correspondents were proofread less frequently by supervisors and was done at the correspondents' desks, dropping verification from 100% to 10%. (Previously, all correspondents' letters had been checked by the supervisor.)	A
The secretaries could be rotated through units handling different customers, and then sent back to their own units.	Production was discussed, but only in terms such as "a full day's work is expected." As time went on, this was no longer mentioned. (Before, the group had been constantly reminded of the number of letters that needed to be answered.)	D
	Outgoing mail went directly to the mailroom without going over supervisors' desks. (The letters had always been routed through the supervisors.)	A
	Correspondents were encouraged to answer letters in a more personalized way. (Reliance on the form-letter approach had been standard practice.)	C
	Each correspondent was held personally responsible for the quality and accuracy of letters. (This responsibility had been the province of the supervisor and the verifier.)	B, E

contribution. The job is to be changed, and it is the content that will produce the motivation, not attitudes about being involved or the challenge inherent in setting up a job. That process will be over shortly, and it is what the employees will be doing from then on that will determine their motivation. A sense of participation will result only in short-term movement.

8. In the initial attempts at job enrichment, set up a controlled experiment. At least two equivalent groups should be chosen, one an experimental unit in which the motivators are systematically introduced over a period of time, and the other one a control group in

which no changes are made. For both groups, hygiene should be allowed to follow its natural course for the duration of the experiment. Pre- and post-installation tests of performance and job attitudes are necessary to evaluate the effectiveness of the job enrichment program. The attitude test must be limited to motivator items in order to divorce employees' views of the jobs they are given from all the surrounding hygiene feelings that they might have.

9. Be prepared for a drop in performance in the experimental group for the first few weeks. The changeover to a new job may lead to a temporary reduction in efficiency.

10. Expect your first-line supervisors to experience some anxiety and hostility over the changes you are making. The anxiety comes from their fear that the changes will result in poorer performance for their unit. Hostility will arise when employees start assuming what the supervisors regard as their own responsibility for performance. The supervisor without checking duties to perform may then be left with little to do.

After successful experiment, however, the supervisors usually discover the supervisory and managerial functions that they have neglected, or that were never theirs because all their time was given over to checking the work of their subordinates. For example, in the R&D division of one large chemical company I know of, the supervisors of the laboratory assistants were theoretically responsible for their training and evaluation. These functions, however, had come to be performed in a routine, unsubstantial fashion. After the job-enrichment program, during which the supervisors were not merely passive observers of the assistants' performance, the supervisors actually were devoting their time to reviewing performance and administering thorough training.

What has been called an employee-centered style of supervision will come about not through education of supervisors, but by changing the jobs that they do.

——— CONCLUDING NOTE

Job enrichment will not be a one-time proposition, but a continuous management function. The initial changes should last for a very long period of time. There are a number of reasons for this:

- The changes should bring the job up to the level of challenge commensurate with the skill that was hired.
- Those who have still more ability eventually will be able to demonstrate it better and win promotion to higher-level jobs.
- The very nature of motivators, as opposed to hygiene factors, is that they have a much longer-term effect on employees' attitudes. Perhaps the job will have to be enriched again, but this will not occur as frequently as the need for hygiene.

Not all jobs can be enriched, nor do all jobs need to be enriched. If only a small percentage of the time and money that is now devoted to hygiene, however, were given to job enrichment efforts, the return in human satisfaction and economic gain would be one of the largest dividends that industry and society have ever reaped through their efforts at better personnel management.

The argument for job enrichment can be summed up quite simply: if you have employees on a job, use them. If you can't use them on the job, get rid of them, either via automation or by selecting someone with lesser ability. If you can't use them and you can't get rid of them, you will have a motivation problem.

* * *

Nineteen years after this reading's original publication, the author wrote the following commentary.

———— RETROSPECTIVE COMMENTARY

I wrote this article at the height of the attention on improving employee performance through various (contrived) psychological approaches to human relations. I tried to redress industrial social scientists' overconcern about how to treat workers to the neglect of how to design the work itself.

The first part of the article distinguishes between motivation and movement, a distinction that most writing on motivation misses. Movement is a function of fear of punishment or failure to get extrinsic rewards. It is the typical procedure used in animal training and its counterpart, behavioral modification techniques for humans. Motivation is a function of growth from getting intrinsic rewards out of interesting and challenging work.

While the immediate behavioral results from movement and motivation appear alike, their dynamics, which produce vastly different long-term consequences, are different. Movement requires constant reinforcement and stresses short-term results. To get a reaction, management must constantly enhance the extrinsic rewards for movement. If I get a bonus of $1,000 one year and $500 the next, I am getting extra rewards both years, but psychologically I have taken a $500 salary cut.

Motivation is based on growth needs. It is an internal engine, and its benefits show up over a long period of time. Because the ultimate reward in motivation is personal growth, people don't need to be rewarded incrementally. I write a book—a big accomplishment. Then I write an article—a lesser accomplishment, but nevertheless an addition to my personal growth.

For this article, I invented the acronym KITA (kick in the ass) to describe the movement technique. The inelegance of the term offended those who consider good treatment a motivating strategy, regardless of the nature of the work itself. In this plain language I tried to spotlight the animal approach to dealing with human beings that characterizes so much of our behavioral science intervention.

EXHIBIT 7
How the Hygiene-Motivator Factors Affect Job Attitudes in Six Countries

	All factors contributing to job dissatisfaction	All factors contributing to job satisfaction
Percentage	100% 80 60 40 20	0 20 40 60 80 100%
Japan	61	8
	39	92
India	70	34
	30	66
South Africa	72	20
	28	86
Zambia	86	15
	12	85
Italy	69	38
	31	62
Israel	60	33
	40	67

Hygiene   Motivators

The article's popularity stems in great part from readers' recognition that KITA underlies the assumed benevolence of personnel practices. If I were writing "One More Time" today, I would emphasize the important, positive role of organizational behaviorists more than I did in 1968. We can certainly learn to get along better on the job. Reduced workplace tension through congenial relations is a necessary ingredient of a pleasant environment.

The second part of the article describes my motivation-hygiene theory. It suggests that environmental factors (hygienes) can at best create no dissatisfaction on the job, and their absence creates dissatisfaction. In contrast, what makes people happy on the job and motivates them are the job content factors (motivators). The controversy surrounding these concepts continues to this day.

While the original 12 studies were mostly American (they also included Finnish supervisors and Hungarian engineers), the results have been replicated throughout the world. A sampling of recent foreign investigations, which the reader can compare with the first American studies detailed in *Exhibit 1*, appears in *Exhibit 7*. The similarity of the profiles is worth noting.

EXHIBIT 8
Sensory Ingredients of Job Enrichment

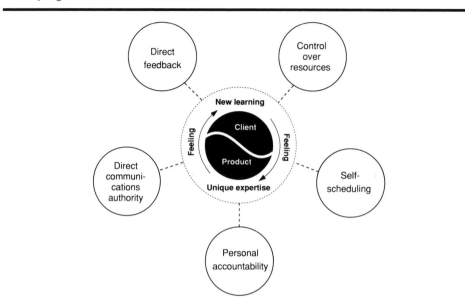

The 1970s was the decade of job enrichment (discussed in the third part of the article), sometimes called job design or redesign by opponents of the motivation-hygiene theory. Since the first trial-and-error studies at AT&T, experience has produced refinements of the procedures for job enrichment and the goals for achieving it. I like to illustrate them in the wheel shown in *Exhibit 8*.

This diagram reflects my conviction that the present-day abstraction of work has shut out feelings from the job content. Finance, for example, has become the focus of attention in most businesses, and nothing is more abstract and devoid of feeling. Part of the blame can be laid to electronic communication, which promotes detachment and abstraction. Job enrichment grows out of knowing your product and your client with feeling, not just intellectually.

With reference to the motivator ingredients discussed in the 1968 article, "recognition for achievement" translates into "direct feedback" in *Exhibit 8*. The wheel in *Exhibit 8* shows this feedback to come chiefly from the client and product of the work itself, not from the supervisor (except in the case of new hires). The motivator factor "responsibility" translates into a number of ingredients: self-scheduling, authority to communicate, control of resources, and accountability. Finally, the motivator factors "advancement" and "growth" translate into the central dynamic of new learning leading to unique expertise. The feeling of satisfaction is also indicated as a dynamic of learning from clients and products.

The key to job enrichment is nurture of a client relationship rather than a functional or hierarchical relationship. Let me illustrate with a diagram of

EXHIBIT 9
Client Relationships in an Air Force Function

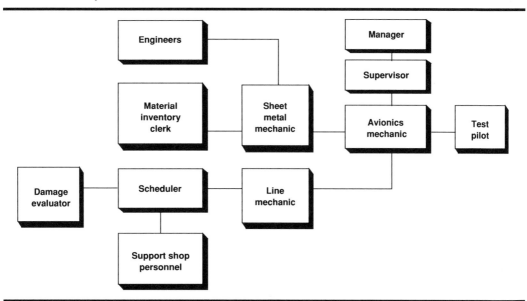

relationships in an airplane overhaul project carried out for the U.S. Air Force (*Exhibit 9*). The avionics mechanic's external client is the test pilot, and although he reports to his supervisor, his supervisor serves him. The sheet metal mechanic and the line mechanic serve the avionics mechanic. And so on back into the system.

By backing into the system, you can identify who serves whom—not who reports to whom—which is critical in trying to enrich jobs. You identify the external client, then the core jobs, or internal client jobs, serving that client. You first enrich the core job with the ingredients shown in *Exhibit 8* and then enrich the jobs that serve these internal clients.

During the 1970s, critics predicted that job enrichment would reduce the number of employees. Ironically, the restructuring and downsizing of U.S. companies during the 1980s have often serendipitously produced job enrichment. With fewer employees performing the same tasks, some job enrichment was inevitable. But the greater efficiency of enriched jobs ultimately leads to a competitive edge and more jobs.

Today, we seem to be losing ground to KITA. It's all the bottom line, as the expression goes. The work ethic and the quality of worklife movement have succumbed to the pragmatics of worldwide competition and the escalation of management direction by the abstract fields of finance and marketing—as opposed to production and sales, where palpable knowledge of clients and products resides. These abstract fields are more conducive to movement than to motivation. I find the new entrants in the world of work on the whole a passionless lot intent on serving financial indexes rather than clients and products. Motivation encompasses passion; movement is sterile.

To return to "One More Time": I don't think I would write it much differently today, though I would include the knowledge gained from recent job enrichment experiments. The distinction between movement and motivation is still true, and motivation-hygiene theory is still a framework with which to evaluate actions. Job enrichment remains the key to designing work that motivates employees.

DISCUSSION QUESTIONS

1. Give an example from your work history of factors that contributed to your job satisfaction and factors that contributed to any feeling of job dissatisfaction that you may have had.
2. Does motivation or job enrichment discussed in this reading apply to all jobs or only to jobs at a certain level in the organization?
3. The author gives several principles of vertical job loading. Are there other principles you could add? Do you see any potential drawbacks to the principles listed?
4. In the original reading, the author did not find much value in the behavioral science philosophy of personnel management. In his retrospective comments, the author states that he "would emphasize the important, positive role of organizational behaviorists." Why do you suppose he has made this shift?
5. Have developments that you are aware of in the areas of organizational design and human resource management tended to support or oppose the author's approach to motivation? Explain.

Pygmalion in Management 12

J. STERLING LIVINGSTON

This reading focuses on the power of managers' expectations in training, teaching, and preparing subordinates for more responsible and rewarding positions. Because the early years of people's careers deeply influence their self-image and future performance, it is crucial that managers be sensitive to their own behavior and its impact on subordinates. Enthusiasm and interest are key; discouragement, low expectations, and lack of involvement by executives lead to poor employee performance and low self-esteem. A retrospective commentary outlines the author's recent perspectives on the power of self-fulfilling managerial prophecies.

In George Bernard Shaw's *Pygmalion*, Eliza Doolittle explains:

You see, really and truly, apart from the things anyone can pick up (the dressing and the proper way of speaking, and so on), the difference between a lady and a flower girl is not how she behaves but how she's treated. I shall always be a flower girl to Professor Higgins because he always treats me as a flower girl and always will; but I know I can be a lady to you because you always treat me as a lady and always will.

Some managers always treat their subordinates in a way that leads to superior performance. But most managers, like Professor Higgins, unintentionally treat their subordinates in a way that leads to lower performance than they are capable of achieving. The way managers treat their subordinates is subtly influenced by what they expect of them. If managers' expectations are high, productivity is likely to be excellent. If their expectations are low, productivity is likely to be poor. It is as though there were a law that caused subordinates' performance to rise or fall to meet managers' expectations.

The powerful influence of one person's expectations on another's behavior has long been recognized by physicians and behavioral scientists and, more recently, by teachers. But heretofore the importance of managerial expectations for individual and group performance has not been widely understood. I have documented this phenomenon in a number of case studies prepared during the past decade for major industrial concerns. These cases and other evidence available from scientific research now reveal the following:

- Managers' expectations and treatment of their subordinates largely determine the subordinates' performance and career progress.
- A unique characteristic of superior managers is the ability to create high performance expectations that subordinates fulfill.
- Less-effective managers fail to develop similar expectations, and as a consequence, the productivity of their subordinates suffers.
- Subordinates, more often than not, appear to do what they believe they are expected to do.

——— IMPACT ON PRODUCTIVITY

One of the most comprehensive illustrations of the effect of managerial expectations on productivity is recorded in studies of the organizational experiment undertaken in 1961 by Alfred Oberlander, manager of the Rockaway district office of the Metropolitan Life Insurance Company. He had observed that outstanding insurance agencies grew faster than average or poor agencies and that new insurance agents performed better in outstanding agencies than in average or poor agencies, regardless of their sales aptitude. He decided, therefore, to group his superior agents in one unit to stimulate their performance and to provide a challenging environment in which to introduce new salespeople.

Accordingly, Oberlander assigned his six best agents to work with his best assistant manager, an equal number of average producers to work with an average assistant manager, and the remaining low producers to work with the least able manager. He then asked the superior group to produce two-thirds of the premium volume achieved by the entire agency during the previous year. He describes the results as follows:

> Shortly after this selection had been made, the people in the agency began referring to this select group as a "superstaff" because of their high esprit de corps in operating so well as a unit. Their production efforts over the first 12 weeks far surpassed our most optimistic expectations . . . proving that groups of people of sound ability can be motivated beyond their apparently normal productive capacities when the problems created by the poor producer are eliminated from the operation.
>
> Thanks to this fine result, our overall agency performance improved by 40%, and it remained at this figure.
>
> In the beginning of 1962 when, through expansion, we appointed another assistant manager and assigned him a staff, we again used this same concept, arranging the agents once more according to their productive capacity.
>
> The assistant managers were assigned . . . according to their ability, with the most capable assistant manager receiving the best group, thus playing strength to strength. Our agency overall production again

improved by about 25% to 30%, and so this staff arrangement remained in place until the end of the year.

Now in this year of 1963, we found upon analysis that there were
so many agents . . . with a potential of half a million dollars or more
that only one staff remained of those people in the agency who were
not considered to have any chance of reaching the half-million-dollar
mark.

Although the productivity of the "superstaff" improved dramatically,
it should be pointed out that the productivity of those in the lowest unit, "who
were not considered to have any chance of reaching the half-million-dollar
mark," actually declined, and that attrition among them increased. The performance of the superior agents rose to meet their managers' expectations, while
that of the weaker ones declined as predicted.

Self-fulfilling Prophecies   The "average" unit, however, proved to be an
anomaly. Although the district manager expected only average performance
from this group, its productivity increased significantly. This was because the
assistant manager in charge of the group refused to believe that she was less
capable than the manager of the superstaff or that the agents in the top group
had any greater ability than the agents in her group. She insisted in discussions
with her agents that every person in the middle group had greater potential
than those in the superstaff, lacking only their years of experience in selling
insurance. She stimulated her agents to accept the challenge of outperforming
the superstaff. As a result, in each year the middle group increased its productivity by a higher percentage than the superstaff did (although it never attained
the dollar volume of the top group).

It is of special interest that the self-image of the manager of the average
unit did not permit her to accept others' treatment of her as an average manager,
just as Eliza Doolittle's image of herself as a lady did not permit her to accept
others' treatment of her as a flower girl. The assistant manager transmitted her
own strong feelings of efficacy to her agents, created mutual expectancy of high
performance, and greatly stimulated productivity.

Comparable results occurred when a similar experiment was made at
another office of the company. Further confirmation comes from a study of the
early managerial success of 49 college graduates who were management-level
employees of an operating company of AT&T. David E. Berlew and Douglas T.
Hall of the Massachusetts Institute of Technology examined the career progress
of these managers over a period of five years and discovered that their relative
success, as measured by salary increases and the company's estimate of each
one's performance and potential, depended largely on the company's expectations of them.

The influence of one person's expectations on another's behavior is by
no means a business discovery. More than half a century ago, Albert Moll
concluded from his clinical experience that subjects behaved as they believed
they were expected to. The phenomenon he observed, in which "the prophecy

causes its own fulfillment," has recently become a subject of considerable scientific interest. For example:

- In a series of scientific experiments, Robert Rosenthal of Harvard University has demonstrated that a "teacher's expectation for a pupil's intellectual competence can come to serve as an educational self-fulfilling prophecy."
- An experiment in a summer Headstart program for 60 preschoolers compared the performance of pupils under two groups: teachers who had been led to expect relatively slow learning by their children, and teachers who had been led to believe that their children had excellent intellectual ability and learning capacity. Pupils of the second group of teachers learned much faster.[1]

Moreover, the healing professions have long recognized that a physician's or psychiatrist's expectations can have a formidable influence on a patient's physical or mental health. What takes place in the minds of the patients and the healers, particularly when they have congruent expectations, may determine the outcome. For instance, the havoc of a doctor's pessimistic prognosis has often been observed. Again, it is well known that the efficacy of a new drug or a new treatment can be greatly influenced by the physician's expectations—a result referred to by the medical profession as a "placebo effect."

Pattern of Failure   When salespersons are treated by their managers as superpeople, as the superstaff was at the Metropolitan Rockaway district office, they try to live up to that image and do what they know supersalespersons are expected to do. But when the agents with poor productivity records are treated by their managers as *not* having any chance of success, as the low producers at Rockaway were, this negative expectancy also becomes a managerial self-fulfilling prophecy.

Unsuccessful salespersons have great difficulty maintaining their self-image and self-esteem. In response to low managerial expectations, they typically attempt to prevent additional damage to their egos by avoiding situations that might lead to greater failure. They either reduce the number of sales calls they make or avoid trying to close sales when that might result in further painful rejection, or both. Low expectations and damaged egos lead them to behave in a manner that increases the probability of failure, thereby fulfilling their managers' expectations. Let me illustrate:

Not long ago I studied the effectiveness of branch bank managers at a West Coast bank with over 500 branches. The managers who had had their lending authority reduced because of high rates of loss became progressively less effective. To prevent further loss of authority, they turned to making only safe loans. This action resulted in losses of business to competing banks and a

---

1. The Rosenthal and Headstart studies are cited in Robert Rosenthal and Lenore Jacobson, *Pygmalion in the Classroom* (New York: Holt, Rinehart, and Winston, Inc., 1968), p. 11.

relative decline in both deposits and profits at their branches. Then, to reverse that decline in deposits and earnings, they often reached for loans and became almost irrational in their acceptance of questionable credit risks. Their actions were not so much a matter of poor judgment as an expression of their willingness to take desperate risks in the hope of being able to avoid further damage to their egos and to their careers.

Thus, in response to the low expectations of their supervisors who had reduced their lending authority, they behaved in a manner that led to larger credit losses. They appeared to do what they believed they were expected to do, and their supervisors' expectations became self-fulfilling prophecies.

——— POWER OF EXPECTATIONS

Managers cannot avoid the depressing cycle of events that flow from low expectations merely by hiding their feelings from subordinates. If managers believe subordinates will perform poorly, it is virtually impossible for them to mask their expectations because the message usually is communicated unintentionally, without conscious action.

Indeed, managers often communicate most when they believe they are communicating least. For instance, when they say nothing—become cold and uncommunicative—it usually is a sign that they are displeased by a subordinate or believe that he or she is hopeless. The silent treatment communicates negative feelings even more effectively, at times, than a tongue-lashing does. What seems to be critical in the communication of expectations is not what the boss says so much as the way he or she behaves. Indifferent and noncommital treatment, more often than not, is the kind of treatment that communicates low expectations and leads to poor performance.

Common Illusions   Managers are more effective in communicating low expectations to their subordinates than in communicating high expectations to them, even though most managers believe exactly the opposite. It usually is astonishingly difficult for them to recognize the clarity with which they transmit negative feelings. To illustrate again:

- The Rockaway district manager vigorously denied that he had communicated low expectations to the agents in the poorest group who, he believed, did not have any chance of becoming high producers. Yet the message was clearly received by those agents. A typical case was that of an agent who resigned from the low unit. When the district manager told the agent that he was sorry she was leaving, the agent replied, "No you're not; you're glad." Although the district manager previously had said nothing to her, he had unintentionally communicated his low expectations to his agents through his indifferent manner. Subsequently, the agents who were assigned to the lowest unit interpreted the assignment as equivalent to a request for their resignation.

- One of the company's agency managers established superior, average, and low units, even though he was convinced that he had no superior or outstanding subordinates. "All my assistant managers and agents are either average or incompetent," he explained to the Rockaway district manager. Although he tried to duplicate the Rockaway results, his low opinions of his agents were communicated—not so subtly—to them. As a result, the experiment failed.

Positive feelings, however, often do not come through clearly enough. Another insurance agency manager copied the organizational changes made at the Rockaway district office, grouping the salespeople she rated highly with the best manager, the average salespeople with an average manager, and so on. Improvement, however, did not result from the move. The Rockaway district manager therefore investigated the situation. He discovered that the assistant manager in charge of the high-performance unit was unaware that his manager considered him to be the best. In fact, he and the other agents doubted that the agency manager really believed there was any difference in their abilities. This agency manager was a stolid, phlegmatic, unemotional woman who treated her agents in a rather pedestrian way. Because high expectations had not been communicated to them, they did not understand the reason for the new organization and could not see any point in it. Clearly, the way managers *treat* subordinates, not the way they organize them, is the key to high expectations and high productivity.

EXHIBIT
The Relationship of Motivation to Expectancy

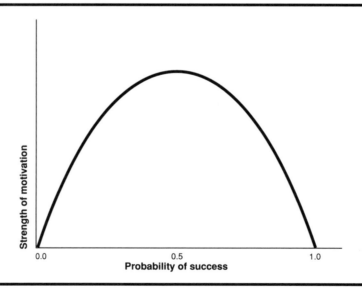

Impossible Dreams   Managerial expectations must pass the test of reality before they can be translated into performance. To become self-fulfilling prophecies, expectations must be made of sterner stuff than the power of positive thinking or generalized confidence in one's subordinates—helpful as these concepts may be for some other purposes. Subordinates will not be motivated to reach high levels of productivity unless they consider the boss's high expectations realistic and achievable. If they are encouraged to strive for unattainable goals, they eventually give up trying and settle for results that are lower than they are capable of achieving. The experience of a large electrical manufacturing company demonstrates this. The company discovered that production actually declined if production quotas were set too high, because the workers simply stopped trying to meet them. In other words, the practice of dangling the carrot just beyond the donkey's reach, endorsed by many managers, is not a good motivational device.

Scientific research by David C. McClelland of Harvard University and John W. Atkinson of the University of Michigan has demonstrated that the relationship of motivation to expectancy varies in the form of a bell-shaped curve (see the *Exhibit*).[2]

The degree of motivation and effort rises until the expectancy of success reaches 50%, then begins to fall even though the expectancy of success continues to increase. No motivation or response is aroused when the goal is perceived as being either virtually certain or virtually impossible to attain.

Moreover, as Berlew and Hall have pointed out, if subordinates fail to meet performance expectations that are close to their own level of aspirations, they will lower personal performance goals and standards, performance will tend to drop off, and negative attitudes will develop toward the activity or job.[3] It is therefore not surprising that failure of subordinates to meet the unrealistically high expectations of their managers leads to high rates of attrition, either voluntary or involuntary.

Secret of Superiority   Something takes place in the minds of superior managers that does not occur in the minds of those who are less effective. While superior managers are consistently able to create high performance expectations that their subordinates fulfill, weaker managers are not successful in obtaining a similar response. What accounts for the difference?

The answer, in part, seems to be that superior managers have greater confidence than other managers in their own ability to develop the talents of their subordinates. Contrary to what might be assumed, the high expectations of superior managers are based primarily on what they think about themselves—about their own ability to select, train, and motivate their subordinates.

---

2. *See* John W. Atkinson, "Motivational Determinants of Risk-Taking Behavior," *Psychological Review*, vol. 64, no. 6 (1957): 365.

3. David E. Berlew and Douglas T. Hall, "The Socialization of Managers: Effects of Expectations on Performance," *Administrative Science Quarterly* (September 1966): 208.

What managers believe about themselves subtly influences what they believe about their subordinates, what they expect of them, and how they treat them. If they have confidence in their ability to develop and stimulate them to high levels of performance, they will expect much of them and will treat them with confidence that their expectations will be met. But if they have doubts about their ability to stimulate them, they will expect less of them and will treat them with less confidence.

Stated in another way, the superior managers' record of success and their confidence in their ability give their high expectations credibility. As a consequence, their subordinates accept these expectations as realistic and try hard to achieve them.

The importance of what a manager believes about his or her training and motivational ability is illustrated by "Sweeney's Miracle," a managerial and educational self-fulfilling prophecy.

James Sweeney taught industrial management and psychiatry at Tulane University, and he also was responsible for the operation of the Biomedical Computer Center there. Sweeney believed that he could teach even a poorly educated man to be a capable computer operator. George Johnson, a former hospital porter, became janitor at the computer center; he was chosen by Sweeney to prove his conviction. In the mornings, George Johnson performed his janitorial duties, and in the afternoons Sweeney taught him about computers.

Johnson was learning a great deal about computers when someone at the university concluded that to be a computer operator one had to have a certain I.Q. score. Johnson was tested, and his I.Q. indicated that he would not be able to learn to type, much less operate a computer.

But Sweeney was not convinced. He threatened to quit unless Johnson was permitted to learn to program and operate the computer. Sweeney prevailed, and he is still running the computer center. Johnson is now in charge of the main computer room and is responsible for training new employees to program and operate the computer.[4]

Sweeney's expectations were based on what he believed about his own teaching ability, not on Johnson's learning credentials. What managers believe about their ability to train and motivate subordinates clearly is the foundation on which realistically high managerial expectations are built.

────── THE CRITICAL EARLY YEARS

Managerial expectations have their most magical influence on young people. As subordinates mature and gain experience, their self-image gradually hardens, and they begin to see themselves as their career records imply. Their own aspirations and the expectations of their superiors become increasingly

---

4. *See* Rosenthal and Jacobson, *Pygmalion in the Classroom*, p. 3.

controlled by the reality of their past performance. It becomes more and more difficult for them and for their managers to generate mutually high expectations unless they have outstanding records.

Incidentally, the same pattern occurs in school. Rosenthal's experiments with educational self-fulfilling prophecies consistently demonstrate that teachers' expectations are more effective in influencing intellectual growth in younger children than in older children. In the lower grade levels, particularly in the first and second grades, the effects of teachers' expectations are dramatic. In the upper grade levels, teachers' prophecies seem to have little effect on children's intellectual growth, although they do affect their motivation and attitude toward school. Although the declining influence of teachers' expectations cannot be completely explained, it is reasonable to conclude that younger children are more malleable, have fewer fixed notions about their abilities, and have less well-established reputations in the schools. As they grow, particularly if they are assigned to "tracks" on the basis of their records, as is now often done in public schools, their beliefs about their intellectual ability and their teachers' expectations of them begin to harden and become more resistant to influence by others.

Key to Future Performance   The early years in a business organization, when young people can be strongly influenced by managerial expectations, are critical in determining future performance and career progress. This is shown by a study at AT&T.

Berlew and Hall found that what the company initially expected of 49 college graduates who were management-level employees was the most critical factor in their subsequent performance and success. The researchers concluded that the correlation between how much a company expects of an employee in the first year and how much that employee contributes during the next five years was "too compelling to be ignored."[5]

Subsequently, the two men studied the career records of 18 college graduates who were hired as management trainees in another of AT&T's operating companies. Again they found that both expectations and performance in the first year correlated consistently with later performance and success.

"Something important is happening in the first year. . . .," Berlew and Hall concluded. "Meeting high company expectations in the critical first year leads to the internalization of positive job attitudes and high standards; these attitudes and standards, in turn, would first lead to and be reinforced by strong performance and success in later years. It should also follow that a new manager who meets the challenge of one highly demanding job will be given subsequently a more demanding job, and his level of contribution will rise as he responds to the company's growing expectations of him. The key . . . is the

---

5. Berlew and Hall, "The Socialization of Managers," p. 221.

concept of the first year as a *critical period for learning,* a time when the trainee is uniquely ready to develop or change in the direction of the company's expectations."[6]

Most Influential Boss   A young person's first manager is likely to be the most influential in that person's career. If managers are unable or unwilling to develop the skills young employees need to perform effectively, the latter will set lower personal standards than they are capable of achieving, their self-images will be impaired, and they will develop negative attitudes toward jobs, employers, and—in all probability—their own careers in business. Because the chances of building successful careers with these first employers will decline rapidly, the employees will leave, if they have high aspirations, in hope of finding better opportunities. If, however, early managers help employees achieve maximum potential, they will build the foundations for successful careers.

With few exceptions, the most effective branch managers at a large West Coast bank were mature people in their forties and fifties. The bank's executives explained that it took considerable time for a person to gain the knowledge, experience, and judgment required to handle properly credit risks, customer relations, and employee relations.

One branch manager, however, ranked in the top 10% of the managers in terms of effectiveness (which included branch profit growth, deposit growth, scores on administrative audits, and subjective rankings by superiors), was only 27 years old. This young person had been made a branch manager at 25, and in two years had improved not only the performance of the branch substantially but also developed a younger assistant manager who, in turn, was made a branch manager at 25.

The assistant had only average grades in college, but in just four years at the bank had been assigned to work with two branch managers who were remarkably effective teachers. The first boss, who was recognized throughout the bank for unusual skill in developing young people, did not believe that it took years to gain the knowledge and skill needed to become an effective banker. After two years, the young person was made assistant manager at a branch headed by another executive, who also was an effective developer of subordinates. Thus it was that the young person, when promoted to head a branch, confidently followed the model of two previous superiors in operating the branch, quickly established a record of outstanding performance, and trained an assistant to assume responsibility early.

For confirming evidence of the crucial role played by a person's first bosses, let us turn to selling, because performance in this area is more easily measured than in most managerial areas. Consider the following investigations:

---

6. David E. Berlew and Douglas T. Hall, "Some Determinants of Early Managerial Success," Alfred P. Sloan School of Management Organization Research Program #81-64 (Cambridge: MIT Press, 1964), p. 13.

- In a study of the careers of 100 insurance salespeople who began work with either highly competent or less-than-competent agency managers, the Life Insurance Agency Management Association found that those with average sales-aptitude test scores were nearly five times as likely to succeed under managers with good performance records as under managers with poor records, and those with superior sales aptitude scores were found to be twice as likely to succeed under high-performing managers as under low-performing managers.[7]
- The Metropolitan Life Insurance Company determined in 1960 that differences in the productivity of new insurance agents who had equal sales aptitudes could be accounted for only by differences in the ability of managers in the offices to which they were assigned. Agents whose productivity was high in relation to their aptitude test scores invariably were employed in offices that had production records among the top third in the company. Conversely, those whose productivity was low in relation to their test scores typically were in the least successful offices. After analyzing all the factors that might have accounted for these variations, the company concluded that differences in the performance of new agents were due primarily to differences in the "proficiency in sales training and direction" of the local managers.[8]
- A study I conducted of the performance of automobile salespeople in Ford dealerships in New England revealed that superior salespersons were concentrated in a few outstanding dealerships. For instance, 10 of the top 15 salespeople in New England were in 3 (out of approximately 200) of the dealerships in this region, and 5 of the top 15 people were in one highly successful dealership. Yet 4 of these people previously had worked for other dealers without achieving outstanding sales records. There was little doubt that the training and motivational skills of managers in the outstanding dealerships were critical.

Astute Selection   Although success in business sometimes appears to depend on the luck of the draw, more than luck is involved when a young person is selected by a superior manager. Successful managers do not pick their subordinates at random or by the toss of a coin. They are careful to select only those who they know will succeed. As Metropolitan's Rockaway district manager, Alfred Oberlander, insisted: "Every man or woman who starts with us is going to be a top-notch life insurance agent, or he or she would not have been asked to join the team."

---

7. Robert T. Davis, "Sales Management in the Field," *Harvard Business Review* (January–February 1958): 91.

8. Alfred A. Oberlander, "The Collective Conscience in Recruiting," address to Life Insurance Agency Management Association annual meeting, Chicago, Illinois (1963), p. 5.

When pressed to explain how they know whether a person will be successful, superior managers usually end up by saying something like, "The qualities are intangible, but I know them when I see them." They have difficulty being explicit because their selection process is intuitive and is based on interpersonal intelligence that is difficult to describe. The key seems to be that they are able to identify subordinates with whom they can probably work effectively—people with whom they are compatible and whose body chemistry agrees with their own. They make mistakes, of course. But they give up on a subordinate slowly because that means giving up on themselves—on their judgment and ability in selecting, training, and motivating people. Less-effective managers select subordinates more quickly and give up on them more easily, believing that the inadequacy is that of the subordinate, not of themselves.

———— DEVELOPING YOUNG PEOPLE

Observing that his company's research indicates that "initial corporate expectations for performance (with real responsibility) mold subsequent expectations and behavior," R. W. Walters, Jr., director of college employment at AT&T, contends that "initial bosses of new college hires must be the best in the organization."[9] Unfortunately, however, most companies practice exactly the opposite.

Rarely do new graduates work closely with experienced middle managers or upper-level executives. Normally they are bossed by first-line managers who tend to be the least experienced and least effective in the organization. Although there are exceptions, first-line managers generally are either old pros who have been judged as lacking competence for higher levels of responsibility, or they are younger people who are making the transition from "doing" to managing. Often these managers lack the knowledge and skill required to develop the productive capabilities of their subordinates. As a consequence, many college graduates begin their careers in business under the worst possible circumstances. Since they know their abilities are not being developed or used, they quite naturally soon become negative toward their jobs, employers, and business careers.

Although most top executives have not yet diagnosed the problem, industry's greatest challenge by far is to rectify the underdevelopment, underutilization, and ineffective management and use of its most valuable resource—its young managerial and professional talent.

Disillusion and Turnover   The problem posed to corporate management is underscored by the sharply rising rates of attrition among young managerial

---

9. "How to Keep the Go-Getters," *Nation's Business* (June 1966): 74.

and professional personnel. Turnover among managers one to five years out of college is almost twice as high now as it was a decade ago, and five times as high as two decades ago. Three out of five companies surveyed by *Fortune* magazine reported that turnover rates among young managers and professionals were higher than five years ago.[10] Although the high level of economic activity and the shortage of skilled personnel have made job-hopping easier, the underlying causes of high attrition, I am convinced, are underdevelopment and underutilization of a work force that has high career aspirations.

The problem can be seen in its extreme form in the excessive attrition rates of college and university graduates who begin their careers in sales positions. Whereas the average company loses about 50% of its new college and university graduates within three to five years, attrition rates as high as 40% in the *first* year are common among college graduates who accept sales positions in the average company. This attrition stems primarily, in my opinion, from the failure of first-line managers to teach new college recruits what they need to know to be effective sales representatives.

As we have seen, young people who begin their careers working for less-than-competent sales managers are likely to have records of low productivity. When rebuffed by their customers and considered by their managers to have little potential for success, the young people naturally have great difficulty in maintaining their self-esteem. Soon they find little personal satisfaction in their jobs and, to avoid further loss of self-respect, leave their employers for jobs that look more promising. Moreover, as reports about the high turnover and disillusionment of those who embarked on sales careers filter back to college campuses, new graduates become increasingly reluctant to take jobs in sales.

Thus ineffective first-line sales management sets off a sequence of events that ends with college and university graduates avoiding careers in selling. To a lesser extent, the same pattern is duplicated in other functions of business, as evidenced by the growing trend of college graduates to pursue careers in more meaningful occupations, such as teaching and government service.

A serious generation gap between bosses and subordinates is another significant cause of breakdown. Many managers resent the abstract, academic language and narrow rationalization characteristically used by recent graduates. As one manager expressed it to me, "For God's sake, you need a lexicon even to talk with these kids." Nondegreed managers often are particularly resentful, perhaps because they feel threatened by the bright young people with book-learned knowledge that they do not understand.

For whatever reason, the generation gap in many companies is eroding managerial expectations of new college graduates. For instance, I know of a survey of management attitudes in one of the nation's largest companies that

---

10. Robert C. Albrook, "Why It's Harder to Keep Good Executives," *Fortune* (November 1968): 137.

revealed that 54% of its first-line and second-line managers believed that new college recruits were "not as good as they were five years ago." Because what managers expect of subordinates influences the way they treat them, it is understandable that new graduates often develop negative attitudes toward their jobs and their employers. Clearly, low managerial expectations and hostile attitudes are not the basis for effective management of new people entering business.

Industry has not developed effective first-line managers fast enough to meet its needs. As a consequence, many companies are underdeveloping their most valuable resource—talented young men and women. They are incurring heavy attrition costs and contributing to the negative attitudes young people often have about careers in business.

For top executives in industry who are concerned with the productivity of their organizations and the careers of young employees, the challenge is clear: to speed the development of managers who will treat subordinates in ways that lead to high performance and career satisfaction. Managers not only shape the expectations and productivity of their subordinates but also influence their attitudes toward their jobs and themselves. If managers are unskilled, they leave scars on the careers of young people, cut deeply into their self-esteem, and distort their image of themselves as human beings. But if they are skillful and have high expectations, subordinates' self-confidence will grow, their capabilities will develop, and their productivity will be high. More often than one realizes, the manager is Pygmalion.

* * *

The author wrote the following commentary nineteen years after this reading was first published.

── RETROSPECTIVE COMMENTARY

Self-fulfilling managerial prophecies were a bit mysterious when I documented the phenomenon 19 years ago. At that time, the powerful influence of managers' expectations on the development, motivation, and performance of their subordinates was not widely understood. Since then, however, the "Pygmalion effect" has become well known.

Recent research has confirmed that effective leaders have the ability to create high performance expectations that their employees fulfill. Every manager should understand, therefore, how the Pygmalion effect works.

What managers think about themselves and their abilities, as I explained in "Pygmalion in Management," is crucial to their effectiveness in creating self-fulfilling prophecies. Warren Bennis and Burt Nanus recently reached a similar conclusion after conducting some 90 interviews with CEOs and top public administrators. They wrote: "Our study of effective leaders strongly suggested that a key factor was . . . what we're calling . . . positive self-regard. . . . Positive self-regard seems to exert its force by creating in others a sense of confidence and high expectations, not very different from the fabled Pygmalion effect."[11]

The way managers develop confidence in their abilities and transmit their feelings of efficacy to their employees is illustrated by the success of Lee A. Iacocca of Chrysler—whom, interestingly, Bennis and Nanus used as a model for their theory of leadership. Iacocca's self-assurance can be traced to his prior success as president of Ford. His subsequent prophecy that Chrysler would be saved was accepted as credible by Chrysler's employees because they saw him as a competent automobile executive. They tried hard to meet his expectations and "behaved as they believed they were expected to," which my article indicated would be normal under the circumstances.

It is highly unlikely, however, that Iacocca could have saved Chrysler if he had been an industry outsider who needed two or three years to learn the automotive business. If he had been an outsider, he could not have moved decisively to do what needed to be done, nor could he have created a strong sense of confidence and high expectations among Chrysler's employees. His success was due to his experience and competence. It is doubtful that a prophecy by a less-qualified executive would have been self-fulfilling. So the message for managers is this: to be a Pygmalion, you must acquire the industry knowledge and job skills required to be confident of your high expectations and to make them credible to your employees.

Your organization can help identify the knowledge and skills you need to perform your job effectively. Your supervisors can give you assignments that will spur your development. But you must assume responsibility for your own development and career growth.

A word of caution may be in order, however. As I explained in my article, managers often unintentionally communicate low expectations to their subordinates, even though they believe otherwise. When they communicate low expectations, they become negative Pygmalions who undermine the self-confidence of their employees and reduce their effectiveness. Managers must be extremely sensitive, therefore, to their own behavior and its impact on their subordinates. They must guard against treating their employees in ways that lower their feelings of efficacy and self-esteem and are unproductive.

If I were writing "Pygmalion in Management" today, I might focus more attention on the problems of the negative Pygmalions because there are more of them than positive Pygmalions in U.S. industry. But the dark side of the Pygmalion effect is distressing, and I prefer to think about the bright side. It is a hopeful concept that can help all managers become more effective.

The difference between employees who perform well and those who perform poorly is not how they are paid but how they are treated. All managers

---

11. Reported in their book *Leaders* (New York: Harper & Row, 1985).

can learn how to treat their employees in ways that will lead to mutual expectations of superior performance. The most effective managers always do.

———— DISCUSSION QUESTIONS

1. Relate in detail, from any period in your life, the effects that another person's positive or negative expectations have had on your self-image and performance.
2. In his retrospective commentary, the author states that "negative" Pygmalions are the rule rather than the exception. Offer specific steps that an organization can take to reverse that trend.
3. This reading stresses the influence a superior has on a subordinate. What are some of the responsibilities a subordinate must assume for his or her development and career growth?
4. The author brings out the importance of the early years in a person's career and of developing young people. What relevance does this reading have to people at mid-life who are changing careers?
5. The author mentions a "generation gap" between nondegreed managers and college-educated subordinates. What are other characteristics of the American work force that might create a "generation gap"? What can management do to remedy them?

Making Performance Appraisal Work   13

MICHAEL BEER

This reading explores some of the reasons why managers and subordinates are often ambivalent about performance appraisal. Both the individual and the organization have their own goals, some of which conflict. The most significant conflict, however, is between the individual and the organization: the individual seeks to confirm a positive self-image and to gain rewards, while the organization wants individuals to be open to criticism so they can improve their performance. The author examines various difficulties that arise from this conflict, particularly the problems of avoidance and defensiveness. He concludes by suggesting solutions to performance appraisal problems. Three possible areas for improvement are the appraisal system itself, the interview process, and the ongoing relationship between the boss and the subordinate.

When performance has been good, when superior and subordinates have an open relationship, when promotions or salary increases are abundant, when there is plenty of time for preparation and discussion—in short, whenever it is a pleasure—performance appraisal is easy to do. Most of the time, however, and particularly when it is most needed and most difficult (e.g., when performance is substandard), performance appraisal refuses to go smoothly.[1]

——— WHAT IS PERFORMANCE APPRAISAL AND WHY IS IT A PROBLEM?

The evaluation of individual performance is an inevitable part of organizational life. Individuals are constantly evaluated by their bosses, peers, and subordinates. Much of the evaluation is informal, but most organizations have a formal appraisal system designed to collect systematic information about the performance of employees. The formal system usually includes a form on which supervisors indicate their evaluations of subordinates' performances. The form may be a blank sheet of paper on which the supervisor notes his or her views,

---

1. Morgan W. McCall and David L. DeVries, "Appraisal in Context: Clashing with Organizational Realities," presented in symposium "Performance Appraisal and Feedback: Flies in the Ointment," at the 84th Annual Convention of the American Psychological Association, Washington D.C., September 5, 1976.

a guide for setting objectives and checking on their attainment (commonly referred to as Management by Objectives or MBO), or a series of ratings on how the subordinate performs on the job. Regardless of the format, appraisals become part of the individual's formal record and are used to make decisions about pay and career. Supervisors usually sit down with the subordinate once a year to discuss the appraisal.

For a number of very important reasons, almost all organizations maintain appraisal systems. They provide data for personnel planning and are a means of influencing employee performance and fulfilling the moral obligation of letting people know where they stand; increasingly, appraisal systems are important as a protection against legal suits by employees who have been fired or demoted.

Managers recognize performance appraisal as a potentially useful tool for improving the performance of subordinates and the effectiveness of their organizational unit; yet they also sense that performance appraisal inherently poses some danger to the motivation of their subordinates and their relationship with them. Like tax payments, performance appraisal is something managers feel obligated to do but would rather avoid. However, subordinates want, and often ask for, feedback about how they are doing, but they prefer feedback that is consistent with their image of themselves as good performers. Thus, both managers and subordinates have ambivalent feelings about performance appraisal and share a natural tendency to underplay or avoid dealing with the negative aspects of the procedure.

Performance appraisal is both a system of papers and procedures designed by the organization for use by its managers (*the appraisal system*) and an interpersonal process in which manager and subordinate communicate and attempt to influence each other (*the appraisal process* or *interview*). Many of the problems in performance appraisal stem from the appraisal system itself—the objectives it is intended to serve, the administrative system in which it is embedded, and the forms and procedures that make up the system. These system-design problems will *not* be discussed in any depth but will be referred to as needed to explain problems in the appraisal process. The focus will be on what is known about this process, the difficulties it presents, and how these might be overcome.

───── **GOALS OF PERFORMANCE APPRAISAL**

Both the organization and the individual employee have goals they wish fulfilled by performance appraisal. In some cases these objectives are compatible, in others not.[2]

---

2. This discussion of performance-appraisal goals draws extensively on Lyman W. Porter, Edward E.Lawler III, and Richard J. Hackman, *Behavior in Organizations* (New York: McGraw-Hill, 1975).

THE ORGANIZATION'S GOALS

Performance evaluation is an important element in the information and control system of most complex organizations. It provides information about the performance of the organization's members, which is used in decisions about placement, promotions, firing, and pay. Not having the right person available to fill an important job can be as serious as not having the money to expand physical facilities or buy equipment. An evaluation system can help track those people who have potential so that they can be placed in developmental positions. The organization's personnel department is usually responsible for coordinating these activities, and the performance appraisal system serves it in this purpose.

Performance appraisal systems, and more important, the discussions between supervisor and subordinate about performance, can also be aimed at influencing the behavior and performance of individuals. This is true of Management by Objectives Systems, as well as various performance-rating systems. The process of influencing behavior is important to the organization's development of future human resources, and it is of utmost importance to managers' efforts to obtain the results for which they are accountable. The performance appraisal process can motivate employees, point out needed change in the way they do things, and help them grow and develop competence needed now and in the future. It is thus a major tool for changing individual behavior.

From the organization's point of view, then, performance appraisal serves the following two sets of goals:

Evaluation Goals

- To give feedback to subordinates so they know where they stand;
- To develop valid data for pay (salary and bonus) and promotion decisions and to provide a means of communicating decisions;
- To help the manager in making discharge and retention decisions and to provide a means of warning subordinates about unsatisfactory performance.

Coaching and Development Goals

- To counsel and coach subordinates so that they will improve their performance and develop future potential;
- To develop commitment to the larger organization through discussion of career opportunities and career planning;
- To motivate subordinates through recognition and support;
- To strengthen supervisor-subordinate relations;
- To diagnose individual and organizational problems.

The most significant observation to draw from this list is that there are many goals and that they are in conflict.[3] When the goal is evaluation, managers

---

3. Michael Beer and Robert A. Ruh, "Employee Growth Through Performance Management," *Harvard Business Review*, July–August 1976.

use the appraisal system as a tool for making difficult judgments that affect a subordinate's future. In communicating these judgments, managers must justify their appraisal in response to or in anticipation of disagreement by the subordinate. The result can be an adversarial relationship, poor listening, and low trust—conditions that work against the coaching and development objectives of performance appraisal. When coaching and development are the goals, managers must play the role of helper. They must listen, draw out subordinates about their problems, and help subordinates understand their weaknesses. The different communication skills required to achieve the conflicting goals of performance appraisal make the process difficult for the manager.

THE INDIVIDUAL'S GOALS

Like the organization, the individual has conflicting goals in performance evaluation. Individuals want feedback about their performance because it helps them learn about themselves.[4] The performance appraisal is an opportunity for them to get feedback and to learn how they are progressing. If this information is favorable, it helps satisfy their needs for competence and psychological success; if it is not, they tend to experience failure, and the feedback is often difficult to accept. Thus, even when people in organizations ask for and sometimes demand feedback, they are hoping for feedback that will affirm their concept of themselves. When rewards such as pay and promotion are tied to the evaluation, employees have a further reason for wanting to avoid unfavorable evaluations. They may gloss over problems, if not deny them. Often without realizing it, the individuals may present themselves in a favorable light to gain valued organizational rewards.

There are obvious conflicts between an individual's desire for personal development and the wish for rewards and feedback consistent with self-image. Self-development requires openness to feedback and receptiveness to alternative approaches to the job. However, this openness may not always serve the subordinate's objective of gaining raises, bonuses, and promotions when these are scarce.

CONFLICTING INDIVIDUAL AND ORGANIZATION GOALS

Because the organization is pursuing the conflicting objectives of evaluation and development, the manager must use performance appraisal

---

4. Leon Festinger et al., *Social Pressures in Informal Groups* (Stanford: Stanford University Press, 1950); T. F. Pettigrew, "Social Evaluation Theory: Convergences and Applications," in J. D. Levine (ed.), *Nebraska Symposium on Motivation* (Lincoln: University of Nebraska Press, 1967).

EXHIBIT 1
Conflicts in Performance Appraisal

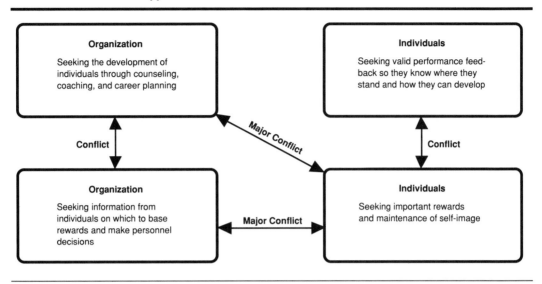

Source: Adapted from Porter, Lawler, and Hackman, *Behavior in Organizations,* 1975.

in two quite contradictory ways. Similarly, individuals have conflicting objectives as they approach a performance appraisal. The most significant conflict, however, is that between the individual and the organization. The individual desires to confirm a positive self-image and to obtain organizational rewards of promotion or higher pay. The organization wants individuals to be open to negative information about themselves so they can improve their performance and also wants individuals to be helpful in supplying this information. The conflict arises over the exchange of valid information. As long as individuals see the appraisal process as having an important effect on their rewards, career, and self-image, they will be reluctant to engage in the open dialogue required for valid evaluation and personal development. The poorer the individual's performance, the worse the potential conflict and the less likely the exchange of valid information. *Exhibit 1* depicts the several kinds of conflict involved in performance appraisal.

PROBLEMS IN PERFORMANCE APPRAISAL

AMBIVALENCE AND AVOIDANCE

Given the inherent conflicts, it is not surprising that supervisors and subordinates are often ambivalent about participating in the performance appraisal process.[5] Superiors are uncomfortable because their organizational role places them in the position of being both judge and jury. They must make decisions that significantly affect people's careers and lives. Furthermore, most managers are not trained to handle the interpersonally difficult situations that often arise with negative feedback. This is particularly a problem because managers would like to maintain good relations with their subordinates in order to carry on with their own jobs. All this leads to uncertainty about their subjective judgments and anxiety about meeting with subordinates to discuss performance. Yet supervisors also know that both the organization and the subordinate want such a discussion to be held. Finally, supervisors often feel personally bound to let people know where they stand. If they are not open with their subordinates, the knowledge that they have been less than truthful keeps them from building a relationship of mutual trust.

At the same time, subordinates are likely to be ambivalent about receiving negative feedback. They may want to discuss negative aspects of their performance so they can improve and develop but will not want to jeopardize promotions, pay, or their own self-image.

The ambivalence of both superiors and subordinates has led to the vanishing performance appraisal.[6] In many organizations, supervisors report that they hold periodic appraisal interviews and give honest feedback, while their subordinates report that they have not had a performance appraisal for many years or that they have heard nothing negative.[7] Probably the supervisors, fearful of the appraisal process, have expressed themselves so that the subordinates do not receive the unwelcome messages. The supervisor may carefully package negative feedback between heavy doses of positive feedback (the sandwich approach) or may make only general statements, without referring to specific problems. That is, supervisors provide negative feedback, but immediately counterbalance it with positive statements when their own anxiety or the subordinate's defensiveness signals potential problems. Because of their fear of awareness that will affect their self-image, subordinates collude with the supervisor in avoiding negative feedback. This sometimes results in long conversations only marginally related to the purpose of the appraisal interview. Sometimes avoidance manifests in small talk or humor that conveys an oblique message, or in the use of phrases that do not have clear meaning to either the supervisor or subordinate. Thus, negative feedback is often not explored in depth and is not fully understood and internalized by the subordinate.

As a result, no real appraisal occurs or, more likely, the appraisal just skims the surface. Both parties collude in meeting the organization requirement for appraisal but avoid the tough issues.

---

5. Douglas T. Hall and Edward E. Lawler III, "Job Design and Job Pressures as Facilitators of Professional-Organization Integration," *Adminstrative Science Quarterly*, 15 (1970), pp. 271–281.

6. Porter et al., *Behavior in Organizations*.

7. Hall and Lawler, "Job Design and Job Pressures."

FEEDBACK AND DEFENSIVENESS

The conflict between the organization's evaluation objectives and its coaching and development objectives tends to place the manager in the incompatible roles of judge and helper. Some managers feel obligated to fulfill their organizational role as judge by communicating to the subordinates all facets of the evaluation. They want to be sure they fulfill their obligation of letting subordinates know where they stand by detailing all shortcomings in performance. This naturally can elicit resistance from subordinates as they defend against threats to their self-esteem. The defensiveness may take various forms.[8] Subordinates may try to blame their unsatisfactory performance on others or on uncontrollable events; they may question the appraisal system itself or minimize its importance; they may demean the source of the data; they may apologize and promise to do better in the hope of shortening their exposure to negative feedback; or they may agree too readily to the feedback while inwardly denying its validity or accuracy.

Supervisors find themselves giving negative feedback while trying to create an open dialogue that will lead to information exchange and development. The defensiveness that results may be expressed as open hostility and denial or may be masked by passivity and surface compliance. In neither case does the subordinate really accept or understand the feedback. Thus, the very subordinates who need development most may learn least.

AVOIDANCE AND DEFENSIVENESS COMBINED

The worst situation is one in which the problems created by ambivalence and avoidance of performance appraisal combine with the problems of feedback and defensiveness. This can happen when managers go through a pro forma performance appraisal simply to fulfill their duty as supervisors. Their ambivalence leads them to avoid direct and meaningful talk about performance. However, because of their need to fulfill their role, they go through a mechanical yet complete review of the evaluation form. Without going deeply into problems of subordinates' performance, they nevertheless elicit defensive behavior by covering the evaluation form in detail. Thus, neither the benefits of avoidance (i.e., maintenance of good relations and personal comfort), nor the benefits of accurate feedback (i.e., clear understanding and development) are realized, while all the problems of avoidance and defensiveness remain.

---

8. Alvin Zander, "Research on Self-Esteem, Feedback and Threats to Self-Esteem," in A. Zander (ed.), *Performance Appraisals: Effects on Employees and Their Performance* (Ann Arbor, Mich.: The Foundation for Research in Human Behavior, 1963).

EXHIBIT 2
Factors Influencing Appraisal Outcomes

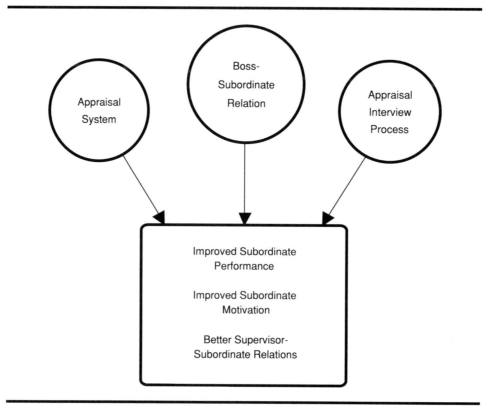

NONEVALUATIVE EVALUATION

The central dilemma in the appraisal process is how to have an open discussion of performance that meets the individual's need for feedback and the organization's personnel development objectives while preventing damage to the individual's self-esteem and confidence about organizational rewards.

—— POTENTIAL SOLUTIONS TO APPRAISAL PROBLEMS

Several approaches to the problems are possible. A manager seeking to improve performance appraisal should examine each of the three major factors influencing appraisal outcomes (*Exhibit 2*), to see where changes might be helpful. First, the appraisal system can be designed to minimize negative dynamics. The manager often has only marginal control over these matters. Second, the ongoing relationship between boss and subordinate will have a major influence on the appraisal process and outcome. Third, the quality of the communication during the interview process can help minimize problems.

THE APPRAISAL SYSTEM

Uncoupling Evaluation and Development   Less defensiveness and a more open dialogue are likely if the manager distinguishes his or her roles as helper and judge.[9] Two separate performance appraisal interviews can be held: one focused on evaluation and the other on coaching and development. The open, problem-solving dialogue required for building a relationship and developing subordinates comes at a different time of the year from the meeting in which the supervisor informs the subordinate of the overall evaluation and its implications for retention, pay, and promotion. This split recognizes that a manager cannot be simultaneously a helper and a judge, because the behavior required by one role interferes with the behavior required by the other.

Choosing Appropriate Performance Data   A manager can minimize defensiveness and avoidance by narrowly focusing feedback on specific behaviors or specific performance goals. For example, an unsatisfactory rating on a characteristic as broad as motivation is likely to be perceived as a personal attack and could threaten self-esteem. Individuals are more likely to attend to feedback about specific incidents or aspects of job performance than to broad generalizations. Specific feedback is also more helpful to the individual in terms of changing behavior. Thus, an appraisal discussion that relies on a report-card rating of traits or performance is doomed to failure because it leads the supervisor into general evaluative statements that threaten the subordinate.

Fortunately, some appraisal techniques can guide the supervisor toward more specific behavioral observations. A behavioral rating scale, for example, asks supervisors to indicate the degree to which subordinates fulfill certain behavioral requirements of their job (e.g., participating actively in meetings or communicating sufficiently with other departments). In the Critical Incident Method, the supervisor records important examples of effective or ineffective performance.[10] Similarly, various Management by Objectives (MBO) techniques can help guide the appraisal discussion toward reviewing specific accomplishments. Some experts on performance appraisal have suggested that a comprehensive performance management system should include both MBO and behavioral ratings.[11] They see these techniques as complementary tools in managing and appraising performance: MBO is a means of managing *what* employees should do, while behavioral ratings are a means of helping them see *how* they should do it.

---

9. Herbert Henry Meyer, Emanuel Kay, and John R. P. French Jr., "Split Roles in Performance Appraisal," *Harvard Business Review*, January–February 1965; Beer and Ruh, "Employee Growth."

10. John C. Flanagan and Robert K. Burns, "The Employee Performance Record," *Harvard Business Review*, September–October 1955.

11. Beer and Ruh, "Employee Growth."

Upward Appraisal One of the appraisal dynamics that contributes most to both defensiveness and avoidance is the authoritarian character of the supervisor-subordinate relationship. The simple fact that one person is the boss and is responsible for evaluation places him or her in a dominant role and induces submissive behavior in the subordinate. Furthermore, the boss holds and controls rewards. To develop the open two-way dialogue required for coaching and employee development, power must be equalized or at least brought into better balance during the interview. Physical arrangements can contribute to this goal, but the adoption of an upward, or rate-your-boss, appraisal process may be even more effective. Before the interview, the subordinate is given a form on which to rate the supervisor's performance, with a clear understanding that the ratings will be discussed in the appraisal meeting.

An upward appraisal can help a supervisor create the conditions needed for an effective performance appraisal interview. This gives subordinates a real stake in the appraisal interview and an opportunity to influence a part of their environment that ultimately affects their performance. Thus, upward appraisal makes subordinates more equal, less dependent, and more likely to enter the appraisal process with an open mind. The supervisor also has an opportunity to model nondefensive behavior and to demonstrate a willingness to engage in a real two-way dialogue.

Most organizations do not have such rate-your-boss forms, but supervisors can develop their own or seek informal feedback sometime during the appraisal interview.

SUPERVISOR-SUBORDINATE RELATIONS

Not surprisingly, the quality of the appraisal process depends on the nature of the day-to-day boss-subordinate relationship. In an effective relationship, the supervisor is providing ongoing feedback and coaching. Thus, the appraisal interview is merely a review of issues that have already been discussed. Moreover, expectations for the appraisal interview are likely to be shaped by the broader supervisor-subordinate relationship of which the appraisal is only a small part. If a relationship of mutual trust and supportiveness exists, subordinates are more apt to be open in discussing performance problems and less defensive in response to negative feedback.

There are no easy techniques for changing a boss-subordinate relationship, but the appraisal interview itself, if appropriately conducted, can help build a relationship of mutual trust.

THE APPRAISAL INTERVIEW

The best techniques for conducting a particular appraisal interview depend on the mix of objectives pursued and the characteristics of the subordinate. Employees differ in age, experience, sensitivity to negative feedback, attitude toward the supervisor, and desire for influence and control over their destiny. If the subordinate is young, inexperienced, and dependent, and looks up to the supervisor, and if the supervisor's objective is to let the subordinate know that performance improvement is needed, it may be appropriate to have the supervisor do most of the talking. However, if the subordinate is older, more experienced, sensitive about negative feedback, and has a high need for controlling his or her destiny, a less directive approach to the interview will better meet the objectives.

Norman Maier describes three types of appraisal interviews, each with a specific and slightly different objective.[12] The differences are important in determining the skills required by the supervisor and the outcomes for employee motivations and supervisor-subordinate relationships. The three methods—termed *tell and sell, tell and listen,* and *problem-solving*—can be combined if several objectives must be met by the same interview.

The Tell-and-Sell Method   The aim of the tell-and-sell method is to communicate to employees their evaluation as accurately as possible. The fairness of the evaluation is assumed and the manager seeks (a) to let the subordinates know how they are doing, (b) to gain their acceptance of the evaluation, and (c) to get them to follow the manager's plan for improvement. In the interview, supervisors are in complete control; they do most of the talking. They decide what subordinates need to do to improve and attempt to persuade subordinates that their observations and recommendations are valid. Clearly, this method can lead to defensiveness, lack of trust, lack of open communication, and exchange of invalid information. Supervisor-subordinate relations can be hurt because the employees feel hostile and angry when they must accept a supervisor's views that are inconsistent with their self-perceptions. This method may not motivate employees to change because they are placed in a dependent position and do not contribute to the plan.

Nevertheless, there may be situations in which this approach is the only way. For example, a supervisor may decide to use this approach for an employee who remains resistant to change after less directive approaches have been used.

The Tell-and-Listen Interview   The purpose of this interview method is to communicate the evaluation to the subordinate and then let him or her respond to it. The supervisor describes the subordinate's strengths and weaknesses during the first part of the interview, postponing points of disagreement until later. The second part of the interview is devoted to exploring the subordinate's feelings about the evaluation. Thus, the supervisor functions as a judge but also listens to objections from the subordinate without refuting

---

12. Norman R. F. Maier, "Three Types of Appraisal Interviews," *Personnel*, March–April 1958.

them. In fact, the supervisor encourages the subordinate to disagree in order to drain off any negative feelings the appraisal arouses. The verbal expression of frustration is assumed to reduce the hostility resulting from negative feedback.

The tell-and-listen interview differs substantially from the tell-and-sell method in how disagreement and resistance are handled. Although both interviews start with a one-way communication from the supervisor to the employee, in the tell-and-listen interview the supervisor then sits back and assumes the role of a nondirective counselor.[13] This role requires the supervisor to (a) *listen actively*—accepting and trying to understand the employee's attitudes and feelings; (b) *make effective use of pauses*—waiting patiently without embarrassment for the subordinate to talk; (c) *reflect feelings*—responding to and restating feelings in a way that shows understanding of them; and (d) *summarize feelings*—helping subordinates understand themselves. This approach is not intended to communicate agreement or disagreement with subordinates. Rather, it acknowledges the subordinates' viewpoints and helps them decide which part of the feedback to accept.

The tell-and-listen approach is apt to result in better understanding between supervisor and subordinate than is the tell-and-sell. The subordinate is less likely to be defensive and therefore more likely to accept feedback. Through listening supervisors can learn a great deal about subordinates. However, the interview may not give subordinates a clear understanding of where they stand and how to improve, and may not inspire a commitment to improving behavior.

The Problem-Solving Interview   This interview approach takes the manager out of the role of judge and puts him or her in the role of helper. The objective is to help subordinates discover their own performance deficiencies and lead them to take the initiative in developing a joint plan for improvement. The problem-solving interview is best suited to coaching and development objectives. It has no provision for communicating the supervisor's evaluation. The assumption is that subordinates' self-understanding and motivation to improve performance can best be achieved in a climate of open communication and mutual influence.

Because the objective is to allow subordinates to discover their own developmental needs, the manager cannot specify areas for improvement—that would be an evaluative judgment. The supervisor helps employees examine themselves and their jobs and must be willing to consider their ideas for performance improvement. In this regard, the skills required in the problem-solving interview are similar to those required in the latter half of the tell-and-listen interview. However, the objective is to go well beyond listening and help subordinates discover and explore alternative solutions to problems identified. Supervisors may suggest their own ideas for solution but in the pure problem-

---

13. Carl R. Rogers, "Releasing Expression," *Counseling and Psychotherapy* (Cambridge: Houghton Mifflin Co., 1942).

solving interview, the supervisor works from the subordinates' initiatives. Supervisors may stimulate subordinate initiative by asking questions about how to eliminate a job problem. The questions should not put subordinates on the spot but should indicate an interest in helping them develop the best plan. Maier gives the following examples:

"Can this plan of yours deal with an emergency situation, if one arises?"
"Would you have other people at your level participate in the plan?"
"What kinds of problems do you anticipate in a changing market?"[14]

Exploratory questions can draw the person out, help clarify thinking, and direct analysis to areas that may have been overlooked.

The problem-solving interview eliminates defensiveness because the issues raised and the ideas for solution are primarily the subordinate's. He or she is therefore more willing to accept problems and better motivated to accomplish personal and job-related plans for improvement. This interview method also encourages creative thinking by the subordinate, and both supervisor and employee are more likely to arrive at new discoveries about the job and themselves. Thus, there is the potential for changes in the job, the organization, and the supervisor's own style. All of these can affect an individual's performance.

The Mixed-Model Interview   These three interview models are a convenient way of categorizing stylistic strategies for an appraisal interview. As noted earlier, the ideal way of dealing with the inherent conflict between evaluation (judging) and development (helping) is to separate the interviews and choose the appropriate method for each. If this were done, the tell-and-sell or tell-and-listen interview would be used for evaluation and the problem-solving interview would be used for developmental objectives. However, such factors as time, organizational practice, and subordinate expectations may dictate that one interview serve both purposes.

The most effective way to implement a mixed-model appraisal interview is to begin with the open-ended problem-solving interview and end with the more directive tell-and-sell or tell-and-listen approach. The reverse order is unlikely to work.[15] If the supervisor starts off with one-way communication, two-way communication and in-depth exploration of personal and job performance issues are unlikely to follow. Thus, as *Exhibit 3* shows, the interview should start with an open-ended exploration of perceptions and concerns, with the subordinate taking the lead, and finish with a more narrowly defined agreement on what performance improvements are expected. If a mutual

14. Maier, "Three Types of Appraisal Interviews."
15. Ibid.; Herbert H. Meyer, "The Annual Performance Review Discussion—Making It Constructive," unpublished and undated paper, University of South Florida.

EXHIBIT 3
Mixed-Model Interview

Interview Begins

Open-ended discussion and
exploration of problems.
The subordinate leads
and the supervisor listens.

Problem-solving interview.
The subordinate leads, but the
supervisor takes a
somewhat stronger role.

Agreement on performance
problems and a plan
for improvements needed.

The supervisor summarizes
his or her views, using
tell-and-listen or tell-and-sell
methods if the subordinate
has not dealt
with important issues.

Interview Ends

agreement on performance problems and improvements is not possible, ultimate responsibility for telling the subordinate what is expected rests with the supervisor.

A mixed-model interview can be implemented in many ways. One possible pattern for an effective appraisal interview with multiple purposes is outlined here. This procedure, which assumes an interview similar to that shown in *Exhibit 3*, makes the climate of the interview more conducive to coaching and problem solving but also allows the supervisor to play a directive role if needed. The goal is to improve employee performance and motivation as well as boss-subordinate relations, while leaving subordinates with a clear understanding of what is expected and where they stand. The 10 steps are described in order.

1. *Scheduling.* Notify the subordinate well before the meeting date that an appraisal discussion is scheduled. The time of the interview should be such that both parties are alert and undisturbed by external organizational or family matters. The side effects of unrelated upsetting events can affect the interview process needlessly.
2. *Agreeing on content.* Discuss with the subordinate the nature of the interview, and work toward agreement on what will be discussed

in the interview (i.e., rating forms to be used or performance issues to be discussed). This gives the subordinate a chance to prepare for the meeting (including rating the supervisor if this is to be part of the session), and to come into the interview on a more equal footing with the boss.

3. *Agreeing on process.* Before the interview, agree with the subordinate on the process for the appraisal discussion. For example, agreement should be reached on the sequencing of interview phases (e.g., an open exploratory discussion, followed by problem solving, action planning, and upward appraisal). Similarly, ground rules for communication can be established that will ensure constructive feedback and good listening. The important point is that both parties understand and agree to the interview process before the interview starts.

4. *Location and space.* If possible, meet on neutral territory or in the subordinate's office. This helps establish a relationship of more equal power, which is crucial to open communication. Using the supervisor's office gives him or her an edge. Similarly, it is best that the supervisor not sit behind a desk, which often symbolizes authority and can be a barrier to communication.

5. *Opening the interview.* Review the objectives of the appraisal interview as previously agreed to. This sets the stage and allows supervisor and subordinate to prepare themselves psychologically. It is a warm-up for the more important communication to come.

6. *Starting the discussion.* Give the initiative to the subordinate in the discussion that follows the opening statement. Specifically, start the discussion by asking, "How do you feel things are going on the job? What's going well and what problems are you experiencing? How do you see your performance?" Such general questions will stimulate the subordinate to take the initiative in identifying and solving problems. A useful technique may be to ask the subordinate to appraise his or her own performance on the form provided by the organization. (It has been found that subordinates usually evaluate themselves and their performance realistically.) If the manager starts by expressing views about the employee's performance, the interview almost inevitably develops into a tell-and-sell session in which the subordinate participates very little. Only an unusually strong and skilled subordinate could regain the initiative.

7. *Exchanging feedback.* Follow well-accepted ground rules for giving and receiving feedback.[16] A supervisor who models these methods for effective communication encourages the exchange of valid information. In giving feedback, a supervisor can reduce employee defensiveness by being specific about the performance and behavior causing the problems. Citing examples of observed behavior and describing the effects of that behavior on others,

---

16. John Anderson, "Giving and Receiving Feedback," Procter & Gamble Co., unpublished paper.

on the supervisor's feelings, and on the performance of the department can help an employee identify what needs to be changed. Following this procedure allows the supervisor to give feedback without being overly evaluative. To prevent defensive reactions, the supervisor should avoid blaming, accusing, making general statements, and imputing motives to behavior (e.g., you aren't committed).

The supervisor should also model and encourage the subordinate to follow ground rules for receiving feedback. When signs of defensiveness appear in the receiver of negative feedback, the giver will often pull back from the process and thus hold back important information. Active listening, however, can enhance the value of negative feedback. Receivers of feedback can maintain openness and keep information coming by exploring negative feedback and showing a willingness to examine themselves critically. They can paraphrase what is being said, request clarification, and summarize the discussion periodically. In contrast, justifying actions, apologizing, blaming others, explaining, or building a case tends to cut off feedback and reduce understanding.

It is impossible and undesirable, of course, to prevent receivers of feedback from giving any explanation of their behavior. The timing of explanations is critical, however, in signaling openness versus defensiveness. Active listening should precede explanations. The communication in an appraisal interview can be much improved if both boss and subordinate follow these ground rules, which should be agreed to before the interview begins.

8. *The manager's views.* Provide a summary of the subordinate's major needs for improvements based on the previous discussion. This summary sets the agenda for jointly developing plans for improvement. This should also include the subordinate's strengths—those assets that should be maintained.

9. *Developing a plan for improvement.* Let the subordinate lead with what he or she thinks is an adequate plan for improvement, given the previous discussion and summary. The supervisor is more likely to prevent defensiveness by reacting to and perhaps expanding on the subordinate's plans for changing rather than by making such suggestions directly. A problem-solving rather than blame-placing approach should be maintained. However, if the subordinate cannot formulate good action plans, or seems to be unmotivated to do so, the supervisor can take a more directive approach at this point. The interview should end with a concrete plan for performance improvement; otherwise, no change is likely to occur. A plan may include certain task assignments, training programs, subordinate experimentation with new approaches in specific settings, a change in the subordinate's role, working closely with others who are skilled in a certain area, or a shift of goals and objectives.

10. *Closing the discussion.* Close the interview by discussing what the future might hold for the individual. (This assumes that opportunities for promotion exist and the employee clearly has potential, or that the individual raises the issue.) If the employee needs to be told where he or she stands, this should occur at the very end of the interview by way of a summary of the appraisal discussion. As stated earlier, such a judgment should ideally be delivered in a separate interview or review.

This proposed interview sequence assumes that the primary objective of the appraisal discussion is counseling and coaching, with a secondary goal of letting subordinates know where they stand. It is also assumed that the appraisal interview is a culmination of ongoing performance discussions. The most effective coaching of behavior takes place immediately and directly on a day-to-day basis. The formal interview is an attempt to improve working relations, encourage upward communication, develop deeper understanding, and define developmental plans.

GUIDELINES FOR ASSESSING THE APPRAISAL PROCESS INTERVIEW

After the interview, participants should ask themselves several questions as a check on the effectiveness of the appraisal process. Indeed, an effective appraisal interview should probably also include at least one examination of the process sometime during the interview. The following questions might be helpful:

At the beginning

1. Did the supervisor create an open and accepting climate?
2. Was there agreement on the purpose and process for the interview?
3. Were both parties equally well prepared?

During the interview

4. To what extent did the supervisor really try to understand the employee?
5. Were broad and general questions used at the outset?
6. Was the supervisor's feedback clear and specific?
7. Did the supervisor learn some new things—particularly about the feelings and values of the subordinate?
8. Did the subordinate disagree with and confront the supervisor?
9. Did the interview end with mutual agreement and understanding about problems and goals for improvement?

Appraisal outcomes

10. Did the appraisal session motivate the subordinate?
11. Did the appraisal build a better relationship?

12. Did the subordinate come out with a clear idea of where he or she stands?
13. Did the supervisor arrive at a fairer assessment of the subordinate?
14. Did he or she learn something new about the subordinate?
15. Did the subordinate learn something new about the supervisor and the pressures he or she faces?
16. Does the subordinate have a clear idea of what actions to take to improve performance?

——— SUMMARY

This reading has explored the underlying causes of problems organizations experience with performance appraisal. The main barriers to effective appraisals are avoidance by the supervisor and defensiveness in the subordinate. This reading has illustrated how supervisors and subordinates can overcome these problems by discussing performance evaluations in a nonevaluative manner.

——— DISCUSSION QUESTIONS

1. Can you name any drawbacks or flaws to performance appraisal other than the difficulties mentioned in the reading? Do you think performance appraisals are necessary? Is there a better solution to evaluating performance?
2. This reading touches on the latent hostility that can exist within an organization. What are some ways that an organization can prevent the buildup of such hostilities?
3. The concept of subordinates evaluating their supervisors is mentioned in the reading. Do you think this is a useful practice? How much weight should such a concept be given in an organization that decides to operate that way?
4. According to the reading, effective performance appraisal is "an inevitable part of organizational life." In organizations where you have been employed, have managers been well prepared to deliver effective evaluations? What can organizations do to ensure that their managers possess this important skill?

Managing Interpersonal Conflict   14

JAMES WARE AND LOUIS B. BARNES

This reading explores the nature, sources, and dynamics of interpersonal conflict. After setting forth some definitions to guide the discussion, the authors consider positive and negative outcomes, substantive and emotional issues, and underlying and background contributors to conflict. They suggest three approaches for managing conflict—bargaining, controlling, and constructive confrontation—and offer a set of action questions to use in developing a strategy to manage conflict.

Few managers enjoy dealing with conflicts that involve themselves, their bosses, peers, or subordinates. Whether the conflict is openly hostile or subtly covert, strong personal feelings may be involved. Furthermore, there are often valid veiwpoints on both sides, making the process of finding an acceptable solution mentally exhausting and emotionally draining. Yet the ability to productively manage such conflict is critical to managerial success. Interpersonal differences often become sharpest when the organizational stakes seem to be high, but almost all organizations include their share of small issues blown into major conflicts. The manager's problem is to build on human differences of opinion, while not letting them jeopardize overall performance, satisfaction, and growth.

——— ASSUMPTIONS AND DEFINITIONS

Interpersonal conflict typically involves a relationship in which a sequence of conditions and events moves toward aggressive behavior and disorder. Conflict can also be viewed, however, in terms of its background conditions, the perceptions of the parties involved, their feelings, their actual behavior, and the consequences or outcomes of their behavior.

Conflict is an organizational reality that is inherently neither good nor bad. It can be destructive, but it can also play a productive role both within a person and between persons. Problems usually arise when potential conflict is artificially suppressed, or when it escalates beyond the control of the adversaries or third-party intermediaries. Whereas most managers will seek to reduce conflict when it occurs, because of its negative repercussions, some will seek to use it for its positive effects on creativity, motivation, and performance. The management of conflict usually entails maintaining a delicate balance between these positive and negative attributes.

There is no one best way for managing interpersonal conflict, either as an involved adversary or as a third party. Rather, there are a number of strategies and tactics involving the external conditions, differing perceptions, internal feelings, behavior, and outcomes. The present relationships of the parties involved (superior–subordinates, peers, representatives) and their past histories as adversaries, allies, or relatively neutral third parties, are other key variables. The relative power of the parties involved is another factor to consider in deciding whether to withdraw from conflict, to compromise, to work toward controlling a conflict within certain boundaries, to seek constructive confrontations, to force conflict into a win/lose pattern, to smooth it over with friendly acts, or to try other subtle or forceful approaches.

Conflict experienced as an involved participant is emotionally different from conflict seen as a relatively objective third party. One advantage of third parties is their ability to add a different perspective to the perceptions, feelings, and behavior of the involved adversaries. This reading examines the management of conflict from the vantage points of both the involved adversaries and an outside third party, which might be a boss, colleague, friend, or subordinate. Each of these different roles has its own strengths and weaknesses.

QUESTIONS FOR THE ANALYSIS OF CONFLICT

A manager may become concerned about conflict when it leads to lower productivity, satisfaction, or growth, be it individual or organizational. The manager might begin an analysis of the conflict by examining such consequences or outcomes. A second area for analysis includes the behavior patterns of the involved parties. A third area entails differing feelings and perceptions. A fourth area consists of underlying or background conditions that helped initiate and now perpetuate the conflict. Each area provides an appropriate point for dealing with a conflict situation. A manager might pose these four questions, which are discussed in the sections that follow:

1. What are the important personal and organizational consequences of the conflict? What are possible future consequences?
2. What behavior patterns characterize the conflict?
3. What substantive issues are involved? To what extent are they colored by each side's perceptions and feelings? Who in the organization might be an objective third party?
4. What are the underlying or background conditions leading to the conflictual feelings, perceptions, behavior, and outcomes?

OUTCOME CONSIDERATIONS

Conflicts generally have both positive and negative consequences. An awareness of both kinds of outcomes complicates the diagnosis but can lead to more effective intervention decisions.

Positive Outcomes   The competitiveness within a conflict can increase the participants' motivation and creativity. A manufacturing manager who becomes angry at being pushed around by a sales vice president, for example, may respond by trying harder to produce a workable production schedule ("just to show that I can do it"). This competitive dynamic—the urge to win—often leads to innovative breakthroughs, because of the effort and willingness to consider new approaches. Interpersonal conflicts frequently clarify persistent underlying organizational problems. Furthermore, intense conflict can focus attention on basic issues and lead to the resolution of long-standing difficulties that can no longer be smoothed over or easily avoided.

Involvement in a conflict can also sharpen an individual's personal approaches to bargaining, influencing, and competitive problem solving. In addition, participants often increase their understanding of their own values and positions on important issues. For example, a manager may clarify an idea by explaining it to someone who clearly disagrees with it.

Thus conflicts can be useful, or at least can lead to positive outcomes, for the organization and for one or more of the individuals involved. There are often negative consequences, however, and conflict can escalate to a level where negative outcomes outweigh the positive ones.

Negative Outcomes   Interpersonal conflicts are often unpleasant emotional experiences for the individuals involved. A subordinate who suppresses anger with a boss, a pair of managers who exchange angry words with each other, two colleagues who avoid each other because of previous tensions, two other associates who "play games" by not sharing relevant and important information—all of these patterns penalize the organization and have an emotional impact on the people involved. The organizational landscape is littered with managers who could not get along with their bosses, colleagues, or subordinates. In one sense, they were not good people managers, but we could also say that the firm had failed to help them develop effective procedures for dealing with conflict.

When a person is involved in a conflict relationship, negative outcomes spill out as emotions of anger, frustration, fear of failure, and a sense of personal inadequacy. Careers can be sidetracked or ruined. The stress of conflictual relationships can make life miserable for people, disrupt patterns of work, and consume an inordinate amount of time for those involved as well as for those affected or indirectly concerned. The direct loss of productivity is but one negative business outcome; the danger of continued poor decision making because of withheld information is yet another. The irony is that the parties determined to win their own limited battles often cause major losses for themselves and the organization.

Short-term negative outcomes can also lead to worsening relationships unless some remedial action is taken. Both the involved and third-party managers have the problem of deciding when to act. Although managers sometimes maintain tensions over time for their positive outcomes, most managers try to change the situation before the schisms become too great. Before they can take appropriate steps, however, managers need to understand the behavior taking place.

BEHAVIOR PATTERNS

Interpersonal conflicts tend to develop patterns. That is, the two parties first engage in open conflict over a particular issue, then separate and gather forces before coming together and going at each other again. Often an organizational procedure, such as budgeting, scheduling, or assigning work, precipitates the conflict and serves as part of the background. Sometimes an apparently trivial issue sets off one party against the other. There may even be periods of time when two people seem to work relatively well together or are effectively buffered from one another. Then, once again, some event or change in circumstances sets them off. Although these events are not always predictable, they often follow an identifiable pattern. Poor listening, one-upmanship, power plays for resources, perceived putdowns, and overcontrolling comments can all serve as triggering devices. The initial behaviors can set in motion the reactions and reciprocal behaviors that start a conflict cycle. Careful attention to when and how a conflict heats up is an important part of developing a conflict-management strategy.

Equally important is how the principals involved express their differences. When the conflict is open and active, the conflictual behaviors are usually obvious: shouting, sulking, repeated sniping, heated debate, unwillingness to listen, hardening of positions, and so on. When the conflict is latent, however, or underground, the signs are not so evident. Then the behaviors are usually more subtle: writing memos to avoid face-to-face contact, delaying decisions to block the other party, interacting through subordinates or third parties, avoiding direct exchanges, or changing times of daily arrivals and departures to avoid meeting. Detecting suppressed conflict requires great sensitivity but is important because many conflicts are expressed indirectly.

Understanding the behavior patterns in a particular conflict is an important prelude to planning its management. If particular events trigger open conflict, then those events may be either stopped or actively constrained. Understanding behavior patterns can also help participants or third parties make more effective choices about when and where to enter the conflict. Finally, the patterns of a conflict can provide important clues to the underlying reasons for the conflict.

SUBSTANTIVE ISSUES, PERCEPTIONS, AND FEELINGS

Most conflicts include two distinctively different kinds of issues. Substantive issues involve disagreements over policies, procedures, decisions, use of resources, roles and responsibilities, or other organizational practices. Emotional issues, in contrast, involve the highly personal perceptions and feelings that people can have about each other and about the substantive issues in contention. Because social customs and the norms of most organizations discourage open expression of negative personal feelings, intense emotional conflicts are often expressed and rationalized as substantive issues. People often drum up disagreements on trivial issues to provide justification for an emotional conflict with another individual.

This tendency to distort and magnify differences means that conflicts often escalate rapidly in intensity and importance. Each person builds a grievance list of real and perceived problems. People seek support wherever they can find it, repeatedly citing evidence to justify their feelings as a means of gaining sympathy. Worse yet, people attribute all kinds of negative motives and intentions to other persons, while thinking of themselves as the injured "good guys."

Conflicts also escalate because each time the two people interact they may try to "score points," and each interaction then becomes part of the history of the conflict. Whenever a person thinks that he or she has lost one round, the effort to win the next one can become even more intense as the following example demonstrates.

> A product manager and an inventory control manager had to meet regularly to review and update sales forecasts. Their interests conflicted somewhat because the product manager wanted to minimize unit costs and avoid stockouts, while the inventory control manager wanted to minimize total purchasing costs and inventory levels. When their forecasts became inaccurate, the two managers had several disagreements over the forecasting procedures and their divergent goals. Gradually, the two managers lost sight of each other's different basic assumptions and organizational needs; rather, they began to personalize their differences. Each felt threatened and attacked by the other, and these feelings intensified each time they interacted. Their growing distrust and lack of respect spilled over into personal antagonism, with each manager seeing ulterior motives and unpleasant personality traits in the other. Hostilities escalated with personal threats, name-calling, and accusations of stupidity, self-interest, and dishonesty. Thus, a legitimate set of substantive differences became transformed into the vicious cycle of an emotional battle.

Some managers involved in a dispute are determined to work out an agreement, through bargaining, control procedures, constructive confrontation, or other forms of negotiation. Still other managers will see conflict as something to avoid, withdraw from, or smooth over. Colleagues and bosses are probably more willing to take the first approach than are subordinates, who may feel forced to fall back on the second approach; and all parties may prefer a third-party mediator. A manager's choice has much to do with individual tolerance for conflict and the accompanying uncertainties. Through experience, managers can learn how much to trust their own perceptions and feelings during such stressful times. Although a certain amount of stress may be a productive motivator, most people have difficulty remaining open-minded and flexible during times of high stress. In addition, performance shortcomings may challenge one's assumptions about personal abilities and self-concept. The most natural response is to look elsewhere for a scapegoat—"If they would give me more accurate sales forecasts, I wouldn't have all this excess inventory." It is much easier to change perceptions about someone else's ability ("she just doesn't know how to forecast") or motives ("he's feeding me false data to make me look bad") than it is to admit personal failure or the need for help. Scapegoating is thus another personal characteristic that contributes to escalation in a conflict.

The advantage of third parties, trusted by both adversaries, is that their outside perceptions and feelings can serve as a reality check for both adversaries. If the third party can help work out a procedure for coping with the conflict, then that may be a major step toward further agreement or resolution. A boss acting as a third party has the added power of being able to arbitrate or to tip the power balance one way or the other; however, even this apparent advantage can have negative effects in the long run if the boss is perceived as taking sides too often. One of the hardest yet most important challenges for the third party is to stay in touch with the perceptions and feelings of both adversaries and simultaneously maintain his or her own views; that is, the third party must deal with the conflict *relationship* rather than be pulled toward either adversarial viewpoint.

UNDERLYING AND BACKGROUND CONDITIONS

The underlying causes of interpersonal conflict are just as numerous and varied as the ways in which conflicts are expressed. Assessing the factors causing or reinforcing a particular conflict is difficult because multiple forces are usually involved. Separating out the primary causes is often impossible because most serious conflicts become self-reinforcing: These conflicts have such a powerful history and have become so personalized that their original sources are irrelevant to the present situation. Nevertheless, attempts to understand a conflict must consider the forces behind the adversaries' actions. Managing the conflict then means changing the situational factors surrounding it, or altering the ways in which the adversaries respond to the situation and to each other.

These causal factors are divided into two categories: (1) situational or external characteristics and (2) personal or internal characteristics. These distinctions are somewhat arbitrary, however, and will be treated more distinctively here than they usually are in practice.

Situational—External Characteristics This category includes all of the external conditions surrounding the two people—the organizational rules and procedures that affect their interactions; the pressures of time and deadlines; competition for budgetary funds, staff, organizational influence, and other scarce resources; performance pressures from bosses, peers, and other departments; and promotion opportunities.

When two people from different departments (such as the market analyst and inventory control manager described earlier) must interact, they may represent and reflect their own reference group's differences in goals, values, and priorities. Thus *interdepartmental* conflict frequently becomes *interpersonal* conflict unless the two representatives can rise above the special interests of the groups they represent.

But even two people from the same department can become competitive for scarce resources, whether these are budgetary funds, subordinates, control over key procedures and decisions, office space, or the boss's time or job. The pressure to perform can make the personal stakes so high that individual managers become inflexible and defensive. These stakes are particularly important when middle managers must compete for promotion opportunities that include individual responsibilities and rewards. Because most organizations reward successful managers both formally (promotions and salary increases) and informally (influence, status, credibility), the social pressures to compete and win can be extremely intense.

Personal—Internal Factors The personal goals, styles, and abilities of two people in conflict can also affect their behavior and their relationship. Personal career goals and ambitions can develop in response to the organizational pressures just described. People may experience feelings of rivalry and interpersonal competition, however, even when there is little external basis for such emotions. Sometimes there is a poor fit between a person and the job requirements, and his or her poor performance may create serious problems for someone else. More frequently, however, conflict erupts and escalates because one manager sees another manager as actively blocking a personally important goal. Whether that perception is accurate or not is almost irrelevant. The resulting anger, frustration, and anxiety contribute to the emotional escalation of conflict. These kinds of feelings are often strong among ambitious, competitive, achievement-oriented individuals.

"Bad chemistry" between two people is also spoken of as a cause of conflict. If people have different personal values, styles, or work habits, then they may also disagree on how to accomplish important tasks. Consider the possible tensions between an aggressive, high-energy manager and a careful, methodical analyst; or between a talkative, easy-going plant manager and a quiet, reserved manufacturing manager. Sometimes personal styles are complementary, but sometimes they are basically incompatible. When the people involved feel strongly about their ways of doing things, conflict is almost inevitable.

One of the most critical personal characteristics feeding a conflict is a limited capacity for coping with stress. When personal and organizational stakes are high, people may develop "short fuses" and become intolerant of others' mistakes or even of their legitimate needs. When two people under extreme pressure must interact frequently, they may find it difficult to avoid blaming each other for the problems they are experiencing.

When a high-pressured situation is exacerbated by each person's internal anxieties and stress, conflict usually surfaces in the areas of perception, feeling, and behavior. Confronted with these conditions and with the outcomes of a conflict, a manager—either as adversary or as onlooker—must face a series of choices. The first is whether to avoid the conflict or to try to manage it. Although the choice may seem clear-cut on paper—managers should manage—many managers are better at conflict avoidance, or smoothing over, than they are at conflict management. The skills and strength for managing a conflict, either as an involved participant or as a third party, do not come easily for most people. At the same time, there are instances when avoidance or smoothing over stress and negative outcomes makes sense, if satisfaction is valued more highly than performance or growth. This is often true in family businesses and in close partnerships. But in situations where management is trying to optimize the balance of the three outcomes—performance, satisfaction, and growth—there is a greater need for managing conflict.

── MANAGING THE CONFLICT

A manager who chooses to manage a conflict and not withdraw or smooth it over must first of all take stock of his or her place in the situation: adversary or third party? boss or subordinate? representative or free agent? with power and dependencies or, relatively speaking, without them? Any one of these roles poses its own set of demands and choices. Some of these demands and choices also depend on the manager's comfort with using power in this fashion and willingness to take on this conflict. The following sections briefly discuss three general approaches to conflict management and then raise several questions that a manager might ask before choosing an approach.[1]

The three approaches can be roughly categorized as (1) bargaining, (2) controlling, and (3) confrontation. *Bargaining behavior* is probably most prevalent under conditions of required interdependence and a rough balance of power. *Controlling behavior* is more apt to be used when one party or the other (including the third party) has relatively higher power and when the interdependence requirements are more flexible. *Confrontation behavior* may be used under either of the above conditions but appears to depend more on the personal attributes of the parties involved and on the assumptions they make about the setting and time pressures. (Confrontation behavior may be intended to be either destructive or constructive. The focus here is on constructive confrontation.) As each of these approaches is discussed, the assumption is made that the acting manager understands the conflict situation's outcomes and consequences; the behavior, the perceptions and feelings related to the substantive issues; and the underlying background conditions. Each approach offers an entry point for either an adversary or a third-party mediator, but the choice of approach depends on the individual's position, skills, and personal preferences.

BARGAINING

For a manager involved in a conflict, as either adversary or mediator, negotiating or bargaining on the substantive issues often appears to be the reasonable approach. The assumption here is that the conflict involves a situation in which one party would gain at the other's expense. If the two parties come to the bargaining table in union-management fashion, however, they signal that they will consider new ways to resolve the conflict.

The advantage of a bargaining approach is that the motive of compromise provides an incentive to go beyond conflict. In approaching the bargaining table, the two parties, with or without a third-party mediator, usually prepare to lose as well as to win some points. The goal is to reach a solution acceptable to both sides. Many bargaining situations, however, involve games such as bluffing, behind-the-scenes negotiations, an attempt to marshal outside power sources, a tendency to overstate one's initial demands, and the heavy use of legalistic procedures that preserve the appearance of a rational process. Each of these bargaining tactics involves risks as well as rewards. Another problem with a bargaining approach is that the parties often place a higher premium on

---

1. Ideas in this section are drawn from the following sources: Richard Walton, *Interpersonal Peacemaking* (Reading, MA: Addison-Wesley, 1969); Louis R. Pondy, "Organizational Conflict: Concepts and Models," *Administrative Science Quarterly* (vol. 12, no. 2, September 1967), pp. 296–320; Robert R. Blake and Jane S. Mouton, *The New Managerial Grid* (Houston: Gulf Publishing Co., 1978).

acceptable compromises than on sound solutions. A manager who engages in a bargaining approach, either as an adversary or as a third party, can lose sight of the organization's well-being and become consumed in the limited goal of reaching an acceptable solution.

CONTROLLING

There are four strategies for controlling interpersonal conflict. They may come into play when a power imbalance enables one party to exert pressure on the situation. Other times, two adversaries will tire of the controls or a third party will appear who gains the trust of both adversaries. Conflict control can also be a temporary approach used until the crisis is over or conditions improve enough to permit bargaining or confrontation. The four strategies are (1) preventing interaction or reducing its frequency, (2) structuring the forms and patterns of interaction, (3) reducing or changing the external situational pressures, and (4) personal counseling to help the two parties accept and deal with the process and realities of the conflict. This last strategy, counseling, is different from mediation and can be used with bargaining and confrontation approaches.

Preventing Interaction or Reducing Its Frequency   This strategy is often useful when emotions are high. It controls conflict by reducing the possibility of triggering events. If the two people are physically separate and no longer need to interact with each other, then there is little opportunity for them to express differences. Although the differences continue to exist, the intense feelings are likely to dissipate without recurring run-ins, or at least to cool down enough to permit other approaches.

There are many ways to reduce or eliminate interaction. Sometimes operating procedures can be modified to eliminate the necessity of two people working together. If that option is impossible, then peers or subordinates can substitute for one or both parties. If the conflict stems from an underlying conflict of interest, however, it is just as likely to flare up in the new relationship. One or both of the people could be transferred to a new job or even to a new physical location.

Several of these options are relatively expensive and time-consuming. They may be useful, however, if there is no other way to work out the differences, or if the hostility has reached a level where confrontation would be either impossible or inordinately drawn out. Separating the two parties may create more serious long-term problems or only delay an eventual confrontation. When adversaries are separated, their hostilities sometimes merely go underground and may become more intense because of the absence of an opportunity to express them. When that happens, the eventual confrontation may be even more serious, as the pent-up emotions finally come tumbling out. In these instances, trusted third parties can help judge whether reducing interaction makes sense.

Structuring the Forms of Interaction   The separation options listed above are sometimes not feasible. When the two parties must continue to interact, the conflict can be controlled by adopting clear guidelines of behavior. These procedures can be as specific and narrow as the parties wish. For example, the procedures might specify the time and place of meetings, the allowable discussion topics, the specific information to be provided by each individual, or even the types of questions or comments not allowed. Alternatively, the procedures might specify or imply new channels of communication: meetings could be replaced with memos, messages, or telephone calls.

How these ground rules are established depends on the specific situation and on the relationships between the people involved. A manager can generally impose these kinds of procedures on subordinates or on other adversaries with less organizational authority. In the absence of such a clear mandate, however, the ground rules are often arrived at by negotiation or mutual agreement or with the help of a third party.

This strategy permits the continued exchange of vital information and prevents the exchange of hostile and judgmental emotions that would interfere with needed communication. Like physical separation, this strategy should be a temporary strategy, since the suppression of strong emotions can easily lead to more violent and destructive flare-ups later on. Involved adversaries may find that their own perspectives need the objectivity of outsiders to reduce distortion in making judgments and to help learn when to use and when to abandon this approach.

Reducing or Changing External Pressures   Changing the conditions that feed the conflict is often more effective than focusing on the interactions that characterize the conflict. When situational factors are largely responsible for the problem, dealing with those factors directly can control the conflict or even eliminate it.

The factors that should be changed will depend on the specific circumstances, each manager's power to affect the critical factors, and the organizational consequences of the changes (sometimes a change that might control the conflict would not be appropriate for other, more important reasons). Situational factors that could be changed include extending deadlines, adding new project personnel, modifying organizational policies or making temporary exceptions, setting up periodic informational meetings, increasing budget allocations, and protecting the principals from harassment by peers or by organizational superiors. Sometimes these mechanisms are in the hands of one of the adversaries and can be acted upon; at other times they need actions from outside or from above the conflict.

Personal Counseling   In contrast to the other control strategies, this approach does not address the conflict itself but focuses on how the two people are reacting to it. The underlying assumption here is that providing counseling, reassurance, and emotional support will help make their conflict more tolerable. In addition, the process of ventilating feelings about an adversary to a colleague or friend usually releases pent-up tensions and may become a first step toward discovering new ways to deal directly with the conflict. Alternatively, talking out the problem with the third party can lead an individual to invent new procedures or personal goals that make him or her less dependent on the other party, thus reducing the inherent stress in the conflict.

Controlling a conflict can be a useful short-term strategy, because it often brings about positive changes in either the situation or the parties. When this approach is not likely to succeed or when interdependence needs are high, managers should think about ways to constructively confront the conflict.

CONSTRUCTIVE CONFRONTATION

Constructive confrontation is potentially the most difficult and the most rewarding of all the approaches to conflict management. It should begin with a serious and well-communicated attempt to understand and explore the other party's perceptions and feelings. A third party can aid this process by helping to build an exploratory climate. This party must be careful to avoid the initial temptation to support one of the two adversaries. It is important to remember that a constructive confrontation does not usually begin with a confrontation but with an attempt to understand.

Constructive confrontation has the advantage, once a climate of exploration has been established, of conveying the possibility of a win/win solution. It seeks an exchange of information—substantive as well as perceptions and feelings—that provides new definitions of the problem and new motives for a common solution. Both mediators and adversaries need skill, patience, persistence, and commitment to listening to each other while constantly looking for ways to move out of a deadlock. Asking the simple question What if . . . ? can be helpful in searching for new alternatives.

A confrontation may initially have to move carefully while the two adversaries seek ways to release their emotions and feelings. Once again a third party can help legitimize these expressions while monitoring the ways in which negative or hostile feelings are expressed. For example, the third party—or even one of the adversaries—may suggest that the parties agree to express and explore feelings that result from actual behavior rather than those based upon inference and speculation of the other's motives and perceptions. Without these ground rules for the expression of feelings, confrontation can easily become more destructive than constructive. Such ground rules help the parties involved move to new stages of exchanging information and problem solving.

——— SOME RELEVANT ACTION QUESTIONS

A manager involved either as an adversary or as a third party in a conflict might use the following questions in deciding on an approach for conflict management. These questions are especially important when considering a confrontation strategy, but they are also applicable to the other approaches.

1. To what extent is there a productive level of tension and motivation in the conflict relationship? Or has the conflict become highly destructive?

If conflict resolution is to be successful, there typically must be enough stress in the situation for the participants to desire a resolution, but not so much that they are unable to deal with the issues or each other. Too little tension may require alerting participants to the personal or organizational outcomes that make the latent conflict dangerous or dysfunctional. Too much tension may require cooling-off steps or temporary controlling measures.

Interpersonal conflict often persists because only one party is motivated to do anything about it. When this happens, little can be done until the tension level is again high enough for both adversaries to at least say they want to work toward a resolution. Such stated motivation can serve as a starting point.

2. What are the balances of status and power positions among the two or three parties?

The balance of power configurations can play a big part in determining appropriate paths to conflict resolution or avoidance. For example, there may be less chance for successful resolution when one party in a two-party relationship is much more powerful or influential than the other. It is often harder to get third-party involvement in such situations, paticularly when the power imbalance involves a superior and a subordinate. At the same time, third-party mediation can be most helpful in these instances, because it can help rebalance the power equation. The advantage for controlling is clearly on the side of the person with higher status, whether that person is an adversary or a third party, although constructive confrontation will more likely thrive when a rough power balance is achieved.

3. To what extent are time and flexible resources available?

Conflict resolution in almost any form can require considerable time, new procedures, off-site meetings, outside help, painful adjustments, restructuring of relationships, and tolerance for uncertainties. As conflict conditions develop and change, so might the participants' needs for time and resources. It may be easier to change situational or external variables, such as new procedures, than it is to change the internal perceptions of all parties in the conflict arena, particularly those who identify with or support the two adversaries. Under these conditions, active counseling by a number of managers may be useful to provide new perspectives throughout the conflict arena. Changing the feelings and perceptions of the two adversaries may not be enough if their supporters will not allow them to relinquish the conflict. The conflict-resolution process may need more time to work for all involved parties.

▬▬ CONCLUSION

Managers must recognize that interpersonal conflict is inevitable in any human organization. It can be both a constructive and a destructive force. A manager's first choice is whether to ignore or avoid such realities or whether to find ways to manage the complexities of the conflict. The first alternative is often easier in the short run but more costly in the long run. The management of conflict requires some understanding of its outcomes, its destructive behavior and reciprocity patterns, the perceptions and feelings that drive the behavior, and the underlying and background conditions that help to perpetuate the conflict. Each of these areas provides an entry point for managing the conflict— whether the approach is bargaining, controlling, confronting, or some combination. Understanding these areas can help a manager explore his or her options in handling the realities of a conflict. Most managers will have ample opportunity to view conflict both as outsiders and as involved adversaries.

▬▬ DISCUSSION QUESTIONS

1. The authors suggest several ways of managing conflict such as bargaining, controlling, and confronting. What other ways of managing conflict can you suggest?
2. Give an example of a conflict situation (either real or imagined) that has a win-win solution. Now think of a situation (again, real or imagined) that has a win-lose outcome. How might this situation have been managed to achieve a win-win result?
3. The authors mention the idea of conflict enhancing the participants' motivation and creativity. Give an example from your experience in which conflict increased your motivation and creativity.
4. The authors focus on the potential gains that conflict can have for individuals. What benefits might an organization gain from conflict?
5. Give an example when conflict avoidance or smoothing over might be more beneficial than conflict management.

Managing Your Boss 15

JOHN J. GABARRO AND JOHN P. KOTTER

It is just as important to manage your relationship with your boss as it is to manage subordinates, products, markets, and technologies, argue these authors. If the relationship is rocky, neither managers nor their bosses can do their jobs effectively; the responsibility for the relationship should not and cannot rest entirely with the boss. This reading offers suggestions for ways that managers can develop and maintain healthy working relationships with their bosses.

To many the phrase *managing your boss* may sound unusual or suspicious. Because of the traditional top-down emphasis in organizations, it is not obvious why you need to manage relationships upward—unless, of course, you would do so for personal or political reasons. But in using the expression managing your boss, we are not referring to political maneuvering or apple-polishing. Rather, we are using the term to mean the process of consciously working with your superior to obtain the best possible results for you, your boss, and the company.

Studies suggest that effective managers take time and effort to manage not only relationships with their subordinates but also those with their bosses.[1] These studies show as well that this aspect of management, essential though it is to survival and advancement, is sometimes ignored by otherwise talented and aggressive managers. Indeed, some managers who actively and effectively supervise subordinates, products, markets, and technologies, nevertheless assume an almost passively reactive stance vis-à-vis their bosses. Such a stance practically always hurts these managers and their companies.

If you doubt the importance of managing your relationship with your boss or how difficult it is to do so effectively, consider for a moment the following sad but telling story:

Frank Gibbons was an acknowledged manufacturing genius in his industry and, by any profitability standard, a very effective executive. His strengths propelled him into the position of vice president of manufacturing for the second-largest and most profitable company in its industry. Gibbons was

---

1. *See*, for example, John J. Gabarro, "Socialization at the Top: How CEOs and Their Subordinates Develop Interpersonal Contracts," *Organizational Dynamics* (Winter 1979); and John P. Kotter, *Power in Management*, AMACOM (1979).

not, however, a good manager of people. He knew this, as did others in his company and his industry. Recognizing this weakness, the president made sure that those who reported to Gibbons were good at working with people and could compensate for his limitations. The arrangement worked well. Two years later, Philip Bonnevie was promoted into a position reporting to Gibbons. In keeping with the previous pattern, the president selected Bonnevie because he had an excellent track record and a reputation for being good with people. In making that selection, however, the president neglected to notice that, in his rapid rise through the organization, Bonnevie himself had never reported to anyone who was poor at managing subordinates. Bonnevie had always had good-to-excellent bosses. He had never been forced to manage a relationship with a difficult boss. In retrospect, Bonnevie admits he had never thought that managing his boss was a part of his job.

Fourteen months after he started working for Gibbons, Bonnevie was fired. During that same quarter, the company reported a net loss for the first time in seven years. Many of those who were close to these events say that they don't really understand what happened. This much is known, however: while the company was bringing out a major new product—a process that required its sales, engineering, and manufacturing groups to coordinate their decisions very carefully—a whole series of misunderstandings and bad feelings developed between Gibbons and Bonnevie.

For example, Bonnevie claims Gibbons was aware of and had accepted Bonnevie's decision to use a new type of machinery to make the new product; Gibbons swears he did not. Furthermore, Gibbons claims he made it clear to Bonnevie that introduction of the product was too important to the company in the short run to take any major risks.

As a result of such misunderstandings, planning went awry: a new manufacturing plant was built that could not produce the new product designed by engineering, in the volume desired by sales, at a cost agreed on by the executive committee. Gibbons blamed Bonnevie for the mistake. Bonnevie blamed Gibbons.

Of course, one could argue that the problem here was caused by Gibbons's inability to manage his subordinates. But one can make just as strong a case that the problem was related to Bonnevie's inability to manage his boss. Remember, Gibbons was not having difficulty with any other subordinates. Moreover, given the personal price paid by Bonnevie (being fired and having his reputation within the industry severely tarnished), there was little consolation in saying the problem was that Gibbons was poor at managing subordinates. Everyone already knew that.

We believe that the situation could have turned out differently had Bonnevie been more adept at understanding Gibbons and at managing his relationship with him. In this case, an inability to manage upward was unusually costly. The company lost $2 to $5 million, and Bonnevie's career was, at least temporarily, disrupted. Many less costly cases like this probably occur regularly in all major corporations, and the cumulative effect can be very destructive.

───── MISREADING THE BOSS-SUBORDINATE RELATIONSHIP

People often dismiss stories like the one we just related as being merely cases of personality conflict. Because two people can on occasion be psychologically or temperamentally incapable of working together, this can be an apt description. But more often, we have found, a personality conflict is only a part of the problem—sometimes a very small part.

Bonnevie did not just have a different personality from Gibbons, he also made or had unrealistic assumptions and expectations about the very nature of boss-subordinate relationships. Specifically, he did not recognize that his relationship to Gibbons involved *mutual dependence* between two *fallible* human beings. Failing to recognize this, a manager typically either avoids trying to manage his or her relationship with a boss or manages it ineffectively.

Some people behave as if their bosses were not very dependent on them. They fail to see how much the boss needs their help and cooperation to do his or her job effectively. These people refuse to acknowledge that the boss can be severely hurt by their actions and needs cooperation, dependability, and honesty from them.

Some see themselves as not very dependent on their bosses. They gloss over how much help and information they need from the boss in order to perform their own jobs well. This superficial view is particularly damaging when a manager's job and decisions affect other parts of the organization, as in Bonnevie's situation. A manager's immediate boss can play a critical role in linking the manager to the rest of the organization, in making sure the manager's priorities are consistent with organizational needs, and in securing the resources the manager needs to perform well. Yet some managers need to see themselves as practically self-sufficient, as not needing the critical information and resources a boss can supply.

Many managers, like Bonnevie, assume that the boss will magically know what information or help their subordinates need and provide it to them. Certainly, some bosses do an excellent job of caring for their subordinates in this way, but for a manager to expect that from all bosses is dangerously unrealistic. A more reasonable expectation for managers to have is that modest help will be forthcoming. After all, bosses are only human. Most really effective managers accept this fact and assume primary responsibility for their own careers and development. They make a point of seeking the information and help they need to do a job instead of waiting for their bosses to provide it.

Thus, it seems to us that managing a situation of mutual dependence among fallible human beings requires the following:

- You must have a good understanding of the other person and yourself, especially regarding strengths, weaknesses, work styles, and needs.
- You must use this information to develop and manage a healthy working relationship—one that is compatible with both persons' work styles and assets, is characterized by mutual expectations, and meets the most critical needs of the other person. And that is essentially what we have found highly effective managers doing.

——— UNDERSTANDING THE BOSS AND YOURSELF

Managing your boss requires that you gain an understanding of both the boss and his context as well as your own situation and needs. All managers do this to some degree, but many are not thorough enough.

THE BOSS'S WORLD

At a minimum, you need to appreciate your boss's goals and pressures, his or her strengths and weaknesses. What are your boss's organizational and personal objectives, and what are the pressures on him, especially those from his boss and others at his level? What are your boss's long suits and blind spots? What is his or her preferred style of working? Does he or she like to get information through memos, formal meetings, or phone calls? Does your boss thrive on conflict or try to minimize it?

Without this information, a manager is flying blind when dealing with his boss, and unnecessary conflicts, misunderstandings, and problems are inevitable.

Goals and Pressures   In one situation we studied, a top-notch marketing manager with a superior performance record was hired into a company as a vice president "to straighten out the marketing and sales problems." The company, which was having financial difficulties, had been recently acquired by a larger corporation. The president was eager to turn it around and gave the new marketing vice president free rein—at least initially. Based on previous experience, the new vice president correctly diagnosed that greater market share was needed and that strong product management was required to bring that about. As a result, the vice president made a number of pricing decisions aimed at increasing high-volume business.

When margins declined and the financial situation did not improve, however, the president increased pressure on the new vice president. Believing that the situation would eventually correct itself as the company gained back market share, the vice president resisted the pressure.

When by the second quarter margins and profits had still failed to improve, the president took direct control over all pricing decisions and put all items on a set level of margin, regardless of volume. The new vice president began to be shut out by the president, and their relationship deteriorated. In fact, the vice president found the president's behavior bizarre. Unfortunately, the president's new pricing scheme also failed to increase margins, and by the fourth quarter both the president and the vice president were fired.

What the new vice president had not known until it was too late was that improving marketing and sales had been only *one* of the president's goals. The most immediate goal had been to make the company more profitable—quickly.

Nor had the new vice president known that the boss was invested in this short-term priority for personal as well as business reasons. The president had been a strong advocate of the acquisition within the parent company, and the boss's personal credibility was at stake.

The vice president made three basic errors. Taking information at face value, the vice president made assumptions in certain areas despite having no information, and—most damaging—never actively tried to clarify what the boss's objectives were. As a result, the vice president ended up taking actions that were actually at odds with the president's priorities and objectives.

Managers who work effectively with their bosses do not behave this way. They seek out information about the boss's goals and problems and pressures. They are alert for opportunities to question the boss and others around him or her to test their assumptions. They pay attention to clues in the boss's behavior. Although it is imperative that they do this when they begin working with a new boss, effective managers also continue to do this because they recognize that priorities and concerns change.

Strengths, Weaknesses, and Work Style   Being sensitive to a boss's work style can be crucial, especially when the boss is new. For example, a new president who was organized and formal in approach replaced someone who was informal and intuitive. The new president worked best with written reports and also preferred formal meetings with set agendas.

One of the division managers realized this need and worked with the new president to identify the kinds and frequency of information and reports the president wanted. This manager also made a point of sending background information and brief agendas for their discussions. The manager found that with this type of preparation their meetings were very useful. With adequate preparation, the new boss was even more effective at brainstorming problems than the boss's more informal and intuitive predecessor had been.

In contrast, another division manager never fully understood the new boss's work style, objecting to its excessive control. As a result, the manager seldom sent the new president the necessary background information, and the president never felt fully prepared for meetings with the manager. In fact, the president spent a great deal of time when they met trying to get what should have been supplied beforehand. The boss experienced these meetings as frustrating and inefficient, and the subordinate often was thrown off guard by the questions that the president asked. Ultimately, this division manager resigned.

The difference between the two division managers just described was not so much one of ability or even adaptability. Rather, the difference was that one of them was more sensitive to the boss's work style than the other and to the implications of the boss's needs.

YOU AND YOUR NEEDS

The boss is only half of the relationship. You are the other half, as well as the part over which you have more direct control. Developing an effective working relationship requires, then, that you know your own needs, strengths and weaknesses, and personal style.

Your Own Style   You are not going to change either your basic personality structure or that of your boss. But you can become aware of what it is about you that impedes or facilitates working with your boss and, with that awareness, take actions that make the relationship more effective.

For example, in one case we observed, a manager and his superior ran into problems whenever they disagreed. The boss's typical response was to harden his position and overstate it. The manager's reaction was then to raise the ante and intensify the forcefulness of his argument. In doing this, he channeled his anger into sharpening his attacks on the logical fallacies in his boss's assumptions. His boss in turn would become even more adamant about holding his original position. Predictably, this escalating cycle resulted in the subordinate avoiding whenever possible any topic of potential conflict with his boss.

In discussing this problem with his peers, the manager discovered that his reaction to the boss was typical of how he generally reacted to counterarguments—but with a difference. His response would overwhelm his peers, but not his boss. Because his attempts to discuss this problem with his boss were unsuccessful, he concluded that the only way to change the situation was to deal with his own instinctive reactions. Whenever the two reached an impasse, he would check his own impatience and suggest that they break up and think about it before getting together again. Usually when they renewed their discussion, they had digested their differences and were more able to work them through.

Gaining this level of self-awareness and acting on it are difficult but not impossible. For example, by reflecting over his past experiences, a young manager learned that he was not very good at dealing with difficult and emotional issues where people were involved. Because he disliked those issues and realized that his instinctive responses to them were seldom very good, he developed a habit of touching base with his boss whenever such a problem arose. Their discussions always surfaced ideas and approaches the manager had not considered. In many instances, they also identified specific actions the boss could take to help.

Dependence on Authority Figures   Although a superior-subordinate relationship is one of mutual dependence, it is also one in which the subordinate is typically more dependent on the boss than the other way around. This dependence inevitably results in the subordinate feeling a certain degree of frustration, sometimes anger, when his or her actions or options are constrained by the boss's decisions. This is a normal part of life and occurs in the best of relationships. The way in which a manager handles these frustrations largely depends on his or her predisposition toward dependence on authority figures.

Some people's instinctive reaction under these circumstances is to resent the boss's authority and to rebel against the boss's decisions. Sometimes a person will escalate a conflict beyond what is appropriate. Seeing the boss almost as an institutional enemy, this type of manager will often, without being conscious of it, fight with the boss just for the sake of fighting. The manager's reactions to being constrained are usually strong and sometimes impulsive. He or she sees the boss as someone whose role is to hinder progress, an obstacle to be circumvented or at best tolerated.

Psychologists call this pattern of reactions counterdependent behavior. Although a counterdependent person is difficult for most superiors to manage and usually has a history of strained relationships with superiors, this sort of manager is apt to have even more trouble with a boss who tends to be directive or authoritarian. When the manager acts on his or her negative feelings, often in subtle and nonverbal ways, the boss sometimes *does* become the enemy. Sensing the subordinate's latent hostility, the boss will lose trust in the subordinate or his or her judgment and behave less openly.

Paradoxically, a manager with this type of predisposition is often a good manager of his or her own people. The manager will often go out of the way to get support for them and will not hesitate to go to bat for them.

At the other extreme are managers who swallow their anger and behave in a very compliant fashion when the boss makes what they know to be a poor decision. These managers will agree with the boss even when a disagreement might be welcome or when the boss would easily alter his or her decision if given more information. Because they bear no relationship to the specific situation at hand, their responses are as much an overreaction as those of counterdependent managers. Instead of seeing the boss as an enemy, these people deny their anger—the other extreme—and tend to see the boss as if he or she were an all-wise parent who should know best, should take responsibility for their careers, train them in all they need to know, and protect them from overly ambitious peers.

Both counterdependence and overdependence lead managers to hold unrealistic views of what a boss is. Both views ignore that most bosses, like everyone else, are imperfect and fallible. They don't have unlimited time, encyclopedic knowledge, or extrasensory perception; nor are they evil enemies. They have their own pressures and concerns that are sometimes at odds with the wishes of the subordinate—and often for good reason.

Altering predispositions toward authority, especially at the extremes, is almost impossible without intensive psychotherapy (psychoanalytic theory and research suggest that such predispositions are deeply rooted in a person's personality and upbringing). However, an awareness of these extremes and the range between them can be very useful in understanding where your own predispositions fall and what the implications are for how you tend to behave in relation to your boss.

If you believe, on the one hand, that you have some tendencies toward counterdependence, you can understand and even predict what your reactions and overreactions are likely to be. If, on the other hand, you believe you have some tendencies toward overdependence, you might question the extent to which your overcompliance or inability to confront real differences may be making both you and your boss less effective.

DEVELOPING AND MANAGING THE RELATIONSHIP

With a clear understanding of both your boss and yourself, you can— usually—establish a way of working together that fits both of you, that is characterized by unambiguous mutual expectations, and that helps both of you to be more productive and effective. We have already outlined a few traits such a relationship consists of, which are itemized in the *Exhibit*, and here are a few more.

COMPATIBLE WORK STYLES

Above all else, a good working relationship with a boss accommodates differences in work style. For example, in one situation we studied, a manager (who had a relatively good relationship with the boss) realized that during meetings the boss would often become inattentive and sometimes brusque. The subordinate's own style tended to be discursive and exploratory. The manager would often digress from the topic at hand to deal with background factors, alternative approaches, and so forth. The boss, instead, preferred to discuss problems with a minimum of background detail and became impatient and distracted whenever the subordinate digressed from the immediate issue.

Recognizing this difference in style, the manager became terser and more direct during meetings with the boss. To prepare to do this, before meetings with the boss the manager would develop brief agendas to be used as a guide. Whenever a digression was needed, the manager explained why. This small shift in personal style made these meetings more effective and far less frustrating for them both.

EXHIBIT
Managing the Relationship with Your Boss

Make sure you understand your boss and the boss's context, including his or her:
Goals and objectives
Pressures
Strengths, weaknesses, blind spots
Preferred work style

Assess yourself and your needs, including:
Your own strengths and weaknesses
Your personal style
Your predisposition toward dependence on authority figures

Develop and maintain a relationship that:
Fits both your needs and styles
Is characterized by mutual expectations
Keeps your boss informed
Is based on dependability and honesty
Selectively uses your boss's time and resources

Subordinates can adjust their styles in response to their bosses' preferred method for receiving information. Peter Drucker divides bosses into "listeners" and "readers." Some bosses like to get information in report form so that they can read and study it. Others work better with information and reports presented in person so that they can ask questions. As Drucker points out, the implications are obvious. If your boss is a listener, you brief him or her in person, *then* follow it up with a memo. If your boss is a reader, you cover important items or proposals in a memo or report, *then* discuss them with him or her.

Other adjustments can be made according to a boss's decision-making style. Some bosses prefer to be involved in decisions and problems as they arise. These are high-involvement managers who like to keep their hands on the pulse of the operation. Usually their needs (and your own) are best satisfied if you touch base with them whenever necessary. A boss who has a need to be involved will become involved one way or another, so there are advantages to including him or her at your initiative. Other bosses prefer to delegate—they don't want to be involved. They expect you to come to them with major problems and inform them of important changes.

Creating a compatible relationship also involves drawing on each other's strengths and making up for each other's weaknesses. Because he knew that his boss—the vice president of engineering—was not very good at monitoring his employees' problems, one manager we studied made a point of doing it himself. The stakes were high: the engineers and technicians were all union members, the company worked on a customer-contract basis, and the company had recently experienced a serious strike.

The manager worked closely with his boss, the scheduling department, and the personnel office to ensure that potential problems were avoided. He also developed an informal arrangement through which his boss would review with him any proposed changes in personnel or assignment policies before taking action. The boss valued his advice and credited his subordinate for improving both the performance of the division and the labor-management climate.

MUTUAL EXPECTATIONS

The subordinate who passively assumes that he or she knows what the boss expects is in for trouble. Of course, some superiors will spell out their expectations very explicitly and in great detail. But most do not. And although many corporations have systems that provide a basis for communicating expectations (such as formal planning processes, career planning reviews, and performance appraisal reviews), these systems never work perfectly. Also, between these formal reviews expectations invariably change.

Ultimately, the burden falls on the subordinate to find out what the boss's expectations are. These expectations can be both broad (regarding, for example, what kinds of problems the boss wishes to be informed about and when) as well as very specific (regarding such things as when a particular project should be completed and what kinds of information the boss needs in the interim).

Getting a boss who tends to be vague or nonexplicit to express his expectations can be difficult. But effective managers find ways to get that information. Some will draft a detailed memo covering key aspects of their work and then send it to their bosses for approval. They then follow this up with a face-to-face discussion in which they go over each item in the memo. This discussion often surfaces virtually all of the boss's relevant expectations.

Other effective managers will deal with an inexplicit boss by initiating an ongoing series of informal discussions about "good management" and "our objectives." Still others find useful information more indirectly through those who used to work for the boss and through the formal planning systems in which the boss makes commitments to his or her superiors. Which approach you choose, of course, should depend on your understanding of your boss's style.

Developing a workable set of mutual expectations also requires that you communicate your own expectations to the boss, find out if they are realistic, and influence the boss to accept the ones that are important to you. Being able to influence the boss to value your expectations can be particularly important if the boss is an overachiever. Such a boss will often set unrealistically high standards that need to be brought into line with reality.

A FLOW OF INFORMATION

How much information a boss needs about what a subordinate is doing will vary significantly depending on the boss's style, the situation the boss is in, and the confidence the boss has in the subordinate. But it is not uncommon for a boss to need more information than the subordinate would naturally supply or for the subordinate to think the boss knows more than he or she really does. Effective managers recognize that they probably underestimate what the boss needs to know and make sure they find ways to keep the boss informed through a process that fits his or her style.

Managing the flow of information upward is particularly difficult if the boss does not like to hear about problems. Although many would deny it, bosses often give off signals that they want to hear only good news. They show great displeasure—usually nonverbally—when someone tells them about a problem. Ignoring individual achievement, they may even evaluate more favorably subordinates who do not bring problems to them.

Nevertheless—for the good of the organization, boss, and subordinate— a superior needs to hear about failures as well as successes. Some subordinates deal with a good-news-only boss by finding indirect ways to get the necessary information to him, such as a management information system in which there is no messenger to be killed. Others see to it that potential problems, whether in the form of good surprises or bad news, are communicated immediately.

DEPENDABILITY AND HONESTY

Few things are more disabling to bosses than subordinates on whom they cannot depend, whose work they cannot trust. Almost no one is intentionally undependable, but many managers are inadvertently so because of oversight or uncertainty about the boss's priorities. A commitment to an optimistic delivery date may please a superior in the short term but be a source of displeasure if not honored. It's difficult for a boss to rely on a subordinate who repeatedly slips deadlines. As one president described a subordinate: "When he's great, he's terrific, but I can't depend on him. I'd rather he be more consistent even if he delivered fewer peak successes—at least I could rely on him."

Nor are many managers intentionally dishonest with their bosses. But it is so easy to shade the truth a bit and play down concerns. Current concerns often become future surprise problems. It's almost impossible for bosses to work effectively if they cannot rely on a fairly accurate reading from their subordinates. Because it undermines credibility, dishonesty is perhaps the most troubling trait a subordinate can have. Without a basic level of trust in a subordinate's word, a boss feels constrained to check all of a subordinate's decisions, which makes it difficult to delegate.

GOOD USE OF TIME AND RESOURCES

Your boss is probably as limited in his or her store of time, energy, and influence as you are. Every request you make of your boss uses up some of these resources. For this reason, common sense suggests drawing on these resources with some selectivity. This may sound obvious, but it is surprising how many managers use up their boss's time (and some of their own credibility) over relatively trivial issues.

In one instance, a vice president went to great lengths to get his boss to fire a meddlesome secretary in another department. His boss had to use considerable effort and influence to do it. Understandably, the head of the other department was not pleased. Later, when the vice president wanted to tackle other more important problems that required changes in the scheduling and control practices of the other department, he ran into trouble. He had used up many of his own as well as his boss's blue chips on the relatively trivial issue of getting the secretary fired, thereby making it difficult for him and his boss to meet more important goals.

—— WHOSE JOB IS IT?

No doubt, some subordinates will resent that on top of all their other duties, they also need to take time and energy to manage their relationships with their bosses. Such managers fail to realize the importance of this activity and how it can simplify their jobs by eliminating potentially severe problems. Effective managers recognize that this part of their work is legitimate. Seeing themselves as ultimately responsible for what they achieve in an organization, they know they need to establish and manage relationships with everyone on whom they are dependent, and that includes the boss.

—— DISCUSSION QUESTIONS

1. This reading focuses on what an individual can do to manage his or her relationship with the boss. What can an organization do to incorporate the concept of managing bosses into its culture?
2. The *Exhibit* in the reading advises you to assess yourself and your needs. What are your strengths and weaknesses when working with a boss? What is your personal style? What is your predisposition toward dependence on authority figures?
3. Describe a situation in which you felt empowered by managing the relationship with your boss. Explain how you managed the relationship in this situation. Describe a situation in which you neglected to manage the relationship with your boss. What would you have done differently?
4. What can a boss do to encourage his or her subordinates to manage the relationship between them constructively?

MANAGING GROUP EFFECTIVENESS

A Framework for Analyzing Work Groups

16

MICHAEL B. MCCASKEY

The author describes work groups as those groups to which a manager may be assigned as either a leader or a member. Using a case example to illustrate the concepts presented, the author explores the features of work groups and the factors that influence their behavior and performance. Topics covered include the significance of context and the role of people, tasks, and formal organization in influencing group design and group culture.

Work groups can be a forum for enhancing self-identity, a protection against excessive stress and uncertainty, and a home base in an otherwise impersonal corporation. However, more often, managers complain about the time wasted in committee meetings, the indecisiveness of the other person's work group and the red tape of one's own. Throughout this reading, the question addressed is What do managers need to know about groups? The concern is on what managers need to know to participate effectively in, as well as lead, work groups.

Work groups here refer to those groups that a manager might be assigned to as either a leader or a member, including such diverse gatherings as a company's sales force and a division operating committee. Membership can number from three up to dozens of people, but not every collection of people is a group.

The factors that can influence a group's behavior and performance include the people in the group, the task(s) they are asked to perform, the organizational constraints placed on the group, and so forth. To assist the reader, an actual work group situation will be presented here and analyzed: The Merit Corporation case will be given in several installments, thus providing a continuous example to ground the concepts of how work groups operate.[1] You may want to move back and forth between the case and the concepts, letting each enrich your understanding of the other.

---

1. The Merit Corporation case used as an illustration is a revised version of a case written by Anthony G. Athos and Diana Barrett. It is meant to serve as the basis for class discussion rather than to illustrate either effective or ineffective handling of an administrative situation.

——— MERIT CORPORATION: PART 1

The Merit Corporation was a medium-sized firm that manufactured and sold children's furniture nationally. From its inception the company had been family owned and operated, and John Kirschner was now the president of Merit. His grandfather and uncle had started the company, and control eventually passed to his father and then to him. At age 54 Kirschner was considering early retirement but was still actively involved with every aspect of the company's operations. He felt that it was time for a close look at his organization.

Merit's headquarters and the largest of its three manufacturing plants were located in an industrial park 10 miles outside of Boston. Merit shared the building with a number of other firms and had offices on the second and third floors of the six-story building. All employees worked a 40-hour, five-day week. Work began promptly at 8:30 A.M. and ended at 4:30 P.M. Coming in early or leaving late was generally considered to be a sign of ineffectiveness by Kirschner. He set the pattern himself (just as his father and grandfather had before him), parking his car next to the front entrance of the building at precisely 8:30 A.M. and, with rare exception, leaving at 4:30 P.M.

In a departure from the company's conservative philosophy and practice, Kirschner had brought in new managers from outside. Some of them had MBAs, and most had backgrounds in plastics or in consumer marketing. Kirschner emphasized continuing technical and managerial education and sent a number of his top people to Harvard's Advanced Management Program. Kirschner also advocated managing by committee, and he shared the CEO function with two other executives. Merit had generous fringe benefits and a pension plan that was a model in its area. Thus labor disputes had never been a significant problem. Turnover was generally low, and employee morale was high. Merit enjoyed a dominant position in the juvenile furniture market. Kirschner felt that the company's only troubling problem was the development of new products.

New products had traditionally been developed by a series of temporary task forces. On a rotating basis, managers would spend six months on a task force to develop a new product. This system had been used for years, since Kirschner's father and grandfather had both felt that line managers should have experience in the new-products area.

Over the past 10 years, however, several changes warranted a new look at an area so fundamental to Merit's success. The birth rate was declining, and people seemed less inclined to spend a great deal of money on juvenile furniture. The consumers' movement was vocal about product imperfections and poor design features, such as sharp corners and toxic paints. Responding to these concerns increased production costs. The field had also become increasingly competitive as manufacturers of household furniture began to use their excess capacity to produce children's furniture. As a result of these and other factors, obtaining adequate financing had become increasingly difficult. The higher cost of debt had led to price increases, which did not help attract customers in a highly competitive market where product differentiation was difficult. The company's sales had leveled off at approximately $120 million.

Kirschner had always been especially interested in the new-products area because he had started there at Merit. He decided that before retiring he wanted to improve significantly the new-products area because strength here would help ensure the firm's continued success.

After giving the matter considerable thought and briefly discussing it with his top managers, Kirschner decided that a radical change was necessary. He decided to form a group of six to eight people with diverse and possibly even unorthodox backgrounds to work full time on developing new products. Kirschner felt that if he could find the right people and give them a good deal of encouragement, the company would strengthen its new-products development. Consequently, he set about finding and hiring the kind of people who could give real impetus to the company's new-products development. Kirschner also began looking for office space to house the new group. Although no space was available on the second and third floors, some office space was available on the fourth floor. It seemed desirable for the group to have an area of its own.

─── GROUP CONTEXT

Whatever actions Kirschner takes in initiating a group at Merit will occur within the context of the existing organization and its wider environment. Even though he is the company's president, he does not have complete freedom. Any changes made must recognize the existing structure and people, the company's history and traditions, what the economy and competitors are doing, and many other features as well. If Kirschner wants to initiate a new group, background factors such as these will influence the size, independence, and behavior of the group. To study how a work group operates, the following aspects of the context or background should be considered:

- Purposes for which the group was created
- Physical setting in which the group works
- Company size, nature of business, location, past history, and proposed future
- Competitors, suppliers, and regulators
- Political, social, economic, and legal systems.

Background factors like these will influence efforts by Kirschner to begin a new group. For example, some of the older executives might value their experience on the rotating task forces of line managers that Merit had used to develop new products and therefore resist any changes in existing procedures.

This does not appear to be the case at Merit, but if such feelings and outlooks arise, Kirschner will have to deal with them. Failing to do so would endanger the ability of the group to carry out its mission or to survive after Kirschner retires.

Contextual factors, then, are the background factors out of which a group arises and in which a group operates. Context will affect the way a group behaves, and these factors must be part of any analysis of how a work group operates. Turning to the case, what do you notice about Merit? What features are likely to be important for how the new work group or any other group performs at Merit?

One of the primary considerations affecting the proposed group is the purpose it will serve. Kirschner seems to like to introduce changes; his assessment of the company's strengths and weaknesses leads him to feel that the new-products area is where the company needs the most improvement. He would like to retire and may want to leave a vital new-products group as a legacy. Since the proposed group will have his support, it may enjoy unusual advantages in securing information and getting resources, but the group's success is not guaranteed. If there is a contest among aspirants to succeed Kirschner as president, some competitive dynamics may endanger or support the fledgling group.

Locating the group on a different floor from the rest of the corporation headquarters may also turn out to be important. The group's mission will be to create new products, and it may want to set up procedures different from those geared to produce and sell existing lines. The physical separation of the group may allow for this.

The company's history of being family owned and managed through three presidents may influence other executives to go along with Kirschner's wishes. He has successfully introduced other changes, and this record may also provide *social capital,* the credibility necessary to introduce further changes. At the same time the leveling off of company growth, and the expectations of future development created by bringing MBAs into the firm, may fuel a desire to create new and better products. Pride in being #1 in its industry and the threat of new competition from general-purpose furniture manufacturers may also fuel a willingness to break with Merit's ways of developing new products. These contextual factors will influence the degree and kind of support group members are likely to receive from the rest of the organization.

——— MERIT CORPORATION: PART 2

Within six months Kirschner hired eight new people, described below, who he felt had diversity of background, intelligence, enthusiasm, and imagination. They were all between the ages of 27 and 29 and had been educated at some of the country's best technical and liberal arts schools.

Christopher Kane, 28, BA Math, Tufts; MBA, Stanford
Worked for McKinsey & Co. in a variety of areas, including marketing diversification and systems analysis.

Andrew Jacobson, 29, BS Math, M.I.T.
Systems Analyst for Mitre Corp. for one year. Founder of a Public Interest Research Group under the auspices of Ralph Nader. Heavily involved with environmental and consumer issues.

John O'Hara, 28, BA, Oberlin
Sculptor and painter. Had a one-artist show at the Cleveland Art Museum. Taught art and metal sculpting in United States and abroad.

Robert Vidreaux, 28, BA Social Relations, Harvard
Led two archeological digs to Iran and spent two years working at the Museum of Natural History in New York. Has three patents and a variety of inventions in the area of water filtration and purification.

Susanne Tashman, 27, BA English, Hollins; JD, Yale
Worked for Davis, Marshall and Polk, a law firm, for two years, specializing in Securities and Exchange Commission work.

Joan Waters, 27, BA Chemistry, Wellesley; MBA, Harvard
Worked for Sloan-Kettering Laboratories in New York City for two years in the area of chromosomal aberrations and viruses. After receiving MBA, worked in the financial office of Lily Laboratories on long-range planning for one year.

Matthew Kiris, 29, BS Chemistry, Cal Tech
Spent three years investigating the effect of high concentrations of pesticides in tidal regions both in the U.S. and in the Far East. Was a consultant in the Dept. of Public Health both in the U.S. and in Japan.

Raynor Carney, 29, BA Political Science, Northwestern; MBA Columbia
Has had extensive political experience, organizing a major gubernatorial campaign and fund raising for the state Democratic party. Served as the primary developer and contractor for modular low-cost housing project in Maryland.

Kirschner wanted one person reporting directly to him but decided against imposing any further structure on the group. He appointed Kane as group head, partly because he was the first to be hired and partly because Kane had made such a positive impression.

When the eight people began work at Merit, they did not know each other, and they did not know what they would be doing on a day-to-day basis. Their training and skills were very different. For example, Jacobson, who had worked as a systems analyst and was also interested in consumer and environmental issues, tended to be comfortable about the implications of the data in light of his other interests. His previous experience in a large company had led him to expect a way of doing things that he guessed was probably quite different from what others in the group expected. O'Hara, for his part, had never worked in a business environment, and although he was used to working long hours and being committed to a project for an extended length of time, he brought fewer expectations than Jacobson did about the job at Merit. Vidreaux, on the other hand, because of his interest in inventing new ways of doing things, tended to approach a procedure by first looking for other ways in which it might be done.

Not only were their backgrounds and interests very different but their personal characteristics were also quite varied. Kane, who had always worn a coat and tie to work, contrasted sharply with O'Hara, who was more comfortable in jeans. Tashman had worked in a law firm before coming to Merit, and thus she had become quite comfortable dressing more formally every day. In contrast, Waters preferred to dress informally; she saw the opportunity to dress even more informally as a major advantage of her new job.

The work styles of the eight were also quite different. O'Hara was extremely untidy and could work comfortably only with stacks of paper cluttering his desk and immediate area. Meanwhile, Jacobson, as he put it, was "compulsively neat." Kiris felt that he worked better with low music in the room, while both Waters and Tashman had strong preferences for quiet when working.

Kirschner believed that the new group would be creative if given lots of freedom and encouragement. He made it clear that his only requirements of the group were a biweekly progress report for the executive committee and a monthly financial report. Kirschner emphasized that group members were free to work as they wished, as long as they focused their energies on developing new products that met the need for durable, but inexpensive, multipurpose children's furniture.

——— GROUP DESIGN FACTORS

In part 2 of the Merit case, several factors appear that are important to the behavior developing in the New Products Development (NPD) group. These factors include the people who formed the group, the tasks they are required to perform, and the formal structure and operating mechanisms of the organization where they work. Part of a manager's job in managing a group is to arrange these factors in such a way as to enhance an organization's effectiveness.

The task for the NPD group is to develop new products that meet the need for durable, but inexpensive, multipurpose children's furniture. Kirschner has hired people he thinks are suited to this task. He also has set the group apart from the rest of the organization, both physically and in their reporting relationship to him. So Kirschner is making decisions about what have been called the three *design factors*—people, task requirements, and formal organization. He is trying to fit these design factors together in the strongest combination to increase the group's chances of success.

PEOPLE

First, there are the people who have been named to the NPD group; they are a diverse collection of people, many without much business experience. Because human beings are composed of a myriad of subtle and shifting characteristics, the possibilities for categorizing them are endless. Research on group behavior and organizational design, however, has found some characteristics more useful to focus on than others:

- Skills and interests possessed by individual members of the group;
- What the members' learning styles are. Some people learn by actually doing things, while others learn by reflecting and analyzing;
- Values and assumptions individual members hold. Particularly important in a group setting are members' expectations about leadership;
- Members' preferences for variety, for definition and structure, and for individual challenge. Some people feel more comfortable with loosely structured situations, where they have a great deal of autonomy. Other people strongly prefer clarity and definition in tasks and roles.

To effectively manage the NPD group, Kirschner will need to consider the rich mix of people and how they might best work together. Included among the eight are people who have sculpted, invented, performed research, and organized campaigns. They are all young and well educated and so may expect to work together in a more or less democratic style. Leadership may emerge slowly and is unlikely ever to be dictatorial.

It may also make a difference to the group's operation that O'Hara and Jacobson have quite different working styles. One is exploratory and messy, the other systematic and neat. Jacobson and Tashman are used to a corporate way of doing things; O'Hara, the sculptor, is not. Vidreaux, who has spent time on archeological digs and inventing, may well be a maverick on procedures. These dispositions and skills must be taken into account in trying to manage the group effectively.

TASK REQUIREMENTS

The second major design factor that influences a group's behavior is the tasks that individuals or the group must perform. Research on designing social systems has identified a group's task requirements:

- Interactions required among people
- Variety of activities involved
- Novelty or routineness of the tasks
- Degree to which the work pace is under an individual's control.

Kirschner has deliberately kept the list of task requirements short and open-ended for the NPD group: develop new products for children's furniture within certain constraints. The fact that the group is to be innovative means that the task is more novel than routine and calls for a breadth of skills. The new product must appeal to parents, not offend consumer watchdogs, be low in cost and durable, and capable of being manufactured by Merit.

Kirschner has not specified or required any pattern of interaction among the eight group members, but the nature of the task suggests they will probably have to interact with those who know marketing and with those who understand engineering and manufacturing. O'Hara, Kane, Waters, and others will have to find ways to divide up the work and then bring all the parts together. Group members have high individual control over their work pace and work activities because the task is relatively unspecified when compared, for example, with an assembly line work group.

FORMAL ORGANIZATION

The third factor is the organizational structure and operating systems, or the formal organization within which the group operates, including

- Hierarchy of authority
- Pattern of reporting relationships
- Formal measurement, evaluations, and control systems
- Reward systems
- Selection and recruitment procedures.

Because he wants to foster innovation, Kirschner has taken special pains to shield the NPD group from most of the structure and procedures that apply to the rest of the organization. He has appointed Kane to be head of the group for reporting purposes, and the only required reviews are a progress report every other week and a monthly financial report. The group reports directly to him and not, as might be true in other organizations, to a vice president of research and development or marketing vice president. Kirschner personally recruited and selected the eight members of the group into the organization, thus making it clear to the rest of the organization that this is a special project, high on his list of priorities. Although little is known about other organizational systems that might affect the NPD group, the point here is that there are few organizational procedures and very little structure to constrain or guide the group's behavior.

Care must be taken not to presume that a manager can readily change structure and procedures. Because Kirschner is the company's president and is starting up a new group, he has more freedom than most managers. However, even he must operate within the context of company history and traditions, the economic outlook, competitors' behavior, and so forth.

In a given situation a manager will have varying degrees of control over the three design factors, depending on his or her formal authority. He or she may influence those things that a manager (1) has complete control over; (2) requires help from others to change; and (3) has little or no control over. In the case of the NPD group, for example, Kane is unlikely to have direct control over how the members of the group are rewarded or where it reports to in the organization hierarchy. But he can go to Kirschner and argue for changes in these factors. For a wide range of other matters, Kane and the group have a great deal of control. This is due to the newness of the group, Kirschner's shielding efforts, and the fact that the task is relatively unspecified on required activities and interactions. In other, well-established groups, long embedded in a particular organizational structure, the degrees of freedom about division of activities, required interactions, pace of the work, and so forth, will often be substantially less. In analyzing what a manager *should do* versus what a manager *can do* to improve the performance of a work group, these three levels of control should be kept firmly in mind.

The eight people named to the NPD group are not yet a group; rather, they are a collection of people who will have to build a group. They are required to perform certain activities and interactions, such as developing a new product and reporting on their progress every other week. However, beyond a few minimal requirements, the eight are free to evolve whatever patterns of thought and behavior meet their needs. The emergence of those patterns is one of the most interesting and, for a manager, important aspects of group life. In reading the next installment of the Merit case, keep close track of behaviors that emerge—those activities, interactions, and rules that are not required but that group members devise over time. Keep track also of how these emerging activities and interactions might affect the group's performance.

———— MERIT CORPORATION: PART 3

On January 2 the eight members of the NPD group arrived at Merit and reported to Kirschner's office. Kirschner had planned an informal orientation day. He presented each person with a packet of information about the company, data about the products that Merit manufactured, and information about compensation and fringe benefits. Then they toured the offices and the plant with "Mr. K.," as they quickly came to call Kirschner.

After lunch, which was held in a restaurant a few miles away, the group members were introduced to the executives with whom they would come into contact. Then Kirschner took them to the fourth floor of the building, where he had rented three offices next to one another. He explained that they would have one secretary who would be working directly with them and that they could use additional support staff if necessary. He apologized for the condition of the offices, which were sparsely furnished and not air-conditioned. He encouraged the group members to get to know one another and to organize the space as they wished.

After Kirschner left, the group spent the rest of the afternoon organizing the work space. The three offices were adjacent to one another and were interconnected. Each office had enough room for two or three desks. The middle office was the largest and contained three desks and a large table. Kane, whom Kirschner introduced as the group's head for reporting and administrative purposes, moved into the first office. Carney took the next desk because he wanted to be near a window. Tashman and Waters had already discovered the middle office. Kiris took the remaining desk in this room because he thought he would occasionally work at the large table. The three others shared the last office where the group decided to put the coffee machine that Jacobson had found in a storage closet (see *Exhibit 1* for a diagram of the office layout).

The group members spent the next few weeks familiarizing themselves with the company. Kirschner usually came upstairs once or twice a week, and he often brought new information that he thought the members might be able to use. They informally organized themselves into functional areas, on the basis of individual interest, training, and expertise. For example, although the group as a whole developed cash flow projections, Tashman usually took responsibility for coordinating this activity. O'Hara used his artistic ability to translate ideas into three-dimensional drawings. And Jacobson proved to be particularly adept at synthesizing complex data because of his background in systems analysis. Vidreaux was first seen as an antagonist, because of the disorderly way in which he worked. Then others began to see him as very helpful because his background and interest in social relations enabled him to bring up potentially disruptive issues about the group's process of working together. Kane was the nominal group head, but Waters soon became a coleader, partly because she had the technical expertise to communicate with engineers in the production department and also because of the organizational ability she had acquired in her MBA training.

The group quickly developed some routines. Group members got into the habit of bringing their lunch and eating around the large table in the middle room. Almost daily over lunch they would brainstorm to elicit new ideas. Anyone could start a lunch session; however, because Waters, Tashman, and Kiris shared the middle office, they tended to initiate the sessions. Because the physical layout brought the eight in contact with one other so easily, they interacted regularly.

Although working an eight-hour day was not specifically required of the group, individuals tended to come in at 8:30 A.M. and leave at 4:30 P.M. As ideas were gradually turned into viable products, however, they began working after hours and on weekends. After a while some of them began to come in late in the mornings and work until 6 P.M. or 7 P.M., while others preferred to come in before work hours and leave early. It became the norm to work late or on

EXHIBIT 1
Office Layout

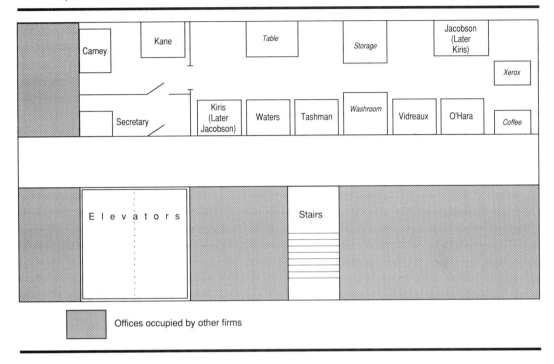

Offices occupied by other firms

weekends if a task was left unfinished. People were almost always in the office between 10 A.M. and 3 P.M., since it was during these hours that the brainstorming sessions and lunch tended to occur. As subgroups formed, and people tended to work together in twos or threes, tension and sometimes friction occurred.

One source of tension was Carney, who preferred to work alone much of the time. He was often in the middle of something when the other members of the group wanted to begin a brainstorming session. Carney felt that it was more important to finish what he was doing than to work with the group. He eventually missed so many sessions that the other group members kidded him about his antisocial behavior. When this seemed to have no effect, they began to exclude him from informal conversations. At lunch one day when Carney was absent, Vidreaux suggested that the group discuss the purpose and frequency of the sessions and the importance of everyone being present. As a result of this discussion, group members realized that exceptions to regular attendance could be made without affecting productivity. Subsequently, Carney was included in more informal conversations, but he still remained at the edge of the group.

A similar incident occurred around the issue of work space. O'Hara was extremely untidy and could work comfortably only in the midst of clutter. Jacobson, one of his office mates, was very orderly and found the clutter disturbing. Considerable antagonism developed between the two until

Vidreaux kiddingly brought up the issue at a group session. As a result of the discussion, Jacobson agreed to change places with Kiris, who was indifferent to messiness.

GROUP CULTURE

Part 3 of the Merit case shows the eight people of the NPD group busy with the process of building a group. Individuals are finding out who they can be in the group, what aspects of self others will value and confirm. Simultaneously, each person is confirming certain aspects of others' self-presentation and also learning the particular social and task skills others bring to the group. The eight are dividing the work, developing patterns of interacting, and establishing norms for behaving. In short, they are building a group culture.

PATTERNS EMERGE

The patterns of behavior and values that members create for themselves constitute a group's culture. These are the ways of thinking and behaving that a group evolves over time. Even in the first weeks of their being together, members of the NPD group developed several characteristic patterns that were not required of them. These emerging patterns of behavior are the members' interpretation of what they have been asked to do. More important, the emerging patterns of behavior are the members' inventions to fit their individual needs to the task and social context. For example, they have developed a pattern of working as many hours as needed to complete their tasks, even if it means coming in on weekends or staying late. They have also developed patterns of mutual helping on the job. These activities and interactions are not required, but nonetheless, they affect the group's performance for better or worse.

Because the group members are young and close in age, it is not surprising that informal, loosely structured interaction has emerged. The members interact frequently and easily and do not seem to emphasize status differences, although some are emerging. They have found lunchtime brainstorming sessions useful, and these sessions are becoming a pattern. Some who previously never brought lunch to work now regularly do to visit and eat together as a group.

NORMS

The patterns outlined are emerging, and some are being enforced as norms of the group. *Norms* are the expectations and guidelines that are shared by group members for how members should behave. Over time, group members define what is fair and what is appropriate behavior. Almost all groups will develop their own norms given enough time. Not to follow the group's norm threatens the cohesiveness of the group, and people who deviate from the group's norms will suffer some form of social censure. For example, in the NPD group, Carney prefers working alone to attending many of the group's brainstorming sessions. At first he is kidded; when this proves ineffective for changing his behavior, he is excluded more and more from ordinary social contact. This could become a serious clash, but Vidreaux initiates explicit discussion. The result is that Carney remains on the periphery of the group, a deviant from the group's norms. The episode illustrates a group's attempt to bring a member's behavior into line. In some groups kidding may even be followed by physical intimidation, and eventually one may be totally cut off from the group's social life. This ultimate sanction treats such a member as a social isolate.

Even though they are enforced by group members, norms are not applied monolithically; they are far more subtle than that. Not all behaviors are covered by norms, and norms do not apply equally to everyone. Some members may be given leeway because of their personal needs or unique contribution. At Merit, Carney is allowed some deviation from group norms, although at the cost of remaining on the social periphery. Research on groups shows that leaders, more than other group members, tend to embody the group's central values and norms. Leaders may be allowed some exceptions from group norms because of their high status, but in so doing they use up a certain amount of the social capital they have accumulated. If, as happens in most groups, members largely conform to the group's norms, the norms help regularize interactions between members. It is much easier, for example, for everyone in the NPD to attend impromptu brainstorming sessions if everyone follows the norm of being in the office between 10 A.M. and 3 P.M.

This does not mean that a manager entering a group for the first time has to conform absolutely to the group's norms. It does mean that he or she must approach the task of possibly changing group norms with care and understanding of how they work.

Take David King, the new principal of Robert F. Kennedy High School, as another example. In his first staff meeting he was surprised that people, who in private meetings with him were highly critical of one another, were extremely polite and considerate with each other in a public meeting. King was uncovering a norm for courteous conduct and the avoidance of open conflict. When King pushed against this norm in his first meeting with his staff, some group members reacted explosively. Norms serve an important function for group members in stabilizing their interactions along predictable paths. When a manager decides that some norms are blocking group effectiveness, he or she must examine the purpose the norms serve before attempting to change them. Similarly, other features of group culture, such as roles, help give stability and predictability to the interactions of group members.

ROLES

A *role* is the characteristic and expected social behavior of an individual. In addition to the role of formally appointed group leader, other informal roles may also develop. For example, Waters has emerged as an *informal coleader* of the group. And Carney has become a *deviant* because of his unwillingness to follow an important norm of the group. Carried further, a member who fails to follow several group norms where other members are less tolerant, may become a *social isolate*. Roles such as these are often helpful in defining what the norms are in a group. At one end of the continuum, informal leaders are likely to adhere to group norms, while at the other end, extreme social isolates violate some, perhaps many, of the group's norms.

In the NPD group several roles have developed based on the special skills and interests of different members. For example, Tashman coordinates the development of cash flow projections and O'Hara does the drawings. Less is known about roles connected to how the group works, except that Kane and Waters are coleaders—Kane is the formal leader and Waters is an informal leader. Vidreaux has become another informal leader because he raises process issues for discussion and can successfully conclude discussions.

People in a group develop patterns of behavior that contribute or detract from the group's ability to achieve its social and task functions. Take a group, for example, where one person consistently cracks a joke to break tensions and to reharmonize relationships. In the same group another person often supplies technical information, while a third person typically keeps an eye on the clock and returns the group to its agenda when discussion strays too far. Behaviors like these, often bundled into specialized roles, are important to the level of effectiveness a group achieves.

RITUALS, STORIES, AND LANGUAGE

As part of its cultural ways, a work group may also develop rituals, stories about past deeds, and language shorthand. In the NPD group, members already have one ritual in the lunchtime discussions along with a norm of consistent attendance. This young group does not have sagas or myths to relate about previous heroic efforts, but when those develop, they will also serve to reinforce the social ties among members. As is typical of work groups, members of the NPD group use their own language shorthand to talk about different parts of their world, such as Mr. K., brainstorming, and antisocial behavior. Language shorthand offers clues to what is emotionally significant in a group's way of working together, or what shared sentiments help hold the group together. For example, *Mr. K.* conveys a mixture of deference and special relationship to the company's president, especially if no one else in the company addresses him this way. It may signal their feeling that, if they are refused a hearing lower down in the organization, they can take their case to the top. Quite likely, members of the NPD group have other phrases and code words that make sense to themselves but are puzzling to outsiders. Like rituals and stories, special language conventions serve to draw boundaries around the group, differentiating group members from others.

MAPS

One feature of group culture is the most invisible and often the most difficult for group members to articulate. It is the *map* that group members create of what is important to notice in the world around them. The eight people in the NPD group do not face a predefined reality that is fixed, objective, and composed of hard facts. Their work world consists of much that is overwhelming. Like individuals who must selectively perceive the world, group members must also selectively perceive aspects of their world. Furthermore, out of what they notice they must build some kind of coherent picture that makes sense to themselves and provides a common base of understanding within the group. Rather quickly, group members tacitly evolve agreements on what is most important and on what the cause-and-effect linkages are. The process of formulating a shared map is not always smooth, and some group members can map only part of their world in common. This version of reality is treated as real; it is real for group members and is slow to change.

A map guides a group member's daily decisions about what to do and how to interact with others, and it facilitates predicting the likely outcomes of one action versus another. With the information provided so far about the NPD group, we know little about its map. But the map of a sales group, for example, may stress the importance of frequently "pressing the flesh" with customers because it appears to be important in a customer's continuing willingness to buy the product. Mapping is the mental process by which members of the group interactively comprehend and deal with the world around them. For a new member coming into a group, this means that a group has the power to influence how she or he sees the world.

Thus far several features of group culture have been distinguished. Its components—emergent activities, norms, roles, rituals, stories, language, and mapping—are an ongoing social construction of reality. The group's culture is not immediately obvious but can be inferred through change in its major outlines, as over time the group makes small modifications and adjustments. What is most important to know for managing groups is that the culture a group forms is outside the direct control of a manager. It can only be influenced by the manager's actions, example, and the arrangement of the various design factors. Appreciating the constructed quality of group culture, however, opens new possibilities for leading and participating in groups. It separates what is easily changed from what is not, and focuses attention on what a manager can directly influence and what is more in the province of group members. Because group culture is closely connected to group performance, managers need to understand the process of forming a group culture and develop the ability to analyze it.

—— MERIT CORPORATION: PART 4

After the NPD group had been operating for six months, Kirschner and the executive committee saw that the group had developed a variety of innovative and unique product ideas. They could also see that group members were enthusiastic about their work. At the end of the first year the group came out with a new product. Within six months the product had won a 20% share of an extremely competitive market and had been widely acclaimed for its low manufacturing costs, durability, and consumer appeal. To celebrate, the group had lunch away from the office one Friday, and the celebration lasted all afternoon.

—— OUTCOMES AND FEEDBACK

Although managers may be tempted to think of what a group produces solely in terms of its work productivity, the outcomes of a group are actually multidimensional. Consider the various outcomes that a group produces under three headings: (1) productivity, (2) satisfaction, and (3) individual growth.

The productivity of the NPD group was quite high. The group produced a variety of new product ideas and successfully introduced a new product into a competitive marketplace. The group had achieved its major purpose.

Beyond work productivity, an important outcome for the group was its sense of satisfaction with how it operated and what it achieved. The term *satisfaction* is a shorthand for the rich mixture of feelings that a member can experience as a result of being part of a successful group. These feelings can include strong negative as well as positive, ambivalent, and sometimes even contradictory emotions. They are part of what fuels each member's participation or lack of it in the group. Think, for a moment, of the groups in which you have especially enjoyed working. What were the characteristics of those groups? How did you feel during the group meetings? How did that add to the amount and the quality of the work you did?

Emotions, feelings of satisfaction or dissatisfaction, can be powerful stimuli for behavior in groups. As some scholars have phrased it, groups run on emotion. The feelings that result from a period of work have reinforcing effects on existing aspects of group life. As group members see the group producing certain outcomes, this reinforces or weakens features in the group culture. For example, those in the NPD group who championed the product idea that proved to be a market success probably saw their standing increased. The success of the group and the attendant positive feelings reinforced the map and the group's norms about what was to be valued and what was not. In addition, feedback can reinforce or weaken the patterns of interaction between people, task, and formal organization. Because the feedback in this instance is positive, patterns are strengthened. If the outcomes had been negative, the pattern of working together, which the group had evolved, would be questioned.

Crucial for managing the group's long-term health is the extent to which individuals feel they are learning and growing. No direct information exists on the NPD group, but it appears that many of the eight see themselves as learning and growing. O'Hara and Kiris, with nonbusiness backgrounds, are learning to operate successfully in a business setting. In exercising leadership skills, Waters is growing and developing as a manager. Such individual growth keeps a member involved and committed to the group's activities and provides a basis for even better performance over the long run. If individual commitment were found lacking, the manager of a group would have to resort to increasingly heavy external pressures that would eventually be self-defeating.

——— WORK-GROUP BEHAVIOR MODEL

The concepts introduced to this point can now come together in a model of work-group behavior. This model, devised for managers, focuses on the dominant features of how a group operates and the action available to a manager for managing a group. The model does not aim for conceptual elegance, nor is it totally inclusive; rather, it tries to distill the number of categories down to those that accurately portray the main features of group life (see *Exhibit 2* for the major elements of the model).

The model indicates that what a group produces, its outcomes, are influenced by a set of factors called group culture. Group culture refers to the patterns of behaving and thinking that develop in the group. Group culture arises from the interaction of the three design factors—the people in the group, the tasks they are required to perform, and the structure and systems of the organization in which the group operates. The design factors and how they interact are in turn shaped by a set of factors called context. The company, its history and traditions, its size and economic clout, the physical setting in which the group works, the state of the economy, government action, consumer attitudes, the actions of competitors are all contextual factors that could ultimately affect a given work group. Theoretically, arrows could be drawn between all parts of the model. Group behavior is a complex and subtle phenomenon in which everything, to some degree, is interconnected. But

EXHIBIT 2
Model for Analyzing a Work Group

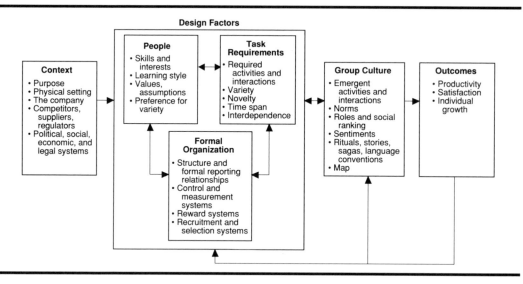

because it is more useful to concentrate on the typical patterns of interaction, arrows describe only the most important relationships.

It is important to note that the whole system is dynamic. Changes in any part of the model can eventually lead to changes throughout the model. For example, when the economy hits a severe downturn (a change in a contextual factor), top management may decide to lay off people. Some of these will be members of a work group. Remaining members may respond by attempting to increase production and lower costs, or they may go on strike or look for other jobs. In response to a downturn, organizational systems, particularly budgeting and auditing systems, are likely to be tightened. This will affect the group's norms about how much they should try to produce and how efficiently. It may well alter patterns of interaction and give new prominence to those group members who have special skills for dealing with the crisis. All the changes and adjustments percolate through and result in altered outcomes—perhaps higher productivity, higher or lower satisfaction, and a mixture of other feelings. The outcomes are multidimensional and have effects on the group culture and on design factors.

You should be able to fill out a chart for the NPD group, using the major categories—context, design factors, group culture, outcomes—of the model in *Exhibit 2*. More important, you should also understand some of the interrelationships between the concepts.

Few social systems stand still, and events continued to change at Merit. Part 5 describes what happened to the NPD group over the next several months. Partway through the case history, there will be a chance to test your understanding of the model.

——— MERIT CORPORATION: PART 5

Three months later Kirschner retired. The executive committee brought in Joe Donaldson as vice president of marketing, a man with 15 years of experience in a large consumer-product organization. The NPD group would now report to him.

Donaldson was extremely interested in the work the group had done, but he was concerned that no additional new products appeared to be imminent. Two months after his arrival at Merit, Donaldson asked Kane to come down to his office to discuss this problem. Kane explained that it had taken some time for the group to adjust to Merit but that things seemed to be going quite well; in fact, Kane was enthusiastic about the group's future. Donaldson continued to express concern about the viability of such a group at Merit. Kane, somewhat flustered, finally told him that he could attribute some of the problems to the poor secretarial help and the lack of support staff on the fourth floor. Kane also stressed that creativity in work groups tends to occur in cycles. He was confident that the group was in a trough now and would soon be out of it.

Two weeks after Donaldson's meeting with Kane, the group heard of his decision. The NPD group would move downstairs with the rest of the staff. Donaldson hoped that with better administrative assistance, closer contact with line executives, and with his personal involvement, the group could repeat its first success.

Within 30 days of Donaldson's decision the NPD group moved downstairs to the second floor and reported directly to Donaldson. Although the offices could not be located next to one another, they were redecorated, and each person was given ample secretarial and administrative help. In addition, Donaldson encouraged the group to increase expenses if necessary to quickly bring out another new product. The group was also encouraged to work an 8:30 A.M. to 4:30 P.M. day, because the occupants of the adjoining offices might resent their unpredictable schedules.

Before reading further, use the model shown in *Exhibit 2* to predict what will happen.

——— MERIT CORPORATION: PART 5 *(CONTINUED)*

At first, the new offices and novel atmosphere made up for the distance between offices. Those who preferred to dress informally, however, began to feel quite uncomfortable and changed to more traditional business attire. Within a few weeks, patterns of interaction that had proved successful as well as personally satisfying to individual members had fallen away. Because group members could no longer easily enter and leave each other's offices and because they had no place to hold brainstorming sessions, their sense of what they ought to do on a given day became vague. Certain individuals, especially Carney, were more uncomfortable than others. Carney began to issue working papers on what the competition was likely to do and on social issues, neither of which was seen as particularly relevant to the group's work. Soon he was ostracized from the group. Without a comfortable and accessible place to have lunch together, people began to go out to restaurants in subgroups. It became the exception rather than the rule for the group to meet informally. Individuals began to feel increasingly dissatisfied with their jobs and felt surrounded by people with different personal values. At the same time, the old roles seemed quite inappropriate in the new environment. During an infrequent group lunch at a nearby restaurant, numerous complaints were voiced, ranging from feelings of inadequacy, to a sense of boredom, to dissatisfaction with the rigid work hours.

Within two months, O'Hara left Merit to be married and to live on the West Coast; Tashman and Carney also left. Kane suggested recruiting new people, but Donaldson decided that it would be best to disband the group, assigning the remaining individuals to regular departments and reinstituting the task-force system that had earlier been used for new-product development. After three months, every member of the group had resigned except for Kane.

On one of his rare visits to the office, Kirschner asked Kane what had gone wrong. Kane was reluctant to describe what he thought Donaldson's effect had been, so he told Kirschner that it was difficult to maintain a creative group over a long time and that most members had personal reasons for leaving. Kirschner seemed to accept the explanation and did not pursue the matter further.

Donaldson looked at the NPD group and saw reduced outcomes. In his eyes, the absence of a new product in two months was cause for trying to change the group. He changed the location and work schedule of the group, without careful consideration of what the group's culture was and how it worked. Unknowingly, he disrupted the culture that group members had devised to fit their diverse personalities to the task Kirschner had given them. The map, norms, and roles the group had established broke down. Carney and others became uncertain about what to do. Their previous excitement, satisfaction, and sense of purpose turned to confusion and hostility. The group as a social system floundered and became a collection of individuals once again. Several people quit and eventually the group was disbanded.

Donaldson used a deficient model of how groups operate. His actions seriously weakened and then broke the links between design and culture and between culture and outcomes. He implicitly linked those things he could directly control—such as work schedule, reporting relationships, and physical setting—to group performance. He seemed unaware of the intervening role played by group culture and of how outcomes were multiple in nature. Using a model that overlooked important features of how a group operates led him to make a number of ill-conceived changes.

One of the aims of presenting a managerial mode of group behavior is to focus attention on the intelligent selection of action to be taken:

1. Look at the outcomes of a group. Why do they perform the way they do?
2. Look at the culture of the group. What are their norms and values? What do they do that is not required but nonetheless affects their performance for better or worse? Why is the culture the way it is?
3. Look at the design factors. Which of these are under your direct control and which can you only indirectly influence? How can the design factors be changed in a desirable direction to produce the outcomes you are trying to achieve?
4. Look at the context within which the group operates. Are the proposed changes consonant with contextual factors? Where should you anticipate difficulties?

Had Donaldson thought through such an analysis for the NPD group, he would not have been guaranteed a success. Skills are needed to carry out any plans suggested by analysis. However, Donaldson would have increased his chances of successfully intervening and eventually achieving the results he sought.

—— CONCLUSION

The model of group behavior presented here captures much of what happens in a work group and provides a platform for building further knowledge. Looking at groups in this way allows the reader to identify the multiple causes of a group's behavior and performance. Furthermore, the model in its attention to managerial action, and what is and is not under a manager's control, suggests a way to think about participating in and leading a work group.

By showing how leadership functions can be distributed in a group and how a map is interactively constructed, the model provides a new way to think about leadership in work groups. An informal, or unappointed, leader of a group can help build a culture that brings together members, tasks, and organization. In high-performing groups several members usually share the behaviors that maintain a group socially and those that move it toward task accomplishment. Likewise, although the first attempt usually falls to the formal leader, informal leaders can play a major role in formulating or reformulating the map that guides a group's efforts.

The culture constructed by group members represents their stance vis-à-vis the rest of the world and influences their effectiveness. They act out the various aspects of their emerging culture and subsequent outcomes provide feedback for further action. Feedback from the rest of the world leads to reinforcing, modifying, or in unusual cases, abandoning the map, norms, and roles that make up the group culture. The revised patterns of thinking and interacting go through additional cycles throughout the group's life. A group might continue its growth and development or settle into established routines.

In summary, group culture is closely connected to the outcomes that the group produces, and yet culture is beyond the direct control of a manager. A manager works through three design factors—people, tasks, and formal organization—to influence culture. These are the most readily available areas for actions influencing group behavior. However, managerial action should occur only after a careful analysis of how the culture of the group will be affected and what the consequences will be for the group. It is a mistake to be concerned with productivity without also being concerned about emotional and individual growth. To improve a work group's performance, a manager must understand the multiple causes of the group's behavior. This model provides a practical starting point for acquiring such an understanding.

——— DISCUSSION QUESTIONS

1. The author mentions a feature of group culture known as maps. Consider the groups that you've belonged to. What were their maps? How did you feel as a new member? How long did it take you to feel like a group member? How did you relate to the members that were there before you? To those that came after you?

2. What has been the context for the groups that you've belonged to? Do you join groups? In what situations? If you don't join groups on your own, how do you feel when you are required to join a group? If you wanted to accomplish a goal, whether at work or elsewhere, and you could only accomplish this goal with group support, how would you go about gaining the support you need?

3. Consider your behavior in a group. Do you interact easily or tend to shy away from interactions? What personal compromises do you make? What personal compromises don't you make?

4. Name five different groups you have been part of that have had an important influence on your life either directly or indirectly. Explain the nature of the influence.

5. The author states that an effective group has several leaders. Does your experience of effective groups agree with the author's assertion? What does the presence of multiple leaders imply—concerning leadership theories?

Problem Solving and Conflict Resolution in Groups

JAMES WARE

This reading begins by describing the strengths and weaknesses of groups as problem solvers. According to the author, the decision to use a group for problem solving is determined by balancing the characteristics of a particular problem against the characteristics of a group. The reading also identifies and compares three modes of conflict resolution: smoothing and avoidance, bargaining and forcing, and confronting and problem solving. Interdepartmental conflict and the difficult position of department representatives are also examined. The author closes with a reminder of the importance of careful diagnosis and with several suggestions for managers on how to constructively influence group behavior.

Management groups deal with organizational problems in a wide variety of ways. Clearly, some styles of problem solving are more effective than others, and some management groups are much more capable of handling and resolving internal conflict than others are. Because group decision making is so common in organizations, effective managers must be highly skilled at influencing group processes.

This reading examines the characteristics of managerial groups that enhance and detract from their effectiveness in problem solving and describes the most common ways in which groups handle conflict. The reading explains how styles of problem solving and conflict resolution affect the nature and quality of group decisions. The dynamics of interdepartmental conflict are also examined because most important organizational problems involve two or more departments with differing goals, priorities, and needs. Although many of the ideas covered here refer primarily to interactions in face-to-face meetings, the same processes generally apply to group behavior over extended periods of time.[1]

---

1. The next two sections on the strengths and weaknesses of groups as problem solvers draw heavily, although not exclusively, on "Assets and Liabilities in Group Problem Solving," by Norman R.F. Maier, *Psychological Review* (July 1967): 239–49. The article is a systematic review of research on group problem-solving behavior and effectiveness in a wide variety of contexts.

—— STRENGTHS OF GROUPS AS PROBLEM SOLVERS

Group problem solving has some distinct advantages over individual problem solving in organizations. The most compelling reasons for using a management group to deal with organizational problems are as follows:

Diversity of Problem-Solving Styles   Different people have different ways of thinking about problems. Although almost any problem can be viewed from several different perspectives, most people have relatively fixed patterns of thinking. Some people (e.g., engineers and accountants) rely on highly quantitative techniques. Other people (e.g., architects and designers) think graphically, using pictures and diagrams, while others (e.g., entrepreneurs and commodity traders) tend to rely on feelings and intuition about what will work in a given situation.

Individual problem solvers too often fall into ruts that prevent them from seeing other productive ways of dealing with a particular problem. When people with different styles interact with others in a group, however, they can stimulate one another to try new ways of approaching the problem.

More Knowledge and Information   Individuals also bring different specialized knowledge and current experiences to a problem-solving discussion. Even when some group members are much more highly skilled or formally educated than others, the diversity of the knowledge, skills, and thinking styles in the group can lead to more innovative solutions than the experts could produce working alone. For example, a sales manager who has worked closely with customers may be able to suggest product-design modifications that would not have occurred to a product engineer.

Furthermore, by exchanging tentative ideas as they explore the problem and possible solutions, group members can challenge and improve one another's thinking. During a discussion, one person's comment often triggers a new idea for someone else. This process of sharing and building increases both the number and the quality of solution ideas.

Greater Understanding and Commitment   By participating in the deliberations that lead to a decision, people gain a more thorough understanding of the problem. Furthermore, even if they disagree with the decision, they are more likely to accept it if they have had an opportunity to express their disagreement during the decision process. Participation is one of the main reasons that task forces are so often successful in achieving organizational changes.

—— WEAKNESSES OF GROUPS AS PROBLEM SOLVERS

Many management groups develop patterns of behavior that seriously detract from their problem-solving effectiveness. Among the most important weaknesses of group problem solving are the following:

Use of Organizational Resources   Group decision making consumes more time and resources than does individual problem solving. After all, a one-hour meeting of eight people requires as much time as one person working all day on the problem. Furthermore, achieving an equal and adequate understanding of the problem by all members of the group can be difficult and time-consuming.

Pressure to Conform   Groups often develop such strong norms of conformity that members spend more time and energy figuring out the party line than they do analyzing a problem. Agreeing becomes more important than being right, and conforming to the majority point of view becomes a requirement for remaining part of the group. Conformity is a particular danger in management groups whose members differ in their levels of authority, status, and power. Less-powerful members may find it especially difficult to confront or disagree with their organizational superiors.

Extensive research on group decision making has repeatedly shown that the solution or argument mentioned most frequently in a group is almost always the one finally chosen, regardless of its validity. This valence effect is particularly pervasive in overly conforming groups.

Advocacy and Individual Domination   Perhaps the most common weakness of problem-solving groups is their susceptibility to control by individuals or small coalitions. Decision making turns into a contest in which winning becomes more important than being right. Individuals advocate their own points of view, vying for leadership to satisfy personal needs or to achieve organizational influence that benefits one group or department rather than the total organization.

Although a group discussion may appear to focus on substantive issues and the pros and cons of each alternative, the debates may involve underlying issues of power, prestige, and influence. If a domination attempt is being made based on information or ideas directly related to the focal problem, the group may actually benefit. Often, however, those who argue loudest and strongest do so precisely because of the logical weaknesses of their positions.

Diffusion of Responsibility   Group members often lose their individual identities and sense of responsibility during problem-solving deliberations. Discussion may move so swiftly that members forget who initiated certain ideas; most finished ideas are combinations of several peoples' recommendations. Although this process can be highly creative, it also can lead to a group's reaching riskier decisions than any of its members would have agreed to individually. Under these circumstances, a group can make poor decisions. Individual members will usually deny personal responsibility for the decisions and their consequences.

Groups Are Solution Oriented   Most people feel unsettled by problems and dislike being faced with them. Thus, many management groups tend to short-circuit problem analysis, jumping quickly to solution proposals. Experienced managers often feel sure they know what the problem is and thus are opposed to spending time exploring its underlying causes. Often, of course, the problem as it is first defined is only a symptom of a much bigger and more complex situation. Yet when problem-solving groups are formed, they rarely spend enough time exploring the problem.

—— WHEN TO USE A GROUP

In many organizational situations, a manager has little choice about whether to handle a problem alone, assign it to a single subordinate, or involve a group. Organizational traditions frequently restrict the manager's options; almost every company has standing committees, regular staff meetings, and other settings that bring together specialists from different functional or geographic areas to address both recurring and isolated problems. In other situations, the pressures of time and individual responsibility, the need for specific expertise, or the requirements of confidentiality clearly point to an individually determined decision. Between these two extremes, however, are situations in which a manager must decide whether an individual or a group effort will be more productive.

The choice of when to refer a particular problem to a management group depends upon both the characteristics of the problem and the skills and interests of the group. The most important factors in each of these areas are discussed in the following sections.

CHARACTERISTICS OF THE PROBLEM

The nature of the problem and the organizational requirements for a solution define the primary criteria for determining whether to use a group problem-solving process.

Complexity, Uncertainty, and Conflict   Organizational problems can usually be described as involving uncertainty, complexity, or conflict. *Uncertain* problems are those in which the problem solver lacks information about underlying causes, potential solutions, or even solution criteria. *Complex* problems are those in which more is known about related causes and possible choices; however, so many factors affect the situation that their interactions and consequences are difficult to trace and to understand. *Conflict* problems are those in which different individuals or subgroups have differing priorities or goals that cannot be mutually satisfied. In conflict situations both the choices and their consequences may be very clear; the difficulty lies in choosing among the alternatives and in determining how to make that choice when competing goals and interests are at stake.

Most real-world problems involve all three of these elements, although in varying degrees. Defining the problem in terms of its uncertainty, complexity, and conflict potential helps clarify what additional information is needed, who possesses it, and who is affected by the problem (or will be affected by its solution). Generally, the more uncertain, the more complex, and the more conflictful the problem, the more likely it is that involving others in developing a solution will be appropriate and effective.

Business Stakes   The more important the problem, the more appropriate it is to involve others in its solution. Problems with higher organizational stakes (whether tangible outcomes, such as costs, profits, and market share, or intangible ones, such as public reputation, status, and power) call for more thorough analysis, wider awareness of issues, and shared responsibility for solutions and their consequences. A group process is much more likely to be effective when the risks and potential payoffs are large because group members will pay more attention, take more time, and devote more energy to finding a widely acceptable solution.

Task Interdependence   When a work procedure or information system crosses department boundaries, procedural changes are almost impossible without bringing together people from all the affected departments. Imagine a materials-control manager attempting to modify an inventory-control system without involving sales, accounting, purchasing, manufacturing, and production control. Each department will be affected by the system changes and can influence the success of the implementation effort. The problem cannot be resolved by one manager in one functional area.

Need for Acceptance and Commitment   Another reason for using a group process is that those people who have been involved in the group deliberations will better understand the problem and its solution and will more readily accept and support the group decision. This aspect of group problem solving is especially important when the solution includes an implementation effort involving several people. When many of those people are not direct subordinates of the manager who is responsible for making the change, their acceptance and commitment is doubly important.

Deadline Pressures   Group processes consume more managerial time and related organizational resources than does individual problem solving. If a decision deadline is too immediate, involving others may be impossible even though the problem is substantive and calls for their inclusion. However, a tight deadline may be a compelling reason for bringing in more people. If their understanding of the problem is adequate, the group members can divide up the work and attack several aspects of it simultaneously.

To summarize, a group problem-solving process is generally called for when

- the problem is uncertain or complex, and has potential for conflict
- the problem requires interdepartmental or intergroup cooperation and coordination
- the problem and its solution have important personal and organizational consequences
- there are significant but not immediate deadline pressures
- widespread acceptance and commitment are critical to successful implementation.

CHARACTERISTICS OF THE GROUP

Organizational problems do not develop in a vacuum, and management groups differ in their abilities to work on various kinds of problems. Several important characteristics of problem-solving groups also influence the decision to use a group process.

Relevant Knowledge and Skills   The most obvious criterion is whether the group possesses the knowledge and skills to solve the problem productively. This is not a simple issue, however, because individuals often have greater problem-solving capabilities than they have previously demonstrated. Furthermore, groups develop problem-solving skills primarily through practice.

Unfortunately, the immediate need to solve a problem and stabilize the organization often overshadows the longer-term developmental needs of a group. Managers frequently justify individual problem solving through lack of time, group work overload, and the group's lack of knowledge and experience. However, when developing the group's problem-solving skills is an important objective, the manager should consciously submit to the group those problems whose nature might otherwise suggest individual attention.

Current Work Load   If a group is already working at or near its normal capacity, then adding another important problem to the group's agenda will generally be ineffective. Not only would the problem receive inadequate attention and effort, but other group tasks will probably suffer as well. An overloaded group is generally characterized by high levels of stress, and high stress typically leads to brief and shallow diagnosis, a preference for solutions that are simple and certain (rather than creative and effective), and unusually severe and inflexible conflict. Overloaded groups are not effective problem solvers.

Group Expectations   Company norms sometimes value group participation in certain kinds of decisions, regardless of whether that participation improves the quality of the solution. In fact, many of the tensions that develop between managers and subordinates derive from differing assumptions about the appropriateness of group participation in certain types of decisions. Thus, a manager must be concerned not only with the substance of a problem but also with its emotional components. If a group feels strongly about its right to be involved in a decision, the manager must take that into account, whether or not he or she agrees with the group.

Norms for Conflict Resolution Perhaps the most critical aspect of a group's problem-solving capacity is its approach to handling conflict. Group decision making is especially difficult when group members have different and/or conflicting goals and needs. If the problem can potentially create serious and heated controversy and the group is not skilled at confronting its differences, a group solution will probably not be effective. A group that has developed healthy confronting norms, however, can be an appropriate forum for reviewing an issue with many alternative solutions.

Because conflict-resolution skills are critical to group problem-solving effectiveness, the next section describes alternative modes for handling conflict.

Thus, a management group is more likely to develop an effective solution to an organizational problem if

- group members possess the required knowledge and analytic skills or are capable of developing them
- the group is not already overloaded with other work
- the group's expectations about involvement are taken into account
- the group is skilled at resolving conflict and is characterized by open, confronting norms.

The manager's task is to find the most workable fit between the problem and the problem-solving group. Neither element can be addressed in isolation, and none of the specific characteristics described earlier can be treated independently of the others. Because an ideal fit almost never occurs on its own, much of the manager's work involves trying to modify one or more of these characteristics. Finding the leverage points is not simple, and there are no formulas that will substitute for careful diagnosis of the most important elements in each situation.

───── MODES OF CONFLICT RESOLUTION

Because styles of problem solving and conflict resolution are such important variables in determining group effectiveness, they are among the most frequently studied aspects of group behavior. The literature on management groups contains numerous models of problem solving, group and intergroup conflict, bargaining, and techniques for managing conflict.

Research on styles of group problem solving suggests that there are three primary modes of conflict resolution: bargaining and forcing, smoothing and avoiding, and confronting and problem solving. As the labels indicate, confronting and problem solving is by far the most effective approach (though by no means the most common). This assertion draws on a substantial body of research. For example, Lawrence and Lorsch, in their extensive study of product innovation groups in several different industries, found that the management groups of the more-profitable firms invariably employed confronting styles of decision making more than other modes and generally did so more often than did the management groups of less-profitable competitors.[2] In fact, the mode of conflict resolution that characterized a company's management groups was found to be the most consistent variable that discriminated between profitable and unprofitable companies in the different industries.

The remainder of this section describes each of these three modes in some detail and suggests their relative strengths and weaknesses as styles of conflict resolution.

SMOOTHING AND AVOIDANCE

A group employing smoothing tactics is more interested in maintaining harmony and agreement than in confronting the problem or the individual members' differences. Group members assume that conflict is destructive; because they value membership in the group, they avoid confronting their differences out of fear that the resulting conflict will split the group irreparably. People who favor smoothing over their differences often have little confidence in their own ability to articulate their reasoning or to persuade others of their position. They also assume that the group is generally incapable of dealing with problems that involve conflict.

Groups that develop a smoothing-and-avoidance style tend to favor the status quo; they work on maintaining an even keel and not rocking the boat. Such groups often redefine the problems they face so that minimum disagreement occurs; they develop powerful norms of avoiding conflict, withdrawing from controversial issues, and withholding critical comments. Members of a smoothing group describe their beliefs by quoting proverbs such as "Soft words win hard hearts," "Kill your enemies with kindness," and "Smooth words make smooth ways." (These and similar sayings were actually used to identify smoothing-and-avoiding groups in the Lawrence and Lorsch research and in earlier studies as well.[3])

Group members may privately express sharp criticisms of each other and even of the way they work as a group; however, these criticisms are kept private. Meetings are often perfunctory and always polite, although a sensitive observer can usually pick up nonverbal signals that contrast sharply with the surface verbal behavior. Even when the stakes are high for some members on a

---

2. Paul R. Lawrence and Jay W. Lorsch, *Organization and Environment* (Homewood, Illinois: Richard D. Irwin, 1969).

3. Robert R. Blake and Jane S. Mouton, *The Managerial Grid* (Houston: Gulf Publishing Company, 1964).

particular issue, the pattern of smoothing is hard to break. Membership in a smoothing group can be extremely frustrating, especially for persons interested in making changes or improving organizational performance.

BARGAINING AND FORCING

In a group characterized by bargaining and forcing, the participants view each other as adversaries and define the problems in terms of what each person, subgroup, or department stands to gain or lose. Decision making is viewed as a win/lose proposition in which it is clearly better to win than to lose. Groups operating in this mode develop norms that justify pushing for one's own point of view regardless of the merits of others' views; forcing when one has an advantage and seeking compromise when one does not; concealing unfavorable information; and digging for data that the opponent is hiding.

The proverbs that typify a bargaining-and-forcing climate include "Tit for tat is fair play," "Might overcomes right," and "You scratch my back, I'll scratch yours." Conflict is viewed as inevitable, necessary, and even desirable; however, it is treated almost like a poker game in which one bluffs, conceals data, and seeks to scare the other participants out of the game. Most decisions are reached by making a series of compromises and trade-offs or by powerful parties forcing the issue. Participants assume the worst about each other, and each party seeks to maximize its own share of the "pot."

The poker analogy is important and appropriate because groups operating in this mode seldom try to increase the total size of the pot or find a solution in which everyone wins. Attention tends to be concentrated on how to divide up limited resources, whether they are budgetary funds, sales territories, management bonuses, or intangibles such as prestige and status.

CONFRONTING AND PROBLEM SOLVING

Groups operating in a confronting mode assume that disagreements are healthy if they are worked through in pursuit of a solution that is good for the total organization. The basic difference between this orientation and the preceding ones is that here the individual parties recognize that their goals are interdependent and that it's to everyone's advantage in the long run if the total organization benefits. A confronting group believes that the solution will be better if each party is open about its needs and objectives and the differences causing the conflict. Emphasizing these differences clarifies goals and interests and leads to creative solutions. Confronting the differences helps individuals find areas of common interest as well; the parties explicitly search for ways to increase the total payoff so that everyone can win rather than merely argue over the relative shares of a fixed outcome.

The proverbs that typify this mode include "Come now and let us reason together," "Try and trust will move mountains," and "By digging and digging the truth is discovered."

A problem-solving group focuses on the needs and objectives of the total organization as well as on those of each member. It also focuses on the relationships between the members, not on the individuals or their personalities. Group members recognize that the problem lies in their differences and interdependencies, rather than with any individuals or their positions. Furthermore, emphasis is on resolving the problem, not on merely accommodating different points of view.

A confronting style is risky and requires participants to challenge one another's underlying values and assumptions and to share personal concerns and criticisms. Trust and integrity are essential to an effective confronting-and-problem-solving climate.

COMPARISONS AMONG THE THREE MODES

The three modes are, of course, prototypes or even stereotypes: Actual management groups often act in ways that contain elements of two or even all three of these modes. Most groups develop a predominant style, but typically each group has its own mixture of styles, which may vary over time or from problem to problem.

The *Exhibit* provides a shorthand means of comparing these three styles. Each style is characterized briefly in terms of the group's way of defining the problem, the role of conflict, the attitudes of the participants, and the nature of the outcomes. The bottom two rows describe characteristic norms and representative proverbs that capture the beliefs and values implicit in the norms.

As noted earlier, the confronting-and-problem-solving mode is generally most effective for resolving group conflicts. However, there are also situations in which either a smoothing or a bargaining orientation is necessary. Consider a group faced with an unavoidable deadline and a decision that involves several mutually exclusive alternatives. The group may be forced to reach a decision without fully confronting all of the individual members' positions and needs. Even if the members are adept at productive confrontation, the group leader may explicitly suppress conflict to reach a quick decision.

Clearly, however, there is a difference between a one-time, short-term strategy of avoiding differences in order to meet a deadline and the longer-term development of norms that continually suppress conflict. Using successive short-term crises to justify a smoothing leadership style can be dangerous: just a few short-term crises can create a long-term pattern.

Bargaining is probably the most common (though not necessarily the most effective) form of conflict resolution when the problem involves scarce resources and two or more departments in an organization. Budgets and sales

EXHIBIT
Modes of Conflict Resolution

	SMOOTHING AND AVOIDING	CONFRONTING AND PROBLEM SOLVING	BARGAINING AND FORCING
Problem	Define to minimize differences	Define relative to total organization's needs	Define in terms of stakes for each subgroup
Role of Conflict	Destructive	Can be healthy	Good to win; bad to lose
Participants	Accommodators	Collaborators	Adversaries
Outcomes	Maintain status quo	Interdependent; all benefit when total group benefits	Win/lose
Typical Norms	Withdraw when attacked	Confront differences	Push when you have the advantage
	Avoid conflict	Be open and fair	Compromise when you do not
	Keep your tongue in check	Decide questions by reason, not by power	Maximize your own share
Representative Proverbs	Soft words win hard hearts	Come now, and let us reason together	Tit for tat is fair play
	Kill your enemies with kindness	Try and trust will move mountains	Might overcomes right
	Smooth words make smooth ways	By digging and digging the truth is discovered	You scratch my back; I'll scratch yours

Source: Adapted from unpublished materials developed by John J. Gabarro

territories *are* limited; organizational resources that go to one department obviously cannot go to another. In the absence of clear organizational priorities, bargaining is often the only means for resolving interdepartmental conflict. Bargaining can be particularly useful for groups that meet infrequently, when members do not know each other well or when the overall organization does not have a definite direction.

All too often, however, the bargaining climate degenerates into the kinds of forcing tactics described earlier. The game and winning become more important than achieving the best solution. The interests of the total group (and even of the subgroups) are lost in the battle to acquire scarce resources or to achieve organizational prominence.

Thus, even under these special circumstances, an open, confronting climate remains a desirable goal. It is an elusive goal, however, because an active confrontation of differences requires skillful participants. Open discussion of important differences is inherently stressful and productive only when group members possess both analytic and interpersonal skills. An effective problem-solving group continually risks falling apart in disagreement; creative problem solving is almost impossible without creative tension.

INTERGROUP AND INTERDEPARTMENTAL DECISION MAKING

Managing group problem solving effectively is a challenge under any circumstances. The process is especially complex when the group is temporary and composed of people from several different primary groups. Most of the difficulties are heightened versions of those that arise within a single group; however, the differing orientations and goals of people from various departments complicate the process significantly.

INTERDEPARTMENTAL CONFLICT

The major sources of interdepartmental conflict include vying for scarce resources; differing interests and priorities; and different personal values, orientations, and styles of thinking and problem solving. Problem-solving groups composed of people from various functional areas clearly begin with a wider range of goals and opinions about the problem. In addition, the stakes are usually higher; the problems are usually more complicated, and individuals' positions on most issues are much less flexible.

Interdepartmental conflict stems from more than just differing goals and priorities, however. Natural differences in departmental size and power also affect the problem-solving process. Larger, more-powerful departments generally exercise greater control over joint operations and decision making. If one department depends on another for a critical resource (raw materials, information, or even people), it may often defer to that department to avoid losing critical resources. This kind of power imbalance frequently leads to decisions being determined by political clout rather than by their merits, and the company suffers as a result. Furthermore, one-sided control usually leads to resentment by the weaker department, and working relationships deteriorate as a result.

Differences in departmental work loads and stress can also contribute to conflict. An overworked department will generally be less open to change, and its members will be especially resentful of other departments' comparative lack of pressure. Furthermore, overworked departments are apt to resort either to bargaining-and-forcing or to smoothing-and-avoidance strategies. They do not have the time to work through differences more carefully.

DEPARTMENT REPRESENTATIVES

Given so many potential sources of conflict, it is easy to understand how difficult interdepartmental problem solving and decision making can be. In most situations what holds the group together is the recognition of a common overriding interest in the success of the total organization. Often, however, that success is so taken for granted that individual departmental interests and prestige become more important. In interdepartmental decision making each group member acts as a representative of his or her home department. This role creates particular difficulties for the representatives, and these difficulties in turn affect their behaviors in the interdepartmental group.

Individual Problems of Department Representatives   Each representative experiences internal conflict as he or she attempts to balance commitments to the home department with those to the interdepartmental group. To maintain membership in both groups each representative must conform to two sets of norms and expectations. Department representatives usually learn rather quickly how to vary their behavior and language depending on the group they are currently interacting with, but there are often times when conforming with one group's expectations places the representative directly at odds with the other group. For example, membership on a task force developing new sales forecasting methods may require a product manager to share marketing department data and procedures that reflect poorly on her own staff. More significantly, the marketing department may have a history of resolving internal conflict via hard-nosed bargaining, while the task-force group is being managed in a more open, confronting style. The product manager is caught in the middle: If she shares data openly with the task force, she risks being ostracized by her own department; yet, if she reflects her department's bargaining stance, she will antagonize other task-force members and perhaps weaken her influence (and thus the marketing department's influence) on the task force's recommendations.

This dual membership problem puts a great deal of stress on department representatives. They must not only live with dual (and often conflicting) sets of goals, norms, and values but must also answer to two constituent groups for the actions they take and the decisions they make. Even when the representative disagrees with the position taken by one group, he or she must offer an explanation to the other group. Furthermore, each constituent group typically holds the representative responsible for *all* the actions and decisions of the other group. The representative is pressured by each group not only to explain its own position to the other group but also to influence the other group. Thus, each representative is a target for influence attempts from both directions, at the same time that he or she is trying to influence both the home department and the problem-solving group.

Relationship Problems of Department Representatives   This internal conflict also contributes to several kinds of relationship problems for department representatives. The pressures they feel often lead them to interpret challenges or criticisms of their home departments as personal attacks. In fact, many managers do express procedural criticisms in a personal fashion. Because the representatives view each other as symbols of their respective departments, substantive departmental conflicts often escalate quickly into emotional interpersonal disputes.

Another relationship problem arises when the representatives feel different levels of commitment to their two constituencies. Although some representatives remain oriented primarily toward their home departments, others develop more loyalty to the interdepartmental group. Group members may also differ in the degree of independence they have to make commitments on behalf of their departments and in the willingness of their departments to accept decisions of the interdepartmental group. These differences in orientation and influence further complicate the way the representatives are able to work with one another.

Personal Skills of Department Representatives   The group and interpersonal skills of the individual department representatives will also affect their ability to work together. The greater the role conflict, the more important personal skills become. Perhaps the most essential characteristic for a representative is a high tolerance for stress, ambiguity, and conflict. Individuals who cannot live with competing goals, irreconcilable values, and unresolved organizational problems should probably avoid interdepartmental assignments. Representatives also must be good listeners. Understanding the needs and motives of others is an essential prerequisite to effective problem solving. Similarly, representatives must be able to explain their own positions and needs articulately and persuasively, and they must be capable of making quick, on-the-spot judgments. Interdepartmental groups usually make decisions that have major implications for individual departments; group members must be able to trace out the consequences of new ideas rapidly in order to influence group decisions as they occur.

───── MANAGERIAL IMPLICATIONS

This reading has identified an extensive and diverse set of ideas for understanding group problem-solving behavior. Up to this point there have been few specific suggestions for how individual managers can develop and reinforce healthy problem-solving norms in groups. The reading has stressed the importance of careful diagnosis because the appropriateness of any particular action depends on the group's present skills and existing norms. However, several basic strategies for effectively influencing group behavior exist and can be employed by managers.

Understand the Sources of Current Behavior   Both individuals and groups develop patterns of behavior that are useful to them. Thus, to change someone's behavior, you must first understand the reasons why that behavior is functional for that person. A manager cannot always change underlying conditions and personal characteristics; however, it is futile to try to influence current behavior without understanding its sources and without considering how it benefits the individuals involved.

Demonstrate Desired Behavior Yourself   Serving as a role model is a powerful way that a manager can affect his or her subordinates' behavior. An obviously capable and successful manager can have a significant impact on peers, and even on superiors, in the organization.

Concerning problem-solving behavior, this principle suggests demonstrating your own commitment to making decisions based on facts and objective criteria. Furthermore, if you stress your own interest in finding solutions that maximize the goals of the total organization, others will also become more aware of their common objectives. You can model problem-solving behavior in the following ways: Suggest several solution alternatives rather than just one; do your homework and present factual support for your suggestions; avoid becoming involved in coalitions and compromises; and define your underlying assumptions so that you and others can question their validity.

Underlying this suggestion is the assumption that a problem-solving orientation will in fact lead to effective decision making. Your own success will encourage others to act similarly and will lead to a more open, confronting set of decision-making norms and procedures.

Monitor the Decision-Making Process   By increasing your sensitivity to the dynamics of a group's decision making, you can improve your ability to influence how the group works together. The counterpart of modeling problem-solving behavior is to insist on it in others as well. Press group members for factual evidence to back up their assertions; do not let minority views get squeezed out; work on achieving a balance of participation, and so on.

One of the most important aspects of group management is varying your style according to the particular phase of problem solving. During problem definition and solution finding, encourage open, nonevaluative exploration. Later, when a decision is required, press individuals to make personal commitments, and again make sure that minority concerns are fully aired before the group decision is considered final.

Although these suggestions are easiest to implement if you are the formal leader of the group, most of them can also be acted on by other members of the group. It may be more difficult for a member to influence group norms, but it is by no means impossible. The principles of effective problem solving that have been discussed in this reading have considerable legitimacy in our society; acting on these ideas will rarely be viewed as inappropriate behavior. In fact, just the opposite is true: By appealing to group members' personal values, you will generally gain much respect. Even when confronting strongly held opinions, you can succeed if you have done your own homework and know you stand on solid ground.

——— DISCUSSION QUESTIONS

1. What cultural concepts might work against the practice of confronting and problem solving as a mode of conflict resolution?
2. Consider your personality, and using traits that you know define you best, decide which mode of conflict resolution you are most comfortable adopting. Ask your peers for feedback. (Do they see you as you see yourself?)
3. If a company discovered that its approaches to conflict resolution did not include confronting and problem solving, what steps might the organization take to include this mode in its culture?
4. According to the author, there are three modes of conflict resolution. Give an example when it might be advantageous to use smoothing and avoiding. Do the same for confronting and problem solving and for bargaining and forcing.
5. The reading mentions that confronting and problem solving as a mode of conflict resolution is an important characteristic of profitable companies. Why might this behavior characterize a successful organization?

Understanding and Influencing Group Process   18

JOHN J. GABARRO AND ANNE HARLAN

This reading focuses on group process, *or how a group goes about achieving its formal tasks. Observing this process, according to the authors, enables a manager to spot the group's covert and overt dynamics and to gain insights that will help make the group's interactions more productive. The authors identify seven aspects of group behavior that indicate how effectively a group is functioning. Suggestions are also given for interventions that a group leader or group member can use to improve group performance.*

A camel is a horse put together by a committee" is a saying frequently applied to group decision making. Why are so many groups inefficient, slow, and frustrating, rather than effective in combining the insights and expertise of their members? To some extent the answer may be found in the formal group design. Perhaps the people chosen were not the ones who should have been included in such a group, or perhaps the group's goal was simply unattainable. More often, however, the difficulties encountered have less to do with content of task issues than with the *group process,* or how the group is going about achieving its formal tasks.[1]

Each group member is a unique individual, bringing certain expectations, assumptions, and feelings to the group, not only about his or her own role but also about the roles of other members in the group. As a result of these expectations certain interrelationships develop. These patterns may become either beneficial or detrimental to the group's purpose. Spotting detrimental patterns is the first key to understanding and improving the functioning of any group, but often these patterns are hard to identify because you cannot read each person's mind. For instance, how do you know that everyone understands what the agenda is, or that person X understands it but is likely to deviate from it if possible, or whether person X has the leverage to change the agenda if he or she wants to? By being attentive to what is happening among group members, you can develop a greater awareness of what is and what is not likely to

---

1. Portions of this reading were excerpted from a working paper by Eric H. Nielsen on influencing groups.

happen in a group and of what the group is or is not capable of doing at a given meeting.

Being able to observe and understand a group's process is important for two reasons. First, it enables you to understand what is taking place covertly as well as overtly in the group's behavior. Second, it can provide you with insights into what you and others can do to make the group's interactions more productive.

Listed below are seven aspects of group behavior that can furnish valuable clues on how effectively a group functions. It is unlikely that all of these will be relevant to your concerns at a given point in time, or that you can attend to them all simultaneously. The more adept you are at observing and assessing them, however, the more likely it is that you will spot potential difficulties early and act on them to improve the group's effectiveness.

───── PARTICIPATION

Participation—who participates, how often, when, and to what effect— is the easiest aspect of group process to observe. Typically, people who are higher in status, more knowledgeable, or simply more talkative, tend to participate more actively. Those who are newer, lower in status, uninformed, or not inclined to express their feelings and ideas verbally, generally speak less frequently. Even in groups composed of people of equal status and competence, some people will speak more than others; this variation is to be expected and is not necessarily a sign of an ineffective group. When great disparity exists among the contributions of individual members, however, it is usually a clue that the process is not effective—particularly when individuals or coalitions dominate the group's discussion.

There are many reasons why unequal participation can reduce a group's effectiveness. Low participators often have good ideas to offer but are reluctant to do so or cannot contribute their ideas because they are squeezed out by high participators who dominate the meeting. This imbalance can be a potential problem because those ideas receiving the most attention inevitably become the ones that are most seriously considered when it is time to make a decision. Considerable research shows that the most frequently stated ideas tend to be adopted by the group, regardless of their quality. Maier calls this the valence effect,[2] and it is one of the reasons groups often make poor decisions. Thus, large imbalance in participation can result in potentially good ideas being underrepresented in the discussion, or perhaps not even expressed.

Another negative consequence of uneven participation, understood through common sense as well as research, is that low participators are likely to tune out, lose commitment to the task, or become frustrated and angry—

2. Norman R. F. Maier, "Assets and Liabilities in Group Problem Solving: The Need for an Integrative Function," *Psychological Review,* vol. 74, no. 4 (July 1967), pp. 239–248.

especially if they have tried to enter the discussion but have been ignored or cut off by high participators. These negative attitudes result not only in poorer quality decisions but also in less commitment to implementing the group's decision.

Several factors contribute to uneven participation. One is that people who have the most at stake in a given issue (and may therefore be the least objective) are more motivated to participate than others who may have better ideas to offer. Another is that different people have different internal standards on which they judge whether one of their ideas is worth offering to the group. Thus, people with higher internal standards may be less likely to contribute than those with lower internal standards. The negative consequences for the quality of the group's discussion are obvious.

A marked change in a person's participation during a meeting is also a clue that something important may be going on. If a person suddenly becomes silent or withdraws during part of a meeting, it could suggest a number of possibilities (depending on the person's nonverbal behavior). For example, it might simply mean that the person has temporarily withdrawn to mull over the comments of a prior speaker. It may also be that the person has tuned out, or it may be a sign of hostility or frustration.

Here are some questions to consider in observing participation:

1. Who are the high participators? Why? To what effect?
2. Who are the low participators? Why? To what effect?
3. Are there any shifts in participators, such as an active participator suddenly becoming silent? Do you see any reason for this in the group's interaction, such as a criticism from a higher-status person or a shift in topic? Is it a sign of withdrawal?
4. How are silent people treated? Is their silence taken by others to mean consent? Disagreement? Disinterest? Why do you think they are silent?
5. Who talks to whom? Who responds to whom? Do participation patterns reflect coalitions that are impeding or controlling the discussion? Are the interaction patterns consistently excluding certain people who need to be supported or brought into the discussion?
6. Who keeps the discussion going? How is this accomplished? Why does the group leader want the discussion to continue in such a vein?

Interventions   There are several simple and unobtrusive process interventions that you can make, either as a group leader or as a group member, to bring about a better balance in participation. These interventions are particularly important if you think that potentially valuable minority views are not getting their share of time, that certain people have not had a chance to develop their ideas fully, or that some group members are not part of the discussion. One intervention is to try to *clarify* a point that someone had made earlier and that seemed to fall through the cracks—by saying something like "Tom, let me see if I understood what you said a moment ago." A related technique is to *reinforce* a prior point by asking the person to elaborate on it—"Dana, I was interested in what you were saying earlier; can you elaborate on it?" Similarly, a very direct technique for bringing out silent people is to simply *query* them— "Maria, you haven't said a word during this discussion; what are your ideas on it?" or to make a comment as direct as "We've heard a lot from the marketing people but very little from production scheduling. What do you folks think about the problem?"

——— INFLUENCE

Influence and participation are not the same thing. Some people may speak very little, yet capture the attention of the whole group when they do speak. Others may talk frequently but go unheard. Influence, like participation, is often a function of status, experience, competence, and to some degree personality. It is normal for some people to have more influence on a group's process than others, and this fact is not necessarily a sign that a group is ineffective. However, when one individual or subgroup has so much influence on a discussion that others' ideas are rejected out of hand, it is usually a clue that the group's effectiveness will suffer and that the discussion will fail to probe alternatives. This imbalance is particularly dangerous when minority views are systematically squelched without adequate exploration.

An asymmetry in influence can have several negative consequences on a group's effectiveness. As already noted, it can result in the suppression of potentially valuable minority views; it can contribute to imbalanced participation, and it will inevitably result in hostility and lack of commitment by group members who feel that they have been left out. As with participation, considerable research on group behavior and alienation shows that the more influence people feel they have had on a group's discussion, the more committed they are likely to be to its decisions, regardless of whether their own points of view have been adopted by the group.

One way of checking relative influence is to watch the reactions of the other group members. Someone who has influence is not only likely to have others listening attentively but is also less likely to be interrupted or challenged by the others. He or she may also be physically seated at or near the head of the table or near the center of a subgroup.

Struggles for influence and leadership often characterize the early stages of a group's life, especially in temporary groups such as task forces, project teams, or committees. To some extent these struggles occur in most groups, although usually mildly covert. Vying for leadership can become a problem, however, when it disrupts the group's ability to deal with the task at hand. The disruption occurs when being dominant is an important need for those who are vying for leadership. Under these circumstances, the competition gets played out indirectly with one person disagreeing with the other because of his or her need to establish dominance, regardless of the relative merits of the other's arguments. The hidden agenda then becomes scoring points rather than working on the problem. Often two people engaged in such a power struggle are not even aware of their hidden motives and genuinely think that they are arguing about the problem at hand.

In assessing influence patterns within a group, you may find the following questions useful:

1. Which members are listened to when they speak? What ideas are they expressing?
2. Which members are ignored when they speak? Why? What are their ideas? Is the group losing valuable inputs simply because some are not being heard?
3. Are there any shifts in influence? Why?
4. Is there any rivalry within the group? Are there struggles among individuals or subgroups for leadership?
5. Who interrupts whom? Does this reflect relative power within the group?
6. Are minority views consistently ignored regardless of possible merit?

Interventions   If you observe that the opinions of an individual or subgroup of people appear to be unduly influencing a group's progress, you can intervene to open up the discussion. One strategy is simply to *support or reinforce* the views of minority members—"I think there is some merit to what Jenna was saying earlier, and I'd like to elaborate on it," or "I think that we're not giving enough thought to Jenna and Carlos's position, and I think we should explore it further before dropping it." Another intervention is to actually *point out* that the opinions of certain people are dominating the discussion—"Mary, you've made your point quite forcefully and clearly, but I'd also like to hear the other side of the question before we go further." Similarly, another technique is to ask the group to *open up* the discussion—"So far we've spent a lot of time talking about Jenna and Bill's proposal, but I'd like to hear some differing opinions," or "The managers seem to agree strongly on what needs to be done, but I'd like to hear more about what the customer representatives think are the problems."

─── GROUP CLIMATE

Members bring with them many assumptions of how groups ought to function generally and how their particular group should function. Frequently, these assumptions will be quite different from one member to another. One person may feel that the way for a group to work effectively is to be strictly business—no socializing and with tight leader control over the group. Others may feel that the only way a group can work creatively is to give each person equal time for suggestions, get together informally, and use relatively loose leadership. After group members have tested each others' assumptions early on in the group, a climate or atmosphere becomes established that may or may not facilitate effective group functioning. Different group climates are effective in different situations.

For example, if the problem to be solved is one that demands a creative, new solution and the collaboration of several experts, then a climate of openness in which everyone has an equal opportunity to participate will be most effective. In other situations, however, a more competitive or structured group climate might encourage a higher-quality solution, especially if expertise is not distributed equally among all group members. To gauge a group's climate, you should make certain observations:

1. Do people prefer to keep the discussion friendly and congenial? Do people prefer conflict and disagreement?
2. Do people seem involved and interested? Is the atmosphere one of work? Play? Competition? Avoidance?
3. Is there any attempt to suppress conflict or unpleasant feelings by avoiding tough issues?

For most task groups an unstructured, laissez-faire, or conflict-free climate is not effective: Important issues and conflicts are not explored sufficiently, and the quality of the group's work is sacrificed for the maintenance of friendly and smooth relations. Conversely, a highly structured climate can impede effective problem solving because members do not allow each other enough freedom to explore alternatives or consider creative solutions. A highly competitive climate can also be dysfunctional; competition can impede thoughtful deliberation and exchange, resulting in failure to build on other people's ideas.

Interventions   Intervening to alter a group's climate is more difficult than the interventions previously described. It can be done, however, by reinforcing and supporting desirable behavior, as well as by raising the issue directly. Where a group is smoothing over and avoiding important problems, for example, a useful intervention would be, "We seem to have a lot of agreement, but I wonder if we have really tackled some of the tougher underlying issues." When a group seems to be tied up by its own structure, often a comment as simple as the following will suffice: "I think that maybe we're looking at the problem too narrowly, and it might be useful to discuss whether we should also consider X, which isn't on the agenda but seems relevant to what we're talking about."

MEMBERSHIP

A major concern for group members is their degree of acceptance or inclusion in the group. Different patterns of interaction may develop in the group, providing clues to the degree and kind of membership. You can use these questions to examine the patterns of interaction:

1. Is there any subgrouping? Sometimes two or three members may consistently agree and support each other or consistently disagree and oppose one another.
2. Do some people seem to be outside the group? Do other members seem to be insiders? How are outsiders treated?
3. Do some members move physically in and out of the group—for example, lean forward or backward in their chairs or move their chairs in and out? Under what conditions do they come in or move out?

The problem of in-groups and out-groups is closely related to the earlier discussion of influence within the group. The interventions described earlier—supporting, querying, and opening up the discussion—are also useful for bringing in marginal members.

───── FEELINGS

During any group discussion, interactions among members frequently generate feelings. These feelings, however, are seldom talked about. When observing, you will often have to use tone of voice, facial expressions, gestures, and other nonverbal cues to make guesses about feelings:

1. What signs of feelings (anger, irritation, frustration, warmth, affection, excitement, boredom, defensiveness, competitiveness, etc.) do you observe in group members?
2. Are group members overly nice or polite to each other? Are only positive feelings expressed? Do members agree with each other too readily? What happens when members disagree?
3. Do you see norms operating about participation or the kinds of questions that are allowed (e.g., "If I talk, you must talk")? Do members feel free to probe each other about their feelings? Do questions tend to be restricted to intellectual topics or events outside of the group?

Most groups in business develop norms that allow for the expression of only positive feelings or feelings of disagreement and not anger. The problem with suppressing strong negative feelings is that they usually resurface later. For example, a person who is angry about what someone said earlier in the meeting gets back at that person later in the discussion by disagreeing or by criticizing his or her idea regardless of the idea's merit. The person's hidden motive becomes getting even, and he or she will do so by resisting ideas, being stubborn, or derailing the discussion. This retaliation is usually disguised with substantive issues and often has an element of irrationality to it. It is often more effective to bring out the person's anger in the first place and deal with it then.

──── TASK FUNCTIONS

For any group to function adequately and make maximum progress on the task at hand, certain task functions must be carried out. First, there must be *initiation*—the problem or goals must be stated, time limits laid out, and some agenda agreed upon. This function most frequently falls to the leader but may be taken on by other group members. Next, there must be both *opinion* and *information* seeking and giving on various issues related to the task. One of the major problems affecting group decisions and commitments is that groups tend to spend insufficient time on these phases. *Clarifying* and *elaborating* are vital not only for effective communication but also for creative solutions. *Summarizing* includes a review of ideas to be followed by *consensus testing*—making sure that all the ideas are on the table and that the group is ready to enter into an evaluation of the various ideas produced. The most effective groups follow this order rather than the more common procedure of evaluating each idea or alternative as it is discussed. Different group members may take on these task functions, but each must be covered. Use the following questions to check:

1. Are suggestions made as to the best way to proceed or tackle the problem?
2. Is there a summary of what has been covered? How effectively is this done? Who does it?
3. Is there any giving or asking for information, opinions, feelings, feedback, or searching for alternatives?
4. Is the group kept on target? Are topic jumping and going off on tangents prevented or discouraged?
5. Are all the ideas out before evaluation begins? What happens if someone begins to evaluate an idea as soon as it is produced?

──── MAINTENANCE FUNCTIONS

Groups cannot function effectively if cohesion is low or if relationships among group members become strained. In the life of any group, there will be periods of conflict, dissenting views, and misunderstandings. It is the purpose of maintenance functions to rebuild damaged relations and bring harmony back to the group. Without these processes, group members can become alienated, resulting in the group's losing valuable resources.

Two maintenance activities that can serve to prevent these kinds of problems are *gate keeping*, which ensures that members wanting to make a contribution are given the opportunity to do so, and *encouraging*, which helps create a climate of acceptance.

Compromising and *harmonizing* are two other activities that have limited usefulness in the actual task accomplishment, but they are sometimes useful in repairing strained relations.

When the level of conflict in a group is so high that effective communication is impaired, it is often useful for the group to suspend the task discussion and examine its own processes in order to define and attempt to solve the conflicts. The following questions will focus attention on a group's maintenance functions:

1. Are group members encouraged to enter into the discussion?
2. How well do members get their ideas across? Are some members preoccupied and not listening? Are there any attempts by group members to help others clarify their ideas?
3. How are ideas rejected? How do members react when their ideas are rejected?
4. Are conflicts among group members ignored or dealt with in some way?

▬ PROCESS OBSERVATION AND FEEDBACK

This reading has covered seven important aspects of group process that can influence a group's effectiveness. The interventions suggested are relatively simple and can be made naturally and unobtrusively during the normal progress of a meeting. The more people in a group skilled at making process observations, the greater the likelihood that the group will not bog down, waste valuable time, or make poor decisions. For this reason an increasing number of U.S. and foreign firms have developed norms that encourage open discussions of group process. In many companies, meetings are ended with a brief feedback session on the group's process, during which group members evaluate the meeting's effectiveness.

You need not be in such a firm or use terms such as *process feedback* to contribute to a group's effectiveness. Most of the ideas presented in this reading are based on common sense; practicing them does not require using the terms described here. The ideas described are more important than specific labels applied to them.

——— DISCUSSION QUESTIONS

1. Describe your participation in work groups to which you've belonged. Has your participation varied within the same group? From group to group? Why or why not?
2. Relate an experience you've had influencing a group. Explain the important aspects of your personal approach to influence in a group setting. If you've never felt as if you've influenced a group, explain why not.
3. What factors—other than those mentioned in the reading—might affect group process?
4. This reading focuses on group dynamics within a single group. Would these same principles apply to the dynamics between two groups? What would be the same? What would be different?

How to Run a Meeting   19

This reading delineates the practical details of running a meeting—"the most overused and underutilized of all management tools." According to the author, careful preparation is essential and includes setting objectives, selecting participants, planning the agenda, collecting relevant information, and setting a time and place for the meeting. The author offers strategies and suggestions for beginning the meeting, encouraging problem solving, keeping the discussion on track, reaching a decision, and ending the meeting.

Meetings are among the most overused and underutilized of all management tools. One study of managerial behavior found that many executives spent over two-thirds of their time in scheduled meetings. More significantly, important organizational decisions are almost always reached in management meetings or as a result of one or more meetings. Given their importance and the amount of management time they consume, it is indeed a tragedy that so many meetings are inefficient and, worse, ineffective.

Yet planning and conducting a meeting is not a difficult task. Although there are no magic formulas to guarantee success, there are a number of simple procedures that effective managers employ to improve the quality of their meetings.

There are, of course, many different kinds of meetings, ranging from two-person interchanges all the way up to industrywide conventions with thousands of participants. Most management meetings, however, involve relatively small groups of people in a single organization. This reading will concentrate on a number of techniques for running these kinds of management meetings more effectively. For further simplicity, the primary focus will be on scheduled meetings of managers who are at approximately the same level in the organization and who have known each other and worked together before.

The suggestions that follow are divided into planning activities to carry out before the meeting and leadership activities to engage in during the meeting. Both kinds of work are essential: The most thorough preparation in the world will be wasted if you are careless during the meeting, while even outstanding meeting leadership rarely overcomes poor planning.

——— PREPARING FOR THE MEETING

Perhaps the most useful way to begin is to sit down with a blank sheet of paper and think through what the meeting will be like. Write down all the issues that are likely to come up, what decisions need to be made, what you want to happen after the meeting, and what things have to happen before the meeting can take place. Although the circumstances surrounding each meeting are unique, your planning should include the following activities:

Setting Objectives   Most managers call meetings either to exchange information or to solve organizational problems. Generally your reasons for calling the meeting are fairly obvious, especially to you. It is worth being very explicit about your purposes, however, because they have major implications for who should attend, which items belong on the agenda, when and where you hold the meeting, and what kinds of decision-making procedures you should use.

An information-exchange meeting can be an efficient mechanism if the information to be shared is complex or controversial, if it has major implications for the meeting participants, or if there is symbolic value in conveying the information personally. If none of these conditions is present, it may be more efficient, and just as effective, to write a memo or make several telephone calls.

Problem-solving meetings provide an opportunity to combine the knowledge and skills of several people at once. The ideas that evolve out of an open-ended discussion are usually richer and more creative than what the same people could produce working individually.

The two different objectives—information exchange and problem solving—call for very different kinds of meetings. Thus, you should make your goals clear both to yourself and to the other meeting participants.

Selecting Participants   Invite people to the meeting who will either contribute to, or be affected by, its outcome. Select individuals who have knowledge or skills relevant to the problem or who command organizational resources (time, budgets, other people, power, and influence) that you need to tap.

As you build your participant list, also give thought to the overall composition of the group. Identify the likely concerns and interests of the individual managers and the feelings they have about each other. Try to obtain a rough balance of power and status among subgroups or probable coalitions (unless you have clear reasons for wanting one group to be more powerful).

Do everything you can to keep the size of the group appropriate to your objectives. Although an information-exchange meeting can be almost any size, a problem-solving group should not exceed 10 people if at all possible.

Planning the Agenda   Even if you are planning an informal exploratory meeting, an agenda can be a valuable means of controlling the discussion and of giving the participants a sense of direction. The agenda defines the meeting's purpose for participants and places boundaries between relevant and irrelevant discussion topics. Furthermore, the agenda can serve as an important vehicle for premeeting discussions with participants.

Some important principles of building an agenda are listed here:

- Sequence items so they build on one another if possible.
- Sequence topics from easiest to most difficult or controversial.
- Keep the number of topics within reasonable limits.
- Avoid topics that can be better handled by subgroups or individuals.
- Separate information exchange from problem solving.
- Define a finishing time as well as a starting time.
- Depending on meeting length, schedule breaks at specific times when they will not disrupt important discussions.

Not every meeting requires a formal written agenda. Often you simply cannot predict where a discussion will lead or how long it will take. However, focusing your attention on these issues can help you anticipate controversy and be prepared to influence it in a productive manner. Even if you do not prepare a public written agenda, you should not begin the meeting without having a tentative private one.

Doing Your Homework   Your major objective in preparing for the meeting is to collect all relevant information you can and consider its implications. Some of this data may be in written documents, but much of it will probably be in other people's heads. The more important and the more controversial the subject, the more contact you should have with other participants before the actual meeting.

These contacts will help you anticipate issues and disagreements that may arise during the meeting. As you talk with the other participants, try to learn all you can about their personal opinions and objectives concerning the meeting topic. These personal objectives—often called hidden agendas—can have as big an impact on what happens during the meeting as your formal explicit agenda. Thus, the more you can discover about the other participants' goals for the meeting, the better prepared you will be to lead an effective discussion.

These premeeting contacts also give you an opportunity to encourage the other participants to do their homework. If there is enough time before the meeting to collect and circulate relevant data or background materials, the meeting itself will proceed much more quickly. Few events are as frustrating as a meeting of people who are unprepared to discuss or decide the issues on the agenda.

As part of your preparation you may want to brief your boss and other executives who will not be at the meeting but who have an interest in its outcomes.

Finally, circulate the agenda and relevant background papers a day or two before the meeting if you can. These documents help clarify your purposes and expectations and encourage the other participants to come to the meeting well prepared. Keep your demands on their time reasonable, however. People are more likely to read and think about brief memos than about long comprehensive reports.

Setting a Time and Place   The timing and location of your meeting can have a subtle but significant impact on the quality of the discussion. These choices communicate a surprising number of messages about the meeting's importance, style, and possible outcomes.

What time of day is best for your meeting? Often the work flow in the organization will constrain your freedom of choice. For example, you could not meet simultaneously with all of a bank's tellers during the regular business hours or with all the order-entry clerks just as the mail arrives. Within these kinds of constraints, however, you often have a wide choice of meeting times. How should you decide?

Early in the day participants will usually be fresher and will have fewer other problems on their minds. In contrast, late-afternoon meetings can be more leisurely, because there will usually be nothing else on anyone's schedule following your meeting. Perhaps the best question to ask is what the participants will be doing after the meeting. Will they be eager to end the meeting so they can proceed to other commitments, or will they be inclined to prolong the discussion? Which attitude better suits your purposes? There is no best time for a meeting, but you should consider which times would be most suitable for your particular objectives.

Two other factors may also influence when you schedule the meeting. First, try to ensure that there will be an absolute minimum of interruptions. Second, gear your starting time to the meeting's probable, or desirable, length. For example, if you want the meeting to last only one hour, a good time to schedule it is at 11 A.M.

Try not to plan meetings that last more than 90 minutes. Most people's endurance—or at least their creative capacity—will not last much longer than that. For complex or lengthy subjects that require more time, be sure to build in coffee-and-stretch breaks at least every 90 minutes.

Another key decision is where to hold the meeting. The setting can have a marked influence on the discussion's tone and content. Consider the difference between calling three subordinates to your office or meeting them for lunch in a restaurant. Each setting implies a particular level of formality and signals the kind of discussion you expect to have. Similarly, if you are meeting with several peers, a conference room provides a more neutral climate than would any of your offices. In each case, the appropriate setting depends on your purposes, and you should choose your location accordingly.

The discussion climate will also be affected by the arrangement of the furniture in the meeting room. In your office, you can stay behind your desk and thereby appear more authoritative or use a chair that puts you on a more equal basis with the other participants. In a conference room, you can sit at the head of the table to symbolize your control or in the center to be one of the group.

You should also be sure to arrange for any necessary mechanical equipment, such as an overhead or slide projector, an easel, or a blackboard. These visual aids can facilitate both information-exchange and problem-solving discussions.

Summary   These suggestions are intended to help you convene a meeting of people who have a common understanding of why they have come together and are prepared to contribute to the discussion. Of course, this kind of thorough preparation is often simply impossible. Nevertheless, the more preparation you do, the more smoothly the meeting will go. Although you can never anticipate *all* the issues and hidden agendas, you can clearly identify the major sources of potential disagreement. That anticipation enables you to control the meeting rather than be caught off guard. Even if you have to schedule a meeting only an hour in advance, you can still benefit from systematic attention to these kinds of details.

——— CONDUCTING THE MEETING

If you have done your homework, you probably have a good idea of where you want the group to be at the end of the meeting. However, remember that you called the meeting because you need something from the other participants—either information relevant to the problem or agreement and commitment to a decision. Your success in achieving those goals now depends not so much on what you know about the problem as on what you and the others can learn during the discussion. Thus, your primary concern as you begin the meeting should be with creating a healthy problem-solving atmosphere in which participants openly confront their differences and work toward a joint solution.

The following suggestions and leadership techniques should help you achieve that goal.

Beginning the Meeting   If you are well prepared, the chances are that no one else has thought as much about the meeting as you have. Thus, the most productive way to begin is with an explicit review of the agenda and your objectives. This discussion gives everyone an opportunity to ask questions, offer suggestions, and express opinions about why they are there. Beginning with a review of the agenda also signals its importance and gets the meeting going in a task-oriented direction.

Be careful not to simply impose the agenda on the group; others may have useful suggestions that will speed up the meeting or bring the problem into sharper focus. They may even disagree with some of your plans, but you will not learn about that disagreement unless you clearly signal that you consider the agenda open to revision. The more the others participate in defining the meeting, the more committed they will be to fulfilling that definition.

This initial discussion also permits participants to work out a shared understanding of the problem that brought them together and of what topics are and are not appropriate to discuss in the meeting.

Encouraging Problem Solving   As the formal leader of the meeting, you can employ a wide variety of techniques to keep the group in a problem-solving mode. Your formal authority as chairperson gives you a great deal of power to influence the group's actions. Often a simple comment, a pointed look, or even a lifted eyebrow is all you need to indicate approval or disapproval of someone's behavior.

Perhaps your best tool is simply your own style of inquiry. If you focus on facts and on understanding points of disagreement, to the exclusion of personalities, others will generally do the same. As the discussion progresses, try to keep differing points of view in rough balance. Do not let a few individuals dominate; when you sense an imbalance in participation, openly ask the quieter members for their opinions and ideas. Never assume that silence means agreement; more often, it signals some disagreement with the dominant theme of the discussion.

Effective problem-solving meetings generally pass through several phases. Early in the discussion, the group will be seeking to understand the nature of the problem. At that point you need to encourage factual nonevaluative discussion that emphasizes describing symptoms and searching for all possible causes. As understanding is gained, the focus will shift to a search for solutions. Again, you must discourage evaluative comments until the group has explored all potential alternatives. Only then should the discussion become evaluative, as the group moves toward a decision.

By being sensitive to the stages of problem solving (describing symptoms, searching for alternatives, evaluating alternatives, selecting a solution), you can vary your leadership style to fit the current needs of the group. At all times, however, keep the discussion focused on the problem, not on personalities or on unrelated issues, no matter how important they may be. Make your priorities clear, and hold the group to them. Finally, maintain a climate of honest inquiry in which anyone's assumptions (including yours) may be questioned and tested.

Keeping the Discussion on Track   When the meeting topic is controversial, with important consequences for the group members, you will have to work hard to keep the discussion focused on the issues.

Controversy makes most people uncomfortable, and groups will often avoid confronting the main issue by finding less important or irrelevant topics to talk about. If the discussion wanders too far from the agenda, bring the group back to the major topics.

Use your judgment in making these interventions, however. If the group is on the verge of splitting up in anger or frustration, a digression to a safe topic may be a highly functional way of reuniting. Generally, such digressions are most beneficial when they follow, rather than precede, open controversy. If you think the group has reached a decision on the main issue, even if it is only an implicit one, you may want to let the digression go on for a while. However, if the discussion is clearly delaying a necessary confrontation, then you will have to intervene to bring the discussion back to the main issue.

If you began the meeting with an explicit discussion of the agenda, you will find this focusing task easier to carry out. Often a simple reminder to the group, with a glance at the clock, is enough. Another useful technique for marking progress is periodically to summarize where you think the group has been and where it seems to be going. Again, treat your summaries as tentative and ask the group to confirm your assessments.

If the discussion seems to bog down or to wander too far afield, the group may need to take a short break. Even two minutes of standing and stretching can revitalize people's willingness to concentrate on the problem. The break also serves to cut off old conversations, making it easier to begin new ones.

Do everything you can to keep the discussion moving on schedule so that the meeting ends on time. The clock can be a useful taskmaster, and busy managers rarely have the luxury of ignoring it. If you have set a specific ending time, and everyone knows you mean it, members will be less likely to digress.

Controlling the Discussion   How authoritatively should you exercise control over the discussion? The answer depends so much on specific circumstances that a general response is almost impossible. The appropriate level of formality depends on the discussion topic, on the specific phase of the problem-solving cycle, and on your formal and informal relationships with the other participants. You will normally want to exercise greater control under the following circumstances:

- The meeting is oriented more toward information exchange;
- The topic generates strong, potentially disruptive feelings;
- The group is moving toward a decision;
- Time pressures are significant.

There are a whole range of techniques you can use to exert more formal control. For example, if you permit participants to speak only when you call on them or if you comment on or summarize each statement, direct confrontations between other individuals will be minimal. If you use a flip chart or blackboard to summarize ideas, you will also increase the level of formality and reduce the number of direct exchanges. In some circumstances, you may even want to employ formal parliamentary procedures, such as requiring motions, limiting debate, taking notes, and so on. These procedures might be appropriate, for example, in meetings of a board of directors, in union-management contract negotiations, or in policy-setting sessions that involve managers from several different parts of the organization.

Many of these techniques are clearly inappropriate for, and rarely used in, smaller management meetings. Although these techniques can give you a high degree of control, they cannot prevent participants from developing strong feelings about the issues—feelings that often become strong precisely because you have not permitted them to be openly expressed.

Thus, it is possible to control a meeting in a way that minimizes conflict. However, one result of that control may be increased tension and even hostility between the participants, leading to more serious future problems. Yet, if tension levels are already so high that a rational discussion will not evolve on its own, some of these controlling techniques may be essential.

Reaching a Decision   Many management groups fall into decision-making habits without thinking carefully about the consequences of those habits. The two major approaches to reaching a group decision are voting and reaching a consensus. Each strategy has its advantages and disadvantages.

Voting is often used when the decision is important and the group seems deadlocked. A major benefit of taking a vote is that it guarantees you will get a decision. However, voting requires public commitment to a position and creates a win/lose situation for the group members. Some individuals will be clearly identified as having favored a minority position. Losers on one issue often try to balance their account on the next decision, or they may withdraw their commitment to the total group. Either way, you may have won the battle but lost the war.

Reaching a group consensus is generally a much more effective decision-making procedure. It is often more difficult, however, and is almost always more time-consuming. Working toward a genuine consensus means hearing all points of view and usually results in a better decision. This also results in greater individual commitment to the group decision, a condition that is especially important when the group members are responsible for implementing the decision. Even when individuals do not fully agree with the group decision, they are more likely to support it (or less likely to sabotage it) if they believe their positions have had a complete hearing.

Ending the Meeting   Most important at the end of the meeting is to clarify what happens next. If the group has made a major decision, be certain all agree on who is responsible for its implementation and on when the work will be completed.

If the group has to meet again, you can save considerable time by scheduling your next meeting then and there. Have everyone check calendars and mark down the date and time of the next meeting.

Depending on the discussion topic and the decisions that have been made, either you or someone else should follow the meeting with a brief memo summarizing the discussion, the decisions, and the follow-up commitments each participant has made. This kind of document serves not only as a record of the meeting but also as a reminder to the participants of what they decided and what they committed themselves to doing.

If you can, spend the last several minutes of the meeting discussing how the meeting went. Although most managers are not accustomed to self-critiques, this practice can contribute significantly to improvements in group problem solving. The best time to share reactions to a meeting is right after it has ended. You evaluate the effectiveness of other management techniques all the time; why not apply the same criteria to your meetings?

——— SUMMARY

Management meetings occur frequently and have a significant impact on organizational productivity. By applying these techniques carefully, with sensitivity to the combination of people and problems you have brought together, you can make your meetings more effective and more interesting. The techniques are simple and require little more than systematic preparation before the meeting and sensitive observation and intervention while the meeting is in progress.

——— DISCUSSION QUESTIONS

1. Name other procedures that you can think of that would enhance the effectiveness of a meeting.
2. State your general opinion about meetings as well as the effectiveness of the meetings that you have attended. What have been their assets and drawbacks?
3. Should the structure of a meeting reflect the structure of the organization? For example, should a hierarchical company have hierarchically structured meetings?
4. What has been the most disruptive incident at a meeting that you have attended? How was it handled? What could have been done to prevent the disruption from occurring? What was done to control its effects?
5. What is your opinion about routine, regularly scheduled meetings? What might prevent them from being effective? How can they maintain their effectiveness?

20   Managing a Task Force

JAMES WARE

This reading describes how to establish, organize, and manage an effective task force. The author guides the reader through each stage of a task force's life cycle: starting up, conducting the first meeting, running the task force, and completing the project. He provides practical advice on how to achieve an outcome that serves the interests of task-force members as well as those of the organization itself.

Companies establish task forces to work on problems and projects that cannot be easily handled by the regular organization. Typically the problems cut across existing departmental boundaries or are simply so time-consuming that working on them would disrupt routine department tasks.

A task force can be a powerful management tool for resolving complex and challenging problems. Several factors contribute to this strength:

- The group is usually very task oriented because it was formed to solve a specific problem or achieve a well-defined outcome. When the problem is solved or the task is accomplished, the group disbands.
- If the task force brings together managers from the affected functional areas, it will possess a diversity of skills and understanding that can potentially produce a high-quality solution.
- If group members are selected on the basis of their individual competence relative to the problem, there is rarely any deadwood.

These same characteristics, however, can present a task-force leader with several difficult managerial problems:

- Because the group represents an inherent criticism of the regular organization's failure to deal with the problem, there may be significant tensions and even battles between members and non-members.
- Individual task-force members who come from different parts of the organization usually bring with them a wide diversity of viewpoints, goals, and loyalties. The task force can become a battleground for fighting out long-standing departmental conflicts.
- The temporary nature of the task force may limit members' willingness to commit personal time and energy to the project.

- Managers who are personally ambitious often view a task-force assignment as a major opportunity to impress upper management. These private agendas can seriously interfere with the group's problem-solving effectiveness.
- If the group members do not know each other well or are competing with each other either personally or as departmental representatives, the leader will find it difficult to create the shared sense of purpose and mutual respect necessary for issue-oriented problem solving.

Clearly, the success of a task force's efforts depends heavily on the way its activities are managed. This reading suggests some operating guidelines for increasing the effectiveness of any temporary management group. These suggestions have been grouped into four categories, based on the sequence in which the leader will confront the problems:

- Starting up the task force,
- Conducting the first meeting,
- Running the task force,
- Completing the project.

The guidelines apply primarily to a task-force leader. Often, however, the most effective groups are those in which several members carry out the leadership activities. Thus, you may find many of these ideas useful even in groups where you do not have formal leadership responsibilities.

——— STARTING UP THE TASK FORCE

Your work as task-force leader begins the moment you accept responsibility for chairing the group. The period before the first formal meeting presents several opportunities for making decisions that will affect many of the group's later activities. Early attention to details will pay dividends as the group confronts tough issues during its deliberations. In fact, these front-end activities probably represent your greatest opportunity for defining the group's working style.

These start-up activities should focus on the following sequence of tasks:

1. Clarify Why the Task Force Is Being Formed   Although the specific circumstances of each project will be unique, most task forces are established to accomplish one or more of the following general objectives:

- Investigate a poorly understood problem.
- Recommend and/or implement a high-quality solution to a recognized problem.
- Respond to a crisis that results from a sudden change in the organization's business conditions.

- Bring together people with the knowledge and skills to work on the problem.
- Gain commitment to a decision by involving the people who will be affected by its implementation.
- Develop managers by providing them with exposure to other functional areas and people.
- Force resolution of a long-standing problem, or work around an obstacle (such as a particular individual or group).

Usually the commissioning executives will have several purposes in mind. (*Commissioning executives* refers to the upper-level management group that determines a task force should be established.) For example, a new-product-development project can also be an excellent training experience for junior marketing managers. Similarly, a study of excessive inventories could be part of a strategy to reduce the power of an ineffective but well-entrenched purchasing manager.

Often, however, multiple objectives are incompatible, because one objective may be attainable only at the expense of another. Additionally, the various commissioning executives may have different objectives or different priorities for conflicting objectives. In many instances these differences will not be openly expressed or even recognized.

Thus, one of your first critical tasks will be to meet with the commissioning executives and with other managers who have an interest in the project's outcome. In those meetings you will want to explore the relevance and relative importance of each possible objective. You may even find it necessary to define alternative objectives and possible conflicts yourself. You can be an active participant in the process of clarifying the task force's mission.

You must also determine whether the task force will be expected to conduct a preliminary investigation, to engage in problem solving and decision making, or to implement an already agreed-upon change. The choice of emphasis will obviously depend upon the history and nature of the particular problem, but you should seek an explicit statement about the boundaries of the project.

The nature of the task will help determine who should be on the task force and what kinds of operating and decision-making procedures will be appropriate.

For example, an exploratory investigation of a customer-service department's efficiency would require very different analytic skills and working procedures than would the installation of a computerized invoicing and inventory-control system. Consequently, you will want to select task-force members whose skills match the project requirements.

A useful technique for confronting these issues is to write out a proposed statement of purpose and then to ask the commissioning executives how well your statement reflects their expectations. As the executives help you revise the statement, they will develop personal commitment to it and thus to the task force's success.

2. Define General Operating Procedures

- Will members be assigned to the group full-time or part-time?
- When should the task be completed?
- What will the group's budget be?
- What organizational reports and other information will be available to the group?
- How much decision-making power is being delegated to the group?
- What information should be reported to functional managers and how often?

You will not be able to anticipate all the procedural issues that the group will face, and many of those that can be anticipated will have to be worked out by the whole task-force group. Again, however, you should discuss these questions in advance with the executives who are establishing the task force. It is far better to be told explicitly that some topics and decisions are beyond the group's charter than to discover those boundaries only by crossing over them.

One of the most important procedural issues to be resolved is the way in which the group will make task-related decisions. The more exploratory and open-ended the basic project is, the more open and participative the decision-making procedures should be. Considerable research evidence suggests that task-oriented groups prefer relatively directive leaders and that decision making is usually more efficient in a structured climate. However, if the problem requires an imaginative or wholly new perspective, then a more unstructured climate will generally produce more innovative ideas.

You should discuss leadership and decision-making styles with both the commissioning executives and prospective task-force members; however, this is not a decision to make once for the entire project. The effectiveness of each style depends very much on the nature of the current problem, and you will probably want to vary your procedures as the project progresses.

3. Determine Who Should Be on the Task Force   As much as possible, individuals who are asked to join the task force should be people who

- Possess knowledge and skills relevant to the task,
- Are personally interested in the problem,
- Have, or can make, the time to devote to the task force,
- Enjoy working in groups and are effective in group settings,
- Will not dominate the meetings or decisions solely with their personality or power.

Although individual competence is important, it is not an adequate basis for constructing the project group. Equally important is the overall composition of the group. Does each member possess organizational credibility and influence relative to the problem? Are all the functional areas that will be affected by the group's work represented? The exclusion of important departments will not only generate resentment and resistance but also may reduce both the quality of the task force's recommendations and the probability that the recommendations will eventually be implemented.

A major dilemma in membership selection is whether to include persons who are likely to obstruct the group's investigations and slow down progress toward a consensus solution. Although including such individuals may reduce problem-solving efficiency, it will increase substantially the probability of their later supporting (or at least not actively opposing) the group's recommendations. Lowered efficiency in early deliberations is usually more than compensated for by a smoother implementation process. In addition, when individual resistance is based on valid information or experience, a solution that ignores the sources of that resistance is likely to be suboptimal or even unworkable.

It is vital that you be involved in the membership selection process. You may have information about prospective members that will have a direct bearing on the appropriateness of their involvement. In addition, your participation in the selection process adds your personal commitment to the group's effectiveness. Finally, your involvement in selecting task-force members provides you with another opportunity to learn about upper management's expectations for the task force.

4. Contact Prospective Members   Your first contact with each prospective task-force member is an opportunity to begin defining not only the problem the group will be addressing but also the procedures it will be using. Whenever possible, make this contact in person. Try to include the prospective member's functional boss in the same meeting so that all three of you can agree on the basic purpose of the task force and on the prospective member's level of involvement.

These first contacts also provide an opportunity for you to explore each person's current knowledge and feelings about the problem and to build a productive personal relationship if one does not already exist. This information and experience can prove invaluable as you prepare for the first full task-force meeting.

5. Prepare for the First Meeting   Because the first meeting sets the tone for all later activities, you will want to prepare a careful agenda. There are two major objectives for this first meeting:

- Reaching a common understanding of the group's task,
- Defining working procedures and relationships.

Because the most important function of the first meeting will be to define the problem and the organization's expectations for the group's output, the commissioning executives should attend the meeting if at all possible. Before the meeting, review everything you have learned about the problem and the group members with your boss.

You probably will not be able to carry out all these start-up activities as thoroughly as you would like. Time pressures, physical separation of group members, and prior relationships may prevent the kind of thorough, rational analysis these suggestions imply. In addition, the commissioning executives may find it difficult to give you a clear statement of the problem. After all, most task forces are established because the organization does not fully understand the nature of its problem.

You have to accept some of the responsibility for defining the problem. But you also have to know when to stop discussing and start doing. That is a difficult managerial judgment that you can make only within the context of a specific situation. These suggestions can get you off to a good start, but you may not be able to follow them all. Often you will have no choice; other decisions will limit your alternatives. But you can become aware of the risks you incur by omitting a preparatory step and thereby be more alert to potential future problems.

CONDUCTING THE FIRST MEETING

This meeting is important not only because it is the first time all task-force members will be together but also because patterns of interactions begun here will influence later group activities.

The two major objectives for this meeting are discussed here:

Reaching a Common Understanding of the Group's Task This goal is clearly the most important item on the agenda; yet in most instances, it will be the most difficult to accomplish. Few of the other members will have devoted as much time or attention to the task as you have. Until they get "up to speed" and see the problem in the same general terms that you do, they will be a group in name only.

Each manager will come to this meeting feeling a responsibility to represent his or her own department's interests. Each will interpret the problem in terms of those interests, and each will possess a unique combination of ideas and information about the problem. Furthermore, many of the group members will be feeling highly defensive, as they anticipate that other managers will blame their departments for the problems. These feelings are common and are often based on past personal experiences. If you know or suspect that such feelings exist within the group, try to find a positive way to bring them to the surface. Encourage group members to participate by expressing their opinions and offering their suggestions, but ask them to withhold judgments until all the relevant information has been heard. You can serve as a role model for other group members by asking questions that focus on facts, by maintaining strict neutrality on the issues, and by eliciting ideas from all members.

At this point the group probably does not possess enough information to achieve a deep understanding of the problem and its causes. Indeed, a lack of information and understanding is generally one of the major reasons for establishing a task force. Nevertheless, it is essential for the group to acknowledge the problem and to agree on its boundaries.

Your most difficult task at this first meeting, however, may be to prevent a premature consensus on an appropriate solution. Most experienced managers are sure they know what the problems are and what actions are required. Thus, although you are seeking some agreement on the nature of the *problem,* you do not want the group to settle on a *solution* yet.

You *do* want group members to develop a sense of their joint responsibilities and to begin considering the appropriate next steps. Be explicit about areas in which group members differ. A task-focused discussion of this kind will generate commitment to the group and its general goals, even when differences of opinion as to appropriate strategies exist and are openly recognized.

Defining Working Procedures and Relationships   The second topic for the first meeting is the question of how the group will work on its task. Among the issues that require explicit attention are the following:

- Frequency and nature of full task-force meetings,
- Structure of subgroups,
- Ground rules for communication and decision making within the task force between meetings,
- Ground rules or norms for decision making and conflict resolution,
- Schedules and deadlines for accomplishing subtasks and for completing the final report,
- Ground rules for dealing with sensitive issues; agreement on which ones require involving other managers,
- Procedures for monitoring and reporting progress to members of the task force and to functional area managers,
- Explicit processes for evaluating and modifying task-force working procedures.

Spending time on these procedural issues serves two primary purposes. First, the discussion will help group members form clear expectations concerning their projected activities and working relationships. These expectations will reduce the tensions inherent in an otherwise very unstructured situation. Second, the process of reaching agreement on procedural matters can become a model of how the task force will resolve other problems.

Resolution of these issues at the first meeting can provide all participants with a positive experience associated with the group; however, you may need to carry some of these topics over into subsequent meetings. Try to end the first meeting on a note of agreement: If you can achieve a solid consensus on some portion of these procedural matters, you will have taken a big step toward a successful project no matter how deeply divided the group is on substantive issues.

RUNNING THE TASK FORCE

Once you have completed front-end work, you should focus on keeping the project moving and on monitoring and reporting the group's progress. Although specific circumstances will vary, there are several general principles to keep in mind:

Hold Full Task-force Meetings Frequently Enough to Keep All Members Informed About Group Progress   Though each meeting should have a specific purpose, periodic meetings should be scheduled well in advance, and all members should be required to attend. A meeting can always be canceled if there is nothing substantial to discuss. However, full meetings do have an important symbolic value. They are the only time the full group is physically together, and anything said there is heard simultaneously by everyone. Very often the most valuable and creative discussions are those that evolve spontaneously in response to someone's raising a nonagenda item. For example, the most successful fund-raising project in the history of public television (the cast party following the final episode of *Upstairs, Downstairs*) grew out of two spontaneous comments during an informal staff meeting at WGBH in Boston.

Although you cannot plan that kind of creativity, you *can* create opportunities for unstructured exploratory discussions.

Unless the Task Force Is Very Small (Fewer Than 5 to 7 Members), Dividing Up into Groups Will Be Mandatory   You must manage this process carefully, however. Dividing the project into separate tasks that can be worked on simultaneously can be an efficient mechanism for achieving rapid progress. But remember that one of the virtues of the task-force approach is the synergy that results from new combinations of individuals investigating problems in areas that are unfamiliar to them. If you permit the task-force members to work only in their own areas or with persons they already know and work well with, you are throwing away an important advantage.

Of course, when managers go poking around in parts of the company that are unfamiliar to them, they may ask questions that insult or unintentionally threaten the functional managers with whom they work. Warn your group members of this danger, and then be prepared to spend some of your time telling functional managers about your group's work and smoothing ruffled feathers as they occur.

You must also recognize that working in subgroups can cause individuals to lose their overall perspective. If the task force becomes too differentiated, the various subgroups may form their own identities and develop an advocacy style of pushing for their own solutions. The more the total job is broken down for subgroup work, the more you must encourage formal intergroup sharing of problems, findings, and ideas as the project moves along.

Be Careful Not to Align Yourself Too Closely with One Position or Subgroup Too Early This principle is particularly important if there are clearly opposing and mutually exclusive sides to the issue. Although you will eventually have to commit to a plan of action, you will serve the group most effectively by being as concerned with the problem-solving *process* as you are with the specific outcomes of that process.

Set Interim Project Deadlines and Demand Adherence to Them When you are in charge of the schedule and know how arbitrarily some of the key checkpoints were set, it becomes far too easy to assume you can make up lost time later. No matter how arbitrary the interim deadlines are, however, if you miss them, you will miss your final deadline too.

Insistence on meeting deadlines is doubly important when the task-force members are assigned to the project only on a part-time basis. If they are continuing to carry out functional responsibilities, they will feel pressures to spend their time on tasks with immediate outcomes. The pressure to accomplish immediate tasks will always outweigh the needs of longer-range task-force projects. Part-time task-force members face a real dilemma and will be under continual stress. As the project leader, you must be prepared to spend a large portion of your time prodding group members to complete their tasks on schedule. At the same time, however, you must remain sympathetic with the legitimate needs of the functional areas and be careful not to antagonize either your members or their functional bosses. Your task will be especially delicate in situations where you have no formal authority over these part-time members or where the lines of authority are vague.

Be Sensitive to the Conflicting Loyalties Created by Belonging to the Task Force As task-force members work together in group activities, they normally begin to develop commitments to the project and to each other. These commitments often become another source of stress, as members feel loyalties to both the task force and to their own departments. On the one hand, they continue to feel responsible for representing the interests of their functional areas, and on the other, they feel growing pressures to help the task force accomplish its goals.

Assisting the task force frequently requires group members to share confidential information with you or with other members. You must recognize the risk that this sharing involves. Whenever feasible, the source of confidential information should remain anonymous. As task-force leader you may be able to play a valuable intermediary role. But remember that once someone has entrusted you with confidential information, that person has become dependent on your integrity. If you are ever indiscreet, you are unlikely to be so trusted again, and your value to the organization will be seriously diminished.

Your Most Important Leadership Role Is That of Communicating Information Among Task-force Members and Between the Task Force and the Rest of the Organization   This communications role is time-consuming but essential to the success of the project. You must take personal responsibility for monitoring group progress, for bringing appropriate subgroups together to share information and ideas, and for reporting both progress and problems to your own boss and to the functional managers in whose areas the task force is working.

Very often your most important activities will involve listening to individual managers, passing information from one task-force member to another, and bringing together managers who must exchange or share information and ideas. Although these activities often seem inordinately time-consuming, they form the glue that binds the individual task-force members together. As individuals and subgroups pursue their investigative tasks, you will probably become the only manager who retains an overall understanding of the total project. Communicating that understanding to others and reminding them of their interdependence are critical responsibilities.

—— COMPLETING THE PROJECT

The work of an investigative task force typically culminates with a written report and a summary presentation of findings and recommendations to upper management. An implementation task force will normally have results that are more concrete to demonstrate its accomplishments, but even so, there is often a formal meeting at which the task force officially relinquishes its responsibilities to an operating group.

The written report documents the work of the task force, but its importance lies in the decision-making process it generated. In fact, the preparation of the final report can provide a structure and focus for the task force's concluding activities. You should prepare a tentative outline of this report early in the project and circulate it widely among group members. This outline can actually serve as a guide to the development of specific recommendations. The need to write the report will force the group to reach specific decisions.

Drafts of the report thus often become the basis for working out any differences remaining among the task-force members. Except in highly charged situations with major organizational consequences, you should strive to reach a group consensus before presenting any recommendations to upper management. Unless your group members agree on what actions are needed, you can hardly expect management acceptance or approval of the report.

The formal presentation of findings and recommendations to management is just as important as the task force's first meeting. The presentation should be carefully organized, with explicit attention to who will say what, in what sequence, and with what visual aids. If the recommendations are surprising, controversial, or expensive, these preparations need even greater attention.

You should brief your own boss and other key executives before the formal presentation. This briefing does not necessarily require their approval or agreement, but their advance understanding can help to prevent defensive reactions or categorical rejections of your group's recommendations. This kind of briefing can be especially important if your recommendations involve major changes in organization structure, budget allocations, or strategic focus for any of the executives who will be present at the formal presentation.

Although important, this formal presentation rarely constitutes an adequate wrap-up of the task-force project. Only if the recommendations are very straightforward and noncontroversial will the management group be able to understand and act on them at one sitting. A more-effective strategy will be to plan two meetings. In the first, you summarize the findings and recommendations and distribute the formal report. At the end of this presentation, you then schedule a second, decision-making meeting for the near future. The time period between the two meetings gives the executives an opportunity to read the report and consider its implications.

This period will be a busy time for the task-force members, who can meet individually and in subgroups with key executives to clarify the report. Only when the report has been acted upon can the task force consider its work actually finished.

▬▬ DISCUSSION QUESTIONS

1. Considering the changes taking place in the business world of the 1990s, do you think the task-force form of organization has more, less, or the same importance?

2. Describe the personality needed to manage a task force. What are some of the important qualities? What type of personality would be ill-suited to manage a task force?

3. What are the advantages and disadvantages of an in-house task force versus outside consultants? Does one seem preferable? If so, under what circumstances?

4. The reading gives four stages in the "life cycle" of a task force (e.g., starting up a task force). The reading provides management guidelines for each stage. Would you add any other guidelines?

5. Think of an instance from your professional experience when a task force might have been useful, but was never established. Why wasn't a task force used in that particular circumstance? What course of action was taken instead? Knowing what you now know, do you think that a task force would have resolved the problem more efficiently? Why or why not?

PART THREE

MANAGING ORGANIZATIONAL EFFECTIVENESS

DESIGNING ORGANIZATIONS FOR EFFECTIVENESS

Organization Design   21

JAY W. LORSCH

This reading focuses on how managers use organization design to influence subordinates to work toward a firm's goals. It begins by describing the origins and elements of organizational contingency theory; it then examines the design issues managers face in the functional unit and in the single-business organization. The reading concludes by discussing leadership style and company culture—two other factors that play a role in how an organization influences its members.

Managers influence subordinates to work toward the goals of the firm in three primary ways: by personal contact (their actions and words in meetings and one-on-one sessions, their speeches, their tours of the plant); by substantive decisions about the allocation of resources; and by decisions about the definition of jobs, their arrangement on organization charts, measurement-and-reward schemes, selection criteria for personnel, and so forth. The latter set of decisions is the focus of this reading and is referred to as organization design.

To be more precise, the *organization design* consists of the structure, rewards, and measurement practices intended to direct members' behavior toward the organization's goals, as well as the criteria used to select persons for the organization. Structure means the pattern of job definition, authority, and communication relationships represented in organization charts, position descriptions, and so on. Rewards refer to financial compensation and benefits as well as career opportunities, interesting work, and even meaningful personal relationships. The criteria that managers use to select new employees are also important. Measurement includes the control and management-information system—that is, the procedures by which plans are made and results are measured and reported.

How much time and effort managers devote to decisions about these design elements depends upon the size of the firm and their own level in the hierarchy. As managers move up in the hierarchy, and/or as the size of their organization grows, they become more concerned with issues of organization design. With more subordinates, managers are less able to rely on personal contact to influence subordinates; therefore, they have to rely more on the organization-design elements of structure, rewards, measurement, and selection criteria. The focus here is more on issues of structure than on the other design elements.

—— THE GOALS OF ORGANIZATION DESIGN

Managers are concerned with three related goals when they make design decisions:

1. To create an organization design that provides a permanent setting in which managers can influence individuals to do their particular jobs.
2. To achieve a pattern of collaborative effort among individual employees, which is necessary for successful operations.
3. To create an organization that is cost effective—one that achieves the first two goals with a minimum of duplication of effort, payroll costs, and so on.

—— A BRIEF HISTORICAL PERSPECTIVE

Managers' concerns with these goals and the issues of organization design are not new. Many of the earliest management writers—Fayol, Urwick, Gulick—wrote about these matters in the first half of the twentieth century. What is new, however, is the increased understanding of organizations and their operations. Those early writers generalized from their own experiences as practitioners in a few basic industries—such as railroads, mining, and automobiles—and concluded that the principles they learned in those industries were applicable to other industries at other points in time. Furthermore, they believed that people are motivated solely by money. Researchers and practitioners since then have learned that employees' needs at work are more varied and complex. The goals of organization design discussed earlier are based on this recognition of the full range of rewards that motivate people to work. More recent studies have also indicated that there is no one best way for a firm to organize; the appropriate organizational form depends upon the human and business situation facing the firm.

Although it is easy to find flaws in the ideas of early management writers, it has not been easy for managers to discard the so-called principles that those early authors laid down: the span of control should be between six and nine subordinates; one boss for each man; authority must equal responsibility; the line does, the staff advises; and so on. Such statements have become part of the folklore of management, at least in the United States. Thus, many managers, when confronted with an organization-design decision, intuitively fall back on those early ideas. This tendency is not surprising, because the simplicity of the ideas gives them an intuitive appeal. It is a dangerous practice, however, because the principles ignore the infinitely varied and complex human, technological, and market conditions for which organizations must be designed. Recent managerial experience and organizational research have provided an approach for thinking about organization-design issues.

THE CONTINGENCY APPROACH

This approach emphasizes that the characteristics of an organization are contingent upon the nature of the environment in which it operates, the tasks that members must perform to accomplish the firm's strategy in this environment, and the psychological characteristics of the members.

DEFINITIONS

To be more precise, four terms need to be defined:

1. *Environment* refers to the forces and objects outside the firm with which its members must deal to achieve the organization's purposes. These may include competitors' actions, customer requirements, financial constraints, scientific and technological knowledge, and so forth. They are information that must be considered when making and implementing decisions inside the organization.
2. The organization's *strategy* is a statement of the environment(s) or business(es) relevant to the organization, the purposes of the organization within that context, and the specific means for achieving these goals. In a sense, then, the strategy defines the environment in which an organization operates. A strategy may be explicitly stated and even written down, or it may simply exist as an implicit idea based on the actions of the organization's managers over time.
3. *Task* refers to the activities that members must perform to achieve the organization's strategic goals in a particular environment. This reading generally uses task to refer to the activities of a particular set of individuals in dealing with the environment— that is, the task of a sales unit or the task of division general managers, and so on.
4. *Psychological characteristics of members* are the factors in an individual's personality that lead him or her to behave in a consistent fashion over time. It is not necessary to debate here whether these should be labeled needs, values, interests, or all three. The important point is that different individuals have different characteristics, and organization-design decisions must take these differences into account.

EXHIBIT 1
The Concept of Fit

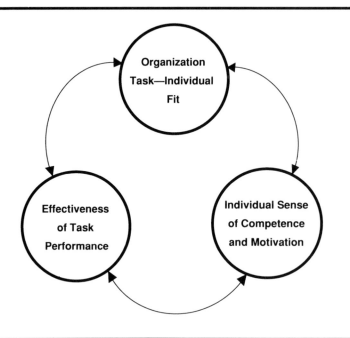

FIT

The first concept to be discussed is *fit*. If there is a three-way fit between an individual's psychological makeup, the nature of the task he or she is performing, and the organization design, the individual will be motivated to perform that task effectively (see *Exhibit 1*). Two examples illustrate the point:

> A production supervisor, such as a foreman, has a job in which his activities are well defined by the technology and product specifications. In essence, his job is to make sure that his subordinates do the same thing well today that they did yesterday. In this sense, the work is highly certain and predictable. Results here can be measured on a daily or possibly more frequent basis. This supervisor has a bachelor's degree in industrial engineering. He likes working with his supervisor, who provides him with clear directions and enjoys his frequent contact with other supervisors. The routine and the predictable work are also attractive to him. In fact, he is upset by too much ambiguity and confusion. For this manager and his colleagues, given their predictable tasks, an organization design that emphasizes tight control and procedures is appropriate. Tight spans of supervisory control, well-specified operating procedures, and specific and frequent measurement of results make sense in this situation.

A group leader in a research laboratory in a consumer products company has a job where results are *not* highly predictable. Her subordinates, who are Ph.D.'s, and their technical assistants are working on problems in food technology. Their progress is hard to measure, and meaningful results may take months or even years. The group leader, who is a Ph.D. biochemist herself, shares many personal characteristics with her subordinates. She likes to work with minimum direction and maximum autonomy and prefers to work alone. She also likes to work on complex and uncertain problems. These tasks and personal characteristics require an organization design with a wide span of management control and with infrequent measurement in relation to general progress. Detailed procedures, job descriptions, and so forth, are out of place here because so little of the work can be preprogrammed. An organization design that has these characteristics should be motivating for this technical manager, as well as her subordinates, and it should also lead to effective results for the laboratory.

As these two examples and *Exhibit 1* illustrate, the three-way fit produces two outcomes—motivation for the individual and performance for the organization. These results are interconnected. As individuals perform their jobs well and receive feedback, their needs for mastery are satisfied, which in turn encourages them to continue working to maintain these positive feelings. There is also a fit required between individual and task characteristics—that is, to be effective, the individual must have interests, skills, and needs that are consistent with the work required. One way to ensure this fit is to select personnel using criteria based on the need for fit. Finally, such a fit also enables the individual to achieve other goals, such as earning money, having an appropriate amount of social contact, and so on.

DIFFERENTIATION

The concept of *differentiation* follows from the notion of fit. It can be defined as the differences among the several units of the organization in organization design and members' behavior. These differences arise because of the variety of tasks various organizational units must accomplish to cope successfully with the firm's total environment. As each unit's organization is designed to achieve a fit with its task and the characteristics of its members, it becomes differentiated from the other units with their own tasks and members; how differentiated depends upon how similar the tasks of the several units are and how similar their members are.

Differentiation has positive and negative consequences simultaneously. Because differentiation stems from the fact that the several units in an organization have achieved a fit with their task and human situations—and this leads to motivation and performance—some degree of differentiation is critical to the effective functioning of organizations. This differentiation among units results from differences in their tasks or members and is therefore appropriate. (Differentiation, of course, can result from management action that is inappropriate to the units' tasks and members; in this instance, too much differentiation might be a liability.) The negative side is that the greater the differentiation among units of an organization, the more difficult it becomes for members to communicate across unit boundaries. For example, a factory supervisor may have great difficulty dealing with a laboratory group leader: One thinks in the short term, the other in the long term; one is concerned with costs and productivity, the other with innovation and knowledge building; one believes in an orderly unambiguous organization, the other relishes ambiguity and autonomy, and so on. Such differences between the individuals impede their understanding of each other's concerns and will probably lead to conflicting ideas about how to solve mutual problems. The fact that differentiation leads to such conflicts is connected to the third concept—integration.

INTEGRATION

Integration is the state of collaboration among organizational units. Integration usually manifests itself in specific conversations between the representatives of units. In thinking about organization design, however, it is possible and necessary to generalize about the state of integration required for the organization to be effective. To do this, we must consider various aspects of integration.

The first is the number and patterns of units that must collaborate to achieve the organization's purposes. In *Organizations in Action*, Thompson identifies one useful way to think about these patterns (see *Exhibit 2*).[1] *Pooled integration* is the simplest pattern, where the various subsidiary units (B,C,D) have no need for integration among themselves. They are all linked together only through their contact with the central unit (A). A holding company typically has this pattern of integration among its major components. *Sequential integration* is where each unit must integrate its activities only with units that precede or follow it in a process or task flow. Factories with work flow across departmental lines provide a good example of this pattern. *Reciprocal integration* means that collaboration is in both directions among all units; for this reason it is the most complex pattern. The integration required among marketing, research development, and manufacturing personnel in developing new products often follows this pattern. As one moves from the pooled to the sequential to the reciprocal pattern, achieving integration becomes more difficult.

---

1. James D. Thompson, *Organizations in Action* (New York: McGraw-Hill, 1967), p. 54.

EXHIBIT 2
Patterns of Required Integration

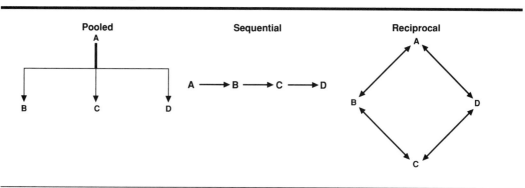

Note: These diagrams are the author's concepts based on Thompson's ideas.

Although this way of thinking can be useful, it is important to recognize that in the real world these pure types rarely exist.

A second aspect of integration is the frequency with which collaboration is necessary. For example, a sales organization usually requires a relatively low frequency of integration among various regional units. The national sales manager may want the regional units to collaborate occasionally in a national program, but generally the regions conduct their sales activity independently. In contrast, consider the electronic engineering and power systems departments of an aerospace firm that is trying to develop a new rocket for NASA. These engineers need to be in frequent contact across departmental lines to make certain that the components they are each developing for the total system will work in harmony.

Closely connected to the frequency of integration required is the importance of achieving it, but these two aspects are not necessarily identical. For example, the sales and manufacturing departments may meet only semiannually to develop an integrated production schedule, but the success of this decision making may have a major impact on the firm's success.

Another aspect of integration that must be considered in thinking about design issues is the certainty and predictability of the information involved. If the matters requiring integration are highly predictable, the managers can use plans and preestablished procedures to achieve integration; then, only infrequent face-to-face contact is necessary. If the information is uncertain and complex, however, more face-to-face contact, as in the aerospace example, may be necessary.

As the examples suggest, organization design can be used to achieve integration in several ways—for example, management hierarchy, regular meetings, coordinating roles such as product or program managers, incentives that reward integrative behavior, and so forth. Managers do have a choice about how much they orient their organization-design decisions to

EXHIBIT 3
Factors Affecting the Difficulty of Achieving Integration

DIFFICULTY OF ACHIEVING INTEGRATION	LOW	HIGH
Degree of differentiation	Small	Large
Number of units requiring integration	Few	Many
Pattern of integration	Pooled	Reciprocal
Frequency of integration required	Infrequent contact	Frequent contact daily or more often
Importance of integration to organization's strategy	Marginal	Critical
Complexity and uncertainty of information	Simple and highly certain	Uncertain and highly complex

achieving integration. To understand the appropriate choice, they need to answer the questions suggested by the factors just discussed:

- How many units require integration and in what pattern?
- How frequently is integration required?
- How important is integration among any set of these units?
- How complex and uncertain is the information being considered?

As *Exhibit 3* illustrates, the answers to these questions can be a rough guide to the difficulty of achieving the necessary integration and therefore to the proper mix of design elements devoted to achieving integration. For example, the more units that must be integrated and the more they are involved in reciprocal relationships, the more the organization design must provide mechanisms, such as teams' coordinating roles, plans, and so forth, to facilitate this integration. This, of course, assumes that achieving integration is important to the company's goals. Whether face-to-face contact or a formal planning scheme is the better means to achieve this integration depends on the complexity and uncertainty of the information that must be handled. If the data are relatively simple and predictable, a predetermined plan might be suitable, but if the information is more uncertain and complex, the organization design will have to provide mechanisms for integration that encourage more face-to-face contact.

Exhibit 3 includes one other issue that affects the difficulty of achieving integration—the degree of differentiation among units. The more differentiated the units are, the more difficult it becomes to achieve integration. Because differentiation and integration have this complex relationship, they are important to understand as tools for thinking about organization design. Together with the concept of fit, they give managers powerful tools for analyzing specific organization-design problems.

In dealing with organization-design issues, the suggested approach involves three steps. First, managers need to use the concepts of fit, differentiation, and integration to understand and assess what the environmental and human situations require of their organization. Second, they need to make design choices to meet these requirements. Finally, they need to consider how to implement necessary changes. (This reading emphasizes the first two steps.)

To illustrate how managers can deal with these diagnosis and design steps, the reading next focuses on some of the design issues managers face at two organizational levels—the functional unit and the single-business organization. This choice of examples is made for two reasons. First, most business firms build their organizations from functional units up. Second, managers at each of these levels of organization are faced with different design problems; therefore, the conceptual ideas discussed earlier must be applied somewhat differently at each level.

——— ORGANIZATION DESIGN IN FUNCTIONAL UNITS

Functional units are not only the basic building blocks on which larger organizations are constructed but also the home of most organization members. In fact, functional units are so pervasive in the business world that they have become institutionalized in the specialized training offered by business administration and engineering schools. Undergraduates and graduate students become specialized; they enter organizations with careers in these function areas as their goals. The average employee may spend an entire career in one function, but even the rising star on a fast career track to general management is likely to spend his or her early years in one function.

EMPLOYEE MOTIVATION

One of the major issues facing a functional manager is to create an organization design that provides a viable set of rewards for subordinates, including compensation and benefits, professionally stimulating work, and meaningful career opportunities. The concept of fit among task and individual characteristics and organization design is a useful way of thinking about how to create a psychological contract acceptable to both the members of a functional unit and the employing organization. It is a potent tool to ensure that the measurements, rewards, and structure of a unit together accomplish the goal of motivating employees to work toward the purposes of the firm.

DIVISION OF WORK

Another important aspect of achieving such a fit is the question of job design and the division of work within the function. Earlier, the reading examined job-design issues as they affected motivation. Job-design decisions also have an important bearing upon a second design goal—creating a cost-effective organization. For example, designing sales jobs to reduce an employee's travel time creates a more cost-effective organization; similarly, adding a second and/or third shift to a factory can ensure maximum machine utilization and lower manufacturing costs. As these examples suggest, the subunits within a function can be created on the basis of occupational specialty, time of workday, or territorial responsibility. The major rationale for occupationally based units is to maintain a differentiated home for specialized expertise. The major reason for creating geographic or temporal subunits is to bring down costs, as the prior examples also suggest.

Regardless of the basis for dividing work, differences in behavior and organization design may exist among members of different subunits within the same function. For example, the controller's function in many firms is made up of a diverse set of subunits, ranging from computer programmers and systems analysts dealing with relatively complex problem-solving tasks to clerical operations with routine and repetitive tasks. Similarly, within a manufacturing function, there are not only line manufacturing supervisors but also industrial engineers, production schedulers, quality control specialists, computer programmers, and so on. Although these different specialists all share some goals and behavior patterns common to their function, they may also have differentiated approaches to these issues, and their tasks and personal characteristics may make a somewhat different organization design appropriate. As functional managers consider the issues of job design and division of work, they must think about achieving a fit that will lead to a motivated and efficient organization. They should also consider how this will affect differentiation within the function and the potential difficulties of achieving integration.

ACHIEVING INTEGRATION

Such difficulties can be managed if the organization design provides a way of achieving integration among those subunits that must work together. Within most functional units the primary device for this is the management hierarchy. The hierarchy is not only a mechanism for directing the activities of individual subunits but also a means for achieving the integration required within the function. For example, if the industrial engineers and mechanical engineers within a manufacturing function have difficulty agreeing upon the production methods for a new product, their common boss would be expected to resolve the dispute.

EXHIBIT 4
Stratified Structures—Product Divisions' Structure

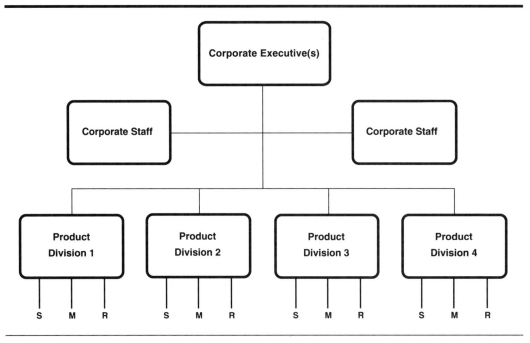

Note: S = Sales; M = Manufacturing; R = Research

Although the management hierarchy is usually capable of handling the information and decision making required for integration within a function, occasionally other means are also necessary. These other means must be employed when the difficulty of achieving integration becomes too great for the hierarchy to manage. This can happen because of any combination of factors mentioned previously and displayed in *Exhibit 4*. Perhaps the hierarchy must be supplemented because the impending start-up of a new-generation computer has increased the need for integrating a controller function; therefore, a special project team is created. Perhaps new pricing regulations make it necessary to create a new position of pricing coordinator on the national sales manager's staff to coordinate pricing decisions across all regions.

APPLYING DESIGN TOOLS

The specific issues that have been discussed show how the three major concepts of fit, differentiation, and integration can help functional managers think about the design problems they face. Before considering how these concepts can be used in single-business organizations, two other points, which apply to all that follows, should be emphasized:

1. *Creative invention can be very useful in solving design problems once they are understood.* An example of this is a factory that experienced difficulty with the integration of its three shifts, each of which operated seven days a week. The management tried all the standard remedies—log books, foremen meeting before the shift, the factory superintendent visiting all shifts, and so on. A more careful review revealed that the problem had arisen because foremen did not have time to grasp the situation on the production floor and then direct their workers. The solution was to put the foremen on a schedule that brought them into work early and allowed them to leave two hours before their subordinates. Thus, the foremen were on a schedule that allowed them time to grasp the problems of the prior shift before a new shift started. This simple scheduling change enabled the management hierarchy to become an effective integrative tool. Such a solution may seem obvious in retrospect; however, given the number of plants that have struggled with the same issue, it is clear that creativity is a necessary ingredient in handling such organizational issues.

2. *The design elements of structure, measurement, and reward need to be thought of as a package.* Changes in one may have to be accompanied by changes in others. If they do not give consistent signals to employees about what management expects, the results can range from confusion to chaos.

——— ORGANIZING THE SINGLE BUSINESS

Single-business organizations are those organizations that are in one primary business. They may be the product division of a multibusiness firm, or they may be a financially independent enterprise. In either case, the organization consists of a set of interrelated functional units whose activities aim at developing, producing, and marketing a common product or service to a particular set of customers.

DIFFERENTIATION OF FUNCTIONS

Because each function needs to achieve a fit with its particular task and human situation to be effective, one of the design issues facing managers of single-business organizations is to maintain and/or achieve the degree of differentiation among functions that is appropriate to their several tasks. If functional managers are allowed to handle the design issues facing them without interference, the necessary differentiation might be a natural consequence of their independent actions. The general managers of single businesses often feel compelled, however, to limit such independent action on the part of their functional managers for two reasons. First, they become concerned about the issue of equity and fairness across functions. Second, uniformity and standardization of practice make it easier for the manager to administer and be certain of what is happening in the organization. Although it is important to maintain a sense of equity in compensation and benefits among various occupational groups in an organization, too much emphasis on standardization can reduce differentiation and harm the organization's effectiveness.

For example, higher management often imposes the same rigid working hours on research scientists that are required of production personnel. Coming and going on time makes sense when the personnel involved are operating a highly interdependent factory where scheduling is critical. In the case of research scientists, however, their problem solving and creative activity does not adhere to any schedule. Thus, the focus on regular hours is inappropriate, and the scientist may become annoyed with such unnecessary rules. The scientist's attitude is then expressed: "If they are so insistent about my being here on time, I'll be sure to quit on time. No more working at night or on weekends to finish experiments." This example is typical of the problems managers can encounter if they do not understand the importance of maintaining differentiation among the functions in their business.

The amount of differentiation required among functions will vary, of course, depending upon the nature of the organization's environment. In most cases, however, the differences across functions will be much more pronounced than those within functional units. The following examples may help the reader understand the range of such cross-functional differentiation.

As an example of minimal differentiation required across functions, consider a firm in the business of producing corrugated containers—boxes or cartons. Only two major functions are involved in this business—selling and manufacturing—and they have different goals: The sales personnel focus on prompt customer delivery and high quality as well as on competitive pricing. The manufacturing managers are concerned with low cost and want to avoid quality and delivery requirements that adversely affect costs. Beyond these varying goals, there are few differences between these two functions. Both are focused on short-term results and are involved in relatively predictable tasks. Thus, a more formal organization design and directive leadership would make sense for both production and sales personnel.

Next, consider a business requiring greater amounts of differentiation—a basic plastic materials business (polystyrene, polyvinylchloride). Here the functions are sales, manufacturing, research, and technical services. The manufacturing personnel, like those in the previous example, are primarily concerned with near-term results in the areas of cost and quality. But because they are operating a more capital-intensive technology, they may be less flexible than their counterparts in other businesses about interrupting product flows or process changes. The sales personnel are concerned with customer relations, competitive pricing, and so forth. Again, their focus is largely on the near term, but they also attend to the future and new products. The technical-services group focuses on providing technical service to the customer in support of the sales force, and thus is concerned with immediate results. At the same time, this group has responsibility for applied research aimed at developing new and improved products and processes; therefore, it also may be focused on the long term. Members of the research unit are involved in more basic research—understanding the structure of the materials and using this understanding to improve existing products and processes and develop entirely new ones. Their time horizon may extend over several years. These units will need widely different organization designs and management styles, which allow each to match its highly differentiated task and members.

These examples demonstrate the range of differences that occurs in different businesses. Although they are all drawn from manufacturing enterprises, similar examples can be found in service industries. Of course, these illustrations are overly simplified. The financial function has been omitted, for example, even though any joint decision involving the functions mentioned will also involve discussions of the appropriate allocation of financial resources.

Using these concepts, managers need to look at each function and determine what characteristics of organization design and behavior are necessary for that function to be performed, and what will motivate the individuals who work in it. From this analysis of each function, the pattern of differences among the functions will become apparent. These questions can be useful when making such an analysis:

- What are the goals that each unit should focus upon?
- What is the time period for each unit to obtain some definitive feedback about the results of its members' efforts?
- What pattern of leadership behavior is appropriate for each unit?
- What pattern of structure, measurement, and rewards will encourage behavior directed toward the goals, time horizon, and other aspects of the unit's task, while also meeting the members' personal expectations?

If managers concern themselves with how much differentiation they want to encourage in their organizations, they will find a useful starting point in considering these questions.

GROUPING FUNCTIONS

The issue of differentiation has an important bearing on another design issue that concerns the manager of a single-business organization—what functions to group together under a common manager. In thinking about this issue, like other design questions, managers often tend to rely on conventional wisdom and/or to emulate what other firms do.

Managers consider grouping activities together for two essential reasons: either they want to get similar activities under a manager who understands them or they want to place activities requiring close integration under one manager to facilitate collaboration. Therefore, the concepts of differentiation and integration can be helpful tools for such decisions. Just by being aware of these concepts, one is forced to ask, "Am I considering grouping these activities together because I want to encourage integration among them, or because they are similar (not highly differentiated), or for both reasons?" If the answer to this question is "both," clearly the decision to group activities together is a sound and easy one. However, if the answer to all parts of the question is "no," one does not want to group the units together.

The more frequently encountered and more difficult problems occur with low differentiation and few requirements for integration or with a large amount of differentiation but also a great need for integration. Here, the organizational designer must make a trade-off about what is to be accomplished. Should the hierarchy be used to achieve integration in this instance? Or should similar activities be grouped together, perhaps facilitating their differentiation from other activities and certainly easing the job of supervisors? In the latter instance, other means would have to be found to achieve integration between the units grouped together and those parts of the organization with which they needed to be integrated.

INTEGRATION OF FUNCTIONS

Using the hierarchy is only one of several means to facilitate integration. Even in single-business units, however, the hierarchy is often the fundamental mechanism for achieving integration. In fact, in businesses with low differentiation and relatively simple integrative requirements (e.g., the corrugated container business), the hierarchy may be the only integrative device necessary. As the requirements for differentiation and integration become greater, however, other integrative devices must supplement the hierarchy. Thus, greater differentiation and a more complex requirement for integration might call for product managers who play an integrating role, and/or a management committee made up of the heads of the several functions.

As with most organization-design issues, there are no simple rules to define what mix of integrative devices is appropriate in a particular situation. Thinking of an organization as a system for taking in bits of information from the business environment and then combining the information to reach and implement decisions can help clarify when certain integrative devices will be appropriate. From this perspective, a review of the factors identified in *Exhibit 3* that affect the difficulty of achieving integration follows:

- Number of units requiring integration,
- Pattern of integration (pooled, sequential, reciprocal),
- Frequency of integration required,
- Importance of integration to organizational results,
- Complexity and uncertainty of information,
- Degree of differentiation.

All of these factors, in theory, could affect the flow of information among functional units, which in turn would affect the difficulty of achieving integration. The more problems these factors suggest, the more supplements the hierarchy will need. Just what form these other devices should take will depend upon the frequency of integration required and the complexity and uncertainty of information. Both of these factors, which frequently are closely connected, will have important influence on whether face-to-face contact is necessary to achieve integration or whether predetermined plans, schedules, and so on, once arrived at, will allow units to operate in an integrated fashion without such direct contact.

There are two types of integrative devices that allow face-to-face contact:

1. *Integrating roles* include positions such as product managers, brand managers, program managers, project managers, account executives, and so on. A major responsibility of these employees is to integrate their activities with those of their peers in other functions. Such an approach makes sense when the information is sufficiently certain and simple so that one person can achieve integration with his or her counterparts on a one-to-one basis.
2. *Cross-functional groups of managers* may be labeled teams, committees, task forces, and so on. Such groups make sense as integrative devices when the information is so complex and uncertain that representatives from the several functions need to sit down together to understand each other's data and reach joint decisions.

Individual integrating positions and cross-functional groups are not mutually exclusive. In some organizations, where the requirements for integration are particularly acute, both devices are used simultaneously. Another reason for establishing a cross-functional group, in addition to an individual integrating role, is that the group builds commitment to the success of integrated effort among the functional specialists assigned to it. For example, artists, copywriters, market information specialists, and others assigned to an account team in an advertising agency become concerned with the overall goals of serving the account, in addition to their own particular functions.

Besides these structural devices, reward and measurement practices can also be utilized to encourage integration. The most common example of this is tying the compensation of functional executives not just to the results of their function but also to business profits.

——— CULTURE AND LEADERSHIP STYLE—THE MISSING LINKS

This reading has used three major concepts—fit, differentiation, and integration—to consider organization-design issues. The focus has been on designing organizations to be consistent with the environment, strategy, and tasks of the organization on the one hand, and the members' characteristics on the other. Such an emphasis is consistent with the present state of knowledge (see *Exhibit 5*). The clearest knowledge exists about the relationship between these factors and organization design. Even in these areas, however, knowledge is limited, and there is still room for managerial judgment and creativity. The shaded area of *Exhibit 5* includes two other major factors about which much less is known but which also must be considered if the organization-design variables are to have their intended impact on members' behavior. In a broad sense the organization design must also be compatible with the style and experience of top management and the company's traditional culture.

MANAGERIAL STYLE

The manager in charge of any organization has a persistent style of leading others with which he or she is comfortable and presumably has had some success. This style is a direct outgrowth of his or her personality and is not likely to be altered easily. Therefore, although there has been little

EXHIBIT 5
Organization-Design Considerations

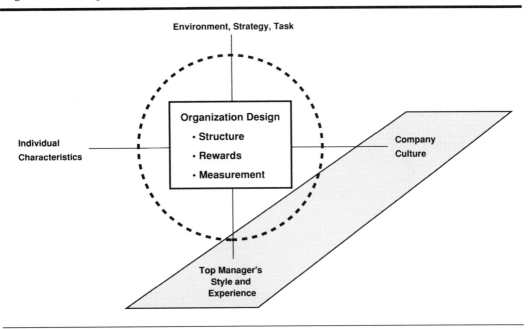

Note: Shading indicates those areas where little systematic research has been completed.

systematic research in this direction, it seems clear that whatever design choices are made must not only fit the external conditions facing the firm and the expectations of its members but also be consistent with the style of the person(s) leading the organization.

The organization design must also be compatible with the experience and talents of the top manager(s). The organization designer should start by using the ideas discussed here; however, the resulting design may have to be altered to accommodate the strengths and weaknesses of available top managers. This approach is preferable to the alternative—tailoring the organization to the style and experience of top managers with little or no regard to the other factors.

COMPANY CULTURE

Company culture consists of the shared implicit and explicit assumptions that members make about what is legitimate behavior in the organization. For example, some organizations place a value on being self-reliant and making decisions alone. Others place more emphasis on holding meetings to reach decisions. As a manager in one such company said, "Here, work is attending meetings." The culture includes not only such norms about how people should behave but also the values they are expected to hold. Further, it includes general understandings about the corporate pecking order. For example, in some companies the technical-research people have high status and influence, while in other firms the product manager reigns. Similarly, in some companies the president of a particular division is understood to be the heir apparent to the presidency of the corporation, and others treat him or her with the deference due such status. Although such expectations are not written down in procedure manuals or drawn on organization charts, they can have an important impact on people's behavior in a particular company. Some researchers have labeled such sets of expectations as the informal organization. This label may suggest, however, that there is a choice between the formal and informal organization and that these organizations are in opposition. In fact, the opposite appears to be true: Organization-design changes can have more immediate impact if they are consistent with the existing culture. Of course, changing the organization design in a way that is inconsistent with the existing culture can be one way of trying to bring about change in an organization's culture, but such efforts are likely to encounter stiff resistance from organization members.

—— DISCUSSION QUESTIONS

1. The reading describes the concept of fit and gives two examples of successful fits. Give an example from your personal experience of a fit that worked. Give an example of one that didn't work. Using the examples in the reading as a guide, provide specifics about what worked and didn't work for you.

2. Name other design issues besides those discussed in this reading that you feel are important or that you have experienced in your professional life.

3. Are design issues always under the control of management? Give an example from your experience in which design was not responsive to management. What are the implications of such situations for company managers?

4. Identify social issues that have surfaced in the 1980s that have had an effect on organization design. Suggest others that may surface in the 1990s.

22   Organization Design: Fashion or Fit?

HENRY MINTZBERG

This reading argues that many organizations fall into one of five configurations: the simple structure, the machine bureaucracy, the professional bureaucracy, the divisionalized form, and the adhocracy. When managers and organizational designers try to mix and match elements of different configurations, they may emerge with a misfit—an organization whose design is no longer suited to its task. The key to organizational design, says the author, is consistency and coherence. He concludes by considering how the five configurations can serve as tools in diagnosing organizational problems.

- **A** conglomerate takes over a small manufacturer and tries to impose budgets, plans, organizational charts, and untold systems on it. The result: declining sales and product innovation—and near bankruptcy—until the division managers buy back the company and promptly turn it around.
- Consultants make constant offers to introduce the latest management techniques. Years ago LRP and OD were in style, later QWL and ZBB.
- A government sends in its analysts to rationalize, standardize, and formalize citywide school systems, hospitals, and welfare agencies. The results are devastating.

These incidents suggest that a great many problems in organizational design stem from the assumption that organizations are all alike: mere collections of component parts to which elements of structure can be added and deleted at will, a sort of organizational bazaar.

The opposite assumption is that effective organizations achieve a coherence among their component parts, that they do not change one element without considering the consequences to all of the others. Spans of control, degrees of job enlargement, forms of decentralization, planning systems, and matrix structure should not be picked and chosen at random. Rather, they should be selected according to internally consistent groupings. And these groupings should be consistent with the situation of the organization—its age and size, the conditions of the industry in which it operates, and its production technology. In essence, like all phenomena from atoms to stars, the characteristics of organizations fall into natural clusters, or *configurations*. When these characteristics are mismatched—when the wrong ones are put together—the organization does not function effectively, does not achieve a natural harmony.

If managers are to design effective organizations, they need to pay attention to the fit.

If we look at the enormous amount of research on organizational structuring in light of this idea, a lot of the confusion falls away and a striking convergence is revealed. Specifically, five clear configurations emerge that are distinct in their structures, in the situations in which they are found, and even in the periods of history in which they first developed. They are the simple structure, machine bureaucracy, professional bureaucracy, divisionalized form, and adhocracy.

——— DERIVING THE CONFIGURATIONS

An adaptable picture of five component parts (see part A, *Exhibit 1*) descibes the five configurations. An organization begins with a person who has an idea. This person forms the strategic apex or top management. He or she hires people to do the basic work of the organization, in what can be called the operating core. As the organization grows, it acquires intermediate managers between the chief executive and the workers. These managers form the middle line. The organization may also find that it needs two kinds of staff personnel. First are the analysts who design systems concerned with the formal planning and control of the work; they form the technostructure. Second is the support staff, providing indirect services to the rest of the organization—everything from the cafeteria and the mail room to the public relations department and the legal counsel.

These five parts together make the whole organization (see part B, *Exhibit 1*). Not all organizations need all of these parts. Some use few and are simple, others combine all in rather complex ways. The central purpose of structure is to coordinate the work divided in a variety of ways; how that coordination is achieved—by whom and with what—dictates what the organization will look like (see *Exhibit 2*):

- In the simplest case, coordination is achieved at the strategic apex by direct supervision—the chief executive officer gives the orders. The configuration called *simple structure* emerges, with a minimum of staff and middle line.
- When coordination depends on the *standardization of work*, an organization's entire administrative structure—especially its technostructure, which designs the standards—needs to be elaborated. This gives rise to the configuration called *machine bureaucracy*.
- When, instead, coordination is through the *standardization of skills* of its employees, the organization needs highly trained professionals in its operating core and considerable support staff to back them up. Neither its technostructure nor its middle line is very elaborate. The resulting configuration is called *professional bureaucracy*.

- Organizations will sometimes be divided into parallel operating units, allowing autonomy to the middle-line managers of each, with coordination achieved through the *standardization of outputs* (including performance) of these units. The configuration called the *divisionalized form* emerges.
- Finally, the most complex organizations engage sophisticated specialists, especially in their support staffs, and require them to combine their efforts in project teams coordinated by *mutual adjustment.* This results in the *adhocracy* configuration, in which line and staff as well as a number of other distinctions tend to break down.

The elements of structure include the following:

- Specialization of tasks.
- Formalization of procedures (job descriptions, rules, and so forth).

EXHIBIT 1
The Five Basic Parts of the Organization

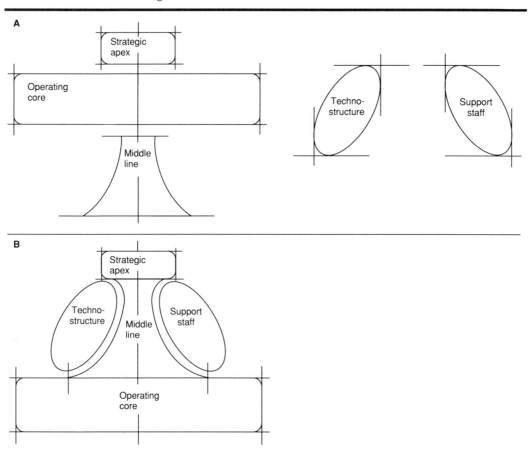

- Formal training and indoctrination required for the job.
- Grouping of units (notably by function performed or market served).
- Size of each of the units (that is, the span of control of its manager).
- Action planning and performance control systems.
- Liaison devices, such as task forces, integrating managers, and matrix structure.

EXHIBIT 2
The Five Configurations

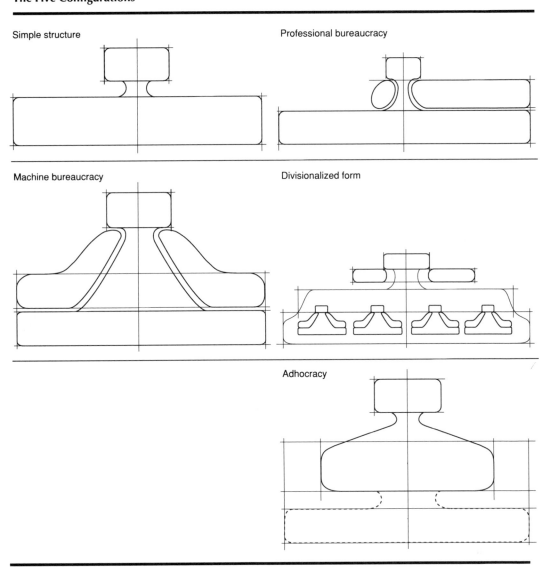

Simple structure

Professional bureaucracy

Machine bureaucracy

Divisionalized form

Adhocracy

- Delegation of power down the chain of authority (called *vertical decentralization*).
- Delegation of power out from that chain of authority to nonmanagers (called *horizontal decentralization*).

I describe how all of these elements cluster into the five configurations in the sections that follow and summarize these descriptions in *Exhibit 3*, where all the elements are displayed in relation to the configurations. In the discussion of each configuration, it should become evident how all of its elements of structure and situation form themselves into a tightly knit, highly cohesive package. No one element determines the others; rather, all are locked together to form an integrated system.

SIMPLE STRUCTURE

The name tells all, and *Exhibit 2* shows all. The structure is simple—not much more than one large unit consisting of one or a few top managers and a group of operators who do the basic work. The most common simple structure is, of course, the classic entrepreneurial company.

What characterizes this configuration above all is what is missing. Little of its behavior is standardized or formalized, and minimal use is made of planning, training, or the liaison devices. The absence of standardization means that the organization has little need for staff analysts. Few middle-line managers are hired because so much of the coordination is achieved at the strategic apex by direct supervision. That is where the real power in this configuration lies. Even the support staff is minimized to keep the structure lean and flexible—simple structures would rather buy than make.

The organization must be flexible because it operates in a dynamic environment, often by choice because that is the one place it can outmaneuver the bureaucracies. And that environment must be simple, as must the organization's system of production, so that the chief executive can retain highly centralized control. In turn, centralized control makes the simple structure ideal for rapid, flexible innovation, at least of the simple kind. With the right chief executive, the organization can turn on a dime and run circles around the slower-moving bureaucracies. That is why so much innovation comes not from the giant mass producers but from small entrepreneurial companies. But where complex forms of innovation are required, the simple structure falters because of its centralization. As we shall see, that kind of innovation requires another configuration, one that engages highly trained specialists and gives them considerable power.

Simple structures are often young and small, in part because aging and growth encourage them to bureaucratize but also because their vulnerability causes many of them to fail. They never get a chance to grow old and large. One heart attack can wipe them out—as can a chief executive so obsessed with innovation that he or she forgets about the operations, or vice versa. The corporate landscape is littered with the wrecks of entrepreneurial companies whose leaders encouraged growth and mass production yet could never accept the transition to bureaucratic forms of structure that these changes required. Yet some simple structures have managed to grow very large under the tight control of clever, autocratic leaders, the most famous example being the Ford Motor Co. in the later years of its founder.

Almost all organizations begin their lives as simple structures, granting their founding chief executives considerable latitude to set them up. And most revert to simple structure—no matter how large or what other configuration normally fits their needs—when they face extreme pressure or hostility in their environment. In other words, systems and procedures are suspended as power reverts to the chief executive to give him or her a chance to set things right.

The heyday of the simple structure probably occurred during the period of the great American trusts, late in the nineteenth century. Although today less in fashion and to many a relic of more autocratic times, the simple structure remains a widespread and necessary configuration—for building up most new organizations and for operating those in simple, dynamic environments and those facing extreme, hostile pressures.

MACHINE BUREAUCRACY

Just as the simple structure is prevalent in pre-Industrial Revolution industries such as agriculture, the machine bureaucracy is the offspring of industrialization, with its emphasis on the standardization of work for coordination and its resulting low-skilled, highly specialized jobs. *Exhibit 2* shows that, in contrast to simple structure, the machine bureaucracy elaborates its administration. First, it requires many analysts to design and maintain its systems of standardization—notably those that formalize its behaviors and plan its actions. And by virtue of the organization's dependence on these systems, these analysts gain a degree of informal power, which results in a certain amount of horizontal decentralization.

A large hierarchy emerges in the middle line to oversee the specialized work of the operating core and to keep the lid on conflicts that inevitably result from the rigid departmentalization, as well as from the alienation that often goes with routine, circumscribed jobs. That middle-line hierarchy is usually structured on a functional basis all the way up to the top, where the real power of coordination lies. In other words, machine bureaucracy tends to be centralized in the vertical sense—formal power is concentrated at the top.

And why the large support staff shown in *Exhibit 2*? Because machine bureaucracies depend on stability to function (change interrupts the smooth functioning of the system), they tend not only to seek out stable environments in which to function but also to stabilize the environments they find themselves in. One way they do this is to envelop within their structures all of the support services possible, ones that simple structures prefer to buy. For the same reason they also tend to integrate vertically—to become their own suppliers and

EXHIBIT 3
Dimensions of the Five Configurations

	SIMPLE STRUCTURE	*MACHINE BUREAUCRACY*	*PROFESSIONAL BUREAUCRACY*	*DIVISIONAL-IZED FORM*	*ADHOCRACY*
Key Means of Coordination	Direct supervision	Standardization of work	Standardization of skills	Standardization of outputs	Mutual adjustment
Key Part of Organization	Strategic apex	Technostructure	Operating core	Middle line	Support staff (with operating core in operating adhocracy)
STRUCTURAL ELEMENTS					
Specialization of Jobs	Little specialization	*Much horizontal and vertical specialization*	*Much horizontal specialization*	Some horizontal and vertical specialization (between divisions and headquarters)	*Much horizontal specialization*
Training and Indoctrination	Little training and indoctrination	Little training and indoctrination	*Much training and indoctrination*	Some training and indoctrination (of division managers)	Much training
Formalization of Behavior— Bureaucratic/ Organic	*Little formalization— organic*	*Much formalization— bureaucratic*	*Little formalization— bureaucratic*	Much formalization (within divisions)— bureaucratic	*Little formalization— organic*
Grouping	Usually functional	*Usually functional*	Functional and market	*Market*	Functional and market
Unit Size	Wide	Wide at bottom, narrow elsewhere	Wide at bottom, narrow elsewhere	Wide at top	Narrow throughout
Planning and Control Systems	Little planning and control	Action planning	Little planning and control	*Much performance control*	Limited action planning (esp. in administrative adhocracy)
Liaison Devices	Few liaison devices	Few liaison devices	Liaison devices in administration	Few liaison devices	*Many liaison devices throughout*
Decentraliza-tion	*Centralization*	*Limited horizontal decentralization*	*Horizontal and vertical decentralization*	*Limited vertical decentralization*	*Selective decentralization*

EXHIBIT 3
Dimensions of the Five Configurations (Continued)

	SIMPLE STRUCTURE	MACHINE BUREAUCRACY	PROFESSIONAL BUREAUCRACY	DIVISIONAL-IZED FORM	ADHOCRACY
SITUATIONAL ELEMENTS					
Age and Size	Typically young and small	Typically old and large	Varies	Typically old and very large	Typically young (operating adhocracy)
Technical System	Simple, not regulating	Regulating but not automated, not very complex	Not regulating or complex	Divisible, otherwise like machine bureacracy	Very complex, often automated (in administrative adhocracy), not regulating or complex (in operating adhocracy)
Environment	Simple and dynamic; sometimes hostile	Simple and stable	Complex and stable	Relatively simple and stable; diversified markets (esp. products and services)	Complex and dynamic; sometimes disparate (in administrative adhocracy)
Power	Chief executive control; often owner man-aged; not fashionable	Technocratic and external control; not fashionable	Professional operator control; fashionable	Middle-line control; fashionable (esp. in industry)	Expert control; very fashionable

Note: Italic type in columns 2–6 indicates key design parameters.

customers. And that of course causes many machine bureaucracies to grow very large. So we see the two-sided effect of size here: size drives the organization to bureaucratize ("We do that every day; let's standardize it!"), but bureaucracy also encourages the organization to grow larger. Aging also encourages this configuration; the organization standardizes its work because "we've done that before."

To enable the top managers to maintain centralized control, both the environment and the production system of the machine bureaucracy must be fairly simple. In fact, machine bureaucracies fit most naturally with mass production, where the products, processes, and distribution systems are usually rationalized and thus easy to comprehend. And so machine bureaucracy is most common among large, mature mass-production companies, such as automobile manufacturers, as well as the largest of the established providers of mass services, such as insurance companies and railroads. Thus McDonald's is a classic example of this configuration—achieving enormous success in its simple industry through meticulous standardization.

Because external controls encourage bureaucratization and centralization, this configuration is often assumed by organizations that are tightly controlled from the outside. That is why government agencies, which are subject to many such controls, tend to be driven toward the machine bureaucracy structure regardless of their other conditions.

The problems of the machine bureaucracy are legendary—dull and repetitive work, alienated employees, obsession with control (of markets as well as workers), massive size, and inadaptability. These are machines suited to specific purposes, not to adapting to new ones. For all of these reasons, the machine bureaucracy is no longer fashionable. Bureaucracy has become a dirty word. Yet this is the configuration that gets the products out cheaply and efficiently. And here too there can be a sense of harmony, as in the Swiss railroad system whose trains depart as the second hand sweeps past the twelve.

In a society consumed by its appetite for mass-produced goods, dependent on consistency in so many spheres (how else to deliver millions of pieces of mail every day?), and unable to automate a great many of its routine jobs, machine bureaucracy remains indispensable—and probably the most prevalent of the five configurations.

PROFESSIONAL BUREAUCRACY

This bureaucratic configuration relies on the standardization of skills rather than work processes or outputs for its coordination and so emerges as dramatically different from the machine bureaucracy. It is the structure hospitals, universities, and accounting firms tend most often to favor. Most important, because it relies for its operating tasks on trained professionals—skilled people who must be given considerable control over their own work—the organization surrenders a good deal of its power not only to the professionals themselves but also to the associations and institutions that select and train them in the first place. As a result, the structure emerges as very decentralized; power over many decisions, both operating and strategic, flows all the way down the hierarchy to the professionals of the operating core. For them this is the most democratic structure of all.

Because the operating procedures, although complex, are rather standardized—taking out appendixes in a hospital, teaching the American Motors case in a business school, doing an audit in an accounting firm—each professional can work independently of his or her colleagues, with the assurance that much of the necessary coordination will be effected automatically through standardization of skills. Thus a colleague of mine observed a five-hour open-heart operation in which the surgeon and anesthesiologist never exchanged a single word!

As can be seen in *Exhibit 2*, above the operating core we find a unique structure. Since the main standardization occurs as a result of training that takes place outside the professional bureaucracy, a technostructure is hardly needed. And because the professionals work independently, the size of operating units can be very large, and so few first-line managers are needed. (I work in a business school where 55 professors report directly to one dean.) Yet even those few managers, and those above them, do little direct supervision; much of their time is spent linking their units to the broader environment, notably to ensure adequate financing. Thus to become a top manager in a consulting firm is to become a salesperson.

On the other hand, the support staff is typically very large in order to back up the high-priced professionals. But that staff does a very different kind of work—much of it the simple and routine jobs that the professionals shed. As a result, parallel hierarchies emerge in the professional bureaucracy—one democratic with bottom-up power for the professionals, a second autocratic with top-down control for the support staff.

Professional bureaucracy is most effective for organizations that find themselves in stable yet complex environments. Complexity requires that decision-making power be decentralized to highly trained individuals, and stability enables these individuals to apply standardized skills and so to work with a good deal of autonomy. To further ensure that autonomy, the production system must be neither highly regulating, complex, nor automated. Surgeons use their scalpels and editors their pencils; both must be sharp but are otherwise simple instruments that allow their users considerable freedom in performing their complex work.

Standardization is the great strength as well as the great weakness of professional bureaucracy. That is what enables the professionals to perfect their skills and so achieve great efficiency and effectiveness. But that same standardization raises problems of adaptability. This is not a structure to innovate but one to perfect what is already known. Thus, so long as the environment is stable, the professional bureaucracy does its job well. It identifies the needs of its clients and offers a set of standardized programs to serve them. In other words, pigeonholing is its great forte; change messes up the pigeonholes. New needs arise that fall between or across the slots, and the standard programs no longer apply. Another configuration is required.

Professional bureaucracy, a product of the middle years of this century, is a highly fashionable structure for two reasons. First, it is very democratic, at least for its professional workers. And second, it offers them considerable autonomy, freeing the professionals even from the need to coordinate closely with each other. To release themselves from the close control of administrators and analysts, not to mention their own colleagues, many people seek to have themselves declared "professional"—and thereby turn their organizations into professional bureaucracies.

DIVISIONALIZED FORM

Like the professional bureaucracy, the divisionalized form is not so much an integrated organization as a set of rather independent entities joined together by a loose administrative overlay. But whereas those entities of the professional bureaucracy are individuals—professionals in the operating core—in the divisionalized form they are units in the middle line, called divisions.

The divisionalized form differs from the other four configurations in one central respect: it is not a complete but a partial structure, superimposed on others. Those others are in the divisions, each of which is driven toward machine bureaucracy.

An organization divisionalizes for one reason above all—because its product lines are diversified. (And that tends to happen most often in the largest and most mature organizations, those that have run out of opportunities or become stalled in their traditional markets.) Such diversification encourages the organization to create a market-based unit, or division, for each distinct product line (as indicated in *Exhibit 2*) and to grant considerable autonomy to each division to run its own business.

That autonomy notwithstanding, divisionalization does *not* amount to decentralization, although the terms are often equated with each other. Decentralization is an expression of the dispersal of decision-making power in an organization. Divisionalization refers to a structure of semiautonomous market-based units. A divisionalized structure in which the managers at the heads of these units retain the lion's share of the power is far more centralized than many functional structures where large numbers of specialists get involved in the making of important decisions.

In fact, the most famous example of divisionalization involved centralization. Alfred Sloan adopted the divisionalized form at General Motors to *reduce* the power of the different units, to integrate the holding company William Durant had put together. That kind of centralization appears to have continued to the point where the automotive units in some ways seem closer to functional marketing departments than true divisions.[1]

But how does top management maintain a semblance of control over the divisions? Some direct supervision is used—headquarters managers visit the divisions periodically and authorize some of their more important decisions. But too much of that interferes with the necessary autonomy of the divisions. So headquarters relies on performance control systems or, in other words, on the standardization of outputs. It leaves the operating details to the divisions and exercises control by measuring their performance periodically. And to design these control systems, headquarters creates a small technostructure. It

---

1. *See* Leonard Wrigley, "Diversification and Divisional Autonomy," DBA thesis, Harvard Business School, 1970.

also establishes a small central support staff to provide certain services common to the divisions (such as legal counsel and external relations).

This performance control system has an interesting effect on the internal structure of the division. First, the division is treated as a single integrated entity with one consistent, standardized, and quantifiable set of goals. Those goals tend to get translated down the line into more and more specific subgoals and, eventually, work standards. In other words, they encourage the bureaucratization of structure. And second, headquarters tends to impose its standards through the managers of the divisions, whom it holds responsible for divisional performance. That tends to result in centralization within the divisions. And centralization coupled with bureaucratization gives machine bureaucracy. That is the structure that works best in the divisions.

Simple structures and adhocracies make poor divisions because they abhor standards—they operate in dynamic environments where standards of any kind are difficult to establish. And professional bureaucracies are not logically treated as integrated entities, nor can their goals be easily quantified. (How does one measure cure in a psychiatric ward or knowledge generated in a university?)

This conclusion is, of course, consistent with the earlier argument that external control (in this case, from headquarters) pushes an organization toward machine bureaucracy. The point is invariably illustrated when a conglomerate takes over an entrepreneurial company and imposes a lot of bureaucratic systems and standards on its simple structure.

The divisionalized form was created to solve the problem of adaptability in machine bureaucracy. By overlaying another level of administration that could add and subtract divisions, the organization found a way to adapt itself to new conditions and to spread its risk. But there is another side to these arguments. Some evidence suggests that the control systems of these structures discourage risk taking and innovation, that the division head who must justify his or her performance every month is not free to experiment the way the independent entrepreneur is.[2]

Moreover, to spread risk is to spread the consequences of that risk; a disaster in one division can pull down the entire organization. Indeed, the fear of this is what elicits the direct control of major new investments, which is what often discourages ambitious innovation. Finally, the divisionalized form does not solve the problem of adaptability of machine bureaucracy, it merely deflects it. When a division goes sour, all that headquarters seems able to do is change the management (as an independent board of directors would do) or divest it. From society's point of view, the problem remains.

Finally, from a social perspective, the divisionalized form raises a number of serious issues. By enabling organizations to grow very large, it leads to the concentration of a great deal of economic power in a few hands. And there is some evidence that it sometimes encourages that power to be

---

2. *See* Wrigley, "Diversification and Divisional Autonomy."

used irresponsibly. By emphasizing the measurement of performance as its means of control, a bias arises in favor of those divisional goals that can be operationalized, which usually means the economic ones, not the social ones. That the division is driven by such measures to be socially unresponsive would not seem inappropriate—for the business of the corporation is, after all, economic.

The problem is that in big businesses (where the divisionalized form is prevalent) every strategic decision has social as well as economic consequences. When the screws of the performance control system are turned tight, the division managers, in order to achieve the results expected of them, are driven to ignore the social consequences of their decisions. At that point, *un*responsive behavior becomes *ir*responsible.[3]

The divisionalized structure has become very fashionable in the past few decades, having spread in pure or modified form through most of the *Fortune* "500" in a series of waves and then into European companies. It has also become fashionable in the nonbusiness sector in the guise of "multiversities," large hospital systems, unions, and government itself. And yet it seems fundamentally ill suited to these sectors for two reasons.

First, the success of the divisionalized form depends on goals that can be measured. But outside the business sector, goals are often social in nature and nonquantifiable. The result of performance control, then, is an inappropriate displacement of social goals by economic ones.

Second, the divisions often require structures other than machine bureaucracy. The professionals in the multiversities, for example, often balk at the technocratic controls and the top-down decision making that tends to accompany external control of their campuses. In other words, the divisionalized form can be a misfit just as can any of the other configurations.

ADHOCRACY

None of the structures discussed so far suits the industries of our age—industries such as aerospace, petrochemicals, think-tank consulting, and filmmaking. These organizations need above all to innovate in complex ways. The bureaucratic structures are too inflexible, and the simple structure is too centralized. These industries require "project structures" that fuse experts drawn from different specialties into smoothly functioning creative teams. Hence they tend to favor our fifth configuration, adhocracy, a structure of interacting project teams.

Adhocracy is the most difficult of the five configurations to describe because it is both complex and nonstandardized. Indeed, adhocracy contra-

---

3. For a full discussion of the problems of implementing social goals in the divisionalized form, *see* Robert W. Ackerman, *The Social Challenge to Business* (Cambridge: Harvard University Press, 1975).

dicts much of what we accept on faith in organizations—consistency in output, control by administrators, unity of command, strategy emanating from the top. It is a tremendously fluid structure, in which power is constantly shifting and coordination and control are by mutual adjustment through the informal communication and interaction of competent experts. Moreover, adhocracy is the newest of the five configurations, the one researchers have had the least chance to study. Yet it is emerging as a key structural configuration, one that deserves a good deal of consideration.

These comments notwithstanding, adhocracy is a no less coherent configuration than any of the others. Like the professional bureaucracy, adhocracy relies on trained and specialized experts to get the bulk of its work done. But in its case, the experts must work together to create new things instead of working apart to perfect established skills. Hence, for coordination adhocracy must rely extensively on mutual adjustment, which it encourages by the use of the liaison devices—integrating managers, task forces, and matrix structure.

In professional bureaucracy, the experts are concentrated in the operating core, where much of the power lies. But in adhocracy, they tend to be dispersed throughout the structure according to the decisions they make—in the operating core, middle line, technostructure, strategic apex, and especially support staff. Thus, whereas in each of the other configurations power is more or less concentrated, in adhocracy it is distributed unevenly. It flows, not according to authority or status but to wherever the experts needed for a particular decision happen to be found.

Managers abound in the adhocracy—functional managers, project managers, integrating managers. This results in narrow "spans of control" by conventional measures. That is not a reflection of control but of the small size of the project teams. The managers of adhocracy do not control in the conventional sense of direct supervision; typically, they are experts too who take their place alongside the others in the teams, concerned especially with linking the different teams together.

As can be seen in *Exhibit 2,* many of the distinctions of conventional structure disappear in the adhocracy. With power based on expertise instead of authority, the line/staff distinction evaporates. And with power distributed throughout the structure, the distinction between the strategic apex and the rest of the structure also blurs. In a project structure, strategy is not formulated from above and then implemented lower down; rather, it evolves by virtue of the multitude of decisions made for the projects themselves. In other words, the adhocracy is continually developing its strategy as it accepts and works out new projects, the creative results of which can never be predicted. And so everyone who gets involved in the project work—and in the adhocracy that can mean virtually everyone—becomes a strategy maker.

There are two basic types of adhocracy, operating and administrative. The *operating* adhocracy carries out innovative projects directly on behalf of its clients, usually under contract, as in a creative advertising agency, a think-tank consulting firm, a manufacturer of engineering prototypes. Professional bureaucracies work in some of these industries too, but with a different orientation. The operating adhocracy treats each client problem as a unique one to be solved in creative fashion; the professional bureaucracy pigeonholes it so that it can provide a standard skill.

For example, there are some consulting firms that tailor their solutions to the client's order and others that sell standard packages off the rack. When the latter fits, it proves much cheaper. When it does not, the money is wasted. In one case, the experts must cooperate with each other in organic structures to innovate; in the other, they can apply their standard skills autonomously in bureaucratic structures.

In the operating adhocracy, the operating and administrative work blend into a single effort. That is, the organization cannot easily separate the planning and design of the operating work—in other words, the project—from its actual execution. So another classic distinction disappears. As shown above the dotted lines in *Exhibit 2*, the organization emerges as an organic mass in which line managers, staff, and operating experts all work together on project teams in ever-shifting relationships.

The *administrative* adhocracy undertakes projects on its own behalf, as in a space agency—NASA, for example, during the Apollo era—or a producer of electronic components. In this type of adhocracy, in contrast to the other, we find a sharp separation of the administrative from the operating work—the latter shown by the dotted lines in *Exhibit 2*. This results in a two-part structure. The administrative component carries out the innovative design work, combining line managers and staff experts in project teams. And the operating component, which puts the results into production, is separated or "truncated" so that its need for standardization will not interfere with the project work.

Sometimes the operations are contracted out altogether. Other times, they are set up in independent structures, as in the printing function in newspapers. And when the operations of an organization are highly automated, the same effect takes place naturally. The operations essentially run themselves, while the administrative component tends to adopt a project orientation concerned with change and innovation, with bringing new facilities on line. Note also the effects of automation—a reduction in the need for rules, since these are built right into the machinery, and a blurring of the line/staff distinction, since control becomes a question more of expertise than authority. What does it mean to supervise a machine? Thus the effect of automation is to reduce the degree of machine bureaucracy in the administration and to drive it toward administrative adhocracy.

Both kinds of adhocracy are commonly found in environments that are complex as well as dynamic. These are the two conditions that call for sophisticated innovation, which requires the cooperative efforts of many different kinds of experts. In the case of administrative adhocracy, the production system is also typically complex and, as noted, often automated. These production systems create the need for highly skilled support staffers, who must be given a good deal of power over technical decisions.

For its part, the operating adhocracy is often associated with young organizations. For one thing, with no standard products or services, organizations that use it tend to be highly vulnerable, and many of them disappear at an early age. For another, age drives these organizations toward bureaucracy, as the employees themselves age and tend to seek an escape from the instability of the structure and its environment. The innovative consulting firm converges on a few of its most successful projects, packages them into standard skills, and settles down to life as a professional bureaucracy; the manufacturer of prototypes hits on a hot product and becomes a machine bureaucracy to mass-produce it.

But not all adhocracies make such a transition. Some endure as they are, continuing to innovate over long periods of time. We see this, for example, in studies of the National Film Board of Canada, famous since the 1940s for its creativity in both films and the techniques of filmmaking.

Finally, fashion is a factor associated with adhocracy. This is clearly the structure of our age, prevalent in almost every industry that has grown up since World War II (and none I can think of established before that time). Every characteristic of adhocracy is very much in vogue today—expertise, organic structure, project teams and task forces, diffused power, matrix structure, sophisticated and often automated production systems, youth, and dynamic, complex environments. Adhocracy is the only one of the five configurations that combines some sense of democracy with an absence of bureaucracy.

Yet, like all the others, this configuration too has its limitations. Adhocracy in some sense achieves its effectiveness through inefficiency. It is inundated with managers and costly liaison devices for communication; nothing ever seems to get done without everyone talking to everyone else. Ambiguity abounds, giving rise to all sorts of conflicts and political pressures. Adhocracy can do no ordinary thing well. But it is extraordinary at innovation.

—— CONFIGURATIONS AS A DIAGNOSTIC TOOL

What in fact are these configurations? Are they (1) abstract ideals, (2) real-life structures, one of which an organization had better use if it is to survive, or (3) building blocks for more complex structures? In some sense, the answer is a qualified yes in all three cases. These are certainly abstract ideals, simplifications of the complex world of structure. Yet the abstract ideal can come to life too. Every organization experiences the five pulls that underlie these configurations: the pull to centralize by the top management, the pull to formalize by the technostructure, the pull to professionalize by the operators, the pull to balkanize by the managers of the middle line, and the pull to collaborate by the support staff.

Where one pull dominates—where the conditions favor it above all—then the organization will tend to organize itself close to one of the configurations. I have cited examples of this throughout my discussion—the entrepreneurial company, the hamburger chain, the university, the conglomerate, the space agency.

But one pull does not always dominate; two may have to exist in balance. Symphony orchestras engage highly trained specialists who perfect their skills, as do the operators in professional bureaucracy. But their efforts must be tightly coordinated, hence, the reliance on the direct supervision of a leader—a conductor—as in simple structure. Thus a hybrid of the two configurations emerges that is eminently sensible for the symphony orchestra (even if it does generate a good deal of conflict between leader and operators).

Likewise, we have companies that are diversified around a central theme that creates linkages among their different product lines. As a result, they continually experience the pull to separate, as in the divisionalized form, and also integrate, as in machine bureaucracy or perhaps adhocracy. And what configuration should we impute to an IBM? Clearly, there is too much going on in many giant organizations to describe them as one configuration or another. But the framework of the five configurations can still help us to understand how their different parts are organized and fit together—or refuse to.

The point is that managers can improve their organizational designs by considering the different pulls their organizations experience and the configurations toward which they are drawn. In other words, this set of five configurations can serve as an effective tool in diagnosing the problems of organizational design, especially those of the *fit* among component parts. Let us consider four basic forms of misfit to show how managers can use the set of configurations as a diagnostic tool.

ARE THE INTERNAL ELEMENTS CONSISTENT?

Management that grabs at every structural innovation that comes along may be doing its organization great harm. It risks going off in all directions: yesterday long-range planning to pin managers down, today Outward Bound to open them up. Quality of working life programs as well as all those fashionable features of adhocracy—integrating managers, matrix structure, and the like—have exemplary aims: to create more satisfying work conditions and to increase the flexibility of the organization. But are they appropriate for a machine bureaucracy? Do enlarged jobs really fit with the requirements of the mass production of automobiles? Can the jobs ever be made large enough to really satisfy the workers—and the cost-conscious customers?

I believe that in the fashionable world of organizational design, fit remains an important characteristic. The *hautes structurières* of New York—the consulting firms that seek to bring the latest in structural fashion to their clients—would do well to pay a great deal more attention to that fit. Machine bureaucracy functions best when its reporting relationships are sharply defined and its operating core staffed with workers who prefer routine and stability. The nature of the work in this configuration—managerial as well as operating—is rooted in the reality of mass production, in the costs of manual labor compared with those of automated machines, and in the size and age of the organization.

Until we are prepared to change our whole way of living—for example, to pay more for handcrafted instead of mass-produced products and so to consume less—we would do better to spend our time trying not to convert our machine bureaucracies into something else but to ensure that they work effectively as the bureaucracies they are meant to be. Organizations, like individuals, can avoid identity crises by deciding what it is they wish to be and then pursuing it with a healthy obsession.

ARE THE EXTERNAL CONTROLS FUNCTIONAL?

An organization may achieve its own internal consistency and then have it destroyed by the imposition of external controls. The typical effect of those controls is to drive the organization toward machine bureaucracy. In other words, it is the simple structures, professional bureaucracies, and adhocracies that suffer most from such controls. Two cases of this seem rampant in our society: one is the takeover of small, private companies by larger divisionalized ones, making bureaucracies of entrepreneurial ventures; the other is the tendency for governments to assume increasingly direct control of what used to be more independent organizations—public school systems, hospitals, universities, and social welfare agencies.

As organizations are taken over in these ways—brought into the hierarchies of other organizations—two things happen. They become centralized and formalized.[4] In other words, they are driven toward machine bureaucracy. Government administrators assume that just a little more formal control will bring this callous hospital or that weak school in line. Yet the cure—even when the symptoms are understood—is often worse than the disease. The worst way to correct deficiencies in professional work is through control by technocratic standards. Professional bureaucracies cannot be managed like machines.

In the school system, such standards imposed from outside the classroom serve only to discourage the competent teachers, not to improve the weak ones. The performance of teachers—as that of all other professionals—depends

---

4. There is a good deal of evidence for this conclusion. *See,* for example, Yitzhak Samuel and Bilha F. Mannheim, "A Multidimensional Approach Toward a Typology of Bureacracy," *Administrative Science Quarterly* (June 1970): 216; Edward A. Holdaway, John F. Newberry, David J. Hickson, and R. Peter Heron, "Dimensions of Organizations in Complex Societies: The Educational Sector," *Administrative Science Quarterly* (March 1975): 37; D. S. Pugh, D. J. Hickson, C. R. Hinnings, and C. Turner, "The Context of Organization Structures," *Administrative Science Quarterly* (March 1969): 91; Bernard C. Reimann, "On the Dimensions of Bureaucratic Structure: An Empirical Reappraisal," *Administrative Science Quarterly* (December 1973): 462.

primarily on their skills and training. Retraining or, more likely, replacing them is the basic means to improvement.

For almost a century now, the management literature—from time study through operations research to long-range planning—has promoted machine bureaucracy as the "one best way." That assumption is false; it is one way among a number suited to only certain conditions.

IS THERE A PART THAT DOES NOT FIT?

Sometimes an organization's management, recognizing the need for internal consistency, hives off a part in need of special treatment—establishes it in a pocket off in a corner to be left alone. But the problem all too often is that it is not left alone. The research laboratory may be built out in the country, far from the managers and analysts who run the machine bureaucracy back home. But the distance is only physical.

Standards have a long administrative reach: it is difficult to corner off a small component and pretend that it will not be influenced by the rest. Each organization, not to mention each configuration, develops its own norms, traditions, beliefs—in other words, its own ideology. And that permeates every part of it. Unless there is a rough balance among opposing forces—as in the symphony orchestra—the prevailing ideology will tend to dominate. That is why adhocracies need especially tolerant controllers, just as machine bureaucracies must usually scale down their expectations for their research laboratories.

IS THE RIGHT STRUCTURE IN THE WRONG SITUATION?

Some organizations do indeed achieve and maintain an internal consistency. But then they find that it is designed for an environment the organization is no longer in. To have a nice, neat machine bureaucracy in a dynamic industry calling for constant innovation or, alternately, a flexible adhocracy in a stable industry calling for minimum cost makes no sense. Remember that these are configurations of situation as well as structure. Indeed, the very notion of configuration is that all the elements interact in a system. One element does not cause another; instead, all influence each other interactively. Structure is no more designed to fit the situation than situation is selected to fit the structure.

The way to deal with the right structure in the wrong environment may be to change the environment, not the structure. Often, in fact, it is far easier to shift industries or retreat to a suitable niche in an industry than to undo a cohesive structure. Thus the entrepreneur goes after a new, dynamic environment when the old one stabilizes and the bureaucracies begin to move in. When a situation changes suddenly—as it did for oil companies some years ago—a rapid change in situation or structure would seem to be mandatory. But what of a gradual change in situation? How should the organization adapt, for example, when its long-stable markets slowly become dynamic?

Essentially, the organization has two choices. It can adapt continuously to the environment at the expense of internal consistency—that is, steadily redesign its structure to maintain external fit. Or it can maintain internal consistency at the expense of a gradually worsening fit with its environment, at least until the fit becomes so bad that it must undergo sudden structural redesign to achieve a new internally consistent configuration. In other words, the choice is between evolution and revolution, between perpetual mild adaptation, which favors external fit over time, and infrequent major realignment, which favors internal consistency over time.

In his research on configuration, Danny Miller found that effective companies usually opt for revolution. Forced to decide whether to spend most of their time with a good external fit or with an established internal consistency, they choose consistency and put up with brief periods of severe disruption to realign the fit occasionally. It is better, apparently, to maintain at least partial configuration than none at all. Miller called this process, appropriately enough, a "quantum" theory of structural change.[5]

—— FIT OVER FASHION

To conclude, consistency, coherence, and fit—harmony—are critical factors in organization design, but they come at a price. An organization cannot be all things to all people. It should do what it does well and suffer the consequences. Be an efficient machine bureaucracy where that is appropriate and do not pretend to be highly adaptive. Or be an adaptive adhocracy and do not pretend to be highly efficient. Or create some new configuration to suit its own needs. The point is not really *which* configuration; it is *that* configuration is achieved.

---

5. Danny Miller, *Revolution and Evolution: A Quantum View of Organizational Adaptation,* working paper, McGill University, 1980.

—— DISCUSSION QUESTIONS

1. Are there other organizational configurations besides the five described in this reading? If so, are they specific to an industry or a particular type of work?
2. What is the relationship between a firm's configuration and its strategy?
3. Choose a company that you know well and identify its configuration, according to Mintzberg's types. Does the configuration seem coherent? If not, how would you modify it to achieve "fit"?
4. The author refers to "the pull to centralize by . . . top management." What are the advantages of centralization? How would you balance this tendency in order to achieve a harmonious configuration?

Functional Integration: Getting All the Troops to Work Together   23

BENSON P. SHAPIRO

This reading begins by explaining the need for functional integration. The focus then turns to cross-functional coordination and the six approaches necessary to achieve it: a strategy, the structural hierarchy, the management processes and systems, the management information system, the informal social systems and culture, and the selection and promotion of employees. The author next examines the four groups of people, in addition to the functional line manager, who contribute to interfunctional coordination: the staff engineering group, cost accounting experts, human resource managers, and top-level general management. The reading concludes with a word about the total system versus "the home team."

Sales is customer oriented. Marketing takes a more long-term perspective, but operations, by definition, needs to keep all systems functioning. Manufacturing wants the product out the door; engineering's interest is to develop new technologically exciting and sophisticated products; but field service wants to keep the customers' earlier purchases running. These line-operating departments, or functions, have different objectives, perspectives, and even cultures. Furthermore, each group, the manager and the workers, often has its own predilections, interests, and culture. It is no wonder that the functions have problems with integration.

Many company decisions can be made only with input from several different functional departments. Making good product-design decisions, for example, requires information from all departments. More important, the inputs cannot be provided sequentially but must occur simultaneously and interactively. Otherwise, effective trade-offs and compromises cannot be made. Engineering may overdesign a product in response to its understanding of customer desires as reported by sales. Had sales recognized the added cost of the attributes it requested, its request might have been different. Desires and constraints, approaches and solutions must constantly be discussed and shared; however, this sharing is difficult to achieve.

The following section describes where interfunctional coordination is most needed. The next section discusses the nature of coordination. The final sections present six different approaches to achieving integration and four adjudicating roles.

——— WHERE IS FUNCTIONAL INTEGRATION NEEDED?

The importance of functional integration is determined by the company and decisions it makes. Some companies need more functional integration than others; unfortunately, functional integration is generally hardest to achieve in the companies that need it most.

The more dispersed the functions, the harder they are to integrate. The dispersion may be organizational: Different functions may reside in different operating units, profit centers, or divisions. It is more difficult to coordinate a sales function in one division with an engineering function in another than to coordinate sales and engineering functions in the same division. Each time a jurisdictional boundary is crossed, a "coordination toll" must be paid. If the two functional departments to be coordinated are in the same jurisdiction, there is only one boundary to cross and one toll to pay.

Geographical distance, even within the same country, but particularly across national borders, adds to problems in functional integration. National cultural differences amplify functional cultural differences; suspicion festers and miscommunication becomes more routine. The logistics of communication also grow more difficult with geographical distance as travel becomes harder and time-zone differences disrupt easy telephone communication. Although voice and electronic mail can help, problems can still remain.

Functional integration is also more problematic in larger companies. There are larger groups of people, and more of them, to pull together and generally greater differences in culture and location among groups. Communication becomes exponentially more difficult as the number of people or groups who must communicate grows.

A company's products and markets have a significant influence on the importance of functional integration. Specialty products require much more intimate cross-functional integration than do commodity products.[1] By and large, specialities depend upon value-added features provided through close functional cooperation. Commodity businesses are generally run in a "lean-and-mean" fashion, which does not require as much cross-functional integration. In addition, the tight margins of a commodity business cannot generously provide for cross-functional integration.

Companies that market systems or programs whose different parts must work together also need exceptional levels of cross-functional integration. A company selling capital equipment through a program based on strong

---

1. For further information, *see* "Specialties vs. Commodities: The Battle for Profit Margins," Harvard Business School Case No. 9-587-120.

service must effectively coordinate engineering, manufacturing, and field service around repair problems and their avoidance; it must also coordinate sales, with its close customer contact, and service so that the customer feels important. A system works only if the individual products are designed in conjunction with one another; however, sometimes parts are engineered and/or produced in different operating units or divisions. Thus, simultaneous cross-division and cross-functional integration is needed for the sales function in one division to talk to the engineering function in another.

Finally, service companies often require more interdepartmental coordination than do product companies because the customer is especially dependent upon it. Many services are performed in the presence of the customer and under intense time pressure. Interfunctional conflicts can become obvious and have immediate and dramatic competitive impact.

By their nature some decisions demand much more functional integration than others. Product-policy decisions are among those requiring the highest degree of functional integration. Each function has a major impact upon product-policy decisions, and as mentioned earlier, the impact must be simultaneous rather than sequential.

Functional integration is also needed in the order-fulfillment cycle, which consists of sales forecasting and capacity planning, shipping, installation, service and repair, and billing. The receipt and entry of the order alone often involves three different functions: Sales accepts the order and hands it over to the customer-service department for credit checking and entry, which hands it over to operations and/or production for scheduling. To make the organizational situation even more complex, the customer-service function, which sits amidst all the order activity, is typically low in status and powerless. Particular activities or parts of the order-fulfillment cycle have traditionally generated exceptional interdepartmental conflict.

Effective cross-functional communication about short-term promotions, for example, can make policies and programs much more profitable. If the sales department, either alone or with the marketing department, schedules promotions without considering their impact on warehouse and factory, the promotions will be suboptimal. Because promotions create a short-term peak in sales, often preceded and followed by an exaggerated trough, they must be carefully integrated into inventory management and production scheduling. Ideally, promotions enable the warehouse and factory to be more efficient, not less. If planning is done separately by function, the promotions will invariably result in lower profits.

Cross-functional policies regarding human resources management will also decrease cross-functional jealousy and backbiting and make transferring individuals across functional jurisdictions easier. When each function designs its own personnel policies, cultural differences among various functions are highlighted. Of course, optimal corporatewide personnel policies can be created only with input from the various functions.

Finally, all operating functions should participate in developing a basic company strategy. If the marketing function mandates that the company will have a strong field-service component in its basic strategy, the field-service department must be committed to developing such strength. A major flaw in the design, and certainly the execution, of many corporate strategies is the absence of some critical functions that have insufficient power to take part in strategy development. Field service and other, generally smaller, functions, such as customer service or order processing, are examples. Few top-level executives spend much thought on order processing; yet ineffective order processing can destroy the finest corporate strategy and waste the work of even the best sales force.

To summarize, interfunctional coordination is most important for specialty products and companies that market systems and programs. Interfunctional coordination is most difficult to achieve in large and/or dispersed companies. It is most necessary when dealing with product-policy decisions, the order-fulfillment cycle, basic human resources policies, and broad corporate strategies.

——— TYPES OF CROSS-FUNCTIONAL COORDINATION

Most people intuitively divide coordination in a company into vertical and horizontal components. The vertical component involves issues such as leadership and delegation. That form of coordination, though important, is not the subject of this reading.

The horizontal dimension of integration and communication typically includes lateral cross-functional aspects. How can sales and manufacturing work together to develop a delivery schedule for a particular customer, for example? Most of this reading will focus on lateral, cross-functional communication and integration. This type of coordination, though simple on paper, is difficult to accomplish.

Other types of cross-functional integration are generally even harder to accomplish. One type is diagonal cross-functional integration, where the people involved reside simultaneously in different functions and at different levels in the organization. This type of coordination involves both vertical communication and lateral cross-functioning. Diagonal communication is fairly common in companies operating in specialty markets. The regional sales manager, for example, might need to talk to a bench engineer, a shipping clerk, or a field-service technician about a particular problem. Or, an engineering manager may want to discuss a particular customer need with a salesperson. The vertical component of the communication makes coordination even harder than when the communication is merely cross-functional.

Finally, as briefly described above, some cross-functional communication must also break through other jurisdictional barriers—for example, those of integrated or partially integrated profit centers or such boundaries as country operating units. Sometimes the communication might involve people in the same function who reside in different divisions—for example, two engineers from different divisions who design components that eventually combine into a finished product or system. At other times, communication is both cross-functional and cross-jurisdictional. One division might provide field-service or technical support for the products of another division. Here, the salesperson of the receiving division might make requests of the technicians of the supplying division. Situations also arise in which the communication is cross-functional, cross-jurisdictional, or cross-divisional, and vertical. For example, an engineering or a manufacturing manager in one division might need to talk with salespeople in other divisions.

In general, as the number of jurisdictional boundaries and the number of levels to be crossed increase so does the difficulty of coordination. The next section shows how cross-functional coordination can be achieved.

THE SIX APPROACHES

There are six approaches to achieving cross-functional coordination:

- A unified, holistic strategy;
- The organization structure or management hierarchy;
- Management processes and systems;
- The management information system and related electronic communications systems;
- The informal social systems and culture;
- The selection and promotion of employees.

These six approaches appear in every organization. Every company has a strategy, for example—even if it is not explicit or written. The point here, however, is to harness these approaches to improve interjurisdictional coordination. These approaches can be "mixed and matched," but this can only happen by first making clear and explicit the role of each in interjurisdictional coordination and the relationships among the six. Most managers, because of their proclivities or experience, tend to depend more heavily on one of the six approaches than on the others. Making trade-offs among the different approaches and among specific elements within each approach is important. In addition, integrating the six approaches is imperative; otherwise, each approach will contribute to interfunctional warfare rather than to coordination. If all the troops are to pull in the same direction, the approaches involved must also pull in the same direction.

A UNIFIED HOLISTIC STRATEGY

Functional coordination begins with the creation of "marching orders" and priorities—the unified, holistic strategy. The strategy is unified because all functional departments have contributed to its development; it is holistic because it describes each major function's role. The strategy document becomes a map as the company threads its way through the competitive maze. Each department understands its role in the strategy and how that role relates to its sibling functions. An effective document offers clear priorities so that all functions share a set of objectives. Limitations, such as resource constraint, should also be clear. Thus, each department has reasonable expectations about what it will receive from other departments and what human and financial resources will be available.

An effective strategy document begins with a clear statement about which customers the unit will serve and which customer needs it will address. These customers and needs will be ranked; because different customers have varying and often conflicting needs, the document must include priorities. When the customer base is small, individual customers can be dealt with. When the customer base is large, the customers must be considered in groups or segments. Customer selection and ranking is probably the most important single topic in the strategy document. It defines the nature and importance of functional contributions and, if done properly, leads to a sustainable, distinctive competitive competence.

The customer-ranking process, though difficult, must be part of a strategy session; it certainly will never happen in the day-to-day hassle of customer complaints, salesperson and customer service lobbying, production and operations expediting, and logistics and service limitations. The clearer the strategy, the customer priorities, and the functional expectations are, the more likely each function will be able to understand and respond to its strategic role.

The strategy-development process offers a wonderful opportunity for introducing and inculcating the concept of cross-jurisdictional coordination. A deliberate, open, and equitable process can be emblematic of the day-to-day interaction to be encouraged among functions, divisions, and other jurisdictions.

Finally, the strategy document and the development process are the foundation upon which to build appropriate organizational structure and management processes. If the strategy is fuzzy, the remaining coordination approaches will not be well defined and smoothly applied.

THE ORGANIZATION STRUCTURE OR MANAGEMENT HIERARCHY

The traditional approach to functional-integration issues has been the organization structure. The organization structure is indeed a powerful way to encourage integration—so powerful that it creates problems. People are anxious about organization structure because it defines their position, and in fact, has a large impact on their power and privileges. The issue thus becomes highly political, with each person typically supporting the structure that most benefits him or her. In addition, executives often analyze structures for the impact they have on organizational protégés and friends. This, combined with the apparent clarity and symbolism of the organization structure, often leads to heated discussions and battles. Consultants may be brought in to provide a more balanced and unbiased view. Though they sometimes succeed, other times they too become embroiled in political wars.

The stakes in structuring decisions have been particularly high in the past because restructuring was relatively infrequent. People feared they would be placed in a permanent, or close to permanent, position. Lately, as companies more frequently restructure in response to more rapid environmental and strategic change, the stakes seem lower, the battles less intense, and companies somewhat more supple organizationally.

In addition to its political sensitivity, the organization structure has major limitations as an integrating mechanism. A natural adversarial relationship seems to exist between specialization and integration, for example. The more specialized two functions are, the more difficult it is to integrate them. Specialization will be necessary when a function must create its own culture, skills, or operating methods that are substantially different from those of other functions. Thus, in many senses, specialization is good. However, increased specialization almost invariably leads to decreased integration.[2]

Nonetheless, the management hierarchy can be used to improve functional coordination. One approach is to separate large functional organizations into parts, which are then grouped around products, geography, or divisions. Thus, a company might be organized to have separate sales and manufacturing functions within each product division. This solution is not perfect because each function does not develop the strong specialization that can make it more efficient. The company might have five different manufacturing functions instead of one more powerful, perhaps better-run, manufacturing department. Furthermore, it is often impossible to separate functions into smaller pieces and still have them well coordinated within the function across operating units and above minimum-efficient scale. Let us look briefly at sales and manufacturing as examples.

Within the sales function, it is important to coordinate all the salespeople calling on a particular account or person.[3] If the company has a single sales force, obtaining that coordination is easier. However, the large single sales force is in direct counterpoint to the concept of having separate sales forces within separate divisions for each product or geography. Choosing between the single sales force and multiple sales forces is difficult and complex. Furthermore, the political sensitivities and personal ambitions of high-level sales executives make it hard to approach this decision in a deliberate and unbiased fashion.

---

2. Jay W. Lorsch and Paul R. Lawrence, "Organizing for Product Innovation," *Harvard Business Review* (January–February 1965): 114–115.

3. Frank V. Cespedes, Stephen X. Doyle, and Robert J. Freedman, "Teamwork for Today's Selling," *Harvard Business Review* (March–April 1989): 44.

The manufacturing function faces much the same problem, although in a somewhat different form. It is often most economical to operate high-speed specialized equipment that requires a substantial product flow. If divisions have their own manufacturing operations, each of the smaller manufacturing operations may fall below this minimum-efficient scale. In addition, divisions often end up being suppliers or customers to one another for components and parts, a situation that opens up new problems of transfer pricing and cross-divisional coordination. Thus, divisionalizing is not a full-blown integration solution. It is merely another partial approach in which compromise and trade-off are necessary.

Another integration technique, the interfunctional coordinating unit, can be used when functions are quite specialized. The interfunctional unit attempts to tie together two functions. Consumer-packaged-goods companies often have sales-promotion groups to connect the sales force and the marketing people (product managers). Some interfunctional groups operate well because they understand both cultures and address a limited number of issues. In other situations, the interfunctional group becomes another group of people to be coordinated. Instead of sales and marketing working together, sales, marketing, and the sales-promotion group must work together. Sometimes, in fact, the coordinating unit adds organizational distance between the two departments it is supposed to coordinate. And, the proliferation of coordinating units can add new jurisdictional boundaries leading to more, rather than fewer, coordination problems. Interfunctional coordinating units must be introduced with careful attention to clarity of objectives, structural design, and streamlined operating procedures.

Another approach is matrix management, an attempt to gain some of the advantages of both the functional and the divisional organization. It arose in the defense industry where project managers formed one side of the matrix and functional managers the other. The hope was that specialization would be nurtured within the functions and integration within the projects. For many companies and industries this approach has been good; for others, it has been an unmitigated disaster. When it has been applied in a true system sense, utilizing sensible management processes and systems, the informal social systems, and the right people, it has tended to work. When used as a panacea, it has tended to fail. The matrix by itself will not solve all the problems of interfunctional or interdivisional conflict.

Because a matrix structure is so hard to work within, it should be used only when a company already has an organization structure that works fairly effectively. Although change to a matrix structure can sometimes improve a strong organization, it will only stress and confound a weak, ineffective organization.

Although the organization structure is a powerful tool for promoting interfunctional coordination, changing the hierarchy frequently, particularly in cultures not used to upheaval, can be difficult. Some companies have found that constant changes help to prevent the creation of oversized barriers between different operating functions and to make the whole structure limber and supple. Other companies have found that frequent organization change leads to constant turmoil. It takes time for each manager and each person to understand where they fit in the new structure. If the structure is constantly changing, people have little chance to learn their jobs.

Finally, there is no perfect organization structure, only important trade-offs and temporary optimums. It is impossible to obtain all the benefits of specialization and integration at the same time, using only the management hierarchy. A move in one direction invariably means that a company gains some things and loses others. If the organization is to be responsive to the environment and to its own strategy, it must change as the environment and strategy change. Thus, even an optimum approach is only a temporary optimum.

The strategy and the structure provide a basis for the application of a rich set of formal management processes and systems, which are presented in the next section.

MANAGEMENT PROCESSES AND SYSTEMS

Formal management process and systems and the informal social system (discussed later) are the two most underused interfunctional coordination approaches among the six. Formal management processes and systems include everything a company can formally do outside of the organization structure and all the people within the organization structure. This section includes only a few of the many ways of using this approach.

The goal-setting process and the system for measuring performance and allocating rewards are closely related. If manufacturing is rewarded for having low inventory levels, while sales is rewarded for obtaining additional sales based on good customer service and high inventory levels, the differing rewards for the two departments will generate intense arguments over inventory and service levels. The explicit differences in the goal-setting process, the measurement system, and the rewards system are much easier to identify then other subtle, more cultural aspects of an organization. At the same time, the goal-setting process, measurement system, and rewards system tend to make the culture and tone of the organization more tangible by emphasizing either cross-functional goals and rewards or single-department goals and rewards. To the extent that the goals and rewards are interfunctional, they tend to foster coordination across departments.

Task forces and committees are other management processes and systems related to the organization structure. A task force tends to be temporary, while a committee can be permanent. Both encourage people from different parts of the organization to come together and jointly solve problems or take advantage of an opportunity.

If the task forces and committees become a focal point of rancor, they may contribute to interfunctional warfare rather than to coordination. Membership, agendas, and processes must be carefully determined if task forces and committees are to work well. Putting a group of people in a room, locking the door, and telling them to work together does not ensure that they will. The task must be clear, and mechanisms must be developed to bring ideas as well as people together.

Another formal management process and system that contributes to interfunctional coordination is career paths. In many companies an individual moves from function to function, gaining background and perspective along the way. In addition, someone who has worked in functions will have political connections there. People in these career paths can help turn a formal system into an effective informal social network.

The interfunctional career path can be overdone, however. A manager who constantly changes function, with no clear progression in one or two primary departments, almost invariably becomes a "jack-of-all-trades but master of none" with little functional depth. An organization staffed with such people tends to lack the subtle judgment and well-honed skills that come from extensive experience in one function. Thus, the interfunctional-career-path approach should include deep experience in one or two functions complemented by broadening exposure to one or perhaps two others. The combinations should make sense for the individual and be related to the natural grouping of functions in the business.

As the interfunctional-career-path approach indicates, some management processes and systems can be a double-edged sword. Each approach and component must be used with moderation and care because each has advantages and disadvantages. The overuse of interfunctional career paths is no better than the underutilization.

THE MANAGEMENT INFORMATION SYSTEM

One formal management process, the information system, has become so pervasive and powerful that it deserves separate attention as the fourth coordination approach. The information system helps the corporation to define what is important and to frame how different departments and divisions view one another and the whole company. Often, the information system is structured to provide functional managers with information in a format customized to their function. This customization tends to exacerbate the cultural differences among functions and to encourage managers in each function to focus on different key success factors. By the same token, the information system can harmonize perspectives of different jurisdictions. A unified information system can be particularly useful to top-level functional managers, encouraging them to focus on the whole company rather than on their individual areas.

The information system is also a powerful communications tool and a potent aid in managing important interfunctional activities, such as order fulfillment. Communication methods, such as shared databases using computer networks, electronic mail, voice mail, and teleconferencing, reduce the barriers of distance, time, and jurisdictional boundaries. Voice mail enables workers and managers in different time zones to share thoughts and keep each other informed. A teleconference has some of the feel and tone of a face-to-face meeting without the travel and hassle. Such technology can foster a sense of unification and togetherness that is otherwise hard to develop in a large multinational, multidivisional organization.

Of course, electronic connectors do not replace the human warmth and feel of a face-to-face meeting; often, electronic get-togethers are more structured and formal. But, they are important and efficient links to face-to-face gatherings and allow the organization to operate without time delays. With electronic communication, the day-to-day flow of information goes faster and more smoothly, thereby diminishing annoyance and irritation.

Finally, the information system is critical to the order-fulfillment process, which is often a primary source of interdepartmental conflict. As the order flows from the sales department, to customer service, to finance/credit, to operations, to logistics, to service, and finally to the finance/billing department, objectives, cultures, evidence, thought processes, and outlooks easily clash. An integrated order-fulfillment system with a shared database can identify points of likely conflict earlier so more time for resolution is available. Shared databases can minimize arguments over the quality of evidence and different people's views of the same situation. Important policy-level issues can be highlighted for high-level decision making. A good order-fulfillment system can also eliminate problems that arise from poor communication and faulty or outdated information.

Much like a strategy document, an integrated order-fulfillment system enables functions to work together with some relief from the tension of on-line decision making. Even the analysis needed to develop the system encourages sharing views and mutual understanding.

The information system is one of the most important tools for coping with the increasing complexity of customer relationships and functional coordination and with the vast growth in transaction volume. And, it has not yet reached its limit as a jurisdictional integrator.

INFORMAL SOCIAL SYSTEMS AND CULTURE

When asked about interfunctional coordination, managers think naturally of organization structure and formal management processes and systems; these approaches are visible, tangible, and enforceable. However, the informal social system can also be helpful. It is an old and effective method of encouraging the parts of an organization to work together.

Geography is important to the information social system. By and large, people tend to work most closely with those who are near them. Thus, a strong way to encourage interfunctional coordination is to move the offices of the people in different functions close to one another. Of course, there are physical limits as well as conflicting pulls to keep the members of a single department close together because they must cooperate to accomplish everyday work.

However, even joint cafeteria facilities, parking lots, restrooms, coffee pots, and water fountains have a big impact on the informal social system. Whenever people see one another or congregate informally, they can converse about business or other joint interests. Such constant, low-key communication is very useful in building interfunctional coordination, and informal goodwill can help limit the work-related conflicts.

Other forms of team building exist, some more subtle than others. At the company picnic, for example, a volleyball game of sales against manufacturing tends to hinder interfunctional coordination. If, however, the two teams each have players from sales and manufacturing, coordination and a sense of working together are engendered. Identifying a wide range of opportunities for such informal team building is possible with careful and creative thought. If the sales vice president and manufacturing vice president go on a series of plant tours and customer visits together, they will tend to work better together over time. In addition, the symbolism is powerful. Their subordinates will understand that working cross-functionally is acceptable and admirable. In fact, it is vital for top functional managers to be seen together publicly; it helps set the culture and tone of the organization.

Many formal management processes have informal social-system consequences that are relevant to interfunctional coordination. For example, as corporate life has grown more complex, corporate training and development programs have increased. Some are designed to help participants learn about other parts of the company and the company's strategy and culture. This formal mechanism helps engender interfunctional coordination and a holistic sense of the firm. However, perhaps most powerful from an interfunctional perspective are the relationships and networks that arise in such settings. By sharing travel, meals, discussion groups, and occasional recreational activities, the representatives of different departments build valuable contacts and resources throughout the organization; their viewpoints broaden. They also have colleagues to contact when they need information or help from other jurisdictions. Almost all face-to-face corporate meetings allow information networks to develop, and these opportunities should be carefully and deliberately nurtured.

A major part of an organization's culture and tone comes from how interfunctional coordination is considered and accomplished. If the president turns to functional subordinates and says, "Work it out among yourselves" and walks away from interfunctional contention, the tone of the meeting is likely to be negative and adversarial. If the president makes all the interfunctional decisions, various top functional managers will not learn how to work together. However, if the president actively brings the various functional leaders together and helps them work out their problems in a constructive, mutually beneficial way, the culture of interfunctional cooperation will be encouraged. Even informal slurs greeted as humor can add to the problem. Top general management must help different functions understand, rather than attack, one another.

THE SELECTION AND PROMOTION OF EMPLOYEES

Culture is set and decisions are made by people. One critical way to encourage interfunctional cooperation is by choosing people with broad perspectives, interfunctional experience, and the ability to work together toward a common vision. All too often, managers are promoted solely on their ability to perform their jobs within their functions. Instead, promotions and hiring should be based not only on functional competence but also on an ability to coordinate and cooperate across jurisdictional boundaries and to engender such behavior from subordinates. Not only will the organization be populated with interdepartmental team players but also a tone of interfunctional communication and working together will be encouraged. In essence, the promotion process becomes part of the formal reward system.

Promotions are related to the reward system and also to career paths. If a company makes a conscious effort to develop people with interfunctional perspectives, it will have a stockpile of promotable managers with broad views and interfunctional experience.

Unfortunately, some people cannot deal psychologically with the conflict accompanying interfunctional coordination. These people do not see conflict as healthy and natural but avoid it at all costs and force their subordinates to do the same. It is most difficult to help such "team destroyers" embrace the need for open communication, honest dissent, and joint compromise.[4] These people can harm an organization; however, should their skills be necessary, they can be placed in special nonmanagement positions. Some companies create positions for those with great functional talent but limited coordination ability.

At a minimum, the people an organization hires must be competent in their own functions. If they are not, the organization will suffer interjurisdictional coordination problems because people coordinate best with those who are able and respected. Functional incompetence breeds interfunctional problems.

—— THE FOUR ADJUDICATORS

In addition to the functional line managers, there are four groups of people that can contribute to interfunctional coordination: the staff engineering group, cost-accounting experts, human resource managers, and top-level

---

4. The term *team destroyers* was coined by Suzanne Wetlaufer in "Anatomy of a 'Team Destroyer'," Harvard Business School Case No. 9-589-038.

general management. The engineers can help by providing clear technical trade-offs that illuminate conflicting points of view and encourage an intellectual dialogue rather than a power struggle. Sometimes, creative engineering ideas can resolve apparently conflicting goals. The engineers can inform people and affect outcomes if they are willing to participate in business decisions. They cannot run from the important issues by hiding behind a veil of formulas and purely technical contributions. Similarly, the line functions must be willing to welcome staff engineering input and to help the engineers incorporate business concerns into their technical analyses.

Cost-accounting experts can also give carefully formed opinions on heated conflicts. Good cost accounting, which focuses on realistic accuracy rather than imagined precision, can help line-operating managers weigh the impact of different options and understand the real cost of various approaches. The cost accountants must understand the economic consequences of decisions and be able to communicate them if they are to be useful in decision making. Most important, they must understand the whole business, and how each function operates. A unified cost system can be an important integrative tool.

Human resources managers can identify and attract to the company highly competent people capable of cross-functional integration. In addition, they can participate in the development of formal management systems and processes and organization structures that contribute to integration. Among these should be training and development programs that include exposure and respect for differing functional responsibilities and perspective. Human resources specialists can also demonstrate a continuing commitment to building a team spirit and mediating functional conflicts. As respected neutral parties, often privy to confidential and sensitive personal information, they can help each line function to understand differing objectives and perspectives.

Staff functions, such as staff engineering, cost accounting, and human resources, are a potentially influential force in interdepartmental coordination. If the staff people see their job as bringing the operating departments together, they can be very helpful. If they believe their power increases when the line functions must deal through them, rather than directly, the staff groups can be very disruptive. It is difficult yet important to inculcate staff values that nurture cooperation with and among line-operating departments.

Finally, top-level general managers can have a great impact on interfunctional coordination. Only they can provide a clear statement of a unified strategy and explicit policies for accomplishing it. The strategy becomes the core of shared goals that supersede individual department goals for the good of the total business. General managers can consistently demonstrate their commitment to building a unified interfunctional team through assignments that foster cooperation, meetings that stress sharing and cooperation, a tone of equity, and an orientation toward results rather than politics and internal power. Finally, top-level general managers can set high standards of competence for high-level functional managers.

——— THE TOTAL SYSTEM

No single aspect or approach to interfunctional coordination is as important as the total system. Over the years different companies have developed a wide variety of techniques, such as particular organizational structures and management processes for engendering interfunctional coordination. Many of these techniques have failed because they were not part of a total system. If top management makes interfunctional coordination a major priority, it can become a part of the strategy, culture, and tone and will be supported by the organization structure, formal management processes and information systems, informal social systems, and the choice of people. All this, however, must be managed continually. Interfunctional coordination is not a problem to be solved; it is constantly being challenged by new environmental demands, new strategic imperatives, and the desire to form closed units. People, and perhaps particularly Americans, tend to "root for the home team." Thus, the members of a function can easily become insular and make themselves the home team.

Top general management must constantly provide the focus, rewards, and systems that inculcate interfunctional coordination, particularly for companies determined to provide specialties and not commodities.

Top management tends to be preoccupied with leadership, but perhaps as important as leadership, which implies a vertical dimension in working within the organization, is team building, which concerns the horizontal dimension. Some managers seem more eager to develop teams than do others. However, if the strategy and the environment require interfunctional coordination, a manager could not find a more worthwhile activity than team building.

——— BIBLIOGRAPHY

Aicklen, Chad, "Development Team Approach to New Product Introductions," *Business Marketing* (November 1985) , p. 114.

Bartlett, Christopher A., and Sumantra Ghoshal, *Managing Across Borders: The Transnational Solution,* (Boston, Mass.: Harvard Business School Press, 1989).

Couretas, John, "The Challenge to Marketing of Integrated Manufacturing Databases," *Business Marketing* (March 1985), p. 40.

Davis, Stanley M., *Future Perfect,* (Reading, Mass.: Addison-Wesley, 1987).

Davis, Stanley M., and Paul R. Lawrence, *Matrix,* (Reading, Mass.: Addision-Wesley, 1977).

Dyer, William G., *Team Building: Issues and Alternatives,* (Reading, Mass.: Addison-Wesley, 1977).

Eccles, Robert G., and Dwight B. Crane, *Doing Deals: Investment Banks at Work,* (Boston, Mass.: Harvard Business School Press, 1988).

Flood, Robert L., and Ewart R. Carson, *Dealing with Complexity: An Introduction to the Theory and Application of Systems*, (New York: Plenum Press, 1988).

Galbraith, Jay, *Designing Complex Organizations*, (Reading, Mass.: Addision-Wesley, Inc., 1973).

Gemmill, Gary R., and David L. Wilemon,"The Product Manager as an Influence Agent," *Journal of Marketing*, Vol 36 (January 1972), pp. 26–33.

Gupta, Ashok K., Raj S.P. Gupta, and David L. Wilemon, "The R & D-Marketing Interface in High-Technology Firms," *Journal of Product Innovation Management*, 2:12–24 (New York: Elsevier Science Publishing Co., Inc., 1985).

Kanter, Rosabeth Moss, "When a Thousand Flowers Bloom: Structural, Collective, and Social Conditions for Innovation in Organizations," Division of Research, Harvard Business School, Working Paper, No. 87-018.

Kanter, Rosabeth Moss, *When Giants Learn to Dance: Mastering the Challenges of Strategy, Management, and Careers in the 1990s*, (New York: Simon and Schuster, 1989).

Lawrence, Paul R., and Jay W. Lorsch, *Developing Organizations: Diagnosis and Action*, (Reading, Mass.: Addison-Wesley, 1969).

Lawrence, Paul R., and Jay W. Lorsch, "New Management Job: The Integrator," *Harvard Business Review* (November–December 1967), pp. 142–151.

Lawrence, Paul R., and Jay W. Lorsch, *Organization and Environment Managing Differentiation and Integration*, (Boston, Mass.: Harvard Business School Press, 1967).

Lorsch, Jay W., "Note on Organization Design," Harvard Business School, Case No. 476-094 (1975).

Lorsch, Jay W., and Paul R. Lawrence, "Organizing for Product Innovation," *Harvard Business Review* (January–February 1965), pp. 109–122.

Mitchell, Russell, "How Ford Hit the Bull's-Eye with Taurus," *Business Week*, (June 30, 1986), p. 69.

Nadler, David, and Michael Tushman, *Strategic Organization Design: Concepts, Tools, Processes*, (Glenview, Ill.: Scott, Foresman and Company, 1988).

Peters, Tom, "The Destruction of Hierarchy," *Industry Week* (August 15, 1988), p. 33.

Ruekert, Robert W., and Orville C. Walker, Jr., "Marketing's Interaction with Other Functional Units: A Conceptual Framework and Empirical Evidence," *Journal of Marketing*, Volume 51 (January 1987), pp. 1–19.

Ruekert, Robert W., Orville C. Walker, Jr., and Kenneth J. Roering, "The Organization of Marketing Activities: A Contingency Theory of Structure and Performance," *Journal of Marketing*, Volume 49 (Winter 1985), pp. 13–25.

Seiler, John A., "Diagnosing Interdepartmental Conflict," *Harvard Business Review* (September–October 1963), pp. 121–132.

Shapiro, Benson P., "Can Marketing and Manufacturing Coexist?," *Harvard Business Review* (September–October 1977), pp. 104–114.

Stefflre, Volney, "Organization Obstacles to Innovation: A Formulation of the Problem," *Journal of Product Innovation Management*, 2:3–11, (New York: Elsevier Science Publishing Co., 1985).

Tekeuchi, Hirotaka, and Ikujiro Nonaka, "The New Product Development Game," *Harvard Business Review* (January–February 1986), pp. 137–146.

Venkatesh, Alladi, and David L. Wilemon, "Interpersonal Influence in Product Management," *Journal of Marketing* (October 1976), pp. 33–40.

Walker, Arthur H., and Jay W. Lorsch, "Organizational Choice: Product vs. Function," *Harvard Business Review* (November–December 1968), pp. 129–138.

Walton, Richard E., *Up and Running: Integrating Information Technology and the Organization,* (Boston, Mass.: Harvard Business School Press, 1989).

Ware, James, "Managing a Task Force," Harvard Business School, Case No. 478-002 (1977).

Wetlaufer, Suzanne, "Anatomy of a 'Team Destroyer'," Harvard Business School, Case No. 589-038 (1988).

—— DISCUSSION QUESTIONS

1. Is functional integration appropriate, to the degree suggested by this reading, for all organizations? When is functional integration beneficial? When is it harmful?

2. Some organizations operate by the philosophy of each tub on its own bottom. Would this interfere with functional integration? Explain whether or not an individualistic style can be just as effective as a highly cooperative style.

3. Are certain societies more culturally suited to functional integration than other societies? Compare and contrast two societies and how you think they would be more or less responsive to functional integration. For example, near the end of the reading the author states, "People, and perhaps particularly Americans, tend to 'root for the home team.'" What might be some of the aspects of the cultures that you have chosen that would encourage or hinder functional integration?

4. Considering the trends that some business authorities see developing—a lessening of hierarchy and a broader dispersion of authority and responsibility—what are the implications for integration as a management concern? Under the influence of these trends, will integration become easier or more difficult?

24   Matrix Management: Not a Structure, a Frame of Mind

CHRISTOPHER A. BARTLETT AND SUMANTRA GHOSHAL

In many companies, argue these authors, strategic thinking has outdistanced organizational capability. These companies adopt elaborate organizational matrices that actually impair their ability to implement sophisticated strategies. Keeping a company strategically agile while still coordinating its activities across divisions, functions, and even continents means eliminating parochialism, improving communication, and weaving the decision-making process into the company's social fabric.

This reading describes techniques that successful companies have used to manage complex strategies. The key is to build a matrix of corporate values and priorities in the minds of managers and let them make the judgments and negotiate the deals that make the strategy pay off.

Top-level managers in many of today's leading corporations are losing control of their companies. The problem is not that they have misjudged the demands created by an increasingly complex environment and an accelerating rate of environmental change, nor even that they have failed to develop strategies appropriate to the new challenges. The problem is that their companies are organizationally incapable of carrying out the sophisticated strategies they have developed. Over the past 20 years, strategic thinking has far outdistanced organizational capabilities.

All through the 1980s, companies everywhere were redefining their strategies and reconfiguring their operations in response to such developments as the globalization of markets, the intensification of competition, the acceleration of product life cycles, and the growing complexity of relationships with suppliers, customers, employees, governments, even competitors. But as companies struggled with these changing environmental realities, many fell into one of two traps—one strategic, one structural.

The strategic trap was to implement simple, static solutions to complex and dynamic problems. The bait was often a consultant's siren song promising to simplify or at least minimize complexity and discontinuity. Despite the new demands of overlapping industry boundaries and greatly altered value-added chains, managers were promised success if they would "stick to their knitting." In a swiftly changing international political economy, they were urged to rein in dispersed overseas operations and focus on the triad markets, and in an increasingly intricate and sophisticated competitive environment, they were encouraged to choose between alternative generic strategies—low cost or differentiation.

Yet the strategic reality for most companies was that both their business and their environment really *were* more complex, while the proposed solutions were often simple, even simplistic. The traditional telephone company that stuck to its knitting was trampled by competitors who redefined their strategies in response to new technologies linking telecommunications, computers, and office equipment into a single integrated system. The packaged-goods company that concentrated on the triad markets quickly discovered that Europe, Japan, and the United States were the epicenters of global competitive activity, with higher risks and slimmer profits than more protected and less competitive markets such as Australia, Turkey, and Brazil. The consumer electronics company that adopted an either-or generic strategy found itself facing competitors able to develop cost and differentiation capabilities at the same time.

In recent years, as more and more managers recognized oversimplification as a strategic trap, they began to accept the need to manage complexity rather than seek to minimize it. This realization, however, led many into an equally threatening organizational trap when they concluded that the best response to increasingly complex strategic requirements was increasingly complex organizational structures.

The obvious organizational solution to strategies that required multiple, simultaneous management capabilities was the matrix structure that became so fashionable in the late 1970s and the early 1980s. Its parallel reporting relationships acknowledged the diverse, conflicting needs of functional, product, and geographic management groups and provided a formal mechanism for resolving them. Its multiple information channels allowed the organization to capture and analyze external complexity. And its overlapping responsibilities were designed to combat parochialism and build flexibility into the company's response to change.

In practice, however, the matrix proved all but unmanageable—especially in an international context. Dual reporting led to conflict and confusion; the proliferation of channels created informational log-jams as a proliferation of committees and reports bogged down the organization; and overlapping responsibilities produced turf battles and a loss of accountability. Separated by barriers of distance, language, time, and culture, managers found it virtually impossible to clarify the confusion and resolve the conflicts.

In hindsight, the strategic and structural traps seem simple enough to avoid, so one has to wonder why so many experienced general managers have fallen into them. Much of the answer lies in the way we have traditionally thought about the general manager's role. For decades, we have seen the general manager as chief strategic guru and principal organizational architect. But as the competitive climate grows less stable and less predictable, it is harder for one person alone to succeed in that great visionary role. Similarly, as formal, hierarchical structure gives way to networks of personal relationships that work through informal, horizontal communication channels, the image of top management in an isolated corner office moving boxes and lines on an organization chart becomes increasingly anachronistic.

Paradoxically, as strategies and organizations become more complex and sophisticated, top-level general managers are beginning to replace their historical concentration on the grand issues of strategy and structure with a focus on the details of managing people and processes. The critical strategic requirement is not to devise the most ingenious and well-coordinated plan but to build the most viable and flexible strategic process; the key organizational task is not to design the most elegant structure but to capture individual capabilities and motivate the entire organization to respond cooperatively to a complicated and dynamic environment.

——— BUILDING AN ORGANIZATION

Although business thinkers have written a great deal about strategic innovation, they have paid far less attention to the accompanying organizational challenges. Yet many companies remain caught in the structural-complexity trap that paralyzes their ability to respond quickly or flexibly to the new strategic imperatives.

For those companies that adopted matrix structures, the problem was not in the way they defined the goal. They correctly recognized the need for a multidimensional organization to respond to growing external complexity. The problem was that they defined their organizational objectives in purely structural terms. Yet the term *formal structure* describes only the organization's basic anatomy. Companies must also concern themselves with organizational physiology—the systems and relationships that allow the lifeblood of information to flow through the organization. They also need to develop a healthy organizational psychology—the shared norms, values, and beliefs that shape the way individual managers think and act.

The companies that fell into the organizational trap assumed that changing their formal structure (anatomy) would force changes in interpersonal relationships and decision processes (physiology), which in turn would reshape the individual attitudes and actions of managers (psychology).

But as many companies have discovered, reconfiguring the formal structure is a blunt and sometimes brutal instrument of change. A new structure creates new and presumably more useful managerial ties, but these can take months and often years to evolve into effective knowledge-generating and decision-making relationships. And because the new job requirements will frustrate, alienate, or simply overwhelm so many managers, changes in individual attitudes and behavior will likely take even longer.

As companies struggle to create organizational capabilities that reflect rather than diminish environmental complexity, good managers gradually stop searching for the ideal structural template to impose on the company from the top down. Instead, they focus on the challenge of building up an appropriate set of employee attitudes and skills and linking them together with carefully developed processes and relationships. In other words, they begin to focus on building the organization rather than simply on installing a new structure.

Indeed, the companies that are most successful at developing multi-dimensional organizations begin at the far end of the anatomy-physiology-psychology sequence. Their first objective is to alter the organizational psychology—the broad corporate beliefs and norms that shape managers' perceptions and actions. Then, by enriching and clarifying communication and decision processes, companies reinforce these psychological changes with improvements in organizational physiology. Only later do they consolidate and confirm their progress by realigning organizational anatomy through changes in the formal structure.

No company we know of has discovered a quick or easy way to change its organizational psychology to reshape the understanding, identification, and commitment of its employees. But we found three principal characteristics common to those that managed the task most effectively:

1. They developed and communicated a clear and consistent corporate vision.
2. They effectively managed human resource tools to broaden individual perspectives and to develop identification with corporate goals.
3. They integrated individual thinking and activities into the broad corporate agenda by a process we call co-option.

——— BUILDING A SHARED VISION

Perhaps the main reason managers in large, complex companies cling to parochial attitudes is that their frame of reference is bounded by their specific responsibilities. The surest way to break down such insularity is to develop and communicate a clear sense of corporate purpose that extends into every corner of the company and gives context and meaning to each manager's particular roles and responsibilities. We are not talking about a slogan, however catchy and pointed. We are talking about a company vision, which must be crafted and articulated with clarity, continuity, and consistency. We are talking about clarity of expression that makes company objectives understandable and meaningful; continuity of purpose that underscores their enduring importance; and consistency of application across business units and geographical boundaries that ensures uniformity throughout the organization.

Clarity   There are three keys to clarity in a corporate vision: simplicity, relevance, and reinforcement. NEC's integration of computers and communications—C&C—is probably the best single example of how simplicity can make a vision more powerful. Top management has applied the C&C concept so effectively that it describes the company's business focus, defines its distinctive source of competitive advantage over large companies like IBM and AT&T, and summarizes its strategic and organizational imperatives.

The second key, relevance, means linking broad objectives to concrete agendas. When Wisse Dekker became CEO at Philips, his principal strategic concern was the problem of competing with Japan. He stated this challenge in martial terms—the U.S. had abandoned the battlefield; Philips was now Europe's last defense against insurgent Japanese electronics companies. By focusing the company's attention not only on Philips's corporate survival but also on the protection of national and regional interests, Dekker heightened the sense of urgency and commitment in a way that legitimized cost-cutting efforts, drove an extensive rationalization of plant operations, and inspired a new level of sales achievements.

The third key to clarity is top management's continual reinforcement, elaboration, and interpretation of the core vision to keep it from becoming obsolete or abstract. Founder Konosuke Matsushita developed a grand, 250-year vision for his company, but he also managed to give it immediate relevance. He summed up its overall message in the "Seven Spirits of Matsushita," to which he referred constantly in his policy statements. Each January he wove the company's one-year operational objectives into his overarching concept to produce an annual theme that he then captured in a slogan. For all the loftiness of his concept of corporate purpose, he gave his managers immediate, concrete guidance in implementing Matsushita's goals.

Continuity   Despite shifts in leadership and continual adjustments in short-term business priorities, companies must remain committed to the same core set of strategic objectives and organizational values. Without such continuity, unifying vision might as well be expressed in terms of quarterly goals.

It was General Electric's lack of this kind of continuity that led to the erosion of its once formidable position in electrical appliances in many countries. Over a period of 20 years and under successive CEOs, the company's international consumer-product strategy never stayed the same for long. From building locally responsive and self-sufficient "mini-GEs" in each market, the company turned to a policy of developing low-cost offshore sources, which eventually evolved into a de facto strategy of international outsourcing. Finally, following its acquisition of RCA, GE's consumer electronics strategy made another about-face and focused on building centralized scale to defend domestic share. Meanwhile, the product strategy within this shifting business emphasis was itself unstable. The Brazilian subsidiary, for example, built its TV business in the 1960s until it was told to stop; in the early 1970s, it emphasized large appliances until it was denied funding, then it focused on housewares until the parent company sold off that business. In two decades, GE utterly dissipated its dominant franchise in Brazil's electrical products market.

Unilever, by contrast, made an enduring commitment to its Brazilian subsidiary, despite volatile swings in Brazil's business climate. Company chairman Floris Maljers emphasized the importance of looking past the latest political crisis or economic downturn to the long-term business potential. "In those parts of the world," he remarked, "you take your management cues from the way they dance. The samba method of management is two steps forward then one step back." Unilever built—two steps forward and one step back—a profitable $300 million business in a rapidly growing economy with 130 million consumers, while its wallflower competitors never ventured out onto the floor.

Consistency   The third task for top management in communicating strategic purpose is to ensure that everyone in the company shares the same vision. The cost of inconsistency can be horrendous. It always produces confusion and, in extreme cases, can lead to total chaos, with different units of the organization pursuing agendas that are mutually debilitating.

Philips is a good example of a company that, for a time, lost its consistency of corporate purpose. As a legacy of its wartime decision to give some overseas units legal autonomy, management had long experienced difficulty persuading North American Philips (NAP) to play a supportive role in the parent company's global strategies. The problem came to a head with the introduction of Philips's technologically first-rate videocassette recording system, the V2000. Despite considerable pressure from world headquarters in the Netherlands, NAP refused to launch the system, arguing that Sony's Beta system and Matsushita's VHS format were too well established and had cost, feature, and system-support advantages Philips couldn't match. Relying on its legal independence and managerial autonomy, NAP management decided instead to source products from its Japanese competitors and market them under its Magnavox brand name. As a result, Philips was unable to build the efficiency and credibility it needed to challenge Japanese dominance of the VCR business.

Most inconsistencies involve differences between what managers of different operating units see as the company's key objectives. Sometimes, however, different corporate leaders transmit different views of overall priorities and purpose. When this stems from poor communication, it can be fixed. When it's a result of fundamental disagreement, the problem is serious indeed, as illustrated by ITT's problems in developing its strategically vital System 12 switching equipment. Continuing differences between the head of the European organization and the company's chief technology officer over the location and philosophy of the development effort led to confusion and conflict throughout the company. The result was disastrous. ITT had difficulty transferring vital technology across its own unit boundaries and so was irreparably late introducing this key product to a rapidly changing global market. These problems eventually led the company to sell off its core telecommunications business to a competitor.

But formulating and communicating a vision—no matter how clear, enduring, and consistent—cannot succeed unless individual employees understand and accept the company's stated goals and objectives. Problems at this level are more often related to receptivity than to communication. The development of individual understanding and acceptance is a challenge for a company's human resource practices.

——— DEVELOPING HUMAN RESOURCES

Although top managers universally recognize their responsibility for developing and allocating a company's scarce assets and resources, their focus on finance and technology often overshadows the task of developing the scarcest resource of all—capable managers. But if there is one key to regaining control of companies that operate in fast-changing environments, it is the ability of top management to turn the perceptions, capabilities, and relationships of individual managers into the building blocks of the organization.

One pervasive problem in companies whose leaders lack this ability— or fail to exercise it—is getting managers to see how their specific responsibilities relate to the broad corporate vision. Growing external complexity and strategic sophistication have accelerated the growth of a cadre of specialists who are physically and organizationally isolated from each other, and the task of dealing with their consequent parochialism should not be delegated to the clerical staff that administers salary structures and benefit programs. Top managers inside and outside the human resource function must be leaders in the recruitment, development, and assignment of the company's vital human talent.

Recruitment and Selection   The first step in successfully managing complexity is to tap the full range of available talent. It is a serious mistake to permit historical imbalances in the nationality or functional background of the management group to constrain hiring or subsequent promotion. In today's global marketplace, domestically oriented recruiting limits a company's ability to capitalize on its worldwide pool of management skill and biases its decision-making processes.

After decades of routinely appointing managers from its domestic operations to key positions in overseas subsidiaries, Procter & Gamble realized that the practice not only worked against sensitivity to local cultures—a lesson driven home by several marketing failures in Japan—but also greatly under-utilized its pool of high-potential non-American managers. (Fortunately, our studies turned up few companies as shortsighted as one that made overseas assignments on the basis of *poor* performance, because foreign markets were assumed to be "not as tough as the domestic environment.")

Not only must companies enlarge the pool of people available for key positions, they must also develop new criteria for choosing those most likely to succeed. Because past success is no longer a sufficient qualification for increasingly subtle, sensitive, and unpredictable senior-level tasks, top management must become involved in a more discriminating selection process. At Matsushita, top management selects candidates for international assignments on the basis of a comprehensive set of personal characteristics, expressed for simplicity in the acronym SMILE: specialty (the needed skill, capability, or knowledge); management ability (particularly motivational ability); international flexibility (willingness to learn and ability to adapt); language facility; and endeavor (vitality, perseverance in the face of difficulty). These attributes are remarkably similar to those targeted by NEC and Philips, where top executives also are involved in the senior-level selection process.

Training and Development   Once the appropriate top-level candidates have been identified, the next challenge is to develop their potential. The most successful development efforts have three aims that take them well beyond the skill-building objectives of classic training programs: to inculcate a common vision and shared values; to broaden management perspectives and capabilities; and to develop contacts and shape management relationships.

To build common vision and values, white-collar employees at Matsushita spend a good part of their first six months in what the company calls "cultural and spiritual training." They study the company credo, the "Seven Spirits of Matsushita," and the philosophy of Konosuke Matsushita. Then they learn how to translate these internalized lessons into daily behavior and even operational decisions. Culture-building exercises as intensive as Matsushita's are sometimes dismissed as innate Japanese practices that would not work in other societies, but in fact, Philips has a similar entry-level training practice (called "organization cohesion training"), as does Unilever (called, straightforwardly, "indoctrination").

The second objective—broadening management perspectives—is essentially a matter of teaching people how to manage complexity instead of merely to make room for it. To reverse a long and unwieldy tradition of running its operations with two- and three-headed management teams of separate technical, commercial, and sometimes administrative specialists, Philips asked its training and development group to de-specialize top management trainees. By supplementing its traditional menu of specialist courses and functional programs with more intensive general management training, Philips was able to begin replacing the ubiquitous teams with single business heads who also appreciated and respected specialist points of view.

The final aim—developing contacts and relationships—is much more than an incidental byproduct of good management development, as the comments of a senior personnel manager at Unilever suggest: "By bringing managers from different countries and businesses together at Four Acres [Unilever's international management-training college], we build contacts and create bonds that we could never achieve by other means. The company spends as much on training as it does on R&D not only because of the direct effect it has on upgrading skills and knowledge but also because it plays a central role in indoctrinating managers into a Unilever club where personal relationships and informal contacts are much more powerful than the formal systems and structures."

Career-Path Management   Although recruitment and training are critically important, the most effective companies recognize that the best way to develop new perspectives and thwart parochialism in their managers is through personal experience. By moving selected managers across functions, businesses, and geographic units, a company encourages cross-fertilization of ideas as well as the flexibility and breadth of experience that enable managers to grapple with complexity and come out on top.

Unilever has long been committed to the development of its human resources as a means of attaining durable competitive advantage. As early as the 1930s, the company was recruiting and developing local employees to replace the parent-company managers who had been running most of its overseas subsidiaries. In a practice that came to be known as "-ization," the company committed itself to the Indianization of its Indian company, the Australization of its Australian company, and so on.

Although delighted with the new talent that began working its way up through the organization, management soon realized that by reducing the transfer of parent-company managers abroad, it had diluted the powerful glue that bound diverse organizational groups together and linked dispersed operations. The answer lay in formalizing a second phase of the -ization process. While continuing with Indianization, for example, Unilever added programs aimed at the "Unileverization" of its Indian managers.

In addition to bringing 300 to 400 managers to Four Acres each year, Unilever typically has 100 to 150 of its most promising overseas managers on short- and long-term job assignments at corporate headquarters. This policy not only brings fresh, close-to-the-market perspectives into corporate decision making but also gives the visiting managers a strong sense of Unilever's strategic vision and organizational values. In the words of one of the expatriates in the corporate offices, "The experience initiates you into the Unilever Club and the clear norms, values, and behaviors that distinguish our people—so much so that we really believe we can spot another Unilever manager anywhere in the world."

Furthermore, the company carefully transfers most of these high-potential individuals through a variety of different functional, product, and geographic positions, often rotating every two or three years. Most important, top management tracks about 1,000 of these people—some 5% of Unilever's total management group—who, as they move through the company, forge an informal network of contacts and relationships that is central to Unilever's decision-making and information-exchange processes.

Widening the perspectives and relationships of key managers as Unilever has done is a good way of developing identification with the broader corporate mission. But a broad sense of identity is not enough. To maintain control of its global strategies, Unilever must secure a strong and lasting individual commitment to corporate visions and objectives. In effect, it must co-opt individual energies and ambitions into the service of corporate goals.

———— CO-OPTING MANAGEMENT EFFORTS

As organizational complexity grows, managers and management groups tend to become so specialized and isolated and to focus so intently on their own immediate operating responsibilities that they are apt to respond parochially to intrusions on their organizational turf, even when the overall corporate interest is at stake. A classic example, described earlier, was the decision by North American Philips's consumer electronics group to reject the parent company's VCR system.

At about the same time, Philips, like many other companies, began experimenting with ways to convert managers' intellectual understanding of the corporate vision—in Philips's case, an almost evangelical determination to defend Western electronics against the Japanese—into a binding personal commitment. Philips concluded that it could co-opt individuals and organizational groups into the broader vision by inviting them to contribute to the corporate agenda and then giving them direct responsibility for implementation.

In the face of intensifying Japanese competition, Philips knew it had to improve coordination in its consumer electronics among its fiercely independent national organizations. In strengthening the central product divisions, however, Philips did not want to deplete the enterprise or commitment of its capable national management teams.

The company met these conflicting needs with two cross-border initiatives. First, it created a top-level World Policy Council for its video business that included key managers from strategic markets—Germany, France, the United Kingdom, the United States, and Japan. Philips knew that its national companies' long history of independence made local managers reluctant to take orders from Dutch headquarters in Eindhoven—often for good reason, because much of the company's best market knowledge and technological expertise resided in its offshore units. Through the council, Philips co-opted their support for company decisions about product policy and manufacturing location.

Second, in a more powerful move, Philips allocated global responsibilities to units that previously had been purely national in focus. Eindhoven gave NAP the leading role in the development of Philips's projection television and asked it to coordinate development and manufacture of all Philips television sets for North America and Asia. The change in the attitude of NAP managers was dramatic.

A senior manager in NAP's consumer electronics business summed up the feelings of U.S. managers: "At last, we are moving out of the dependency relationship with Eindhoven that was so frustrating to us." Co-option had transformed the defensive, territorial attitude of NAP managers into a more collaborative mind-set. They were making important contributions to global corporate strategy instead of looking for ways to subvert it.

In 1987, with much of its TV set production established in Mexico, the president of NAP's consumer electronics group told the press, "It is the commonality of design that makes it possible for us to move production globally. We have splendid cooperation with Philips in Eindhoven." It was a statement no NAP manager would have made a few years earlier, and it perfectly captured how effectively Philips had co-opted previously isolated, even adversarial, managers into the corporate agenda.

▬▬▬ THE MATRIX IN THE MANAGER'S MIND

Since the end of World War II, corporate strategy has survived several generations of painful transformation and has grown appropriately agile and athletic. Unfortunately, organizational development has not kept pace, and managerial attitudes lag even farther behind. As a result, corporations now commonly design strategies that seem impossible to implement, for the simple reason that no one can effectively implement third-generation strategies through second-generation organizations run by first-generation managers.

Today the most successful companies are those where top executives recognize the need to manage the new environmental and competitive demands by focusing less on the quest for an ideal structure and more on developing the abilities, behavior, and performance of individual managers. Change succeeds only when those assigned to the new transnational and interdependent tasks understand the overall goals and are dedicated to achieving them.

One senior executive put it this way: "The challenge is not so much to build a matrix structure as it is to create a matrix in the minds of our managers." The inbuilt conflict in a matrix structure pulls managers in several directions at once. Developing a matrix of flexible perspectives and relationships within each manager's mind, however, achieves an entirely different result. It lets individuals make the judgments and negotiate the trade-offs that drive the organization toward a shared strategic objective.

——— DISCUSSION QUESTIONS

1. What aspects of American culture support participation in a shared vision? What aspects of American culture might hinder a company's employees from participation in a company's shared vision?

2. An international company is encouraged to create loyalty to the organization among its managers. What are some of the difficulties an organization might encounter from its overseas managers? Within the world at large, what social implications, both positive and negative, might result from creating a matrix of the mind?

3. The authors state that matrix management is a way of thinking. What are some possible disadvantages to this approach that relies heavily on developing an organization's human resource?

4. Does this reading suggest that the organization is taking a place similar to that of a country in the loyalties of its managers? Explain why or why not.

25   In Praise of Hierarchy

ELLIOTT JAQUES

Hierarchy, the most effective organizational form that a big company can employ, has been widely misunderstood and abused, according to this author. Pay grades are confused with real layers of responsibility, for example, and incompetent bosses abound. Nevertheless, the key to organizational success is individual accountability, and hierarchy preserves unambiguous accountability for getting work done. This reading describes the uses and misuses of hierarchy, demonstrating that it can serve as a powerful tool for understanding how an organization ought to work and how it ought to perform.

At first glance, hierarchy may seem difficult to praise. Bureaucracy is a dirty word even among bureaucrats, and in business there is a widespread view that managerial hierarchy kills initiative, crushes creativity, and has therefore seen its day. Yet 35 years of research have convinced me that managerial hierarchy is the most efficient, the hardiest, and in fact the most natural structure ever devised for large organizations. Properly structured, hierarchy can release energy and creativity, rationalize productivity, and actually improve morale. Moreover, I think most managers know this intuitively and have only lacked a workable structure and a decent intellectual justification for what they have always known could work and work well.

As currently practiced, hierarchy undeniably has its drawbacks. One of business's great contemporary problems is how to release and sustain among the people who work in corporate hierarchies the thrust, initiative, and adaptability of the entrepreneur. This problem is so great that it has become fashionable to call for a new kind of organization to put in place of managerial hierarchy, an organization that will better meet the requirements of what is variously called the Information Age, the Services Age, or the Post-Industrial Age.

As vague as the description of the age is the definition of the kind of new organization required to suit it. Theorists tell us it ought to look more like a symphony orchestra or a hospital or perhaps the British raj. It ought to function by means of primus groups or semiautonomous work teams or matrix overlap groups. It should be organic or entrepreneurial or tight-loose. It should hinge on skunk works or on management by walking around or perhaps on our old friend, management by objective.

All these approaches are efforts to overcome the perceived faults of hierarchy and find better ways to improve morale and harness human creativity. But the theorists' belief that our changing world requires an alternative to hierarchical organization is simply wrong, and all their proposals are based on an inadequate understanding of not only hierarchy but also human nature.

Hierarchy is not to blame for our problems. Encouraged by gimmicks and fads masquerading as insights, we have burdened our managerial systems with a makeshift scaffolding of inept structures and attitudes. What we need is not simply a new, flatter organization but an understanding of how managerial hierarchy functions—how it relates to the complexity of work and how we can use it to achieve a more effective deployment of talent and energy.

The reason we have a hierarchical organization of work is not only that tasks occur in lower and higher degrees of complexity—which is obvious—but also that there are sharp discontinuities in complexity that separate tasks into a series of steps or categories—which is not so obvious. The same discontinuities occur with respect to mental work and to the breadth and duration of account-ability. The hierarchical kind of organization we call bureaucracy did not emerge accidentally. It is the only form of organization that can enable a company to employ large numbers of people and yet preserve unambiguous accountability for the work they do. And that is why, despite its problems, it has so doggedly persisted.

Hierarchy has not had its day. Hierarchy never did have its day. As an organizational system, managerial hierarchy has never been adequately de-scribed and has just as certainly never been adequately used. The problem is not to find an alternative to a system that once worked well but no longer does; the problem is to make it work efficiently for the first time in its 3,000-year history.

—— WHAT WENT WRONG . . .

There is no denying that hierarchical structure has been the source of a great deal of trouble and inefficiency. Its misuse has hampered effective man-agement and stifled leadership, while its track record as a support for entre-preneurial energy has not been exemplary. We might almost say that successful businesses have had to succeed despite hierarchical organization rather than because of it.

One common complaint is excessive layering—too many rungs on the ladder. Information passes through too many people, decisions through too many levels, and managers and subordinates are too close together in experi-ence and ability, which smothers effective leadership, cramps accountability, and promotes buck passing. Relationships grow stressful when managers and subordinates bump elbows, so to speak, within the same frame of reference.

Another frequent complaint is that few managers seem to add real value to the work of their subordinates. The fact that the breakup value of many large corporations is greater than their share value shows pretty clearly how much value corporate managers can *subtract* from their subsidiary businesses, but in fact few of us know exactly what managerial added value would look like as it was occurring.

Many people also complain that our present hierarchies bring out the nastier aspects of human behavior, like greed, insensitivity, careerism, and self-importance. These are the qualities that have sent many behavioral scientists in search of cooperative, group-oriented, nonhierarchical organizational forms. But are they the inevitable companions of hierarchy, or perhaps a product of the misuse of hierarchy that would disappear if hierarchy were properly understood and structured?

————— . . . AND WHAT CONTINUES TO GO WRONG

The fact that so many of hierarchy's problems show up in the form of individual misbehavior has led to one of the most widespread illusions in business, namely, that a company's managerial leadership can be significantly improved solely by doing psychotherapeutic work on the personalities and attitudes of its managers. Such methods can help individuals gain greater personal insight, but I doubt that individual insight, personality matching, or even exercises in group dynamics can produce much in the way of organizational change or an overall improvement in leadership effectiveness. The problem is that our managerial hierarchies are so badly designed as to defeat the best efforts even of psychologically insightful individuals.

Solutions that concentrate on groups, on the other hand, fail to take into account the real nature of employment systems. People are not employed in groups. They are employed individually, and their employment contracts—real or implied—are individual. Group members may insist in moments of great esprit de corps that the group as such is the author of some particular accomplishment, but once the work is completed, the members of the group look for individual recognition and individual progression in their careers. It is not groups but individuals whom the company will hold accountable. The only true group is the board of directors, with its corporate liability.

None of the group-oriented panaceas face this issue of accountability. All the theorists refer to group authority, group decisions, and group consensus, none of them to group accountability. Indeed, they avoid the issue of accountability altogether, for to hold a group accountable, the employment contract would have to be with the group, not with the individuals, and companies simply do not employ groups as such.

To understand hierarchy, first you must understand employment. To be employed is to have an ongoing contract that holds you accountable for doing work of a given type for a specified number of hours per week in exchange for payment. Your specific tasks within that given work are assigned to you by a person called your manager (or boss or supervisor), who *ought to be held accountable* for the work you do.

If we are to make our hierarchies function properly, it is essential to place the emphasis on *accountability for getting work done*. This is what hierarchical systems ought to be about. Authority is a secondary issue and flows from accountability in the sense that there should be just that amount of authority needed to discharge the accountability. So if a group is to be given authority, its members must be held accountable as a group, and unless this is done, it is very hard to take so-called group decisions seriously. If the CEO or the manager of the group is held accountable for outcomes, then in the final analysis, he or she will have to agree with group decisions or have the authority to block them, which means that the group never really had decision-making power. Alternatively, if groups are allowed to make decisions without their manager's seal of approval, then accountability as such will suffer, for if a group does badly, the group is never fired. (And it would be shocking if it were.)

In the long run, therefore, group authority *without* group accountability is dysfunctional, and group authority *with* group accountability is unacceptable. So images of organizations that are more like symphony orchestras or hospitals or the British raj are surely nothing more than metaphors to express a desired feeling of togetherness—the togetherness produced by a conductor's baton, the shared concern of doctors and nurses for their patients, or the apparent unity of the British civil service in India.

In employment systems, after all, people are not mustered to play together as their manager beats time. As for hospitals, they are the essence of everything bad about bureaucratic organization. They function in spite of the system, only because of the enormous professional devotion of their staffs. The Indian civil service was in many ways like a hospital, its people bound together by the struggle to survive in a hostile environment. Managers do need authority, but authority based appropriately on the accountabilities they must discharge.

▬▬ WHY HIERARCHY?

The bodies that govern companies, unions, clubs, and nations all employ people to do work, and they all organize these employees in managerial hierarchies, systems that allow organizations to hold people accountable for getting assigned work done. Unfortunately, we often lose sight of this goal and set up the organizational layers in our managerial hierarchies to accommodate pay brackets and facilitate career development instead. If work happens to get done as well, we consider that a useful bonus.

But if our managerial hierarchical organizations tend to choke so readily on debilitating bureaucratic practices, how do we explain the persistence and continued spread of this form of organization for more than 3,000 years? And why has the determined search for alternatives proved so fruitless?

The answer is that managerial hierarchy is and will remain the *only* way to structure unified working systems with hundreds, thousands, or tens of thousands of employees, for the very good reason that managerial hierarchy is the expression of two fundamental characteristics of real work. First, the tasks we carry out are not only more or less complex but they also become more complex as they separate out into discrete categories or types of complexity. Second, the same is true of the mental work that people do on the job, for as this work grows more complex, it too separates out into distinct categories or types of mental activity. In turn, these two characteristics permit hierarchy to meet four of any organization's fundamental needs: to add real value to work as it moves through the organization, to identify and nail down accountability at each stage of the value-adding process, to place people with the necessary competence at each organizational layer, and to build a general consensus and acceptance of the managerial structure that achieves these ends.

───── HIERARCHICAL LAYERS

The complexity of the problems encountered in a particular task, project, or strategy is a function of the variables involved—their number, their clarity or ambiguity, the rate at which they change, and overall, the extent to which they are distinct or tangled. Obviously, as you move higher in a managerial hierarchy, the most difficult problems you have to contend with become increasingly complex. The biggest problems faced by the CEO of a large corporation are vastly more complex than those encountered on the shop floor. The CEO must cope not only with a huge array of often amorphous and constantly changing data but also with variables so tightly interwoven that they must be disentangled before they will yield useful information. Such variables might include the cost of capital; the interplay of corporate cash flow; the structure of the international competitive market; the uncertainties of Europe in the next decade; the future of Pacific Rim development; social developments with respect to labor; political developments in Eastern Europe, the Middle East, and the Third World; and technological research and change.

That the CEO's and the lathe operator's problems are different in quality as well as quantity will come as no surprise to anyone. The question is—and always has been—where does the change in quality occur? On a continuum of complexity from the bottom of the structure to the top, where are the discontinuities that will allow us to identify layers of hierarchy that are distinct and separable, as different as ice is from water and water from steam? I spent years looking for the answer, and what I found was somewhat unexpected.

My first step was to recognize the obvious, that the layers have to do with manager-subordinate relationships. The manager's position is in one layer and the subordinate's is in the next layer below. What then sets the necessary distance between? This question cannot be answered without knowing just what it is that a manager does.

The managerial role has three critical features. First, and *most* critical, every manager must be held accountable not only for the work of subordinates but also for adding value to their work. Second, every manager must be held accountable for sustaining a team of subordinates capable of doing this work. Third, every manager must be held accountable for setting direction and getting subordinates to follow willingly, indeed enthusiastically. In brief, every manager is accountable for work and leadership.

In order to make accountability possible, managers must have enough authority to ensure that their subordinates can do the work assigned to them. This authority must include at least these four elements:

1. The right to veto any applicant who, in the manager's opinion, falls below the minimum standards of ability;
2. The power to make work assignments;
3. The power to carry out performance appraisals and, within the limits of company policy, to make decisions—not recommendations—about raises and merit rewards;
4. The authority to initiate removal—at least from the manager's own team—of anyone who seems incapable of doing the work.

But defining the basic nature of the managerial role reveals only part of what a managerial layer means. It cannot tell us how wide a managerial layer should be, what the difference in responsibility should be between a manager and a subordinate, or most important, where the break should come between one managerial layer and another. Fortunately, the next step in the research process supplied the missing piece of the puzzle.

—— RESPONSIBILITY AND TIME

This second step was the unexpected and startling discovery that the level of responsibility in any organizational role—whether a manager's or an individual contributor's—can be objectively measured in terms of the target completion time of the *longest* task, project, or program assigned to that role. The more distant the target completion date of the longest task or program, the heavier the weight of responsibility is felt to be. I call this measure the responsibility time span of the role. For example, a supervisor whose principal job is to plan tomorrow's production assignments and next week's work schedule but who also has ongoing responsibility for uninterrupted production supplies for the month ahead has a responsibility time span of one month. A foreman who spends most of the time riding herd on this week's production quotas but who must also develop a program to deal with the labor requirements of next year's retooling has a responsibility time span of a year or a little more. The advertising vice president who stays late every night working on next week's layouts but who also has to begin making contingency plans for the expected launch of two

EXHIBIT 1
Managerial Hierarchy in Fiction and in Fact

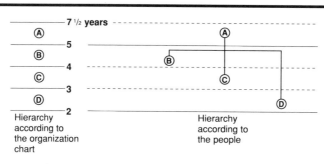

new local advertising media campaigns three years away has a responsibility time span of three years.

To my great surprise, I have found, over the past 35 years, that in all types of managerial organizations in many different countries, people in roles that have the same time spans experience the same weight of responsibility and declare the same level of pay to be fair, regardless of their occupation or actual pay. The time-span range runs from a day at the bottom of a large corporation to more than 20 years at the top, while the felt-fair pay ranges from $15,000 to $1 million and more.

Armed with my definition of a manager and my time-span measuring instrument, I then bumped into the second surprising finding—repeatedly confirmed—about layering in managerial hierarchies: the boundaries between successive managerial layers occur at certain specific time-span increments, just as ice changes to water and water to steam at certain specific temperatures. And the fact that everyone in the hierarchy, regardless of status, seems to see these boundaries in the same places suggests that the boundaries reflect some universal truth about human nature.

Exhibit 1, "Managerial Hierarchy in Fiction and in Fact," shows the hierarchical structure of part of a department at one company I studied, along with the approximate responsibility time span for each position. The longest task for manager A was more than five years, while for B, C, and D, the longest tasks fell between two and five years. Note also that according to the organization chart, A is the designated manager of B, B of C, and C of D.

In reality, the situation was quite different. Despite the managerial roles specified by the company, B, C, and D all described A as their "real" boss. C complained that B was "far too close" and "breathing down my neck." D had the same complaint about C. B and C also admitted to finding it very difficult to manage their immediate subordinates, C and D respectively, who seemed to do better if treated as colleagues and left alone.

In short, there appeared to be a cutoff at five years, such that those with responsibility time spans of less than five years felt they needed a manager with a responsibility time span of more than five years. Manager D, with a time span of two to three years, did not feel that C, with a time span of three to four, was distant enough hierarchically to take orders from. D felt the same way about B. Only A filled the bill for *any* of the other three.

As the responsibility time span increased in the example from two years to three to four and approached five, no one seemed to perceive a qualitative difference in the nature of the responsibility that a manager discharged. Then, suddenly, when a manager had responsibility for tasks and projects that exceeded five years in scope, everyone seemed to perceive a difference not only in the scope of responsibility but also in its quality and in the kind of work and worker required to discharge it.

I found several such discontinuities that appeared consistently in more than 100 studies. Real managerial and hierarchical boundaries occur at time spans of three months, 1 year, 2 years, 5 years, 10 years, and 20 years.

These natural discontinuities in our perception of the responsibility time span create hierarchical strata that people in different companies, countries, and circumstances all seem to regard as genuine and acceptable. The existence of such boundaries has important implications in nearly every sphere of organizational management. One of these is performance appraisal. Another is the capacity of managers to add value to the work of their subordinates.

The only person with the perspective and authority to judge and communicate personal effectiveness is an employee's accountable manager, who in most cases, is also the only person from whom an employee will accept evaluation and coaching. This accountable manager must be the supervisor one real layer higher in the hierarchy, not merely the next higher employee on the pay scale.

As I suggested earlier, part of the secret to making hierarchy work is to distinguish carefully between hierarchical layers and pay grades. The trouble is that companies need two to three times as many pay grades as they do working layers, and once they've established the pay grades, which are easy to describe and set up, they fail to take the next step and set up a different managerial hierarchy based on responsibility rather than salary. The result is too many layers.

My experience with organizations of all kinds in many different countries has convinced me that effective value-adding managerial leadership of subordinates can come only from an individual one category higher in cognitive capacity, working one category higher in problem complexity. By contrast, wherever managers and subordinates are in the same layer—separated only by pay grade—subordinates see the boss as too close, breathing down their necks, and they identify their "real" boss as the next manager at a genuinely higher level of cognitive and task complexity. This kind of overlayering is what produces the typical symptoms of bureaucracy in its worst form—too much passing problems up and down the system, bypassing, poor task setting, frustrated subordinates, anxious managers, wholly inadequate performance appraisals, "personality problems" everywhere, and so forth.

——— LAYERING AT COMPANY X

Companies need more than seven pay grades—as a rule, many more. But seven hierarchical layers is enough or more than enough for all but the largest corporations.

Let me illustrate this pattern of hierarchical layering with the case of two divisions of Company X, a corporation with 32,000 employees and annual sales of $7 billion. As shown in *Exhibit 2,* the CEO sets strategic goals that look ahead as far as 25 years and manages executive vice presidents with responsibility for 12- to 15-year development programs. One vice president is accountable for several strategic business units, each with a president who works with critical tasks of up to 7 years duration.

One of these units (Y Products) employs 2,800 people, has annual sales of $250 million, and is engaged in the manufacture and sale of engineering products, with traditional semiskilled shop-floor production at Layer I. The other unit (Z Press) publishes books and employs only 88 people. Its funding and negotiations with authors are in the hands of a general editor at Layer IV, assisted by a small group of editors at Layer III, each working on projects that may take up to 18 months to complete.

So the president of Y Products manages more people, governs a greater share of corporate resources, and earns a lot more money for the parent company than does the president of Z Press. Yet the two presidents occupy the same hierarchical layer, have similar authority, and take home comparable salaries. This is neither coincidental nor unfair. It is natural, correct, and efficient.

It is the level of responsibility, *measured in terms of time span,* that tells you how many layers you need in an enterprise—not the number of subordinates or the magnitude of sales or profits. These factors may have a marginal influence on salary; they have no bearing at all on hierarchical layers.

——— CHANGES IN THE QUALITY OF WORK

The widespread and striking consistency of this underlying pattern of true managerial layers leads naturally to the question of why it occurs. Why do people perceive a sudden leap in status from, say, 4½ years to 5 and from 9 to 10?

The answer goes back to the earlier discussion of complexity. As we go higher in a managerial hierarchy, the most difficult problems that arise grow increasingly complex, and as the complexity of a task increases, so does the

EXHIBIT 2
Two Divisions of Corporation X

	Layer	Time Span	Felt Fair Pay*
CEO	VII	20 years	$1,040
EVP EVP EVP EVP	VI	10 years	520
President President President	V	5 years	260
General Manager General Editor General Manager General Manager	IV	2 years	130
Unit Managers Editors	III	1 year	68
First-Line Managers	II	3 months	38
Technicians and Operators Typists	I	1 day	20

*(In thousands of dollars)

complexity of the mental work required to handle it. What I found when I looked at this problem over the course of 10 years was that this complexity, like responsibility time span, also occurs in leaps or jumps. In other words, the most difficult tasks found within any given layer are all characterized by the same type or category of complexity, just as water remains in the same liquid state from 0° to 100° Celsius, even though it ranges from very cold to very hot. (A few degrees cooler or hotter and water changes in state, to ice or steam.)

It is this suddenly increased level of necessary mental capacity, experience, knowledge, and mental stamina that allows managers to add value to the work of their subordinates. What they add is a new perspective, one that is broader, more experienced, and most important, one that extends further in time. If the Z Press editors at Layer III find and develop manuscripts into books with market potential, it is their general editor at Layer IV who fits those books into the press's overall list, who thinks ahead to their position on next year's list and later allocates resources to their production and marketing, and who makes projections about the publishing and book-buying trends of the next two to five years.

It is also this sudden change in the quality, not just the quantity, of managerial work that subordinates accept as a natural and appropriate break in the continuum of hierarchy. It is why they accept the boss's authority and not just the boss's power.

So the whole picture comes together. Managerial hierarchy or layering is the only effective organizational form for deploying people and tasks at complementary levels, where people can do the tasks assigned to them, where the people in any given layer can add value to the work of those in the layer below them, and finally, where this stratification of management strikes everyone as necessary and welcome.

What we need is not some new kind of organization. What we need is managerial hierarchy that understands its own nature and purpose. Hierarchy is the best structure for getting work done in big organizations. Trying to raise efficiency and morale without first setting this structure to rights is like trying to lay bricks without mortar. No amount of exhortation, attitudinal engineering, incentive planning, or even leadership will have any permanent effect unless we understand what hierarchy is and why and how it works. We need to stop casting about fruitlessly for organizational Holy Grails and settle down to the hard work of putting our managerial hierarchies in order.

───── DISCUSSION QUESTIONS

1. Hierarchy or bureaucracy has always been a feature of organizational life, and according to the author, hierarchy has never been adequately used. In the rush for innovation in the business world, what other traditional aspects of organizational life are being considered a problem when indeed they may be the solution?

2. The author addresses the issue of accountability. What are some of the factors that contribute to a lack of accountability in many businesses?

3. In your opinion, how effectively does the author make the case for hierarchy? Do his ideas about hierarchy hold up for the organization of the 1990s? How does his argument hold up against those promoting flatter organizations?

4. Relate your work experience in a hierarchical organization. In your experience, what have the positive aspects of hierarchy been? The negative aspects?

5. Would you rather work in a hierarchical or a flat organization? Explain the basis of your preference.

MANAGING ORGANIZATIONAL CHANGE

Choosing Strategies for Change　　26

JOHN P. KOTTER AND LEONARD A. SCHLESINGER

As the business environment becomes more competitive, organizations cannot afford not to change; yet, people in organizations understandably fear and resist change. A major task of managers is to implement change, which means overcoming the resistance. The authors of this reading describe four basic reasons why people resist change and offer various methods for dealing with the different types of resistance.

In 1973, The Conference Board asked 13 eminent authorities to speculate what significant management issues and problems would develop over the next 20 years. One of the strongest themes that runs through their subsequent reports is a concern for the ability of organizations to respond to environmental change. As one person wrote: "It follows that an acceleration in the rate of change will result in an increasing need for reorganization. Reorganization is usually feared, because it means disturbance of the status quo, a threat to people's vested interests in their jobs, and an upset to established ways of doing things. For these reasons, needed reorganization is often deferred, with a resulting loss in effectiveness and an increase in costs."[1]

Subsequent events have confirmed the importance of this concern about organizational change. Today, more and more managers must deal with new government regulations, new products, growth, increased competition, technological developments, and a changing work force. In response, most companies or divisions of major corporations find that they must undertake moderate organizational changes at least once a year and major changes every four or five.[2]

Few organizational change efforts tend to be complete failures, but few tend to be entirely successful either. Most efforts encounter problems; they often take longer than expected and desired; they sometimes kill morale, and they often cost a great deal in terms of managerial time or emotional upheaval. More than a few organizations have not even tried to initiate needed changes because

---

1. Marvin Bower and C. Lee Walton, Jr., "Gearing a Business to the Future," in *Challenge to Leadership* (New York: The Conference Board, 1973), p. 126.

2. For recent evidence on the frequency of changes, *see* Stephen A. Allen, "Organizational Choice and General Influence Networks for Diversified Companies," *Academy of Management Journal,* September 1978, p. 341.

the managers involved were afraid that they were simply incapable of successfully implementing them.

In this reading, we first describe various causes for resistance to change and then outline a systematic way to select a strategy and set of specific approaches for implementing an organizational change effort. The methods described are based on our analyses of dozens of successful and unsuccessful organizational changes.

——— DIAGNOSING RESISTANCE

Organizational change efforts often run into some form of human resistance. Although experienced managers are generally all too aware of this fact, surprisingly few take time before an organizational change to assess systematically who might resist the change initiative and for what reasons. Instead, using past experiences as guidelines, managers all too often apply a simple set of beliefs—such as "engineers will probably resist the change because they are independent and suspicious of top management." This limited approach can create serious problems. Because of the many different ways in which individuals and groups can react to change, correct assessments are often not intuitively obvious and require careful thought.

Of course, all people who are affected by change experience some emotional turmoil. Even changes that appear to be "positive" or "rational" involve loss and uncertainty.[3] Nevertheless, for various reasons, individuals or groups can react very differently to change—from passively resisting it, to aggressively trying to undermine it, to sincerely embracing it.

To predict what form their resistance might take, managers need to be aware of the four most common reasons people resist change. These include a desire not to lose something of value, a misunderstanding of the change and its implications, a belief that the change does not make sense for the organization, and a low tolerance for change.

PAROCHIAL SELF-INTEREST

One major reason people resist organizational change is that they think they will lose something of value as a result. In these cases, because people focus on their own best interests and not on those of the total organization, resistance often results in "politics" or "political behavior."[4] Consider these two examples:

---

3. For example, *see* Robert A. Luke, Jr., "A Structural Approach to Organizational Change," *Journal of Applied Behavioral Science*, September–October 1973, p. 611.

4. For a discussion of power and politics in corporations, *see* Abraham Zaleznik and Manfred F. R. Kets de Vries, *Power and the Corporate Mind* (Boston: Houghton Mifflin, 1975), Chapter 6; and Robert H. Miles, *Macro Organizational Behavior* (Pacific Palisades, Calif.: Goodyear, 1978), Chapter 4.

After several years of rapid growth, the president of an organization decided that its size demanded the creation of a new staff function—New-Product Planning and Development—to be headed by a vice president. Operationally, this change eliminated most of the decision-making power that the vice presidents of marketing, engineering, and production had over new products. Inasmuch as new products were very important in this organization, the change also reduced the vice presidents' status which, together with power, was very important to them.

During the two months after the president announced his idea for a new-product vice president, the existing vice presidents each came up with six or seven reasons why the new arrangement might not work. Their objections grew louder and louder until the president shelved the idea.

A manufacturing company had traditionally employed a large group of personnel people as counselors and "father confessors" to its production employees. This group of counselors tended to exhibit high morale because of the professional satisfaction they received from the helping relationships they had with employees. When a new performance-appraisal system was installed, every six months the counselors were required to provide each employee's supervisor with a written evaluation of the employee's emotional maturity, promotional potential, and so forth.

As some of the personnel people immediately recognized, the change would alter their relationships from a peer and helper to more of a boss and evaluator with most of the employees. Predictably, the personnel counselors resisted the change. While publicly arguing that the new system was not as good for the company as the old one, they privately put as much pressure as possible on the personnel vice president until he significantly altered the new system.

Political behavior sometimes emerges before and during organizational change efforts when what is in the best interests of one individual or group is not in the best interests of the total organization or of other individuals and groups.

Although political behavior sometimes takes the form of two or more armed camps publicly fighting things out, it usually is much more subtle. In many cases, it occurs completely under the surface of public dialogue. Although initiators of power struggles are sometimes scheming and ruthless individuals, more often than not they are people who view their potential loss from change as an unfair violation of their implicit, or psychological, contract with the organization.[5]

---

5. *See* Edgar H. Schein, *Organizational Psychology* (Englewood Cliffs, N.J.: Prentice-Hall, 1965), p. 44.

MISUNDERSTANDING AND LACK OF TRUST

People also resist change when they do not understand its implications and perceive that it might cost them much more than they will gain. Such situations often occur when trust is lacking between the person initiating the change and the employees.[6] Here is an example:

> When the president of a small midwestern company announced to his managers that the company would implement a flexible working schedule for all employees, it never occurred to him that he might run into resistance. He had been introduced to the concept at a management seminar and decided to use it to make working conditions at his company more attractive, particularly to clerical and plant personnel.
>
> Shortly after the announcement, numerous rumors began to circulate among plant employees—none of whom really knew what flexible working hours meant and many of whom were distrustful of the manufacturing vice president. One rumor, for instance, suggested that flexible hours meant that most people would have to work whenever their supervisors asked them to—including evenings and weekends. The employee association, a local union, held a quick meeting and then presented the management with a nonnegotiable demand that the flexible hours concept be dropped. The president, caught completely by surprise, complied.

Few organizations can be characterized as having a high level of trust between employees and managers; consequently, it is easy for misunderstandings to develop when change is introduced. Unless managers surface misunderstandings and clarify them rapidly, they can lead to resistance. And that resistance can easily catch change initiators by surprise, especially if they assume that people only resist change when it is not in their best interest.

DIFFERENT ASSESSMENTS

Another common reason people resist organizational change is that they assess the situation differently from their managers or those initiating the change and see more costs than benefits resulting from the change, not only for themselves but for their company as well. For example:

> The president of one moderate-size bank was shocked by his staff's analysis of the bank's real estate investment trust (REIT) loans. This complicated analysis suggested that the bank could easily lose up to $10 million, and that the possible losses were increasing each month by 20%. Within a week, the president drew up a plan to reorganize the

---

6. *See* Chris Argyris, *Intervention Theory and Method* (Reading, Mass.: Addison-Wesley, 1970), p. 70.

part of the bank that managed REITs. Because of his concern for the bank's stock price, however, he chose not to release the staff report to anyone except the new REIT section manager.

The reorganization immediately ran into massive resistance from the people involved. The group sentiment, as articulated by one person, was, "Has he gone mad? Why in God's name is he tearing apart this section of the bank? His actions have already cost us three very good people [who quit], and have crippled a new program we were implementing [which the president was unaware of] to reduce our loan losses."

Managers who initiate change often assume both that they have all the information required to conduct an adequate organization analysis and that those who will be affected by the change have the same facts, when neither assumption may be correct. In either case, the difference in information that each group works with often leads to different analyses, which in turn can lead to resistance. Moreover, if the analysis made by those not initiating the change is more accurate than that derived by the initiators, resistance is obviously "good" for the organization. But this likelihood is not obvious to some managers who assume that resistance is always bad and therefore always fight it.[7]

LOW TOLERANCE FOR CHANGE

People also resist change because they fear they will not be able to develop the new skills and behavior that will be required of them. All human beings are limited in their ability to change, with some people much more limited than others.[8] Organizational change can inadvertently require people to change too much, too quickly.

Peter F. Drucker has argued that the major obstacle to organizational growth is managers' inability to change their attitudes and behavior as rapidly as their organizations require.[9] Even when managers intellectually understand the need for changes in the way they operate, they sometimes are emotionally unable to make the transition.

It is because of people's limited tolerance for change that individuals will sometimes resist a change even when they realize it is a good one. For example, those who receive significantly more important jobs as a result of an organizational change will probably be very happy. But it is just as possible for such people to also feel uneasy and to resist giving up certain aspects of the current situation. New and very different jobs will require new and different

7. *See* Paul R. Lawrence, "How to Deal with Resistance to Change," *Harvard Business Review* (May–June 1954): 49; reprinted as *Harvard Business Review Classic* (January–February 1969): 4.

8. For a discussion of resistance that is personality based, *see* Goodwin Watson, "Resistance to Change," in *The Planning of Change*, eds. Warren G. Bennis, Kenneth F. Benne, and Robert Chin (New York: Holt, Rinehart, and Winston, 1969), p. 489.

9. Peter F. Drucker, *The Practice of Management* (New York: Harper and Row, 1954).

behaviors, new and different relationships, as well as the loss of some satisfactory current activities and relationships. If the changes are significant and the tolerance for change is low, people might begin actively to resist the change for reasons even they do not consciously understand.

People also sometimes resist organizational change to save face; to go along with the change would be, they think, an admission that some of their previous decisions or beliefs were wrong. Or they might resist because of peer group pressure or because of a supervisor's attitude. Indeed, there are probably an endless number of reasons why people resist change.[10]

Assessing which of the many possibilities might apply to those who will be affected by a change is important because it can help a manager select an appropriate way to overcome resistance. Without an accurate diagnosis of possibilities of resistance, a manager can easily get bogged down during the change process with very costly problems.

────── DEALING WITH RESISTANCE

Many managers underestimate not only the variety of ways people can react to organizational change but also the ways they can positively influence specific individuals and groups during a change. And, again because of past experiences, managers sometimes do not have an accurate understanding of the advantages and disadvantages of the methods with which they are familiar.

EDUCATION AND COMMUNICATION

One of the most common ways to overcome resistance to change is to educate people about it beforehand. Communication of ideas helps people see the need for and the logic of a change. The education process can involve one-on-one discussions, presentations to groups, or memos and reports. For example:

> As a part of an effort to make changes in a division's structure and in measurement and reward systems, a division manager put together a one-hour audiovisual presentation that explained the changes and the reasons for them. Over a four-month period, she made this presentation no less than a dozen times to groups of 20 or 30 corporate and division managers.

---

10. For a general discussion of resistance and reasons for it, *see* Chapter 3 in Gerald Zaltman and Robert Duncan, *Strategies for Planned Change* (New York: John Wiley, 1977).

An education and communication program can be ideal when resistance is based on inadequate or inaccurate information and analysis, especially if the initiators need the resistors' help in implementing the change. But some managers overlook the fact that a program of this sort requires a good relationship between initiators and resistors or that the latter may not believe what they hear. It also requires time and effort, particularly if a lot of people are involved.

PARTICIPATION AND INVOLVEMENT

If the initiators involve the potential resistors in some aspect of the design and implementation of the change, they can often forestall resistance. With a participative change effort, the initiators listen to the people the change involves and use their advice. To illustrate:

> The head of a small financial services company once created a task force to help design and implement changes in his company's reward system. The task force was composed of eight second- and third-level managers from different parts of the company. The president's specific charter to them was that they recommend changes in the company's benefit package. They were given six months and asked to file a brief progress report with the president once a month. After they had made their recommendations, which the president largely accepted, they were asked to help the company's personnel director implement them.

We have found that many managers have quite strong feelings about participation—sometimes positive and sometimes negative. That is, some managers feel that there should always be participation during change efforts, while others feel this is always a mistake. Both attitudes can create problems for a manager, because neither is very realistic.

When change initiators believe they do not have all the information they need to design and implement a change or when they need the wholehearted commitment of others to do so, involving others makes very good sense. Considerable research has demonstrated that, in general, participation leads to commitment, not merely compliance.[11] In some instances, commitment is needed for the change to be a success. Nevertheless, the participation process does have its drawbacks. Not only can it lead to a poor solution if the process is not carefully managed, but also it can be enormously time consuming. When the change must be made immediately, it might take too long to involve others.

---

11. *See*, for example, Alfred J. Marrow, David F. Bowers, and Stanley E. Seashore, *Management by Participation* (New York: Harper and Row, 1967).

FACILITATION AND SUPPORT

Another way that managers can deal with potential resistance to change is by being supportive. This process might include providing training in new skills or giving employees time off after a demanding period or simply listening and providing emotional support. For example:

> Management in one rapidly growing electronics company devised a way to help people adjust to frequent organizational changes. First, management staffed its human resource department with four counselors who spent most of their time talking to people who were feeling burnt out or who were having difficulty adjusting to new jobs. Second, on a selective basis, management offered people four-week minisabbaticals that involved some reflective or educational activity away from work. And, finally, it spent a great deal of money on in-house education and training programs.

Facilitation and support are most helpful when fear and anxiety lie at the heart of resistance. Seasoned, tough managers often overlook or ignore this kind of resistance, as well as the efficacy of facilitative ways of dealing with it. The basic drawback of this approach is that it can be time consuming and expensive and still fail.[12] If time, money, and patience are not available, then using supportive methods will not be very practical.

NEGOTIATION AND AGREEMENT

Another way to deal with resistance is to offer incentives to active or potential resistors. For instance, management could give a union a higher wage rate in return for a rule change; it could increase an individual's pension benefits in return for an early retirement. Here is an example of negotiated agreements:

> In a large manufacturing company, the divisions were very interdependent. One division manager wanted to make some major changes in her organization. Yet, because of the interdependence, she recognized that she would be forcing some inconvenience and change on other divisions as well. To prevent top managers in other divisions from undermining her efforts, the division manager negotiated a written agreement with each manager. The agreement specified the outcomes the other division managers would receive and when, as well as the kinds of cooperation that she would receive from them in return during the change process. Later, whenever the division managers complained about her changes or the change process itself, she could point to the negotiated agreements.

---

12. Zaltman and Duncan, *Strategies for Planned Change,* Chapter 4.

Negotiation is particularly appropriate when someone is going to lose out as a result of a change, and his or her power to resist is significant. Negotiated agreements can be a relatively easy way to avoid major resistance though, like some other processes, they may become expensive. And once a manager makes it clear that he or she will negotiate to avoid major resistance, the manager is vulnerable to the possibility of blackmail.[13]

MANIPULATION AND CO-OPTATION

In some situations, managers also resort to covert attempts to influence others. Manipulation, in this context, normally involves the very selective use of information and the conscious structuring of events.

One common form of manipulation is co-optation. Co-opting an individual usually involves giving him or her a desirable role in the design or implementation of the change. Co-opting a group involves giving one of its leaders, or someone it respects, a key role in the design or implementation of a change. This is not a form of participation, however, because the initiators do not want the advice of the co-opted, merely his or her endorsement. For example:

> One division manager in a large multibusiness corporation invited the corporate human relations vice president, a close friend of the president, to help him and his key staff diagnose some problems the division was having. Because of his busy schedule, the corporate vice president was not able to do much of the actual information gathering or analysis himself, thus limiting his own influence on the diagnoses. But his presence at key meetings helped commit him to the diagnoses as well as the solutions the group designed. The commitment was subsequently very important because the president, at least initially, did not like some of the proposed changes. Nevertheless, after a discussion with his human relations vice president, he did not try to block them.

Under certain circumstances co-optation can be a relatively inexpensive and easy way to gain an individual's or a group's support (cheaper, for example, than negotiation and quicker than participation). Nevertheless, it has its drawbacks. If people feel they are being tricked into not resisting, are not being treated equally, or are being lied to, they may respond unfavorably. More than one manager has found that, by his effort to give some subordinate a sense of participation through co-optation, he created more resistance than if he had done nothing. In addition, co-optation can create a different kind of problem if those co-opted use their ability to influence the design and implementation of changes in ways that are not in the best interests of the organization.

---

13. For an excellent discussion of negotiation, *see* Gerald I. Nierenberg, *The Art of Negotiating* (Birmingham, Ala.: Cornerstone, 1968).

Other forms of manipulation have drawbacks also, sometimes to an even greater degree. Most people are likely to greet what they perceive as covert treatment and/or lies with a negative response. Furthermore, if a manager develops a reputation as a manipulator, it can undermine his ability to use needed approaches such as education/communication and participation/involvement. At the extreme, it can even ruin his career.

Nevertheless, people do manipulate others successfully—particularly when all other tactics are not feasible or have failed.[14] Having no other alternative and not enough time to educate, involve, or support people and without the power or other resources to negotiate, coerce, or co-opt them, managers have resorted to manipulating information channels in order to scare people into thinking there is a crisis coming which they can avoid only by changing.

EXPLICIT AND IMPLICIT COERCION

Finally, managers often deal with resistance coercively. Here they essentially force people to accept a change by explicitly or implicitly threatening them (with the loss of jobs, promotion possibilities, and so forth) or by actually firing or transferring them. As with manipulation, using coercion is a risky process because inevitably people strongly resent forced change. But in situations where speed is essential and where the changes will not be popular, regardless of how they are introduced, coercion may be the manager's only option.

Successful organizational change efforts are always characterized by the skillful application of a number of these approaches, often in very different combinations. However, successful efforts share two characteristics: managers employ the approaches with a sensitivity to their strengths and limitations (see *Exhibit 1*) and appraise the situation realistically.

The most common mistake managers make is to use only one approach or a limited set of them regardless of the situation. A surprisingly large number of managers have this problem. This would include the hard-boiled boss who often coerces people, the people-oriented manager who constantly tries to support and involve people, the cynical boss who always manipulates and co-opts others, the intellectual manager who relies heavily on education and communication, and the lawyerlike manager who usually tries to negotiate.[15]

A second common mistake that managers make is to approach change in a disjointed and incremental way that is not a part of a clearly considered strategy.

---

14. *See* John P. Kotter, "Power, Dependence, and Effective Management," *Harvard Business Review* (July–August 1977): 125.

15. Ibid., p. 135.

EXHIBIT 1
Methods for Dealing with Resistance to Change

APPROACH	COMMONLY USED IN SITUATIONS	ADVANTAGES	DRAWBACKS
Education + communication	Where there is a lack of information or inaccurate information and analysis	Once persuaded, people will often help with the implementation of the change	Can be very time consuming if many people are involved
Participation + involvement	Where the initiators do not have all the information they need to design the change and where others have considerable power to resist	People who participate will be committed to implementing change, and any relevant information they have will be integrated into the change plan	Can be very time consuming if participators design an inappropriate change
Facilitation + support	Where people are resisting because of adjustment problems	No other approach works as well with adjustment problems	Can be time consuming, expensive, and still fail
Negotiation + agreement	Where someone or some group will clearly lose out in a change and where that group has considerable power to resist	Sometimes it is a relatively easy way to avoid major resistance	Can be too expensive in many cases if it alerts others to negotiate for compliance
Manipulation + co-optation	Where other tactics will not work or are too expensive	It can be a relatively quick and inexpensive solution to resistance problems	Can lead to future problems if people feel manipulated
Explicit + implicit coercion	Where speed is essential and the change initiators possess considerable power	It is speedy and can overcome any kind of resistance	Can be risky if it leaves people mad at the initiators

CHOICE OF STRATEGY

In approaching an organizational change situation, managers explicitly or implicitly make strategic choices regarding the speed of the effort, the amount of preplanning, the involvement of others, and the relative emphasis they will give to different approaches. Successful change efforts seem to be those where these choices both are internally consistent and fit some key situational variables.

The strategic options available to managers can be usefully thought of as existing on a continuum (see *Exhibit 2*).[16] At one end of the continuum, the

---

16. *See* Larry E. Greiner, "Patterns of Organization Change," *Harvard Business Review* (May–June 1967): 119; and Larry E. Greiner and Louis B. Barnes, "Organization Change and Development," in *Organizational Change and Development,* eds. Gene W. Dalton and Paul R. Lawrence (Homewood, Ill.: Irwin, 1970), p. 3.

EXHIBIT 2
Strategic Continuum

FAST	SLOWER
Clearly planned	Not clearly planned at the beginning
Little involvement of others	More involvement of others
Attempt to overcome any resistance	Attempt to minimize any resistance

Key Situational Variables

The amount and type of resistance anticipated

The position of the initiators vis-à-vis the resistors (in terms of power, trust, etc.)

The locus of relevant data for designing the change and of needed energy for implementing it

The stakes involved (e.g., the presence or lack of presence of a crisis, the consequences of resistance and lack of change)

change strategy calls for a very rapid implementation, a clear plan of action, and little involvement of others. This type of strategy mows over any resistance and, at the extreme, would result in a fait accompli. At the other end of the continuum, the strategy would call for a much slower change process, a less clear plan, and the involvement of many people other than the change initiators. This type of strategy is designed to reduce resistance to a minimum.[17]

The further to the left one operates on the continuum in *Exhibit 2*, the more one tends to be coercive and the less one tends to use the other approaches—especially participation; the converse also holds.

Organizational change efforts that are based on inconsistent strategies tend to run into predictable problems. For example, efforts that are not clearly planned in advance and yet are implemented quickly tend to become bogged down owing to unanticipated problems. Efforts that involve a large number of people, but are implemented quickly, usually become either stalled or less participative.

SITUATIONAL FACTORS

Exactly where a change effort should be strategically positioned on the continuum in *Exhibit 2* depends on four factors:

17. For a good discussion of an approach that attempts to minimize resistance, *see* Renato Tagiuri, "Notes on the Management of Change: Implication of Postulating a Need for Competence," in John P. Kotter, Vijay Sathe, and Leonard A. Schlesinger, *Organization* (Homewood, Ill.: Irwin, 1979).

1. *The amount and kind of resistance that is anticipated.* All other factors being equal, the greater the anticipated resistance, the more difficult it will be simply to overwhelm it, and the more a manager will need to move toward the right on the continuum to find ways to reduce some of it.[18]
2. *The position of the initiator vis-à-vis the resistors, especially regarding power.* The less power the initiator has with respect to others, the more the initiating manager *must* move to the right on the continuum.[19] Conversely, the stronger the initiator's position, the more he or she can move to the left.
3. *The person who has the relevant data for designing the change and the energy for implementing it.* The more the initiators anticipate that they will need information and commitment from others to help design and implement the change, the more they must move to the right.[20] Gaining useful information and commitment requires time and the involvement of others.
4. *The stakes involved.* The greater the short-run potential for risks to organizational performance and survival if the present situation is not changed, the more one must move to the left.

Organizational change efforts that ignore these factors inevitably run into problems. A common mistake some managers make, for example, is to move too quickly and involve too few people despite the fact that they do not have all the information they really need to design the change correctly.

Insofar as these factors still leave a manager with some choice of where to operate on the continuum, it is probably best to select a point as far to the right as possible for both economic and social reasons. Forcing change on people can have too many negative side effects over both the short and the long term. Change efforts using the strategies on the right of the continuum can often help develop an organization and its people in useful ways.[21]

In some cases, however, knowing the four factors may not give a manager a comfortable and obvious choice. Consider a situation where a manager has a weak position vis-à-vis the people whom she thinks need a change and yet is faced with serious consequences if the change is not implemented immediately. Such a manager is clearly in a bind. If she somehow is not able to increase her power in the situation, she will be forced to choose some compromise strategy and to live through difficult times.

---

18. Jay W. Lorsch, "Managing Change," in *Organizational Behavior and Administration*, eds. Paul R. Lawrence, Louis B. Barnes, and Jay W. Lorsch (Homewood, Ill.: Irwin, 1976), p. 676.
19. Ibid.
20. Ibid.
21. Michael Beer, *Organization Change and Development: A Systems View* (Santa Monica, Calif.: Goodyear, 1980).

IMPLICATIONS FOR MANAGERS

Managers can improve their chance of success in an organizational change effort by doing the following:

1. *Conducting an organizational analysis that identifies the current situation, problems, and the forces that are possible causes of those problems.* The analysis should specify the actual importance of the problems, the speed with which the problems must be addressed if additional problems are to be avoided, and the kinds of changes that are generally needed.

2. *Conducting an analysis of factors relevant to producing the needed changes.* This analysis should focus on questions of who might resist the change, why, and how much; who has information that is needed to design the change, and whose cooperation is essential in implementing it; and what is the position of the initiator vis-à-vis other relevant parties in terms of power, trust, normal modes of interaction, and so forth.

3. *Selecting a change strategy, based on the previous analysis.* This analysis should specify the speed of change, the amount of preplanning, and the degree of involvement of others; select specific tactics for use with various individuals and groups; and be internally consistent.

4. *Monitoring the implementation process.* No matter how good a job one does of initially selecting a change strategy and tactics, something unexpected will eventually occur during implementation. Only by carefully monitoring the process can one identify the unexpected in a timely fashion and react to it intelligently.

Interpersonal skills, of course, are the key to using this analysis. But even the most outstanding interpersonal skills will not make up for a poor choice of strategy and tactics. And in a business world that continues to become more and more dynamic, the consequences of poor implementation choices will become increasingly severe.

—— DISCUSSION QUESTIONS

1. The reading mentions education and communication as "one of the most common ways to overcome resistance to change." What are the positive attitudes about change that you would want to instill in employees? What are negative attitudes toward change that you would want to acknowledge?

2. Considering your personal temperament, what method of dealing with resistance to change suggested by the authors would you be prone to choose? What action would you take to verify your decision?

3. What steps can an organization take to incorporate healthier attitudes toward change in its corporate culture?

4. Resistance to change is not necessarily wrong. Give an example— hypothetical or one from your own experience—when resistance could actually be the proper outcome to a proposed change.

5. What are changes that American businesses need to make to remain competitive? What aspects of American culture promote change? What aspects resist change?

6. Compare and contrast factors that might influence (1) a national company versus a multinational company regarding change; (2) a single business versus multibusiness; and (3) a manufacturing business versus a service business.

27 Evolution and Revolution as Organizations Grow

LARRY E. GREINER

This author maintains that growing organizations move through five distinguishable phases of development, each of which contains a calm period of growth that ends with a management crisis. He argues, moreover, that because each phase is strongly influenced by the previous one, a management with a sense of its own organization history can anticipate and prepare for the next developmental crisis. This reading provides a prescription for appropriate management action in each of the five phases, and it shows how companies can turn organizational crises into opportunities for future growth.

A small research company chooses too complicated and formalized an organization structure for its young age and limited size. It flounders in rigidity and bureaucracy for several years and is finally acquired by a larger company.

Key executives of a retail store chain hold on to an organization structure long after it has served its purpose, because their power is derived from this structure. The company eventually goes into bankruptcy.

A large bank disciplines a "rebellious" manager who is blamed for current control problems, when the underlying causes are centralized procedures that are holding back expansion into new markets. Many younger managers subsequently leave the bank, competition moves in, and profits are still declining.

The problems of these companies, like those of many others, are rooted more in past decisions than in present events or outside market dynamics. Historical forces do indeed shape the future growth of organizations. Yet management, in its haste to grow, often overlooks critical developmental questions such as Where has our organization been? Where is it now? And what do the answers to these questions mean for where we are going? Instead, management's gaze is fixed outward toward the environment and the future—as if more precise market projections will provide a new organizational identity.

Companies fail to see that many clues to their future success lie within their own organizations and their evolving states of development. Moreover, the inability of management to understand its organization-development problems can result in a company becoming frozen in its current stage of evolution or, ultimately, in failure, regardless of market opportunities.

My position in this reading is that the future of an organization may be determined less by outside forces than it is by the organization's history. In stressing the force of history on an organization, I have drawn from the legacies of European psychologists (their thesis being that individual behavior is determined primarily by previous events and experiences, not by what lies ahead). Extending this analogy of individual development to the problems of organization development, I shall discuss a series of developmental phases through which growing companies tend to pass. But, first, let me provide two definitions:

- The term *evolution* is used to describe prolonged periods of growth where no major upheaval occurs in organization practices.
- The term *revolution* is used to describe those periods of substantial turmoil in organization life.

As a company progresses through developmental phases, each evolutionary period creates its own revolution. For instance, centralized practices eventually lead to demands for decentralization. Moreover, the nature of management's solution to each revolutionary period determines whether a company will move forward into its next stage of evolutionary growth. As I shall show later, there are at least five phases of organization development, each characterized by both an evolution and a revolution.

——— KEY FORCES IN DEVELOPMENT

During the past few years a small amount of research knowledge about the phases of organization development has been building. Some of this research is very quantitative, such as time-series analyses that reveal patterns of economic performance over time.[1] The majority of studies, however, are case-oriented and use company records and interviews to reconstruct a rich picture of corporate development.[2] Yet both types of research tend to be heavily empirical without attempting more generalized statements about the overall process of development.

A notable exception is the historical work of Alfred D. Chandler, Jr., in his book *Strategy and Structure*.[3] This study depicts four very broad and general phases in the lives of four large U.S. companies. It proposes that outside market opportunities determine a company's strategy, which in turn determines the company's organization structure. This thesis has a valid ring for the four companies examined by Chandler, largely because they developed in a time of

---

1. *See*, for example, William H. Starbuck, "Organizational Metamorphosis," in *Promising Research Directions*, edited by R. W. Millman and M. P. Hottenstein (Tempe, Arizona: Academy of Management, 1968), p. 113.

2. *See*, for example, the *Grangesberg* case series, prepared by C. Roland Christensen and Bruce R. Scott, IMEDE, Lausanne, Switzerland.

3. *Strategy and Structure: Chapters in the History of the American Industrial Enterprise* (Cambridge, Mass., The M.I.T. Press, 1962).

explosive markets and technological advances. But more recent evidence suggests that organization structure may be less malleable than Chandler assumed; in fact, structure can play a critical role in influencing corporate strategy. It is this reverse emphasis on how organization structure affects future growth which is highlighted in the model presented in this reading.

From an analysis of various studies, five key dimensions emerge as essential for building a model of organization development:[4]

1. The age of the organization
2. The size of the organization
3. The stages of evolution
4. The stages of revolution
5. The growth rate of the industry

Each of these elements will be discussed separately, but first note their combined effect as illustrated in *Exhibit 1*. Note especially how each dimension influences the other over time; when all five elements begin to interact, a more complete and dynamic picture of organizational growth emerges.

After describing these dimensions and their interconnections, each evolutionary/revolutionary phase of development will be discussed. Next the reading will discuss how each stage of evolution breeds its own revolution and how management solutions to each revolution determine the next stage of evolution.

AGE OF THE ORGANIZATION

The most obvious and essential dimension for any model of development is the life span of an organization (represented as the horizontal axis in *Exhibit 1*). All historical studies gather data from various points in time and then make comparisons. From these observations, it is evident that the same organization practices are not maintained throughout a long time span. This makes a most basic point: management problems and principles are rooted in time. The concept of decentralization, for example, can have meaning for describing corporate practices at one time period but loses its descriptive power at another.

---

4. I have drawn on many sources for evidence: a) numerous cases collected at the Harvard Business School; b) *Organization Growth and Development*, edited by William H. Starbuck (Middlesex, England: Penguin Books, Ltd., 1971), where several studies are cited; and c) articles published in journals, such as Lawrence E. Fouraker and John M. Stopford, "Organization Structure and the Multinational Strategy," *Administrative Science Quarterly*, Vol. 13, No. 1 (1968): 47; and Malcolm S. Salter, "Management Appraisal and Reward Systems," *Journal of Business Policy*, Vol. 1, No. 4 (1971).

EXHIBIT 1
Model of Organization Development

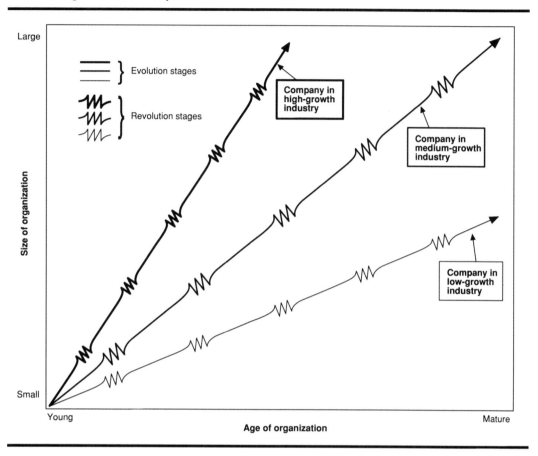

The passage of time also contributes to the institutionalization of managerial attitudes. As a result, employee behavior becomes not only more predictable but also more difficult to change when attitudes are outdated.

SIZE OF THE ORGANIZATION

This dimension is depicted as the vertical axis in *Exhibit 1*. A company's problems and solutions tend to change markedly as the number of employees and sales volume increase. Thus, time is not the only determinant of structure; in fact, organizations that do not grow in size can retain many of the same management issues and practices over lengthy periods. In addition to increased size, however, problems of coordination and communication magnify, new functions emerge, levels in the management hierarchy multiply, and jobs become more interrelated.

STAGES OF EVOLUTION

As both age and size increase, another phenomenon becomes evident: the prolonged growth that I have termed the evolutionary period. Most growing organizations do not expand for two years and then retreat for one year; rather, those that survive a crisis usually enjoy four to eight years of continuous growth without a major economic setback or severe internal disruption. The term *evolution* seems appropriate for describing these quieter periods because only modest adjustments appear necessary for maintaining growth under the same overall pattern of management.

STAGES OF REVOLUTION

Smooth evolution is not inevitable; it cannot be assumed that organization growth is linear. *Fortune's* "500" list, for example, has had significant turnover during the last 50 years. Thus we find evidence from numerous case histories that reveals periods of substantial turbulence spaced between smoother periods of evolution.

I have termed these turbulent times the periods of revolution because they typically exhibit a serious upheaval of management practices. Traditional management practices, which were appropriate for a smaller size and earlier time, are brought under scrutiny by frustrated top managers and disillusioned lower-level managers. During such periods of crisis, a number of companies fail—those unable to abandon past practices and effect major organization changes are likely either to fold or to level off in their growth rates.

The critical task for management in each revolutionary period is to find a new set of organization practices that will become the basis for managing the next period of evolutionary growth. Interestingly enough, these new practices eventually sow their own seeds of decay and lead to another period of revolution. Companies therefore experience the irony of seeing a major solution in one time period become a major problem at a later date.

GROWTH RATE OF THE INDUSTRY

The speed at which an organization experiences phases of evolution and revolution is closely related to the market environment of its industry. For example, a company in a rapidly expanding market will have to add employees rapidly; hence, the need for new organization evolutions to accommodate large staff increases is accelerated. While evolutionary periods tend to be relatively short in fast-growing industries, much longer evolutionary periods occur in mature or slowly growing industries.

Evolution can also be prolonged, and revolutions delayed, when profits come easily. For instance, companies that make grievous errors in a rewarding industry can still look good on their profit-and-loss statements; thus, they can avoid a change in management practices for a longer period. The aerospace industry in its infancy is an example. Yet revolutionary periods still occur, as one did in aerospace when profit opportunities began to dry up. Revolutions seem to be much more severe and difficult to resolve when the market environment is poor.

──── PHASES OF GROWTH

With the foregoing framework in mind, let us now examine in depth the five specific phases of evolution and revolution. As shown in *Exhibit 2*, each evolutionary period is characterized by the dominant *management style* used to achieve growth, while each revolutionary period is characterized by the dominant *management problem* that must be solved before growth can continue. The patterns presented in *Exhibit 2* seem to be typical for companies in industries with moderate growth over a long time period; companies in faster-growing industries tend to experience all five phases more rapidly, while those in slower-growing industries encounter only two or three phases over many years.

It is important to note that *each phase is both an effect of the previous phase and a cause for the next phase*. For example, the evolutionary management style in Phase 3 of the exhibit is "delegation," which grows out of and becomes the solution to demands for greater "autonomy" in the preceding Phase 2 revolution. The style of delegation used in Phase 3, however, eventually provokes a major revolutionary crisis that is characterized by attempts to regain control over the diversity created through increased delegation.

The principal implication of each phase is that management actions are narrowly prescribed if growth is to occur. For example, a company experiencing an autonomy crisis in Phase 2 cannot return to directive management for a solution—it must adopt a new style of delegation in order to move ahead.

PHASE 1: CREATIVITY

In the birth stage of an organization, the emphasis is on creating both a product and a market. Here are the characteristics of the period of creative evolution:

- The company's founders are usually technically or entrepreneurially oriented, and they disdain management activities; their physical and mental energies are absorbed entirely in making and selling a new product.
- Communication among employees is frequent and informal.
- Long hours of work are rewarded by modest salaries and the promise of ownership benefits.
- Control of activities comes from immediate marketplace feedback; the management acts as the customers react.

The Leadership Crisis   All of the foregoing individualistic and creative activities are essential for the company to get off the ground. But therein lies the problem. As the company grows, larger production runs require knowledge about the efficiencies of manufacturing. Increased numbers of employees cannot be managed exclusively through informal communication; new employees are not motivated by an intense dedication to the product or organization. Additional capital must be secured, and new accounting procedures are needed for financial control.

Thus the founders find themselves burdened with unwanted management responsibilities. So they long for the good old days, still trying to act as they did in the past. And conflicts between the harried leaders grow more intense.

EXHIBIT 2
The Five Phases of Growth

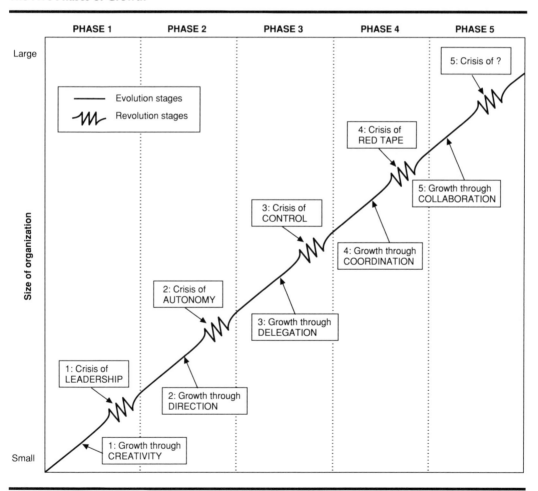

At this point a crisis of leadership occurs, which is the onset of the first revolution. Who is to lead the company out of confusion and solve the managerial problems confronting it? Quite obviously, a strong manager is needed who has the necessary knowledge and skill to introduce new business techniques. But this is easier said than done. The founders often hate to step aside even though they are probably temperamentally unsuited to be managers. So here is the first critical developmental choice—to locate and install a strong business manager who is acceptable to the founders and who can pull the organization together.

PHASE 2: DIRECTION

Those companies that survive the first phase by installing a capable business manager usually embark on a period of sustained growth under able and directive leadership. Here are the characteristics of this evolutionary period:

- A functional organization structure is introduced to separate manufacturing from marketing activities, and job assignments become more specialized.
- Accounting systems for inventory and purchasing are introduced.
- Incentives, budgets, and work standards are adopted.
- Communication becomes more formal and impersonal as a hierarchy of titles and positions builds.
- The new manager and his or her key supervisors take most of the responsibility for instituting direction, while lower-level supervisors are treated more as functional specialists than as autonomous decision-making managers.

The Autonomy Crisis   Although the new directive techniques channel employee energy more efficiently into growth, they eventually become inappropriate for controlling a larger, more diverse and complex organization. Lower-level employees find themselves restricted by a cumbersome and centralized hierarchy. They have come to possess more direct knowledge about markets and machinery than do the leaders at the top; consequently, they feel torn between following procedures and taking initiative on their own.

Thus the second revolution is imminent as a crisis develops from demands for greater autonomy on the part of lower-level managers. The solution adopted by most companies is to move toward greater delegation. Yet it is difficult for top managers who previously were successful at being directive to give up responsibility. Moreover, lower-level managers are not accustomed to making decisions for themselves. As a result, numerous companies flounder during this revolutionary period, adhering to centralized methods while lower-level employees grow more disenchanted and leave the organization.

PHASE 3: DELEGATION

The next era of growth evolves from the successful application of a decentralized organization structure. It exhibits these characteristics:

- Much greater responsibility is given to the managers of plants and market territories.
- Profit centers and bonuses are used to stimulate motivation.
- The top executives at headquarters restrain themselves to managing by exception, based on periodic reports from the field.
- Management often concentrates on making new acquisitions that can be lined up beside other decentralized units.
- Communication from the top is infrequent, usually by correspondence, telephone, or brief visits to field locations.

The delegation stage proves useful for gaining expansion through heightened motivation at lower levels. Decentralized managers with greater authority and incentive are able to penetrate larger markets, respond faster to customers, and develop new products.

The Control Crisis   A serious problem eventually evolves, however, as top executives sense that they are losing control over a highly diversified field operation. Autonomous field managers prefer to run their own shows without coordinating plans, money, technology, and personnel with the rest of the organization. Freedom breeds a parochial attitude.

Hence, the Phase 3 revolution is under way when top management seeks to regain control over the total company. Some top management teams attempt a return to centralized management, which usually fails because of the vast scope of operations. Those companies that move ahead find a new solution in the use of special coordination techniques.

PHASE 4: COORDINATION

During this phase, the evolutionary period is characterized by the use of formal systems for achieving greater coordination and by top executives taking responsibility for the initiation and administration of these new systems, for example:

- Decentralized units are merged into product groups.
- Formal planning procedures are established and intensively reviewed.
- Numerous staff members are hired and located at headquarters to initiate companywide programs of control and review for line managers.
- Capital expenditures are carefully weighed and parceled out across the organization.

- Each product group is treated as an investment center where return on invested capital is an important criterion used in allocating funds.
- Certain technical functions, such as data processing, are centralized at headquarters, while daily operating decisions remain decentralized.
- Stock options and companywide profit sharing are used to encourage identity with the firm as a whole.

All of these new coordination systems prove useful for achieving growth through more efficient allocation of a company's limited resources. They prompt field managers to look beyond the needs of their local units. Although these managers still have much decision-making responsibility, they learn to justify their actions more carefully to a watchdog audience at headquarters.

The Red-Tape Crisis   A lack of confidence gradually builds between line and staff and between headquarters and the field, however. The proliferation of systems and programs begins to exceed its utility; a red-tape crisis is created. Line managers, for example, increasingly resent heavy staff direction from those who are not familiar with local conditions. Staff people, on the other hand, complain about uncooperative and uninformed line managers. Together both groups criticize the bureaucratic paper system that has evolved. Procedures take precedence over problem solving, and innovation is dampened. In short, the organization has become too large and complex to be managed through formal programs and rigid systems. The Phase 4 revolution is under way.

PHASE 5: COLLABORATION

The last observable phase in previous studies emphasizes strong interpersonal collaboration in an attempt to overcome the red-tape crisis. Where Phase 4 was managed more through formal systems and procedures, Phase 5 emphasizes greater spontaneity in management action through teams and the skillful confrontation of interpersonal differences. Social control and self-discipline take over from formal control. This transition is especially difficult for those experts who created the old systems as well as for those line managers who relied on formal methods for answers.

The Phase 5 evolution, then, builds around a more flexible and behavioral approach to management. Here are its characteristics:

- The focus is on solving problems quickly through team action.
- Teams are combined across functions for task-group activity.
- Headquarters staff experts are reduced in number, reassigned, and combined in interdisciplinary teams to consult with, not to direct, field units.
- A matrix-type structure is frequently used to assemble the right teams for the appropriate problems.

- Previous formal systems are simplified and combined into single multipurpose systems.
- Conferences of key managers are held frequently to focus on major problem issues.
- Educational programs are utilized to train managers in behavioral skills for achieving better teamwork and conflict resolution.
- Real-time information systems are integrated into daily decision making.
- Economic rewards are geared more to team performance than to individual achievement.
- Experiments in new practices are encouraged throughout the organization.

The Crisis   What will be the revolution in response to this stage of evolution? Many large U.S. companies are now in the Phase 5 evolutionary stage, so the answers are critical. Although there is little clear evidence, I imagine the revolution will center around the psychological saturation of employees who grow emotionally and physically exhausted by the intensity of teamwork and the heavy pressure for innovative solutions.

My hunch is that the Phase 5 revolution will be solved through new structures and programs that allow employees to periodically rest, reflect, and revitalize themselves. We may even see companies with dual organization structures: a "habit" structure for getting the daily work done, and a "reflective" structure for stimulating perspective and personal enrichment. Employees then could move back and forth between the two structures as their energies are dissipated and refueled.

One European organization has implemented just such a structure. Five reflective groups have been established outside the regular structure for the purpose of continuously evaluating five task activities basic to the organization. They report directly to the managing director, although their reports are made public throughout the organization. Membership in each group includes all levels and functions, and employees are rotated through these groups every six months.

Other concrete examples now in practice include providing sabbaticals for employees, moving managers in and out of "hot-spot" jobs, establishing a four-day workweek, ensuring job security, building physical facilities for relaxation during the working day, making jobs more interchangeable, creating an extra team on the assembly line so that one team is always off for reeducation, and switching to longer vacations and more flexible working hours.

The Chinese practice of requiring executives to spend time periodically on lower-level jobs may also be worth a nonideological evaluation. For too long U.S. management has assumed that career progress should be equated with an upward path toward title, salary, and power. Could it be that some vice presidents of marketing might just long for, and even benefit from, temporary duty in the field sales organization?

IMPLICATIONS OF HISTORY

Let me now summarize some important implications for practicing managers. First, the main features of this discussion are depicted in *Exhibit 3,* which shows the specific management actions that characterize each growth phase. These actions are also the solutions that ended each preceding revolutionary period.

In one sense, I hope that many readers will react to my model by calling it obvious and natural for depicting the growth of an organization. To me this type of reaction is a useful test of the model's validity.

But at a more reflective level I imagine some of these reactions are more hindsight than foresight. Those experienced managers who have been through a developmental sequence can empathize with it now, but how did they react when in the middle of a stage of evolution or revolution? They can probably recall the limits of their own developmental understanding at that time. Perhaps they resisted desirable changes or were even swept emotionally into a revolution without being able to propose constructive solutions. So let me offer some explicit guidelines for managers of growing organizations to keep in mind.

Know Where You Are in the Developmental Sequence   Every organization and its component parts are at different stages of development. The task of top management is to be aware of these stages; otherwise, it may not recognize when the time for change has come, or it may act to impose the wrong solution.

Top leaders should be ready to work with the flow of the tide rather than against it; yet they should be cautious, because it is tempting to skip phases out of impatience. Each phase results in certain strengths and learning experiences in the organization that will be essential for success in subsequent phases. A child prodigy, for example, may be able to read like a teenager, but he cannot behave like one until he ages through a sequence of experiences.

I also doubt that managers can or should act to avoid revolutions. Rather, these periods of tension provide the pressure, ideas, and awareness that afford a platform for change and the introduction of new practices.

Recognize the Limited Range of Solutions   In each revolutionary stage it becomes evident that this stage can be ended only by certain specific solutions; moreover, these solutions are different from those that were applied to the problems of the preceding revolution. Too often it is tempting to choose solutions that were tried before, which makes it impossible for a new phase of growth to evolve.

Management must be prepared to dismantle current structures before the revolutionary stage becomes too turbulent. Top managers, realizing that their own managerial styles are no longer appropriate, may even have to take themselves out of leadership positions. A good Phase 2 manager facing Phase 3 might be wise to find another Phase 2 organization that better fits his or her talents, either outside the company or with one of its newer subsidiaries.

EXHIBIT 3
Organization Practices During Evolution in the Five Phases of Growth

CATEGORY	PHASE 1	PHASE 2	PHASE 3	PHASE 4	PHASE 5
Management Focus	Make and sell	Efficiency of operations	Expansion of market	Consolidation of organization	Problem solving and innovation
Organization Structure	Informal	Centralized and functional	Decentralized and geographical	Line-staff and product groups	Matrix of teams
Top Management Style	Individualistic and entrepreneurial	Directive	Delegative	Watchdog	Participative
Control System	Market results	Standards and cost centers	Reports and profit centers	Plans and investment centers	Mutual goal setting
Management Reward Emphasis	Ownership	Salary and merit increases	Individual bonus	Profit sharing and stock options	Team bonus

Finally, evolution is not an automatic affair; it is a contest for survival. To move ahead, companies must consciously introduce planned structures that not only are solutions to a current crisis but also are fitted to the *next* phase of growth. This requires considerable self-awareness on the part of top management, as well as great interpersonal skill in persuading other managers that change is needed.

Realize That Solutions Breed New Problems   Managers often fail to realize that organizational solutions create problems for the future, such as when a decision to delegate eventually causes a problem of control. Historical actions are very much determinants of what happens to the company at a much later date.

An awareness of this effect should help managers to evaluate company problems with greater historical understanding instead of pinning the blame on a current development. Better yet, managers should be in a position to *predict* future problems, and thereby to prepare solutions and coping strategies before a revolution gets out of hand.

A management that is aware of the problems ahead could well decide *not* to grow. Top managers may, for instance, prefer to retain the informal practices of a small company, knowing that this way of life is inherent in the organization's limited size, not in their congenial personalities. If they choose to grow, they may do themselves out of a job and a way of life they enjoy.

And what about the managements of very large organizations? Can they find new solutions for continued phases of evolution? Or are they reaching a stage where the government will act to break them up because they are too large?

───── CONCLUDING NOTE

Clearly, there is still much to learn about processes of development in organizations. The phases outlined here are only five in number and are still only approximations. Researchers are just beginning to study the specific developmental problems of structure, control, rewards, and management style in different industries and in a variety of cultures.

One should not, however, wait for conclusive evidence before educating managers to think and act from a developmental perspective. The critical dimension of time has been missing for too long from our management theories and practices. The intriguing paradox is that by learning more about history we may do a better job in the future.

───── DISCUSSION QUESTIONS

1. The author states that growth through collaboration or teamwork characterizes evolution in Phase 5. Social control and self-discipline mark the transition. Based on cultural history, what are possible difficulties that Americans might have with this approach? What characteristics of American culture support this approach?

2. The author has provided a scenario for the next revolution. Do you agree? If you do, what do you see as the next scenario for the revolution arising out of this evolution? If you disagree, what scenario would you propose as an alternative to the one the author has suggested?

3. How could the phases of organization development based on evolution and revolution be used to assist human resource management in its hiring decisions? In the reassignment of personnel? In other practices?

4. The author stresses the force of history on an organization. Give examples from your work life when you have been influenced by the force of your own work history. How have you changed? Were the changes you made internal (new behaviors or outlooks) or external (new careers or companies)?

5. Is it possible to apply the theory of evolution and revolution to a country's competitive position? For example, compare American and Japanese competitiveness based on this theory.

28   Leading Change

MICHAEL BEER

Dissatisfaction with the status quo is the source of motivation for change. This reading describes how company leaders can "create" dissatisfaction in their organization and define a vision of how the organization can improve both its internal and competitive performance. Change is inevitably painful and must be carried out with care and deliberation. The author offers a variety of insights on managing transitions effectively, emphasizing the importance of helping individuals and groups understand the reasons for the change as well as involving them in its implementation.

Leading change has become a crucial competence for managers. International competition and deregulation have forced corporations to seek and adopt more effective approaches to management, strategic planning, marketing, and manufacturing. In many firms these changes amount to major shifts in the culture, or in the basic behavior and belief system, of the organization.

This reading presents a conceptual formula incorporating the critical dimensions of change that must be considered by managers.[1] The formula can be summarized as follows:

$$\text{Amount of Change} = (\text{Dissatisfaction} \times \text{Model} \times \text{Process}) > \text{Cost of Change}$$

DISSATISFACTION

For change to take place, key organization members must be dissatisfied with the status quo and lack confidence in themselves and their organization. This dissatisfaction is the source of energy or motivation for the change. That energy is essential because change demands extraordinary commitment.

What conditions lead executives to be dissatisfied with the status quo? A survey of the contemporary business scene quickly leads to the conclusion that crisis is the most frequent condition that energizes change. But must companies approach the precipice before major adaptation to new conditions

---

1. This change formula was developed by me based on discussions with Dr. Alan Burns many years ago. I subsequently learned that the formula came from David Gleicher. It is also discussed in Michael Beer, *Organization Change and Development: A Systems View* (Santa Monica, Calif.: Goodyear, 1980).

is possible? Are the human and economic costs of a crisis an inevitable by-product of major change? The answer to these questions is no. Change can be stimulated and managed without crisis, though managers should be ready to use external crisis, when it presents itself, as a vehicle for managing planned change.

What, then, is the alternative to crisis as the stepping-stone to change? If dissatisfaction is necessary for change, then corporate leaders must create dissatisfaction in their organizations. They may use one or more of the following methods:

1. Managers can use information about the organization's competitive environment to generate discussions of current or prospective problems. Top management often does not understand why employees are not as concerned as it is about productivity, customer service, or cost. Often this situation is created because management has not provided employees with the same data that have led to management dissatisfaction. Sometimes this information is kept from employees because it is thought to be confidential. Companies trying to be more competitive have begun communicating this information to employee groups and union leaders.

2. Similarly, information about the concerns of employees and their perceptions about how the company is being run can be a powerful tool for creating dissatisfaction among managers. Just as competitive information can be a tool for creating dissatisfaction downward so attitude surveys (through interviews and questionnaires) can be a powerful tool for creating dissatisfaction upward. Consider managers who do not know their subordinates feel uninvolved because these managers control too closely, or top management that does not understand how the vitality of the organization is being sapped by overmanagement from corporate staff groups.

3. There must be a dialogue between managers and employees about the meaning of the data. Through dialogue, managers and employees can inform each other about their underlying assumptions and reach a joint understanding of the organization's problems. A shared explanation of root causes is key to a process of mutual adaptation by all stakeholders.

4. Managers can also create the energy for change by setting high, but realistic, standards and expecting employees to meet them. The managerial act of stating expectations is an effective means of creating dissatisfaction as long as the manager is trusted and seen as credible. Although managers often state expectations for profit performance, they rarely demand specific behaviors, even when the behaviors necessary to turn a situation around are known. Specifying organizational and individual behaviors is important to successful change.

These methods can individually or in concert unleash discontent and mobilize energy for change. But if managers are to channel this discontent into focused efforts, they must concern themselves with the model in the change formula.

—— MODEL

A vision of the future state of the organization—its behaviors and attitudes as well as structure and systems—is necessary for change to occur. Such a vision not only serves the purpose of energizing change but also provides a model toward which employees and managers can work. Management should design the model based on its own diagnosis of root causes of organizational problems, examples of excellent practice observed in visits to other companies, and the ideas of leading consultants and academics.

The envisioned state should reflect the multidimensionality of organizations. The model should specify hard aspects of organization design, strategy, structure, and systems, as well as the soft elements of style, staff, skills, and shared values.[2] Too often, change efforts to improve the organization specify only one or two of these dimensions, usually strategy and structure, and ignore the behaviors, attitudes, and competencies required for the new organization to work. Moreover, the specification of a multidimensional model forces managers to examine the fit between elements. Ignoring the multiple elements of organization is one of the reasons for failure to change organizational behavior and culture.

The multidimensional model must also fit the diagnosis of the organization's problems. The organizational arrangements contemplated for the future should induce those behaviors that are keys to its success. Much theory and experience support the proposition that organizational arrangements (structure, systems, style, etc.) differ for companies that compete through low cost as compared with companies that compete through innovation and differentiation. At the same time, the organizational arrangements contemplated must match the needs and expectations of employees and the social culture of the country in which the company is embedded. Through analysis and discussion, the designers of the model must determine that their vision of the future is viable.

As the change effort unfolds, it is extremely beneficial to have an organizational unit within the firm that represents successful application of the new practice from which others can learn and become convinced. Most companies undergoing transformations toward employee involvement have at least one leading-edge plant that serves as their model. Prospective change managers visit these plants or are transferred into them for a period of time so that they

---

2. Waterman, Robert, T. Peters, and J. Philips, "Structure Is Not Organization," *Business Horizons,* June 1980.

can learn new management approaches and apply them in their own assignments as change managers.

——— PROCESS

Organizational change is not instantaneous. A model of how the organization is to be structured does not quickly translate into change in the
behaviors of large aggregates of employees. Managers sometimes make the
mistake of assuming that announcing the change is the same as making it
happen. How often is a Friday memorandum expected to translate into change
on Monday morning?

The process for change is a sequence of events, speeches, meetings,
educational programs, personnel decisions, and other actions aimed at helping
employees, including top management, learn new perspectives, skills, attitudes,
and behaviors. The elements of the process required to gain commitment
and/or compliance need attention. Although commitment is clearly the more
desirable means for achieving change, doses of compliance are inevitably part
of the change process even when employees have been involved in developing
the new model. Often change that starts with compliance becomes change to
which individuals become committed as they engage in the new management
practice.

All things being equal, people will become committed to that which they
help create. Effective processes of change involve those affected in planning the
change and executing it. The direction of the change may be set by the general
manager, but many significant aspects of the change can be determined by
individuals at lower levels. Executives often underestimate the amount of
involvement in change employees can constructively undertake or the types of
decisions in which employees can participate.

Despite the possibilities for participation when trust exists, the politics
of change must be understood and managed. Even individuals who want to put
the interest of the organization ahead of their own, succeed in doing so only
partially and only some of the time. It is, therefore, important for managers to
recognize the realities of self-interest and to cultivate support from individuals
and groups. Coalitions must be formed to support change and the voice of
support must be louder than the voice of resistance to change. Managers
succeed in making participation work by placing supporters on key task forces
or committees and by developing sufficient political support for them to be
taken seriously by those who might otherwise resist.

Because behavioral change is required, the process of organizational
change demands that change managers discuss ineffective or inappropriate
behavior with managers and workers. In effective organizational transformation, change managers confront ineffective or inappropriate behavior early.
That discussion leads to adaptation or replacement. Too often, however,

managers who are leading a change do not confront these difficult problems, thus calling into question management's commitment to the new model.

Difficult personnel decisions are an important part of every major cultural change. When participation, politics, and performance appraisal fail, replacement becomes the only option if momentum is to be maintained. The transfer or termination of some individuals and the promotion of others who fit the new model is common in most organizational changes. The consistency of this finding leads to this rule of thumb: if no replacements are taking place, there is probably no major cultural change occurring.

More important, effective change requires careful planning for succession. Are the candidates for promotion consistent with the new model? If they are not, how can the corporation hire or develop these types of managers? How can the corporation most effectively use the limited number of managers who fit the new model?

Major organizational change is a matter of years—not days or months. Therefore, the capacity of the change manager to be patient and persistent is a key ingredient in managing change. Transforming an organization can be frustrating; other problems are always demanding attention. Managers often lose the will to confront difficult problems that arise or to continue expending the necessary energy for keeping the change effort alive. The proper time perspective helps as does the development of a change process that can maintain focus, organize the activities that are part of the effort, and provide emotional support for change leaders. Developing a network of change managers who periodically meet and consult with each other is one way to persist.

▬▬▬ THE COST OF CHANGE

The change formula suggests that if organizational change is to occur, D, M, and P must all be present in sufficient strength to overcome the cost of change. The cost of change is the *losses* employees and other stakeholders anticipate as a result of the change. What are the typical losses incurred?

Power   Major change involves a shift in power. That power may be from manufacturing to marketing, from first-line supervisors to production workers, from staff to line, or from distributors to the direct sales force. Groups and their managers who will be losing power typically resist such shifts because of the implications for influence, careers, and status in the organization.

Competence   New models require new competencies and make old ones obsolete. A shift in marketing focus from the sale of products to the sale of systems will require systems-oriented salespersons and will make narrower-product salespeople obsolete. A shift to more participative management will devalue the skills of first-line supervisors who rely on technical competence to direct others. A new set of people and process skills will be required. The fear of losing competencies relied on to be successful can be very threatening; people feel a loss of mastery and dignity.

Relationships   Security and comfort in daily work come from a network of dependable relationships. Changes in organizational arrangement typically require new relationships and therefore make obsolete this network of people.

Rewards   Most major organizational changes involve the reassignment of individuals, changes in title and perquisites, changes in pay grades, and consequently, changes in actual compensation. Thus, major change threatens the tangible and intangible rewards of some individuals. A smaller office, the loss of a vice president's title, the loss of points, the loss of a company car, the loss of a private parking space, exclusion from eligibility for a bonus—all these can cause resistance to the change. This may occur even when the change is not intended to signal demotion.

Identity   Many of these losses amount in whole or in part to a change in the role of the individual manager or worker in the organization's social fabric. Thus, changes in the workplace often mean a crisis in personal identity. Managers and other professionals for whom work is central to a concept of self are particularly vulnerable to this loss of self-esteem.

——— BALANCING DRIVING FORCES WITH REDUCTION OF LOSSES

The fear of losses is the cause of resistance to change. The change formula, *Change = (D × M × P) > Cost*, suggests that the greater the potential losses, the stronger the $D \times M \times P$ must be. Major changes require considerable dissatisfaction, a clear vision of the future model, and a well-planned process. Alternatively, change momentum may be increased by working on the loss side of the equation, by reducing resistance through a reduction in perceived losses. How might losses be reduced?

Losses of competence may be reduced by strong efforts to develop employees in the newly required skills. Development means not only training but also counseling and coaching from supervisors and human resource professionals. The development of new career paths that support the change can also pave the way. If all this is done well before the actual rearrangement of the organization, the threat of the change can be reduced. Similarly, people can be helped to establish new relationships before having to permanently break the old.

These efforts require substantial deviation from the accepted practice of announcing the change and making it immediately. Corporations usually do not provide an interim period when people are still in their old jobs but know what their new positions will be and with whom they will work. Allowing people to participate in planning changes is, of course, another way to establish new relationships and develop competencies. As people discuss the future, they begin to make necessary adaptations in attitude and to anticipate competencies required.

Losses in power and rewards are harder to face. Nevertheless, a manager can help individuals adapt to these losses through empathy and listening and by helping them reorient their perceptions of themselves. By emphasizing the value of the new role, a manager can help an employee develop a new professional identity. Individuals who experience losses can adapt to them faster if they are allowed a legitimate outlet for their initial anger and then are helped, through dialogue, to go through a rationalization process, which will help them create meaning out of their new circumstances.

The role of losses in creating resistance to change has implications for the design of adaptive organizations. Organizations that have fewer distinctions in power and rewards—in other words, more egalitarian organizations—give people fewer things to lose. In such organizations people are more willing to take jobs and roles called for by the changes in competitive circumstances. Similarly, losses in relationships and competence are less likely to be experienced in organizations that have high trust and that naturally encourage lateral job mobility, collaboration, and integration. Finally, change will be less threatening to a sense of competence if employees have multiple skills and a broad corporate perspective developed through cross-functional career paths.

Leading change is not easy and cannot be reduced to simple or quick fixes. Change leaders must persist over a long time in involving many individuals and groups in understanding why change is needed, formulating a new approach to organizing and managing, and selecting and developing employees who fit the vision.

——— DISCUSSION QUESTIONS

1. Do you agree with the formula for change offered in this reading? Are there elements that you would change, leave out, or add? Apply this model to your own personal experience with a change in your life.

2. There are inevitable changes facing companies in the 1990s, such as the changing demographics of the work force. Give an example of a change that is not inevitable but that a company might decide to make rather than *have to* make.

3. Imagine that you are working for a company and you hit upon an idea for change that would make your organization more effective. There is no crisis, you are ahead of your time. Discuss how you would approach handling this change as the company's president, as a middle manager, and as a line worker or regular employee.

4. The reading mentions elements of design that are important for organizational change. What might an organization's design look like when it is successfully implementing change? Can an organization have a different design and still implement successful change?

5. In the past, tradition has been considered important to an organization's identity and unity. What is the role of tradition in an organization that is leading change?

Speed, Simplicity, Self-Confidence: An Interview with Jack Welch

NOEL TICHY AND RAM CHARAN

Jack Welch, chairman and CEO of General Electric, believes that a large company must operate with the flexibility and agility of a small company. In this interview, he discusses the companywide drive he has implemented to eliminate unproductive work and energize employees. The centerpiece of Welch's transformation process is Work-Out—a program through which representatives of GE's 14 businesses meet regularly to identify and resolve problems. In describing his goals for GE and his means of attaining them, Welch offers a variety of insights into the qualities of effective leaders and effective organizations.

John F. Welch, Jr., chairman and CEO of General Electric, leads one of the world's largest corporations. It is a very different corporation from the one he inherited in 1981. GE is now built around 14 distinct businesses—including aircraft engines, medical systems, engineering plastics, major appliances, NBC television, and financial services. They reflect the aggressive strategic redirection Welch unveiled soon after he became CEO.

By now the story of GE's business transformation is familiar. In 1981, Welch declared that the company would focus its operations on three "strategic circles"—core manufacturing units such as lighting and locomotives, technology-intensive businesses, and services—and that each of its businesses would rank first or second in its global market. GE has achieved world market-share leadership in nearly all of its 14 businesses. In 1988, its 300,000 employees generated revenues of more than $50 billion and net income of $3.4 billion.

GE's strategic redirection had essentially taken shape by the end of 1986. Since then, Welch has embarked on a more imposing challenge: building a revitalized "human engine" to animate GE's formidable "business engine."

His program has two central objectives. First, he is championing a companywide drive to identify and eliminate unproductive work in order to energize GE's employees. It is neither realistic nor useful, Welch argues, to expect employees of a decidedly leaner corporation to complete all the reports, reviews, forecasts, and budgets that were standard operating procedure in more forgiving times. He is developing procedures to speed decision cycles, move information through the organization, provide quick and effective feedback, and evaluate and reward managers on qualities such as openness, candor, and self-confidence.

Second, and perhaps of even greater significance, Welch is leading a transformation of attitudes at GE—struggling, in his words, to release "emotional energy" at all levels of the organization and encourage creativity and feelings of ownership and self-worth. His ultimate goal is to create an enterprise that can tap the benefits of global scale and diversity without the stifling costs of bureaucratic controls and hierarchical authority and without a managerial focus on personal power and self-perpetuation. This requires a transformation not only of systems and procedures, he argues, but also of people themselves.

What makes a good manager?

Jack Welch: I prefer the term "business leader." Good business leaders create a vision, articulate the vision, passionately own the vision, and relentlessly drive it to completion. Above all else, though, good leaders are open. They go up, down, and around their organization to reach people. They don't stick to the established channels. They're informal. They're straight with people. They make a religion out of being accessible. They never get bored telling their story.

Real communication takes countless hours of eyeball to eyeball, back and forth. It means more listening than talking. It's not pronouncements on a videotape, it's not announcements in a newspaper. It is human beings coming to see and accept things through a constant interactive process aimed at consensus. And it must be absolutely relentless. That's a real challenge for us. There's still not enough candor in this company.

What do you mean by "candor"?

I mean facing reality, seeing the world as it is rather than as you wish it were. We've seen over and over again that businesses facing market downturns, tougher competition, and more demanding customers inevitably make forecasts that are much too optimistic. This means they don't take advantage of the opportunities change usually offers. Change in the marketplace isn't something to fear; it's an enormous opportunity to shuffle the deck, to replay the game. Candid managers—leaders—don't get paralyzed about the fragility of the organization. They tell people the truth. That doesn't scare them because they realize their people know the truth anyway.

We've had managers at GE who couldn't change, who kept telling us to leave them alone. They wanted to sit back, to keep things the way they were. And that's just what they did—until they and most of their staffs had to go. That's the lousy part of this job. What's worse is that we still don't understand why so many people are incapable of facing reality, of being candid with themselves and others.

But we are clearly making progress in facing reality, even if the progress is painfully slow. Take our locomotive business. That team was the only one we've ever had that took a business whose forecasts and plans were headed straight up, and whose market began to head straight down, a virtual collapse, and managed to change the tires while the car was moving. It's the team that forecast the great locomotive boom, convinced us to invest $300 million to renovate its plant in Erie, and then the market went boom all right—right into a crater. But when it did, that team turned on a dime. It reoriented the business.

Several of our other businesses in the same situation said, "Give it time, the market will come back." Locomotive didn't wait. And today, now that the market *is* coming back, the business looks great. The point is, what determines your destiny is not the hand you're dealt; it's how you play the hand. And the best way to play your hand is to face reality—see the world the way it is—and act accordingly.

What makes an effective organization?

For a large organization to be effective, it must be simple. For a large organization to be simple, its people must have self-confidence and intellectual self-assurance. Insecure managers create complexity. Frightened, nervous managers use thick, convoluted planning books and busy slides filled with everything they've known since childhood. Real leaders don't need clutter. People must have the self-confidence to be clear, precise, to be sure that every person in their organization—highest to lowest—understands what the business is trying to achieve. But it's not easy. You can't believe how hard it is for people to be simple, how much they fear being simple. They worry that if they're simple, people will think they're simpleminded. In reality, of course, it's just the reverse. Clear, tough-minded people are the most simple.

Soon after you became CEO, you articulated GE's now-famous strategy of "number one or number two globally." Was that an exercise in the power of simplicity?

Yes. In 1981, when we first defined our business strategy, the real focus was Japan. The entire organization had to understand that GE was in a tougher, more competitive world, with Japan as the cutting edge of the new competition. Nine years later, that competitive toughness has increased by a factor of 5 or 10. We face a revitalized Japan that's migrated around the world—to Thailand, Malaysia, Mexico, the United States—and responded successfully to a massive yen change. Europe is a different game today. There are great European business people, dynamic leaders, people who are changing things. Plus you've got all the other Asian successes.

So being number one or number two globally is more important than ever. But scale alone is not enough. You have to combine financial strength, market position, and technology leadership with an organizational focus on speed, agility, and simplicity. The world moves so much faster today. You can be driving through Seoul, talking to France on the phone and making a deal, and have a fax waiting for you when you get back to the United States with the deal in good technical shape. Paolo Fresco, senior vice president of GE International, has been negotiating around-the-clock for the past two days on a deal in England. Last night I was talking with Larry Bossidy, one of our vice chairmen, who was in West Germany doing another deal. We never used to do business this way. So you can be the biggest, but if you're not flexible enough to handle rapid change and make quick decisions, you won't win.

How have you implemented your commitment to simplicity at the highest levels of GE, where you can have the most direct impact on what happens?

First, we took out management layers. Layers hide weaknesses. Layers mask mediocrity. I firmly believe that an overburdened, overstretched executive is the best executive because he or she doesn't have the time to meddle, to deal in trivia, to bother people. Remember the theory that a manager should have no more than 6 or 7 direct reports? I say the right number is closer to 10 or 15. This way you have no choice but to let people flex their muscles, let them grow and mature. With 10 or 15 reports, a leader can focus only on the big important issues, not on minutiae.

We also reduced the corporate staff. Headquarters can be the bane of corporate America. It can strangle, choke, delay, and create insecurity. If you're going to have simplicity in the field, you can't have a big staff at home. We don't need the questioners and the checkers, the nitpickers who bog down the process, people whose only role is to second-guess and kibitz, the people who clog communication inside the company. Today people at headquarters are experts in taxes, finance, or some other key area that can help people in the field. Our corporate staff no longer just challenges and questions; it assists. This is a mind-set change; staff essentially reports to the field rather than the other way around.

So many CEOs disparage staff and middle management—you know, "If only those bureaucrats would buy into my vision." When you talk about "nitpickers" and "kibitzers," are you talking about lousy people or about good people forced into lousy jobs?

People are not lousy, period. Leaders have to find a better fit between their organization's needs and their people's capabilities. Staff people, whom I prefer to call individual contributors, can be tremendous sources of added value in an organization. But each staff person has to ask, How do I add value? How do I help make people on the line more effective and more competitive? In the past, many staff functions were driven by control rather than adding value. Staffs with that focus have to be eliminated. They sap emotional energy in the organization. As for middle managers, they can be the stronghold of the organization. But their jobs have to be redefined. They have to see their roles as a combination of teacher, cheerleader, and liberator, not controller.

You've dismantled GE's groups and sectors, the top levels of the corporate organization to which individual strategic business units once reported. That certainly makes the organization chart more simple—you now have 14 separate businesses reporting directly to you or your two vice chairmen. How does the new structure simplify how GE operates on a day-to-day basis?

Cutting the groups and sectors eliminated communications filters. Today there is direct communication between the CEO and the leaders of the 14 businesses. We have very short cycle times for decisions and little interference by corporate staff. A major investment decision that used to take a year can now be made in a matter of days.

We also run a Corporate Executive Council, the CEC. For two days every quarter, we meet with the leaders of the 14 businesses and our top staff people. These aren't stuffy, formal strategic reviews. We share ideas and information candidly and openly, including programs that have failed. The important thing is that at the end of those two days everyone in the CEC has seen and discussed the same information. The CEC creates a sense of trust, a sense of personal familiarity and mutual obligation at the top of the company. We consider the CEC a piece of organizational technology that is very important for our future success.

Still, how can it be "simple" to run a $50 billion enterprise? Doesn't a corporation as vast as GE need management layers, extensive review systems, and formal procedures—if for no other reason than to keep the business under control?

People always overestimate how complex business is. This isn't rocket science; we've chosen one of the world's more simple professions. Most global businesses have three or four critical competitors, and you know who they are. And there aren't that many things you can do with a business. It's not as if you're choosing among 2,000 options.

You mentioned review systems. At our 1986 officers' meeting, which involves the top 100 or so executives at GE, we asked the 14 business leaders to present reports on the competitive dynamics in their businesses. How'd we do it? We had them each prepare one-page answers to five questions: What are your market dynamics globally today, and where are they going over the next several years? What actions have your competitors taken in the last three years to upset those global dynamics? What have you done in the last three years to affect those dynamics? What are the most dangerous things your competitor could do in the next three years to upset those dynamics? What are the most effective things you could do to bring your desired impact on those dynamics?

Five simple charts. After those initial reviews, which we update regularly, we could assume that everyone at the top knew the plays and had the same playbook. It doesn't take a genius. Fourteen businesses each with a playbook of five charts. So when Larry Bossidy is with a potential partner in Europe, or I'm with a company in the Far East, we're always there with a competitive understanding based on our playbooks. We know exactly what makes sense; we don't need a big staff to do endless analysis. That means we should be able to act with speed.

Probably the most important thing we promise our business leaders is fast action. Their job is to create and grow new global businesses. Our job in the executive office is to facilitate, to go out and negotiate a deal, to make the acquisition, or get our businesses the partners they need. When our business leaders call, they don't expect studies—they expect answers.

Take the deal with Thomson, where we swapped our consumer electronics business for their medical equipment business. We were presented with an opportunity, a great solution to a serious strategic problem, and we were able to act quickly. We didn't need to go back to headquarters for a strategic analysis and a bunch of reports. Conceptually, it took us about 30 minutes to decide that the deal made sense and then a meeting of maybe two hours with the Thomson people to work out the basic terms. We signed a letter of intent in five days. We had to close it with the usual legal details, of course, so from beginning to end it took five months. Thomson had the same clear view of where it wanted to go—so it worked perfectly for both sides.

Another of our jobs is to transfer best practices across all the businesses, with lightning speed. Staff often put people all over the place to do this. But they aren't effective lightning rods to transfer best practice; they don't have the stature in the organization. Business leaders do. That's why every CEC meeting deals in part with a generic business issue—a new pay plan, a drug-testing program, stock options. Every business is free to propose its own plan or program and present it at the CEC, and we put it through a central screen at corporate, strictly to make sure it's within the bounds of good sense. We don't approve the details. But we want to know what the details are so we can see which programs are working and immediately alert the other businesses to the successful ones.

You make it sound so easy.

Simple *doesn't* mean easy, especially as you try to move this approach down through the organization. When you take out layers, you change the exposure of the managers who remain. They sit right in the sun. Some of them blotch immediately; they can't stand the exposure of leadership.

We now have leaders in each of the businesses who *own* those businesses. Eight years ago, we had to sell the idea of ownership. Today the challenge is to move that sense of ownership, that commitment to relentless personal interaction and immediate sharing of information, down through the organization. We're very early in this, and it's going to be anything but easy. But it's something we have to do.

From an organizational point of view, how are the 14 businesses changing? Are they going through a delayering process? Are their top people communicating as the CEC does?

In addition to locomotives, which I've already discussed, we've had major delayering and streamlining in almost all of our businesses, and they have made significant improvements in total cost productivity.

The CEC concept is flowing down as well. For example, each of the businesses has created its own executive committee to meet on policy questions. These committees meet weekly or monthly and include the top staff and line people from the businesses. Everyone in the same room, everyone with the same information, everyone buying into the targets. Each business also has an operations committee. This is a bigger group of maybe 30 people for each business: 5 staffers, 7 people from manufacturing, 6 from engineering, 8 from marketing, and so on. They get together every quarter for a day and a half to thrash out problems, to get people talking across functions, to communicate with each other about their prospects and programs. That's 30 people in 14 businesses, more than 400 people all together, in a process of instant communication about their businesses and the company.

You see, I operate on a very simple belief about business. If there are six of us in a room, and we all get the same facts, in most cases, the six of us will reach roughly the same conclusion. And once we all accept that conclusion, we can force our energy into it and put it into action. The problem is, we don't get the same information. We each get different pieces. Business isn't complicated. The complications arise when people are cut off from information they need. That's what we're trying to change.

> *That brings us to Work-Out, which you've been championing inside GE since early this year. Why are you pushing it so hard?*

Work-Out is absolutely fundamental to our becoming the kind of company we must become. [See the *Appendix* at end of reading for an example of Work-Out.] That's why I'm so passionate about it. We're not going to succeed if people end up doing the same work they've always done, if they don't feel any psychic or financial impact from the way the organization is changing. The ultimate objective of Work-Out is so clear. We want 300,000 people with different career objectives, different family aspirations, different financial goals, to share directly in this company's vision, the information, the decision-making process, and the rewards. We want to build a more stimulating environment, a more creative environment, a freer work atmosphere, with incentives tied directly to what people do.

Now, the business leaders aren't particularly thrilled that we're so passionate about Work-Out. In 1989, the CEO is going to every business in this company to sit in on a Work-Out session. That's a little puzzling to them. "I own the business, what are you doing here?" they say. Well, I'm not there to tell them how to price products, what type of equipment they need, whom to hire; I have no comments on that.

But Work-Out is the next generation of what we're trying to do. We had to put in a process to focus on and change how work gets done in this company. We have to apply the same relentless passion to Work-Out that we did in selling the vision of number one and number two globally. That's why we're pushing it so hard, getting so involved.

What is the essence of Work-Out, the basic goal?

Work-Out has a practical and an intellectual goal. The practical objective is to get rid of thousands of bad habits accumulated since the creation of General Electric. How would you like to move from a house after 112 years? Think of what would be in the closets and the attic—those shoes that you'll wear to paint next spring, even though you know you'll never paint again. We've got 112 years of closets and attics in this company. We want to flush them out, to start with a brand new house with empty closets, to begin the whole game again.

The second thing we want to achieve, the intellectual part, begins by putting the leaders of each business in front of 100 or so of their people, 8 to 10 times a year, to let them hear what their people think about the company, what they like and don't like about their work, about how they're evaluated, about how they spend their time. Work-Out will expose the leaders to the vibrations of their business—opinions, feelings, emotions, resentments, not abstract theories of organization and management.

Ultimately, we're talking about redefining the relationship between boss and subordinate. I want to get to a point where people challenge their bosses every day: "Why do you require me to do these wasteful things? Why don't you let me do the things you shouldn't be doing so you can move on and create? That's the job of a leader—to create, not to control. Trust me to do my job, and don't make me waste all my time trying to deal with you on the control issue."

Now, how do you get people communicating with each other with that much candor? You put them together in a room and make them thrash it out.

These Work-Out sessions—and I've already done several of them—create all kinds of personal dynamics. Some people go and hide. Some don't like the dinner in the evening because they can't get along with the other people. Some emerge as forceful advocates. As people meet over and over, though, more of them will develop the courage to speak out. The norm will become the person who says, "Dammit, we're not doing it. Let's get on with doing it." Today the norm in most companies, not just GE, is not to bring up critical issues with a boss, certainly not in a public setting, and certainly not in an atmosphere where self-confidence has not been developed. This process will create more fulfilling and rewarding jobs. The quality of work life will improve dramatically.

It's one thing to insist that the people who report directly to you, or who work one or two layers below you, become forceful advocates and criticize the status quo. They've got your support. But what about people lower in the organization, people who have to worry how their bosses will react?

You're right on the hottest issue—when a boss reacts to criticism by saying, "I'll get that guy." Now, hopefully, that guy is so good he quits that same week and shows the boss where that attitude gets him. That's not the best result for GE, of course, but that's what it may take to shake people up.

It's not going to be easy to get the spirit and intent of Work-Out clear throughout the company. I had a technician at my house to install some appliances recently. He said, "I saw your videotape on Work-Out. The guys at my level understand what you're talking about: we'll be free to enjoy our work more, not just do more work, and to do more work on our own. But do you know how our supervisors interpreted it? They pointed to the screen and said, 'You see what he's saying, you guys better start busting your butts.'" We have a long way to go!

The potential for meanness in an organization, for a variety of reasons, is often in inverse proportion to level. People at the top have more time and resources to be fair. I wasn't trained to be a judge, but I spend a lot of time worrying about fairness. The data I get generally favor the manager over the employee. But we have two people at headquarters, fairness arbitrators so to speak, who sift the situation. So when I get a problem, I can smell it and feel it and try to figure out what's really happening. Managers down in the organization don't have the time or help for that. They too often say, "This is how we do it here, go do it." Work-Out is going to break down those attitudes. Managers will be in front of their people, challenged in a thousand different ways, held to account.

> *To change behavior, you must also change how people are compensated and rewarded. Are those systems being changed at GE?*

We let every business come up with its own pay plan. It can create bonus plans in any way that makes sense. We're also doing all kinds of exciting things to reward people for their contributions, things we've never done before. For example, we now give out $20 to $30 million in management awards every year—cash payments to individuals for outstanding performance. We're trying desperately to push rewards down to levels where they never used to be. Stock options now go to 3,000 people, up from 400 ten years ago, and that's probably still not enough.

> *Another way to influence behavior is to promote people based on the characteristics you want to encourage. How can you evaluate executives on qualities as subjective as candor and speed?*

Not only can we do it, we *are* doing it. Again, we're starting at the top of the company and, as the new systems prove themselves, we'll drive them down. We took three years to develop a statement on corporate values, what we as a company believe in. It was a brutal process. We talked to 5,000 people at our management development center in Crotonville. We sweated over every word. This will be the first year that our Session C meetings, the intensive process we use to evaluate the officers of the company, revolve around that value statement. We've told the business leaders that they must rank each of their officers on a scale of one to five against the business and individual characteristics in that statement (see the *Exhibit*). Then I, Larry Bossidy, and Ed Hood, our other vice chairman, will rate the officers and see where we agree or disagree with the business leaders.

We had a long discussion about this in the CEC. People said just what you said: "How can you put a number on how open people are, on how directly they face reality?" Well, they're going to have to—the best numbers they can come up with, and then we'll argue about them. We have to know if our people are open and self-confident, if they believe in honest communication and quick action, if the people we hired years ago have changed. The only way to test our progress is through regular evaluations at the top and by listening to every audience we appear before in the company.

> *All corporations, but especially giant corporations like GE, have implicit social and psychological contracts with their employees—mutual responsibilities and loyalties by which each side abides. What is GE's psychological contract with its people?*

Like many other large companies in the United States, Europe, and Japan, GE has had an implicit psychological contract based on perceived lifetime employment. People were rarely dismissed except for cause or severe business downturns, like in Aerospace after Vietnam. This produced a paternal, feudal, fuzzy kind of loyalty. You put in your time, worked hard, and the company took care of you for life.

That kind of loyalty tends to focus people inward. But given today's environment, people's emotional energy must be focused outward on a competitive world where no business is a safe haven for employment unless it is winning in the marketplace. The psychological contract has to change. People at all levels have to feel the risk-reward tension.

My concept of loyalty is not "giving time" to some corporate entity and, in turn, being shielded and protected from the outside world. Loyalty is an affinity among people who want to grapple with the outside world and win. Their personal values, dreams, and ambitions cause them to gravitate toward each other and toward a company like GE that gives them the resources and opportunities to flourish.

The new psychological contract, if there is such a thing, is that jobs at GE are the best in the world for people who are willing to compete. We have the best training and development resources and an environment committed to providing opportunities for personal and professional growth.

> *How deeply have these changes penetrated? How different does it feel to be a GE manager today versus five years ago?*

It depends how far down you go. In some old-line factories, they probably feel it a lot less than we would like. They hear the words every now and then, but they don't feel a lot of difference. That's because the people above them haven't changed enough yet. Don't forget, we built much of this company

EXHIBIT
GE Value Statement

BUSINESS CHARACTERISTICS	*INDIVIDUAL CHARACTERISTICS*

Lean

What – Reduce tasks and the people required to do them.
Why – Critical to developing world cost leadership.

Agile

What – Delayering.
Why – Create fast decision making in rapidly changing world through improved communication and increased individual response.

Creative

What – Development of new ideas—innovation.
Why – Increase customer satisfaction and operating margins through higher-value products and services.

Ownership

What – Self-confidence to trust others. Self-confidence to delegate to others the freedom to act while, at the same time, self-confidence to involve higher levels in issues critical to the business and the corporation.
Why – Support concept of more individual responsibility, capability to act quickly and independently. Should increase job satisfaction and improve understanding of risks and rewards. Although delegation is critical, there is a small percentage of high-impact issues that need or require involvement of higher levels within the business and within the corporation.

Reward

What – Recognition and compensation commensurate with risk and performance—highly differentiated by individual, with recognition of total team achievement.
Why – Necessary to attract and motivate the type of individuals required to accomplish GE's objectives. A #1 business should provide #1 people with #1 opportunity.

Reality

What – Describe the environment as it is—not as we hope it to be.
Why – Critical to developing a vision and a winning strategy, and to gaining universal acceptance for their implementation.

Leadership

What – Sustained passion for and commitment to a proactive, shared vision and its implementation.
Why – To rally teams toward achieving a common objective.

Candor/Openness

What – Complete and frequent sharing of information with individuals (appraisals, etc.) and organization (everything).
Why – Critical to employees knowing where they, their efforts, and their business stand.

Simplicity

What – Strive for brevity, clarity, the "elegant, simple solution"—less is better.
Why – Less complexity improves everything, from reduced bureaucracy to better product designs to lower costs.

Integrity

What – Never bend or wink at the truth, and live within both the spirit and letter of the laws of every global business arena.
Why – Critical to gaining the global arenas' acceptance of our right to grow and prosper. Every constituency: shareowners who invest; customers who purchase; community that supports; and employees who depend on, expect, and deserve our unequivocal commitment to integrity in every facet of our behavior.

Individual Dignity

What – Respect and leverage the talent and contribution of every individual in both good and bad times.
Why – Teamwork depends on trust, mutual understanding, and the shared belief that the individual will be treated fairly in any environment.

in the 1950s around the blue books and POIM: plan, organize, integrate, measure. We brought people in buses over to Crotonville and drilled it into them. Now we're saying, "Liberate, trust," and people look up and say, "What?" We're trying to make a massive cultural break. This is at least a 5-year process, probably closer to 10.

What troubles you about what's happened to date?

First, there's a real danger of the expectation level getting ahead of reality. I was at Crotonville recently, talking about Work-Out, and someone said, "I don't feel it yet." Well, we're only a few months into it, it's much too early.

No matter how many exciting programs you implement, there seems to be a need for people to spend emotional energy criticizing the administration of the programs rather than focusing on the substance. I can sit in the Crotonville pit and ask, "How many of you are part of a new pay plan?" More than half the hands go up. "How many of you have received a management award in the last year?" More than 90% of the hands go up. "How many of you are aware of stock options?" All the hands go up. And yet many of these people don't see what we're trying to do with the programs, why we've put them in place. The emotional energy doesn't focus often enough on the objectives of the bonus plan or the excitement of the management award; it focuses on the details. The same is true of Work-Out. We'll have too much discussion on the Work-Out "process" and not enough on the "objective" to instill speed, simplicity, and self-confidence in every person in the organization.

When will we know whether these changes have worked?
What's your report card?

A business magazine recently printed an article about GE that listed our businesses and the fact that we were number one or number two in virtually all of them. That magazine didn't get one complaint from our competitors. Those are the facts. That's what we said we wanted to do, and we've done it.

Ten years from now, we want magazines to write about GE as a place where people have the freedom to be creative, a place that brings out the best in everybody. An open, fair place where people have a sense that what they do matters, and where that sense of accomplishment is rewarded in both the pocketbook and the soul. That will be our report card.

———————————

APPENDIX
Work-Out: A Case Study

GE Medical Systems (GEMS) is the world leader in medical diagnostic imaging equipment, including CT scanners, magnetic resonance equipment, and X-ray mammography. Its more than 15,000 employees face formidable international competition. Despite positive financial results, GEMS is working to transform its human organization. Work-Out is designed to identify sources of frustration and bureaucratic inefficiency, eliminate unnecessary and unproductive work, and overhaul how managers are evaluated and rewarded.

Work-Out began last fall when some 50 GEMS employees attended a five-day offsite session in Lake Lawn, Wisconsin. The participants included senior vice president and group executive John Trani, his staff, six employee relations managers, and informal leaders from technology, finance, sales, service, marketing, and manufacturing. Trani selected these informal leaders for their willingness to take business risks, challenge the status quo, and contribute in other key ways to GEMS. We participated as Work-Out faculty members and have participated in follow-up sessions that will run beyond 1989.

The Lake Lawn session took place after two important preliminary steps. First, we conducted in-depth interviews with managers at all levels of GEMS. Our interviews uncovered many objections to and criticisms of existing procedures, including measurement systems (too many, not focused enough on customers, cross-functional conflicts); pay and reward systems (lack of work goals, inconsistent signals); career development systems (ambiguous career paths, inadequate performance feedback); and an atmosphere in which blame, fear, and lack of trust overshadowed team commitments to solving problems. Here are some sample quotes from our interviews:

- I'm frustrated. I simply can't do the quality of work that I want to do and know how to do. I feel my hands are tied. I have no time. I need help on how to delegate and operate in this new culture.

- The goal of downsizing and delayering is correct. The execution stinks. The concept is to drop a lot of 'less important' work. This just didn't happen. We still have to know all the details, still have to follow all the old policies and systems.

- I'm overwhelmed. I can and want to do better work. The solution is not simply adding new people; I don't even want to. We need to team up on projects and work. Our leaders must stop piling on more and help us set priorities.

Second, just before the first Work-Out session, Jack Welch traveled to GEMS headquarters for a half-day roundtable with the Work-Out participants. Here are some sample quotes from middle managers:

APPENDIX
Work-Out: A Case Study (Continued)

- To senior management: "Listen! Think carefully about what the middle managers say. Make them feel like they are the experts and that their opinions are respected. There appear to be too many preconceived beliefs on the part of Welch and Trani."

- To senior management: "Listen to people, don't just pontificate. Trust people's judgment and don't continually second-guess. Treat other people like adults and not children."

- About themselves: "I will recommend work to be discontinued. I will try to find 'blind spots' where I withhold power. Any person I send to speak for me will 'push' peers who resist change."

- About themselves: "I will be more bold in making decisions. I will no longer accept the status quo. I will ask my boss for authority to make decisions. In fact, I will make more decisions on my own."

The five-day Work-Out session was an intense effort to unravel, evaluate, and reconsider the complex web of personal relationships, cross-functional interactions, and formal work procedures through which the business of GEMS gets done. Cross-functional teams cooperated to address actual business problems. Each functional group developed a vision of where its operations are headed.

John Trani participated in a roundtable where he listened and responded to the concerns and criticisms of middle managers. Senior members of the GEMS staff worked to build trust and more effective communication with the functional managers. All the participants focused on ways to reorganize work and maximize return on organization time, on team time, and on individual time.

The five-day session ended with individuals and functional teams signing close to 100 written contracts to implement the new procedures. There were contracts between functional teams, contracts between individuals, contracts between function heads an their staffs, and businesswide contracts with John Trani and his staff.

Work-Out has picked up steam since Lake Lawn. Managers from different product lines have participated in workshops to review and implement the attitudes, values, and new work procedures discussed at Lake Lawn. A Work-Out steering committee has held cross-functional information meetings for field employees around the world. Managers throughout GEMS are reviewing and modifying their reward and measurement systems. And Welch continues to receive regular briefings on Work-Out's progress.

No two GE businesses approach Work-Out in the same way; a process this intensive can't be cloned successfully among vastly different businesses. But Work-Out at GEMS offers a glimpse of the change process taking place throughout General Electric.

──── DISCUSSION QUESTIONS

1. Jack Welch mentions the importance of candor, which he defines as "facing reality, seeing the world as it is rather than as you wish it were." Do you feel that American businesses are practicing candor? Why or why not? What contribution can an individual make in a corporation that isn't facing reality?

2. What do you think Welch means by simplicity? Why is it important?

3. What changes in the business world have created the need for a leader with Welch's philosophy? What conditions could make his leadership style obsolete? What philosophy could replace his? Compare Welch with another dynamic business leader that you admire.

4. "GE has had an implicit psychological contract based on perceived lifetime employment," states Welch. Discussing GE's new psychological contract he says, " . . . jobs at GE are the best in the world for people who are willing to compete. . . . [they] provid[e] opportunities for personal and professional growth." Do you believe that this psychological contract is more appropriate in today's business context? Why or why not?

5. Do you think Welch has the formula that will keep American business competitive? Choose two or three of Welch's ideas on maintaining competitiveness and comment on why you either agree or disagree with them.

PART FOUR

MANAGING THE HUMAN RESOURCE

Planning with People in Mind 30

D. QUINN MILLS

This reading focuses on the need for companies to incorporate human resource planning into their long-term strategy making. It provides a firsthand report on the changes occurring in the management of human resources. Drawing on a survey of human resource activities at large companies as well as experience in the field, the author analyzes current practice, illustrates the diversity that characterizes the planning processes at sophisticated companies, and provides an inside view of people planning that works. As the author shows, top-level officers at the companies studied are likely to credit people planning for its part in raising morale, improving performance, and boosting profits.

General Electric had been engaged in formal business planning for several years before it began to take a longer-term view of human resources. In the interim, GE had faced a big problem as its business plans directed corporate resources to new products and technologies. "I didn't realize it at the time [that is, in 1970]," Reginald Jones, GE's former chairman, told me, "but we were a company with 30,000 electromechanical engineers becoming a company that needed electronics engineers. We didn't plan for this change in 1970, and it caused us big problems by the mid-1970s." Partly as a result of this experience, in the late 1970s GE began to ask its managers to plan for its human resource needs.

Similar costly hitches attributable to a lack of "people planning" are easily found. Consider, for example, the experience of a large multinational aluminum company planning to build a sophisticated computerized smelter in Brazil. The new technology had been a great success in the company's home country. But management ultimately realized that in Brazil it would be unable to find or train the computer technicians and service people needed to run such a facility. Plans were then revised at considerable cost to adapt the facility to the local labor force.

A large defense company faced its "people" crisis when it received a demanding government contract for which it had done little personnel planning. The company was forced to drain engineers and managers from other divisions, give them responsibilities far above their competence, and mount a costly rapid-hiring effort. The project survived, but the excess strain and high costs led top management to include a human resource component in its business plans. Since then, the company has also used human resource planning to avoid abrupt layoffs that could adversely affect the whole community.

Partly because of experiences like these, many American companies have begun to plan for their professional, managerial, and technical personnel. The scope of this activity varies widely, of course, and at some companies planning still means little more than head-count forecasts and a succession plan for the CEO. But a growing number of senior executives have been rethinking their companies' human resource planning in two important regards. First, they are supplementing familiar hiring and promotion activities with innovative efforts to enhance corporate performance and boost employee morale. And second, they are forging new links between these activities and their long-term business goals.

How a company forges these links depends in large part on how its management views planning. As we will see, some executives like informal methods, while others prefer written memos and plans. But whatever form the process takes, the most critical element is management's appreciation for the ways in which its human resource decisions affect the company's ability to achieve its business plans—and vice versa. Thus corporate blueprints, however roughly drawn, are likely to contain some version of the feedback loops that characterize my model of the people-planning process.

In the pages that follow, I will examine instances of successful people planning and discuss its implications at greater length. First, however, let us review current practice in the field.

—— WHY COMPANIES PLAN FOR PEOPLE

The trend toward human resource planning emerges clearly from my survey of planning practices in large companies as well as from other studies and conversations with corporate officers.[1] (See *Exhibit 1*.)

Among respondents to my survey, 40% include a human resource component in their long-term business plans. A somewhat larger group, just below 50%, draws up a formal management-succession plan, and a similar proportion prepares training and development plans for managerial employees. In contrast, only 15% of the respondents reported that they do no people planning at all.

Typically, planning horizons fall into industry-related patterns, with formal human resource plans following the time line established by a company's business plan. (Some 89% of the respondents prepare a long-term business plan.) Business plans in construction and service companies, for example, tend to be short term, while in mining, transportation, communications, and utilities,

---

1. *See,* for example, Harriet Gorlin and Lawrence Schein, *Innovations in Managing Human Resources* (New York: Conference Board, 1984).

EXHIBIT 1
A Survey of Human Resource Planning in Large Companies

To ensure that the sample would be characteristic of large American companies as a whole, I chose approximately 11% of the 2,625 U.S. parent companies listed in Dun's *Directory of American Corporate Families*. Each of the randomly selected 291 companies in the sample reported sales of $50 million or more, conducted business from 10 or more locations, and had a controlling interest in one or more subsidiaries.

Because I also wished to minimize the possibility that professional attachments would color the respondents' replies, I directed the survey mostly to line managers, as the following breakdown indicates:

President	28.6%
Vice president—operations	23.7%
Vice president—manufacturing	14.3%
Senior executive vice president	10.7%
Vice president—planning or business development	9.4%
Vice president—personnel	5.3%
Vice president—sales administration or finance	8.0%

Executives at the sample companies received telephone calls during the summer of 1983. Some 77% replied to inquiries in 20- to 30-minute conversations. While this rate of response would be high in any case, it is especially striking in contrast to the 14% to 50% response rates usually registered in surveys.

managers are likely to plan five or more years ahead. (*Exhibit 2* gives the planning horizons by industry for companies in the survey.)

I based the survey on the notion that people planning is mainly a matter of challenge and response: companies facing occupational shortages or anticipating major business changes would respond by taking a careful look at their human resource needs. So in interviews I asked managers about their expectations. Were personnel shortages anticipated? Were competitors pressing hard on the company's heels? Were technological changes altering the skills their people needed? If so, then planning would surely follow.

And to a degree this hypothesis is correct: managers who anticipate competitive and technological challenges do plan for the effects of these changes on their people. But other managers, equally aware of coming changes, do not engage in people planning. Challenge alone is not enough to elicit a response.

Corporate size and strategic intent also fail to differentiate companies that plan from those that do not. Larger companies are no more likely to plan than smaller ones; and companies pursuing rapid growth are no more likely to plan than those that are simply trying to hold their own. What then explains the difference?

The explanation, I find, lies less in how a company's managers perceive the challenges facing them than in how they perceive planning. The companies engaged in people planning do it because their top executives are convinced it gives them a competitive advantage in the marketplace. Thus they adopt

EXHIBIT 2
Business Plan Horizons for Sample Companies

	TWO YEARS	THREE TO FIVE YEARS	MORE THAN FIVE YEARS
Mining		67%	33%
Construction	17%	83	
Nondurable-goods manufacturing	2	88	10
Durable-goods manufacturing		88	12
Transportation, communication, utilities*		67	27
Wholesale trade		88	12
Retail trade		95	5
Finance, insurance, real estate		89	11
Services	8	84	8

*6% not applicable.

planning because they believe it makes their company more flexible and entre-preneurial, not because the environment forces it on them.

Managers involved in human resource planning have difficulty under-standing how other companies can do without it. "Our growth is related to talent and training," said one executive. "We prepare for the future to eliminate surprises," added another. "It is basic to the planning process," said a third, "because it is easier to save capital than people." "It is our number-one priority," said a bank president, "absolute, unquestioned. It is the most important thing we do in terms of our productivity. How can a company be successful without people planning?"

In contrast, managers who resist planning do so because they believe it is costly and ineffective. They often associate planning with bureaucracy, and many remember unhappy planning experiences from years past. "I've told my staff to quit talking to me about human resource planning," said one executive. "We can't plan for people because we do a miserable job of business planning. And I don't want another nest of strategic planners in the company."

When planning gives the wrong directions or becomes too bureaucratic, of course it deserves to be condemned. But companies that do the best job of people planning usually avoid these problems by keeping the process as infor-mal as possible and leaving the responsibility in the hands of line officers. Moreover, managers who dismiss people planning out of hand may be short-changing their companies and their employees.

During the 1981–1982 recession, for example, more than half the com-panies in the survey had to lay off middle managers. But those companies in which people planning is most developed minimized these reductions, partly through hiring freezes, attrition, and other forms of advance action.

Similarly, 72% of the survey respondents who practice human resource planning are certain that it improves profitability. And 39%, or more than half of the human resource planners, insist that they can measure the difference on the bottom line. (It is probably no surprise that the companies doing the most wide-range planning are also the most likely to measure quantitatively the impact of their human resource efforts.)

Survey data also allowed me to analyze the profitability of the companies that include human resource goals in their business plans compared with those that do not. Profitability rests on many factors other than planning, of course. Yet on balance, when I compared companies in the same broad industrial categories, those that have such goals in their business plans are the more profitable. Thus the survey corroborates the intuitive judgment of those who link people with profits.

——— EVOLVING PROCESSES

For comparative purposes, I grouped the sample companies into five stages, based on three criteria: 1) the number of people-planning elements used in the company, 2) the degree to which human resource plans are integrated into the business plan, and 3) the expressed amount of interest in and commitment to the planning process. The greater the number of elements, the degree of integration, and the degree of interest, the higher the stage to which I assigned the company.

Each stage represents a point along a continuum. At one end are the companies that do little or no people planning; at the other are those that integrate long-range human resource planning into their strategic business plans. The majority of the survey companies fall between these two extremes, as *Exhibit 3* indicates.

Stage 1 companies have no long-term business plans, and they do little or no human resource planning. Several are family companies and tend to be run paternalistically. Their managers often build morale by traditional methods such as parties and picnics and show little interest in planning. "There are plenty of people in the local labor market," said one executive, "We go on faith."

Senior managers at Stage 2 companies tend to be skeptical of human resource planning, even though each of their companies has a long-term business plan. Some, especially those "managing for survival" in declining industries, think people planning is not very realistic, while others see it in limited terms and equate it with head-count forecasts. "To most companies, human resource planning is basically forecasting," said one executive. Still, a number of Stage 2 company managers see that people planning is becoming more important and believe there is a need to do more.

Respondents at all Stage 3 companies cited several people-planning components in addition to longer-term staff forecasts that project human resource

EXHIBIT 3
Five Stages in Human Resource Planning

	NUMBER OF COMPANIES	PERCENT OF RESPONDENTS	CHARACTERISTIC ACTIVITIES
Traditional			
1	34	15%	Company picnic
2	81	36	Short-term head-count forecasting
Moderate			
3	60	27	Longer-term head-count forecasting
Advanced			
4	27	14	Skills inventories and succession planning as part of a long-term business plan
5	18	8	Scenarios, trend analysis, management development, morale management

needs three to five years out. For the most part, however, they do not integrate these activities into the long-range business plan.

Stage 4 companies do a good deal of people planning, and their senior managers typically are enthusiastic about the process. "People are our principal asset," said one. "Without good people our company can't do a thing." "A well-managed company *must* emphasize it," said another. "We should be doing more. We often fall short of having qualified people ready when we need them." All Stage 4 companies practice long-term planning, and 87% have at least one human resource component integrated into the long-range plan.

At Stage 5 companies, human resource components are an important part of the long-term business plan. Almost all do formal management-succession planning, and 94% engage in forecasting activities of some kind. Predictably, all these companies are highly enthusiastic about human resource planning. As one corporate executive commented, "HRP is our number-one priority—the most important thing we do relative to productivity. To get people involved, HRP has to be alive and credible."

To illustrate the differences among companies at various stages, consider the pattern that emerges from the respondents' replies to questions about their hiring and retraining practices. As *Exhibit 4* indicates, there is a quite steady progression from Stage 1 companies' focus on hiring and training as needed to Stage 5 companies' emphasis on anticipatory action.

Thus managers at Stage 1 and 2 companies tend to hire or retrain people only when they have immediate vacancies, while those at Stage 4 and 5 companies often look as far as three to six years ahead. These differences are marked for scientific and technical positions, and they are even more dramatic for

EXHIBIT 4
Time Frames for Personnel Decisions

Human resource planning stage	*HIRE OR RETRAIN TO FILL SCIENTIFIC AND TECHNICAL POSITIONS* *Percent of Respondents*			
	As needed	*Six months to one year in advance*	*Two years in advance*	*Three to six years in advance*
1	66%	31%	0%	3%
2	63	26	4	7
3	49	36	2	13
4	47	40	0	13
5	44	19	6	31
	HIRE OR RETRAIN TO FILL MANAGERIAL AND PROFESSIONAL POSITIONS *Percent of Respondents*			
1	55%	26%	0%	19%
2	34	33	1	32
3	36	24	5	35
4	23	27	3	47
5	11	25	6	58

managerial and professional personnel. For example, some large companies have recruited a number of graduating electronics engineers, with the expectation that the payoff from their contributions will come in 5 to 10 years. Thus the managers at these Stage 5 companies seem to be applying the same time frame to their human resource investments that they have commonly used for research and development projects and large-scale capital investments.

Succession planning, or the identification of people to fill key administrative positions, is probably the most widely used building block in human resource planning. And it, too, reflects a full range of responses. At one extreme are the companies that do no succession planning other than replacement planning. At the other are Stage 4 and Stage 5 companies that gain competitive advantage from planning for all their employees, not just top executives.

Despite the widespread use of formal and informal succession plans, only about one company in ten integrates succession into its long-term strategic plan. Apparently many executives conceive of succession plans as nothing more than a way of coping with possible crises such as resignations or serious illnesses. If these executives thought about the plans' potential for orderly career advancement, however, the wisdom of incorporating them in their business plans (which identify opportunities and therefore promotion possibilities) would be obvious.

Beyond preparing for disasters, succession planning has two important advantages. First, it spotlights people in the ranks, potentially enhancing their careers by calling them to top management's attention. Second, and even more critical, it identifies and directs management's attention to possible costly vacancies that cannot readily be filled.

Like all aspects of planning, succession planning has its pitfalls, of course, including the possibility that a key subordinate will be listed for several management slots. But these snares should not deter executives from using them to develop a more competitive work force.

VIEW FROM WITHIN

Although I have used human resource policies and practices as criteria for categorizing companies, these activities are only building blocks for individual systems. In practice, people planning has many sources and takes various forms, as companies develop distinctive ways to meet their needs, experience, and business strategies.

The ways in which companies link people planning to long-term strategic business planning vividly reflect these differences. For example, some companies request formal human resource plans from their division managers and review them at regional or group-level corporate planning meetings. At other companies, where people planning is woven into day-to-day operations, the link may be nothing more formal than the fact that the corporate vice president of personnel sits in on strategic planning meetings and raises human resource issues.

Even companies that do the most advanced people planning show considerable divergence in their planning processes. Some carefully build the process around sophisticated components, such as computerized personnel-data systems, skills inventories, career and organizational development plans, environmental-scanning and trend analyses, competitive work force analyses, and alternative-future scenarios. In other companies, however, the process may focus on one or two components, such as succession planning or executive selection and development. (The range of planning practices among Stage 5 companies is described in *Exhibit 5*.)

Whatever form a company's people planning takes, however, the involvement of line managers is a must. People planning may benefit significantly from staff support, of course. Usually, in the best-organized processes, staff people analyze problems and identify options. But in the end, people planning is a line responsibility.

"People and Productivity," a study published by the New York Stock Exchange in 1982, suggests one reason for line managers' involvement. Based primarily on a survey of American industrial corporations, the report identifies 15 common human resource activities. Although some are training matters, a

EXHIBIT 5
No One Way to Plan

People planning takes many forms. Some Stage 5 companies find an informal and decentralized approach best suited to their needs, while others opt for more structure. What matters most is achieving a fit between top management's style and the planning process it chooses so that the company's human resource activities mesh with its culture.

To illustrate, consider these two examples of sophisticated people planning.

The James Company is a large, decentralized multinational with divisions and subsidiaries throughout the world. Each operating company does its own planning, while the CEO has the job of conceptualizing corporate strategy. A small staff with expertise in finance, technology, and personnel turns these concepts into plans.

The company's human resource planning is likewise decentralized and informal; discussions and minimal reporting constitute the planning process. An international skills group works with company and regional personnel to coordinate skills inventories. And people planners from each division and subsidiary meet all over the world through the company's personnel network to discuss human resource issues.

Human resource planning at the corporate level focuses on policy development in three key areas: 1) the identification and appointment of senior managers to implement business strategies, 2) the incorporation of people-related information into strategic, operational, and succession planning, and 3) the design and review of personnel policies to support strategy implementation.

Human resource building blocks used at the corporate level and by the individual companies include head-count planning and forecasting, environmental monitoring, and training and development programs. These are not formally related to the strategic-planning process, which focuses on management-succession planning and the worldwide skills inventory only.

Rising managers receive profit-and-loss responsibilities early in their careers, and their candidacy for high-level, general management positions is measured by how well the units perform.

The planning process at Webb Company, a large, successful high-tech company, is highly centralized and carefully structured. Formal links between the human resource function and the strategic-

large number, such as individual goal setting, appraisal and feedback, job redesign, quality circles, and so forth, affect the organization's day-to-day relations with its employees. Thus line management has to be part of the people-planning system.

Involvement can occur in different ways, however. Line management may submit a business plan to the corporate staff analysts who then request modifications. Alternatively, the staff may prepare reports on expected developments (such as occupational shortages and surpluses, life-style changes that could affect attitudes and performance, and government regulations) that it circulates to division managers. Then these line officers, with their staff, prepare a plan to deal with the identified issues and send it back to corporate staff for review.

EXHIBIT 5
No One Way to Plan (Continued)

planning process go back to the late 1960s, when management devised a concurrence/nonconcurrence option for corporate personnel. Under this system, personnel is a decision-pushing function with real influence on decision making. If the corporate staff disagrees strongly with a business strategy, it can stop the plan until the issues are resolved by top management. By using the "silver bullet" of nonconcurrence, the staff can even kill an unfit program; if it chooses not to do so, it commits itself to the plan by default.

The company separated strategic and operational planning during the mid-1970s and in 1982 introduced a new business-planning system to encourage entrepreneurship and minimize bureaucracy. With this reorganization strategic planning became a corporate-level, top-down process, limited in detail and focused on the investment-planning cycle. At the same time, the company replaced its old divisional operating blueprints with bottom-up, detailed commitment plans. Proposals developed by the divisions in the commitment-planning process go to all major functional vice presidents for review. The human resources staff retains its concurrence option and prepares strategy reviews to identify disadvantages. If it finds issues that cannot be resolved informally, personnel sends the plan to the top-level business operations committee for resolution.

To give promising executives wide exposure to the company, Webb rotates them through varied assignments that can include staff positions designed to give them a look at top-level management. Its commitment to getting, keeping, and developing the very best people is evident in a recent decision to authorize yearly hiring of the top 5% of new graduates in certain engineering specialties. This philosophy is also reflected in the company's full-employment no-layoff policy for full-time permanent employees. This policy, in turn, is an important feature in other decisions, such as the ongoing need to find new projects for talented employees.

Among Webb's well-executed human resource activities are management-succession planning, extensive management-development efforts, and training programs in effective management. The company is also beginning to apply strategic thinking to its compensation systems so that they support its business goals, strategies, and culture.

Getting operating managers to invest time in the planning process can be difficult. Helping managers look beyond numbers or head-counts to development, morale, and performance issues, breaking away from job descriptions in thinking about future skill needs, and escaping the tyranny of sales forecasts with their implicit message that people are simply a derived demand are among the problems senior executives cite. To make human resource plans more than shallow appendages to the strategic business plan, however, managers must master these difficulties.

Identifying the payoff from human resource planning in improved organizational performance is one way to try to overcome resistance. If line executives see plans as "a graphics exercise," in GE Chairman John Welch's words, they simply will not support the process.[2] Also, managers need adequate information about legal developments, employee mores, and other external factors to plan intelligently for hiring, motivation, performance, and morale.

Significantly, companies that show the highest commitment to human resource planning are also those that share the most information with their managers and are the most likely to help them make sense of their environment. For example, managers at Stage 1 companies reported that, for the most part, they try to keep up with legal, legislative, and life-style trends on their own. Conversely, 77% of those at Stage 5 companies rely on their organizations for half or even most of their information.

PEOPLE PLANNING THAT WORKS

Many companies incorporate human resource goals in their long-term business planning, and about half of those surveyed require staffing forecasts. But few include the development activities and costs that are a crucial part of long-term staffing strategies. Thus the people-planning process is often seriously incomplete.

When planning stops with objectives and short of implementation, the business advantages it provides are likely to be lost. Consider, therefore, how one high-tech company avoided this common pitfall in its approach to a crucial sales-force planning issue.

For years this big company had prospered by hiring large numbers of young liberal arts graduates and giving them extensive training. As product technology advanced, however, salespeople lacking a technical background were less and less able to grasp it. By 1983 management faced an important decision: In the years ahead should the company alter its strategy and recruit more heavily among technical college graduates? If so, how fast should the company move, and how should the transition be managed?

Representatives from marketing, field sales, product development, and personnel formed a task force to devise a program for identifying future sales-force candidates. The assignment proved extraordinarily complicated, and days of discussion followed. A flow chart, prepared to assist the task force's deliberations, demonstrated the complexity of careful human resource planning and the virtue of organizing the process into a series of manageable steps (see *Exhibit 6*).

The task force began by identifying the chief factors that were determining future salespeople's capabilities. It then used these factors to establish the

---

2. John F. Welch, Jr., "Managing Change," dedication convocation, Fuqua School of Business, Duke University, April 21, 1983.

company's needs and to determine objectives for the sales force. At this point, too, the task force requested an inventory of the company's current sales team to see how it balanced against the identified needs.

Having determined that the company lacked the people it needed, the task force identified its alternatives. This brainstorming phase was a logical follow-up to the forecasting, modeling, and data collection that had gone on before, and it represented the task force's entry into the decision stage. However, at the same time the alternatives made further analysis essential. For example, because hiring from the outside was one alternative, the company had to survey the available job seekers. And because internal development was another avenue, the task force had to know more about the company's willingness to retrain and relocate its employees.

At this point, the task force faced crucial "make-or-buy" decisions. What should it recommend? The decision to look outside for more technically trained people could be easily implemented. But, as the task force realized, its options were also constrained by previous decisions. New hires could strengthen the sales force, but they could not substitute for it. The company had a large number of salespeople already and could not seriously think about replacing them in a short time. What, then, could the company do?

The task force recommended that the company detail technically trained people to sales and supplement them with a large-scale retraining program for the existing staff. Options such as reorganization of the company's sales efforts, job redesign, and changes in the compensation system were held for further study. Implementation of the task force's recommendations occurred during the next three years.

EXHIBIT 6
The Planning Process for a Sales Force Change

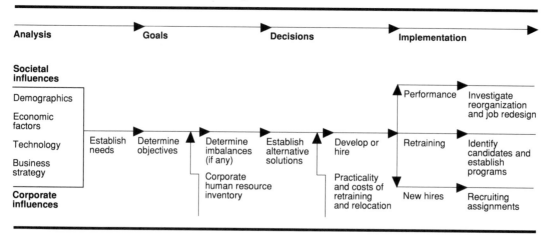

MODEL PROCESS

Every company organizes its people-planning process in its own way, and some use only parts of the model shown in *Exhibit 7*. Yet this sequential and idealized version of the people-planning process both accurately reflects current practice at several highly successful companies and reveals the logical order that ties these activities together.

As the model makes clear, the most important development in human resource planning is not the creation of many elements but rather their integration into a decision-making process that combines three important activities: 1) identifying and acquiring the right number of people with the proper skills, 2) motivating them to achieve high performance, and 3) creating interactive links between business objectives and people-planning activities.

Thinking ahead begins with a company's multiyear business plan, which establishes both its overall organization structure and goals and objectives for each business. Then the planning process divides to reflect the two factors that make any business successful in human terms.

A company's skill and staffing forecasts are set by both its organization structure and its business goals. Then company managers must decide whether to meet forecasted needs by hiring new people or retraining and reassigning the

EXHIBIT 7
The Human Resource Planning Process

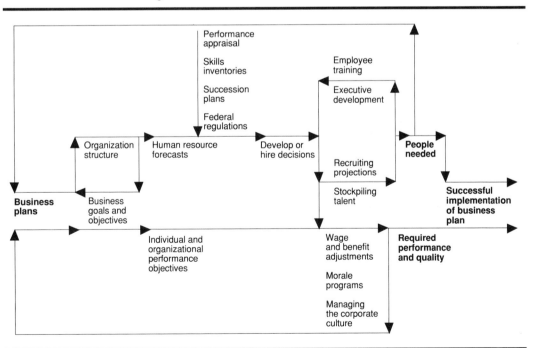

current staff. Performance appraisals, skills inventories, management succession plans, and equal opportunity programs all provide input for this choice. For current personnel, employee training and executive-development programs come into play, while recruiting projections, advance hiring, and even stockpiling of key talent are used for new hires.

Business goals also generate the productivity and quality requirements that are translated into performance objectives for individuals and organizational units. Designing and strengthening work programs, assessing the corporate culture, and, if necessary, modifying or reinforcing it from the top are among the ways human resource planners target performance objectives. They also adjust wages and benefits as necessary to preserve morale and promote recruiting and retention of employees.

Companies that have the people in place to meet their performance objectives are well-equipped to implement their business plans successfully. If, however, the right people are unavailable or if the performance goals cannot be met, the plans themselves may require revision, as the feedback loops in the model show. Many companies would have spared themselves embarrassing marketplace failures if they had first recognized that the human resource implications of their strategic plans were unrealizable. And in fact, astute managers no longer assume that every plan is doable, nor do they simply derive their people plans from their long-term business plans.

Personnel and skills forecasts are common in business organizations, and this aspect of people planning has received much attention in recent years. Newer and quite important are the human resource activities designed to evoke high performance from individuals and groups within the company. This morale management bodes well for the future, since it is people's performance and productivity that help create the lower costs and higher quality essential for profitability.

The people-planning process described here is taking shape in many companies throughout the country. In some it has evolved, beginning with one or two components and the gradual addition of others. In a smaller group of companies it began in reaction to environmental challenges. But in the largest group by far, people planning has resulted from the leadership, vision, and purpose of top management.

—— **DISCUSSION QUESTIONS**

1. The reading points out how people planning benefits companies. How might it benefit individuals? How might people planning influence an individual's career development? What other benefits might this approach to planning have for the individual?

2. This reading focuses on the advantages of people planning. What might be some drawbacks to people planning?

3. Few companies involve themselves in people planning. What message does this send to employees of companies? Does the scarcity of people planning reveal particular attitudes that companies hold toward the work force?

4. As an employee of a company that does not take the approach to planning advocated in the reading, would your job performance be affected in any way? Would your commitment to the company be stronger, weaker, or unaffected?

31 Career Systems and Strategic Staffing

JEFFREY A. SONNENFELD AND MAURY A. PEIPERL

This reading begins by defining career systems as the sets of policies and procedures firms use to provide staff to meet human resource requirements. It examines the basic elements of career systems and explains how human resource management policy relates to the overall strategy of a firm. The authors discuss the three stages of a career system: entry, development, and exit. They then describe the two fundamental properties of career systems: supply flow and assignment flow. Also covered are different methods that groups use to maintain membership: the academy, the club, the baseball team, and the fortress. This four-cell typology of career systems links staffing policy with business strategy.

A small but successful software company faces a severe turnover problem. Because its labor market is so competitive, employees whom it has spent hundreds of hours and thousands of dollars recruiting and training are leaving more rapidly than it can replace them. Besides the obvious personnel shortage, the firm is receiving little or no return for its substantial investment in these employees' development.

A second firm—a retailer—finds that its staff is mismatched to its needs: It has too many merchandisers and not enough store-operations personnel. Should the firm—already running on extremely tight margins—retrain and relocate its employees or cut its surplus merchandisers and try to bring in experienced operations talent?

A third firm—a professional-services company—is experiencing a drop in productivity as both its technical and sales managers reach performance plateaus. Although there is room for growth in its market, the firm is unable to take advantage of these external opportunities without further developing and revitalizing its people. How does it approach this task?

All three of these companies face strategic staffing problems that depend on the firm's career system for solutions. A *career system* is the set of policies and practices an organization uses to provide staff to meet its human resource requirements. The firm is a production system as well as a social system. Three general system events—input, throughput, and output—are the basic dynamics behind entry, development, and exit. Within these areas, specific career-system functions include the hiring and firing of employees, training and development, performance evaluation, succession planning, and retirement provisions. Career systems may be the result of careful planning and construction, or they may be de facto products of organizational evolution.

Why study career systems? The successful manager recognizes that human resource management is not merely the assignment of the right people to the right jobs, but that it also includes responsibility for helping employees manage their careers within (and occasionally beyond) the company's career system.

HUMAN RESOURCE FLOWS: THREE BASIC STAGES

Career systems involve the flow of people through the organization.[1] As in any system, the flows take place in three stages: entry, development, and exit. In a career system, entry corresponds to recruitment and selection; development to assignment, promotion, and training; and exit to layoff, firing, retirement, or resignation.

ENTRY

Recruitment is the means of attracting candidates for hire, while *selection* is the process of evaluating the fit of the candidate to the position and the firm. Because these processes go hand in hand, they are frequently managed together. The first step in the recruitment and selection process is the determination of human resource requirements. The firm must decide what sort of people are required to support current and future strategic directions. Firms will vary, for example, in their needs for technological expertise and management skill. Firms organized along product lines and functional areas may recruit by product or function with fairly specialized criteria. More diversified or regionally organized firms may require more general talent with greater variation in recruiting criteria.

Having decided on the human resource requirements behind recruitment, the firm must next consider which executives should be involved in the selection process. Often senior managers become involved in specifications but not in the initial screening process. The initial phases are generally guided by professional recruiters. These recruiters disseminate information about the firm and manage the initial contact and follow-through. The better informed the recruiters are about organizational needs, the higher the quality of the recruitment decision.

Firms must then decide on recruitment methods. These will depend on the type of recruit desired. Executive search firms are usually used to fill senior

---

1. Jeffrey A. Sonnenfeld, *Managing Career Systems: Channeling the Flow of Executive Careers* (Homewood, Ill.: Richard D. Irwin, 1984), Chapter 1.

positions when the labor market is tight. Technical experts are most effectively located through word-of-mouth channels and professional associations. Employee referrals are also an important source of information and candidates.

After a pool of candidates has been recruited, the final selection occurs. Although this process may include sophisticated procedures, such as assessment centers and physical and/or psychological examinations, the more common procedure for selection is a series of interviews with department heads, peers, and likely bosses. It is important that, during this process, candidates not become the victims of internal feuds, biases derived from initial impressions (e.g., physical attractiveness, sex, religion, race), or poor listening skills on the part of interviewers.

Interviews in the final stage often blend into early socialization, in an effort to provide candidates with realistic job previews. Meetings with current employees, site visits, job descriptions, and company literature on its history, performance, and career paths can supplement the more costly and more time-consuming interview process.

DEVELOPMENT

Assignment and promotion are two key elements of the development process. Research has shown that initial job assignments significantly affect a manager's later career; thus, a new employee's first assignment should be neither too easy nor too difficult. Employees spend much of their time in the first assignment adjusting to the realities of the workplace and the culture.

Competition for promotion may begin early. Those who fail in early tournament competitions are not likely to be included in later contests. Although the losers of promotion contests may not travel much farther on the career path, they may still face peer-level contests in order to maintain the same position. Their immobility may make them feel stagnant and frustrated. Monitoring the direction and pace of individual careers can help minimize problems of immobility. Companies such as IBM, which pace people through career paths, can ensure that one undesirable or dead-end post does not block an employee's further development.

Career momentum, the pace at which people advance, varies by company. Culture and strategy influence what constitutes being "on, ahead of, or behind schedule." Overall company growth and strategy will affect employees' opportunities for career growth by helping to determine how many and what kinds of jobs are open, and with what frequency. Also, different types of individuals will seek different types of mobility. For instance, younger, early-career workers may be disappointed with lateral movement, while older ones may prefer lateral moves to hierarchical moves that would require relocating.

Organizations can assist their members in their career planning through formal career-development programs that take some of the control away from the supervisor. Firms with centralized career programs can (1) minimize hoarding of talent, (2) reduce drifts toward obsolescence, and (3) improve equal-opportunity provisions for women and minorities. Often career-development programs include an employee self-assessment and a developmental review with the boss. Yet in order to have effective career-development programs, companies must go beyond the self-assessment tools and employee-superior meetings. They must assess themselves to determine the changing human resource needs of the company and the career paths likely to be followed by those who will fill those needs in the future.

Training programs are the other half of the development process. They can serve many purposes. Most generally they serve as key interventions in large organizational changes or as individual development efforts designed to improve the immediate performance or longer-term preparedness of particular workers. Examples of training for organizational change include teaching new techniques and explaining new products; individual development programs might include new-employee orientation, functional-skills training, and preparation for retirement or outplacement.

The steps in developing training programs are, first, to assess the organization's training goals and the training requirements of individuals; second, to plan a curriculum, taking into account the time frame (will the training have immediate or longer-term applicability?); and third, to choose pedagogical techniques appropriate to the people being trained and the ideas being taught. Techniques might include self-study workbooks, videos, lectures, class discussions, group work, and intergroup competitions. Fourth, the firm must select instructors appropriate to the material and the audience. Lastly, the firm must evaluate the success of the training effort: Was the proper material taught? Were the right people involved? Did the training address the immediate needs of the firm? The long-term needs? Company training staffs can play critical roles as educational brokers or intermediaries, and with managers, as evaluators of the training process.

EXIT

Organizational exit is typically the single worst-managed process in the career system. Even when the reasons for exit are logical and clear-cut—a plant closing, a retirement, a resignation in order to pursue a better opportunity—the processes are unnecessarily destructive to the departing individual and the organization he or she leaves behind.

Losing or leaving a job can be extremely difficult on an individual, whose life in some degree revolves around the job. The change spills over into other life sectors; the loss of a work identity often shatters one's self-confidence in dealing with future challenges. People suffer from job loss as much from the way the event transpires as from its actual occurrence. Managers who lack the courage to address the facts surrounding the firing of a subordinate allow a cloud of suspicion about one's honesty or competence to haunt an employee upon dismissal. The lack of directness, the anger, and the abruptness may reflect a manager's fear of reprisal from friends of the fired employee. Such behavior may also reflect a manager's own feelings of guilt. Such poor management of organizational exit not only damages the lives and careers of those departing but also hurts the internal culture of the firm.

To manage exits effectively, firms must understand the reason for a worker's departure. High turnover may be symptomatic of underlying problems in the organization (alternatively, it may be typical of certain industries or markets). Exit interviews and research on resignations may help determine causes. When an employee is dismissed, firms must learn whether the firing was fair, appropriate, and necessary. Was the employee consistently receiving honest performance feedback?

Firms must also be certain which workers they are better off losing and which are hard to replace. Carefully tailored approaches to exits can improve a firm's ability to keep the employees it needs and remove those it does not. Selective salary cuts, job redesign, changes in hours, and retraining of experienced and motivated personnel may all be more effective than broad-based exit plans in management of the workforce.

Finally, managing exits means easing the transition. Advance notice and outplacement counseling can better prepare employees for their disengagement. If the explanation for the termination is clear and assistance is genuine, the likelihood of retaliation and sabotage is not greater than for any other source of disgruntlement. Programs for flextime, job sharing, part-time employment, and phased retirement allow workers to learn and become increasingly involved in activities outside of the firm.

——— CAREER SYSTEMS: AN ORGANIZATIONAL PERSPECTIVE

A firm's labor supply is subject to the external environment in the basic processes of entry and exit and is internally interdependent among its components in the process of development.[2] This approach implies two fundamental properties of career systems: first, the movement into and out of the firm, the *supply flow*; and second, the movement across job assignments and through promotions within the firm, the *assignment flow*. By positioning firms along these two dimensions, many of the variations in career systems can be profiled.

---

2. Jeffrey A. Sonnenfeld and Maury A. Peiperl, "Staffing Policy as a Strategic Response: A Typology of Career Systems," *Academy of Management Review* (October 1988): 588–600.

SUPPLY FLOW

The supply-flow dimension is measured by the openness of the career system to the external labor market at other than entry levels. For example, IBM has an almost total reliance on its internal labor market, creating a closed supply flow except at the entry level. In contrast, most semiconductor, advertising, broadcasting, and entertainment firms rely on extensive mid-career recruitment; therefore, positions other than those at entry level are more open to outside supply. It follows that these firms also see a higher level of mid-career exits or outflow. Supply flow thus reflects the degree to which a firm staffs itself from external sources. It can be seen in the level of employment security and loyalty to long-service employees on the one hand, and receptiveness to new members and turnover on the other.

ASSIGNMENT FLOW

The assignment-flow dimension describes the criteria by which assignment and promotion decisions are made. It reflects the pace and pressure in the career pipeline and the criteria for promotion: technical versus political. The vacancy rate, growth rate, and demographics also affect this dimension. In particular, the choice of individuals for assignments can be made primarily on the basis of their individual performance or on the basis of their contribution to the general group. Although some career systems favor the star performer, others prefer the solid contributor.

The *Exhibit* on the next page displays these two dimensions and the resultant four-cell typology, with entry, development, and exit characteristics for each cell. The cells have been given distinctive labels that evoke groups with distinctly different methods of maintaining membership.

THE ACADEMY

The key career-system objective of an academy is development. The academy is often a dominant or core competitor. Workers in these firms see themselves as members of a modern guild. They see professional growth as a personal goal and a community obligation. They value skillful teamwork rather than solo performance. Important to these systems are such contextual qualities as task uncertainty, firm-specific knowledge, related job sequences, and competition for scarce skills. These systems seek to develop and retain their own talent.

Within the academy, IBM is a good example. At IBM, point of entry is restricted to early-career positions. An employee entering any given management group has an 80% chance of staying with IBM through to retirement. By contrast, at a major New York City bank that same individual would have an

EXHIBIT
Models of Career Systems

	FORTRESS—Retrenchment	BASEBALL TEAM—Recruitment
External	*Entry*	*Entry*
	Passive recruitment	Primary human resources practice
	Drawn to industry by own interests/background	Emphasis on credentials, expertise
	Selective turnaround recruitment	Recruit at all career stages
	Development	*Development*
	Effort to retain core talent	On-the-job
		Little formal training
		Little succession planning
	Exit	*Exit*
	Layoffs frequent	High turnover
	Respects seniority	Cross-employer career paths
SUPPLY FLOW	CLUB—Retention	ACADEMY—Development
	Entry	*Entry*
	Early career	Strictly early career
	Emphasis on reliability	Ability to grow
	Development	*Development*
	As generalists	Primary human resources practice
	Slow paths	Extensive training for specific jobs
	Required steps	Tracking and sponsorship of high-
	Emphasis on commitment	potential employees
		Elaborate career paths/job ladders
	Exit	*Exit*
	Low turnover	Low turnover
	Retirement	Retirement
		Dismissal for poor performance
Internal		

Group Contribution	ASSIGNMENT FLOW ──────────▶	Individual Contribution

80% chance of quitting by the end of his or her first decade of employment. To understand the reasons behind these kinds of statistics, keep in mind that disparate corporate objectives have resulted in a wide variety of career-systems policies.

THE CLUB

The key career-system task for a club is retention. Security and membership are the essence of commitment. Status attainment prior to employment, such as schooling, contributes to an employee's perceived value. The club is frequently shielded by regulatory buffers or a monopoly situation. Workers often see their employer (e.g., a public utility) as an institution with a mission—to serve the public interest—that transcends marketplace concerns.

THE BASEBALL TEAM

A baseball team's career system focuses on recruitment. In firms where innovation is at a premium, the lack of employment security heightens the pressure for creativity. The pool of risk takers is not limited to the internal labor market. The spirit in the baseball team is upbeat; employees see themselves as minor celebrities, each with a shot at becoming a true star. Commitment is at a lower level than in either academies or clubs. When complacency sets in at baseball types of firms (such as advertising, broadcasting, or semiconductor companies), professional networks, trade associations, and recruiters seek new talent.

THE FORTRESS

A fortress career system focuses on retrenchment. The fortress is in a struggle for survival. This type of firm may have hired and fired in reaction to market conditions. These may be firms never in control of their strategic environment because of the intense competition or the shortage of key resources. They may also be firms caught in crises, facing turnaround challenges. Sometimes such crises are intentionally brought to a head by a shift in career systems. For instance, a commercial bank attempting to shed the people and businesses acquired during a different regulatory environment may lead the firm into a fortress career system as a planned transitional phase. Similarly, a film studio or advertising firm with long-service, but poor-performing, talent may elect to streamline before restaffing in ways that resemble its baseball-team competitors. Workers in these fortress industries may have been attracted to the presumed glamour in the business (e.g., publishing, hotels, retail). They may also have joined the firms in a healthier period. Or, they may have backed in by mistake. Employees here see themselves as soldiers locked in combat.

STRATEGIC CHOICE AND CAREER SYSTEMS

The differing management practices of each career-system profile are frequently the product of strategic intentions. To create the needed pool of labor to accomplish distinct missions, firms will vary in their emphasis upon such membership qualities as professional expertise, competitiveness, loyalty, flexibility, and company-specific knowledge.

Each of the four strategic types corresponds to a different set of career-system practices that provides the requisite degree of skill and continuity in the workforce. Academies, for example, survey their context carefully and inventory their internal resources before plunging into new activities. They are most skillful at execution and rarely lead the market with new ideas. Their career systems must be anticipatory so that they have the infrastructure to ensure reliable delivery upon their commitments. The more feisty baseball teams attract innovative talent that often has a more cosmopolitan commitment to the occupation or profession than to the firm. The clubs are concerned more with maintaining their strategic domain than with seeking new expansion. Regulatory protection and general community support are often important. Hence, their employment practices are often managed in ways that promote their identity as benevolent public institutions. Finally, the fortresses' strategic style suggests that they have lost control over their environment. These firms may be academies, clubs, or baseball teams that failed at their mission. Many firms may pass through this style while retrenching or turning themselves around. Some spend a long time as fortresses before reviving; others institute quick and drastic changes; still others never break out of fortress mode. Although persisting in a boom-or-bust fashion may be natural in certain industries (e.g., retail), it may indicate a performance problem in others.

Thus the staffing difficulties experienced by the three firms at the beginning of this reading may be better understood in light of the models just described. The software company that keeps investing in people only to lose them is an example of a baseball team, where people regularly move from firm to firm. Rather than pouring money into employees' development, this company should consider buying the skills it needs in the open labor market. Of course, it will have to ensure that its reward systems address the pay-for-performance expectations of its workforce, or else it may not be able to keep any employees for long. The retailer is probably a fortress, under so much competitive pressure that it cannot afford the costs of job security and retraining. It may find it necessary to lay off its surplus merchandisers and hire operations talent from outside. The mature professional-services company may want to be an academy but is finding itself more like a club. To foster the continued development of its plateaued managers, the company should focus more on pay-for-performance and targeted training. Only by aligning career systems with overall corporate strategy can firms achieve satisfactory management of human resource flows.

Copyright © 1988; revised 1991.

—— DISCUSSION QUESTIONS

1. Should a company be concerned with the three stages of human resource flows? Why not simply focus on the stage best suited for that particular company?
2. What is a more effective philosophy for a company's career planning system—one based on paternalism or one based on each employee for himself or herself? Does this depend on certain factors such as the kind of business or industry in which a company is engaged?
3. Given your career choices, what sort of company would you be attracted to as described in the *Exhibit*—the fortress, the baseball team, the club, or the academy? Explain why.

32   Reward Systems and the Role of Compensation

MICHAEL BEER AND RICHARD E. WALTON

This reading examines reward systems and their effects on employee satisfaction and motivation. It explores how employees' and management's attitudes toward money make designing a reward system problematic. It then considers systems for maintaining pay equity, internally and externally, as well as the advantages and disadvantages of determining pay levels by evaluating the worth of a job or an individual's abilities and skill level. Seniority and pay for performance are also considered as the bases for rewards.

The design and management of reward systems present the general manager with one of the most difficult HRM (human resource management) tasks. This HRM policy area contains the greatest contradictions between the promise of theory and the reality of implementation. Consequently, organizations sometimes go through cycles of innovation and hope as reward systems are developed, followed by disillusionment as these reward systems fail to deliver.[1]

REWARDS AND EMPLOYEE SATISFACTION

Gaining an employee's satisfaction with the rewards given is not a simple matter. Rather, employee satisfaction is a function of several factors that organizations must learn to manage:

- *The individual's satisfaction with rewards is, in part, related to what is expected and how much is received.* Feelings of satisfaction or dissatisfaction arise when individuals compare their input—job skills, education, effort, and performance—with output—the mix of extrinsic and intrinsic rewards they receive.
- *Employee satisfaction is also affected by comparisons with other people in similar jobs and organizations.* In effect, employees compare their own

---

1. This reading consists of material adapted from *Managing Human Assets* by Michael Beer, Bert Spector, Paul Lawrence, D. Quinn Mills, and Richard Walton (New York: The Free Press, 1984).

input/output ratio with that of others. People vary considerably in how they weigh various inputs in that comparison. They tend to weigh their strong points more heavily, such as certain skills or a recent incident of effective performance. Individuals also tend to give their own performance a higher rating than the one they receive from their supervisors. The problem of unrealistic self-ratings exists partly because supervisors in most organizations do not communicate a candid evaluation of their subordinates' performances to them. Such candid communication to subordinates, unless done skillfully, seriously risks damaging self-esteem. The bigger dilemma is that failure by managers to communicate a candid appraisal of performance makes it difficult for employees to develop a realistic view of their own performance, thus increasing the possibility of dissatisfaction with the pay they are receiving.

- *Employees often misperceive the rewards of others.* Evidence shows that individuals tend to overestimate the pay of fellow workers doing similar jobs and to underestimate their performance (a defense or self-esteem-building mechanism). Misperceptions of the performance and rewards of others also occur because organizations do not generally make available accurate information about the salary or performance of others.

- *Overall satisfaction results from a mix of rewards rather than from any single reward.* The evidence suggests that both intrinsic rewards and extrinsic rewards are important and cannot be directly substituted for each other. Employees who are paid well for repetitious, boring work will be dissatisfied with the lack of intrinsic rewards, just as employees who are paid poorly for interesting, challenging work may be dissatisfied with extrinsic rewards.

REWARDS AND MOTIVATION

From the organization's point of view, rewards are intended to motivate certain behaviors. But under what conditions will rewards actually motivate employees? To be useful, rewards must be seen as timely and tied to effective performance.

One theory suggests that the following conditions are necessary for employee motivation:[2]

- Employees must believe effective performance (or certain specified behavior) will lead to certain rewards. For example, attaining certain results will lead to a bonus or approval from others.
- Employees must feel that the rewards offered are attractive. Although some employees may desire promotions because they seek

---

2. Edward E. Lawler, *Pay and Organizational Effectiveness: A Psychological View* (New York: McGraw-Hill, 1971): 267–272.

power, others may want a fringe benefit, such as a pension, because they are older and want retirement security.

- Employees must believe a certain level of individual effort will lead to achieving the corporation's standards of performance.

As indicated, motivation to exert effort is triggered by the prospect of desired rewards: money, recognition, promotion, and so forth. If effort leads to performance and performance leads to desired rewards, the employee is satisfied and motivated to perform again.

As previously mentioned, rewards fall into two categories: extrinsic and intrinsic. *Extrinsic rewards* come from the organization as money, perquisites, or promotions or from supervisors and co-workers as recognition. *Intrinsic rewards* accrue from performing the task itself and may include the satisfaction of accomplishment or a sense of influence. The process of work and the individual's response to it provide the intrinsic reward. But the organization seeking to increase intrinsic rewards must provide a work environment that allows these satisfactions to occur; therefore, more organizations are redesigning work and delegating responsibility to enhance employee involvement.

EQUITY AND PARTICIPATION

The ability of a reward system to both motivate and satisfy depends on who influences and/or controls the system's design and implementation. Even though considerable evidence suggests that participation in decision making can lead to greater acceptance of decisions, participation in both the design and administration of reward systems is rare. Such participation is time-consuming.

Perhaps a greater roadblock is that pay has been one of the last strongholds of managerial prerogatives. Concerned about employee self-interest and compensation costs, corporations do not typically allow employees to participate in pay-system design or decisions. Thus, it is not possible to test thoroughly the effects of widespread participation on acceptance of and trust in reward systems.

——— COMPENSATION SYSTEMS: THE DILEMMAS OF PRACTICE

A body of experience, research, and theory has been developed about how money satisfies and motivates employees. Virtually every study on the importance of pay compared with other potential rewards has shown that pay is important. It consistently ranks among the top five rewards. Many factors, however, affect the importance of pay and other rewards. Money, for example, is likely to be viewed differently at various points in one's career, because the need for money versus other rewards (status, growth, security, and so forth) changes at each stage. National culture is another important factor. U.S. managers and employees emphasize pay for individual performance more than do their European or Japanese counterparts. European and Japanese companies, however, rely more on slow promotions and seniority as well as some degree of employment security. Even within a single culture, shifting national forces may alter people's needs for money versus other rewards.

Companies have developed various compensation systems and practices to achieve pay satisfaction and motivation. In manufacturing firms, payroll costs can run as high as 40% of sales revenues, whereas in service organizations payroll costs can top 70%. General managers, therefore, take an understandable interest in payroll costs and how these dollars are spent.

The traditional view of managers and compensation specialists is that the right system would solve most problems. This assumption is not plausible because there is no one right answer or objective solution to what or how someone should be paid. What people will accept, be motivated by, or perceive as fair is highly subjective. Pay is a matter of perceptions and values that often generate conflict.

MANAGEMENT'S INFLUENCE ON ATTITUDES TOWARD MONEY

Many organizations are caught in a vicious cycle that they partly create. In their recruitment and internal communications, firms often emphasize compensation levels and a belief in individual pay for performance. This is likely to attract people with high needs for money as well as to heighten that need in those already employed. Thus, the meaning employees attach to money is partly shaped by management's views. If merit increases, bonuses, stock options, and perquisites are held out as valued symbols of recognition and success, employees will come to see them in this light even more than they might have at first. Having heightened money's importance as a reward, management must then respond to employees who may demand more money or better pay-for-performance systems.

Firms must establish a philosophy about rewards and the role of pay in the mix of rewards. Without such a philosophy, the compensation practices that happen to be in place will continue to shape employees' expectations, and those expectations will sustain the existing practices. If money has been emphasized as an important symbol of success, that emphasis will continue even though a compensation system with a slightly different emphasis might have equal motivational value with fewer administrative problems and perhaps even lower cost. Money is important, but its degree of importance is influenced by the type of compensation system and philosophy that management adopts.

PAYROLL STRATIFICATION: A ONE- OR TWO-CLASS SOCIETY?

An organization with different compensation systems for different levels of the organization that offer different fringe benefits, pay-for-performance rewards, and administrative procedures is sending employees a message about more than just the specific behavior the compensation system is intended to reward. That message is that there are differences in the company's expectations of the commitment and role of employees at different levels and the degree to which they are full and responsible members of the organization.

Several understandable reasons exist for these differences. To circumvent the intended effects of progressive tax laws, corporations pay managers in a form different from that of lower-level employees. Deferred compensation, stock options, and various perquisites protect executives from taxation that reduces the value of their rewards.

In the United States, all organizations must distinguish between *exempt employees* (those who, according to the wage-and-hour laws, have significant decision-making responsibility—typically, managers and professional employees) and *nonexempt employees* (all other regular members of the organization—typically clerical white-collar and hourly blue-collar employees). Federal law requires nonexempt employees to receive overtime pay for a workweek that exceeds 40 hours; exempt employees are, as the name implies, exempt from such legislative protection. Because of this legal requirement, organizations must maintain records of time worked by nonexempt employees, which often results in the use of time clocks. These groups are also given different payroll labels: salaried payroll for exempt employees and hourly payroll for production employees. Thus, a two-class language is created.

Federal law governing overtime pay for nonexempt employees was created in the 1930s to protect employees from exploitation by management. It can, and often does, have the unintended result of creating or reinforcing certain assumptions made by managers about their employees' commitment to the organization. It might also affect employees' perceptions of their roles in the organization and thereby alter their commitment. A two-class society is subtly reinforced within the organization.

All-Salaried System   Some organizations have attempted to overcome this legislated division of the work force through an all-salaried compensation system. Workers traditionally paid by the hour join management in receiving a weekly or monthly salary (nonexempt employees are still paid on an hourly basis for overtime work).

Although an all-salaried system cannot eliminate the legislated distinction between exempt and nonexempt employees, it can at least remove one symbolic, but nonetheless important, difference: Workers join managers in having more flexibility, because time can be taken off from work with no loss in pay. Thus, workers can be given more responsibility for their hours. Such treatment, in turn, could increase their commitment and loyalty to the organization.

Some managers fear that adopting a salaried system across the board will lead to greater absenteeism, but this does not appear to have happened. Such a system by itself will not increase commitment; nevertheless, as part of an overall shift in corporate philosophy and style, it can play an important supporting role. Companies such as Hewlett-Packard and IBM as well as participative nontraditional plants at Procter & Gamble, Dana, TRW, and Cummins Engine have successfully used the all-salaried payroll in this way.

SYSTEMS FOR MAINTAINING EQUITY

To maintain employee satisfaction with pay, corporations have developed systems to maintain pay equity with comparable internal and external persons and groups.

The consequences of inequity in employee pay regarding the external labor markets are potentially severe for a corporation, which would be unable to attract and keep the talent required. The costs of maintaining that equity, however, are also high. Meeting all competitive wage offers obtainable by employees—the extreme form of maintaining external equity—can encourage employees to search for the highest job offers to convince management to increase their pay. This results in a market system for determining compensation much like the free-agent system in sports—a time-consuming and expensive proposition for employers that can lead to internal inequities. It can also lead an employee to a self-centered orientation toward career and pay.

Some companies, such as IBM, intentionally position their total compensation package at the high end of the market range. High total compensation does not, however, ensure that the best employees are retained. To keep them, a company must also pay its better performers more than it pays poorer performers, and the difference must be significant in the judgment of individual employees.

The potential consequences of internal pay inequity are employee dissatisfaction, withholding of effort, and lack of trust in the system. Internal inequity can result in conflict within the organization, which consumes the time and energy of managers and personnel. Maintaining high internal equity, however, can result in overpaying some people compared to the market, while underpaying others—thus destroying external equity.

There is continual tension in an organization between concerns for external and internal equity. Line personnel may be willing to sacrifice corporate internal equity to attract and keep the talent they want for their departments. Because they perceive efforts to pay whatever is needed to attract a candidate as a threat to internal equity, human resource personnel, with their corporate perspectives, often oppose such efforts by line managers. Human resource personnel insist on the integrity of the job-evaluation and wage-survey systems to avoid the costly conflicts that they fear will result from numerous exceptions to the job-evaluation system. This dilemma remains insoluble; no new system will eliminate it. The balance must be continually managed to reduce problems and maintain a pay system that yields equity and cost effectiveness.

Job Evaluation   In the United States, most firms determine pay levels by evaluating the worth of a job to the organization through a job-evaluation system.

Job evaluations begin by describing the various jobs within an organization. Then jobs are evaluated by considering several job factors: working conditions, necessary technical knowledge, required managerial skills, and importance to the organization. A rating for each factor is made on a standard scale, and the total rating points are used to rank jobs. Next, a salary survey identifies comparable jobs in other organizations and learns what those organizations are paying for similarly rated jobs.

The salary survey and other considerations—such as legislation, job-market conditions, and the organization's willingness to pay—establish pay ranges for jobs. (The tighter the labor market, the more closely wages will be tied to the going rate. In a loose labor market, the other factors will tend to dominate.) Jobs may then be grouped into a smaller number of classifications and assigned a salary range. The level of the individual employee within his or her particular range is determined by a combination of job performance, seniority, and experience or any other combination of factors selected by the organization.

Job-evaluation plans, along with wage surveys, have been used in wage-and-salary administration for over 50 years. They have proved useful for maintaining internal and external equity.

Even if these steps are taken, however, no job-evaluation system can solve the problem of salary compression, or inequities, that inevitably occur when new employees are hired. To recruit successfully in the labor market, firms must offer competitive wages, and these competitive wages sometimes create inequities with the salaries of employees who have been with the firm for some time. These inequities occur because corporations usually do not raise the salaries of incumbents when salary surveys result in an upward movement of the salary range. To do so would be costly; not doing so also allows the firms to keep the pay of poorer performers behind the market by denying merit increases.

Some analysts argue that companies should solve inequities due to compression by regularly raising wages for everyone when salary surveys so indicate and by managing poor performers through other means. Some companies ask managers to position their subordinates within the appropriate pay range according to performance, providing larger increases for good performers over several years so they will be near the top of their range and giving poor performers lower increases or no increases to keep them at the bottom of the range.

The conflicting objectives of keeping costs down and rewarding good performers—not the job-evaluation system itself—cause inequity and dissatisfaction. Of these objectives, cost effectiveness is the critical factor, because good performance can be rewarded and poor performance discouraged in other monetary and nonmonetary ways. General managers must decide if the cost of across-the-board increases is worth the benefits of greater internal and external equity. To solve the equity problems, they must clarify their philosophy and make choices between objectives of cost and equity, a process determined more by values and financial constraints than by systems.

Pay systems structured by job evaluation have special problems. Salary ranges associated with jobs limit the pay increases an individual can obtain. Thus, significant advancements in status and pay can come only through promotions. This need for promotion can cause technical people to seek promotions to management positions, even though their real skills and interests might be in technical work. If no promotions are available, individuals' needs for advancement and progress are frustrated.

Additionally, job-evaluation systems cause a certain loss of flexibility in transferring people within an organization. If that transfer is to a job with a lower pay grade, fear of lower pay and status will reduce the individual's willingness to transfer. Although companies usually make an exception and maintain the individual's salary above the range of the new job, the perception of loss and the reality of an actual loss of pay over time makes such a transfer difficult.

To solve problems of job-evaluation systems, some companies have come up with an alternative: a person- or skill-based evaluation system. This system promises to solve the flexibility and limited growth problem of job evaluation, but it does not solve all the equity problems already discussed.

Person/Skill Evaluation   Person- or skill-based evaluation systems base salary on the person's abilities. Pay ranges are arranged in steps, from least skilled to most skilled. Employees come into the organization at an entry-level pay grade and, after demonstrating competence at that level, begin to move up the skill-based ladder. Such a system should lead to higher pay for the most skilled individuals and encourage the acquisition of new skills.

Skill-based systems generally allow more flexibility in moving people from one job to another and in introducing new technology. A skill-based compensation system can also change management's orientation. Rather than limit assignments to be consistent with job level, managers must try to utilize the available skills of people, since employees are being paid for those skills. Moreover, a skill-based evaluation system's greatest benefit is that it communicates to employees a concern for their development. This concern leads management to develop competence and utilize it, resulting in greater employee well-being and organizational effectiveness.

Person-based evaluation systems that have been applied to technical personnel in R&D organizations are often called *technical ladders*. Technical ladders could be applied to other technical specialists, such as lawyers, sales personnel, and accountants. Their use might encourage good specialists to stay in these roles rather than seek management jobs that pay more but for which they may not have talent. The organizations would avoid losing good technical specialists and gaining poor managers.

Skill-based pay systems have also been applied to production-level employees. In some of their more progressive plants, companies such as Procter & Gamble, General Motors, and Cummins Engine have introduced plans that pay workers for the skills they possess rather than for the jobs they hold. The benefits of flexibility and employee growth and satisfaction, mentioned earlier, have been experienced in these plants.

Some problems exist in a person- or skill-based approach, however. For example, many individual employees may, after several years, reach the top skill level and find themselves with no place to go. At this point, the organization might consider some type of profit-sharing scheme to encourage these employees to continue to seek ways of improving organizational effectiveness. Another problem is that a skills-evaluation program calls for a large investment in training, because pay increases depend upon the learning of new skills. Furthermore, external equity is more difficult to manage. Because each organization has its own unique configurations of jobs and skills, it is unlikely that individuals with similar skills can be found elsewhere, particularly in the same community, which is where production workers typically look for comparisons. This is less of a problem for professional employees whose jobs are more similar across companies. Because skill-based systems emphasize learning new tasks, employees may come to feel that their higher skills call for higher pay than the system provides, particularly when they compare their wages with those of workers in traditional jobs. Without effective comparisons expectations could rise, unchecked by a good reality test.

The most difficult problem facing a skills-evaluation plan is its administration. To make the system work properly, attention must be paid to the skill level of every employee. Some method must be devised, first, to determine how many and what new skills must be learned to receive a pay boost and, second, to determine whether or not the individual employee has, in fact, mastered those new skills. The ease with which the first point is achieved depends on how measurable or quantifiable the necessary skills are. Identification of particular skills is more easily accomplished for lower-level positions than for top management or professional positions.

Skill-based pay systems hold out some promise of improving competence in a cost-effective way and enhancing both organizational effectiveness and employee well-being. They are not solutions for all situations and depend heavily on solving the problem of measuring and assessing skills or competencies. Only an organization with a climate of trust is likely to use the system successfully. Moreover, skill-based compensation systems work only in those organizations where skilled workers are essential and where flexibility is required. They are also hard to introduce in organizations where a traditional job-evaluation system exists.

SENIORITY

Seniority has been accepted as a valid criterion for pay in some countries. Japanese companies, for instance, use seniority-based pay along with other factors, such as slow-but-steady promotion, to help achieve a desired organizational culture. In the United States, proponents of a seniority-based pay system tend to be trade unions. Distrustful of management, unions often feel that any pay-for-performance system will end up increasing paternalism, unfairness, and inequities. Thus, unions often prefer a strict seniority system. Many U.S. managers, however, feel that seniority runs contrary to the country's individualistic ethos, which maintains that individual effort and merit should be rewarded above all else.

PAY FOR PERFORMANCE

Some reasons organizations pay their employees for performance are as follows:

- Under the right conditions, a pay-for-performance system can motivate desired behavior.
- A pay-for-performance system can help attract and keep achievement-oriented individuals.
- A pay-for-performance system can help to retain good performers while discouraging the poor performers.
- In the United States, at least, many employees, both managers and workers, prefer a pay-for-performance system, although white-collar workers are significantly more supportive of the notion than are blue-collar workers.

However, there is a wide gap between the desire to devise a pay-for-performance system and the ability to make such a system work.

The most important distinction among various pay-for-performance systems is the level of aggregation at which performance is defined—individual, group, and organization-wide.[3] The *Exhibit* summarizes several pay-for-performance systems.

Historically, pay for performance has meant pay for individual performance. Piece-rate incentive systems for production employees and merit salary increases or bonus plans for salaried employees have been the dominant means of paying for performance. In the past, piece-rate incentive systems have dramatically declined because managers have discovered that such systems result in dysfunctional behavior, such as low cooperation, artificial limits on

---

3. Edward E. Lawler, *Pay and Organization Development* (Reading, Mass.: Addison-Wesley, 1981): 82–85.

EXHIBIT
Pay-for-Performance Systems

INDIVIDUAL PERFORMANCE	GROUP PERFORMANCE	ORGANIZATION-WIDE PERFORMANCE
Merit system	Productivity incentive	Profit sharing
Piece rate	Cost effectiveness	Productivity sharing
Executive bonus		(Scanlon Plan)

production, and resistance to changing standards. Similarly, more questions are being asked about individual bonus plans for executives as top managers discover their negative effects.

Meanwhile, organization-wide incentive systems are becoming more popular, particularly because managers are finding that these systems foster cooperation, which leads to productivity and innovation. To succeed, however, these plans require certain conditions. A review of the key considerations for designing a pay-for-performance plan and a discussion of the problems that arise when these considerations are not observed follow.

Individual Pay for Performance   The design of an individual pay-for-performance system requires an analysis of the task. Does the individual have control over the performance (result) that is to be measured? Is there a significant effort-to-performance relationship? For motivational reasons already discussed, such a relationship must exist. Unfortunately, many individual bonus, commission, or piece-rate incentive plans fall short in meeting this requirement. An individual may not have control over a performance result, such as sales or profit, because economic cycles or competitive forces beyond his or her control affect that result. Indeed, few outcomes in complex organizations are not dependent on other functions or individuals, and fewer still are not subject to external factors.

Choosing an appropriate measure of performance on which to base pay is a related problem incurred by individual bonus plans. For reasons discussed earlier, effectiveness on a job can include many facets not captured by cost, units produced, or sales revenues. Failure to include all activities that are important for effectiveness can lead to negative consequences. For example, sales personnel who receive a bonus for sales volume may push unneeded products, thus damaging long-term customer relations, or they may push an unprofitable mix of products just to increase volume. These same salespeople may also take orders and make commitments that cannot be met by manufacturing. Instead of rewarding salespeople for volume, why not reward them for profits, a more inclusive measure of performance? The obvious problem with this measure is that sales personnel do not have control over profits.

These dilemmas are constantly encountered and have led to the use of more subjective but inclusive behavioral measures of performance. Why not observe whether the salesperson or executive is performing all aspects of the job well? Most merit salary increases are based on subjective judgments and so are some individual bonus plans. Subjective evaluation systems, though they can be all-inclusive if based on a thorough analysis of the job, require deep trust in management, good manager-subordinate relations, and effective interpersonal skills. Unfortunately, these conditions are not fully met in many situations, though they can be developed if judged to be sufficiently important.

Group and Organization-wide Pay Plans   Organizational effectiveness depends on employee cooperation in most instances. An organization may elect to tie pay, or at least some portion of pay, indirectly to individual performance. Seeking to foster teamwork, a company may tie an incentive to some measure of group performance, or it may offer some type of profit- or productivity-sharing plan for the whole plant or company.

Gain-sharing plans have been used for years and in many varieties. The real power of a gain-sharing plan comes when it is supported by a climate of participation.[4] Various structures, systems, and processes involve employees in decisions that improve the organization's performance and result in a bonus throughout the organization. The Scanlon Plan is one such example. When the plan is installed in cooperation with workers and unions, a management-labor committee is created. Then committees seek and review suggestions for reducing costs. Payout is based on improvements in the sales-to-cost ratio of the plant compared to some agreed-upon base period before the adoption of the plan.

Organization-wide incentive plans that are part of a philosophy of participation require strong labor-management cooperation in design and administration. For example, the Scanlon Plan requires a direct employee vote with 75% approval before implementation. Without joint participation, commitment to any organization-wide incentive plan system will be low, and its symbolic and motivational value will be minimal.

Several critical decisions influence the effectiveness of a gain-sharing plan:

- Who should participate in the plan's design and administration, and how much participation will be allowed by management and union?
- What will be the size of the unit covered? Small units obviously offer easier identification with the organization's performance and the bonuses that result.
- What standard will be used to judge performance? Employees, the union (if involved), and management must agree on this for strong commitment. There are inevitable disagreements.
- How will the gains be divided? Who shares in the gains? What percentage of the gains goes to the company and what percentage to employees?

---

4. Christopher S. Miller and Michael H. Schuster, "Gain-sharing Plan: A Comparative Analysis," *Organizational Dynamics* (Summer 1987): 44–67.

When management and employees have gone through a process of discussion and negotiation, allowing a consensus to emerge on these questions, a real change in management-employee and union relations can occur. A top-down process would not yield the same benefits. Gain-sharing approached participatively can create a fundamental change in the psychological and economic ownership of the firm. Therein lies its primary motivational and satisfactional value; however, only a management that embraces values consistent with participation can make it work.

—— DISCUSSION QUESTIONS

1. In the United States, future employees may earn less than those currently working. How will this affect the design of reward systems and the role of compensation?
2. What business conditions might cause a company to redesign its reward system?
3. As observed in the reading, there are many different ways to design reward systems. Is there a design not mentioned in the reading that you can suggest?
4. Name a company and describe its reward system that you believe should be emulated. Explain why the system is effective in the organization.
5. How have you felt about the compensation you've received for the work you've done? Have you felt overpaid, underpaid, or fairly paid? How important is compensation to you relative to the other factors of your career? What is the source of your view?

From Control to Commitment in the Workplace   33

RICHARD E. WALTON

The author of this reading focuses on two different strategies for managing a work force. One is based on imposing control; the other relies on eliciting the commitment of workers. The traditional control model attempts to "establish order, exercise control, and achieve efficiency." In the commitment strategy, jobs are designed more broadly; planning and implementation are combined; operations are upgraded, not simply maintained; individual responsibilities vary as conditions vary; the focus is on teams rather than on the individual; and the organization is flatter. Workers are encouraged to fulfill their potential, and the company offers employees the assurance of security.

Eliciting worker commitment—and providing the environment in which it can flourish—pays tangible dividends for the individual and for the company. The author describes these opposing strategies toward employees and points out the key challenges in moving from one to the other.

The larger shape of institutional change is always difficult to recognize when one stands right in the middle of it. Today, throughout American industry, a significant change is under way in long-established approaches to the organization and management of work. Although this shift in attitude and practice takes a wide variety of company-specific forms, its larger shape—its overall pattern—is already visible if one knows where and how to look.

Consider, for example, the marked differences between two plants in the chemical products division of a major U.S. corporation. Both make similar products and employ similar technologies, but that is virtually all they have in common.

The first, organized by businesses with an identifiable product or product line, divides its employees into self-supervising 10- to 15-person work teams that are collectively responsible for a set of related tasks. Each team member has the training to perform many or all of the tasks for which the team is accountable, and pay reflects the level of mastery of required skills. These teams have received assurances that management will go to extra lengths to provide continued employment in any economic downturn. The teams have also been thoroughly briefed on such issues as market share, product costs, and their implications for the business.

Not surprisingly, this plant is a top performer economically and rates well on all measures of employee satisfaction, absenteeism, turnover, and safety. With its employees actively engaged in identifying and solving problems, it operates with fewer levels of management and fewer specialized departments than do its sister plants. It is also one of the principal suppliers of management talent for these other plants and for the division manufacturing staff.

In the second plant, each employee is responsible for a fixed job and is required to perform up to the minimum standard defined for that job. Peer pressure keeps new employees from exceeding the minimum standards and from taking other initiatives that go beyond basic job requirements. Supervisors, who manage daily assignments and monitor performance, have long since given up hope for anything more than compliance with standards, finding sufficient difficulty in getting their people to perform adequately most of the time. In fact, they and their workers try to prevent the industrial engineering department, which is under pressure from top plant management to improve operations, from using changes in methods to "jack up" standards.

A management campaign to document an "airtight case" against employees who have excessive absenteeism or sub-par performance mirrors employees' low morale and high distrust of management. A constant stream of formal grievances, violations of plant rules, harassment of supervisors, wildcat walkouts, and even sabotage has prevented the plant from reaching its productivity and quality goals and has absorbed a disproportionate amount of division staff time. Dealings with the union are characterized by contract negotiations on economic matters and skirmishes over issues of management control.

No responsible manager, of course, would ever wish to encourage the kind of situation at this second plant, yet the determination to understand its deeper causes and to attack them at their root does not come easily. Established modes of doing things have an inertia all their own. Such an effort is, however, in process all across the industrial landscape. And with that effort comes the possibility of a revolution in industrial relations every bit as great as that occasioned by the rise of mass production the better part of a century ago. The challenge is clear to those managers willing to see it—and the potential benefits, enormous.

—— APPROACHES TO WORK-FORCE MANAGEMENT

What explains the extraordinary differences between the plants just described? Is it that the first is newer and the other old? Yes and no. Not all new plants enjoy so fruitful an approach to work organization; not all older plants have such intractable problems. Is it that one plant is not unionized and the other is? Again, yes and no. The presence of a union may institutionalize conflict and lackluster performance, but it seldom causes them.

At issue here is not so much age or unionization but two radically different strategies for managing a company's or a factory's work force, two incompatible views of what managers can reasonably expect of workers and of the kind of partnership they can share with them. For simplicity, I will speak of these profound differences as reflecting the choice between a strategy based on imposing *control* and a strategy based on eliciting *commitment*.

THE 'CONTROL' STRATEGY

The traditional—or control-oriented—approach to work-force management took shape during the early part of this century in response to the division of work into small, fixed jobs for which individuals could be held accountable. The actual definition of jobs, as of acceptable standards of performance, rested on "lowest common denominator" assumptions about workers' skill and motivation. To monitor and control effort of this assumed caliber, management organized its own responsibilities into a hierarchy of specialized roles buttressed by a top-down allocation of authority and by status symbols attached to positions in the hierarchy.

For workers, compensation followed the rubric of "a fair day's pay for a fair day's work" because precise evaluations were possible when individual job requirements were so carefully prescribed. Most managers had little doubt that labor was best thought of as a variable cost, although some exceptional companies guaranteed job security to head off unionization attempts.

In the traditional approach, there was generally little policy definition with regard to employee voice unless the work force was unionized, in which case damage-control strategies predominated. With no union, management relied on an open-door policy, attitude surveys, and similar devices to learn about employees' concerns. If the work force was unionized, then management bargained terms of employment and established an appeal mechanism. These activities fell to labor relations specialists, who operated independently from line management and whose very existence assumed the inevitability and even the appropriateness of an adversarial relationship between workers and managers. Indeed, to those who saw management's exclusive obligation to be to a company's shareowners and the ownership of property to be the ultimate source of both obligation and prerogative, the claims of employees were constraints, nothing more.

At the heart of this traditional model is the wish to establish order, exercise control, and achieve efficiency in the application of the work force. Although it has distant antecedents in the bureaucracies of both church and military, the model's real father is Frederick W. Taylor, the turn-of-the-century "father of scientific management," whose views about the proper organization of work have long influenced management practice as well as the reactive policies of the U.S. labor movement.

Recently, however, changing expectations among workers have prompted a growing disillusionment with the apparatus of control. At the same time, of course, an intensified challenge from abroad has made the competitive obsolescence of this strategy clear. A model that assumes low employee commitment and that is designed to produce reliable if not outstanding performance simply cannot match the standards of excellence set by world-class competitors. Especially in a high-wage country like the United States, market success depends on a superior level of performance, a level that, in turn, requires the deep commitment, not merely the obedience—if you could obtain it—of workers. And as painful experience shows, this commitment cannot flourish in a workplace dominated by the familiar model of control.

THE 'COMMITMENT' STRATEGY

Over the past 20 years, companies have experimented at the plant level with a radically different work-force strategy. The more visible pioneers—among them, General Foods at Topeka, Kansas; General Motors at Brookhaven, Mississippi; Cummins Engine at Jamestown, New York; and Procter & Gamble at Lima, Ohio—have shown how great and productive the contribution of a truly committed work force can be. For a time, all new plants of this sort were nonunion, but by 1980 the success of efforts undertaken jointly with unions—GM's cooperation with the UAW at the Cadillac plant in Livonia, Michigan, for example—was impressive enough to encourage managers of both new and existing facilities to rethink their approach to the work force.

Local managers and union officials increasingly talk about common interests, working to develop mutual trust, and agreeing to sponsor quality-of-work-life (QWL) or employee involvement (EI) activities. Although most of these ventures have been initiated at the local level, there have been major exceptions.

More recently, a growing number of manufacturing companies have begun to remove levels of plant hierarchy, increase managers' spans of control, integrate quality and production activities at lower organizational levels, combine production and maintenance operations, and open up new career possibilities for workers. Some corporations have even begun to chart organizational renewal for the entire company. Cummins Engine, for example, has ambitiously committed itself to inform employees about the business, to encourage participation by everyone, and to create jobs that involve greater responsibility and more flexibility.

In this commitment-based approach to the work force, jobs are designed to be broader than before, to combine planning and implementation, and to include efforts to upgrade operations, not just maintain them. Individual responsibilities are expected to change as conditions change, and teams, not individuals, often are the organizational units accountable for performance. With management hierarchies relatively flat and differences in status minimized, control and lateral coordination depend on shared goals, and expertise rather than formal position determines influence.

Under the commitment strategy, performance expectations are high and serve not to define minimum standards but to provide "stretch objectives," emphasize continuous improvement, and reflect the requirements of the marketplace. Accordingly, compensation policies reflect less the old formulas of job evaluation than the heightened importance of group achievement, the expanded scope of individual contribution, and the growing concern for such questions of "equity" as gain sharing, stock ownership, and profit sharing.

Equally important to the commitment strategy is the challenge of giving employees some assurance of security, perhaps by offering them priority in training and retraining as old jobs are eliminated and new ones are created. Guaranteeing employees access to due process and providing them the means to be heard on such issues as production methods, problem solving, and human resources policies and practices is also a challenge. In unionized settings, the additional tasks include making relations less adversarial, broadening the agenda for joint problem solving and planning, and facilitating employee consultation.

Underlying all these policies is a management philosophy, often embodied in a published statement, that acknowledges the legitimate claims of a company's multiple stakeholders—owners, employees, customers, and the public. At the center of this philosophy is a belief that eliciting employee commitment will lead to enhanced performance. The evidence shows this belief to be well-grounded. In the absence of genuine commitment, however, new management policies designed for a committed work force may well leave a company distinctly more vulnerable than would older policies based on the control approach. The advantages—and risks—are considerable.

—— THE COSTS OF COMMITMENT

Because the potential leverage of a commitment-oriented strategy on performance is so great, the natural temptation is to assume the universal applicability of that strategy. Some environments, however, especially those requiring intricate teamwork, problem solving, organizational learning, and self-monitoring, are better suited than others to the commitment model. Indeed, the pioneers of the deep commitment strategy—a fertilizer plant in Norway, a refinery in the United Kingdom, a paper mill in Pennsylvania, a pet-food-processing plant in Kansas—were all based on continuous process technologies and were all capital- and raw-material intensive. All provided high economic leverage to improvements in workers' skills and attitudes, and all could offer considerable job challenge.

Is the converse true? Is the control strategy appropriate whenever—as with convicts breaking rocks with sledgehammers in a prison yard—work can be completely prescribed, remains static, and calls for individual, not group,

EXHIBIT
Work-Force Strategies

	CONTROL	TRANSITIONAL	COMMITMENT
Job Design Principles	Individual attention limited to performing individual job.	Scope of individual responsibility extended to upgrading system performance, via participative problem-solving groups in QWL, EI, and quality circle programs.	Individual responsibility extended to upgrading system performance.
	Job design deskills and fragments work and separates doing and thinking.	No change in traditional job design or accountability.	Job design enhances content of work, emphasizes whole task, and combines doing and thinking.
	Accountability focused on individual.		Frequent use of teams as basic accountable unit.
	Fixed job definition.		Flexible definition of duties, contingent on changing conditions.
Performance Expectations	Measured standards define minimum performance. Stability seen as desirable.		Emphasis placed on higher, "stretch objectives," which tend to be dynamic and oriented to the marketplace.
Management Organization: Structure, Systems, and Style	Structure tends to be layered, with top-down controls.	No basic changes in approaches to structure, control, or authority.	Flat organization structure with mutual influence systems.
	Coordination and control rely on rules and procedures.		Coordination and control based more on shared goals, values, and traditions.
	More emphasis on prerogatives and positional authority.		Management emphasis on problem solving and relevant information and expertise.
	Status symbols distributed to reinforce hierarchy.	A few visible symbols change.	Minimum status differentials to de-emphasize inherent hierarchy.

effort? In practice, managers have long answered yes. Mass production, epitomized by the assembly line, has for years been thought suitable for old-fashioned control.

But not any longer. Many mass producers, not least the automakers, have recently been trying to reconceive the structure of work and to give employees a significant role in solving problems and improving methods. Why?

EXHIBIT
Work-Force Strategies (Continued)

	CONTROL	*TRANSITIONAL*	*COMMITMENT*
Compensation Policies	Variable pay where feasible to provide individual incentive.	Typically no basic changes in compensation concepts.	Variable rewards to create equity and to reinforce group achievements: gain sharing, profit sharing.
	Individual pay geared to job evaluation.		Individual pay linked to skills and mastery.
	In downturn, cuts concentrated on hourly payroll.	Equality of sacrifice among employee groups.	Equality of sacrifice.
Employment Assurances	Employees regarded as variable costs.	Assurances that participation will not result in loss of job.	Assurances that participation will not result in loss of job.
		Extra effort to avoid layoffs.	High commitment to avoid or assist in reemployment.
			Priority for training and retaining existing work force.
Employee-Voice Policies	Employee input allowed on relatively narrow agenda. Attendant risks emphasized. Methods include open-door policy, attitude surveys, grievance procedures, and collective bargaining in some organizations.	Addition of limited, ad hoc consultation mechanisms. No change in corporate governance.	Employee participation encouraged on wide range of issues. Attendant benefits emphasized. New concepts of corporate governance.
	Business information distributed on strictly defined "need to know" basis.	Additional sharing of information.	Business data shared widely.
Labor-Management Relations	Adversarial labor relations; emphasis on interest conflict.	Thawing of adversarial attitudes; joint sponsorship of QWL or EI; emphasis on common fate.	Mutuality in labor relations; joint planning and problem solving on expanded agenda.
			Unions, management, and workers redefine their respective roles.

For many reasons, including to boost in-plant quality, lower warranty costs, cut waste, raise machine utilization and total capacity with the same plant and equipment, reduce operating and support personnel, reduce turnover and absenteeism, and speed up implementation of change. In addition, some managers place direct value on the fact that the commitment policies promote the development of human skills and individual self-esteem.

The benefits, economic and human, of worker commitment extend not only to continuous process industries but to traditional manufacturing industries as well. What, though, are the costs? To achieve these gains, managers have had to invest extra effort, develop new skills and relationships, cope with higher levels of ambiguity and uncertainty, and experience the pain and discomfort associated with changing habits and attitudes. Some of their skills have become obsolete, and some of their careers have been casualties of change. Union officials, too, have had to face the dislocation and discomfort that inevitably follow any upheaval in attitudes and skills. For their part, workers have inherited more responsibility and, along with it, greater uncertainty and more open-ended possibility of failure.

Part of the difficulty in assessing these costs is the fact that so many of the following problems inherent to the commitment strategy remain to be solved.

EMPLOYMENT ASSURANCES

As managers in heavy industry confront economic realities that make such assurances less feasible and as their counterparts in fiercely competitive high-technology areas are forced to rethink early guarantees of employment security, pointed questions await.

Will managers give lifetime assurances to the few, those who reach, say, 15 years' seniority, or will they adopt a general no-layoff policy? Will they demonstrate by policies and practices that employment security, though by no means absolute, is a higher-priority item than it was under the control approach? Will they accept greater responsibility for outplacement?

COMPENSATION

In one sense, the more productive employees under the commitment approach deserve to receive better pay for their better efforts, but how can managers balance this claim on resources with the harsh reality that domestic pay rates have risen to levels that render many of our industries uncompetitive internationally? Already, in such industries as trucking and airlines, new domestic competitors have placed companies that maintain prevailing wage rates at a significant disadvantage. Experience shows, however, that wage freezes and concession bargaining create obstacles to commitment, and new approaches to compensation are difficult to develop at a time when management cannot raise the overall level of pay.

Which approach is really suitable to the commitment model is unclear. Traditional job classifications place limits on the discretion of supervisors and encourage workers' sense of job ownership. Can pay systems based on employees' skill levels, which have long been used in engineering and skilled crafts, prove widely effective? Can these systems make up in greater mastery, positive motivation, and workforce flexibility what they give away in higher average wages?

In capital-intensive businesses, where total payroll accounts for a small percentage of costs, economics favors the move toward pay progression based on deeper and broader mastery. Still, conceptual problems remain with measuring skills, achieving consistency in pay decisions, allocating opportunities for learning new skills, trading off breadth and flexibility against depth, and handling the effects of "topping out" in a system that rewards and encourages personal growth.

There are also practical difficulties. Existing plants cannot, for example, convert to a skill-based structure overnight because of the vested interests of employees in the higher classifications. Similarly, formal profit- or gain-sharing plans like the Scanlon Plan (which shares gains in productivity as measured by improvements in the ratio of payroll to the sales value of production) cannot always operate. At the plant level, formulas that are responsive to what employees can influence, that are not unduly influenced by factors beyond their control, and that are readily understood, are not easy to devise. Small stand-alone businesses with a mature technology and stable markets tend to find the task least troublesome, but they are not the only ones trying to implement the commitment approach.

TECHNOLOGY

Computer-based technology can reinforce the control model or facilitate movement to the commitment model. Applications can narrow the scope of jobs or broaden them, emphasize the individual nature of tasks or promote the work of groups, centralize or decentralize the making of decisions, and create performance measures that emphasize learning or hierarchical control.

To date, the effects of this technology on control and commitment have been largely unintentional and unexpected. Even in organizations otherwise pursuing a commitment strategy, managers have rarely appreciated that the side effects of technology are not somehow "given" in the nature of things or that they can be actively managed. In fact, computer-based technology may be the least deterministic, most flexible technology to enter the workplace since the industrial revolution. As it becomes less hardware-dependent and more software-intensive and as the cost of computer power declines, the variety of ways to meet business requirements expands, each with a different set of human implications. Management has yet to identify the potential role of technology policy in the commitment strategy, and it has yet to invent concepts and methods to realize that potential.

SUPERVISORS

The commitment model requires first-line supervisors to facilitate rather than direct the work force, to impart rather than merely practice their technical and administrative expertise, and to help workers develop the ability to manage themselves. In practice, supervisors are to delegate away most of their traditional functions—often without having received adequate training and support for their new team-building tasks or having their own needs for voice, dignity, and fulfillment recognized.

These dilemmas are even visible in the new titles many supervisors carry—"team advisers" or "team consultants," for example—most of which imply that supervisors are not in the chain of command, although they are expected to be directive if necessary and assume functions delegated to the work force if they are not being performed. Part of the confusion here is the failure to distinguish the behavioral style required of supervisors from the basic responsibilities assigned them. Their ideal style may be advisory, but their responsibilities are to achieve certain human and economic outcomes. With experience, however, as first-line managers become more comfortable with the notion of delegating what subordinates are ready and able to perform, the problem will diminish.

Other difficulties are less tractable. The new breed of supervisors must have a level of interpersonal skill and conceptual ability often lacking in the present supervisory work force. Some companies have tried to address this lack by using the position as an entry point to management for college graduates. This approach may succeed where the work force has already acquired the necessary technical expertise, but it blocks a route of advancement for workers and sharpens the dividing line between management and other employees. Moreover, unless the company intends to open up higher-level positions for these college-educated supervisors, they may well grow impatient with the shift work of first-line supervision.

Even when new supervisory roles are filled—and filled successfully—from the ranks, dilemmas remain. With teams developed and functions delegated, to what new challenges do they turn to utilize fully their own capabilities? Do these capabilities match the demands of the other managerial work they might take on? If fewer and fewer supervisors are required as their individual span of control extends to a second and third work team, what promotional opportunities exist for the rest? Where do they go?

UNION-MANAGEMENT RELATIONS

Some companies, as they move from control to commitment, seek to decertify their unions and, at the same time, strengthen their employees' bond to the company. Others pursue cooperation with their unions, believing that they need their active support.

These developments open up new questions. Where companies are trying to preserve the nonunion status of some plants and yet promote collaborative union relations in others, will unions increasingly force the company to choose? After General Motors saw the potential of its joint QWL program with the UAW, it signed a neutrality clause and then an understanding about automatic recognition in new plants. If forced to choose, what will other managements do? Further, where union and management have collaborated in promoting QWL, how can the union prevent management from using the program to appeal directly to the workers about issues, such as wage concessions, that are subject to collective bargaining?

And if, in the spirit of mutuality, both sides agree to expand their joint agenda, what new risks will they face? Do union officials have the expertise to deal effectively with new agenda items like investment, pricing, and technology? To support QWL activities, they already have had to expand their skills and commit substantial resources at a time when shrinking employment has reduced their membership and thus their finances.

—— THE TRANSITIONAL STAGE

Although some organizations have adopted a comprehensive version of the commitment approach, most initially take on a more limited set of changes, a "transitional" stage or approach. The challenge here is to modify expectations, to make credible the leaders' stated intentions for further movement, and to support the initial changes in behavior. These transitional efforts can achieve a temporary equilibrium, provided they are viewed as part of a movement toward a comprehensive commitment strategy.

The cornerstone of the transitional stage is the voluntary participation of employees in problem-solving groups like quality circles. In unionized organizations, union-management dialogue leading to a jointly sponsored program is a condition for this type of employee involvement, which must then be supported by additional training and communication and by a shift in management style. Managers must also seek ways to consult employees about changes that affect them and to assure them that management will make every effort to avoid, defer, or minimize layoffs from higher productivity. When volume-related layoffs or concessions on pay are unavoidable, the principle of "equality of sacrifice" must apply to all employee groups, not just the hourly work force.

As a rule, during the early stages of transformation, few immediate changes can occur in the basic design of jobs, the compensation systems, or the management system itself. It is easy, of course, to attempt to change too much too soon. A more common error, especially in established organizations, is to make only "token" changes that never reach a critical mass. All too often managers try a succession of technique-oriented changes one by one: job enrichment, sensitivity training, management by objectives, group brainstorming, quality circles, and so on. Whatever the benefits of these techniques, their value to the organization will rapidly decay if the management philosophy—and practice—does not shift accordingly.

A different type of error—"overreaching"—may occur in newly established organizations based on commitment principles. In one new plant, managers allowed too much peer influence in pay decisions; in another, they underplayed the role of first-line supervisors as a link in the chain of command; in a third, they overemphasized learning of new skills and flexibility at the expense of mastery in critical operations. These design errors by themselves are not fatal, but the organization must be able to make mid-course corrections.

RATE OF TRANSFORMATION

How rapidly is the transformation in work-force strategy occurring? (See the *Exhibit* on pages 492–493 for a summary of work-force strategies.) Early change focused on the blue-collar work force and on those clerical operations that most closely resemble the factory. Although clerical change has lagged somewhat—because the control model has not produced such overt employee disaffection, and because management has been slow to recognize the importance of quality and productivity improvement—there are signs of a quickened pace of change in clerical operations.

Only a small fraction of U.S. workplaces today can boast of a comprehensive commitment strategy, but the rate of transformation continues to accelerate, and the move toward commitment via some explicit transitional stage extends to a still larger number of plants and offices. This transformation may be fueled by economic necessity, but other factors are shaping and pacing it—individual leadership in management and labor, philosophical choices, organizational competence in managing change, and cumulative learning from change itself.

DISCUSSION QUESTIONS

1. Is a commitment strategy economically feasible for most firms? What are the hidden costs of implementing such a strategy?
2. Are some elements of the traditional control strategy still essential to competitiveness? Would a mix of the two strategies better serve some companies, or should all firms seek to move from control to commitment?
3. With a commitment strategy, "Compensation policies reflect less the old formulas of job evaluation than the heightened importance of group achievement . . ." Does a commitment strategy remove individual incentive to perform well?
4. Should a commitment strategy change the way managers approach their work? Would it affect their perceived status?

From Affirmative Action to Affirming Diversity

34

R. ROOSEVELT THOMAS, JR.

To compete globally, America needs to create workplaces that tap the full potential of every employee, says this author. Affirmative action programs, although appropriate, fail to deal with the root causes of prejudice and inequality and do little to develop people and strengthen organizations. In this reading, the author examines affirmative action programs and their shortcomings, contrasting them with more suitable contemporary approaches that affirm and make full use of an openly multicultural workplace.

Sooner or later, affirmative action will die a natural death. Its achievements have been stupendous, but if we look at the premises that underlie it, we find assumptions and priorities that look increasingly shopworn. Thirty years ago, affirmative action was invented on the basis of these five appropriate premises:

1. Adult, white males make up something called the U.S. business mainstream.
2. The U.S. economic edifice is a solid, unchanging institution with more than enough space for everyone.
3. Women, blacks, immigrants, and other minorities should be allowed in as a matter of public policy and common decency.
4. Widespread racial, ethnic, and sexual prejudice keeps them out.
5. Legal and social coercion are necessary to bring about the change.

Today all five of these premises need revising. Over the past six years, I have tried to help some 15 companies learn how to achieve and manage diversity, and I have seen that the realities facing us are no longer the realities affirmative action was designed to fix.

To begin with, more than half the U.S. work force now consists of minorities, immigrants, and women, so white, native-born males, though undoubtedly still dominant, are themselves a statistical minority. In addition, white males will make up only 15% of the increase in the work force over the next 10 years. The so-called mainstream is now almost as diverse as the society at large.

Second, while the edifice is still big enough for all, it no longer seems stable, massive, and invulnerable. In fact, American corporations are scrambling, doing their best to become more adaptable, to compete more successfully for markets and labor, foreign and domestic, and to attract all the talent they can find. (*Exhibits 1* to *5* show what a number of U.S. companies are doing to manage diversity.)

Third, women and minorities no longer need a boarding pass, they need an upgrade. The problem is not getting them in at the entry level; the problem is making better use of their potential at every level, especially in middle-management and leadership positions. This is no longer simply a question of common decency, it is a question of business survival.

Fourth, although prejudice is hardly dead, it has suffered some wounds that may eventually prove fatal. In the meantime, American businesses are now filled with progressive people—many of them minorities and women themselves—whose prejudices, where they still exist, are much too deeply suppressed to interfere with recruitment. The reason many companies are still wary of minorities and women has much more to do with education and perceived qualifications than with color or gender. Companies are worried about productivity and well aware that minorities and women represent a disproportionate share of the undertrained and undereducated.

Fifth, coercion is rarely needed at the recruitment stage. There are very few places in the United States today where you could dip a recruitment net and come up with nothing but white males. Getting hired is not the problem—women and blacks who are seen as having the necessary skills and energy can get *into* the work force relatively easily. It's later on that many of them plateau and lose their drive and quit or get fired. It's later on that their managers' inability to manage diversity hobbles them and the companies they work for.

In creating these changes, affirmative action had an essential role to play and played it very well. In many companies and communities it still plays that role. But affirmative action is an artificial, transitional intervention intended to give managers a chance to correct an imbalance, an injustice, a mistake. Once the numbers mistake has been corrected, I don't think affirmative action alone can cope with the remaining long-term task of creating a work setting geared to the upward mobility of *all* kinds of people, including white males. It is difficult for affirmative action to influence upward mobility even in the short run, primarily because it is perceived to conflict with the meritocracy we favor. For this reason, affirmative action is a red flag to every individual who feels unfairly passed over and a stigma for those who appear to be its beneficiaries.

Moreover, I doubt very much that individuals who reach top positions through affirmative action are effective models for younger members of their race or sex. What, after all, do they model? A black vice president who got her job through affirmative action is not necessarily a model of how to rise through the corporate meritocracy. She may be a model of how affirmative action can work for the people who find or put themselves in the right place at the right time.

If affirmative action in upward mobility meant that no person's competence and character would ever be overlooked or undervalued on account of

EXHIBIT 1
Out of the Numbers Game and into Decision Making

Like many other companies, Avon practiced affirmative action in the 1970s and was not pleased with the results. The company worked with employment agencies that specialized in finding qualified minority hires, and it cultivated contacts with black and minority organizations on college campuses. Avon wanted to see its customer base reflected in its work force, especially at the decision-making level. But while women moved up the corporate ladder fairly briskly—not so surprising in a company whose work force is mostly female—minorities did not. So in 1984, the company began to change its policies and practices.

"We really wanted to get out of the numbers game," says Marcia Worthing, the corporate vice president for human resources. "We felt it was more important to have five minority people tied into the decision-making process than ten who were just heads to count."

First, Avon initiated awareness training at all levels. "The key to recruiting, retaining, and promoting minorities is not the human resource department," says Worthing. "It's getting line management to buy into the idea. We had to do more than change behavior. We had to change attitudes."

Second, the company formed a Multicultural Participation Council that meets regularly to oversee the process of managing diversity. The group includes Avon's CEO and high-level employees from throughout the company.

Third, in conjunction with the American Institute for Managing Diversity, Avon developed a diversity-training program. For several years, the company has sent racially and ethnically diverse groups of 25 managers at a time to Institute headquarters at Morehouse College in Atlanta, where they spend three weeks confronting their differences and learning to hear and avail themselves of viewpoints they initially disagreed with. "We came away disciples of diversity," says one company executive.

Fourth, the company helped three minority groups—blacks, Hispanics, and Asians—form networks that crisscrossed the corporation in all 50 states. Each network elects its own leaders and has an adviser from senior management. In addition, the networks have representatives on the Multicultural Participation Council, where they serve as a conduit for employee views on diversity issues facing management.

---

race, sex, ethnicity, origins, or physical disability, then affirmative action would be the very thing we need to let every corporate talent find its niche. But what affirmative action means in practice is an unnatural focus on one group, and what it means too often to too many employees is that someone is playing fast and loose with standards in order to favor that group. Unless we are to compromise our standards, a thing no competitive company can even contemplate, upward mobility for minorities and women should always be a question of pure competence and character unmuddled by accidents of birth.

And that is precisely why we have to learn to manage diversity—to move beyond affirmative action, not to repudiate it. Some of what I have to say may strike some readers—mostly those with an ax to grind—as directed at the majority white males who hold most of the decision-making posts in our economy. But I am speaking to all managers, not just white males, and I certainly don't mean to suggest that white males somehow stand outside diversity. White males are as odd and as normal as anyone else.

—— THE AFFIRMATIVE ACTION CYCLE

If you are managing diverse employees, you should ask yourself this question: Am I fully tapping the potential capacities of everyone in my department? If the answer is no, you should ask yourself this follow-up: Is this failure hampering my ability to meet performance standards? The answer to this question undoubtedly will be yes.

Think of corporate management for a moment as an engine burning pure gasoline. What's now going into the tank is no longer just gas, it has an increasing percentage of, let's say, methanol. In the beginning, the engine will still work pretty well, but by and by it will start to sputter, and eventually it will stall. Unless we rebuild the engine, it will no longer burn the fuel we're feeding it. As the work force grows more and more diverse at the intake level, the talent pool we have to draw on for supervision and management will also grow increasingly diverse. So the question is: Can we burn this fuel? Can we get maximum corporate power from the diverse work force we're now drawing into the system?

Affirmative action gets blamed for failing to do things it never could do. Affirmative action gets the new fuel into the tank, the new people through the front door. Something else will have to get them into the driver's seat. That something else consists of enabling people, in this case minorities and women, to perform to their potential. This is what we now call managing diversity. Not appreciating or leveraging diversity, not even necessarily understanding it. Just managing diversity in such a way as to get from a heterogeneous work force the same productivity, commitment, quality, and profit that we got from the old homogeneous work force.

The correct question today is not, How are we doing on race relations? or Are we promoting enough minority people and women? but rather, Given the diverse work force I've got, am I getting the productivity, does it work as smoothly, is morale as high, as if every person in the company was the same sex and race and nationality? Most answers will be, Well, no, of course not! But why shouldn't the answer be, You bet!?

When we ask how we're doing on race relations, we inadvertently put our finger on what's wrong with the question and with the attitude that underlies affirmative action. So long as racial and gender equality is something we grant to minorities and women, there will be no racial and gender equality. What we must do is create an environment where no one is advantaged or disadvantaged, an environment where "we" is everyone. What the traditional approach to diversity did was to create a cycle of crisis, action, relaxation, and disappointment that companies repeated over and over again without ever achieving more than the barest particle of what they were after.

Affirmative action pictures the work force as a pipeline and reasons as follows: If we can fill the pipeline with *qualified* minorities and women, we can solve our upward mobility problem. Once recruited, they will perform in accordance with our promotional criteria and move naturally up our regular developmental ladder. In the past, where minorities and women have failed to progress, they were simply unable to meet our performance standards. Recruiting qualified people will enable us to avoid special programs and reverse discrimination.

This pipeline perspective generates a self-perpetuating, self-defeating, recruitment-oriented cycle with six stages:

1. Problem Recognition   The first time through the cycle, the problem takes this form—We need more minorities and women in the pipeline. In later iterations, the problem is more likely to be defined as a need to retain and promote minorities and women.

2. Intervention   Management puts the company into what we may call an Affirmative Action Recruitment Mode. During the first cycle, the goal is to recruit minorities and women. Later, when the cycle is repeated a second or third time and the challenge has shifted to retention, development, and promotion, the goal is to recruit *qualified* minorities and women. Sometimes, managers indifferent or blind to possible accusations of reverse discrimination will institute special training, tracking, incentive, mentoring, or sponsoring programs for minorities and women.

3. Great Expectations   Large numbers of minorities and women have been recruited, and a select group has been promoted or recruited at a higher level to serve as highly visible role models for the newly recruited masses. The stage seems set for the natural progression of minorities and women up through the pipeline. Management leans back to enjoy the fruits of its labor.

4. Frustration   The anticipated natural progression fails to occur. Minorities and women see themselves plateauing prematurely. Management is upset (and embarrassed) by the failure of its affirmative action initiative and begins to resent the impatience of the new recruits and their unwillingness to give the company credit for trying to do the right thing. Depending on how high in the hierarchy they have plateaued, alienated minorities and women either leave the company or stagnate.

5. Dormancy   All remaining participants conspire tacitly to present a silent front to the outside world. Executives say nothing because they have no solutions. As for those women and minorities who stayed on, calling attention to affirmative action's failures might raise doubts about their qualifications. Do

EXHIBIT 2
"It Simply Makes Good Business Sense"

Corning characterizes its 1970s affirmative action program as a form of legal compliance. The law dictated affirmative action and morality required it, so the company did its best to hire minorities and women.

The ensuing cycle was classic: recruitment, confidence, disappointment, embarrassment, crisis, more recruitment. Talented women and blacks joined the company only to plateau or resign. Few reached upper-management levels, and no one could say exactly why.

Then James R. Houghton took over as CEO in 1983 and made the diverse work force one of Corning's three top priorities, alongside Total Quality and a higher return on equity. His logic was twofold:

First of all, the company had higher attrition rates for minorities and women than for white males, which meant that investments in training and development were being wasted. Second, he believed that the Corning work force should more closely mirror the Corning customer base.

In order to break the cycle of recruitment and subsequent frustration, the company established two quality-improvement teams headed by senior executives, one for black progress and one for women's progress. Mandatory awareness training was introduced for some 7,000 salaried employees—a day and a half for gender awareness, two-and-a-half days for racial awareness. One goal of the training is to identify unconscious company values that work against minorities and women. For example, a number of awareness groups reached the conclusion that working late had so much symbolic value that managers tended to look more at the quantity than at the quality of time spent on the job, with predictably negative effects on employees with dependent-care responsibilities.

The company also made an effort to improve communications by printing regular stories and articles about the diverse work force in its in-house newspaper and by publicizing employee success stories that emphasized diversity. It worked hard to identify and publicize promotion criteria. Career-planning systems were introduced for all employees.

With regard to recruitment, Corning set up a nationwide scholarship program that provides renewable grants of $5,000 per year for college in exchange for a summer of paid work at some Corning installation. A majority of program participants have come to work for Corning full-time after graduation, and very few have left the company so far, though the program has been in place only four years.

The company also expanded its summer intern program, with an emphasis on minorities and women, and established formal recruiting contacts with campus groups such as the Society of Women Engineers and the National Black MBA Association.

Corning sees its efforts to manage diversity not only as a social and moral issue but also as a question of efficiency and competitiveness. In the words of Mr. Houghton, "It simply makes good business sense."

they deserve their jobs, or did they just happen to be in the right place at the time of an affirmative action push? So no one complains, and if the company has a good public relations department, it may even wind up with a reputation as a good place for women and minorities to work.

If questioned publicly, management will say things like "Frankly, affirmative action is not currently an issue," or "Our numbers are okay," or "With respect to minority representation at the upper levels, management is aware of this remaining challenge."

In private and off the record, however, people say things like "Premature plateauing is a problem, and we don't know what to do," and "Our top people don't seem to be interested in finding a solution," and "There's plenty of racism and sexism around this place—whatever you may hear."

6. Crisis   Dormancy can continue indefinitely, but usually it is broken by a crisis of competitive pressure, government intervention, external pressure from a special interest group, or internal unrest. One company found that its pursuit of a Total Quality program was hampered by the alienation of minorities and women. Senior management at another corporation saw the growing importance of minorities in their customer base and decided they needed minority participation in their managerial ranks. In another case, growing expressions of discontent forced a break in the conspiracy of silence even after the company had received national recognition as a good place for minorities and women to work.

Whatever its cause, the crisis fosters a return to the Problem Recognition phase, and the cycle begins again. This time, management seeks to explain the shortcomings of the previous affirmative action push and usually concludes that the problem is recruitment. This assessment by a top executive is typical:

> The managers I know are decent people. While they give priority to performance, I do not believe any of them deliberately block minorities or women who are qualified for promotion. On the contrary, I suspect they bend over backward to promote women and minorities who give some indication of being qualified.
>
> However, they believe we simply do not have the necessary talent within those groups, but because of the constant complaints they have heard about their deficiencies in affirmative action, they feel they face a no-win situation. If they do not promote, they are obstructionists. But if they promote people who are unqualified, they hurt performance and deny promotion to other employees unfairly. They can't win. The answer, in my mind, must be an ambitious new recruitment effort to bring in quality people.

And so the cycle repeats. Once again blacks, Hispanics, women, and immigrants are dropped into a previously homogeneous, all-white, all-Anglo, all-male, all native-born environment, and the burden of cultural change is placed on the newcomers. There will be new expectations and a new round of frustration, dormancy, crisis, and recruitment.

EXHIBIT 3
Turning Social Pressures into Competitive Advantage

Like most other companies trying to respond to the federal legislation of the 1970s, Digital Equipment Corp. started off by focusing on numbers. By the early 1980s, however, company leaders could see it would take more than recruitment to make Digital the diverse workplace they wanted it to be. Equal Employment Opportunity (EEO) and affirmative action seemed too exclusive—too much "white males doing good deeds for minorities and women." The company wanted to move beyond these programs to the kind of environment where every employee could realize his or her potential, and Digital decided that meant an environment where individual differences were not tolerated but valued, even celebrated.

The resulting program and philosophy, called Valuing Differences, has two components:

First, the company helps people get in touch with their stereotypes and false assumptions through what Digital calls Core Groups. These voluntary groupings of 8 to 10 people work with company-trained facilitators whose job is to encourage discussion and self-development and, in the company's words, "to keep people safe" as they struggle with their prejudices. Digital also runs a voluntary two-day training program called "Understanding the Dynamics of Diversity," which thousands of Digital employees have now taken.

Second, the company has named a number of senior managers to various Cultural Boards of Directors and Valuing Differences Boards of Directors. These bodies promote openness to individual differences, encourage younger managers committed to the goal of diversity, and sponsor frequent celebrations of racial, gender, and ethnic differences such as Hispanic Heritage Week and Black History Month.

In addition to the Valuing Differences program, the company preserved its EEO and affirmative action functions. Valuing Differences focuses on personal and group development, EEO on legal issues, and affirmative action on systemic change. According to Alan Zimmerle, head of the Valuing Differences program, EEO and Valuing Differences are like two circles that touch but don't overlap—the first representing the legal need for diversity, the second the corporate desire for diversity. Affirmative action is a third circle that overlaps the other two and holds them together with policies and procedures.

Together, these three circles can transform legal and social pressures into the competitive advantage of a more effective work force, higher morale, and the reputation of being a better place to work. As Zimmerle puts it, "Digital wants to be the employer of choice. We want our pick of the talent that's out there."

——— TEN GUIDELINES FOR LEARNING TO MANAGE DIVERSITY

The traditional American image of diversity has been assimilation: the melting pot, where ethnic and racial differences were standardized into a kind of American puree. Of course, the melting pot is only a metaphor. In real life, many ethnic and most racial groups retain their individuality and express it energetically. What we have is perhaps some kind of American mulligan stew; it is certainly no puree.

At the workplace, however, the melting pot has been more than a metaphor. Corporate success has demanded a good deal of conformity, and employees have voluntarily abandoned most of their ethnic distinctions at the company door.

Now those days are over. Today the melting pot is the wrong metaphor even in business, for three good reasons. First, if it ever was possible to melt down Scotsmen and Dutchmen and Frenchmen into an indistinguishable broth, you can't do the same with blacks, Asians, and women. Their differences don't melt so easily. Second, most people are no longer willing to be melted down, not even for eight hours a day—and it's a seller's market for skills. Third, the thrust of today's nonhierarchical, flexible, collaborative management requires a ten- or twentyfold increase in our tolerance for individuality.

So companies are faced with the problem of surviving in a fiercely competitive world with a work force that consists and will continue to consist of *unassimilated diversity*. And the engine will take a great deal of tinkering to burn that fuel.

What managers fear from diversity is a lowering of standards, a sense that anything goes. Of course, standards must not suffer. In fact, competence counts more than ever. The goal is to manage diversity in such a way as to get from a diverse work force the same productivity we once got from a homogeneous work force, and to do it without artificial programs, standards—or barriers.

Managing diversity does not mean controlling or containing diversity, it means enabling every member of your work force to perform to his or her potential. It means getting from employees, first, everything we have a right to expect, and, second—if we do it well—everything they have to give. If the old homogeneous work force performed dependably at 80% of its capacity, then the first result means getting 80% from the new heterogeneous work force too. But the second result, the icing on the cake, the unexpected upside that diversity can perhaps give as a bonus, means 85% to 90% from everyone in the organization.

For the moment, however, let's concentrate on the basics of how to get satisfactory performance from the new diverse work force. There are few adequate models. So far, no large company I know of has succeeded in managing diversity to its own satisfaction. But any number have begun to try.

On the basis of their experience, here are my 10 guidelines:

1. Clarify Your Motivation   A lot of executives are not sure why they should want to learn to manage diversity. Legal compliance seems like a good reason. So does community relations. Many executives believe they have a social and moral responsibility to employ minorities and women. Others want to placate an internal group or pacify an outside organization. None of these are bad reasons, but none of them are business reasons, and given the nature and scope of today's competitive challenges, I believe only business reasons will supply the necessary long-term motivation. In any case, it is the business reasons I want to focus on here.

In business terms, a diverse work force is not something your company ought to have; it's something your company does have, or soon will have. Learning to manage that diversity will make you more competitive.

2. Clarify Your Vision   When managers think about a diverse work force, what do they picture? Not publicly, but in the privacy of their minds?

One popular image is of minorities and women clustering on a relatively low plateau, with a few of them trickling up as they become assimilated into the prevailing culture. Of course, they enjoy good salaries and benefits, and most of them accept their status, appreciate the fact that they are doing better than they could do somewhere else, and are proud of the achievements of their race or sex. This is reactionary thinking, but it's a lot more common than you might suppose.

Another image is what we might call heightened sensitivity. Members of the majority culture are sensitive to the demands of minorities and women for upward mobility and recognize the advantages of fully utilizing them. Minorities and women work at all levels of the corporation, but they are the recipients of generosity and know it. A few years of this second-class status drives most of them away and compromises the effectiveness of those that remain. Turnover is high.

Then there is the coexistence-compromise image. In the interests of corporate viability, white males agree to recognize minorities and women as equals. They bargain and negotiate their differences. But the win-lose aspect of the relationship preserves tensions, and the compromises reached are not always to the company's competitive advantage.

Diversity and equal opportunity is a big step up. It presupposes that the white male culture has given way to one that respects difference and individuality. The problem is that minorities and women will accept it readily as their operating image, but many white males, consciously or unconsciously, are likely to cling to a vision that leaves them in the driver's seat. A vision gap of this kind can be a difficulty.

In my view, the vision to hold in your own imagination and to try to communicate to all your managers and employees is an image of fully tapping the human resource potential of every member of the work force. This vision sidesteps the question of equality, ignores the tensions of coexistence, plays down the uncomfortable realities of difference, and focuses instead on individual enablement. It doesn't say, "Let *us* give *them* a chance." It assumes a diverse work force that includes us and them. It says, "Let's create an environment where everyone will do their best work."

Several years ago, an industrial plant in Atlanta with a highly diverse work force was threatened with closing unless productivity improved. To save their jobs, everyone put their shoulders to the wheel and achieved the results they needed to stay open. The senior operating manager was amazed.

EXHIBIT 4
Discovering Complexity and Value in P&G's Diversity

Because Procter & Gamble fills its upper-level management positions only from within the company, it places a premium on recruiting the best available entry-level employees. Campus recruiting is pursued nationwide and year-round by line managers from all levels of the company. Among other things, the company has made a concerted—and successful—effort to find and hire talented minorities and women.

Finding first-rate hires is only one piece of the effort, however. There is still the challenge of moving diversity upward. As one top executive put it, "We know that we can only succeed as a company if we have an environment that makes it easy for all of us, not just some of us, to work to our potential."

In May 1988, P&G formed a Corporate Diversity Strategy Task Force to clarify the concept of diversity, define its importance for the company, and identify strategies for making progress toward successfully managing a diverse work force.

The task force, composed of men and women from every corner of the company, made two discoveries: First, diversity at P&G was far more complex than most people had supposed. In addition to race and gender, it included factors such as cultural heritage, personal background, and functional experience. Second, the company needed to expand its view of the value of differences.

The task force helped the company to see that learning to manage diversity would be a long-term process of organizational change. For example, P&G has offered voluntary diversity training at all levels since the 1970s, but the program has gradually broadened its emphasis on race and gender awareness to include the value of self-realization in a diverse environment. As retiring board chairman John Smale put it, "If we can tap the total contribution that everybody in our company has to offer, we will be better and more competitive in everything we do."

P&G is now conducting a thorough, continuing evaluation of all management programs to be sure that systems are working well for everyone. It has also carried out a corporate survey to get a better picture of the problems facing P&G employees who are balancing work and family responsibilities and to improve company programs in such areas as dependent care.

For years he had seen minorities and women plateauing disproportionately at the lower levels of the organization, and he explained that fact away with two rationalizations. "They haven't been here that long," he told himself. And "This is the price we pay for being in compliance with the law."

When the threat of closure energized this whole group of people into a level of performance he had not imagined possible, he got one fleeting glimpse of people working up to their capacity. Once the crisis was over, everyone went back to the earlier status quo—white males driving and everyone else sitting back, looking on—but now there was a difference. Now, as he put it himself, he had been to the mountaintop. He knew that what he was getting from minorities and women was nowhere near what they were capable of giving. And he wanted it, crisis or no crisis, all the time.

3. Expand Your Focus   Managers usually see affirmative action and equal employment opportunity as centering on minorities and women, with very little to offer white males. The diversity I'm talking about includes not only race, gender, creed, and ethnicity but also age, background, education, function, and personality differences. The objective is not to assimilate minorities and women into a dominant white male culture but to create a dominant heterogeneous culture.

The culture that dominates the United States socially and politically is heterogeneous, and it works by giving its citizens the liberty to achieve their potential. Channeling that potential, once achieved, is an individual right but still a national concern. Something similar applies in the workplace, where the keys to success are individual ability and a corporate destination. Managing disparate talents to achieve common goals is what companies learned to do when they set their sights on, say, Total Quality. The secrets of managing diversity are much the same.

4. Audit Your Corporate Culture   If the goal is not to assimilate diversity into the dominant culture but rather to build a culture that can digest unassimilated diversity, then you had better start by figuring out what your present culture looks like. Because what we're talking about here is the body of unspoken and unexamined assumptions, values, and mythologies that make your world go round, this kind of cultural audit is impossible to conduct without outside help. It's a research activity, done mostly with in-depth interviews and a lot of listening at the water cooler.

The operative corporate assumptions you have to identify and deal with are often inherited from the company's founder. "If we treat everyone as a member of the family, we will be successful" is not uncommon. Nor is its corollary "Father Knows Best."

Another widespread assumption, probably absorbed from American culture in general, is that "cream will rise to the top." In most companies, what passes for cream rising to the top is actually cream being pulled or pushed to the top by an informal system of mentoring and sponsorship.

Corporate culture is a kind of tree. Its roots are assumptions about the company and about the world. Its branches, leaves, and seeds are behavior. You can't change the leaves without changing the roots, and you can't grow peaches on an oak. Or rather, with the proper grafting, you *can* grow peaches on an oak, but they come out an awful lot like acorns—small and hard and not much fun to eat. So if you want to grow peaches, you have to make sure the tree's roots are peach friendly.

5. Modify Your Assumptions   The real problem with this corporate culture tree is that every time you go to make changes in the roots, you run into terrible opposition. Every culture, including corporate culture, has root guards that turn out in force every time you threaten a basic assumption.

Take the family assumption as an example. Viewing the corporation as a family suggests not only that father knows best; it also suggests that sons will inherit the business, that daughters should stick to doing the company dishes, and that if Uncle Deadwood doesn't perform, we'll put him in the chimney corner and feed him for another 30 years regardless. Each assumption has its constituency and its defenders. If we say to Uncle Deadwood, "Yes, you did good work for 10 years, but years 11 and 12 look pretty bleak; we think it's time we helped you find another chimney," shock waves will travel through the company as every family-oriented employee draws a sword to defend the sacred concept of guaranteed jobs.

But you have to try. A corporation that wants to create an environment with no advantages or disadvantages for any group cannot allow the family assumption to remain in place. It must be labeled dishonest mythology.

Sometimes the dishonesties are more blatant. When I asked a white male middle manager how promotions were handled in his company, he said, "You need leadership capability, bottom-line results, the ability to work with people, and compassion." Then he paused and smiled. "That's what they say. But down the hall there's a guy we call Captain Kickass. He's ruthless, mean-spirited, and he steps on people. That's the behavior they really value. Forget what they say."

In addition to the obvious issue of hypocrisy, this example also raises a question of equal opportunity. When I asked this young middle manager if he thought minorities and women could meet the Captain Kickass standard, he said he thought they probably could. But the opposite argument can certainly be made. Whether we're talking about blacks in an environment that is predominantly white, whites in one predominantly black, or women in one predominantly male, the majority culture will not readily condone such tactics from a member of a minority. So the corporation with the unspoken kickass performance standard has at least one criterion that will hamper the upward mobility of minorities and women.

Another destructive assumption is the melting pot I referred to earlier. The organization I'm arguing for respects differences rather than seeking to smooth them out. It is multicultural rather than culture blind, which has an important consequence: When we no longer force people to "belong" to a common ethnicity or culture, then the organization's leaders must work all the harder to define belonging in terms of a set of values and a sense of purpose that transcend the interests, desires, and preferences of any one group.

6. Modify Your Systems   The first purpose of examining and modifying assumptions is to modify systems. Promotion, mentoring, and sponsorship comprise one such system, and the unexamined cream-to-the-top assumption I mentioned earlier can tend to keep minorities and women from climbing the corporate ladder. After all, in many companies it is difficult to secure a promotion above a certain level without a personal advocate or sponsor. In the context of managing diversity, the question is not whether this system is maximally

EXHIBIT 5
The Daily Experience of Genuine Workplace Diversity

Chairman David T. Kearns believes that a firm and resolute commitment to affirmative action is the first and most important step to work-force diversity. "Xerox is committed to affirmative action," he says. "It is a corporate value, a management priority, and a formal business objective."

Xerox began recruiting minorities and women systematically as far back as the mid-1960s, and it pioneered such concepts as pivotal jobs (described later). The company's approach emphasizes behavior expectations as opposed to formal consciousness-raising programs because, as one Xerox executive put it, "It's just not realistic to think that a day-and-a-half of training will change a person's thinking after 30 or 40 years."

On the assumption that attitude changes will grow from the daily experience of genuine workplace diversity, the Xerox Balanced Work Force Strategy sets goals for the number of minorities and women in each division and at every level. (For example, the goal for the top 300 executive-level jobs in one large division is 35% women by 1995, compared with 15% today.) "You *must* have a laboratory to work in," says Ted Payne, head of Xerox's Office of Affirmative Action and Equal Opportunity.

Minority and women's employee support groups have grown up in more than a dozen locations with the company's encouragement. But Xerox depends mainly on the three pieces of its balanced strategy to make diversity work.

First are the goals. Xerox sets recruitment and representation goals in accordance with federal guidelines and reviews them constantly to make sure they reflect work-force demographics. Any company with a federal contract is required to make this effort. But Xerox then extends the guidelines by setting diversity goals for its upper-level jobs and holding division and group managers accountable for reaching them.

The second piece is a focus on pivotal jobs, a policy Xerox adopted in the 1970s when it first noticed that minorities and women did not have the upward mobility the company wanted to see. By examining the backgrounds of top executives, Xerox was able to identify the key positions that all successful managers had held at lower levels and to set goals for getting minorities and women assigned to such jobs.

The third piece is an effort to concentrate managerial training not so much on managing diversity as on just plain managing people. What the company discovered when it began looking at managerial behavior toward minorities and women was that all too many managers didn't know enough about how to manage anyone, let alone people quite different from themselves.

---

efficient but whether it works for all employees. Executives who only sponsor people like themselves are not making much of a contribution to the cause of getting the best from every employee.

Performance appraisal is another system where unexamined practices and patterns can have pernicious effects. For example, there are companies where official performance appraisals differ substantially from what is said informally, with the result that employees get their most accurate performance feedback through the grapevine. So if the grapevine is closed to minorities and women, they are left at a severe disadvantage. As one white manager observed, "If the blacks around here knew how they were really perceived, there would be a revolt." Maybe so. More important to your business, however, is the fact that without an accurate appraisal of performance, minority and women employees will find it difficult to correct or defend their alleged shortcomings.

7. Modify Your Models   The second purpose of modifying assumptions is to modify models of managerial and employee behavior. My own personal hobgoblin is one I call the Doer Model, often an outgrowth of the family assumption and of unchallenged paternalism. I have found the Doer Model alive and thriving in a dozen companies. It works like this:

Because father knows best, managers seek subordinates who will follow their lead and do as they do. If they can't find people exactly like themselves, they try to find people who aspire to be exactly like themselves. The goal is predictability and immediate responsiveness because the doer manager is not there to manage people but to do the business. In accounting departments, for example, doer managers do accounting, and subordinates are simply extensions of their hands and minds, sensitive to every signal and suggestion of managerial intent.

Doer managers take pride in this identity of purpose. "I wouldn't ask my people to do anything I wouldn't do myself," they say. "I roll up my sleeves and get in the trenches." Doer managers love to be in the trenches. It keeps them out of the line of fire.

But managers aren't supposed to be in the trenches, and accounting managers aren't supposed to do accounting. What they are supposed to do is create systems and a climate that allow accountants to do accounting, a climate that enables people to do what they've been charged to do. The right goal is doer subordinates, supported and empowered by managers who manage.

8. Help Your People Pioneer   Learning to manage diversity is a change process, and the managers involved are change agents. There is no single tried-and-tested "solution" to diversity and no fixed right way to manage it. Assuming the existence of a single or even a dominant barrier undervalues the importance of all the other barriers that face any company, including, potentially, prejudice, personality, community dynamics, culture, and the ups and downs of business itself.

While top executives articulate the new company policy and their commitment to it, middle managers—most or all of them still white males, remember—are placed in the tough position of having to cope with a forest of problems and simultaneously develop the minorities and women who represent their own competition for an increasingly limited number of promotions. What's more, every time they stumble they will themselves be labeled the major barriers to progress. These managers need help, they need a certain amount of sympathy, and most of all, perhaps, they need to be told that they are pioneers and judged accordingly.

In one case, an ambitious young black woman was assigned to a white male manager, at his request, on the basis of her excellent company record. They looked forward to working together, and for the first three months, everything went well. But then their relationship began to deteriorate, and the harder they worked at patching it up, the worse it got. Both of them, along with their superiors, were surprised by the conflict and seemed puzzled as to its causes. Eventually, the black woman requested and obtained reassignment. But even though they escaped each other, both suffered a sense of failure severe enough to threaten their careers.

What could have been done to assist them? Well, empathy would not have hurt. But perspective would have been better yet. In their particular company and situation, these two people had placed themselves at the cutting edge of race and gender relations. They needed to know that mistakes at the cutting edge are different—and potentially more valuable—than mistakes elsewhere. Maybe they needed some kind of pioneer training. But at the very least they needed to be told that they were pioneers, that conflicts and failures came with the territory, and that they would be judged accordingly.

9. Apply the Special Consideration Test   I said earlier that affirmative action was an artificial, transitional, but necessary stage on the road to a truly diverse work force. Because of its artificial nature, affirmative action requires constant attention and drive to make it work. The point of learning once and for all how to manage diversity is that all that energy can be focused somewhere else.

There is a simple test to help you spot the diversity programs that are going to eat up enormous quantities of time and effort. Surprisingly, perhaps, it is the same test you might use to identify the programs and policies that created your problem in the first place. The test consists of one question: Does this program, policy, or principle give special consideration to one group? Will it contribute to everyone's success, or will it only produce an advantage for blacks or whites or women or men? Is it designed for *them* as opposed to *us*? Whenever the answer is yes, you're not yet on the road to managing diversity.

This does not rule out the possibility of addressing issues that relate to a single group. It only underlies the importance of determining that the issue you're addressing does not relate to other groups as well. For example, management in one company noticed that blacks were not moving up in the organization. Before instituting a special program to bring them along, managers conducted interviews to see if they could find the reason for the impasse. What blacks themselves reported was a problem with the quality of supervision. Further interviews showed that other employees too—including white males—were concerned about the quality of supervision and felt that little was being done to foster professional development. Correcting the situation eliminated a problem that affected everyone. In this case, a solution that focused only on blacks would have been out of place.

Had the problem consisted of prejudice, on the other hand, or some other barrier to blacks or minorities alone, a solution based on affirmative action would have been perfectly appropriate.

10. Continue Affirmative Action   Let me come full circle. The ability to manage diversity is the ability to manage your company without unnatural advantage or disadvantage for any member of your diverse work force. The fact remains that first you must have a work force that is diverse at every level, and if you don't, you're going to need affirmative action to get from here to there.

The reason you then want to move beyond affirmative action to managing diversity is because affirmative action fails to deal with the root causes of prejudice and inequality and does little to develop the full potential of every man and woman in the company. In a country seeking competitive advantage in a global economy, the goal of managing diversity is to develop our capacity to accept, incorporate, and empower the diverse human talents of the most diverse nation on earth. It's our reality. We need to make it our strength.

──── DISCUSSION QUESTIONS

1. Examine your attitudes toward people who are different. In the workplace, what are your attitudes toward people of another race or the other gender?
2. As a general manager, would you consider it important to encourage diversity in your work force? Explain your principal reasons for your position, pro or con.
3. Do the issues that this reading addresses apply only to large corporations? Should smaller businesses also strive for diversity?
4. The reading touches on modifying assumptions about the corporate culture. What assumptions do you have about the workplace culture, or what assumptions have you had to modify since you began working?
5. Should affirming diversity be an issue that is addressed by other institutions besides business corporations? If so, what other institutions can help to promote diversity?

35 Management Women and the New Facts of Life

FELICE N. SCHWARTZ

Women managers cost more to employ than men, asserts this author. Management women range from those whose careers come first—often to the exclusion of family—to those who try to balance family and career. The chances are that turnover among women managers will be higher and that they will be more likely to interrupt their careers.

In this reading, the author explores ways to retain the best women and eliminate the extra cost of employing them. She advocates a combination of opportunity and flexibility. Opportunity means judging and promoting ambitious women on the same terms as men. Flexibility means allowing women to share jobs or work part-time while their children are young.

The cost of employing women in management is greater than the cost of employing men. This is a jarring statement, partly because it is true, but mostly because it is something people are reluctant to talk about. A new study by one multinational corporation shows that the rate of turnover in management positions is 2½ times higher among top-performing women than it is among men. A large producer of consumer goods reports that one half of the women who take maternity leave return to their jobs late or not at all. And we know that women also have a greater tendency to plateau or to interrupt their careers in ways that limit their growth and development. But we have become so sensitive to charges of sexism and so afraid of confrontation, even litigation, that we rarely say what we know to be true. Unfortunately, our bottled-up awareness leaks out in misleading metaphors ("glass ceiling" is one notable example), veiled hostility, lowered expectations, distrust, and reluctant adherence to Equal Employment Opportunity requirements.

Career interruptions, plateauing, and turnover are expensive. The money corporations invest in recruitment, training, and development is less likely to produce top executives among women than among men, and the invaluable company experience that developing executives acquire at every level as they move up through management ranks is more often lost.

The studies just mentioned are only the first of many, I'm quite sure. Demographic realities are going to force corporations all across the country to analyze the cost of employing women in managerial positions, and what they will discover is that women cost more.

But here is another startling truth: The greater cost of employing women is not a function of inescapable gender differences. Women *are* different from men, but what increases their cost to the corporation is principally the clash of their perceptions, attitudes, and behavior with those of men, which is to say, with the policies and practices of male-led corporations.

It is terribly important that employers draw the right conclusions from the studies now being done. The studies will be useless—or worse, harmful—if all they teach us is that women are expensive to employ. What we need to learn is how to reduce that expense, how to stop throwing away the investments we make in talented women, how to become more responsive to the needs of the women that corporations *must* employ if they are to have the best and the brightest of all those now entering the work force.

The gender differences relevant to business fall into two categories: those related to maternity and those related to the differing traditions and expectations of the sexes. Maternity is biological rather than cultural. We can't alter it, but we can dramatically reduce its impact on the workplace and in many cases eliminate its negative effect on employee development. We can accomplish this by addressing the second set of differences, those between male and female socialization. Today, these differences exaggerate the real costs of maternity and can turn a relatively slight disruption in work schedule into a serious business problem and a career derailment for individual women. If we are to overcome the cost differential between male and female employees, we need to address the issues that arise when female socialization meets the male corporate culture and masculine rules of career development—issues of behavior and style, of expectation, of stereotypes and preconceptions, of sexual tension and harassment, of female mentoring, lateral mobility, relocation, compensation, and early identification of top performers.

The one immutable, enduring difference between men and women is maternity. Maternity is not simply childbirth but a continuum that begins with an awareness of the ticking of the biological clock, proceeds to the anticipation of motherhood, includes pregnancy, childbirth, physical recuperation, psychological adjustment, and continues on to nursing, bonding, and child rearing. Not all women choose to become mothers, of course, and among those who do, the process varies from case to case depending on the health of the mother and baby, the values of the parents, and the availability, cost, and quality of child care.

In past centuries, the biological fact of maternity shaped the traditional roles of the sexes. Women performed the home-centered functions that related to the bearing and nurturing of children. Men did the work that required great physical strength. Over time, however, family size contracted, the community assumed greater responsibility for the care and education of children, packaged foods and household technology reduced the work load in the home, and technology eliminated much of the need for muscle power at the workplace.

Today, in the developed world, the only role still uniquely gender related is childbearing. Yet men and women are still socialized to perform their traditional roles.

Men and women may or may not have some innate psychological disposition toward these traditional roles—men to be aggressive, competitive, self-reliant, risk taking; women to be supportive, nurturing, intuitive, sensitive, communicative—but certainly both men and women are capable of the full range of behavior. Indeed, the male and female roles have already begun to expand and merge. In the decades ahead, as the socialization of boys and girls and the experience and expectations of young men and women grow steadily more androgynous, the differences in workplace behavior will continue to fade. At the moment, however, we are still plagued by disparities in perception and behavior that make the integration of men and women in the workplace unnecessarily difficult and expensive.

Let me illustrate with a few broadbrush generalizations. Of course, these are only stereotypes, but I think they help to exemplify the kinds of preconceptions that can muddy the corporate waters.

Men continue to perceive women as the rearers of their children so they find it understandable, indeed appropriate, that women should renounce their careers to raise families. Edmund Pratt, CEO of Pfizer, once asked me in all sincerity, "Why would any woman choose to be a chief financial officer rather than a full-time mother?" By condoning and taking pleasure in women's traditional behavior, men reinforce it. Not only do they see parenting as fundamentally female, they see a career as fundamentally male—either an unbroken series of promotions and advancements toward CEOdom or stagnation and disappointment. This attitude serves to legitimize a woman's choice to extend maternity leave and even, for those who can afford it, to leave employment altogether for several years. By the same token, men who might want to take a leave after the birth of a child know that management will see such behavior as a lack of career commitment, even when company policy permits parental leave for men.

Women also bring counterproductive expectations and perceptions to the workplace. Ironically, although the feminist movement was an expression of women's quest for freedom from their home-based lives, most women were remarkably free already. They had many responsibilities, but they were autonomous and could be entrepreneurial in how and when they carried them out. And once their children grew up and left home, they were essentially free to do what they wanted with their lives. Women's traditional role also included freedom from responsibility for the financial support of their families. Many of us were socialized from girlhood to expect our husbands to take care of us, while our brothers were socialized from an equally early age to complete their educations, pursue careers, climb the ladder of success, and provide dependable financial support for their families. To the extent that this tradition of freedom lingers subliminally, women tend to bring to their employment a sense that they can choose to change jobs or careers at will, take time off, or reduce their hours.

Finally, women's traditional role encouraged particular attention to the quality and substance of what they did, specifically to the physical, psychological, and intellectual development of their children. This traditional focus may explain women's continuing tendency to search for more than monetary reward—intrinsic significance, social importance, meaning—in what they do. This too makes them more likely than men to leave the corporation in search of other values.

The misleading metaphor of the glass ceiling suggests an invisible barrier constructed by corporate leaders to impede the upward mobility of women beyond the middle levels. A more appropriate metaphor, I believe, is the kind of cross-sectional diagram used in geology. The barriers to women's leadership occur when potentially counterproductive layers of influence on women—maternity, tradition, socialization—meet management strata pervaded by the largely unconscious preconceptions, stereotypes, and expectations of men. Such interfaces do not exist for men and tend to be impermeable for women.

One result of these gender differences has been to convince some executives that women are simply not suited to top management. Other executives feel helpless. If they see even a few of their valued female employees fail to return to work from maternity leave on schedule or see one of their most promising women plateau in her career after the birth of a child, they begin to fear there is nothing they can do to infuse women with new energy and enthusiasm and persuade them to stay. At the same time, they know there is nothing they can do to stem the tide of women into management ranks.

Another result is to place every working woman on a continuum that runs from total dedication to career at one end to a balance between career and family at the other. What women discover is that the male corporate culture sees both extremes as unacceptable. Women who want the flexibility to balance their families and their careers are not adequately committed to the organization. Women who perform as aggressively and competitively as men are abrasive and unfeminine. But the fact is, business needs all the talented women it can get. Moreover, as I will explain, the women I call career-primary and those I call career-and-family each have particular value to the corporation.

Women in the corporation are about to move from a buyer's to a seller's market. The sudden, startling recognition that 80% of new entrants in the work force over the next decade will be women, minorities, and immigrants has stimulated a mushrooming incentive to "value diversity."

Women are no longer simply an enticing pool of occasional creative talent, a thorn in the side of the EEO officer, or a source of frustration to corporate leaders truly puzzled by the slowness of their upward trickle into executive positions. A real demographic change is taking place. The era of sudden population growth of the 1950s and 1960s is over. The birth rate has dropped about 40%, from a high of 25.3 live births per 1,000 population in 1957, at the peak of the baby boom, to a stable low of a little more than 15 per 1,000 over the last 16 years, and there is no indication of a return to a higher rate. The tidal wave of baby boomers that swelled the recruitment pool to overflowing seems to have been a one-time phenomenon. For 20 years, employers had the pick of a very large crop and were able to choose males almost exclusively for the executive track. But if future population remains fairly stable while the economy continues to expand and if the new information society simultaneously creates a greater need for creative, educated managers, then the gap between supply and demand will grow dramatically and, with it, the competition for managerial talent.

The decrease in numbers has even greater implications if we look at the traditional source of corporate recruitment for leadership positions—white males from the top 10% of the country's best universities. Over the past decade, the increase in the number of women graduating from leading universities has been much greater than the increase in the total number of graduates, and these women are well represented in the top 10% of their classes.

The trend extends into business and professional programs as well. In the old days, virtually all MBAs were male. I remember addressing a meeting at the Harvard Business School as recently as the mid-1970s and looking out at a sea of exclusively male faces. Today, about 25% of that audience would be women. The pool of male MBAs from which corporations have traditionally drawn their leaders has shrunk significantly.

Of course, this reduction does not have to mean a shortage of talent. The top 10% is at least as smart as it always was—smarter, probably, because it's now drawn from a broader segment of the population. But it now consists increasingly of women. Companies that are determined to recruit the same number of men as before will have to dig much deeper into the male pool, while their competitors will have the opportunity to pick the best people from both the male and female graduates.

Under these circumstances, there is no question that the management ranks of business will include increasing numbers of women. There remains, however, the question of how these women will succeed—how long they will stay, how high they will climb, how completely they will fulfill their promise and potential, and what kind of return the corporation will realize on its investment in their training and development.

There is ample business reason for finding ways to make sure that as many of these women as possible will succeed. The first step in this process is to recognize that not all women are alike. Like men, they are individuals with differing talents, priorities, and motivations. For the sake of simplicity, let me focus on the two women I referred to earlier, on what I call the career-primary woman and the career-and-family woman.

Like many men, some women put their careers first. They are ready to make the same trade-offs traditionally made by the men who seek leadership positions. They make a career decision to put in extra hours, to make sacrifices in their personal lives, to make the most of every opportunity for professional development. For women, of course, this decision also requires that they remain single or at least childless or, if they do have children, that they be satisfied to have others raise them. Some 90% of executive men but only 35% of executive women have children by the age of 40. The *automatic* association of all women with babies is clearly unjustified.

The secret to dealing with such women is to recognize them early, accept them, and clear artificial barriers from their path to the top. After all, the best of these women are among the best managerial talent you will ever see. And career-primary women have another important value to the company that men and other women lack. They can act as role models and mentors to younger women who put their careers first. Because upwardly mobile career-primary women still have few role models to motivate and inspire them, a company with women in its top echelon has a significant advantage in the competition for executive talent.

Men at the top of the organization—most of them over 55, with wives who tend to be traditional—often find career women "masculine" and difficult to accept as colleagues. Such men miss the point, which is not that these women are just like men but that they are just like the *best* men in the organization. And there is such a shortage of the best people that gender cannot be allowed to matter. It is clearly counterproductive to disparage in a woman with executive talent the very qualities that are most critical to the business and that might carry a man to the CEO's office.

Clearing a path to the top for career-primary women has four requirements:

1. Identify them early.
2. Give them the same opportunity you give to talented men to grow and develop and contribute to company profitability. Give them client and customer responsibility. Expect them to travel and relocate, to make the same commitment to the company as men aspiring to leadership positions.
3. Accept them as valued members of your management team. Include them in every kind of communications. Listen to them.
4. Recognize that the business environment is more difficult and stressful for them than for their male peers. They are always a minority, often the only woman. The male perception of talented, ambitious women is at best ambivalent, a mixture of admiration, resentment, confusion, competitiveness, attraction, skepticism, anxiety, pride, and animosity. Women can never feel secure about how they should dress and act, whether they should speak out or grin and bear it when they encounter discrimination, stereotyping, sexual harassment, and paternalism. Social interaction and travel with male colleagues and with male clients can be charged. As they move up, the normal increase in pressure and responsibility is compounded for women because they are women.

Stereotypical language and sexist day-to-day behavior do take their toll on women's career development. Few male executives realize how common it is to call women by their first names while men in the same group are greeted with surnames, how frequently female executives are assumed by men to be secretaries, how often women are excluded from all-male social events where business is being transacted. With notable exceptions, men are still generally more comfortable with other men, and as a result women miss many of the career and business opportunities that arise over lunch, on the golf course, or in the locker room.

The majority of women, however, are what I call career-and-family women, women who want to pursue serious careers while participating actively in the rearing of children. These women are a precious resource that has yet to be mined. Many of them are talented and creative. Most of them are willing to trade some career growth and compensation for freedom from the constant pressure to work long hours and weekends.

Most companies today are ambivalent at best about the career-and-family women in their management ranks. They would prefer that all employees were willing to give their all to the company. They believe it is in their best interests for all managers to compete for the top positions so the company will have the largest possible pool from which to draw its leaders.

"If you have both talent and motivation," many employers seem to say, "we want to move you up. If you haven't got that motivation, if you want less pressure and greater flexibility, then you can leave and make room for a new generation." These companies lose on two counts. First, they fail to amortize the investment they made in the early training and experience of management women who find themselves committed to family as well as to career. Second, they fail to recognize what these women could do for their middle management.

The ranks of middle managers are filled with people on their way up and people who have stalled. Many of them have simply reached their limits, achieved career growth commensurate with or exceeding their capabilities, and they cause problems because their performance is mediocre but they still want to move ahead. The career-and-family woman is willing to trade off the pressures and demands that go with promotion for the freedom to spend more time with her children. She's very smart, she's talented, she's committed to her career, and she's satisfied to stay at the middle level, at least during the early child-rearing years. Compare her with some of the people you have there now.

Consider a typical example, a woman who decides in college on a business career and enters management at age 22. For nine years, the company invests in her career as she gains experience and skills and steadily improves her performance. But at 31, just as the investment begins to pay off in earnest, she decides to have a baby. Can the company afford to let her go home, take another job, or go into business for herself? The common perception now is yes, the corporation can afford to lose her unless, after six or eight weeks or even three months of disability and maternity leave, she returns to work on a full-time schedule with the same vigor, commitment, and ambition that she showed before.

But what if she doesn't? What if she wants or needs to go on leave for six months or a year or, heaven forbid, five years? In this worst-case scenario, she works full-time from age 22 to 31 and from 36 to 65—a total of 38 years as opposed to the typical male's 43 years. That's not a huge difference. Moreover, my typical example is willing to work part-time while her children are young, if only her employer will give her the opportunity. There are two rewards for companies responsive to this need: higher retention of their best people and greatly improved performance and satisfaction in their middle management.

The high-performing career-and-family woman can be a major player in your company. She can give you a significant business advantage as the competition for able people escalates. Sometimes too, if you can hold on to her, she will switch gears in mid-life and reenter the competition for the top. The price you must pay to retain these women is threefold: you must plan for and manage maternity, you must provide the flexibility that will allow them to be maximally productive, and you must take an active role in helping to make family supports and high-quality, affordable child care available to all women.

The key to managing maternity is to recognize the value of high-performing women and the urgent need to retain them and keep them productive. The first step must be a genuine partnership between the woman and her boss. I know this partnership can seem difficult to forge. One of my own senior executives came to me recently to discuss plans for her maternity leave and subsequent return to work. She knew she wanted to come back. I wanted to make certain that she would. Still, we had a somewhat awkward conversation, because I knew that no woman can predict with certainty when she will be able to return to work or under what conditions. Physical problems can lengthen her leave. So can a demanding infant, a difficult family or personal adjustment, or problems with child care.

I still don't know when this valuable executive will be back on the job full-time, and her absence creates some genuine problems for our organization. But I do know that I can't simply replace her years of experience with a new recruit. Since our conversation, I also know that she wants to come back, and that she *will* come back—part-time at first—unless I make it impossible for her by, for example, setting an arbitrary date for her full-time return or resignation. In turn, she knows that the organization wants and needs her and, more to the point, that it will be responsive to her needs in terms of working hours and child care arrangements.

In having this kind of conversation it's important to ask concrete questions that will help to move the discussion from uncertainty and anxiety to some level of predictability. Questions can touch on everything from family income and energy level to child care arrangements and career commitment. Of course you want your star manager to return to work as soon as possible, but you want her to return permanently and productively. Her downtime on the job is a drain on her energies and a waste of your money.

For all the women who want to combine career and family—the women who want to participate actively in the rearing of their children and who also want to pursue their careers seriously—the key to retention is to provide the flexibility and family supports they need in order to function effectively.

Time spent in the office increases productivity if it is time well spent, but the fact that most women continue to take the primary responsibility for child care is a cause of distraction, diversion, anxiety, and absenteeism—to say nothing of the persistent guilt experienced by all working mothers. A great many women, perhaps most of all women who have always performed at the highest levels, are also frustrated by a sense that while their children are babies they cannot function at their best either at home or at work.

In its simplest form, flexibility is the freedom to take time off—a couple of hours, a day, a week—or to do some work at home and some at the office, an arrangement that communication technology makes increasingly feasible. At the complex end of the spectrum are alternative work schedules that permit the woman to work less than full-time and her employer to reap the benefits of her experience and, with careful planning, the top level of her abilities.

Part-time employment is the single greatest inducement to getting women back on the job expeditiously and the provision women themselves most desire. A part-time return to work enables them to maintain responsibility for critical aspects of their jobs, keeps them in touch with the changes constantly occurring at the workplace and in the job itself, reduces stress and fatigue, often eliminates the need for paid maternity leave by permitting a return to the office as soon as disability leave is over, and, not least, can greatly enhance company loyalty. The part-time solution works particularly well when a work load can be reduced for one individual in a department or when a full-time job can be broken down by skill levels and apportioned to two individuals at different levels of skill and pay.

I believe, however, that shared employment is the most promising and will be the most widespread form of flexible scheduling in the future. It is feasible at every level of the corporation except at the pinnacle, for both the short and the long term. It involves two people taking responsibility for one job.

Two red lights flash on as soon as most executives hear the words "job sharing": continuity and client-customer contact. The answer to the continuity question is to place responsibility entirely on the two individuals sharing the job to discuss everything that transpires—thoroughly, daily, and on their own time. The answer to the problem of client-customer contact is yes, job sharing requires reeducation and a period of adjustment. But as both client and supervisor will quickly come to appreciate, two contacts means that the customer has continuous access to the company's representative, without interruptions for vacation, travel, or sick leave. The two people holding the job can simply cover for each other, and the uninterrupted, full-time coverage they provide together can be a stipulation of their arrangement.

Flexibility is costly in numerous ways. It requires more supervisory time to coordinate and manage, more office space, and somewhat greater benefits costs (though these can be contained with flexible benefits plans, prorated benefits, and, in two-paycheck families, elimination of duplicate benefits). But the advantages of reduced turnover and the greater productivity that results from higher energy levels and greater focus can outweigh the costs.

A few hints:

- Provide flexibility selectively. I'm not suggesting private arrangements subject to the suspicion of favoritism but rather a policy that makes flexible work schedules available only to high performers.
- Make it clear that in most instances (but not all) the rates of advancement and pay will be appropriately lower for those who take time off or who work part-time than for those who work full-time. Most career-and-family women are entirely willing to make that trade-off.
- Discuss costs as well as benefits. Be willing to risk accusations of bias. Insist, for example, that half time is half of whatever time it takes to do the job, not merely half of 35 or 40 hours.

The woman who is eager to get home to her child has a powerful incentive to use her time effectively at the office and to carry with her reading and other work that can be done at home. The talented professional who wants to have it all can be a high performer by carefully ordering her priorities and by focusing on objectives rather than on the legendary 15-hour day. By the time professional women have their first babies—at an average age of 31—they have already had nine years to work long hours at a desk, to travel, and to relocate. In the case of high performers, the need for flexibility coincides with what has gradually become the goal-oriented nature of responsibility.

Family supports—in addition to maternity leave and flexibility—include the provision of parental leave for men, support for two-career and single-parent families during relocation, and flexible benefits. But the primary ingredient is child care. The capacity of working mothers to function effectively and without interruption depends on the availability of good, affordable child care. Now that women make up almost half the work force and the growing percentage of managers, the decision to become involved in the personal lives of employees is no longer a philosophical question but a practical one. To make matters worse, the quality of child care has almost no relation to technology, inventiveness, or profitability but is more or less a pure function of the quality of child care personnel and the ratio of adults to children. These costs are irreducible. Only by joining hands with government and the public sector can corporations hope to create the vast quantity and variety of child care that their employees need.

Until quite recently, the response of corporations to women has been largely symbolic and cosmetic, motivated in large part by the will to avoid litigation and legal penalties. In some cases, companies were also moved by a genuine sense of fairness and a vague discomfort and frustration at the absence of women above the middle of the corporate pyramid. The actions they took were mostly quick, easy, and highly visible—child care information services, a three-month parental leave available to men as well as women, a woman appointed to the board of directors.

When I first began to discuss these issues 26 years ago, sometimes I was able to get an appointment with the assistant to the assistant in personnel, but it was only a courtesy. Over the past decade, I have met with the CEOs of many large corporations, and I've watched them become involved with ideas they had never previously thought much about. Until recently, however, the shelf life of that enhanced awareness was always short. Given pressing, short-term concerns, women were not a front-burner issue. In the past few months, I have seen yet another change. Some CEOs and top management groups now take the initiative. They call and ask us to show them how to shift gears from a responsive to a proactive approach to recruiting, developing, and retaining women.

I think this change is more probably a response to business needs—to concern for the quality of future profits and managerial talent—than to uneasiness about legal requirements, sympathy with the demands of women and minorities, or the desire to do what is right and fair. The nature of such business motivation varies. Some companies want to move women to higher positions as role models for those below them and as beacons for talented young recruits. Some want to achieve a favorable image with employees, customers, clients, and stockholders. These are all legitimate motives. But I think the companies that stand to gain most are motivated as well by a desire to capture competitive advantage in an era when talent and competence will be in increasingly short supply. These companies are now ready to stop being defensive about their experience with women and to ask incisive questions without preconceptions.

Even so, incredibly, I don't know of more than one or two companies that have looked into their own records to study the absolutely critical issue of maternity leave—how many women took it, when and whether they returned, and how this behavior correlated with their rank, tenure, age, and performance. The unique drawback to the employment of women is the physical reality of maternity and the particular socializing influence maternity has had. Yet to make women equal to men in the workplace we have chosen on the whole not to discuss this single most significant difference between them. Unless we do, we cannot evaluate the cost of recruiting, developing, and moving women up.

Now that interest is replacing indifference, there are four steps every company can take to examine its own experience with women:

1. Gather quantitative data on the company's experience with management-level women regarding turnover rates, occurrence of and return from maternity leave, and organizational level attained in relation to tenure and performance.
2. Correlate these data with factors such as age, marital status, and presence and age of children, and attempt to identify and analyze why women respond the way they do.
3. Gather qualitative data on the experience of women in your company and on how women are perceived by both sexes.
4. Conduct a cost-benefit analysis of the return on your investment in high-performing women. Factor in the cost to the company of

women's negative reactions to negative experience, as well as the probable cost of corrective measures and policies. If women's value to your company is greater than the cost to recruit, train, and develop them—and of course I believe it will be—then you will want to do everything you can to retain them.

We have come a tremendous distance since the days when the prevailing male wisdom saw women as lacking the kind of intelligence that would allow them to succeed in business. For decades, even women themselves have harbored an unspoken belief that they couldn't make it because they couldn't be just like men, and nothing else would do. But now that women have shown themselves the equal of men in every area of organizational activity, now that they have demonstrated that they can be stars in every field of endeavor, now we can all venture to examine the fact that women and men are different.

On balance, employing women is more costly than employing men. Women can acknowledge this fact today because they know that their value to employers exceeds the additional cost and because they know that changing attitudes can reduce the additional cost dramatically. Women in management are no longer an idiosyncrasy of the arts and education. They have always matched men in natural ability. Within a very few years, they will equal men in numbers as well in every area of economic activity.

The demographic motivation to recruit and develop women is compelling. But an older question remains: Is society better for the change? Women's exit from the home and entry into the work force has certainly created problems—an urgent need for good, affordable child care; troubling questions about the kind of parenting children need; the costs and difficulties of diversity in the workplace; the stress and fatigue of combining work and family responsibilities. Wouldn't we all be happier if we could turn back the clock to an age when men were in the workplace and women in the home, when male and female roles were clearly differentiated and complementary?

Nostalgia, anxiety, and discouragement will urge many to say yes, but my answer is emphatically no. Two fundamental benefits that were unattainable in the past are now within our reach. For the individual, freedom of choice—in this case the freedom to choose career, family, or a combination of the two. For the corporation, access to the most gifted individuals in the country. These benefits are neither self-indulgent nor insubstantial. Freedom of choice and self-realization are too deeply American to be cast aside for some wistful vision of the past. And access to our most talented human resources is not a luxury in this age of explosive international competition but rather the barest minimum that prudence and national self-preservation require.

━━━ DISCUSSION QUESTIONS

1. The reading quotes a CEO asking the author, "Why would any woman choose to be a chief financial officer rather than a full-time mother?" Do you think that this is a commonly asked question? If someone were to ask you the same question, how would you respond?

2. Do you think that special provisions ought to be made in order to keep working mothers in the work force? Why or why not?

3. Can you think of other groups of people who would also benefit from the types of considerations and policies that the author discusses?

4. Is it possible that the use of special policies within an organization might cause hostility among employees? Explain. How would you manage the situation if hostility *did* develop?

Business and the Facts of Family Life
36

FRAN SUSSNER RODGERS AND CHARLES RODGERS

The shift of women out of the home and into the workplace has not been matched by an adjustment in business policies and practices. Gradually, however, organizations are becoming more interested in work-and-family issues. This reading examines the reasons why companies must find ways to help employees balance their professional and personal responsibilities and reports on the progress some companies have made in addressing these concerns.

Business is a good thing. Family is also a good thing. These are simple, self-evident propositions.

Yet the awkward fact is that when we try to combine these two assertions in the new labor force, they stop being safe, compatible, and obvious and become difficult, even antagonistic. Sometimes the most complex and controversial challenges we face have commonsense truths at their roots.

Consider these variations on the same theme:

- Our economy needs the most skilled and productive work force it can possibly find in order to remain competitive.
- That same work force must reproduce itself and give adequate care to the children who are the work force of the future.
- People with children—women especially—often find themselves at a serious disadvantage in the workplace.
- Among Western democracies, the United States ranks number three in dependence on women in the work force, behind only Scandinavia and Canada.

In short, we value both business and family, and they are increasingly at loggerheads.

────── THE FAMILY AS A BUSINESS ISSUE

At one time, women provided the support system that enabled male breadwinners to be productive outside the home for at least 40 hours every week. That home-based support system began to recede a generation ago and is now more the exception than the rule. The labor force now includes more than 70% of all women with children between the ages of 6 and 17 and more than half the women with children less than 1 year old. This new reality has had a marked effect on what the family requires of each family member—and on what employers can expect from employees. It is not only a question of who is responsible for very young children. There is no longer anyone home to care for adolescents and the elderly. There is no one around to take in the car for repair or to let the plumber in. Working families are faced with daily dilemmas: Who will take care of a sick child? Who will go to the big soccer game? Who will attend the teacher conference?

Yet employees from families where all adults work are still coping with rules and conditions of work designed, as one observer put it, to the specifications of Ozzie and Harriet. These conditions include rigid adherence to a 40-hour workweek, a concept of career path inconsistent with the life cycle of a person with serious family responsibilities, notions of equity formed in a different era, and performance-evaluation systems that confuse effort with results by equating hours of work with productivity.

Despite the growing mismatch between the rules of the game and the needs of the players, few companies have made much effort to accommodate changing lifestyles. For that matter, how serious can the problem really be? After all, employees still get to work and do their jobs. Somehow the plumber manages to find the key. We know that children and the elderly are somewhere. Why start worrying now? Women's entry into the labor force has been increasing for 20 years, and the system still appears to function.

Nevertheless, we are seeing a rapidly growing corporate interest in work-and-family issues. There are four principal *business* reasons:

First, work-force demographics are changing. Most of the increase in the number of working women has coincided with the baby boom. Any associated business fallout—high turnover, lost productivity, absenteeism—occurred in the context of a large labor surplus. Most people were easily replaced, and there was plenty of talent willing to make the traditional sacrifices for success—such as travel, overtime work, and relocation. With the baby boom over and a baby bust upon us, there are now higher costs associated with discouraging entry into the labor force and frustrating talented people who are trying to act responsibly at home as well as at work. In some parts of the country, labor is already so scarce that companies are using progressive family policies as a means of competing for workers.

Second, employee perceptions are changing. Unless we rethink our traditional career paths, the raised aspirations of many women are now clearly on a collision course with their desire to be parents. Before the emergence of the women's movement in the 1960s, many suburban housewives thought their frustrations were uniquely their own. Similarly, for 20 years corporate women who failed to meet their own high expectations considered it a personal failing. But now the invisible barriers to female advancement are being named, and the media take employers to task for their inflexibility.

This shift in women's perceptions greatly changes the climate for employers. Women and men in two-career and single-parent families are much better able to identify policies that will let them act responsibly toward their families and still satisfy their professional ambitions. Companies that don't act as partners in this process may lose talent to companies that do rise to the challenge. No one knows how many women have left large companies because of cultural rigidity. It is even harder to guess at the numbers of talented women who have never even applied for jobs because they assume big companies will require family sacrifices they are unwilling to make.

And it's not just women. In two studies at Du Pont, we found that men's reports of certain family-related problems nearly doubled from 1985 to 1988. (Interestingly, on a few of these items, women's reported problems decreased proportionally, which suggests that one reason women experience such great difficulty with work-and-family issues is that men experience so little.)

In fact, men's desire for a more active role in parenting may be unacceptable to their peers. Numerous reports show that few men take advantage of the formal parental leave available to them in many companies. Yet a recent study shows that many men do indeed take time off from work after the birth of a child, but that they do so by piecing together other forms of leave—vacation, personal leave, sick leave—that they see as more acceptable.[1]

A third reason why more companies are addressing work-and-family issues is increasing evidence that inflexibility has an adverse effect on productivity. In a study at Merck in 1984, employees who perceived their supervisors as unsupportive on family issues reported higher levels of stress, greater absenteeism, and lower job satisfaction.[2] Other studies show that supportive companies attract new employees more easily, get them back on the job more quickly after maternity leave, and benefit generally from higher work-force morale.[3]

Fourth, concern about America's children is growing fast. Childhood poverty is up, single-parent families are on the increase, SAT scores are falling, and childhood literacy, obesity, and suicide rates are all moving in the wrong direction.

So far, the business community has expressed its concern primarily through direct efforts to improve schools. Yet in our studies, one-third to one-half of parents say they do not have the workplace flexibility to attend teacher conferences and important school events. It is certainly possible that adapting work rules to allow this parent-school connection—and trying to

---

1. Joseph Pleck, "Family-Supportive Employer Policies and Men's Participation," Wheaton College (1989), unpublished paper.

2. From research conducted by Ellen Galinsky at Merck and Company, Rahway, New Jersey, 1983, 1984, and 1986.

3. Terry Bond, *Employer Supports for Child Care,* report for the National Council of Jewish Women, Center for the Child, New York (August 1988).

influence schools to schedule events with working parents in mind—might have as great a positive effect on education as some direct interventions.

For companies that want to use and fully develop the talents of working parents and others looking for flexibility, the agenda is well defined. There are three broad areas that require attention:

- Dependent care, including infants, children, adolescents, and the elderly.
- Greater flexibility in the organization, hours, and location of work, and creation of career paths that allow for family responsibility as well as professional ambition.
- Validation of family issues as an organizational concern by means of company statements and manager training.

Few companies are active in all three areas. Many are active in none. The costs and difficulties are, after all, considerable, and the burden of change does not fall only on employers. There is plenty for government to do. Individual employees too will have to take on new responsibilities. Corporate dependent-care programs often mean purchasing benefits or programs from outside providers and may entail substantial community involvement. Workplace flexibility demands reexamination of work assumptions by employees as well as employers and often meets with line resistance. A corporate commitment to family takes time to work its way down to the front-line supervisory levels where most of the work force will feel its effects.

━━━ DEPENDENT CARE

Dependent care is a business issue for the obvious reason that employees cannot come to work unless their dependents are cared for. Study after study shows that most working parents have trouble arranging child care, and that those with the most difficulty also experience the most frequent work disruptions and the greatest absenteeism. Moreover, the lack of child care is still a major barrier to the entry of women into the labor force.

Child-care needs vary greatly in any employee population, and most companies have a limited capacity to address them. But, depending on the company's location, financial resources, the age of its work force, and the competitiveness of its labor market, a corporate child-care program might include some or all of the following:

- Help in finding existing child care and efforts to increase the supply of care in the community, including care for sick children.
- Financial assistance for child care, especially for entry-level and lower-level employees.
- Involvement with schools, Ys, and other community organizations to promote programs for school-age children whose parents work.

- Support for child-care centers in locations convenient to company employees.
- Efforts to move government policies—local and federal—toward greater investment in children.

Existing child care is often hard to find because so much of the country's care is provided by the woman down the street, who does not advertise and is not usually listed in the yellow pages or anywhere else. Even where lists do exist—as the result, say, of state licensing requirements—they are often out-of-date. (Turnover in family day care, as this form of child care is called, is estimated at 50% per year.) And lists don't give vacancy information, so parents can spend days making unsuccessful phone calls. Sometimes existing care is invisible because it operates in violation of zoning rules or outside of onerous or inefficient regulatory systems.

In other places—suburban neighborhoods where many women work outside the home or where family income is so high that few need the extra money—there is virtually no child care. Often, too, land prices make centers unaffordable. Infant care is especially scarce because it requires such a high ratio of adults to children. Care for children before and after school and during the many weeks when school is out is in short supply just about everywhere, as is care for "off hour" workers such as shift workers, police officers, and hospital employees.

In addition to the difficulty of finding child care, quality and affordability are always big questions. Cost depends greatly on local standards. In Massachusetts, for example, infant care in centers runs from $150 to more than $200 per week per child due to a combination of high labor costs and strict state licensing standards. Even the highest standards, however, still mean that an infant-care staff member has more to do all day—and more responsibility—than a new parent caring for triplets. In states with lower standards, one staff member may care for as many as eight infants at a time. Up to now, child care in many places has been made affordable by paying very low wages—the national average for child-care staff is $5.35 an hour—and by reducing the standards of quality and safety below what common sense would dictate.[4]

Given all these problems, is it any wonder the companies that want to help feel stymied? Although few companies provide significant child-care support today, a very large number are exploring the possibility. We think that number will increase geometrically as the competition for labor grows and more members of the labor force need such support.

One increasingly popular way for companies to address these issues is through resource and referral services. Typically, such services do three things: they help employees find child care suited to their circumstances; they make an

---

4. Marcy Whitebook, Carollee Howes, and Deborah Phillips, "Who Cares: Child Care Teachers and the Quality of Care in America," National Child Care Staffing Study, Child Care Employee Project, Oakland, California (1989).

effort to promote more care of all types in the communities where employees live; and they try to remove regulatory and zoning barriers to care facilities. Resource and referral services (R&Rs) meet standards of equity by assisting parents regardless of their incomes and their children's ages. And R&Rs work as well for a few workers as for thousands. When the service is delivered through a network of community-based R&Rs, moreover, corporate involvement also can strengthen the community at large.

Although R&R programs can be very helpful, they have limitations. By themselves, they have little effect on affordability, for example, and only an indirect effect on quality, primarily through consumer education and provider training. Also, R&Rs cannot dig up a supply of care where market conditions are highly unfavorable.

A small but growing number of companies provide, subsidize, or contract with outside providers to operate on-site or near-site centers that are available to employees at fees covering at least most of the cost. A North Carolina software company, SAS Institute Inc., provides child care at an on-site center at no cost to employees. The company reports that its turnover rates are less than half the industry average and feels the center's extra expense is justified because it decreases the extremely high cost of training new workers.[5]

Companies that get involved with child-care centers, however, find themselves making difficult trade-offs as a result of the high cost of good care. Many companies won't associate themselves even indirectly with any child care that doesn't meet the highest standards, which means that without a subsidy, only higher-income employees can afford the service. But if a company does subsidize child care, it must justify giving this considerable benefit to one group of parents while other parents, who buy child care in some other place or way, get none. One way of avoiding this dilemma is to give child-care subsidies to all lower-income employees as an extension of the R&R service, the approach recently announced by NCNB, the banking corporation.

Companies sometimes capitalize centers by donating space or land along with renovation costs or by providing an initial subsidy until the centers are self-supporting. In this way, Du Pont helped a number of community not-for-profit organizations establish and expand existing child-care centers in Delaware. Of course, costs can vary hugely. If a building is already available, renovation and startup costs could be as low as $100,000. In most cases, the bill will run from several hundred thousand to several million dollars.

Businesses also are working more closely with schools to encourage before-school, after-school, and vacation care programs. Such a partnership has been established between the American Bankers Insurance Group and the Dade

---

5. "On-site Child Care Results in Low Turnover at Computer Firm," *National Report on Work and Family*, vol. 2, no. 13 (Washington, D.C.: Buraff Publications, June 9, 1989): 3.

County, Florida, school system. The school system actually operates a kindergarten and a first- and second-grade school in a building built by the insurance company. In Charlotte, North Carolina, the 19 largest employers have joined forces with the public sector to expand and improve the quality of care.

In any case, employee interest in child care is great, and employees often fix on the issue of on-site care as a solution to the work-and-family conflicts they experience. But helping employees with child care, given the enormity of the problem in the society at large, is a complicated question. More and more companies are taking the kinds of steps described here, but as the pressure grows, business as a whole is likely to focus more attention on public policy.

Of course, dependent care is not just a question of care for children. Studies at Travelers Insurance Company and at IBM show that 20% to 30% of employees have some responsibility for the care of an adult dependent. Traditionally, the wife stayed home and cared for the elderly parents of both spouses, but as women entered the work force, this support system began to disappear. Because the most recent growth in the female work force involves comparatively younger women whose parents are not yet old enough to require daily assistance, the workplace has probably not yet felt the full effects of elder-care problems.

As in the case of child care, studies show that productivity suffers when people try to balance work and the care of parents. Some people quit their jobs entirely. The most immediate need is for information about the needs and problems of the aging and about available resources. Most young people know nothing at all about government programs like Medicare and Medicaid. More often than not, children know very little about their own parents' financial situations and need help simply to open communication.

Unlike child care, elder care is often complicated by distance. In our experience with some 12,000 employees with elderly dependents, more than half lived more than 100 miles from the person they were concerned about. Crises are common. The elderly suffer unexpected hospitalizations, for example, and then come out of the hospital too weak to care for themselves. A service that can help with referrals and arrangements in another city can spare employees time, expense, and anguish. Also, people often need to compare resources in several states where different siblings live in order to make decisions about such things as where parents should live when their health begins to deteriorate.

—— CONDITIONS OF WORK

A study at two high-tech companies in New England showed that the average working mother logs in a total workweek of 84 hours between her home and her job, compared with 72 hours for male parents and about 50 hours for married men and women with no children. In other words, employed parents—

women in particular—work the equivalent of two full-time jobs.[6] No wonder they've started looking for flexible schedules, part-time employment, and career-path alternatives that allow more than one model of success. For that matter, is it even reasonable to expect people who work two jobs to behave and progress along exactly the same lines as those with no primary outside responsibilities?

Until now, most companies have looked at job flexibility on a case-by-case basis and have offered it sparingly to valued employees as a favor. But increasing competition for the best employees will make such flexibility commonplace. A smaller labor supply means that workers will no longer have to take jobs in the forms that have always been offered. Companies will have to market their own employment practices and adapt their jobs to the demands of the work force.

We all know that the way we did things in the past no longer works for many employees. Our research shows that up to 35% of working men and women with young children have told their bosses they will not take jobs involving shift work, relocation, extensive travel, intense pressure, or lots of overtime. Some parents are turning down promotions that they believe might put a strain on family life. Women report more trade-offs than men, but even the male numbers are significant and appear to be increasing. In our study, nearly 25% of men with young children had told their bosses they would not relocate.

Interestingly enough, few employees seem angry about such trade-offs. They value the rewards of family life, and by and large, they don't seem to expect parity with those willing to sacrifice their family lives for their careers. Nevertheless, they are bothered by what they see as unnecessary barriers to success. Most believe they could make greater contributions and go farther in their own careers—despite family obligations—if it weren't for rigid scheduling, open-ended expectations, and outmoded career definitions. They long for alternative scenarios that would allow them more freedom to determine the conditions of their work and the criteria for judging their contributions.

The question is whether a willingness to sacrifice family life is an appropriate screen for picking candidates for promotions. It would be wrong to suppose that these employees are any less talented or less ambitious than those who don't make the family trade-off. One study we conducted at NCNB showed no evidence of any long-term difference in ambition between people with and without child-care responsibilities. Because fewer and fewer people in our diverse labor force are willing to pay the price for traditional success, to insist on it is only to narrow the funnel of opportunity and, eventually, to lower the quality of the talent pool from which we draw our leaders.

---

6. Dianne Burden and Bradley Googins, *Boston University Balancing Job and Homelife Study* (Boston: Boston University School of Social Work, 1986).

FLEXIBLE SCHEDULES

In addition to time away from work to care for newborn or newly adopted children, employees with dependent-care responsibilities have two different needs for flexibility. One is the need for working hours that accommodate their children's normal schedules and their predictable special requirements such as doctor's appointments, school conferences, and soccer championships. The other is the need to deal with the emergencies and unanticipated events that are part and parcel of family life—sudden illness, an early school closing due to snow, a breakdown in child-care arrangements.

The most common response to both needs has been flextime. Flextime can be narrowly designed to permit permanent alterations of a basically rigid work schedule by, say, half an hour or an hour, or it can be more broadly defined to allow freewheeling variations from one workday to the next.

Pioneered in this country by Hewlett-Packard, flextime is now used by about 12% of all U.S. workers, while half the country's large employers offer some kind of flextime arrangement. Its effects on lateness, absenteeism, and employee morale have been highly positive.[7] The effects on the family are not as easily measured, but most employees say they find it helpful, and the more scheduling latitude it offers, the more helpful they seem to find it.

A number of companies are considering ways of further expanding the notion of flextime. One alternative, called *weekly balancing*, lets employees set their own hours day-to-day as long as the weekly total stays constant. In Europe, some companies offer monthly and yearly balancing. Clearly, this is most difficult to do in situations where production processes require a predictable level of staffing.

In November 1988, Eastman Kodak announced a new work-schedule program that permits four kinds of alternative work arrangements:

1. Permanent changes in regular, scheduled hours.
2. Supervisory flexibility in adjusting daily schedules to accommodate family needs.
3. Temporary and permanent part-time schedules at all levels.
4. Job sharing.

Aetna Life and Casualty also recently launched an internal marketing effort and training program to help its supervisors adapt to, plan for, and implement unconventional work schedules.

Employees also must assume new roles. In the job-sharing program at Rolscreen Company, for example, employees are responsible for locating compatible partners for a shared job and for ensuring that the arrangement

---

7. Kathleen Christensen, *A Look at Flexible Staffing and Scheduling in U.S. Corporations* (New York: Conference Board, 1989); and Jon L. Pierce et al., *Alternative Work Schedules* (Newton, Mass.: Allyn and Bacon, 1988).

works and that business needs are met.[8] Also, employees are often expected to make themselves available when business emergencies arise. In the best flexible arrangements, employers and employees work as partners.

PART-TIME EMPLOYMENT

Studies show that a third to half of women with young children want to work less than full time for at least a while, despite the loss of pay and other benefits. Yet we have found in our work with dozens of companies that managers at all levels show firm resistance to part-time work. They seem to regard the 40-hour week as sacred and cannot imagine that anyone working fewer hours could be doing anything useful. Even in companies that accept the need for part-time work, we see managers who refuse to believe it will work in their own departments. Indeed, even the term "part-time" seems to have a negative connotation.

Research on part-time productivity is sometimes hard to interpret, but the studies we've seen indicate that the productivity of part-time workers is, in certain cases, better than their full-time counterparts and, in all cases, no worse. One study comparing part-time and full-time social workers found that, hour for hour, the part-time employees carried greater caseloads and serviced them with more attention.[9]

Part-time is not necessarily the same as half-time, as many managers assume. Many parents want 4-day or 30-hour workweeks. Many other assumptions about less than full-time employment are also unwarranted. For example, managers often insist that customers will not work with part-time employees, but few have asked their customers if this is true.

Another axiom is that supervisory and managerial personnel must always be full-time, because it is a manager's role to "be there" for subordinates. This article of faith ignores the fact that managers travel, attend meetings, close their doors, and are otherwise unavailable for a good part of every week.

CAREER-PATH ALTERNATIVES

It takes a lot of ingenuity and cultural adaptability to devise meaningful part-time work opportunities and to give employees individual control of their working hours. But an even greater challenge is to find ways of fitting these flexible arrangements into long-term career paths. If the price of

---

8. *Work and Family: A Changing Dynamic* (Washington, D.C.: Bureau of National Affairs Special Report, 1986): 78–80.

9. *Part-Time Social Workers in Public Welfare* (New York: Catalyst, 1971), cited in *Alternative Work Schedules*, p. 81.

family responsibility is a label that reads "Not Serious About Career," frustrations will grow. But if adaptability and labor-market competitiveness are the goals, then the usual definition of fast-track career progression needs modification.

The first step, perhaps, is to find ways of acquiring broad business experience that are less disruptive to the family. For example, Mobil Oil has gradually concentrated a wide range of facilities at hub locations, partly in order to allow its employees a greater variety of work experience without relocation.

Another essential step is to reduce the tendency to judge productivity by time spent at work. Nothing is more frustrating to parents than working intensely all day in order to pick up a child on time, only to be judged inferior to a coworker who has to stay late to produce as much. For many hardworking people, hours certainly do translate into increased productivity. Not for all. And dismissing those who spend fewer hours at the workplace as lacking dedication ignores the fact that virtually all employees go through periods when their working hours and efficiency rise or fall, whether the cause is family, health, or fluctuating motivation.

———— CORPORATE MISSION

Fertility in the United States is below replacement levels. Moreover, the higher a woman's education level, the more likely she is to be employed and the less likely to have children. The choice to have a family is complex, yet one study shows that two-thirds of women under 40 who have reached the upper echelons in our largest companies and institutions are childless, while virtually all men in leadership positions are fathers.[10] If we fail to alter the messages and opportunities we offer young men and women and if they learn to see a demanding work life as incompatible with a satisfying family life, we could create an economy in which more and more leaders have traded family for career success.

There are four steps a company needs to take in order to create an environment where people with dependents can do their best work without sacrificing their families' welfare:

- Develop a corporate policy that it communicates to all its employees;
- Train and encourage supervisors to be adaptable and responsible;
- Give supervisors tools and programs to work with;
- Hold all managers accountable for the flexibility and responsiveness of their departments.

---

10. *The Corporate Woman Officer* (Chicago, Ill.: Heidrick and Struggles, Inc., 1986); *Korn/Ferry International's Executive Profile: Corporate Leaders in the Eighties* (New York: Korn/Ferry International, 1986).

The key people in all this are first-line managers and supervisors. All the policies and programs in the world don't mean much to an employee who has to deal with an unsupportive boss, and the boss is often unsupportive because of mixed signals from above.

We have seen companies where the CEO went on record in support of family flexibility but where supervisors were never evaluated in any way for their sensitivity to family issues. In one company, managers were encouraged to provide part-time work opportunities, yet head-count restrictions reckoned all employees as full-time. In another, maternity leave was counted against individual managers when measuring absenteeism, a key element in their performance appraisals. As a general rule, strict absenteeism systems designed to discourage malingerers often inadvertently punish the parents of young children. Yet such systems coexist with corporate admonitions to be flexible. Where messages are mixed and performance measurement has not changed since the days of the "give them an inch, they'll take a mile" personnel policy, it is hardly surprising that supervisors and managers greet lofty family-oriented policy statements with some cynicism.

Training is critical. IBM, Johnson & Johnson, Merck, and Warner-Lambert have all established training programs to teach managers to be more sensitive to work-and-family issues. The training lays out the business case for flexibility, reviews corporate programs and policies, and presents case studies that underline the fact that there are often no right answers or rule books to use as guides in the complicated circumstances of real life.

Perhaps the thorniest issue facing businesses and managers is that of equity. Most managers have been trained to treat employees identically and not to adjudicate the comparative merits of different requests for flexibility. But what equity often means in practice is treating everyone as though they had wives at home. On the other hand, it is difficult to set up guidelines for personalized responses, since equity is a touchstone of labor relations and human resource management. Judging requests individually, on the basis of business and personal need, is not likely to lead to identical outcomes.

Seniority systems also need rethinking. Working second or third shift is often the only entry to a well-paying job for nonprofessional employees, but for a parent with a school-age child, this can mean not seeing the child at all from weekend to weekend. Rotating shifts wreak havoc with child-care arrangements and children's schedules. Practices that worked fine when the labor force consisted mostly of men with wives at home now have unintended consequences.

Finally, the message top management sends to all employees is terribly important. In focus groups at various large companies, we hear over and over again a sense that companies pay lip service to the value of family and community but that day-to-day practice is another story altogether. We hear what we can only describe as a yearning for some tangible acknowledgment from top management that family issues are real, complex, and important.

EXHIBIT
Companies That Lead the Way

For years, IBM has steadily increased its efforts to adapt to family needs. It pioneered child-care and elder-care assistance programs. A national resource and referral service network originally put together for IBM in 1984 now serves about 900,000 employees of more than 35 national companies. In 1988, IBM expanded its flextime program to allow employees to adjust their workdays by as much as two hours in either direction and adopted an extended leave-of-absence policy permitting up to a three-year break from full-time employment with part-time work in the second and third years. The company has also been experimenting with work-at-home programs. And earlier this year, it introduced family-issues sensitivity training for more than 25,000 managers and supervisors.

Johnson & Johnson recently announced an extremely broad work-and-family initiative that includes support for elder care and child care, greater work-time flexibility, management training, and a change in its corporate credo.

AT&T recently negotiated a contract with two of its unions that established a dependent-care referral service and provides for leaves of up to one year, with guaranteed reinstatement, for new parents and for workers with seriously ill dependents.

At NCNB, a program called Select Time allows employees at all levels in the company, including managers, to reduce their time and job commitments for dependent-care purposes without cutting off current and future advancement opportunities.

Apple Computer operates its own employee-staffed child-care center and gives "baby bonuses" of $500 to new parents. Du Pont has helped to establish child-care centers in Delaware with contributions of money and space. Eastman Kodak has adopted new rules permitting part-time work, job sharing, and informal situational flextime.

For reasons partly societal and partly strategic, these and scores of other businesses are building work environments that let people give their best to their jobs without giving up the pleasures and responsibilities of family life.

Johnson & Johnson, which sees its 40-year-old corporate credo as central to its culture, recently added the statement, "We must be mindful of ways to help our employees fulfill their family obligations." Du Pont has developed a mission statement that commits it, in part, to "making changes in the workplace and fostering changes in the community that are sensitive to the changing family unit and the increasingly diverse work force." (See the *Exhibit*.)

Throughout Europe, governments have required companies to treat the parenting of babies as a special circumstance of employment and have invested heavily in programs to support the children of working parents. In this country, recent surveys indicate almost universal popular support for parental leave. But our instincts oppose government intervention into internal business practices. We leave decisions about flexibility and the organization of work to individual companies, which means that the decisions of first-line managers in large part create our national family policy.

In this, the United States is unique. But then we are also unique in other ways, including the depth of our commitment to business, to fairness, to equal opportunity, to common sense. Many of our young women now strive to become CEOs. No one intended that the price for business success should be indifference to family or that the price of having a family should be to abandon professional ambition.

━━━ DISCUSSION QUESTIONS

1. In your opinion, can an individual be both an involved family member and an active, committed participant in the work force? Why or why not?

2. Imagine that your company is moving to another state and your supervisor tells you that you must relocate in order to keep your job. Assume also that this new situation conflicts with the needs of your family. What would you decide to do? What factors would influence your decision?

3. How have the organizations you have worked for accommodated the needs of employees who have dependents? Could these organizations have done more to accommodate the needs of families? Should they do more?

4. The authors state that "Women and men in two-career and single-parent families are much better able to identify policies that will let them act responsibly toward their families and still satisfy their professional ambitions." They stress that employees and management must work together to create flexible policies. Do you find leaders in the organizations you have worked for open to suggestions from employees? Has management been open to this type of collaboration with employees? How would you foster this approach as a senior manager in a company?

Beyond Testing: Coping with Drugs at Work

37

JAMES T. WRICH

Drug abuse costs American business billions of dollars a year in lost productivity. Many companies have adopted drug-testing initiatives as a way of identifying drug abusers for treatment or disciplinary action. But these initiatives often create more problems than they solve.

This reading explores a more effective method for dealing with chemical dependency—employee assistance programs. It describes their history, how they work, and what they can accomplish. Acknowledging that "a drug-free workplace in a drug-filled society is an illusion," the author offers hope rather than a panacea.

It is hard to overestimate the impact of substance abuse on the workplace. Even the most conservative estimates are staggering. The National Institute on Drug Abuse (NIDA) and the National Institute on Alcohol Abuse and Alcoholism (NIAAA) estimate that at least 10% of the work force is afflicted with alcoholism or drug addiction. Another 10% to 15% is affected by the substance abuse of an immediate family member. Still more bear the scars of having grown up with an addicted or alcoholic parent.

All in all, even after eliminating duplicates, at least 25% of any given work force suffers from substance abuse—their own or someone else's. As a chronic alcoholic from the ages of 15 to 27, I have personal experience with the problem and know the devastation it can cause. Managers are right to be apprehensive about drugs in the workplace, but a punitive response is inappropriate. Drug testing may be necessary where compelling issues of safety or national security are involved, but drug testing alone will not make the problem go away. Inexplicably, our efforts to deal with drug abuse ignore nearly 50 years of experience in the workplace treatment of alcoholism. We have had Broadbrush employee assistance programs for more than 15 years, and they continue to be used with great effectiveness to reduce absenteeism, promote recovery, minimize relapse, cut treatment costs, and improve productivity among drug abusers as well as alcoholics.

——— ASSESSING THE PROBLEM

For practical purposes, alcoholics and addicts are not two groups of people but one. Alcoholics cannot safely use drugs, and drug addicts cannot safely use alcohol. Moreover, treatment centers have reported for at least 10 years that a majority of patients under the age of 40 are dually addicted to alcohol and at least one other drug. Because it is legal, we seem to find alcohol less frightening, but the effects of alcoholism are at least as devastating.

A recent estimate by the Alcohol, Drug Abuse and Mental Health Administration indicates that alcohol and drug abusers together cost the country more than $140 billion annually, including $100 billion in lost productivity. And these are only the direct costs. If we include family members in our calculation, the total will rise still higher.

An NIDA survey indicates that 19% of Americans over the age of 12 have used illicit drugs during the past year. Among 18- to 25-year-olds—the population now entering the work force—65% have used illicit drugs, 44% in the past year.

Given these figures, it is hardly surprising that many companies have opted for hardball methods, heeding the law and conventional notions of human rights only when faced with unequivocal prohibitions. In general, managers are not only extremely concerned about drugs, they are also convinced that fast action can solve the problem quickly and that they have the muscle and the means to do it. They have been encouraged by the attorney general's drug-testing initiative and by testimony from the commissioner of baseball claiming that the drug problem in the major leagues has been resolved. First Lady Nancy Reagan's "Just Say No!" slogan gave the effort an appealing simplicity that encouraged everyone to overlook the complexities involved. In essence, many *managers* just said "No!" They resolved to get drug abusers out of the workplace one way or another, and drug-testing initiatives (DTIs) became their weapon of choice (see *Exhibit 1*).

Drug-testing initiatives usually employ the following sequence of elements. The company does the following:

1. Prepares a written policy and procedure statement;
2. Trains supervisors to recognize the signs and symptoms that would justify reasonable suspicion of drug use;
3. Instructs supervisors to refer employees for testing if these criteria are met;
4. Obtains and tests a sample of the employee's urine;
5. Confirms all positive test results with a second, more accurate test;
6. Gives those who are confirmed positive a second time the choice between treatment and disciplinary action up to and including termination;
7. Requires retesting without notice for those who complete treatment;
8. Establishes serious disciplinary measures, often termination, for those who test positive after undergoing treatment.

More than 35% of the country's largest companies have DTIs, and the number is growing fast. This overwhelming response may be seen as a clear indication that business is ready to tackle the problem. Nevertheless, I believe these programs are based on a number of questionable assumptions, many of which were proven false by programs instituted as long ago as the 1940s to deal with alcoholism. Drug-testing initiatives make the following assumptions.

- We can adequately train supervisors to recognize the telltale signs and symptoms of substance abuse.
- Supervisors will find reasonable suspicion an adequate basis for referral.
- Supervisors can be motivated to make such referrals.
- Testing will be accurate.
- The positive tests will be accurately interpreted.
- The imposition of treatment or disciplinary action will be appropriate, and employees will respond appropriately to whichever course is pursued.

——— OUR EXPERIENCE WITH ALCOHOLISM

Substance abuse is nothing new. Heroin was once considered a wonder drug to cure morphine addiction in soldiers returning from Civil War hospitals.

EXHIBIT 1
When DTIs Are Called For

The value of drug testing is so questionable and the drawbacks so great that no organization should even consider a DTI without compelling safety or national security reasons. An airline, for example, might decide to saddle itself with a DTI to increase the safety of its passengers, and a defense contractor might consider weapons secrets worth the small extra protection that an expensive and troublesome DTI could provide. Even in such cases, however, careful planning and administration are essential if the DTI is to solve more problems than it creates.

To set up a workable drug-testing program, an organization should

1. Have an effective employee assistance program already in place.

2. Familiarize itself with the technical and legal limitations of a DTI and consider the possible negative effect on employee relations.
3. Place control and direction of the DTI in the hands of its human resource department, with input from its legal department—not the other way around.
4. Convince supervisors and employees of the need for drug testing and give them reason to trust and support the program.
5. Require drug testing of everyone in the organization from the CEO on down.
6. Establish criteria in advance for maintaining confidentiality and evaluating effectiveness.

Cocaine was first used in the United States in the 1880s—not the 1980s—and was outlawed in 1914, whereupon amphetamines more or less took its place until recently.

Alcohol, our national legal drug of choice, has been with us practically forever and, with 11 million alcoholics and another 7 million alcohol abusers, is by far our most serious chemical dependency. Employers who recognized the problems that alcohol creates in the workplace have tried a number of remedies over the past 45 years. Employee assistance programs have been the most effective.

Until the 1970s, the great majority of companies addressed employee alcoholism with an informal policy of concealment and denial. When the alcoholic employee's condition became so severe as to be obvious to everyone, he or she was fired or retired or died. Some companies have tried to weed out alcoholics before they reached that stage, but managerial naivete and a lack of supervisory cooperation have usually thwarted such efforts.

The problem has always been twofold: how to identify afflicted employees and what to do with them. The success of identification programs depended greatly on what the work force perceived to be the consequences to the employee. Progressive companies such as Eastman Kodak and the Northern Pacific Railroad (now part of the Burlington Northern) launched formal efforts decades ago to help alcoholics. Program staff usually consisted of a recovering alcoholic and sometimes a sympathetic company doctor or nurse who encouraged the employee to attend meetings of Alcoholics Anonymous.

These early efforts greatly helped those few alcoholics who were referred, but the vast majority went unidentified and untreated. Naturally, employees were concerned about confidentiality, job security, the possible stigma, and the quality of case handling.

Experience brought other problems to light through the 1940s and 1950s. Training was difficult to deliver, and its impact was short-lived. In the course of their regular work, supervisors had scant opportunity to practice what little they had learned. The training taught them to look for bloodshot eyes, slurred speech, and the smell of alcohol on the breath, but supervisors were neither comfortable nor proficient as amateur sleuths and pseudo-diagnosticians. Much of the current DTI training to help supervisors establish "reasonable suspicion" resembles those early efforts to cope with alcoholism.

In those early programs, the training was seldom offered to managers above the supervisory level, and instructional anecdotes focused almost exclusively on nonmanagement employees, which implied that no one above that level had a problem. Addicted supervisors rarely saw the problem anywhere. Supervisors with a strong bias against alcohol tended to see it everywhere.

All the while, the alcoholic senior manager remained completely hidden. These inconsistencies did not go unnoticed by employees and unions. They are also analogous to situations found in many of today's DTIs. It is rare for company officers to be tested, even though the problem is certainly present at that level.

Finally, there was the dimension of the disease that still amazes experts—the alcoholic's profound capacity for denial and deception. By the time addicted people were confronted, they had often spent years developing their alibi systems and their unique capacity to manipulate. Matching an alcoholic against a supervisor with one or two hours of training in late-stage symptoms was usually no contest. Moreover, when alcoholic employees learned what supervisors were looking for, they stopped displaying those symptoms, at least until the very latest stages when they completely lost control. When today's addicted employees learn their company's criteria for "reasonable suspicion," they too will work hard to avoid such behavior. Today's addicts are at least as cunning as yesterday's.

In the 1960s, programs shifted their focus from symptoms to job performance. Because supervisors were so often outmaneuvered, the experts decided to take the game out of the alcoholic's ballpark and put it into the supervisor's. Job performance became the principal criterion for referral. Supervisors were told to stop diagnosing and, moreover, not even to discuss alcohol. Of course if they thought an employee had a drinking problem, they were to refer him or her to the company program.

This ambiguous message confused everyone. Obviously, if supervisors did not make some kind of diagnosis, however amateurish, they certainly were not going to refer the employee to an alcoholism program.

On the positive side, these programs were sincere efforts at rehabilitation, recovery rates were encouraging, and the testimonials of participants were glowing. Even so, feelings of suspicion ran high among employees. Confidentiality was so often compromised that laws were later written to safeguard it. Supervisors disliked the confrontational role, and they feared sending someone to the program who wasn't really an alcoholic, thus hurting the employee and damaging their own credibility. A 1976 review showed that only one-third of 1% of all employees made use of such programs each year. In addition, those who used the programs tended to be in late stages of the disease and had already experienced great personal suffering and productivity loss. Because of the denial inherent in the disease, and because coercion as a method of referral so closely resembled punitive action, there seemed little hope of seeing significant numbers of self-referrals without a change in approach.

Ironically, had there then been a test to prove conclusively that an employee had been drinking on the job, it is doubtful that it would have improved overall program effectiveness. Then, as now, you can't test what you can't refer; you can't refer what you can't find; you can't find what you're not trained to find; and training alone will not inspire those with a vested interest in the status quo. Experience indicates that a disproportionate number of chemically dependent employees end up working for others who are addicts, substance abusers, or the untreated adult children of alcoholics. Such individuals—perhaps as many as a third of all supervisors—are unlikely to do well as police officers.

———— BROADBRUSH EMPLOYEE ASSISTANCE PROGRAMS

In 1972, NIAAA launched a new workplace alcoholism program called the Broadbrush approach and sent 100 program consultants, of whom I was one, into the field to sell the idea to management and labor.

The Broadbrush approach—what we now call employee assistance programs or EAPs—took into account the limitations of earlier efforts as well as the nature of addiction. Knowing that alcoholic denial and manipulation were more than the typical supervisor could learn to cope with, it likewise stressed that supervisors were not to diagnose.

But for the first time, it also provided a structure for implementation. Rather than focus only on alcoholism, the program was broadened to cover a wide range of personal problems including emotional, marital, family, and financial difficulties, and of course, drug abuse. The alcoholic label was no longer automatically attached to anyone using the program. The new approach not only reduced the stigma but also encouraged supervisors to refer a troubled employee without first trying to figure out the nature of the problem. Previously, when alcoholic employees argued that the problem wasn't really drinking but a bad marriage, say, or indebtedness, they generally got off the hook. Now there was a program that dealt with these other, "respectable" issues as well. EAP staff assessed the nature and severity of problems, referred employees to appropriate care in the community, and followed up (see *Exhibit 2*).

EXHIBIT 2
Developing an Effective EAP

Building an effective EAP requires time, insight, and a lot of work. We cannot simply slap together a few outmoded ideas, dress them up with word processors, add a testing gimmick, and peddle them as a package.

For the most part, an EAP should be custom designed for its specific workplace. To be effective, it should see and refer for drug-abuse treatment at least 1% of the work force each year. To do this, the program must be properly staffed. Generally this means one full-time equivalent assessment and referral (A&R) resource professional for every 3,500 to 4,200 employees, plus adequate clerical support.

The A&R staff must have considerable training and experience working with chemically dependent people. Whatever their academic degrees, professionals without vast experience working with alcoholics and drug addicts can do as much harm as good. Resourceful addicts and alcoholics often can deceive them, which leads to inappropriate care and drives up employee health-care costs without solving the problem.

A sufficient budget, an effective training and communications program, a good management information system, a valid outcome evaluation program, a credible benefit-to-cost analysis, an appropriately designed benefits package, ongoing education for EAP staff, and lots of attention and support from senior management are among the other key ingredients for a successful EAP.

By the late 1970s, employees could get help even without a documented job performance problem. In addition, EAP professionals had developed new outreach and intervention techniques to generate referrals by peers and to identify substance abusers at an earlier stage of their dependency. For the first time, self-referrals began to outnumber referrals from supervisors.

The results were gratifying. Employees were getting experienced, professional help, and getting it sooner, which reduced both personal suffering and productivity losses. Earlier treatment also meant lower costs, because someone in the later stages of any problem is less likely to respond to outpatient care. Both diagnosis and treatment were confidential. Managers liked the idea of attacking a wider range of problems, because their goal was to reduce losses in productivity regardless of their cause. Many managers had wanted to address alcoholism more aggressively for years but had hesitated because previous approaches so often looked like witch-hunts.

Most important, the programs were reaching nearly three times as many alcoholics as before. Burlington Northern changed from a straight alcoholism program to the Broadbrush approach and achieved utilization rates of more than 1% for alcohol and 2% to 3% for other problems. This meant that the time required to reach a number of alcoholics equivalent to the population at risk had been reduced to as little as seven years in some programs. We thought we had discovered pure gold.

The new approach had its detractors, of course. Some alcoholism professionals feared that alcoholism would get lost in the shuffle if it weren't the sole focus of the program. Some managers disdained rehabilitation as an organized form of coddling undesirables. Some unions thought that EAPs infringed on their turf. But EAPs worked, and by 1979, more than half of the country's largest companies had EAPs in one form or another, and about 80% of new programs were some variation of the Broadbrush approach.

My own experience is representative. From 1978 to 1984, I was director of the EAP at United Airlines. Of the first 5,100 employees using the program, 65% came in on their own or on the encouragement of their family, friends, or unions. About 2,000 of these were in trouble with alcohol or drugs, often both. Of the 35% referred by management, less than half had developed job-performance problems. Our evaluation showed the following:

- Absenteeism among program participants, measured from one year before entering the program to one year after, went down 74% in Chicago and 80% in San Francisco, to cite two cities.
- Recovery rates the first time through the program were 74% for ground employees, 82% for flight attendants, and 92% for pilots and copilots.
- Recovery rates for those who relapsed and reentered the program were about 40%.
- The benefit-to-cost ratio, based on reduction in sick leave and including cost of program operations, treatment, and time off work while receiving treatment, was 7 to 1 projected over five

years and nearly 17 to 1 when projected over the expected career of participants.

- Job performance improvement, rated by supervisors on an 11-point scale ranging from -5 to +5, was 3.5 points on average.

Other companies have reported equally encouraging results.

- Kimberly-Clark documented a 43% reduction in absenteeism and a 70% reduction in accidents among a sample of employees who had participated in its employee assistance program.
- Chairman Roger Smith of General Motors announced in 1983 that, of some 60,000 employees who had taken part in its EAP, between 60% and 70% were still abstaining from alcohol or drugs one year later.
- Phillips Petroleum reported that its EAP had netted more than $8 million a year in reduced accidents and sick leave, and in higher productivity.
- The Kelsey-Hayes EAP tracked 58 plant workers involved in its program and documented the recovery of 18,325 hours in one year, an average of 316 hours per employee.
- An AT&T study in 1982 showed declines of 78% in overall absenteeism, 87% in absence due to disability, 81% in on-the-job accidents, and 58% in off-the-job accidents.

THE SOLUTION THAT ACTS LIKE A PROBLEM

In our eagerness to attack the current crop of devastating drugs—particularly cocaine—we have ignored not only the pitfalls of the past but also the effectiveness of our present employee assistance programs. We have somehow convinced ourselves that the solution should be easy—an inference easily drawn from the Reagan administration's simplistic approach and the blandishments of those consultants who market DTIs.

But solving tough problems is seldom easy. Even a superficial study of past efforts suggests a number of hard questions. It was difficult to train supervisors to identify late-stage alcoholics whose drug was familiar and whose problems developed slowly. How difficult will it be to train supervisors in the various effects of a wide spectrum of unfamiliar drugs that can cause extreme problems in the course of a few months? If it was difficult for supervisors to overcome their fear of stigmatizing subordinates with an alcoholic label, how hard will they find it to refer employees for possible termination? If the alcoholic supervisors of the past failed to refer alcoholic subordinates for fear of exposing themselves, what are the chances today that a supervisor who abuses illegal drugs will refer an employee for testing?

The basic approach and underlying philosophy of many DTIs pose serious obstacles to their effectiveness. Although EAPs generally assure employees that only substandard performance or rule violations—not EAP participation—will jeopardize their jobs, drug testing can mean job loss even where performance problems and rules violations are not evident. DTIs are essentially punitive and therefore legalistic in tone and approach. They are often based on several misjudgments.

For example, we take it for granted that supervisors will support tough tactics because the problem is so serious, but experience shows that supervisors often identify more closely with the subordinates they work with every day than they do with top management.

We figure that if we can make examples of the worst offenders, others will change their behavior. This may work with some people, but not with alcoholics and other addicts. Addicts believe they can get away with it because they nearly always do. Until the late stages of the illness, their deception skills will be much more effective than the detection skills of the company.

We assume that a positive or negative test result will help us to identify problems and limit their effects. But the tests in use today are not entirely reliable, and many practiced drug abusers know how to beat them. Even a true positive can mean many things. The employee could be an addict, an abuser, an occasional user, or merely someone who likes a sandwich on a poppy-seed roll. Moreover, a nonaddicted employee who smoked marijuana 10 days ago could test positive, while a chronic alcoholic who was drunk 10 hours ago might very well test negative. Even error-free test results would need professional assessment (see *Exhibit 3*).

We argue that cocaine and other drugs require special attention and effort because they are against the law, but alcohol is legal and does no less damage in the workplace. The problem for businesses and their employees is chemical dependency, and fortunately, that is a problem we know how to address with EAPs.

We tell ourselves that drug testing can't hurt so we may as well try it. But if drug testing ignores the human element and damages employee relations, it can hurt greatly. Worst of all may be the mistaken belief that something of value has been done.

Finally, we tend to assume that as long as drug testing is legal, it is all right. But the tone, approach, and perceived objectives of DTIs are adversarial, and the courts and legislatures have not yet spoken their final words on the subject. Drug-test procedures are essentially legal treatises designed to defend the company in a grievance hearing or courtroom, but that is the last place anyone but a lawyer wants to be.

The fact that DTIs emphasize "reasonable suspicion" as a basis for referral reveals the essential combativeness of such programs and explains why they are so ineffective. Establishing reasonable suspicion requires a focus on the more obvious, late-stage symptoms—the more conclusive the evidence, the safer the process legally. But winning in court is not the same as winning in the workplace. Later and fewer referrals mean a return to the intake levels of the 1940s.

Moreover, skewing tests to avoid the legal fallout of false positives will only produce more false negatives. And these particular false negatives are

EXHIBIT 3
The Medical Case Against Drug Testing

A drug's detectability depends on many variables: dosage, absorption rate, location of entry, drug purity, individual metabolism, frequency of use, and whether drugs are consumed singly or in combination. A urine test does not test for the presence or absence of the drug, but for a critical quantity of it. If the concentration drops below a certain level, the test usually will not detect it. Knowing how long it takes for abstinence to reduce concentrations below these critical thresholds—2 to 4 days for cocaine, heroin, and amphetamines; 3 to 10 days for occasional use of marijuana; 5 to 13 hours for alcohol—allows chronic users to feign illness and postpone their tests long enough to free their bodies of the drug and its metabolites.

Abstinence is not the only way to beat the tests. Employees have been known to smuggle in clean urine (and to keep it at body temperature to fool the medical attendant), to drink large quantities of water to dilute their samples, even to obtain prescriptions for legal drugs known to test positive in order to provide themselves with a "legitimate" explanation of their own more genuine positives. Marijuana users can add salt, sweat, or Drano to increase the pH of their urine samples. Besides, there is a 5% to 10% chance that drug abusers will falsely test negative despite the drugs in their bodies.

There is also a chance that positive tests will be false. Even if the test is accurate, the mere indication of the drug does not tell us whether the employee has used the drug once or a hundred times—or at all.

Most laboratories screen for illegal drugs with the so-called EMIT method, which is hardly foolproof. A number of harmless—or in any case legal—substances have molecular and electrochemical patterns similar to the hard drugs EMIT was designed to identify. Over-the-counter cough and cold preparations may test positive for amphetamines. The opiate-like drugs and alcohol found in other legal medications may also confound test findings. Poppy seeds eaten in quantity may produce a trace opiate indication. Some herbal teas have been associated with positive tests for various illegal drugs.

Ibuprofen, a painkiller found in Advil, Datril, Rufen, and other over-the-counter medications, can cause a false positive result for marijuana. Ephedrine, an ingredient of Nyquil, can test positive for amphetamines. Dextromathorphon, found in many cough suppressants, has tested positive for opiates. False positives may also result from laboratory errors such as mislabeling urine or transposing results, or from improperly cleaned equipment, incompetence, or out-and-out fraud.

Several years ago, the Navy found that more than 30% of positives were erroneous. In one methadone maintenance program, accuracy was no better than 50%. In a litigious society, employers are well-advised to do two confirmatory tests. Even so, they run the risk of lawsuits. In May 1987, San Diego Gas and Electric lost a court case to a "false positive." The cost of defending the suit, settlement, and other fees was publicly stated as $80,000.

Even without litigation, testing is expensive. Besides the costs of the tests, companies must add the costs of administration, supervision, and lost work time. Last but hardly least, the cost to employee morale cannot be measured.

– David Bearman, M.D.

likely to render the DTI ineffective, because the people we most want to catch in a drug-testing net are the very people who are most skilled at achieving negative or ambiguous results by devious means.

Drug testing, even when necessary, should not be seen as a program in itself but rather as one element in a larger effort, an effort that begins with a properly designed and staffed EAP.

Our leaders suggest that we may be able to eliminate this problem in two or three years if we really get tough. But until we find a way to prevent 10% of the population from becoming addicted, the problem will continue. If all employers were able to prescreen with 100% accuracy, the resulting rise in unemployment would be staggering, and we would also find an increase in the suffering and disruption of other family members still in the work force. By the same token, if all employed alcoholics and addicts could be identified in the next three years, our current treatment capacity could not possibly handle the load.

Creation of a drug-free workplace in a drug-filled society is an illusion. It emphasizes supply rather than demand. It suggests that eradication of cocaine and other hard drugs will solve the problem generally. It insists that drug addicts and alcoholics are separable groups, the former far more intractable than the latter.

Our goal should be an *addiction-free* workplace. That means focusing on all addictive substances, not just those portrayed in the scariest colors. It means treatment of the whole problem, not just punitive measures for the small portion currently in the spotlight. It means concern for all employees at all levels, not just those in the lower echelons. We could have a drug-free workplace today if that were the only freedom we valued. We certainly would not be free of addiction. Untreated addiction will always resurface in some new and equally destructive form.

——— DISCUSSION QUESTIONS

1. What should a corporation's policy be regarding employees' personal problems? How involved should a company become in the personal problems of its employees?
2. Suppose you've discovered that your boss or a coworker has a serious drinking/drug problem. What action would you take?
3. What steps can a company take to educate employees about such issues as drug abuse? What other issues that affect an employee's productivity might a company want to address?
4. Do you think that companies and organizations in the future will become more or less involved with the general well-being of their employees, or will their involvement remain the same? Explain the reasons for your view.

INDEX

Absenteeism
  family issues and, 531
  flextime and, 537
  salaried system and, 478
Academy (career-system model),
    469–470, 472
Acceptance, group problem-solving
    and, 267
Accountability, hierarchy and, 384–385
Accounting system, at Semco, 79–80
Achievement, motivation and, 163, 164
Ackerman, Robert W., 344n
Addiction, 553. *See also* Alcoholism;
    Drug abuse
Adhocracy, 334, 338–339, 344–347
Administrative adhocracy, 346–347
Aetna Life and Casualty, 537
Affirmative action, 499–505
  at Corning, 504
  cycle in, 503, 505
  at DEC, 506
  managing diversity and, 501, 502,
    515
Agenda, for meeting, 290–291
Agenda control, as motivation, 67

Agreement, change resistance overcome
    by, 402–403, 405
Aguilar, Francis J., 15n
Alan Patricof Associates, 119
Albrook, Robert C., 191n
Alcan, 59
Alcoholism, 543–544, 546–547
  Broadbrush employee assistance
    programs for, 548–550
  drug testing and, 550–553
Aligning of people, 107–109
Allen, Stephen A., 395n
Allis-Chalmers Corp., 79, 80
All-salaried compensation system,
    478–479
Alternative career paths, 538–540
Alternative work schedules, career-and-
    family women and, 524. *See also*
    Flexible scheduling
Ambiguity, leadership pattern and, 133
Ambivalence, in performance appraisal,
    199–200
American Bankers Insurance Group,
    534–535
American Express, 58, 106–107

Anderson, John, 209n
Andrews, Kenneth R., 18n
Apple Computer, 120, 541
Appraisal process or interview, 196, 204–211
  guidelines for assessing, 211–212
Appraisal system, 196, 203–204. *See also* Performance appraisal or evaluation
Apprenticeship, in leadership development, 97–98
Argyris, Chris, 133n, 398n
Assignment (human resources), 466
Assignment flow (human resources), 468, 469
Athos, Anthony G., 241n
Atkinson, John W., 185n
AT&T Co., 176, 541, 550
Authority
  accountability and, 385
  dependence and, 36
  formal, 42
  in leadership pattern, 127–128, 132
Authority figures, relationship with boss and, 233
Autonomy crisis, 417
Avoidance
  in group conflict resolution, 270–271, 272, 273
  in performance appraisal, 199–200, 201
Avon Products, Inc., 501

Banc One, 58
Banfield, Edward C., 48, 48n
Bargaining
  in group conflict resolution, 271, 272–273
  interpersonal conflict and, 221–222
Barnard, Chester I., 65, 145
Barnes, Louis B., 92n, 405n, 407n
Barrett, Diana, 241n
Baseball team (career-system model), 470, 471, 472
Bass, Bernard, 116n
Beech-Nut Nutrition Corporation, 149
Beer, Michael, 197n, 203n, 407n, 424n, 474n
Behavioral modification, 174

Behavioral science, personnel management and, 166–167
Behavior model, of work-group, 257–258, 261
Benne, Kenneth F., 399n
Bennis, Warren G., 192, 193, 399n
Berlew, David E., 181, 185n, 187, 187n, 188n
Blake, Robert R., 221n, 270n
Bond, Terry, 531n
Bossidy, Larry, 434, 436, 441
Boss-imposed time, 50
Bower, Marvin, 395n
Bowers, David F., 401n
Brazil, Semco in, 70
Bridge club, as participative mechanism, 118
Broadbrush employee assistance programs, 548–550
Brophy, Paul, 143n
Buchanan, Paul C., 137n
Budgeting, 103
  at Semco, 80
Burden, Dianne, 536n
Bureaucracy. *See also* Hierarchy
  machine, 333, 337–340, 349
  professional, 333, 338–339, 340–341, 346
Burlington Northern Railroad, 546, 549
Burnham, David H., 48n
Burns, Alan, 424n
Burns, James McGregor, 116n
Burns, Robert K., 203n
Burns, Tom, 16n
Business plans, human resources planning and, 450–451, 452
Buy-make decision. *See* Make-or-buy decision

Candor
  in GE value statement, 442
  Welch on GE and, 433–434
Capital budgeting, managerial decisions and, 24
Caplan, Frieda, 118–119, 121
Career momentum, 466
Career paths
  alternatives in, 538–540

interfunctional coordination and, 362, 365
management of, 378
mentors in, 98–99, 511–512
temporary lower-level jobs, 420
for women, 521, 522–523, 530
Career system, 464–465
assignment flow, 468, 469
basic stages, 465–468
strategic choice and, 471–472
supply flow, 468, 469
typology of groups defined through, 469-471
Carlson, Sune, 15n
Carlzon, Jan, 104
Carnegie, Andrew, 98
Cartwright, Dorwin, 38n
CEOs, contacts of, 20–21, 22. *See also* Senior managers
Cespedes, Frank V., 359n
Chandler, Alfred D., 411–412
Change, 395–396
choice of strategy for, 405–408
cost of, 428–429
dealing with resistance to, 400–405
diagnosing resistance to, 396–400
formula for, 424–430
leadership and, 103
in managerial work, 57–62
quantum theory of, 351
in society, 138–139
women's opportunities and, 124
Chemical dependency. *See* Alcoholism; Drug abuse
Chew, Pat, 143n
Child care, 525, 532–535
Chin, Robert, 399n
Choran, Irving, 16n
Christensen, C. Roland, 411n
Christensen, Kathleen, 537n
Chrysler Corp., 193
Circle, organizational, 73
Civil disobedience, 75
Civil rights movement, leadership pattern and, 138
Clarifying, in group process, 286
Clarity, in corporate vision, 373–374
Cloherty, Patricia M., 119

Club (career-system model), 470–471, 472
Coaching, performance appraisal and, 197, 203
Coercion, change resistance overcome by, 404, 405
Coleman, Debi, 120
Collaboration period of organizational growth, 419–420, 422
Collaborative ventures, 64
Commissioning executives, 300
Commitment
of followers, 147–148
group problem-solving and, 267
group-process influence and, 282
new management work and, 69
Commitment strategy in work-force management, 490–497, 498
Communication
aligning as, 107–108
change resistance overcome by, 400–401, 405
cross-functional, 356–357; *see also* Interfunctional coordination
informational roles and, 21–22
of managerial expectations, 183–186
motivation and, 162–163
preferences on forms of, 235
two-way, 163
Welch on, 433
Communications media, managers' use of, 16–18
Communications role, of task-force leader, 307
Company culture, 330
Compensation systems, 476–477. *See also* Rewards and rewards systems
equity and, 479–482
management philosophy and, 477
pay-for-performance, 483–486
payroll stratification, 477–478
seniority and, 483
wages as motivation, 161
Competence
change and, 428–429
of followers, 148
Complexity, group problem-solving and, 266–267
Compromising, in group process, 286

Computer, managers' work procedures and, 18, 30

Conditions of work. *See* Working conditions

Confidence in subordinates, 133

Confidential information, task force and, 306

Configurations, organization design. *See* Organization design configurations

Conflict
adjudicators of, 365–366
group problem-solving, 266–267
interdepartmental, 274
in interfunctional coordination, 365
in task forces, 298, 306

Conflict, interpersonal, 213–220
action questions, 225–226
managing, 214, 220–225
managing your boss and, 229; *see also* Managing your boss

Conflict resolution in groups. *See* Group conflict resolution

Confrontation
authority vs. issues, 100
constructive, 221, 224–225
in group conflict resolution, 271–272, 273

Confronting norms, 269

Connor, Fox, 98

Consensus testing, in group process, 286

Consistency, in corporate vision, 375

Consumer movement, leadership pattern and, 138

Context, group, 243–244

Contingency approach, to organization design, 315–321

Continuity, in corporate vision, 374–375

Continuum of leadership behavior, 128–130, 138, 139

Continuum of manager-nonmanager behavior, 140–141

Control
as configuration element, 338
external (over divisions), 340, 342–343, 349–350
in growth phases, 422
vs. motivation, 109–110

Control crisis, 418

Controlling
actual managerial work and, 13
interpersonal conflict and, 221, 222–224

Control strategy in work-force management, 489–490, 492–493

Co-opting
change resistance, 403–404, 405
management efforts, 379–380

Coordinating, actual managerial work and, 13

Coordination, interfunctional or cross-functional. *See* Interfunctional coordination

Coordination period of organizational growth, 418–419, 422

Copeman, George H., 16n

Corning Glass Works, 504

Corporate Executive Council (General Electric), 436, 437–438

Corporate mission, family concerns and, 539–542

Corporation Man (Jay), 72

Cost-accounting experts, as interfunctional adjudicators, 366

Counseling
interpersonal conflict and, 224
motivation and, 163

Counterdependence, 233–234

Courage, of followers, 149

Crandall, Bob, 108–109

Creativity
in GE value statement, 442
organizational design and, 324

Creativity period in organizational development, 415–417, 422

Critical Incident Method, 203

Cross-functional coordination. *See* Interfunctional coordination

Cross-functional groups of managers, 328

Culture
group, 252–256, 257, 260, 261–262
of leadership, 111–114
managerial, 86

Culture, company or corporate, 330
diversity and, 510
interfunctional coordination and, 363–365

Culture, national, compensation systems and, 476–477
Cummins Engine Co., 479, 482, 490
Customer-ranking process, 358

Dalton, Gene W., 92n, 405n
Dana Corp., 479
Data bank, in managers' minds, 18, 26
Davis, Robert T., 16n, 189n
Deadlines, task–force membership and, 306
Decentralization
    as configuration element, 338
    vs. divisionalization, 342
    horizontal, 336
    leadership development and, 112
    vertical, 336
Decisional roles, 23
    disturbance handler, 23–24
    entrepreneur, 23
    negotiator, 24
    resource allocator, 24
Decision making
    in continuum of leadership behavior, 128
    delegation of, 18, 64–65, 131, 152
    in group problem-solving, 277
    intergroup and interdepartmental, 274–276
    in meeting, 296
Decision-making style, managing your boss and, 235
Defensiveness, in performance appraisal, 201
de Gaulle, Charles, 91
Dekker, Wisse, 374
Delegation
    followership encouragement, 152
    hierarchy and, 64–65
    information dilemma, 18
    risk, 131
Delegation period of organizational growth, 418, 422
Democracy, in leadership pattern, 127–128, 132
Democracy, work-force. See Employee involvement; Participation
Department representatives, 274–276

Dependability, in managing your boss, 237
Dependency
    leadership and, 87
    mutual, 229–230
    perception of, 40–42, 43, 44–45
Dependency relationships of manager, 34–38
Dependent care, 532–535
Design, organization. See Organization design
Design tools, 323–324
Development
    of managers, 377–378
    performance appraisal and, 197, 203
DeVries, David L., 195n
Differentiation, 317–318
    of single-business organizations, 324–328
Digital Equipment Corp. (DEC), 58, 506
Direction period of organizational growth, 417, 422
Direction-setting, leadership as, 103, 104–105
Discretionary time, 50
Dissatisfaction, change and, 424–426
Disseminator role, 22
Disturbance handler role, 23–24
Diversity, managing, 502, 506–515. See also Women managers
    affirmative action and, 501, 502, 515; see also Affirmative action
    at Avon, 501
    at DEC, 506
    family concerns in, 529–542
    future work-force entrants and, 519
    inability at, 500
Divisionalized form, 334, 338–339, 342–344
Division of work, 322
Donner, Frederic G., 88
Doyle, Stephen X., 359n
Dress code, Semco abolition of, 75–76
Drucker, Peter F., 235, 399, 399n
Drug abuse, 543–544
    Broadbrush employee assistance programs, 548–550
Drug testing, 543, 544–545
    medical case against, 552

Drug testing (continued)
  obstacles to, 550–551
  senior managers and, 546
  unreliability of, 551–553
Dual membership problem, 275–276
Duncan, Robert, 400n, 402n
du Pont, Pierre, 88, 90
Du Pont (E. I.) De Nemours and Co.,
  531, 534, 541
Durant, William, 342

Eastman Kodak Co., 59, 108–109, 537,
  541, 546
Ecology, leadership pattern and, 138
Education. *See also* Training
  change resistance overcome by,
    400–401, 405
  of managers, 29
Einstein, Albert, 97
Eisenhower, Dwight D., 97–98, 98n
Elaborating, in group process, 286
Elder care, 535
Electronic mail, 363
Elliott, Susan S., 119, 120–121
Emotional issues, 217
  in relationship with boss, 232–233
Empathy, 64, 93
Employee assistance programs (EAPs),
  Broadbrush, 548–550
Employee involvement (EI). *See also*
  Participation
  commitment strategy, 490
  at Semco, 72–75
Employee motivation, organization
  design and, 321
Employees, at Semco, 75–77
Employee satisfaction, rewards and,
  474–475
Empowerment, through aligning, 108
Engineers, as interfunctional adjudi-
  cators, 366
Entrepreneurial company, as simple
  structure, 336
Entrepreneur role, 23
Environment, 315
  as configuration element, 339
  organization design and, 350–351

Equity
  child care and, 534
  family concerns and, 540
  systems for maintaining, 479–482
Ethics, followership and, 149
Evaluation
  job, 480–481
  person/skill, 481–482
Evaluation goals, of performance
  appraisal, 197
Evolution, as growth period, 411, 414
Exempt employees, 478
Exit from firm, 467–468
Expectations
  group, 268–269
  in managing your boss, 236
Expectations by managers, 179–181
  communication of, 183–186
  early years, 186–190
  new hires, 190–192
  as Pygmalion effect, 192–193
  realistic vs. unrealistic, 185
  as self-fulfilling prophecies, 181–183,
    186, 187
Expertise, power and, 39, 43, 44
Extrinsic rewards, 476

Face-to-face influence, 42–45
Facilitation, change resistance overcome
  by, 402, 405
Family and business, 529–532. *See also*
  Women; Women managers
  corporate mission and, 539–542
  dependent care, 532–535
  working conditions, 535–539
Fayol, Henri, 13, 314
Feedback
  firing of employee and, 468
  for followership, 151
  in groups, 257, 287
  in performance appraisal, 200, 201,
    209
Feelings
  in appraisal interview, 206
  group process and, 285
Festinger, Leon, 198n
Figurehead role, 19–20
Firing of employees, 467–468

Fit in organization design, 106, 315–317, 348–349
Flanagan, John C., 203n
Flexible scheduling
  career-and-family women and, 524–525
  family concerns and, 536, 537–538
  at Semco, 77
Flextime
  family concerns and, 537
  outside activities and, 468
  at Semco, 76
Focus, of followers, 148
Followers, 143–146
  cultivating, 150–153
  qualities of, 146–149
Forcing, in group conflict resolution, 271, 272–273
Ford Motor Co., 337
Formal authority, 42
Formal organization, as group design factor, 248–249
Formal structure, 372
Fortress (career-system model), 470, 471, 472
Fouraker, Lawrence E., 412n
Freedman, Robert J., 359n
French, John R. P., Jr., 38n, 203n
Fresco, Paolo, 434
Freud, Sigmund, 40
Frieda's Finest, 118–119
Fringe benefits, motivation and, 162
Functional integration. *See* Interfunctional coordination; Integration
Functional units, organization design in, 321–324

Gabarro, John J., 227n, 273
Gain-sharing plans, 485–486
Galinsky, Ellen, 531n
Gate keeping, in group process, 286
General Electric Co., 67–68, 112, 374, 432–445, 449
  continuity lacking in, 374
  Corporate Executive Council, 436, 437–438
  decentralization, 112
  human resources, 449

as training ground, 67–68
  Value statement, 442
  Welch interview on, 432–445
  Work-Out program, 438–440, 443, 444–445
General Foods Corp., 64, 490
General Motors Corp., 65, 90, 342, 482, 490, 497, 550
Gerstner, Lou, 106–107
Glass ceiling, 516, 519
Gleicher, David, 424n
Goals
  in boss's world, 230–231
  managers vs. leaders, 88–89
  social vs. economic, 344
Googins, Bradley, 536
Gorlin, Harriet, 450n
Grapevine, diversity and, 512–513
Grayson, C. Jackson, Jr., 19n
Great Western Forum, 119
Greiner, Larry E., 405n
Group climate, group process and, 283–284
Group conflict resolution, 269–270
  bargaining and forcing, 271, 272–273
  confronting and problem solving, 271–272, 273
  smoothing and avoidance, 270–271, 272, 273
Group culture, 252–256, 257, 260, 261–262
Group effectiveness, leadership pattern and, 135
Grouping of functions, for single-business organizations, 326–327
Group process, 279–287
Groups, work, 241
  behavior model of, 257–258, 261
  context of, 243–244
  design factors, 246–249
  interdepartmental, 274–276
  leaderless, 152
  Merit Corp. case, 241–243, 244–246, 249–252, 256, 259–261
  outcomes, 256–257
  as problem solvers, 264–269, 276–277
  at Semco, 77
  task forces, 298–308
  with temporary and rotating leadership, 152

Growth, organizational, 410–411
  implications of history of, 421–422
  key forces in, 411–415
  phases, 415–420
Guest, Robert H., 14n, 20, 21
Gulick, Charles A., Jr., 314

Hackman, Richard J., 196n, 199
Half-time employment, 538
Hall, Adrienne, 120
Hall, Douglas T., 181, 185n, 187, 187n,
  188n, 200n
Harmonizing, in group process, 286
Hawthorne Effect and experiment, 163,
  169
Hecht, Lee, 65
Hekimian, James S., 28n
Heron, R. Peter, 349n
Hewlett-Packard Co., 112, 479, 537
Hickson, David J., 349n
Hierarchy, 382–383, 392. *See also*
  Bureaucracy
  delegation and, 64–65
  faults, 383–385
  intellectual complexity, 390–391
  layers, 386–387
  managerial change and, 58, 59, 60, 63
  new managerial work and, 65
  vs. participatory management, 74
  reason for, 385–386
  responsibility time span, 387–390
Hinnings, C. R., 349n
Hodgson, Richard C., 25n
Hoffmann, Inge, 91, 91n
Hoffmann, Stanley, 91, 91n
Holdaway, Edward A., 349n
Homans, George C., 21, 21n
Honesty, in managing your boss, 237
Hood, Ed, 441
Horizontal job loading, 167–168, 172
Hottenstein, M. P., 411n
Houghton, James R., 504
Howes, Carollee, 533n
HRM. *See* Human resources manage-
  ment
Hubris, 100
Human relations training, motivation
  and, 162

Human resources management
  assignment, 466
  career systems, 464–472
  diversity and, 502, 506–515; *see also*
    Diversity, managing of
  exit, 467–468
  family concerns and, 529–542
  organizational psychology and,
    376–379
  planning, 449–462
  promotion, 466–467; *see also* Promotion
  recruitment, 376, 465–466, 500
  rewards, 474–486; *see also* Rewards
    and reward systems
  selection, 365, 376–377, 466
  training, 29, 150–151, 377–378, 467
  women managers and, 115–118,
    124–125, 516–527; *see also* Women
    managers
Human resources managers, as interfunctional adjudicators, 366
Hygiene vs. motivators, 164–166, 173

Iacocca, Lee A., 193
IBM Corp., 59, 72, 76, 469–470, 479, 535,
  540, 541
Identification, with manager, 40, 43
Identity, change and, 429, 430
Implementation, dissident individuals
  and, 302
Incentives, innovative types of, 67
Incentive system, 483–486
  as motivation, 160
Indirect influence methods, 43, 45–46
Industrial engineering, personnel management and, 166–167
Industrial revolution, big-group functioning and, 72
Influence, 42
  face-to-face, 42–45
  in group process, 282–283
  indirect, 43, 45–46
  managerial ways of, 313
  as necessary, 48
Informal relationships. *See also* Networks
  coordination through, 110–111
  interfunctional coordination and,
    363–365

Information
   confidential, 306
   hard vs. soft, 17
   privileged, 26
   women managers as sharing, 120–121
Information access, at Semco, 71, 78–80
Information Age, 382
Informational roles, 21–22
Information-exchange meeting, 290
Information flow, managing your boss
      and, 236–237
Information seeking, in group process,
      286
Information system, 16, 362–363
Initiative, 54, 55
Insight, of managers, 25
Inspiration, through leadership, 104
Integrating roles, 328
Integration, 318–321, 353–356. *See also*
      Interfunctional coordination
   functional units and, 322–323
   in single-business organizations,
      327–328
Interactive leadership
   vs. command-and-control, 125
   by women, 118–122, 123, 124–125
Interdepartmental conflict, 274
Interdependence, 105–106
   in forces affecting leadership pattern,
      139
   group problem-solving and, 267
Interfunctional (cross–functional)
      coordination, 356–357
   adjudicators in, 365–366
   through informal social systems and
      culture, 363–365
   through management information
      system, 362–363
   through management processes or
      systems, 361–362
   through organization structure
      or management hierarchy,
      358–361
   through selection and promotion,
      365
   total system and, 367
   unified holistic strategy for,
      357–358
International Women's Forum, 116

Interpersonal conflict. *See* Conflict,
      interpersonal
Interpersonal roles, 19
   figurehead, 19–20
   leader, 20
   liaison, 20–21
Intrinsic rewards, 476
Involvement, change resistance over-
      come by, 401, 405
Issues, substantive vs. emotional, 217
ITT Corp., 375

Jacobson, Lenore, 182n, 186n
James, William, 95, 95n
Jay, Antony, 72, 77
Job design, 176
   work-force strategies and, 492
Job enlargement, 167
Job enrichment, 167, 173–174,
      176–178
   steps, 170–173
   successful experiment in, 168–170
Job evaluation, 480–481
Job loading, 167–168, 172
Job participation. *See* Participation
Job rotation, at Semco, 76
Job satisfaction
   family issues and, 531
   motivation vs. hygiene, 164
Job security, at Semco, 76
Job sharing
   for career-and-family women, 524
   outside activities and, 468
Johnson, George, 186
Johnson & Johnson, 112, 540, 541
Jones, Reginald, 449

Kay, Emanuel, 203n
Kearns, David T., 512
Kelsey-Hayes, 550
Kennedy, John F., 91–92
Kets de Vries, Manfred F. R., 97n,
      396n
Kettering, Charles, 90
Kimberly-Clark Corp., 550
KITA, as motivator, 159–164, 174–175
Kotter, John P., 227n, 404n, 406n

Labor force, demographic change and, 519–520, 530

Labor-management relations, workforce strategies and, 493, 496–497

Land, Edwin, 89

Language, in group culture, 254–255

Lawler, Edward E. III, 196n, 199, 200n, 475n, 483n

Lawrence, Paul R., 270, 270n, 359n, 399n, 405n, 407n, 474n

Leader role, 20

Leaders, group norms and, 253

Leadership, 85, 126–127

  command-and-control type, 125

  creating culture of, 111–114

  deciding on pattern of, 132–136

  democracy vs. authority in, 127–128, 132

  development, 96–100

  followers and, 143–153

  in GE value statement, 442

  group process and, 282

  human needs and, 110

  insight and, 137

  interactive, 118–122, 123, 124–125

  key questions, 130–132

  long-run strategy and, 136–137

  need for, 102

  range of behavior in, 128–130

  social changes and, 138–141

  vs. technical ability (Semco), 74

  transformational, 117, 125

  by women, 115–125; *see also* Women managers

Leadership crisis, 416–417

Leadership-management differences, 102–104

  alignment of people vs. organizing or staffing, 105–109

  in attitudes toward goals, 88–89

  direction-setting vs. planning, 103, 104–105

  motivating vs. control or problem solving, 109–111

  in personality, 86–88

  relations with others, 92–95

  senses of self, 95–96

  in work conceptions, 89–92

Learning

  cognitive vs. skills, 29

  as motivational tool, 67–68

Levine, J. D., 198n

Levinson, Daniel J., 25n

Levitt, Theodore, 86, 86n

Liaison role, 20–21

LiCari, Jerome, 149

Life Insurance Agency Management Association, 189

Lifetime employment, Welch on, 441

Livingston, J. Sterling, 29n

Lorsch, Jay W., 270, 270n, 359n, 407n

Loyalty, Welch on, 441

Luke, Robert A., Jr., 396n

McAllister, Daniel, 116

McCall, Morgan W., 195n

McClelland, David, 48n, 185

McDonald's Corp., 340

Machine bureaucracy, 333, 337–340

  external control and, 340, 349

McWhinney, Will, 140

Maier, Norman R. F., 205, 205n, 207n, 263n, 280, 280n

Maintenance functions, group process and, 286–287

Make-or-buy decision

  on human resources, 460

  simple structure and, 336

Maljers, Floris, 375

Management by Objectives (MBO), 196, 203

Management hierarchy, interfunctional coordination and, 358–361

Management information system (MIS), 16, 362–363

Management-leadership differences. *See* Leadership-management differences

Management processes and systems, 361–362

Management time, 50. *See also* Subordinate-imposed time

Management training. *See* Training

Managerial culture, 86

Managerial expectations. *See* Expectations by managers

Managerial style, 329–330
  in growth phases, 422
Managerial work, 13–14
  change in, 57–62; *see also* New managerial work
  decisional roles in, 23–24
  description of, 19
  folklore vs. fact, 14–19
  ignorance, 13–14, 31
  informational roles, 21–22
  integration of roles, 25
  interpersonal roles, 19–21
  issues in effectiveness of, 25–28
  managers vs. leaders and, 89–92; *see also* Leadership-management differences
  two faces of, 30–31
Managers
  development and training, 29, 376–379
  expectations of, 179–194
  regular duties, 15–16
  vs. technical experts (Semco), 74
  Welch on, 433
Managing your boss, 227–229
  boss's world, 230–232
  developing relationship, 234–238
  misreading boss-subordinate relationship, 229–230
  own needs and, 232–234
Manipulation, change resistance overcome by, 403–404, 405
Manipulation of environment, 43, 45–46
Mannheim, Bilha F., 349n
Maps, in group culture, 255–256
Marrow, Alfred J., 401n
Massarik, Fred, 132n
Maternity, women managers and, 517–518
Maternity leave, 526
Matrix management, 360, 371, 372, 380
Matsushita, 377
Matsushita, Konosuke, 374, 377
Mechlin, Ellen, 143n
Mechlin, Stuart, 143n
Meetings
  conducting, 293–297
  preparing for, 290–293
Membership, in group process, 284–285

Mentors, 98–99
  diversity and, 511–512
Merck & Co., Inc., 531, 540
Merit Corp. case, 241–243, 244–246, 249–252, 256, 259–261
Messages, vs. signals, 94
Metropolitan Life Insurance Co., 189
Meyer, Herbert Henry, 203n, 207n
Miles, Robert H., 396n
Miller, Christopher S., 485n
Miller, Danny, 351, 351n
Millman, R. W., 411n
Mills, D. Quinn, 474n
Minorities, affirmative action and, 500
Mintzberg, Henry, 14n, 28n, 36n
MIS (management information system), 16, 362–363
Mission, as motivational tool, 67
Mixed-model interview, 207–211
Mobil Oil, 539
Models
  mental, 17
  as specialists, 28
Moll, Albert, 181–182
Monitor role, 22
Monkey-on-the-back analogy, 51–56
Moore, Leo, 130n
Motivation
  conditions necessary for, 475–476
  vs. control, 109–110
  employee (organization design), 321
  expectancy and, 184, 185
  in high-producing group, 180
  vs. hygiene, 164–166, 173
  through job enrichment, 167, 168–174, 176–178
  KITA as, 159–164, 174–175
  through leadership, 104; *see also* Leadership
  vs. movement, 174
  myths, 161–164
  new managerial work and, 66–69
  at Procter & Gamble, 112–113
  rewards and, 475–476
  snake-oil speculation on, 159
  by women managers, 122
Mouton, Jane S., 221n, 270n
Multicultural Participation Council (Avon), 501

Nanus, Burt, 192, 193
National Film Board of Canada, 347
NCNB, 534, 536, 541
NEC, 377
Needs
  biological vs. psychological, 164
  leadership as satisfying, 110
Negative physical KITA, 160
Negative psychological KITA, 160
Negotiation, change resistance overcome by, 402–403, 405
Negotiator role, 24
Networks. *See also* Informal relationships
  coordination through, 110–111
  new managerial work and, 63, 65
Neustadt, Richard E., 17, 17n, 22, 22n, 41n
Newberry, John F., 349n
New managerial work, 57–62
  motivation sources and, 66–69
  power bases and, 62–66
New-venture teams, 65
New York Stock Exchange, "People and Productivity" study by, 456
Nicolosi, Richard, 112–113
Nielsen, Eric H., 279n
Nierenberg, Gerald I., 403n
Nonexempt employees, 478
Nontraditional leadership style, 124
Nonverbal cues, in group process, 285
Nordin, Janet, 143n
Nordstrom's, 152
Norms
  confronting, 269
  in group culture, 252–253, 265
North American Philips Corp. (NAP), 375, 379–380
Northern Pacific Railroad, 546

Oberlander, Alfred, 180, 189, 189n
Obligation
  managerial effectiveness and, 28
  power and, 38–39, 43, 47
One Enterprise program (American Express), 58
One-to-one relationships, 100
Open-system theory, 139

Operating adhocracy, 345–346, 347
Operating systems, as group design factor, 248–249
Opinion seeking, in group process, 286
Order-fulfillment system, integrated, 363
Organizational change. *See* Change
Organizational circle, 73
Organizational growth. *See* Growth, organizational
Organizational psychology, 372, 373
  co-opting and, 379–380
  human resource development and, 376–379
  shared vision and, 373–376
Organizational pyramid, 73
Organizational structure
  for followership encouragement, 151–153
  as group design factor, 248–249
  in growth phases, 422
  interfunctional coordination and, 358–361
  and organizational psychology, 372–373
  at Semco, 77
  strategic requirements, 370–371
  work-force strategies and, 492
Organizational theory, personnel management and, 166–167
Organization design, 313
  coherence, 332
  company culture and, 330
  consistency, 348–349, 351
  contingency approach to, 315–321
  external controls and, 349–350
  in functional units, 321–324
  goals, 314
  historical perspective on, 314
  hived-off parts in, 350
  managerial style and, 329–330
  single businesses and, 324–328
  and situation, 350–351
Organization design configurations, 332–336, 338–339
  adhocracy, 334, 338–339, 344–347
  as diagnostic tool, 347–348
  divisionalized form, 334, 338–339, 342–344

machine bureaucracy, 333, 337–340, 349

professional bureaucracy, 333, 338–339, 340–341, 346

simple structure, 333, 336–337, 338

Organizations

conservatism of, 85–86

leadership development and, 99–100

Organizing, 103–104

actual managerial work and, 13

vs. aligning, 106

Outplacement counseling, 468

Overreaching, commitment strategy and, 498

Parental leave, 526, 531

Participation. *See also* Employee involvement

change and, 401, 405, 427

in group process, 280–282

in interactive leadership, 118–120

motivation and, 163

in reward systems, 476

Part-time employment

family concerns and, 524, 538

outside activities and, 468

Patricof, Alan, Associates, 119

Payne, Ted, 512

Pay for performance, 483–486

Payroll stratification, 477–478

Peer training, 99

Peiperl, Maury A., 468n

People, as group design factor, 247

People planning, 449–462. *See also* Human resources

Performance appraisal or evaluation, 195–196

ambivalence and avoidance, 199–200

appraisal interview and, 196, 204–211

appraisal system, 196, 203–204

combined avoidance and defensiveness in, 201

diversity and, 512–513

factors influencing outcomes, 202

feedback and defensiveness, 201

for followership, 151

goals, 196–199

nonevaluative evaluation as dilemma, 202

overall supervisor-subordinate relations and, 204

Performance control systems, 342–343

Personal relations

change and, 429

managers vs. leaders, 92–95

Personnel management, general philosophies of, 166–167. *See also* Human resources management

Person/skill evaluation, 481–482

Persuasion, 36, 43

Peters, Tom, 31, 426n

Pettigrew, T. F., 198n

Philips Industries, N.V., 99, 374, 375, 377, 379

Philips, J., 426n

Phillips, Deborah, 533n

Phillips Petroleum Company, 550

Piece-rate incentive systems, 483–484

Pierce, Jon L., 537n

Placebo effect, 182

Planning, 103

actual managerial work and, 13, 14–15

as configuration element, 338

for human resources, 449–462

vs. setting direction, 104, 105

Planning dilemma, 28

Pleck, Joseph, 531n

Polaroid, 89

Pondy, Louis R., 221n

Pooled integration, 318

Porter, Lyman W., 196n, 199, 200n

Positive KITA, 160–161

Postentrepreneurial corporation, 57, 62–69

Post-industrial Age, 382

Power, 33–34

belief in manager's expertise and, 39, 43, 44

change and, 428, 430

as configuration element, 339

dependence and, 36–38

through identification with manager, 40

influencing others through, 42

investing of, 48

Power (continued)
  new managerial work and, 58, 62–66
  perceived dependence on manager
      and, 40–42, 43, 44–45
  sense of obligation and, 38–39, 43
  use of, 47–48
  women managers as sharing, 120–121
Pratt, Edmund, 518
Predictability, leadership pattern and,
    133
Prejudice, decline of, 500
Presidents, U.S., information-collecting
    habits, 17, 21–22
Pressures, in boss's world, 230–231
Privileged information, sharing, 26
Problem-solving
  in group conflict resolution, 271–272,
      273
  by groups, 264–269, 276–277
  interview, 206–207
  managers vs. leaders, 109
  manager's presence and, 131, 277
  meetings and, 290, 294
Process observation, group process
    and, 287
Procter & Gamble Co., 65, 112–113, 376,
    479, 482, 490, 509
Productivity
  expectancy and, 181
  vs. time at work, 539
Professional bureaucracy, 333, 338–339,
    340–341
  operating adhocracy and, 346
Professions, management and, 18
Profit sharing, 485
  at Semco, 71, 77–78, 80
Promotion of employees, 466–467
  diversity and, 511–512
  family life and, 536
  interfunctional coordination through,
      365
Psychological saturation, 420
Psychology, organizational. *See*
    Organizational psychology
Pugh, D. S., 349n
Pygmalion (Shaw), 179
Pygmalion effect, 192–193
Pyramid, organizational, 73

Quality circles, 497
Quality-of-work-life (QWL), 138, 177
  commitment strategy and, 490
  at GM, 497

Raven, Bertram, 38n
Raytheon Co., New Products Center,
    63
Reagan administration, drug abuse
    and, 550
Reagan, Nancy, 544
Reciprocal integration, 318
Recruitment, 465–466
  affirmative action and, 500
  of managers, 376
Red-tape crisis, 419
Reflective structure, 420
Reimann, Bernard C., 349n
Relations, personal. *See* Personal
    relations
Representatives, department, 274–276
Reputation, as motivator, 68
Resource allocator role, 24
Resource and referral services (R&Rs),
    534
Resources
  affecting perceptions of, 41–42
  finding and acquiring, 40–41
  in managing your boss, 237–238
Responsibility, in groups, 265
Responsibility time span, 387–390
Retirement, phased, 468
Revolution, as growth period, 411,
    414
Rewards and reward systems
  change and, 429, 430
  compensation systems, 161, 476–486;
      see also Compensation systems
  employee satisfaction and, 474–475
  followership and, 152
  in GE value statement, 442
  in growth phases, 422
  motivation and, 475–476
  participation in, 476
Rituals, in group culture, 254–255
Rockefeller, John D. 3rd, 85–86, 86n
Rogers, Carl R., 206n

Roles, 254
  communications (task force), 307
  decisional, 23–24
  in group culture, 253–254
  informational, 21–22
  as integrated whole, 25
  integrating, 328
  interpersonal, 19–21
  responsibility time span of, 387–389
Rolscreen Co., 537
Roosevelt, Franklin, 22
Rosenthal, Robert, 182, 182n, 186n, 187
Rothman, Claire, 119, 121, 122
Ruh, Robert A., 197n, 203n
Rynd, Mary Jane, 119–120, 121–122

Salter, Malcolm S., 412n
Samuel, Yitzhak, 349n
San Diego Gas and Electric Co., 552
SAS Institute Inc., 534
Sather, Vijay, 406n
Satisfaction, employee, 474–475
Sayles, Leonard R., 23, 23n, 34n
Scandinavian Airline Systems (SAS),
    104–105
Scanlon Plan, 484, 485, 495
Schedules, alternate or flexible,
    524–525, 536, 537–538
Schein, Edgar H., 397n
Schein, Lawrence, 450n
Schlesinger, Leonard A., 406n
Schmidt, Warren H., 137n
Schuster, Michael H., 485n
Science, management and, 18
Scientific management, 489
Scott, Bruce R., 411n
Scott, Thomas A., 98
Seashore, Stanley E., 401n
Seckler, Howard, 143n
Second American Revolution, The
    (Rockefeller), 85
Security, of employment vs. employ-
    ability, 69
Security Pacific National Bank, 58
Selection of employees, 466
  interfunctional coordination through,
    365
Selection of managers, 376–377

Selection of subordinates, 189–190
Self, senses of, managers vs. leaders
    and, 95–96
Self-esteem, managers' effect on, 192,
    193
Self-image
  manager's effect on, 192, 193
  productivity and, 181
Self-imposed time, 50
Self-interest, change and, 396–397, 427
Self-management, followership and,
    146–147
Self-worth, woman managers as
    enhancing, 121–122
Semco, 70–80
Seniority, 483
  family concerns and, 540
Senior (top-level) managers
  alcoholism testing and, 546
  interfunctional coordination and,
    364–365, 366
  in leadership development, 113–114
  organizational tasks, 372
  organization design and, 330
Sensitivity training, motivation and,
    162
Sequential integration, 318
Shariq, Syed, 143n
Shaw, George Bernard, Pygmalion, 179
Signals, vs. messages, 94
Simple structure, 333, 336–337, 338
Single-business organizations, 324–328
Sloan, Alfred P., Jr., 88, 88n, 90, 342
SMILE (specialty, management ability,
    international flexibility, language
    facility, endeavor), 377
Smoothing, in group conflict resolution,
    270–271, 272, 273
Social changes, and leadership,
    138–141
Social consequences, and divisionalized
    form, 344
Socialization process
  leaders and, 96
  women managers and, 122, 123
Social systems, interfunctional coordina-
    tion and, 363–365
Sonnenfeld, Jeffrey A., 465n, 468n
Special consideration test, 514

Specialization
  as configuration element, 338
  integration and, 359
Spector, Bert, 474n
Spokesperson role, 22
Sponsorship, diversity and, 511–512
Stability, leadership pattern and, 133
Staffing, 103–104, 106
Staffs
  interdepartmental coordination and, 366
  Welch on, 435
Stakeholders, commitment strategy and, 491
Starbuck, William H., 411n, 412n
Stephens, Gregory, 116
Stewart, Rosemary, 15n, 16n, 20, 34n
Stopford, John M., 412n
Stories, in group culture, 254–255
Strategic choice, and career systems, 471–472
Strategy, 315
  leadership pattern and, 136–137
  organizational structure and, 370, 371–372, 380
Strategy document, 357–358
Stress, family issues and, 531
Structure, formal, 372
Style, in relationship with boss, 231–232, 234–236
Subordinate-imposed time, 50–51
  monkey-on-the-back analogy and, 51–56
Subordinates
  firing, 467–468
  as followers, 143–153
  generation gap and, 191
  GE Work-Out program and, 439
  leader role of managers and, 20
  managers' influence on, 313
  managing of boss by, 227–238
  selection of, 189-190
Substance abuse, 543, 545–546. *See also* Alcoholism; Drug abuse
Substantive issues, 217
Succession planning, 455–456
Summarizing, in group process, 286
Superficiality, managerial work and, 27, 31

Supervisors
  in commitment strategy, 496
  drug-abuse measures and, 545, 546–547, 550, 551
Supply flow (human resources), 468, 469
Support, change resistance overcome by, 402, 405
Sweeney, James, 186
System-imposed time, 50
System Service Enterprises, 119

Tannenbaum, Robert, 132n
Task, 315
Task forces, 298–299
  first meeting of, 303–305
  project completion and, 307–308
  running of, 305–307
  start-up activities, 299–303
Task functions, in group process, 286
Task requirements, as group design factor, 247–248
Taylor, Frederick W., 489
Team destroyers, 365
Team management, problems of, 25
Technical ladders, 481
Technology, commitment strategy and, 495
Teknowledge, Inc., 65
Teleconferencing, 363
Tell-and-listen interview, 205–206
Tell–and–sell method in appraisal interview, 205
Termination of employment, 467–468
Thompson, James D., 318, 318n, 319
3M Co. (Minnesota Mining & Mfg. Co.), 112
Time pressure
  leadership pattern and, 136
  managing your boss and, 237–238
Time span, responsibility, 387–390
Top-level managers. *See* Senior managers
Total information system, 16
Training, 467
  for followership, 150–151
  of managers, 29, 76, 377–378
Trani, John, 444, 445

Transformational leadership, 117, 125

Transitional stage in work-force management, 492–493, 497–498

Travelers Insurance Co., 535

Travel Related Services (TRS) arm of American Express, 106–107

Trowbridge, Chuck, 108–109

Trust, change and, 398

TRW Inc., 479

Turner, C., 349n

Uncertainty
  group problem-solving and, 266–267
  leadership pattern and, 133

Unilever, 375, 377–379

Union-management relations. See Labor-management relations

United Airlines, 549

Upward appraisal, 204

Urwick, Lyndall, 314

Valence effect, 280

Value creation, sharing of, 67

Value statement, GE, 442

Value system, leadership continuum and, 132–133

Valuing Differences program (DEC), 506

Varieties of Religious Experience, The (James), 95

Vertical job loading, 167, 168, 172

Vietnam War, leadership excess and, 92

Viteles, Morris S., 137n

Voice mail, 363

Wages, motivation and, 161. See also Compensation system

Walters, R. W., Jr., 190

Walton, C. Lee, Jr., 395n

Walton, Richard, 221n, 474n

Warner-Lambert Co., 540

Waterman, Robert, 31, 426n

Watson, Goodwin, 399n

Watson, Thomas, 76

Weber, Max, 38n

Weekly balancing, 537

Welch, John F., Jr., 432–445, 458–459, 459n

Wetlaufer, Suzanne, 365n

WGBH, 305

Whitebook, Marcy, 533n

Whyte, William F., 21n

Win-win situation, 93–94

Women. See also Diversity, managing of
  affirmative action and, 500; see also Affirmative action
  family and, 530–531; see also Family and business
  work-plus-home burden, 535–536

Women managers, 115–118, 124–125, 516–527
  career-primary vs. career-and-family, 519, 520–523
  child care and, 525
  flexible scheduling and, 524–525
  interactive leadership by, 118–122, 123, 124–125
  maternity and, 517–518
  as part-time workers, 538
  in paths of least resistance, 122–123
  societal issues concerning, 527

Work, division of, 322

Work ethic, decline of, 177

Work-force democracy. See Employee involvement; Participation

Work-force management, 487–498
  commitment strategy in, 490–497, 498
  control strategy in, 489–490, 492–493
  transitional stage in, 492–493, 497–498

Work groups. See Groups, work

Working conditions
  alternate or flexible schedules, 524–525, 536, 537–538
  employee involvement in, 72–75, 490; see also Participation
  family concerns and, 535–539
  job enrichment, 167, 168–174, 176–178
  quality-of-work-life (QWL), 138, 177, 490, 497
  at Semco, 75–76
  three philosophies of, 166–167

Work-Out (GE program), 438–440, 443, 444–445

Work schedules, alternate or flexible, 524–525, 536, 537–538
Work style, in relationship with boss, 231–232, 234–236
Work time, motivation and, 161
Worthing, Marcia, 501
Wrapp, H. Edward, 17n
Wrigley, Leonard, 342n, 343n

Xerox Corp., 512

Youth revolution, leadership pattern and, 138

Zaleznik, Abraham, 25n, 92n, 97n, 396n
Zaltman, Gerald, 400n, 402n
Zandler, Alvin, 38n, 201n
Zimmerle, Alan, 506

Presidents of the United States

1789–1797	1. George Washington	none
1797–1801	2. John Adams	Federalist
1801–1809	3. Thomas Jefferson	Democratic-Republican
1809–1817	4. James Madison	Democratic-Republican
1817–1825	5. James Monroe	Democratic-Republican
1825–1829	6. John Quincy Adams	Democratic-Republican
1829–1837	7. Andrew Jackson	Democratic
1837–1841	8. Martin Van Buren	Democratic
1841	9. William Henry Harrison	Whig
1841–1845	10. John Tyler	Whig
1845–1849	11. James K. Polk	Democratic
1849–1850	12. Zachary Taylor	Whig
1850–1853	13. Millard Fillmore	Whig
1853–1857	14. Franklin Pierce	Democratic
1857–1861	15. James Buchanan	Democratic
1861–1865	16. Abraham Lincoln	Republican/Union
1865–1869	17. Andrew Johnson	Union
1869–1877	18. Ulysses S. Grant	Republican
1877–1881	19. Rutherford B. Hayes	Republican
1881	20. James A. Garfield	Republican
1881–1885	21. Chester A. Arthur	Republican
1885–1889	22. Grover Cleveland	Democratic
1889–1893	23. Benjamin Harrison	Republican
1893–1897	24. Grover Cleveland	Democratic
1897–1901	25. William McKinley	Republican
1901–1909	26. Theodore Roosevelt	Republican
1909–1913	27. William Howard Taft	Republican
1913–1921	28. Woodrow Wilson	Democratic
1921–1923	29. Warren G. Harding	Republican
1923–1929	30. Calvin Coolidge	Republican
1929–1933	31. Herbert Hoover	Republican
1933–1945	32. Franklin Delano Roosevelt	Democratic
1945–1953	33. Harry S. Truman	Democratic
1953–1961	34. Dwight D. Eisenhower	Republican
1961–1963	35. John F. Kennedy	Democratic
1963–1969	36. Lyndon B. Johnson	Democratic
1969–1974	37. Richard M. Nixon	Republican
1974–1977	38. Gerald Ford	Republican
1977–1981	39. James E. Carter	Democratic
1981–1989	40. Ronald Reagan	Republican
1989–1993	41. George H. W. Bush	Republican
1993–2001	42. William J. Clinton	Democratic
2001–2009	43. George W. Bush	Republican
2009–2017	44. Barack Obama	Democratic
2017–2021	45. Donald Trump	Republican
2021–	46. Joseph R. Biden	Democratic

BVT Publishing

Publisher and Managing Director: Richard Schofield
Production and Fulfillment Manager: Janai Escobedo
Textbook Specialist: Christina Davies

Front Cover Image: "The Spirit of '76" by Archibald Willard; Public Domain

eBookPlus ISBN: 978-1-5178-1217-1
Soft Cover ISBN: 978-1-5178-1216-4

Understanding
American Politics

Seventh Edition

Robert J. Bresler
Pennsylvania State University

Robert J. Friedrich
Franklin and Marshall College

Joseph J. Karlesky
Franklin and Marshall College

D. Grier Stephenson Jr.
Franklin and Marshall College

Charles C. Turner
California State University, Chico

(Getty Images)

Brief Contents

Chapter 01
The Constitution of the United States   3

Chapter 02
Federalism: States in the Union   33

Chapter 03
Civil Liberties & Civil Rights   63

Chapter 04
Political Ideologies   105

Chapter 05
Public Opinion & Political Participation   131

Chapter 06
Politics & the Media   163

Chapter 07
Interest Groups & Political Parties   199

Chapter 08
Campaigns & Elections   237

Chapter 09
Congress   275

Chapter 10
The Presidency   307

Chapter 11
Bureaucracies   347

Chapter 12
The Supreme Court & American Judiciary   379

Chapter 13
Government & Public Policy   407

Chapter 14
Public Policy & Economics   427

Chapter 15
Domestic Policy   453

Chapter 16
Foreign Policy   485

Table of Contents

Preface   **xvii**

Introduction   **xxvii**

Chapter 01

The Constitution of the United States   3

1.1	**What Is a Constitution?**	**4**
	1.1a	Constitutionalism
	1.1b	Constitutional Functions
1.2	**The Road to Nationhood**	**5**
	1.2a	The Declaration of Independence: The Idea of Consent
	1.2b	The Articles of Confederation: The Idea of Compact
1.3	**The Making of the Constitution**	**9**
	1.3a	Prelude to Philadelphia
	1.3b	The Philadelphia Convention
	1.3c	Ratification
1.4	**Features of the Constitution**	**16**
	1.4a	Republicanism, Divided Powers, and Federalism
	1.4b	A Single and Independent Executive
	1.4c	Adaptability
	1.4d	Amendment of the Constitution
1.5	**Judicial Review Comes to the Supreme Court**	**24**
	1.5a	*Marbury v. Madison:* The Case of the Undelivered Commissions
	1.5b	The Significance of *Marbury*
	1.5c	Judicial Review and the Framers

Chapter 02

Federalism: States in the Union   33

2.1	**The Idea of Federalism**	**34**
	2.1a	Confederate, Unitary, and Federal Forms of Government
	2.1b	Unity and Diversity in the Federal System
	2.1c	A Comparative Perspective on Federalism
2.2	**States in the Constitutional System**	**38**
	2.2a	The Rise of the National Government
	2.2b	Express and Implied Powers
	2.2c	Reserved Powers: What Do the States Do?
	2.2d	Local Government: A Political Landscape of Contrasts

2.3   Government Relationships in the Federal System   48
        2.3a   Models of Federalism
        2.3b   Legal Relationships
        2.3c   Fiscal Relationships
        2.3d   Political Relationships

2.4   **Federalism Today**   56

Chapter 03
Civil Liberties & Civil Rights   63

3.1   **The Bill of Rights: Securing the Blessings of Liberty**   64
        3.1a   Applying the Bill of Rights to the States
        3.1b   The Fragility of Civil Liberties

3.2   **Free Expression: Speech, Press, and Assembly**   66
        3.2a   The Value of Free Expression
        3.2b   The Test of Freedom
        3.2c   Gags
        3.2d   Obscenity and Libel
        3.2e   Freedom of Assembly and Symbolic Speech

3.3   **Religious Freedom**   70
        3.3a   Religion and the Constitution
        3.3b   Aid to Sectarian Schools
        3.3c   Prayer in Public Schools
        3.3d   Religious Observances in Official Settings
        3.3e   Free Exercise of Religion

3.4   **Fundamentals of American Criminal Justice**   74
        3.4a   Presumption of Innocence and Notice of Charges
        3.4b   Limits on Searches and Arrests
        3.4c   Assistance of Counsel and Protection Against Self-Incrimination
        3.4d   Limits on Punishment

3.5   **A Right to Privacy**   79
        3.5a   The Abortion Controversy
        3.5b   Personal Autonomy, Sexual Orientation, and LGBT Rights

3.6   **Racial Equality**   83
        3.6a   Equality: A Concept in Dispute
        3.6b   The Legacy: Slavery and Third-Class Citizenship
        3.6c   The Counterattack
        3.6d   Putting *Brown* to Work: The Law and Politics of Integration
        3.6e   The Continuing Effects of *Brown*
        3.6f   Affirmative Action
        3.6g   Voting Rights

3.7   **Sexual Equality**   92
        3.7a   The Legacy
        3.7b   Gender to the Forefront

3.8   Other Americans and Civil Rights   93
        3.8a   American Indians
        3.8b   Latinx
        3.8c   Immigrants
        3.8d   Americans with Disabilities

3.9   Liberties and Rights in the Constitutional Framework   96

Chapter 04

Political Ideologies   105

4.1   American Political Ideologies   106

4.2   Liberalism   107
        4.2a   Classical Liberalism: Thomas Jefferson and Andrew Jackson
        4.2b   Populism and Progressivism: The Repudiation of Classical Liberalism
        4.2c   Contemporary Liberalism: The Welfare State and Beyond
        4.2d   Neoliberalism: Adjusting Liberalism to the Twenty-First Century

4.3   Conservatism   114
        4.3a   Early American Conservatism: John Adams
        4.3b   Conservatism and the Industrial Age: Herbert Spencer and William
                Graham Sumner
        4.3c   Contemporary Conservatism: A Response to the Welfare State
        4.3d   Neoconservatism in the Twenty-First Century

4.4   Ideological Challenges to the Status Quo   121
        4.4a   Democratic Socialism: A Radical Challenge to American Capitalism
        4.4b   Libertarianism: A Revival of Classical Liberalism

Chapter 05

Public Opinion & Political Participation   131

5.1   Public Opinion: What Americans Think About Politics   132
        5.1a   The Character of Public Opinion
        5.1b   How Much Americans Care and Know About Politics
        5.1c   What Americans Hold in Common
        5.1d   Where Americans Differ

5.2   The Sources of Public Opinion: Political Socialization   143
        5.2a   The Processes of Political Socialization
        5.2b   The Agents of Political Socialization
        5.2c   The Development of a Political Self
        5.2d   Diversity in Socialization

5.3   Political Participation   149
        5.3a   Motives for Political Participation
        5.3b   Forms of Participation
        5.3c   Differences in Participation
        5.3d   The Impact of Political Participation
        5.3e   The Rationality of Political Participation

Chapter 06

Politics & the Media — 163

6.1   The "Fifth Branch" — 164

6.1a   The Dynamics of an Industry

6.1b   The Constitutional Basis of the Press

6.1c   The Federal Communications Commission

6.1d   The Equal-Time Rule

6.1e   The Fairness Doctrine

6.1f   Regulating the Internet

6.2   Politics and the Press — 177

6.2a   Direct Communication: The Media as Vehicles

6.2b   Political Knowledge and Attitudes: The Media as Gatekeepers

6.2c   Issue Making and Issue Reporting: The Media as Spotlights

6.2d   Candidates and Campaigns: The Media as Talent Scouts

6.2e   Believability

6.3   Tools of the Trade: Politicians and the "Fifth Branch" — 181

6.3a   Access

6.3b   Public Announcements

6.3c   Other Media Events

6.3d   A Right to Know?

6.4   Are the Media Biased? — 184

6.4a   The Journalists

6.4b   Deciding What Becomes News

6.4c   Deciding How the News Appears

6.4d   The Impact of the Visual

6.4e   A Public Trust

Chapter 07

Interest Groups & Political Parties — 199

7.1   Interest Groups in American Politics — 200

7.1a   Characteristics of Interest Groups

7.1b   What Interest Groups Do

7.1c   Major Interest Groups

7.2   Perspectives on Interest Groups — 212

7.2a   Interest Groups as the Foundation of Democracy

7.2b   Interest Groups Versus the Public Interest

7.2c   Interest Group Gridlock

7.3   Political Parties — 214

7.3a   What Parties Do

7.4   Basic Characteristics of the American Party System — 217

7.4a   A Two-Party System

7.4b   A Complex Party Structure

7.5   **American Political Parties: Past, Present, and Future**   223

     7.5a   Parties Past

     7.5b   Parties Present

     7.5c   Parties Future

Chapter 08

Campaigns & Elections   237

8.1   **The Voter's Perspective: To Vote or Not to Vote**   238

     8.1a   Voting Requirements and Eligibility

     8.1b   Who Votes?

     8.1c   Declining Turnout

8.2   **The Voter's Perspective: How to Vote**   245

     8.2a   Parties

     8.2b   Candidates

     8.2c   Issues

8.3   **The Candidate's Perspective: Running for President**   249

     8.3a   Who Runs for President?

     8.3b   The Media Campaign

     8.3c   Campaign Finance

     8.3d   Getting Nominated

     8.3e   The Electoral College

     8.3f   Campaign Strategies

8.4   **The Candidate's Perspective: Running for Congress**   264

     8.4a   Campaign Finance

     8.4b   Incumbency

     8.4c   Parties, Candidates, and Issues

Chapter 09

Congress   275

9.1   **The Constitutional Powers of Congress**   276

9.2   **The Members of Congress**   278

     9.2a   Who Are They?

     9.2b   How Do They See Their Roles?

     9.2c   How Long Do They Stay?

     9.2d   How Much Do They Do?

     9.2e   What Do They Do?

     9.2f   How Do They See Each Other?

9.3   **The Structure of Congress**   284

     9.3a   Party Leadership: The House

     9.3b   Party Leadership: The Senate

     9.3c   The Committee System

     9.3d   Subcommittees

     9.3e   Congressional Staff and Agencies

9.4 **Congressional Procedures: How a Bill Becomes a Law**   293

    9.4a   Committee to Floor Debate

    9.4b   Floor Debate: The House

    9.4c   Floor Debate: The Senate

    9.4d   The Conference Committee: Resolving Senate-House Differences

9.5 **Congress and the Political System**   297

    9.5a   Lobbies

    9.5b   The Bureaucracy

9.6 **What Role for a Changing Congress?**   299

Chapter 10

The Presidency   307

10.1 **The President and Symbolic Leadership**   308

10.2 **The President and the Constitution**   311

    10.2a   Executive Power

    10.2b   The Power of Appointment

    10.2c   The Removal Power

    10.2d   The Power to Pardon

10.3 **The President and the Executive Branch**   315

    10.3a   The Cabinet

    10.3b   The White House Staff

    10.3c   The Executive Office of the President

    10.3d   The Vice President

    10.3e   Presidential Succession

10.4 **The President and Congress: Foreign Policy**   324

    10.4a   Negotiating Treaties

    10.4b   Executive Agreements

10.5 **The President and Congress: The War Power**   326

    10.5a   The Mexican and Civil Wars

    10.5b   The Two World Wars

    10.5c   The Cold War

    10.5d   The Vietnam Trauma

    10.5e   The War Powers Resolution

    10.5f   The Iraq War

10.6 **The President and Congress: Domestic Policy**   330

    10.6a   Legislative Skills

    10.6b   The Presidential Veto

    10.6c   Executive Privilege

    10.6d   Impeachment

    10.6e   The Clinton Impeachment

    10.6f   The Trump Impeachments

10.7 **The President and the Media**   339

    10.7a   Phases of the Relationship

    10.7b   The Imperial President Versus the Imperial Media

Chapter 11

Bureaucracies 347

11.1 **Bureaucracies as the Fourth Branch of Government** 348
11.1a Bureaucracies: Translating Ideas into Action
11.1b Who Are the Bureaucrats?
11.1c Distinguishing Characteristics of Bureaucracies

11.2 **Executive Branch Organization: Types of Bureaucracies** 352
11.2a The Executive Office of the President
11.2b Executive Departments
11.2c Independent Agencies
11.2d Independent Regulatory Commissions
11.2e Government Corporations

11.3 **The Search for Competence in the Civil Service** 355
11.3a The Spoils System
11.3b The Pendleton Act and the Merit Principle
11.3c The Civil Service Reform Act of 1978

11.4 **The Search for Bureaucratic Responsiveness: The Political Environment of Bureaucracies** 358
11.4a The President
11.4b Congress
11.4c The Case of the Veto
11.4d Interest Groups
11.4e The Courts

11.5 **Bureaucrats and Government Regulation** 362
11.5a Regulation in Perspective
11.5b Regulatory Agencies and Types of Regulations
11.5c The Regulatory Process
11.5d The Ebb and Flow of Regulatory Debate

11.6 **Bureaucracies: Targets and Mirrors of Conflict** 370

Chapter 12

The Supreme Court & American Judiciary 379

12.1 **The National Court System** 380
12.1a Cases: Raw Material for the Judiciary
12.1b Fifty-one Judicial Systems
12.1c State and Local Courts
12.1d United States District Courts
12.1e United States Courts of Appeals
12.1f Special Courts
12.1g The Supreme Court of the United States
12.1h Federal Judicial Selection

12.2 **What Courts Do** 389

    12.2a   Constitutional Interpretation

    12.2b   Statutory Interpretation

    12.2c   Fact Determination

    12.2d   Clarification of the Boundaries of Political Authority

    12.2e   Education and Value Application

    12.2f   Legitimization

12.3 **The Supreme Court at Work** 394

    12.3a   Petition for Review

    12.3b   Briefs on the Merits

    12.3c   Oral Argument

    12.3d   Conference and Decision

    12.3e   Assignment and Writing of Opinions

    12.3f   Law Clerks

12.4 **The Supreme Court and American Government: An Assessment** 398

    12.4a   Judicial Review and Democracy

    12.4b   Influences on Supreme Court Decision-Making

    12.4c   Checks on Judicial Power

Chapter 13

Government & Public Policy   407

13.1 **Public Policy in the Political Process** 407

    13.1a   Conflict Over the Ends of Government

    13.1b   Perspectives on Policy Making

    13.1c   Stages in the Policy Process

13.2 **The Purposes and Presence of the National Government** 419

    13.2a   Views of Public Policy

13.3 **Politics and Economic Self-Interest** 420

    13.3a   Categories of National Government Policies

Chapter 14

Public Policy & Economics   427

14.1 **Government and Economic Policy** 428

    14.1a   Basic Issues of Economic Policy

    14.1b   Fiscal and Monetary Policy

14.2 **The Deficit and the National Budget** 432

    14.2a   The Deficit as a Political Issue

    14.2b   Major Components of the National Budget

    14.2c   Mandatory Programs in the Budget

14.3   **The President and Congress in the Budgeting Process**   **439**

14.3a   The Stages of Budgeting

14.3b   The President in the Budget Process

14.3c   Congress and Budgeting

14.4   **The Search for Better Budget Procedures**   **444**

Chapter 15

Domestic Policy   453

15.1   **Debates Over Public Purposes**   **454**

15.1a   Social Welfare Policies

15.2   **The Development of Federal Social Welfare Policy**   **457**

15.2a   The Philosophy of Social Darwinism

15.2b   The Progressive Era

15.2c   The New Deal Policy Revolution

15.2d   Expansion of the National Role in the Great Society

15.3   **The National Government as Social Insurer**   **461**

15.3a   Social Security

15.3b   Medicare

15.3c   Unemployment Compensation

15.4   **Public Policy and Economic Inequality**   **466**

15.4a   Measures of Economic Inequality

15.4b   Poverty as a Political and Social Problem

15.4c   Temporary Assistance for Needy Families

15.4d   Supplemental Security Income

15.4e   Medicaid

15.4f   The Supplemental Nutrition Assistance Program

15.4g   Social Welfare Policy and Future Challenges

15.5   **Environmental Policy**   **475**

15.5a   Environmentalism on the Policy Agenda

15.5b   The Environmental Protection Agency and Government Regulation

15.5c   The Future of Environmental Policy

Chapter 16

Foreign Policy   485

16.1   **America's Role in the World**   **486**

16.1a   The Cold War and the Post–Cold War Era

16.2   **The Policy Machinery**   **492**

16.2a   Department of State

16.2b   Central Intelligence Agency

16.2c   Department of Defense

16.2d   The Role of Congress

16.3   **Domestic Policy and National Security**   **501**
     16.3a   Public Moods and Foreign Policy
     16.3b   Multinational Corporations and Banks
     16.3c   The Military-Industrial Complex

16.4   **Current Issues in Foreign and Defense Policy**   **505**
     16.4a   9/11 and the Ongoing War on Terrorism
     16.4b   International Organization and the Developing World

Appendix 01
The Declaration of Independence   513

Appendix 02
The Constitution of the United States   517

Appendix 03
Glossary   535

Appendix 04
Index   557

Appendix 05
Supplementary Materials   565

Preface

The need persists for widespread mastery of the political system John Quincy Adams once described as "the most complicated on the face of the globe." Adams was writing nearly two hundred years ago, and things certainly haven't become less complicated since then. In the early 2000s, we experienced a number of political complications, including several close and contentious presidential elections that geographically and ideologically divided our nation into "red" and "blue" states. We suffered a devastating terrorist attack on our own soil, plunging the nation into an open-ended and contentious "War on Terror." We went to war with Iraq for the second time in a dozen years. We saw the national economy reach great heights and disturbing lows, causing unemployment and recession in the private sector and a return of enormous deficit spending in the public sector. We began to recognize the need for significant changes to deal with persistent and systemic racial injustices. We faced a deadly pandemic that forced us to restructure many aspects of our lives. How do we make sense of all these ups and downs of economics, ideology, and politics? We think the best approach is to take seriously our understanding of the political system in which all of these events take place. To that end, we offer today's students a comprehensive, readable, and balanced study of the context, structure, and process of American politics.

(Getty Images)

"Always vote for principle, though you may vote alone, and you may cherish the sweetest reflection that your vote is never lost." *John Quincy Adams*

(Shutterstock)

Economics, Ideology, and Politics

A distinguishing feature of this book is the explicit recognition that economics and ideology significantly influence American politics. No student or instructor in a course on American government is immune to the ideological and economic forces that help shape the perennial pursuit of power in a democracy. Nor is any class or instructor untouched by recurring problems ranging from budget deficits and health care to unemployment and the underclass. Economics and ideology, in one way or another, intersect nearly all of them.

This text highlights, in several ways, the importance of economics and ideology in the context of American government. The chapter on public policy and economics explores the relationship between politics and economics, as does a series of "Politics and Economics" boxes (described later) found throughout the book. Students see how economic decisions have political consequences and how political decisions affect the economy. This is essential information in a day when economic topics frequently dominate electoral campaigns, television and internet news, and conversation both at the dinner table and via social media. However, the text assumes no prior knowledge of economics, and references to economic policy are free of confusing jargon.

Understanding differences among political beliefs is likewise essential at a time when the labels "liberal" and "conservative," "left" and "right" are hurled about. Such terms can be baffling, particularly because their meanings have not been consistent. Consequently, the text underscores the importance of political ideology—the ideas people have about what government should or should not do and what kind of government they should have. This emphasis is reflected in a series of "Politics and Ideas" boxes (described later) that appear throughout the text. The chapter on political ideologies is nearly unique among shorter volumes on American government because it draws a road map that guides students through intellectual debates, past and present, in American politics. Additionally, the chapter that deals with civil liberties and civil rights probes ideological distinctions among Americans concerning fundamental freedoms. Such an encompassing survey of the spectrum of political ideas encourages students both to comprehend and to tolerate points of view other than their own, enabling them to gain further insight into political differences that exist nationwide.

New to the Eleventh Edition

American politics is a constantly changing montage of people and events, of facts and opinions. To keep up with our changing environment, and to make sure students have the most up-to-date information available, each new edition of *Introduction to American Government* undergoes a vigorous process of fact-checking and updating. In this edition, for example, readers will find revised weblinks and readings for further study; more critical thinking questions; and discussions of the latest events in American government, such as the 2020 presidential election, the Trump presidency and impeachments, the recent racial justice movements, the Barrett Supreme Court nomination and important recent Court decisions, the government's response to wildfires and other disasters, and numerous discussions of the relationship between the US government and the COVID-19 pandemic. In addition, each chapter contains important new material and the most current available facts and figures.

Pedagogical Features

This textbook is not a "theme," or point-of-view, book. Aside from emphasizing the importance of politics and political involvement, the book embraces no single ideological perspective; it does not attempt to make readers Democrats or Republicans, liberals or conservatives. To ensure a single voice in this presentation, one author has served as general editor.

The goals are knowledge of and critical thinking about American politics and government. Accordingly, we have designed the book to encourage students to engage the material. Passive reading is not enough; understanding so important and complex a subject necessitates active intellectual involvement.

To aid in learning, this textbook incorporates several serviceable pedagogical features.

Chapter Objectives

Each chapter begins with a brief overview of topics to be covered. Reading the information provided in the chapter objectives cues students' critical thinking and analytical thought processes before they dig into the chapter itself.

e-Resources

Beyond the pages of this textbook lies a wealth of information about the American government concepts described here. Each chapter identifies online resources specific to the subject matter being presented. These resources offer students an opportunity to further explore topics from the text to gain an even more comprehensive experience.

Figures and Tables

Tables, graphs, and maps appear throughout the text to display both quantitative and conceptual data. Some illustrations present new data, while others summarize information covered in the body of the chapter.

Special Boxed Features

Politics and Ideas

These boxes, appearing throughout the text, explore ideological topics in depth. They demonstrate how ideological divisions generate different political consequences. The text includes the following Politics and Ideas boxes:

- Whose Constitution Is It?
- Changing State Constitutions
- Millennials, Gen Z, and Political Ideology
- Textbooks and Children's Ideas About American Politics
- Confidentiality of News Sources and Information
- Pluralism and Elitism
- Campaign and Electoral Reform: A Comparative Perspective
- Midterm Elections: Reflection and Change
- Two Ideologues Leave the House
- A Six-Year Term for Presidents?
- A "New Kind of War"—The Ongoing War on Terrorism
- Immigration Reform: Laws and Executive Orders
- The Politics of Judicial Vacancies
- Gun Violence: The Search for Solutions
- Political Ideologies and the Welfare State
- Contrasting Approaches to Foreign Policy: Idealism, Realism, and Isolationism
- Can Presidents Take the Country to War on Their Own Authority?

Politics and Economics

These boxes, appearing throughout the text, highlight special economics topics, illustrating the relationship between economics and politics. The text includes the following Politics and Economics boxes:

- Handling a Wildfire: Federalism and Disaster Relief
- Economic Status and Ideology
- Media Monopolies?
- Economic Status and Party Identification
- Regulation and Cost-Benefit Analysis
- The Supreme Court and Economic Policy
- The Road to a New Cabinet Department
- The President and Economic Policy Making
- The Ideology of Economic Policy
- Corporations and the Economy

Political Controversies

These boxes are present in several chapters to illustrate how the subject matter covered in the chapter carries over into disputes that divide the nation. The text includes the following Political Controversies boxes:

- America Responds: Government Action and COVID-19
- How Much Affirmative Action?
- Race and (In)Justice: Law Enforcement, Homicide, and Change
- Public Opinion and Terrorism: American Government in the Eyes of the World
- Can Political News Be Entertaining, Social, and Informative?
- Turnout, Choice, and Economic Status
- An Election Gone Wrong?
- Low Voter Turnout: A Comparative Perspective
- Congress Shows Several Members the Door
- Election 2020: A Presidential Election Breaks New Ground
- Donald Trump: An Unconventional President
- The Supreme Court and "Obamacare"
- Nuclear Power and the Environment
- The US vs. ISIS: A New Direction in the War on Terror?

Study Questions

Each special boxed feature includes study questions to encourage critical thinking and further inquiry.

End-of-Chapter Material

Each chapter concludes with a chapter review, a list of key terms, readings for further study, a list of sources used in the chapter, and a pop quiz.

- The chapter review contains, in numbered form, the main points presented in the chapter.
- Key terms are in boldface and are defined in the margins at the point at which they are introduced in the chapter.
- Readings for further study are widely available primary and secondary sources that students may consult in pursuing topics in the chapter.
- The pop quiz offers students an opportunity to do a quick check of their knowledge retention. Similar to questions found on a test, these quiz questions can help students see if they are on the right track or if there are elements of a chapter's content they need to review further.

Supplements and Resources

Instructor Supplements

A complete teaching package is available for instructors who adopt this book. This package includes an **online lab**, **instructor's manual**, **exam bank**, **PowerPoint™ slides**, **LMS Integration**, and **LMS exam bank files**.

Online Lab	BVT's online lab is available for this textbook on two different platforms—BVT*Lab* (at www.BVT*Lab*.com), and LAB BOOK™ (at www.BVTLabBook.com). These are described in more detail in the corresponding sections below. Both platforms allow instructors to set up graded homework, quizzes, and exams.
Instructor's Manual	The Instructor's Manual helps first-time instructors develop the course, while also offering seasoned instructors a new perspective on the materials. Each section of the Instructor's Manual coincides with a chapter in the textbook. The user-friendly format begins by providing a chapter summary, learning objectives, and detailed outlines for each chapter. Then, the manual presents lecture discussions, key terms, class activities, and sample answers to the end-of-chapter review questions. Lastly, additional resources—books, articles, websites, and videos—are listed to help instructors review the materials covered in each chapter.
Exam Bank	An extensive exam bank is available to instructors in both hard-copy and electronic form. Each chapter has approximately one hundred multiple-choice, twenty-five true/false, fifteen short-answer, and five essay questions ranked by difficulty and style. Each question is referenced to the appropriate section of the text to make test creation quick and easy.
PowerPoint Slides	A set of PowerPoint slides includes about thirty slides per chapter, including a chapter overview, learning objectives, slides covering all key topics, key figures and charts, and summary and conclusion slides.
LMS Integration	BVT offers basic integration with Learning Management Systems (LMSs), providing single-sign-on links (often called LTI links) from Blackboard, Canvas, Moodle (or any other LMS) directly into BVT*Lab*, eBook^Plus or the LAB BOOK platform. Gradebooks from BVT*Lab* and the LAB BOOK can be imported into most LMSs.
LMS Exam Bank Files	Exam banks are available as Blackboard files, QTI files (for Canvas), and Respondus files (for other LMSs) so they can easily be imported into a wide variety of course management systems.

Student Resources

Student resources are available for this textbook on both the BVT*Lab* platform and the LAB BOOK platform, as described below. These resources are geared toward students needing additional assistance, as well as those seeking complete mastery of the content. The following resources are available:

Practice Questions	Students can work through hundreds of practice questions online. Questions are multiple choice or true/false in format and are graded instantly for immediate feedback.
Flashcards	BVT*Lab* includes sets of flashcards that reinforce the key terms and concepts from each chapter.
PowerPoint Slides	For a study recap, students can view all of the instructor PowerPoint slides online.
Additional LAB BOOK Resources	On the LAB BOOK platform, comprehension questions are sprinkled throughout each chapter of the eBook, and detailed section summaries are included in the lab. Study tools such as text highlighting and margin notes are also available. These resources are not available in BVT*Lab*.

LAB BOOK

LAB BOOK is a web-based eBook platform with an integrated lab providing comprehension tools and interactive student resources. Instructors can build homework and quizzes right into the eBook. LAB BOOK is either included with eBOOK[Plus] or offered as a stand-alone product.

Course Setup	LAB BOOK uses the BVT*Lab* interface to allow instructors to set up their courses and grade books and to replicate them from section to section and semester to semester.
Grade Book	Using an assigned passcode, students register into their section's grade book, which automatically grades and records all homework, quizzes, and tests.
Advanced eBook	LAB BOOK is a mobile-friendly, web-based eBook platform designed for PCs, MACs, tablets and smartphones. LAB BOOK allows highlighting, margin notes and a host of other study tools.
Student Resources	All student resources for this textbook are available in the LAB BOOK, as described in the **Student Resources** section above.
Online Classes	A host of instructor resources and tools to support digital learning environments.

Customization

BVT's Custom Publishing Division can help you modify this book's content to satisfy your specific instructional needs. The following are examples of customization:

- Rearrangement of chapters to follow the order of your syllabus
- Deletion of chapters not covered in your course
- Addition of paragraphs, sections, or chapters you or your colleagues have written for this course
- Editing of the existing content, down to the word level
- Customization of the accompanying student resources and online lab
- Addition of handouts, lecture notes, syllabus, etc.
- Incorporation of student worksheets into the textbook

All of these customizations will be professionally typeset to produce a seamless textbook of the highest quality, with an updated table of contents and index to reflect the customized content.

About the Authors

Charles C. Turner

Charles C. Turner is a professor of political science at California State University, Chico. His PhD is from Claremont Graduate University. He has taught at Chico State since 2000 and has served as department chair and as president of the Chico chapter of the California Faculty Association. Turner's published research focuses on the political behavior of Congress and the Supreme Court, as well as on the scholarship of teaching and learning.

D. Grier Stephenson Jr.

Donald Grier Stephenson Jr. is a Charles A. Dana Professor of Government at Franklin & Marshall College. He is general editor of ABC-CLIO's *America's Freedoms Series,* author of *Campaigns and the Court: The U.S. Supreme Court in Presidential Elections,* and co-author of *American Constitutional Law,* 15th edition.

Robert J. Bresler

Robert J. Bresler received his AB degree from Earlham College and his PhD from Princeton University. He has taught at the University of Wisconsin–Green Bay, the University of Delaware, and Penn State University–Harrisburg, where he completed a thirty-two-year career. During his time at Penn State, Professor Bresler served for some years as the director of the School of Public Affairs. He has been a visiting professor at the U.S. Army War College and the Franklin & Marshall College and a Senior Fulbright Fellow at the National University of Singapore. He was the recipient of the James A. Jordan Award for Teaching Excellence and the Outstanding Civilian Award from the Department of the Army.

Professor Bresler is the National Affairs Editor of *USA Today: The Magazine of the American Scene,* where he writes a regular column on American politics. His books include *Us vs. Them: American Political and Cultural Conflict from WWII to Watergate* and *Freedom of Association: Civil Rights and Liberties Under the Law.* His articles have appeared in *Political Science Quarterly, Politics and Society, Bulletin of Atomic Scientists, Commonweal, Inquiry, The Nation, Intellect,* and *Telos.*

Robert J. Friedrich

Robert J. Friedrich is an associate professor in the Department of Government at Franklin & Marshall College, where he teaches courses in American government, public opinion and mass political behavior, political ideology, and research methods. His research interests are in electoral politics and electoral institutions, particularly the relationship between seats and votes in legislative elections, and in political values and ideology. He has reviewed manuscripts for the *American Political Science Review,* the *American Journal of Political Science,* and the *Journal of Politics,* for which he also served on the editorial board. Dr. Friedrich received his bachelor's degree from the University of Colorado and his master's and doctor of philosophy degrees from the University of Michigan.

Joseph J. Karlesky

Joseph J. Karlesky is the Honorable and Mrs. John C. Kunkel Professor of Government. He received his Bachelor's degree from La Salle College and his PhD in public law and government from Columbia University. He is co-author of *The State of Academic Science: The Universities in the Nation's Research Effort* and of *American Government,* an American government textbook. He has also authored the monograph "Thinking About Environmental Policy."

He has been a guest scholar at the Brookings Institution in Washington, DC, and has served as a consultant for the Commonwealth of Pennsylvania on home rule for municipalities and on academic science policy for the state of Montana. He has served as associate dean for academic affairs at Franklin & Marshall and as codirector of the University of Pennsylvania Master of Governmental Administration Program in Harrisburg.

His teaching and research interests focus on public policy, particularly the interrelationships between public policy and science and technology and the consequences of these interrelationships for policies in energy and health. He is currently doing research on decision-making models and dry cask storage of spent nuclear fuel. He regularly teaches courses in American government, understanding public policy, public policy implementation, and a seminar on health policy.

Acknowledgments

The authors would like to express their appreciation to the many individuals who have offered helpful suggestions and criticisms for previous editions of this text. An introductory American government book can never hope to cover every important topic, but many generous reviewers have helped us make sure that not too many crucial issues were left unexplored.

We would also like to acknowledge the fine team at BVT Publishing that has made this book possible. We are especially grateful to Richard Schofield and Janai Escobedo for managing this project and to Regina Roths for her diligent work as copy editor.

Finally, we would like to acknowledge our families, who have provided the inspiration and support necessary to see this project through to its completion. Specifically, we thank Jessica Bresler, Lin Carvell, and Jordan and Greg Rogoe; Rebecca, Philip, and Elizabeth Friedrich; Audrey, Christopher, and Matthew Karlesky; Ellen, Todd, and Claire Stephenson; and Wesley, Hudson, and Meghan Turner.

Charles C. Turner
D. Grier Stephenson Jr.
Robert J. Bresler
Robert J. Friedrich
Joseph J. Karlesky

(Shuttertock)

Introduction

This book is an introduction to American politics and government. Its objective is not to convince readers that a particular political position is "best." It does not celebrate the virtues of capitalism or socialism, the unfettered free market, or a government-guided economy. Nor does this book argue that taxes are too high or too low, abortion is right or wrong, social welfare policies are too generous or too stingy, or government is too big or too small. This book is not designed to create more liberals or conservatives or capitalists or socialists. Its task is to examine the American political system and to stimulate informed critical thinking about politics and government.

The two fundamental goals of this book are (1) to explain why understanding politics and government is crucial to being an engaged citizen in our complex society and (2) to clarify how the actions of politicians and the consequences of governmental decisions affect people's lives. The book highlights the importance of ideas and economic concerns in the resolution of political issues. Toward this end, every chapter contains one or more of the following special feature boxes: "Politics and Economics," "Politics and Ideas," and "Contemporary Controversies."

What Is Politics?

What exactly is politics? For many people the word evokes negative feelings. "It's just politics," people say when they don't like a decision that's been made or when a friend loses out on a promotion. The very mention of the word often conjures up a picture of a smooth-talking "wheeler-dealer" who uses cash to influence votes, or a corrupt office-holder who exploits his or her position for financial gain. However, politics is not all graft and kickbacks. Despite much of the current disillusionment with the political process, politics can be an honorable and noble profession. At its best, it is a moral activity reconciling social and economic differences and constructing a way of governing society without chaos, tyranny, or undue violence.[1]

The ancient Greek philosopher Aristotle once called politics the "master science." He did not mean that politics explained all the mysteries of human life and nature. Rather, Aristotle meant that politics provides the means by which a community of people with differing views and interests can strive for collective survival and advancement. The drama of the American Civil War illustrates the importance of politics as a means of resolving differences without resorting to violence. All societies inevitably have differences; the issue is how a society copes with those differences. In this sense, politics is better described as the "necessary science."

(Shutterrock)

Politics is better described as a "necessary science," as its purpose is to allow for a community of people with differing views and interests to strive for collective survival and advancement.

With over 330 million people, the United States of America is a diverse nation. Some people are white, and some are African American. Some Americans were born in other countries, and some have an American ancestry that dates back centuries. Some are religious fundamentalists and others liberal humanists. Some are young, paying Social Security taxes; and some are old, receiving Social Security benefits. Some earn high incomes, and others have little or no income at all. Some live in fashionable townhouses or suburbs, and others live in blighted inner cities or on declining farms. Some make their living in high-tech industries, and others in traditional smokestack industries.

The point need not be belabored. The US is a complex, multicultural society in which consensus is often difficult to achieve. Different groups want different things and have different values. Such differences are at the root of the political process. In its best-known and most straightforward definition, **politics** is the study of "who gets what, when, and how."[2] Put another way, politics is the process of peacefully reconciling social and economic differences.

Politics and Economics

Many of the conflicts that arise in a society—who has and who has not, who gives and who gets, who gains and who loses—are economic in their origins or their manifestations. Because money and material resources are limited and because human wants and demands are almost limitless, the need to make choices about spending money and using scarce resources becomes inevitable. Many government decisions are economic in nature because they affect the production, distribution, and consumption of wealth.

Even though our national government spends close to $4 trillion annually—and far more in years like 2020, when it faces threats such as recession and high unemployment—it still does not have enough capital to satisfy all the demands and expectations placed on it. Every year the president and Congress

Former President Franklin D. Roosevelt

(Courtesy of Library of Congress Prints and Photographs Division Washington, DC, circa 1941, via Wikimedia)

wrestle over the budget. Should we increase the funding for military operations or spend more on Medicare coverage? Not all programs can be funded to the complete satisfaction of their supporters, nor will all agree on who should provide the tax revenue to pay for these programs.

Politicians must make these choices under the pressure of people who clamor to advance their own interests. The elderly are likely to press for increases in Social Security, while the young are more likely to be interested in higher student aid grants and loans for college expenses. Steel and autoworkers may favor tariffs on foreign imports. Farmers who depend on the export market may fear such tariffs because foreign governments might retaliate against our agricultural products. Of course, not everyone takes predictable positions on every issue, nor is everyone motivated entirely by economic self-interest. Some of the wealthy are willing to pay higher taxes to help the poor, and some of the poor oppose higher social welfare spending. In general, when economic or occupational consequences are at stake, most people press for programs that serve their self-interests. Politicians must resolve the resulting conflicts.

politics
The process of peacefully reconciling social and economic differences

In the face of scarcity, this task is difficult. Not all people will be satisfied; and few, if any, will be satisfied completely. Politics produces decisions that are almost guaranteed to be imperfect. Although the American system leaves most decisions about economics to the marketplace, it has never considered economic liberty an absolute right. Nor has America practiced any pure form of **capitalism**—an economic system based on private ownership of property and free economic competition among individuals and businesses. Minimum wage laws, child labor laws, and environmental regulations are a few examples of government restrictions on the functioning of the marketplace. From the beginning of the nation, government has provided certain infrastructural services (schools, roads, hospitals) in order for capitalism to flourish. Since President Franklin D. Roosevelt's New Deal in the 1930s, the government has provided benefits for the elderly, the poor, and the unemployed. The American experience, particularly over the past century, has been witness to a strong central government that complements, coexists with, and regulates an economy largely in private hands. In the United States, economic and political powers have historically been divided; however, the line is always fluid and often hotly contested.

The genius of the American political experience comes from our ability, with the notable exception of the Civil War, to compromise claims and resolve differences without wrenching the system apart. As the country grows more complex and diverse, that challenge becomes more formidable.

capitalism

An economic system based on private ownership of property and free economic competition among individuals and businesses

(nyker / Shutterstock)

Known as a symbol of capitalism and prosperity, the Charging Bull is a Wall Street icon and popular tourist attraction located in downtown Manhattan.

Politics and Ideas

Money and its uses have a magnetic attraction. Even if the supply of money were infinite (which it clearly is not), conflict would still be present. Political systems are continually buffeted by debates over issues in which money and economic goods may be involved, but in which they do not play a central role. Such debates focus on the question of which political ideas and values should be reflected in a nation's laws and political institutions. In other words, many political disputes are ideological in origin. **Ideology** (used interchangeably in this book with the term *political ideas*) refers to the kind of government people think they should have. Ideology may also include ideas about the economic system. The prevailing political ideas have a lot to do with shaping the kind of life Americans enjoy, and ideological differences among Americans spark many political controversies.

For example, should abortion be allowed or banned? What pro-choice groups see as the constitutional right of women to control their own bodies, pro-life groups see as the murder of innocents. Other examples of disputes over values include debates about LGBT[3] rights, the necessity and morality of capital punishment, the balance between protecting the rights of gun ownership and reducing the prevalence of gun violence, and the teaching of evolution and sex education in public schools.

Opposition to the sums of money spent on public health insurance programs, therefore, comes not just from the people who are concerned about the costs but also from those who believe that mandating health coverage is an inappropriate role for the government. Likewise, others call for increased government aid to the homeless because they believe providing such aid is the humane thing to do.

No amount of money can bring people together on these issues, which involve fundamentally different views about what is right and just. In these matters, as in economic issues, politicians must get people to settle for less than their ideal in this imperfect world. Politicians are the brokers of the claims we make and the values we insist on. Politics becomes the art of reaching compromises when none seem possible.

Why Government?

People often use the words politics and government interchangeably. However politics is a process, and **government** is the set of organizations within which much of that process takes place.

Why government? What is its purpose? No better answer to these questions can be found than in the Preamble to the Constitution of the United States. In 1787, the framers summarized the answer in one sentence:

> *We the People of the United States, in Order to form a more perfect Union, establish Justice, insure domestic Tranquility, provide for the common defense, promote the general Welfare, and secure the Blessings of Liberty to ourselves and our Posterity, do ordain and establish this Constitution for the United States of America.*

ideology
A set of ideas concerning the proper political and economic system in which people should live

government
The political and administrative organization of a state, nation, or locality

"To Establish Justice, Insure Domestic Tranquility ... and Secure the Blessings of Liberty"

Government is essential to civilization. Restraint and decency among people are necessary prerequisites of a civilized society. To government falls the task of trying to ensure such behaviors. "Taxes," Justice Oliver Wendell Holmes (1902–1932)[4] wrote, "are what we pay for civilized society."[5] The English philosopher **Thomas Hobbes** wrote that in the absence of "the sovereign" or government, life among individuals would be "solitary, poor, nasty, brutish, and short."

Sovereign power is essential for protecting people from one another, by force if necessary. If people attempt to kill one another or steal from one another or assault one another, government must intervene. If it does not, civilization is simply not possible. People could not enjoy the fundamental pleasures of life—such as a walk in the park, a baseball game, a concert—if their physical well-being were constantly threatened by others whose violent acts went unhindered or unpunished. Although anarchists would disagree, government is essential to human liberty.

Yet government cannot by itself guarantee civil behavior. Civilization is a precious and fragile state of human existence that must be continually buttressed by the supporting values and beliefs of individuals in a society. Hobbes saw civilization as a thin veneer, beneath which surged a boiling cauldron of human impulses.

Thomas Hobbes

Seventeenth-century English political philosopher who wrote about the basis of sovereignty residing in a social contract

(Emily Taner/Shutterstock)

People could not enjoy certain pleasures of life—such as an outdoor music festival—if their physical well-being were constantly threatened, either by a pandemic like COVID-19 or by other humans whose violent acts went unhindered or unpunished.

Even in contemporary society the veneer is occasionally pierced. When civil tensions reach a breaking point, as they did during the chaotic aftermath of the killing of unarmed African American George Floyd by a white police officer in 2020, antisocial forms of behavior frequently emerge. In addition to the peaceful and lawful protests of the majority, some citizens and some officers committed uncivil acts—vandalism, assault, or battery. These threats to civil behavior must be resisted, and it is government that does the resisting.

"To Provide for the Common Defense"

Government must also protect its citizens against threats from other societies or governments. National defense is among the most important and visible functions of government. National security is essential to a society's preservation. The common defense has a long history, as any recounting of this nation's wars over the last two centuries will suggest. One of the principal concerns of the framers of the Constitution in 1787 was the creation of a stronger national government that could grapple more easily with the external threats and dangers of an uncertain world.

People may debate whether the government spends enough or too much on defense, but few will deny that the national government must be capable of defending the nation. Any organization or group calling itself a government that does not possess that capability may be a symbol or a wish—but it is not a government.

(Courtesy of US Army, via Wikimedia)

Although the American people may debate whether the government spends enough or too much on defense, few can deny that the US government must be capable of defending the nation.

"To Promote the General Welfare"

Government also exists to organize cooperative public efforts. Although some people believe in the adage "the government that governs least, governs best," few believe that government should do nothing. Throughout history government has subsidized railroads, constructed dams, protected the wilderness, provided for the needy, established schools, and built space shuttles. Such enterprises are **collective goods**, available for the benefit of all citizens whether or not they paid taxes to support them. These enterprises are generally too massive for private undertaking. They require a government that can tax and spend on a large scale.

The ideological debate over the size and scope of governmental enterprises has endured since the founding of our nation. Advocates of the **positive state** argue that government should play an active role in providing the goods, services, and conditions for a prosperous and equitable society. Adherents of the **minimalist state** argue that government is too inefficient and coercive and should be restricted to producing only goods that individuals themselves cannot provide.

collective goods

Something of value that, by its nature, can be made available only to everybody or not to anyone at all

positive state

A government that helps provide the goods, services, and conditions for a prosperous, equitable society

minimalist state

A government that restricts its activities to providing only goods that the free market cannot produce

What Is Democracy?

It is a basic axiom of American society that a government cannot be accountable merely to itself. The legitimacy of government in America rests on the consent of the governed. The Preamble to the Constitution states, "We the people of the United States … do ordain and establish this Constitution." We live in a representative **democracy**, a system of government in which political authority is vested in the people. The underlying ideology of a representative democracy supposes that people are capable of controlling their own destiny, selecting their own leaders, and cooperating in creating a peaceful and wholesome society. Alexander Hamilton, a delegate from New York to the Constitutional Convention in 1787, thought the new American nation could answer "the important question whether societies … are really capable or not of establishing good government from reflection and choice, or whether they are forever destined to depend … on accident and force."[6]

Democratic Values and Goals

What makes a government democratic? Democracy requires a system of government based on four precepts:

1. *Majority rule* expressed in free, periodic elections

2. Full protection of *minority rights* against an irrational or tyrannical majority

3. Protection of *individual rights* to freedom of speech, press, religion, petition, and assembly

4. *Equality* before the law for all citizens, regardless of race, creed, color, gender, national origin, or other immutable characteristics

These four objectives can be reached in different ways. Governments can vary in form and still be labeled democratic. In the United States, the head of state and the head of government are combined in one president, elected by the people. In other lands these roles may be vested in two people.

These four objectives are also, to a degree, in conflict with one another. The achievement of one can entail limits on another. Minority rights limit the kinds of laws that majorities in Congress or in the state legislatures may pass. Being in control of government in the United States does not give unlimited power to a majority. If, for example, the Republicans lose an election to the Democrats, the latter have no authority to seize the property of the former or to say that Republicans no longer have the right to vote. Nor can members of a majority silence their critics (as much as they might like to) simply because they won an election.

Likewise, the command of equality before the law places limits on what a majority may do. Democratic governments may not design election laws so that some people have more votes than others, but the rule that everyone's vote counts equally does not guarantee everyone the same influence in public affairs. Citizens with money to contribute to the campaigns of certain candidates often have more influence than those who have less or who choose not to contribute. Equality before the law is often difficult to achieve in the face of economic inequality. For example, wealthier school districts often provide a better education than poorer districts. Educational opportunities relate to one's income potential and full development as an informed citizen.

democracy

A system of government based on majority rule, protection of minority and individual rights, and the equality of all citizens before the law

(Shutterstock)

Efforts to achieve equality may also involve restraints on individual liberty. Laws banning certain forms of racial and gender discrimination—thus ensuring equal treatment for employees in the workplace—decrease the liberty of employers to hire and fire whomever they please. In turn, the protection of certain liberties may result in economic inequalities. For example, the liberty to keep one's property and earnings (subject, of course, to taxation) may result in vast disparities in wealth and income.

So American-style democracy is not only, in Lincoln's immortal words, "government of the people, by the people, for the people." As we shall see in Chapter 1, American democracy also involves **constitutionalism**—the principle of limiting governmental power by a written charter. Our Constitution restricts the power of the state. It also establishes the basic idea that no official, no matter how high, is above the law. This point is reaffirmed on Inauguration Day each time a president promises to "preserve, protect, and defend the Constitution of the United States."

Making Democracy Work

For a democracy to function effectively, the people and their leaders must be willing to accept compromise and the notion that no one group will get all it desires. They must also accept democratic values and goals such as majority rule and minority rights. For democracy to work, the public must support the process by which agreement is reached. As one political scientist described it, "The American way is by compromise in little bits, by persuasion, by much talk and little bitterness."[7]

constitutionalism

The belief in limiting governmental power by a written charter

Through the avenues of open debate and free elections, those who lose a political battle generally get another opportunity. Minority factions in a democracy are more likely to accept defeat today if they know the way is open for them to become a majority tomorrow.

Why Do Politics and Government Matter?

Although Americans have had political institutions since colonial days, the nature of government in the United States has undergone radical change. Today, government at all levels—state, local, and especially the national government—plays a much larger role in the life of the average citizen than it did 230 years ago during President Washington's administration, or even 160 years ago during President Lincoln's time.

Today, the national government pervades society, the economy, and the lives of its citizens. Its actions affect people all over the globe. Its $4 trillion budget creates work for about 2.7 million federal civilian employees. Governmental involvement is pervasive, regulating products from prescription drugs to toys. It insures banks, protects the air and drinking water, and warns against cigarette smoking.

With so broad a reach, the national government dwarfs every other organization in American society, including huge corporations like ExxonMobil and Walmart. Everyone who makes money must send some portion of it to the government in the form of taxes. In short, few people can get through a single day without being touched by the actions of the national government. These actions result from the process called politics. As the chapters that follow show, politics pervades American society, economy, and culture.

CHAPTER REVIEW

1. Politics is about the resolution of conflict in society. Conflicts frequently arise over resource allocation and value preferences. Politicians, at their best, find compromises between these issues when none seem available.

2. Government is essential to a civilized society. Its tasks are to ensure a peaceful society, to provide for the national defense, to secure basic freedoms, and to undertake cooperative enterprises for the general welfare.

3. American democracy provides for a government based on the consent of the governed, the protection of individual rights, and the equality of rights before the law. The Constitution, the basic charter of our government, preserves the principle of government under law.

4. In contemporary America, the tasks of government are extensive and varied. The national government spends about $4 trillion per year, and its activities pervade society. All Americans are directly affected by the policies and choices of government.

KEY TERMS

capitalism xxx	ideology xxxi
collective goods.......................... xxxiii	minimalist state xxxiii
constitutionalism xxxv	politics xxix
democracy xxxiv	positive state xxxiii
government xxxi	Thomas Hobbes.......................... xxxii

READINGS FOR FURTHER STUDY

Two classic discussions of politics can be found in Harold Lasswell, *Politics: Who Gets What, When, How* (Whitefish, MT: Literary Licensing, 2011), and Bernard Crick, *In Defence of Politics* (New York: Continuum International, 2001).

Much of the political theory underlying the American political system can be found in philosophical treatises such as *Leviathan* by Thomas Hobbes (New York: Penguin Classics, 2017), *Two Treatises of Government* by John Locke (New York: Cambridge University Press, 1988), and *The Spirit of the Laws* by Montesquieu (New York: Cambridge University Press, 1989).

Richard Hofstadter's *The American Political Tradition* (New York: Vintage Books, 1989) remains a landmark study in American political history.

A searching examination of American politics in theory and practice can be found in Samuel P. Huntington, *Who Are We? The Challenges to America's National Identity* (New York: Simon and Shuster, 2005).

NOTES

1. Bernard Crick, *In Defence of Politics* (New York: Continuum International, 2001), ch. 1.

2. Harold Lasswell, *Politics: Who Gets What, When, How* (Whitefish, MT: Literary Licensing, 2011) (originally published 1936).

3. LGBT, which stands for lesbian, gay, bisexual, and transgender, is the most widely used term for describing this community.

4. Throughout this book, dates in parentheses following the names of presidents and justices of the Supreme Court indicate their years in office.

5. *Campanio de Tobacos v. Collector*, 275 U.S. 87, 100 (1904).

6. *Federalist*, No. 1.

7. Frank Tannenbaum, "On Certain Characteristics of American Democracy," *Political Science Quarterly, 60*(1945): 350.

INTRODUCTION TO

American Government

Chapter

01

(Shutterstock)

THE CONSTITUTION OF THE UNITED STATES

In This Chapter

1.1   What Is a Constitution?
1.2   The Road to Nationhood
1.3   The Making of the Constitution
1.4   Features of the Constitution
1.5   Judicial Review Comes to the Supreme Court

Chapter Objectives

A nation's politics is given a special cast by the kind of government it has as well as by the values of its citizens. This country is no exception. The Constitution and the institutions that document summoned into being have shaped American politics mightily.

This chapter reviews the purposes of a constitution and traces the origins of our Constitution from the Revolutionary War and the first experiment with a national government under the Articles of Confederation to judicial review and the Supreme Court. Attention to the Philadelphia Convention of 1787 sheds light on what the framers of the Constitution wanted to avoid as well as what they wanted to achieve. Did they want to establish a democracy? What was the significance of dividing governmental authority among legislative, executive, and judicial branches? What is the unique relationship between the Supreme Court and the Constitution? How can a piece of parchment from the eighteenth century fit American needs in the twenty-first century?

Exploring such questions is essential to understanding American government today, particularly when one considers that the Constitution of the United States is the oldest written national charter still in force.

What Is a Constitution?

"What is a constitution?" asked Supreme Court Justice William Paterson (1793–1806) over two centuries ago. "It is," he answered, "the form of government, delineated by the mighty hand of the people, in which certain first principles of fundamental laws are established." Like Paterson and his contemporaries, most Americans embrace **constitutionalism**: the belief in limiting governmental power by a written charter. This makes a constitution a very special document.

1.1a Constitutionalism

Constitutionalism has long been important in American politics. Each of the fifty states has a constitution. In January 2021, President Joe Biden—like all his predecessors back to George Washington (1789–1797)—took an oath to "preserve, protect, and defend" the Constitution. Constitutionalism has also been contagious. Almost every country on earth has a constitution, but constitutions take different forms in different lands. Most, like the United States Constitution, are single documents, usually with amendments. A few, like the British Constitution, are made up of a series of documents and scattered major acts of Parliament (the British lawmaking body) that time and custom have endowed with paramount authority. The major difference between American-style constitutionalism and British-style constitutionalism is that the British Constitution can be changed by an act of Parliament. As described later in this chapter, the American Constitution can be formally altered only by an elaborate amendment procedure that includes the states—not Congress alone.

American style or British style, a constitution is more than a piece of paper. It is a living thing that embodies much more than mere words can convey—it embodies intangibles that enable it to work and to survive. Moreover, it provides clues to the political ideas that are dominant in a nation. The United States Constitution, for example, includes a cluster of values in its Preamble: "to form a more perfect *Union,* establish *Justice,* insure domestic *Tranquility,* provide for the common *defense,* promote the general *Welfare,* and secure the Blessings of *Liberty.*"

1.1b Constitutional Functions

Constitutions matter because of what they do (or do not do) and what they are. First, a constitution *outlines the organization of government.* The outline may be long or short, detailed or sketchy, but it answers key questions about the design of a government. Are executive duties performed by a monarch, prime minister, president, or ruling committee? Who makes the laws? A constitution probably won't answer all of the structural questions about a political system, however. The American Constitution, for instance, makes no mention of political parties; yet a picture of American politics without them would be woefully incomplete. Thus, while knowledge about constitutions may be a good starting place for a student of politics, it is hardly the finishing point.

Second, a constitution *grants power.* Governments exist to do things; and under the idea of constitutionalism, governments need authority to act. For example, Article I of the Constitution (reprinted in the Appendix) contains a long list of topics on which Congress may legislate, from punishing counterfeiters and regulating commerce "among the several States" to declaring war.

constitutionalism

The belief in limiting governmental power by a written charter

Grants of power imply limits on power. This is the principle of constitutional government in America: Rulers are bound by the ruled to the terms of a written charter. Thus, a constitution can also be a *mainstay of rights*. Constitutions commonly include a bill of rights or a declaration of personal freedoms that lists some of the things that governments may not do and proclaims certain liberties to be so valued that a society enshrines them in fundamental law.

Finally, a constitution may serve as a *symbol of the nation*—a repository of political values. When this happens, a constitution becomes more than the sum of its parts. More than a document that organizes, authorizes, and limits, it becomes an object of veneration. Americans have probably carried constitution veneration further than people of any other nation. Such emphasis on the Constitution has had an impact on the political system that can hardly be exaggerated. Frequently, people debate policy questions, not just in terms of whether something is good or bad, wise or foolish, but also whether it is *constitutional*. Debate may rage over the meaning of the Constitution, but contending forces accept the document as the fundamental law of the land. One group might argue that the Constitution bans state limitations on carrying concealed weapons, for example, while another might argue just as vehemently that the Constitution permits such restrictions.

1.2 **The Road to Nationhood**

In order to reach a better understanding of how America developed such a relationship with its Constitution, it is important to first understand the origins of that document. American government does not begin with the Constitution. Prior to 1787, there were many years of British rule, followed by the turbulence of revolution and an experiment with national government under the Articles of Confederation.

1.2a   The Declaration of Independence: The Idea of Consent

England first began developing **colonies** in North America in the early 1600s. By the mid-1700s, many British colonies had been established, thirteen of which were geographically contiguous along the eastern seaboard. While the colonies were profitable for Britain, there were also associated costs—such as defending British territory claims against Native American tribes and the claims of other European countries. At least thirteen years before the revolution, British leaders in London attempted to bring the American colonies under more direct control. Among other things, they wanted the colonists to pay a larger share of defense expenses and developed a series of tax and military policies to that end. These policies, however, ran head-on into colonial self-interest, revolutionary ideas, and a feeling of a new identity—an American identity as opposed to a purely British one. A series of events between 1763 and 1776 encouraged organized resistance to British authority and

colony

A territory under the direct control of a parent state

culminated in independence. Politics and reasoned debate within the British Empire soon gave way to armed revolt against it. Near the end of this period, colonial political leaders—meeting as the Second Continental Congress—considered a resolution moved by Richard Henry Lee of Virginia on June 7, 1776: "Resolved, that these United Colonies are, and of right ought to be, free and independent states." A declaration embodying the spirit of Lee's resolution and largely reflecting Thomas Jefferson's handiwork soon emerged from committee. Twelve states (New York abstaining) accepted it on July 2, with approval by all thirteen coming on July 4.

At one level, the Declaration of Independence (reprinted in the Appendix) itemized and publicized the colonists' grievances against British rule, personified in King George III. The revolutionists felt obliged to justify what they had done. Reprinted in newspapers up and down the land, the document was one the revolutionists hoped might, with luck, rally support at home and abroad to the cause of independence—especially for the military conflict underway. There was, after all, no unanimity within the colonies in 1776 on the wisdom of declaring independence. Loyalists were an active and hostile minority. Even among those who favored the break with England, some opposed fighting a war. Others were plainly indifferent.

In its goal of making the cause seem just and worth great sacrifice, the Declaration at another level said much about political thinking at the time. The authors of the Declaration were steeped in the thinking of English and Scottish natural rights philosophers, such as **John Locke**, who were trying to find a new source of legitimacy for political authority. Formerly, justification of authority stemmed from the belief that governments were ordained by God. Consequently, rulers governed on the basis of a covenant with the Deity, which implied limits to power, or on the basis of "divine right," which did not. If government were to have a secular basis, however, rulers could govern only by consent—not as an agent of God on earth but as an agent of the people.

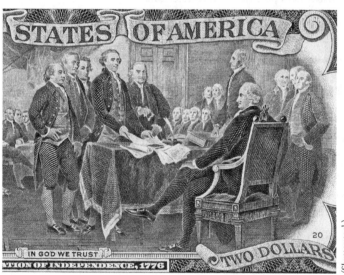

(Shutterstock)

A depiction of the signing of the Declaration of Independence as seen on the back of a $2 bill.

American leaders were also aware of precedents for rebellion in British history. Tensions between the Crown and Parliament had climaxed in the Glorious Revolution of 1688, which secured the supremacy of Parliament over the monarchy. They knew also of the series of political battles, large and small, over the centuries that had won particular rights for English subjects. They were familiar with the writings of the seventeenth-century English jurist Sir Edward Coke (whose name rhymes with *look*), who maintained that even actions of Parliament had to conform to "common right and reason" as embodied in the law of the land. Ironically, Coke's ideas eventually took root in America but not in England.

The Declaration of Independence drew heavily on these traditions. At least four themes emerge from its text:

John Locke

English political philosopher whose ideas about political legitimacy influenced the American founders

1. **Humankind shares equality.** All persons possess certain rights by virtue of their humanity. The Declaration called them "unalienable rights" and mentioned three specifically: "Life, Liberty, and the Pursuit of Happiness." These rights were bestowed by the Creator and were "self-evident."

2. **Government is the creation and servant of the people.** It is an institution deliberately brought into being to protect the rights that all naturally possess. It maintains its authority by consent of the governed. When government is destructive of the rights it exists to protect, citizens have a duty to revolt when less drastic attempts at reform fail. Citizens would, then, replace a bad government with a good one.

3. **The rights that all intrinsically possess constitute a higher law binding government.** Constitutions, statutes, and policies must be in conformity with this higher law. That is, they must promote the ends that government was created to advance. Natural rights would become civil rights.

4. **Governments are bound by their own laws.** These laws must be in conformity with the higher law. No officer of government is above the law. To make this point, the authors of the Declaration detailed violations, by the king, of English law in a list that consumes more than half the text.

(Chris Nesseth/Shutterstock)

A far-right rally held at the justice center, in Portland, Oregon, ended with bear mace, paintballs, and live rounds directed towards Black Lives Matter protestors. (August 15, 2020)

By eighteenth-century standards, the Declaration of Independence advanced objectives that were far removed from reality. Some newspapers of 1776 reprinted the Declaration alongside advertisements for slaves. Moreover, as a statement of American ideology, the Declaration's objectives remain unattained even today.

1.2b   The Articles of Confederation: The Idea of Compact

Even if the Declaration of Independence proclaimed separation from England, it did little to knit the former colonies into a nation. Central political control disappeared in 1776. Something would now have to take its place for successful execution of the war and for development of the nation once liberty was won. Only eight days after the adoption of the Declaration of Independence, a committee of Congress chaired by John Dickinson placed before the entire body a plan of union. The **Articles of Confederation** became the first American national constitution. Meeting in York, Pennsylvania—a safe distance from the British who occupied Philadelphia—Congress approved Dickinson's Articles in amended form in November 1777 and referred them to the states for approval. All states, save one, gave assent by May 1779 (with Maryland holding out until March 1781 because of a land dispute).

The main provisions of the Articles of Confederation are summarized in Table 1.1. Several features distinguished the document. First, *the Articles preserved state autonomy.* The document read more like a treaty between nations than a device to link component states. Describing the compact as "a firm league of friendship," the Articles stated clearly that "each state retains its sovereignty, freedom and independence, and every power, jurisdiction and right which is not by this Confederation expressly delegated to the United States in Congress assembled." The word *confederation* accurately described the arrangement: It was a loose union of separate states.

Articles of Confederation

This first plan of a national government for the thirteen American states was replaced by the Constitution; under the Articles, the states retained most political power

Second, *the Articles guaranteed equal representation for the states.* Congress represented the states, not the people. While a state's delegation could range in size from two to seven, each state had only one vote. The delegates were to be appointed "in such manner as the legislature of each state shall direct," and the states reserved the right to recall and replace their delegates at any time.

Table 1.1   An Overview of the Articles of Confederation

The Articles of Confederation provided for the dominance of the states in the political system and granted only a few powers to Congress.

Article I	Name of the confederacy: the United States of America
Article II	Guaranteed the powers of the member states, except where the states expressly delegated powers to Congress
Article III	Stated the purpose of the confederation: the defense and protection of the liberties and welfare of the states
Article IV	Stated that, as they traveled from state to state, citizens of the several states were to enjoy the privileges each state accorded its own citizens and granted freedom of trade and travel between states
Article V	Specified the processes of selection of delegates to Congress by state legislatures and of voting by states in Congress
Article VI	Prohibited states from engaging in separate foreign and military policies or using duties to interfere with treaties; recognized that each state would maintain a militia and a naval force
Article VII	Specified the appointment by state legislatures of all militia officers of or under the rank of colonel
Article VIII	Specified that national expenses were to be paid by states to Congress, in proportion to the value of the land in each state; states retained sole power to tax citizens
Article IX	Placed the sole power to make peace and war in Congress; restricted treaty-making power; designated Congress the "last resort" in all disputes between states; spelled out procedures for settling such disputes; gave the power to establish a postal system and to regulate the value of money issued by state and central governments to Congress; made provision for an executive committee of Congress, called a "Committee of the States," to manage the government; stipulated that most major pieces of legislation would require the affirmative vote of nine states
Article X	Authorized the Committee of the States to act for Congress when Congress was not in session
Article XI	Provided a provision for Canada to join the United States
Article XII	Deemed debts previously incurred by Congress to be obligations of the government under the Articles of Confederation
Article XIII	Specified the obligation of each state to abide by the provisions of the Articles of Confederation and all acts of Congress; provided for amendment by consent of the legislatures of every state

Third, *the Articles granted the central government only a few important powers.* The central government was given control over foreign affairs and military policy; however, it was denied taxing power completely, as well as the authority to regulate most trade. Revenues instead would be supplied by the states. If a state failed to make its proper payment, the Articles offered no remedy. Furthermore, most appropriations and laws of any significance required the affirmative vote of nine states.

Fourth, *the Articles provided for no separate executive branch and no national courts.* The rights of citizens lay in the hands of state courts. Congress was supposed to be the arbiter of last resort in disputes between states. Officers appointed by Congress performed the few executive duties permitted under the Articles.

Fifth, *the Articles made amendment almost impossible.* Changes in the terms of the Articles needed approval not only by Congress but also by the "legislatures of every state." For example, a single state could block any realignment of the balance the Articles struck between central direction and local autonomy. The states seemed destined to hold the dominant position for a long time to come.

1.3 The Making of the Constitution

Defects in the Articles of Confederation soon became apparent. Citizens who wanted change built their case on either of two deficiencies, and often on both. First was *an absence of sufficient power in the central government.* Absence of national taxation meant that Congress was hard pressed to carry out even the limited responsibilities it had, such as national defense. Absence of control over interstate commerce meant trade wars between the states, with some states prohibitively taxing imports from others. Congress could do little to promote a healthy economic environment. Absence of power to compel obedience by the states meant that foreign countries had no assurance that American states would comply with treaties to which the national government agreed.

Why did the founders call for a constitutional convention?

See for yourself by comparing the Constitution printed in the Appendix to this web version of the Articles of Confederation, which also includes earlier draft versions of the text.

http://www.bvtlab.com/K67c8

The second deficiency often mentioned was *the presence of too much power in the hands of the state governments.* Local majorities, unchecked by national power, could infringe on an individual's property rights. Of particular concern were the "cheap money" parties that had been victorious in some of the states. The decade of the 1780s was generally one of economic depression. In the wake of the ravages of war and the loss of British markets, times were hard. In response, state legislatures suspended debts or provided for payment of debts in kind, not cash. Added to this was the circulation of different currencies issued by the states, even though the national government was supposed to have monetary power. Printing additional money drove down its value, aiding debtors and hurting creditors. The economic picture was unsettled at best—chaotic at worst.

1.3a   Prelude to Philadelphia

A revolt of farmers led by Daniel Shays in Massachusetts in 1786–1787, known as **Shays' Rebellion**, was one of many events that heightened concerns about the Articles of Confederation. When farmers in the Berkshire Hills failed to get the debt relief they had demanded from the legislatures, they closed local courts and forced the state supreme court at Springfield to adjourn before they were finally routed by a state military contingent of 4,400 men. Although it was a military failure, the rebellion demonstrated that the central government under the Articles was powerless to protect the nation from domestic violence. Other issues, such as the refusal of states to provide the national government with the funds it needed to pay debts, further emphasized the shortcomings of the Articles.

In September 1786, on the eve of Shays' Rebellion, delegates from five states attended the **Annapolis Convention** in Maryland to consider suggestions for improving commercial relations among the states. Alexander Hamilton was a delegate from New York. Along with Virginia's James Madison, Hamilton persuaded the gathering to adopt a resolution calling for a convention of all states to meet in Philadelphia the following May to "render the Constitution of the Federal Government adequate to the exigencies of the Union." In February 1787, Congress authorized the convention. All the states except Rhode Island selected delegates; those delegates, however, were limited to considering amendments to the Articles of Confederation.

Even though the Constitution soon replaced the Articles, the nation's first experiment with central government was not a complete failure. In June 1787, in one of its last actions, the Congress established by the Articles enacted the **Northwest Ordinance**. This statute provided for the government and future statehood of the lands west of Pennsylvania, laid the basis for a system of public education, and banned slavery in that territory.

1.3b   The Philadelphia Convention

To appreciate fully what happened in Philadelphia in 1787, one must visualize America two centuries ago. Doing so may not be easy. Today our nation is a global power—economically, militarily, and politically—with a population exceeding 330 million people in fifty states, stretching from the Atlantic into the Pacific.

By contrast, the America of 1787 was a sparsely settled, weakly defended, and internationally isolated nation of thirteen coastal states with a combined population of under four million. Philadelphia boasted a population of 30,000, making it the largest city in the land. Virginia and Massachusetts were the most populous states, with 747,000 and 473,000 inhabitants, respectively. Rhode Island and Delaware were the smallest, with populations of only 68,000 and 59,000, respectively. Three other states had fewer than 200,000 inhabitants. The slave population, found mostly in the states from Maryland southward, numbered 670,000—or about 17 percent of the total population.

It was in this context that the Philadelphia Convention assembled. By modern standards, the convention was not a large body; the legislatures of twelve states had selected seventy-four delegates, and fifty-five eventually took their seats. Of these, fewer than a dozen did most of the work. Quality amply compensated for quantity, however. Probably no other American political gathering has matched the convention in talent and intellect.

Who were the framers? Twenty-nine were college graduates, and the remaining twenty-six included notables such as George Washington and Benjamin Franklin. The youngest delegate, Jonathan Dayton of New Jersey, was 26. Franklin, of Pennsylvania, was the oldest at 81. Thirty-four were lawyers; others were farmers and merchants. Some names were prominent by their absence. Thomas Jefferson was abroad. John Jay of New York was not chosen, even though he had been foreign affairs secretary for the Articles

Shays' Rebellion
A revolt by farmers from Massachusetts in 1786–1787 over the lack of economic relief, which led many to believe that a stronger central government was necessary

Annapolis Convention
The meeting of delegates from five states, held in Annapolis, Maryland, in 1786, to consider a common policy for trade among the American states; it resulted in a recommendation for a constitutional convention the following year

Northwest Ordinance
This major statute, enacted by Congress in 1787 under the Articles of Confederation, provided for the development and government of lands west of Pennsylvania

Table 1.2   Comparing the Articles of Confederation and the U.S. Constitution

	Articles of Confederation	Constitution
Location of sovereign power	States	Federal government
Basis of representation	All states equally	Combination of state equality and population
Taxation power	States only	States and federal government
Trade regulation	States	Federal government
Approval of appropriations and other major legislation	Supermajority of states (9 of 13)	Simple majority of House and Senate, plus approval of president
Federal executive	None	President
Federal courts	None	U.S. Supreme Court and federal court system
Revision/amendment	Unanimous state approval	Three-quarters of states' approval

Congress. Patrick Henry of Virginia was chosen but declined because he "smelt a Rat." Richard Henry Lee, also of Virginia, and Samuel Adams of Massachusetts were likewise suspicious of what might happen and stayed away. Ten delegates were also members of the Articles Congress. Eight delegates had signed the Declaration of Independence, and the signatures of six appeared on the Articles of Confederation; but on balance, this was not a reassembling of the generation that had set the revolution in motion. Rather, the delegates came from a pool of men who were fast gaining a wealth of practical experience in the political life of the young nation. Most were also committed to making changes to the Articles of Confederation—otherwise they would not have sacrificed the time and effort to attend.

The appointed day for meeting was May 14, 1787, but the ten delegates who convened that day at the Pennsylvania statehouse (now called Independence Hall) could do nothing until more arrived. Not only did the convention need its quorum of states, but each state delegation also needed a quorum because voting would be by state. Finally, on May 25, the Philadelphia Convention began its work. From then until September 17 the delegates conferred almost without pause, formally at the statehouse and informally at the City and Indian Queen taverns, short walks away.

In one of their first actions, the delegates adopted a rule of secrecy. The delegates even closed the windows during the steamy Philadelphia summer to discourage eavesdroppers. Without secrecy, it is doubtful whether

(Shutterstock)

The historic Independence Hall in Philadelphia, Pennsylvania the group could have succeeded. With secrecy came the freedom to maneuver, explore, and compromise. Because no verbatim stenographic account was made at the time, knowledge of the proceedings has had to be re-created piece by piece over the years.[1] The official journal of the convention was not made public until 1818. James Madison's notes on the proceedings, which are the most extensive account of what occurred, were not published until 1840.

On May 29, the Virginia delegation, led by Governor Edmund Randolph, seized the high ground for the discussion to follow. His fifteen resolutions—largely Madison's handiwork—made it increasingly evident that replacement, not tinkering, awaited the Articles of Confederation. Called the **Virginia Plan** and depicted in Table 1.3, the resolutions proposed a substantially stronger national government and a Congress based on numerical representation. This plan generated a counterproposal put forward by William Paterson of New Jersey. Known as the **New Jersey Plan** (see Table 1.3), it called for only modest changes to the Articles of Confederation, keeping the state governments dominant. What divided the delegates most was the issue of representation, because legislative representation translates into power. Would some states and interests have more votes than others in Congress? In late June and early July, the convention was deadlocked between delegates who favored representation in proportion to a state's population and those who wanted to keep equality between the states. Without settling this matter, the convention could not proceed.

Virginia Plan

The first plan of union proposed at the Constitutional Convention in 1787; it called for a strong central government

New Jersey Plan

Introduced in the Constitutional Convention in opposition to the Virginia Plan, it emphasized the dominance of the states

Table 1.3 The Virginia Plan, the New Jersey Plan, and the Constitution

In the form signed by the framers on September 17, 1787, the Constitution reflected some features of both the Virginia and New Jersey plans. Other features of the two plans were discarded during the summer's debates. The Great Compromise settled the issue of representation, drawing from both plans.

Virginia Plan	New Jersey Plan	Constitution of 1787
A two-house legislature, with numerical representation, where popularly elected lower house elects upper house	A one-house legislature, with equal state representation	A two-house legislature, with numerical representation in popularly elected House and equal state representation in state-selected Senate
Broad but undefined legislative power, with absolute veto over laws passed by state legislatures and taxing power	Same legislative power as under Articles, plus power to levy some taxes and to regulate commerce	Broad legislative power, including power to tax and to regulate commerce
Single executive elected by legislature for fixed term	Plural executive, removable by legislature on petition from majority of state governors	Single executive, chosen by electoral college
National judiciary elected by the legislature	Judiciary, appointed by executive, to hear appeals on violations of national laws in state courts	National judiciary, appointed by president and confirmed by Senate
Council of Revision, composed of the executive and judiciary, to review laws passed by national legislature	A "supremacy clause" similar to that found in Article VI of present Constitution	Supremacy clause; no Council of Revision

This division is sometimes seen as the less-populous states versus the more-populous ones (small against large). True, a state such as Delaware would lose voting strength in the national legislature if population became the basis for representation, but the divisions of opinion were not always based solely on state size. A majority of the New York delegation, for example, opposed numerical representation in either house because other states could lay claim to extensive western lands with the potential for significant population growth. Besides, the Virginia Plan meant a greatly reduced role *for states as states* in the Union. Local leaders viewed centralizing tendencies as a threat to their own influence, regardless of their state's population.

Credit for a breakthrough goes to Dr. William Samuel Johnson and Oliver Ellsworth, both delegates from Connecticut. Known as the **Great Compromise** or the Connecticut Compromise, their plan called for numerical representation in the lower house and equal state representation in the upper house. This compromise broke the deadlock, permitting the delegates to move along to other matters, and it forms the basis of congressional representation today: by population in the House of Representatives and by states in the Senate.

There were other compromises as well. The most notorious was the **three-fifths compromise**, which permitted slave states to count each slave as three-fifths of a person, thus enhancing these states' representation in the House while denying slaves—who were legally classified as property—the right to vote. Moreover, the Constitution let each state decide who could vote in national as well as state elections. As a result, a majority of people in the US (women and all slaves) were denied basic rights of political participation for years to come. Property qualifications that existed in some states for a time barred the poorest white males from the polling places as well.

1.3c   Ratification

The formal signing of the Constitution took place on September 17, 1787—109 days after the convention first met. Thirty-nine names appear on the document. Three delegates (Elbridge Gerry of Massachusetts and George Mason and Edmund Randolph of Virginia) refused to sign. Others, such as New York's Robert Yates, had gone home early because the Constitution included too many changes.

Approval by the country was surely on the framers' minds. Just as the delegates had taken liberty with their instructions to revise the Articles of Confederation, they proposed to bypass the rule of legislative unanimity for amendment. Article VII of the Constitution stipulated, in revolutionary fashion, that the new government would go into effect when *conventions* in *nine* states gave their assent. On September 28, 1787, the Articles Congress resolved unanimously—though noncommittally—that the Constitution should be handed over to the state legislatures "to be submitted to a convention of Delegates chosen in each state by the people thereof." Ironically, approval by popularly elected conventions meant that ratification of the Constitution would be a more democratic process than adoption of either the Declaration of Independence or the Articles of Confederation.

Supporters of the proposed Constitution called themselves **Federalists** and dubbed the nonsupporters **Antifederalists**, thus scoring a tactical advantage by making it seem that opponents of ratification were against union altogether. Because ratification meant persuasion, both sides engaged in a great national debate in the months after the Philadelphia Convention adjourned. Not since the eve of the revolution had there been such an outpouring of pamphlets and essays. Most prominent among the tracts was *The Federalist*, a collection of eighty-five essays written by Alexander Hamilton, John Jay, and James Madison under the pen name Publius, which originally appeared between October 27, 1787, and August 15, 1788, in New York state newspapers. One of

Great Compromise

An agreement at the Constitutional Convention in 1787, arranged by the delegation from Connecticut, proposing to accept representation by population in the House and by states in the Senate; sometimes called the Connecticut Compromise

three-fifths compromise

A temporary resolution to the controversy over slavery, this agreement allowed slaveholding states to count each slave as three-fifths of a person for purposes of congressional representation

Federalists

A term for persons who advocated ratification of the Constitution in 1787 and 1788 and generally favored a strong central government; it was also the name of the dominant political party during the administrations of Presidents George Washington and John Adams

Antifederalists

In the first years of government under the Constitution, Antifederalists in Congress were persons who opposed ratification of the Constitution in 1787 and 1788 and opposed policies associated with a strong central government such as a national bank

The Federalist

A series of eighty-five essays written by Alexander Hamilton, John Jay, and James Madison and published in New York newspapers in 1787 and 1788, urging ratification of the Constitution

("Portrait of John Jay," by Gilbert Stuart, 1794, oil on canvas. Courtesy of the National Gallery of Art via Wikimedia)

(Portrait of Alexander Hamilton by John Trumbull, 1805, oil on canvas. Courtesy of New York City Hall via Wikimedia)

(Portrait of James Madison by John Vanderlyn, 1816, oil on canvas, courtesy of The White House Historical Association, via Wikimedia)

John Jay, Alexander Hamilton , and James Madison (Top–Bottom) wrote *The Federalist,* a collection of eighty-five essays, as an authoritative commentary on the Constitution.

the most important expositions of American political theory, *The Federalist* achieved early recognition as an authoritative commentary on the Constitution.

Who were the Antifederalists? Most were not opposed to all change in the government. Some fought ratification because the Constitution was to become the supreme law of the land in an illegal manner, replacing the Articles of Confederation in violation of the Articles' own amendment procedure. For many, the Constitution was unacceptable because it would severely weaken state governments, leading eventually to a loss of local authority. Other opponents believed that individual liberty could be preserved only in "small republics," or states. If states were subordinated in the new government, it was only a matter of time before liberty would be lost—especially since the Constitution contained no bill of rights. As the governments closest to the people, states offered the best chance for self-government and so would promote, Antifederalists thought, a virtuous citizenry. Conversely, a distant government endangered not just popular rule but also citizenship itself. Moreover, the Constitution seemed designed to promote a commercial empire. This prospect threatened the agrarian values many of the Antifederalists shared.

The Antifederalists were not actually opposed to the concept of federalism, but their views on the nature of power differed from those of the Federalists. You can read some of the original *Federalist* papers here:

http://www.bvtlab.com/sA9cs

For a time, ratification by the requisite number of states was in doubt, causing John Quincy Adams to observe a half-century afterward that the Constitution "had been extorted from the grinding necessity of a reluctant nation."[2] Not until June 21, 1788, did the ninth state (New Hampshire) ratify. Practically, however, the new government could not have succeeded had the important states of Virginia and New York not signed on. These states ratified on June 25 and 26, respectively—the latter by the close vote of 30–27. Some states ratified only on the promise that a bill of rights would soon be added to the Constitution, which it was (see Chapter 3).

Meeting on September 13, 1788, the Articles Congress acknowledged ratification, set a date in February for electors to choose a president, and designated "the first Wednesday in March next ... for commencing proceedings under the said Constitution." The new House and Senate transacted their first business on April 2 and April 5, 1789, respectively, with George Washington's inauguration as president following on April 30. On September 24, Washington signed legislation creating the Supreme Court and setting February 1, 1790, as the day of its first session. Confirmation by the Senate of the first Supreme Court justices followed on September 26, 1789.

The Constitution is reprinted in the Appendix. The main provisions of the Constitution (without amendments) are summarized in Table 1.4. Amendments, including the Bill of Rights, are summarized in Table 1.5.

Table 1.4   An Overview of the Constitution of 1787

In the form in which it left the hands of the framers in 1787, the Constitution stressed the powers of the national government and did not include a bill of rights.

Article I	Establishment of legislative departments; description of organizations; list of powers and restraints; election of legislators
Article II	Establishment of executive department; powers, duties, restraints; election of the president and vice president
Article III	Establishment of judicial departments; jurisdiction of Supreme Court and other courts established by Congress; definition of *treason;* appointment of judges
Article IV	Relation of the states to the national government and to one another; guarantees of the states; provision for territories and statehood
Article V	Amendment of the Constitution; assurance of equal representation of the states in the Senate
Article VI	Guarantee of national debts; supremacy of the national constitution, laws, and treaties; obligation of national and state officials under the Constitution; no religious test for national office
Article VII	Ratification of the Constitution

Table 1.5   Amendments to the Constitution by Subject

Since the Bill of Rights (Amendments 1–10) was added in 1791, only seventeen formal changes have been made to the Constitution. Most have occurred in periods of reform and have affected the manner in which officials are elected and the operation and powers of the national government.

Individual rights

I	(1791)	Free expression
II	(1791)	Bearing arms
III	(1791)	No quartering of troops
IV	(1791)	Searches, seizures, and warrants
V	(1791)	Criminal procedure and fair trial
VI	(1791)	Criminal procedure and fair trial
VII	(1791)	Jury trials in civil suits
VIII	(1791)	No cruel and unusual punishment
IX	(1791)	Recognition of rights not enumerated
XIII	(1865)	Abolition of slavery

XIV	(1868)	Restrictions on state interference with individual rights; equality under the law; also altered nation–state relations

Political process

XII	(1804)	Separate voting by electors for president and vice president
XV	(1870)	Removal of race as criterion for voting
XVII	(1913)	Popular election of US senators
XIX	(1920)	Removal of gender as criterion for voting
XXIII	(1961)	Enfranchisement of District of Columbia in voting for president and vice president
XXIV	(1964)	Abolition of poll tax in federal elections
XXVI	(1971)	National voting age of eighteen in all elections

Nation–state relations

X	(1791)	Powers of the states
XI	(1798)	Restriction of jurisdiction of federal courts

Operation and powers of national government

XVI	(1913)	Income tax
XX	(1933)	Shift of start of presidential term from March to January; presidential succession
XXII	(1951)	Two-term presidency
XXV	(1967)	Presidential disability and replacement of vice president
XXVII	(1992)	Limitation on timing of change in congressional salaries

Miscellaneous

XVIII	(1919)	Prohibition of alcoholic beverages
XXI	(1933)	Repeal of Eighteenth Amendment

1.4 Features of the Constitution

Several features, implicit or explicit, in the document of 1787 (plus its Bill of Rights) suggest why the Constitution was important to the framers. More pertinent, these features help explain how the Constitution shapes American government today.

1.4a Republicanism, Divided Powers, and Federalism

republican (or representative) government

A style of government in which people elect representatives to make decisions in their place

The framers deliberately chose a **republican (or representative) government** with divided powers. They feared the excesses of democracy, or pure majority rule, that they had seen in the politics of their own states. At the same time, recalling the Declaration's insistence on "the consent of the governed," they knew that government had to be generally responsive to the people if ratification were to occur and revolution to be avoided. So, the Constitution

blended democratic and antidemocratic elements: popular election (voters, as qualified by their states, directly elected only the members of the House of Representatives); indirect popular election (state legislatures chose members of the Senate, while specially designated electors selected the president); and appointment (the president picked the national judiciary with the approval of the Senate).

In addition, the Constitution placed limits on what government can do. Implicit in the idea of a written constitution is that a government does not have unlimited power. As described later in this chapter, courts in the United States have assumed the role of deciding what those limits are and when they have been crossed. The Bill of Rights contains some of those restrictions; Sections 9 and 10 of Article I contain others.

The Constitution also diffused and dispersed power. Clearly concerned with the necessity of strengthening government, the framers divided power even as they added it. They were aware of an old dilemma: How does one construct a government with sufficient strength without endangering the freedom of individuals? Madison put it this way in *Federalist* No. 51: "In framing a government ... the greatest difficulty lies in this: you must first enable the government to control the governed; and in the next place oblige it to control itself." The solution, thought the framers, lay in design: dividing power both horizontally among the different parts of the national government and vertically between the national government and the states.

(Getty Images)

To be avoided at all costs was tyranny, which Madison defined as "the accumulation of all powers, legislative, executive, and judiciary, in the same hands, whether of one, a few, or many, and whether hereditary, self-appointed, or elective." This threat could take at least two forms: domination of the majority by a minority, or domination of a minority by the majority, with the latter running roughshod over the former in disregard of its rights. Ordinarily, the ballot box would give ample protection. The vote, after all, was the primary check on rulers. Madison, however, saw the "necessity of auxiliary precautions."

The division of responsibilities at the national level among the three branches of government (Congress, the president, and the Supreme Court) would help, but that would not be enough. What was to keep one branch from grabbing all of the power from the other two? Words on paper ("parchment barriers," Madison called them) would be inadequate—especially because experience had taught that the legislature might be too responsive to the popular will. The solution lay in juxtaposing power—"contriving the interior structure of the government, as that its several constituent parts may, by their mutual relations, be the means of keeping each other in their proper places." Rather than counting on noble motives to ward off tyranny, the Constitution assumed the existence of less noble motives. "Ambition," wrote Madison, "must be made to counteract ambition."

This is the constitutional arrangement commonly called **checks and balances**. Power is checked and balanced because the separate institutions of the national

checks and balances

The system of separate institutions sharing some powers that the Constitution mandates for the national government; its purpose is to keep power divided among the three branches: legislative, executive, and judicial

government—legislative, executive, and judicial—share some powers. As depicted in Figure 1.1, no one branch has exclusive dominion over its sphere of activity.

For example, a proposed law may pass both houses of Congress only to run headlong into a presidential veto, itself surmountable only by a two-thirds vote of each house. After scaling that obstacle, the law in question might well encounter a negative from the Supreme Court using its power of judicial review. Judicial review is not explicitly mentioned in the Constitution, but it soon joined the roster of Madison's "auxiliary precautions." Even the president's powers of appointment and treaty making require Senate cooperation; and although the president is designated commander in chief of the armed forces, Congress must declare war and appropriate money to finance the president's policies.

Figure 1.1   The Constitutional System of Checks and Balances

The framers designed the Constitution not just to divide governmental function among three branches but also to create a tension among the branches by allowing each one influence over the other two. American constitutional government means not just a separation of powers but also separate institutions sharing certain powers. The objective was to safeguard liberty by preventing a concentration of power.

President
(Shutterstock modified by BVT Publishing)

Congress
(Shutterstock modified by BVT Publishing)

Supreme Court
(Shutterstock modified by BVT Publishing)

President	Congress	Supreme Court
Appoints all federal judges	(Each house may veto the other)	Lifetime appointment
Enforces court decisions	Has general lawmaking power	No reduction in salary
Proposes legislation	Appropriates all funds	May declare actions of president and subordinates unconstitutional
May veto legislation passed by Congress	Creates executive departments	
Convenes Congress	Declares war	May declare acts of Congress unconstitutional
Appoints many administrative officials	Approves certain executive appointments (Senate only)	
Serves as commander in chief of armed forces	Ratifies treaties (Senate only)	
Conducts foreign relations	Removes president and federal judges by impeachment	
	Defines Supreme Court's appellate jurisdiction	
	Sets size of Supreme Court	
	Creates lower federal courts and their jurisdictions	

Securing liberty was also to be helped by federalism, the vertical division between national and state governments (explained in Chapter 2). The Constitution left the states with ample regulatory or police power—that is, control over the health, safety, and welfare of their citizens. As associate justice of the Supreme Court John Marshall Harlan II (1955–1971) argued many years later, "We are accustomed to speak of the Bill of Rights and the Fourteenth Amendment as the principal guarantees of personal liberty. Yet it would surely be shallow not to recognize that the structure of our political system accounts no less for the free society we have." Harlan echoed Alexander Hamilton's observation in *Federalist* No. 84 that the Constitution, even without amendments, "is itself, in every rational sense, and to every useful purpose, a Bill of Rights."

Coupled with divided power at the top, federalism was useful in guarding against majority tyranny. Some of the framers worried about "factions"—today we would call them tightly knit political parties or interest groups. The most productive source of factions, Madison acknowledged in *Federalist* No. 10, was economic inequality—rich versus poor, creditors versus debtors, and so forth. The Constitution was designed, in part, to limit the influence of factions. Minority factions could be outvoted. Majority factions would, with luck, exhaust themselves trying to fuse together what the Constitution had diffused. The Constitution would ultimately not prevent the majority from attaining its objectives, but the effort would have to be both long and hard. Short of this, the Constitution would work to insulate national policy from political fads that might capture majority sentiment in one or two states. The framers were especially concerned about movements like Shays' Rebellion that threatened the rights of political minorities.

Power was divided horizontally and vertically in order to check human ambition run amok. Measured by this standard, the Constitution has been largely successful, yet the scheme is by no means foolproof. The vaccination against tyranny has had some unpleasant side effects. First, the arrangements that held off the threats to the nation that Madison feared have sometimes made dealing with threats to individual liberty in the states more difficult. As Chapter 3 describes, even after the central government took a stand against continued racial and gender discrimination, fragmented powers and federalism hindered steps to alleviate existing wrongs. All checks, primary and auxiliary, failed to work for a long time. Second, the constitutional legacy of the framers has sometimes made the task of governing the nation (more than 230 years later) a difficult one. Separate national institutions and federalism have contributed to weak political parties, all of which combine to tax the skills of any leader (including the president) who calls for concerted action. Sometimes power has to be amassed, it seems, in spite of the Constitution. The advantage tends to lie with those who would delay, deflect, or derail. The framers institutionalized tension within the government. Yet on balance, the benefits of fragmented power have been worth the costs, as American constitutional government is now in its third century.

1.4b   A Single and Independent Executive

Although few doubted that the Philadelphia Convention would make provision for a legislature, controversy converged on issues such as representation and manner of selection for that legislature. What is perhaps astonishing about the Constitution is that it provided for a single *and* independently elected executive. Neither the Virginia Plan nor the New Jersey Plan offered both, as Table 1.3 illustrates. After 1776, executive authority was understandably suspect; determining the kind of executive branch to implement in the new government was thus a topic of debate throughout the summer. State constitutions of the day typically enhanced legislative power and kept governors on a short leash.

POLITICAL CONTROVERSIES

America Responds: Government and Covid-19

In 2020, America changed. The year started out normally enough, but by the end of January the first case of a novel coronavirus, dubbed COVID-19, had been confirmed in the United States. While the highly communicable respiratory infection originated elsewhere, it spread rapidly in this country, infecting millions and killing hundreds of thousands. Though one might see the disease as primarily a concern of health scientists, an issue of this magnitude and severity requires a government response.

So, while medical advice and individual behavior certainly changed, our government changed as well. Nearly every aspect of American government addressed in the pages of this textbook felt the impact of COVID-19. The Constitution (Chapter 1) has long protected Americans' rights, such as a right to privacy. But as the pandemic took hold, 61 percent of Americans said preventing the spread of the coronavirus was more important than protecting individuals' medical privacy. The emergency relief efforts that followed the outbreak raised federalism questions, as they required coordination of local, state, and national agencies, with many of the decisions regarding rules for businesses and behaviors in public spaces falling to state governors (Chapter 2). The protection of civil rights and liberties became a concern as government officials and citizens weighed the trade-off between restricting freedom—through social distancing and mask requirements, for example—and providing

New York Governor Andrew Cuomo makes an announcement and holds a media briefing at his 3rd Avenue office in Manhattan. (July 1, 2020)

(lev radin / Shutterstock)

Americans with a greater sense of safety (Chapter 3). Political ideologies temporarily lost some significance when congressional leaders—liberal and conservative alike—passed a nearly unanimous CARES Act (Coronavirus Aid, Relief, and Economic Security Act) and multiple additional bills to fund research and support the battered economy (Chapter 4). The public's response included large numbers identifying COVID-19 as the "most important problem" facing the country (45 percent) and remaining confident that their social distancing practices were saving lives (87 percent) (Chapter 5). Media outlets responded by changing their programming to increase coverage of both the spread of the virus and responses to it, with 99 percent of individuals reporting having heard or read about the virus by mid-March (Chapter 6). While both major political parties took the pandemic seriously, divisions emerged over strategy as President Trump's downplaying of the virus led many Republicans to take the threat less seriously, while many Democrats criticized this approach. For example, in July 2020 one poll found 86 percent

of Democrats, but only 15 percent of Republicans believed the coronavirus situation was "getting a lot worse" (Chapter 7). In many states primary elections that had been scheduled between April and June had to be postponed or adjusted due to social distancing guidelines (Chapter 8).

The institutions of American government responded to change as well. In addition to passing multiple bills, totaling trillions of dollars in federal spending, the U.S. Congress took the unusual step of adjusting its own voting rules in an effort to reduce health risks for those working in the Capitol. On May 15, 2020, the House of Representatives authorized remote voting by members for the first time in its history (Chapter 9). President Trump wielded both formal and informal powers of the presidency to address the pandemic, signing an executive order to restrict immigration in response to lower labor demands and invoking the Defense Production Act to contract for hundreds of millions of face masks, as well as using press briefings to make his own statements about the pandemic to the American people (Chapter 10). Many pieces of

America's vast bureaucracy came into play as well: the Centers for Disease Control and Prevention issued public health guidelines and collected data on the spread of the virus, while the Small Business Administration and the Internal Revenue Service coordinated the CARES Act's efforts to provide financial relief to millions of Americans and businesses (Chapter 11). Even the Supreme Court addressed the pandemic, deciding a case that challenged how mail-in ballots should be counted in Wisconsin's primary election (Chapter 12).

Finally, the government responded to COVID-19 through multiple acts of public policy, a process that was greatly sped up due to the urgency of the issue (Chapter 13). The nation's budget, in a year that began with a strong economy, quickly found its deficits expanding as trillions of dollars in supplemental appropriations were approved to help pay for recovery and response efforts (Chapter 14). One of the key components of the relief effort was to expand the social safety net, by extending unemployment benefits as jobless numbers skyrocketed and by sending direct payments to the vast majority of Americans (Chapter 15). In foreign policy, President Trump became upset with what he considered the World Health Organization's slow response to the pandemic and took action to stop American payments to the international body and to formally withdraw American membership (Chapter 16).

Indeed, just as no American was left untouched by the COVID-19 pandemic, no aspect of American government emerged unscathed either. How did these events affect you or your family, and how have they affected your interactions with the American government? What further changes do you expect in the future?

SOURCE: The Gallup Organization, "Americans Rank Halting COVID-19 Spread Over Medical Privacy," May 15, 2020; "COVID-19 Quickly Becomes Most Important U.S. Problem," April 21, 2020; "Americans Highly Confident Social Distancing Saves Lives," May 8, 2020; "U.S. COVID-19 Outlook Deteriorates as Infections Spike," July 24, 2020. NBC News/*Wall Street Journal* Survey, March 11-13, 2020, https://assets.documentcloud.org/documents/6810602/200149-NBCWSJ-March-Poll-Final-3-14-20-Release.pdf. CNN, "Majority of Americans Now Say the Government Has Done a Poor Job of Preventing Coronavirus Spread," April 8, 2020; *Republican National Committee v. Democratic National Committee*, 589 U.S. (U.S. Supreme Court, 2020).

Some delegates to the Philadelphia Convention favored a plural executive or a single executive responsible to a council or to Congress.

The framers in Philadelphia finally reached a compromise about the selection of a president at the end of the convention. Their creation of the Electoral College, discussed in Chapter 8, meant that the delegates could avoid direct election by the people (a plan that allowed for too much democracy), election by Congress (a plan that would make the executive subservient to the legislature), and election by state legislatures (a plan that might make the executive a puppet of state governments). By allowing for selection of a single individual by specially chosen electors, the Constitution provided independence, strength, and eventually a popular base of power for the president.

1.4c Adaptability

The Constitution today is a living charter that plays a significant role in government. Yet eighteenth-century men, with eighteenth-century educations, wrote the Constitution for an obscure and fragile eighteenth-century nation. Formal amendment of the document, a process that we will discuss shortly, has taken place only seventeen times since the ratification of the Bill of Rights in 1791. How, then, does a document written in a bygone era by a fledgling nation fit the needs of a world power in the twenty-first century? The answer is that the Constitution is adaptable. It is adaptable both because of particular characteristics built into it and because of the way the document has been regarded by successive generations.

The first factor in its adaptability is *brevity*. Including all twenty-seven amendments, the Constitution of the United States contains fewer than six thousand words, resulting in a shortage of detail and an absence of reference to many things the framers could conceivably have included. (By contrast, the constitutions of the fifty states today tend to be long and detailed; many are also short-lived.) Tactically, brevity was wise in the face of the ratification debate—the less said, the less to arouse opposition. Later generations would have to flesh out the full potential of the document through interpretation

and practice. For example, the "executive power" that Article II vests in the president is largely undefined.

Second, there is *elasticity* in the language of the Constitution. Some words and phrases do not have a precise meaning. Among Congress's powers listed in Section 8 of Article I is the regulation of foreign and interstate commerce. But what does "commerce" include? In the 1960s, Congress prohibited racial discrimination in hotels, restaurants, and other places of public accommodation. Its authority? The power to regulate commerce.[3] Broadly speaking, to regulate commerce is to regulate the economic environment, particularly the buying and selling of goods and services. This meant a fairly narrow range of policies in the 1790s, but the **commerce clause** includes a much broader set of congressional policies today.

Following the list of Congress's powers is the **necessary and proper clause**, which authorizes Congress to pass "all Laws which shall be necessary and proper for carrying into Execution the foregoing Powers." Thus, an indefinite reservoir of implied powers was added to the scope of congressional authority. In different periods of American history this clause—often referred to as the "elastic clause"—has enabled government to meet new challenges and the needs of a changing nation. For instance, as explained in Chapter 2, the Supreme Court long ago relied on the elastic clause to uphold Congress's authority to charter a national bank. According to Chief Justice John Marshall (1801–1835), the Constitution was "intended to endure for ages to come, and consequently to be adapted to the various crises of human affairs."[4] Today, Congress uses that power to extend its reach into issues of public safety, environmental protection, and social welfare that were not contemplated by the very small national government of the late eighteenth century. That being said, the necessary and proper clause is not an infinite power—laws must be related to the prescribed authority, the legislature. When Congress attempts to stretch the elastic clause too far, the Supreme Court exercises its check of judicial review (described below) to rein in legislative overreaching.

Third, the Constitution exalts *procedure* over substance, containing far more about how policies are to be made than about what policies are to be chosen. The Constitution stresses means over ends. The result has been to avoid tying the Constitution, for long periods of time at least, to a certain way of life—whether agrarian, industrial, or technological—or to a certain economic doctrine.

1.4d Amendment of the Constitution

The framers knew that the Constitution must allow for change in its terms if it were to be an enduring force. The near impossibility of amending the Articles of Confederation, after all, drove the framers to scrap the rule of unanimity that the Articles had required. Formal amendment is thus another means of ensuring adaptability.

Yet of the more than five thousand amendments that have been introduced in Congress, only twenty-seven amendments have been added to the document since 1789 (see Table 1.5). Article V of the Constitution mandates that only three-fourths of the states are needed to ratify an amendment to the Constitution. Compared with the Articles of Confederation, amending the Constitution is easier; however, it is still not an easy process. The national constitution is amended much less frequently than are state constitutions.

As shown in Figure 1.2, the Constitution specifies two different tracks for its own amendment: initiation by Congress and initiation by state legislatures. Only the first has been employed successfully. Since 1789 Congress has submitted thirty-three amendments to the states for ratification. Until 1992, all but seven had been approved. Of those to fail, the two most recent were the District of Columbia Amendment, which would

commerce clause

Found in Article I, Section 8, of the Constitution, this clause gives Congress the authority to regulate the country's economic environment

necessary and proper clause

The "elastic clause" of Article I, Section 8, of the Constitution; this is the source of "implied powers" for the national government, as explained in *McCulloch v. Maryland* [17 U.S.(4 Wheaton) 316 (1819)]

have given the district voting representation in Congress, and the Equal Rights Amendment, which would have banned discrimination by government on the basis of gender.

On May 7, 1992, the Twenty-seventh Amendment—long known as the "lost amendment"—became part of the Constitution upon ratification by Michigan, the thirty-eighth state (two additional states ratified it later in May). The Twenty-seventh Amendment declares: "No law, varying the compensation for the services of the Senators and Representatives, shall take effect, until an election of Representatives shall have intervened."

Ironically, this newest amendment is actually one of the oldest. It was among the twelve amendments Congress submitted to the states in 1789. (Ten of this group of amendments became the Bill of Rights. Another,

Prior to the amendment of the Constitution, not all citizens were guaranteed the right to vote. Today, anyone at least eighteen years of age, of any race, gender, or class, is free to vote.

dealing with apportionment of the House of Representatives, was never ratified and is obsolete.) By December 1791, when the Bill of Rights amendments were ratified, only six states had approved the pay amendment. Only one additional state ratified it during all of the nineteenth century, but a drive to revive the amendment began in the late 1970s as many people became increasingly frustrated with Congress.

Today, Congress sets a time limit for ratification—usually seven years. An amendment that fails to obtain the required three-fourths approval by the specified date then "dies." No such limit applied to the early amendments. Critics say that accepting the lost amendment as part of the Constitution is a dangerous precedent because allowing the ratification process to be spread over so long a period of time does not guarantee a contemporary national consensus. Others reply that the amendment would not have been

Figure 1.2   Formal Amendment of the Constitution

Article V of the Constitution prescribes the formal amendment procedure beginning with a proposal and ending with ratification.

The Four Pathways from Proposal to Ratification

Proposal

Proposal by two-thirds vote of both houses of Congress	
Proposal by two-thirds vote of national convention called by Congress on request of two-thirds of state legislatures	

Used for 26 amendments ⟶

Used once for Amendment 21

Not yet used ⟶

Not yet used ⟶

Ratification

Passage by three-quarters of state legislatures	
Passage by three-quarters of special state conventions	

revived had there not been such support for setting the limits on congressional powers mandated by the amendment.[5]

The second track for amendment is the closest the Constitution comes to popular initiation of amendments. As depicted in Figure 1.2, the legislatures of two-thirds of the states first make application to Congress for an amendment. Congress then calls a convention, which in turn submits the amendment for ratification by the legislatures (or conventions) of three-fourths of the states. From time to time, people have attempted to amend the Constitution by campaigning for a second convention when Congress declined to propose the desired amendment in the usual way. Recently, efforts to obtain an amendment that would mandate a balanced budget for Congress proceeded along this second and untraveled track. By 1993, thirty-two states—two short of the required number—had petitioned Congress for a convention to propose such an amendment. This thrust from the states led the House of Representatives to pass a balanced-budget amendment on multiple occasions in the 1990s, most recently in March 1997. Had the proposal not fallen one vote short of a two-thirds majority in the Senate, the amendment would have been submitted to the states for ratification. Although some legislators continue to introduce a similar amendment from time to time, since 1997 bipartisan agreements to reduce spending have largely derailed the movement for the amendment. In this instance, Congress used track one of the amendment process to head off the drive along track two. The issue may again rise to the forefront of public debate, as evidenced by the fact that the Ohio legislature voted to petition Congress for this amendment in late 2013 and Michigan followed suit the next year. By 2020, five states had called for a convention to reform campaign finance laws.

Grave doubts persist over the wisdom of summoning a second convention. Many questions understandably remain unanswered. *Must* Congress call a convention when two-thirds of the states request one? Would such a convention be limited to proposing the amendment sought by the petitioning states, or could a convention propose other changes in the Constitution? Would the delegates vote as individuals, or would they cast the vote of a state, as was done in 1787? The Constitution does not answer any of these questions.

Aside from formal amendment and judicial interpretation (which we will discuss next), the political system has also changed by custom. Even without changing the words in the Constitution, the public's expectations of governmental institutions continue to evolve. Democratic values, socioeconomic conditions, industrialization, urbanization, and technology have all influenced attitudes and practices. For example, political parties—which developed early in our political history—are not mentioned in the Constitution. An even more obvious example of change by custom is the pledge of presidential electors to support their party's ticket, a practice the Constitution does not require. For a very long time, members of the Electoral College have been expected to register the choice of the voters on election day, rather than to exercise an independent choice for president and vice president (voters would feel both anger and betrayal if the latter occurred).

1.5 Judicial Review Comes to the Supreme Court

Most changes to the Constitution since its inception have resulted not in adding or deleting words but in applying new meaning to existing words—a task that has largely

fallen to the Supreme Court. Through its interpretative powers, the Supreme Court is rather like an ongoing constitutional convention. Thus, we must often look to court cases to interpret the meaning of various parts of the Constitution. Whether the framers intended the Court to occupy a place of such prominence in the political system is uncertain. For more about the Supreme Court and its power of judicial review, see Chapter 12.

1.5a *Marbury v. Madison:* The Case of the Undelivered Commissions

Following the presidential election of November 1800, the nation witnessed the modern world's first peaceful electoral transfer of political power from one party to another.[6] The "out group" of Democratic-Republicans led by Thomas Jefferson (1801–1809) captured the presidency and Congress, displacing the "in group" of Federalists led by President John Adams (1797–1801). Partisan tensions ran high.

In the wake of Adams's defeat, Oliver Ellsworth (1796–1800) resigned as the third chief justice of the U.S. Supreme Court. If Adams moved swiftly, he—and not Jefferson— would be able to make the new appointment. Adams offered the job to John Jay (1789– 1795), who had been the first chief justice; Jay declined because he doubted that the Court would ever amount to much. Adams turned next to his secretary of state, John Marshall, who accepted.

Several weeks before the switch in administrations, the Federalist-dominated Congress passed the District of Columbia Act, which authorized the appointment of forty-two new justices of the peace. President Adams made the appointments, much to the displeasure of the Jeffersonians waiting in the wings. This series of events was possible because Congress convened annually in December in those days, which meant that members defeated in the November election (the "lame ducks") were still on hand to make laws. The newly elected Congress would not convene until after the presidential inauguration in March of the following year, a practice that was not changed until ratification of the Twentieth Amendment in 1933.

The role of the Supreme Court in governing the nation is one of the distinguishing characteristics of the American government.

(Erik Cox Photography / Shutterstock)

In the waning hours of the Adams administration, John Marshall—who was still serving as secretary of state—failed to deliver all of the commissions of office to the would-be justices of the peace. Upon assuming office on March 4, 1801, Jefferson held back delivery to some of Adams's appointees and substituted a few of his own. Later that year, William Marbury and three others whom Adams had named as justices of the peace filed suit against Secretary of State James Madison in the Supreme Court. They wanted the Supreme Court to issue a *writ of mandamus* to Madison, directing him to hand over the undelivered commissions. (A writ of mandamus is an order issued by a court to a public official, directing performance of a ministerial, or nondiscretionary, act.) Thus, a case was initiated that tested the power of the Supreme Court over another branch of government.

When the Court heard the arguments in the case of *Marbury v. Madison* in February 1803, the Jefferson administration displayed its hostility to Marshall and the other

writ of mandamus
Order by a court to a public official to perform a nondiscretionary or ministerial act

Marbury v. Madison
Landmark decision [5 U.S. (1 Cranch) 137 (1803)] by the Supreme Court in 1803 establishing the Supreme Court's power of judicial review

POLITICS AND IDEAS

Whose Constitution Is It?

What standard should guide justices of the Supreme Court in deciding what the Constitution means? One approach criticizes the justices for too often substituting their own values in place of those the Constitution explicitly contains. Because the Constitution says nothing about abortion, for instance, and because there is no evidence that those who wrote either the document of 1787 or later amendments intended to include abortion as a protected liberty, they believe the Court was plainly wrong when it ruled in *Roe v. Wade* (1973) that the Constitution protects the right to abortion (see Chapter 3). In place of excessive judicial creativity, the Court relies on "original intent."[1] According to this view, the Supreme Court's task is to give the Constitution the meaning intended by those who wrote it. Whether abortions should be legal thus becomes a question for voters and legislators, not judges.

Others disagree and advance a different approach. Often the original intent is neither knowable nor clear, they argue. Even if it is, whose intent is supposed to matter most—those who wrote the words in the Constitution, those who voted on them at the Philadelphia Convention or (with respect to amendments) in Congress, or those in state ratifying conventions and legislatures? These questions aside, must the nation always be locked into an old way of thinking until the Constitution is formally amended? The Fourteenth Amendment, for example, commands that no state deny to any person the "equal protection of the laws." In its historic decision in *Brown v. Board of Education of Topeka* (1954), discussed in Chapter 3, the Supreme Court concluded that these words prohibited racial segregation in public schools. Yet the same Congress that wrote and proposed the Fourteenth Amendment almost a century earlier also mandated racially segregated schools for the District of Columbia. It is hard to argue that the framers of the Fourteenth Amendment intended to ban a practice they were themselves requiring. Does this mean that the 1954 decision was wrong? No—because the Constitution must be adaptive. According to opponents of "originalism," the Court's task should be one of applying principles, not specific intents. This approach sees in the Constitution the general principle of human dignity. One generation's understanding of human dignity will probably not be the same as another's. The question becomes not what the words meant in 1787 or 1868, but what the words mean in our own time.[2]

Even many proponents of original intent do not disagree with the result of *Brown.* Rather, they say that the Court can be faithful to the intent of the Fourteenth Amendment and still invalidate laws that require racial segregation because the framers of the Fourteenth Amendment, in laying down a command of "equal protection," did not foresee the harmful consequences of forced segregation.

If justices of the Supreme Court interpret the Constitution according to their understanding of the basic principles that the Constitution contains, how do they discover those principles? Why is their view of the values protected by the Constitution somehow superior to the views of state legislators or members of Congress? Should the fundamental law of the land be developed by elected representatives or by appointed judges?

1. Robert H. Bork, *The Tempting of America* (New York: Free Press, 1990), 143–160.

2. William J. Brennan Jr., "The Constitution of the United States: Contemporary Ratification," *American Constitutional Law,* 16th ed., edited by Alpheus T. Mason and D. Grier Stephenson Jr. (New York: Longman, 2011).

Federalist justices by boycotting the proceeding.[7] By then it was apparent that Marshall and the five associate justices were in a predicament. If the Court issued the writ, Jefferson and Madison would probably disregard it. There would be no one to enforce the order, and the Court would seem powerless and without authority. For the Court to decide that Marbury and the others were not entitled to their judgeships would be an open acknowledgment of weakness and error.

Marshall's decision skillfully avoided both dangers and claimed added power for the Supreme Court, even though Marbury walked out the door empty-handed. First, in a lecture on etiquette to his cousin the president, Marshall made it clear that Marbury was entitled to the job. Second, he ruled that courts could examine the legality of the actions of the head of an executive department. Third, and dispositive, Marshall announced

that Marbury was out of luck because the writ of mandamus he requested was not the proper remedy.

Why? Marshall acknowledged that Section 13 of the 1789 Judiciary Act gave the Supreme Court authority to issue a writ as part of the Court's original, as opposed to appellate, jurisdiction. (A court has **original jurisdiction** when a case properly starts in that court and **appellate jurisdiction** when the case begins elsewhere and comes to a higher court for review.) Marshall pointed out that the Supreme Court's original jurisdiction was specified in Article III of the Constitution and included no mention of writs of mandamus. By adding to the Court's original jurisdiction, Section 13 appeared unwarranted by the Constitution. Was the Court to apply an unconstitutional statute? No. To do so would make the statute (and Congress) superior to the Constitution. Section 13, therefore, was void, and the Court was obliged to say so.

1.5b The Significance of *Marbury*

Marbury v. Madison remains important because of what Chief Justice Marshall said about the Constitution and the Supreme Court. First, officers of the government were under the law and could be called to account in court. Second, statutes contrary to the Constitution were not valid laws. Third, the Court claimed for itself the authority to decide what the Constitution means and to measure the actions of other parts of the government against that meaning. This is the power of **judicial review**: Judges holding lifetime appointments can block an electorally responsible agency of government. Alternatively, the lawmaking body (Congress) would be the judge of its own authority. Fourth, Marshall was answering the rumblings of dissent heard in the **Kentucky and Virginia Resolutions** of 1798. Written, respectively, by Jefferson and Madison (the latter had by now become a foe of strong central government) as an attack on Federalist Party policies, these resolutions claimed for the states final authority to interpret the Constitution. In the words of those resolutions lay the seeds for dismemberment of the Union. Marshall's reply was that the Court would have the final say on the meaning of the Constitution.

1.5c Judicial Review and the Framers

The novelty of the *Marbury* case is that it marked the first instance in which the Supreme Court declared an act of Congress to be in violation of the Constitution. Did the framers intend the Court to have such power? The question cannot be answered with certainty. Some members of the Philadelphia Convention seemed to assume that the Court could set aside laws that ran counter to the Constitution. In *Federalist* No. 78, Alexander Hamilton made an argument in support of judicial review that Marshall followed closely in his *Marbury* ruling. References to judicial review abound in the records of the state ratifying conventions, and some state courts made use of the power well before Marshall did. Moreover, several Supreme Court decisions prior to *Marbury* assumed the existence of judicial review but neither explained nor applied it. Still, if the Court were to possess such a potentially important power, it is strange that the Constitution would not mention it. Neither does the Constitution say anything about how its words are to be interpreted— a question that still divides political leaders and legal scholars. (See "Politics and Ideas: Whose Constitution Is It?")

It is probably safe to say that Marshall's opinion in Marbury would not have come as a great surprise to the authors of the Constitution; however, it is also probably true that they did not envision the Court becoming a major policy maker—a role that the doctrine of judicial review makes possible and that the Court enjoys today, as Chapters 3 and 12

original jurisdiction

Authority of a court over cases that begin in that court; courts of general jurisdiction have original jurisdiction over most criminal offenses, the original jurisdiction of the U.S. Supreme Court is very small

appellate jurisdiction

Includes cases a court receives from lower courts; Congress defines the appellate jurisdiction of the U.S. Supreme Court

judicial review

The authority of courts to set aside a legislative act as being in violation of the Constitution

Kentucky and Virginia Resolutions

A challenge to national supremacy, these state documents declared states to be the final authority on the meaning of the Constitution

show. In fairness to Marshall, he viewed judicial review as a modest power. Whereas Marshall was not hesitant to strike down state laws that he felt conflicted with the Constitution, it was not until the infamous *Dred Scott* case in 1857—twenty-two years after Marshall's death—that the Supreme Court again set aside an act of Congress as violating the Constitution.[8] (Inflaming abolitionist sentiment on the eve of the Civil War, this decision denied congressional authority to prohibit slavery in the territories and asserted that African Americans were not intended to be citizens under the Constitution.)

Because of judicial review, the changes wrought by custom and formal amendment, and the needs of an expanding nation, what Americans mean by "the Constitution" today is vastly different from the document that emerged from the convention in Philadelphia in 1787. Yet the Constitution, coupled with a commitment to constitutionalism, continues to play a vital role in the third century of American government.

CHAPTER REVIEW

1. The Constitution of the United States is a living document—the charter of the nation—and thus has a presence that gives it a special place in American government.

2. The Declaration of Independence attempted to justify revolution against Great Britain by explaining the purposes of government. The Articles of Confederation represented the first effort at establishing a central government for the newly independent states, but the plan proved to be defective.

3. The Philadelphia Convention in 1787 produced a plan for a new national government that had to be approved by conventions in nine states before going into effect.

4. The Constitution was designed to achieve both effective and limited government: effective by granting powers sufficient for a strong union and limited by restraining and arranging those powers to protect liberty.

5. The possibility of amendment helps explain how the Constitution remains current in its third century. The Constitution has also been remade through interpretation by the courts and through custom and usage.

6. *Marbury v. Madison* brought judicial review to the Constitution in 1803. As a result, the Supreme Court sits as the final authority on the meaning of the Constitution.

KEY TERMS

Annapolis Convention 10

Antifederalists. 13

appellate jurisdiction. 27

Articles of Confederation 7

checks and balances. 17

colony 5

commerce clause. 22

constitutionalism 4

Federalists. 13

Great Compromise 13

John Locke. 6

judicial review 27

Kentucky and Virginia Resolutions. 27

Marbury v. Madison 25

necessary and proper clause 22

New Jersey Plan 12

Northwest Ordinance. 10

original jurisdiction. 27

republican (or representative) government. 16

Shays' Rebellion 10

The Federalist 13

three-fifths compromise. 13

Virginia Plan 12

writ of mandamus. 25

READINGS FOR FURTHER STUDY

A Machine That Would Go of Itself, by Michael Kammen (Piscataway, NJ: Transaction, 2006), explores the role of constitutionalism in American life.

Decisions of the Supreme Court interpreting the Constitution are readily found in edited form in casebooks such as Lee Epstein, Kevin T. McGuire, and Thomas G. Walker, *Constitutional Law for a Changing America: A Short Course,* 8th ed. (Washington, DC: CQ Press, 2020).

An explanation of the Constitution, section by section, appears in Sue Davis and J. W. Peltason, *Corwin and Peltason's Understanding the Constitution,* 17th ed. (Belmont, CA: Wadsworth, 2008).

Useful insight into American political thought in the founding era can be gleaned from Gordon S. Wood, *The Creation of the American Republic, 1776–1787* (Chapel Hill: University of North Carolina Press, 1998).

The Federalist essays are widely available in several editions.

The best collection of antifederalist literature is Herbert J. Storing, ed., *The Complete Anti-Federalist,* 3 vols. (Chicago: University of Chicago Press, 2007).

A wide range of writings from the founding era is collected in Bruce Frohnen, ed., *The American Republic: Primary Sources* (Indianapolis: Liberty Fund, 2002).

Constitutional development since colonial days is the subject of Alfred H. Kelly, Winfred A. Harbison, and Herman Belz, *The American Constitution,* 7th ed., 2 vols. (New York: Norton, 1991).

NOTES

1. See Max Farrand, *The Records of the Federal Convention of 1787,* 4 vols. (New Haven, CT: Yale University Press, 1911).

2. John Quincy Adams, *The Jubilee of the Constitution* (New York: Samuel Colman, 1839), p. 55.

3. *Heart of Atlanta Motel v. United States,* 379 U.S. 274 (1964). This is a citation to a Supreme Court decision. "U.S." stands for the *United States Reports,* the official publication containing decisions by the Supreme Court. The number 379 preceding "U.S." and the number 274 following "U.S." indicate the volume and page, respectively, of the *reports* in which the case can be found. For more information about Supreme Court decisions, see Chapter 12.

4. *McCulloch v. Maryland,* 17 U.S. (4 Wheaton) 316, 415 (1819) (emphasis deleted). "Wheaton" was the name of the Supreme Court's reporter of decisions at this time. Until 1875, when the use of "U.S." became the rule, citations to Supreme Court decisions contained the reporter's name. Hence, this case was in volume 4 of the reports published by Henry Wheaton.

5. Marcia Coyle, "No Set Procedure for Amendments," *National Law Journal,* June 1, 1992, p. 10.

6. Richard Hofstadter, *The Idea of a Party System* (Berkeley: University of California Press, 1969), p. 128.

7. *Marbury v. Madison,* 5 U.S. (1 Cranch) 137 (1803).

8. *Scott v. Sanford,* 60 U.S. (19 Howard) 393 (1857).

POP QUIZ

1. The Declaration of Independence contains a strong belief that government is the creation and servant of the _____ .

2. Under the Articles of Confederation, the _____ retained most political power.

3. Supporters of the proposed Constitution called themselves _____ .

4. The _____ authorizes Congress to pass laws allowing it to carry into execution its expressed powers.

5. The British Constitution can be changed by an act of Parliament.   T   F

6. Virtual unanimity existed in the colonies in favor of declaring independence in 1776.   T   F

7. One of the few successes of Congress under the Articles of Confederation was the Northwest Ordinance.   T   F

8. As written, the Constitution facilitates the political parties and interest groups, called *factions* by Madison.   T   F

9. The Constitution of the United States is longer than most state constitutions.   T   F

10. Prior to the American Revolution, what did British leaders in London do?
    A) attempted to force the colonies to raise armies for self defense
    B) repealed the Townshend Acts, allowing the colonies to tax
    C) gave the colonies power to appoint their own governors
    D) attempted to bring the colonies under more direct control

11. Which of the following is not a major theme of the Declaration of Independence?
    A) Humankind shares equality.
    B) Government is a divinely ordained compact between people and God.
    C) The rights that all people intrinsically possess constitute a higher law binding government.
    D) Governments are bound by their own laws.

12. Which of the following was one of the major deficiencies of the Articles of Confederation?
    A) too great a policy-making role for the national courts
    B) the ability of the states to declare war separately
    C) the ease by which the Articles could be amended by the states
    D) the absence of sufficient power in the central government

13. One of the few successes of the Articles of Confederation was the _____ .
    A) Annapolis Convention
    B) Northwest Ordinance
    C) Townshend Acts
    D) three-fifths compromise

14. In order for the new Constitution to go into effect, it had to be approved by which of the following?
    A) all of the state legislatures
    B) seven of the thirteen state legislatures
    C) popularly elected conventions in nine states
    D) popularly elected conventions in all of the states

15. The Kentucky and Virginia Resolutions of 1798 did which of the following?
    A) called for the Supreme Court to have the power of judicial review
    B) favored decentralized over centralized judicial review
    C) claimed for the states the final authority to interpret the Constitution
    D) called for Congress to have the power of judicial review

Answers:
1. people 2. states 3. Federalists
4. necessary and proper (or elastic clause)
5. T 6. F 7. T 8. F 9. F 10. D
11. B 12. D 13. B 14. C 15. C

Chapter

02

FEDERALISM: STATES IN THE UNION

In This Chapter

2.1   The Idea of Federalism
2.2   States in the Constitutional System
2.3   Government Relationships in the Federal System
2.4   Federalism Today

Chapter Objectives

The Constitution established a national government with power dispersed among separate branches. The document also created a second kind of power diffusion: the sharing of power between the national government and individual states. This sharing of power is the principal characteristic of a "federal" system. At its root, federalism is the product and symbol of the continuing struggle between the value of unity and the value of diversity as they compete for dominance in the political system.

This chapter considers the meaning of federalism and why comprehending it is crucial to a full understanding of American government. Continuing tension between national and state governments requires a look at the place of state governments in the Constitution and their role in American politics. The chapter discusses the legal, fiscal, and political relationships among national, state, and local governments.

The national government has progressively become more dominant, but the chapter concludes by reviewing federalism as a complex, adaptable system of relationships in which states have begun to assume a more energetic and vigorous role in domestic policy.

2.1 The Idea of Federalism

Federalism is a system of government in which the national government and state governments share power within the same political system. As the terrorist attacks on the World Trade Center and Pentagon in 2001, the devastation of Hurricane Katrina in 2005, the COVID-19 pandemic, and the ongoing tragedy of mass shootings have all demonstrated, a single event may trigger action by officials at both levels of government.

In a federal system, both the national and state governments have jurisdiction over individuals. For example, in preparation for the tax-filing deadline each year, individual citizens perform tasks resulting directly from the existence of a federal system. Taxpayers must file returns with the national government; in most states (those that choose to have income taxes), they must also file returns with state governments. The duty of filing national and state tax returns illustrates an important point about federalism: Individuals receive services both from Washington, DC, and their state capitals, and they must consequently send money to two different levels of government.

The federal system is a compromise between a strong central government and a league of separate states. Because the states ultimately had to approve any change to the new constitution being created in 1787, the challenge for the framers was clear: How could a stronger national government be created without, at the same time, instilling so much fear in the states that the proposed new structure would be rejected? The states, after all, were already in place. The framers pressed for change, but not so much change that their efforts would fail. The result was a federal system.

2.1a Confederate, Unitary, and Federal Forms of Government

As Figure 2.1 illustrates, the powers of states and the powers of a central or national government can assume different combinations in different political systems. A **confederation** is a loose collection of states in which principal power lies at the level of the individual state rather than at the level of the central or national government. Individual states, not the central government, have jurisdiction over individuals. As discussed in Chapter 1, the Articles of Confederation made up such a system when they were in force during the decade before the Philadelphia Convention of 1787. Under the Articles, the states retained many important powers.

In contrast to a confederation, a **unitary system** of government is one in which principal power within the political system lies at the level of a national or central government rather than at the level of some smaller unit, such as a state or province. Individual citizens have direct allegiance to the national or central government, which possesses ultimate power to make all political choices and determine public policy. The government of France is an example of a unitary system. The fifty American states are themselves unitary governments with respect to their own local governments. As later discussion in this chapter will make clear, principal power *within* each state lies with the state government rather than with local governments.

Confederations are founded on the political idea of diversity and local control. Such structures allow individual states to pursue diverse approaches to policy matters. On the matter of voting rights, for example, one state might allow every citizen over the age of eighteen to vote, another might require that voters own property, and a third might make the right to vote contingent on passing a literacy test. According to the idea of diversity,

federalism

A system of government in which both the national and state governments share power within the same political system

confederation

A loose association of states in which dominant political power lies with the member states and not with the central government

unitary system

A system of government in which principal power lies at the level of a national or central government rather than at the level of some smaller unit (a state or a province) within the political system

individual states know best their own people and their own needs. Consequently, individual states ought to have their own powers to pursue individual approaches to the problems they face. On the issue of voter eligibility, consider this: The state of North Dakota does not require its citizens to register to vote. The government of that state has determined that this system is effective at encouraging residents to vote without creating any unintended problems. This is possible, in part, due to a relatively sparse population that allows for very small voting precincts. The much more populous state of New York, on the other hand, has determined that registration twenty-five days before an election is necessary to avoid potential problems with voter fraud. The federal nature of American government allows for such diversity.

Unitary structures rest on the value of unity. Such structures assume that there is a national interest in meeting needs and problems in a particular way. Individuals are citizens of the nation (not of separate states); procedures and approaches to policy problems ought to be uniform rather than individualized and disparate. In the voting rights example, voter qualifications would be determined at the central level in the interest of a unified voting rights policy for all citizens of the nation.

Figure 2.1   Unitary, Federal, and Confederate

The central government has jurisdiction over individuals in a unitary government. If states or provinces exist, they are symbolic or administrative units with no real power. In a confederation, states are dominant and have jurisdiction over individuals. In a federal system, the central and state governments both have jurisdiction over individuals.

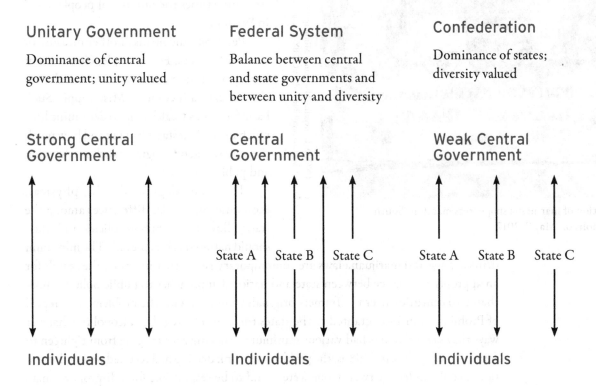

In creating a federal system, the framers of the Constitution sought to change the political structure of a loose collection of states so that the value of unity might be more easily achieved. Although they were moved by a mix of considerations in the move to a national government, the most important were probably the economy, foreign policy, and the military.[1] Foreign and military policies are areas in which centralized approaches are essential to success. Diverse approaches in these areas (e.g., if North Carolina and Massachusetts were to conduct their own foreign policies) would surely make any kind of union among the states impossible. Indeed, this was a major fault of the Articles of Confederation. The weak central government provided by the Articles had no real way to prevent the states from going in separate directions. At the same time, the framers had to acknowledge the continuing existence of diverse states—and their diverse approaches to some areas of public policy.

2.1b   Unity and Diversity in the Federal System

Diversity among the states can be measured in numerous dimensions. States differ in historical traditions, unemployment rates, economic development, ethnic composition, social welfare spending, federal funding, age distributions, religious affiliations, voter turnout rates, degrees of political party competitiveness, and even physical environments.[2] That states differ in physical size and population is readily evident. For example, Rhode Island is a state of just over 1,000 square miles; Alaska, by far the largest state, comprises more than 570,000 square miles. About 541 Rhode Islands could fit into Alaska. California, a state with 39 million people, has about sixty-nine times the number of people living in Wyoming.

Per capita income is another measure of state differences. For example, Connecticut has a per capita income that is about double the per capita income of Mississippi.[3] Such basic factors as wealth help to determine how much individual states can tax and how much they can spend on programs such as education and public assistance.

To what degree should physical, economic, and social differences among the states allow diverse public policies, and when should national values prevail? The minimum drinking age and marijuana laws are contemporary issues that illustrate the search for an appropriate balance between state and national approaches to public policy—more than two centuries after the framers originally wrestled with the problem. The repeal of Prohibition in 1933 granted to the states the power to regulate alcohol in whatever ways they saw fit. States had various minimum drinking ages ranging from eighteen to twenty-one. By the early 1980s, the problem of drunk driving had received national attention. People under age twenty-one were found to be responsible for a disproportionate number of alcohol-related traffic fatalities and injuries. In response to growing pressure from groups such as Mothers Against Drunk Driving (MADD), Congress enacted a measure withholding a portion of national highway funds from individual states unless the states raised their minimum drinking age to twenty-one. Whether there should be a

Legalization of marijuana supporters march in South Minneapolis on May 7, 2017.

("MN NORML - Legalize Marijuana - Minneapolis MayDay Parade 2017" by Tony Webster, available under a CC BY-SA 2.0 license via Wikimedia.)

national drinking age or whether the individual states ought to decide their own minimum drinking age is a classic example of the types of debates that arise in a federal system. Is the value of unity (a national approach) more or less important than the value of diversity (individual state approaches) in a matter that had been the states' own prerogative for more than half a century?

Debate over the decriminalization or legalization of marijuana for medicinal or recreational use illustrates the same question. Although national laws prohibiting the use of certain narcotics have existed since 1914, it was not until the early 1970s that the national "War on Drugs" took its present form, with the establishment of a comprehensive drug policy and creation of the federal Drug Enforcement Administration. Concerns about high enforcement and incarceration costs, lack of effective prevention efforts, and questions surrounding the costs and benefits of marijuana for some medicinal uses led several states to balk at the federal policy. In 1996, California voters passed a law making it legal—under state law—for residents to possess marijuana for personal medicinal use. Since then, thirty-two other states and the District of Columbia have passed similar laws, creating an awkward situation where medical marijuana use is a violation of federal law, but not state law, in two-thirds of the country. Eleven states, as well as Washington, DC, have approved marijuana for both recreational and medical use. The Supreme Court has upheld the federal government's authority to regulate marijuana, but the tension between federal and state law has made marijuana decriminalization a hot political issue in the twenty-first century. While the Obama administration largely avoided enforcing federal marijuana laws, the Trump administration took a more oppositional stance toward state legalization of marijuana. Should there be a uniform national law on marijuana use, or should states decide for themselves the acceptable use of this drug within their borders?

2.1c   A Comparative Perspective on Federalism

Federalism is not unique to the United States. Other countries that have federal constitutional systems include Australia, Brazil, India, Malaysia, Nigeria, Pakistan, Switzerland, and Venezuela. Although such countries may differ in size, wealth, and military power, what is common among them is their attempt to pull together disparate groups while at the same time acknowledging the groups' separate identities. The search for the appropriate balance in power between the states and the national government in the United States resonates in other federal systems as well.

Daniel Elazar, the renowned federalism scholar, wrote that "[f]ederalism has to do with the need of people and polities to unite for common purposes yet remain separate to preserve their respective integrities. It is rather like wanting to have one's cake and eat it too."[4] Groups in federal systems might be cultural or language minorities, people living in geographical units whose history predates the creation of the federal system, or different religious denominations in which no single one is dominant. Federal systems have pulled together, or tried to, French and English speakers, Lithuanians and Ukrainians, and Pennsylvanians and New Yorkers. Such groups get together for purposes such as a common defense or a common currency, but they retain their separate identities for other purposes, such as education or law enforcement.

The relative power of the central government and constituent groups will vary among countries, but federal

Despite their name, the Antifederalists actually favored federalism. A collection of their views on the need for strong state governments can be found within the timeline at this site:

http://www.bvtlab.com/78q88

systems generally have a dynamic quality in which there is a continuing search for the appropriate balance between national purposes and group needs. Some of the world's great political conflicts are essentially struggles to define this balance. For example, debate over the political status of French-speaking Quebec—the only one of Canada's ten provinces with a French majority—has strained Canadian politics for years. Whether Quebec can, or will, go it alone remains a troubling issue for Canada.

The dissolution of the Soviet Union is an illustration of how changes in a federal system can have momentous implications for world politics. The Soviet Union, a military superpower, comprised fifteen republics held together by the Communist Party and backed by the threat of military force. Unchallenged central control made the system federal in name only. Worsening economic conditions, the emergence of ethnic demands, and attempts at liberal reforms showed cracks in the system. After an attempted coup by Communist Party hard-liners failed in 1991, the central government's power over the fifteen Soviet republics dwindled sharply. Individual republics declared their independence, and what was left of the Soviet Union quickly unraveled. The Soviet government officially disbanded several months after the failed coup and was replaced by the Commonwealth of Independent States in which the republics retained their independent status.[5] Today, the former Soviet republics are largely autonomous states, allying themselves when appropriate via international treaties and organizations, but displaying few traces of the once forced federal relationship.

2.2 States in the Constitutional System

That there are fifty states is a historical accident. If wars had been lost instead of won, if treaties and land purchases had not been made, if rivers coursed through different areas, the number, names, and sizes of states would be different. States are integral parts of our social and political consciousness. State boundaries are superimposed on satellite pictures of weather patterns. State universities enjoy great attention through the exploits of their athletic teams, and children in elementary schools throughout the land spend time trying to memorize the names of state capitals. The existence of states is a ubiquitous part of American life.

States play a crucial role in the American political system. They administer social welfare policies, grapple with regional problems, amend the Constitution, and shape electoral contests at the national level. States act in some measure as administrative units to help carry out national social welfare programs substantially funded by Congress, such as the Supplemental Nutrition Assistance Program (SNAP), Medicaid, and Temporary Assistance

(USDA.gov)

State governments act as administrators to carry out national social welfare policies such as welfare benefits, SNAP, EBT (Electronic Benefit Transfer), Medicaid, and TANF programs.

for Needy Families (TANF). Through the device of the **interstate compact**, states can enter into formal agreements with other states to deal with policy problems that cross state lines. An example is the agreement between New York and New Jersey to establish the New York Port Authority to regulate transportation in the New York City area. States also play a role in the process of formally amending the Constitution. Although controversy between states has raged over a variety of proposed amendments—involving issues like abortion, flag burning, and a balanced budget—no formal change to the Constitution can be made without the states considering, debating, and voting on the issue.

With the exception of the president and vice president of the United States, every elected official in the country is chosen either by all the voters in a particular state (the governor or a US senator) or by voters in part of a state (US representatives or state legislators). Every elected official, except for the president and vice president, has a geographic constituency that is either a state or part of a state, such as a county or a congressional district. This simple but crucial fact helps to explain much legislative behavior at the national level, such as when members of Congress press for national legislation that helps industries in their home states or oppose the closing of military bases in their districts.

The **Electoral College**, a political institution that—following the mandate in the Constitution—determines the winner in presidential elections, is another illustration of the role of the states. (As the Electoral College is both an important facet of American federalism and the key to understanding presidential elections, your text will discuss its features both here and in Chapter 8.) Presidents are elected not by a plurality (the highest number) of votes cast by voters throughout the United States, but by a majority of Electoral College votes. Each state has a number of electoral votes equal to the number of its members in the House and Senate combined. Because the number of representatives is determined by population, the states with larger numbers of people have a larger number of electoral votes. California, for example, has fifty-five electoral votes, whereas Delaware has only three. In every state but two, the presidential candidate receiving the largest number of popular votes in that state receives all of that state's electoral votes.[6]

In effect, on the day of the presidential election, fifty-one separate elections are taking place (in the fifty states and the District of Columbia). Voters choose among slates of electors committed to one or another of the candidates. When the popular votes in each state are counted, state-by-state Electoral College vote totals are combined to determine the presidential victor. After the election, victorious electors officially cast their presidential votes in their respective state capitals. From the perspective of federalism, the important point is that states as states play a crucial role in electing the person who holds the most important political office in the land. Presidential candidates must appeal not to an amorphous mass of citizens but to Texans, North Carolinians, Californians, and Virginians.

The center of the US population changes as more and more people follow the sun and move to the South and the West. Florida, California, and Texas have gained population, while New York, Ohio, Pennsylvania, Illinois, and Michigan have suffered relative losses. Such population changes have implications for power shifts in the U.S. House and in the Electoral College. Table 2.1 shows the shifts in regional power between 1950 and 2020. Since the 2010 census, more than one in four members of the U.S. House come from California, Texas, or Florida, and the presidential candidate winning California receives 20 percent of the electoral votes needed to win the presidency.

interstate compact

A formal agreement between states designed to solve a problem faced by more than one state when such an agreement is necessary because political problems are not limited by geographic boundaries

Electoral College

Institution established by the Constitution for electing the president and vice president and whose members—electors chosen by the voters—actually elect the president and vice president

Table 2.1 Shifts in Regional Power: 1950 and 2020, as Measured by the Size of State Delegations in the U.S. House of Representatives

Shifts and changes in population between 1950 and 2020 meant that over the past seventy years, parts of the East and the Midwest have lost seats in the House of Representatives, while the West and South have gained seats. The apportionment of the 435 House seats is calculated for each state following the census every ten years. A state may increase its population but lose a seat if the rate of gain in other states is much greater.

Region/State	1950	2020
Mountains and Plains	29	36
Montana	2	1
Wyoming	1	1
North Dakota	2	1
South Dakota	2	1
Nebraska	4	3
Kansas	6	4
New Mexico	2	3
Arizona	2	9
Utah	2	4
Idaho	2	2
Colorado	4	7

Region/State	1950	2020
Midwest	117	85
Minnesota	9	8
Wisconsin	10	8
Michigan	17	14
Iowa	8	4
Illinois	26	18
Indiana	11	9
Ohio	23	16
Missouri	13	8

Region/State	1950	2020
East	127	87
Maine	3	2
New Hampshire	2	2
Vermont	1	1
Massachusetts	14	9
Connecticut	6	5
Rhode Island	2	2
New York	45	27
Pennsylvania	33	18
New Jersey	14	12
Maryland	6	8
Delaware	1	1

Region/State	1950	2020
South	128	152
West Virginia	6	3
Virginia	9	11
Oklahoma	8	5
Arkansas	7	4
Kentucky	9	6
North Carolina	12	13
Tennessee	10	9
South Carolina	6	7
Texas	21	36
Louisiana	8	6
Mississippi	7	4
Alabama	9	7
Georgia	10	14
Florida	6	27

Region/State	1950	2020
West	34	75
Washington	6	10
Oregon	4	5
California	23	53
Nevada	1	4
Alaska	N/A	1
Hawaii	N/A	2

N/A = not applicable

2.2a The Rise of the National Government

As Chapter 1 made clear, the states were clearly dominant under the Articles of Confederation. The national government quite literally started out from nothing; yet we have today a national government whose actions—from delivering Social Security checks to regulating the safety of toys and power plants—pervade the daily lives of citizens. How did this change come about? Massive technological, communication, and economic changes have transformed the nation over the past two centuries. War and depression have made their own contributions to the shift in focus of demands and expectations.

The conflict between unity and diversity, which gave birth to the federal system, also shaped the relationships between the national and state governments in the early decades of the new nation. The national government cooperated with the states in a variety of areas. Because economic development was among the highest of priorities for the new nation, the national government provided funds and technical assistance to the states for construction of roads and canals. Land grants to states in the West for educational purposes signaled greater cooperation between the national government and the states to come.[7]

Despite the cooperation, however, sharp conflicts also occurred between the national government and the states in the early decades of the Republic. The Kentucky and Virginia Resolutions, adopted by the legislatures of those states in 1798, held that the Constitution created a compact among the states and that the power of the national government was sharply limited by the states. In 1819 the state of Maryland contested the right of the national government to establish a national bank (leading to the Supreme Court case *McCulloch v. Maryland,* discussed in the following section), and in 1832 the South Carolina legislature declared a national tariff law null and void. The very existence of national power was at issue in these instances of nation/state conflict.

The federal system was ultimately tested in war. The early skirmishes between the national government and the states paled in significance compared to the Civil War. At one level, the war was about the question of slavery; at another level, the war was about the question of federalism. Could a state (or several states) leave the Union and, in effect, unravel the work of the Constitutional Convention of 1787? From the perspective of federalism, the most important consequence of the war was preservation of the Union. President Lincoln is best known as emancipator of the slaves, but his sharp and unyielding refusal to allow dissolution of the Union was crucial in the evolution of federalism. The significance of Lincoln's stance cannot be overstated. Lincoln, the chief executive in a national government that had not even existed a century earlier, used *national* resources in a major war effort to resist by brute force the claims of the seceding states—four of which predated the national government itself.

("Young Texas mother," photographed by Dorothea Lange, 1935. Courtesy of the Library of Congress.)

A twenty-two-year-old mother with her children, camped in a resettlement camp for migrants during the Great Depression.

The end of the Civil War marked the beginning of a rapid change in the character of the nation's economy. Transcontinental railroads pulled the nation together and brought farmers, producers, and sellers closer to buyers and consumers. Major new industries—such as steel, oil, and, later, the automobile—began to emerge. With them came new forms of economic organization.

Corporations crossed state boundaries in their activities and their effects. Control and regulation of economic matters increasingly eluded the grasp of any single state, resulting in political demands by the states that the national government confront the problems that economic monopolies left in their trail.

Later, in the twentieth century, the economy plunged into the Great Depression of the 1930s. Farm and industrial prices collapsed, factories closed, banks failed, homes were foreclosed, and unemployment rates rose dramatically. State and local governments were overwhelmed by the needs and demands of millions of Americans who clearly needed help to survive. National problems seemed to require national solutions. As never before, the national government embarked on a series of social welfare policies—known as the New Deal—that both improved the economic conditions of many and generated expectations that the national government could solve a variety of social problems in the future. Today many domestic programs administered by the states or their localities are funded by the national government.

Finally, the national government is responsible for national security and relations with other nations. In the twentieth century, the Cold War and the increasing interdependence of the world economy combined to make the national government's conduct of foreign affairs important on a continuing basis. Although the Cold War has ended, demands for a revitalized military establishment remain strong; and the need for national government policies to enhance the nation's competitiveness in the global economy have become more acute.

The seemingly inexorable rise in the power of the national government has been accompanied by political demands that state and local governments assume a larger presence in the making of policy decisions affecting them. For example, **New Federalism**—a term most closely associated with the Republican administrations of Richard Nixon (1969–1974) and Ronald Reagan (1981–1989)—calls for state and local governments to assume a much greater role than they traditionally had during the explosions of national policy initiatives that took place during the Democratic administrations of Franklin Roosevelt (1933–1945) (the New Deal) and Lyndon Johnson (1963–1969) (the Great Society).[8] New Federalism took on a new life during the George W. Bush (2001–2009) administration, this time in the form of calling for state self-reliance during crises and scaling back federal environmental regulations. New Federalism holds that not only should state and local governments be entrusted with greater responsibilities but that they should also be allowed to follow their own best judgment in making decisions. Giving state and local governments more discretion in how they spend national grant money is an illustration. This view of federalism dovetails with the traditional Republican Party "grassroots" philosophy that the government in the best position to make good policy choices is the government "closest" to the people. Whether nationally defined policy goals, such as the amelioration of poverty, can (or should) accommodate state and local policies that may diverge from those goals is an old question in federalism. A recent example of this tension has been the balance between national and state leadership in responding to the COVID-19 pandemic. While the national government declared a national emergency and established limitations on international travel and immigration, states and localities developed rules and guidelines for closing schools and businesses and limiting public gatherings.

New Federalism

A view of federalism that posits an expanded role for state and local governments and holds that state and local governments should be entrusted with greater responsibilities

2.2b Express and Implied Powers

The search for the right balance between state and national power remains an enduring issue in the federal system. What powers do the states have in their relationships to each other and to the national government? What powers does the national government

have over the states? The Republic has struggled with these questions since 1787. The Constitution prohibits the exercise of some powers by one or both levels of national and state governments; for example, states may not coin money. In addition, national and state governments share some concurrent powers, such as the power each has to tax the same individual's income. However, the most important point about national and state powers is the distinction between *delegated* and *reserved* powers.

Keep up to date on the latest developments in state politics at the Council of State Governments website.

http://www.bvtlab.com/727EB

In accepting the Constitution, the people in the states—through the ratification process—delegated important powers to the new national government. The statement of these powers is contained in Article I, Section 8, of the Constitution (see the Appendix). **Delegated powers** are ordinarily divided into two types: express powers and implied powers. **Express powers** are specifically enumerated as belonging to Congress. Among these are the powers to levy and collect taxes, to borrow money, to regulate interstate commerce, to coin money, to declare war, and to raise and support armies.

However, the last statement of power listed in Article I, Section 8, also delegates to the national government **implied powers**, which by their very nature have been subject to intense dispute. As discussed in Chapter 1, this provision is also known as the elastic or necessary and proper clause and delegates to Congress the power "to make all Laws which shall be necessary and proper for carrying into Execution the foregoing Powers, and all other Powers vested by this Constitution in the Government of the United States, or in any Department or Officer thereof." Obviously, what is "necessary and proper" in a particular circumstance is a matter open to varying interpretations. A narrow interpretation would constrict the powers of the national government, whereas a broad interpretation would enlarge them.

The first time the clause was specifically interpreted was in *McCulloch v. Maryland*, one of the most famous and consequential Supreme Court decisions ever made.[9] The case represented an ideological division over the powers of the national government and the place of the states in the Union. Conflicting political objectives were sought in terms of opposing theories of federalism. Congress had chartered a national bank. Some states opposed the bank because it competed with state-chartered banks. Hoping to put the national bank out of business, Maryland imposed a tax on the new bank. McCulloch, its cashier, refused to pay. As part of its case, Maryland argued not only that a state could tax a nationally chartered bank but also that Congress had no authority to charter a bank in the first place because banking was not a power delegated to Congress. Instead, Maryland claimed, banking was a power the Constitution reserved for the states.

Contrary to Maryland's claims, Chief Justice John Marshall (1801–1835) declared that Congress possessed ample constitutional authority to charter a bank, even though such a power was not expressly listed in the Constitution. In Marshall's view, the power to establish a bank was implied in the express powers, such as the powers to tax and to coin money. A bank was a means to achieving the ends spelled out in the Constitution. Marshall's interpretation of the necessary and proper clause clearly allowed expansive power to the national government. In his memorable words,

> Let the end be legitimate, let it be within the scope of the Constitution, and all means which are appropriate, which are plainly adapted to that end, which are not prohibited, but consistent with the letter and spirit of the constitution, are constitutional.

delegated powers

Legal authority that the people in the states granted to the national government for certain purposes by ratifying the Constitution; can be either express or implied

express powers

Powers specifically enumerated in the Constitution as belonging to the national government

implied powers

Powers of national government that are not specifically cited in the Constitution but that are implicit in powers expressly granted by the Constitution

McCulloch v. Maryland

Supreme Court case in 1819 that established the constitutionality of a national bank and solidified national power by confirming that the federal government can exercise implied powers to carry out legitimate and otherwise constitutional ends

Furthermore, Marshall held that Maryland could not tax the bank because it was an instrument of the national government. In a conflict between an act of Congress and a state law, the former would prevail. No single part of the political community could be allowed to subvert a policy undertaken by the whole community represented in Congress.

Because of the brevity of the Constitution, many of its clauses and phrases are ambiguous and give little or no direction as to what is "legitimate" in a particular circumstance. The framers could not address every problem or clarify every uncertainty. According to Marshall's decision in *McCulloch,* the Constitution created a stronger national government by delegating to it express and implied powers. Exactly how strong it was to be or how it would evolve was left for later generations to decide.

2.2c   Reserved Powers: What Do the States Do?

If the new government was to be more powerful and the states were, nonetheless, to continue to exist, what powers were left to the states? Although simpler in theory than in practice, the principle is that states can do all things not specifically prohibited to them and not delegated exclusively to the national government. These remaining powers are known

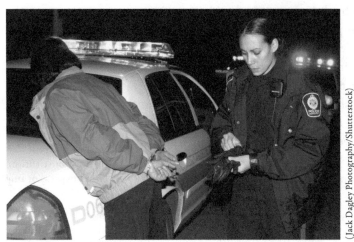

(Jack Dagley Photography/Shutterstock)

as **reserved powers**. State and local governments are responsible for delivering the vast majority of public services. About 2.7 million civilian employees work for the national government, a number that has decreased slightly since a peak of 3.1 million in 1990. However, growth in government employment has occurred at the state and local levels. The most recently reported figures, in 2018, indicate that state and local governments employ just over 19 million people—about seven times the number of civilian employees working for the national government.[10] This number of employees indicates that states and localities play a large role in providing public services.

State officers, such as police and sheriffs, track down suspected criminals—rapists, murderers, thieves, burglars, muggers, and assorted swindlers. These suspects are tried and prosecuted primarily in state courts and incarcerated primarily in state prisons.

The **Tenth Amendment** states that "the powers not delegated to the United States by the Constitution, nor prohibited by it to the States, are reserved to the States respectively, or to the people." Politicians and groups whose political ideas are served by advocating "states' rights" have frequently pointed to the Tenth Amendment as support for their claims. However, that amendment, unlike the Articles of Confederation, does not contain the word *expressly* in citing powers delegated to the national government. Such delegated powers therefore include the implied powers cited by Chief Justice Marshall in *McCulloch v. Maryland.*

Among powers reserved for the states are "police" responsibilities for the health, safety, and welfare of citizens. For civilized life to be possible, people must be able to carry on their day-to-day activities with the reasonable assurance that physical threats to their health and well-being are kept to an absolute minimum. For example, among the health responsibilities of states are those such as dealing with outbreaks of contagious diseases, the disposal of wastes, cleanliness in public eating establishments, and the administration of networks of state hospitals and mental institutions.

reserved powers

Powers not specifically prohibited to the states and not delegated to the national government by the Constitution

Tenth Amendment

Amendment ratified in 1791 that reserves to the states powers not prohibited to them and not delegated to the national government by the Constitution

In one of their most visible roles, the states also have primary responsibility for preventing and prosecuting criminal activities. Most of this work occurs at the level of local governments whose organization, powers, and functions are constitutionally subject to control by state governments. Some crimes—such as airline hijacking, kidnapping, tampering with US mail, and counterfeiting money—are violations of national law enforced by the national government. However, most law enforcement officers in the country are state agents and local personnel who act as agents of the state. From state police officers to county sheriffs who track down suspected criminals to the local police who deal with matters such as burglary and domestic violence, most law enforcement responsibilities lie at the state and local levels. Most suspected rapists, murderers, thieves, burglars, muggers, and assorted swindlers are pursued only by state and local law enforcement personnel, prosecuted only in state courts, and incarcerated only in state prisons.

Sometimes these state police powers and national policy interests come into conflict. The Constitution grants the national government control over immigration via the power to "establish a uniform Rule of Naturalization" in Article I, Section 8. Despite a thorough set of federal immigration laws, some states, frustrated by increases in illegal immigration, have enacted their own statutes. In 2010 Arizona passed a law making it a state crime to be in the country illegally, banning undocumented immigrants from working in the state, authorizing police to arrest individuals they suspect of having committed a deportable offense upon probable cause, and requiring police to check the immigration status of everyone they detain. In the 2012 case Arizona v. United States, the Supreme Court held the first three of these provisions to be unconstitutional because they are preempted by federal laws and sent the fourth back for further review by the lower courts.[11]

Most individuals encounter state power in a direct and personal way many times in their lives. A variety of inoculations and vaccinations may be required by the state before entrance into the elementary school system. To drive a car, you must apply for a state driver's license and pass a driver's test administered by a state officer. Individuals who wish to marry must apply for a state marriage license, and the ceremony is performed either by a state public official (such as a justice of the peace) or by an individual (often a religious leader, like a minister, priest, or rabbi) who acts as an agent of the state in performing the ceremony. In divorce, the contesting parties must go through some state judicial proceeding to legally dissolve the relationship; and when the custody of children is at issue, state courts are called on to make the decision.

States also play a regulatory role in a variety of matters having to do with business and commerce within the state. From laws on safety to zoning practices to requirements for filing periodic tax and information reports—practically no enterprise can escape the touch of the state. Entrance into many professions is controlled by state licensing boards, which set rules, regulations, and standards that are supposed to ensure the quality of services delivered to citizens, but which also serve to limit entry into the profession. Such licensing procedures touch barbers, lawyers, medical specialists, dietitians, cosmetologists, real estate agents, and even taxidermists.

Perhaps the most visible and pervasive role of the state is in the area of public education. State policies of universal education have emerged from a belief in the importance of schools for improving literacy, inculcating civic and cultural values, and generally enhancing the capabilities of citizens. In administering educational systems, local school districts are agencies of the state. Curricula, certification of teachers, length of the school year, and policy on truancy are all matters of state power and concern. Some of the great policy debates of the past generation have focused on the role of the states in education. Should prayers be said aloud in the schools, or should a moment of silence for "meditation" be allowed at the beginning of each school day? Should schools be desegregated, and if so, how? Should the busing of schoolchildren be required to achieve integration?

Should states be required to equalize expenditures among wealthier and poorer school districts? The *national* government can pursue *national* approaches, but its stress on unity can limit or threaten diversity among the states. Educational policy debates illustrate the vitality of the federal system. When should the national government have its way, and when should the states be allowed to go their separate ways? In recent years, the federal No Child Left Behind law and, more recently, the Every Student Succeeds Act, have challenged traditional answers to these questions.

POLITICS AND ECONOMICS

Handling a Wildfire: Federalism and Disaster Relief

On the morning of November 8, 2018, in rural northern California, a metal hook on a power transmission line broke, sparking a fire. Strong winds, canyon geography, and drought conditions turned this small fire into an inferno in short order. What would become known as the Camp Fire (due to the name of the road nearest to where it ignited) would take at least 85 lives and burn more than 153,000 acres, destroying 19,000 homes and other structures before eventually being extinguished more than two weeks later. The Camp Fire destroyed the town of Paradise, California, and smaller nearby communities, displacing tens of thousands of residents, with financial damages in excess of $16 billion. Two years after the fire, many of those affected remained without adequate housing, and many communities had not been rebuilt.

The emergency response to the Camp Fire, as is the case with many large-scale wildfires each year, involved dozens of government agencies. Due

to our federal system of government, agencies at all three levels—national, state, and local—were involved in the rescue and recovery efforts. Initially a matter of local responsibility, the scope of this disaster quickly led the national government to declare a federal disaster and to instruct the Federal Emergency Management Agency (FEMA) to take the lead. An agency within the Department of Homeland Security, FEMA has as its mission "to lead America to prepare for, prevent, respond to and recover from disasters." In this case, that responsibility included coordinating the efforts of numerous agencies, such as the U.S. Small Business Association, as well as cooperating with state and local agencies like the

California Office of Emergency Services, and nongovernmental agencies like the American Red Cross.

The difficulty of coordinating all of these agencies—each with its own goals, training, and procedures—can lead to inefficiencies, redundancies, and criticism. After Hurricane Katrina in 2005, for example, many questioned whether or not FEMA had mishandled the relief efforts, in effect making the situation worse than it should have been. Politicians and media pundits accused then-FEMA Director Michael Brown of incompetence, and the director soon resigned under pressure. In contrast, most saw FEMA's handling of the Camp Fire in a much more positive light. Blame in this case fell not on those who led the

A neighborhood devastated by fire in Paradise, California.

relief efforts, but on the company the state of California would soon find responsible for causing the fire: Pacific Gas and Electric (PG&E), one of the state's largest energy service providers. Facing lawsuits from those harmed by the fire, in January 2019, PG&E filed for bankruptcy protection in federal court. Over the course of the next two years both the federal and state court systems would effectively coordinate efforts to aid individuals and local governments in receiving financial relief from the company responsible for the fire, while approving a plan for PG&E to emerge from bankruptcy

What is the proper balance of responsibility between federal, state, and local levels of government in disaster relief? Should the federal government's superior financial resources supersede concerns about overcentralization? Should the federal government foot the bill but then defer to the potentially greater expertise of state and local agencies when it comes to implementation? How did the public react to this emergency? Some have argued that wildfires, hurricanes, and other natural disasters in recent years have been exacerbated by climate change. What role should governments play in attempting to reduce climate change?

SOURCES: NBC News, "Head of California electric utility quits amid fallout from deadly wildfires," January 13, 2019, https://www.nbcnews.com/news/us-news/head-california-electric-utility-quits-amid-fallout-deadly-wildfires-n958241 (July 27, 2020); "About FEMA," June 3, 2019, https://www.fema.gov/about-agency (July 27, 2020).

2.2d Local Government: A Political Landscape of Contrasts

One of the reserved powers of the states is their control over the structure and powers of local governments. The Constitution makes no mention of city or other local governments, only of the nation's capital, the "Seat of Government." This fact makes local governments "creatures of the state." The relationships between state legislatures (traditionally with a rural bias) and local governments, especially those of larger cities, have frequently been stormy. Through much of the nineteenth century, state legislatures kept local governments on a tight leash by determining with great specificity their powers, functions, and procedures. In the late nineteenth century and the first half of the twentieth century, however, many local governments—particularly those of larger cities—were granted **home rule**: the power to determine, within broad limits, their own powers and functions. In the 1960s local governments (again, those of larger cities, in particular) increasingly developed relationships—generally created by flows of cash—directly with the national government. Nonetheless, all local governments are, according to the Constitution, agents of the state, performing what are constitutionally state functions.

As shown in Table 2.2, more than ninety thousand local governments exist in the United States. These local governments perform many of the unglamorous services essential to civilized life, such as collecting trash, pursuing criminals, putting out fires, and providing drinking water. Local governments range in size from huge cities like New York with more than eight million people (more than in forty entire states) to small villages and hamlets with fewer than one hundred inhabitants. Governments at the local level differ in their structure. Some have a **mayor-council** form of government, which mirrors the executive-legislative structure at the state and national levels. Others have a **council-manager** form in which appointed managers look after the day-to-day operations of the government. Still others have a commission form of government in which power is diffused, and no single individual is in charge. Some local governments are "general purpose"—that is, they are responsible for a wide variety of functions, including police protection, housing, social services, and parks administration. School districts and special districts overlap these general-purpose governments and are limited to a single function, such as education, mosquito control, fire protection, or transportation.

home rule

A legal status in which local governments, especially large cities, can determine for themselves within broad parameters their own powers and functions without interference from the state government

mayor-council

A form of government at the local level that mirrors the executive-legislative structure at the state and national levels where the mayor has executive powers and the council has legislative powers

council-manager

A form of government at the local level where an elected council exercises legislative powers and hires a city manager to perform executive and administrative duties

Table 2.2 Governmental Units in the Federal System

The federal system contains many governments, but they do not all do the same things. The national government, all state governments, and many local governments are general-purpose governments; that is, they perform a wide variety of functions. A city government, for example, will typically provide police protection and numerous social services. School districts and special districts geographically overlap with general-purpose governments and perform only a single function, such as education, water distribution, fire protection, or sewage treatment. The largest growth in number of governmental units in recent years has occurred in special districts, due to the fact that they enable local areas to collectively provide services that they could not afford individually. Moreover, the particular tasks of special districts often stretch beyond the boundaries of local general-purpose governments. Finally, some local governments, such as towns or townships, have not been given power by their state constitutions and governments to perform such functions.

1	National government
50	State governments
90,075	Local governments
3,031	Counties (called parishes in Louisiana)
16,253	Towns and townships
19,495	Municipal governments
12,754	School districts
38,542	Special districts

SOURCE: U.S. Census Bureau, 2017 Census of Governments, October 2019.

Although residents do not usually pay much attention to local government, they can and do get intensely interested during a local crisis or controversy. For example, when the water supply becomes polluted with toxic waste, citizens get involved. School board meetings can be drab affairs, but they can become arenas of excitement and drama when matters such as sex education programs or higher taxes to fund a new school are at stake. Similarly, most local zoning board hearings are routine and sparsely attended, but proposals such as a hamburger chain seeking to locate near a predominantly residential area, or the efforts of a chemical company to place a toxic waste facility in or near a town, are issues that practically guarantee action by affected residents. In terms of size, structure, function, and degree of citizen interest, local governments are a mosaic of contrasts.

2.3 Government Relationships in the Federal System

The existence of different levels of government within a federal system means that federalism is about *relationships* among governments.[12] Because these governmental relationships are intangible and constantly shifting and changing, trying to understand them is

not an easy task. Unlike the presidency, for example, federalism is not an institution with a physical place where its work is done; however, one way to understand federalism is to picture it as a series of *legal, fiscal,* and *political* relationships among levels of government.

2.3a Models of Federalism

The federal system can at first appear to be a jumble of intangible relationships without obvious order or meaning. The effort to create models is an attempt to create pictures or portraits that bring some order to the complexity and chaos. Two models are particularly important.

The first is **dual federalism**, a model positing the view that national and state governments are separate and independent from each other, with each level exercising its own powers in its own jurisdiction. This model, supporting the rights of the states, was important as a judicial theory of federalism in the nineteenth and early twentieth centuries. In *Hammer v. Dagenhart*[13] (a decision the justices later overturned) the Supreme Court ruled that Congress could not ban shipment across state lines of products made with child labor because labor regulation was a state power only.

Dual federalism was never a completely realistic description of the relationship between the nation and the states. For example, in the nineteenth century the national government gave land to the states to use for educational purposes. Indeed, some of the nation's great universities today are among the "land grant" institutions that resulted from this policy. The model does reflect, however, the fact that the state and national governments in much of the nineteenth and early twentieth centuries did not interact with each other with the regularity taken for granted today. Dual federalism is also known as the "layer cake" model because the separate levels of government in the model are likened to distinct layers of a cake.

The second model is **cooperative federalism**. In this model, national and state governments share a number of tasks that had previously been the exclusive domain of only one level of government. Cooperative federalism is sometimes called "marble cake" federalism because it is a view of federalism that likens the intertwining relationships between the national and state and local governments to the intertwining flavors in a marble cake.[14] Cooperative federalism best describes the system that developed as a result of the expansion of national government roles in the twentieth century, particularly after implementation of the New Deal and Great Society programs. Across a wide range of public policies, despite occasional conflict, all levels of government work closely with one another. Minnesotans and Georgians are also Americans, and that fact helps to explain the intermingling of governmental functions. Interstate highways are largely funded by federal grants, but the highways are built and patrolled by the states. National and state governments jointly fund medical care for the poor. National, state, and local law enforcement authorities regularly combine forces in pursuit of criminals such as drug smugglers, bank robbers, and suspected murderers whose escape routes take them across state lines. State and local health authorities call on the expert services of the national Centers for Disease Control and Prevention when outbreaks of contagious or mysterious diseases threaten communities, such as with the COVID-19 outbreak in 2020. State emergency services agencies work with national units, such as the Federal Emergency Management Agency, when national disasters such as hurricanes or wildfires strike.

The relationships are not always smooth and free of conflict. State and local officials criticize the national government for cuts in funding; FBI agents may run up against local police policies that, in the agents' view, hinder efficient law enforcement work; state and local officials may confront national regulations that they see as either pointless or

dual federalism
A model of federalism in which national and state governments are separate and independent from each other, with each level exercising its own powers in its own jurisdiction

cooperative federalism
A model of federalism that features intertwining relationships and shared areas of responsibility between the national and state and local governments

unnecessarily encumbering. In recent years, tensions between local, state, and national approaches to tightened airport security and other homeland security measures have been emblematic of this ongoing struggle. Nonetheless, cooperative federalism is a portrait of the federal system in which officials from different levels of government work together regularly.

2.3b   Legal Relationships

One consequence of having different levels of government in the same political system is the potential for conflict over who has the power to do what. Legal conflicts between the national and state governments have both a rich past and a continuing vibrancy. The Supreme Court has played a major role in answering the questions that such conflicts raise.

The Court has interpreted the Constitution to mean that utilizing diverse approaches among the states in some matters is constitutionally unacceptable. It has generally supported the national government and national constitutional values in conflicts with the states. Its interpretation of the interstate commerce clause is a good example. The "regulation of interstate commerce" is one of the most important powers that the Constitution grants to Congress. This provision has allowed Congress to shape national economic and even social policy. States do have a role to play. They can enact legislation affecting commerce to protect the health and safety of citizens. States can also act in the absence of congressional action or when not prohibited by Congress. When Congress does act, the Supreme Court has generally allowed wide latitude to national legislation that limits state power in interstate commerce. For example, upholding the reach of congressional power in the Civil Rights Act of 1964, the Court held that hotels and local restaurants could not discriminate on the basis of race in their services because travelers and food served were part of interstate commerce.[15] More recently, however, the Court has indicated a willingness to restrict the definition of interstate commerce, thereby limiting congressional power to create gun-free school zones, for example, or to limit violence against women.[16] In 2012, the Court refused to accept the national government's argument that the commerce clause gave Congress the power to require individuals to purchase health insurance, though the Court majority concluded that the Patient Protection and Affordable Care Act (see discussion in Chapter 12) was constitutional as a result of Congress's taxing powers.[17] In 2019, however, the Court held that the state of Tennessee created a trade barrier that violated the federal government's interstate commerce powers by placing a two-year residency requirement on individuals seeking liquor store licenses.[18]

Through its interpretation of the due process clause of the Fourteenth Amendment, the Court has also applied most of the limitations on the power of the national government contained in the first eight amendments to the activities of the states themselves. These amendments were added to the Constitution in the early years of the new government to assuage fears that the new national government might be a powerful threat to individual liberties. Ironically, the Court has applied these limitations to the states as well. For example, states must now provide counsel for people accused of crimes and may not sponsor prayer in the public schools.[19]

The Court's interpretation of the Fourteenth Amendment's equal protection clause has also limited state power. For example the Court's reapportionment decision, which required equal populations in state legislative districts, shifted political power from rural to urban areas.[20] The Court has even shaped the structure of local government. As an example, the Court found New York City's Board of Estimate—a local government body with substantial powers over land use, the city's budget, and other matters—in violation of its "one person, one vote" rulings.[21] The five boroughs of New York had equal

representation on the board, despite great population differences among the boroughs. The Court's decision was the impetus behind the elimination of the Board of Estimate and a major restructuring of New York City's government.

Using the equal protection clause, the Court has also held that the states cannot exclusively determine for and by themselves the shape of their own school systems—even though public education has been traditionally among the reserved powers of the states. In *Brown v. Board of Education*,[22] the Court unanimously declared that racially segregated school systems are unconstitutional. Thus, some constitutional values have been deemed so important that they must be nationally determined and, if necessary, enforced by national power.

Despite the support the Court has generally given to the national government, the constitutional power of the states in conflicts with the national government is not a predetermined issue. In some recent cases the Court has weakened the power of the states and slighted the principle of federalism; in others the Court has asserted a constitutional role for the states, protecting them from incursions of congressional power. The issue of who should set minimum wages and maximum hours for the employees of state governments and their political subdivisions is an example of a case that has gone back and forth with regard to who has jurisdiction. Although the Court upheld that private employers could set wages and hours a half-century ago, it declared in 1976 that states were immune to such requirements. The Court reversed itself, however, in 1985 by ruling in *Garcia v. San Antonio Metropolitan Transit Authority* that Congress may apply minimum-wage and maximum-hour legislation to state employees.[23] Three years later, in *South Carolina v. Baker,* the Court ruled that Congress could tax state and local government bearer bonds,[24] a decision that limits the tax immunity of state and local governments. The *Garcia* and *South Carolina* decisions made state and local officials wonder whether the Court had "abandoned" Tenth Amendment protection of state powers.[25]

However, assuaging such fears, the Court ruled in 1991 that a congressional statute banning age discrimination does not overrule a provision in the Missouri Constitution requiring state judges to retire at age seventy. In other words, the state of Missouri can reasonably determine for itself mandatory retirement policies for state officials.[26] The Court also ruled, in 1992, that Congress cannot require a state to "take title" to radioactive waste produced within its borders if the state does not make provision for its disposal.[27] Additionally, in 1997 the Court struck down a congressional attempt to require local law enforcement officials to perform background checks on handgun purchasers and, in 2000, ruled unconstitutional Congress's effort to prevent states from disclosing a driver's personal information without the driver's consent.[28]

Looming on the forefront of federalism for several years was the issue of same-sex marriage—a legal arrangement that some state supreme courts ruled must be permitted under their constitutions. Though marriage has traditionally been in the domain of state law, the national attention this issue gained in recent years led some groups on both sides of the debate to push for national uniformity. The Court's decisions on this issue in 2013, while striking down a federal law that defined marriage as only a union between a man and

While marriage has traditionally been in the domain of state law, regional variation and conflict regarding the rights of same-sex couples to marry led the Supreme Court in 2015 to recognize marriage as a federally protected fundamental right.

(Bikeworldtravel/Shutterstock)

a woman, maintained that marriage rules are properly an area of state law. These cases indicated that states continued to draw on powers reserved for them in the Constitution.[29] But in 2015, facing contradictory rulings in appellate courts that threatened to create untenable regional divisions in federal law, the Supreme Court finally faced the issue directly. In *Obergefell v. Hodges,* a Court majority declared that marriage is a fundamental right and that the equal protection and due process clauses of the Fourteenth Amendment require states to preserve this right for same-sex couples.[30] The search for the proper legal balance between state and national power continues to be a point of contention; the line between them has not disappeared.

POLITICS AND IDEAS

Changing State Constitutions

In contrast to the U.S. Constitution, state constitutions are newer, longer, and more frequently changed. Of the forty-five states admitted to the union before 1900, thirteen adopted one or more constitutions in the twentieth century. Of the fifty states, thirty-one have adopted two or more constitutions, with Louisiana having approved its eleventh in 1975. Among the most recent is the Georgia constitution (the state's tenth) adopted in 1983. Only one state constitution still in force— Massachusetts's, adopted in 1780— predates the U.S. Constitution.

With about 8,300 words, only Vermont's constitution is nearly as short as the U.S. Constitution. Alabama's has 350,000 words, Texas's over 100,000, and Oklahoma's about 94,000. Much of the length of state constitutions is due to amendments. The length of state constitutions means that they are usually far more detailed than the U.S. Constitution. The abundant detail is explained by a fundamental difference in the way Americans view their national and state constitutions. The former has been largely concerned with the structure, operation, and powers of the

government. Since the early nineteenth century the latter have reflected battles within the states over economic and social issues—matters of less interest to the national government before 1890. State constitutions also reflect struggles over legislative apportionment and the franchise. Since constitutions were more permanent than statutes, contending political groups attempted to write their preferred policies into a state's higher law. Moreover, state courts could not invalidate a constitutional provision as being in conflict with the state's constitution. This is why many state constitutions today read more like statutes.

The detail in state constitutions also means that they are changed frequently. The California constitution has been amended over five hundred times, and even the new Georgia constitution had eighteen amendments added within six years of its adoption. Since 1776, some 233 constitutional conventions have been held by the states to propose new constitutions or major alterations to existing ones. Between 1900 and 1997, forty-three of the fifty states took some kind of official action to amend their constitutions, resulting in the adoption of 644 constitutional amendments—an average of nearly 13 per state. Approximately one-sixth of the 644 were "local" amendments that affected only part of a state, but the remaining amendments had statewide

applications. In both categories, the amendments typically involved finance, taxation, and debt.

States vary in the way constitutional amendments are proposed, although each state makes proposing an amendment a separate step from ratifying it. While all allow the legislature (like Congress) to propose amendments, eighteen permit a constitutional initiative. This allows voters to begin the process of constitutional change by collecting the required number of signatures on a petition. Some states, however, restrict the kind of amendment that may be proposed by an initiative. Amendments may also be proposed by convention. Indeed, the constitutions of fourteen states now require the periodic submission to the voters of the question of whether a constitutional convention should be held. By whatever means proposed, ratification of amendments in almost all states occurs following a majority vote by the electorate.

This chapter explains that much of the change in the national constitution has come about not through formal amendment but by judicial interpretation. Should Americans prefer more frequent change of the national Constitution by amendment, as is now done in the states? Should the people vote directly on changes to the national Constitution as they routinely do on changes to state constitutions?

2.3c   Fiscal Relationships

Federalism is about more than just legal relationships. Cooperative fiscal relationships have become the single most important characteristic of federalism in the twentieth and twenty-first centuries, with money acting as a kind of glue that binds the different levels of government together. It is now commonplace to cite the ratification of the **Sixteenth Amendment** in 1913, which granted Congress the power to tax incomes, as a significant event contributing to the national government's unparalleled capacity to raise revenue. This capacity to raise funds reinforced the unprecedented emergence of public expectations for national government action in the Great Depression. The national government was cast in the role of banker, doling out money to deal with social and economic ills that states had either ignored or found too large for local solutions.

Terms and conditions vary enormously from one program to another, but cash grants from the national government to state and local governments are usually divided into two groups: categorical grants-in-aid and block grants. A **categorical grant-in-aid**, the predominant form of national aid, is a transfer of cash from the national government to state or local governments for some specific purpose—usually with the accompanying requirement that state and local governments match the national money with some funds of their own. The purposes of these grants are determined by the national government, and state and local governments have little or no discretion or flexibility in how the funds can be spent. If the money is given for highways, it cannot be spent on libraries or airports. Some of these grants are given to state and local governments on the basis of formulas that take into account factors such as population, poverty, and income levels. Others distribute money for specific projects in response to applications from state or local governments.

Categorical grants are available in practically every policy area, including highways, health, education, and nutrition. The federal government's *Assistance Listings* catalog reports that there are 2,262 grant programs;[31] however, a small number of grants make up a large proportion of total grant dollars. The grants for health programs, including Medicaid (medical benefits for the poor), and income security programs (such as welfare payments) will make up over 76 percent of the grant total in 2021.[32]

A **block grant** is a transfer of cash from the national government to state and local governments that allows the recipients greater discretion in its use. Instead of defining with great specificity how the money must be spent, the national government permits expenditures in some broad policy area, such as community development, social services, or criminal justice. An increase in this type of grant has been a major federalism priority of Republican administrations because block grants allow greater discretion at the state and local levels. State and local governments prefer the flexibility allowed by block grants to the more rigid procedural requirements that accompany categorical grants.

In 1922, the national government granted to the states the relatively paltry sum of $122 million, the major proportion of which was spent on highway construction.[33] Figure 2.2 shows the sharp increase in such aid over the past several decades. Reflecting the explosion of Great Society grant programs in the 1960s, national aid in current dollars almost quintupled between 1965 and 1975, from $11 billion to $50 billion, and it almost tripled again in the decade and a half after 1975.

Figure 2.2 shows that national aid continued to rise in the 2000s; however, the growth area in national government dollars is in programs providing payments for individuals, such as Medicaid. In 1960, only 35 percent of federal grant dollars were spent on payments for individuals.

Sixteenth Amendment

Amendment to the Constitution, ratified in 1913, that gave Congress the power to tax incomes and thereby massively increase the potential revenue available to the national government

categorical grant-in-aid

Transfers of cash from the national to state and/or local governments for some specific purpose, usually with the accompanying requirement that state and local governments match the national money with some funds of their own

block grant

Transfers of cash from the national to state and local governments in which state and local officials are allowed discretion in spending the money within some broad policy area, such as community development or social services

Figure 2.2   National Aid to State and Local Governments since 1960, in Current and Constant Dollars, in Billions

National aid to state and local governments rose sharply after 1960 to a high in 1980 of $283.7 billion in constant 2012 dollars; it then fell in constant dollars through the 1980s. In the early 1990s, aid began to rise again, in both current and constant dollars. In 2021, the amount in constant dollars is estimated at $694 billion, which is more than twelve times the amount of aid in 1960.

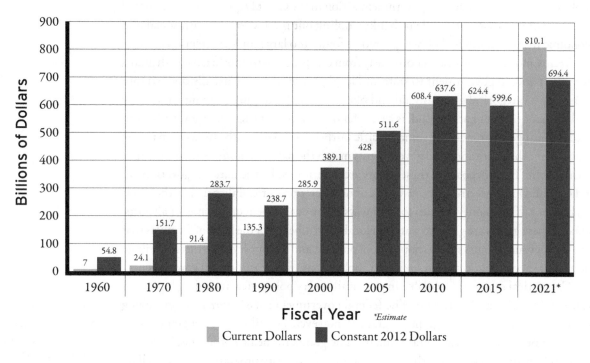

Fiscal Year *Estimate*

■ Current Dollars   ■ Constant 2012 Dollars

DATA SOURCE: Office of Management and Budget, Budget of the United States Government, Fiscal Year 2021, Analytical Perspectives: Special Topics, Aid to State and Local Governments, https://www.whitehouse.gov/wp-content/uploads/2020/02/ap_14_state_and_local_fy21.pdf

By 2021, that proportion increased to about 73 percent.[34] The proportional drop in grant programs that allow state and local governments to spend money, such as funding for capital projects, forced those governments to depend increasingly on their own resources to support programs that had previously been aided by Congress.

2.3d   Political Relationships

The federal system can be viewed as a series of legal and fiscal relationships. However, a third way to look at the federal system is to see it as an arena for political relationships among officials at all levels of government who lobby and cajole one another and who bargain and negotiate with one another. The cast of political players includes members of Congress representing states and local districts, the president, governors, state legislators, mayors, county and township commissioners, and national, state, and local bureaucrats. These officials band together into groups such as the National Governors Association, the National Conference of State Legislatures, and the United States Conference of Mayors—all of which participate in federal system politics.

The range and variety of political relationships are enormous because officials at all levels in the federal system press for their own interests as they see them. Scarce resources,

the search for the appropriate balance between state and national power, and social and economic differences among the states all drive these political relationships. Sometimes local or state officeholders will make demands on the national government as a group. In the competition for dollars, for example, mayors want more federal money. In the battle over which level of government has the power to do what, governors want fewer federal regulations and more state flexibility in deciding regulatory policy.

Many of the political relationships in the federal system derive from economic differences between regions and states and their localities as they compete with each other to press their individual interests. Economic development and the creation of new jobs are always among the highest priorities of state officials. New businesses and jobs can bolster tax collections, help political incumbents keep their posts, and make the state more attractive to outsiders. Understandably, states are in constant competition with each other to attract new industry and to retain the industry they have. Domestic and foreign corporations that are planning new plant sites are wooed by governors, economic development staffs, and local officials, all of whom cite favorable tax provisions, excellent physical facilities, and a skilled and dependable workforce as reasons the new plant should be located in their state.

State officials lobby to get what they see as their fair share of the huge budget expenditures of the national government. Associations of state and city officials and organizations such as the Northeast-Midwest Institute promote the economic interests of the regions they represent. Members of Congress want for their states and districts the "plums" of national policy, such as military contracts, but not the undesirable consequences of national policy, such as nuclear waste dumps. Competition among the states for national defense dollars is especially keen. Military installations and work on new weapons systems may bring millions of dollars into a state each year, and efforts to close facilities or cut weapons development meet with predictable opposition from state officials and congressional representatives. Understandably, Mississippi's members of Congress think that naval ships built in Mississippi are better than ships built in Virginia.

Other policy examples—beyond the struggle for money—also illustrate the conflicts between states, and between states and the national government. The long history of slavery and discrimination against African Americans in the South created epic battles between the Southern states and the national government. Fights over school integration over the past generation illustrate the durability of the struggle. The issue did not reach the same intensity in states with different traditions and different avenues of economic development. Some of the great battles in Congress over environmental policy are conflicts between members of Congress trying to represent the interests of their states. Californians want stricter auto emissions

(Shutterstock)

Members of Congress come into conflict over many issues, including environmental policy. These policies affect protected areas of the United States, such as Yellowstone National Park.

standards to ameliorate their problem of dirty air, but autoworkers in Michigan fear the economic consequences of stricter standards for their industry. As these illustrations suggest, political relationships in the federal system shape many public policies.

The Supreme Court created a political hot potato for all three levels of government in 2005 when it clarified and, by doing so, expanded the governmental power of eminent domain in the case *Kelo v. City of New London*.[35] The takings clause of the Fifth Amendment has long been interpreted to provide governments the power to seize private property for public use in exchange for just compensation. In the *Kelo* case, however, the Court presented a very broad interpretation of "public use" that enables governments to take private property and resell it to other private entities as long as there is a "public purpose." Fearing this decision would lead cities to condemn private homes in favor of shopping malls (which produce more tax revenue), citizens of many states and localities demanded that their governments pass laws or ordinances to limit the use of this broad power.

2.4 Federalism Today

In the third decade of the twenty-first century, the federal system appears to be a curious blend of contrasts, as each level of government asserts its role. The states are now innovators in a variety of public policy areas, including education, welfare, and the environment. Policy innovation is not a new role for the states. States had, in the past, experimented with new ideas that were later accepted as national policy. For example, a variety of states enacted old-age pension laws several years before Congress mandated Social Security as a national policy in 1935. Similarly, the state of Wisconsin had a program of unemployment compensation that predated national policy on the matter.[36]

Some states are now experimenting with market-like approaches in public education by allowing parents to choose the schools their children will attend; other state courts are mandating more equal educational expenditures across school districts. The latest round of welfare reform (requiring welfare recipients to work) was actually presaged by states that had already begun to experiment with such programs.[37] Across a range of environmental policies—including auto and power plant emissions, recycling, and water quality—some states have set more stringent standards than the national government. Federal budget cuts help to explain this increased vigor of the states. As the national government has wrestled with its own budget deficit, the states have expanded their policy role.

During the early 1990s, tensions grew between the national and state and local governments. The national government cut funding going to state and local governments, while, at the same time, it increased the number of regulations applied to state and local governments. Critics of this strategy called the national actions "unfunded mandates." Examples of these regulations, which result in higher costs that state and local governments must pay, include the federal mandate that local school districts remove asbestos materials from school buildings and the requirement that municipalities monitor a large list of pollutants in drinking water.[38] Protecting water supplies and the health of schoolchildren are worthwhile objectives, but which level of government should pay to meet the costs of national policy mandates?[39] States were being asked to do more to achieve policy objectives set by the national government—but with fewer federal resources. By 1995, however, the national government seemed to have gotten the message. Congress passed the Unfunded Mandates Reform Act that year; though not a panacea, the legislation led

to the review of over 350 intergovernmental mandates during its first five years of operation. The Congressional Budget Office reports that the number of mandates that could be defined as unfunded declined steadily over that time period.[40]

Governors, state legislators, and mayors are more active than they used to be; many of them believe, however, that the national government is curtailing their powers and responsibilities and denying them sufficient resources to perform the tasks they are asked to do. The national government has increasingly preempted state and local action in a variety of areas. For example, the national government has told the states to stay out of the economic regulation of buses, trucks, and airlines. The rise in federal demands and the scarcity of dollars at all levels have increased tensions among governments in the federal system. State and local governments have assumed a prominent role in policy making; yet the lively debate over which level of government should have the power to do what, whether national or state action is more appropriate, and who should pay the costs in light of budget deficits illustrates the continuing vitality of the federal system.

CHAPTER REVIEW

1. Federalism is a system of government in which a central or national government and regional or state governments exercise governmental power within the same political system. Federalism is a compromise between a confederation, in which states hold principal power, and a unitary form of government, in which a central government is dominant. Countries throughout the world have federal systems, and some of the most bitter and consequential conflicts in other countries are battles to redefine the shape of federal systems.

2. In policy, the amendment process, and elections, states play an important role; but the national government has become more dominant in the federal system over the past two centuries. The Constitution delegates express powers to the national government, and the Supreme Court has given expansive interpretation to the implied powers clause in the document. Powers not delegated to the national government are reserved for the states and include police powers, ensuring the health, safety, and education of citizens. Also among state powers is control over local governments, which vary greatly in size, structure, and functions.

3. Two models of the federal system are dual federalism and cooperative federalism. The federal system can be seen as a series of legal, fiscal, and political relationships among governments. Through its interpretation of the Constitution, the Supreme Court has generally supported national constitutional values and the national government. At the expense of support for capital and other programs, an increasingly greater proportion of national aid to state and local governments goes to payments for individuals. Officials at all levels press for the interests of their governments in political relationships with other officials in the federal system.

4. States are now vigorous policy innovators, but budget deficits and the rise in national regulations have increased tensions in the federal system.

KEY TERMS

block grant 53

categorical grant-in-aid 53

confederation. 34

cooperative federalism. 49

council-manager 47

delegated powers. 43

dual federalism 49

Electoral College 39

express powers. 43

federalism. 34

home rule 47

implied powers 43

interstate compact 39

mayor-council 47

McCulloch v. Maryland 43

New Federalism 42

reserved powers. 44

Sixteenth Amendment 53

Tenth Amendment 44

unitary system. 34

READINGS FOR FURTHER STUDY

Laurence J. O'Toole and Robert K. Christensen, eds., *American Intergovernmental Relations: Foundations, Perspectives, and Issues,* 5th ed. (Washington, DC: CQ Press, 2012) offers a contemporary view of federalism.

Federalism and the Making of America, 2nd ed. (New York: Routledge, 2017) by David Bryan Robertson places contemporary US federalism in its historical context.

The Council of State Governments (Lexington, Kentucky) publishes biennially *The Book of the States,* a compendium of demographic, structural, and policy data about the states.

Articles describing and analyzing state and local governments in the federal system can be found in the journals *Publius and National Civic Review* and in the magazine *Governing.*

Thomas O. Hughlin and Alan Fenna offer a comparative perspective on federalism in *Comparative Federalism: A Systematic Inquiry,* 2nd ed. (Toronto: University of Toronto Press, 2015).

David Osborne provides case studies of policy vigor in the states in *Laboratories of Democracy: A New Breed of Governor Creates Models for National Growth* (New York: McGraw-Hill, 1990).

David Osborne's and Ted Gaebler's *Reinventing Government* (New York: Plume, 1993) presents an entrepreneurial approach to state and local governance that has been successful in providing policy makers with workable approaches in contemporary federalism.

Politics in the American States: A Comparative Analysis, 11th ed. (Los Angeles: Sage/CQ Press, 2017), edited by Virginia Gray, Russell L. Hanson, and Thad Kousser, is one of the best scholarly comparisons of state policy.

Alice Rivlin's *Reviving the American Dream: The Economy, the States, and the Federal Government* (Washington, DC: The Brookings Institution, 1993) presents provocative proposals to reorder policy responsibilities between the national and state governments.

Robert F. Nagel's *The Implosion of American Federalism* (New York: Oxford University Press, 2002) offers a critical look at contemporary American federalism.

NOTES

1. John P. Roche, "The Founding Fathers: A Reform Caucus in Action," *American Political Science Review* 55 (1961): 804; William H. Riker, *Federalism: Origin, Operation, Significance* (Boston: Little, Brown, 1964).

2. For a seminal discussion of different political cultures among the states, see Daniel J. Elazar's *American Federalism: A View from the States*, 3rd ed. (New York: Harper & Row, 1984), pp. 114–142.

3. Bureau of Economic Analysis, U.S. Department of Commerce, Interactive Data, https://www.bea.gov /data/income-saving/personal-income-by-state (June 6, 2020).

4. Daniel J. Elazar, *Exploring Federalism* (Tuscaloosa: University of Alabama Press, 1987), p. 33.

5. See Gregory Gleason's *Federalism and Nationalism: The Struggle for Republican Rights in the USSR* (Boulder, CO: Westview Press, 1990) for discussion of Soviet federalism prior to the creation of the Commonwealth of Independent States.

6. The two exceptions are Maine and Nebraska, which allocate electoral votes on the basis of candidate victories in congressional districts.

7. See Daniel J. Elazar's "Federal-State Cooperation in the Nineteenth-Century United States," *Political Science Quarterly* 79 (1964): 248–265.

8. For an examination on the differences between the Nixon and Reagan approaches to New Federalism, see Timothy Conlan's *New Federalism: Intergovernmental Reform from Nixon to Reagan* (Washington, DC: Brookings Institution, 1988).

9. *McCulloch v. Maryland,* 17 U.S. (4 Wheaton) 316 (1819).

10. U.S. Bureau of Labor Statistics, https://www.bls.gov/ (June 7, 2020).

11. *Arizona v. United States,* 567 U.S. 387 (2012).

12. For a comprehensive view of government relationships in the federal system on which this section draws, see Laurence J. O'Toole and Robert K. Christensen, eds., *American Intergovernmental Relations: Foundations, Perspectives, and Issues*, 5th ed. (Washington, DC: CQ Press, 2012).

13. *Hammer v. Dagenhart,* 247 U.S. 251 (1918).

14. The classic statement of the model can be found in Morton Grodzins, "The Federal System," in *President's Commission on National Goals, Goals for Americans* (Englewood Cliffs, NJ: Prentice-Hall, 1960), pp. 265–282.

15. See *Heart of Atlanta Motel v. United States,* 379 U.S. 274 (1964), and *Katzenbach v. McClung,* 379 U.S. 294 (1964).

16. See *United States v. Lopez,* 514 U.S. 549 (1995), and *United States v. Morrison,* 529 U.S. 598 (2000), respectively.

17. *National Federation of Independent Businesses v. Sebelius,* 567 U.S. 519 (2012).

18. *Tennessee Wine and Spirits Retailers Assn. v. Thomas,* 588 U.S. ___ (2019).

19. *Gideon v. Wainwright,* 372 U.S. 335 (1963); *Engel v. Vitale,* 370 U.S. 421 (1962).

20. *Baker v. Carr,* 369 U.S. 186 (1962); *Reynolds v. Sims,* 377 U.S. 533 (1964).

21. *Morris v. Board of Estimate,* 489 U.S. 103 (1989).

22. *Brown v. Board of Education,* 347 U.S. 483 (1954).

23. *National League of Cities v. Usery,* 426 U.S. 833 (1976); *Garcia v. San Antonio Metropolitan Transit Authority,* 469 U.S. 528 (1985).

24. *South Carolina v. Baker,* 485 U.S. 505 (1988).

25. See, for example, David E. Nething, "States Must Regain Their Powers," *State Government* 63 (January–March 1990): 6–7.

26. *Gregory v. Ashcroft,* 501 U.S. 452 (1991).

27. *New York v. United States,* 505 U.S. 144 (1992).

28. See *Printz v. United States,* 521 U.S. 898 (1997), and *Reno v. Condon,* 528 U.S. 141 (2000).

29. See Charles Wise and Rosemary O'Leary, "Is Federalism Dead or Alive in the Supreme Court? Implications for Public Administrators," *Public Administration Review* 52 (November–December 1992): 559–572.

30. *Obergefell v. Hodges,* 576 U.S. ___ (2015).

31. Assistance Listings, https://beta.sam.gov/ (June 9, 2020).

32. Office of Management and Budget, *Analytical Perspectives, Budget of the United States Government, Fiscal Year 2021*, https://www.whitehouse.gov/omb /analytical-perspectives/ (June 9, 2020).

33. Advisory Commission on Intergovernmental Relations, *Categorical Grants: Their Role and Design* (Washington, DC: Government Printing Office, 1978), p. 16.

34. Office of Management and Budget, *Analytical Perspectives, Fiscal Year 2021*, p. 202.

35. *Kelo v. New London,* 545 U.S. 469 (2005).

36. Arthur M. Schlesinger Jr., *The Coming of the New Deal* (Boston: Houghton Mifflin, 1965), pp. 301–303.

37. Elaine Stuart, "Roaring Forward," *State Government News* (January/February 1999): 10–14.

38. Ibid., 28–29.

39. Timothy J. Conlon, "And the Beat Goes On: Intergovernmental Mandates and Preemption in an Era of Deregulation," *Publius 21* (Summer 1991): 50–53.

40. Congressional Budget Office, *CBO's Activities Under the Unfunded Mandates Reform Act, 1996–2000* (May 2001).

POP QUIZ

1. The fifty American states are themselves _____ governments because the principal power within each state lies with the state government.

2. The Supreme Court case of _____ v. _____ interpreted the necessary and proper clause as allowing expansive power to the national government.

3. A model of federalism that views national and state governments as separate and independent from each other is called _____ .

4. The most predominant form of national aid to the states takes the form of _____ .

5. The federal system is a compromise between a strong central government and a league of separate states.   T   F

6. States act in some measure as administrative units to carry out national social welfare programs.   T   F

7. Among the powers reserved for the states is the responsibility for preventing and prosecuting criminal activities.   T   F

8. Studies have shown that citizen interest in the affairs of local government is almost nonexistent.   T   F

9. Through a process of cooperative agreements, the states have the power to regulate interstate commerce.   T   F

10. Federalism is the product and symbol of the continuing ideological struggle between the values of _____ and _____ .
    A) freedom, equality
    B) unity, diversity
    C) justice, protection
    D) individualism, nationalism

11. The government of France is a _____ system.
    A) confederate
    B) unitary
    C) federal
    D) decentralized

12. Federal systems are found in _____ .
    A) Africa
    B) South Asia
    C) North America
    D) All of the above

13. The states play a crucial role in all except which of the following activities?
    A) administering social welfare policies
    B) regulating interstate commerce
    C) amending the Constitution
    D) shaping electoral contests at the national level

14. The Supreme Court case of McCulloch v. Maryland confirmed the national government's _____ powers.
    A) delegated
    B) express
    C) implied
    D) reserved

15. According to the text, the most visible and pervasive role of the state is in the area of _____ .
    A) interstate commerce
    B) education
    C) health
    D) business regulation

Chapter
03

(Andrea Izzotti / Shutterstock)

CIVIL LIBERTIES & CIVIL RIGHTS

In This Chapter

3.1   The Bill of Rights: Securing the Blessings of Liberty

3.2   Free Expression: Speech, Press, and Assembly

3.3   Religious Freedom

3.4   Fundamentals of American Criminal Justice

3.5   A Right to Privacy

3.6   Racial Equality

3.7   Sexual Equality

3.8   Other Americans and Civil Rights

3.9   Liberties and Rights in the Constitutional Framework

Chapter Objectives

Chapter 1 explained that a constitution can be a mainstay of rights. Beyond organizing and granting authority, constitutions place limits on what governments may do. Collectively, these limits are known as civil liberties and civil rights. Civil liberties are legally enforceable freedoms to act or not to act and to be free from unwarranted official intrusion into one's life. They include (but are not limited to) the First Amendment's guarantees of free expression and religious freedom and the Fourth, Fifth, Sixth, and Eighth Amendments' strictures governing police and courts in fighting crime.

Civil rights relate to participation—citizens' rights under the law to take part in society on an equal footing with others. They embrace the guarantees of the three Civil War amendments to the Constitution (the Thirteenth, Fourteenth, and Fifteenth), as well as laws passed to give those amendments meaning and force.

Civil rights are assurances that people are not penalized because of criteria (such as race or gender) that society decides should be irrelevant in making public policy. Yet, even after more than 240 years' experience as a nation, we continue to disagree over what liberty and equality mean in practice. Which rights and liberties do you exercise most frequently? Are there any that deserve more protection than they are currently afforded? What happens when civil rights and liberties come into conflict with one another?

3.1 The Bill of Rights: Securing the Blessings of Liberty

As explained in Chapter 1, when the Constitution left the hands of the framers in 1787 there appeared to be too few restrictions on what the national government could do, leaving individual liberty without sufficient protection. Several of the state conventions that ratified the proposed Constitution did so with the provision that a "bill of rights" would soon be added. In 1791, the Bill of Rights, comprising the first ten amendments, was ratified (see Table 3.1).

3.1a Applying the Bill of Rights to the States

Nearly 180 years elapsed before most of the rights spelled out in the Bill of Rights applied fully to state governments. This was because, as Chief Justice John Marshall (1801–1835) held for the Supreme Court, the Bill of Rights was not intended to apply to the states.[1] As a result, at first disputes between states and their citizens were controlled by the federal constitution to only a small degree. For most abuses of power, citizens had recourse only to their state constitutions and state courts; the ratification of the **Fourteenth Amendment** (see Appendix) in 1868, however, laid the groundwork for a drastic change in the nature of the Union. First, the amendment's language is directed to *state* governments, so aggrieved persons have the federal Constitution as an additional shield between themselves and their state governments. Second, the words of the amendment are ambiguous. What, for instance, is the "liberty" the amendment protects?

The Supreme Court was initially hesitant to use the Fourteenth Amendment as a vehicle through which to make the Bill of Rights applicable to the states. Within a century, however, the Court did just that. Without an additional formal amendment of the Constitution, the Court "incorporated" or absorbed the Bill of Rights into the Fourteenth Amendment in a series of about two dozen cases, beginning in 1897 and largely concluding in 1969. Then, in the first part of the twenty-first century, the Court lurched forward again with the incorporation process. First, in 2010, the Court incorporated the Second Amendment's right to bear arms.[2] Then, in a pair of 2019 decisions, the Court added two more previously unincorporated rights to the growing list. In the case *Timbs v. Indiana* a unanimous bench declared the Eighth Amendment's Excessive Fines Clause incorporated via the Fourteenth Amendement. In the civil forfeiture case, the the state of Indiana had tried to seize a defendant's vehicle that was worth several times more than the maximum fine he could have received.[3] Finally, a few months later, the Court declared that the Sixth Amendment's right to a trial by jury included a requirement of unanimous verdicts in state courts.[4]

Fourteenth Amendment
Ratified in 1868, the amendment altered the nature of the Union by placing significant restraints on state governments

Table 3.1   Content of the Bill of Rights

Consisting of barely 450 words, the Bill of Rights (Amendments I through X) was intended to remedy a defect critics found in the Constitution of 1787. In September 1789, Congress proposed twelve amendments for approval by the states. As the eleventh state (three-fourths of fourteen), Virginia's ratification in December 1791 made the Bill of Rights officially part of the Constitution. The remaining three states—Connecticut, Georgia, and Massachusetts—did not ratify until the 150th anniversary of the Bill of Rights in 1941. One amendment was never ratified. It dealt with apportionment of the House of Representatives and is now obsolete. The other amendment was not ratified until 1992—more than two hundred years after it was proposed! The Twenty-seventh Amendment—called the "lost amendment"—delays any increase in congressional salaries until a congressional election has intervened.

Amendment I	Nonestablishment of religion; free exercise of religion; freedoms of speech, press, petition, and peaceable assembly
Amendment II	Keep and bear arms
Amendment III	No quartering of troops
Amendment IV	No unreasonable searches and seizures; standards for search warrants
Amendment V	Indictment by grand jury; no double jeopardy or self-incrimination; no deprivation of life, liberty, or property without due process of law; compensation for taking of private property
Amendment VI	Speedy and public trial by impartial jury in state and district where crime was committed; nature and cause of accusation; confrontation of accusers; compulsory process for witnesses; assistance of counsel
Amendment VII	Jury trial in certain civil cases
Amendment VIII	No excessive bail or fines; no cruel and unusual punishments
Amendment IX	Recognition of the existence of rights not enumerated
Amendment X	Reserved powers of the states

Today almost all of the provisions in the first eight amendments—whether involving free speech or the rights thought necessary for a fair trial—apply with equal rigor to both state and national officials and the laws they make. Only the Sixth Amendment's stipulation about a trial's location, the Seventh's stipulation for a jury trial in most civil suits, the Eighth's ban on excessive bail, and the Third Amendment still apply only to the national government. Of these, only the Eighth is substantively important (the Ninth and Tenth Amendments, although part of the Bill of Rights, do not lend themselves to absorption into the Fourteenth Amendment).

3.1b   The Fragility of Civil Liberties

Charters of liberty, like a bill of rights, are commonplace today in the constitutions of many governments. Yet even a casual observer of world affairs knows that civil liberties are more likely to be preserved (or suspended) in some countries than in others. Even in the United States, the liberties enshrined in the Bill of Rights have meant more in some years than in others because of changing interpretations by the Supreme Court. For example, the Fourth Amendment's ban on "unreasonable searches and seizures" did not apply for a long time to electronic surveillance unless police physically trespassed on

a suspect's property. This meant that state and federal agents could eavesdrop electronically in many situations without fear of violating the Constitution. In 1967, however, the Court ruled that the Fourth Amendment covered most electronic searches too, as long as there was a "reasonable expectation of privacy."[5] In 2014, the Court specifically extended this privacy right to cover the data stored on cell phones.[6] In 2018, the Court further noted that the location-tracking information that cell phones provide to carriers is private and can only be searched if a warrant is first secured.[7] The words in the Bill of Rights have not changed, but the meaning attributed to those words has changed in the context of Supreme Court decisions.

Exactly why civil liberties thrive in one place or time and not another is a complex phenomenon. However, this much is certain: Civil liberties are fragile. The most frequent and sometimes the most serious threats to civil liberties have come not from people intent on throwing away the Bill of Rights but from well-meaning and overzealous people who find the Bill of Rights a temporary bother, standing in the way of objectives—often laudatory ones—they want to reach. Put another way, constitutional protections are sometimes worth the least when they are needed most. When public opinion calls for a "crackdown" on certain rights, such demands are felt in judicial chambers just as they are heard in legislative halls. Unsupported, courts and the Bill of Rights alone cannot defend civil liberties.

3.2   Free Expression: Speech, Press, and Assembly

Since the Bill of Rights was enacted, freedom of speech has been, and still remains, a subject of controversy.

(Christopher Penler / Shutterstock)

The place of the **First Amendment** in the Bill of Rights is symbolic. Its liberties are fundamental because they are essential to the kind of nation the framers envisioned.

3.2a   The Value of Free Expression

Free expression serves several important objectives. First, *free expression is necessary to the political process set up by the Constitution*. It is difficult to imagine government being responsive to a majority of the political community if the members of that community are afraid of saying what they think. It is even more difficult to imagine members of a political minority trying to persuade the majority without the right to criticize political officeholders. For democratic politics to work, free speech must prevail.

Second, in politics, as in education, *free expression allows the dominant wisdom of the day to be challenged*. Open discussion and debate aid the search for truth and thus foster intelligent policy-making. Whether the question is safeguarding the environment or systemic racism, free speech encourages both investigation of the problem and examination of possible solutions.

First Amendment

The part of the Bill of Rights containing protections for political and religious expression

Third, *free expression aids self-development.* Intellectual and artistic expression may contribute to realizing one's full potential as a human being. If government has the authority to define what kind of art is "acceptable," other kinds will be discouraged or suppressed altogether. Freedom of expression does not guarantee success as a poet, artist, or composer, but it does guarantee each person's right to try.

Free expression has its risks, however. There are no assurances that open debate and discussion will produce the "correct" answer or the wisest policy. Letting people speak their minds freely will surely stretch out the time it takes for a political community to decide what to do. Free speech can also threaten social and political stability. Although there are risks in silencing dissent, risks exist in permitting it, also. Nations in upheaval rarely tolerate vocal dissent against official policy. On balance, however, the American people—through their public officials and judges—seem willing to accept these risks most of the time.

3.2b   The Test of Freedom

Even though the First Amendment has been part of the Constitution from almost the beginning, freedom's record has not been free of blemishes. The ink had hardly dried on the Bill of Rights when Congress passed the Sedition Act of 1798, making it a crime to publish "false, scandalous, and malicious" statements about government officials. The law was not challenged in the Supreme Court even though at least ten individuals were convicted before it expired in 1801. Scattered instances of suppression occurred on both sides during the Civil War, but the next major nationwide attacks on speech were directed at virtually anyone or anything pro-German during World War I and on socialist ideas during the "Red Scare" that followed. Only then did the Supreme Court first interpret the free speech clause of the Constitution.

During World War I, Charles Schenck was found guilty of violating the Espionage Act by printing and circulating materials designed to protest and obstruct the draft. Announcing the **clear and present danger test**, Justice Oliver Wendell Holmes (1902–1932) ruled that the First Amendment provided no shield for Schenck's words: "The question ... is whether the words are used in such circumstances and are of such a nature as to create a clear and present danger that they will bring about the substantive evils that Congress has a right to prevent. It is a question of proximity and degree."[8]

Although Schenck lost his case, Holmes's reasoning remained important. Only when harmful consequences of speech were imminent could government act to suppress it. As Justice Louis Brandeis (1916–1939) later declared, "If there be time to expose through discussion the falsehood and fallacies, to avert the evil by the processes of education, the remedy to be applied is more speech, not enforced silence."[9] Since 1969 the clear and present danger test has evolved into the **incitement test**, stressing the Court's insistence that harmful consequences (such as a riot) be exceedingly imminent.[10]

Some settings and speech content also allow for limitations on First Amendment speech rights. In a 2007 case, the Supreme Court held that the characteristics of the school environment made it constitutionally permissible for school administrators to demand that students remove a banner reading "BONG HiTS 4 JESUS" from a public forum without infringing on the students' speech rights.[11] On the other hand, the Court has held that concern about a lack of decency and respect in location choice does not limit free expression protections. In the 2011 case *Snyder v. Phelps,* the Court concluded that the hateful signs that members of the Westboro Baptist Church display at military funerals are protected from liability claims by the First Amendment.[12] Of course, these guarantees only protect individuals from government constraints, not from private entities. The

clear and present danger test

Guideline devised by the Supreme Court in *Schenck v. United States* [249 U.S. 47 (1919)] to determine when speech could be suppressed under the First Amendment

incitement test

The Court's current test for First Amendment restrictions that asks whether a speech act attempts or is likely to incite lawless action

Court stressed this point in 2019 when it held that a corporation regulating public access television channels is not a government actor and, therefore, not subject to the requirements of the First Amendment.[13]

3.2c   Gags

Of the possible restrictions on speech today, the Court is least likely to approve a **prior restraint**. This is official censorship *before* something is said or published, or censorship that halts publication already under way. Prior restraints are especially dangerous to free expression because government does not have to go to the trouble of launching a prosecution and convicting someone at a trial. Even when the *New York Times* and the *Washington Post* reprinted verbatim parts of a purloined classified study of the Defense Department's decision-making on Vietnam, the Supreme Court (in the "Pentagon Papers" case) refused to ban further publication.[14] Most of the justices admitted that the government could make it a crime to publish such materials, but concluded that there could be no restraints in advance. Likewise, the justices will only rarely approve a pretrial gag on media reports about a crime, even if such suppression would help protect another constitutional right: the right to a fair trial.

3.2d   Obscenity and Libel

Descriptions and depictions of various sexual acts have presented a special problem. Unlike cases involving other types of speech, the Court has required no evidence that obscene materials are in fact harmful. Yet the Court steadfastly regards **obscenity** as unprotected speech because of the widespread public view that exposure to obscenity is deleterious. The justices have had a hard time writing a clearly understood definition of what is obscene. Justice Potter Stewart (1958–1981) once admitted, "I know it when I see it." Under the current standard, the Court will uphold an obscenity conviction if

> (a) "the average person, applying contemporary community standards," would find that the work, taken as a whole, appeals to the prurient interest ...
> (b) ... the work depicts or describes, in a patently offensive way, sexual conduct specifically defined by the applicable state law, and (c) ... the work, taken as a whole, lacks serious literary, artistic, political, or scientific value.[15]

The target seems to be "hard-core" pornography. Within limits, the "community" to which the Court refers is local and not national, making the definition of obscenity variable. The policy thus allows one locale to suppress sexually explicit materials while another tolerates them. For example, the Court upheld a city ordinance that prohibited nudity in public places, including erotic-dancing establishments.[16] Obscenity continues to trouble the nation. Films, videos, and magazines portraying explicit sex are big business. Many think the Supreme Court's definition is both too lax and insufficiently enforced. Although reluctant to advocate censorship, some feminists object to obscenity because it degrades women and may even contribute to sexual crimes against women. The Court, however, continues to err on the side of liberty in this issue—even when ruling on a subject as universally condemned as child pornography. In a series of recent cases, the Court held that the federal Child Online Protection Act and its revisions (measures designed to restrict child pornography on the internet) have been too sweeping, failing to meet the Court's "least restrictive means" test for limiting free speech.[17] Moving beyond pornography, a majority of justices applied similar logic to video games in 2011 when they struck down a California law banning the sale of violent video games to minors.[18] The Court

prior restraint

Official censorship before something is said or published, or censorship that halts publication already under way is usually judged unconstitutional today under the First Amendment

obscenity

As applied by the Supreme Court, certain pornographic portrayals of sexual acts not protected by the First Amendment (The Supreme Court's current definition of the legally obscene appeared in *Miller v. California* [413 U.S. 5 (1973)].)

held that video games are protected by the First Amendment, and that the law was not narrowly tailored and failed to provide a compelling state interest to limit their sale. Social media is another electronic front where the Court is still sketching out the reach of First Amendment rights. In 2017, a majority struck down a North Carolina law that prevented registered sex offenders from accessing social media sites that can be visited by minors, finding that the law forbade too vast a scope of speech and was not narrowly tailored to prevent crime.[19] Finally, even the seemingly mundane field of trademark law has become a battleground between obscenity and protected speech. In 2019, the Court found that a law seeking to prohibit registration of "immoral" or "scandalous" trademarks violated the First Amendment, siding with the owner of a clothing company called FUCT.[20]

Like obscenity, the First Amendment does not protect **libel**. Involving published defamation of a person's character or reputation, libel may subject a publisher or television network to damage suits involving thousands or even millions of dollars. Beginning in 1964, however, the Supreme Court made it very difficult for public figures and public officials to bring successful libel suits against their critics because the court felt that the democratic process needs robust and spirited debate, which might be muted by threat of legal action. In such situations, public figures and officials initiating libel suits must be able to prove "actual malice"—that is, that the author published information knowing it was false or not caring whether it was true or false.[21]

3.2e   Freedom of Assembly and Symbolic Speech

People often convey ideas and attempt to build support for a cause by holding a meeting or a rally. This is an example of the freedom of assembly that the First Amendment protects. Sometimes assembly involves **symbolic speech** in which words, pictures, and ideas are not at issue, but action is. A person may *do* something to send a message, usually in a dramatic, attention-getting manner. It might be a sit-in at the mayor's office to protest a budget cut, or a sit-down on a public road leading to an oil pipeline under construction. In some instances, demonstrators may be constitutionally punished for such nontraditional forms of expression—not because of the ideas expressed but because of the harm that results from the *mode* of expression. It is not the message but the medium that can be the basis of a legitimate arrest.

Yet in a 1989 decision that generated a storm of controversy, the Supreme Court overturned the conviction of Gregory Lee Johnson for burning the American flag in violation of a Texas law.[22] In a demonstration at Dallas City Hall during the Republican National Convention in 1984, protesters chanted, "America, the red, white, and blue, we spit on you," as Johnson doused the flag with kerosene and set it ablaze. Short of a protest that sparks a breach of the peace or causes some other kind of serious harm, the Court held (5–4) that a state could not criminalize the symbolic act of flag burning. The Court's reasoning was that government protects the physical integrity of the flag because the flag is a symbol of the nation. Just as people may verbally speak out against what they believe

libel

Defamation of a person's character or reputation, not protected by the First Amendment (*New York Times Co. v. Sullivan* [376 U.S. 254 (1964)] makes it difficult for public figures and officials to bring successful libel suits against their critics.)

symbolic speech

A speech act that centers on action or performance to communicate a point rather than on words

(AP Photo / Marcio Jose Sanchez, File)

In 2016, several professional athletes protested during the United States national anthem. The protests began in the National Football League (NFL), after Colin Kaepernick of the San Francisco 49ers sat during the anthem, as opposed to the tradition of standing, before his team's third preseason game of 2016.

(Everett Collection / Shutterstock)

The Supreme Court has overturned lower court rulings that outlawed certain forms of symbolic hate speech, such as cross burnings.

the nation "stands for," they may also express the same thought by defacing or destroying the symbol of the nation. The following year, the Court held that the First Amendment also barred Congress from criminalizing flag burning, a decision that sparked a renewed drive to amend the Constitution.[23] The drive failed in 1990 when Congress failed to pass a constitutional amendment by the required two-thirds vote in both houses.

The Court has also invalidated a city ordinance that outlawed cross burning and other forms of symbolic hate speech directed against certain minorities.[24] The ordinance was defective because it was content-based. Some, not all, hate messages were banned. The decision may be far-reaching because it calls into question the constitutionality of similar bans at public universities. In 2014, the Court struck down a Massachusetts law that attempted to limit speech near women's health clinics. The Court held that the law's attempt to create a buffer zone around the clinics was overbroad and violated the speech rights of those wishing to make known their views on abortion.[25] On the other hand, the Court has also held that a state does not have to aid citizens in promoting speech that it finds hateful. In 2015, the justices upheld the refusal of the state of Texas to create specialty license plates featuring the Confederate battle flag, which had been requested by a heritage group.[26]

3.3   Religious Freedom

Guarantees of religious freedom form the first lines of the First Amendment. Ahead of other protections are an assurance of free exercise and a prohibition of an established religion. Removing religion from the reach of political majorities reflected practical needs in 1791. The United States was already one of the world's most religiously diverse countries.

3.3a   Religion and the Constitution

The Constitution is intentionally a nonsectarian document. It had to be if the framers were to secure ratification after 1787 and if the new government were to avoid the religious divisiveness that had plagued Europe before and after the Protestant Reformation, as well as the American colonies. Even though a few states still maintained established (state-supported) churches in 1791, the First Amendment said that the nation could not have one.

The United States is even more religiously diverse today. Over two-thirds of the population identifies with a particular religion.[27] More than twenty-five distinct religious groups claim more than one million members each, with dozens more having smaller memberships.[28] Within this context, the religion clauses have the same objectives, but they work in different ways. The **free exercise clause** preserves a sphere of religious practice free of interference by government. The idea is that people should be left to follow their

free exercise clause

Provision of the First Amendment guaranteeing religious freedom

own dictates of belief or nonbelief. The **establishment clause** keeps government from becoming the tool of one religious group against others. Government cannot be a prize in a nation of competing faiths.

Even though both religion clauses work to guard religious freedom, they concern different threats and so at times seem to pull in opposite directions. Rigorous protection of free exercise may appear to create an established religion. Rigorous enforcement of the ban on establishment may seem to deny free exercise.[29]

3.3b   Aid to Sectarian Schools

The Supreme Court has never limited the First Amendment's ban on the literal establishment of an official state church. How much involvement between church and state is too much, however? Coins, for example, display the motto "In God We Trust." A troublesome area for almost a half-century has been public financial support for sectarian schools. The current standard for determining when government has violated the establishment clause in this context dates from a 1971 decision by the Supreme Court.[30] To pass scrutiny under the *Lemon* **test**, a law must have, first of all, a *secular purpose.* Second, the primary effect of the law must be *neutral,* neither hindering nor advancing religion. Third, the law must not promote *excessive entanglement* between church and state by requiring government to become too closely involved in the affairs of a religious institution. Using these criteria, the Court has upheld some, but not most, forms of state aid that have been challenged. Generally, direct grants of money from a government agency to a religious institution are the least likely to be found acceptable under the Constitution. However, in 2011—drawing a distinction between direct and indirect state contributions—the Supreme Court let stand an Arizona law that provided tax credits for individual contributions to religiously affiliated schools.[31] In 2017, the Court used the free exercise clause to determine that Missouri had improperly found a Lutheran preschool ineligible for a grant for playground materials that had been made available to nonreligious schools.[32] In 2020 the Court heard a case where one side argued the free exercise clause required a law to be repealed while the other side argued that the establishment clause required the law to remain in place. At issue was Montana's private school scholarship program, which forbade the use of funds from going to religion-based schools. The Court sided with the free exercise advocates, concluding that if a state chose to create such a program, it had to treat all schools equally regardless of religious mission.[33]

3.3c   Prayer in Public Schools

Whether or not religious observances can take place in public schools is another thorny issue. Even though we don't tend to think of schools as part of the government, public schools are funded through tax dollars and are governed by elected school boards— they are government-run institutions. Because of strong emotions on both sides of the prayer in schools issue, the Court's decisions have stirred up controversy. In 1962, the justices outlawed a nondenominational prayer prescribed by the Board of Regents for opening daily exercises in the public schools of New York State. The following year, a Pennsylvania statute mandating daily Bible readings in public schools met a similar fate.[34] Reactions in Congress and the nation to these decisions were anything but dispassionate. After the New York prayer case, the U.S. House of Representatives unanimously passed a resolution to have the motto "In God We Trust" placed behind the Speaker's desk in the House chamber. The motto is still there for all to see during televised sessions of Congress.

establishment clause

Provision of the First Amendment barring government support of religion

Lemon **test**

A standard announced in *Lemon v. Kurtzman* [403 U.S. 602 (1971)] to determine when a statute violates the establishment clause (The law in question must have a secular purpose and a neutral effect and must avoid an excessive entanglement between church and state.)

(Shutterstock)

The Supreme Court has held that state-sponsored religious activities in public schools are unconstitutional.

Of course, the Supreme Court has never said that students cannot pray in school—students have been doing that before exams for years—but the Court has remained firm in its opposition to state-sponsored religious activities in public schools. For example, an Alabama statute authorizing a period of silence at the start of the school day for "meditation or voluntary prayer" was seen by most justices as constitutionally defective because the law endorsed religion as a preferred activity.[35] A bare majority of the Court even found an invocation offered by a rabbi at a public middle school commencement constitutionally objectionable. Although student attendance at the ceremony was optional, the prayer nonetheless carried "a particular risk of indirect coercion" of religious belief, according to Justice Anthony Kennedy.[36] For the four dissenters, Justice Antonin Scalia asserted that the nation's long tradition of prayer at public ceremonies was a compelling argument that the school had not violated the establishment clause. In 2000, the Court maintained course by finding a student-led prayer played over a public address system prior to a school football game to be in violation of the establishment clause.[37]

3.3d Religious Observances in Official Settings

Because of the impressionable nature of children, the Court has been quickest to strike down religious influences in elementary and secondary schools. Elsewhere, the justices sometimes look the other way. In 1983, the Court approved Nebraska's practice of paying the state legislature's chaplain out of public funds.[38] In a narrowly decided 2014 case, the Court upheld ceremonial invocations at the beginning of local government meetings—even though plaintiffs in the case objected to the specifically Christian nature of most of these prayers.[39] (Both houses of the United States Congress also have chaplains who pray at the beginning of each day's session.) In 1984, a bare majority allowed city officials in Pawtucket, Rhode Island, to erect a municipally owned Christmas display, including a crèche, in a private park. However, the Court has placed some limits on official observances of religious holidays, finding unacceptable a privately owned crèche displayed in the county courthouse in Pittsburgh, Pennsylvania. Above the crèche was a banner proclaiming *"Gloria in Excelsis Deo"* (Latin for "Glory to God in the highest"). Yet in the same case, the Court found acceptable a nearby display that combined an eighteen-foot menorah and a forty-five-foot tree decorated with holiday ornaments. The justices explained that the crèche and banner impermissibly "endorsed" religion, but that the menorah and tree only "recognized" the religious nature of the winter holidays.[40]

In 2004, a Californian named Michael Newdow brought suit on behalf of his daughter to oppose the recitation of the Pledge of Allegiance and its phrase "under God" in a public school setting. Although the Court dismissed the case without deciding its merits, the issue sparked renewed public debate over the boundaries of church and state.[41] In 2005 the Court held that a display of the Judeo-Christian Ten Commandments in a Kentucky courthouse violated the establishment clause because it violated the requirement of government neutrality. Employing the *Lemon* test, the majority of justices found that the display

lacked a primary secular purpose.[42] On the same day, however, the Court handed down another decision in which it found acceptable a display of the Ten Commandments at the Texas state capitol.[43] The justices found the passive nature of the display and its location and historical presence to be the key factors distinguishing it from the Kentucky case. The *Lemon* test was in the news again in 2019 when the Court found that a large memorial cross that had stood on public land in Maryland for nearly a century did not violate the Constitution because its primary purpose was to commemorate soldiers who died during World War I, not to advance religion.[44] Such varied decisions point to the difficulty in deciding how much separation the establishment clause commands between government and religion.

3.3e Free Exercise of Religion

Contemporary free exercise problems typically arise from the application of a law that by its own words has nothing to do with religion, yet that causes hardship for some religious groups by commanding them to do something that their faith forbids (or by forbidding them to do something that their faith commands). This kind of conflict often occurs with small separatist groups whose interests are overlooked when laws are made. Relying on the free exercise clause, they ask to be exempted on religious grounds from obeying the law. For example, a nearly unanimous bench in 1972 exempted members of the Old Order Amish and the Conservative Amish Mennonite churches from Wisconsin's compulsory school attendance law.[45] Like most states, Wisconsin required school attendance until age sixteen. The Amish were religiously opposed to formal schooling beyond the eighth grade. The justices found a close connection between the faith of the Amish and their simple, separatist way of life. The law not only compelled them to do something at odds with their religious tenets but also threatened to undermine the Amish community. On balance, in the Court's view, the danger to religious freedom outweighed the state's interest in compulsory attendance.

At other times, however, the Court has been less hospitable to free exercise claims. In 1990, the justices ruled against two members of the American Indian Church who were fired from their jobs as drug counselors in a clinic in Oregon after they ingested peyote (a hallucinogen) as part of a religious ritual. Oregon officials then denied them unemployment compensation because their loss of employment resulted from "misconduct." Under state law, peyote was a "controlled substance" and its use was forbidden. The two ex-counselors cited scientific and anthropological evidence that the sacramental use of peyote was an ancient practice and was not harmful. The Court, however, decided that Oregon had not violated the First Amendment. When action based on religious belief runs afoul of criminal law, the latter prevails.[46] Even though Congress attempted to reverse this ruling with the Religious Freedom Restoration Act in 1993, the Court found that this act exceeded congressional authority.[47]

More recently, the Court defended the free exercise rights of a private company when it decided the case *Burwell v. Hobby Lobby*.[48] In a 5–4 decision, the Court ruled that the Affordable Care Act could not compel businesses to provide employees with insurance coverage for certain types of contraception over the religious objections of the business owners. In 2015, the Court held that corrections officials in Arkansas violated the free exercise of religion when they forbade Muslim inmates from growing beards.[49] In the much anticipated 2018 case of *Masterpiece Cakeshop v. Colorado Civil Rights Commission*, the Court held that Colorado was impermissibly biased against a baker's religious beliefs when it sanctioned him for refusing to make a cake for a same-sex wedding.[50]

3.4 Fundamentals of American Criminal Justice

The system of criminal justice in the US insists not simply that a person be proved guilty but that the guilt is proved in the legally prescribed way. This is the concept of **legal guilt**, inherent in the idea of "a government of laws and not of men."[51] Courts sit not just to make sure that wrongdoers are punished but also to see that law enforcement personnel obey the commands of the Bill of Rights. The precise meaning of these commands at a given time represents the prevailing judgment on the balance to be struck between two values: the liberty and the safety of each citizen. The first focuses on fairness to persons accused of crimes and emphasizes that preservation of liberty necessitates tight controls on law enforcement officers, even if some guilty persons go unpunished. The second focuses on crime control, emphasizing that too many rules hamstring police and judges, give lawbreakers the upper hand, and disserve honest citizens. Tension between the two values persists.

Inconvenient as they may be, the strictures of the Bill of Rights deliberately make government's crime-fighting tasks harder to perform. Yet, holding police to standards of behavior set by the Constitution protects the liberty of everyone. Otherwise, officials would have the power to do whatever they wanted to whomever they wanted, whenever they wanted. Without limits to authority, the US would be a far different place in which to live.

3.4a Presumption of Innocence and Notice of Charges

The idea that a person is "innocent until proved guilty" is often misunderstood. It does not mean that the police and prosecuting attorney think that the accused person is innocent, for putting obviously innocent people through the torment of a criminal trial would be a gross injustice. Instead, the **presumption of innocence** lays the burden of proof on the government. It is up to the state to prove the suspect's guilt "beyond a reasonable doubt." Along with a convincing case of factual guilt, the prosecution must also demonstrate criminal intent, or *mens rea*.

A suspect is entitled to know what the state intends to prove and, therefore, what he or she must defend against. The state must go beyond saying merely that someone is a thief. The charge must explain, among other things, (1) what was stolen, (2) approximately when it was stolen, (3) by whom, and (4) from whom it was stolen. This principle also means that criminal laws must be as specific as possible so that citizens can have fair notice of what conduct is prohibited. The greater the vagueness in a law, the greater the danger of arbitrary arrests and convictions.

The basic fairness component of advance notice is why the Constitution prohibits **ex post facto laws**, criminal laws that apply retroactively. The Constitution also forbids a bill of attainder for a similar reason. A **bill of attainder** is a law that imposes punishment but bypasses the procedural safeguards of the legal process. Thus, a person might not have the opportunity for even a simple defense.

legal guilt
The concept that a defendant's factual guilt be established in accordance with the laws and the Constitution before criminal penalties can be applied

presumption of innocence
A concept in criminal procedure that places the burden of proof in establishing guilt on the government

ex post facto laws
Laws that make an act a crime after it was committed or increase the punishment for a crime already committed—prohibited by the Constitution

bill of attainder
A law that punishes an individual and bypasses the procedural safeguards of the legal process—prohibited by the Constitution

3.4b   Limits on Searches and Arrests

The **Fourth Amendment** denies police unbounded discretion to arrest and search people and their possessions. Many searches and some arrests cannot take place at all until a judge has issued a **warrant**, or official authorization. To obtain a warrant, the police must persuade a judge that they have very good reason (called **probable cause**) for believing that someone has committed a crime or that evidence exists in a particular location. Warrantless searches of arrested suspects or automobiles are permitted in certain circumstances, but police officers who have made a warrantless search must still convince a judge afterward that they had probable cause to act. In 2009, the Court clarified that warrantless automobile searches are permissible only if there are safety concerns or if there is a reasonable belief that the car contains evidence relevant to the specific crime for which the suspect is being arrested.[52] In 2013, the Court concluded that the use of a trained police dog (for the purpose of detecting narcotics) on a person's front porch was also the type of search that required a warrant.[53] A pair of 2018 cases concluded that warrants are generally needed for searching vehicles parked near a private residence and for rental vehicles, even when being driven by unauthorized drivers.[54] And a 2019 case found that subjecting an unconscious driver to a blood test to determine their blood alcohol concentration was a constitutionally acceptable warrantless search due to the "exigent circumstances" involved.[55] In other words, the evidence of the crime— driving while impaired—would have disappeared had the officers waited to obtain a warrant.

(Shutterstock)

Advances in surveillance technology continue to push the boundaries of the Fourth Amendment.

Electronic surveillance is usually considered to be a search, in the constitutional sense. Under current law, practically all such "bugging" must be done on the authority of a warrant—except for exceptional situations involving agents of foreign powers.[56] Advances in surveillance technology continue to push the boundaries of the Fourth Amendment. In 2001, the Court held that heat-sensing equipment that detects whether a private home is radiating abnormal levels of heat (which might indicate the use of heat lamps for growing marijuana plants) could not be used without a warrant.[57] Similarly, in 2012 a Court majority held that police could not install a GPS device on a vehicle in order to track its owner without a warrant.[58]

Once a valid arrest has been made, however, police have a right to search a detained individual. In a 2012 case, the Court ruled that a man arrested for failing to appear at a court hearing to pay a fine could be subjected to a strip search.[59] This search was found acceptable in order to ensure the safety of the correctional facility where he was being detained, regardless of the reason for the initial arrest. The following year the Court extended the logic of diminished privacy rights for those held in custody when it upheld the constitutionality of a Maryland law that allows officers to collect DNA samples from those charged with violent crimes.[60]

Fourth Amendment

Part of the Bill of Rights that prohibits unreasonable searches and seizures of persons and their property

warrant

Official authorization for government action

probable cause

A standard used in determining when police can conduct arrests and searches

What happens when a judge concludes that police officers have acted improperly when making an arrest or conducting a search? In such instances, the **exclusionary rule** may come into play. This judge-made rule puts teeth into the Fourth Amendment by denying government, in many situations, the use of evidence gained as a result of the violation of the suspect's rights. The rule lies at the heart of the clash between the values of fairness and crime control.[61]

3.4c   Assistance of Counsel and Protection Against Self-Incrimination

Other constitutional restraints are at work in the police station and in the courtroom. As interpreted by the Supreme Court, the Fifth Amendment denies government the authority to coerce confessions from suspects or to require suspects to testify at their own trials. These restraints conform to presumption of innocence. The state must make its case—it may not compel the suspect to do its work. Under *Miranda v. Arizona,*[62] judges exclude almost all confessions, even if no physical coercion is present, unless police have first performed the following actions:

1. Advised the suspect of his or her right to remain silent (that is, the right not to answer questions)

2. Warned the suspect that statements he or she might make may be used as evidence at a trial

3. Informed the suspect of his or her right to have a lawyer present during the interrogation

4. Offered the services of a lawyer free of charge during the interrogation to suspects financially unable to retain one

If a suspect refuses to talk to the police, the police may not continue the interrogation. If a suspect waives these *Miranda* **rights** and agrees to talk, the state must be prepared to show to a judge's satisfaction that the waiver was done "voluntarily, knowingly, and intelligently." As it is, many defendants decide that it is in their interest to accept a **plea bargain**—a deal with the prosecutor to obtain fewer or lesser charges or a lighter sentence in exchange for a guilty plea. Guilty pleas allow most criminal cases to be settled without going to trial, so the legal use of confessions continues. In 2010, the Court clarified that simply remaining silent for a period of time is not the same as invoking the right to remain silent; therefore, law enforcement can continue to question a suspect even if he or she does not initially respond.[63]

For a long time, the **Sixth Amendment**'s assurance of counsel, or legal assistance, remained more promise than substance. Many defendants simply could not afford to hire an attorney, and some courts provided free counsel for the poor only in **capital cases** (cases in which the death penalty might be imposed). Until the 1970s, for example, 75 percent of people accused of **misdemeanors** (less serious offenses, punishable by a jail term of less than one year) went legally unrepresented. Since the 1930s the Supreme Court has greatly expanded the Sixth Amendment right. Today all persons accused of **felonies** (serious offenses, punishable by more than one year in jail) and all accused of misdemeanors for which a jail term is imposed must be offered counsel, at the government's expense if necessary.[64]

The ongoing war on terrorism has led to a reexamination of several of these criminal defense concerns. In 2004, the Court handed down a series of decisions that among other things, concluded that the government may detain enemy combatants indefinitely during

exclusionary rule

Rule developed in *Mapp v. Ohio* [367 U.S. 643 (1961)] that prevents the state from bringing evidence against a defendant when that evidence was obtained illegally

Miranda rights

Requirements announced in *Miranda v. Arizona* [384 U.S. 436 (1966)] to protect a suspect during a police interrogation

plea bargain

A deal with the prosecutor to obtain fewer or lesser charges or a lighter sentence

Sixth Amendment

Provision of the Bill of Rights assuring, among other things, the right to counsel

capital case

A criminal proceeding in which the defendant is on trial for his or her life

misdemeanor

Less serious criminal offense, usually punishable by not more than one year in jail

felony

A serious criminal offense, usually punishable by more than one year in prison

times of war, but that those being held, whether US citizens or foreign nationals, must be given the opportunity to challenge their detention in court.[65] In 2008 the Court exercised its power of judicial review in finding that parts of the Detainee Treatment Act of 2005 and the Military Commissions Act had unconstitutionally denied the writ of habeas corpus to foreign nationals detained in the American facilities at Guantanamo Bay.[66] In 2019 the Court dismissed a case that again sought to challenge indefinite detention, allowing the remaining Guantanamo prisoners—some of whom had already been held for over seventeen years—to remain imprisoned without formal charge.[67] The ongoing and contentious nature of these cases speaks to the currency and importance of establishing clear and fair rules for the criminally accused.

Still, none of the right-to-counsel rulings create full equality in access to legal assistance. The Constitution, after all, does not guarantee a "perfect" trial, only a "fair" one. The indigent must be content with public defenders and court-appointed attorneys paid from public funds. Public defenders carry heavy caseloads; their time is spread thin; and compared to others in their profession, they are underpaid. In federal courts they are now responsible for over half of all defense work. They can cope with their caseloads only with the help of plea bargains. Defendants retaining counsel at their own expense also fare differently. Only a few can afford the best.

3.4d Limits on Punishment

Guilty verdicts by juries or through guilty pleas usually result in the punishment of the accused. Generally the Constitution leaves the particulars of the sentence to legislators and judges, subject to the **Eighth Amendment**'s prohibition of "**cruel and unusual punishment.**" In the Supreme Court's view, this means first that certain kinds of penalties (torture, for example) may not be imposed at all; second, that certain acts or conditions (such as alcoholism) may not be made criminal;[68] and third, that penalties may not be imposed capriciously. Indeed, the Eighth

(Photo courtesy of Shane T. McCoy, U.S. Navy, via Wikimedia)

The Supreme Court found that the foreign nationals detained at the Guantanamo Bay facilities were unconstitutionally denied the writ of habeas corpus.

Amendment comes into play most frequently when someone has been sentenced to death. In only a few noncapital cases has the Court overturned a sentence because it was too extreme.[69] Most recently, in 2012, the Court found that sentencing a juvenile to life in prison without parole violated the Eighth Amendment.[70] More typically, though, the Court is reluctant to find the length of sentences to be cruel and unusual; in 2003 the Court upheld the use of "three strikes" laws (by which criminals are given long sentences, such as twenty-five years to life) for a third felony offense, regardless of its severity.[71]

Between 1930 and mid-2020 there were approximately 5,383 legal executions in the United States, with about 72 percent of these occurring before 1972. Today, twenty-eight of the fifty states—as well as the federal government—allow capital punishment; however, states vary widely in terms of the number of executions carried out, as Figure 3.1 shows. The US government executed ten people in 2020, marking the first federal executions in seventeen years. Nationally, about 2,620 persons were on "death row" as of mid-2020.[72] Opponents of the death penalty would like the Supreme Court to impose more restrictions on the states, as they find it inherently cruel and increasingly unusual. Death penalty opponents claimed a rare victory in 2005 when the Court held that the execution of defendants under the age of eighteen was a cruel and unusual punishment.[73] Even if executions are not inherently "cruel and unusual," many believe that they are racially discriminatory because African Americans are more likely than whites to be sentenced

Eighth Amendment

The part of the Bill of Rights that prohibits "cruel and unusual punishment," which is often at issue in death penalty cases

cruel and unusual punishment

Prohibited by the Eighth Amendment—at issue in capital cases

Figure 3.1 Executions by State, 1976–2020*

In *Furman v. Georgia,* 408 U.S. 238 (1972), the Supreme Court ruled 5–4 that the death penalty, as then administered, was cruel and unusual punishment in violation of the Eighth Amendment. Too much discretion in the hands of juries and judges had made application of the death penalty capricious. Most states then reinstated capital punishment (as did Congress for aircraft hijacking) with more carefully drawn statutes to meet the Court's objections in *Furman.* In *Gregg v. Georgia,* 428 U.S. 152 (1976), a majority of the Supreme Court concluded that the death penalty was not inherently cruel and unusual and upheld a two-step sentencing scheme designed to set strict standards for trial courts. A jury would first decide the question of guilt and then in a separate proceeding impose punishment. Of the twenty-eight states that now permit capital punishment, one (Kansas) executed no one between 1976 and 2020. Texas, Virginia, Oklahoma, and Florida accounted for approximately 60 percent of the executions during that time span. Twenty states executed 98 convicted capital felons in 1999—the largest number of executions in a single year since 1951, when 105 persons were put to death.

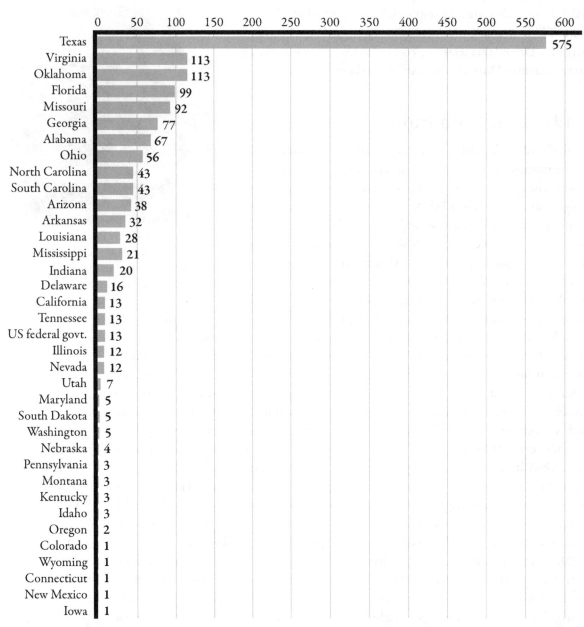

* Data are current through December 18, 2020.
SOURCE: Data from Death Penalty Information Center.

to die, as are killers of whites versus killers of African Americans.[74] In 2016, the Court overturned a death penalty conviction on the grounds that prosecutors had improperly used race as a reason to exclude African American jurors.[75] Other death penalty critics conclude that the sentencing process is fundamentally flawed because it results in caprice. One study found little or no difference between the facts of murder cases in which the death penalty was imposed and in which it was not.[76]

The constitutionality of capital punishment remains a contentious issue. In 2008, the Court rejected an argument that lethal injection as a method of capital punishment subjected the condemned to cruel and unusual punishment. The justices extended this reasoning in 2015 when they concluded that lethal injection is not cruel and unusual even when the drugs injected cause extreme pain.[77] However, the Court overturned a Louisiana law that allowed for the death penalty as a punishment for the rape of a child because "evolving standards of decency" preclude death as a punishment for a crime that does not itself cause a death.[78] As of 2020, 36 percent of Americans think the death penalty is the best punishment for murder, while 60 percent think life imprisonment with no possibility of parole is better.[79]

3.5   A Right to Privacy

Some liberties people in the US enjoy are not specifically mentioned in the Constitution, as the **Ninth Amendment** cautions. One such judicially discovered civil liberty is the right to privacy, announced in 1965.[80] With far-reaching implications, this decision invalidated a Connecticut statute that prohibited the use of birth control devices.

3.5a   The Abortion Controversy

Several decisions that followed led to *Roe v. Wade,*[81] the landmark abortion case. Throwing out the abortion laws of almost all the states, the Court recognized a woman's interest in terminating her pregnancy, the state's interest in protecting her health, and the state's interest in protecting "prenatal life." According to the seven-justice majority, the Constitution prohibited virtually all restrictions on abortions during the first trimester of pregnancy, allowed reasonable medical regulations to guard the woman's health in the second trimester (but no outright prohibitions of abortion), and permitted the state to ban abortions only in the third trimester after the point of fetal "viability" (except when the pregnancy endangered the woman's life). For fifteen years after *Roe,* Congress and some state legislatures tried to limit the availability of abortion and to discourage its use; however, the Supreme Court invalidated most restrictions, reasoning that the right to an abortion was a fundamental right, and thus the government had to show compelling reasons when the right was curtailed.

In 1989, opponents of abortion won a significant victory in the Supreme Court. In a case from Missouri, five justices upheld (among other things) a requirement for fetal viability testing prior to the twenty-fourth week of pregnancy—something the Court previously would doubtlessly have struck down.[82] Moreover, the Court discarded Roe's trimester-based analysis of the abortion right, but stopped short of overruling *Roe.* In 1992, the Court upheld parts of a Pennsylvania statute that imposed several conditions before a woman could obtain an abortion.[83] These included informed consent provisions, a twenty-four-hour waiting period, parental consent for minors, and record-keeping

Ninth Amendment

Part of the Bill of Rights that cautions that the people possess rights not specified in the Constitution

Roe v. Wade

Supreme Court decision [410 U.S. 113 (1973)] establishing a constitutional right to abortion

POLITICAL CONTROVERSIES

How Much Affirmative Action?

Suppose that a school board and a teachers union agree to increase the number of minority faculty members in public schools. In this district there has been no prior racial discrimination; the union and the school officials simply conclude that it is good publicity to hire more minority teachers. Suppose, also, that the agreement protects minority teachers by providing that if layoffs become necessary, the percentage of minority teachers would not be reduced. Next assume that budget reductions force layoffs, with the result that white teachers with greater seniority are laid off before minority teachers with less. In a 1986 case with similar facts from Jackson, Michigan,[1] the Supreme Court ruled that racially preferential firing was not permissible unless identifiable victims of past discrimination were being protected. Most justices thought the Michigan plan went too far by imposing undue burdens on particular individuals in order to achieve the laudable objective of racial equality. Yet, a majority believed that racially preferential hiring was permissible

under certain circumstances. According to Justice Sandra Day O'Connor, "A public employer, consistent with the Constitution, may undertake an affirmative action program which is designed to further a legitimate remedial purpose and which implements that purpose by means that do not impose disproportionate harm on the interests, or unnecessarily trammel the rights, of innocent individuals."

In another situation, suppose that a city government requires contractors receiving city business to subcontract out a certain percentage of the dollar amount of each contract to one or more minority-owned businesses. Called a set-aside quota, the plan is designed to assist minorities by overcoming their exclusion in past years from the construction trade. Modeling its program on a 10 percent set-aside mandated by Congress and upheld by the Supreme Court in 1980,[2] the city council in Richmond, Virginia, adopted a 30 percent set-aside plan in 1983. In 1989, however, the Supreme Court ruled that the quota violated the Fourteenth Amendment's equal protection clause.[3] According to Justice O'Connor, "To accept Richmond's claim that past societal discrimination alone can serve as a basis for rigid racial preferences would be to open the door to competing claims for 'remedial relief' for every disadvantaged group. The dream of a Nation of

equal citizens in a society where race is irrelevant to personal opportunity and achievement would be lost in a mosaic of shifting preferences based on inherently unmeasurable claims of past wrongs." The ruling in the *Richmond* case has had a widespread impact—36 states and 190 cities had similar remedial programs.

In a situation like the Michigan case, should consideration of race be permitted in hiring but not in firing? In his dissent in the layoff case, Justice John Paul Stevens compared the Michigan plan to a contract that gives added job protection to computer science or foreign-language teachers. Should race-based classifications be regarded differently from those that are skill-based? In the Richmond case, do you agree with the Court's decision? Should it make any difference that a bare majority of Richmond's city council was African American at the time the council adopted the set-aside quota? The Court has also addressed affirmative action in college admissions (see the section titled "Affirmative Action" later in this chapter). Do your views on affirmative action differ depending on whether it involves school or work? Why or why not?

1. *Wygant v. Jackson Board of Education*, 476 U.S. 267 (1986).

2. *Fullilove v. Klutznick*, 448 U.S. 448 (1980).

3. *Richmond v. J. A. Croson Co.*, 488 U.S. 469 (1989).

regulations for medical personnel. However, the Court refused to accept a requirement for spousal notification because it imposed an "undue burden" on the abortion right.

The decisions in the Missouri and Pennsylvania cases have led to four conclusions. First, abortion is no longer a fundamental right, but it does enjoy modest constitutional protection. Second, and as a consequence of the first, total or near-total bans on abortion are almost certainly unconstitutional. Third, it remains to be seen what additional abortion regulations the Court is prepared to accept. Fourth, except for outright bans, a woman's freedom to terminate a pregnancy now depends largely on what her state legislature, Congress, and the executive branch allow. That being said, in 2000 the Court further defined the scope of legislative restrictions by ruling unconstitutional a Nebraska

statute that criminalized late-term abortions that used a specific medical procedure (called "partial birth" by its opponents).[84] In a follow-up case in 2007, however, the Court refused to strike down a more narrowly worded federal law banning the procedure.[85] The right to choose abortion again came into play in 2010, when antiabortion legislators threatened to block passage of the health-care reform bill until they were assured that limits on federal funding of abortion would be kept in place.[86] In the latest development, the Court in 2020 struck down a Louisiana law that required abortion-providing doctors to have admitting privileges at a local hospital. The Court

Anti-abortion protesters march around the Texas capitol on January 23, 2016.

(stock_photo_world / Shutterstock)

majority concluded that the law was politically, rather than medically, motivated and would have had the effect of closing every abortion-providing clinic in the state, effectively denying women in the state the constitutional protection established in *Roe*.[87]

3.5b   Personal Autonomy, Sexual Orientation, and LGBT Rights

For many people, the principle of personal autonomy, which lies at the heart of privacy cases, suggests that government should leave people alone in their choices about sexual relations. Nonetheless, all states today have laws regulating private behavior and personal relations to some extent. Sexual privacy has been an issue of particular concern among members of the LGBT community (those who identify as lesbian, gay, bisexual, or transgender), which has been the group most frequently affected by state forays into sexual privacy. In some locales, same-sex couples may not adopt or have legal custody of children. While over half of the states and numerous cities banned at least some discrimination based on gender identity and/or sexual orientation, it remained legal in many places to engage in sexual-orientation discrimination in housing and employment practices.[88] These discriminatory practices were dealt a serious blow, however, in 2020. In the case *Bostock v. Clayton County* the Court ruled 6–3 that discrimination based on sexual orientation or gender identity was inherently discrimination based on sex—a practice outlawed by the federal government in Title VII of the 1964 Civil Rights Act.[89] This sweeping ruling is likely to result in additional legal challenges to discriminatory practices against LGBT individuals in years to come.

The two most salient issues regarding government regulation of sexual orientation have been anti-sodomy laws and laws recognizing or banning same-sex marriages and domestic partnerships. Before 2003, five states outlawed sodomy (oral or anal sex) between persons of the same gender, and twelve more states outlawed sodomy regardless of gender. Although the Supreme Court found such policies acceptable under the Constitution in 1986, ten years later it found that a Colorado constitutional amendment that prohibited laws barring discrimination against homosexuals was in violation of the equal protection clause of the Fourteenth Amendment.[90] In 2003, the Court went a step further, directly overturning the 1986 decision and declaring that laws prohibiting sexual acts between same-sex partners violated the due process clause of the Fourteenth Amendment.[91]

Regarding same-sex marriage, in 1996 Congress passed the Defense of Marriage Act, which provided a federal definition of marriage that specifically excluded same-gender

(Shutterstock)

In some areas, same-sex couples may not adopt or have legal custody of children.

couples. Forty-one states passed similar laws, many of which were challenged in the courts.[92] In 2004, the Massachusetts Supreme Judicial Court brought more attention to this controversy when it held that a proposed state law creating civil unions for same-sex couples was discriminatory and that the state must give same-sex couples the same marriage rights as opposite-sex couples. In reaction to this decision, eleven states modified their statutes or constitutions in November 2004 to specifically forbid same-sex marriage. In May 2008, the California Supreme Court found the state's ban on same-sex marriage to be unconstitutional, and the state began issuing marriage licenses to same-sex couples in June of that year. However, in November 2008, California voters went to the polls and a narrow majority voted for a ballot initiative that revised the state constitution in order to reinstitute the ban. The initiative was subsequently challenged in federal court on the grounds that it served no legitimate state interest and that gays and lesbians should be treated as a protected class with constitutional protections from discrimination. The trial court decided that the law was unconstitutional, and when the governor and attorney general refused to defend the law, the Supreme Court held that the district court decision must stand, making same-sex marriage legal in the nation's largest state.[93]

In 2011, New York joined New Hampshire, Massachusetts, Connecticut, Iowa, and Vermont as states legalizing same-sex marriage. President Barack Obama (2009–2017) made headlines in May 2012 when he became the first president to take a public position in favor of same-sex marriage. Then, in 2013, a big change occurred. In the case *United States v. Windsor,* the Supreme Court held the federal Defense of Marriage Act unconstitutional.[94] Finding that this law resulted in discrimination against a class of persons that many states sought to protect, the Court majority concluded that it must be invalidated on equal protection grounds. Although that case settled the federal question, it left standing more than a dozen state laws that prevented the performance and recognition of same-sex marriages. The issue was finally put to rest nationwide in 2015, when a Court majority held in *Obergefell v. Hodges* that marriage is a fundamental right and that both the equal protection and due process clauses of the Fourteenth Amendment guarantee a right of same-sex couples to marry and have their marriages recognized throughout the United States.[95] The case had immediate and practical impacts, with the percentage of cohabitating same-sex couples who were legally married rising from 38 percent to 61 percent within two years of the decision.[96]

As a growing majority of Americans now believe same-sex marriages should be recognized by the law as valid, and as other states and the federal government grapple with their own laws and constitutional amendments, this issue promises to be one of evolving debate in the years to come. It also appears to be an issue of generational divide. While 67 percent of people in the US overall support legal same-sex marriage, that figure rises to 77 percent among the eighteen- to thirty-four-year-old demographic.[97]

Unless foes of equality can muster the support for a constitutional amendment—which seems unlikely—the marriage issue seems to be a settled one. That being said, the fight for equality and acceptance continues for LGBT individuals. In 2016, the state of North Carolina passed a law to prevent transgender people from using public restrooms

that do not correspond to their biological sex. Although the federal government warned the state that it was in violation of federal law, the persistence of state-level efforts to discriminate against members of LGBT communities suggests that this area of civil rights will continue to face challenges as people in the US struggle with fully realizing the demands of equality and equal protection under the law.

3.6 Racial Equality

The United States is racially and ethnically wealthy because of centuries of immigration from virtually every part of the globe. The nation's motto *(E Pluribus Unum*—"out of many, one") symbolizes this coming together of peoples as much as it does the union of the states. Some groups have encountered massive discrimination, however; racial, religious, and ethnic stigmas have been real barriers for many. Perhaps because of color—and certainly because of centuries of slavery—African Americans have had the biggest challenge overcoming discrimination in the US. Latinx, whose numbers in this nation have increased in recent years, have faced some of the same obstacles to equality.

3.6a   Equality: A Concept in Dispute

A word like *equality* can mean different things to different people. For believers in **equality of opportunity**, it is enough if government removes barriers of discrimination that have existed in the past. If life is like a marathon, all people should be allowed to participate by having a number and a place at the starting line. Others think government should promote **equality of condition**. To do this, policies should seek to reduce or even eliminate handicaps that certain runners face because of the lingering effects of past discriminations. The marathon can hardly be fair, they say, if some runners start out with their shoelaces tied together or have to wear ill-fitting shoes. Accordingly, the government will have to redistribute income and resources, collecting from those who have more and giving to those who have less. Head Start programs for preschool children and need-based scholarships for college students are obvious devices intended to further equality of condition. Some find such policies inadequate. The effects of inequality, whether of wealth or race or gender, are too strong and pervasive. Government must, therefore, pursue **equality of result**. In the marathon, government may have to carry some runners to the finish line if they are to get there at all. Some affirmative action programs are aimed at achieving equality of result.

3.6b   The Legacy: Slavery and Third-Class Citizenship

Shortly after the Civil War ended, in 1865, ratification of the **Thirteenth Amendment** banished slavery and "involuntary servitude" from the country. Following quickly were ratification of the Fourteenth and Fifteenth Amendments in 1868 and 1870 and passage of several civil rights acts. Collectively these conferred rights of citizenship on the newly freed slaves and officially removed race as a criterion for voting. Especially significant was the **equal protection clause** of the Fourteenth Amendment: "Nor shall any State deny to any person within its jurisdiction the equal protection of the laws" (see Table 3.2).

equality of opportunity
A standard that calls for government to remove barriers of discrimination, such as segregation laws or racially exclusive hiring practices, that have existed in the past

equality of condition
A standard, beyond equality of opportunity, that requires policies (such as redistribution of income and other resources) that seek to reduce or eliminate the effects of past discrimination

equality of result
A standard, beyond equality of condition, that requires policies such as affirmative action or comparable worth that place some people on an equal footing with others

Thirteenth Amendment
The first of the Civil War amendments to the Constitution; adopted in 1865, it banned slavery throughout the United States

equal protection clause
Part of the Fourteenth Amendment that is the source of many civil rights and declares that no state shall deny to any person "the equal protection of the laws"

Table 3.2 Chronology of Major Civil Rights Decisions, Laws, and Amendments

The drive for political equality for all Americans has been a long process and remains incomplete. Congressional statutes and Supreme Court decisions since the Civil War have been important in achieving equality.

1865	Thirteenth Amendment abolishes slavery and "involuntary servitude"
1868	Fourteenth Amendment prohibits state action denying any person "the equal protection of the laws"
1870	Fifteenth Amendment removes race as a qualification for voting
1875	Civil Rights Act bans racial discrimination in places of public accommodation
1883	Civil Rights cases hold 1875 statute unconstitutional
1896	*Plessy v. Ferguson* upholds constitutionality of state law requiring racial segregation on trains in "separate but equal" facilities
1920	Nineteenth Amendment extends franchise to women
1954	*Brown v. Board of Education of Topeka* declares unconstitutional racially segregated public schools; Plessy v. Ferguson reversed
1957	Congress establishes the Civil Rights Commission
1963	Congress passes the Equal Pay Act
1964	Congress passes the Civil Rights Act: Title II outlaws racial discrimination in places of public accommodation; Title IV allows the Justice Department to sue school districts on behalf of African American students seeking integrated education; Title VI bans racial discrimination in federally funded programs; Title VII prohibits most forms of discrimination (on the basis of race or gender) in employment and creates the Equal Employment Opportunity Commission; Twenty-fourth Amendment eliminates poll taxes in federal elections
1965	Congress passes the Voting Rights Act; President Johnson bans racial discrimination by federal contractors
1968	Civil Rights Act's Title VIII prohibits most forms of discrimination in sale or rental of housing
1971	Twenty-sixth Amendment lowers national voting age to 18
1972	Congress submits Equal Rights Amendment to states for ratification
1978	*Regents v. Bakke* invalidates a medical school admissions program that reserved a specific number of seats for minority applicants
1979	*Steelworkers v. Weber* upholds legality of a voluntary affirmative action plan for industrial apprenticeships that gives preference to African American workers over white workers with greater seniority
1982	Ratification of Equal Rights Amendment fails; Congress extends and amends Voting Rights Act; Title IX of Educational Amendments bars sex discrimination in "any education program or activity receiving Federal financial assistance"
1989	*Richmond v. J. A. Croson Co.* invalidates a municipally mandated 30 percent set-aside quota for racial minorities

1990	Congress enacts the National Hate Crimes Statistics Act, which requires the Justice Department to gather data on crimes motivated by prejudice about race, religion, ethnicity, or sexual orientation; the Americans with Disabilities Act becomes law
1991	Congress enacts a civil rights bill designed to modify several 1989 Supreme Court decisions that had made on-the-job discrimination more difficult to prove, and affirmative action plans easier to challenge in court
2003	The Supreme Court finds the University of Michigan's law school admission process, which uses race as affirmative criteria, acceptable because it is narrowly tailored
2006	Congress reauthorizes the Voting Rights Act for an additional twenty-five years
2011	President Obama certifies the congressional act repealing the military's "Don't Ask, Don't Tell" policy (This allows gay men, lesbians, and bisexuals to serve openly in the military for the first time.)
2015	*Obergefell v. Hodges* establishes marriage as a fundamental right and guarantees marriage equality for same-sex couples

By the end of the nineteenth century, however, it was clear that the nation had abandoned the promise of full citizenship for the former slaves. Enforcement of civil rights laws became lax, and the Supreme Court made it clear that the Constitution would not stand in the way of racially discriminatory policies. In *Plessy v. Ferguson,* for example, the Court announced the **separate-but-equal doctrine** in upholding a Louisiana law that required racial segregation on trains.[98] As long as racially separate facilities were "equal," the Court maintained, the Constitution had not been violated.

(Courtesy of Robert L. Knudsen, White House Photograph Office, National Archives, via Wikimedia)

Lady Bird Johnson, the First Lady, reading to children enrolled in Project Head Start at Kemper School in Washington, DC.

Three kinds of policies then developed that denied many African Americans their rights until after the middle of the twentieth century. First, the law racially segregated virtually every aspect of life in the South (the region of the nation in which most African Americans lived). Segregation existed elsewhere, too, but it was enforced more by custom than by law. No section of the nation was immune to racist attitudes and racially motivated violence, including riots and lynchings. Segregated neighborhoods became fixtures in the North and South alike.

Second, Southern politicians systematically excluded African Americans from the political process. To get around the Fifteenth Amendment, legislatures turned to devices such as poll taxes, good-character tests, and literacy tests to keep African Americans away from the ballot box. Until its use was declared unconstitutional by the Supreme Court,[99] the "grandfather clause" allowed whites to vote who would otherwise have been disfranchised by those same barriers. Of all the discriminatory devices, the white primary was probably the most effective. Because one party (the Democrats) was dominant in the region after 1900, the real electoral choices in state, local, and congressional races were made in the primary—not in the general election. White Democrats thus excluded African Americans from meaningful political participation by adopting party rules that allowed only whites to vote in the Democratic primaries. Even though the white primary

separate-but-equal doctrine

The standard announced by the Supreme Court in *Plessy v. Ferguson* in 1896 that allowed racially separate facilities on trains (and by implication in public services such as education), as long as the separate facilities were equal (overturned by *Brown v. Board of Education of Topeka* in 1954)

seems an affront to the Fifteenth Amendment, it was not until 1944 that the Supreme Court ruled that such deception violated the Constitution.[100] Still, for two decades afterward most African Americans were kept from voting in many places.

Third, without the vote African Americans were shortchanged across the board in the delivery of public services such as education. Favors are rarely extended to entire groups that are permanently disfranchised, especially when they bear racial or religious stigmas as well. Thus, the spirit of *Plessy* was honored only in part; although separate, services and facilities were rarely equal.

3.6c   The Counterattack

Opponents of racism saw little hope of victory through the legislative process. At the local level, African Americans were politically powerless in the areas in which segregation was most pervasive. At the national level, Congress operated racially segregated schools in Washington, DC, and provided separate eating and working places for African American civil servants. Even Uncle Sam's toilets were marked "Whites Only" and "Colored." The armed forces remained racially segregated until President Harry Truman (1945–1953) ordered an end to the practice in 1948.

Thus, the counterattack against racism looked to the federal judiciary and was led principally by the National Association for the Advancement of Colored People. Known by its initials, the **NAACP** was founded in 1909 to improve the social, economic, and political condition of African Americans. A separate division for litigation, called the Legal Defense Fund (LDF), began work in 1939 and had the primary responsibility of pressing the desegregation drive in courtrooms in the 1940s, 1950s, and 1960s. One prominent African American attorney in the LDF was Thurgood Marshall, later the first African American justice on the Supreme Court (1967–1991).

The National Civil Rights Museum was established in Memphis, Tennessee, in 1991. Visit this website for an interactive tour of the museum:

http://www.bvtlab.com/3833V

The assault on racial segregation reached a climax in the landmark decision of May 17, 1954: ***Brown v. Board of Education of Topeka***.[101] "Does segregation of children in public schools solely on the basis of race, even though the physical facilities and other 'tangible' factors may be equal, deprive the children of the minority group of equal educational opportunities?" asked Chief Justice Earl Warren (1953–1969). "We believe that it does. ... In the field of public education," he concluded, "the doctrine of 'separate but equal' has no place. Separate educational facilities are inherently unequal." *Plessy* was overruled.

3.6d   Putting *Brown* to Work: The Law and Politics of Integration

The Court had made its decision. What was to happen? Rather than order an immediate end to segregation, the justices announced that integration was to proceed "with all deliberate speed."[102] In most places "deliberate speed" proved to be a turtle's pace. A decade after the Court's historic pronouncement, less than 1 percent of the African American children in the states of the old Confederacy were attending public school with white children. In six border states and the District of Columbia the figure was much higher: 52 percent.

NAACP

National Association for the Advancement of Colored People; an organization founded to improve the social, economic, and political condition of African Americans

Brown v. Board of Education of Topeka

Landmark Supreme Court decision [347 U.S. 483 (1954)] that overturned the separate-but-equal standard of *Plessy v. Ferguson* [163 U.S. 537 (1896)] and began an end to racial segregation in public schools

Chapter 03 Civil Liberties & Civil Rights

Several factors severely hampered quick implementation of *Brown,* making the 1954 decision a test case of the Supreme Court's power. First, some federal judges in the South were themselves opposed to integration. They did little to press for *Brown's* speedy implementation. Second, state legislatures and local school boards usually reflected strong white opposition to *Brown's* enforcement. Third, fear of hostile reaction by the local white community discouraged litigation. It was economically and physically risky for parents of African American children to sue local officials. Fourth, the Court received little initial support from Congress, the White House, and a large part of the organized legal community.

Significant enforcement of *Brown* and the lowering of other racial barriers did not come until civil rights activists, such as Martin Luther King Jr., riveted the nation's attention on the injustices that persisted and called for action. Congress then enacted two important pieces of legislation: the **Civil Rights Act of 1964** and the Elementary and Secondary Education Act of 1965. The importance of the first act for *Brown* came in Title VI: Every federal agency that funded local programs through grants, loans, or contracts was required to press for an end to racial discrimination. The 1965 school aid act was the first massive federal appropriation for local school systems; to keep the money, however, school systems had to move swiftly on integration. The 1964 act was the hook, and the 1965 act was the bait. Ironically, public schools in the South are now among the most integrated in the nation, whereas schools in the Northeast are among the most segregated.

(Courtesy of John Vachon, 1938, via Library of Congress)

Segregated drinking fountains symbolized the separate worlds of the South until the 1960s.

3.6e   The Continuing Effects of *Brown*

Supreme Court decisions about school integration since 1971 have come largely from states outside the South. Non-Southern school systems had segregated schools, but rarely had law segregated them recently. The racial composition of these schools reflected decades of residential segregation that had resulted from economic inequities and private discrimination. This kind of "unofficial" segregation was called **de facto segregation**; but in a pair of decisions from Ohio in 1979,[103] the Supreme Court decided that "racially identifiable schools" in any district probably resulted from school board policy. What many had thought to be de facto segregation was now considered **de jure segregation**: racial separation caused by government policy. Because of the 1979 ruling, local officials now have the affirmative duty of redrawing attendance zones and busing pupils from one part of town to another.

Busing itself remains controversial. Many parents—African American and white alike—object to having their children transported farther than seems necessary. Many prefer neighborhood schools. Aside from achieving integration, scholars disagree on the effects of busing and similar measures on the schoolchildren involved, debating whether integration improves the educational performance of African American students. Although integrated schools often mean that African American parents lose control over schools in African American neighborhoods, integrated education probably better prepares all students for living in a racially diverse society. Moreover, many believe

Civil Rights Act of 1964
Comprehensive legislation to end racial segregation in access to public accommodations and in employment in the public and private sectors

de facto segregation
Programs or facilities that are racially segregated by private choice or private discrimination, not because of law or public policy

de jure segregation
Programs or facilities that are racially segregated because of law or public policy

that "green follows white"—that the presence of white students assures more generous economic support of a school by local officials. Nonetheless, the Supreme Court has now taken the position that once a school district has eliminated segregation, the district ceases to be under a constitutional obligation to continue the policies that produced the integrated system, even if "re-segregation" might result.[104]

Whatever the progress has been with school integration, social segregation remains a fact in many areas of the nation. Even though the Civil Rights Acts of 1964 and 1968, respectively, prohibit racial discrimination in employment and in the sale or rental of housing (as do the laws in most states and hundreds of municipalities), African Americans remain the most segregated minority group—the group most isolated from whites. This ongoing segregation in many metropolitan areas and elsewhere continues to have a negative economic impact—measured by income, crime rates, and educational attainment—on all residents of the racially segregated regions, regardless of race.[105]

3.6f   Affirmative Action

Many people believe that ending discrimination is not enough. They believe that positive steps called **affirmative action** are also needed to overcome the residual effects of generations of racial bias. Others oppose affirmative action if it involves preferential treatment for minorities. They argue that jobs and university scholarships, for example, are finite. To give to one means to withhold from someone else. They make the case that the nonminority applicant who loses out because of race has been hurt in much the same way as a minority applicant in earlier years who was kept out because of race.

If a national consensus has developed against racial discrimination in its old forms, no firm consensus exists on affirmative action. A recent poll indicates that 61 percent of people in the US favor affirmative action programs for racial minorities, but 30 percent oppose them; however, only 31 percent of people in the US believe race should be taken into account in college admissions.[106] Even the Supreme Court has been divided, as *Regents of the University of California v. Bakke*[107] illustrates. In this landmark affirmative action case, the Supreme Court invalidated the use of a racial quota for medical school admissions at the Davis campus of the University of California, but it said that race could still be taken into account. Admissions officers may use race as one of several criteria in evaluating the record of an applicant but may not admit or exclude solely on the basis of race. In 2003, twenty-five years after *Bakke,* the Court again took up the issue, holding that the University of Michigan's undergraduate admission system unfairly allowed race to play too decisive a role because it failed to treat applicants as individuals rather than merely group members.[108] On the other hand, the Court found Michigan's law school admission process acceptable because its use of race as affirmative criteria was narrowly tailored.[109] In two additional cases, the Court has held that admissions policies can consider race only if the university can meet the "strict scrutiny" standard of showing a compelling state interest; moreover, it is permissible for a state constitutional amendment to ban the use of race-conscious admissions policies entirely.[110] Finally, in a University of Texas case in 2016, the Court approved of the university's admission policy, which considers academic performance alone in a first round of admissions and then considers academics and race among several factors in a second round.[111] The Court majority determined that the policy did not violate the equal protection clause because its pursuit of a diverse student body served a compelling interest for the state.

In other cases, the Court has allowed governments and private businesses wide latitude in personnel decisions. Title VII of the Civil Rights Act of 1964 bans job discrimination on the basis of "race, color, religion, sex, or national origin." The Court has reasoned that

affirmative action

Positive steps taken by public or private institutions to overcome the remaining effects of racial or sexual bias (Affirmative action programs attempt to achieve equality of result.)

POLITICAL CONTROVERSIES

Race and (In) Justice: Law Enforcement, Homicide, and Change

Seven minutes and forty-six seconds on May 25, 2020, transformed the focus of American politics in the summer of 2020, leading to a racial justice movement that called for significant and permanent change to our society. This is how long a white police officer in Minneapolis, Minnesota, knelt on the neck of handcuffed African American George Floyd (who was suspected of using a counterfeit $20 bill), causing his death. While an outrageous act by itself, its presence as part of a larger pattern of abuse of African Americans at the hands of law enforcement officers made it even more significant. The event crystallized for many the ongoing struggles and tensions our nation experiences when it comes to race. In the days and months following the killing of George Floyd, peaceful protests and demands for justice took place in cities throughout the country. There were also curfews, clashes between citizens and law enforcement, accusations, and frustrations. While some people caused damage to local businesses or committed violent acts, the actions by most were by-and-large lawful, focused, and well-received—with 65 percent of people in the US stating their support of the racial justice protests.

Dozens of major corporations made their support known as well, voicing the phrase "Black Lives Matter" via advertising and social media. Many cities addressed resolutions to "defund the police"—an idea that gained currency via the protests and that largely focused on reducing spending on the more militarized aspects of policing, redirecting those funds to less confrontational methods of ensuring public safety, such as de-escalation training and the hiring of more mental health experts. Other outcomes were symbolic and wide-ranging. Cities and states took action on removing statues of Confederate leaders and renaming public spaces that had honored the Confederacy, and the Mississippi state legislature finally acted to remove the Confederate battle standard from its state flag. The Washington, DC, professional football team changed its nickname (which had been a racial slur toward American Indians) and musicians changed the names of their bands to avoid glorifying the pre-Civil War South; The Dixie Chicks became simply The Chicks and Lady Antebellum became Lady A. Along with these symbolic acts came promises of sustained, long-term reform from nearly all levels of government.

Why was this event so significant? What made George Floyd's death an issue of national, not just personal, tragedy? One answer has to do with systemic racism and the reality of stark differences in the criminal justice system in the US. African American teenagers are twenty-one times more likely to be shot and killed by police officers than white teens. Moreover, African Americans and Latinx make up 32 percent of the total US population, but 56 percent of those incarcerated in our nation's prisons and jails. If these trends continue, one in three African American males born today will be imprisoned over the course of his lifetime, but only one in seventeen white men will suffer that fate. On the other side of the equation, we have a law enforcement system that is largely white: 72 percent of local police officers are white.

Another reason the events in Minneapolis, Minnesota, became a part of the national conversation is that perceptions of the facts described above differ markedly. In the weeks following the killing of Floyd, people in the US of all races agreed nearly unanimously on some issues: law enforcement officers should be punished for abuses, fired for multiple abuses, and be required to have good relations with the community they serve. But support for other reforms has differed sharply by race: 72 percent of African Americans, but only 44 percent of white Americans, believe police officers should not be in charge of enforcing nonviolent crimes; 70 percent of African Americans, but only 41 percent of white Americans, believe police budgets should be reduced and the money shifted toward social programs.

Racial profiling, use of force, and the militarization of domestic law enforcement are also issues Americans often view differently depending on their own ascriptive identities. More than half (60 percent) of white Americans trust the ability of police to protect them from violent crime, but fewer than half of nonwhite Americans feel the same way. Similar double-digit racial differences exist when people in the US are polled about their confidence in the police or the criminal justice system generally. And what causes the disparate outcomes described in the previous paragraph? Fifty percent of African Americans say the cause is mostly discrimination, but only 19 percent of white Americans agree.

What do wrongful deaths of African Americans at the hands of police officers mean for American politics? Among other things, they remind us that the processes and policies of our system of government

have very real consequences for us. The politicians we vote for in federal, state, and local elections shape our communities and our justice system. The choices we have made over centuries and that we continue to make today have created an imperfect system that we must continue to improve. When America was founded, we endeavored to (among other things) "form a more perfect Union, establish Justice, [and] insure domestic Tranquility." The killing of George Floyd reminds us of how hard we still need to work to attain those goals.

How did you experience the racial justice protests in 2020? How would you describe the relationship between people in your community and law enforcement? What changes would you like to see in that relationship?

SOURCES: The Gallup Organization, "Two in Three Americans Support Racial Justice Protests," July 28, 2020; "Most Americans Say Policing Needs 'Major Changes,'" July 22, 2020; "Nonwhites Less Likely to Feel Police Protect and Serve Them," November 17, 2014. ProPublica, "Deadly Force in Black and White," October 10, 2014, https://www.propublica.org/article/deadly-force-in-black-and-white. NAACP, "Criminal Justice Fact Sheet," https://www.naacp.org/criminal-justice-fact-sheet/ (July 29, 2020). *The Washington Post*, "In urban areas, police are consistently much whiter than the people they serve," June 4, 2020, https://www.washingtonpost.com/nation/2020/06/04/urban-areas-police-are-consistently-much-whiter-than-people-they-serve/?arc404=true (July 29, 2020).

a law intended to end discrimination against racial minorities and women should not be used to prohibit programs designed to help those groups.[112] What, then, are the limits to affirmative action under the law? There is no clear answer to this question. Generally, policies by an employer to overcome the effects of its past discrimination are permissible; indeed, they may be required. Even some policies by an employer to alleviate general "societal discrimination" for which the employer is not responsible are permissible. Hiring policies that look like "quotas" or admissions policies that assign point values to one's race have the greatest chance of being struck down.[113]

3.6g Voting Rights

Two centuries ago most Americans were denied the right to vote. The Constitution left voting qualifications to the states, with the result that women, African Americans, and even some white adult males were left out. Since the 1820s, the national trend has been to chip away at these restrictions so that today almost all adult citizens in the United States have the right to vote.

As late as 1964, however, African Americans in particular were systemically denied the right to vote in most parts of the South. The response to this situation was the **Voting Rights Act of 1965**—the most important voting legislation ever enacted by Congress. Besides removing many barriers to voting, the act required that any change in a "standard, practice, or procedure with respect to voting" in certain parts of the United States (most of them being in the South) could take effect only after being cleared by the attorney general of the United States or by the United States District Court for the District of Columbia. The Supreme Court interpreted "standard, practice, or procedure" to include any change in a locale's electoral system. This advance clearance requirement was satisfied only if the proposed change had neither the *purpose* nor the *effect* of "denying or abridging the right to vote on account of race or color." This meant that African American voting power could in no way be weakened or diluted by any change in local election practices.

Voting Rights Act of 1965
Major legislation designed to overcome racial barriers to voting, primarily in the Southern States; it was extended again in 2006 for twenty-five years

Congress made an important change in the law in 1982, banning existing electoral arrangements with a racially discriminatory effect anywhere in the United States. Conceivably, this addition to the law may produce a realignment of political power in sections of the country in which African Americans and Latinx amount to at least a sizable minority of the population, and in which local political practices dilute the political influence of these minorities. More recently, the Court ruled in 1993 that reapportionment schemes may violate the equal protection clause if they are drawn based

solely on race—even when the intent is to increase racial minority representation.[114] Evidence that the Voting Rights Act continues to be controversial can be found in the 2006 congressional debates over renewing the act. Southern Republicans opposed extending the provisions requiring some states (mostly in the South) to obtain preclearance before altering their voting laws, and other legislators balked at extending requirements to provide ballots in multiple languages.[115] Ultimately, the act was extended for another twenty-five years, with some portions being made permanent. President George W. Bush signed the reauthorization act into law on July 27, 2006.

(Photo courtesy of Yoichi Okamoto, 1965, via Wikimedia.)

President Lyndon B. Johnson meets with Martin Luther King Jr. at the signing of the Voting Rights Act of 1965. The legislation provided African Americans the right to vote without discrimination and was the most important voting legislation ever enacted by Congress.

Provisions of this reauthorization faced legal challenges, though, and in 2009 the Supreme Court unanimously ruled that the law's "preclearance" provisions can be challenged by individual communities ("political subdivisions") seeking permanent exemption based on the argument that discrimination is no longer a concern in their locality.[116] Then, in 2013, a narrowly divided Court weakened the power of the Voting Rights Act still further. Finding the formula that identified those jurisdictions to be anachronistic and an overreach of federal power, it struck down the provision listing preclearance jurisdictions entirely. Stating that the nation had changed greatly since the act's initial passage, the Court insisted that legislation must address current conditions.[117] As a result of this decision some jurisdictions, such as Texas, have adopted new voter ID laws and redistricting maps that may not have been approved by the federal government had preclearance still been in effect. The long-term effects on voter registration and turnout remain to be seen.

The Voting Rights Act has had a far-reaching impact. African Americans in the Southern states now vote at a rate approximating that of whites. In the 2020 election for the U.S. House of Representatives, voters nationally chose at least fifty-nine African American and forty-five Latinx members—a number that amounts to about 24 percent of the chamber. At the time of writing, there are currently three African Americans and five Latinx serving in the U.S. Senate. There are also eighteen Asian Americans serving in the House of Representatives and three in the Senate. Of course, it goes without saying that the 2008 presidential election was a landmark for African Americans in electoral politics. Illinois Senator Barack Obama, the son of a black father and white mother, became the first African American identified presidential nominee of a major party when he was chosen as the Democratic nominee after a hard-fought primary season. He made history again in November 2008, when he was elected as the first African American president. One of the most significant acts of President Obama's first year in office was to appoint Sonia Sotomayor to the Supreme Court, making her the first Latina Supreme Court justice. In 2020, California Senator Kamala Harris became the first African American and first Asian American to be elected vice president.

3.7　Sexual Equality

Because the political system has been a battleground for so many years in the fight for racial equality, it is easy to suppose that sexual equality has occupied the attention of Congress and the courts for just as long. However, such has not been the case. Making the nation free of discrimination based on gender has been a national priority for only about five decades.

3.7a　The Legacy

Until recently, the legal status of women in the United States was one of substantial inequality. A wife had no legal existence apart from her husband. Without his consent, she could make no contracts that bound either of them. In response to such attitudes, the first convention on women's rights was held in 1848 in Seneca Falls, New York. Change in attitudes came slowly, however. Even the Fourteenth Amendment spoke of "male inhabitants." The **Nineteenth Amendment**, extending the franchise to women, was not ratified until 1920, after a long and turbulent suffrage movement. Not until 1971 did the Supreme Court first invalidate a law because it discriminated against women,[118] and as late as 1973 there were nine hundred gender-based federal laws still on the books.

(Getty Images)

The Nineteenth Amendment prohibits state and federal governments from denying citizens the right to vote because of their gender.

3.7b　Gender to the Forefront

Attacks on racial discrimination during the 1950s helped to turn attention to laws that penalized women because they were women. Sex discrimination became a political issue few politicians could ignore after the publication of books such as Betty Friedan's *Feminine Mystique* in 1963 and Kate Millett's *Sexual Politics* in 1971, and after the formation of the National Organization for Women (NOW) in 1966. At about the same time, the female half of the postwar "baby boom" entered college, graduate schools, and the workforce. There were more women than ever before who were at an age and place in life and career when questions of gender discrimination were very important.

Responding to inequities that had become obvious, Congress passed the Equal Pay Act in 1963, which commanded "equal pay for equal work." Title VII of the Civil Rights Act of 1964 outlawed sexual (as well as racial) bias in employment and promotion practices. Title IX of the 1972 Educational Amendments banned sex discrimination in education programs and activities at colleges receiving federal financial aid. (Title IX remains contentious because of its applicability to how universities allocate dollars between male and female athletic teams.)

As a result of changes in both laws and attitudes, sex-based retirement plans, for example, may no longer require women to make higher contributions or to receive lower

Nineteenth Amendment

Amendment ratified in 1920 that prohibits limitations on voting based on sex

monthly benefits than men just because women as a group live longer than men as a group.[119] States may no longer operate single-sex schools of nursing (and probably any other kind), even if coeducational public nursing schools also exist.[120] In the workplace, not only has sexual harassment been judged to be a violation of Title VII, but the Supreme Court also holds employers responsible under the law for not taking steps to prevent it.[121] Despite such remedies, sexual harassment and misconduct continue to be a problem in many settings, as contemporary movements such as #MeToo demonstrate.

Many people believe that real economic equality between the sexes will not be achieved without **comparable worth** (equal pay for jobs of equal value), a policy not required by federal law. Otherwise, they say, full-time female workers will continue to earn less on average than full-time male workers in many fields. According to the latest figures from the U.S. Bureau of Labor Statistics, women currently earn only about eighty-one cents for every $1 that men earn.[122]

The American Civil Liberties Union is a nonprofit and nonpartisan organization that fights vigorous court battles to defend the civil rights and liberties guaranteed by the Constitution. To find out more about the organization and the issues they are currently addressing, visit this website.

http://www.bvtlab.com/7Ud79

3.8   Other Americans and Civil Rights

Discrimination against women and African Americans has occupied a prominent place on the public agenda in recent years, but discrimination has claimed other victims as well. American Indians, Asian Americans, Latinx, immigrants, and Americans with disabilities have all demanded—with varying degrees of success—that public officials take steps to remedy years of neglect and unequal treatment. Sexual orientation and gender identity have also been the basis for discrimination by governments, businesses, and individuals, and were discussed as aspects of privacy earlier in this chapter.

3.8a   American Indians

From an estimated sixteenth-century population of perhaps 2 million or more[123] (no one knows for certain), American Indians (also called Native Americans) numbered barely 500,000 in 1900 as war, disease, and systematic slaughter took their toll. Today, there are over 6 million, about 2 percent of the total US population. As a group, American Indians suffer disproportionately high rates of sickness, poverty, illiteracy, and unemployment. Not until 1924 did Congress recognize them as citizens.

Many American Indians have understandably resisted assimilation into the rest of the population, insisting instead on preserving their culture and heritage. Approximately one-quarter live on 325 semiautonomous reservations and, in Alaska, in 223 native villages under the supervision of the Bureau of Indian Affairs in the Department of the Interior. The Indian Self-Determination and Education Assistance Act of 1975 granted American Indians greater control over their own affairs, and the Indian Bill of Rights of 1968 gave American Indians living on reservations protections similar to those found in the Constitution.

comparable worth

An employment policy designed to overcome the economic inequities of sexual discrimination, mandating that persons holding jobs of equal responsibility and skill be paid the same

(Shutterstock)

Congress recognized American Indians as citizens since 1924.

Recent policy reflects resurgent ethnic pride and new political awareness that began in the 1960s and 1970s and has been asserted by activist groups such as the National Indian Youth Council and the American Indian Movement. Such groups have not only protested inadequate national assistance and the plight of the reservation population but also have attempted, with some success, to recover through litigation ancient tribal fishing and land rights sometimes worth millions of dollars. In recent decades, several American Indian tribes have been granted state authorization to operate gaming facilities on reservation land, providing an important source of revenue for their communities. With this success, though, has come a backlash. Though tribes have historically operated largely autonomously of state control, state compacts authorizing gaming have resulted in large profits that the non-Indian populations of these states have seen as potential tax revenue, leading some states to seek tax rates on casino profits well in excess of standard business tax rates.

3.8b Latinx

Numbering almost 60 million and making up about 19 percent of the population, Latinx are the nation's fastest-growing minority. In the most recent census, the number of Americans identifying themselves as Latino or Latina was larger than the number identifying as African American. A majority originally came from Mexico; most of the others came from Puerto Rico, South America, and parts of Central America. Historically, Mexican Americans resided mainly in the Southwest, Cuban Americans in Florida, and Puerto Ricans in the Northeast; today, Latinx live in significant numbers throughout much of the country.

For decades, Latinx have encountered the same discriminations in voting, education, housing, and employment that have confronted African Americans, compounded by a language barrier. Amendments to the Voting Rights Act of 1965 require ballots to be printed in Spanish as well as English in areas in which Spanish-speaking people number more than 5 percent of the population. Partly as a result of this act, Latinx voter registration jumped dramatically nationwide between 1972 and 2010, rising to over 51 percent of eligible Latinx voters; yet Latinx are still less likely than African Americans and whites to register to vote.[124] Despite lower registration rates, by 2020 there were over 32 million eligible Latinx voters—comprising about 13 percent of the electorate.[125] Moreover, Title VI of the Civil Rights Act of 1964 requires public schools to provide bilingual instruction to students deficient in English. Both education and political participation are important to any group seeking to maintain ethnic identity in a diverse culture. Policies to lower language barriers have sparked a backlash among those who see non-English-speaking (particularly Spanish-speaking) persons as a threat to an American cultural identity.

3.8c Immigrants

As the Statue of Liberty signifies, America is a land of immigrants—but some have been more welcome than others. Until 1921 entry into the United States was virtually unlimited; but in that year Congress established the first of a series of ceilings on immigration that discriminated against persons from Eastern Europe and Asia, a bias not eliminated until 1965. Today the law sets a ceiling of 675,000 immigrants per year, including those admitted because of job skills and family relationships. Exceptions to the ceiling for refugees and others mean that the total number of immigrants admitted annually exceeds 1 million.

Thousands more—no one knows the exact number—successfully enter or remain in the country illegally, putting pressure on public services and, some say, taking jobs from citizens and others who legally reside in the United States. About 11 million immigrants reside in the United States illegally today. In response to these issues, Congress passed the Immigration Reform and Control Act in 1986. Among other things, the law requires employers to verify the American citizenship or legal status of all job applicants and provides stiff penalties for employers who hire undocumented workers. The 1986 law has had an unintended consequence: discrimination against persons of Latinx or Asian descent. A study by the General Accounting Office (an investigatory agency of Congress, now called the Government Accountability Office) found that one in five of the 4.6 million employers surveyed admitted that the law encouraged them to discriminate against job applicants who were "foreign-appearing" or "foreign-sounding."[126] Arizona sparked immigration controversy in 2010 when it passed a law requiring law enforcement officials to determine the immigration status of anyone they reasonably suspected of being an illegal alien. Supporters argued that this misdemeanor offense merely enforces existing federal law, while opponents contended it would lead to discriminatory racial profiling.[127] In 2012, the Supreme Court struck down most of the law on federalism grounds, but let stand the provision that requires state law enforcement officials to check the immigration status of people they arrest.[128] Frustrated by a congressional stalemate on the issue, President Obama tackled immigration reform in 2014 via an executive action that would have deferred many deportations (see "Immigration Reform: Laws and Executive Orders" in Chapter 10). In 2016, however, the Court did not overturn an appellate decision that held that these actions exceeded the president's constitutional authority.[129] Immigration issues took center stage in the 2016 presidential campaign when Republican candidate Donald Trump claimed he would build a wall between the United States and Mexico that he would force Mexico to pay for. He also claimed he would ban all immigration by Muslims to the United States as an anti-terrorism measure. As president, Trump continued lobbying Congress to support building his wall, and he successfully imposed a ban on travel from several majority-Muslim nations, which the Supreme Court concluded was a lawful exercise of his power.[130] In May 2020, in response to the COVID-19 pandemic, President Trump signed an executive order temporarily suspending most immigration to the US. While many of President Trump's supporters were vocal advocates of his anti-immigrant stance, 76 percent of Americans view immigration as

The number of immigrants entering the United States was virtually unlimited until 1921.

("Statue of Liberty from Ellis Island." National Park Service, 1930, via Library of Congress.)

a good thing for the country today.[131] Such sentiments, coupled with the continued influx of immigrants, guarantees that "immigration reform" will continue to be an important political topic for the foreseeable future.

3.8d Americans with Disabilities

One of the nation's largest minority groups consists of the more than 61 million Americans with a physical or mental disability. The Civil Rights Act of 1964, the most comprehensive antidiscrimination legislation ever enacted by Congress, did not cover disabled Americans—long victims of bias in both the public and private sectors.

In 1990, Congress passed the Americans with Disabilities Act, which bans discrimination in employment (in businesses with more than fifteen employees) and in places of public accommodation (including not only restaurants and hotels but also establishments as varied as physicians' offices, zoos, sports arenas, and dry cleaners). Called a "bill of rights for Americans with disabilities," the law also stipulates that newly manufactured buses and railroad cars be accessible to persons in wheelchairs and that telephone companies provide service for those with hearing and speech impairments. The law's definition of Americans with disabilities goes beyond those who rely on wheelchairs or who have difficulty seeing or hearing—it includes people with mental disorders and those with AIDS (acquired immune deficiency syndrome) and HIV (the virus that causes AIDS), but not those who use illegal drugs or who abuse legal drugs such as alcohol. Although in 2001 the Supreme Court ruled that the Americans with Disabilities Act required the PGA (Professional Golfers Association) to allow disabled persons to use golf carts during the PGA tour, the act suffered a major setback when the Court held that state employees could not sue states for failing to comply with the act.[132]

3.9 Liberties and Rights in the Constitutional Framework

Civil rights and liberties, the subjects of this chapter, are part of the framework of American constitutional government. Freedoms of political and religious expression, limits on the police, protection of privacy—all examples of civil liberties—are not only essential components of the political process but also help to define the quality of life people in the US enjoy. Civil rights in turn are inspired by the bold assertion of the Declaration of Independence that "all men are created equal." Against a legacy of toleration of inequality, much of what government and private citizens have done in recent decades has been driven by an intolerance of inequality. Through application of constitutional provisions, laws, and policies, many people have tried to make the Declaration's words a reality, for women as well as men, for African Americans as well as whites. Their efforts employ the tools of politics and the major institutions of government, described in the chapters that follow.

CHAPTER REVIEW

1. Civil liberties are freedoms, protected by law, to act or not to act and to be free from unwarranted governmental intrusion in one's life. Civil rights encompass participation in society on an equal footing with others.

2. Initially the Bill of Rights restrained only the national government; however, using the Fourteenth Amendment, the Supreme Court has applied most of the protections of the Bill of Rights to the states.

3. Free expression is necessary to the democratic political process. Only in rare instances today will the Court approve restrictions on the content of what a person says.

4. The free exercise and establishment clauses have two main objectives: separation of church and state and toleration of different religious faiths.

5. Other parts of the Bill of Rights guard liberty by placing limits on what officials may do in the process of fighting crime.

6. By interpretation, the Constitution includes a right to privacy, giving people the right to make basic decisions about procreation without undue interference by government. Abortion continues to be a divisive national issue.

7. Only since the landmark case of *Brown v. Board of Education of Topeka* in 1954 has the nation made significant progress toward removing discrimination on the basis of race from life in the US. The Voting Rights Act of 1965 has enabled African Americans (as well as others) to participate more equitably in the political process.

8. Most discrimination based on sex is generally forbidden by statute and by the Supreme Court's interpretation of the Fourteenth Amendment.

9. LGBT individuals, American Indians, Latinx, immigrants, and Americans with disabilities are other groups who face discrimination and present special needs.

KEY TERMS

affirmative action 88

bill of attainder 74

Brown v. Board of Education of Topeka 86

capital case 76

Civil Rights Act of 1964 87

clear and present danger test 67

comparable worth 93

cruel and unusual punishment 77

de facto segregation 87

de jure segregation 87

Eighth Amendment 77

equality of condition 83

equality of opportunity 83

equality of result 83

equal protection clause 83

establishment clause 70

exclusionary rule 76

ex post facto laws 74

felony 76

First Amendment 66

Fourteenth Amendment 64

Fourth Amendment 75

free exercise clause 71

incitement test 67

legal guilt	74	presumption of innocence	74
Lemon test	71	prior restraint	68
libel	69	probable cause	75
Miranda rights	76	*Roe v. Wade*	79
misdemeanor	76	separate-but-equal doctrine	85
NAACP	86	Sixth Amendment	76
Nineteenth Amendment	92	symbolic speech	69
Ninth Amendment	79	Thirteenth Amendment	83
obscenity	68	Voting Rights Act of 1965	90
plea bargain	76	warrant	75

READINGS FOR FURTHER STUDY

The Bill of Rights by Irving Brant (American Council of Learned Societies History E-Book Project, 2008) remains one of the best treatments of the origins of the liberties protected in the Constitution.

The rapidly changing field of criminal procedure and criminal justice can be followed in *Criminal Justice: A Brief Introduction,* 13th ed., by Frank J. Schmallenger (New York: Pearson, 2020).

Efforts to achieve racial equality are fully described in Richard Kluger's *Simple Justice* (New York: Vintage, 2004).

A great resource for tracing the statistical history of minority politics is Mart Martin's *The Almanac of Women and Minorities in American Politics 2002* (Boulder, CO: Westview Press, 2001).

Lisa Garcia Bedolla examines Latinx politics in *Latino Politics,* 2nd ed. (Boston: Polity, 2016), and Ed Morales provides another useful account in *Latinx: The New Force in American Politics and Culture* (New York: Verso, 2019). Matt Barreto and Gary M. Segura provide another important look at this issue in *Latino America: How America's Most Dynamic Population Is Poised to Transform the Politics of the Nation* (New York: PublicAffairs, 2014).

American Indian politics is discussed in John M. Meyer, ed., *American Indians and U.S. Politics* (Westport, CT: Praeger, 2002), and in David E. Wilkins and Heidi Kiiwetinepinesiik Stark, *American Indian Politics and the American Political System,* 4th ed. (Lanham, MD: Rowman & Littlefield, 2017).

The emerging field of sexual diversity and politics is well-covered in *Beyond the Politics of the Closet: Gay Rights and the American State Since the 1970s,* by Jonathan Bell (Philadelphia: University of Pennsylvania Press, 2020); in *LGBTQ Americans in the U.S. Political System: An Encyclopedia of Activists, Voters, Candidates, and Officeholders,* edited by Jason Pierceson (Santa Barbara: ABC-CLIO, 2019); in Victory: *The Triumphant Gay Revolution,* by Linda Hirshman (New York: HarperCollins, 2017); and in *The Gay Revolution: The Story of the Struggle,* by Lillian Faderman (New York: Simon & Schuster, 2016).

NOTES

1. *Barron v. Baltimore,* 32 U.S. (7 Peters) 243 (1833).

2. *McDonald v. Chicago,* 561 U.S. 742 (2010).

3. 586 U.S. ___ (2019).

4. *United States v. Haymond,* 588 U.S. ___ (2019).

5. *Katz v. United States,* 389 U.S. 347 (1967), overruling *Olmstead v. United States,* 277 U.S. 438 (1928).

6. *Riley v. California,* 573 U.S. ___ (2014).

7. *Carpenter v. United States,* 585 U.S. ___ (2018).

8. *Schenck v. United States,* 249 U.S. 47 (1919).

9. *Whitney v. California,* 274 U.S. 357, 377 (1927), Justice Brandeis concurring.

10. *Brandenburg v. Ohio,* 395 U.S. 444 (1969).

11. *Morse v. Frederick,* 551 U.S. 443 (2007).

12. *Snyder v. Phelps,* 562 U.S. (2011).

13. *Manhattan Community Access Corporation v. Halleck,* 587 U.S. ___ (2019).

14. *New York Times Co. v. United States,* 403 U.S. 713 (1971).

15. *Miller v. California,* 413 U.S. 15 (1973).

16. *Erie v. Pap's A.M.,* 529 U.S. 277 (2000).

17. *Reno v. ACLU,* 521 U.S. 844 (1997); *Ashcroft v. ACLU,* 535 U.S. 564 (2002); *Ashcroft v. ACLU,* 542 U.S. 656 (2004).

18. *Brown v. Entertainment Merchants Association,* 564 U.S. 786 (2011).

19. *Packingham v. North Carolina,* 582 U.S. ___ (2017).

20. *Iancu v. Brunetti,* 588 U.S. ___ (2019).

21. *New York Times Co. v. Sullivan,* 376 U.S. 254 (1964).

22. *Texas v. Johnson,* 491 U.S. 397 (1989).

23. *United States v. Eichman,* 496 U.S. 310 (1990).

24. *R.A.V. v. City of St. Paul,* 505 U.S. 377 (1992).

25. *McCullen v. Coakley,* 573 U.S. ___ (2014).

26. *Walker v. Texas Division, Sons of Confederate Veterans,* 576 U.S. ___ (2015).

27. The Gallup Organization, "Religion," https://news.gallup.com/poll/1690/Religion.aspx (June 11, 2020).

28. *Statistical Abstract of the United States,* Table 76, 2012. https://www.census.gov/library/publications/2011/compendia/statab/131ed/population.html

29. For example, see *Westside Community Schools v. Mergens,* 496 U.S. 226 (1990).

30. *Lemon v. Kurtzman,* 403 U.S. 602 (1971).

31. *Arizona Christian School Tuition Organization v. Winn,* 563 U.S. 125 (2011).

32. *Trinity Lutheran Church of Columbia, Inc. v. Comer,* 582 U.S. ___ (2017).

33. *Espinoza v. Montana Department of Revenue,* 591 U.S. ___ (2020).

34. *Engel v. Vitale,* 370 U.S. 421 (1962); *School District of Abington Township v. Schempp,* 374 U.S. 203 (1963).

35. *Wallace v. Jaffree,* 472 U.S. 38 (1985).

36. *Lee v. Weisman,* 505 U.S. 577 (1992).

37. *Santa Fe Independent School Dist. v. Doe,* 530 U.S. 290 (2000).

38. *Marsh v. Chambers,* 463 U.S. 783 (1983).

39. *Town of Greece v. Galloway,* 572 U.S. 565 (2014).

40. *Allegheny County v. American Civil Liberties Union,* 492 U.S. 573 (1989).

41. *Elk Grove Unified School District v. Newdow,* 542 U.S. 1 (2004).

42. *McCreary County v. American Civil Liberties Union of Kentucky,* 545 U.S. 844 (2005).

43. *Van Orden v. Perry,* 545 U.S. 677 (2005).

44. *American Legion v. American Humanist Association,* 588 U.S. ___ (2019).

45. *Wisconsin v. Yoder,* 406 U.S. 205 (1972).

46. *Oregon Employment Division v. Smith,* 494 U.S. 872 (1990).

47. *City of Boerne v. Flores,* 521 U.S. 507 (1997).

48. *Burwell v. Hobby Lobby Stores, Inc.,* 573 U.S. ___ (2014).

49. Holt v. Hobbs 574 U.S. ___ (2015).

50. 584 U.S. ___ (2018).

51. This phrase was popularized by John Adams shortly before the Revolutionary War and was later incorporated into the Massachusetts Constitution, the oldest of the American state constitutions still in force.

52. *Arizona v. Gant,* 556 U.S. 332 (2009).

53. *Florida v. Jardines,* 569 U.S. 1 (2013).

54. *Collins v. Virginia,* 584 U.S. ___ (2018); *Byrd v. United States,* 584 U.S. ___ (2018).

55. *Mitchell v. Wisconsin,* 588 U.S. ___ (2019).

56. *United States v. U.S. District Court,* 407 U.S. 297 (1972).

57. *Kyllo v. United States,* 533 U.S. 27 (2001).

58. *U.S. v. Jones,* 566 U.S. 400 (2012).

59. *Florence v. Board of Chosen Freeholders,* 566 U.S. 318 (2012).

60. *Maryland v. King,* 569 U.S. 435 (2013).

61. See *Mapp v. Ohio,* 367 U.S. 643 (1961), and United States v. Leon, 468 U.S. 897 (1984).

62. 384 U.S. 436 (1966). See also *Dickerson v. United States,* 530 U.S. 428 (2000).

63. *Berghuis v. Thompkins,* 560 U.S. 370 (2010).

64. *Powell v. Alabama,* 287 U.S. 45 (1932); *Gideon v. Wainwright,* 372 U.S. 335 (1963); *Scott v. Illinois,* 440 U.S. 367 (1979).

65. *Hamdi v. Rumsfeld,* 542 U.S. 507 (2004); *Rasul v. Bush,* 542 U.S. 466 (2004).

66. *Boumediene v. Bush,* 553 U.S. 723 (2008).

67. Ariane de Vogue, "Supreme Court rejects Guantanamo Bay detention challenge," CNN.com, June 10, 2019. https://www.cnn.com/2019/06/10/ politics/supreme-court-guantanamo-indefinite-detention/index.html.

68. *Robinson v. California,* 370 U.S. 660 (1962).

69. *Weems v. United States,* 217 U.S. 349 (1910); *Solem v. Helm,* 463 U.S. 277 (1983). *Harmelin v. Michigan,* 501 U.S. 957 (1991), which upheld a mandatory sentence of life imprisonment without the possibility of parole for possession of more than 650 grams of a substance containing cocaine; means that legislatures have almost complete discretion in setting punishments for noncapital offenses.

70. *Miller v. Alabama,* 567 U.S. 460 (2012).

71. *Lockyer v. Andrade* 538 U.S. 63 (2003).

72. Death Penalty Information Center, "Facts About the Death Penalty," June 11, 2020. https://files. deathpenaltyinfo.org/documents/pdf/FactSheet. f1591881221.pdf

73. *Roper v. Simmons,* 543 U.S. 551 (2005.)

74. David C. Baldus, George Woodworth, and Charles Pulanski, "Comparative Review of Death Sentences: An Empirical Study of the Georgia Experience," *Journal of Criminal Law and Criminology* 74 (1983): 661; see *McCleskey v. Kemp,* 481 U.S. 279 (1987).

75. *Foster v. Chatman* 578 U.S. ___ (2016).

76. Victor L. Streib, "Executions Under the Post-Furman Capital Punishment Statutes," *Rutgers Law Journal* 15 (1984): 443.

77. Glossip v. Gross 576 U.S. _____(2015).

78. *Baze v. Rees,* 553 U.S. 35 (2008); *Kennedy v. Louisiana,* 554 U.S. 407 (2008).

79. The Gallup Organization, "Death Penalty," https:// news.gallup.com/poll/1606/Death-Penalty.aspx, (June 11, 2020).

80. *Griswold v. Connecticut,* 381 U.S. 479 (1965).

81. *Roe v. Wade,* 410 U.S. 113 (1973).

82. *Webster v. Reproductive Health Services,* 492 U.S. 490 (1989).

83. *Planned Parenthood of Southeastern Pennsylvania v. Casey,* 505 U.S. 833 (1992).

84. *Stenberg v. Carhart,* 530 U.S. 914 (2000).

85. *Gonzales v. Carhart,* 550 U.S. 124 (2007).

86. CNN.com, "Obama Signs Executive Order on Abortion Funding Limits," March 24, 2010. http://www.cnn.com/2010/POLITICS/03/24 /obama.abortion/index.html

87. *June Medical Services v. Russo,* 591 U.S. ____ (2020).

88. Wayne van der Meide, *Legislating Equality: A Review of Laws Affecting Gay, Lesbian, Bisexual, and Transgendered People in the United States* (Washington, DC: Policy Institute of the National Gay and Lesbian Task Force, 2000); National Gay and Lesbian Task Force, "State Nondiscrimination Laws in the U.S.," May 21, 2014. http://www .thetaskforce.org/nondiscrimination-laws-map/; *USA Today,* "'Shocking' numbers: Half of LGBTQ adults live in states where no laws ban job discrimination," October 8, 2019, https://www.usatoday.com /story/news/nation/2019/10/08/lgbt-employment -discrimination-half-of-states-offer-no-protections /3837244002/.

89. 590 U.S. ___ (2020).

90. *Bowers v. Hardwick,* 478 U.S. 186 (1986), and *Romer v. Evans,* 517 U.S. 620 (1996).

91. *Lawrence v. Texas* 539 U.S. 558 (2003).

92. Schacter, James, "Courts and the Politics of Backlash: Marriage Equality Litigation, Then and Now," *Southern California Law Review* 82, no 1153 (February 2010): 1153–1223.

93. *Hollingsworth v. Perry,* 570 U.S. 693 (2013).

94. ibid.

95. *Obergefell v. Hodges,* 576 U.S. ___ (2015).

96. The Gallup Organization, "In U.S., 10.2% of LGBT Adults Now Married to Same-Sex Spouse," June 22, 2017. https://news.gallup.com/poll /212702/lgbt-adults-married-sex-spouse.aspx

97. The Gallup Organization, "Americans Still Unclear on Public Support for Gay Marriage," June 10, 2020, https://news.gallup.com/poll/312524/americans -unclear-public-support-gay-marriage.aspx.

98. *Plessy v. Ferguson,* 163 U.S. 537 (1896).

99. *Guinn v. United States,* 238 U.S. 347 (1915).

100. *Smith v. Allwright,* 321 U.S. 649 (1944).

101. *Brown v. Board of Education of Topeka,* 347 U.S. 483 (1954).

102. *Brown v. Board of Education of Topeka (II),* 349 U.S. 294 (1955).

103. *Columbus Board of Education v. Penick,* 443 U.S. 449 (1979); *Dayton Board of Education v. Brinkman,* 443 U.S. 526 (1979).

104. *Freeman v. Pitts,* 503 U.S. 467 (1992).

105. Henry Grabar, "If the Moral Imperative to End Segregation Wasn't Enough, Here's Some Economic Data," *Slate,* March 28, 2017, http://www.slate.com /blogs/moneybox/2017/03/28/new_report_details _costs_of_segregation_in_chicago.html.

106. The Gallup Organization, "The Harvard Affirmative Action Case and Public Opinion," October 22, 2018. https://news.gallup.com/opinion/polling-matters /243965/harvard-affirmative-action-case-public -opinion.aspx; "Americans' Support for Affirmative Action Programs Rises," February 27, 2019. https://news.gallup.com/poll/247046/americans -support-affirmative-action-programs-rises.aspx

107. *Regents of the University of California v. Bakke,* 438 U.S. 265 (1978).

108. *Gratz v. Bollinger* 539 U.S. 244 (2003).

109. *Grutter v. Bollinger* 539 U.S. 306 (2003).

110. *Fisher v. University of Texas at Austin,* 570 U.S. 297 (2013); *Schuette v. Coalition to Defend Affirmative Action,* 572 U.S. 291 (2014).

111. *Fisher v. University of Texas at Austin* 579 U.S. ___ (2016).

112. For example, see *United Steelworkers of America v. Weber,* 443 U.S. 193 (1979), and *Johnson v. Transportation Agency,* 480 U.S. 616 (1987).

113. *Richmond v. J.A. Croson Co.,* 488 U.S. 469 (1989).

114. *Shaw v. Reno,* 509 U.S. 630 (1993).

115. Associated Press, "House Delays Vote on Voting Rights Act Renewal", June 21, 2006, http://www.cnn.com/2006/POLITICS/06/21 /voting.rights.act.ap/index.html (June, 21 2006).

116. *Northwest Austin Municipal Utility District Number One v. Holder,* 557 U.S. 193 (2009).

117. *Shelby County v. Holder,* 570 U.S. 529 (2013).

118. *Reed v. Reed,* 404 U.S. 71 (1971).

119. *City of Los Angeles v. Manhart,* 435 U.S. 702 (1978); *Arizona Governing Committee v. Norris,* 463 U.S. 1073 (1983).

120. *Mississippi University for Women v. Hogan,* 458 U.S. 718 (1982).

121. *Mentor Savings Bank v. Vinson,* 477 U.S. 57 (1986).

122. U.S. Bureau of Labor Statistics, "Women in the labor force: a databook," December 2019, https://www.bls.gov/opub/reports/womens -databook/2019/home.htm.

123. *Historical Atlas of the United States* (Washington, DC: National Geographic Society, 1988), p. 34.

124. Mark Hugo Lopez, *The Latino Electorate in 2010: More Voters, More Non-Voters* (Washington, DC: Pew Hispanic Center, April 26, 2011).

125. NBC News, "Latinos on track to become largest share of nonwhite voters in 2020, Pew says," January 30, 2019, https://www.nbcnews.com/news/latino/first -time-latinos-be-largest-non-white-share-eligible -voters-n964571 (June 14, 2020).

126. Paul M. Barrett, "Immigration Law Found to Promote Bias by Employers," *Wall Street Journal,* March 30, 1990, p. A18.

127. CNN.com, "Thousands Descend on Phoenix to Protest Immigration Law," May 29, 2010, http://www.cnn.com/2010/US/05/29/arizona. immigration.march/ (June 8, 2010).

128. *Arizona v. United States,* 567 U.S. 387 (2012).

129. *United States v. Texas,* 579 U.S. ___ (2016).

130. *Trump v. Hawaii,* 585 U.S. ___ (2018).

131. Gallup Organization, "Immigration," June 16, 2019, https://news.gallup.com/poll/1660/Immigration. aspx (June 14, 2020).

132. *PGA TOUR, Inc. v. Martin,* 532 U.S. 355 (2001); *Board of Trustees of University of Alabama v. Garrett,* 531 U.S. 356 (2001).

POP QUIZ

1. The purpose of protecting _____ is to place certain practices beyond government's reach.

2. Of the possible restrictions on speech today, the Supreme Court is least likely to approve a _____ .

3. The _____ clause keeps government from becoming the tool of one religious group against others.

4. A deal with a prosecutor to obtain a lesser charge or lighter sentence in exchange for a guilty plea is called a _____ .

5. Affirmative action programs are often aimed at achieving equality of _____ .

6. For the most part, the Supreme Court considers obscenity as unprotected speech. T F

7. The establishment clause forbids the creation of an official state religion. T F

8. A police officer must always present a warrant before any search is made. T F

9. The Supreme Court has required the states to formulate uniform policies toward capital punishment. T F

10. Civil rights refers exclusively to one's specific constitutional rights. T F

11. Which of the following statements does not reflect an important objective of free expression?
    A) It is necessary to the political process set up by the Constitution.
    B) It contributes to social and political stability.
    C) It allows the dominant wisdom of the day to be challenged.
    D) It aids self-development.

12. An example of symbolic speech is _____ .
    A) a sit-in
    B) libel
    C) obscenity
    D) defamation of character

13. The Supreme Court has approved all except which of the following?
    A) paying a state legislature's chaplain out of public funds
    B) letting the Amish take their children out of school after the eighth grade
    C) the formation of a religious club at a public high school
    D) exempting from state law members of the American Indian Church who ingest peyote as part of a religious ritual

14. The exclusionary rule does which of the following?
    A) allows retroactive application of criminal laws in certain cases
    B) bypasses the procedural safeguards of the legal process when meting out punishment
    C) denies government the use of evidence gained as a result of the violation of the suspect's rights
    D) allows the police to search a suspect without a warrant

15. According to the Supreme Court, segregation between school districts is unconstitutional when which of the following occurs?
    A) Each district is composed of over 85 percent of one race.
    B) It is accompanied by large economic inequalities between the districts.
    C) There is evidence that school boards have caused the segregation between districts.
    D) Educational opportunities are substantially different between the districts.

Answers:
1. civil liberties   2. prior restraint
3. establishment   4. plea bargain   5. result
6. T   7. T   8. F   9. F   10. F   11. B
12. A   13. D   14. C   15. C

Chapter
04

I AM NOT AN ADVOCATE FOR FREQUENT
CHANGES IN LAWS AND CONSTITUTIONS.
BUT LAWS AND INSTITUTIONS MUST GO
HAND IN HAND WITH THE PROGRESS
OF THE HUMAN MIND. AS THAT BECOMES
MORE DEVELOPED, MORE ENLIGHTENED,
AS NEW DISCOVERIES ARE MADE, NEW
TRUTHS DISCOVERED AND MANNERS AND
OPINIONS CHANGE, WITH THE CHANGE
OF CIRCUMSTANCES, INSTITUTIONS
MUST ADVANCE ALSO TO KEEP PACE
WITH THE TIMES. WE MIGHT AS WELL
REQUIRE A MAN TO WEAR STILL THE
COAT WHICH FITTED HIM WHEN A BOY
AS CIVILIZED SOCIETY TO REMAIN
EVER UNDER THE REGIMEN OF THEIR
BARBAROUS ANCESTORS.

POLITICAL IDEOLOGIES

In This Chapter

4.1   American Political Ideologies
4.2   Liberalism
4.3   Conservatism
4.4   Ideological Challenges to the Status Quo

Chapter Objectives

Politics is about power and influence—who gets what, when, and how; but also, politics is about ideas. A political ideology is an integrated set of political ideas about what constitutes the most equitable and just political order. Political ideologies are concerned with the proper function of government, the issues of liberty and equality, and the distribution of goods and services.

All of the ideological perspectives discussed in this chapter, and given any serious attention by Americans, accept the basic ideas of democracy—representative government and individual liberty. They do not question the fundamental precepts of American political life, but they differ on matters of emphasis and degree. Although most Americans do not think in rigid ideological terms, ideology does influence how Americans think about political leaders. Politicians and policies tend to be labeled liberal, conservative, radical, or reactionary; and with some frequency we hear the terms *neoconservative* and *neoliberal* (neo being Greek for "new"). This chapter introduces the landscape of contemporary American political ideas and movements—liberal, conservative, neoliberal, neoconservative, socialist, and libertarian.

4.1 American Political Ideologies

Ideology "spells out what is valued and what is not, what must be maintained, and what must be changed."[1] Most political leaders and most Americans share elements of or identify with mainstream ideologies. Generally identified as *liberal* or *conservative,* these ideological positions do not challenge the existing political order. Neither liberals nor conservatives want to make major changes in our political and social order. They accept capitalism American-style as a successful economic system, and the economic marketplace

A political ideology is an integrated set of political ideas that influences how Americans think about political leaders.

("Living U.S. Presidents 2009" by Pete Souza, Obama-Biden Transition Project, available under a CC 2.0 license via Wikimedia)

as the chief instrument for the distribution of economic goods. At the same time, liberals and conservatives accept most of the economic reforms of the New Deal (explained later in this chapter)—Social Security, unemployment insurance, and agricultural subsidies—as a permanent part of our political system. Their differences are over matters of emphasis and degree.

By contrast, radical ideologies—such as *democratic socialism* and *libertarianism*—challenge much of the existing social and political order. Democratic socialists do not accept the capitalist system or what they consider to be the inordinate power of the big corporations. Socialists want to remove most of the major economic decisions on investments, wages, and prices from the private sector and place them in the hands of government. Libertarians seek to establish an economic system free of governmental interference and regulation and to dismantle most of the existing welfare state programs. These ideologies challenge many of the existing arrangements in our political system.

Exotic as socialism or libertarianism may seem to most Americans, these ideologies and movements operate within the framework of our democratic system. Democratic socialists and libertarians believe in peaceful change and accept the rules of the game. They frequently enter candidates in elections—although those candidates rarely win, and then typically just at the state and local levels. (An important exception to this general rule was the campaign of Senator Bernard Sanders (I-VT)* for the Democratic presidential nomination in the 2016 and 2020 presidential contests. The avowed socialist won many state primaries and finished a close second to eventual nominee Hillary Clinton in 2016 and a more distant second to Joe Biden in 2020.) Because their ideas challenge the dominant ideologies of our time, it is important to understand their criticisms and their prescriptions for the future, just as it is important to understand beliefs that are more widely held.

---

* "I" is a journalistic designation used for members of the U.S. Senate and House of Representatives: "D" or "R" or "I" indicates political party (Democratic, Republican, or Independent), followed by the member's home state.

4.2   Liberalism

One influential American ideology is **liberalism**. Liberalism begins with the assumption that individuals are, in the main, rational beings capable of overcoming obstacles to progress without resorting to violence. The roots of liberalism can be traced to the great English philosopher John Locke (1632–1704). Locke, who believed in the natural goodness of human beings, developed the **contract theory** of the state. According to Locke's theory, the state gains its legitimacy from the consent of the governed and is formed primarily to protect individuals' rights to life, liberty, and property. Locke's ideas of limited government, resting on the consent of the governed, became the textbook of the American Revolution. Locke was an inspiration to Thomas Jefferson, one of the most important early American liberal thinkers.

4.2a   Classical Liberalism: Thomas Jefferson and Andrew Jackson

Contemporary American liberalism is vastly different from what was known in the nineteenth century as **classical liberalism** (see Table 4.1). Liberals of that time, going back to Thomas Jefferson and Andrew Jackson, believed that a government that governed least governed best. Those nineteenth-century liberals felt that government should step out of the way so that the new entrepreneurs of the young Republic—the small business owners and farmers—could have an opportunity to compete in the economic system. Jefferson shared Locke's view that government must treat property rights with particular care. Jefferson had high praise for Adam Smith's *Wealth of Nations* (1776), the bible of capitalism. In his first inaugural address, Jefferson stated:

> A wise and frugal government, which shall restrain men from injuring one another, shall leave them otherwise free to regulate their own pursuits of industry and improvement and shall not take from the mouth of labor the bread it has earned. This is the sum of good government.[2]

President Andrew Jackson's (1829–1837) struggle against the wealth and power of a national bank was a classic example of the nineteenth-century liberal creed in action. Jackson also opposed extensive government expenditures on roads and canals. He believed that such expenditures "would make the federal government a partner with business in the financial prosperity of the upper class."[3] Speaking for the liberal reformers of his day, Jackson declared that a strong central government "is calculated to raise around the administration a moneyed aristocracy dangerous to the liberties of the country."[4] Like Jefferson, Jackson believed that liberty was the absence of government interference in the rights of all citizens to enjoy the fruits of their labor and prosperity.

4.2b   Populism and Progressivism: The Repudiation of Classical Liberalism

In the latter part of the nineteenth century, liberal attitudes toward government began to change. In the decades following the Civil War, American farmers—the backbone of support for Jeffersonian and Jacksonian liberalism—suffered through a perpetual economic crisis. Agricultural prices fell and interest rates rose. The target of liberal

liberalism

An ideology that regards the individual as a rational being capable of overcoming obstacles to a better world and supporting changes in the political and economic status quo

contract theory

Theory holding that the state gains its legitimacy from the consent of the governed and is formed primarily to protect the rights of individuals to life, liberty, and property

classical liberalism

A view, dating from the nineteenth century, that government should play a minimal role in society and should permit maximum economic freedom for the individual

Table 4.1 Key Ideas of American Ideologies

Different forms of liberalism and conservatism have defined much of the ideological debate in American politics; other ideologies challenged and influenced mainstream ideas.

Ideology	Key Ideas and Policies
Liberalism	
Classical Liberalism	Minimal government; protection of property rights
Populism	Democratization of government; economic reform
Progressivism	Social programs to cope with problems caused by industrialization; public limits on private corporate power
Contemporary Liberalism	The positive state; faith in solving problems collectively through government; programs to provide for the economic well-being of the nation, including the basic material needs of each individual; tolerance of various lifestyles
Neoliberalism	Creation, not redistribution, of wealth; free trade; reform of entitlement programs; a strong but economical defense
Conservatism	
Early American Conservatism	Sanctity of private property; distrust of unchecked popular rule; duty of government to promote a healthy economic environment and a virtuous citizenry
Industrial Age Conservatism	Laissez-faire economics; individualism; social Darwinism
Contemporary Conservatism	Reduced spending on social programs; revamping tax policies to encourage economic growth; strong military defense; little positive action to redress racial and gender discrimination; duty of government to promote a virtuous citizenry
Neoconservatism	Skepticism of government's ability to solve social and economic problems; acceptance of a modest welfare state; opposition to racial and gender quotas to redress discrimination; creation, not redistribution, of wealth; assertive foreign policy
Challenges to the Status Quo	
Democratic Socialism	Public ownership of basic industries, banks, agricultural enterprises, and communications systems; wage and price controls; redistribution of wealth to achieve true economic equality; expanded welfare programs
Libertarianism	Minimal government; protection of property rights and freedom of individuals; no governmental regulation of the economy; noninterventionist foreign policy; drastic reduction in defense spending

reform became the railroads and the banks, not the government. Out of this turmoil evolved a new liberal movement, known as **populism**. The populists, who formed their own political party in the 1880s, called for further democratization of government through the secret ballot, direct election of senators, and voter initiatives and referenda.

They also advocated fundamental economic reforms that would strengthen government's role, including nationalization of the railroads and the telegraph, a graduated income tax, free coinage of silver, and a vastly expanded supply of paper money. The Populist Party did not supplant either of the two major parties; however, its ideas—particularly with the nomination of William Jennings Bryan as the Democratic presidential candidate in 1896—profoundly affected the Democratic Party in the twentieth century.

In urban America, among the middle classes, there was also a growing movement for social and economic reform known as **progressivism**. Progressives supported government programs to ease the problems of industrialization, including worker's compensation, a ban on child labor, regulation of corporations, and a minimum wage. Progressives achieved their major successes during the presidential administrations of Theodore Roosevelt (1901–1909) and Woodrow Wilson (1913–1921). During Roosevelt's years in office, Congress passed the Hepburn Act, which regulated the railroads, and the Pure Food and Drug Act and the Meat Inspection Act, which eliminated many of the unhealthy practices of food and drug industries.

("Fast food workers on strike for higher minimum wage and better benefits" by Fibonacci Blue, available under a CC 2.0 license via Wikimedia)

Progressives support government programs, including worker's compensation, to ease the problems of industrialization. Fast food workers are shown striking for a higher minimum wage and better benefits.

Woodrow Wilson proposed a program called New Freedom and signed into law bills regulating the banking industry, restricting unfair business competition, and establishing an eight-hour day for railroad workers. The populist and progressive belief that government could remedy the economic ills of the nation by limiting the power and wealth of private corporations and banks had a profound effect on American liberalism. The rise of populism and progressivism signaled a decline in the faith of liberalism in laissez-faire (minimal government regulation of economic affairs) and began a new era of belief in the power and virtues of a strong central government.

Wilson felt that Jefferson would have understood the need for a more activist government. He said,

> If Jefferson were living in our day, he would see what we see: that the individual is caught in a great confused nexus of all sorts of complicated circumstances, and that to let him alone is to leave him helpless.[5]

4.2c Contemporary Liberalism: The Welfare State and Beyond

The administration of President Franklin D. Roosevelt (1933–1945) took the concerns of the populists and progressives a step further. Roosevelt's New Deal program reflected the change in the constituency of liberalism. In contrast to the nineteenth-century liberal, who

populism

A political movement that sets the interests of the masses or common people against those of the political elite or the wealthy

progressivism

An urban reform movement of the late nineteenth and early twentieth centuries that called for direct primaries, restrictions on corporations, and improved public services and that was influential in the administrations of Theodore Roosevelt and Woodrow Wilson

addressed the needs of the entrepreneurial class, New Deal liberals were concerned about the farmers, the unemployed, and the labor union movement. Carrying on the populist and progressive tradition, liberals no longer saw government as a threat to liberty or as the inevitable partner of the rich and powerful. In a complex industrial age—particularly one racked by the Great Depression of the 1930s—liberals believed that government action should ensure the economic well-being of the nation and should provide basic material guarantees (food, shelter, health care, and education) for every individual. The New Deal included programs to ensure protection for the unemployed, pensions for the elderly, and guaranteed prices for the farmers. It symbolized the idea of the positive or interventionist state, which became the hallmark of contemporary liberalism.

In the 1960s, President Lyndon Johnson's Great Society moved beyond the New Deal. Civil rights laws protected the rights of minorities; Medicare and Medicaid laws provided health insurance for the elderly and the poor; and funds aided impoverished elementary and secondary school districts. In the 1970s, liberals proposed a broad range of programs to protect the environment, to assist consumers, and to expand welfare benefits through the food stamp program.

Liberals today believe that a strong central government is necessary to protect individuals from the inequities of a modern industrial and technological society, and that the growth of government has enhanced—not diminished—individual freedom. Although the positive state is central to the contemporary liberal creed, liberals do not believe that government should displace private enterprise. Most liberals are capitalists, if not forthrightly so. In fact, many argue that American capitalism has survived because government has humanized the industrial order, and that Franklin Roosevelt's New Deal saved capitalism from repudiation during the 1930s. Liberals argue that the positive state cushions the inequalities of power and wealth that arise in any capitalist system. They see government as correcting the injustices of the marketplace, not supplanting it. Liberals recognize that in any society there will be some inequalities of wealth and income, but they feel that government must intervene to redress the most excessive inequalities. Thus, in debates over tax laws, liberals frequently support shifting more of the burden to people in the upper income brackets.

The idea of a benevolent government that offers services to the disadvantaged (unemployment insurance) as well as to the

The World's Smallest Political Quiz is a tool designed to assess one's political ideology. The quiz was created by a Libertarian organization. Does that make it too biased, or is it useful?

Visit this site and decide for yourself.

http://www.bvtlab.com/8GAMr

middle class (Social Security) has been for generations the centerpiece of American liberalism. Liberal ideas fueled the administrations of Presidents Franklin Roosevelt, Harry Truman, John Kennedy, and Lyndon Johnson. Johnson, for one, saw the United States as "an endless cornucopia." His Great Society began a virtual torrent of new government programs: rent supplements for the poor, scholarships for college students, aid to the arts and humanities, higher pensions for government workers and veterans, aid to children with disabilities, and a massive food stamp program. These programs assisted the poor and the disadvantaged as well as many in the middle and upper income brackets.

In the 1970s and early 1980s, the growth rate of the economy declined while the demand for government services continued. Unlike his predecessors, President Jimmy Carter (1977–1981) did not offer a new set of governmental programs and benefits. Hampered by the problems of inflation and an energy shortage, Carter could offer few initiatives. His administration stirred little enthusiasm among liberals.

Liberals remain wedded to the idea of affirmative government. In the early 1980s, some began to discuss the idea of an industrial policy. Championed by liberal economic thinkers such as Robert Reich and Felix Rohatyn, an **industrial policy** involves a partnership in economic decision-making among government officials, labor unions, and public interest groups. President Bill Clinton (1993–2001) endorsed this approach in a slightly modified form in his 1992 election campaign and later named Reich secretary of labor.

In matters involving national security and personal morality, however, liberals seek to restrict the role of government. Liberals extend broad tolerance to different lifestyles and dispute government efforts to impose a single standard of religious practice or sexual morality. Consequently, liberals are at the forefront of opposition to constitutional amendments that might sanction prayer in schools or limit the rights of women to obtain an abortion.

Since the Vietnam War, liberals have backed away from an interventionist, military-oriented foreign policy. In January 1991, most congressional liberals voted against authorizing President George H. W. Bush to use military force in the Persian Gulf and preferred the continuation of economic sanctions against Iraq. Liberals are also critical of large defense budgets and became, in recent years, the most vocal critics of the Iraq and Afghanistan Wars.

In general, liberals favor government programs and budgeting priorities that put domestic social programs before those of the Pentagon. Their belief in a strong activist government concentrates primarily on domestic issues (see Table 4.2). Recently, liberals have been outspoken on the issue of universal health care—health insurance coverage as a right for all Americans—and achieved at least a partial victory in 2010 with the passage of the Patient Protection and Affordable Care Act and the Health Care and Education Reconciliation Act.

industrial policy
Proposals for partnership in economic decision-making among government officials, corporate leaders, union officials, and public interest groups

Table 4.2   Milestones in American Liberalism

1690	John Locke's *Second Treatise on Government* published
1776	Adam Smith's *Wealth of Nations,* Thomas Paine's *Common Sense,* and the Declaration of Independence published
1832	President Andrew Jackson vetoes a bill to recharter the Bank of the United States
1892	First Populist Party convention held
1896	William Jennings Bryan wins Democratic presidential nomination; the Democratic Party adopts much of the Populist program.
1909	Herbert Croly's *Promise of American Life* published; a group of African American leaders, including W. E. B. DuBois, meets at Niagara Falls, Canada, and inaugurates the modern civil rights movement
1913–1916	President Woodrow Wilson proposes his New Freedom program and steers it through Congress
1933–1936	President Franklin Roosevelt's New Deal reforms inaugurate the modern welfare state
1954	The Supreme Court declares racial segregation unconstitutional in *Brown v. Board of Education of Topeka*

1964	Congress passes the landmark Civil Rights Act of 1964
1965	President Lyndon Johnson successfully pushes his Great Society programs through Congress
1972	Liberal Democratic candidate George McGovern loses presidential election to conservative Republican incumbent Richard Nixon in a landslide
1992	Bill Clinton wins the presidency while making universal health care a cornerstone of his campaign
2010	President Barack Obama and a Democratic majority in Congress pass the Affordable Care Act, providing all Americans the opportunity to purchase health insurance
2010	President Barack Obama announces plans to end the Iraq War; US troops leave by end of 2011
2012	President Barack Obama announces his support for same-sex marriage rights

Who are the liberals? They are usually found in the Democratic Party, although historically the Democrats have harbored some conservatives and the Republicans a handful of liberals. Some liberals also support third parties, such as the Green Party. The association of liberals with Democrats is in part due to the fact that the constituency of the Democratic Party—minorities, the labor movement, feminists, and the poor— supports a wide range of liberal welfare programs. **Americans for Democratic Action** (ADA) has historically been the best-known pressure group for contemporary liberalism. Founded in 1947, ADA presidents have included Senators Hubert Humphrey (D-MN) and George McGovern (D-SD), both one-time nominees of the Democratic Party for president. Headquartered in Washington, DC, the ADA is an advocate of legislation designed to reduce economic inequality and defense spending and to protect consumers. It opposes laws that encroach on civil rights and civil liberties. Each year it rates members of Congress on a broad spectrum of liberal issues. In recent years, the popularity of the ADA among liberals has been surpassed by the upstart progressive organization MoveOn. Founded in 1998, MoveOn now boasts a membership of over seven million.

4.2d Neoliberalism: Adjusting Liberalism to the Twenty-First Century

During the administrations of Franklin Roosevelt, Harry Truman, and John Kennedy, liberalism focused on economic issues and emphasized government's obligation to assist those on the lower end of the income scale. In recent decades, liberalism has shifted its focus somewhat and reached into social and foreign policy issues. However, it did so at a political cost. The strong association of liberalism with the civil rights movement hurt the liberal image among Southerners who identified with the old, white-dominated political order and among Northern whites living in urban enclaves who also felt threatened by African American advancement. Many voters also associated liberalism with controversial Supreme Court decisions legalizing abortion and banning school prayer. After the Vietnam War, liberals were highly critical of American military intervention and the level of defense spending, alienating some voters who considered them "soft" on defense.

Americans for Democratic Action

The best-known pressure group for contemporary liberalism

Although liberal candidates were quite successful in congressional and state elections, such negative associations dogged them at the presidential level.

Stunned by these successive presidential defeats, a group of young journalists and elected officials attempted to sharpen and modernize the focus of contemporary liberalism. The leader of the movement was Charles Peters, the editor of the *Washington Monthly* (see Table 4.3), who adopted the label "neoliberal." **Neoliberalism** calls for a shift in the emphasis of liberalism from the redistribution of wealth to the promotion of wealth, for a far less critical attitude toward American capitalism, and for policies that promote greater government and business cooperation.

Table 4.3   A Guide to Contemporary Political Ideas and Leaders

American ideologies are expressed through a variety of journals, writers, and political leaders.

Ideology	Media	Leading Spokesperson	Political Leader
Liberalism	*The American Prospect; HuffPost*	Rachel Maddow	Joe Biden
Neoliberalism	*Washington Monthly; Exponents*	Charles Peters	Pete Buttigieg
Conservatism	*National Review; Fox News*	Rush Limbaugh	Ted Cruz
Neoconservatism	*Commentary; Weekly Standard*	William Kristol	Lindsey Graham
Democratic Socialism	*Dissent; Jacobin*	Cornel West	Bernard Sanders
Libertarianism	*Reason; The Independent Review*	Ron Paul	Justin Amash

---

Neoliberals do not repudiate the New Deal and Great Society legacies; they simply feel that the emphasis of liberal reform should be different. They argue that liberals must confront public distrust of government. As a writer for the *Washington Monthly* put it, "Any time a liberal politician says the word 'program,' most voters hear 'bureaucracy' and right away get turned off."[6]

Neoliberals direct their attention not to the expansion of government services, but to their effective delivery. Neoliberals criticize government unions and the size and costs of government bureaucracy. Neoliberals also call for the reform of entitlement spending programs such as Social Security that go to people who are already well protected by private pensions and their own investments. The neoliberals criticize civil service and military retirement benefits for being far more generous than those in the private sector. They believe that increases in spending for these programs should be based not on the cost of living but on the rate of real growth in the economy.

Traditional liberals take issue with the neoliberal emphasis on government efficiency. They emphasize older liberal issues such as the problem of personal income inequality,

neoliberalism

A pragmatic form of liberalism that emphasizes such beliefs as the promotion of wealth rather than its redistribution and the reform of military practices rather than the simple reduction of military spending

which has become more pronounced in recent decades. Traditional liberals would like to increase the top income tax rate, which is currently 37 percent. They unapologetically champion the cause of affirmative government and the positive state. Arthur Schlesinger Jr., a prominent liberal spokesperson for over a generation, argued for greater government investment in research and development and in education; in the rehabilitation of our bridges, dams, and highways; and in the protection against toxic waste, acid rain, and global warming. "The markets," wrote Schlesinger, "will solve none of these problems."[7]

Some traditional liberals feel that Michael Dukakis's emphasis on competency rather than ideology during the 1988 presidential campaign was, in fact, a neoliberal theme that failed to ignite the electorate. By contrast Bill Clinton, in 1992 and 1996, and Al Gore, in 2000, were able to blend older, more populist ideas—such as raising taxes for the rich—with neoliberal themes such as a partnership between government and business. John Kerry's presidential campaign spotlighted both traditional liberal values, like affordable health care, and neoliberal ideas about fiscal responsibility; but these issues took a backseat to foreign policy in 2004. The year 2008 saw a return to more traditional liberal positions when the Democratic Party nominated Barack Obama (D-IL) as its presidential candidate. An analysis of Senate roll call votes from 2007 led the *National Journal* to identify Obama as the nation's most liberal senator.[8] In contrast, 2016 Democratic nominee Hillary Clinton ran a more centrist campaign and was identified as both a liberal and a neoliberal at various points in her political career. In 2020, Joe Biden was able to draw on both his liberal credentials as Obama's vice president and the more centrist politics of his long Senate career, though his main draw was simply as a more reasonable alternative to the bombastic incumbent Donald Trump.

(Getty Images)

Edmund Burke (1729-1797). Engraved by H. Robinson and published in The National Portrait Gallery Of Illustrious And Eminent Personages encyclopedia, United Kingdom, 1847.

4.3 Conservatism

In contrast to liberalism's confidence in the capacity of individuals to overcome obstacles collectively, political conservatism reflects doubt and distrust. **Conservatism** emphasizes the value of tradition and established practices as guides for the future. It finds its origins in the writings of Edmund Burke (1729–1797), whose most famous work, *Reflections on the Revolution in France* (1790), is considered the first major statement of conservative principles. A leading figure in the British Parliament, Burke was appalled by the excesses of the French Revolution and by its rejection of tradition. Burke was suspicious of any generation's claim that it could remake society, believing that the experience of past generations was the most reliable guide to good government. Customs, traditions, and laws embodied the wisdom of the past and should not be carelessly discarded. Thus, argued Burke, people should act with deliberation, seeking change only when necessary. Burke believed that society grew slowly and with purpose; therefore, the past gave continuity to present and

conservatism

A defense of the political and economic status quo against forces of change, holding that established customs, laws, and traditions should guide society

future generations. Burke was suspicious of the general public and its capacity to appreciate tradition and custom. He believed in government by the propertied class. People were not equal in ability or talent, according to Burke, and should not be so considered when it came to the governing of society. In Burke's view, a natural inequality among people meant that a ruling class of ability and property ought to control government.

4.3a   Early American Conservatism: John Adams

It was difficult to make Burkean conservatism relevant to the American experience, which had no landed aristocracy, no established church, and no royal tradition. American conservatism—although influenced by Burke—found its own voice in John Adams, the second president of the United States, who lived from 1735 to 1826. The excesses of the French Revolution, particularly its executions and confiscation of property, repelled Adams as they did Burke. Adams agreed with Burke unreservedly about the sanctity of private property (see Table 4.1); but unlike Burke, Adams did not associate property rights with a landed aristocracy. Adams believed that property should be widely held and that a propertied class would produce a natural aristocracy of talent.

Although Adams was one of the architects of the American Revolution and a passionate defender of the right of every individual to life, liberty, and property, he distrusted unchecked democratic rule as much as he did excessive power in the hands of the aristocracy. Unlimited rule of the people led to clamor for dictatorship. Adams rejected the Jeffersonian notion of the natural goodness of humankind; he felt that people were neither totally innocent nor totally depraved. Laws and government, in Adams's view, were needed to promote public virtue and to curb private greed. By public virtue Adams meant "a positive passion for the public good, the public interest, honor, power, and glory established in the minds of the people."[9] A properly balanced government could serve to suppress the evils of ambition, selfishness, self-indulgence, and corruption.

John Adams found this balance in the American Constitution. A popularly elected House would represent the people, an indirectly elected Senate would protect the rights of property, and the president would represent the whole. Thus the poor could not confiscate the property of the rich, and the rich would not be able to exploit the poor. Society would retain its balance, and liberty would be safeguarded from both the excesses of democracy and the abuses of an aristocracy. After he had appointed John Marshall, a conservative Federalist, to the Supreme Court in 1801, Adams looked to the judicial branch as the ultimate guarantor of property rights against any attempts by legislatures to compromise them.

In the 1820s, long after he had left the presidency, Adams joined with other American conservatives—including Chief Justice Marshall and Senator Daniel Webster—in opposing the elimination of property qualifications for voting. These conservatives considered *universal suffrage* (and in that era, they debated only universal *white male suffrage*) to be a threat to the Republic. In their opinion, men without property lacked the independence, judgment, and virtue to be voting members of a free republic.[10]

Chancellor James Kent of New York, one of the most famous legal scholars and jurists of the early nineteenth century, argued that "there is a tendency in the majority to tyrannize over the minority and trample down their rights; and in the indolent and profligate to cast the whole burden of society upon the industrious and virtuous."[11] The victory of Jacksonian democracy in the states during the 1820s brought an end to antidemocratic conservatism. Conservatives seemed to realize the finality of their defeat on that issue and concentrated, in the latter part of the nineteenth century, on the defense of property rights and the system of laissez-faire economics.

4.3b   Conservatism and the Industrial Age: Herbert Spencer and William Graham Sumner

Industrialization following the Civil War brought a major change in American conservatism. Although conservatives of the early Republic fervently believed in property rights, the belief that government should play a limited role in the economy did not necessarily follow. Conservatives such as John Adams, John Marshall, and Alexander Hamilton supported a strong central government to defend the propertied classes from the encroachments of the more radical state governments. They defended the Bank of the United States against the attacks of the Jefferson-Jackson liberals.

As America industrialized, conservatives embraced **laissez-faire economics**—an economic system that operated free of government control. Burke and Adams regarded the state as essential to the promotion of public virtue and the protection of property; in the Industrial Age, however, the state became the object of conservative scorn. In stressing individualism, economic growth, and the limited role of government, conservatives seemed closer to Jefferson and Jackson in this regard than to Burke and Adams.

Herbert Spencer (1820–1903), an English social scientist, and William Graham Sumner (1840–1910), an American sociologist, developed the theory of economic individualism that became the keystone of late-nineteenth-century and early-twentieth-century conservatism. The theory was popularly known as **social Darwinism**. Sumner stated the case in a somewhat extreme form: People, Sumner argued, should be free to compete with each other for survival. From this economic competition, the fit will survive and the weak will perish. The result will be the betterment of humankind through the survival of superior individuals. Sumner opposed governmental aid to the needy as inconsistent with his views on social and economic evolution. Government was inefficient by nature, Sumner argued, and should be limited to fundamental concerns. Sumner wrote, "At bottom there are two chief things with which government has to deal. They are, the property of men and the honor of women. These it has to defend against crime."[12]

Although these views were far too extreme—even for the nineteenth century—Spencer and Sumner made a great impact on conservative thinking. Conservatives of the Industrial Age did not emphasize the individual's obligation to the state or the state's obligation to promote public virtue; instead, the emphasis was almost entirely on the individual. If people worked hard, they argued, people could become successful; and economic growth would ensue. The government need only stand out of the way. Many business leaders were attracted to this philosophy, although it did not prevent them from helping themselves to governmental favors (tariff protection or direct subsidies) when the occasion arose. These business leaders invoked conservatism to justify opposition to antitrust laws, bills regulating hours and wages, and a progressive income tax.

In short, conservatism became the ideology of America's business class. As long as most Americans shared somewhat in the growth of the American economy, they were willing to accept most of the tenets of conservatism. From the end of Reconstruction to the New Deal, Americans elected presidents (with the exceptions of Theodore Roosevelt and Woodrow Wilson) who reflected those values.

4.3c   Contemporary Conservatism: A Response to the Welfare State

Conservatism since the 1980s has taken on a more positive cast with an agenda of its own—reducing social spending, reshaping the tax code, and rebuilding national defense.

laissez-faire economics

French for "leave things alone"; the view in economics that government should not interfere in the workings of the economy

social Darwinism

A set of ideas applying Charles Darwin's theory of biological evolution to society and holding that social relationships occur within a struggle for survival in which only the fittest survive

In economic matters, conservatives draw on many of the ideas of nineteenth-century individualism. Conservatism still remains at its core a defense of economic individualism against the growth of the welfare state. Conservatives oppose any increase in the role of the federal government over the general direction of the economy and contend that a vibrant private-sector economy can best create jobs for the poor, immigrants, and minorities. Welfare state programs, conservatives argue, only create a permanent class of the poor who are dependent on the state and have no genuine incentives to enter the working world.

Although many conservatives opposed the major civil rights laws of the 1960s on the grounds that they represented a serious encroachment on states' rights, most now accept these laws as a permanent part of our political landscape. They do, however, challenge the idea of quotas and other affirmative-action policies as a means of enforcing civil rights laws in the areas of jobs, educational opportunities, and access to federal contracts. They argue that civil rights should mean equality of treatment and not equality of results.

On social and cultural issues, conservatives remain close to Burkean ideals. Contemporary conservatives believe that the state must promote virtue and social responsibility and take appropriate measures to improve the moral climate of society. They support constitutional amendments restricting abortion and permitting prayers in public schools. They oppose the concept of civil rights for LGBT individuals in jobs, the military, housing, and marriage. Speaking as a modern-day Burkean, conservative philosopher and syndicated columnist George Will wrote, "Traditional conservatism has not been, and proper conservatism cannot be, merely a defense of industrialism and individualist 'free market' economics. Conservatism is about the cultivation and conservation of certain values or it is nothing."[13]

As conservative causes have gained broader public support, conservatives no longer invoke the suspicion of the masses as they did in John Adams's day (see Table 4.4). Nor do they talk very much about the independence of the judicial branch as a check on the excesses of legislative power. In fact, conservatives have been particularly critical of Supreme Court decisions outlawing prayers in school and legalizing abortion.[14]

Conservatives believe that the state should take part in improving the moral climate of society, such as by promoting prayer in schools.

(Shutterstock)

Conservatives support efforts to have such decisions overturned by constitutional amendment or weakened by legislative action. Direct democracy, so feared by the conservatives of the eighteenth and nineteenth centuries, has become an important tool of contemporary conservatives. Conservatives have successfully employed the popular initiative or referendum process (a device that permits people to vote on policy questions as well as for candidates) in California and Massachusetts as a check on the power of state legislatures to tax their own citizens.

Some conservative causes have generated intense (although not broad) rank-and-file support. In part because of conservative support for reduced taxes, restrictions on abortion, and opposition to LGBT rights and immigration, conservatism has been transformed from an elitist philosophy of the propertied class to a more populist cause of the working and middle classes.

Table 4.4 Milestones in American Conservatism

1790	Edmund Burke's *Reflections on the Revolution in France* published; Alexander Hamilton, first U.S. Treasury secretary, introduces a report recommending a national bank
1851	Herbert Spencer's *Social Statics* published
1883	William Graham Sumner's *What Social Classes Owe to Each Other* published
1905	Supreme Court in *Lochner v. New York* strikes down New York law limiting working hours of bakers as a violation of freedom of contract under the Fourteenth Amendment
1920	Warren Harding elected president, marking the beginning of a new era of conservative dominance lasting until 1932
1955	*National Review* founded, marking the beginning of the intellectual revitalization of post–World War II conservatism
1964	Barry Goldwater receives the Republican presidential nomination, beginning the conservative ascendancy in the party
1981	President Ronald Reagan begins his program of tax reductions, domestic spending cuts, and defense buildup
1994	Newt Gingrich and his "Contract with America" sweep the Republican Party into the majority in both chambers of Congress for the first time in forty years
2000	George W. Bush and Dick Cheney win the electoral vote and embark on an agenda of tax cuts, defense spending, and environmental deregulation
2002	The Bush doctrine of preventive war is announced in National Security Strategy of the United States, with the country embarking on the Iraq War the following year
2010	Bolstered in part by the Tea Party movement, voters return a Republican majority to both chambers of Congress in the midterm elections
2017–8	Aided by a slim Republican majority in the Senate, Donald Trump nominates Neil Gorsuch, Brett Kavanaugh, and Amy Coney Barrett to the Supreme Court, ensuring a solid conservative majority

Who are the conservatives? In most cases their political home is in the Republican Party. Ronald Reagan was the first president since the Great Depression to identify himself openly with conservatism and conservative causes. Previous Republican presidents—Eisenhower, Nixon, and Ford—were men of the center who shunned ideology and ideological labels. Perhaps the best-known conservative journal is *National Review*, founded by William Buckley, who was one of the most prominent conservative spokespersons for over half a century.

Millennials, Gen Z, and Political Ideology

Would you describe yourself as a conservative or a liberal? How do you feel about the economy, climate change, and health-care coverage? How do your views compare to those of your fellow college students? Since 2000, a Harvard University Institute of Politics survey has been asking young people across the country about their political views.[1] Regarding specific issues, the Spring 2020 nationwide survey of eighteen-to twenty-nine-year-olds (the older of whom are often identified as millennials, while those born after 1996 are increasingly labeled Generation Z) found that only 21 percent of respondents believed that the country is headed in the right direction, while 45 percent thought the country was off on the wrong track. Regarding specific issues, 19 percent of respondents listed COVID-19 as their number one political concern, followed by health care (17 percent); the economy and the environment came in third and fourth (14 percent and 9 percent, respectively). When asked whether they agreed or disagreed with the statement "Basic health insurance is a right for all people, and if someone has no means of paying for it, the government should provide it," 63 percent

agreed, and 16 percent disagreed, with the remaining 19 percent undecided.[2]

Regarding political parties, the 2020 survey found that 22 percent of young adults identified themselves as Republicans, 42 percent as Democrats, and 35 percent as Independents. This finding represents an increase in the number of Independents and suggests that it may be important to move beyond partisan labels and take a deeper look at ideology in order to best understand the political beliefs of millennials and Generation Z.

In taking this deeper look, recent Harvard studies discovered that, in addition to the traditional progressive–conservative ideological spectrum, millennial and Gen Z ideologies could also be divided into more specific categories. Based on respondents' answers to fifteen different typology questions, the researchers developed five labels for identifying young adult ideology.

Engaged Progressives is the term given to 18 percent of the respondents. These young people were the most likely to say they would vote in the next election and to support Joe Biden as a presidential candidate. This group was the most likely to have graduated from college and follow politics closely and was the least religious. They see a strong role for government in health care, climate change, and poverty reduction.

Center-Left is the term used to describe 28 percent of the sample. These individuals were the most likely to be female and nearly all consider themselves either moderate or liberal. They are less likely than Engaged Progressives to vote, but also favored Biden and want

more government involvement in health care and climate issues.

Multicultural Moderates are 15 percent of the group, are more likely to be male, and are the most racially and ethnically diverse group. They are likely to be religious, not likely to attend college, and, while they believe in a right to health care and approve of affirmative action, they are also in favor of free trade and reducing taxes.

The MAGA Gen is the term the researchers gave to 11 percent of the respondents. This group was the most likely to approve of President Trump, identify as religious, and to self-identify as patriots and capitalists. They oppose government efforts to provide health care, reduce climate change, and decrease poverty.

The Disengaged are the final group. Comprising 31 percent of the sample population, these individuals are just as likely to identify as Democratic as Republican, though much more likely to identify as moderate or conservative than liberal. Most are not college graduates and they were the least likely group to say they planned on voting in the next election.

What role did the millennial and Gen Z vote play during the 2020 presidential election? How will young adults affect the next election? Do you think these survey findings accurately describe your college campus? Why or why not? Which of the five categories most closely describes your political thinking?

1. Harvard University Institute of Politics, *Survey of Young Americans' Attitudes toward Politics and Public Service 39th Edition: March 11 – March 23, 2020.*

2. Ibid., p. 2.

4.3d Neoconservatism in the Twenty-First Century

In the 1970s, a number of leading American intellectuals, many of them longtime liberals, became openly critical of the drift of contemporary liberalism; thus began the ideology labeled **neoconservatism** in the popular press. Neoconservatives feel that liberals have overestimated the ability of government to solve social problems such as industrial pollution, economic inequality, and racial discrimination. They argue that liberals have gone beyond the initial New Deal concept that government need only provide a "safety net" for the subsistence needs of society's victims—the unemployed, disabled Americans, and the elderly. Contemporary liberalism, the neoconservatives claim, transformed the New Deal's modest welfare state into a more intrusive, paternalistic state. Neoconservatives disagree with such liberal ideas as the use of racial or gender preferences as a means of assuring fairness in hiring, promotion, or acceptance to professional schools. They also reject the idea of forced school busing as a means of achieving racial balance in enrollment. They consider these ideas elitist liberal schemes not supported by the majority of Americans.

Neoconservatives feel that liberals no longer speak for the "average person" but rather for a "new class" of relatively affluent reformers—lawyers, social workers, educators, and city planners—with careers in the expanding public sector. This new liberal class intends "to propel the nation from that modified version of capitalism we call 'the welfare state' toward an economic system so regulated in detail as to fulfill many of the traditional anticapitalist aspirations of the left."[15]

Neoconservatives also argue that liberals emphasize policies (such as higher taxes on the upper class) that are aimed not at creating wealth but only at redistributing it. Skeptical about government's ability to erase economic inequalities, neoconservatives stress policies such as lower taxes on large incomes and less regulation of business to promote economic growth. Such growth, they feel, would more likely broaden economic opportunity and create greater social stability. Likewise, they are suspicious of policies that polarize one class or group against another—such as racial busing that pits the white working-class communities in the large cities against the poor African American community—and gender and racial quotas that place the interests of women and minorities above those of white males.

In short, neoconservatives feel that modern liberals have promised too much to too many groups and that a government that promises too much cannot deliver, becoming "overloaded." As a result, they argue, government loses its authority and cannot govern effectively. Neoconservatives differ from traditional conservatives in that neoconservatives support, in principle and practice, a modest welfare state (Social Security, unemployment insurance, and Medicare). In fact, neoconservatives argue that a properly constructed welfare state strengthens citizens' loyalty to the existing capitalist system and is thus a stabilizing force.

Neoconservatives have engendered some resentment among many members of the Old Right, sometimes dubbed paleoconservatives (*paleo* from the Greek meaning "ancient"), who decry the neoconservative accommodation to the welfare state and remain hostile to government efforts to establish social and economic equality. The paleoconservatives believe that religious traditions embodied in the church and family should be the basis of a stable and ordered society. The welfare state philosophy of the New Deal and Great Society is, according to them, an effort to create a secular moral order. By defending the New Deal legacy, the paleoconservatives charge the neoconservatives with defending not only a misguided political idea but also a religious heresy.

neoconservatism

A belief associated with many former liberal intellectuals that contemporary liberalism has transformed the modest New Deal welfare state into an intrusive, paternalistic state

The sudden collapse of communism in 1989 opened up new fissures in contemporary conservatism. With the unraveling of the Soviet Union, some paleoconservative leaders—such as journalist Patrick Buchanan, who challenged President George H. W. Bush in the 1992 primaries—sounded older conservative themes of isolationism and America first. Neoconservatives, in turn, strongly supported continued American leadership in world affairs. George W. Bush (2001–2009) surrounded himself with a number of neoconservative advisers, such as Paul Wolfowitz, and embarked on his presidency with a promise of "compassionate conservatism." Neoconservatives were among the most vocal critics of the Trump administration, as their support for strong US leadership in the world clashed with President Trump's nationalistic isolationism.[16]

Neoconservatism has emerged as an influential intellectual and political force. Its ideas influenced the Reagan administration and both Bush administrations and have brought about a more respectful hearing for conservatism in general among academics and intellectuals.

4.4   Ideological Challenges to the Status Quo

Not all American ideologies fit comfortably under the rubrics *liberal* and *conservative*. Some challenge dominant opinion and propose policies that are outside today's mainstream. Yet the fact that they represent a minority point of view does not make them unimportant. The history of American political thought is full of examples of "extreme" ideas that gained acceptability and entered the mainstream.

4.4a   Democratic Socialism: A Radical Challenge to American Capitalism

Democratic socialism is an economic system in which the basic industries, banks, agricultural systems, and communication networks are owned and controlled by the government at either the local or national level. While a private sector of the economy may continue to exist under socialism, major industries and corporations would be owned by the state; thus, the government would be responsible for planning and directing the economy. Key decisions concerning investments, prices, and wages would be placed in the hands of public institutions. What separates democratic socialists from communists, who also believe in the principle of public ownership, is that democratic socialists reject the idea of violent revolution. Instead, democratic socialists advocate the adoption of socialism through peaceful and constitutional means; they support the basic democratic rights embodied in our Constitution.

Economic equality is an essential idea in socialism. Socialists argue that capitalism in America—despite its success in creating wealth—has failed to solve the fundamental problem of poverty. Equality of opportunity is not enough, socialists argue. A genuinely democratic society must produce equality of results. Socialists wish to replace a society based on competition with a society based on cooperation. The socialist ideal sees individuals motivated not by profit and personal gain, but by a sense of social responsibility.

democratic socialism

An economic system in which the major industries are owned by a democratically elected government responsible for planning and directing the economy

In short, democratic socialism requires the following:

1. Government ownership and control of the major industries, utilities, and transportation systems

2. A limit on individual wealth and property

3. A welfare system that guarantees all persons decent health care, an education, and adequate food and shelter

4. Extensive governmental regulation of the economy

Democratic socialism was a powerful force in Western Europe throughout the twentieth century; but in the United States, socialism and social democratic parties have had little success. In the early years of the twentieth century, the Socialist Party, headed by Eugene V. Debs and later by Norman Thomas, gained some influence and support. During the Great Depression, the millions of unemployed provided the socialists with a major opportunity. In 1932, in the last significant showing of the Socialist Party in a presidential election, Norman Thomas gained about 2 percent of the popular vote; but the election of Franklin Roosevelt and acceptance of his New Deal welfare measures stole much of the socialists' thunder. Irving Howe, co-chair of the Democratic Socialists of America, admitted in 1984, "The Socialist Party fell apart because it could not come to terms with Roosevelt."[17]

(pio3/Shutterstock)

Among other things, democratic socialism requires government ownership and control of the major industries, utilities, and transportation systems—such as the subway, which is vital in a busy metropolis like New York City.

The Democratic Socialists of America, the successor to the Socialist Party of Debs and Thomas, no longer expects to galvanize broad mass support behind its banners. Instead, it operates within a number of liberal organizations, including the Democratic Party, to influence their ideas and direction (see, for example, the discussion of Bernie Sanders, below). Today, the Democratic Socialists of America number only about 70,000 nationwide, but they can count Congress members Alexandria Ocasio-Cortez (D-NY) and Rashida Tlaib (D-MI) among their members.

The issues that faced the socialist movement in the pre–New Deal days were relatively simple and dramatic: The elderly needed a guaranteed pension; the unions needed government guarantees of their rights to organize and bargain; and the unemployed needed some form of protection. The New Deal established programs to deal with these issues, and the subsequent questions of their financing and administration were no longer dramatic. What, then, is the social democratic program in the post–New Deal, post–welfare state era?

Full employment, guaranteed by the government, has become a major demand of contemporary socialists. This requires a reduction of the workweek from forty to thirty-five hours so that more people can work fewer hours, with the government compensating workers with tax credits for any wages they lose by a reduction of their hours. Socialists call for a massive public works program for rebuilding America's *infrastructure* (roads, bridges, sewage systems) in order to create millions of new jobs for the unemployed. Because full employment can stimulate inflation, the socialists would also employ controls on wages, prices, incomes, rents, and dividends.

Sensitive to the issue that socialism spawns bureaucracy and centralization, American socialists support a system of public ownership characterized by worker-owned or community-controlled businesses and factories. Nevertheless, Americans remain resistant to the idea of socialism, associating it with either the authoritarian communism that plagued Eastern Europe or, in its democratic form, with the sluggish economy that characterized pre-Thatcherite Great Britain. In the present era, socialism presents more of an intellectual challenge to American capitalism than a serious political threat. Nonetheless, in 1990, longtime socialist Bernie Sanders—not running under the Democratic banner—was elected to the House of Representatives from Vermont. He was the first independent socialist elected to Congress in over half a century. In 2004, he returned to Congress for his eighth consecutive term, winning 68 percent of the votes. In 2006, Sanders ran as an independent candidate for the U.S. Senate. Sanders squared off against a Republican candidate for the open seat, and Vermonters elected the independent socialist to the Senate with 65 percent of the vote. He won reelection in 2012 by an even wider margin. Most impressive,

(Dorothea Lange, photographer, 1936. Farm Security Administration—Office of War Information Photograph Collection/Library of Congress)

The "Migrant Mother" photo of destitute thirty-two-year-old Florence Thompson, mother of seven children, has become one of the most recognized documentary-type photographs of the Depression Era, circa 1930.

though, were his bids for the Democratic presidential nomination in 2016 and 2020. Although the senator from Vermont had campaigned as an independent for previous offices, he officially became a Democrat in 2015, and again in 2019. He challenged front-runner Hillary Clinton throughout the primary season in 2016, winning contests in twenty-three states and amassing almost 40 percent of the party's delegates. In 2020 he finished a strong second to Joe Biden, gaining nearly 30 percent of the delegates. He campaigned on a number of economic issues, including reducing income inequality, making college tuition-free, raising the minimum wage, expanding Social Security and Medicare, and placing stricter regulations on Wall Street. This theme resonated well

with many Americans—especially millennials and Gen Z, who found themselves disillusioned with the "politics as usual" approach of more traditional party insiders. Ultimately, his campaign fell short, but it also proved that democratic socialism may have a future as an important voice on the American political scene. If it is to make further inroads, however, socialism will need to overcome the fact that 53 percent of Americans say they would not vote for a socialist for president.[18]

A related recent phenomenon—the international Occupy movement, sometimes called the "99 Percent" movement—started in 2011 in the United States and bore some resemblance to democratic socialism, although it did not call for government ownership of industry the way that socialism does. A protest against

("Day 20 Occupy Wall Street, October 5, 2011, Shankbone 3" by David Shankbone, license via Wikimedia)

Members of National Nurses United labor union show their support for Occupy Wall Street in Foley Square in New York City on October 5, 2011.

the powerful influence of Wall Street and mega-corporations, the growth in income inequality, and what the movement's supporters saw as an increasingly undemocratic government, the Occupy movement had a diverse set of goals and demands. Ultimately, the movement's intentionally nonhierarchical organization precluded success in Occupy's goals of reducing economic inequalities and holding government more accountable to the citizenry.

4.4b Libertarianism: A Revival of Classical Liberalism

Although the Libertarian Party remains on the fringe of American politics, its ideas have stimulated considerable interest. The intellectual roots of libertarianism can be traced to the classical liberal movement of the eighteenth and nineteenth centuries and the ideas of Thomas Jefferson and Andrew Jackson. In the 2016 presidential election, the Libertarian Party candidate, former Republican governor of New Mexico Gary Johnson, polled just over four million votes—about 3.3 percent of the total votes cast. In 2020 the party nominated Jo Jorgensen, a psychology lecturer, who received under two million votes, about 1.2 percent of the total.

Like classical liberalism, **libertarianism** holds that the state must be kept extremely small. The essential role of government should be only the protection of the following human rights:

1. The right to life, by which libertarians mean protection against the use of force by others

2. The right to liberty, meaning the freedoms of speech, press, and assembly and protection against any government restrictions on ideas, books, films, or other means of communication

3. The right to property, by which libertarians support legislation that protects the property rights of individuals against confiscation, robbery, trespass, libel, fraud, and copyright violations[19]

Libertarians also oppose the interference of government in the private lives of citizens. They seek, for example, the repeal of all laws that involve so-called victimless crimes (prostitution, pornography, gambling). They seek an unfettered, free-market economy and oppose laws regulating the price of milk as well as those that prohibit the use of marijuana. Unlike the liberals, who support laws expanding the role of government in the economy, and social conservatives, who support legislation outlawing abortion and pornography, the libertarians oppose with equal fervor laws that regulate either the moral or the economic life of individuals.

Libertarians favor nonintervention in the affairs of other nations. They believe that military alliances and arms aid only lead to war, and that wars and war preparation bring about a vast increase in the power of government. One leading libertarian theorist argued that the United States should revoke all its military and political commitments to other countries.[20]

Libertarians call for a drastic reduction in the defense budget and a defense policy designed solely to defend the territory of the United States. Accordingly, the military draft is considered a form of involuntary servitude. Because proponents of the libertarian movement and the Libertarian Party have no immediate prospect of coming into power, their positions remain free of the need to compromise. In the 2020 presidential campaign, candidate Jo Jorgensen called for a drastic reduction in military spending, an

libertarianism

A belief that the state should regulate neither the economic nor the moral life of its citizens

Are your congressional representatives and senators generally liberal, or are they mostly conservative?

Americans for Democratic Action is an organization that attempts to answer that question by assigning each legislator a "Liberal Quotient" score based on their voting record.

http://www.bvtlab.com/3A8Dp

open immigration policy regulated by the marketplace, simplification of the tax code, a broad expansion of civil liberties, and promotion of nuclear power as a means of reducing carbon emissions.[21]

Although the Libertarian Party remains a minor party, its ideas have influenced both major parties. The Republican Party has taken a much more aggressive stand against the social programs of the 1960s and 1970s. It has also championed the reduction of income tax rates and the deregulation of business and industry. The Democratic Party has supported broader freedom from government interference in the areas of abortion, school prayer, and LGBT issues. Nevertheless, Americans have generally been reluctant to follow radical or revolutionary movements. Perhaps they perceive libertarianism as an interesting criticism, but they are not yet prepared to accept its far-reaching solutions.

The most recent form of libertarianism to capture America's imagination was a blend of conservative and libertarian positions coalescing under the umbrella of the Tea Party movement. Formally founded in 2009 as the Tea Party Patriots, this organization took its name from the Boston Tea Party—the Colonial American rebellion against British-imposed taxes. Sponsoring local chapters in many states throughout the country, Tea Party activists called for "promoting the principles of fiscal responsibility, constitutionally limited government, and free markets."[22] Although not founded to run candidates for office, the movement's popularity and the passion of its adherents were considered to have had a significant effect on the outcome of a number of congressional elections in 2010, 2012, and 2014. Though that movement has faded, one of the candidates it swept into office in 2010—Justin Amash (L-MI)—left the Republican Party for the Libertarian Party in 2020, becoming that party's first member of Congress.

(Shutterstock)

Libertarians feel that the government should not prohibit the use of marijuana or otherwise interfere in the private lives of citizens.

CHAPTER REVIEW

1. People do not simply dispute issues that reflect their own self-interest. They also disagree—sharply, at times—about what constitutes a good society. Since the American and French revolutions, disputes between liberals and conservatives have occupied center stage in Western democracies and in the United States, in particular; but liberalism and conservatism have often changed colors and even exchanged attitudes.

2. Nineteenth-century liberals Thomas Jefferson and Andrew Jackson equated the idea of a powerful state with the protection of the wealthy merchant classes, but liberalism changed in the Industrial Age. Deeply affected by the populist and progressive movements, liberalism saw government as an important vehicle for the protection of the many from exploitation by the few. Liberals and neoliberals today still regard governmental programs and intervention as the key to solving our economic problems; but in matters of personal morality, liberals hark back to an earlier age. Their opposition to governmental interference in matters of abortion and school prayer is reminiscent of Jefferson's concerns.

3. Conservatives in the early days of the American republic were the supporters of a strong government. They believed that only a government of a talented and propertied elite could preserve the sacred rights of all people. As the voting franchise was extended to more and more people, conservatives lost their faith in central government and focused on the rights of property, independent of the state, and the rights of individuals to be free of governmental interference. With their opposition to abortion, pornography, and LGBT rights, conservatives remain true in matters of moral and social policy to the old Burkean belief that the state can promote social virtue. The central controversy between liberals and conservatives today is not over whether government should be strong or weak but when it should be strong or weak.

4. Libertarianism and democratic socialism advocate fundamental alterations in the status quo. Social democrats focus on the good of the whole society and envision a system under which all people will be equal economically and politically. They support a broad program of governmental control that includes ownership of the major corporations and industries. Unlike the libertarians, who see the state as the greatest threat to human liberty, the social democrats see the state as the greatest hope for human equality.

5. Libertarians, in their opposition to the very idea of big government, hark back to the nineteenth-century liberals. They are opposed to government interference in the setting of agricultural price supports as well as in the prohibition of illegal drugs. They believe that government should exist primarily to defend the rights to life, liberty, and property, and to defend the homeland from attack.

KEY TERMS

Americans for Democratic Action........... 112

classical liberalism 107

conservatism 114

contract theory 107

democratic socialism 121

industrial policy 111

laissez-faire economics 116

liberalism 107

libertarianism 124

neoconservatism 120

neoliberalism 113

populism.................................. 109

progressivism............................. 109

social Darwinism 116

READINGS FOR FURTHER STUDY

A broad overview of political ideologies can be found in Roger Eatwell, *Contemporary Political Ideologies.* (New York: Routledge, 2019), and in John Andrew Heywood, *Political Ideologies: An Introduction,* 6th ed. (New York: Palgrave Macmillan, 2017).

Both David F. Ericson and Louisa Bertch Green, eds., *The Liberal Tradition in American Politics* (New York: Routledge, 1999) and Charles W. Dunn and J. David Woodard, *The Conservative Tradition in America* (Lanham, MD: Rowman & Littlefield, 2003) provide a valuable collection of important historical readings.

Alpheus T. Mason and Gordon E. Baker, *Free Government in the Making,* 4th ed. (New York: Oxford University Press, 1985) supplements readings on U.S. political thought with helpful essays.

Readers interested in exploring socialist thought should consult Michael Newman, *Socialism: A Very Short Introduction* (New York: Oxford University Press, 2005).

Those interested in a greater understanding of libertarianism should see Jacob H. Huebert, *Libertarianism Today* (Santa Barbara, CA: Praeger, 2010).

For a discussion of neoliberal and neoconservative thought, consult Matthew Eagleton-Pierce, *Neoliberalism: The Key Concepts* (New York: Routledge, 2016) and Francis Fukuyama, *America at the Crossroads: Democracy, Power, and the Neoconservative Legacy* (New Haven, CT: Yale University Press, 2007).

For an overview of the impact of the contemporary ideological debate on American politics, see Morris P. Fiorina, *Culture War? The Myth of a Polarized America,* 3rd ed. (New York: Pearson Longman, 2010) and Thomas Frank, *What's the Matter With Kansas?* (New York: Henry Holt and Company, 2005).

For an understanding of the Tea Party movement, see Theda Skocpol and Vanessa Williamson, *The Tea Party and the Remaking of Republican Conservatism* (New York: Oxford University Press, 2016).

The Occupy movement is explored in *The Occupy Handbook,* edited by Janet Byrne (New York: Back Bay Books, 2012).

NOTES

1. Roy C. Macridis, *Contemporary Political Ideologies* (Boston: Little, Brown, 1983), p. 9.

2. Quoted in Walter E. Volkomer, ed., *The Liberal Tradition in American Thought* (New York: Capricorn Books, 1969), p. 104.

3. Robert V. Remini, *Andrew Jackson and the Course of American Freedom, 1822–1832,* vol. 2 (New York: Harper & Row, 1981), p. 116.

4. Ibid., p. 33.

5. Quoted in Arthur A. Ekrich Jr., *Progressivism in America* (New York: New Viewpoints, 1974), p. 170.

6. Paul Glastris, "The Phillips Curve," *Washington Monthly* (June 1990): 54.

7. Arthur Schlesinger Jr., "The Liberal Opportunity," *The American Prospect* (Spring 1990): 15.

8. "Obama: Most Liberal Senator in 2007," *National Journal*, January 31, 2008.

9. Quoted in James M. Burns, *The Vineyard of Liberty* (New York: Knopf, 1982), p. 225.

10. Clinton Rossiter, *Conservatism in America*, 2nd ed., rev. (Cambridge, MA: Harvard University Press, 1982), p. 118.

11. Quoted in Jay Sigler, ed., *The Conservative Tradition in American Thought* (New York: Capricorn Books, 1969), p. 118.

12. Quoted in Rossiter, *Conservatism in America*, (Harvard University Press, 1962), p. 138.

13. George Will, *Statecraft as Soulcraft: What Government Does* (New York: Simon & Schuster, 1983), pp. 119–120.

14. *Engel v. Vitale*, 370 U.S. 421 (1962); *Roe v. Wade*, 410 U.S. 113 (1973); *Wallace v. Jaffree*, 472 U.S. 38 (1985).

15. Irving Kristol, *Reflections of a Neoconservative: Looking Back, Looking Ahead* (New York: Basic Books, 1953), p. 212.

16. Conor Lynch, "Why Neocons Really Hate Trump," Salon, February 25, 2018, https://www.salon.com/2018/02/25/why-neocons-really-hate-trump-hes-hastening-the-decline-of-american-empire/.

17. "Voices from the Left: A Conversation Between Michael Harrington and Irving Howe," *New York Times Magazine*, June 17, 1984, p. 28.

18. The Gallup Organization, "Socialism and Atheism Still U.S. Political Liabilities," February 11, 2020, https://news.gallup.com/poll/285563/socialism-atheism-political-liabilities.aspx (June 16, 2020).

19. John Hospers, "What Libertarianism Is," in Tibor Machan, ed., *The Libertarian Alternative: Essays in Social and Political Philosophy* (Chicago: Nelson-Hall, 1974), p. 13.

20. Murray Rothbard, *For a New Liberty: The Libertarian Manifesto*, rev. ed. (New York: Collier, 1978), p. 291.

21. Jorgensen/Cohen 2020, https://joj2020.com/ (June 16, 2020).

22. "Tea Party Patriots Mission Statement and Core Values," http://www.teapartypatriots.org/Mission.aspx (June 8, 2010).

POP QUIZ

1. Classical liberals believed that the government that governed _____ governed _____ .

2. _____ direct their attention not to the expansion of government services but to their effective delivery.

3. Contemporary conservatism remains at its core a defense of economic individualism against the growth of the _____ .

4. Democratic socialists believe that a genuinely democratic society must produce equality of _____.

5. Both liberals and conservatives accept most of the economic reforms of the New Deal.   T   F

6. Populists and progressives advocate economic reforms that would strengthen the government's role.   T   F

7. Neoliberals have repudiated the New Deal and Great Society legacies while emphasizing the promotion of wealth.   T   F

8. Early American conservatives believed that only men who owned property should be allowed to vote.   T   F

9. Democratic socialism essentially supports the democratic process and the ideals of capitalism.   T   F

10. Which of the following is true of radical ideologies such as democratic socialism and libertarianism?
    A) They accept the basic principles of capitalism as a successful economic system.
    B) They challenge much of the existing social and political order.
    C) They function outside of the democratic process.
    D) They have become a major challenge to liberalism and conservatism in America.

11. Classical liberals such as Thomas Jefferson and Andrew Jackson believed which of the following?
    A) in a strong central government
    B) that unregulated capitalism resulted in rule by a moneyed aristocracy
    C) that liberty was the absence of government interference with the rights of citizens
    D) that government expenditures should be limited to infrastructure projects such as roads and canals

12. Which of the following was true of New Deal, contemporary liberalism?
    A) It changed the constituency of liberalism to include the entrepreneurial class.
    B) It is based on the belief that government should provide basic material guarantees for every individual.
    C) It favored a decreased role of government in the economy.
    D) It repudiated the ideals of capitalism.

13. Which of the following is true of neoliberals?
    A) They favor policies that call for greater government and business cooperation.
    B) They support expanding the size and role of government unions.
    C) They prefer reducing defense spending to military reforms.
    D) They favor tying civil service and military benefits to the cost of living.

14. Which of the following is true of neoconservatives?
    A) They support racial and sexual quotas.
    B) They stress policies that lower taxes on large incomes.
    C) They call for more regulation of business to promote economic growth.
    D) They support the idea of the welfare state in principle, but not in practice.

15. The intellectual roots of libertarianism can be traced to which of the following?
    A) populism and progressivism
    B) the philosophy of Edmund Burke
    C) classical liberalism
    D) the New Deal

Answers:
1. least, best   2. Neoliberals   3. welfare state
4. results   5. T   6. T   7. F   8. T   9. F
10. B   11. C   12. B   13. A   14. B   15. C

Chapter
05

PUBLIC OPINION & POLITICAL PARTICIPATION

In This Chapter

5.1   Public Opinion: What Americans Think About Politics
5.2   The Sources of Public Opinion: Political Socialization
5.3   Political Participation

Chapter Objectives

This chapter examines what the American people actually think about politics, how they come to think what they do, and how they translate their thoughts into politically relevant actions. Chapter 4 described the major patterns of American political beliefs in philosophical and historical terms. In this chapter, we concern ourselves with the extent to which the general public actually subscribes to those beliefs—leading into an examination of how people learn to think about politics.

What influences encourage people to become Democrats, independents, or Republicans and determine their opinions on political issues?

These topics are discussed in the sections on political socialization. The chapter concludes with a discussion of how political beliefs are translated into political actions, ranging from voting to protest demonstrations and civil disobedience.

(Joseph Sohm/Shutterstock)

Democratic presidential candidates (L to R) Mayor Mike Bloomberg, Sen. Elizabeth Warren, Sen. Bernie Sanders, former VP Joe Biden, Mayor Pete Buttigieg, Sen. Amy Klobuchar, on February 19, 2020, Las Vegas, Nevada.

5.1   Public Opinion: What Americans Think About Politics

What Americans *think* about politics is important because it determines, in part, how they act politically. The diverse but predominantly moderate character of Americans' political views and the relatively modest intensity with which most people advance their views set the tone for the whole political process. To understand how people think about politics is to understand an essential element of the environment within which the political process functions.

5.1a   The Character of Public Opinion

Public opinion may sound like a simple and stable concept, but it is actually complex and ever changing. **Public opinion** is a combination of the views, attitudes, and ideas held by individuals in a community. There is no single public opinion; there is, rather, a wide variety of viewpoints. Different publics or groups of people think differently about political questions. Some people hold very sophisticated views about politics; others do not. Some people devote their entire lives to politics; others hardly ever think about politics.

Certain facets of public opinion are remarkably constant. Love of country and pride in the nation's accomplishments, for instance, are attitudes that are almost always present and widely shared. Other facets of public opinion are *dynamic*—fluctuating considerably in response to social, political, and economic events. Some opinions are held *intensely;* others seem to be little more than *casual preferences.* An opinion that is intensely held is more likely to influence what a person thinks about political candidates and how that person might get involved politically.

public opinion

The array of beliefs and attitudes that people hold about political and related affairs

The politically sophisticated and the general public observe the same political world. However, much of the public sees it—to borrow an expression from the Bible—"through a glass darkly." Politicians and political commentators can argue at length about what they see as the major political issues of the time, but much of this seems to pass by most of the public. As explained in the following sections, a substantial share of the American public does not care much about politics, knows relatively little about it, and does not think about it in very sophisticated terms. Still, few would say that public opinion is unimportant. Indeed, political analysts and politicians are very concerned about what the public thinks.

5.1b How Much Americans Care and Know About Politics

Polling—the process of using social science methods to get an accurate sense of the public's view on an issue—has been an important facet of American politics since the 1930s. The first public opinion pollsters assumed that the public cared and was reasonably well-informed about politics; however, they were startled to find that many Americans cared little and knew less about what went on in the political arena. More recent surveys have done little to contradict these early findings or show any recent increase in public interest and information—a surprising finding given the rising level of education and the proliferation of the media, particularly television and internet news, over the last few decades.

In a 2020 Gallup poll, 78 percent of Americans said they were at least moderately proud of their country.

This is not to say that the public as a whole is essentially uninterested in politics; indeed, a substantial number of people indicate a considerable degree of interest. For example, a recent survey found that 39 percent of the public said that they followed government and public affairs "most of the time," 35 percent "some of the time," 17 percent "only now and then," and only 8 percent "hardly at all."[1] These results fall short of the democratic ideal of a keenly interested electorate, but are reasonably reassuring in that most people do seem to be at least somewhat interested in politics.

The meaningfulness of such expressions of interest is called into question, however, by the public's level of information about politics. A 2019 survey indicated that 61 percent of Americans did not know what determines a state's number of electoral votes, and 38 percent did not know which political party held a majority in the U.S. Senate.[2] In addition, a 2011 study found that 24 percent of Americans could not name the country from which the United States gained its independence following the Revolutionary War.[3]

5.1c What Americans Hold in Common

On many fundamental political matters, the majority of Americans are in substantial agreement. First of all, Americans are proud of their country and are emotionally attached to it and its symbols. The majority of Americans—about 63 percent—say they are either "extremely proud" or "very proud" to be an American, with another 15 percent identifying as "moderately proud." Only 21 percent of Americans say they are "only a little" or "not at all proud."[4] Studies consistently show that the percentages of people expressing enthusiasm

polling
The process of using social science methods to get an accurate sense of the public's view about an issue or set of issues

and pride for their country are, in fact, higher in the United States than in almost any other country. That being said, these numbers are lower now than they have been in the past. In 2013, the number saying they were extremely or very proud was 85 percent; in 2003, it was 92 percent.[5]

Americans are also positive about their country's political, social, and economic institutions. When asked how much confidence they had in their country's public and private institutions, Americans almost always responded more favorably than citizens from four European democracies (Figure 5.1). Although some Americans are critical of their nation's institutions, what is most striking is that Americans are clearly less critical than people in other countries. Americans consistently have more confidence in even those institutions that are sometimes singled out as objects of public disdain—such as the media, labor unions, and Congress—than do their European counterparts.

Figure 5.1   Confidence in Public Institutions: A Comparative Perspective

Americans typically express greater confidence in their country's political, social, and economic institutions than do citizens of other democratic countries.

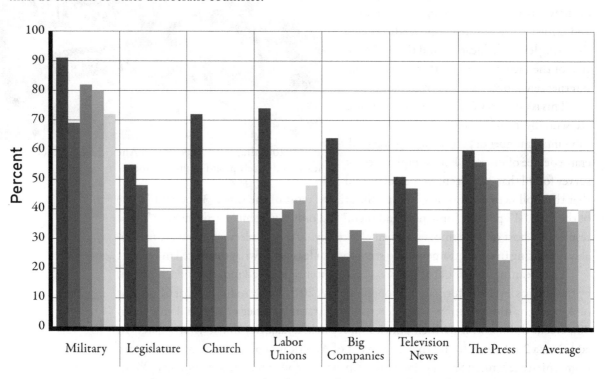

Percentage answering that they trust the institution (Europe) or have "a great deal," "quite a lot," or "some" confidence in it (U.S.)

■ United States   ■ Germany   ■ France   ■ United Kingdom   ■ Spain

DATA SOURCES: The Gallup Organization, "Confidence in Institutions," June 2020, Copyright © 2020 Gallup, Inc., https://news.gallup.com/poll/1597/Confidence-Institutions.aspx (June 18, 2020); European Commission, "Eurobarometer Interactive," October 2005–June 2020, https://ec.europa.eu/commfrontoffice/publicopinion/index.cfm/Survey/index (December 17, 2020).

POLITICS AND IDEAS

Textbooks and Children's Ideas About American Politics

American students typically spend a dozen or more years of their lives poring over textbooks of various sorts. Some of these books have little to do with politics: math books, chemistry books, foreign language books. Many of them, however, do deal directly or indirectly with topics related to politics: social studies books, history books, American government books, economics books, and sociology books.

Because students spend so much time reading them, textbooks seem likely to significantly affect how students think about politics. Further, the books may be particularly influential because of the way students are likely to approach them. Students treat the material in textbooks as information they need to know, rather than as information to be read critically or thought about afterward in depth. Almost as soon as the material is known, it starts to be forgotten. As the specific facts fade, what tends to be remembered is a general impression—a color and tone and feeling that can persist for years.

The influence of textbooks brings up some of the most important and difficult issues of political socialization.[1] Much of political socialization occurs not in sudden and dramatic jumps from ignorance to knowledge or from ambivalence to passion but through a slow, steady gain and loss of political information and impressions. The content of school textbooks is determined by a combination of scholarly, economic, and political factors. The scholars who write the book, the editors and publishers who mold the book to help it sell, and the more or less politically accountable officials who pick the books to be used—all shape the final product. Yet who should decide which textbooks American children should read? Are not school boards democratic institutions? More generally, who should decide what children will be taught? How democratic do we want the education process to be?

Earlier textbooks often presented children with an idealized picture of American history, society, and politics ("sugarcoating," some scholars have called it); recently, however, there has been more sentiment toward giving students the "unvarnished truth." For example, over the past generation textbooks have become more multicultural—featuring more stories and descriptions of ethnic and racial minorities and women.[2] But is there such a thing as "unvarnished truth," or are there just different perspectives? Is there a "best" way to present America's diverse cultural history? Again, who should decide?

Teaching children to think critically about their country, as newer texts tend to do, is certainly an admirable goal; yet it can run counter to the goal of political socialization necessary to promote good citizenship. How does a society create in its children the appropriate balance of respect and skepticism for its basic values? To put it differently, every society wants to instill in its youth favorable feelings toward its values and institutions. Where is the line between socialization and brainwashing?

1. Joseph Moreau, *Schoolbook Nation* (Ann Arbor: University of Michigan Press, 2004).

2. Jesus Garcia, "The Changing Image of Ethnic Groups in Textbooks," *Phi Delta Kappa* 75 (1993): 29–35.

Why are Americans generally so proud of their country and positive about its institutions? One reason is that they have been taught all their lives to think of America as the best (see the section on political socialization later in this chapter); the roots of American pride run deeper than that, however. Americans also take pride in their country because they are generally raised to hold certain basic values and to believe that the United States, among all nations, is particularly dedicated to the fulfillment of those values. The Declaration of Independence exemplifies these values:

WE hold these Truths to be self-evident, that all Men are created *equal,* that they are endowed by their Creator with certain unalienable Rights, that among these are *Life, Liberty, and the Pursuit of Happiness.* That to secure these rights, Governments are instituted among Men, deriving their just *Powers* from the *Consent of the Governed.*

To these three basic values of democracy—equality, freedom, and consent of the governed—can be added most Americans' commitment to capitalism and the free enterprise system.

- **Equality**   The majority of Americans genuinely believe in equality; and whether or not they really think people are equal, about 95 percent believe that the government should treat everyone as if they were equal.[6] That being said, Americans tend to disagree on the best way for the government to treat citizens equally. For example, just 38 percent of Americans believe the government should play a major role in trying to improve the social and economic position of minorities in the United States.[7]

- **Freedom**   Americans believe in their capacity to do what is best for themselves. Hence, they think that individuals should be free to act as they please, with minimal government interference, as long as they do not interfere with other people's freedom. Surveys have long shown a strong commitment to freedom of speech, press, religion, and association.[8] For example, 92 percent of Americans responding to a poll indicated that the First Amendment protection for freedom of speech is either crucial or very important to their own sense of freedom, and more than two-thirds of Americans believe speech offensive to religion or minority groups should be tolerated.[9] Some Americans even value freedom over potential threats to their own health. When asked in 2020 how likely they would be to follow a government recommendation to stay at home for a month in response to a local COVID-19 outbreak, 19 percent of Americans said they would be somewhat or very unlikely to follow the recommendation.[10] On the other hand, when rights come into conflict, Americans are faced with tough choices regarding which freedoms to support. The issue of school prayer often pits those who favor free exercise of religion against those who oppose the establishment of religion. In a recent poll, 61 percent of Americans said they would support daily prayer in public schools, even though the Supreme Court has consistently found such prayer in violation of the First Amendment.[11]

- **Consent of the governed**   Americans see their acceptance of government as voluntary. About 73 percent of Americans believe that periodic elections make the government "pay attention to what the people think" at least some of the time.[12] While only 17 percent responded that they trust the government to do what is right most or all of the time, just 10 percent of Americans said they never trust the government.[13] Americans also believe firmly in the idea that the majority (more than half) of the people should rule in political affairs. At the same time, however, they believe that majorities should not possess unlimited power and that the rights of a minority (less than half) of the people should be protected against the whims of the majority.

- **Capitalism and the free enterprise system**   Americans believe in the value of hard work, in private property, in economic competition, and in profit. In contrast to some other societies, most Americans tend to view hard work as a virtue and laziness as a vice—tenets of the so-called Protestant ethic. They

see private property as an essential element of economic progress. They believe that competition brings out the best in people and that the most successful competitors deserve the greatest rewards. Americans' preference for freedom over equality manifests itself in the economic as well as the political sphere. This particular combination of values fits well with a free-market, entrepreneurial economy. Americans like the idea of a fair competition in which everybody starts out equally but in which they all have the freedom to pursue their self-interest and thus end up unequally well-off, depending on how well they have pursued their self-interest. A series of Gallup polls taken over the past twenty years indicates that a consistent plurality of Americans believes the government "is trying to do too many things that should be left to individuals and businesses."[14] Regarding taxation, 46 percent of Americans polled in 2020 indicated that the amount of federal income tax they have to pay is too high, while 48 percent say the amount is about right.[15] On the other hand, in the very same poll, 59 percent of respondents said the amount of taxes they have

(Debby Wong / Shutterstock)

Americans like the idea of a fair competition in which everybody starts out equally, but in which they all have the freedom to pursue their self-interest and thus end up unequally well-off.

to pay is fair, and in another poll, 59 percent agreed with the statement "the money and wealth in this country should be more evenly distributed among a larger percentage of the people."[16] Polling also found that over 71 percent of respondents agreed that there is either too much or just the right amount of government regulation of business and industry.[17]

Although Americans are proud of their country's system of government and believe in the fundamental values on which it rests, they are not beyond finding fault with it. In fact, since the 1960s the American political system has struggled with a widespread undercurrent of dissatisfaction with the way in which the system is working, fueled by the urban disorder of the 1960s, the Vietnam War, the Watergate scandal, and the nation's ongoing economic problems. Between 1964 and 1994, the percentage of Americans who said they trusted the government to do what was right all or most of the time fell from 76 percent to 21 percent, and the percentage who said that public officials care what "people like me" think declined from 62 percent to 22 percent. This sense of alienation started to turn around somewhat by the beginning of the twenty-first century, however, as the trust-in-government number rose to 47 percent, and the percent who believed government cared about what they think rose to 34 percent by 2004.[18] By late 2008, however, the trust-in-government index had fallen again—this time to 26 percent. Such mood changes may not be entirely unrelated to Americans' pocketbooks. In 2008, due to the economic downturn of the early 2000s, only 8 percent of Americans believed the economy was getting better; 87 percent believed it was getting worse. By 2012, though, a majority of Americans believed that the economy was recovering.[19] These figures coincided

with the public's rising approval ratings for the president (50 percent).[20] As the economic recovery fell short of expectations in 2013 and 2014, so fell President Obama's approval ratings in those years, but then they rose again during his final two years in office as the economy continued to strengthen.[21] Even President Trump, who had consistently low approval ratings, saw some improvement as the economy performed well in 2018. However, in 2020, as the COVID-19 crisis led unemployment numbers to shoot past 16 percent, Trump's approval quickly fell from a then-high of 49 percent to 39 percent over the course of just a couple of weeks.[22] This connection between trust in the government and the success of the economy is an enduring feature of American public opinion.

5.1d Where Americans Differ

Citizens of the United States manifest considerable agreement on the general principles of democracy just described, but consensus is far from complete. The American people differ on the implications of these general principles when applied to particular cases. They also differ in their political ideologies.

The Meaning of Equality

Although Americans profess a belief in equality in the abstract, just what this means and to whom it applies are matters for disagreement. First, as we discussed in Chapter 3, does equality mean equality of opportunity or equality of result? That is, should everybody have an equal chance to pursue an education and earn a high income, or should everybody get the same education and earn the same income? Americans seem to lean away from equality of result. Only 24 percent believe the government should "take active steps in every area it can to try and improve the lives of its citizens."[23]

Second, just which "men" are equal? Some Americans do not believe that men and women are equal. According to a 2008 survey, 7 percent of Americans still agreed that "women's place is in the home rather than business, industry, or government."[24] Even into contemporary times, a substantial percentage of Americans have not regarded African Americans and whites as equals. In a 1990 survey, 78 percent of whites thought that African Americans were more likely to prefer living on welfare than whites; 62 percent thought African Americans less likely to be hardworking; 56 percent thought African Americans more prone to violence; and 53 percent thought African Americans less intelligent. African Americans see this sense of racial inequality from a different perspective. In a 2018 poll, 67 percent of whites thought an African American had as good of a chance as a white American to get a job for which they were qualified, but 69 percent of African Americans felt this was not the case. Additionally, 75 percent of whites believed that African American children have the same chance as white children to get a good education, whereas only 49 percent of African Americans share this view.[25]

Limits of Freedom

Although Americans believe in freedom as a general principle, they do see it as having

(Belltreephotography/Shutterstock)

Flag burning is considered an extension of freedom of speech.

definite limits. More than 95 percent endorse the principle of freedom of expression in the abstract, but percentages drop sharply with the possibility that "bad" or "dangerous" ideas will be expressed.[26] For many Americans, freedom of expression does not extend to speaking, writing, or teaching when the ideas are unpopular ones—for example, anti-religious or racist.[27] Further, some Americans do not agree that people should be able to express their views any way they want. The Supreme Court's decisions in 1989 and 1990 upholding the rights of protesters to burn the American flag set off a bitter national debate. A constitutional amendment to criminalize the act has been introduced in Congress nearly every session since. In the wake of the war on terrorism, Americans have expanded their view on what expressions are potentially dangerous and how restrictive the government should be in response. Some have argued that the 2001 Patriot Act went too far in restricting civil liberties, but by 2006, only 30 percent of Americans thought the act needed major changes or should be eliminated entirely.[28] Even fifteen years after the 9/11 attacks of 2001, 30 percent of Americans responded that the government should take all steps necessary to prevent terrorist acts, even if their "basic civil liberties would be violated."[29]

Majority Rule Versus Minority Rights

The American people's adherence to the ideals of majority rule and minority rights sometimes loses something in the translation to everyday political questions. Slightly more than half of the respondents in one survey held that only people who were well informed about issues should be allowed to vote in elections in which questions relating to "tax-supported undertakings" are at issue, and in a recent survey, 34 percent of respondents held that only people who pay taxes should have the right to vote.[30] The idea that any citizen should be able to grow up to be president is endorsed in the abstract but rejected by some in practice. In April 2008, 35 percent of Americans did not think the country was ready for a woman president and 22 percent did not think the country was ready for a black president.[31] Of course, the Democratic Party put those attitudes to the test when Senators Hillary Clinton (D-NY) and Barack Obama (D-IL) campaigned throughout the entire presidential primary season. By June of that year, Obama had secured enough delegates to become his party's nominee and the first black presidential candidate to represent one of the two main political parties. His election victory in November 2008 may have finally put the question about race to rest, and Hillary Clinton's nomination in 2016 likely did the same for the gender question.

Free Enterprise in Practice

As enamored with the free enterprise system as Americans are, their affection for it still has some limits. About 68 percent of Americans express quite a lot or a great deal of confidence in small business owners, but only about 23 percent have that same degree of confidence in big business.[32] In light of recent financial sector crises, 61 percent of Americans approved of increased government regulation of banks and financial institutions.[33] Americans are particularly wary of big business, with half of respondents in a recent poll saying they would like to see big business have less influence on the nation than it does now and only 5 percent wishing it had more influence.[34]

Political Ideology

Perhaps the most important matter on which Americans differ is political ideology. American politics is often portrayed as a controversy between liberals and conservatives. As discussed in Chapter 4, with the rise of neoconservatism, neoliberalism, and the return to classical liberal principles in libertarianism, particularly in recent years, the reality

has become much more complicated. Commentators have also distinguished among the different dimensions of liberalism and conservatism: economic, social, and cultural. Such debates have certainly occupied the attention of the intellectual elites, but what is striking is how far removed they are from the concerns of most Americans. Even the most basic notions of liberalism and conservatism meet with limited recognition. Only about half of US citizens recognize the terms *liberalism* and *conservatism* and have some general sense of what they mean.[35] In a 2016 national survey, about 18 percent of the respondents declined to place themselves on a liberal–conservative scale when asked to do so because they said they did not know or had not thought that much about it; in a 2020 survey, 36 percent responded that they were moderate—"neither liberal nor conservative" on social issues and 38 percent declared themselves moderate on economic issues.[36] Studies of people's answers to questions raising liberal–conservative issues have long shown little consistency between answers, suggesting that many people do not think about politics in ideologically coherent terms.[37] First of all, such findings are important because they suggest that a good share of the population does not really have a grasp on the debate between liberals and conservatives. Second, the findings raise questions about the meaningfulness of the American public's responses to questions about their political ideology. When people are unsure of what they are being asked, a safe response is often in the middle.

Figure 5.2 shows how over most of the past four decades, more Americans have characterized themselves as conservatives than as moderates or liberals. This trend peaked in 1994, when 36 percent of Americans identified themselves as conservative and only 14 percent as liberal. The years since then have shown a small reversal, with 26 percent of respondents in 2018 identifying as liberal and just 9 percent more as conservative.

What these findings really mean is difficult to interpret without some sense of what the American public means when it uses the words *liberal* and *conservative*. Different people appear to mean different things when they use the terms. When a national election survey asked people what they had in mind when they said that someone's political views were liberal or conservative, the most common responses described liberals as people who are open to change and new ideas, for government action to help solve social problems, allied with working people, inclined to spend government money, and somewhat rash. In contrast, conservatives were viewed as resistant to change, for free enterprise solutions, allied with big business and the rich, against government spending, and cautious.[38]

What about the people who don't think in terms of—or even recognize—liberal and conservative labels? Political scientists have tried to plumb political thinking to get at the mental images of these people. What they have found does not paint an encouraging portrait. Many Americans seem to respond to political issues on an essentially individual basis, without any broad or overarching political philosophy to guide them. Instead, their responses are shaped by their sense of identification with one or another political party or group, by their feelings about whether "it's good times" or "it's hard times," or by their feelings about a particular candidate or public figure.[39]

However, there may be an important qualification: The level of coherence in public thinking may be at least partially dependent on how politicians handle issues in campaign and policy-making discussions. When candidates and public figures address the public on issues, the public does seem to respond by becoming more conscious of and concerned about those issues. For example, in the relatively placid 1950s, candidates and parties did little to bring issue differences to the attention of the public, and the public showed little awareness of issues or coherence in its thinking about them. From the mid-1960s into the 1970s, however, candidates began to discuss compelling issues such as the Vietnam War and urban disorder, and the public seemed to respond with increased awareness and coherence.[40]

Figure 5.2 Americans Rate Themselves on the Liberal–Conservative Scale, 1978–2018

While the number of Americans identifying themselves as conservatives has remained higher than the number identifying themselves as liberals over much of the past forty years, this gap has narrowed recently.

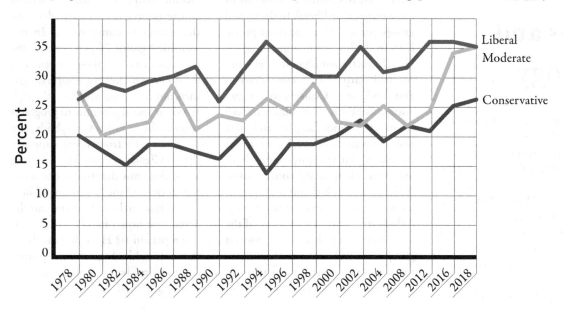

SOURCE: American National Election Studies, 2016, 2020.

More recent research has called into question the degree and meaningfulness of the changes observed in the 1960s and 1970s, suggesting that they may result from changes in the way questions were asked and that much of the research into this area may be fatally flawed. It may be that the public's level of sophistication about politics has always been low and that it has changed little over the last fifty years. Whatever apparent increases in liberal–conservative thinking there have been may result from the public merely parroting the heightened liberal–conservative rhetoric of candidates without really understanding it.[41]

The political beliefs of the American public establish patterns that help to shape politics. The general agreement on principles such as freedom and majority rule defines the boundaries within which the game of American politics is played. These limits help to blunt any potential for political instability or violence. Commitments to ideas such as equal opportunity tend to define the basic objectives of the political system. The relatively low level of ideological thinking provides political leaders with room to maneuver and thereby fosters political stability.

Nevertheless, differences in ideological perspective result in fundamental conflicts that the political process must resolve. For instance, how actively should the government promote the interests of disadvantaged or oppressed groups? Where should the government strike the balance between promoting social change and maintaining social stability? How the public thinks about politics defines, in part, some of the most fundamental principles and problems of American democracy.

POLITICS AND ECONOMICS

Economic Status and Ideology

Conventional wisdom has it that political ideology is closely tied to economic status, with the less well-off holding liberal beliefs and the better-off aligning themselves with a conservative viewpoint. How well does this relationship hold up in America? Figure 5.3 shows the relationship between the respondent's professed political ideology and the respondent's income. The poorest Americans are not the most likely group to identify themselves as liberal. These citizens are more likely to identify as moderate or conservative than liberal. In the second group, conservatives are most prevalent. In the highest income category, liberals reach their highest total—but are still outpaced by conservatives and moderates. Conservative views outnumber both of the others in only the middle income category, and there does not seem to be much support for the claim that wealthier individuals are more likely to be conservative. Additionally, the higher income groups are more likely to express an ideological identity: three times more of the wealthiest group than of the poorest group identified with one of the three categories. One striking feature of these data is the relative weakness of the ideological differences between the income groups. More than 35 percent of the poorest Americans describe themselves as conservative. In the wealthiest group, 26 percent describe themselves as liberal—more than in the other two categories. Surprisingly, then, not everybody who pays (through taxes) for liberal government programs opposes them; and not everybody who might benefit from them supports them. Clearly, economic standing alone does not determine the ideological views of the American public.

What other factors might determine how liberal or conservative a person is? How do you think the other ideological viewpoints discussed in Chapter 4 might relate to economic status?

Figure 5.3   Political Ideology and Income

Poorer people tend to be less ideological and richer people tend to be more moderate, but all income levels have substantial numbers of all three ideologies, and the richest group has the highest percentage of liberals.

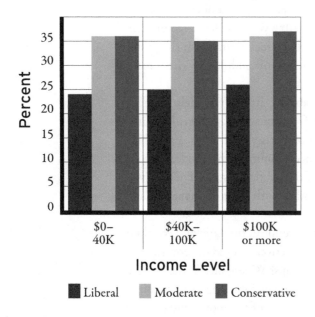

DATA SOURCE: The Gallup Organization, January 9, 2020, Copyright © 2020 Gallup, Inc.
https://news.gallup.com/poll/275792/remained-center-right-ideologically-2019.aspx

The Sources of Public Opinion: Political Socialization

Given the importance of public opinion, it is useful to comprehend why the public thinks as it does about politics. The origins of public opinion lie in history and philosophy, as discussed in Chapter 4. However, knowing where ideas come from does not explain how people come to hold certain beliefs; understanding that phenomenon requires a discussion of political socialization.

Political socialization is the process by which citizens come to think what they do about politics. Through political socialization, citizens internalize—or incorporate into their own thinking—beliefs, feelings, and evaluations (judgments on whether something is good or bad) about the political world in which they live. Think of the tremendous range of knowledge, feelings, and evaluations that people have about politics, and think of the many sources from which they all come; political socialization is obviously a long and complicated process.

Most of what people think and feel about politics has been learned from somebody else, but to leave it at that would deny the dynamic nature of the process and ultimately the possibility of any political change. That is, if all people simply stuck with what they have been taught about politics, nobody would ever think of anything new, and nothing would ever change. Clearly, then, some people break away from rigid adherence to old ideas and put thoughts together in new ways; but even those people start somewhere, building upon what already exists. Thus, political socialization is important to both stability and change in American politics.

5.2a   The Processes of Political Socialization

How do people learn about politics? Psychologists say that people tend to repeat behavior patterns that are rewarded and not to repeat patterns that are not rewarded or that are punished. Much of what people know about politics they learn through explicit teaching. Information is presented to them, and they are either rewarded for learning it (by a higher grade or the praise of teachers or parents, for example) or punished for not learning it (by a lower grade or the criticism of teachers or parents). The mechanisms of learning are really the domain of psychology. Listed below are some of the basic processes that political scientists have identified as important in political socialization.

- **Social learning theory**   People experience subtle rewards and punishments from the psychological attachments they form to particular people around them, some of whom they admire, others of whom they dislike. Because people like to have favorable images of themselves, they may attempt to boost their self-images by acting like people they admire or by avoiding the behavior of those they do not like. Thus, a little boy may parrot his mother's views about the president, or a rebellious teenager may criticize a candidate that her disliked father holds dear.

- **Transfer theory**   People may carry over attitudes developed in a narrower setting, such as the family or school, to the broader political setting. A boy who dislikes his father may rebel against political authority more generally.

- **Cognitive development theory**   What people can learn about politics depends on the stage of their mental development. Some things can be learned only early in life, while others can be learned only later on. An adult immigrant

political socialization

The process by which citizens acquire politically relevant knowledge, beliefs, attitudes, and patterns of behavior

newly arrived in America may never develop the deep emotional attachment to the nation felt by a person who has grown up in this country from birth. By contrast, a first grader lacks the intellectual capacity to master the intricacies of federalism.[42]

These different theories of how people learn about politics are not competing but are rather complementary. Social learning sometimes occurs through explicit teaching. The possibilities of transference, social learning, and explicit teaching probably all vary, depending on the intellectual development of the learner. Political socialization is too complex to be accounted for by any one theory or explanation.

5.2b The Agents of Political Socialization

Agents of socialization are the people and institutions from which we learn. A person growing up in the United States learns about politics from many teachers. A comprehensive list would be too long to include here, but it is possible to identify a few of the most important agents. (Another important agent, the mass media, is discussed in the next chapter.)

- **The family** Under almost any realistic theory of political socialization, the family is uniquely situated to be a potent agent. The young individual who, according to developmental theory, is most vulnerable to socialization spends much time with the family. Thus, the family has the first chance at influencing political development. Psychological attachments are often strong and therefore conducive to the transference of attitudes toward authority, which influences attitudes and behavior relating to participation and partisanship. Although much learning takes place in the family, how much of that learning is political is difficult to pinpoint and varies from family to family. Politics is not of paramount interest to most Americans and thus is not usually at the top of the typical family's agenda for discussion. As such, it is not surprising that children sometimes grow up to be politically different from their parents. Research indicates that the transmission of political attitudes from parents to their children is substantial only when the attitudes relate to topics that regularly come up for discussion in the family.[43]

(Shutterstock)

In school, which is a prime agent of political socialization, many students learn about political participation, knowledgeability, and tolerance.

- **The school** The school is also a prime agent of political socialization. Education can be related to many political orientations—political participation, political knowledgeability, and political tolerance, among others. Certainly the school is the primary explicit teacher of information about politics and government. A good share of the learning fades away, as every student well knows, unless it is periodically reinforced by additional education, exposure to the media, political discussion, or repeated use.

  However, schools involve more than just the presentation of facts; they are complex and diverse bundles of experiences and impressions. Students encounter teachers, books, authority figures and role models (such as principals

agents of socialization

A "teacher" in the process of political socialization, for example, the family, the school, a peer group, or the mass media

and coaches), and their fellow students or peers. Some of the people students encounter may be very much like themselves, and some may be different. Meeting students of different races or religions in the school setting often provides children with their first real encounter with social diversity. Students may involve themselves in low-level political activities: class and club elections, student government, protests against school policies, and so on. They acquire not just facts but also subtle impressions about the way things are and the way things ought to be. They develop feelings about social and political involvement and what they can hope to accomplish through the political process.[44]

(Twin Design/Shutterstock)

- **Peer groups** Peer groups are groups of people, roughly equal in social position, who interact with one another. Students who go to school together, people who work together in an office or factory or bowl on the same team, the neighbors on the block—all are peer groups. Social pressures on group members to conform can be quite powerful.

Peer groups act as agents of political socialization and influence your development and opinions.

Group members adopt "proper" attitudes and behavior because they seek the boost to their self-image that comes with the approval of others—or because they fear that nonconformity will lead to ostracism. Because other things are usually more important, peer groups do not always set norms relating to politics. However, when they do, the political consequences can be significant.[45]

5.2c   The Development of a Political Self

How does political learning actually take place? How do politically blank infants develop into full-blown political beings? Probably the first political thought to blossom in the mind of a small child in the United States is a psychological attachment to America. This is by no means a sense of what America is, just a feeling of belonging to it. In families where partisanship is important, a primitive sense of "I'm a Republican" or "I'm a Democrat" may appear. A sense of an external authority—above the authority of the parents—that must be obeyed also emerges. This is most often attached to two specific figures: the president and the police officer. The president is the focal point of the American political system; thus, it is not surprising that this focused attention influences even very small children. The police officer gains attention as a less remote figure of considerable authority who moves about in a child's world. Perhaps the most striking feature of these early images is their positive character. Small children tend to idealize political authorities, attributing to them all possible virtues.[46]

As children grow, their political orientations evolve. In school, they begin to acquire substantial new knowledge pertinent to politics. Much of this they soon forget, but some of it becomes part of their lasting store of information. Their conceptions of politics become less personal and more institutional. For example, the president is important not so much as a person but as a position. Idealization of political authority fades to realism: Public figures have flaws, they make mistakes, and people criticize them. Once in school, where

POLITICAL CONTROVERSIES

Public Opinion and Terrorism: American Government in the Eyes of the World

As soon as the terrorist attacks hit the United States on September 11, 2001, Americans, governments, and citizens throughout the world began to react to the unfolding events. Many of these reactions were captured in opinion polls conducted by the news media and by independent polling agencies. Although reactions were initially quite uniform, cleavages soon began to emerge around the world.

A majority of Americans supported the government's initial responses. The president's approval ratings (in response to the question "Do you approve or disapprove of the way George W. Bush is handling his job as president?") initially jumped from 51 percent, just prior to September 11, to 86 percent a few days later. This figure rose to 90 percent in the following weeks and remained there for longer than any previous president since the Gallup Organization started measuring approval ratings in the 1940s. Throughout the weeks that followed 9/11, Americans also indicated strong support for Congress (84 percent), military action in Afghanistan (88 percent), and the use of ground troops (80 percent). When it came to the next steps, however, diversity of opinion—a hallmark

of democracy—began to return to American politics. Although support for the government's overall actions was high, about half of the nation (49 percent) believed that the government's repeated warnings about the possibility of further terrorist attacks didn't help but "just scared people." When political leaders began to speculate about the need to restrict personal freedoms, such as personal privacy, in order to prevent future acts of terror, 60 percent of Americans opposed making it easier for legal authorities to read mail and email or tap phones without a person's knowledge.

Around the world reactions have been even more varied. Although countries almost universally condemned the terrorist attacks against the United States, opinions were wide-ranging regarding America's military response. In the weeks following the attacks of September 11 and the October 7 launch of a military response, America's closest traditional allies tended to be the most supportive. British Prime Minister Tony Blair made his nation's support evident, and the British people followed suit: 93 percent favored arresting anyone found to be aiding terrorists, and 70 percent believed the United States and its allies should "be prepared to take military action" against nations harboring the terrorists responsible for the attacks. Britons were wary, however, of the consequences of such actions—78 percent believed any military response would create a wider conflict between "the Western world and the Islamic world."

The people of many other nations were deeply split over support for the military response. The Russians—a newly acquired and still cautious ally—expressed confidence in the Bush administration's ability to handle the situation; only 42 percent approved of the military strikes against Afghanistan, however. The Russian people had experienced firsthand the

misery of a protracted Afghan war in the 1980s, and many (60 percent) believed the actions of the United States would threaten Russian security. Some (54 percent) blamed terrorism and the Taliban regime for the military conflict, but others (30 percent) held American leadership and American society responsible. One of the main concerns expressed in the Russian press and elsewhere was that the United States was engaging in actions that would not solve the problem of terrorism, and was doing so without providing evidence of al Qaeda's guilt to the rest of the world.

Finally, the citizens of several nations stood opposed to nearly all American military efforts, some believing the United States should have pursued a diplomatic solution and others asserting that America's foreign policy and global capitalism were merely reaping what they had sown. Although the official government responses of nations such as Egypt and

Reaction to the American government's initial response to the 9/11 terrorist attacks varied around the world.

Pakistan, for example, were initially supportive of American strikes against Afghanistan, the people of these countries demonstrated opposition through anti-American street protests and peace vigils. Why such a reaction? One factor is that many nations in the Middle East and Asia have large Muslim populations that expressed concerns that an attack on one Muslim nation could spread to others. This was the case in Turkey, where 80 percent of Turkish citizens opposed an American military response in Afghanistan.

In the years since 9/11, this division between the US and the Arab and broader Muslim world deepened as American military efforts turned from Afghanistan to Iraq—with increasing hints that Iran might be a future target, as well. Though attitudes toward the American people and the values of freedom and democracy remained largely favorable, a 2004 survey of six Arab nations indicated declining attitudes, overall, over the previous two years. Opposition to American terrorism policy ranged from 75 to 96 percent and opposition to American Iraq policy ranged from 78 to 98 percent. A 2008 poll indicated that American leadership received only a 17 percent approval rating in the Middle East—the lowest of any region and only about half of the world average. Although still lower than in most parts of the world, and still the only region where more respondents disapprove than approve, approval by Arab nations of American leadership did increase significantly with the election of President Barack Obama, before falling precipitously during the Trump administration.

Do you or your family members remember the 9/11 attacks on America? If so, how did you or your family initially react? If not, how has the "war on terrorism" shaped your perceptions of the world? What policy approaches have you approved of and disapproved of regarding terrorism? How did you react—and how did the world react—to more recent acts of terrorism, such as the Boston Marathon bombing in 2013, the San Bernardino mass shooting in 2015, and the Orlando nightclub massacre in 2016? Are the world's citizens correct to criticize American foreign policy, or are their perspectives too limited by the information they receive? Is there such a thing as an objective, or "correct," view of politics?

SOURCES: The Gallup Organization, "Reactions to the Attacks on America and U.S.-Led Response," October 9, 2001, http://www.gallup.com/poll/releases/pr010914f.asp (November 4, 2001); The Gallup Organization, "Attack on America: Key Trends and Indicators," October 23, 2001, http://www.gallup.com/poll/releases/pr010926c.asp (October 30, 2001); CNN.Com, "World Reacts to War on Terror," http://www.cnn.com/ (November 3, 2001); World Press Review, "After September 11: A New Worldview," http://www.worldpress.org/specials/wtc/front.htm (November 3, 2001); Zogby International, "Impressions of America 2004: How Arabs View America, How Arabs Learn About America," 2004; The Gallup Organization, "U.S. Leadership Approval Lowest in Europe, Mideast," April 2, 2008, http://www.gallup.com/poll/105967/US-Leadership-Approval-Lowest-Europe-Mideast (July 15, 2008); The Gallup Organization, "Global Image of U.S. Leadership Rebounds," April 10, 2014, http://www.gallup.com/poll/168425/global-image-leadership-rebounds.aspx (September 10, 2014); The Gallup Organization, "Image of U.S. Leadership Now Poorer than China's," February 28, 2019, https://news.gallup.com/poll/247037/image-leadership-poorer-china.aspx (June 28, 2020).

---

teachers may try to minimize classroom conflict by downplaying partisan differences, children tend to become less partisan.

As partisanship declines, the ability to deal with the political world on a more abstract level increases. Children develop intellectually and morally to the extent that they can begin to look at politics in a more sophisticated and structured way. The critical age at which political thinking really starts to blossom seems to be about twelve. Within a couple more years, children's thinking becomes nearly as abstract and sophisticated as that of adults. Also, with increasing exposure to the sometimes unattractive facets of political life, realism often fades into cynicism. By the late teens, most individuals have established a political identity.

Political socialization does not end at the age of twenty-one, however; learning about politics continues through adulthood. As people age, their needs and concerns evolve; for example, from their own education to their children's education and, later in life, to their own health care. People's social environments change; their family roles shift from child to parent to grandparent; the school years recede into the past, and peer groups switch from fellow students to fellow workers to fellow retirees. Broader social change affects political learning, too, as large-scale social transformations—such as the civil rights movement and the women's movement—alter the expectations that people have of themselves and of society. Major unresolved issues revolve around how much childhood socialization persists into adulthood, and how much adult political learning is constrained by what has been learned as a child.[47]

5.2d   Diversity in Socialization

Socialization is not an identical process for all Americans. American society includes many subsocieties with their own distinctive political subcultures or shared patterns of political attitudes and behavior—many of which are racially and ethnically based. African Americans constitute one of the largest distinctive subcultures. Although African Americans and white Americans view many issues similarly, significant divisions exist—particularly with regard to equality and the government. For example, 73 percent of whites believe that equal housing opportunities exist for African Americans, but only 40 percent of African Americans hold this view. While 77 percent of African Americans believe they are treated less fairly by the police, only 45 percent of whites believe this is true.[48] When the nation reacted strongly to the killing of African American George Floyd by police officers in Minneapolis, Minnesota, in 2020, it was not surprising that responses differed by race: while 57 percent of all people in the US believe police are more likely to use deadly force against African Americans, 83 percent of African Americans hold this view.[49] Among Americans living in low-income communities, 60 percent of African Americans say they know some or a lot of people who have been treated unfairly by police, but only 31 percent of the white residents of those communities say the same. These disparate life experiences may help explain such differing attitudes.[50]

Latinx and Asian subcultures are harder to characterize, partly because neither is a single subculture but rather a collection of them. The rapidly growing Latinx subculture encompasses the Mexican-oriented culture of the Southwest, the Cuban-oriented culture of south Florida, and the Puerto Rican culture of New York and other large cities. Similarly, the Asian subculture includes the long-established Chinese communities of San Francisco, Los Angeles, and New York City and the more recently established communities of immigrants from Vietnam, Laos, and other Southeast Asian countries.

The different regions of the United States, to some degree, also constitute distinctive subcultures with unique patterns of political thought and behavior. The South is perhaps the most distinct from the others, owing to the continuing legacy of slavery and subsequent racial strife, as well as its more rural, agricultural subculture. Earlier studies of socialization found children in the South to differ from those in the North, but these differences seem to be fading.

In fact, the general trend seems to be away from clear-cut differentiation and toward greater homogeneity. Some attribute this trend to the "nationalization" of American culture and politics, which tends to blur regional differences. Americans in all parts of the country eat the same fast food and buy the same national-brand products. Most important politically, they read the same wire-service news stories, national news magazines, and internet news sites, and they watch the same network and cable news broadcasts. As a result, public opinion in the United States is becoming more and more uniform from region to region.

One other aspect of diversity in political socialization involves gender differences. Much of the early research on political socialization portrayed females as less political than males and traced those differences back to the childhood years.[51] The changing social and economic role of women from the eighteenth century to today is both a cause and a result of changes in the political interest, competence, and involvement of women.[52] The move toward more equal roles for men and women fostered by feminist movements is likely to manifest itself in, and benefit from, less political difference between young males and females.

5.3   Political Participation

So far we have examined what Americans think about politics and why they think what they do. The next step in our discussion is to focus on what Americans do about what they think. In other words, how is public opinion translated into political participation? Of course, putting it in those terms suggests that political participation stems exclusively from political considerations such as concern about issues and ideology. Such considerations are only part of the story.

Keep your finger on the pulse of American public opinion with the latest polls from the Gallup Organization.

http://www.bvtlab.com/a7e8t

5.3a   Motives for Political Participation

The conventional image of political participation is that of concerned citizens trying to advance their views by engaging in political activity. This is no doubt an accurate picture for some people. However, substantial numbers who are relatively unconcerned about politics nevertheless participate, and substantial numbers of people who are concerned about politics do not participate. Obviously, other factors must also motivate political participation.

Some participation is sparked by *political motivations*. **Political efficacy** is a person's sense of being able to accomplish something politically. It involves judgments both about one's own competence in the political arena (sometimes called internal efficacy) and about the responsiveness of the political system to one's efforts (external efficacy). People with a very strong sense of efficacy are more likely to be politically active than those with a weak sense of efficacy. Other citizens are motivated to become involved by a **sense of duty**. They may care less about the issues or be put off by politics, but they have been socialized to think that good citizens get involved in politics. People with a strong sense of duty are more likely to participate politically than those without it.

Party identification, the psychological attachment that many Americans feel toward a particular political party, also provides a strong impetus for political action. The highest rates of political activity are observed among people with a strong commitment to one or another of the political parties. A person who strongly supports programs advocated by the Democratic Party, for example, will probably work to promote a Democratic victory. Yet someone who sees little difference between the parties and who cares little about issues may not even vote.

Other factors spurring people on to political involvement are essentially nonpolitical or social motivations. Many people engage in political activity for its social rewards: meeting people, making friends, and developing new relationships. People low in self-esteem or lacking in confidence may attempt to bolster their self-image by taking on the social opportunities and challenges that political activity offers. In other cases, concern about an issue may initially mobilize a citizen into political involvement; but even when the concern fades away, the social connection keeps the person going.[53] This is not to say that political activity so inspired is of no political consequence; the labor, the money, or the vote of such a person counts the same as that of the most ideological partisan. Rather, the point is that not all political actions can be understood simply in terms of political motives.

political efficacy

A person's sense of being able to accomplish something politically, an important determinant of political participation

sense of duty

A motivating factor, felt by some citizens, to get involved in politics

party identification

Psychological attachment that a citizen may feel toward a particular political party

5.3b   Forms of Participation

Any American who wants to become politically involved has a broad range of options, from merely scrolling through news headlines occasionally all the way to running for president of the United States. Some of these forms of participation are the focus of other chapters in this book. Participation related to campaigns and elections will be discussed in greater detail in Chapter 8. Much political activity occurs within the framework of interest groups and political parties. These facets of participation will be examined closely in Chapter 7. The rest of this section focuses on some of the most important other ways in which Americans can participate politically.

Following Politics

Just paying attention to politics constitutes a simple form of political participation. For many Americans, politics is—if nothing more—an entertaining spectator sport. As noted earlier in this chapter, about three-quarters of Americans say they follow government and public affairs "most" or "some" of the time. How actively they pursue public affairs is suggested by these statistics: 59 percent of the American people say they watch television news, 72 percent receive news via the internet or on a mobile device, and 20 percent read a printed newspaper.[54]

Contacting Public Officials

One of the most direct ways to convey a political message is to deliver it straight to a politician or governmental authority. Not many Americans do this very often, and the numbers seem to be declining. One study indicates that 23 percent fewer citizens wrote to their legislators between the 1970s and 1990s.[55] Another study shows that while 19 percent of respondents had contacted a public official over the past twelve months, only 14 percent had volunteered for a group or cause, and only 8 percent had attended a public rally or demonstration.[56] So where does all that mail to public officials come from? First, an occasional letter from even a small proportion of a large number of constituents can generate a lot of mail—as the caseworker in almost any congressional office can confirm. Beyond that, it appears that a small group of letter writers writes a large number of letters. One study estimated that two-thirds of all mail to public officials comes from just 3 percent of the population.[57]

Direct, face-to-face contact with members of Congress and other public officials is harder to assess. While less than 20 percent of Americans directly contact public officials about an issue or problem, other approaches can be effective as well.[58] Another standard strategy for contacting public officials is the petition—a right protected by the First Amendment. A petition is a written statement, circulated among and signed by a group of citizens, requesting that the government follow some course of action. About 28 percent of Americans claim that they have signed a petition in the last twelve months.[59] Writing letters and signing petitions have both changed significantly in recent years. As the internet and social media have greatly reduced the costs of circulating and sending such messages, participation has increased.[60]

(Getty Images)

Even simply following political progression online can be a form of political participation.

That being said, the interest in and impact of sending and receiving such messages remain a topic deserving of continued study.

Protests Within and Beyond the Law

Abstract theories of representative democracy and the original Constitution itself focus on the election of representatives as the principal means of communication between citizens and government. The First Amendment to the Constitution—in its guarantees of freedom of speech, assembly, and petition—reminds us of other forms of political expression, however. These guarantees reflect a political tradition in which political protest sometimes assumes an important role and embodies the view that at least some such actions are legitimate.

Political protest can assume many different forms, some of which are discussed below.

- **Marches and rallies** Marches and demonstrations have a long-standing tradition in American politics. Perhaps the most famous example was the great March on Washington in August 1963. This landmark event in the civil rights movement, which brought more than 250,000 peaceful demonstrators to the National Mall, culminated with Dr. Martin Luther King Jr.'s historic "I Have a Dream" speech from the steps of the Lincoln Memorial. The Vietnam War brought numerous marchers to Washington, DC, in the late 1960s and early 1970s. In recent years, protesters have taken to the streets of cities across America and to Washington, DC, in support of movements ranging from Black Lives Matter to #MeToo to both sides of the immigration debate.[61] The summer of 2020 saw thousands of protests across the country demanding police reform and an end to systemic racism in the wake of unarmed African American George Floyd's murder at the hands of police.

- **Boycotts** Boycotts, the refusal of citizens to buy a particular product or use a certain service, are another important tool of protest. In the late 1950s, the refusal of African Americans in the South to ride in the rear of buses exerted economic pressure on municipalities and attracted public attention to their cause. Some 25 percent of people in the US say that they have participated in a boycott in the past 12 months.[62]

- **Picketing** Groups of protesters standing in front of a retail store or office building, placards in hand, are a common sight in the American political scene. One of the most frequent uses of picketing in recent years has been for pro-environmental or animal causes—such as pickets in front of World Trade Organization meetings or protests against human use of animal fur or other inhumane animal treatment.

Protest demonstrations are one of the most visible, though certainly not the most common, forms of political participation in America. Accurate estimates of the extent of protest are notoriously difficult to obtain because people are sometimes reluctant to

Boycotts and protests are examples of political expression.

(a katz/Shutterstock)

admit their participation to researchers. That being said, about 36 percent of Americans say they have felt inclined to join a protest rally, march, or demonstration. This is one area in which younger people are more likely than their older peers to be involved. Another survey shows that only 5 percent of those twenty-six and older have protested in the past year, but 11 percent of those twenty-five and younger have.[63]

Estimates of participation are even more difficult when it comes to actions that involve violence and crime.

- **Political violence** On some occasions, American citizens have engaged in violent outbursts with political connotations. At the very founding of the United States, Massachusetts farmers led by Daniel Shays forced the closing of local and state courts before the rebellion was forcibly put down by the state militia. The antidraft riots of the Civil War, the urban ghetto riots of the 1960s, and the antiwar violence of the Vietnam War era resulted in widespread personal injury and destruction of property for political ends. In the spring of 1992, there was large-scale civil unrest in Los Angeles, following the announcement of not-guilty verdicts in the cases of four police officers accused of brutally beating a young African American motorist, Rodney King. The violent actions resulted in the destruction of more than $500 million in property and the loss of more than ninety lives.

- **Politically motivated crimes** Although riots and other violent outbursts have at least the appearance of spontaneity, other politically relevant acts are clearly premeditated criminal violence. The civil rights movement, in particular, spawned a number of violent reactions: the death of four African American children in a fire-bombed church; the murder of three young civil rights workers—Andrew Goodman, James Chaney, and Michael Schwerner—in Mississippi in 1963; and the assassination of Dr. Martin Luther King Jr. in Memphis in 1968. More recently, an assassination attempt on Congresswoman Gabrielle Giffords (D-AZ) in 2011 left the legislator severely injured.

Many types of political protest are perfectly legal—particularly as long as they do not endanger the well-being of others. Peaceful marches and demonstrations certainly fall into this category. Others are clearly illegal: Most people would probably agree that rioting and assassination fall into the latter category because they destroy both life and property. Nevertheless, the line between legitimate and illegitimate political protest is sometimes hard to define. Further, some acts of political protest, even if illegal, are undertaken on the basis of a moral justification. These are acts of **civil disobedience**—deliberate violations of the law as a means of asserting the illegitimacy of the law or calling attention to a higher moral principle. Civil rights activists in the South in the 1950s and 1960s organized sit-ins at lunch counters and other facilities designated for whites only with the explicit intention of being arrested. They saw such action as a way of calling attention to unjust laws and, more generally, to their unjust treatment.

A related strategy is the practice of **passive resistance**, in which protesters do not actively oppose government, but rather refuse to cooperate by doing nothing. For example, protesters may not struggle with angry white citizens or police, but simply lie down in the face of attack or arrest and force the police to drag them off to the police van and jail. Beginning in September 2011, groups of protesters identifying as part of the Occupy movement began using tactics of civil disobedience to protest a wide range of economic disparities in cities throughout the United States. Dr. Martin Luther King Jr. provided a good explanation of the moral legitimacy of an illegal action in a famous letter that he wrote from a Birmingham, Alabama, jail:

civil disobedience

A form of political protest in which advocates of a cause deliberately break a law as a means of asserting its illegitimacy or drawing attention to their cause

passive resistance

A form of civil disobedience in which protesters do not actively oppose government's attempts to control them, but rather refuse to cooperate by doing nothing—for example, by going limp when police try to pick them up or insisting on being carried to a police van rather than walking

I submit that an individual who breaks a law that conscience tells him is unjust, and willingly accepts the penalty by staying in jail to arouse the conscience of the community over its injustice is in reality expressing the very highest respect for law.

Civil disobedience is thus characterized by a moral justification, a willingness to accept whatever penalty the action incurs, and as a critical element, some would add, an intention to avoid physical harm to others. Only a small proportion of Americans (2 percent) say that they have broken the law in a protest for a political or social cause.[64] That small percentage should not be discouraging, though; one political scientist has concluded that protests involving at least 3.5 percent of a population have always been successful in effecting significant political change.[65] However, civil disobedience is widely recognized as an acceptable strategy in extreme circumstances. When asked whether people should obey the law without exception, or whether there are exceptional occasions on which people should follow their consciences even if it means breaking the law, 42 percent of a national sample supported obeying the law, whereas 57 percent opted for following one's conscience.[66]

(Photo courtesy of Transportation Security Administration via Wikimedia)

One of the most tragic politically motivated crimes that our country has known was the terrorist attacks on September 11, 2001. Strong restrictions placed around air travel were a result of that day.

5.3c Differences in Participation

What determines the forms of political participation in which citizens tend to engage? In a classic study that is probably the most thorough examination of political participation in America yet done, Sidney Verba and Norman Nie identified six categories of citizen participation and determined the kinds of people who fell into each.[67]

- **Inactives** These people, making up about 22 percent of the population, take virtually no part in political life. Lower-status social and economic groups, African Americans, women, the youngest, the oldest, and the least concerned about politics are particularly likely to fall into this category.

- **Voting specialists** About 21 percent of the population do little more politically than vote regularly. This group is distinctive primarily due to its strong sense of partisanship. It seems that some citizens who might otherwise be inactive get firmly attached to a party and that connection is enough to bring them to the polls at most elections.

- **Parochial participants** About 4 percent of the population contact public officials when they have a particular personal problem and seek governmental assistance in solving it. Such activity is more common among lower-status groups, Catholics, and urban dwellers than among higher-status, Protestant, and rural citizens. Such people show little partisan or ideological involvement, but they can sometimes make a difference in what government does.

Are you registered to vote?

You can register using the Election Assistance Commission's National Mail Voter Registration form at this website:

http://www.bvtlab.com/78P86

- **Communalists**   Another 20 percent of the population has little involvement in electoral politics apart from voting, but they do engage in group and community activities with the aim of solving social problems. This group is highly involved in politics but decidedly nonpartisan and nonconflictual in its orientation. This group is very much an upper-status group socially and economically, predominantly white, Protestant, and more small-town and rural than urban.

- **Campaigners**   In sharp contrast to the preceding group, this 15 percent of the population engages in little group activity but much campaign activity. This pattern stems, in part, from a highly partisan and more conflictual orientation to politics. The group tends to be of higher status; African Americans and Catholics are campaigners, as are urban and suburban dwellers.

- **Complete activists**   About 11 percent of the population do it all: voting, contacting, group activities, and campaigning. This is a group highly attuned to politics and predominantly upper-status and middle-age.

While this study's specific data come from a previous generation, the categories it identifies remain very relevant and raise an important question—namely, what difference does it make that different groups tend to participate in different ways? Officials are bombarded with messages from the public and people claiming to represent the public. Public officials have preconceptions and make judgments about the forms of political participation to which they need to be most attentive. Because different kinds of people tend to participate in numerous ways, officials get varying impressions of public opinion depending on the forms of participation to which they pay attention. A senator who focuses on constituency service by reading all the mail from parochial participants will get a different sense of the public's mind than one who hobnobs with campaign workers and financial supporters. The people staging a sit-in in front of a congressional representative's district office have very different things on their minds from those who pulled the lever in the voting booth a couple of Novembers earlier. For politicians assessing public opinion, the medium of participation in large measure determines the message.

(Ebony Magazine, circa 1955, via Wikimedia)

The choice is up to you to follow the law or your own conscience when you feel it is necessary. For example, African American Rosa Parks decided to follow her conscience and did not give up her seat on the bus.

5.3d   The Impact of Political Participation

Does political activity really make any difference? The stereotypical notion of democracy is that the people's wishes become the law of the land. However, the democratic process cannot be that simple. On some issues, many people do not know what they want. Even if they do, they may not be moved to express their preferences via the political process. Politicians—whether they are presidents, Senate or House members, or Supreme Court justices—may be attentive to what the "public" wants, but such preferences are rarely the only factors they take into account. First of all, our nation comprises many publics, not just one. Further, constitutional constraints, legal constraints, budgetary constraints, foreign policy constraints on domestic policy, and domestic policy constraints on foreign policy also impact the decisions government officials can make.

Little wonder, then, that most studies of the relationship between public opinion and public policy have found the connection to be a relatively loose one.[68] Public opinion is usually sufficiently amorphous, officials' perceptions of it sufficiently cloudy, and more tangible pressures sufficiently strong to ensure that officials are not severely constrained by public opinion. When there is a clearly expressed body of opinion on a salient issue, the relationship between public opinion and public policy can be substantial, however.[69] For example, growing public concern over drugs in the late 1980s led politicians to move anti-drug legislation to the top of the agenda. In 1989, the much-publicized oil spill from the tanker *Exxon Valdez* into Prince William Sound on the Alaska coast reenergized the flagging environmental movement and sparked a flurry of environmental legislation in the early 1990s. After a series of energy crises in early 2001, 21 percent of Americans in a nationwide poll mentioned energy as the most important problem facing the country.[70] In the wake of recent terrorist attacks, 46 percent of Americans in an October 2001 poll indicated that terrorism was the most important problem.[71] In 2006, Americans named the Iraq War as the most important problem facing the country.[72] From 2008 through 2012, the struggling economy was the number one concern of the largest number of Americans—but noneconomic concerns began to dominate beginning in 2013. Since then, dissatisfaction with government leadership, immigration, and the economy have jockeyed for position as the top problem for Americans, and by 2018, just 1 percent of Americans named the threat of terrorism as the most important problem.[73] The tumultuous events of 2020 contributed to three issues dominating Americans' minds: poor leadership, COVID-19, and race relations.[74]

In 2011–2012, Americans expressed their dissatisfaction with the wealth disparity, generally—and the financial sector, specifically—via the Occupy movement.

(Joe Tabacca / Shutterstock)

5.3e The Rationality of Political Participation

Does it make sense to participate politically? Over sixty years ago, Anthony Downs pioneered a new field of political analysis in an important and influential book called *An Economic Theory of Democracy*.[75] He examined political activity in terms of the so-called **rational actor model**. In this model, a citizen rationally weighs the costs and the benefits of participating. If the benefits exceed the costs, the citizen participates; if not, the citizen does not. Focusing on voting, Downs pointed out that getting registered, keeping informed, and going to the polls all take a substantial amount of time. The benefits, by contrast, are actually quite low. What politicians from one party or the other actually do after an election may not be very different from what their opponents would have done. Even more important, one individual's vote is very unlikely to determine whether his or her favored candidate wins. These factors make the expected benefit of voting relatively small.

A similar analysis could be made of most other individual political actions. When weighed against the low probability of any benefit, the costs of individual political actions make them appear to be of dubious rationality. One possible exception is what Verba and Nie call *parochial participation*. When focused on a narrow personal objective, and with the expenditure of a fair amount of effort directed toward a particular decision maker,

rational actor model

A perspective that looks at politics as a system in which individuals and organizations pursue their self-interests, defined in terms of costs and benefits, and choose to do those things that give them the greatest benefit at the least cost

the individual may stand a fair chance of achieving success.[76] Collective activities may also be more effective. Joining together allows costs to be shared and resources to be pooled. All other things being equal, many citizens will probably be more influential than one.

Finally, even political protest may prove to be a rational strategy. Minority and dissident groups often lack political clout because they lack resources and thus cannot afford the costs of participation. One political scientist has called this the "problem of the powerless."[77] A rational strategy for such people is to attract the attention of those with resources and draw them into the cause. A minimal expenditure of resources is required to engage in unusual or dramatic activities, such as sit-ins and demonstrations, which call public attention to the plight of the protesters. Such activities constitute, to borrow one apt description, the use of "protest as a political resource."[78]

CHAPTER REVIEW

1. Public opinion is complicated because our nation consists of not one public but many, and because opinion varies over time and in intensity and sophistication. Americans differ widely in their interest in and sophistication about politics; most of them have relatively little day-to-day concern with, knowledge about, or real understanding of what goes on in the political world. Americans do agree on certain basic values. However, they disagree about exactly what many of these values mean in particular circumstances and about political ideology.

2. Political socialization is the process by which young Americans are taught about political life in the United States. Through various processes of socialization, young people acquire the information and the ability to reason about politics. The values that they draw on as political actors are learned from their parents, schools, peers, and the mass media.

3. Americans involve themselves in politics in many ways for a variety of reasons. Involvement can range from simply following politics and voting to intense immersion in campaigns, community activities, or more dramatic forms of participation such as protest marches, sit-ins, and demonstrations. The impact of participation on policy is often weak, however; and much political participation is hard to justify in purely rational terms.

KEY TERMS

agents of socialization 144

civil disobedience 152

party identification 149

passive resistance 152

political efficacy 149

political socialization 143

polling 133

public opinion 132

rational actor model 155

sense of duty 149

READINGS FOR FURTHER STUDY

Classic works on public opinion include Walter Lippmann's *Public Opinion* (New York: Free Press, 1997) and one of the first major reports on survey research into public opinion, *Voting: A Study of Opinion Formation in a Presidential Campaign,* by Bernard R. Berelson, Paul F. Lazarsfeld, and William N. McPhee (Chicago: University of Chicago Press, 1986).

Rosalee A. Clawson and Zoe M. Oxley's *Public Opinion: Democratic Ideals, Democratic Practice,* 4th ed. (Washington, DC: CQ Press, 2020) provides a more recent overview of public opinion, and *Polling and the Public,* 9th ed., by Herbert Asher (Washington, DC: CQ Press, 2016) addresses the more scientific aspects of opinion polls.

Perhaps the major contributor to our understanding of basic American political values is Herbert McClosky, who has written (with Alida Brill) *Dimensions of Tolerance* (New York: Russell Sage, 1983) and (with John Zaller) *The American Ethos* (Cambridge, MA: Harvard University Press, 1984).

Cultivating Democracy: Civic Environments and Political Socialization in America (Washington, DC: Brookings Institute, 2003) by James G. Gimpel, J. Celeste Lay, and Jason E. Schuknecht provides a good overview of the topic of political socialization.

An excellent study of civic engagement in America is Robert D. Putnam, *Bowling Alone* (New York: Touchstone, 2000).

Perhaps the best overall empirical studies of political participation in all its facets are *Political Participation in America: Political Democracy and Social Equality* (New York: Harper & Row, 1987) by Sidney Verba and Norman Nie; *Voice and Equality: Civic Volunteerism in American Politics* (Cambridge, MA: Harvard University Press, 2006) by Sidney Verba, Kay Lehman Schlozman, and Henry Brady; and *The Unheavenly Chorus: Unequal Political Voice and the Broken Promise of American Democracy* (Princeton, NJ: Princeton University Press, 2012) by Kay Lehman Schlozman, Sidney Verba, and Henry E. Brady.

How Americans talk to each other about politics is covered in *Talking Together: Public Deliberation and Political Participation in America* (Chicago: University of Chicago Press, 2009) by Lawrence R. Jacobs, Fay Lomax Cook, and Michael X. Delli Carpini.

NOTES

1. Pew Research Center, "Partisan Antipathy: More Intense, More Personal," October 10, 2019, file:///C:/Users/charl/Downloads/10-10-19 -Parties-report.pdf

2. Pew Research Center, "Election News Pathways November 2019 Survey," https://www.journalism. org/dataset/election-news-pathways-november-2019 -survey/ (June 18, 2020).

3. Marist Poll, "Independence Day—Seventeen Seventy When?," July 1, 2011, http://maristpoll.marist.edu /71-independence-day-dummy-seventeen-seventy -when/print/ (August 7, 2014).

4. The Gallup Organization, "U.S. National Pride Falls to Record Low," June 15, 2020, https://news.gallup.com/poll/312644/national -pride-falls-record-low.aspx?utm_source=alert&utm _medium=email&utm_content=morelink&utm _campaign=syndication.

5. Ibid.

6. David Azerrad, "How Equal Should Opportunities Be?" *National Affairs,* Spring 2020, https://www.nationalaffairs.com/publications/detail /how-equal-should-opportunities-be (June 19, 2020).

7. The Gallup Organization 2016.

8. Herbert McClosky and Alida Brill, *Dimensions of Tolerance: What Americans Believe About Civil Liberties* (New York: Russell Sage Foundation, 1983), pp. 48–135.

9. The Gallup Organization, "Question Profile," November 12, 2003, http://brain.gallup.com /documents/question.aspx?question=146243 (October 10, 2006); Pew Research Center, "5 Ways Americans and Europeans Are Different," April 19, 2016, https://www.pewresearch.org/fact-tank /2016/04/19/5-ways-americans-and-europeans -are-different/ (June 28, 2016).

10. The Gallup Organization, "Coronavirus Pandemic," https://news.gallup.com/poll/308222/coronavirus-pandemic.aspx (June 19, 2020).

11. The Gallup Organization, "In U.S., Support for Daily Prayer in Schools Dips Slightly," September 25, 2014, http://www.gallup.com/poll/177401 (June 28, 2016).

12. American National Election Studies, 2016.

13. Pew Research Center, "2019 Political Survey," March 2019, https://www.people-press.org/2019/04/11/little-public-support-for-reductions-in-federal-spending/ (June 19, 2020).

14. The Gallup Organization, "Government," 2009–2020.

15. The Gallup Organization, "Taxes," April 14, 2020.

16. Ibid. The Gallup Organization, April 10, 2016.

17. The Gallup Organization, "Government," September 15, 2019.

18. American National Election Studies, 2008.

19. NBC News/*Wall Street Journal* Poll, June 20–24, 2012.

20. The Gallup Organization, 2012.

21. The Gallup Organization, 2016.

22. The Gallup Organization, Presidential Approval Ratings," June 4, 2020.

23. The Gallup Organization, "Government," 2019.

24. The Gallup Organization, 2007.

25. The Gallup Organization, "Race Relations," 2016, 2018.

26. For perhaps the most thorough analysis of the gap between support for freedom of speech in the abstract and support for it in particular situations, see McClosky and Brill, *Dimensions of Tolerance*, (New York: Russell Sage Foundation, 1983) pp. 48–58.

27. National Opinion Research Center, General Social Survey, 2012, http://www3.norc.org/GSS+Website/Browse+GSS+Variables/Subject+Index/ (July 23, 2012).

28. The Gallup Organization, 2006.

29. The Gallup Organization, "Terrorism in the United States," 2016.

30. James W. Prothro and Charles M. Grigg, "Fundamental Principles of Democracy," *Journal of Politics 22* (1960): 276–294; YouGov, February 20, 2014, "Should Only Taxpayers Have a Vote?" February 20, 2014, https://today.yougov.com/news/2014/02/20/should-only-taxpayers-have-vote/ (August 14, 2014).

31. CNN/*Essence Magazine*/Opinion Research Corporation Poll, April 2008.

32. The Gallup Organization, "Confidence in Institutions," 2019.

33. *USA Today*/Gallup Poll, August 27–30, 2010.

34. The Gallup Organization, 2018.

35. Eric R. A. N. Smith, *The Unchanging American Voter* (Berkeley: University of California Press, 1989), pp. 56–58.

36. American National Election Studies, 2016; The Gallup Organization, "Gallup Poll Social Series: Values and Beliefs," 2020.

37. The path-breaking study on attitude consistency, in particular, and mass political ideology, more generally, is Philip Converse's "The Nature of Belief Systems in Mass Publics," in David Apter, ed., *Ideology and Discontent* (New York: Free Press, 1964). For perhaps the best overview of the long and complicated series of challenges and counterchallenges to Converse's work over the last twenty-five years, see Smith, *The Unchanging American Voter*.

38. American National Election Survey, 1988.

39. Angus Campbell, Philip E. Converse, Warren E. Miller, and Donald E. Stokes, *The American Voter* (New York: Wiley, 1960); Norman H. Nie, Sidney Verba, and John R. Petrocik, *The Changing American Voter*, enlarged ed. (Cambridge, MA: Harvard University Press, 1979).

40. Nie, Verba, and Petrocik, *The Changing American Voter*.

41. The best summary of, and most substantial contribution to, this recent research is Smith, *The Unchanging American Voter*. On the role of political rhetoric, see especially pp. 45–104.

42. Robert D. Hess and Judith V. Torney, *The Development of Political Attitudes in Children* (Garden City, NY: Doubleday/Anchor Books, 1967), pp. 24–26, offer a good overview of psychological theories of socialization.

43. M. Kent Jennings and Richard Niemi, *Generations and Politics* (Princeton, NJ: Princeton University Press, 1981), pp. 76–114.

44. David C. Bricker, *Classroom Life as Civic Education* (New York: Teachers College Press, 1989) provides a discussion of some of these issues.

45. Theodore M. Newcomb, "Persistence and Regression of Changed Attitudes: Long-Range Studies," *Journal of Social Issues 19* (1963): 3–14.

46. Fred I. Greenstein, *Children and Politics* (New Haven, CT: Yale University Press, 1965).

47. Roberta S. Sigel, ed., *Political Learning in Adulthood* (Chicago: University of Chicago Press, 1989) provides a good overview of adult political socialization and research on the topic.

48. The Gallup Organization, "Race Relations," 2020, http://www.gallup.com/poll/1687/Race-Relations (June 28, 2020).

49. CBS NEWS, "Americans' Views Shift on Racial Discrimination," June 4, 2020, https://www.cbsnews.com/news/racial-discrimination-americans-views-shift-cbs-news-poll/?utm_source=link_newsv9&utm_campaign=item_312590&utm_medium=copy (June 28, 2020).

50. The Gallup Organization, "Implications of Inequitable Policing in Fragile Communities," June 16, 2020, https://news.gallup.com/opinion/gallup/312707/implications-inequitable-policing-fragile-communities.aspx (June 28, 2020).

51. See, for example, Fred L. Greenstein, "Sex-Related Political Differences in Childhood," *Journal of Politics* 23 (1961): 353–371.

52. Ethel Klein, *Gender Politics* (Cambridge, MA: Harvard University Press, 1984), pp. 117–119.

53. Samuel J. Eldersveld, *Political Parties: A Behavioral Analysis* (Chicago: Rand McNally, 1964), pp. 290–292.

54. Reuters Institute for the Study of Journalism, "Digital News Report 2020," (June 28, 2020).

55. Robert D. Putnam, *Bowling Alone* (New York: Touchstone, 2000), p. 45.

56. PPRI/The Atlantic 2018 Civic Engagement Survey, https://www.prri.org/research/american-democracy-in-crisis-civic-engagement-young-adult-activism-and-the-2018-midterm-elections/ (June 28, 2020).

57. Philip E. Converse, Aage R. Clausen, and Warren E. Miller, "Electoral Myth and Reality: The 1964 Election," *American Political Science Review 59* (June 1965): 321–336.

58. PPRI/The Atlantic 2018 Civic Engagement Survey, https://www.prri.org/research/american-democracy-in-crisis-civic-engagement-young-adult-activism-and-the-2018-midterm-elections/ (June 28, 2020).

59. Ibid.

60. See American National Election Study, 2016.

61. The Gallup Organization, "One in Three Americans Have Felt Urge to Protest," August 24, 2018.

62. PPRI/The Atlantic 2018 Civic Engagement Survey, https://www.prri.org/research/american-democracy-in-crisis-civic-engagement-young-adult-activism-and-the-2018-midterm-elections/ (June 28, 2020).

63. Lopez et al (2006).

64. Norman Ornstein, Andrew Kohut, and Larry McCarthy, *The People, the Press, and Politics: The Times Mirror Study of the American Electorate* (Boston: Addison-Wesley, 1988).

65. Chenowith, Erica. "The Success of Nonviolent Civil Resistance," November 2013, https://www.nonviolent-conflict.org/resource/success-nonviolent-civil-resistance/ (June 28, 2020).

66. International Social Survey Program: Role of Government III, 1996.

67. Sidney Verba and Norman Nie, *Political Participation in America: Political Democracy and Social Equality* (Chicago: University of Chicago Press, 1987), pp. 56–81. If a particular characteristic is not mentioned, the group is about average for that characteristic.

68. Perhaps the most famous study is Warren E. Miller and Donald E. Stokes, "Constituency Influence in Congress," *American Political Science Review 57* (1963): 45–56.

69. Benjamin L. Page and Robert Y. Shapiro, "Effects of Public Opinion on Policy," *American Political Science Review 77* (1983): 175–190, show how changes in public policy between 1935 and 1979 in the United States related to changes in public opinion, particularly when there were large and enduring changes in public opinion on salient issues.

70. The Gallup Organization, 2001.

71. Ibid.

72. The Gallup Organization, 2006.

73. The Gallup Organization, 2008–2018.

74. The Gallup Organization, "Most Important Problem," 2020.

75. New York: Harper & Row, 1957.

76. Verba and Nie, *Political Participation in America*, pp. 104–106.

77. James Q. Wilson, "The Strategy of Protest: Problems of Negro Civic Action," *Journal of Conflict Resolution* 3 (September 1961): 291.

78. Michael Lipsky, "Protest as a Political Resource," *American Political Science Review 62* (1968): 1144.

POP QUIZ

1. Although Americans profess a belief in equality, they seem to lean away from equality of _____ .

2. Groups of people, roughly equal in social position, that interact with one another are called _____

   _____ .

3. _____ is a person's sense of being able to accomplish something politically.

4. According to the _____

   _____ the expected benefit of voting is relatively small.

5. Americans tend to support equality of opportunity over equality of result.   T   F

6. The effect of school as an agent of political socialization is sudden and dynamic as the child enters grade school.   T   F

7. Once in school, children tend to become less partisan.   T   F

8. The highest rates of political activity are among people with a strong commitment to a political party.   T   F

9. Most studies have shown a strong relationship between public opinion and public policy.   T   F

10. A recent survey found that a plurality of the public says they follow government and public affairs _____ .
    A)   most of the time
    B)   some of the time
    C)   only now and then
    D)   hardly at all

11. In recent years, American public opinion has done which of the following?
    A)   shifted to the right
    B)   shifted to the left
    C)   stayed essentially centrist
    D)   has become less ideologically oriented

12. Which of the following best describes the first political thoughts acquired by a small child?
    A)   a psychological attachment to America
    B)   a primitive sense of party identification
    C)   a sense of external authority above parental authority
    D)   all of the above

13. Acts of civil disobedience have been justified on the basis of _____ .
    A)   legality
    B)   effectiveness
    C)   morality
    D)   popularity

14. According to Verba and Nie, the category of citizen participation that comprises about 4 percent of the population; consists of mainly lower-status groups, Catholics, and urban dwellers; and shows little partisan or ideological involvement is _____ .
    A)   inactives
    B)   parochial participants
    C)   communalists
    D)   campaigners

15. According to the rational actor model, which of the following activities would be considered the most rational and effective form of political participation?
    A)   voting
    B)   letter writing to public officials
    C)   collective activities
    D)   political assassination

Answers:
1. result   2. peer groups   3. Political efficacy
4. rational actor model   5. T   6. F   7. T
8. T   9. F   10. B   11. A   12. D
13. C   14. B   15. C

Chapter

06

(Getty Images)

POLITICS & THE MEDIA

In This Chapter

6.1   The "Fifth Branch"
6.2   Politics and the Press
6.3   Tools of the Trade: Politicians and the "Fifth Branch"
6.4   Are the Media Biased?

Chapter Objectives

Most of the chapters in this book focus on political institutions and leaders and the things they do. This chapter, however, focuses on part of US corporate life called the "mass media." Of special interest are journalists: people who gather, write, edit, report, and produce the news that people read in newspapers, hear on the radio, watch on television, and browse on the internet. So, while the previous chapter addressed the opinions people in the US hold, this chapter focuses on the sources of information that often lead us to form those opinions.

Of course, nobody votes for journalists. They are not public officials. They do not make laws. They do not work for the government. So why do the mass media rate a chapter in a book on American government? The mass media have a chapter all to themselves because newspapers, radio, television, and the internet matter politically. In carving out a specific guarantee for freedom of the press, the First Amendment of the Constitution gives a strong hint that the news media are supposed to matter.

They are the means by which much political information and many political ideas reach the people in the US. They often provide the forums for clashes between ideologies. In short, they help to define political reality for the nation. Understanding the business of print and electronic journalism is now a necessary part of understanding American government.

The job of the White House press secretary is to move information in two directions—from the president to the people and from the people to the president. Kayleigh McEnany, Donald Trump's fourth press secretary, regularly stood before the White House press corps (a select group of respected **journalists**) to describe the president's actions and answer questions, a tradition that continues in the Biden presidency. The press secretary is also responsible for informing and updating the executive branch of the government on the news stories being reported in the press. Few in the White House, on Capitol Hill, or in any statehouse or city hall are unconcerned about or uninterested in the news business. All want to know what has become news and how others have reacted to the news.

Political leaders since George Washington's time have known that access to knowledge and control of communication matter in a democracy. Essential to both today are the **mass media**: newspapers, magazines, radio, television, and the internet. The word *media* in this context refers to the *means* of communication with large numbers of people. In recent years, this has also meant taking a leading role in the development of new media—such as cable and satellite television and radio, websites, and video streaming via the internet. Growing numbers of Americans get up-to-the-minute news via social media and smartphone-based applications. The media now offer people in the US rapid access to large amounts of news about public affairs. Indeed, the distribution of news and opinions is so important that the press occupies a special place in the constitutional system.

6.1 The "Fifth Branch"

The press is sometimes called the **fifth branch** of government—after Congress, the president, the Supreme Court, and the bureaucracy. This classification reflects the fact that the mass media can serve as an additional check on the powers of public officials through their discovery and coverage of news and commentary on events. However, because the media are mainly businesses that exist to make money, it is essential to know something about these commercial enterprises. Like government, the news media have changed greatly over the course of the past two centuries.

6.1a The Dynamics of an Industry

Newspapers have been part of American culture since early colonial days. In an era during which news could travel only as fast as the fastest horse, these were four-page weeklies with type painstakingly set by hand. It was through the medium of these early papers that news about skirmishes with the British at Lexington and Concord and copies of the Declaration of Independence circulated up and down the eastern seaboard in 1775 and 1776. Publication of *The Federalist* and much of the rest of the debate over ratification of the Constitution, discussed in Chapter 2, took place in the press.

Telegraphy, larger and faster presses, lower unit production costs, and improved literacy made possible the rapid growth of newspapers in the nineteenth century. The "penny press" (named for its price) became the main contact for many Americans with events around the nation and the world. No doubt the intensity of feeling about slavery

journalists

People who gather, write, and report the news for newspapers, magazines, radio, television, and the internet

mass media

Instruments such as newspapers, magazines, radio, television, and the internet that provide the means for communicating with large numbers of people in a short period of time

fifth branch

Refers to the press in its role as a check on public officials, after the other four branches (Congress, the president, the Supreme Court, and the bureaucracy)

and secession, in both the North and South, on the eve of the Civil War was due in part to the pervasiveness of the press. Growth of the industry later opened the door to the increased political influence of publishers and editors such as Joseph Pulitzer and William Randolph Hearst.

(Shutterstock)

Yet eighteenth- and nineteenth-century newspapers were distant cousins in size and circulation to today's computer-composed, mass-produced daily papers that frequently fill one hundred pages or more, contain news and photographs transmitted digitally, and have accompanying websites that allow Americans to read the "paper" on their e-readers and smartphones. As Table 6.1 suggests, print journalism has experienced changes brought about by advances in technology; altered lifestyles; competition from television, radio, and the internet; and other economic forces. A typical trend over the past several years for many leading newspapers has been declining print circulation accompanied by increases in digital circulation—though the latter can be difficult to quantify consistently.[1]

Table 6.1 American Daily Newspapers Since 1900

Daily newspaper circulation since 1990 has decreased even as the population has increased. Only about one-quarter of US households seem to have regular access to a daily print or digital newspaper. The 2020 figures include newspapers in both their print and digital forms.

Year	Number of Daily Papers	Circulation	Circulation as Percentage of Number of Households*
1900	2,226	15,102,000	95
1920	2,042	27,791,000	114
1930	1,942	39,589,000	132
1940	1,878	41,132,000	118
1950	1,772	53,829,000	124
1960	1,763	58,882,000	112
1970	1,748	62,108,000	99
1980	1,745	62,200,000	77
1990	1,611	62,300,000	67
2000	1,480	55,800,000	53
2010	1,382	44,421,000	38
2020	1,141	28,600,000	22

* A "household" is the Census Bureau's term for a living unit.

DATA SOURCES: Bureau of the Census, Statistical Abstract of the United States; Pew Research Center, State of the News Media 2019; Editor & Publisher International Yearbook, Library of Congress Newspaper Directory, 2020.

Magazines are another form of print journalism that became popular in the nineteenth century. Over ten thousand periodicals other than newspapers are published in the United States, with a growing number available digitally. While most are small or have little to do with public affairs, political news and opinion are the main content of many. Mass circulation weekly news magazines—in print or digital form—include *Time* and *Newsweek*. Others, such as *Washington Monthly, The American Prospect,* and *National Review* (described in Chapter 4) are journals of opinion and target different political audiences. While nearly all major print magazines also have a web presence, other magazines—such as *Slate, HuffPost,* and *Salon*—are found only on the internet and have never existed in print form.

The year 1920 marked the beginning of radio as a mass medium. Within a decade, as Table 6.2 shows, radios were common household appliances. Only 30 radio stations were transmitting in 1922, but that number grew to 556 in 1923.[2] Not far behind was television; its astonishing growth since 1950 now permits almost all households to be served by many stations. Thanks to cable, satellite, and streaming systems, many homes now have hundreds of stations from which to choose.

Beginning in the 1970s, cable services developed. They did not transmit over the air, like ordinary television stations had; instead, they transmitted by satellite directly to cable companies in hundreds of cities and towns. Over the past fifty years cable, digital satellite, and other subscription services have drastically changed the way Americans view television. Rather than offering only local stations and a few large networks for free, subscription television now provides access to hundreds of stations broadcast from around the world and serves interests ranging from the very broad to the quite narrow.

(lev radin/Shutterstock)

The Daily Show with Trevor Noah is a primary source for political communication to young adults today.

All American television programming completed the switch from analog to digital delivery in 2009. This transition, prompted by the government's Federal Communications Commission and federal law, provides a much more efficient delivery format. Today, while a majority of households are equipped with some type of paid premium service like cable, a growing number subscribe to streaming services (like Netflix or Hulu) either in addition to or in place of cable.

In recent years, the growth of cable has produced several new networks devoted exclusively to news. CNN, MSNBC, CNBC, and Fox News have become worldwide sources for news. Many world leaders, including American presidents, have been known to tune in to these stations, especially when following critical events as they unfold at almost any point on the globe. For example, millions of Americans—including many political leaders—watched the coverage on these news networks nearly around the clock on September 11, 2001, in a search for answers regarding terrorist attacks on the World Trade Center and Pentagon. Government agencies sometimes find cable news a more accurate source of timely information than their own official sources. That so many leaders might rely on the same source at the same time could have a major impact in the management of international crises and in other situations calling for rapid decision-making.

Table 6.2   Growth of Radio and Television in the United States

Nearly half of all American households owned a radio set by 1930, enabling Franklin Roosevelt to become the first "media president." Although World War II delayed the commercial development of television, TV sets are now more common in US homes than refrigerators. The average number of television sets in each American home is 2.8.

(A) Radio

Year	Number of AM Stations	Number of FM Stations	Households with at Least One Radio Set (%)
1922	30	0	0.2
1930	618	0	46.0
1940	847	3	82.8
1950	2,144	753	94.0
1960	3,483	906	95.0
1970	4,288	2,542	99.0
1980	4,689	4,546	99.9
1990	4,977	5,694	99.9
2000	4,783	5,766	99.9
2010	4,786	9,717	99.9
2020	4,570	10,903	99.9

(B) Television

Year	Number of TV Stations*	Households with at Least One TV Set (%)
1950	104	9
1960	626	87
1970	881	95
1980	1,132	98
1990	1,446	98
2000	1,585	98
2010	1,784	98
2020	1,758	98

* Includes commercial and educational stations on VHF and UHF channels.

SOURCES: Bureau of the Census, Statistical Abstract of the United States; Federal Communications Commission.

The impact of cable and satellite television continues to be felt. The proliferation of channels, along with the widespread use of DVD players and subscription streaming-video on-demand services like Netflix and Hulu, is the major reason that the share of the viewing audience claimed by the major broadcast networks (NBC, ABC, CBS, and Fox) has declined steadily. By 2001, cable network news had surpassed the broadcast networks, claiming nearly 60 percent of the total news audience. Today, just over half of Americans say either cable or network television is their main source of news.[3]

As a result of the phenomenal growth of the video industry, television has largely displaced radio as a major source of news. Except for a few all-news stations, the radio industry invests little in national news reporting beyond providing a headline service interspersed in music and talk shows. Indeed, television has surpassed the newspaper as the primary source of national news for most Americans, although newspapers remain the main source for local news.

The average American spends seventy minutes a day with some form of news media. Thirty-two of those minutes are spent watching television news, fifteen are spent listening to the radio, ten are spent reading a print newspaper, and thirteen are spent getting news online.[4] The internet is the news source growing fastest in popularity; in 2016, 65 percent of Americans said they had learned news about the presidential election from digital sources.[5] Of course, when topics beyond just the news are considered, television is the clear winner. The average American watches almost three hours of television per day.[6] Over 98 percent of households have at least one television, and over 80 percent of Americans view television on any given day.[7]

Most Americans get at least some news on a daily basis. Of Americans who regularly consume news, 44 percent prefer listening to news on the television, 24 percent prefer getting news from a news website or application, 14 percent prefer listening to news on the radio, 10 percent prefer getting news from a social media site such as Facebook, and 7 percent prefer reading news in a print newspaper.[8] Easy access to information and entertainment, however, does not guarantee attentiveness to public affairs. While young Americans from 1941 to 1975 knew as much about issues and followed major news events as closely as their elders, this is no longer the case. Younger people are now far less attentive to public affairs. Even though someone who is twenty-one years old is more likely than someone who is fifty years old to have used a computer, to have gone to college, or to currently be reading a book, the younger individual is likely to be substantially less aware of current events and public figures. As Table 6.3 suggests, one implication of such differences is that Americans in different age groups may be consuming different types of news. Older Americans are the most likely to be aware of events reported on televised news, whereas younger Americans are more likely to be aware of news reported online.

6.1b   The Constitutional Basis of the Press

It is not by chance that the media count politically. The Constitution confers on journalists explicit recognition and protection: "Congress shall make no law," the First Amendment declares, "abridging the freedom of ... the press." This restraint has also applied to state and local governments since 1931.[9] As explained in Chapter 3, aside from obscenity and libel, prevailing interpretations of the Constitution by the Supreme Court tolerate almost no restrictions on the content of what editors decide to publish. "A free press is indispensable to the workings of our democratic society," Justice Felix Frankfurter (1939–1962) once declared. The point to remember is that the Constitution creates the *opportunity* for the press to play an active role in public affairs. What the role actually becomes, however, is left up to reporters, editors, and publishers—and to their readers and viewers.

Table 6.3 News Consumption "Yesterday" and Most Common News Source

Younger Americans read newspapers and watch news on television less than older Americans. Younger Americans also "consume" such news far less regularly than they did a few decades ago. In the category of internet news usage, however, Americans under fifty seem to be leading the way. The first four columns refer to news consumption on the previous day, while the last refers to most common source of news.

Read a Newspaper Yesterday/ Most Common	1960	1990	2000	2015	2020
All respondents 21 and older*	71%	44%	46%	20%	3%
Under 35**	67%	30%	29%	8%	1%
35–49***	73%	44%	43%	14%	2%
50+	74%	55%	58%	37%	5%

Watched TV News Yesterday/ Most Common	1960	1990	2000	2015	2020
All respondents 21 and older*	55%	53%	55%	52%	45%
Under 35**	52%	41%	44%	37%	18%
35–49***	52%	49%	51%	46%	34%
50+	62%	67%	67%	60%	65%

Read News Online or Digitally Yesterday/ Most Common	1960	1990	2000	2015	2020
All respondents 21 and older*	--	--	33%	51%	43%
Under 34**	--	--	46%	61%	74%
34–49***	--	--	37%	51%	53%
50+	--	--	20%	39%	23%

* For the years 2015 and 2020, the age range for this category is 18 and older.

** For the years 2000 and 2020, the age range for this category is under 30; for 2015, it is under 34.

*** For the year 2000, the age range for this category is 34–49; for 2020 it is 30–49.

DATA SOURCES: The Age of Indifference: A Study of Young Americans and How They View the News (Washington, DC: Times Mirror Center for The People & The Press, 1990), p. 20; The Pew Research Center for the People and the Press, "In Changing News Landscape, Even Television Is Vulnerable," September 27, 2012, http://www.people-press.org/files/legacy-pdf/2012%20News%20 Consumption%20Report.pdf; U.S. Census Bureau, Statistical Abstract of the United States, 2008; The Pew Research Center, State of the News Media 2016; The Pew Research Center, American News Pathways Project, 2020, Copyright 2020 Pew Research Center.

Protection of the press from most governmental restraints is necessary because its involvement with "the workings of our democratic society" guarantees conflict between journalists and government. "Politics and media are inseparable," veteran CBS correspondent Walter Cronkite observed. "It is only the politicians and the media that are incompatible."[10] The First Amendment anticipates a common failing: the tendency to attempt to silence those who criticize or disagree. In personal relations, this tendency may only be annoying; in political relations between leaders and citizens, it can prove deadly to democracy.

6.1c   The Federal Communications Commission

While the news media enjoy constitutionally protected freedom, some of the media are freer than others. This is because electronic journalism operates under legal restraints that do not (and could not constitutionally) apply to print journalism.

With the development of radio early in the twentieth century, the nation faced a choice. Table 6.4 shows how the political implications of the new medium, soon followed by television, became apparent. The new medium could be left to grow almost unregulated, like newspapers; or it could be operated mainly by government, as is done now in most places in the world

The Federal Communications Commission is responsible for regulating the mass media. You can read about the agency's latest activities and its current priorities at its website:

http://www.bvtlab.com/79F8H

(France and Great Britain, for example) even where some privately owned stations are permitted. Because of the ideological preference for free enterprise, public ownership in the United States was never a serious possibility. Because of the potential for chaos on the airwaves, complete freedom for broadcasters was unacceptable as well. Congress chose a middle route of private ownership under government supervision.

Table 6.4   Radio, Television, the Internet, and Politics: Milestones

Commercial radio has been part of American culture since the 1920s. Television became widespread after World War II ended in 1945. The internet emerged as an important news source in the 1990s. All three media are politically important today.

1920   KDKA in Pittsburgh announces election results in the presidential race between Warren Harding and James Cox.

1923   President Calvin Coolidge's opening address to Congress is broadcast by a series of radio stations, linked by telephone lines, as far west as Dallas.

1927   Congress establishes the Federal Radio Commission, assuring private ownership of the broadcast industry, with government regulation.

1928   General Electric Co. and the Radio Corporation of America begin experimental television transmissions.

1933   President Franklin Roosevelt delivers his first "fireside chat" to Americans via radio.

1934   Congress establishes the Federal Communications Commission, replacing the Federal Radio Commission.

1939   NBC begins limited regular television programming.

1940   The Democratic and Republican conventions are televised.

1943   The FCC requires NBC to sell its second ("blue") network, which becomes ABC.

1947   President Harry Truman's State of the Union message is the first complete presidential address transmitted on television.

1948   President Truman is the first to sit in the White House and watch his opponent nominated on television.

1949   The FCC introduces the fairness doctrine.

1951   The Supreme Court rules that movies qualify for First Amendment protection.

1952   Richard Nixon's "Checkers speech" on television helps convince Dwight Eisenhower to keep him as his running mate; the Republican Party makes first use of TV commercials in a presidential campaign.

1960   Candidates John Kennedy and Richard Nixon meet in the first televised debate between presidential candidates.

1961   President Kennedy institutionalizes "live" televised White House press conferences.

1963   Evening network news programs expand from fifteen to thirty minutes.

1964   Television networks call the results of the presidential election between President Lyndon Johnson and Senator Barry Goldwater before the polls have closed on the West Coast.

1965   The networks provide regular coverage of the Vietnam fighting on the evening news; first regular transmission of television signals via satellite begins.

1979   U.S. House of Representatives approves live television coverage of its sessions (now carried on C-SPAN, a cable channel).

1980   Cable News Network (CNN)—a twenty-four-hour, all-news, cable-only service—begins operation.

1984   TV networks cease "gavel-to-gavel" coverage of presidential nominating conventions.

1986   U.S. Senate approves television coverage of its sessions.

1987   The FCC repeals the fairness doctrine.

1991   Live media coverage of the Persian Gulf War allows Americans a view of the conflict as it unfolds.

1996   Congress passes the Communications Decency Act to regulate internet content. (It was later held unconstitutional, in part, by the Supreme Court.)

2003   Over half of all American households have access to the internet.

2009   All broadcast television stations in the United States stop analog use and begin broadcasting only in a digital format.

2017   The FCC votes to repeal net neutrality rules, which had prevented service provider companies from charging differential rates for internet access or slowing access speeds.

2019   Federal courts rule that FCC cannot stop state and local government efforts to enforce net neutrality.

2020   President Trump signs executive order that attempts to remove internet corporations of legal immunity when regulating content on their platforms.

POLITICS AND ECONOMICS

Media Monopolies?

America today teems with information. As Table 6.1 and Table 6.2 suggest, print and electronic media are within easy reach of almost everyone. However as depicted in Figure 6.1, multiple outlets do not themselves ensure diversity of news and opinion. Indeed, *concentration* is the word that best applies to the mass media today. This economic reality raises questions about the role of the media in a democratic political system.

Most newspapers and radio and television stations rely on relatively few sources of national and international news. Wire services such as the Associated Press and United Press International are indispensable for daily newspapers and for locally produced newscasts. They are often the only sources for news of statewide interest. Only the largest newspapers maintain reporters in Washington, state capitals, and abroad as independent sources. The largest television audiences belong to the more than seven hundred commercial stations affiliated with one of the four major broadcast networks: ABC, CBS, Fox, and NBC. Public television stations—funded by private contributions, state appropriations, and since 1967 the federally chartered and congressionally supported Corporation for Public Broadcasting—divide a much smaller audience. Network programming

---

Figure 6.1   Channels Receivable per TV Household

In 2000, some 69 percent of American households with television sets could receive 26 or more channels. By 2019, the average home received 192 channels, despite regularly watching only 13 of them.

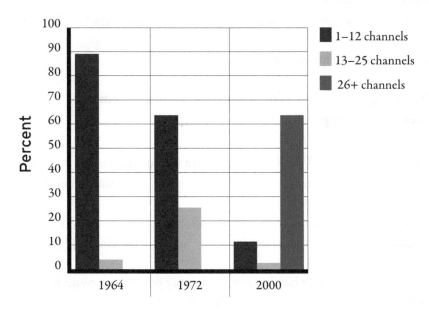

DATA SOURCES: Pew Research Center for the People & the Press; MediaDailyNews, "Forget Cord-Cutting—Nielsen Data Reveals Americans Are Cutting TV Channels, Too," July 30, 2019, https://www.mediapost.com/publications/article/338728/forget-cord-cutting-nielsen-data-reveals-american.html.

typically accounts for about 65 percent of a local station's airtime, with much of the rest consisting of reruns of discontinued network shows.

Among newspapers, competition for reporting news and setting advertising rates has all but disappeared in many sections of the nation. Today, only a dozen or so American cities have separately owned and fully competitive daily newspapers, compared to 502 cities in 1923.

Chain ownership is quickly dominating the newspaper, radio, and television business. Locally owned newspapers and television and radio stations may soon be a thing of the past. Media mergers over the past two decades mean that today just six corporations control 90 percent of the media in America.[1] In 2020, the five largest media companies earned more money than the next ninety largest companies combined. Comcast, Disney, and Netflix alone accounted for well over $200 billion in sales revenue.[2] This consolidation trend is not limited to traditional media. Even the internet has not escaped the move toward mega-media corporations. Between 1999 and 2001, the number of companies controlling 60 percent of online time shrank from 110 down to only 14.[4] Since then, the consolidation of broadband services with cable companies—symbolized by the merger of Charter and Time Warner Cable in 2016 and the subsequent acquisition of Time Warner by AT&T (which rebranded it WarnerMedia)—has led to worries about a lack of competitive pricing and options.[5] Some media corporations own several outlets of the same type—newspapers or television stations. Many stress cross-media ownership, combining newspapers, radio, television, cable, and internet services. WarnerMedia, for example, owns hundreds of magazine publishing companies (DC Comics, *Sports Illustrated*), cable and broadcast television stations (HBO, CNN, CW), and film companies (DC Entertainment, Warner Bros.). Disney owns the ABC network, television stations, radio stations, book and magazine publishing companies, and cable channels.[6]

This consolidation disturbs many Americans. In a 2019 survey, 92 percent of respondents said that they would be very or somewhat concerned about the political views of the owners influencing the fairness of coverage if a large company purchased their local news organization.[7] The government has taken at least some steps to assuage these fears. Aside from antitrust restraints, which apply to all businesses, additional limitations on media concentrations come in the form of regulations issued by the Federal Communications Commission. The most significant of these limitations include rules that prevent a single company's stations from reaching more than 35 percent of viewers and prevent a single company from owning more than one of the four major networks; a rule limiting the number of television stations a company can own across the country; and rules limiting the number of media sources (radio, TV, and newspaper) a company can own in a single market.[8]

Alongside these restrictions is the growth of satellite and cable television and the more recent addition of streaming services, with the former now serving 65 percent of American households and the latter, 69 percent.[9] Satellites decrease the cost of transmitting news over vast distances and increase a local station's news sources. Aside from one of the four major networks, a station may have a contract with CNN, may receive "feeds" direct from government agencies, and may exchange stories with other local stations. For viewers, cable television at first glance means greater choice; yet many of the cable channels are themselves owned by the media conglomerates. Streaming services are becoming even more popular, as they often provide more tailored options for a smaller monthly fee, rather than packages of dozens of channels at a larger price tag, but they are quickly consolidating as well.

If concentrations in ownership are easy to measure, their effects are not. One view argues that an information conglomerate's "most powerful influence … is the power to appoint media leaders" such as editors, producers, and publishers.[10] To what degree does the economic reality of media corporations tend to decrease the diversity of news and opinion that Americans read, see, and hear? Does concentration of ownership increase the political power of these corporations?

1. Ashley Lutz, "These 6 Corporations Control 90% of the Media in America," *Business Insider,* June 14, 2012.

2. "The World's Largest Media Companies of 2020," *Forbes* (May 13, 2020).

3. Ben H. Bagdikian. *The New Media Monopoly,* 7th ed. (Boston: Beacon Press, 2004).

4. Press Release, *Jupiter Media Metrix,* June 4, 2001.

5. "Bye, Bye Time Warner Cable. Hello Charter," CNN.com, May 18, 2016.

6. "Who Owns What," *Columbia Journalism Review,* http://www.cjr.org/owners/ (February 24, 2015).

7. The Gallup Organization, "When It Comes to Local News Mergers, Bias Top Concern," August 15, 2019.

8. Yochi J. Dreazen, "FCC Will Simultaneously Review All of Its Media-Ownership Rules," *Wall Street Journal,* June 18, 2002, http://online.wsj.com /article_email/0SB1024 337625179502320.html.

9. Chris Brantner, "More Americans Now Pay For Streaming Services Than Cable TV," *Forbes,* March 20, 2019, https://www.forbes.com /sites/chrisbrantner/2019/03/20 /americans-now-pay-more-for -streaming-services-than-cable -tv/#22dfff39fcdd (July 13, 2020).

10. Bagdikian, *The New Media Monopoly.*

Initial regulation was in the hands of the Department of Commerce, but Congress created the Federal Radio Commission in 1927 with the power to issue station licenses, allocate frequencies, and fix transmitting power. Present regulation of all wired and wireless communication, including transmission via satellite, is the responsibility of the **Federal Communications Commission (FCC)**, established in 1934 as the successor to the Radio Commission. The FCC has broad rule-making authority, which it has employed to require radio and television stations to operate "in the public interest." For instance, stations are limited in the number of commercials that may be broadcast per hour; a certain amount of time must be set aside for public service and public affairs programming, and obscenity and "filthy words" are prohibited.[11] The justification for such governmental intrusion has been that frequencies (and therefore the number of stations) are finite and that the airwaves are public property.[12]

Today, the FCC is composed of five commissioners appointed by the president and confirmed by the Senate for seven-year terms. Since the 1970s, the FCC has moved toward less regulation of radio and television, adopting the view that the marketplace and not the commissioners should dictate development of the industry, with the commission confining itself to licensing stations, assigning frequencies, and policing their use. Among the regulations, two have been very significant for news reporting.

6.1d The Equal-Time Rule

The **equal-time rule**, from section 315 of the Communications Act of 1934, requires stations to give or sell time to one political candidate if the station has given or sold time to another candidate for the same office. The time must not only be equal in length but must also be at a similar time of the day. A station cannot give a candidate for school board five minutes of airtime at 8:00 a.m. and then relegate an opponent to 2:30 a.m. During the 1980 and 1984 presidential campaigns, for example, television stations had to cease showing old movies starring Ronald Reagan. That would have amounted to free time, which could have been demanded in equal quantities by his Democratic opponents, Jimmy Carter and Walter Mondale. In 1984 the FCC decided that the rule does not apply to televised debates among candidates, thus allowing a station to invite some candidates and not others. This ruling allowed networks to invite only former vice president Joe Biden and incumbent president Donald Trump to the 2020 presidential debates, despite protestations by excluded third-party candidates.

6.1e The Fairness Doctrine

The **fairness doctrine** was an FCC regulation that applied throughout the year, not just during political campaigns. Stations had to devote a "reasonable" percentage of airtime to a discussion of public issues and had to ensure fair coverage for each side. If a station presented only one side of an issue, advocates for the other side had a legal right to be heard. If, in the discussion of an issue, the honor or integrity of a person or group was attacked, the station had to notify the person or group and supply both a transcript of the attack and an opportunity to respond on the air. Moreover, if a station endorsed a candidate for public office, the same requirements for notice and reply applied. It was to avoid conflict with the fairness doctrine that television networks routinely allowed a "Democratic response" following an address by a Republican president, and vice versa, a practice that has survived the demise of the doctrine itself. For a time, public broadcasting stations were treated differently and prohibited by law from editorializing at all on the air, a restriction the Supreme Court voided in 1984.[13]

Federal Communications Commission (FCC)

An agency of the national government that regulates the telecommunications industry in the United States, including the licensing and operation of all radio and television stations

equal-time rule

A provision of the Communications Act of 1934 that requires radio and television stations to give or sell equivalent time to one political candidate if the station has given or sold time to another candidate for that office

fairness doctrine

A regulation of the Federal Communications Commission that required radio and television stations to devote some airtime to a balanced discussion of public issues; abolished in 1987

Given the trend toward deregulation of the broadcast industry, it was not surprising that the FCC repealed the fairness doctrine in 1987. The FCC concluded that the doctrine was unconstitutional and that expansion of cable television had largely undercut the original rationale for treating radio and television stations differently from newspapers. Most communities now have access to more television channels than newspapers, meaning that the potential for competition among viewpoints is now greater in electronic than print journalism. That being said, access to more channels does not necessarily mean access to media owned by a wider variety of individuals or companies. As "Politics and Economics: Media Monopolies?" indicates, fewer regulations on media ownership can have a dampening effect on competition.

The media can help identify and define issues that people regard as important, such as the struggling economy, the health-care law, same-sex marriage, and marijuana legalization.

6.1f   Regulating the Internet

While the FCC is responsible for regulating interstate and international communication within the United States, its jurisdiction only partially extends to global communications such as the internet. One area of regulation in which the FCC has recently ventured is known as net neutrality. In 2015, the commission established net neutrality rules that prevented internet service providers from charging more for accessing particular content or from blocking or slowing access. In 2017, however, the FCC repealed these rules, opening the door for providers to begin using differential pricing and access speeds to favor some content and services (such as those owned by a parent company) over others.[14] In 2020 President Trump, upset at having some of his tweets labeled as misleading, issued an executive order aimed at removing legal immunity from internet companies in issues regarding content. As the internet becomes an increasingly important force in mass media, the federal government will face further challenges in its attempt to regulate internet content.

Efforts to crack down on internet fraud have been handled by the Federal Trade Commission and have met with some degree of success. The Supreme Court, however, has found that the First Amendment protects nearly all nonfraudulent commercial and private uses of this medium. In 1996, Congress passed the Communications Decency Act in an attempt to limit postings of obscene and offensive materials on websites. As discussed in Chapter 3, the Court held that this and subsequent congressional efforts have been overbroad limitations on protected speech. Since efforts to restrict offensive materials have been unsuccessful, any regulation of news content seems highly unlikely to pass constitutional muster. For now, almost anything goes on the internet.

POLITICS AND IDEAS

Confidentiality of News Sources and Information

Government cannot constitutionally prevent reporters from publishing news, but protection of a reporter's news sources and information remains uncertain. The success of much investigative journalism depends on the willingness of people with information to share it with journalists. For a variety of reasons, however, these news sources do not want their identities revealed. Some may fear embarrassment or the loss of a job; in the case of disclosure of criminal wrongdoing, they may be concerned about their physical safety. With no assurance of confidentiality, news sources might dry up, resulting in a loss of news to the public. Moreover, without some legal protection, officials could harass reporters they do not like by hauling them into court.

When it becomes apparent that reporters possess information, such as the names of witnesses, that law enforcement agents do not have, many people believe that journalists should have to testify just like ordinary citizens. Moreover, they say, because government officials rely on the press for a favorable public image, abuses would rarely, if ever, occur. Besides, sources do not disappear simply because the assurance of confidentiality is not absolute. In 1972, the Supreme Court ruled 5–4 in *Branzburg v. Hayes*[1] that the First Amendment does not protect the identity of a reporter's sources, but most states have enacted **shield laws** that give varying degrees of protection to news sources. Some protect only a journalist's sources, while others protect undisclosed information too. Congress has not passed a shield law for federal investigations.

The Supreme Court has also ruled in a case from Stanford University that the First Amendment does not shield newspaper offices from police searches, even when the newspaper, broadcast station, or its staff is not accused of wrongdoing.[2] Following violent demonstrations on the campus, the *Stanford Daily* published photographs of the clash. Police concluded that the newspaper's files might contain other evidence to help identify rioters and searched the premises. In reaction to the Stanford case, Congress passed the Privacy Protection Act of 1980, which prohibits unannounced searches of news media offices and those of authors and researchers by federal, state, and local police departments. There are three exceptions: when a journalist may have committed a crime, when the desired information is classified or otherwise related to national defense, or when someone's physical safety is at risk. The 1980 act has not ended newsroom searches, but it has reduced their frequency.[3]

More recently, news leaks regarding the war on terrorism have led government officials to seek out the informant on their own, rather than going after the journalists. On June 19, 2002, CNN first reported that the National Security Agency had intercepted conversations regarding an imminent terrorist attack prior to September 11, 2001. Since the intelligence community had shared this classified information with only a limited number of individuals—namely, the Senate Intelligence Committee—the FBI investigation focused on the senators rather than the news media.[4]

Another unusual twist on the issue of source confidentiality came in July 2003, when journalist Robert Novak wrote a column for the *Washington Post* in which he identified former ambassador Joseph Wilson's wife, Valerie Plame, as a CIA agent. The revelation was controversial because revealing the identity of an intelligence agent is illegal due to the security risk it creates and because many suspected that members of the Bush administration had leaked the information in retaliation for published criticism by Wilson. Although Novak cooperated with the special prosecutor assigned to investigate the leak, another reporter in possession of the leaked information, Judith Miller, refused to identify her sources and spent almost three months in jail as a result. Eventually, the investigation revealed that three administration officials had provided the classified information on Plame to reporters: President Bush's senior policy adviser Karl Rove, Vice President Dick Cheney's chief of staff I. Lewis "Scooter" Libby, and Deputy Secretary of State Richard Armitage.[5]

Whether in shielding the identity of sources or investigatory material, should journalists have legal protection denied to other citizens? Should government officials be held to different standards? How might threats to national security change your views?

1. 408 U.S. 665 (1972).

2. *Zurcher v. Stanford Daily,* 436 U.S. 547(1978).

3. Jane E. Kirtley, "Dealing with Newsroom Searches," *National Association of Broadcasters* (October/November 1988).

4. Kate Snow, "FBI Seeks Senators' Records in 9/11 Leak Probe," CNN.com, August 24, 2002.

5. "Armitage on CIA Leak: 'I Screwed Up,'" CBS News, September 7, 2006, http://www.cbsnews.com/stories/2006/09/07/eveningnews/main1981433.shtml.

shield laws

Statutes that protect the identity of journalists' news sources or their knowledge of criminal acts

6.2   Politics and the Press

Understanding why the press matters politically requires a look at several roles the media play in American politics. The media serve as *vehicles* of direct communication, as *gatekeepers* of political knowledge and attitudes, as *spotlights* on issues, and as *talent scouts* in campaigns.

6.2a   Direct Communication: The Media as Vehicles

With heavy doses of entertainment and information in abundance, the mass media understandably have real significance for politics and government in the United States. Radio, television, and the internet have become *vehicles,* making it possible for a president or other national political leader to speak simultaneously and directly to virtually everyone in the land. "No mighty king, no ambitious emperor, no pope, no prophet ever dreamt of such an awesome pulpit, so potent a magic wand," observed CBS veteran news director Fred W. Friendly.[15] Former senator J. William Fulbright (D-AR) even claimed that television had changed the constitutional system by doing "as much to expand the powers of the president as would a constitutional amendment formally abolishing the co-equality of the three branches of government."[16]

Among recent presidents, Ronald Reagan and Bill Clinton have appeared the most comfortable communicating directly with the American people via television. Regardless of preferences, circumstances often force presidents into the national spotlight. During his first several months in office, George W. Bush gave relatively few nationally televised addresses—preferring to communicate less formally or through his press secretary at the time, Ari Fleischer. After the 9/11 tragedies, however, Bush was compelled to deliver a series of difficult televised addresses. By many accounts, these tragedies turned a reluctant speechmaker into a formidable public communicator. Although President Donald Trump had his ups and downs with the media, his innovative use of Twitter for directly communicating with the American public—averaging more than twelve tweets per day to more than eighty-three million followers in 2020—demonstrated that the traditional news media may hold less of a monopoly over political communication in the future.[17] Early evidence suggests that President Biden will be a more traditional communicator, though it is unlikely any future presidency will eschew entirely the opportunities for direct communication that social media provides.

6.2b   Political Knowledge and Attitudes: The Media as Gatekeepers

As *gatekeepers,* editors and journalists in newsrooms across the land decide in large measure what people in the US will receive information about. Just because the media report a lot of news, however, does not mean that Americans are always eager to receive it—or even when they are eager recipients, they aren't always successful at remembering most of what they read or see.[18] It was shown in Chapter 5 that many Americans do not know very much about their political leaders and what they do or how the American political system works. In part, this is because most of the time spent watching television, reading newspapers, or browsing the internet is not spent watching or reading the news. Only

(ChameleonsEye/Shutterstock)

President George W. Bush during the welcoming ceremony in Israel on January 9, 2008

about 31 percent of Americans report that they follow national political news very closely on a regular basis.[19] But these numbers can change drastically when big events intervene—in 2020, 89 percent of Americans reported following news about COVID-19 either very or somewhat closely.[20]

Even when people pay attention to the news, they do not retain large amounts of specific information for very long. Given the number of events and situations that are televised, written about, and talked about, one day's news is overtaken by the next.

The mass media also influence political attitudes—what people think about their political leaders and institutions. Of course, the formation of political attitudes is complex, stretching from childhood to old age; and the media are part of this process. News stories contribute to emotions and impressions that can matter politically, apart from whatever facts are transferred from the screen or page to the brain. Feelings of outrage, sadness, pride, trust, or distrust can linger long after the specific content of a news story has been forgotten.

It makes a difference, then, how journalists keep watch over public life when pointing to shortcomings, corruption, failures, and successes. One study of network television news coverage of the White House found that stories reflecting favorably on the president and his policies were outnumbered by those that reflected unfavorably on the administration. The author suggested that this fact accounts for the difficulty recent presidents have had in maintaining their popularity past the initial "honeymoon" stage.[21] President Clinton was an amazing exception to this rule, leaving office after eight years with an approval rating higher than when he started. This was not due to favorable news stories (indeed, a vast number of stories centered on the scandals that led to his impeachment), but rather to a favorable economy. Americans consistently gave high marks to Clinton's job performance but low marks to the president "as a person."[22] The media were initially critical of George W. Bush's job performance but rallied around him after the 9/11 attacks, possibly in response to a perceived need for national unity. Although this supportive media attitude lasted for some time, questions began to emerge about the necessity—and success—of the Iraq War; and the media returned to their more critical role. Much of the media—the exceptions being Fox News and other dedicated conservative outlets—were at odds with Donald Trump from the day he took office, due in part to his irreverence for institutional traditions regarding the relationship between the president and the press. Rather than passively take a drubbing from the media, Trump took them on directly, calling the press the "enemy of the people" and pleasing his base of supporters in doing so.[23]

6.2c Issue Making and Issue Reporting: The Media as Spotlights

Just as the media can act as gatekeepers, they can be *spotlights* as well. Sometimes journalists talk about their work as if television, newspapers, and the internet were mirrors of society. That would mean that life in its many varieties and experiences would be reflected in the programs people watch and the articles they read. Most of the humdrum of daily living, however, goes unnoticed and unreported by the media. Indeed, many people watch

television to escape, not relive, such humdrum. Rather than thinking of the media as "mirroring" society, it is probably more helpful to think about the media as spotlighting or highlighting parts of it.

The media help to identify and define the issues people regard as important. Moreover, prominent coverage of a topic, such as drunk driving, day after day may heighten the importance people assign to it—just as an absence of coverage can lead people to believe that a problem, such as hunger, is no longer serious. Footage of drug sales on street corners in broad daylight, for instance, is almost certain to produce some kind of response from the mayor or police chief. More media attention results, then, because officials are now considering the problem and deciding what action, if any, to take. Journalists and government officials will sometimes collaborate to "manufacture" an issue. For example, the staff of a congressional committee might share information with reporters about waste and cost overruns in the military. The objective is to generate widespread feeling that new policies are needed to cope with a recently "discovered" problem.[24]

Especially when the news is not favorable, journalists may run afoul of officials. When investigating a story on local corruption, for instance, reporters will need "inside" sources to provide information and insight. These sources, understandably, will not want their names made public. Yet if the story leads to arrests by the police, witnesses will have to be called. Should reporters nonetheless be allowed to protect the identity of their sources? This is the question probed in "Contemporary Controversies: Confidentiality of News Sources and Information."

Spotlighting issues may affect political attitudes by **priming** the public. Priming occurs when the news media, especially television, set the terms by which the public judges its leaders. The way in which the media present an issue, such as protecting the environment, can make it appear to be the business of a particular official, such as the president. If viewers and readers then regard the problem as important—as they probably will if it appears to be a problem of presidential magnitude—they are likely to judge officials according to how well they think the latter have responded to the challenge.[25] The media do not tell the people what to think. Rather, American media are significant because they tell the people what (and whom) to think about.

6.2d Candidates and Campaigns: The Media as Talent Scouts

Just as every aspiring singer and shortstop wants to be noticed and taken seriously, candidates for political office want "good press." Political parties have historically been intermediaries, or linkages, between governors and the governed. To a degree, the two major parties still perform these functions; as parties have weakened, however, the media have come to occupy an ever-larger political role in campaigns, partially displacing the parties themselves. Today voters receive more political information from the media than from political parties. More voters can see a presidential candidate simultaneously in a single appearance on television than during a three-week whistle-stop train tour of the nation one hundred years ago. Good reporting can help voters understand a candidate's stand on the issues.

All too often, however, the media treat campaigns as if they were little more than horse races. News stories identify "serious" contenders and "front-runners," those whose campaigns have "momentum," as well as those who have "peaked too soon" or are "has-beens." Candidates want to do well at the start, with their early successes featured in the news.[26] Sometimes this means getting more votes than any of the other candidates, or it may mean getting more votes than journalists expected. In the 2016 presidential

priming

Occurs when the news media, especially television, set the terms by which the public judges its leaders

(Courtesy of the Richard Nixon Presidential Library and Archive, circa 1946, via Wikimedia)

Election flyer for former President Richard Nixon, distributed on behalf of his campaign for Congress in 1946

primaries, for example, the media often provided Republican candidate Donald Trump more coverage than all the other candidates combined, largely because of journalists' shock at Trump's provocative statements and his ability to perform well despite his lack of political experience. The media were also impressed by Democratic contender Pete Buttigieg early in the 2020 race. The gay, thirty-eight-year-old veteran and mayor of South Bend, Indiana, won a surprise victory in the Iowa caucuses and received a great deal of news coverage as a result. News accounts may then affect outcomes in later primaries because they affect the support that flows toward or away from a candidate. Sometimes, as in Trump's case, this can propel a candidate to victory. In other years, the candidate fails to gain traction and fades despite the media attention, as was the case with Buttigieg. On the other side—especially in state and local races, where turnouts are usually lower than in national elections—a lack of media attention can leave voters in the dark about who the candidates are and where they stand on the issues.

Moreover, given the legal constraints on campaign gifts and spending, news stories that place candidates in a favorable light can add up to free advertising. Particularly for campaigns run on a financial shoestring, journalists are indispensable in bringing candidates' views and personalities to the attention of the electorate. Without such "free publicity," for example, third-party candidates like Jo Jorgensen (Libertarian Party) and Howie Hawkins (Green Party) would not have been able to reach as many potential voters. This "free" media attention comes at a price, however. When candidates have to rely on journalists to present their message, they often find themselves at the mercy of the journalists' perspective. Once most mainstream media outlets decided Jorgensen and Hawkins were not serious contenders for the presidency in 2020, they devoted significantly less attention to these candidates, possibly reducing public support for these presidential hopefuls.

6.2e   Believability

Whether functioning as vehicles, gatekeepers, spotlights, or talent scouts, many news media receive respectable marks from the public for "believability"—whether people are inclined to accept what they read and see as true. Thus believability makes news reporting more important politically. Polls done a half-century ago indicated that, at the time, about one person in three thought that the news media were inaccurate. A survey performed in 1986 yielded similar figures.[27] By 2020, however, 58 percent of those polled said they had not very much or no confidence that the news media report the news fairly and accurately.[28] With reference to *particular* news sources, trust is sometimes higher, as Figure 6.2 indicates. Yet nearly 80 percent of Americans see the press as influenced by powerful people and organizations, and 82 percent are either very or somewhat concerned that "fake" or made-up news stories could have an effect on something as important as the presidential election.[29]

Figure 6.2   Trust Ratings for Selected Mass Media

According to a 2020 report, survey respondents were asked whether they trusted or distrusted selected mass media organizations on a scale of 0 (not at all trustworthy) to 10 (completely trustworthy). The graph shows the trustworthiness of various media sources.

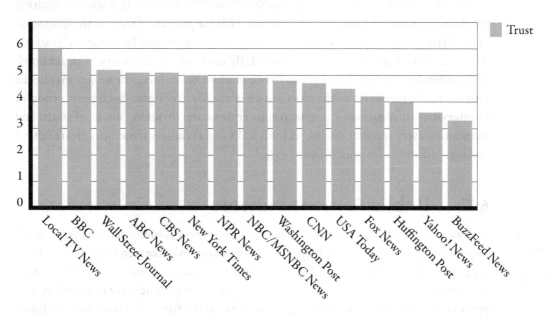

DATA SOURCE: Reuters Institute, "Digital News Report 2020," https://reutersinstitute.politics.ox.ac.uk/sites/default/files/2020-06/DNR_2020_FINAL.pdf (July 15, 2020).

6.3   Tools of the Trade: Politicians and the "Fifth Branch"

If politicians need the mass media, the media also need candidates and officials. The relationship between the two is *symbiotic:* It is advantageous to both, with each contributing something to the needs of the other. In dealing with the media, politicians have several tools that they can use to their own advantage as journalists compete with each other for page space and airtime. "What producers and reporters want more than anything else," admitted Fred Friendly, "is to get on the air."[30]

6.3a   Access

Journalists rely on candidates and officials for access to news and news sources. Access, in turn, promotes their stature and advancement in the profession. For example, reporters assigned to cover the White House—who are usually among the first to learn what is happening, who are called on at presidential news conferences, or who have their telephone calls returned—are envied by their peers and valued by their employers.

Access sometimes takes the form of being the recipient of a **leak**. A leak is rarely accidental. It is a deliberate release of information by an official to a reporter for a specific purpose. Besides doing the journalist a favor, the official may be trying to embarrass a supervisor, impress the journalist, expose bad management or corruption, provide

leak

The deliberate release of information by an official to a journalist for a specific purpose

damaging details to discredit a policy, or test the political waters for a new idea. Leaks can spring from the pettiest personal motives or from the loftiest patriotic sentiments. They counterbalance an agency's tight control of information.

In 1986, for instance, the *Washington Post* angered high officials in the Defense Department by revealing the location, number, cost, and test flight routine of the Air Force's hitherto super-secret stealth bomber—the existence of which the government would not even acknowledge. The story made it clear that this was information the Post had acquired from persons involved with the project.[31] (See also the discussion of the Plame affair in the "Confidentiality of News Sources and Information" feature.) The source of a leak is only rarely revealed. By contrast, the **exclusive** is an acknowledged interview that an official grants to one or more journalists. The subject may be the First Lady, the president, or the chief justice of the United States. Such people consent to interviews infrequently. Being scarce, interviews are, therefore, marks of status and recognition every reporter covets; yet both leaks and exclusives sometimes create ethical and legal dilemmas for journalists.

6.3b Public Announcements

In contrast to leaks and exclusives, news releases, press conferences, and news briefings are aimed at all interested reporters. These devices make news by virtue of their happening. Written by an official's press secretary, the **news release** is a ready-made story distributed for the purpose of attracting media attention to some event or situation. The **press conference** and **news briefing** are similar. In the first, an official or a candidate stands before reporters, cameras, and microphones and answers questions. With his quick wit and disarming smile, President John Kennedy (1961–1963) was the first to make the televised White House press conference a regular event. It was a forum in which he excelled.

In a briefing, an official makes an announcement or attempts to explain a policy. In international hostage situations, for instance, much of the news originates from regular briefings given to reporters at the State Department. **Backgrounders** are like briefings, except that reporters may not cite the source. They permit officials to make statements without having their names attached to what is reported. Each form of public announcement attempts to create a newsworthy event that qualifies for press coverage. Officials may achieve much the same result by agreeing to appear on Sunday interview shows such as *Face the Nation* and *Meet the Press.* Often, statements made on these programs generate front-page stories in Monday's newspapers or become trending topics in social media.

6.3c Other Media Events

Like news releases, letters can make news. Rather than simply letting it be known that a senator is concerned about, say, unfair trade restrictions abroad, the senator can write a letter to the secretary of commerce and release a copy to the press. Reporters might have trouble writing a story about a vague concern, but a letter is concrete. Moreover, like an event, it is something to report.

Designed for television, the **visual** features someone's appearance at an appropriate location. For a state legislator who wants to launch a campaign against potholes, merely complaining may go unheard; but if she stands in a pothole (after alerting camera crews, of course), she will be hard to miss. Television reporters do their own visuals. When a story breaks at the White House, network correspondents take turns doing their "stand-ups" with the lovely mansion as a backdrop.

---

exclusive

An interview that an official or other individual grants to one or more journalists that provides information not generally made available to all media

news release

A story written by a press agent for distribution to the media

press conference

A meeting of journalists and an official or other person at which the latter answers the questions posed by the former

news briefing

An announcement or explanation of policy by an official

backgrounders

News briefings in which reporters may not reveal the identity of the source of their information

visual

An image or series of images representing news in action; a visual depiction of a political act, such as campaigning, which may carry more impact than words alone

Figure 6.3 Sources Vary for Internet News

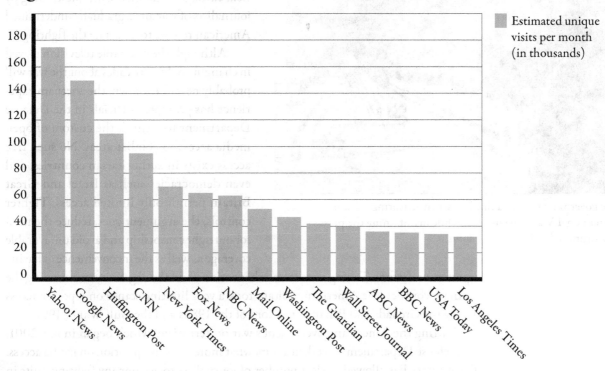

Estimated unique visits per month (in thousands)

DATA SOURCE: "Top 15 Most Popular News Websites," eBizMBA: The eBusiness Guide, February 2020, http://www.ebizmba.com/articles/news-websites (July 15, 2020).

Important for newspapers, but especially so for television, **photo opportunities** are events staged not so much for the purpose of dramatizing an issue as for creating visible activity. They show an official or candidate *doing something*—providing footage for the evening news or a good shot for tomorrow's front page. When a foreign leader comes to Washington to confer with the president, little may be released about what is actually discussed. Instead, viewers will see the two chatting informally over coffee, taking a stroll in the Rose Garden on the White House grounds, or tossing horseshoes at Camp David.

6.3d A Right to Know?

All of these "tools of the trade" involve officials providing news of one kind or another to the media. There are plenty of other occasions, however, when reporters want information but can find no one to provide it. "A free press and a purposeful government are destined always to be involved in a war of sorts," observed one former White House aide.[32] Although the Constitution protects the reporter's right to print news, there is not an equal right in all situations to acquire it. The press "is free to do battle against secrecy and deception in government," Justice Potter Stewart once said, "but the press cannot expect from the Constitution any guarantee that it will succeed."[33]

For instance, how much access should journalists have to ongoing military operations? Traditionally, journalists have witnessed most American military operations, even if dispatches might be delayed or censored for security reasons. The Vietnam War ushered in the first major television coverage of day-to-day combat, with evening news shows displaying in vivid color battle scenes that had occurred within twenty-four hours of airtime. In contrast with World War II, there were virtually no government-imposed

photo opportunity
An event scheduled to give newspaper reporters and television crews a chance to photograph someone

(Dover Air Force Base via Wikimedia)

The government walks a fine line when censoring certain content on TV and the internet while maintaining the press's constitutional rights and freedoms.

restrictions on what could be shown. Some people believe that the daily scenes of battlefield carnage, combined with questioning by journalists of war aims, gradually undermined American resolve to continue the fighting.[34]

Although the exact role television played in changing public attitudes about the war will probably never be known, the Vietnam experience has prompted officials in the Defense Department to rethink the custom of open media access to combat areas. No such free access exists in authoritarian countries, and even democracies such as Israel and Great Britain permit only limited access. Tighter controls, the argument goes, reduce the need for outright censorship and avoid unfavorable coverage as well as the inconvenience of having reporters underfoot. Taking a cue from other nations, and the negativity surrounding the Vietnam conflict, the American military took a very limiting stance on reporter access during the Grenada and Panama invasions of the 1980s and the Gulf War of 1991.

During the American government's war on terrorism, which began in late 2001, the Defense Department has taken a somewhat more inclusive position on media access. The military has allowed a select number of journalists to accompany fighting units in "embedded" positions. In other words, the reporters have observed the conflict directly, alongside troops and with all of the related dangers. While this approach has led to some excellent, up-close coverage, some worry that the Defense Department may be extending an open invitation in certain situations only so that the decision to restrict access elsewhere won't be questioned. This issue made the headlines again during the Iraq War when media outlets were warned against depicting caskets of American soldiers and when efforts were made to restrict photos of prisoner abuse by American soldiers at Abu Ghraib prison. When actions are committed in secret, without press coverage, Americans are prevented from forming objective opinions. As Michael Getler, ombudsman of the *Washington Post*, has remarked, "We don't know what we don't know."[35]

6.4   Are the Media Biased?

Politicians, including most American presidents, have long complained about news coverage. Are the media biased? Most Americans apparently think so. Of Americans polled, 62 percent believe there is political bias in traditional news media coverage, and 80 percent see bias in social media news coverage.[36] That being said, Americans do not agree on the direction of the bias: Polling found that 42 percent believe the media are too liberal and 13 percent say they are too conservative.[37] Some bias is probably unavoidable in reporting the news. The bias is both *personal* and *structural*. It results from the political attitudes of reporters and editors as well as from the nature of the news-reporting business itself.

POLITICAL CONTROVERSIES

Can Political News Be Entertaining, Social, and Informative?

Most of the facts and figures about media used in this chapter are based on nationwide polls of adults in general. It may not surprise you to learn that there are generational differences in preferred news sources. A report by the Pew Research Center found that about twice as many younger people (aged eighteen to thirty-three) than older people (aged fifty and older) got at least some of their political news from comedy shows like *The Colbert Report* (which aired from 2005 to 2014) or *The Daily Show* (1996–present).[1] Perhaps even more important is the trust gap. More young Americans say they trust these shows for information about government and politics than say they distrust them. However, the opposite is true for older Americans.[2]

If you watch *The Daily Show* (with Trevor Noah), *The Late Show* with Stephen Colbert, *Last Week Tonight* (with John Oliver), or *Full Frontal with Samantha Bee,* are you really learning anything about politics? Put another way, is all of this comedy and satire good for young adults? Survey results suggest that, at the very least, it is better than no news at all. Of young viewers, 27 percent indicated that they learned things about the presidential campaign from watching comedy and late-night shows that they had not known before.[3] Although anyone wishing to be an informed citizen should seek out news from a variety of sources, it appears that comedy shows may be a legitimate part of that repertoire. A poll that tested respondents' knowledge of political campaigns found that viewers of *The Daily Show* scored 16 percent higher than respondents who did not watch any late-night comedy programs.[4] The organization conducting the poll, however, was quick to point out that *The Daily Show* was probably not solely responsible for the greater knowledge and that the findings were likely the result of viewers' prior knowledge combined with information learned from the show.

Beyond the traditional television format, more Americans are now turning to social media for political news as well. When these outlets first became popular, younger people led the charge, using Facebook, Twitter, Reddit, YouTube, Snapchat, and other social media platforms to obtain political news at a rate that far outpaced members of the older generation. But now older Americans are starting to catch up—depending on the platform. For Facebook, 34 percent of adults under thirty report using the platform on a weekly basis for political and election news, and 16 percent of those over sixty-five did. The numbers were even closer for Google News—21 and 16 percent respectively. But for Instagram and Reddit, only 1 percent of those over sixty-five were users, while 18 percent of those under thirty were. Twitter is used by 27 percent of the younger cohort and only 4 percent of the older one.[6] Encouragingly, users of social media are likely to seek news from a variety of more traditional sources as well.[7]

What media sources do you turn to for political news? Are they the same sources your parents use? What might be the disadvantages of seeking all of your political news from comedy sources and social media? What are the advantages of seeking news from a variety of sources?

1. The Pew Research Center, "Millennials and Political News," June 1, 2015, http://www.journalism.org /2015/06/01/millennials -political-news/.

2. Ibid.

3. The Pew Research Center, "Cable and Internet Loom Large in Fragmented Political News Universe," January 11, 2004, http://people-press.org/reports/ display.php3?ReportID=200.

4. National Annenberg Election Survey, "*Daily Show* Viewers Knowledgeable About Presidential Campaign, National Annenberg Election Survey Shows," September 21, 2004.

5. The Pew Research Center, "News Use Across Social Media Platforms 2018," September 10, 2018, http://assets.pewresearch.org /wp-content/uploads/sites/13 /2018/09/10103311/PJ _2018.09.10_social-media-news _FINAL.pdf.

6. Pew Research Center's American News Pathways data tool, https://www.pewresearch.org /pathways-2020/ (July 15, 2020).

7. The Pew Research Center, "News Use Across Social Media Platforms in 2016," May 20, 2016, http://www.journalism.org/2016 /05/25/.

6.4a   The Journalists

Vice President Spiro Agnew (1969–1973) once publicly accused the news media of controlling news. "A small group of men, numbering perhaps no more than a dozen anchormen, commentators, and executive producers," argued Agnew, "settle upon the film and commentary that is to reach the public. They decide what forty to fifty million Americans will learn of the day's events in the nation and the world."[38]

Of course the people who write news influence it. Reporters and commentators are not value-free machines that simply grind out a product. Their attitudes and outlooks are bound to affect what Americans read and see, even if journalists make every effort to be accurate. Who are the journalists staffing the major newspapers and network news bureaus? Generally, they tend to come from small towns, largely in the Midwest, rather than the cities and suburban communities of the Northeast or the West. Many of them went to state colleges, not to Ivy League or other highly selective private institutions. They probably majored in journalism or English rather than in philosophy, economics, or political science. Few have been politically active in the sense of strongly identifying with and working for a party and its candidates.

In what direction is your news source biased? This website provides a chart for evaluating many print, television, and internet news sources.

http://www.bvtlab.com/w8a4v

When they vote, journalists overwhelmingly favor Democratic or otherwise liberal candidates. But despite being more liberal in their beliefs than the typical American, there is little evidence this results in bias regarding the stories they present—the gatekeeping function described earlier.[39] Moreover, they tend to be suspicious of most politicians—whether Democratic or Republican, liberal or conservative. As one scholar has concluded, journalists distrust politicians because politicians have to compromise. Compromise "tends not to involve the clear and snappy opposition of right and wrong that is the stuff of television drama." There is a journalistic idea "of the individual good citizen, independent of special interests and party loyalties, making up his own mind about the measures and candidates that will best promote the public good."[40]

Suspicion of politicians, in turn, leads to suspicion of "the establishment"—the people in power. In a campaign, the underdog may be more appealing than the supposed front-runner. With numerous exposés to their credit, uncovering corruption and shady deals by public officials, journalists may see themselves as a permanent "loyal opposition" or "watchdog" apart from the competition between the ins and outs of the two-party system. Surely the important role of newspaper sleuths in uncovering and probing the Watergate scandal during the early 1970s has only strengthened this perception.

Without a watchful press, President Richard Nixon (1969–1974) and "all the president's men" would probably have survived the impeachment controversy that led to his resignation in August 1974.[41] However the press was far less vigilant, collectively, in the late 1980s in reporting the growing insolvency of the savings and loan industry—a fiasco that Americans are continuing to pay for through their tax dollars. Whether because the subject was so complex, involved so many people and institutions, or seemingly lacked drama and interest, journalists initially ignored the topic while Congress, the executive branch, and the regulatory agencies allowed the problem to fester. Finding it to be a more gossipy, attention-grabbing story, the media devoted a great deal of attention to the extramarital scandals of the Bill Clinton presidency during the 1990s.

Other forces tend to compensate for a liberal bias, to the extent it exists in the national press. Editorial endorsements from the "front office" usually go to conservatives, and reporters in towns and small cities may have a more conservative outlook, too. (Still, the more liberal urban papers have larger circulations.) Moreover, reactions of advertisers, viewers, readers, and officials have to be considered. Editors and producers, for example, may want to curry favor with sponsors by avoiding subjects or ideas that sponsors might find offensive. In addition, the media mergers that have occurred over the past two decades mean that a large number of media outlets are owned by a small number of mega-corporations—a trend that may be leading to more favorable coverage of big business and more conservative coverage generally.

(Getty Images)

Another concern is that because journalists rely on officials for access to information, journalists may become "lap dogs" by placing favorable slants on stories they write. Conservative officials and causes may, therefore, get more balanced treatment than they would otherwise receive. Some critics say that these considerations mean that certain issues may be neglected altogether or covered only in a shallow fashion. The result is that people are poorly informed by a bland style of reporting that succeeds only because it is marginally acceptable to most and offensive to only a few. Still, a tradition of journalistic professionalism argues strongly for both *depth* and *evenhandedness* in news coverage.

6.4b Deciding What Becomes News

Since literally thousands of events occur in the world every day, space and time constraints mean that most of them go unreported. Selecting what becomes news—the process of **agenda setting**—is especially critical in television. Approximately twenty minutes are available for news during a thirty-minute news show, allowing for ten to fifteen stories at most. This means that even the major stories are usually allotted only two to three minutes each. The news reported last evening on television could easily fit on the front page of this morning's newspaper. If a "big story" is in the news, other stories are crowded out.

Political cartoons are a part of the mass media that are meant to entertain, inform, and critique. Find your favorite cartoonist at this website.

http://www.bvtlab.com/49KmF

Once cut, these would-be stories may never have a second chance to appear. Expanded coverage is possible only on more lengthy programs such as *PBS NewsHour* on public television.

What factors seem to guide this inevitable selection? Some events seem destined to become news: natural disasters and political "turning points" such as elections, revolutions, and military invasions. Other events or circumstances will become news if they happen to appeal to the people responsible for selecting stories or if they have a high interest among the reading and viewing audience. Still others qualify as news because they are "scoops"—attention-getting stories made public by a single newspaper or station. A day's delay might give the competition the chance to claim a scoop as its own. Aside from scoops, there seems to be substantial agreement among the networks on what constitutes the most newsworthy events. One study found that two of three major networks carried the same lead story on the evening news 91 percent of the time,

agenda setting

The process by which the news media select and focus on a small number of stories from a large number of possibilities—shaping, in part, Americans' opinions about what is important

and in only 7 percent of the programs did two run the same lead story without the third network placing it somewhere in the program.[42]

About half of network news stories originate from or focus on Washington, DC. This is not only because it is the nation's capital—and thus the location of many stories reporters deem important—but also because staff, equipment, and circuits are already there. Reporting stories from Washington is, therefore, relatively easy and cost-efficient. Within Washington, however, news coverage is not equally dispersed. About half the stories deal primarily with the "golden triangle"—the White House, the Department of Defense, and the Department of State. Reporters and technicians assigned just to cover the White House number more than two hundred. Congress receives somewhat less coverage, with the Senate drawing more attention than the House. Regulatory agencies and the Supreme Court receive the least coverage. Moreover, two-thirds of the stories on the presidency—but only half of those on Congress—are accompanied by film or video. Presidential stories typically run more than twice the length of those on Congress and tend to come earlier in the broadcast.[43] Of course, these figures are dependent on the relative levels of congressional and White House initiative, as well as the number of international crises, and are therefore subject to some variation from year to year. Campaign reporting by the media tilts even more sharply toward the presidency.

What accounts for this disparate treatment? It is partly a function of the stories journalists think are most important. Also, the executive branch, though many times larger than Congress, is more easily personified. One can associate the president or the secretaries of state and defense with policies in a way that is not as conveniently done in Congress with its 100 senators and 435 representatives. Moreover, much congressional time is consumed with deliberation. This is often not as dramatic to report as an initial proposal to Congress that originated in the White House or an executive decision based on legislation Congress has passed. Imbalance in coverage between presidential and congressional races on the networks is largely explained by the difficulty ABC, CBS, Fox, and NBC have in holding the interests of viewers (and, therefore, their audiences) in one state when discussing the House and Senate races of another state. The solution for the networks is obvious: ignore most of the congressional races most of the time.

(mark reinstein / Shutterstock)

By 1986, both the House and Senate were finally allowing cameras into their chambers so that news teams could cover debates.

Television coverage of Congress is technically easier now that both the House (since 1979) and Senate (since 1986) permit television cameras in their chambers. Thus coverage of the legislative process has increased, especially on locally produced newscasts. Aside from interviews with individual legislators, networks and local stations can pick up statements from floor debates to include on news programs. This is an opportunity that has not gone unnoticed, as some members have learned to "play" to the cameras, even before a virtually empty room. Indeed, continuous television in Congress now means that floor debates sometimes resemble a video equivalent of the telephone answering machine. Even in the momentous debate in the House and Senate in January 1991 over the use of force in the Persian Gulf crisis, most members with something to say filed into their respective chamber at the designated time, made a speech that was recorded for posterity, and then returned to their offices or homes to watch, on television, their colleagues doing the same.

Yet, just because something can be considered newsworthy is not necessarily reason enough why it should become news. Journalistic ethics play a role too. To what extent, for instance, should journalists probe the private lives of officials and candidates? This was the question posed when the *Miami Herald* published reports in 1987 accusing Democratic presidential front-runner Gary Hart of improprieties in spending a weekend with a woman who was not his wife. When made aware of additional damaging information in the possession of the *Washington Post* a few days later, candidate Hart announced his withdrawal from the race.[44] The media's success with Hart laid the groundwork for their approach to the Monica Lewinsky scandal during the Bill Clinton administration. Issues that would have been deemed "off limits" in a previous generation made their way, for good or ill, into prime-time news coverage. Some people argue that the lives of candidates should be like a "fishbowl" or an "open book." Others say that one's personal life should not be the public's business unless it reflects on a candidate's qualifications to be president or to hold another public office.

6.4c   Deciding How the News Appears

Journalists describe or portray events in different ways, with different emphases. This process of shaping stories is sometimes called **framing**. In one of the televised debates in 1976 between President Gerald Ford (1974–1977) and challenger Jimmy Carter (1977–1981), for example, Ford slipped up by saying that Poland was not under Soviet domination. In surveys immediately after the debate, viewers were almost evenly divided when asked which candidate had done the better job; but over the next twenty-four hours, as news reports about the debate emphasized Ford's blunder, reaction shifted dramatically in Carter's favor. Some people later admitted to changing their minds, saying that the news stories about the debate led them to conclude that their initial judgments (favoring Ford) must have been wrong. The "newsworthy" part of the debate had become Ford's blooper.[45]

Today candidates are reluctant to leave interpretation of events solely to journalists. In the 2020 presidential campaign debates between Democrat Joe Biden and Republican Donald Trump, for example, the candidates had barely begun when the "spin doctors" went to work. Viewers were presented with ample live feedback in the form of tweets and on-screen messages. As soon as each debate ended, there was "post-debate quarterbacking" from officeholders and campaign officials from each party who crowded around the press to provide instant analysis of what "really happened." Unlike the usual press conference, however, there were more interviewees than interviewers. Do the spin doctors make a difference? Unless one candidate commits a major blunder, as Ford did in 1976, most viewers will probably not be greatly swayed by post-debate commentary. Still, it probably shapes the opinions of some, and neither campaign wants to leave the other free to provide an unanswered interpretation of events.

More than print journalism, television news reporting calls for *interpretation* of events, rather than a bare statement of what happened. This is also the case with stories on programs such as *60 Minutes*. Because of the need to hold a viewing audience to a particular channel, television news is purposely designed to be gripping and dramatic. An executive producer of the *NBC Nightly News* once made this point a requirement for his staff:

> Every news story should, without any sacrifice of probity or responsibility, display the attributes of fiction, of drama. It should have structure and conflict, problem and denouement, rising action and falling action, a beginning, middle, and an end. These are not only the essentials of drama; they are the essentials of narrative.[46]

framing

The way that the media present a story, consisting of angle, tone, and point of view

What if an event lacks the elements of fiction, drama, or conflict? The item might be passed over entirely or, if reported, given the added drama it needs. Reporting the news may well mean molding it, too. The irony is that politicians often succeed by managing conflict and reconciling differences among groups. Journalists succeed by capitalizing on conflict and magnifying those differences.[47]

Because news reporting is a business, stations sell time on news programs just as they do during weekend football games and afternoon soap operas. Newspapers, social media, and websites sell ad space. Understandably, media executives are acutely conscious of circulation figures and **Nielsen ratings**. Such numbers largely determine commercial revenue, and therefore profits. Economic considerations understandably dictate that the media attract as many viewers and readers as possible.

6.4d   The Impact of the Visual

Television's unique quality is its capacity to transmit images into virtually every home in the land simultaneously. Thus, television gives a special meaning to the old saying that a picture is worth a thousand words. A news article about a plane crash will not have the same effect as color video of the same scene. Consider, for example, the emotionally moving nature of the photographs and video of the World Trade Center collapse. The tragedy seemed all the more real, and near, because it was on television. Of course, today's widespread use of smartphones and streaming video means that such visual presentations are no longer limited to the home but are, instead, viewed by Americans wherever they are.

The *visual* also becomes a factor in the selection of stories and in the way those stories will be presented. Television news editors prefer stories that can be easily visualized. Similarly, they prefer to cover the parts of a story that display movement. Televised reports on political campaigns, for instance, typically emphasize what candidates are *doing* more than what they are *saying*. Instead of the issues that divide candidates, viewers may get an eyeful of colorful rallies, parades, flag-waving, and handshaking. One may see a lot of activity without necessarily *learning* very much about a candidate or the substance of the campaign. Sometimes, knowledge that voters glean about the candidates is more likely to have come from the candidates' own advertisements than from news reports on their campaigns.

Likewise, television's preference for action shapes the way candidates conduct their campaigns. Appearances must be timed so that coverage can make the evening news. A prepared statement on grain subsidies or interest rates will not draw nearly the attention generated by a ride on a tractor across a wheat field or a visit to the home of a farmer whose house and farm are about to be foreclosed. Including such visuals in newscasts is far easier today than it was a generation ago because of the miniaturization of cameras and other devices that have largely replaced bulkier and more cumbersome equipment. Because television favors images over words, candidates learn to include "sound bites" in

(Official White House Photo by Pete Souza via Wikimedia)

President Barack Obama hugs Stephanie Davies, who helped keep her friend, Allie Young, left, alive after she was shot during the theater shooting on July 20, 2012, in Aurora, Colorado. The president visited patients and family members affected by the shooting on July 22, 2012, at the University of Colorado Hospital.

Nielsen ratings

Surveys conducted by the A.C. Nielsen Company to measure the size of television audiences

their speeches—one or two catchy sentences or phrases designed for the brief coverage television provides. With streaming video on the internet, viewers can now watch these sound bites over and over at their own leisure when visiting media websites. Such use further enhances the value of a good sound bite—and the cost of an embarrassing one.

In politics, television has clearly benefited some political leaders more than others. One of the earliest examples of television's impact occurred in 1960 when Senator John Kennedy (D-MA) debated Vice President Richard Nixon (1953–1961) in the first televised debate between presidential candidates. While transcripts of the debates show plainly how the candidates differed on some of the issues, many viewers were struck more by what they saw than by what they heard. Nixon went into the debate widely perceived as the "candidate of experience" even though both he and Kennedy had entered Congress in the same year. While Kennedy had served in the Senate as well as the House, many thought that he was inexperienced and maybe just a little too youthful and immature for the presidency. The September debate, the first of four that fall, shook both sets of preconceptions. Perhaps the perfect television candidate, Kennedy seemed mature, firm, vigorous, and at ease. Nixon appeared drooped, tired, nervous, and even haggard. In short, Kennedy *looked* presidential and thus achieved on television, in an instant, what it would have otherwise taken weeks of campaigning to accomplish.

It is likely that the televised debates in the 2000 election also helped one candidate and hurt the other, largely due to the inability of each to meet with viewers' and the media's preconceived expectations and the impact of the visual. Vice President Al Gore, assumed to be the more practiced and qualified statesperson, did not dominate his opponent the way many had predicted he would. On the other hand, Governor George W. Bush—depicted in the media as an inexperienced leader with a poor grasp on foreign policy—held his own. Gore's visual image reinforced descriptions of him as stiff and wooden. Bush's expressive face allowed viewers to develop a sense of being personally connected with the candidate. Thus, even though the content of the debates resulted in a draw at best for Bush, the fact that he performed better than many in the media had predicted and provided viewers with a more human visual image led to a boost in his poll numbers following each debate.[48] By the 2004 debates, public expectations of Bush had risen, so when his answers seemed less developed and appealing than his opponent's, viewers concluded that Senator John Kerry (D-MA) was the winner. Ultimately, the debate victory meant little, however, as the election victory went to the perceived loser of the debates for the third time in the last six presidential elections.

The 2008 debates gave both Senators Barack Obama and John McCain an opportunity to talk about their own brands of change. Facing a country mired in financial crisis, and in which only 7 percent of the populace said they were satisfied with the way things were going, both candidates made efforts to distinguish themselves from the unpopular Bush administration. Senator Obama stressed middle-class tax cuts and foreign policy diplomacy, while Senator McCain emphasized offshore oil drilling and reducing wasteful spending.

The 2012 election was, in many ways, a referendum on President Obama's first term, with the president listing his successes and Governor Mitt Romney pointing out the president's failures. Though a majority of viewers felt Obama came up short in the first debate, they saw Obama as the victor in the second and third. This result left many Americans feeling that the overall debate outcome was essentially a tie.

The 2016 presidential election broke new ground in many ways, including its approach to the debates. Former Secretary of State Hillary Clinton and businessman Donald Trump squared off in a series of three debates characterized by interruptions, fact-checking, and claims of victory by both sides. Though most mainstream media outlets reported that Donald Trump made more false statements and interrupted his opponent much more

often, and that Hillary Clinton was regarded as the winner in post-debate opinion polls, the Trump campaign touted only sources showing its candidate to be the winner. Whether or not this strategy was completely honest, the confidence Trump exuded during the debates and throughout the campaign—despite polls consistently showing him behind—was likely a factor in his surprising victory in the general election.

The 2020 debates took an unusual turn, coming in the midst of the COVID-19 pandemic. Indeed, incumbent President Trump was diagnosed with the coronavirus shortly after the first debate. This led to the cancellation of the second debate, and a final debate that included greater social distance between President Trump and former Vice President Joe Biden. At the end of the day, despite these controversies, the debates themselves likely changed few minds. Most potential voters had already made up their minds, and millions had already returned their mail-in ballots.

While reactions to a debate do not necessarily translate into votes, a televised debate presents an opportunity for voters to sense which candidate they would rather see as the nation's leader during the next four years. As voters form impressions of candidates, few doubt that the visual component of television plays an important role.

6.4e   A Public Trust

If bias exists in news reporting, does this mean that journalists have somehow betrayed a trust? Are journalists worthy of the protections accorded them by the First Amendment? If Americans of President Washington's time were alive today, they would probably confess that they expected bias in the news. The press then, as well as throughout the nineteenth century, was far more biased, inaccurate, partisan, and vitriolic than almost any mainstream news site widely available today.

The First Amendment does not assume a bias-free press any more than the Constitution assumes pure and ambition-free politicians. Recall the constitutional system of checks and balances discussed in Chapter 1. At the heart of this arrangement, the media amount to another kind of check and balance. Just as the Constitution allows ambition to counter ambition, so the First Amendment allows one opinion to combat another; one claim of truth, perspective, and opinion to compete with another. In this way, the media best serve democratic politics.

CHAPTER REVIEW

1. The media today are characterized by less diversity in ownership and in the production of news. While people in the US have access to more television channels than ever before, most national news originates from several networks and major newspapers. Moreover, the number of daily newspapers is declining. The First Amendment makes possible an important role for the media by prohibiting most restrictions on what is published. The electronic media, however, are subject to special kinds of regulations that do not apply to the print media. That being said, a constitutional method of regulating new media sources, such as the internet, has proved more elusive.

2. The mass media—newspapers, magazines, radio, television, and the internet—are vital links between citizens and their government. As observers of the political arena, the media serve as vehicles, gatekeepers, spotlights, and talent scouts.

3. The relationship between politics and media is symbiotic. While officials need the media, individual reporters depend on candidates and officeholders for access to news sources and newsmakers.

4. Bias in journalism may result from the political views of the people who report, publish, and broadcast the news and from the structure of the news media. Half of network news stories focus on Washington, and of these about half deal mainly with the executive branch. The visual nature of television not only influences which events will be deemed newsworthy but also influences the ways political campaigns are conducted and the ways officials attempt to gain publicity.

KEY TERMS

agenda setting 187

backgrounders 182

equal-time rule 174

exclusive 182

fairness doctrine 174

Federal Communications Commission (FCC) . . . 174

fifth branch 164

framing 189

journalists 164

leak 181

mass media 164

news briefing 182

news release 182

Nielsen ratings 190

photo opportunity 183

press conference 182

priming 179

shield laws 176

visual 182

READINGS FOR FURTHER STUDY

Two good texts that approach the topic of American politics through the lens of the mass media are Amber E. Boydstun's *Making the News: Politics, the Media, and Agenda Setting* (Chicago: University of Chicago Press, 2013) and *Making Sense of Media and Politics* by Gadi Wolfsfeld (New York: Routledge, 2011).

Two of the leading contemporary researchers in the field of politics and the media are Doris Graber and Shanto Iyengar. Graber's recent works include *Mass Media and American Politics,* 10th ed. (with Johanna Dunaway, Washington, DC: CQ Press, 2017) and *Media Power in Politics,* 6th ed. (Washington, DC: CQ Press, 2010). Iyengar wrote *News That Matters: Television and American Opinion,* rev. ed. (Chicago: University of Chicago Press, 2010), with Donald R. Kinder and Benjamin I. Page, and *Media Politics: A Citizen's Guide,* 4th ed. (New York: Norton, 2018).

The Boys on the Bus (New York: Random House, 2003) by Timothy Crouse is a classic case study of journalists in the 1972 presidential contest.

A more recent look at journalists is provided by Beth J. Harpaz's *The Girls in the Van* (New York: St. Martin's Press, 2002), which follows Hillary Clinton's 2000 Senate campaign.

For details on legal regulation of both print and electronic journalism, see T. Barton Carter, Marc A. Franklin, Amy Kristin Sanders, and Jay B. Wright's *The First Amendment and the Fourth Estate: The Law of Mass Media,* 12th ed. (Mineola, NY: Foundation Press, 2016) and The First Amendment and the Fifth Estate: Regulation of Electronic Mass Media, 7th ed. (Mineola, NY: Foundation Press, 2007).

Michael Parenti's *Inventing Reality: The Politics of News Media,* 2nd ed. (New York: St. Martin's Press, 1993) argues that journalism is the tool of established economic and political interests in the United States.

Ben H. Bagdikian's *The New Media Monopoly,* rev. ed. (Boston: Beacon Press, 2014) addresses some of the problems associated with media consolidation.

The Power of the Press: The Birth of American Political Reporting by Thomas C. Leonard (New York: Oxford University Press, 2000) is a study of the rise of political journalism in the nineteenth century.

In *Democracy and the News* (New York: Oxford University Press, 2004), Herbert J. Gans explores the relationship between democracy and the news media in light of new media developments such as cable and satellite television and the internet. Also see *After Broadcast News: Media Regimes, Democracy, and the New Information Environment* by Bruce A. Williams and Michael X. Delli Carpini (New York: Cambridge University Press, 2012).

Finally, the writers of the satirical news program *The Daily Show* have written *America: The Book* (New York: Warner Books, 2006) as a parody of an American government textbook. Not to be outdone, the following year, Stephen Colbert followed up with *I Am America (And So Can You!)* (New York: Grand Central, 2007) and then in 2014, *America Again: Re-becoming the Greatness We Never Weren't* (New York: Grand Central, 2014).

NOTES

1. Sam Kirkland, "Digital Circulation Figures Are an Absolute Mess," Poynter.org, May 5, 2014, http://www.poynter.org/latest-news/mediawire /250218/digital-circulation-figures-are-an -absolute-mess/ (September 19, 2014).

2. John Edward Hasse, "Remembering the Radio Revolution," *The Wall Street Journal,* November 6, 2020, https://www.wsj.com/articles/remembering -the-radio-revolution-11604689751

3. The Pew Research Center, "News Use Across Social Media Platforms 2018."

4. The Pew Research Center for the People and the Press, "Americans Spending More Time Following the News," September 12, 2010, http://www.people-press.org/2010/09/12/americans -spending-more-time-following-the-news/ (August 2, 2012).

5. The Pew Research Center, "State of the News Media 2016."

6. U.S. Bureau of Labor Statistics, *American Time Use Survey*, June 28, 2018.

7. Bureau of Labor Statistics, "Television Capturing America's Attention at Prime Time and Beyond," September 2018, https://www.bls.gov/opub/btn /volume-7/television-capturing-americas-attention .htm#:~:text=With%20nearly%2080%20percent %20of,leisure%20activity%20for%20many%20 Americans (July 12, 2020).

8. The Pew Research Center, "American Trends Panel, 2018."

9. *Near v. Minnesota*, 283 U.S. 697 (1931).

10. James F. Fixx, ed., *The Mass Media and Politics* (New York: Arno Press, 1972), p. ix.

11. *Federal Communications Commission v. Pacifica Foundation*, 438 U.S. 726 (1976).

12. *Red Lion Broadcasting Co. v. Federal Communications Commission*, 395 U.S. 367 (1969).

13. *Federal Communications Commission v. League of Women Voters*, 468 U.S. 364 (1984).

14. Reuters, "U.S. Regulators Ditch Net Neutrality Rules as Legal Battles Loom," December 14, 2017, https://www.reuters.com/article/us-usa-internet /u-s-regulators-ditch-net-neutrality-rules-as-legal -battles-loom-idUSKBN1E81CX.

15. Quoted in Newton Minnow, et al., *Presidential Television* (New York: Basic Books, 1973), p. vii.

16. U.S. Congress. Senate. Committee on Commerce. Subcommittee on Communication. *Hearings on S.J. Res. 209*. 91st Cong. 2nd Sess. 1970, p. 15.

17. Twitter Counter, https://twittercounter.com /realDonaldTrump (September 16, 2018); https://twitter.com/realDonaldTrump (July 13, 2020).

18. Charles Atkin, "A Conceptual Model for Information Seeking, Avoiding, and Processing," in *New Models for Mass Communication Research*, ed. Peter Clarke (Beverly Hills, CA: Sage, 1973), pp. 205–242.

19. The Gallup Organization, 2018.

20. The Gallup Organization, 2020.

21. Fred Smoller, "The Six O'Clock Presidency," *Presidential Studies Quarterly 26* (1986): 42–44.

22. The Gallup Organization, "Clinton Leaves Office with Mixed Public Reaction," January 12, 2001, http://www.gallup.com/poll/releases/pr010112.asp (September 14, 2002).

23. Brett Samuels, "Trump ramps up rhetoric on media, calls press 'the enemy of the people,'" The Hill, April 5, 2019, https://thehill.com/homenews /administration/437610-trump-calls-press-the -enemy-of-the-people.

24. Fay Lomax Cook, et al., "Media and Agenda Setting: Effects on the Public, Interest Group Leaders, Policy Makers, and Policy," *Public Opinion Quarterly 47* (1983): 32–33.

25. Shanto Iyengar and Donald R. Kinder, *News That Matters* (Chicago: University of Chicago Press, 1987), pp. 98–111.

26. Richard Joslyn, *Mass Media and Elections* (Reading, MA: Addison-Wesley, 1984), p. 215.

27. *The People and the Press* (Los Angeles: Times Mirror, 1986), p. 20.

28. The Gallup Organization, "Media Use and Evaluation," 2020.

29. The Pew Research Center for the People and the Press, "Widely Criticized, but Trusted More Than Other Information Sources," September 22, 2011, http://www.people-press.org/2011/09/22/press -widely-criticized-but-trusted-more-than-other -institutions/ (August 3, 2012); The Pew Research Center, "Concern about influence of made-up news on the election is lowest among those paying the least attention," February 19, 2020, https://www.journalism.org/2020/02/19/concern -about-influence-of-made-up-news-on-the-election -is-lowest-among-those-paying-the-least-attention/ (July 15, 2020).

30. "The New Face of TV News," *Time,* February 25, 1980.

31. *Washington Post*, August 22, 1986, p. A1. For a discussion of leaks prior to the American raid on Libya in 1986, see David C. Martin and John Walcott, *Best Laid Plans: The Inside Story of America's War Against Terrorism* (New York: Harper & Row, 1988), pp. 269–271.

32. Douglass Cater, *Power in Washington* (New York: Random House, 1964), p. 235.

33. Potter Stewart, "Or of the Press," *Hastings Law Journal 26* (1975): 634.

34. Edward J. Epstein, *Between Fact and Fiction: The Problems of Journalism* (New York: Random House/ Vintage Books, 1975), pp. 210–232.

35. "Press Coverage and the War on Terrorism: Assessing the Media and the Government," Brookings/Harvard Forum transcript, January 9, 2002, http://www.brook .edu/dybdocroot/comm/transcripts/20020109.htm (September 15, 2002).

36. The Gallup Organization, "Americans: Much Misinformation, Bias, Inaccuracy in News," June 20, 2018, https://news.gallup.com/opinion /gallup/235796/americans-misinformation-bias -inaccuracy-news.aspx (September 16, 2018).

37. The Gallup Organization, 2019.

38. *Collected Speeches of Spiro Agnew* (New York: Audubon Books, 1971), p. 89.

39. The Conversation, "Claims of ideological bias among the media may be overblown," May 18, 2020, https://theconversation.com/claims-of-ideological -bias-among-the-media-may-be-overblown-135617 (July 15, 2020).

40. Austin Ranney, "The Cook Lectures: Politics in the Television Age," *Law Quadrangle Notes 26* (1982): 19. See also Austin Ranney, *Channels of Power* (New York: Basic Books, 1983), pp. 55–63.

41. Carl Bernstein and Bob Woodward, *All the President's Men* (New York: Simon and Schuster, 1974).

42. Joe Foote and Michael Steele, "Degree of Conformity in Lead Stories in Early Evening Network TV Newscasts," *Journalism Quarterly 63* (1986): 21.

43. Lynda Kaid and Joe Foote, "How Network Television Coverage of the President and Congress Compare," *Journalism Quarterly 62* (1985): 59.

44. Paul Taylor, "Hart to Withdraw from Presidential Campaign," *Washington Post*, May 8, 1987, p. Al. Hart later reentered the race and competed in some of the 1988 primaries before withdrawing again.

45. Frederick T. Steeper, "Public Responses to Gerald Ford's Statements on Eastern Europe in the Second Debate," in *The Presidential Debates: Media, Electoral, and Policy Perspectives*, eds. George F. Bishop, et al. (New York: Praeger, 1978), pp. 81–101.

46. Reuven Frank, quoted in Edward Jay Epstein, *News from Nowhere* (New York: Random House/Vintage Books, 1973), pp. 4–5.

47. Herbert Schmertz, "The Media and the Presidency," *Presidential Studies Quarterly 26* (1986): 21.

48. The Gallup Organization, "Major Turning Points in 2000 Election: Primary Season, Party Conventions, and Debates," November 7, 2000, http://www.gallup.com/poll/releases/pr001107c.asp (September 16, 2002).

POP QUIZ

1. People who gather, write, and report the news for the mass media are called _____ .

2. The equal-time rule requires _____ and _____ stations to give or sell equivalent time to a political candidate if the station has given or sold time to another candidate for the same office.

3. The _____ was a regulation of the FCC that required radio and television stations to devote some airtime to a balanced discussion of public issues.

4. Priming occurs when the news media, especially _____ , set the terms by which the public judges its leaders.

5. A news release is a story written by a press agent for distribution to the _____ .

6. Visuals allow the public to see political candidates and their characteristics.   T   F

7. Journalistic ethics do not play a role in the bias of the media.   T   F

8. Economics plays a role in what stories the media will cover.   T   F

9. The bias of the media is affected by the attitudes and outlooks of journalists.   T   F

10. A visual is a scheduled event to give newspaper reporters and television crews a chance to photograph someone.   T   F

11. An announcement or explanation of policy to the media is called a _____.
    A) news briefing
    B) press conference
    C) news release
    D) news framing

12. When candidates answer questions given by journalists, they are at a _____.
    A) news briefing
    B) press conference
    C) news release
    D) news framing

13. Favorable stories equal free advertising for _____.
    A) candidates
    B) journalists
    C) television
    D) radio

14. Since the 1960s, _____ have been using the media to directly communicate with the American people.
    A) presidents
    B) mayors
    C) journalists
    D) executives

15. The _____ requires radio and television stations to give or sell equivalent time to one political candidate if the station has given or sold time to another candidate for that office.
    A) equal-time rule
    B) fair candidate rule
    C) airtime doctrine
    D) fairness doctrine

Answers:
1. journalists   2. radio and television
3. fairness doctrine   4. television   5. media
6. T   7. F   8. T   9. T   10. F   11. A
12. B   13. A   14. A   15. A

Chapter

07

(worthavisual / Shutterstock)

INTEREST GROUPS & POLITICAL PARTIES

In This Chapter

7.1   Interest Groups in American Politics
7.2   Perspectives on Interest Groups
7.3   Political Parties
7.4   Basic Characteristics of the American Party System
7.5   American Political Parties: Past, Present, and Future

Chapter Objectives

People get involved in politics not just as individuals but also as groups. This chapter examines the uniquely important role that two kinds of groups—interest groups and political parties—play in the American political system. The first part of the chapter focuses on interest groups, their activities, and the reasons behind differences in their effectiveness. This discussion sets the stage for an examination of some of the major interest groups on the American political scene today and an evaluation of the role that interest groups play.

The second part of the chapter focuses on parties, which differ from interest groups in that political parties run candidates for public office. By trying to elect members to office, the party serves a variety of important political functions, for example, channeling and clarifying political consensus and conflict, training political leaders, and organizing elections and government.

The American parties form a loosely organized two-party system, a system that is in transition. Are the parties in trouble? What does the future hold for them? These questions are considered in this chapter.

7.1 Interest Groups in American Politics

Interest groups are associations of people who hold common views and who work together to influence what government does. Their interest is in a position, benefit, or advantage (such as favorable treatment under the tax laws) that they want to protect and perhaps

AFL-CIO headquarters in Washington, DC

enlarge. Interest groups look out for their members' political interests by campaigning for policies that promote their goals and by opposing policies that work against those goals. The American Federation of Labor and Congress of Industrial Organizations (AFL-CIO), one of the largest groups of unionized labor in the nation, obviously seeks to win favorable wage and job benefits from companies employing its members; however, it also exists to ensure that government protects its unionizing activities and adopts policies on issues such as trade, interest rates, and education that promote the well-being of its members.

Interest groups have been a prominent feature of American politics since the earliest years of the Republic. During the thick of the public debate over the adoption of a new constitution in 1787, James Madison wrote in *Federalist* No. 10 about the divisions he saw as naturally developing in a society:

> A zeal for different opinions concerning religion, concerning government, and many other points ... have, in turn, divided mankind into parties, inflamed them with mutual animosity, and rendered them much more disposed to vex and oppress each other than to cooperate for the common good. ... The regulation of these various and interfering interests forms the principal task of modern legislation and involves the spirit of party and faction in the necessary and ordinary operations of government.

Compared to other countries, interest groups in the United States play a particularly prominent role in political life. Chapter 5 reported Verba and Nie's finding that roughly 30 percent of Americans (communalists and complete activists) engage in group activities and that joining and working through groups to solve community problems is more common in the United States than in other democracies. It is not surprising, therefore, that scholars studying the American social and political system have focused on interest groups as a uniquely important element of American life. As noted in "Politics and Ideas: Pluralism and Elitism," many see these groups as the basic building blocks of American political life. Perhaps the dominant view is of America as a **pluralist democracy**: American society is made up of many different groups, each looking to secure its members' interests. The principal task of government is, therefore, one of managing the interplay of group interests.

Why American society and politics should be so group-conscious is hard to say. Probably the best explanation is that America is the coming together of so many diverse groups—the **"melting pot"** of different races, nationalities, religions, cultures, and languages—that the variety itself constantly calls attention to the existence and the activities of groups. Beyond being one of the most universally identified features of American

interest groups

Associations of people who hold common views and who work together to influence what government does

pluralist democracy

A system in which the people rule and have their interests protected through the interaction of many different social, political, and economic groups, and in which the principal task of government is to manage group conflict and cooperation

melting pot

Characterization of America as the coming together of a wide variety of racial, ethnic, and religious groups

politics and society, interest groups are also among the most controversial. Interest groups have long been praised as one of the most important contributors to the success of American democracy. As interest groups have become more visible, more sophisticated in their tactics, and more powerful, they are now sometimes condemned as one of the greatest threats to the continuing viability of the American political system. These are concerns that we will return to later.

7.1a   Characteristics of Interest Groups

A stunning variety of organizations fit under the general definition of interest group. The different forms and features that interest groups assume can have an impact on a group's political effectiveness. Of course, no determinant of effectiveness is absolute. A group's influence must be measured relative to the groups with which it contends. Several major characteristics distinguish interest groups and affect their influence.

One of the most obvious characteristics is size. Interest groups vary dramatically in size. All other things being equal, the bigger the group, the more effective it is likely to be. Large groups can mobilize more members, raise more money to support lobbying activities and favored political candidates, and swing more votes in an election. Although, as will be seen shortly, being large is not an unequivocal advantage for an interest group, given a democracy's reliance on plurality and majority decision-making being large is generally better than being small. Sometimes, when an interest group is large or a number of interest groups band together in a common cause, the result is referred to as a **movement**, as in the civil rights movement, environmental movement, feminist movement, or Tea Party movement.

Interest groups vary in membership procedures. Some groups enroll members formally, as when labor unions ask workers to join and pay dues. Other groups rest on a more informal notion of membership in which people just think of themselves as belonging. People may never go to church but nevertheless think of themselves as Catholics. Even this informal sense of membership can vary. Some groups evoke in their membership a very strong sense of identification with the group, whereas others do so only weakly. For still other groups, membership is not even a choice of the individual involved. For instance, African Americans and women are often identified as important interest groups, but most African Americans and most women belong to no race- or gender-based organization. They may not even think of themselves as belonging to some large group. Rather, they are labeled as a member of the group simply because they possess a particular characteristic. Generally speaking, the stronger the bonds of the individual members to the group, the more effective the group will be.[1]

(U.S. Air Force photo by Tech. Sgt. Keith Brown, via Wikimedia)

Membership in some interest groups can be involuntary, with people belonging simply by sharing a particular characteristic, such as women in the military.

Groups also differ in how well they are organized, and the success of an interest group in advancing its interests depends in some measure upon this criteria. A strong network of communication and control can amplify the power of one group, whereas poor internal organization and an inability to coordinate common efforts can dissipate the influence of another. Groups also differ in how democratic they are. Some groups are run as virtual

movement

An effort to attain an end through an organized set of actions and individuals

POLITICS AND IDEAS

Pluralism and Elitism

Pluralism is one of the fundamental ideas of American politics. It is hard to appreciate this unique American contribution to political thought without understanding a little about the political perspective with which it so sharply contrasts. Elitism holds that power in a society is concentrated in the hands of a small group of powerful people, a ruling class. This "elite" is often seen as exercising its power in ways that work to its own benefit and to the disadvantage of those whom it rules, the "masses." Other commentators portray elites as more benevolent, using their power to improve the lot of the less fortunate and to promote democratic values.

The major American contributor to elitist theory was C. Wright Mills.[1] He saw real power in the United States as concentrated in the hands of the highest political, military, and corporate leaders. Mills did not argue for malevolent conspiracy. Rather, he saw the leaders of these institutions as coming from similar backgrounds, sometimes trading positions, interacting with one another, and therefore tending to hold similar values. Foremost among them was a belief in a strong and stable society.

Pluralism, in contrast, sees power as dispersed among many different centers of power, the leaders of various groups that make up society: labor organizations, professional associations, veterans, industries, and the like. Sometimes these centers of power are in agreement, but other times they are not. In any case, collective action is difficult without a reasonable amount of consensus among the

groups about what should be done. This need for consensus compels politics to be moderate and stable. For example, laws passed since the early 1970s to reduce harmful automobile emissions were not imposed on the nation by a single small elite. The laws do not represent a "perfect" solution but rather a compromise among many groups: environmentalists, health-care specialists, automobile manufacturers and dealers, labor unions, and petroleum companies.

What evidence of a power elite do you see in US society? Who is in it? To what ends does it use its power? What evidence do you see of pluralism in US society? What are the dominant groups? How do they use their power? How do the recent Tea Party and Black Lives Matter movements fit into this discussion?

1. *The Power Elite* (Oxford: Oxford University Press, 2000).

---

autocracies with the leadership exerting almost dictatorial control over the group; others are very democratic. The relationship between how democratic a group is and its effectiveness is an uncertain one. Groups run democratically may benefit from the additional commitment that broad membership participation engenders, as long as members can reach substantial consensus in the group. When a lack of consensus hinders decision-making, however, the group may suffer from a lack of common purpose. Conversely, groups run by narrow elites may benefit from singleness of purpose but suffer a lack of support if members feel estranged from the leadership.

How connected a group is to politics can also affect its influence. Some interest groups have little if any connection to politics. They are generally not concerned with political issues or involved in political activity. A town's bowling league rarely has anything to do with politics. Indeed, it would probably suffer as an organization if it became embroiled in partisan political struggles. Its political significance lies in its potential to become politically active should its interests somehow be threatened in the political arena. Legislation to outlaw bowling as an immoral pastime would undoubtedly inspire it to take up the cudgels of politics. However, under normal circumstances it stands completely aside from the political fray. Other interest groups exist solely to pursue political ends. A political action committee, which is discussed later, exists in most cases solely for the purpose of channeling money to political candidates sympathetic to the interests of the group. Between these two extremes reside many organizations that are involved in politics to a

greater or lesser degree. The more closely a group is tied to political issues, personalities, and organizations, the more likely it is to be effective politically.

Finally, groups differ in terms of their adherence to the essentially mainstream views of society. Some groups pursue a course outside the American mainstream. For example, the American Nazi Party leaned to the right of the mainstream and the Communist party to the left of it. Where a group stands in relation to the consensus of American politics has considerable effect on how influential it will be. The most passionate, best-organized interest group in the country will make little headway if it pursues policies that are far off the beaten track of American politics. Groups that argue for complete elimination of income taxes, for example, are likely to make less headway than those that argue for modest reform in the current system.

7.1b   What Interest Groups Do

Interest groups engage in a broad range of activities to protect and advance the well-being of their members. Foremost among these activities is the attempt to influence public opinion. Many interest groups try to create public support or sympathy for their political goals. The major channel for accomplishing this is the mass media. When a group's political interests are threatened, representatives of the group use the media to make the group's views known. Interviews on radio and television news broadcasts, quotations in newspaper and magazine articles, letters to the editor, social media posts, and essays for newspaper op-ed pages are all tools of influence for interest groups. In recent years, interest groups have developed the use of an individual (as opposed to mass) medium to influence public opinion. This is the **direct mail** method, in which computers generate thousands of personally addressed letters soliciting support and financial contributions from potentially sympathetic citizens. Even more recently, savvy interest groups have begun targeted electronic advertising and direct email efforts—targeting potential donors, providing them with a secure method of payment, and saving them a stamp in the process.

Interest groups, of course, are involved in the electoral process through the votes their members cast. More important, interest group members can work in the campaigns of their favored candidates. In recent years, interest groups have been deeply involved in the financing of political campaigns, usually through **political action committees** or **PACs**. PACs are organizations devoted to channeling money from members of interest groups to political candidates sympathetic to the groups' policy preferences. By law, PACs must register with the Federal Election Commission (FEC), have at least fifty contributors, and make contributions to at least five candidates for federal office. No contributor can give any one PAC more than $5,000 per calendar year, and no PAC can give any one candidate more than $5,000 per election. Until recently, individuals were limited in their total contributions to candidates, parties, and committees to $123,200 over a two-year campaign cycle. In 2014, however, the Supreme Court case *McCutcheon v. FEC* held that limiting an individual's overall contributions was a violation of First Amendment freedom of speech guarantees.[2] So, while per-candidate limits still exist, individuals can give money to as many different candidates and PACs as they choose. One study estimated that this ruling could allow a single donor to contribute over $700,000 to candidates and parties in a single election cycle.[3] There is also no limit on how much PACs may raise or give in total. Nor is there any limit on the total amount that a candidate can accept from different PACs. In addition to making direct contributions to candidates, PACs may also spend as much money as they want on independent activities on behalf of one or more candidates, usually purchasing advertising in the broadcast or print media.

direct mail

Method of contacting citizens by mail, rather than through personal contact or the mass media

political action committee (PAC)

Political organization set up to channel campaign money from a group to political candidates sympathetic to the group's political views

PACs blossomed as a result of the **Federal Election Campaign Act**, passed in 1971 and amended significantly in 1974 in an attempt to prevent the misuse of campaign funds brought to light in the Watergate scandal. A few PACs existed previously; but the 1974 act, by setting limits of $1,000 on individual contributions and $5,000 on group contributions, made group contributions more attractive and led to a proliferation of PACs. From 1974 to 2020, the number of PACs increased from about 600 to over 7,000 (see Figure 7.1). During the same period, the amount of money spent by PACs rose from about $10 million to well over $1 billion. PACs have become a controversial issue in American politics, with many questioning whether the post-Watergate reforms have not been a cure that is worse than the disease.

In an effort to rein in what many perceived as out-of-control campaign spending, Congress passed the Bipartisan Campaign Reform Act in 2002 (also known as BCRA or the McCain-Feingold Act, after its sponsors). Among the notable features of this law were a disclaimer rule that required candidates to verbally acknowledge their approval of radio and television advertisements created on their behalf and a "Millionaire's Amendment" that allowed increased contribution limits for candidates running against wealthy opponents. The Supreme Court, in the case of *Davis v. FEC* (2008), held that this amendment was unconstitutional. The Court found the burden imposed on wealthy candidates is not justified by a compelling government interest in lessening corruption. The most controversial feature of the BCRA has been its effort to control "soft money" (unregulated) donations. Although the law closed some loopholes for PACs, it spawned a rise of "527" organizations—so called because they are defined by section 527 of the Internal Revenue Code. These organizations are not permitted any communication with a candidate or allowed to expressly attempt to elect or defeat a particular candidate; but since they are not regulated by the FEC, many contributors have used them as a way to influence politics free from monetary limitations by making independent expenditures. Again, the effort for reform seems to have been thwarted by the desire to use money to influence political outcomes.

Efforts to regulate campaign spending were dealt a blow in 2010 when the Supreme Court held in *Citizens United v. FEC* that prohibiting corporations and labor organizations from independently spending money to advocate for or against candidates for federal office was a violation of the First Amendment's free speech protections.[4] This decision has led to the rise of "super PACs"—organizations that are able to collect and spend money with practically no limitation or regulation, as long as they do not coordinate their efforts directly with political parties or candidates. In the 2014 and 2016 campaign cycles, this often led to super PACs far outspending the campaign organizations of individual candidates. By October 2020, about 5,000 super PACs were registered with the FEC.

Lobbying, the attempt to influence the shape of legislation emanating from the U.S. Congress and other political decision-making bodies, has traditionally been a mainstay of interest group activity. Lobbying involves more than just hobnobbing with legislators; in many cases, lobbyists

("National Association of Realtors building (Washington, D.C.)" by TheAgency, available under a CC BY-SA 3.0 license via Wikimedia)

The National Association of Realtors building in Washington, DC, houses one of the largest lobbying groups in the United States.

Federal Election Campaign Act

Law that regulates campaign financing, requiring full disclosure of sources and uses of campaign funds, and limits contributions to political candidates

lobbying

Attempting to influence legislation under consideration, particularly through personal contact by group representatives

Figure 7.1 The Proliferation of PACs, 1974-2020

The number of political action committees has soared since the post-Watergate campaign reforms made them the preferred vehicle for channeling money from interest group members to political candidates. The recent rapid growth in nonconnected PACs, also known as super PACs, is a result of the Supreme Court's *Citizens United v. FEC* decision.

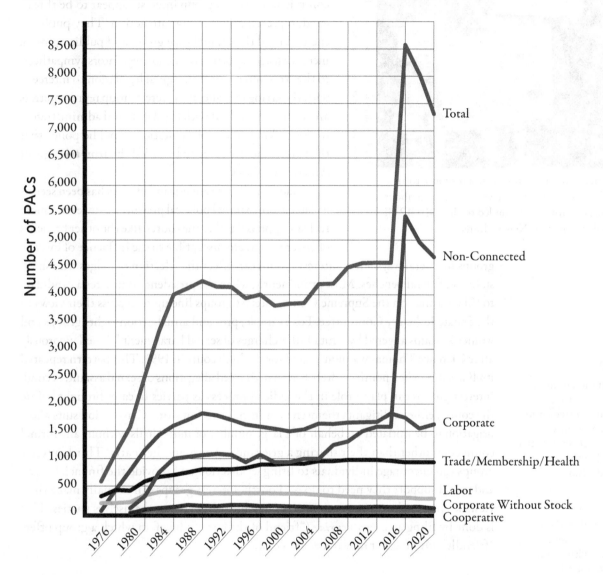

DATA SOURCE: Federal Election Commission, 2020.

are a major source of reliable information for the legislature. Lobbyists provide published materials and advisory letters and testify before congressional committees. They sometimes become deeply involved in the actual process of writing legislation by collaborating with members of Congress and their staffs on the drafting of bills or amendments. In some cases, they may even draft legislation themselves and pass it on to a senator or representative willing to introduce it on the floor. Modern lobbyists are a far cry from the shady figures of folklore. Some are among the most highly paid, respected, and influential figures in Washington.

("BP Oil Spill Protest Jax Square Sunshine" by Infrogmation of New Orleans, available under a CC BY-SA 3.0 license via Wikimedia)

Some special interest groups are a response to an immediate issue or concern, such as protests about how the government responded to the 2010 BP oil spill and its effect on New Orleans.

iron triangle

The combination of interest group representatives, legislative committees, and government administrators seen as extremely influential in determining the outcome of political decisions

class action suit

Legal action initiated on behalf of a large number of individuals without any common interest other than their grievance against the person or institution being sued

***amicus curiae* brief**

Latin for "friend of the court"—persons, government agencies, or groups that are not parties to a case but nonetheless have an interest in its outcome can make their views known by filing this brief with the court

The idea of lobbying extends beyond the corridors and offices of Capitol Hill. The effect of a law depends not just on how the legislation is written but also on how it is translated into action. Therefore, interest group representatives keep close watch on the rules and regulations set by the many agencies of the executive branch of government and the various independent regulatory commissions. When group interests appear to be threatened, representatives swing into action. They publicize the potential threat, mobilize group and public opinion, meet with agency officials, and ask legislators sympathetic to the "true intent" of the original legislation to intercede with the erring bureaucrats. Interest group representatives are so closely involved with legislators and administrators in the making and implementation of public policy that the threesome has come to be called the **iron triangle** of American politics.

Traditionally, the American judiciary has been seen as isolated from external political pressures. However, a more realistic appraisal is that the courts, like the other branches of government, are susceptible to the influence of interest groups in several ways. First, interest groups can affect the selection of judges who sit on state and federal benches. Most prominently, when the president nominates a candidate to fill a vacancy on the Supreme Court, interest groups line up to express their views to the Senate Judiciary Committee. For example, pro- and antiabortion rights groups and women's groups angered by Anita Hill's charges of sexual harassment lobbied vigorously after Clarence Thomas was nominated for the high court in 1991. This pattern repeated itself in 2018, when nominee Brett Kavanaugh faced allegations of sexual assault. Second, interest groups can play a role in the judicial process as parties in cases brought before the courts, either as litigants themselves or in **class action suits**. Class action suits allow litigation to be initiated on behalf of a large number of individuals without any formal connection other than their sharing a grievance against another party. Third, interest groups can encourage individuals to bring legal action and provide the financial, legal, and moral support they need to do so. Fourth, interest groups can formally make their views known to the courts, even in cases in which they are not themselves parties. This is done by filing an *amicus curiae* ("friend of the court") **brief**, in which a group offers "friendly" advice about how to decide a case.

7.1c   Major Interest Groups

Americans belong to a myriad of interest groups. As noted, some are members of more than one group. The *Encyclopedia of Associations*, which confines itself to formal organizations, lists over 24,000 different national groups and over 100,000 state and local organizations. There is even a lobby for lobbyists: the Association of Government Relations Professionals. Taking into account all of the uncounted formal groups and the multitude of informal groups, there are tens of thousands more. Interest groups can be categorized by their characteristics, goals, tactics, and degrees of success. Major groups usually fit into economic, social, religious, ideological, or issue categories. Table 7.1 summarizes the major concerns of different types of interest groups and gives examples of each type of group.

Table 7.1　Types of Major Interest Groups

The table includes only a few of the thousands of groups that exist. In addition, note that a group may be of more than one type. This occurs when economic groups, for example, make statements about social and ideological questions.

Type	Concerns	Examples
Economic	Business, labor, agriculture, and professions	National Association of Manufacturers; American Federation of State, County, and Municipal Employees; American Bar Association; American Farm Bureau Federation
Social	Gender, race, and ethnic discrimination; economic advancement	National Organization for Women; National Association for the Advancement of Colored People; Mexican American Legal Defense and Educational Fund; National Congress of American Indians
Religious	Religious freedom; values reflected in public policy	U.S. Catholic Conference; National Council of Churches; American Jewish Committee; Mennonite Central Committee
Ideological	Political impact of specific public policy	Americans for Democratic Action; People for the American Way; Heritage Foundation; MoveOn
Single Issue	Narrow agenda; limited political goals	Environmental Defense Fund; National Right to Life Committee; National Abortion Rights Action League
Public Interest	Broadly defined consumer and general welfare goals	Common Cause; Public Citizen; Consumers Union; Equal Justice Foundation; League of Women Voters

Economic Groups

Interest groups frequently form around economic issues. In *Federalist* No. 10, Madison wrote, "The most common and durable source of factions has been the various and unequal distribution of property." The various ways in which people gain their livelihood lead to great diversity in the array of groups that form.

Business groups are among the most powerful of all interest groups. Perhaps business's most prominent advocate is the Chamber of Commerce of the United States, which pursues efforts to influence government on a broad front. It engages in extensive **grass roots lobbying** by encouraging its members across the country to contact their elected officials about issues of concern. However, its effectiveness is sometimes diminished, due to the fact that the breadth of its membership makes it difficult for it to take stands that are satisfactory to all its members.

Business interests combine into other, larger organizations based on their special concerns. Large manufacturing companies, for example, have come together in the National Association of Manufacturers. A vast array of industry-wide trade associations, such as the American Iron and Steel Institute and the American Gas Association, represent more particular interests. At the other end of the spectrum are small businesses—the

grass roots lobbying

Attempting to influence members of Congress by encouraging citizens in the home district or state to contact their legislators

hundreds of thousands of small manufacturing concerns, neighborhood TV repair shops, and "mom and pop" grocery stores. The National Federation of Independent Business is one of the best-known small business-oriented groups. Particular professions are represented by important organizations such as the American Medical Association (the leading organization of doctors), the National Association of Realtors, and the American Bar Association. Business groups do not always speak with one voice, however, because political issues sometimes pit one business interest against another. For example, in the early 2000s, many software companies found themselves at odds with industry giant Microsoft when the latter fought against federally imposed antitrust actions.

When people think of labor as an interest group, they usually think first of its more visible side, labor as organized into unions. Individual unions themselves function as independent interest groups. The United Auto Workers, the Teamsters, and the American Federation of State, County, and Municipal Employees are just a few of the many unions recognized as politically active. The AFL-CIO is an umbrella organization of unions with a total membership of approximately 11 million that spearheads political activity on behalf of organized labor. Disagreements over strategy led several member unions to split from this parent organization in 2005 and form their own umbrella organization of about 5.5 million workers called the Change to Win federation. Organized labor was once seen as a monolithic mainstay of the Democratic coalition; but in recent years its influence has diminished, primarily because the share of the labor force belonging to unions has dropped considerably in the last fifty years. The creation of Change to Win indicates a redirection of political efforts in light of this decline in union membership.

Labor has another side that is less visible but numerically larger than the unionized contingent. The majority of American working people do not belong to unions. In fact, workers in the new high-technology industries are much less likely to be unionized than workers in the old smokestack industries they are supplanting. The nonunion workers' lack of organization limits their political influence. Although their more organized counterparts advance some of their interests, their opportunities for political representation are often limited to the actions of their individual members.

Farmers have long been a potent force in American politics. Even today, agriculture is a huge industry. Long-standing organized groups include the American Farm Bureau Federation and the National Grange. They lobby furiously as Congress, once every five years, revises the rules governing agricultural subsidies. Dwindling numbers and hard economic times, however, have conspired to reduce the political power of agricultural interests. In 1930, more than 25 percent of all people in the US lived on farms; today that number has fallen to less than 1 percent. Such pressures have spawned several more-radical and aggressive farm groups, such as the National Farmers Organization and the American Agriculture Movement. The heyday of the farm lobby is over, but agriculture remains a sector that cannot be ignored.

Social Groups

Birth, not choice, determines membership in some interest groups. One of these groups, women, composes one of the potentially largest interest groups in the United States. Slightly more than half of the US population is female, but relatively few belong to politically relevant women's organizations. The most prominent organization is the National Organization for Women (NOW), which presses for economic and political equality for women and, particularly, freedom of choice on abortion. NOW has over 500,000 members, about one out of every three hundred women in the US. Within such a group, the sense of identification can run strong, although it may not run as strong in the female population as a whole.

The women's movement is closely tied to politics in that many of its goals relate to political issues. The increasing number of female candidates running for public office has also strengthened ties. For many years the legitimacy of female involvement in politics was impugned by the old saying that "a woman's place is in the home," but today women are equal participants in the American political process. Perhaps the best indication of change is the growing number of women who have been elected to public office in the past forty years (see Figure 7.2). The nomination of the first major-party female candidate for president or vice president occurred in 1984, when

(Rachael Warriner/Shutterstock)

Washington DC/USA, November 13, 2018: Alexandria Ocasio-Cortez and student activists with the Sunrise Movement occupy Nancy Pelosi's office to demand that she and the Democrats act on climate change.

Geraldine Ferraro was the Democratic candidate for vice president. Senator Hillary Clinton's (D-NY) bid for the Democratic Party's presidential nomination in 2008 came up just short, but it solidified her position as a key contender and led to her eventual nomination in 2016. Kamala Harris made history in 2020, becoming the first woman, as well as the first woman of color, elected vice president. In 2021, there were at least 117 women in the House of Representatives and twenty-four in the Senate. The percentage of female state legislators was 29.3 percent in 2020, more than five times what it was in 1971.

Figure 7.2 Female, African American, and Latinx National and State Legislators and Executives, 1975–2021

The increasing numbers of women, African Americans, and Latinx elected to public offices such as the U.S. Senate and House and state legislatures and to state executive offices in the past forty years demonstrates how the political process has opened up to members of these groups.

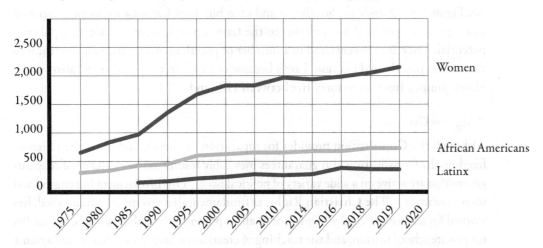

DATA SOURCES: Statistical Abstract of the United States, 2012; Center for the American Woman and Politics, 2020; NALEO Educational Fund, 2020 Vital Statistics on American Politics, 4th ed., 1999–2000; Pew Research Center, 2020; National Conference of State Legislatures, 2020.

Certainly the most prominent of all biologically based interest groups in recent American history is the African American population. Whereas African Americans constitute only about 13 percent of the American population, they gain considerable influence from two sources: their strong sense of group identification and the close ties between the group and the world of politics. Shut out from the social and economic establishments, African Americans had little recourse but to pursue advancement through the political system, which in itself has given their cause a special political legitimacy. Further, forceful African American leaders, such as Dr. Martin Luther King Jr. and the Reverend Jesse Jackson, have not hesitated to spur African Americans to political action. The National Association for the Advancement of Colored People (NAACP) remains perhaps the most visible African American interest organization. Although only a small percentage of African Americans (less than 2 percent) belong to the NAACP, it is the most widely recognized formal African American organization in America, with a membership of about 500,000.

Although the United States is far from total resolution of its racial problems, the African American civil rights movement has, over the long term, met with considerable success. This success is at least partly due to the fact that the movement's goals are not an attack on fundamental values but rather a push for broader realization of traditional American social, political, and economic equality. In recent years, a major effort has been aimed at encouraging African Americans to use their hard-won right to vote and get more African Americans elected to public office. Including positions in local governments, the United States now has more than 9,000 elected African American officials.[5] The number of African Americans in the House of Representatives rose from seventeen in 1981 to at least fifty-nine in 2021.

Another prominent ethnic group is the growing Latinx segment of the American population—primarily Mexican Americans, Cuban Americans, and Puerto Ricans. Although Latinx in the United States currently number nearly 60 million, they confront a situation similar to what African Americans faced forty years ago. Like African Americans, Latinx lag in educational level and are only now developing a strong sense of collective political identity. Fewer Latinx are registered to vote (only 54 percent of the 29 million eligible Latinx); and those who are registered do not always vote (40 percent, compared to 55 percent for whites and 51 percent for African Americans in 2018).[6] Those who cast ballots do not necessarily vote for Latinx candidates. Latinx lack a cohesive national organization on the order of the NAACP. As a result, there are fewer elected Latinx leaders (see Figure 7.2). Outside the Southwest and a few big cities, Latinx are seldom recognized as a significant political bloc. However, the Latinx people have considerable political potential. They are concentrated in a number of populous states that can be critical to victory in a presidential election. Partly because of this fact, the number of Latinx in the House jumped from six to forty-five between 1981 and 2021.

Religious Groups

Although the Constitution provides for separation of church and state, the religious freedom the Constitution also guarantees inevitably results in the existence of religious groups that are active on a wide variety of political issues. This involvement has engendered some controversy. The **Christian Right**, as fundamentalist groups are often called, has worked for a constitutional amendment to allow prayer in the public schools, tax credits for private school tuition, and the teaching of creationism in public schools, and against laws favoring the rights of women and LGBT individuals and the teaching of anything but abstinence in sex education.

Christian Right

Conservative, religion-based groups that involve themselves in the political process

The religious right loomed as a major factor in American politics through the early 1980s; however, its visibility receded in the late 1980s after revelations of sexual and financial misconduct by such well-known figures as Jim and Tammy Bakker and Jimmy Swaggart. Since then, though, conservative Christians have been working quietly but diligently around the country to elect their adherents to state and local offices and have virtually taken over the Republican Party organization in several states. Perhaps the most prominent organization spearheading this activity is television evangelist Pat Robertson's

Christian Coalition. The Christian Right was credited with playing an important role both in the election of a Republican congressional majority in 1994 and the election of President George W. Bush in 2000 and 2004. In 2008, Christian conservatives made former Arkansas Governor Mike Huckabee a viable candidate in the Republican presidential primary. Other more socially liberal denominations such as the United Church of Christ—in effect an emerging "Christian Left"—have involved themselves in controversies over arms control, human rights abroad, and US policy in Central America, among others.

No issue in recent years has drawn religious groups more into the political fray than abortion. The Catholic Church and the Christian Right have both worked hard to make abortion a political issue through support of sympathetic candidates and demonstrations outside abortion clinics. A particularly dramatic example by the Roman Catholic Church was its use of the threat of excommunication against Catholics who support or even tolerate abortion.

Rush Limbaugh is a conservative political commentator. Conservatism is an ideological political group.

(Official White House Photo by Joyce N. Boghosian via Wikimedia)

Ideological Groups

Some groups pursue an explicitly political agenda almost exclusively. When that agenda is broad, the group is characterized as an ideological one. Such groups typically have a clear philosophy of governmental action and evaluate public policy proposals in those terms. Perhaps the best example is the Americans for Democratic Action (ADA), a relatively small group with about 65,000 members that has long espoused a liberal perspective on American politics. Thus, it has become a beacon to those on the American left and an enemy to those on the right. The ADA is best known for the ratings of members of the House and the Senate, which it publishes every year as a way of calling attention to individual legislators' fidelity to liberal values. In recent election cycles, the organization MoveOn has played a growing role in supporting progressive causes by making use of the internet and electronic mailing lists to build a network of supporters and contributors. At the other end of the political spectrum, Tea Party organizations around the country have backed an array of conservative or libertarian candidates and causes, with a particular focus on reducing taxes and budget deficits.

Single-Issue Groups

In contrast to the broad political agenda of ideological groups, single-issue groups have narrower agendas and more limited political goals. One of the most visible of all the

narrow single-issue groups has been the antiabortion, or right-to-life, movement. Groups such as the National Right to Life Committee have been single-minded in their attempts to ban abortion. These groups regard the issue of abortion as the overriding issue of contemporary politics—a so-called litmus test of whether a candidate should be supported.

("Chipotle Brandon" by User:proshob, available under a CC BY-SA 3.0 license via Wikimedia)

Chipotle Mexican Grill closed forty-three restaurants in Washington and Oregon in response to the initial outbreak of *E. coli* in early November 2015. Public interest groups focus on issues of product safety and the effectiveness of government regulation of public utilities and industry.

The uncompromising position of antiabortion groups has spawned some similarly uncompromising reactions from single-interest abortion-rights groups. The most prominent among these groups is the National Abortion and Reproductive Rights Action League, which claims some 250,000 members.

Single-issue groups are a controversial political phenomenon. Advocates contend that there are indeed some overriding moral issues that people should rightly pursue to the exclusion of everything else. Others see single-issue groups as a threat to democracy because they refuse the compromise that helps to make a democratic system work.

Public Interest Groups

With so many interest groups vying for advantage in the political arena, it sometimes seems that everybody's individual political interests get served, but not the public's as a whole. Thus, organizations have formed to represent broad-based notions of the public's interest. These groups focus on issues such as product safety and the effectiveness of government regulation of public utilities and industry. Perhaps the most prominent such group is Common Cause, the self-styled "citizens' lobby" founded in 1970. It has taken on a broad range of issues, including that of campaign financing.

7.2 | Perspectives on Interest Groups

Given the visibility and the pervasiveness of interest groups in American democracy, it is not surprising that they evoke strong reactions from both the general public and political experts. Some citizens view interest groups in highly positive terms, seeing them as essential elements of a successful democracy. Others take a dimmer view, finding them to be perpetual and inevitable dangers to the common good.

7.2a | Interest Groups as the Foundation of Democracy

Classical democratic theory demands that citizens be interested in politics, informed about politics, rational in their political judgments, and active in the political process. As Chapter 5 made clear, many people fall short of these expectations. The question is how American democracy can continue to function, and even prosper, in the face of this disparity.

Some observers see interest groups as the answer. As noted earlier, the United States is a pluralist society. Most Americans belong to at least one formal group as well as to a number of other groups. The leaders of these various interest groups act on behalf of their members to protect and advance their causes. Because there are so many groups, sheer force of competition prevents any single group or handful of groups from dominating the others. Thus, every member of society has his or her interests protected without having to be politically active. Democracy functions through representation—not just formal representation via elected officials, but also representation of individual citizens by the leaders of the interest groups.

Further, because most Americans belong to several groups, political disputes seldom run along the same lines. To illustrate, one woman may be a white, Catholic homemaker, whereas her neighbor is a white, Protestant public schoolteacher. The two will probably agree about property taxes but disagree about tuition tax credits for parents with children in private schools. Political scientists call this tendency for different coalitions to form on different issues **cross-cutting cleavage** and see it as a brake on polarizing conflict in society. These two elements, competition between interest groups and cross-cutting cleavages, contribute to an equitable and stable society. Indeed, some scholars laud the pluralistic character of American society as an essential factor in the success of its democratic system.[7]

Not surprisingly, critics have found flaws in this flattering portrait of American politics. Not every citizen belongs, in any meaningful way, to a significant interest group; and group leaders do not necessarily represent the best interests of all the group members. In fact, the structure of some interest groups may be very undemocratic. Also, pure competition cannot exist among all the interest groups in a society. Some groups are big and powerful and can dominate; others are small and weak and can be dominated. After all, with what does a small and powerless interest group have to bargain? It is very hard for a group to enter into negotiations with nothing and emerge with something. Thus, pluralist democracy may, in reality, turn out to be **interest group elitism**. The elites within interest groups pursue their own interests rather than their members' interests; and the elite interest groups—the biggest and most powerful groups—pursue their interests at the expense of the small and powerless groups.

7.2b   Interest Groups Versus the Public Interest

Interest groups are most widely reviled when they are seen as using the political process to achieve selfish objectives. A manufacturing group that resists regulation by the Consumer Product Safety Commission may claim that it is only defending the public's right to buy whatever it wants at the lowest possible price. Instead, the public may perceive the group as demanding the right to make money by producing shoddy and unsafe goods. This kind of spectacle is no doubt one of the greatest frustrations of democratic government and has caused many people to favor tighter regulation of lobbying and other interest group activities. What is the "common good"? Who gets to define it? Should the common good never be impaired in the slightest, even to do a great good for a small number? Does a common good exist, in fact, apart from the outcome of the democratic process that defines it?

Interest group obstructionism of the majority may seem indefensible until it is our own interests upon which that majority is about to trample. A person might protest loudly when import quotas on automobiles make imported cars more expensive and push up prices of domestic models. That same person would probably think differently if he or she worked in a Detroit auto assembly plant or owned a Ford dealership. The real quarrel of those who decry interest group activities may not be with interest groups themselves

cross-cutting cleavage
The overlapping of interest group membership from individual to individual, with the result that society rarely finds the same people lined up on opposite sides on all the issues and is thus protected against political polarization

interest group elitism
The idea that the leaders of interest groups may act in ways that promote their own interests rather than the interests of the broader membership of the group

(Ken Durden / Shutterstock)

The health-care bill was an example of interest group gridlock.

but rather with the political processes that strike the balance between majority and minority interests.

7.2c Interest Group Gridlock

Pluralist theory envisions a myriad of interests doing battle in the political arena and the government emerging with policies that, although probably not ideal for any, are acceptable to all. What if no consensus could be reached, however? Critics charge that a pluralistic system could arrive at a virtual state of paralysis, in which an overabundance of interest groups develops, each refusing to compromise. One commentator has called this situation *interest group gridlock,* analogous to the traffic gridlock that often develops in large cities.[8] In an analogy to the clogged arteries that threaten many people's health, another commentator has characterized these stalemates as "demosclerosis"—a state in which the political process is so clogged by the piling up of numerous permanent commitments to interest groups that the government lacks the resources to deal with new problems that arise.[9] Interest group gridlock and demosclerosis may be stark warnings of the dangers of pluralism run amok. The hope of democracy is that good "traffic regulation" by public officials and a more moderate diet for interest groups can help to smooth the way for the successful development of public policy.

7.3 Political Parties

A **political party** is an organization that seeks to influence public policy by putting its own members into positions of governmental authority. In the United States and other democratic nations where most important public officials are chosen by popular election, this means placing a party member's name on the ballot, identifying the candidate as a member of that party, and then working to elect the party member to the office. Parties and interest groups are alike in that their members may share common political views or objectives and may engage in collective political activities. They differ in that interest groups do not run their own candidates for public office. Further, there are many interest groups, each with narrower agendas; however, there are just two major parties, each with a broader agenda.

7.3a What Parties Do

In the pursuit of elective office, parties can perform several important functions that help to bring order to the electoral process and coherence to government. First, by making themselves visible actors on the stage of politics and trying to gain public support, parties accomplish several important **socialization functions**. Because people tend to identify with political parties, parties provide a psychological hook that pulls people into the world of politics. Parties also help to structure people's perceptions of politics.

political party

A group that seeks to influence public policy by placing its own members in positions of governmental authority

socialization functions

With reference to political parties, the ways in which parties, by seeking to win elections, help to socialize voters into politics and form public opinion

They provide important cues to citizens as they perceive and try to make sense of the political world around them. Parties educate citizens about politics and mobilize them into political action. In their attempts to attract voters to their causes, parties tell voters about what is going on in politics, how it affects them, and why they should get involved. Finally, whereas candidates and issues come and go from one election to the next, parties tend to persist. By providing relatively fixed reference points in a changing political scene, parties help people keep their political bearings and thus help to maintain political and social stability.

Jo Jorgensen speaking with supporters at a campaign rally at Eldorado Park in Scottsdale, Arizona

Winning elective office requires getting votes. Given the wide range of voters' interests, a single issue will probably not appeal to enough voters to win. The party, therefore, must put together a package of positions on a variety of issues that will attract sufficient numbers of voters. In doing so, parties accomplish four important **electoral functions**. The first is to integrate interests. It is unlikely that any one candidate will offer everything that every voter seeks; however, candidates who satisfy needs common to large numbers of voters will receive their support. Second, the set of alternatives from which voters can pick is simplified. Because substantial numbers of voters find their views reflected by one or the other of the coalition candidates, fewer candidates are needed on the ballot. Third, the parties complement the legally established process for choosing public officials. By setting up procedures for determining who will represent a party in a campaign and for supporting these candidates in the election, parties fill important gaps in the selection process. Finally, parties are a prime means of recruiting and training political leaders. Parties provide many people with an entry into politics and opportunities to develop their political skills.

Once a political party achieves electoral victory, it confronts the task of governing. By trying to achieve what they have proposed during the campaign, parties accomplish two important **governmental functions**. First, they organize government and give coherence to governmental policy. Because the founders saw centralized political power as a threat to individual freedom, the Constitution dispersed power to avoid the tyranny of the majority. Power was broken up by function in the separation of powers in the federal system and by geography. Experience soon showed, however, that this fragmentation of power led to a lack of coordination, stagnation, and even paralysis in government. Political parties evolved as a new source of coordination in the political system. With like-minded individuals pursuing common objectives dispersed throughout the executive, legislative, and judicial branches of the national and state governments, coherence and coordination were restored to policy-making.[10]

Second, parties help make government responsible to the people. Because parties are stable features on the American political scene, the electorate can reward a party that does a good job of governing and punish a party that does not. Thus, even though the public is not in a position to supervise every detail of governmental action, parties allow the public to exert some degree of oversight and control over what the government does.

electoral functions

With reference to political parties, the ways in which parties, by seeking to win elections, help to bring order to campaigns and elections

governmental functions

With reference to political parties, the ways in which parties, by seeking to win elections, help to organize the government, give coherence to public policy, and make government responsible to the people

POLITICS AND ECONOMICS

Economic Status and Party Identification

Traditional wisdom portrays the Democrats as the party of the economically less well-off and the Republicans as the party of the more economically successful. How well does this image square with current reality? Figure 7.3 shows the relationship between party identification and income. Interestingly, a small number of Americans at every income level identify themselves as purely independent—not leaning toward the Democrats or the Republicans. Apart from this fact, the trends anticipated by the traditional image of the parties do appear. Far more of the poorest people are Democrats than Republicans, and more of the wealthier people are Republicans than Democrats—though not in the highest income category included here. However, a significant number of the poorest people are Republicans, and an even larger number of the wealthiest people are Democrats. Thus, economic status has some effect, but party choice in the United States is not made on the basis of economic self-interest alone.

Why is the Democratic Party traditionally associated with the less well-off and the Republican Party with the better-off? Why does party affiliation not divide more clearly along economic lines—that is, why are some poorer people Republicans and some richer people Democrats?

Figure 7.3   Party Identification by Income

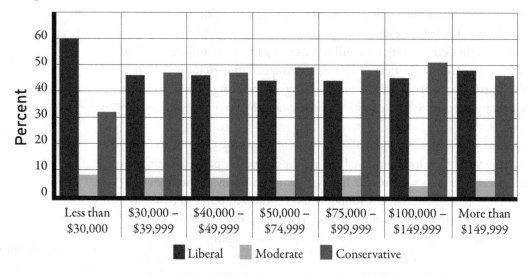

*This figure groups respondents who indicated they "leaned toward" a particular party with that party.

DATA SOURCE: Pew Research Center, "2016 Party Identification Detailed Tables," September 13, 2016.

7.4 Basic Characteristics of the American Party System

Political parties exist under almost every form of government. However, the particular shape a party system assumes varies from one country to another. In the United States, the party system is characterized by having just two major parties and a loose relationship between the national, state, and local parties and the three components that make up the party: the formal party organization, the party in the electorate, and the party in the government.

7.4a   A Two-Party System

From its beginnings, the United States has had a two-party system. Never have there been more than two large and enduring political organizations at the same time. Party fortunes, of course, have ebbed and flowed. At some times, minor parties have flourished. At other times, some people have feared that one party would rule the nation unchallenged; but the minor parties have always faded, the party with the overwhelming majority has faltered, or the opposition party has rebounded.

Why does this pattern consistently recur? One theory is based on the old saying that "there are two political parties because there are two sides to every question." This explanation sounds good, but many political questions have more than two sides. Also, unless there are fewer sides to political questions in the United States than in other countries, every country should have a two-party system. Many of them do not.

Both major political parties draft statements of beliefs, called platforms, every presidential election year. You can find the most recent Democratic and Republican platforms at the below websites.

Republican platform

http://www.bvtlab.com/QqM67

Democratic platform

http://www.bvtlab.com/96WR7

Another old adage may come closer to the truth: "There are two political parties because there are two sides to every office—inside and outside." In the American system, where most offices are contested on an individual basis (i.e., one person wins a single office such as mayor or governor or congressional representative), winning usually requires simply getting more votes than anybody else. This is called **plurality election**. Plurality elections contrast with **majority elections**, in which the victor must receive more than half of all the votes. A **run-off election** is required under a system of majority elections if more than two candidates run and none gets a majority. With plurality or majority elections, most electoral contests in the United States have a single winner and one or more losers—one "in" and one or more "outs." Because the only way for an outsider to displace an insider is to win more votes, the natural tendency is for political organizations to form around those in power and those out of power.

An alternative electoral system is **proportional representation**, whereby offices, such as seats in a legislature, are awarded in proportion to the percentage of votes a party receives. Proportional representation may encourage the growth of more than two parties because a party may place third or fourth in an election and still win seats. Proportional

plurality election

Election in which a candidate wins simply by getting more votes than any other candidate, even if it is less than a majority of the votes

majority election

Election in which a candidate wins by getting more than one-half of the votes cast

run-off election

An election pitting the leading candidates of a previous election against each other when the previous election has not produced a clear-cut winner

proportional representation

A system for allocating seats in a legislative body in which the number of seats a party gets out of the total is based on the percentage of votes that the party receives in an election

representation is relatively rare in the United States; it is more common in other countries, such as France and Italy.

The plurality election system is not the only reason the United States has a two-party system. Undoubtedly other factors enter in as well, including the predominantly centrist distribution of opinion, the impact of history, and the absence of consistently intense ethnic and religious divisions that might lead to chronic political fragmentation. However, the electoral system has certainly played a significant role in shaping the basic structure of the American party system.

This discussion of the two-party system should not obscure the fact that third parties do have a place in the American political system. As shown in Figure 7.4, third parties have existed for a long time. Although most third parties have been little more than temporary vehicles for a particular candidate or issue, they nevertheless have played an important role in influencing the actions of the major parties. They have raised issues that the major parties were eventually forced to address. For example, the abolitionist parties of the mid-nineteenth century forced slavery onto the agendas of the major political parties. Persistent advocacy of egalitarian ideas such as female suffrage, government regulation of big business, Social Security, and low-cost health care by the Populists, Progressives, and Socialists laid the groundwork for much of the New Freedom of Woodrow Wilson, the New Deal of Franklin Roosevelt, and the Great Society of Lyndon Johnson.

In a few cases, the presence of third parties in the field has tipped the balance from one of the major parties to the other. In 1912, in the middle of a long period of Republican dominance, former President Theodore Roosevelt's Bull Moose Party garnered 27 percent of the popular vote and eighty-eight electoral votes, siphoning off enough votes from the Republican incumbent William Howard Taft to give the Democrat Woodrow Wilson the victory. (This was, by the way, the only time in American history that a **third party** actually outpolled one of the major parties in a presidential election.) In 1968, American Independent candidate George Wallace won 14 percent of the popular vote and forty-six electoral votes, probably drawing off enough votes from Democrat Hubert Humphrey to give Republican Richard Nixon the victory.

In 1992, independent presidential candidate Ross Perot, running under the banner of his United We Stand movement, garnered 19 percent of the popular vote, making his the most successful third-party movement in recent American history. Because Perot seemed to draw votes almost equally from Bush and Clinton, it is unlikely that he changed the outcome of the election. However, Perot participated in the three presidential debates and was instrumental in making deficit reduction and economic revival major issues in the campaign. Perot ran again in 1996, but only managed to gain about half of the total vote that he had earned in 1992. In 2000, Pat Buchanan ran on the Reform Party ticket, and Ralph Nader ran as a Green Party candidate. The two combined to garner over 3.3 million votes in a very tight election. Since Nader, who generated about 2.9 million of those votes, was a decidedly liberal candidate, some have suggested that he cost Al Gore the election. Such conclusions, however, overlook the fact that many Nader voters were disenchanted with the two-party system and might not have voted at all if George W. Bush and Gore were the only choices available. The lesson Americans took away from that election, though, may have been that it is risky to vote for a minor party candidate during a close presidential race. In 2004, Pat Buchanan backed the incumbent Republican president and the Green Party refused to nominate Ralph Nader, choosing to go instead with a candidate who vowed to campaign only in states where the outcome was not expected to be close. Ultimately, less than 1 percent of the popular vote went to minor party candidates in 2004. Given the many contrasts between the two major party candidates, voters largely stuck with the Democratic and Republican choices in 2008 and 2012, continuing the trend of not providing more than 1 percent of the vote for any third-party candidate. In 2016, faced

third party

In the American political context, a minor party that attracts only a small share of the electorate's vote and is a party other than the two major parties that have dominated politics through most of American history

Figure 7.4   American Political Parties Since 1789

The chart indicates the years during which parties either ran presidential candidates or held national conventions. The life span for many political parties can only be approximated because parties existed at the state or local level before they ran candidates in presidential elections and continued to exist at local levels after they ceased running presidential candidates. For example, in the year 2020, at least a dozen parties ran a candidate for president in one or more states, but only five candidates were on the ballot in over ten states: Donald Trump (Republican), Joe Biden (Democrat), Jo Jorgensen (Libertarian), Howie Hawkins (Green), and Don Blankenship (Constitution).

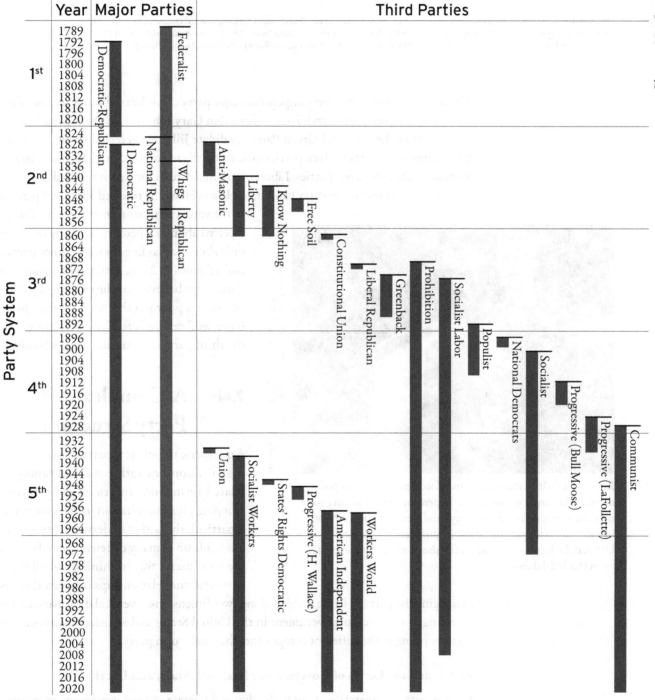

Figure continued on next page.

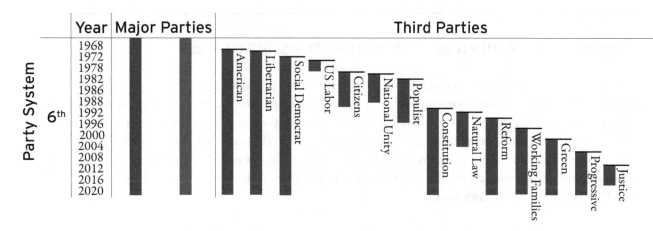

Party System	Year	Major Parties	Third Parties
6th	1968 1972 1978 1982 1986 1988 1992 1996 2000 2004 2008 2012 2016 2020		American · Libertarian · Social Democrat · US Labor · Citizens · National Unity · Populist · Constitution · Natural Law · Reform · Working Families · Green · Progressive · Justice

DATA SOURCES: Congressional Quarterly's Guide to the U.S. Elections, 2nd ed. (Washington, DC: Congressional Quarterly, 1985), p. 224; Congressional Quarterly Weekly Report, November 5, 1988, p. 3184; Federal Election Commission, "1992 Official Presidential General Election Results," Press Release, January 14, 1993; Federal Election Commission, http://www.fec.gov/; Ballotpedia, https://ballotpedia.org.

with a choice between two very unpopular major party candidates, about 5 percent of the vote went to minor party candidates. Libertarian Gary Johnson led the way with about 3.3 percent of the vote, and Green Party candidate Jill Stein received about 1 percent, with write-ins and other minor parties making up the remainder. In 2020, voters largely focused on the two major parties. Libertarian candidate Jo Jorgensen received about 1.2 percent of the vote, Green Party candidate Howie Hawkins received about 0.2 percent of the vote, and other minor party candidates received about 0.3 percent, resulting in a total only about half as large as what minor parties had achieved in 2016. Although a majority of Americans believe that the two major parties "do such a poor job that a third major party is needed," relatively few have been enticed by the third-party options that currently exist.[11]

("Gary Johnson by Gage Skidmore 4" by Gage Skidmore, available under a CC BY-SA 3.0 license via Wikimedia)

In August 2016, Libertarian candidate Gary Johnson's poll numbers began to approach the 15 percent threshold necessary to make him the first third-party candidate since Ross Perot in 1992 to participate in broadcast presidential debates. Ultimately, Johnson's numbers fell short, and he was excluded from the fall debates.

7.4b A Complex Party Structure

An American political party is not a single organization but rather a broad family of related formal organizations and informal groupings. It is complex, not in the sense that it is particularly hard to understand, but in that it is made up of many different parts. Perhaps the most useful way to think about all these parts and the relationships between them is to imagine the party as being divided along two dimensions: a vertical dimension corresponding to the levels of government in the United States and a horizontal dimension corresponding to the different components that make up a party.

Parties and the Levels of Government: National, State, and Local

Because party organizations tend to develop and operate around institutions of government, it is only natural that their structure tends to parallel that of government. One of

the most important divisions of government in the United States is the federal system. Just as the American government is divided into national, state, and local institutions, so also are parties divided into national, state, and local organizations and groupings. As in the government, the relationship among the levels is not a strictly hierarchical one; each level retains some level of independence and autonomy from the others.

Parties and Their Components: Formal, Electoral, and Governmental

Even at any one level of government, a political party is not just a single organization. Rather, it has at least three distinguishable sectors or components: the formal party organization, the party in the electorate, and the party in the government.[12] The **formal party organization** is the party narrowly construed and that which most people would think of if asked to define the political party. It consists of the people who actually work for the party as leaders or followers, professionals or volunteers, and members of committees or attendees of meetings.

The formal structure of American parties parallels the structure of federalism. Power is vested at both the national and state levels. Ultimate authority lies with the party's **national convention**, which meets prior to the presidential election every four years. Because political parties exist to contest elections, most of what the convention does is related to the upcoming presidential campaign: writing a **platform** (a statement of the party's proposed program) and selecting the party's candidates for president and vice president. These activities are discussed in more detail in Chapter 8.

Some of the convention's activities have a more strictly organizational slant. The convention is the ultimate authority in setting the party's rules; and it formally designates the **national committee**, the permanent body that oversees the party's affairs on an ongoing basis. Each state's members on the national committee are usually selected by state party organizations in conventions or primaries. The national committee, in turn, formally elects the party chairperson. The national chairperson supervises the work of the headquarters staff, a role that has become more significant in recent years, for reasons to be seen shortly. From 2011 until the end of July 2016, the Democratic Party chairperson was Debbie Wasserman Schultz, a member of Congress from Florida. Schultz resigned just prior to the Democrats' national convention after leaked emails indicated that she had actively sought support for candidate Hillary Clinton and attempted to discredit the Bernie Sanders campaign. A party chair's role is to remain neutral until the party's voters have decided on their candidate. Schultz was replaced temporarily by Donna Brazile, a former campaign manager. In 2017, the Democrats selected former Secretary of Labor Tom Perez as their chairperson. The Republican Party was led by Reince Priebus, an attorney and former chair of the Wisconsin Republican Party. After the 2016 election, President Trump named Priebus as his first chief of staff, and the Republicans elected Ronna Romney McDaniel as his replacement.

For years, state and local parties were the bedrock of the American party system, often due to the influence of state and local "political machines." A **political machine** is a political organization that recruits and controls its membership through the use of its governmental authority to bestow benefits on its supporters and withhold them from its opponents. This patronage includes benefits such as obtaining government jobs, government contracts, and "favors." To gain benefits, people had to support the machine by voting for its candidates and campaigning for the machine. The great urban political

What issues affect the public in your state?

The Public Interest Research Group's website is a good starting point for answering this question.

http://www.bvtlab.com/BH8T9

formal party organization
One of the three components or distinguishable sectors of a political party; the official structure of a political party and includes people who officially belong to it, elected and appointed officers, and committees

national convention
The quadrennial meeting of an American political party that focuses on the upcoming presidential election

platform
A broad statement of the philosophy and program under which a party's candidates run for election

national committee
The body responsible for guiding political party organization on an ongoing basis

political machine
Political organization that recruits and controls its membership through the use of its governmental authority to give benefits (jobs, contracts, etc.) to its supporters and deny them to its opponents

machines, in large part, have faded from the American political scene, although the use of public power to perpetuate partisan dominance lives on in many municipalities and some states.

The structure of the state and local parties is, in many respects, similar to that of the national parties with state party conventions and **state committees** that are usually made up of representatives from the state's counties or congressional districts. The party typically elects a state chairperson, who is in charge of the day-to-day operations of the party. Underlying the statewide party organization is a hierarchy of county, city, ward (or district), and precinct committees and chairpersons. In some locales this organization constitutes a formidable political force, while elsewhere the structure is moribund, with many of the positions not even filled.

state committee
The body responsible for guiding a state political party organization on an ongoing basis

There is more to a party than just its formal organization. A party includes, not in any formal sense but psychologically and socially, the citizens in the electorate who support it. This **party in the electorate** can be viewed in two different ways. At the individual level, the defining component of the connection of an individual to a party is party identification, "a psychological identification" or "sense of individual attachment to a party," independent of "legal recognition or even without a consistent [voting] record of party support."[13] Appropriate to the definition, party identification has typically been measured simply by asking people whether they think of themselves as Republicans, Democrats, independents, and so on, and following up with questions about strength of feeling. Thus, the party in the electorate is really defined by people who claim to think of themselves as belonging to the party. Figure 7.5 shows how the distribution of party identification has varied over the last sixty years.

party in the electorate
The individual citizens throughout the country who identify with a political party

Figure 7.5 Party Identification of the American Electorate, 1960–2020

The Democratic Party held a substantial edge in party identification from the 1960s into the 1970s, but Republican resurgence beginning in the 1980s eroded that edge. Today, Democrats maintain the advantage over Republicans, but more Americans identify as independents than with either party.

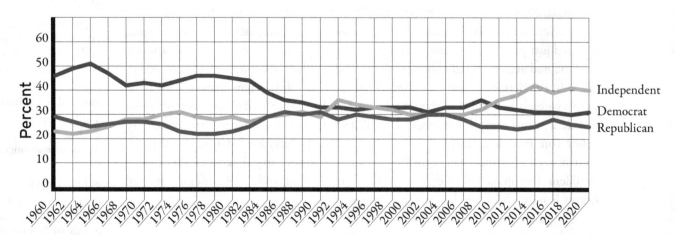

DATA SOURCE: American National Election Studies, 2006; The Gallup Organization, 2020. Copyright © 2020 Gallup, Inc.

Individuals who identify with a party relate to it, not just as individuals, but also as members of the various groups to which they belong. Parties, in other words, can be seen as coalitions of the various social, economic, regional, and religious groups. The Democratic Party was traditionally seen as the party of the working class, the rural and southern constituents, and Catholics, whereas the Republican Party has been seen as the party of the upper classes, big businesses, and Protestants. These relationships have changed in recent years as new political battles have reshaped party lines, but the fact remains that both parties must rely on their appeal to large groups of the electorate to maintain their appeal. Thus, the party in the electorate also includes these groups that are thought of as belonging to the party's **coalition**.

Finally, there is the **party in the government**. Once a party's candidates are elected, the elected officials (at least in theory) need to organize themselves and work together to implement the policies on the basis of which they campaigned. Thus, the party in government consists of the elected candidates of a party—president, governors, mayors, senators, members of the House, state legislators, city council members—as well as the organizations these officials establish and the leaders they designate to help carry out their work. The most visible of these are the legislative party meetings (caucuses, as the Democrats call them, and conferences, as the Republicans call them), the congressional campaign committees, and the majority and minority leaders and whips. The party in government also includes, however, the less visible and informal *executive party* created by the president and governors who tend to appoint members of their own party to administrative positions, and even the shadowy *judicial party* suggested by patterns of party-oriented bloc voting in some courts.[14]

7.5 American Political Parties: Past, Present, and Future

The health of the American party system has been one of the most talked-about political subjects over the past fifty years. To understand the current state of the American party system and what its future may be, it is necessary to understand a little about the history of the American party system.

7.5a Parties Past

Political parties emerged early in the history of the American republic and have existed ever since. American history up through 1968 can be divided into six major **party systems** (see Figure 7.3). The first party system (1789–1824), which developed from the pre-Revolutionary alignment of parties paralleling the British system of the period (conservative Tories and progressive Whigs), pitted Federalists against Antifederalists. The two parties disagreed primarily on whether the new government should be relatively centralized and elite (the Federalist view) or decentralized and democratic (the Antifederalist view). The Federalist Party faded away after 1800; but the Democratic Republicans, as the Antifederalists came to be called, continued on to govern through a period of comparatively little national political conflict between 1815 and 1825, called the Era of Good Feelings.

coalition
A subgroup of a party, based on common social, economic, and religious characteristics

party in the government
One of the three components or sectors of a political party: the party as embodied in those of its members who have been elected or appointed to public office, the organizations they establish, and the leaders they choose to help them carry out their work

party system
Period during which the pattern of support for political parties based on a particular set of important political issues remains reasonably stable

(iStock)

Andrew Jackson, as depicted on the $20 bill, was the founder of the Democratic Party. Founded in the mid-1820s, the U.S. Democratic Party is still active, making it the oldest in the world today.

By the mid-1820s, the weak framework of the Democratic Republican Party began to fall apart. Andrew Jackson emerged from this factional conflict as the founder of the Democratic Party, which continues as an active party today, making it the oldest party in the world. The Democrats confronted a new Whig party in the second party system (1824–1860). The Democrats were the party of lower-class rural and urban "working people" and old-fashioned machine politics, whereas the Whigs were the party of business and political reform. Slavery destroyed the Whig–Democratic party alignment; through the 1850s, both parties split into northern and southern branches over the issue that would soon tear apart the nation as well.

Beginning in 1860, under the third-party system (1860–1896), former Whigs, led by Abraham Lincoln of Illinois, combined with some progressive remnants of the northern Democrats to form the new Republican Party, built on opposition to slavery and also on the idea of government as a promoter of commerce. The Democratic Party receded into the Confederacy during the Civil War. After the war and the restoration of the union, the Democrats reemerged on the national scene to compete vigorously with the Republicans for the favor of business. The pro-business tilt of the third-party system fostered progressive and populist sentiment for more regulation of big business and protection of common people's interests.

These sentiments, fired by a series of disastrous recessions and depressions, came to a head in the presidential election of 1896, when the populist Democrat William Jennings Bryan challenged the candidate of the business establishment, Republican William McKinley. The failure of the populist challenge marked the beginning of the fourth party system (1896–1932), throughout which the Republicans dominated the national political scene and allowed the capitalist system free rein. Only when former Republican President Teddy Roosevelt's progressive Bull Moose Party split Republican ranks were the Democrats able to put their candidate, Woodrow Wilson, into the White House from 1912 to 1920.

The onset of the Great Depression in 1929, in part the result of the lack of restraint placed on the free enterprise system, drove Republican President Herbert Hoover from office. Franklin Delano Roosevelt swept into the White House in 1932 on a flood tide of national discontent and despair. In a bold effort to use the power of the federal government to end the Depression and restore economic prosperity, he ushered in a new era of governmental involvement in economic affairs and government responsibility for ensuring the people's basic well-being. FDR also initiated a period of Democratic dominance that constituted the fifth party system (1932–1968).

In each of these years—1824, 1860, 1896, and 1932—a new party system evolved from an old one in a relatively short period of turmoil and change called *realignment*. **Realignment** occurs when a reasonably stable pattern of party support, based on a particular set of important political issues, is replaced by a new pattern of party support based on a new set of issues. Because realignments are such landmark events in the American party system, scholars have devoted much effort to determining when and why they occur. They have identified a number of significant changes that seem to accompany realignment, most notable of which is the period before each realignment in which the

realignment

A major change in the pattern of support for political parties and the important issues on which that pattern of support is based

old party structure seems to fall apart, or **dealign**. Why do realignments occur? As the preceding discussion suggests, the single most important factor may be the emergence of some new issue that cuts across the existing party lines and divides the electorate in some new way—for example, slavery in the third-party system, and the Great Depression and the role of the federal government in the economy in the fifth party system. Also, quite clearly, realignments tended to come at approximately thirty-six-year intervals.

7.5b　Parties Present

Beginning in the mid-1960s, the fifth party system began to falter. This was most evident in the woes of the Democratic Party, whose long-standing dominance began to unravel. Consistent with the pattern of a major partisan shift every thirty-six years, the Democratic Party, which had won the White House in every election over the thirty-six years from 1932 to 1968 except 1952 and 1956—seven of nine elections—lost the 1968 election; and over the next twenty years it would win only one of five more. The only bright spot for the Democrats was that they did manage, mostly, to hold on to their majorities in the House and Senate throughout the period; the one exception being the Republicans' majority in the Senate from 1981 to 1987, which primarily was a result of Ronald Reagan's victory in 1980.

That exception alone set political analysts abuzz. Dealignment was clearly underway. While some saw realignment into a new Republican majority in the offing, others worried that the party system was confronting an even more fundamental crisis—the possibility of complete collapse.

Certainly, beginning in the 1960s, both parties were beset by signs of deterioration. At the national level, the party headquarters, chairperson, and committee seemed increasingly irrelevant to the course of American politics and to political campaigns, specifically. Their principal function seemed to be to organize the national party convention once every four years. The title of a study published in 1964 seemed to sum up their plight, "Politics Without Power: The National Party Committees."[15]

The party in the electorate, the mass base of the political parties, also showed signs of weakening. Through the early 1960s, more than 75 percent of the American people said that they identified strongly or weakly with one or the other of the parties and less than 25 percent described themselves as independents. Beginning about 1964, attachments to parties started to weaken substantially. By the late 1970s only about 60 percent said that they

Ronald Reagan's presidential inauguration, 1981

(Photo by White House Photographic Office, 1981, courtesy of the National Archives and Records Administration)

identified with a party, and more than a third said they were independents. Not only were people less likely to identify with the parties, voters were also less likely to see the parties in favorable terms and to vote according to their party identification.

Trouble loomed, as well, for the other aspect of the party in the electorate, the party coalitions. The coalitions that had supported the major parties, particularly the Democratic coalition, seemed to be coming apart. At its peak in the Johnson landslide, the Democratic Party had expanded to encompass not just the Roosevelt New Deal coalition of the working class, unions, the poor, urban residents, citizens of the South, Catholics,

dealignment

Period during which the partisan ties of the public diminish and the party system breaks down

Jews, and liberals, but also African Americans. The Republican Party was left as the party of the upper class, big business, and people residing in the suburbs. Clearly through the 1970s and peaking in 1980, the Democratic coalition fell into disarray, as working-class people, Catholics and some Jews, and white Southerners were drawn away in the Reagan landslide and left the Democratic Party looking more and more like the party of liberals and African Americans—two groups too small to have much of a future as a winning coalition for the party.

The parties in government also suffered their own difficulties through the 1970s and 1980s as party discipline and coordination seemed to deteriorate. Party discipline seemed to sag in the Congress, as members less dependent on the party for help in getting reelected increasingly broke party ranks when local needs or special interest groups dictated.[16] Party coordination between the executive branch and the legislative branch suffered as presidents and members of their own party in Congress were often at odds on legislation.

(Alex Brandon / AP Photo)

President Donald Trump speaks from the South Lawn of the White House on the fourth day of the Republican National Convention, Thursday, Aug. 27, 2020.

What caused the parties to go into **decline**? A number of governmental, electoral, and socialization changes seem to have contributed to the deteriorating condition of American political parties since the mid-1960s. As noted earlier, patronage was one of the traditional reservoirs of party strength. It provided party leaders with bargaining chips to use in the game of politics, but reformers intent on reducing the power of the bosses and increasing the competence and integrity of public employees pushed for the establishment of a system of civil service. As more public jobs fell under civil service, politicians found themselves with fewer "goodies" to give out and were, thus, less able to marshal political support.

Another governmental change that hurt the parties was the rise of the public welfare system. The parties of earlier years built support by serving as a kind of informal welfare system for their supporters. A faithful party member in financial trouble could seek help in the form of money, food, or shelter from the neighborhood party organization. People came to owe the party. With the rise of the modern welfare system, the government itself formally began to ensure a minimal level of well-being among citizens. Consequently, the party lost its exclusive role as a source of help and its ability to put people in its debt.

Electoral changes played an important part in hurting the parties, as well. In earlier years, political parties were an essential part of the electoral apparatus of the United States. To get a message to the electorate, a candidate needed an army of workers to fan out over the constituency—buttonholing passersby, knocking on doors, handing out party literature, and twisting arms. Modern technology provides less labor-intensive alternatives. Nowadays, with a string of appearances on television news programs and in campaign advertisements, a candidate can make more frequent and seemingly more "personal" contact with far more voters than could an army of party workers on the streets. Computerized direct mailing and emailing techniques and smart use of social media like Facebook and Twitter can yield large sums of money, which can be used to buy more television time and internet advertisements and to send out more mail, all of which can generate more money, and so on. Simply put, candidates no longer need to rely as much on parties and party workers to serve as their intermediaries with the public.

decline

The idea that the American political parties are collapsing and may, perhaps, eventually disappear

Traditionally, parties have also been important sources of campaign funds for their candidates. Today, however, presidential and congressional candidates benefit from the support of the PACs and unaffiliated super PACs. Access to these new sources of money has made candidates less dependent on parties for help and has, consequently, contributed to the weakening of the parties. Also, in an earlier era, parties tightly controlled the process by which candidates for public office were selected. Party leaders got together in party **caucuses** (meetings) or conventions to pick the party's candidates. However, political reformers fought to open up the nomination process to represent a broader cross section of the population, leading to selection of convention delegates by open conventions or primary elections.

Parties long existed as standing armies of campaign workers, ready to step into political battle on behalf of the party candidates. Now, more and more candidates are relying not on the party machinery but on their own personal organizations for campaign assistance. Although candidates obviously want to capitalize on their party's name, many run without the aid of the party machinery. Once in office, they are likely to feel little obligation to help the party. Single-issue groups also pose a challenge to the existing party system by threatening to siphon off precious campaign resources and public support. The antiabortion movement is perhaps the most prominent recent example.

Finally, most people acquire their sense of party identification through socialization by their parents, but that process of transmission has appeared to break down in recent years. Between the 1950s and the 1970s, the percentage of young people adopting the same party as their parents dropped by about 15 percent. Expansion of the Vietnam War tarnished both parties, the Republican Party was scarred by the Watergate scandal, and the Democratic Party suffered from the economically difficult Carter years. Party disenchantment in one generation sows party disenchantment in the next. Thus, it is not hard to understand why the ranks of the party faithful dwindled and the ranks of the independents swelled.

Many of these changes were viewed with concern; analysts were not clear whether what was occurring was dealignment leading toward realignment or dealignment leading toward collapse. The deeper concern was that the weakening or disappearance of political parties might impair the functioning of our democratic system. Think of all the valuable functions parties perform, and then think about what might happen if the parties were not around to perform them.

Just as the idea that the parties were dead or dying began to gain widespread currency, a new group of commentators rose to argue that the parties were making a comeback. Led by Xandra Kayden and Eddie Mahe Jr.'s *The Party Goes On: The Persistence of the Two-Party System in the United States*,[17] a number of new studies found evidence of the parties in **resurgence**. The major center of revitalization in the formal party organizations has been within the national party organizations, particularly the national party headquarters supervised by the national chairperson and operated on a day-to-day basis by an increasingly professional, sophisticated, and well-paid staff. These staff employ modern data technology to gather and analyze polling results, conduct direct mail and email campaigns, and raise money.

Although the American public has not flooded back to embrace the political parties, the trend against them has at least been arrested, perhaps even slightly reversed. There is also some evidence that the party coalitions are reforming along somewhat different lines. The Democratic Party has suffered from the loss of the white South and some working-class Catholic and union support, but it has gained a new constituency in female and racial and ethnic minority voters. For example, according to a recent poll, millennial women (those born between 1981 and 1996) identify with the Democratic Party over the

caucus

A meeting of members of a political party or the members of a party in a legislature—also referred to as a party caucus; in some states used to select delegates to the national conventions, which nominate presidential candidates

resurgence

The idea that American political parties, following a period of decline from the 1960s to the early 1980s, are now making a comeback, gaining in organizational, electoral, and governmental strength

Republican Party 70 percent to 23 percent.[18] The Republican Party, on the other hand, has gained substantially among working-class whites and in the South.

The primary reason for party resurgence is that the parties, instead of standing on the sidelines and allowing themselves to be kept out of the game, have at last recognized the changing environment of the American political system and adjusted their activities accordingly. For example, they have recognized that modern political campaigns depend less on armies of party volunteers tramping from door to door and more on money and the media. Thus, they have moved to become a major source of political money, in effect not fighting the PACs but joining them. They have seen how candidates must rely on a modern media campaign and have moved to provide candidates with the training and production services that they need to conduct such campaigns. They know that candidates want to use polling results and social media, so they share polling results and social media strategies and technologies.

7.5c Parties Future

Realignment, dealignment, and resurgence—it is hard enough to say where the American party system is now, much less where it is going. The Democrats' victory in the 1992 presidential election did not make the task any easier. Certainly some sort of realignment took place in the transition from the fifth party system's clear Democratic dominance to what seemed to be a sixth party system starting in 1968 of divided government—Republican domination of the presidency and Democratic domination of Congress. Was 1992 a return to Democratic dominance? Events since 1992 suggest that, despite Bill Clinton's victory in 1992, we were still very much in the era of divided government. United Democratic governance lasted only until the 1994 midterm elections when the Republican Party won majorities in both the House and Senate. Clinton won reelection in 1996; his last six years in office were a continuation of the dealignment era's divided government pattern, although this time with a Democratic president and Republican Congress.

At first, the 2000 election looked to be another opportunity for realignment as the Republicans gained unified control of the government for the first time since the Eisenhower administration. George W. Bush's opportunity to lead a united Congress, however, was even shorter-lived than Clinton's had been. After the election, the Senate stood evenly divided, with fifty Democrats and fifty Republicans. The Republicans maintained a procedural majority because Vice President Dick Cheney, in his role as president of the Senate, could break any tie votes. In May 2001, however, Jim Jeffords, a third-term senator from Vermont, left the Republican Party and became an independent. This action provided Democrats with a fifty to forty-nine majority and returned the nation to divided party government. The Republicans reestablished their majority in 2002, so the 2004 election was seen by many as a potential turning point. Republican victory would solidify arguments for the party's resurgence, while a Democratic victory in the presidential race could spell a return to divided government. Although the campaign was neck and neck up to the very end, the Republican Party emerged victorious, winning the presidency and strengthening majorities in both the House and Senate. The year 2006 spelled a reversal of fortune for the Republicans with Democrats regaining the majority in both the House and the Senate for the first time in a dozen years. The Democratic victory created another period of divided government, once again calling into question the future direction and momentum of American political parties.

The 2008 campaign was another important moment for the two political parties. Barack Obama and the Democratic Party rode to victory on a wave of dissatisfaction with a faltering economy. Gaining support from new voters and younger voters, turnout was

the highest it had been in four decades; and the Democrats gained seats in both the House and Senate, as well as claiming a decisive victory in the presidential race. The Republican Party's only modest success was in maintaining at least forty Senate seats—the number required to make a viable filibuster threat.

Partly as a result of the 2008 election, and partly in reaction to "big government" proposals to stimulate a stalled economy, a movement adopting the moniker "tea party" emerged in 2009. By mid-2010, an organization called the Tea Party Patriots could boast of hundreds of local chapters and over 100,000 members nationwide. The organization identified its core values as fiscal responsibility, constitutionally limited government, and free markets.[19] Was this "party" more like a political party, or more like an interest group?

People watch Democratic presidential candidate and former Vice President Joe Biden speak at a watch party for the Democratic National Convention at Dunkin' Donuts Park, home of the minor league baseball team the Hartford Yard Goats, Thursday, Aug. 20, 2020.

They campaigned on behalf of (or against) particular candidates, but did not seek recognition on the ballot. Officially, the Tea Party remained nonpartisan, but the movement's priorities likely helped the Republicans gain a majority in the House of Representatives in 2010. The movement was not well-represented by either candidate in the 2012 presidential election—where President Obama handily defeated Mitt Romney. Tea Party adherents did play a role in securing some Republican seats in the 2014 midterm elections, but some of the Republican primary candidates they supported held extreme positions that likely worked to the advantage of the Democrats in other districts. Those losses were the beginning of the end for what turned out to be a fairly short-lived movement.

The impact of the 2016 elections on both political parties will likely be debated for years to come. The success of Donald Trump—a political outsider who had very weak ties to the party and its platform—in securing the Republican presidential nomination seemed to epitomize the power of individual candidates in a weak party system. On the Democratic side, the nearly successful primary campaign of Senator Bernie Sanders (I–VT)—who had spent years as an independent and identified as a socialist—pointed to a similar party weakness. Donald Trump's victory served to highlight both the power of individual candidates and the necessity of party. Though Trump clearly called the shots during his campaign for the White House, he would not have emerged the victor if the Republican party structure and a large percentage of Republicans in the electorate had not backed him. Individuals may lead the charge, but they need a well-organized party apparatus to support them. Moreover, the electorate's treatment of the Republican Party in the 2018 midterm elections was, for many voters, a referendum on the Republican president's performance.

The 2020 election featured an intense battle between the two parties and their candidates presenting starkly contrasting visions of the country. By this point in his presidency, Donald Trump had solidified his control over the Republican party. About 72 million voters cast ballots for his vision of the country, which championed an "America First" economy and foreign policy, while downplaying the dangers of COVID-19. Despite Trump's strong showing, a broad coalition of over 77 million voters chose the Democratic candidate, former vice president Joe Biden, who called for greater civility, attention to climate change, taking the racial justice movement seriously, and a more comprehensive response to the pandemic. Though many independents, and even a group of outspoken

Republicans dissatisfied with Trump's crude and bombastic demeanor, helped elect Biden, the Democratic Party lost seats in the House of Representatives, though it did gain just enough seats in the Senate to achieve Democratic control. This resulted in a unified Democratic government for the first time in a decade.

Is the recent resurgence of the parties just the last gasp of a dying system? Some critics think that it is and that the two-party system is really on its last legs;[20] however, the parties' comeback probably represents a broader and more permanent change. Through much of American history, political parties were decentralized because political power in the United States was decentralized. Political power has become more centralized; and parties, although slow to react, have now adapted to that new reality with stronger central party organizations. It makes little sense to think that parties will move again toward decentralization unless the government does—and that does not appear to be in the offing. Similarly, the resurgence of the national party organizations occurred in response to the rise of the modern media campaign and the increased demand for campaign money. It would make sense to think that the organizations would again wither away only if the media and money somehow became less important, but there is no sign that such changes are on the immediate horizon.

Of course, this analysis does not take into account the many other factors that might change and affect the parties, either strengthening or weakening them. The recent episode of decline and resurgence, though, does teach us something about parties that is useful when contemplating their future: The parties have demonstrated an ability to adapt to changing circumstances—not always quickly, not always entirely successfully, but eventually and sufficiently. Unforeseen social and political changes involving circumstances hardly envisioned in this chapter may occur and lay the parties low again; past experience, however, suggests that parties—perhaps not exactly as we know them today, but parties nevertheless—will adapt again.

CHAPTER REVIEW

1. Groups are an essential element in the functioning of the American democratic system. A group's political effectiveness depends on its size, the strength of its members' identification, its proximity to politics, its internal organization, and its closeness to the broader societal consensus.

2. Interest groups engage in a wide array of politically relevant activities. They press their views on their own membership, the general public, and the political elites of the legislative, executive, and judicial branches. One of their most potent weapons of late has been the political action committee (PAC).

3. Some of the major group participants in the American political process are based on different interests: economically based groups, such as the Chamber of Commerce of the United States and the AFL-CIO; socially based groups, such as the National Organization for Women (NOW) and the National Association for the Advancement of Colored People (NAACP); ideological groups, such as the liberal Americans for Democratic Action; single-issue groups, such as the right-to-life and pro-choice movements; and public interest groups, such as Common Cause, the "citizens' lobby."

4. The role that interest groups play in a democratic society is as controversial as it is pervasive. Pluralistic theory sees interest groups as working to overcome the deficiencies of individual citizens and to perpetuate a functioning democracy. Other perspectives see interest groups as failing to serve their own members' interests, the public interest, or both.

5. In a democracy, political parties try to influence public policy by backing members as candidates in elections to public offices. In the course of getting their members elected to public office, political parties perform a number of important functions for the system of government: socializing citizens, pulling together the diverse interests contending in a society, simplifying the alternatives confronting the voters, structuring campaigns and elections, recruiting and training political leaders, and organizing and coordinating government.

6. The American party system is a two-party system, probably due primarily to the plurality election system commonly used in the United States and the generally centrist distribution of political beliefs in America. The parties are characterized by a relatively loose relationship among their component parts—divided into national, state, and local at one level and into formal party organization, the party in the electorate, and the party in the government at another level.

KEY TERMS

amicus curiae brief 206

caucus 227

Christian Right..............................210

class action suit 206

coalition 223

cross-cutting cleavage 213

dealignment................................225

decline.....................................226

direct mail 203

electoral functions 215

Federal Election Campaign Act..............204

formal party organization 221

governmental functions 215

grass roots lobbying........................207

interest group elitism........................213

interest groups..............................200

iron triangle.................................206

lobbying 204

majority election............................217

melting pot.................................200

movement...................................201

national committee 221

national convention.........................221

party in the electorate 222

party in the government.....................223

party system................................223

platform 221

pluralist democracy 200

plurality election............................217

political action committee (PAC) 203

political machine 221

political party 214

proportional representation..................217

realignment 224

resurgence..................................227

run-off election.............................217

socialization functions 214

state committee.............................222

third party 218

READINGS FOR FURTHER STUDY

James Madison's *Federalist* No. 10 remains mandatory reading for anyone interested in exploring the role of groups in American political life.

A more modern, yet classic, study is *The Governmental Process* (Berkeley, CA: Public Policy Press, 1993) by David Truman.

Interest groups are important elements in the pluralist perspective on American democracy. Robert A. Dahl sets out that perspective most clearly in *Who Governs?* 2nd ed. (New Haven, CT: Yale University Press, 2005). Another important work is Allan J. Cigler, Burdett A. Loomis, and Anthony J. Nownes eds., *Interest Group Politics*, 10th ed. (Lanham, MD: Rowman & Littlefield, 2019).

As a central feature of American politics, parties are one of the most written-about of all American political institutions. V. O. Key Jr. provides a classic description of the role that parties play in the American political system in *Politics, Parties, and Pressure Groups*, 5th ed. (New York: Crowell, 1964).

Jeffrey M. Stonecash's *Political Parties Matter: Realignment and the Return of Partisan Voting* (Boulder, CO: Lynne Rienner, 2005) offers a historical perspective on the parties, centering on the notion of realignment, and his *Understanding American Political Parties* (New York: Routledge, 2012) provides a contemporary look at their strategic choices.

Good overviews of the changing role of American parties are John C. Green and Daniel J. Coffey, eds., *The State of the Parties 2018*, 8th ed. (Lanham, MD: Rowman & Littlefield, 2018), and Marjorie Randon Hershey's *Party Politics in America*, 17th ed. (New York: Routledge, 2017).

Theda Skocpol and Caroline Tervo give an account of a the most recent party and interest group phenomenon in *Upending American Politics: Polarizing Parties, Ideological Elites, and Citizen Activists from the Tea Party to the Anti-Trump Resistance* (New York: Oxford, 2020).

A good account of the future of political parties and how they change is Michael Barone, *How America's Political Parties Change (and How They Don't)* (New York: Encounter, 2019). Lee Drutman debates the advantages and disadvantages of a two-party system in *Breaking the Two-Party Doom Loop: The Case for Multiparty Democracy in America* (New York: Oxford, 2020).

NOTES

1. The ideas in this section and the next are drawn in part from the seminal discussion of group influences in politics in Angus Campbell, Philip E. Converse, Warren E. Miller, and Donald E. Stokes, *The American Voter* (New York: Wiley, 1960), pp. 295–332.

2. *McCutcheon v. Federal Election Commission*, 572 U.S. 185 (2014).

3. Peter Overby, "How Hillary Clinton Could Ask a Single Donor for Over $700,000," NPR, December 28, 2015.

4. *Citizens United v. FEC*, 558 U.S. 50 (2010).

5. *Statistical Abstract of the United States, 2012.*

6. U.S. Census Bureau, "Voting and Registration," https://www.census.gov/data/tables/time-series /demo/voting-and-registration/p20-583.html (June 30, 2020).

7. The leading advocate of this point of view is Robert A. Dahl. See, for example, his classic book *Who Governs?* (New Haven, CT: Yale University Press, 1961).

8. Robert J. Samuelson, "Interest Group Gridlock," *National Journal* (September 25, 1982): 1642.

9. Jonathan Rauch, "Demosclerosis," *National Journal* (September 5, 1992): 1998–2003.

10. V. O. Key Jr., *Politics, Parties, and Pressure Groups*, 5th ed. (New York: Crowell, 1964), p. 656.

11. The Gallup Organization, "Majority in U.S. Still Say a Third Party is Needed," October 26, 2018, https://news.gallup.com/poll/244094/majority-say -third-party-needed.aspx, (July 4, 2020).

12. This distinction is another legacy of V. O. Key Jr., originated in his *Politics, Parties, and Pressure Groups*. (It has now been widely adopted by students of the American party system. See, for example, Frank J. Sorauf and Paul Allen Beck, *Party Politics in America*, 6th ed. (Glenview, IL: Scott, Foresman, 1988).

13. Campbell, et al., *The American Voter*, pp. 121–122.

14. Sorauf and Beck, *Party Politics in America*, pp. 396–446.

15. Cornelius P. Cotter and Bernard C. Hennessy (New York: Atherton, 1964).

16. William J. Keefe, *Parties, Politics, and Public Policy in America* (Hinsdale, MN: Dryden Press, 1976), pp. 139–140; Barbara Sinclair Deckard, "Political Upheaval and Congressional Voting: The Effects of the 1960s on Voting Patterns in the House of Representatives," *Journal of Politics 38* (1976): pp. 326–345.

17. New York: Basic Books, 1985.

18. The Partisan Gender Gap Among Millennials is Staggeringly Large, *Vox,* March 22, 2018, https://www.vox.com/policy-and-politics/2018 /3/22/17146534/millennial-gender-gap-partisan, (September 23, 2018).

19. Tea Party Patriots, "Mission Statement and Core Values," http://www.teapartypatriots.org /Mission.aspx (June 14, 2010).

20. Theodore Lowi, "The Party Crasher," *The New York Times Magazine* (August 23, 1992): 28–33.

POP QUIZ

1. Interest groups, legislators, and administrators are sometimes called the _____ of American politics.

2. America has been known as the _____ society because it consists of people of all races and nationalities.

3. The tendency for different coalitions to form on different issues is called _____ .

4. One of the _____ functions of parties is to educate citizens and mobilize them into political action.

5. The increase in party identification since 1978 has primarily benefited the _____ Party.

6. Most PACs are registered with the Federal Election Commission.   T   F

7. The influence of the Christian Right declined dramatically in the late 1980s.   T   F

8. Political parties are formally sanctioned in Article III, Section 4 of the Constitution.   T   F

9. Third parties have had very little influence on the American political system.   T   F

10. The increase in the number of single-issue interest groups has contributed to the resurgence of political parties based on new coalitions.   T   F

11. The major means by which interest groups try to create public support or sympathy for their political goals is/are _____ .
    A) the mass media
    B) direct mail
    C) opinion leaders
    D) political action committees

12. The iron triangle of American politics consists of which of the following?
    A) interest group representatives, legislators, and judges
    B) Congress, the presidency, and the Supreme Court
    C) interest group representatives, legislators, and administrators
    D) interest group representatives, PACs, and political candidates

13. In recent years the most important political issue concerning religious groups has been _____ .
    A) the Middle East conflict
    B) abortion
    C) school prayer
    D) poverty

14. When a pluralistic system becomes paralyzed from too many interest groups refusing to compromise, this is known as interest group _____ .
    A) gridlock
    B) anarchy
    C) elitism
    D) cleavage

15. Each party system evolved from its predecessor in a relatively short period of political turmoil and change called _____ .
    A) factionalization
    B) dealignment
    C) realignment
    D) anarchy

Answers:
1. iron triangle   2. melting pot
3. cross-cutting cleavage   4. socialization
5. Republican   6. T   7. T   8. F   9. F
10. F   11. A   12. C   13. B   14. A   15. C

Chapter

08

(Getty Images)

CAMPAIGNS & ELECTIONS

In This Chapter

8.1   The Voter's Perspective: To Vote or Not to Vote
8.2   The Voter's Perspective: How to Vote
8.3   The Candidate's Perspective: Running for President
8.4   The Candidate's Perspective: Running for Congress

Chapter Objectives

In a campaign and the election that concludes it, all the actors in the political process come into vigorous interplay. Parties begin selecting and promoting candidates. Interest groups mobilize their forces to ensure that their interests will be remembered. The mass media put politics more clearly and consistently at center stage. As a result, the public, whose interest in political affairs is generally limited, now turns its attention to the candidates vying for public office.

This chapter examines the process from the perspectives of the two principal types of players in the drama: voters and candidates. For voters, the basic questions are whether to vote and how to vote. Candidates, whether presidential or congressional, must devise strategies that will bring voters to the polls and attract their votes. They must pull together the financial resources and organization needed for a credible campaign, obtain the nomination of their parties, and compete against the other party's candidate in the general election campaign.

8.1 The Voter's Perspective: To Vote or Not to Vote

As discussed in Chapter 5, politics is not usually a matter of concern to most citizens. Their interest is most aroused around Election Day—when they begin to take note of the campaign, think about going to the polls to cast their ballots, and sometimes engage in activities related to the campaign. Many begin to follow it on television or in newspapers and talk about it with family and friends; some try to influence the way in which someone else will vote. A somewhat smaller number wear buttons, display stickers or signs on their cars or houses, post about candidates or positions on social media, and attend campaign meetings, rallies, speeches, or dinners. A few actually work for or give money to a candidate or party. Even with these other kinds of campaign-related activities, voting remains the most frequent act of political participation and the most meaningful act as well. In a representative democracy, voting forges the essential link between the citizens and their government. In the end, then, it comes down to two basic decisions: whether to vote and how to vote.

(Roy Harris / Shutterstock)

Americans are required to register if they wish to vote. The inconvenience of this alone deters many residents from voting at all; therefore, many states have passed legislation to allow same-day registration.

8.1a Voting Requirements and Eligibility

Not everyone is in a position to decide to vote. The law excludes some people. In fact, for more than one hundred years after the founding of the United States, a majority of the American people were not eligible to vote. During that period the states controlled who could or could not vote, and they typically limited the electorate to white males over the age of twenty-one. Since then the United States has made great strides in eliminating restrictions on voting.

Racial barriers to voting began to fall first. The **Fifteenth Amendment** (1870) outlawed denying the right of citizens to vote on the grounds of "race, color, or previous condition of servitude." Nevertheless, after the Civil War the South created a new system of inferior status for African Americans, which came to be called "Jim Crow." Jim Crow included several elements limiting African American voting. One element was the white primary. As discussed in Chapter 3, in the one-party South of the post-Reconstruction era, winning the Democratic primary was equivalent to an election because the general election was nearly always a rout of the disfavored Republicans. The Democratic Party routinely excluded African Americans from its primaries, thus effectively barring them from any meaningful role in the electoral process. The Supreme Court in *Smith v. Allwright* struck down the white primary in 1944.

Another element of Jim Crow was the **poll tax**, which stipulated that in order to vote, citizens had to pay a tax. This tax was often enforced cumulatively, meaning that people had to pay the tax for every previous election in which they had not voted. Because African Americans had not been able to vote in many previous elections, they were confronted

Fifteenth Amendment

Outlawed race-based restrictions on voting

poll tax

A tax on voting, applied discriminatorily to African Americans under "Jim Crow" in the post–Civil War South

with large cumulated poll taxes that they could not pay. Thus, they were excluded from voting. However, the **Twenty-fourth Amendment** prohibited poll taxes in federal elections in 1964, and the Supreme Court's decision in *Harper v. Virginia State Board of Elections*, in 1966, prohibited them in state elections.

A third element of Jim Crow was the literacy test. In order to vote, a person had to demonstrate the ability to read. Many African Americans at that time were illiterate, so they were, thereby, excluded. This requirement was prohibited by the **Voting Rights Act of 1965**, which waived literacy tests for anyone with a sixth-grade education. The Voting Rights Act of 1965 and subsequent amendments in 1982 and 2006 took other important steps to protect African American voting rights, as discussed in Chapter 3.

While African American participation declined under Jim Crow, political pressures to grant **female suffrage**, the right of women to vote, increased. This movement, stirred to life in the early nineteenth century, achieved its first major success when the territory of Wyoming granted suffrage to women in 1869. Activists first coalesced into two competing organizations with somewhat different styles—the more militant National Woman Suffrage Association led by Susan B. Anthony and the more conservative American Woman Suffrage Association led by Lucy Stone. The two groups joined forces in 1890. Final success was not achieved on the national level until 1920, when the states ratified the **Nineteenth Amendment**, which gave women the right to vote.

The last major broadening of the electorate occurred in 1971, when the **Twenty-sixth Amendment** reduced the voting age from twenty-one to eighteen. In the midst of the Vietnam War, the argument that people old enough to die for their country ought to be able to vote in their country's elections was very persuasive. In addition, both Republicans and Democrats hoped to capitalize on the large bloc of new voters. In combination with the coming of age of the post–World War II baby boom generation, the lowering of the voting age produced one of the greatest expansions of the electorate in American history. Although a few municipalities have recently extended voting rights to sixteen-year-olds in local elections, there is not yet widespread support for lowering the national voting age further.[1]

The laws of the United States generally exclude from voting people who are not citizens of this country. Some other voting laws differ widely from state to state. In most states, people who have been convicted of a felony or who are confined in prisons and mental institutions cannot vote. Most jurisdictions also typically exclude citizens who have not resided within their boundaries for a minimum amount of time. This law is intended to ensure that citizens are reasonably permanent residents of the community. Impediments to voting imposed by lengthy **residence requirements** were weakened substantially by the **Voting Rights Act of 1970**, which mandated that states require no more than thirty days' residency to establish eligibility to vote in presidential elections. Today the thirty-day maximum is standard for all elections, even though some states have selected shorter periods.

Beyond meeting the basic qualifications, potential voters in most places in the United States (all states except North Dakota) are required to **register**—that is, to enter their names on the local government's list of those eligible to vote in a particular area, usually by visiting a government office. This requirement poses enough of an inconvenience that many people do not bother. Recent studies have shown, in fact, that the registration requirement may reduce electoral participation by as much as 10 to 15 percent.[2] Because registration reduces voting, it has long been the target of political reformers. Some places now permit registration by mail or via the internet, and a few allow citizens to register on Election Day, even at the same time and place as they vote. Such arrangements seem to make a difference. Twenty-one states have implemented these same-day registration

Twenty-fourth Amendment

Adopted in 1964, forbids the use of poll taxes in federal elections (Since 1966, the Court has applied this proscription to state elections as well.)

Voting Rights Act of 1965

Major legislation designed to overcome racial barriers to voting, primarily in the Southern states—extended in 1982 for twenty-five years and again in 2006

female suffrage

The right of women to vote, which was bestowed nationally by the Nineteenth Amendment in 1920

Nineteenth Amendment

Constitutional amendment of 1920 giving women the right to vote

Twenty-sixth Amendment

Constitutional amendment adopted in 1971 that fixed the minimum voting age at eighteen years

residence requirements

State laws designed to limit the eligible electorate by requiring citizens to have been a resident of the voting district for a fixed period of time prior to an election

Voting Rights Act of 1970

The law that limited residence requirements to thirty days for presidential elections, further ensuring voting rights

register

To place one's name on the list of citizens eligible to vote

laws, with advocates claiming a significant reduction in voters being turned away at the polls for lack of registration.[3]

Recognizing the important role played by registration laws, Congress passed the National Voter Registration Act of 1993, also known as the "Motor Voter" law since it required voter registration to be made available at the state departments of motor vehicles. Over fifteen million Americans registered to vote via their state motor vehicle agency in 1997–98. Partly as a result of this new law, registration rates climbed to over 70 percent in 1998, the highest level in a congressional election year since 1970. It is important to note that this piece of legislation was passed during a period of unified Democratic government. Many prior proposals had failed primarily because of Republican opposition. The historical pattern has been for Republicans to oppose such measures and for Democrats to support them. The Democrats generally emphasize the virtues of higher turnout, whereas the Republicans worry about opening the door to fraud.[4] These positions are also consistent with strategic considerations for each party, as demographic data suggest that increased registration and turnout would help Democrats and hurt Republicans. The issue rose to the forefront again in 2020 as Democrats pushed for greater ballot access and expanded vote-by-mail options during the COVID-19 pandemic, and Republicans worried that such access would lead to increased fraud.

8.1b   Who Votes?

Voting turnout varies with people's social characteristics and psychological and political attitudes, as well as with the circumstances of voting. Voting participation used to vary dramatically across a wide variety of social groupings in the United States. Whites were much more likely to vote than African Americans, men were more likely to vote than women, and so on. In recent years there has been a general convergence in the voting rates among various groups of citizens. This is partly due to the success of the long struggle to ensure equal access to the voting booth. Just as significant, the broader trend toward social and economic equality has tended to promote political equality.

Two social characteristics show the strongest relation to voting turnout: age and education. (A third important factor is discussed in "Politics and Economics: Turnout, Choice, and Economic Status.") The older a person is, the more likely that person is to vote. One reason is that older people move less often and therefore do not need to re-register as often. Young people are more likely to be away from their place of residence—for example, at college or in the military. Because voting by absentee ballot takes more forethought and is perceived as more difficult than voting in person, young people are more likely to be discouraged from voting. They are also more preoccupied with getting a start in life than with relatively remote political concerns. As people grow older, they have more time and inclination to participate in politics and consequently build a habit of voting.

The more educated a person is, the more likely he or she is to vote. Slightly less than 24 percent of US citizens in the voting-age population with less than a high school education reported having voted in the 2016 presidential election, whereas over 71 percent of those with a college degree or graduate-school education reported having voted.[5] Education plays such a big role because it stimulates political interest and provides the information that people need to be effective participants in the political process. Differences in education have undoubtedly contributed to voting differences between social groups in the past. African Americans and women voted less often than white males, in part because they did not enjoy the benefits of education that white males did. With the recent expansion of educational opportunities for minorities and women, levels of voting for these groups have

approached those for white males. In fact, the Census Bureau reported that in the 2016 presidential election women voted at a significantly higher rate than men—58 percent to less than 54 percent.

Psychological influences play a role as well. Not surprisingly, the greater a person's interest in politics, the more likely the person is to vote. The more a citizen thinks he or she can accomplish politically (i.e., the more political efficacy he or she has), the greater the likelihood the person will vote. Partisanship is a powerful motivating force. The stronger a person's attachment to a political party, the more inclined that person will be to vote. Conservatives and liberals are slightly more likely to vote than moderates, probably because they tend to be more interested and partisan. However, some psychological factors thought to have a major impact on turnout really do not. Surprisingly, despite much attention in the late 1960s and early 1970s, trust—defined as reliance on the integrity of public officials—has little effect. Overall, in 2020, almost 67 percent of eligible voters cast a ballot for president.

Finally, primarily as a result of differences in psychological factors, turnout varies substantially across the different types of elections. In elections that the public finds interesting and important, so-called **high-stimulus elections**, turnout is usually relatively high; in less interesting, **low-stimulus elections**, it is usually low.[6] Presidential elections are generally higher stimulus than congressional elections, and general elections are usually higher stimulus than the primary elections that precede them. Turnout in recent presidential elections has averaged between 50 and 60 percent, while turnout in congressional midterm elections has run between 35 and 40 percent. Voting rates in presidential general elections also typically far exceed the turnout rates of 30 percent or less observed in primary elections.

high-stimulus election
Election that the public finds interesting and important

low-stimulus election
Election that the public finds uninteresting or unimportant

POLITICAL CONTROVERSIES

Turnout, Choice, and Economic Status

Economic status influences voter turnout. For example, as Figure 8.1 shows, the higher a citizen's family income, the more likely the citizen is to vote. This pattern emerges, in part, because higher income encourages many of the factors that promote voting, particularly education, political interest, and efficacy.

Voting choice is also influenced by economic status. As Figure 8.2 shows, in 2016, voters in both the lowest and the two highest income categories were more likely to vote for Democrat Hillary Clinton than for Republican Donald Trump. While this meets with expectations for the lowest earners, the highest earners defied expectations in this particular election. The tendency of higher-income people to favor Republican candidates was observed in many previous elections. It results primarily because higher-income people tend to identify with the Republican Party, as discussed in Chapter 7, and because

Republican identifiers tend to vote for Republican candidates.

These two factors can combine to hurt Democratic candidates and help Republican candidates. Democratic candidates have a greater following among lower-income people, but those people turn out to vote less often. Republican candidates typically have a greater following among higher-income people, who vote more often. This is one reason the Republicans, even as the minority party in terms of population, have been so successful in getting their candidates elected to public office.

What other reasons are there for the Republicans' success in winning elections, even though they have been in the numerical minority for so long?

Figure 8.1   Voting Turnout by Family Income

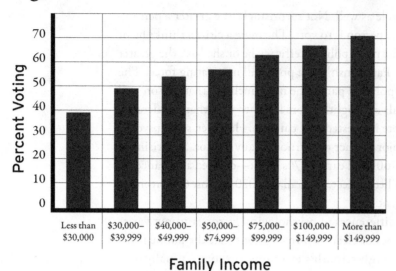

DATA SOURCE: U.S. Census Bureau, "Voting and Registration in the Election of November 2018," April 2019

Figure 8.2   Percent Voting for Candidate by Family Income

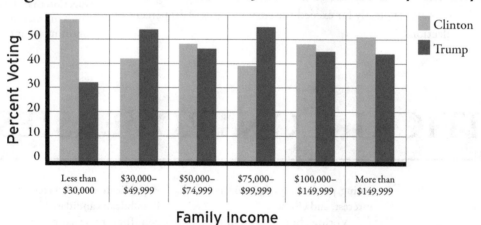

DATA SOURCE: Pew Research Center, "For Most Trump Voters, 'Very Warm' Feelings for Him Endured," August 8, 2018.

8.1c   Declining Turnout

Although presidential voting reached over the 66 percent mark in 2020, the highest level in over a century, there remains a troubling long-term trend toward lower voter turnout in the United States, as shown in Figure 8.3. After an explosion in the early nineteenth century, owing to the expansion of the electorate discussed earlier in this chapter, voter turnout by the 1990s had fallen to one of its lowest points in the last 150 years and had sagged substantially since its post–World War II peak in 1960. Although the long-term trend in turnout is striking, it is not necessarily ominous. The greatest part of the decline took place in the late-nineteenth and early-twentieth centuries. Some theorists attribute this to growing disaffection for the political system,[7] but other factors were probably involved. The widespread imposition of voter registration systems lowered turnout, both by excluding fraudulent votes and by discouraging some honest ones.[8] Moreover, Jim Crow laws in the South wiped out the gains made among African American voters in the years after the Civil War.

The Nineteenth Amendment, which enlarged the electorate by giving women the right to vote, temporarily reduced turnout. Many women had never voted before and did not immediately begin to exercise the right. As women, particularly younger women, got used to the newly opened political world, turnout climbed steadily through the 1930s. World War II disrupted voting interest, but interest bounced back in the 1950s. Demographic and institutional changes reduced voter turnout in the 1960s and 1970s. The maturation of the postwar baby boom and the reduction of the voting age from twenty-one to eighteen added millions of new voters; but because younger citizens are not as likely to vote as older people, this actually decreased the figures for turnout as a percentage of the voting-age population.

(Getty Images)

Many Americans are discouraged by the political world and thus decide not to vote. However, democracy's success depends on the enthusiastic participation of all of its citizens.

Yet many observers still believe that deep-seated psychological inclinations account for some of the contemporary decrease. Some blame political alienation or distrust. They argue that the American people are discouraged by what they see going on in politics and are increasingly inclined, therefore, not to vote. However, as noted earlier, trust does not

Figure 8.3   Turnout in Presidential and Congressional Elections, 1790–2020

Since the end of the nineteenth century, the long-term historical trend for voter turnout has been downward. Turnout for midterm congressional elections is lower than in presidential elections.

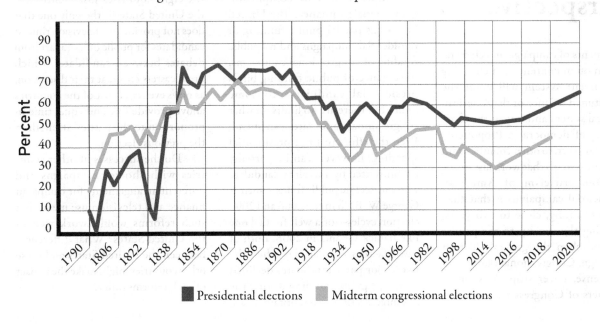

■ Presidential elections   ■ Midterm congressional elections

DATA SOURCES: Harold W. Stanley and Richard G. Niemi, Vital Statistics on American Politics (Washington, DC: CQ Press, 1990); Federal Election Commission; United States Election Project, http://www.electproject.org/home/voter-turnout/voter-turnout-data (December 21, 2020).

seem to have much effect on voting; so an increase in distrust does not necessarily imply a decrease in voting. In fact, many of the new voters in the 2000s seem to have been motivated more by the emergence of national campaigns by the Green Party and Libertarian Party than anything else. On the other hand, decreasing partisanship and external political efficacy clearly relate to voting turnout.[9] Young people are less partisan, and less partisan people are less likely to vote. It may be, therefore, that weakening partisanship is due to the influx of young people into the electorate, resulting in a decline in voting.

Some commentators view the long-term decline in voter turnout with alarm. The success of democracy, they argue, depends on the enthusiastic participation of its citizens; thus, declining electoral involvement is not a good sign. However, other commentators believe that less than total participation may be desirable because it can give a democracy room for compromise and flexibility.[10] Nonvoting may not imply a lack of trust or support for the political system but is perhaps a passive nonvote of confidence. In other words, staying home on Election Day may just be a way of saying that everything is all right.

POLITICS AND IDEAS

Campaign and Electoral Reform: A Comparative Perspective

Opponents of campaign and electoral reform often contend that changing the current system will upset the finely tuned balance of the American political system and impair the functioning of democracy. Proponents point, however, to other countries with different systems that work just fine.

One criticism of American presidential campaigns is that they go on too long, close to two years, counting the run-up to the primaries and then the general election campaign. Congressional campaigns, in a sense, never stop. As soon as members of Congress take office in

January, they must begin to look to the next election "only" twenty-two months away. Clearly other nations, particularly those with parliamentary systems, accomplish the process much more quickly. The best example is Great Britain, where the span from the announcement of an election to the new government's taking office is little more than a month.

Another area of comparison is in campaign finance. The United States has partial public funding of presidential campaigns and no public funding of congressional campaigns. Acceptance of public funding binds presidential candidates to some limits, but there are no limits on what congressional candidates can spend. Even the effort to limit presidential spending, however, can be partially circumvented by a wealthy candidate who can decline public funds—such as George W. Bush in the 2000 and 2004 election cycles—or a well-funded one like Barack Obama in 2008. Both of those factors were at play when the two major party candidates declined to accept public funding during the last three election cycles. Britain, Israel,

and Japan have no public funding whatsoever. Britain and Japan do impose limits on spending while Israel does not. Denmark, France, Italy, and Germany all have public funding based on strength in the previous election or a reimbursement according to strength in the current election.

A third point of comparison is in the use of television in campaigns. Of the eight countries just mentioned, the United States is the only one that does not provide free television time to candidates for public office (apart from debates between candidates, which broadcasters cover, at their discretion, as news events). Most of the countries above provide free and equal time in proportion to the parties' strength in the previous election.

Do the successes of other countries with shorter campaigns and different arrangements for campaign finance and television use mean that such reforms would work well in the United States? What differences between the United States and these other countries might make the impact of such reforms differ?

8.2 The Voter's Perspective: How to Vote

Just as various political, social, and psychological factors contribute to citizens' decisions about whether to exercise their voting rights, different elements help determine for whom they cast their ballots. Analysts have identified three major factors that seem to influence how people vote: parties, candidates, and issues.

8.2a Parties

For many years, affiliation with a political party was regarded as the mainstay of voting decisions in the United States. For some people, all that mattered was that a candidate belonged to "their" party. However, voter allegiance was not the only impact of strong party affiliation. In many instances party identification colored the way in which a voter looked at the pivotal elements of a presidential election. Party continues to play an important role in American electoral behavior. The 2016 presidential race illustrates the strong relationship between how people vote and their sense of partisanship. Eighty-nine percent of Democrats voted for the candidate of their party, while only 9 percent crossed party lines to vote for Trump, according to exit polls. Moreover, 90 percent of Republicans voted for the candidate of their party, while only 7 percent reported defecting to vote for Clinton.[11] In the 2020 election, Trump was again on the ballot, this time as the incumbent, and Republicans voted for him at a rate of 94 percent, with 6 percent choosing Biden. Similarly 94 percent of Democrats voted for Biden and 5 percent chose Trump.[12]

As established in Chapter 7, there can be little doubt that party has weakened as a reference point for many American voters in recent years. As party has become less important to voters, it has become a less important determinant of their voting decisions, which has left more room for candidate characteristics and issues to have an influence, as can be seen in the results described above.

8.2b Candidates

Opinions about the candidates themselves play a powerful role in influencing how voters ultimately vote. Because partisanship is fairly stable, assessments of the candidates are major contributors to changes in presidential voting from one election to the next.[13] When it comes to qualities of the candidate, voters seem to put the greatest weight on three factors:

- **Experience** The public shows a marked preference for someone with substantial political experience. Hence, the public leans very much toward incumbent presidents, vice presidents, senators, and governors from large states. The only recent presidents without substantial national political experience prior to taking office were Dwight Eisenhower (1953–1961), who had extensive military experience, and Jimmy Carter (1977–1981), the governor of a smaller state, Georgia. Although Bill Clinton (1993–2001) was the governor of a small southern state, he had been active on the national scene for many years as a leader in the National Governors Association and the Democratic Leadership Council. In the 2008 campaign, many of John McCain's advertisements focused on the candidate's long tenure in the Senate as compared to his opponent's much shorter tenure. By 2012, however, President Obama could

point to four years in the White House, so lack of experience was no longer an issue. Having served as governor of a populous state, Mitt Romney could boast of political experience as well. Election year 2016 had great contrasts in experience. On the one hand, Hillary Clinton had been a figure in national politics for a quarter of a century, having served as a senator from New York and as US secretary of state, not to mention eight years in the White House as first lady during the Bill Clinton administration. Donald Trump, on the other hand, had no political experience whatsoever, making him the least experienced major party candidate since Wendell Willkie in 1940. As a result, twice as many Americans said Hillary Clinton had the necessary experience to be president as said so about Donald Trump.[14] Yet, when the dust settled on Election Day, Trump emerged victorious, becoming the least experienced president in American history. Whether this was the beginning of a trend or merely an exception that proves the rule remains to be seen. By 2020 Trump had four years as president under his belt, but his challenger, Joe Biden, had served for eight years as vice president and for thirty-six years in the U.S. Senate. Thus, both could claim valuable experience.

- **Leadership**   The public is partial to candidates who seem able to take command of a situation, who do not wallow in pessimism or indecision, and who act when the time is right. President Carter suffered in the 1980 campaign because in the face of economic problems and the Iran hostage crisis, he was not seen as taking decisive and effective action. Twelve years later, in 1992, George H. W. Bush was hurt by the widespread public perception that he had no plan for addressing the economic problems besieging the country. His son must have learned a lesson from this as his efforts to project the image of a strong, decisive leader consistently resulted in high marks on this quality in opinion polls. In 2016, Donald Trump presented himself as a strong business leader, making the case that his skills in the boardroom would translate into the political arena. But by 2020 President Trump had a track record of presidential leadership, which challenger Biden summarily attacked on issues ranging from racial injustice to his handling of the COVID-19 crisis.

- **Personal qualities**   At the same time that voters want someone who will be a strong leader, they are also inclined to want an attractive and "nice" person in the White House. Eisenhower, Kennedy (1961–1963), and Reagan (1981–1989) all benefited from attractive personalities. Bill Clinton's campaign in 1992 mounted a major effort to offset early perceptions of him as dishonest and untrustworthy— "Slick Willy"—with an image-rebuilding effort that campaign insiders dubbed the "Manhattan Project" after the World War II program to develop the atomic bomb.[15] Not only did Bill Clinton overcome negative public perception to win the election in 1992 and reelection in 1996, but when he left office in January 2001, despite eight years of investigation that ultimately led to his impeachment, 65 percent of the American public approved of the way he handled his job as president.[16] In 2008, Barack Obama struck millions of Americans as an inspiring source of positive change, and his powerful speeches created the biggest stir about personality since the Reagan era. In a mid-2012 poll, 81 percent of respondents found Barack Obama "likable," and only 64 percent found Mitt Romney to be so.[17] In 2016, voters were less enamored of their choices. Only 46 percent of Americans said Hillary Clinton was "likable," and just 36 percent said Donald Trump was.[18] Trump's likability continued to remain low, still registering at just 37 percent well into his presidency, and only 36 percent found him "honest and trustworthy" in 2020.[19] Joe Biden, on the other hand, while also facing a very partisan America, had the confidence of 52 percent of the public in his ability to address race relations—an important issue in the 2020 race, and a rating 12 percent higher than his opponent.[20]

8.2c Issues

Today more than ever, issues seem to drive the public toward a particular electoral choice. A 2004 poll suggested that voters saw whether or not a candidate shared their values as the defining issue in the presidential race between Kerry and Bush.[21] In 2012, voters gave that edge to Obama over Romney by a margin of 53 to 45 percent.[22] Even observers who have previously minimized the importance of issues now concede that issues can make a difference when the public knows and cares about them and when the candidates differentiate themselves on issues. Single-issue groups, described in Chapter 7, play a big role in emphasizing particular concerns. Opponents of gun control or tax increases, for example, can "target" an official for defeat. Even without the participation of single-issue groups, social issues such as crime control and foreign policy issues such as military intervention in the Middle East usually receive considerable attention in a campaign.

More often, though, the voter's focus is on economic issues. Year in and year out, the mainspring issue driving most electoral decisions seems to be the economy. Even the earliest voting studies that discovered issues to be relatively unimportant found that bread-and-butter economic issues did make a difference. Personal economic well-being seems to influence how Americans vote. Figure 8.4 relates the percentage of the popular vote for president received by the incumbent party to an indicator of how much a citizen's disposable income had increased during the election year. Clearly, the better off people are during an election year, the more likely they are to vote for the party holding the White House.

Figure 8.4 The Economy and Presidential Voting

The better the economy, the better the candidate of the incumbent party does in the presidential election. The diagonal line shows the basic trend in the relationship—that is, how much, on average, voting is related to improvements in the economy. Of course, in some years, other issues trump the economy, as in 2016, when the incumbent's party lost despite improving economic conditions.

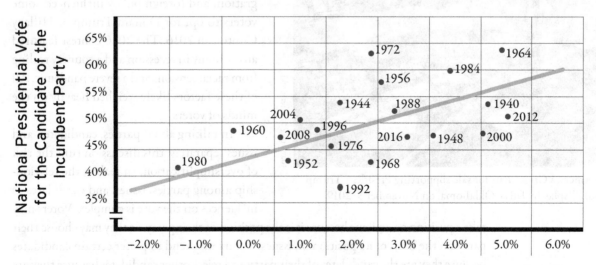

Election-Year Change in Real Disposable Income per Capita

Data Sources: Federal Election Commission, retrieved at https://www.fec.gov/introduction-campaign-finance/election-and-voting-information/; The Cook Political Report, retrieved at https://cookpolitical.com/2020-national-popular-vote-tracker, Copyright 2020 by Cook Political Report, All Rights Reserved; Bureau of Economic Analysis, retrieved at https://www.bea.gov/data/income-saving/disposable-personal-income; Edward Tufte, Political Control of the Economy (Princeton, NJ: Princeton University Press, 1978), p. 123.

(chrisdorney / Shutterstock)

Single-issue groups hold great sway over whether a candidate will gain a citizen's vote. It doesn't matter if a candidate supports or opposes the use of nuclear weapons, abortion, gun control, or other controversial issues; he or she can still be dropped from the race for office.

Some political commentators pointed to Ronald Reagan's celebrated question near the end of his 1980 election debate with Jimmy Carter—"Are you better off now than you were four years ago?"—as the symbolic turning point of that campaign. The statistical evidence suggests that the Reagan campaign may have been right in emphasizing the role of the economy. The same was true for the 1992 presidential election—exit polls showed Bush running far ahead of Bill Clinton (62 percent to 24 percent) among voters who thought their family's financial situation had improved over the preceding four years, and the two candidates were dead even (at 41 percent each) among those who thought things had stayed the same. Clinton outpolled Bush 61 percent to 14 percent among those who felt they were worse off; and fortunately for Clinton, those voters outnumbered by a margin of four to three voters who felt they were better off—enough to give Clinton the victory. Clinton benefited from an economic upturn during his first administration, and the fact that a majority of Americans in the fall of 1996 believed that national economic conditions were improving helped him retain office. However, although an even higher percentage of Americans thought the economy was getting better in fall 2000, Al Gore was unable to translate his connection to the incumbent Democratic administration into electoral victory.[23] In 2008, a national recession allowed Barack Obama to gain ground by distancing himself from the Bush administration in a way that his Republican opponent could not. When the economy began to rebound by 2012, the incumbent Obama was able to take advantage of that change, as well. This is not to say that

(damann / Shutterstock)

"Keep America Great" hats for sale supporting President Trump with gun display in Tulsa, Oklahoma, on November 9, 2019.

economics is the only issue that sways voters. Other issues have some impact. No doubt the candidates' differences on gun control, immigration, and foreign policy influenced some voters to opt for Donald Trump or Hillary Clinton in 2016. The 2020 contest featured an economy in recession and a country reeling from racial tensions and a severe pandemic. All of these factors likely weighed heavily on the minds of voters.

In talking about parties, candidates, and issues separately, this discussion runs the risk of oversimplification. In reality, the relationship among parties, issues, and candidates as influences on the vote is complex. Voters may take a position on an issue because it is the position of their party, or they may choose their party on the basis of its position on issues. Voters may tend to prefer certain candidates because they are the candidates of their party and reject other candidates because they are candidates of the other party; or they may judge a party according to how much they like its candidates. Finally, voters may like candidates because they agree with their positions on certain issues, or voters may adopt certain positions on issues because they like the candidates who advocate them. Thus, voter decision-making is based on the interplay of a number of factors—and not just on those factors alone.

8.3 | The Candidate's Perspective: Running for President

While voters need to decide whether and how to vote, a more complicated set of choices confronts candidates. Their basic decisions include whether or not to run and how to attract enough votes to win. To achieve the latter, contemporary presidential candidates must make scores of strategic decisions, carve out a clear position as a serious contender early on, raise large amounts of money, choose the right campaign consultant, decide which issues to raise, select the primaries and caucuses on which to concentrate, garner enough delegates in the national convention to secure the nomination, choose a running mate, and win states with enough electoral votes to win the electoral college. These tasks are compounded by the fact that a candidate must also outmaneuver opponents who are working equally hard to attract voters.

8.3a   Who Runs for President?

In American political folklore, anyone can grow up to be president whether they have humble beginnings, like Abraham Lincoln, or high social and economic status, like Franklin Roosevelt. Is such folklore actually true? In fact, the Constitution lays down few requirements. The person must be a natural-born citizen of the United States, a resident of the United States for at least fourteen years, and at least thirty-five years of age. The **Twenty-second Amendment** (1951), ratified in the aftermath of Franklin Roosevelt's unprecedented four elections to the presidency, imposes one more restriction: An individual cannot be elected to the presidency more than twice, or more than once if the individual has completed more than two years of another president's term.

Despite the relatively small set of formal qualifications, however, evidence suggests that the path to power is fairly steep and narrow. The key to attaining the highest political office in the United States is to have held other reasonably high political offices. Consider the twenty-seven individuals who have run for the presidency under the banner of the major parties in the last nineteen elections. Eight of them had been governors of their states, nine had previously served as vice president, and fifteen had served in the U.S. Senate. Only two, Dwight Eisenhower and Donald Trump—had never held an elective office. However, the best assurance of being elected president is to already *be* president. In the thirty-one elections in which an incumbent president sought reelection, the incumbent was successful in twenty-one, or 68 percent of the time. This statistic probably stems in part from the incumbent president's unique ability to manipulate events in his favor and the high visibility and name recognition a president enjoys.

What other qualities put an individual in line to be considered for the highest office in the land? Recent history suggests several qualities are prevalent. For one, the presidency was historically a white, male preserve. This was not seriously challenged until 2008, when the Democratic primary elections ensured change by presenting a Caucasian woman (Hillary Clinton) and an African American–identified man (Barack Obama, whose father was a black man from Kenya) as their top two contenders. Obama winning the presidency in 2008 and 2012 and Hillary Clinton winning the popular vote (though not the presidency) in 2016 made it clear the office is no longer a white men's club in the twenty-first century. In addition, most presidents in recent times have been from at least reasonably well-off, Protestant backgrounds and have been reasonably well educated. Not until 1960, with the election of John F. Kennedy, did a Catholic become president;

Twenty-second Amendment

Ratified in 1951, this amendment restricts the president to two terms in office

and there was not another Catholic on a major party ticket until John Kerry in 2004. Joe Biden became the first Catholic elected vice president in 2008, and the Republican nomination of Paul Ryan in 2012 meant both vice-presidential candidates were Catholic that year. Democratic vice-presidential nominee Tim Kaine continued that trend in 2016. No Jew has ever been elected president, and Joe Lieberman became the first Jewish vice-presidential candidate of a major party in 2000. Mitt Romney's 2012 Republican nomination was the first of a Mormon. This growing diversity in nominees for the nation's highest offices reflects changes in both the demographics and the cultural acceptance of diversity in America.

In this age of media politics, an attractive image is clearly an important asset; perhaps, however, the most important quality of all is determination. Securing a major party's presidential nomination nowadays typically takes months, even years, of grinding work. In some cases candidates start campaigning in January of the year before the presidential election year and continue nonstop for almost the next two years. Presidential hopeful Gary Hart vividly illustrated the kind of ordeal that a modern presidential candidate has to endure when he revealed that some mornings, during his 1984 campaign, he would awaken in a strange hotel room and have to reach for the phone book in order to remember what city he was in.

POLITICAL CONTROVERSIES

An Election Gone Wrong?

The Constitution charges the American states with the responsibility of regulating the time, place, and manner of elections. Traditionally, this has meant that each state establishes its own rules and designs its own ballots. Since the presidential election is combined with state and local races, county election boards often end up designing ballots of their own, following state guidelines. Typically this is not an issue of concern; but controversy arose on November 7, 2000, when one county's choice of ballot design seemed to determine the outcome of an extremely close presidential election.

Palm Beach County, Florida, voters were confronted with a "butterfly ballot" (so called because the pages on either side of the center punch card resemble wings) that listed presidential candidate names alternately on both the left and right sides of the holes. The Republican Party candidates were listed first on the left side, and the Democratic Party candidates second; but in between the two, the Reform Party candidates were listed on the *right* side. Many voters claimed to be confused as a result of this ballot—a claim that seemed well-supported by the election results. In Palm Beach County, 5,330 voters punched holes for both Democratic candidate Al Gore and Reform candidate Pat Buchanan. Did some, or even most, of these voters intend to select Al Gore? We will never know for certain. But after careful analysis of the Florida vote, it seems possible that this ballot irregularity cost Al Gore the presidency.

A study commissioned by *USA Today* and several other papers concluded that George W. Bush still would have been victorious even if a hand recount of all the Florida votes had taken place. The study also noted, however, that a majority of Florida voters probably intended to vote for Al Gore. In an election as close as the presidential race in 2000, a poorly designed ballot in a single county can have an enormous effect. As a result of these complications, Congress passed the Help America Vote Act in 2002, which provided funds to states so that they could update and streamline voting and ballot counting procedures.

Should the federal government regulate ballots? Should it provide suggested guidelines to the states? What standards are needed to guarantee a fair and accurate election? What do ballots look like in your county? Do you find them confusing or easy to use?

8.3b   The Media Campaign

The primary determinant of the shape of the modern political campaign is the mass media. Candidates used to be concerned primarily with mobilizing the party organization behind their efforts. Now their principal concern is mobilizing the media, particularly television, to bring their name and "image" before the public. Such efforts assume three principal forms. The first form is the expenditure of most of the campaign treasury on political advertisements. Precious paid television time is generally devoted to short advertisements that focus on simple images and issues, rather than longer speeches that focus on in-depth discussions of public policy. Campaign debates waged in one-minute, thirty-second, and even fifteen-second spots have drawn considerable criticism for oversimplifying campaign issues. Ross Perot's 1992 and 1996 campaigns defied traditional practice by spending millions of dollars on half-hour blocks devoted to detailed discussions of economic problems and solutions—and defied conventional wisdom by drawing large viewing audiences.

(Andrew Cline / Shutterstock)

Former Vice President Joe Biden takes a selfie with voters during a town hall campaign stop in Hampton, N.H., on February 9, 2020.

Another way candidates bring their names before the media is to structure traditional campaign events—such as speeches, rallies, and news conferences—in order to get media attention. These activities, once the core of the traditional political campaign, are now used mainly as "media events," or opportunities to attract coverage by the news media. Republican candidate Donald Trump seemed to have mastered this concept in 2016, when his unconventional candidacy and his ability to make controversial statements attracted media attention almost constantly. According to one study, he had received the equivalent of $2 billion in free media exposure before the primary season even ended.[24]

A third strategy is for candidates to try to get as much free television time as possible on regular news and interview broadcasts. Extended nationally televised appearances on the nightly network news broadcasts, traditional news interview programs such as *Nightline*, and, more recently, the "softer" interview shows such as *The View* are the candidate's dream—but these coveted appearances are hard to come by.

The bread and butter of free television time comes in two forms: the "sound bite" on the national network news broadcasts and the daily stream of interviews on local TV stations as candidates travel around the country. Sound bites are short, taped excerpts from statements that a candidate makes. Candidates hope to get at least one sound bite on the national news broadcasts every night during the course of the campaign and thus attempt to say things in ways that are "sound biteable" to the TV crews covering them.

Another major development of recent years has been the rise of the professional **media consultant**. In the past, candidates tended to rely on party leaders or a personal coterie to plan and execute their campaign strategy. The current trend, however, is toward reliance on professional campaign consultants. Such individuals, while certainly oriented more toward one party or philosophy than another, make themselves available for hire to candidates able to pay for their services. One of the best known and most successful media consultants in recent years is James Carville, who led Bill Clinton's media campaign in 1992 and then served as senior political adviser to President Clinton.

media consultant

An expert hired by a political candidate to give advice on the use of the mass media, particularly television and direct mail, in a campaign for public office

The media typically concentrate not on the issues of the campaign but on the strategies, tactics, and likely outcome of the campaign. Politicians and commentators call such a focus the *horse race.* Poll results are tracked throughout the campaign to see who is in the lead and to test the potential effect of various moves by the candidates. Some critics have argued that the emphasis placed on the polls in the mass media serves to make polls the makers, rather than the measurers, of public opinion. Polling results showing a candidate doing better than expected tend to increase that candidate's credibility, and thereby contribute to further gains in the polls. Polling results showing a candidate lagging far behind may lead the public to write off that candidate as a wasted vote. Also, a poor showing in the polls can cause potential contributors to cut the flow of money to a candidate. Politicians, particularly those trailing in the polls, like to say, "The only poll that counts is the one on Election Day"; yet preelection polls may encourage shifts in opinion that are translated into shifts in voting on Election Day. In 1992, interest in the election was heightened as public opinion polls showed the race between Bush and Clinton tightening in the last two weeks of the campaign, only to have the drama diminish as the apparent Bush surge fell back in the last few days before the voting. In 2000, the race was tight right down to the wire; opinion polls during the last two weeks before the election consistently found the race too close to call. In this case the polls were right. The election turned out to be one of the tightest in recent history, with only a few hundred votes separating Bush and Gore in some key states.

(George Bush: White House photo by Eric Draper, via Wikimedia, 2001)

(Al Gore: White House photo via Wikimedia, 1994)

The 2000 race for the presidency between George W. Bush and Al Gore came down to only a few hundred votes. The news media risked its credibility when it inaccurately claimed Gore to have won Florida's votes. A recount named Bush the winner of the votes in Florida.

In recent years, the media and the polls have become controversial even on Election Day itself. Modern sampling techniques and **exit polls** (interviews with voters leaving the polls) often enable analysts to predict the winner long before polls everywhere have closed. For example, in 1988 CBS and ABC projected George Bush as the victor over Michael Dukakis at 9:20 p.m. Eastern Standard Time, well before many voters in Western states had voted. Do early predictions about who is winning or losing dissuade those who have not yet voted from doing so, create a "bandwagon" effect for the projected winner, or do they incur sympathy votes for the projected loser? The evidence on these questions is mixed, but there are some signs that early projections do reduce turnout. In the 2000 election, the media caused an even bigger uproar, first by declaring Al Gore the winner of Florida's twenty-five electoral votes, then by retracting and declaring Bush the winner of both Florida and the national election, and then—finally—by admitting that the race was too close to call. In its race to break an important story, the news media risked its credibility with the public.

exit poll

A poll of voters taken as they leave a polling place and usually conducted by the media to get an advance indication of voting trends and facilitate analysis of the reasons behind the outcome of the election

As the media have come more and more to shape the modern presidential campaign, and as dissatisfaction with modern campaigns has grown, the media have become the object of blame for the problems and the target of reform. As reasonable and laudable as the proposed media reforms sound, many of them collide with the First Amendment principles of freedom of the press and speech, potentially infringing on broadcasters' rights as journalists and the candidates' rights to express themselves freely. Below are some of the specific proposals that have been advanced in recent years.

- Requiring broadcasters to give more free time to candidates, thus reducing the candidates' need for money to spend on advertising

- Establishing rules for political advertising on television, thus possibly forcing broadcasters and candidates to present only spots of one minute or more and prohibiting any unfair or negative elements

- Conditioning federal campaign funding for presidential candidates on their agreement to participate in at least four televised debates

- Challenging television news organizations to devote more time to the substance of the campaign and less to the horse race

- Prohibiting television news organizations from projecting winners before all polls have closed, or creating, as an alternative, a uniform national poll-closing time

POLITICAL CONTROVERSIES

Low Voter Turnout: A Comparative Perspective

The public debate about low voter turnout in the United States and what to do about it takes place against an international backdrop that offers some unflattering comparisons. As Figure 8.5 shows, the United States ranks near the bottom of democratic countries in the percentage of its voting-age population that actually votes.

All kinds of explanations relating to distrust of government and lack of confidence in American political institutions have been offered to account for the low rate of turnout in the United States. The evidence shows, however, that these factors have little impact and that, in any case, trust and confidence in government are higher in the United States than in many other countries.

Turnout is lower in the United States than elsewhere primarily because there are more obstacles and fewer incentives to vote than elsewhere. The primary obstacle is, of course, the American system of voter registration. In fact, in many other democratic countries, registration is automatic. In Germany, Italy, and Sweden, for example, citizens who move are required to report their new address to the government. Once they do this, their voting rights are automatically canceled at their old polling place and reinstated at their new one. Other countries (for example, Australia, Belgium, Greece, and Spain) have given people an incentive to vote by establishing penalties for nonvoting that, even if rarely enforced, seem to boost turnout by 10 percent. Perhaps the most effective sanctions are found in Italy. Italian citizens who fail to vote have "DID NOT VOTE" stamped on their identification papers, which can be a significant embarrassment and disadvantage in dealing with government officials.[1]

Despite such evidence, solutions to low voter turnout may take time to

materialize. The American government took steps to address the registration concern with passage of the National Voter Registration Act in 1993. Although this effort to simplify the process resulted in higher registration rates, voter turnout in the 2012 presidential election was still less than 54 percent of the voting-age population and was only slightly higher in 2016. The 2020 election broke this trend, with about 62 percent of the voting age population casting a ballot, but it remains to be seen whether such a rate will persist, or whether 2020 was an anomaly.

Voting is the defining act of a democracy. While such problems as voter fraud cannot be ignored, the United States might take a lesson from many of its sister democracies: Low turnout is not an intractable given, but a problem that can be addressed by reducing obstacles and increasing incentives.

1. David Glass, Peverill Squire, and Raymond Wolfinger, "Voter Turnout: An International Comparison," *Public Opinion* (December, 1983): 49–55.

Figure 8.5 Percentage of Voting-Age Population That Votes in Twenty-one Western Countries

The United States ranks near the bottom of democratic countries in the percentage of the voting-age population that actually votes, primarily because it places more obstacles in front of and offers fewer incentives to voters.

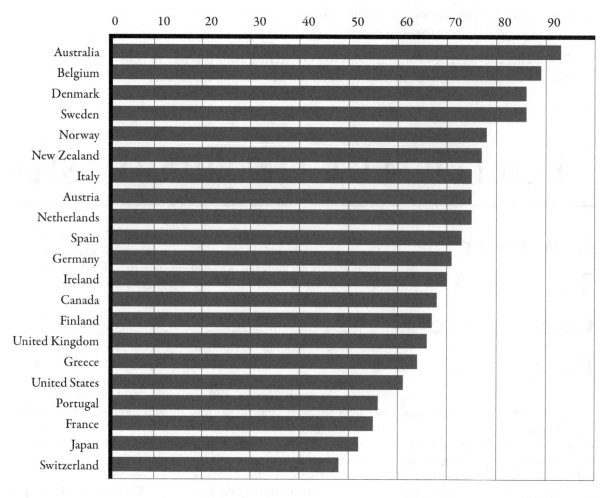

DATA SOURCE: International Institute for Democracy and Electoral Assistance, "Voter Turnout Trends Around the World," https://www.idea.int/sites/default/files/publications/voter-turnout-trends-around-the-world.pdf (September 24, 2018); U.S. Elections Project, 2020 November General Election Turnout Rates, November 4, 2020, http://www.electproject.org/2020g (November 11, 2020).

8.3c Campaign Finance

Financing campaigns has always been an issue for candidates. The rate at which modern, media-based, jet-borne, poll-addicted campaigns consume money has made the problem even greater. The Federal Election Commission (FEC) reports that in congressional races alone candidates spent over $2.7 billion in the 2018 election cycle. The independent Center for Responsive Politics placed the total spending for the presidential contest and all other races in the 2016 election cycle at over $6.4 billion.[25] With the demands for more money have come growing public concern and increased legislative action to prevent political money from tainting the electoral and governmental processes.

In 1971 Congress passed the **Federal Election Campaign Act** (FECA). The unfolding of the Watergate scandal in 1974 and other subsequent developments have led to amendments to FECA. Current campaign finance law requires full disclosure of the sources and uses of campaign funds on the theory that requiring candidates to disclose where their money came from will encourage them to behave more ethically. Thus, candidates must file a complete accounting with the FEC of where they get their money and how they spend it.

The law bans direct contributions to candidates by corporations and labor unions, although such organizations can set up political action committees (PACs) through which their employees or members can contribute. (For more on PACs, see Chapter 7.) The law also places limits on campaign contributions. Currently individuals may give up to $5,200 per candidate in each election cycle, but thanks to a recent Supreme Court ruling there is no longer an overall cap.[26] In other words, a wealthy donor could contribute that full $5,200 to each candidate throughout the nation. An individual cannot give more than $5,000 to a PAC per election per year, and a PAC cannot give more than $5,000 to one candidate in a federal election. However, there are no limits on the total a PAC can contribute to all federal candidates or on the total a candidate can receive from all PACs. National party committees can also spend about six cents per member of the voting population on the presidential election campaign. The largest growth in spending in recent election cycles, however, has been in the so-called super PACs, which are unaffiliated with a particular campaign and are therefore not limited in the amount they can spend or that contributors can donate. An even more disturbing trend is that super PACs have begun using legal loopholes to avoid disclosing the sources of their funding until after an election cycle has concluded.[27]

Where does all the money for a political campaign come from?

Find out who contributes to your favorite (or least favorite!) candidates at the Center for Responsive Politics.

http://www.bvtlab.com/6Y8RN

The Revenue Act of 1971 created a system of public financing for presidential campaigns. Every taxpayer had the option of earmarking $1 of federal income tax for the **Presidential Election Campaign Fund**. This earmark has since been raised to $3. The money generated is distributed directly to presidential candidates according to specific formulas that tie amounts that can be spent to the rate of inflation. Before the party conventions, candidates are eligible for federal matching funds. To receive these funds, candidates must raise at least $5,000 in each of at least twenty states. Contributions are limited to $250 per contributor. Once a candidate has qualified, the federal government will match all individual contributions up to a specified amount if the candidate agrees to hold total spending under a limit. After the party conventions, major-party candidates who give up the right to accept any contributions from the public whatsoever can opt for federal financing of their campaigns, up to limits set by the law. Since the Revenue Act of 1971 was passed, all major-party presidential candidates opted for federal funding—until 2008, when Senator Barack Obama decided to forgo this option, citing a broken system that needed to be fixed. Senator McCain initially accepted, and then later rejected, the spending limits and the $84.1 million dollars from the federal government that came with it. Neither major-party candidate has accepted public funding since then.

Individual, PAC, and party contributions, as well as federal funds, are not the only money that can be spent on a candidate's behalf. Independent of the official campaign, individuals and PACs can spend as much as they want on behalf of a presidential candidate on such things as their own political advertisements and direct mail. Also, candidates willing to forgo federal funding can spend as much of their own money as they

Federal Election Campaign Act

Law passed in 1971 and amended several times that regulates campaign financing and requires full disclosure of sources and uses of campaign funds and limits contributions to political candidates

Presidential Election Campaign Fund

Pool of money available that is collected from a $3 check-off on the federal income tax form and is available to presidential candidates for campaign expenses

want. In 1992 independent candidate Ross Perot was estimated to have spent at least $60 million of his own money in his bid to win the White House. Surprisingly, though he is a multibillionaire who claimed not to need money from others to run his campaign, Donald Trump spent only about $66 million of his own money on his 2016 campaign—less than 20 percent of the total raised.[28] As the incumbent, Trump spent none of his own money throughout the 2020 primary season. In contrast, former New York City mayor Michael Bloomberg spent over $1 billion of his own money on his short-lived 2020 Democratic primary campaign. Candidates who do opt for federal funding are limited to spending $50,000 of their own money.

The problems concerning PACs have led some recent candidates to reject financial support from them. Many critics now call for the abolition of PACs or for tighter controls on them, but these actions would raise serious questions about freedom of speech. As a result, PACs and super PACs may be a permanent fixture of American politics. How candidates manage their relationships with them, however, is another, less predictable matter. Proposals for PAC reform include increasing the amounts that individuals can give to candidates and restoring tax deductions for political contributions.

The major loophole in the controls on money that can be spent on a candidate's behalf was a seemingly innocuous amendment to the campaign finance laws passed by Congress in 1979—the so-called **soft money** loophole. The tight controls on party spending imposed by the FECA laws in the early 1970s had the effect of drastically reducing the money that the national party could give to state and local parties to help pay for grassroots activities supporting the presidential campaign—handing out buttons and bumper stickers, for example. In 1979 Congress moved to solve this problem by allowing the national parties to raise and spend money, without any restrictions, for state and local parties, routine operating expenses, and "party-building" activities, as long as the expenditures were not directly related to any federal campaign.

The parties soon began to exploit this exception to the hilt. Within the law, they moved to solicit unlimited contributions from individuals, corporations, and unions. Within the law, they cleverly spent the money in ways that technically were not directly associated with federal candidates, but clearly helped the candidates and freed up other party funds to help them. Under the new law, parties have to report virtually nothing about how the money is raised or spent.

Many critics, led by such organizations as Common Cause, see the soft money exception as an evasion of the entire structure of campaign finance law. These organizations have prodded the FEC to scrutinize whether state and local expenditures are too closely tied to federal candidates and to rewrite the rules governing the raising and spending of soft money. The FEC has been slow to make changes; however, one reform that stands some chance of being implemented is fuller disclosure of the sources and uses of soft money—partly because the parties have already begun to do this on a limited, voluntary basis in an attempt to head off more restrictive reforms. Some would like to see the 1979 amendment that opened the soft money loophole repealed, but such repeal seems unlikely given that so many of the legislators voting on the issue benefit from the soft money system. Indeed, the Bipartisan Campaign Reform Act of 2002 closed many loopholes, but its failure to tighten restrictions on uncoordinated expenditures (see Chapter 7) led to the formation of new groups (super PACs) and a new approach to soft money spending.

8.3d Getting Nominated

The modern-day orientation toward the media, supported by unending efforts to raise money, is superimposed over the traditional political events that in the heyday of political

soft money

A category of campaign money that was created by an amendment to the campaign finance laws in 1979, allowing the national parties to raise and spend money, essentially without restriction, for state and local parties, routine operating expenses, and party-building activities, as long as the expenditures are not directly related to any federal campaign

parties were the central mechanisms by which candidates were selected: primaries, caucuses, and conventions.

The most visible part of the presidential nominating process in recent years has been the long string of **primary elections** and party caucuses, extending from the Iowa caucuses and the New Hampshire primary in early February, to the big primaries in such populous states as Illinois and California in March and April, to the latecomers like New Jersey and Montana in June. In 2020 many states had to postpone their contests by a month or more to make social distancing adjustments due to COVID-19. Primary elections are intraparty elections in which a political party selects the candidates it will run for office in the final interparty **general election**. Primary elections differ from state to state in terms of who is allowed to vote. In an **open primary**, any voter regardless of party affiliation can participate in the selection of the party's candidates. In a **closed primary**, only voters registered as members of the party can participate in the selection process for that party. Some states express their presidential preferences in caucuses, or small party meetings. **Caucuses** typically include discussion time before voting, thus giving them a more deliberative character than the simple voting of a primary election. Each state and each party has its own set of rules for caucuses, but the process often includes a series of conversations about the candidates in which efforts are made to come to consensus by persuading the supporters of less popular candidates to join the cause of candidates with greater support. The process continues until one or more candidate(s) reaches a previously agreed to threshold of support, or until the state's delegates are divided proportionately.

The earliest presidential primaries and caucuses are the most important because they quickly sort out the field into contenders and also-rans. Most important in this respect is the New Hampshire primary, which provides the first real electoral test of the candidates' popular appeal. Candidates in the earliest contests run not so much against one another as against the expectations that the press and polls have created about how those candidates should fare. After the early contests shape the field, the political battles move out onto a broader plain.

In 2016, the process took longer than expected for both parties. The Republicans started with an astounding seventeen candidates, with several staying in the race well into the primary season. Not until after political neophyte Donald Trump had secured a majority of delegates on May 3 did Senator Ted Cruz (R-TX) and Ohio Governor John Kasich finally suspend their campaigns. Intraparty opposition to Trump's candidacy—symbolized by the #NeverTrump movement—made the real estate tycoon's nomination a topic of suspense right up until it was made official at the Republican convention in July. While the Democratic field was much smaller, both Hillary Clinton and Bernie Sanders battled it out through the entire season of primaries and caucuses. Many observers attributed the long primary season to the Democratic Party's awarding of state delegates proportionately. Unlike the Republicans' winner-take-all approach in many states, any Democratic candidate securing at least 15 percent of a state's vote is eligible to receive delegates. This process allowed both candidates to continue accruing delegates, even in states where their opponent won the plurality of votes.

In 2020, the nomination worked very differently for the two parties. The Republicans had, in Donald Trump, an incumbent president who was eligible for reelection. So, they did what parties typically do in this case and renominated him. Though there were some intraparty grumblings about Trump no serious challenger emerged, and the sitting president received the party's nomination with little effort. On the Democratic side, however, over two dozen hopefuls vied for the opportunity to be their party's nominee. With multiple people of color, women, and an LGBT candidate, it was an impressively diverse field. In the end, though a number of contests had to be postponed or modified due to the COVID-19 threat, former vice president Joe Biden emerged with the nomination.

primary election
Preliminary election in which a party picks delegates to a party convention or its candidates for public office

general election
Election, which occurs in November, to choose the candidates who will hold public office, following primary elections held during the spring and summer

open primary
A primary election in which any voter, regardless of party affiliation, can participate

closed primary
A primary election in which only the members of the party holding the election are allowed to participate

caucus
A meeting of members of a political party (the members of a party in a legislature are also referred to as a party caucus), used in some states to select delegates to the national conventions, which nominate presidential candidates

The protracted series of primaries and caucuses leading up to the party conventions seems excessive to many observers. The crucial early events, which set the tone for the rest of the campaign, take place in relatively small and unrepresentative states. Some see this as a good thing. A long primary season with many of the early events centered in small states keeps the political process open by giving less well-known candidates with limited resources a chance to break into the political arena. Others see this as a disadvantage. They say the American political process is served less well by the election of obscure outsiders than by that of better-known insiders who understand how to make the system work as soon as they take office.

One reform proposal suggests that the primary process be compressed in time and broadened in representation by instituting either a one-day national primary or a series of regional primaries. Advocates argue that such moves would speed up the nominating process and give the citizens of every state, not just those with early delegate-selection procedures, the opportunity to play a meaningful role in the selection of presidential candidates. The one-day national primary strikes many as a radical change, giving only the best-known and most prosperous candidates a real chance

(Nuno21 / Shutterstock)

Then-Senator Kamala Harris giving a rebuttal response to the Republican National Convention and failure of President Trump on August 27, 2020. In November 2020, Harris became the first female elected to the office of vice president.

at the nomination. A reasonable compromise between the current fragmented system and a single national primary has been proposed—a series of **regional primaries** in different areas of the country, perhaps spaced two weeks apart over two months. Lesser-known candidates would then have the opportunity to build from small beginnings in their home regions.

The state caucuses and primaries culminate in the selection of delegates to the national **party conventions** held in late summer of the presidential election year. It is here that the party nominees are finally selected. In the past, the outcome of the nominating contest was often in doubt as delegates wrangled over disputes about rules, credentials, and party platforms, and as decisions were made in "smoke-filled rooms" by party elites. In recent years conventions have become more sedate. The publicity surrounding the selection of delegates has made the convention process almost perfunctory. The parties have tried hard to settle differences in advance of—or off of—the convention floor, lest public bickering paint an inharmonious picture of the party on television screens across the country. As the parties have tried to control and exploit media coverage of their conventions, the news value of these political events has declined and the television networks have given them less coverage. Despite rumblings of dissatisfaction—and threats of an attempt to block Donald Trump's nomination on the floor of the convention—even the 2016 Republican convention went off without much controversy. The 2020 conventions, facing the challenges of social distancing, were postponed and then conducted largely in online and remote formats with smaller in-person gatherings, though ones which still allowed for televised speeches in prime time.

One of the most important strategic decisions a presidential candidate must make by the end of the convention is selection of a vice-presidential running mate. Much political folk wisdom revolves around this choice, particularly the need to **balance the ticket** geographically or ideologically. The idea is to pick a running mate who differs from the presidential candidate in a way that makes the ticket attractive to a broader range of

regional primary
A primary election held across an entire geographic area (for example, the South or the West) rather than within a single state

party convention
Regularly scheduled general meeting of a political party that is held for the purpose of ratifying party policies and deciding on party candidates

balance the ticket
A political party's effort to appeal to a wider cross-section of voters by providing regional or ideological balance in its nominations for president and vice president

voters. Thus, southern outsider Jimmy Carter picked northern insider Walter Mondale in 1976, western outsider Ronald Reagan picked eastern insider George Bush in 1980, and eastern liberal Michael Dukakis picked southern conservative Lloyd Bentsen in 1988. Bill Clinton broke with this practice in 1992 when he chose Al Gore, a moderate white Southern male like himself, as his running mate. In 2000, Al Gore attempted to purify a candidacy tainted by connection to campaign finance scandals and chose Joe Lieberman, a

Sample ballot from the 2020 presidential election.

senator whose ethical standards were above reproach. George W. Bush, perceived by some as being an intellectual lightweight, chose the more cerebral Dick Cheney to balance his ticket. In 2004, John Kerry of Massachusetts went the regional route, selecting North Carolina Senator John Edwards to provide the ticket with broader appeal in the South. In 2008, Barack Obama selected Delaware Senator Joe Biden to give his ticket more experience in the field of foreign policy. John McCain selected Alaska Governor Sarah Palin in order to shore up support from the more conservative wing of the Republican Party. In 2012, Mitt Romney also catered to conservative Republicans with his choice of running mate, Paul Ryan. Unlike McCain, though, Romney avoided accusations that he had chosen an inexperienced political lightweight by selecting Wisconsin Representative Ryan, a member of Congress since 1999 who had already held important leadership roles, such as chair of the House Budget Committee. In 2016, and again in 2020, Donald Trump picked Indiana governor Mike Pence, both to appeal to the morally conservative wing of his party and to balance his own bombastic style with Pence's more sedate tone. Moreover, it provided the ticket with one member who had held office before. Hillary Clinton chose Tim Kaine, a senator from Virginia who was seen as both likable and unconnected to scandal. Democrat Joe Biden declared early on that he would choose a female running mate in 2020. Ultimately, he stayed true to his word and selected California Senator Kamala Harris. Harris became the third female nominated by a major party for the vice presidency and the first person of African American and Indian descent.

The vice presidency has long been the object of political scorn. Nevertheless, the offer of the vice-presidential nomination is something that few politicians would sneer at. The amenities that go with the job are first-class, and recent presidents have gone to special lengths to see that their seconds have meaningful work. Perhaps most important is the fact that the vice presidency is the most direct stepping-stone to the White House. Of the forty-seven people who have served as vice president, fourteen have gone on to become president. No job in the world gives its holder better odds of becoming president. However, the ascent typically comes by death of the president rather than election. Since 1800, only two incumbent vice presidents have gone on to win a presidential election: Martin Van Buren in 1836 and George Bush in 1988.

8.3e   The Electoral College

The main factor driving strategic decisions in the general election is the **Electoral College**. (Discussed in Chapter 2 as a federalism issue, the topic is revisited here as a key facet of presidential elections.) The election of the president of the United States is an indirect process: Citizens' votes elect electors; and those electors, constituted as the Electoral College, elect the president. Each state gets a number of electors equal to the combined

(The Toidi / Shutterstock)

Electoral College

This institution was established by the Constitution for electing the president and vice president. Electors chosen by the voters actually elect the president and vice president. Each state has a number of electors equal to the total number of its senators and representatives, while the District of Columbia (under the terms of the Twenty-third Amendment) has three electors.

Table 8.1 Electoral Votes, 2020 Presidential Election

State	Trump	Biden	State	Trump	Biden
Alabama	9	--	Nebraska	4	1
Alaska	3	--	Nevada	—	6
Arizona	--	11	New Hampshire	—	4
Arkansas	6	--	New Jersey	--	14
California	--	55	New Mexico	--	5
Colorado	--	9	New York	—	29
Connecticut	--	7	North Carolina	15	—
Delaware	--	3	North Dakota	3	—
Florida	29	--	Ohio	18	--
Georgia	--	16	Oklahoma	7	--
Hawaii	--	4	Oregon	--	7
Idaho	4	--	Pennsylvania	--	20
Illinois	—	20	Rhode Island	--	4
Indiana	11	—	South Carolina	9	--
Iowa	6	--	South Dakota	3	--
Kansas	6	--	Tennessee	11	--
Kentucky	8	--	Texas	38	--
Louisiana	8	--	Utah	6	--
Maine	1	3	Vermont	--	3
Maryland	--	10	Virginia	--	13
Massachusetts	--	11	Washington	--	8
Michigan	--	16	Washington, DC	—	3
Minnesota	--	10	West Virginia	5	--
Mississippi	6	--	Wisconsin	--	10
Missouri	10	--	Wyoming	3	--
Montana	3	--	**TOTAL**	232	306

number of its representatives in the Senate and House. Thus, every state gets at least three electors, with additional electors depending on the size of its population. The District of Columbia currently gets three electors under the terms of the **Twenty-third Amendment** (1961). (Table 8.1 shows the number of electoral votes for each state.) The Electoral College has 538 in all, with 270 needed to win the presidency. There is no constitutional requirement about how states choose their electors; such choices are left to the discretion of each state's legislature. All but two of the states have chosen to award all their electoral votes to the candidate (actually the slate of electors for that candidate) who wins a plurality in the state. The exceptions are Maine and Nebraska, which award two electoral votes to the statewide winner and the rest of their electoral votes by congressional district.

The members of the Electoral College never actually meet in one place. Electors from each state meet in their state capitals to cast their ballots on or about December 15 of the election year. The results are sent to the U.S. Senate; and the president of the Senate (who is, of course, the vice president of the United States) presides over the counting of the results in the presence of the Senate and House of Representatives. A presidential candidate who has a majority (more than 50 percent) of the electoral votes is elected outright. If no candidate has a majority, the House of Representatives—with each state delegation casting a single vote—elects a president by majority from among the top three contenders. If no president can be elected by this process, the vice president becomes acting president. A vice-presidential candidate who has a majority is elected outright. If no candidate has a majority, the Senate picks the vice president from the top two contenders by majority vote of individual members. In the days following the 2000 election, Al Gore found himself with 267 electoral votes and George W. Bush had 246—with disputed Florida returns still in question. The need for the House of Representatives to decide the outcome was averted when the Supreme Court ruled against additional recounts and Bush was declared the winner in Florida, allowing him to clear the threshold with 271 electoral votes. Though still close, the 2004 contest was more decisive, with Bush beating Kerry 286–252. In 2008, Barack Obama claimed 365 electoral votes to McCain's 173, providing the most decisive electoral outcome since 1996. In 2012, Obama was reelected with 332 electoral votes to Romney's 206. In 2016, Hillary Clinton received nearly 3 million more popular votes than Donald Trump but came up short in the Electoral College, receiving only 227 electoral votes to Trump's 304. This unusual outcome was due to Clinton winning big in some heavily populated states and losing narrowly in others. In 2020, Joe Biden racked up over 5 million more popular votes than incumbent Donald Trump and was victorious in the Electoral College 306–232. Though the popular vote was very close in some swing states, and Trump's campaign asked for recounts and filed numerous lawsuits alleging fraud or other improprieties, these challenges were largely found meritless and did not affect the outcome of the contest.

The Electoral College has been, perhaps, the most prominent target of the advocates of electoral reform. Because the number of senators as well as the number of representatives determines a state's representation, small states are represented out of proportion to their populations. Electors are chosen state by state by plurality election, so a winner's advantage and a loser's disadvantage, no matter how slim, are magnified in the extreme. The greatest gains can be made at the smallest cost with narrow victories in big states, so candidates often focus their efforts almost entirely in the larger states. Further, persons chosen as electors for a particular presidential ticket are under no effective legal obligation to actually cast their ballots for that ticket (the **faithless elector** problem). In fact, in 2016, there were seven faithless electors—five refusing to cast a ballot for Clinton and two refusing to vote for Trump. This explains the slightly lower totals for the states of Washington, Texas, and Hawaii. To correct this problem, many states have passed laws

Twenty-third Amendment

Constitutional amendment adopted in 1961 granting the District of Columbia three electors in the Electoral College

faithless elector

A person who is chosen to vote for particular presidential and vice-presidential candidates in the Electoral College but who, nevertheless, votes for different presidential and vice-presidential candidates

that require electors to cast their votes for the winner of the state's popular vote. The Supreme Court affirmed the constitutionality of such laws in 2020.[29]

Worst of all, to some people, is the prospect of a popular-minority president—a president who gets fewer popular votes than the opponent but still wins the presidency. This has happened five times in American history. In 1824 Andrew Jackson received more votes than John Quincy Adams, but the House chose Adams as president. In 1888, popular-vote winner Grover Cleveland lost to Benjamin Harrison. In 1876, the Democratic candidate Samuel J. Tilden outpolled Republican Rutherford B. Hayes; but a Republican-controlled commission appointed to settle a dispute over the electoral votes of three southern states awarded them—and thus the White House—to Hayes. The 2000 presidential contest provides a more recent occurrence, when Gore received 50,992,335 popular votes to George W. Bush's 50,455,156, making Gore the popular-vote winner but electoral-vote loser. Hillary Clinton became the most recent to share this fate in 2016—her popular vote total of 65,853,514 to Trump's 62,984,828 made Donald Trump the most extreme popular-minority president in modern American history.

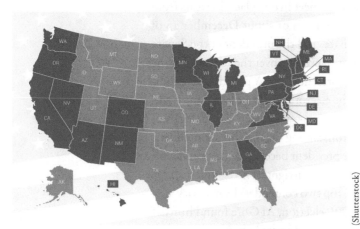

(Shutterstock)

This is how the USA voted in the 2020 presidential election, showing the electoral votes for each state going to the Republicans (red) or to the Democrats (blue).

Given these inadequacies, it should not be surprising that Americans are not generally supportive of the Electoral College. A consistent majority of respondents have favored eliminating it since Gallup began asking this question in its polls in 1948.[30] To repair all these alleged defects, reformers have come up with a variety of changes. The most sweeping proposal is to do away with the Electoral College entirely and to replace it with **direct popular election** of the president and vice president. Thus, whichever candidate received the largest percentage of the total national popular vote would win the White House. Such a process solves all the problems cited so far, but critics of direct national election see it as jeopardizing the delicate balance of the American political system. Simple plurality election would mean that presidents could be elected with the support of far less than half the people. Instituting a requirement of a majority of the votes to be elected might often mean a runoff election. That, in turn, would encourage more candidates to run in the first-round election. The result might be the end of the two-party, middle-of-the-road approach that has so long characterized American politics. Critics of the popular election can easily point to one of the Electoral College's greatest virtues: With only the five exceptions cited, it almost always produces a clear-cut winner.

Seeing problems with both the current Electoral College and direct popular election, moderate reformers propose to steer a course somewhere between the two. One idea for reducing the impact of the statewide winner-take-all system with the resultant candidate emphasis on big states is to move to a winner-take-all system on the level of congressional districts, as Maine and Nebraska have done. This would reduce the tendency of large blocs of votes to be awarded on the basis of narrow popular-vote margins. Solutions to the faithless elector problem propose requiring electors to vote for the presidential candidate under whose banner they were elected or to do away with electors completely and simply tally up electoral votes.

Another call for reform focuses on the problems generated by a president who is compelled to spend the last half of a first term running for a second term. Critics of the current law, which limits a president to two full four-year terms, contend that

direct popular election

Selection of officials on the basis of those receiving the largest number of votes cast, sometimes referring to a proposal to choose the president and vice president on this basis rather than through the Electoral College

single-term presidents do not have enough time to master the job and that first-term presidents who aspire to a second term are diverted from their duties by their efforts to get reelected. Defenders of the status quo argue that the limitation of two four-year terms gives good presidents plenty of time to achieve their objectives and allows the public ample opportunity to vote out poor presidents. A president limited to a single term, they say, would become an instant lame duck. A compromise would be to allow the president one longer term, for example, a term of six years (see "A Six-Year Term for Presidents?" in Chapter 10).[31]

8.3f   Campaign Strategies

Presidential campaigns must pay careful attention to several strategic problems. One such

Look at maps, examine party success over time, and compare vote totals for every presidential election at Dave Leip's *Atlas of U.S. Presidential Elections*.

http://www.bvtlab.com/776aj

problem is that of image. Most candidates seek to establish their image in the public mind. For an incumbent, the choice is usually an easy one: to exploit as much as possible the resources of the presidency. Presidents often try to look fully occupied with governing the country and too busy to engage in partisan politics. For opponents the choices are more difficult. Should the challenger go on the attack against the incumbent president or play the role of the statesperson instead? If the president is popular, the electorate may take the former as an attack on the country; however, the latter course is likely to attract little attention. Neither of these does the challenger much good.

How much focus should be placed on issues is another strategic problem. Should the candidate present specific proposals regarding national problems or instead project a broad and necessarily fuzzy vision of the future? The American people continually decry candidates who do not take clear positions on issues because they deny voters a choice. It is sobering to note, however, that the two candidates in postwar history who gave the public the clearest choices, the conservative Barry Goldwater in 1964 and the liberal George McGovern in 1972, went down in two of the biggest defeats in American electoral history.

Nowhere are the questions of images and issues raised more directly and dramatically than in presidential debates. For an incumbent, a debate is close to a no-win proposition. It gives publicity to the opponent, puts the challenger on an equal footing with the president, and risks embarrassment either by an inadvertent slip or by an aggressive challenger. Only the desire not to appear intimidated keeps a president from opting out of debates completely. As a result, incumbents usually want as few debates and as much structure as possible. For a nonincumbent, a debate represents perhaps the best strategic opportunity of the campaign. It provides the greatest media exposure, "presidential" standing, a

George Bush and Bill Clinton shake hands just after the 1993 inaugural ceremonies at the U.S. Capitol.

chance to flush the president (if the incumbent is the opponent) out of the Rose Garden, and an opportunity to display one's intellectual, political, and rhetorical wares.

The 1992 debates provided a case study on many of these issues. George Bush, as an incumbent tied to a weak economy facing an experienced and articulate debater in Bill Clinton, initially tried to avoid debates as long as possible. Clinton's taunts that Bush was afraid to debate (accompanied by Clinton supporters dressed in chicken suits haunting Bush campaign appearances) and Clinton's persistent lead in the polls forced Bush campaign advisers to go with a heavy debate schedule as one of their few hopes of turning the election around.

In the debates, Clinton appeared presidential and Bush failed to deliver either a negative knockout punch or a positive vision of his plans for a second term. In fact, many saw Bush's fumbling response in the second debate to a young woman's question about how the bad economy had affected him personally as a clear sign that he was not going to be able to turn the election around. Bill Clinton, who followed up with a more articulate and sensitive response to that question, and Ross Perot, who scored overall with his homespun rhetoric and humorous one-liners, emerged as the overall winners.

The questions of campaign strategy are numerous and complex. The most vexing fact, however, is that strategy is always at the mercy of events. An unforeseen event can make a candidate look like a hero or a fool. A serious economic dislocation, a negative revelation about an associate, an outbreak of violence halfway around the world—any of these things can make one candidate look inept and another candidate look "presidential." Because incumbent presidents have the power to take action rather than just talk about events, they generally gain some advantage in such circumstances. If events prove to be intractable, incumbent presidents can suffer badly. Jimmy Carter's futile struggle to free the hostages from the American embassy in Tehran, Iran, during the 1980 campaign; George Bush's poor economic record in 1992; and Donald Trump's inability to develop an effective plan to combat the spread of COVID-19 stand as recent examples. Sometimes there is little anyone, even the president of the United States, can do to overcome events.

8.4   The Candidate's Perspective: Running for Congress

Running for Congress is much like running for president, except the stage is smaller, of course—a state (for the Senate) or a congressional district (for the House) instead of the entire country. The basic strategic elements are the same: the problem of getting money; the two-phase contest of getting the nomination and then winning the election; the impact of party, candidate appeal, and issues; the growing importance of the media; the long hours on the campaign trail; and so on. However, different aspects tend to be particularly problematic.

8.4a   Campaign Finance

Like presidential campaigns, House and Senate elections have become big-money enterprises. Candidates need money for television advertising, direct-mail operations to get their messages across and raise more money, polling to see how their messages are playing, and expensive media consultants. According to Federal Election Commission statistics,

POLITICS AND IDEAS

Midterm Elections: Reflection and Change

On November 6, 2018, American voters went to the polls to cast their ballots in elections for all 435 members of the U.S. House of Representatives and about one-third of the U.S. Senate. Dubbed *midterm* elections, these federal elections come in even-numbered years when there is not a presidential election. Midterm elections are typically characterized by relatively low turnout and serve both as an opportunity for the nation to reflect on the performance of the incumbent president and his or her party and as the beginning of speculation about the upcoming presidential race. The 2018 midterms were no exception to these trends. Even though turnout was higher for a midterm than it had been in decades, only 49.4 percent of eligible voters cast a ballot—as opposed to the 60.1 percent who had voted in the 2016 presidential election.[1] The lack of a presidential race, combined with the lack of competitiveness and voter interest that characterizes many congressional races, produces far fewer voters.

Despite lower turnout, midterm elections often serve as a referendum on the president. In six of the last

seven second-term midterm elections, the president's party lost congressional seats. On average, the opposition party gains six Senate seats and twenty-nine House seats during the sixth year of a presidency. As an example, 2014 was fairly typical in this regard, when President Barack Obama's Democrats lost a total of twenty-two seats in both houses. First-term midterm elections—like the one in 2018—have just as dismal a record. In 2002, George W. Bush was the only president since 1962 to gain seats for his party during a first-term midterm election. President Donald Trump's Republican Party did not deviate from the typical pattern of losing seats. In 2018, Republicans lost nearly forty House seats and gained only two Senate seats, leading to a new Democratic majority in the House of Representatives. These changes meant that President Trump would have a more difficult time achieving his legislative agenda than he had during the first two years of his presidency.

The media attention around midterm elections often focuses on potential contenders for the White House. In this regard, as well, 2018 was no exception. On the Democratic side, the reelection campaigns of Massachusetts Senator Elizabeth Warren and New York Senator Kirsten Gillibrand were spotlighted not because they were in close races—both won easily—but because they were seen as potential precursors to 2020 presidential runs. Texas Senate candidate Beto O'Rourke, even though he lost to Republican incumbent Ted Cruz, also demonstrated his broad

national appeal. On the Republican side, Trump garnered a large amount of media attention throughout the campaign season. Taking pride in the importance of his support, President Trump endorsed several Republican candidates, which gave him an opportunity to speak at campaign rallies despite not being up for reelection himself until 2020. When the smoke had cleared, Trump's endorsement actually resulted in a significant net loss for his party; however, in politics, almost everything is subject to "spin." The president himself presented the election result as a win, boasting via Twitter of receiving "so many Congratulations from so many on our Big Victory."[2]

How did events play out in the 116th Congress (2019–20)? Did the perceived presidential candidates behave accordingly? In retrospect, what should they have done differently? The 115th Congress (2017–19) coincided with the first two years of a new presidency. How did this result in different strategies and expectations from the 116th? How did candidates position themselves for the 2020 elections, and what issues did they focus on?

1. U.S. Election Project, http://www.electproject.org/home/voter-turnout/voter-turnout-data (November 21, 2018).

2. Donald J. Trump (@realDonaldTrump), November 7, 2018, https://twitter.com/realDonaldTrump?ref_src=twsrc%5Etfw%7Ctwcamp%5Etweetem-bed%7Ctwterm%5E1060130202418864129&ref_url=https%3A%2F%2Fwww.vox.com%2F2018%2F11%2F7%2F18071396%2Fmidterm-elections-results-trump-big-victory-twitter (November 21, 2018).

candidates for the House and Senate in the 2018 midterm elections spent more than $2.7 billion on their contests. This figure represents more than a 50 percent increase in spending over the 2010 midterm election cycle.[32]

Although public financing has been an important resource for presidential elections, congressional campaigns continue to operate without it. This leaves, as the primary resources for most congressional campaigns, money donated or spent by individuals,

parties, and PACs. Recent congressional elections have seen widespread efforts by candidates and parties to get around the restrictions imposed by federal campaign finance laws. Foremost among such efforts was the increasing use of independent PAC expenditures to avoid the legal limits on direct contributions to candidates and the use of soft money by parties. Since the Court's 2010 decision in Citizens United, the spending by nonaffiliated independent expenditure groups known as super PACs has shown a dramatic increase.[33]

A key question is whether this money actually helps a candidate. Research suggests that it helps challengers more than officeholders. The more money a challenger spends, the more likely he or she is to defeat the incumbent. Such a tendency is probably due to the fact that money can be used to buy the name recognition and visibility necessary to offset the advantages of incumbency. Incumbents who spend a lot of money, however, do not fare as well as those who spend less. This is probably because incumbents tend to spend a lot of money only when they find themselves facing a serious challenge.[34]

As in presidential campaigns, financing is a frequent target for reform in congressional campaigns. The focuses for reform are similar in some respects—for example, too much PAC money, particularly for incumbents, and too much soft money. However, the problems for congressional elections are exacerbated by the lack of public financing of congressional campaigns. This makes congressional candidates much more dependent than presidential candidates on problematic sources of funds. Thus, the most significant campaign reform in congressional campaigns would be to institute public funding—a change that would be supported by about 50 percent of Americans.[35] Congress has struggled repeatedly over the last several years to institute this reform, but so far it has been unable to arrive at any plan agreeable to both Democrats and Republicans. Many Democrats and Republicans now say they want public financing; the bone of contention lies over whether spending limits should be imposed. Democrats want limits because they fear the wealth and fundraising potential of some Republican candidates. Republicans, on the other hand, oppose limits because they think outspending firmly entrenched Democratic incumbents is the only way to dislodge them.

Even the modest reforms of the Bipartisan Campaign Reform Act of 2002 were struck a blow in 2008, when the Supreme Court found one of its provisions—the so-called "Millionaire's Amendment"—unconstitutional. The Court said the provision, which allowed higher party-contribution limits to candidates whose opponents exceeded certain self-financing thresholds, was an infringement of First Amendment speech rights.[36]

8.4b   Incumbency

Incumbency is even more of an asset to members of Congress than it is to presidents. In 2020, about 95 percent of all representatives who ran for reelection won. In the Senate, incumbency is also an important advantage, although the retention rates are typically somewhat lower. In 2020, the success rate for incumbent senators was about 90 percent. In 2018, incumbents won 93 percent of the time in the House and 86 percent of the time in the Senate. Of course, political movements can challenge the incumbency advantage from time to time. The Tea Party movement and other anti-incumbency sentiment led to the defeat of over sixty incumbent legislators who were seeking reelection during the 2010 midterm elections.

The main reason for the frequent difference between the House and Senate return rates is that about five out of six congressional districts are **safe seats**. That is, House districts tend to be homogeneous, and the division of party affiliation within them is lopsided enough that one or the other party is virtually assured of victory. Because senators represent states, their "districts" are often more heterogeneous, with a more even division

safe seats

Congressional districts in which the division of voters between the parties is so lopsided as to virtually ensure one party of victory

between the parties. For both representatives and senators, incumbents are usually much better known than their challengers.[37]

As described in Chapter 9, incumbents in Congress continually boost themselves by taking credit for every beneficial activity the federal government undertakes in their states and districts. Incumbents, also, generally have a much easier time raising campaign funds. For example, in recent elections, more than 80 percent of all PAC money contributed to House campaigns went to incumbents. In addition, members of Congress are in a good position to use the resources of their offices to get reelected. One of the most valuable resources they have is the franking privilege, the right to send out official mail without any postage. Senators and representatives frequently use this privilege to send out newsletters extolling their activities on behalf of the district or questionnaires soliciting the public's opinion on current issues. In almost every case, the name and face of the legislator are prominently displayed. Another valuable resource is staff. Most members of Congress use much of their staff's time to perform constituency services—mostly running interference through the Washington bureaucracy for constituents with problems. Needless to say, the hope is that the satisfied home voters will remember the favors on Election Day.

Critics charge that the high rates of reelection for incumbents have led to legislative stagnation and unresponsiveness. One solution that has attracted broad attention in recent years is **term limits**, restricting the number of terms a person can serve in the House or Senate (for example, to twelve years). Term limits were on the ballot in fourteen states in 1992 and won in all fourteen. In 1995, the Supreme Court held that these restrictions were unconstitutional at the federal level, although limitations on state-level legislators now exist in about fifteen states.[38] Another solution is to reduce the advantages that come with a seat in the House or Senate, in particular to limit the amount of mail members of Congress may send at public expense under their franking privilege. A series of revisions to the franking privilege in the late 1990s requires members of Congress to deduct franking costs from their official budgets, even though there is no restriction on the amount of their budgets they can use for mailings.

(Shutterstock)

In the 2016 presidential elections, Donald Trump brought attention to the issue of immigration by declaring that, if elected, he would have a wall built along the border with Mexico. This caused the impact of the immigration issue to soar.

8.4c   Parties, Candidates, and Issues

After incumbency, the single most important determinant of voting in congressional races is party. Both party and incumbency provide "low-cost" information cues to people facing a voting decision. The candidate's party is supplied on the ballot. The incumbent's name and generally positive reputation are known. Either may be used with little time and effort in information gathering—and either one may be substituted for the other.[39]

Earlier discussion indicated that the issues themselves usually do not play a major role in presidential campaigns. The same is even truer of congressional campaigns. The major problem is information, or rather a lack of it. If, as in many contests, voters do not even recognize the names of the candidates, they obviously know even less about the candidates' positions and voting records on the issues.[40] Of course, the impact of issues can soar when differences between the candidates are sharp and well publicized on matters

term limits

Laws restricting the number of terms an elected representative may serve—the Court has struck down state efforts to limit terms for federal offices, but has allowed state laws that limit terms for elected officials at the state level

of importance. The only issue that consistently achieves salience with the public is the economy. In both presidential and midterm election years, the better the economy is doing, the better the congressional candidates of the president's party do.[41]

The other major factor in congressional voting, as in presidential voting, is the candidates themselves. Candidates for the House rest their appeal on such general qualities as trust and competence, and voters seem to respond most favorably to them.[42] Senate candidates, in contrast, are evaluated in more specific terms of experience and ability, qualities that are closer to those by which presidential candidates are judged.[43] This difference in factors affecting voting decisions between House and Senate candidates is probably due to the fact that Senate candidates are generally better known than House candidates. Negative campaigning is as much a trend and an issue for congressional campaigns as it is for presidential ones.

The success of the congressional candidates from each party may be affected by the popularity of their party's president or presidential candidate. In the years when congressional elections coincide with a presidential election, a presidential candidate whose popularity appears to give a boost to his party's candidates for the House and Senate is said to have coattails. Ronald Reagan was said to have coattails in 1980 because his appeal seemed to help Republican congressional candidates to do better than had been expected. In contrast, in 1988, George Bush was said to have no coattails because his party picked up no seats. In four of the last seven presidential elections, the winning candidate's party actually lost seats in Congress—an effect known as negative coattails. In midterm elections, the congressional vote is often interpreted as a referendum on how the president is doing. Historically, the president's party has tended to lose congressional seats in midterm elections. A gain or a small loss for the president's party is interpreted as an endorsement of the president and a big loss as repudiation. In the 2006 midterm elections, President Bush's Republican Party lost thirty-four seats; and in the 2010 midterm elections, President Obama's Democratic Party lost sixty-nine seats. The 2010 midterm elections proved to be the largest swing in recent years, with the Republicans gaining seventy seats and regaining the majority in the House of Representatives. The news only got worse for President Obama in the 2014 midterm elections. His party lost its majority in the Senate—and in the House, Republicans made enough gains to secure their largest majority since just after World War II. In the 2018 midterms, President Trump's Republican Party gained two seats in the Senate, where it retained its majority, but lost nearly forty seats in the House of Representatives, where it became the minority party.

Chapter Review

1. The American voter confronts two fundamental decisions on Election Day: whether or not to vote and, if so, how to vote. Qualifications for voting and registration in most states define the boundaries of the electorate. Beyond that, voting turnout varies substantially with social characteristics and psychological outlook toward politics.

2. The voter's decision about how to vote is similarly influenced by a broad range of factors. Throughout much of American history, partisanship has established a baseline in the division of the vote; but in recent years, opinions about candidates and issues have caused voters to break from party lines.

3. Presidential candidates confront a challenge that is difficult in both strategic and physical terms. Strategically, a candidate for president confronts two separate contests: the intraparty race for the nomination and the interparty race for the White House. Physically, the candidate faces a grueling journey that begins not long after one presidential election and ends in elation or disappointment on election night four years later.

4. Congressional candidates confront a similar range of problems in getting elected. Money is an even greater problem because public financing has not yet come to congressional campaigns. Private contributions, particularly from PACs, remain a major source of political lifeblood. Because congressional elections are generally less visible than presidential campaigns, personalities and issues usually count for less and party and incumbency for more.

Key Terms

balance the ticket 258

caucus 257

closed primary 257

direct popular election 262

Electoral College 259

exit poll 252

faithless elector 261

Federal Election Campaign Act 255

female suffrage 239

Fifteenth Amendment 238

general election 257

high-stimulus election 241

low-stimulus election 241

media consultant 251

Nineteenth Amendment 239

open primary 257

party convention 258

poll tax 238

Presidential Election Campaign Fund 255

primary election 257

regional primary 258

register 239

residence requirements 239

safe seats 266

soft money 256

term limits 267

Twenty-fourth Amendment 239

Twenty-second Amendment 249

Twenty-sixth Amendment 239

Twenty-third Amendment 261

Voting Rights Act of 1965 239

Voting Rights Act of 1970 239

READINGS FOR FURTHER STUDY

The voter's side of campaigns and elections is explored in two major works on voting, the classic *The American Voter* by Angus Campbell, Philip E. Converse, Warren E. Miller, and Donald E. Stokes (Chicago: University of Chicago Press, 1980), and in *The Changing American Voter*, rev. ed., by Norman Nie, Sidney Verba, and John Petrocik (Cambridge, MA: Harvard University Press, 1979). The former is based on surveys from the 1950s, and the latter with surveys from the 1960s and 1970s; the latter also updates and challenges, in some cases, the earlier study. The ideas in these volumes have been updated with the publication of *The American Voter Revisited* (Ann Arbor: University of Michigan Press, 2008) by Michael Lewis-Beck, William G. Jacoby, Helmut Norpoth, and Herbert F. Weisberg.

Examinations of more recent elections include *Political Behavior in Midterm Elections* (Washington, DC: CQ Press, 2015), by Elizabeth A. Theiss-Morse, Michael W. Wagner, William H. Flanigan, and Nancy H. Zingale; Elizabeth A. Theiss-Morse and Michael W. Wagner's *2018 Congressional Elections* (Washington, DC: CQ Press, 2019); *Political Behavior of the American Electorate*, 14th ed. (Washington, DC: CQ Press, 2018) by Elizabeth A. Theiss-Morse, Michael W. Wagner, William H. Flanigan and Nancy H. Zingale, and *The American Campaign,* 2nd ed., by James E. Campbell (College Station: Texas A&M University Press, 2008).

Two excellent studies of voting turnout are Raymond Wolfinger and Steven Rosenstone, *Who Votes?* (New Haven, CT: Yale University Press, 1980) and Ruy A. Teixeira *The Disappearing American Voter* (Washington, DC: Brookings, 1992). A recent study on how the electorate can be changed is Lisa Garcia Bedolla and Melissa R. Michelson's *Mobilizing Inclusion: Transforming the Electorate Through Get-Out-the-Vote Campaigns* (New Haven, CT: Yale University Press, 2012).

The literature on presidential campaigns and elections is rich indeed. Virtually every election spawns at least one substantial account of what "really" went on. Most notable is the *Making of the President* series by Theodore H. White—particularly the classic *The Making of the President 1960* (New York: Atheneum, 1988).

An interesting philosophical question is raised in Martin P. Wattenberg's *Is Voting for Young People?*, 5th ed. (New York: Routledge, 2020). Russell J. Dalton takes up a similar theme in *The Good Citizen: How a Younger Generation Is Reshaping American Politics,* 3rd ed. (Washington, DC: CQ Press, 2020).

NOTES

1. "Should 16-Year-Olds be Able to Vote? A Majority of the D.C. Council Thinks So," *The Washington Post,* June 27, 2018, https://www.washingtonpost.com /local/dc-politics/should-16-year-olds-be-able-to -vote-a-majority-of-the-dc-council-thinks-so/2018 /06/27/7ce0cbfc-796c-11e8-93cc-6d3beccdd7a3 _story.html?utm_term=.8c93b09fafd8 (September 24, 2018).

2. Steven Rosenstone and Raymond Wolfinger, "The Effect of Registration Laws on Voter Turnout," *American Political Science Review 72* (1978): 22–45; G. Bingham Powell Jr., "American Voter Turnout in Comparative Perspective," *American Political Science Review 80* (1986): 35; Brennan Center for Justice, *Voting Law Changes in 2012,* http://brennan.3cdn.net/92635ddafbc09e8d88 _i3m6bjdeh.pdf (August 9, 2012).

3. National Conference of State Legislatures, "Same Day Voter Registration," June 28, 2019, https://www.ncsl.org/research/elections-and -campaigns/same-day-registration.aspx (July 5, 2020).

4. Federal Election Commission, *The Impact of the National Voter Registration Act on the Administration of Elections for Federal Office, 1997–1998,* http://www.fec.gov/pages/9798NVRAexec.htm (August 26, 2001).

5. U.S. Census Bureau, "Voting and Registration in the Election of November 2016," May 2017.

6. Angus Campbell, "Surge and Decline: A Study of Electoral Change," in *Elections and the Political Order,* eds. Angus Campbell, Philip E. Converse, Warren E. Miller, and Donald E. Stokes (New York: Wiley, 1966), p. 41.

7.   Walter Dean Burnham, "The Changing Shape of the American Political Universe," *American Political Science Review* 59 (1965): 7–28.

8.   Philip E. Converse, "Change in the American Electorate," in *The Human Meaning of Social Change*, eds. Angus Campbell and Philip E. Converse (New York: Russell Sage Foundation, 1972), pp. 281–286.

9.   Paul Abramson, *Political Attitudes in America* (San Francisco: Freeman, 1983), pp. 291–306.

10. This argument is most often associated with Bernard Berelson, *Voting* (Chicago: University of Chicago Press, 1954), pp. 305–323.

11. "Election 2016: Exit Polls," *The New York Times,* November 8, 2016.

12. "National Exit Polls: How Different Groups Voted," *The New York Times,* November 3, 2020.

13. Donald Stokes, "Some Dynamic Elements of Contests for the Presidency," *American Political Science Review* 60 (1966): 19–28.

14. The Gallup Organization, "Clinton's Biggest Asset, Trump's Biggest Liability: Experience," June 3, 2016.

15. "Manhattan Project, 1992," *Newsweek* special election edition (November/December 1992): 40–56.

16. The Gallup Organization, 2001.

17. The Gallup Organization, "Likeability Top Characteristic for Both Romney and Obama," June 26, 2012.

18. The Gallup Organization, "Clinton's Biggest Asset, Trump's Biggest Liability: Experience," June 3, 2016.

19. The Gallup Organization, "Americans' Views of Trump's Character Firmly Established," June 18, 2020, https://news.gallup.com/poll/312737/americans -views-trump-character-firmly-established.aspx (July 5, 2020).

20. Monmouth University, "More Voters Trust Biden on Race Relations," June 3, 2020, https://www.monmouth.edu/polling-institute /reports/monmouthpoll_us_060320/ (July 7, 2020).

21. The Gallup Organization, 2004.

22. The Gallup Organization, "Likeability Top Characteristic for Both Romney and Obama."

23. The Gallup Organization, 2001.

24. *New York Times,* "$2 Billion Worth of Free Media for Donald Trump," March 15, 2016.

25. OpenSecrets News, "Election 2016: Trump's Free Media Helped Keep Cost Down, but Fewer Donors Provided More of the Cash," April 13, 2017, https:// www.opensecrets.org/news/2017/04/election-2016- trump-fewer-donors-provided-more-of-the-cash/ (September 30, 2018).

26. Maggie Severns, "'Oh, That's Cool—Do That!': Super PACs Use New Trick to Hide Donors," *Politico,* August 17, 2018, https://www.politico. com/story/2018/08/17/super-pacs-hidden-donors- disclosures-741795 (September 30, 2018).

27. Dave Levinthal, "Actions, Not Words, Tell Trump's Political Money Story," Center for Public Integrity, January 19, 2018, https://www.publicintegrity. org/2018/01/19/21480/actions-not-words-tell- trumps-political-money-story (September 30, 2018).

28. *McCutcheon v. Federal Election Commission*, 572 U.S. ___ (2014).

29. *Chiafalo v. Washington,* 591 U.S. ____ (2020).

30. The Gallup Organization, "Gallup Vault: Rejecting the Electoral College," June 14, 2016.

31. Tom Wicker, "Six Years for the President?" *The New York Times Magazine* (June 26, 1983): 16.

32. Federal Election Commission, https://transition.fec .gov/press/campaign_finance_statistics.shtml (July 11, 2020).

33. *Citizens United v. Federal Election Commission*, 558 U.S. 50 (2010).

34. Gary Jacobson, *Money in Congressional Elections* (New Haven, CT: Yale University Press, 1980), p. 49.

35. The Gallup Organization, "Half in U.S. Support Publicly Financed Federal Campaigns," June 24, 2013.

36. *Davis v. FEC*, 554 U.S. 724 (2008).

37. Edie N. Goldenberg and Michael W. Traugott, *Campaigning for Congress* (Washington, DC: Congressional Quarterly, 1984), p. 136.

38. *U.S. Term Limits, Inc. v. Thornton*, 514 U.S. 779 (1995).

39. Barbara Hinckley, *Congressional Elections* (Washington, DC: Congressional Quarterly, 1981), p. 68.

40. Thomas Mann and Raymond Wolfinger, "Candidates and Parties in Congressional Elections," *American Political Science Review 74* (1980): 629.

41. Edward Tufte, *Political Control of the Economy* (Princeton, NJ: Princeton University Press, 1978), pp. 113, 120.

42. Richard Fenno, *Home Style: House Members in Their Districts* (Boston: Little, Brown, 1978), pp. 54–61.

43. Hinckley, *Congressional Elections*, pp. 79–82.

POP QUIZ

1. Two social characteristics that show the strongest relation to voting turnout are _____ and _____.

2. The three virtues that voters seem to consider most important in a candidate are attractive personal qualities, _____, and _____.

3. Today, presidential candidates tend to rely on more professional _____ _____ to plan and execute their campaign strategy.

4. A major loophole in the controls on money that can be spent on a presidential candidate's behalf is the ability of state and local parties to raise _____ _____.

5. A presidential candidate whose popularity appears to give a boost to his party's candidates for the House and Senate is said to have _____.

6. Studies have shown that younger people are more likely to vote than older people.   T   F

7. In recent years, political party affiliation has become a less important determinant of voting decisions.   T   F

8. Candidates tend to favor long television advertisements in order to maximize public exposure and issue formulation.   T   F

9. An incumbent president has little to gain in accepting a debate with his opponent.   T   F

10. Candidates for the House and Senate receive only a small amount of public financing, too little to run a successful campaign.   T   F

11. The two social characteristics that show the strongest relation to voting are _____ and _____.
    A) party identification, income
    B) race, religion
    C) age, education
    D) sex, regional habitat

12. In recent years, which of the following is true of serious contenders for the presidency?
    A) They have most often come from the successful side of mainstream America.
    B) They usually come from the House of Representatives.
    C) They have never, until George Bush, served as vice president.
    D) They have rarely had college educations.

13. Which of the following is true of the Federal Election Campaign Act?
    A) It creates a system of public financing for presidential campaigns through the federal income tax system.
    B) It limits the amount of money a PAC can contribute to all federal candidates.
    C) It requires all contributions to be funneled through the state and local political party.
    D) It requires full disclosure of sources and uses of campaign funds.

14. Which of the following applies to presidential debates?
    A) They are most advantageous for nonincumbents.
    B) They are required by law before a candidate can receive federal funds.
    C) They have had little impact on the outcome of presidential elections.
    D) All of the above

15. Which of the following is true of midterm congressional elections?
    A) They usually result in a gain for the president's party.
    B) They are often viewed as a referendum on how the president is doing.
    C) They usually result in high voter turnout.
    D) They have historically favored the Republican Party.

Answers:
1. age, education   2. experience, leadership
3. campaign consultants   4. soft money
5. coattails   6. F   7. T   8. F   9. T
10. F   11. C   12. A   13. D   14. A   15. B

Chapter

09

(Shutterstock)

Congress

In This Chapter

9.1   The Constitutional Powers of Congress
9.2   The Members of Congress
9.3   The Structure of Congress
9.4   Congressional Procedures: How a Bill Becomes a Law
9.5   Congress and the Political System
9.6   What Role for a Changing Congress?

Chapter Objectives

Thanks to the U.S. Constitution, Congress is the chief lawmaking body in the land. Because it is the branch of government established in Article I of the Constitution, Congress is sometimes called the "first branch." Of the three branches, Congress is also called the "people's branch" because its members are the public officials who seem most immediately responsive to changes in the public's moods and opinions. Americans have demonstrated significant mood changes in recent years. In 1994 voters chose a majority Republican House and Senate for the first time in forty years. In 2006 the public mood swung back in the other direction, creating Democratic majorities in both chambers again. The 2010 midterm elections provided yet another swing. Republicans reduced the Democratic majority in the Senate by several seats and regained a majority in the House of Representatives. In the 2014 midterms, Republicans added to their majority in the House and regained control of the Senate, as well. In 2016, the Democrats gained two seats in the Senate and six in the House, but the Republican Party maintained majorities in both chambers. In 2018, although Republicans took back two Senate seats to add to their majority, they lost nearly forty House seats, making the Democrats the majority party in that chamber. Most recently, the 2020 elections saw the Democrats lose a few seats in the House, but maintain their majority. In the Senate, the Democrats inched closer, even forcing two runoff elections in the state of Georgia. The Democrats' victories in those two contests created an evenly divided Senate, but the Democrats attained majority status due to the tie-breaking role of the vice president.

Congress is also the branch of the national government in which the political ideas of Americans are most visibly represented. Few legislative bodies possess greater authority over the lives, property, and happiness of a nation. Congress makes, or at least ratifies, fundamental decisions about national policy—for instance, whether the United States will have a military draft. Congress determines the fraction of every person's income the government will collect as taxes and the purposes for which that money will be spent.

(Drop of Light / Shutterstock)

Key to understanding the first branch is understanding the 535 individuals who serve in Congress: 435 as members of the House of Representatives and 100 as members of the Senate. Knowing who they are, what their job is like, what forces influence what they do, and how Congress is organized helps explain how laws are passed.

Of the three government branches, Congress is sometimes called the "first branch." It is also called the "people's branch" because its members are the public officials who seem most immediately responsive to changes in the public's moods and opinions.

9.1 The Constitutional Powers of Congress

The very first words of the Constitution declare, "All legislative powers herein granted shall be vested in a Congress which shall consist of a Senate and a House of Representatives." What are those powers? As summarized in Table 9.1, Congress may levy taxes, borrow and spend money, regulate foreign and interstate commerce, coin money, declare war, maintain the armed services, and establish federal courts inferior to the Supreme Court, to name but a few. Perhaps the most important grant of power is in the **necessary and proper clause**, which authorizes Congress to "make all laws which are necessary and proper for carrying into execution the foregoing powers and all other powers vested by this Constitution in the government."

necessary and proper clause

Also called the "elastic clause," Article I, Section 8, of the Constitution, is the source of "implied powers" for the national government, as explained in *McCulloch v. Maryland* [17 U.S. (4 Wheaton) 316 (1819)]

In *McCulloch v. Maryland*,[1] Chief Justice Marshall, speaking for the Supreme Court, found ample power in this clause for Congress to use all appropriate means to achieve its enumerated goals. In this case, discussed in Chapter 2, the Court supported the congressional power to create a national bank, even though this explicit power was not mentioned in the Constitution. Marshall made it clear that the necessary and proper clause added implied powers to those enumerated in the Constitution. With few exceptions, the powers of Congress have been construed broadly ever since. That being said, the current Supreme Court has demonstrated a greater willingness than its recent predecessors to rein in congressional power.[2] Even with these occasional setbacks, however, the powers granted by the necessary and proper clause remain vast.

Table 9.1 The Constitutional Powers of Congress

Article I of the Constitution grants many powers to Congress. In most cases, both houses must act, but in a few instances the Constitution specifies that one house or the other has a special role.

Responsibilities of Both House and Senate	Responsibilities of Senate Only	Responsibilities of House Only
Levy taxes	Try impeachments	Bring impeachments
Borrow and spend money	Ratify treaties	Originate tax bills
Regulate commerce	Confirm all federal judges, ambassadors, cabinet members, and other officials	
Regulate currency		
Establish postal system		
Provide for patents and copyrights		
Establish federal courts below Supreme Court		
Declare war		
Maintain armed forces		
Govern the nation's capital		
Oversee national property		
Make laws "necessary and proper" to carry out above powers		

The Constitution does, however, impose some constraints. First, the enumeration of specific powers limits what Congress can do with those powers and others implied from them. Second, Article I, Section 9, contains eight specific limitations, including a ban on **bills of attainder** (legislative acts that declare an individual guilty and mete out punishment without a trial) and **ex post facto laws** (laws that make an act a crime after it was committed or increase the punishment for a crime already committed). As described in Chapter 3, the Bill of Rights places a set of personal liberties beyond the reach of Congress. For example, Congress cannot establish a state religion or abolish jury trials in criminal cases without violating the First and Sixth amendments. In the area of economic and social policy, Congress is given a wide berth. For example, Congress can decide whether to regulate certain industries or to continue price supports for certain farm commodities.

The Constitution requires Congress to share many of its powers. This is the principle of **checks and balances** discussed in Chapter 1. The Senate ratifies treaties, but the president or his advisers negotiate them. Congress may pass laws, but the president can veto them (and can be overruled by a two-thirds vote in each chamber). The Supreme Court can also declare them unconstitutional. In foreign policy the president and Congress battle for control. Although Congress can declare war, the president commands the armed forces and can send them anywhere on the globe.

Congress also shares power within itself, for it is divided into two chambers—the Senate and the House of Representatives. The House, according to one of the founders, George Mason, "was to be the grand depository of the Democratic principles of government." Each state was granted representation in the House according to its

bill of attainder

A law, prohibited by the Constitution, that punishes an individual and bypasses the procedural safeguards of the legal process

ex post facto law

A law that makes an act a crime after it was committed or increases the punishment for a crime already committed, both of which are prohibited by the Constitution

checks and balances

The system of separate institutions sharing some powers that the Constitution mandates for the national government, the purpose of which is to keep power divided among the three branches: legislative, executive, and judicial

proportion of the national population, and members were selected by direct election. In 1964 the Supreme Court, in *Wesberry v. Sanders*,[3] took the principle a step further, requiring that each congressional district within the states be apportioned on the basis of equal population.

The delegates to the Constitutional Convention assumed that the House, being the most democratic of our institutions, would also be the most impulsive. Thus the Senate was meant to constrain the excesses of popular government. As James Madison put it, "The use of the Senate is to consist in its proceeding with more coolness, with more system, and with more vision than the popular branch."[4]

Apportioned two for each state, senators were originally elected by the state legislatures with the expectation that they would be more conservative and partial to entrenched economic interests. With direct election of senators required in 1913 by the **Seventeenth Amendment**, the Senate also became subject to the mass electorate; and the distinction the founders considered to be so important faded away.

Differences between the House and the Senate remain, however, as Table 9.2 indicates. Almost all members of the House represent only part of a state, whereas each senator represents an entire state. Although the Constitution assigns both equal weight in writing laws, it commands unique duties to each. The Senate has the sole power to try impeachments, to confirm presidential nominations, and to ratify treaties. The House must originate tax bills (and, by custom, appropriation bills) and bring impeachments. Although neither chamber has ever consistently dominated the other, the prestige of a senator is greater than that of a House member. The reasons are obvious—there are fewer senators, and their terms are three times longer (six years versus two years). Representatives frequently give up their House seats to run for the Senate, but the reverse is seldom done.

Speaker of the House Nancy Pelosi (D-CA) speaks to constituents after a healthcare rally at San Francisco City Hall.

(Kim Wilson / Shutterstock)

<table>
<tr><td>9.2</td><td></td></tr>
</table>

9.2 The Members of Congress

The powers that the Constitution bestows on Congress present the opportunity for congressional action and influence on national policy. Much of what Congress actually does, however, is not specified in the Constitution but is largely a product of the values and interests of the 535 members who sit in the House and the Senate.

9.2a Who Are They?

Seventeenth Amendment
Ratified in 1913, provides for the direct popular election of United States senators

The constitutional requirements for membership in Congress are simple. A House member must be twenty-five years old, a US citizen for seven years, and a resident of the state (not the district) he or she represents. A senator must be thirty years of age, a US citizen for nine years, and a resident of the state he or she represents. Although these requirements open the door to most of the adult population of the country, in practice

Table 9.2 Differences Between the House and the Senate

Although the House and the Senate are alike in many ways, differences give each a special character. In addition, the Constitution assigns to the Senate particular confirmation and treaty-ratifying powers and to the House the right to originate tax bills.

Senate	House of Representatives
Senators represent entire states, with each state differing in population from other states.	Members represent only part of a state (unless a state is assigned only one representative); House districts are equal in population.
Senate contains 100 members.	House contains 435 members.
Senators serve six-year terms.	Representatives serve two-year terms.
Floor debate is important in shaping outcome of legislation.	Committee work is important in shaping outcome of legislation.
Unlimited debate	Limited debate
All senators have the ability to shape debate and amendments.	The Rules Committee shapes debate and amendment options.
Riders (nongermane amendments) are permitted.	Riders are prohibited.
More prestige, media coverage, and visibility	Less prestige, media coverage, and visibility
Larger staff for each senator, with size determined by population of state and distance from Washington, DC	Smaller staffs of equal size for each member
Casework less important	Casework more important
Fewer committees	More committees
Source of many presidential aspirants	Few presidential aspirants
Vice president is the presiding officer.	House elects the presiding officer (Speaker).

the people who eventually go to Congress do not represent a cross-section of the adult population. Members of Congress are predominantly white and upper middle class. In the 117th Congress (2021–2022), the majority are lawyers or people who came from banking or business.

From its beginnings, Congress was predominantly a men's club. The percentage of women serving in Congress in 1991 (5.8 percent) was only slightly higher than the percentage serving in 1953 (3 percent). Dubbed "the year of the woman," the 1992 election brought twenty-four new women to the House and four new women to the Senate. More than two decades later, 2015 was the first time that women held more than a hundred legislative seats. In the 117th Congress, women made up about 27 percent of the House and 24 percent of the Senate. These percentages are likely to continue to grow in the coming years as more women are elected to state legislatures, a common launching ground for a congressional race.

A generation ago, African Americans and other minorities were barely represented in Congress. Between 1900 and 1928, no African Americans served in Congress, and until the passage of the Voting Rights Act of 1965, no African Americans represented

(Courtesy of Kristie Boyd, U.S. House Office of Photography via Wikimedia)

(U.S. House Office of Photography via Wikimedia)

Ilhan Omar and Rashida Tlaib, the first two Muslim women elected to Congress.

the South. Judicial interpretation of the Voting Rights Act has required that minorities be given maximum opportunity to elect their own to Congress. By the 1992 election thirteen African Americans and six Latinx won election to the House. In 2006, Minnesota voters sent to Congress Keith Ellison, an African American who became the first Muslim elected to the House of Representatives. By the 116th Congress, the fifty-six African Americans in the House constituted about 12.9 percent of Congress, which was the first time that percentage was on par with the percentage of African Americans in the US population as a whole. In addition, in 2012, Hawaii voters elected Tulsi Gabbard, the first Hindu American in Congress, and Wisconsin voters elected Tammy Baldwin, the first openly gay person in the U.S. Senate. After the 2018 elections, out LGBT legislators numbered in the double-digits for the first time in history.[5] The elections of 2016 saw the first Latina (Catherine Cortez Masto [D-NV]) voted into the Senate and the first Indian American woman (Pramila Jayapal [D-WA]) and Vietnamese American woman (Stephanie Murphy [D-FL]) elected into the House. In 2018, Deb Haaland (D-NM) and Sharice Davids (D-KS) were elected as the first American Indian women in Congress, and Ilhan Omar (D-MN) and Rashida Tlaib (D-MI) became the first Muslim women elected to Congress. The 2020, elections continued to expand diversity. For example, nearly 10 percent of congressional seats are now held by women of color. Table 9.3 profiles members of the 117th Congress by age, gender, and ethnicity.

Table 9.3   Profile of the 117th Congress (2021–2022)

	Senate	House
Average Age	63	58
Men/Women	76/24	318/117
African Americans	3	59
Latinx	5	45
Asian Americans and Pacific Islanders	3	18
Indigenous Americans	0	6

SOURCE: Congressional Research Service, 2020.

9.2b   How Do They See Their Roles?

The great eighteenth-century English political thinker Edmund Burke felt that an elected representative should seek to represent not his constituents' views but rather his own conscience and the broad interests of the nation. "Your representative owes you," said Burke, "not his industry only, but his judgment; and he betrays, instead of serving you, if he sacrifices it to your opinion."[6] Such an understanding is known as the **trustee role**. Those who see themselves as simply voting their constituents' desires perform the **delegate role**. Most legislators combine both roles into what is known as the **politico style** of representation. These members consider both their constituents' opinions and their own view of the national interest in making up their minds. The weight assigned to each varies with the issue involved. On bread-and-butter questions, such as public works and farm supports, members are more likely to follow their constituents' views than on issues they might consider moral questions such as abortion or LGBT rights.

9.2c   How Long Do They Stay?

In the early years, few members considered an actual career in Congress. Washington in the 1800s was a provincial, mosquito-ridden town, and most members lived in boarding-houses. Until after the Civil War it was not uncommon for half the members of the House to be first-timers. Nor was it unusual for a representative or senator to resign midterm to pursue a more lucrative profession. Few served longer than two terms.

Toward the end of the nineteenth century, more members began to see service in Congress as a career. As the role of the national government expanded, the business of Congress seemed more urgent and exciting. Between 1850 and 1950 the average tenure for both senators and representatives increased, and the percentage of first-term members declined. In the 1970s those trends began to flatten. Fewer members seemed interested in a lengthy congressional career, and the number of House members with twenty or more years' service decreased by half. In the 116th Congress, the average House member had served 8.6 years, and the average Senator, 10.1 years. Although voters continue to reelect incumbents, this does not mean that Americans are satisfied with the job of Congress as a whole. Consistently the lowest rated of the three branches of government, Congress reached a historic low in November 2013, when a nationwide poll indicated that only 9 percent of Americans approved of the job the legislature was doing.[7] Though now back in the double digits, congressional approval remained in the range of 15–20 percent—and disapproval hovered around 80 percent—for several years. Only with Congress's important efforts to address the COVID-19 crisis in 2020 did approval again top 30 percent.[8]

9.2d   How Much Do They Do?

Today's legislators work almost eleven hours a day when Congress is in session, which adds up to approximately three hundred working days a year. The business of Congress has expanded in both volume and complexity. No longer does Congress have the luxury to ruminate over the two or three issues of the day. In the Sixteenth Congress, when James Monroe (1817–1825) was president, 480 bills were introduced. In the 116th Congress (2019–2020), more than 14,000 measures were introduced; they were longer and more intricate than those in the past and involved practically every area of our economic and social life. Fewer than 200 of those bills were eventually passed and enacted into law.

trustee role
The concept that legislators should vote on the basis of their consciences and the broad interests of the nation, not simply on the views of their constituents

delegate role
A concept of legislative work as simply voting the desires of one's constituents, regardless of one's own personal views

politico style
A manner of representation in which members of Congress attempt to strike a balance between the interests of their constituents and the dictates of their own judgment and conscience

Franked letter from U.S. Senator Maria Cantwell to a constituent

(Wikimedia / Public Domain)

Legislators' schedules are long, fragmented, and unpredictable. On any particular day they may breakfast with a reporter; attend several committee hearings; meet with constituents, lobbyists, or officials on legislative issues; discuss pending legislation with other members or staff; and attend floor debate. Evenings are often consumed with meetings, receptions, and fundraisers. Most of this is crammed into four working days so that members may return home for a weekend of campaigning. A survey of members showed that one-half had no personal time and one-third had no time for family.[9]

9.2e   What Do They Do?

The imperative of getting reelected motivates most members of Congress; therefore, they must cultivate the support and the trust of their constituents. How they do that is described by political scientist Richard Fenno as a member's *homestyle*, which involves the following: (1) the members' allocation of time and resources to their district, (2) their personal style, and (3) their explanations of their Washington activities. Sophisticated use of the **franking privilege** (free postage for official business) has become an increasingly effective method of members for keeping their constituents informed. By 1990, the cost of the congressional frank exceeded $100 million. Public outrage at such costs led to reform legislation that curtailed the privilege somewhat. In recent years, Congress has spent around $20 million on franking.[10] Critics point out that, while the franking privilege was designed to keep constituents informed, members send a great deal more mail in election years than in nonelection years.

A recent phenomenon is satellite-feed video, whereby members can send prepackaged statements directly to a local television channel or stream them directly to their own websites. Both parties have high-tech studios on Capitol Hill. For example, in the Hart Office Building the Senate Republicans have studios, film-editing rooms, and dishes on the roof so that senators can do call-in shows or interviews for local cable channels.[11] With an advanced copy of the president's State of the Union address, members can send their taped reaction to the speech to local television stations in time for the eleven o'clock news.

Members use a variety of methods to gain recognition and build support back home. They fight hard to see to it that their states or districts get their share of the governmental pie. Known as **pork barrel politics**, the process involves gaining federal funds for such things as sewage plants, housing units, and dams.

As eager as legislators are to denounce the size of the federal budget, they are far more anxious to secure a new federal office building, a bridge, or a hospital in their own districts. One cannot denounce Congress, however, because the public at large shares the hypocrisy. Constituents expect their representatives in Washington both to cut the budget and to gain them a slice of the pork.

Beyond legislative work, each member is also expected to serve as an **ombudsman**, or go-between, who intervenes with the federal bureaucracy on behalf of individual constituents. Such intervention is called **casework** and may include helping a student who requests information on a government scholarship program, a soldier interested in an early discharge, or someone with a tax or immigration problem. The staff usually handles such matters through phone calls to the appropriate agency. If the case is difficult or involves influential people in the state or district, a member will deal with it personally.

franking privilege

A congressional benefit that permits members to send out official mail using their signature rather than postage

pork barrel politics

The effort to enact legislation favoring a legislator's home district, often in the form of costly government spending that may not be advantageous to the country as a whole

ombudsman

A person who intervenes with the bureaucracy on behalf of individual citizens

casework

The congressional task of handling requests by constituents for information or assistance with the federal bureaucracy

POLITICAL CONTROVERSIES

Congress Shows Several Members the Door

Americans often muse about "crooked politicians." In fact, in a Gallup poll, 52 percent of Americans indicated that they believe most members of Congress are corrupt.[1] While "most" is likely an overstatement, Congress seems to have gotten the message and demonstrated its concern for ethics in recent years, with investigations leading to the departure of several scandal-plagued incumbents.

The 116th Congress (2019–20) was certainly not the first to see multiple members resign from office, retire in disgrace, or fail in reelection bids due to scandal, but the volume and variety of ethical failures are notable. Perhaps unsurprisingly, sexual misconduct and financial greed were prominent themes. Married House member Katie Hill (D-CA) resigned during her first term in office after photos and texts of her illicit relationship with a campaign staffer surfaced. Later the same year, Representative Chris Collins (R-NY) pled guilty to federal insider trading charges and resigned his seat.

Of course, ethical issues other than sex and money also challenged some legislators. Interestingly, many of these cases involved campaign finance and the sanctity of elections themselves. Representative Duncan Hunter (R-CA) faced a federal indictment for using more than a quarter million dollars of campaign donations for personal expenses, such as extramarital affairs. Though he won reelection in 2018 in spite of these allegations, in 2020 he pled guilty, resigned from Congress and was sentenced to 11 months in federal prison.

Two other members of Congress became entangled in election fraud charges as well. Mark Walker (R-NC) decided not to run for reelection in 2020 after being linked to an effort to bribe state insurance officials. Finally, Steve Watkins (R-KS) was charged with voter registration felonies for listing a UPS store as his home address in order to vote in a different district. The scandal did not stop Watkins from seeking reelection.

In an effort to address these seemingly never-ending scandals, the House of Representatives adopted a rule in 2019 to require ethics training every year for lawmakers. Time will tell whether such a move will have a positive effect.

What is the proper role for ethics in politics? Are members of Congress held to higher ethical standards than the rest of society? Should they be? Who suffers when a member of Congress leaves office amid scandal? Who suffers when they don't leave?

The Gallup Organization, 2015.

9.2f   How Do They See Each Other?

Legislative norms are the standards or unwritten rules of acceptable behavior in Congress. Some of these norms operate differently in each chamber, and time has altered others. First among the most important norms is **reciprocity**. Members are expected to extend support to other members in the expectation that the favor will be returned. An urban representative may support a farm bill in exchange for a rural member's vote for an affordable housing program. This practice is known as logrolling. Among the general public it is considered vaguely disreputable, but members consider such conduct perfectly acceptable.

During the recent years of large deficits and budget cutbacks, legislation often requires that sacrifices rather than rewards be shared. In a form of negative logrolling, members will accept across-the-board reductions that limit all programs or benefits. If members can claim that everyone is taking their lumps, they can more easily avoid blame.[12]

Second, since political conflict is inherent in Congress, members are expected to extend as much *personal courtesy* to each other as is possible. On the floor of Congress, colleagues refer to each other as "the gentleman from ..." or "the gentlewoman from . ..." Members who engage in personal attacks on their colleagues are frequently rebuked.

legislative norms
The unwritten rules of acceptable behavior in Congress

reciprocity (or logrolling)
A practice whereby two or more members of Congress exchange support for legislation important to each other

Historically, because of the Senate's smaller size, its members have gotten to know each other better than those in the House. This tendency has changed somewhat in recent years. The necessities of dealing with larger staffs, media demands, and frequent traveling have made it difficult for senators to establish close friendships. The Senate's "club-iness" and sense of esprit de corps have consequently declined.[13]

Third, members are expected to specialize in one or two subjects, usually matters within their assigned committees. This gives Congress a degree of expertise on complex issues ranging from defense spending to health care. Specialization also makes a legislator's job manageable, allowing members to allocate their time and energy more efficiently. The degree of specialization is greater in the House than the Senate. Large staffs do an enormous amount of legwork, enabling a Senator to become knowledgeable on a broad range of issues.[14]

In the 1950s, when older, conservative, and generally Southern members dominated Congress, junior members were expected to serve a period of apprenticeship. They were expected to work hard, stay out of floor debates, and defer to their seniors—in brief, they were to be seen and not heard. Today a more independent and outspoken membership rarely observes such deference. The liberal members elected in the 1960s and 1970s and the conservatives elected in the 1980s and 1990s were independent and impatient. In the House, new members who recognize the need for some period of apprenticeship see it as months, not years. Junior senators feel no obligation to serve an apprenticeship, and senior members no longer expect it of them.

9.3 The Structure of Congress

Congress contains a complex network of party organizations, committees, subcommittees, and supporting agencies. Understanding each part of this network is important to comprehending the whole.

9.3a Party Leadership: The House

The **Speaker of the House** is the presiding officer of the House of Representatives. The position, established by the Constitution (Article I, Section 2) is, according to the Presidential Succession Act of 1947, next in line to succeed the president after the vice president. Although formally elected by the entire House membership, the majority party nominates the Speaker; and all majority-party members routinely vote for him or her. When the president and the Speaker are of the same party, the Speaker is expected to mobilize support for the president's program in the House and to represent House opinion to the president, seeing to it that unnecessary clashes are avoided.

The Speaker's power once rivaled that of the president; toward the end of the nineteenth century, the Speaker was frequently referred to as a czar. The office reached its pinnacle under Speaker Joseph Cannon (R–IL; 1903–1911). Cannon had the power to make committee assignments and appoint and remove committee chairpersons. His impact on national policy was unmistakable. A staunch reactionary, Cannon helped to stifle much of President Theodore Roosevelt's (1901–1909) reform program on child labor, lower tariffs, and banking. In the 1910–1911 session of Congress, a rising tide of progressivism (see Chapter 4) swept the House; a revolt arose against Cannon, in particular, and the powers of the Speaker, in general. The Speaker lost the power to make committee

Speaker of the House

The presiding officer of the House of Representatives, who is selected by the majority party

assignments and appoint committee chairpersons; and for some years after the revolt, the Speaker once again became a figurehead.

In 1975 the House Democrats increased the substantive power of the Speaker considerably. The Speaker became the chair of the party's Steering and Policy Committee, with the power to nominate all Democratic members of the **Rules Committee**, which clears major legislation going to the House floor and is generally considered one of the most desirable and powerful committees. During his brief tenure as Speaker, Jim Wright (D-TX; 1987–1989) aggressively exploited the new powers of the office to speed his legislative priorities through the House. He exerted tight control of scheduling and used the Rules Committee to restrict the amendments offered on the House floor. Wright referred pieces of major legislation to multiple committees with strict deadlines for consideration—a device known as "multiple referrals." He oversaw the passage of major trade legislation, a farm credit bill, and catastrophic health insurance. Wright resigned from the House in 1989 under fire for ethics violations. Yet, in two years he had transformed the office from a consensus builder to an agenda setter.[15] When the 2006 midterm elections swept the Democrats back into power in the House, after a period of twelve years of Republican majorities, representatives elected Nancy Pelosi (D-CA) Speaker, making her the first woman to hold that post. Pelosi replaced Denny Hastert (R-IL), who had held this position since 1999. The Republican majority elected in 2010 made John Boehner (R-OH) Speaker, a position he held until late 2015, when his frustrations with ultraconservative members of his own party—known as the Freedom Caucus—led him to resign. House Republicans then made Paul Ryan (R-WI) the youngest Speaker (at age 45) since 1875. When Democrats regained the majority in 2019, Nancy Pelosi returned to the Speaker role.

The **majority leader** is the Speaker's chief deputy and the second most powerful figure in the majority party. Elected by the party caucus, the formal organization of House Democrats and House Republicans, the majority leader is the party's leader on the floor of the House, its chief spokesperson, and defender of the party's record from partisan attacks. He or she assists the Speaker in scheduling legislation and deciding party strategy in floor debates. Owing to their influence with the Speaker, the majority leader can help colleagues schedule legislation for floor consideration. When the president is of the same party, the majority leader confers regularly with the president and frequently works to advance the president's programs. At the outset of the 113th Congress, the majority leader was Eric Cantor (R-VA). But when Cantor lost his party primary to a right-wing challenger in June 2014, Republicans selected Kevin McCarthy (R-CA) to succeed him in that role. Cantor was the first sitting majority leader to lose a primary since the office was created in 1899.[16] McCarthy remained majority leader throughout the 114th and 115th Congresses, but the role was claimed by Steny Hoyer (D-MD) when the Democrats became the majority party starting in 2019.

The leader of the loyal opposition in the House is the **minority leader**, a post filled since the 116th Congress by former majority leader McCarthy. Being the leader of a minority can be dispiriting because one's party does not control the committee agenda and frequently loses votes on the floor.

The **party whip** acts as an assistant majority or minority leader. The party caucus chooses the whips. Although they

Rules Committee
Powerful House committee that clears most important bills for floor consideration and decides the rule under which bills should be considered; also, the committee of a party convention that recommends changes in the way a party conducts its affairs

majority leader (House)
Leader and chief spokesperson for the majority party in the House

minority leader (House)
Leader and chief spokesperson for the minority party in the House

party whip
Member of each party's leadership responsible for party discipline and attendance for key votes

(U.S. Congress via Wikimedia)

Party whips, such as Steve Scalise, act as an assistant majority or minority leader by encouraging party discipline and floor attendance during important votes.

have little independent power, they serve their party leadership by encouraging party discipline and floor attendance during important votes. This makes the whips the heart of the party communication system. They poll members on crucial legislation and, when possible, pressure uncommitted members to follow the party line. They have the major responsibility of ensuring that the necessary members are present during important votes. The House majority whip's office is a large intelligence-gathering organization that includes a chief deputy whip, seven deputy whips, more than thirty at-large whips, and more than twenty assistant whips. In the 116th Congress, Democratic representatives selected Jim Clyburn (D-SC) to be their party whip, and Steve Scalise (R-LA) was the Republicans' choice. Notably, Scalise retained this post despite being sidelined for nearly four months after being shot in the hip by a gunman who opened fire on players practicing for a charity baseball game near the Capitol in June 2017.

The Democratic Caucus, which comprises all Democratic House members, elects Democratic leadership, approves committee assignments, and enforces party rules and discipline. It is composed of a number of task forces that report on important current policy issues. In the 116th Congress, the Democratic Caucus focused on a few key issues, covering topics such as lower prescription drug costs and immigration reform.

The Republican caucus, known as the **Conference**, organizes the Republican membership of the House. The members elect Republican leadership, approve committee assignments, and shape communications and strategy for the party. The major arm of the Conference is the House Republican Policy Committee. This committee, which typically has around sixty members, develops policy and legislative proposals. This work helps guide and focus party priorities for the legislative term.

9.3b   Party Leadership: The Senate

Because the Senate has fewer members, party organization in the Senate is not as elaborate as it is in the House. Moreover, a tradition of independence cuts against attempts to regiment the membership along party lines. The **president of the Senate** and chief presiding officer is the vice president of the United States, but the role is entirely ceremonial. It involves presiding over Senate sessions, which rarely occur, and voting only to break a tie, which happens infrequently. An important exception to this general rule occurred in early 2021, when Vice President Kamala Harris was in a position to cast tie-breaking votes in a Senate that was evenly divided between the parties. In addition to the vice president, the Constitution also provides for a **president pro tempore** who may preside over the Senate in the absence of the vice president. Since reforms passed in 1945, the post of president pro tempore has been regarded as largely honorific and given to the senior majority party member. In practice, the task of presiding over the Senate debates is given to a dozen or so junior senators in the majority party who serve about a half hour each day.

The **majority leader** is the leader of the majority party in the Senate and elected at the beginning of each session. The **minority leader**, who leads the minority party, is also elected by party colleagues; however, the majority leader is the dominant figure. As the floor leader, the majority leader is recognized first in debate, influences who will be recognized, and controls the scheduling of bills for floor consideration. Like the House Speaker, the majority leader may influence committee assignments of new senators and of other senators seeking to gain more desirable committee positions.

The Senate is far more difficult to lead than the House. Its one hundred members, elected for six years, have a strong sense of independence and expect more deference to their wishes from the leadership than do House members. Only by a vote of sixty members can debate be terminated, and most routine Senate business is conducted by

Conference

The Republican leadership committee in the House

president of the Senate

A largely ceremonial role held by the vice president of the United States

president pro tempore

The presiding officer of the Senate in the absence of the vice president—largely honorific post and usually given to the senior majority party member

majority leader (Senate)

Leader and chief spokesperson for the majority party in the Senate

minority leader (Senate)

Leader and chief spokesperson for the minority party in the Senate

unanimous consent. Much of the majority leader's time is spent accommodating the hectic schedules of the individual senators. Rising constituent demands involve more service and visits to home states. The need for aggressive self-promotion and perpetual campaigning requires much from senators. They must not only make frequent home visits but also engage in a constant round of media appearances, speeches, and fundraising activities. Former majority leader Robert Byrd (D-WV) once explained his role as "a traffic cop, babysitter, welfare worker, minister, lawyer, umpire, referee, punching bag, target, lightning rod, and the cement that holds his party group together."[17] Thus, an effective majority leader must be a consummate diplomat—nurturing inflated egos, accommodating individual agendas, and smoothing ruffled feathers in order to pass important legislation.

(U.S. Senate photo, via Wikimedia)

Former majority leader Robert Byrd (D-WV) once explained his role as "a traffic cop, babysitter, welfare worker, minister, lawyer, umpire, referee, punching bag, target, lightning rod, and the cement that holds his party group together."

The function of the party leader goes beyond managing the business of the Senate. The party leader is also a media personality and spokesperson for the party. Senator Harry Reid (D-NV) carried this burden from the beginning of 2007 until the end of 2014. When the Republicans regained the majority in the Senate after the 2014 midterm elections, Senator Mitch McConnell (R-KY) became majority leader and Reid was relegated to the role of Senate minority leader. When Reid retired at the end of 2016, Chuck Schumer (D-NY) became minority leader. McConnell and Schumer switched roles at the beginning of the 117th Congress in 2021.

The whip system in the Senate is smaller and less institutionalized than in the House. The Senate whips basically serve the floor leaders as vote counters and are not major power brokers. Both the Senate majority and minority whips are elected by their caucus on a secret ballot prior to the beginning of each new Congress.

standing committees

The permanent committees of Congress that alone can approve legislation and send it to the floor of the House or Senate

9.3c The Committee System

Contemporary lawmaking involves an understanding of numerous complex subjects. Members of Congress cannot be expected to master the details of the hundreds of bills that come before them. Through the committee system, they can gain specialized knowledge of particular areas of policy and legislation.

There are three classes of committees. **Standing committees** (twenty in the House and sixteen in the Senate—see Table 9.4) are at the center of the congressional process. They alone can approve legislation and send it to the House or Senate floor for consideration. **Joint committees** are permanent committees made up of members from both houses. **Special or select committees** are created periodically to study particular problems or new areas of legislation not covered by the standing committees. For example, in 2019 the House of Representatives established a Select Committee on the Climate Crisis.

The concept of seniority, or privileges based on length of service, permeates Congress and is essential to understanding the committee system. **Congressional seniority** is based on length of continuous service in Congress. Seniority can affect committee assignments, the amount of office space a member is granted, and even the deference shown a member during floor debate. Committee seniority is determined by the years of continuous service on a particular committee. The committee chair is usually the member of the majority

joint committees

Permanent committees of Congress made up of members from both houses

special or select committees

Committees of Congress created periodically to study particular problems or new areas of legislation

congressional seniority

Based on a member's length of continuous service in the Congress, it can affect committee assignments, the amount of office space granted, and even the deference shown a member during floor debate

Table 9.4 Committees in Congress

Standing Committees

House	Senate
Agriculture	Agriculture, Nutrition, and Forestry
Appropriations	Appropriations
Armed Services	Armed Services
Budget	Banking, Housing, and Urban Affairs
Education and the Workforce	Budget
Energy and Commerce	Commerce, Science, and Transportation
Ethics	Energy and Natural Resources
Financial Services	Environment and Public Works
Foreign Affairs	Finance
Homeland Security	Foreign Relations
House Administration	Health, Education, Labor, and Pensions
Judiciary	Homeland Security and Government Affairs
Natural Resources	Judiciary
Oversight and Government Reform	Rules and Administration
Rules	Small Business and Entrepreneurship
Science, Space, and Technology	Veterans' Affairs
Small Business	
Transportation and Infrastructure	
Veterans' Affairs	
Ways and Means	

Special/Select Committees

House	Senate
Permanent Select Committee on Intelligence	Indian Affairs
Select Committee on the Climate Crisis	Caucus on International Narcotics Control
Select Committee on the Modernization of Congress	Select Committee on Ethics
	Select Committee on Intelligence
	Special Committee on Aging

Joint Committees

Joint Economic Committee

Joint Committee on Taxation

Joint Committee on Printing

Joint Committee on the Library

party with the longest consecutive service on the committee. A member who switches committees must start at the bottom of the committee ladder. This adherence to seniority has been challenged and revised in recent years. In 1995, a newly elected Republican majority disregarded seniority in making many of its committee leadership selections.

Members consider desirable committee assignments crucial to their reelection. After each congressional election, freshmen representatives and senators scramble to gain assignments suitable to their political fortunes and interests. Incumbents maneuver to gain more prestigious assignments. Assignments are first

The prime scene of discussion in the Senate regarding the U.S. military is the Armed Services Committee.

(Chad J. McNeeley, U.S. Navy, 2007, via Wikimedia)

handled by a committee or committees in each chamber by each party, approved by the party caucuses (Democrats only), and then, in what is always a formality, approved again by the full Senate and House. Several criteria govern these assignments. For example, House Democrats rarely allow any member serving on what they call the "exclusive" committees (Ways and Means, Rules, and Appropriations) to serve on any other standing committee. Both Republicans and Democrats in the Senate agree that no member will receive two major committee assignments until every member has received one. Almost every senator now has the opportunity to serve on one of the four most prestigious committees (Appropriations, Armed Services, Finance, and Foreign Relations).

Members concerned primarily with reelection seek to join committees whose work has a direct impact on their constituents. A representative or senator from an area with considerable defense installations and large military contracts will probably seek membership on the Armed Services Committee, which handles the defense budget. Westerners are attracted to the House Natural Resources and Senate Energy and Natural Resources committees, whose jurisdictions include mining, government lands, immigration, and environmental laws. Members from states that produce crops heavily dependent on government support programs (wheat, peanuts, tobacco, and sugar) seek membership on the agriculture committees. Those interested in influencing national policy seek membership on committees that consider broad public issues such as education, foreign policy, and civil rights. Some members, as they become more senior and more entrenched at home, seek to expand their influence within their respective chambers. They are drawn to committees that decide matters of importance to practically every member, such as the tax-writing committees (Senate Finance and House Ways and Means, as well as the Joint Taxation Committee), the spending committees (Appropriations and Budget), and, in the House, the scheduling committee (Rules).

Members cannot passively wait for their assignments. They must make their preferences known, urge senior members from their own states to lobby for them, personally meet with the chair or ranking minority member of the committee, and cultivate the support of the party leadership. Election results are barely known in November when senators and representatives descend on Washington to compete for the choicest committee seats. Committee assignments, one of the few benefits the congressional leadership can control, are employed, when

Mike Thompson represents California's 5th Congressional District and is a member of the House Committee on Ways and Means, chairman of the Select Revenue Measures Subcommittee, and a senior member of the Health Subcommittee.

(Courtesy of U.S. House Office of Photography/House Creative Services)

possible, to promote party loyalty and responsibility. At one time, committee chairs gained their position by sheer dint of seniority and ran their committees like feudal baronies. They appointed subcommittee chairs, abolished or created subcommittees, decided whether to call committee meetings, and hired staff. Although the chairs still retain many of these powers (influencing the agenda, hiring staff, controlling committee funds), they are no longer the autocrats of yesteryear.

The reforms of the 1970s limited and defined the chairs' power. In the House, they lost the power to prevent committees from meeting, to designate subcommittee chairs, and to refer legislation to subcommittees. In the Senate, chairs no longer control all staff appointments; consequently, they have lost their influence over this important group of experts. Chairs do not want to appear to be obstructing legislation strongly supported by a majority of the caucus for fear of losing their positions; although it is far from absolute, however, chairs still hold considerable power. To get things done, they must use all their diplomatic and legislative skills. Former House Rules Committee chair Joe Moakley (D-MA) put it this way: "The days of snarling chairmen who look through junior members are long gone. To survive, you have to be gracious even when you say no."[18] Nor can chairs exercise their authority behind closed doors. The Legislative Reorganization Act of 1970 opened up the committee process, which had previously been conducted away from the direct scrutiny of the public and the media (as well as the lobbyists). Open committee hearings are now required in most cases, and committee roll-call votes are available to the public.

POLITICS AND IDEAS

Two Ideologues Leave the House

Ideologues can rarely be called great architects of legislation, although they can have an important effect on a legislative body and on the national political conversation. Consider two recent members of the House of Representatives: John Lewis and Justin Amash. Standing at opposite ends of the political spectrum, Representative John Lewis (D-GA) and Representative Justin Amash (L-MI) were ideologues—people for whom it can be more important to

defend principles than to resolve differences. Lewis served in the House for nearly thirty-four years, from his first election in 1986 until his death in 2020; and Amash served for a decade, deciding not to seek reelection in 2020.

Amash, an Arab American attorney from Michigan, became known for holding some of the most libertarian, anti–big-government views in Congress. In fact, these firmly held convictions often led him to vote "present" rather than to lend his support to either Republican or Democratic bills with which he disagreed and eventually prompted him to leave the Republican Party— becoming the Libertarian Party's first member of Congress in 2020. He even briefly considered seeking the Libertarian nomination for president in 2020. Although Amash ran as a Republican in each of his congressional campaigns, he was never comfortable with the breadth of the Republican

agenda, particularly when he saw it interfering with freedom of thought or with capitalism. Amash was outspoken in his support of free-market policies and decreases in taxes and spending and in his opposition to the death penalty and the war on drugs.

Amash first sought a seat in Congress at the same time the Tea Party movement was emerging in American politics. He aligned himself with that movement and became a co-founder of the House Freedom Caucus and chair of the Liberty Caucus, groups in Congress whose views were often more extreme than those of more mainstream Republicans. Even though his positions on what he saw as basic principles of economics and government often placed him at odds with the majority of the American public and sometimes forced his fellow Republicans into difficult positions, his unwavering stances made him a popular figure amongst Libertarians.

Always more focused on principles than on electoral or legislative success, Amash "retired" from Congress at age 40, but whether and how his political career will continue remain to be seen.

While sharing only a few of Justin Amash's views (although both voted to impeach Donald Trump), liberal Representative John Lewis employed some of the same techniques to bring attention to his causes. Although they were polar opposites on many issues, ranging from environmental regulation to health-care reform, Lewis and Amash were both outspoken critics of colleagues with whom they disagreed, and both mastered the use of media to develop a national following beyond the halls of Congress and the confines of their congressional districts. Growing up the son of sharecroppers in the segregated South, Lewis was drawn to the emerging Civil Rights Movement at a young age. He gained a reputation as a powerful speaker and leader as one of the original Freedom Riders, the head of the Student Nonviolent Coordinating Committee (SNCC), and as an organizer of the Selma marches. He was the youngest speaker at the 1963 March on Washington. Beaten and arrested many times for his nonviolent protests and boycotts, Lewis spent the 1960s and 1970s leading efforts to expand civil rights in the South before turning to politics. Elected to the Atlanta city council in 1981, Lewis was then elected to represent Georgia's Fifth District in Congress in 1986, a position he held until his death thirty-four years later.

In addition to taking liberal positions on legislation, Lewis also used the tactics he had developed during the Civil Rights Movement in the Capitol. In 2016, for example, Lewis led a sit-in on the floor of Congress to call attention to the need for gun safety legislation. This was only one of several times Lewis put his reputation on the line for a cause he believed in; he was arrested during protests and sit-ins numerous times while serving as a member of the House of Representatives, protesting issues ranging from the Iraq War to immigration reform.

Both Amash and Lewis paid a price for their extremism, Lewis sometimes risking his life and Amash risking his political future. Never afraid to stand their ground, they stuck to principle. Some critics say these maverick legislators are more interested in using the House as a platform for their ideas than in forging coalitions and compromises. Do legislators such as Amash and Lewis raise important issues, or do they merely obstruct the business of Congress? Is it more important for a legislator to compromise and pass legislation, or to stick firmly to a principle? What other legislators retired in 2020? What views did they hold?

SOURCES: Adam Shaw, "Rep. Justin Amash announces he is leaving GOP; Trump calls it 'great news,'" *Fox News,* July 4, 2020, https://www.foxnews.com/politics/michigan-rep-justin-amash-quits-gop-says-he-is-frightened-by-party-politics, (August 3, 2020); Chad Pergram, "John Lewis, civil rights icon, congressman for 33 years, dead at 80," *Fox News,* July 18, 2020, https://www.foxnews.com/politics/john-lewis-civil-rights-icon-obituary, (August 3, 2020).

9.3d   Subcommittees

Most of the standing congressional committees are divided into subcommittees. In the 117th Congress there are more than one hundred subcommittees in the House and about sixty-seven in the Senate. House committee chairs previously controlled their subcommittees by packing them with members who would follow their lead. Under such circumstances, subcommittees would rarely report to the full committee legislation that the chair opposed. When the era of the autocratic chair came to an end, however, the trend in the House toward "subcommittee government" began.

In 1973, the House Democratic Caucus adopted a subcommittee "bill of rights." Democrats on every committee were given the authority to select subcommittee chairs, establish subcommittee jurisdiction, and provide the budgets for running the subcommittees. It required that all committees with more than twenty members establish at least four subcommittees, ending the Ways and Means Committee's unique practice of operating without subcommittees. Subcommittee chairs and the ranking minority members were allowed to hire staff to work directly for them on their subcommittee.

Subcommittees assumed greater independence, conducting legislative hearings once held primarily by the full committee. Whereas subcommittees conducted only 30 percent of the legislative hearings in the early 1950s, by the mid-1970s the figure had risen to 90 percent. Subcommittees were also drafting more legislation and frequently gaining full committee approval. Subcommittee chairs were replacing committee chairs as the managers of legislation on the floor.

This movement toward subcommittee government is less prevalent in the Senate, where subcommittees primarily hold hearings and key votes are taken in the full committee. In the Senate Commerce, Judiciary, and Labor committees, subcommittees have gained greater autonomy.[19]

The more democratic subcommittee government came with a cost. As more members exercised initiative and fewer could deliver the votes and call the shots, the committee system became increasingly unwieldy. With additional centers of power in Congress, party leaders had a far more difficult time building coalitions and constructing compromises.

9.3e Congressional Staff and Agencies

One hundred years ago senators and members of Congress performed their duties with only a few clerks, paid from members' own personal funds. In 2021, about thirty thousand people were employed by the legislative branch to work, for instance, on Capitol Hill as personal staff to representatives and senators or as committee staff—all paid from public funds. This burgeoning congressional bureaucracy reflects the complexity of modern government. The issues have grown more intricate, the congressional workload has expanded, and Congress has felt the need to match the expertise of the executive branch. A typical congressional office will include a **legislative assistant (LA)** to analyze bills, draft laws, write speeches, and prepare position papers, and an **administrative assistant (AA)** to act as the legislator's alter ego in dealing with colleagues, constituents, and lobbyists. In addition, most legislators have offices in their home states or districts to provide efficient constituent service and a personal touch.

Who are these staff people? They are relatively young (average age slightly under forty), well educated (close to half have postgraduate or professional degrees), and predominantly male (about 68 percent).[20] In an earlier time they may have been political operatives or cronies of the legislator, but today they are bright university graduates. The experience of being a staffer can be both exhilarating and precarious. Staffers are frequently in the center of dramatic legislative battles, but they have no civil service protection and can be fired by their representative or senator without cause or notice.

Unlike the personal staffers, whose job it is to serve the member and his or her political interest, the *committee staffers* are responsible for developing the legislation that comes from the committees. The committee chair, subcommittee chair, or ranking minority party member appoint these committee staffers. They, in turn, organize hearings, conduct research, assist in the drafting of legislation, and prepare the reports that accompany bills sent out of committee. The chief committee aides—those most familiar with the details of a particular bill—may accompany the committee chair when the bill is debated on the floor. Because a member's time is stretched thin, staffers may act as stand-ins for the legislators themselves, negotiating with lobbyists, executive branch officials, and even other legislators to gain support for a particular bill. Like the rest of the congressional bureaucracy, the congressional committee staffs grew from about four hundred in 1947 to over 2,500 by the 2000s—an increase of over 600 percent.

Has this expansion of staff solved the congressional need for more information? Some argue that members have become too dependent upon committee staff. Frequently, staffers are the only ones who understand increasingly complex legislation, such as the Patient Protection and Affordable Care Act of 2010. Others argue that more staff generate more legislation, diluting a member's ability to concentrate on what is important. Has the Congress simply transferred its dependency for information from the executive branch to its own staff?[21]

legislative assistant (LA)

A congressional aide who analyzes bills, drafts laws, writes speeches, and prepares position papers

administrative assistant (AA)

Top aide to a member of Congress who frequently acts on behalf of the legislator in dealing with staff, colleagues, constituents, and lobbyists

In addition to staff, three agencies provide Congress with research and analysis of policy options:

1. **The Congressional Research Service (CRS)** serves the entire Congress—members, committees, and aides. On request, it conducts legal research and policy analysis and digests and summarizes legislation. Congress created the CRS to remedy the dearth of information at Congress's disposal as compared to the information resources long available to the president.

2. **The Government Accountability Office (GAO)**, known as the watchdog agency, reports to Congress on the efficiency and performance of federal programs. With over 3,000 employees, its task is to determine whether a program is achieving the objectives that Congress has prescribed. Previously known as the General Accounting Office, the name was changed in 2004 to better reflect the agency's activities, which now extend well beyond mere financial audits.

3. **The Congressional Budget Office (CBO)** provides essential analysis of the economy and the federal budget for Congress. Specifically, it provides an assessment of the inflationary impact of major bills, projects the five-year costs of proposed legislation, and forecasts economic trends. The CBO gives Congress an independent base of economic and budgetary expertise to challenge the economic assumptions behind the president's budget.

9.4   Congressional Procedures: How a Bill Becomes a Law

You can search through the full text of federal legislation and track bills through the legislative process at Congress.gov—a service of the Library of Congress.

http://www.bvtlab.com/43k77

Ultimately, Congress impacts American government because it is the chief lawmaking body. Presidents, parties, and interest groups may propose a host of programs; yet unless Congress acts favorably, each proposal remains an idea, not a law. The legislative process in Congress is an obstacle course (see Figure 9.1). A bill can be stalled or defeated at various points along the way, and most are. Of the more than fourteen thousand pieces of legislation introduced in the 116th Congress, fewer than two hundred eventually became law.

9.4a   Committee to Floor Debate

The objective of guiding a bill through Congress is to have both houses pass the bill in identical form. Only then can it go to the president for signing. At the initial stage of the legislative process, only a member of the House or the Senate may introduce a bill, although the proposal frequently originates in the executive branch, an interest group, or a member's staff. Once a bill is introduced, it is sent to the appropriate committee; should a committee refuse to consider the bill, it is consigned to an early death. If the bill is considered, it is usually assigned to a subcommittee for study; and the process begins. The subcommittee may then hold hearings inviting government officials and other experts

mark-up

The process in which a legislative committee sets the precise language and amendments of a bill

Figure 9.1 How a Bill Becomes Law

At each step along the way a bill can be stymied, making this journey a genuine obstacle course.

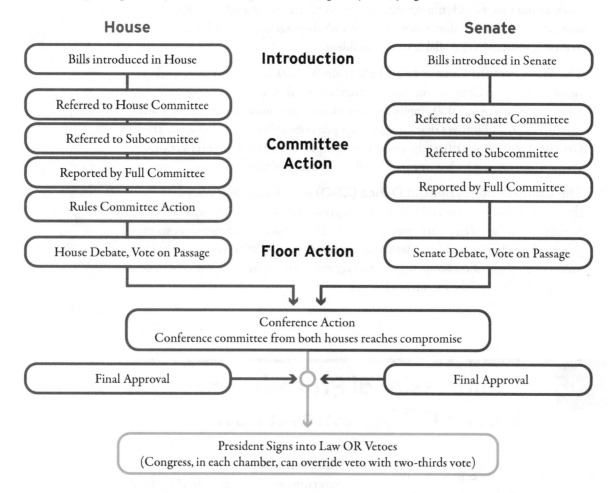

to testify. These hearings serve not only to obtain information but also to test public opinion, build support for the measure, or perhaps delay ultimate consideration. Except in the case of national security matters, most hearings are open to the public. When the hearings are complete, the bill is **marked up**. This is the process whereby the subcommittee decides on the bill's precise language and on amendments. Like hearings, most markup sessions are open to the public.

The bill, if approved by the subcommittee, then goes to the full committee for consideration. If the full committee approves the bill (it may mark up the bill or add its own amendments), it sends the bill to its respective chamber for consideration. Bills voted out of committee are often accompanied by an extensive report that explains the bill's purpose, the committee amendments, its effect on existing law, and its probable costs.

9.4b Floor Debate: The House

Bills finally reported out of committee are listed on one of the House calendars. Tax and appropriation bills are placed on the **Union Calendar**. Nonmoney bills go to the **House Calendar**. Private bills, such as one that granted citizenship to a 111-year-old

Albanian woman so that she could vote in a free election before she died, are placed on the **Private Calendar.**

The Speaker and the majority leader determine when bills are called off the calendar and placed on the House floor. Bills on the Private Calendar can be heard only on certain days of the month; they are brought directly to the floor, usually by unanimous consent, and passed with little debate. The Speaker may also bring other minor bills directly to the floor by a suspension of the rules. Under this procedure, which requires a two-thirds vote of the House, debate is limited to forty minutes; no amendments are allowed. Other matters are considered privileged and can be brought to the House floor at almost any time, but most major bills must take the route from the committee to the House floor via the Rules Committee. The Rules Committee decides the amount of time the House will spend debating a bill and dictates the amending process. The committee may send a bill to the floor with a **closed rule**, prohibiting all amendments except those from the committee that reported the bill; an **open rule**, permitting any amendments from the floor; or

(Courtesy U.S. Senate Photographic Studio, Renee Bouchard, via Wikimedia)

Tammy Duckworth (D-IL), who became the first senator to give birth while in office in 2018.

a **modified rule**, allowing a limited number of amendments. Tax bills, reported out of the Ways and Means Committee, are usually given the privilege of a closed rule. The Speaker appoints all of his or her party's members on the Rules Committee, and the committee is thus an arm of the leadership.

When floor debate begins, the Speaker has a member of the Rules Committee from each party explain the rule under which the bill will be debated and voted. Usually the Rules Committee specifies from one to two hours of debate, but it will grant controversial bills of particular importance up to ten hours. Despite the strictness of these rules, the party leaders may allot themselves virtually unlimited time. In 2018, Minority Leader Nancy Pelosi (D-CA) gave the longest speech in House recorded history—speaking for over eight hours straight in protest of a spending bill's failure to address immigration reform.[22]

Floor debate begins with a statement from the floor manager of the bill, who is by custom the chairperson of the committee or subcommittee that reported the bill. The floor manager has the responsibility of guiding the bill to passage. Frequently debate is conducted in the **Committee of the Whole.** This device allows the House to conduct business more quickly by relaxing the formal rules and allowing a quorum of only 100, instead of the usual 218; but the full House must approve decisions made by the Committee of the Whole before they are official.

After general debate covering the pros and cons of the bill, the amending process begins. Here the fate of a bill may be decided. Opponents of the bill may try to amend it beyond recognition or else add objectionable provisions destined to kill it. The House rules require that amendments be germane to the bill under consideration. Amendments are debated no more than ten minutes—five minutes for the sponsors and five for the opponents.

An electronic voting system, installed in 1973, makes time-consuming roll-call votes unnecessary. Members may insert a plastic card into one of forty voting machines and vote "yes," "no," or "present" (abstaining). The vote is recorded on an electronic display board on the wall of the chamber, and the process takes about fifteen minutes. A series of bells that ring through the halls and offices of Congress alerts members to floor votes. In an effort to cope with the COVID-19 crisis and maintain social distancing, the House adopted a

closed rule

An order from the House Rules Committee that prohibits amendments to a bill under consideration on the House floor

open rule

An order from the House Rules Committee whereby amendments to a bill are permitted on the floor

modified rule

An order from the House Rules Committee allowing a limited number of amendments to a bill during floor consideration

Committee of the Whole

A parliamentary device used by the House of Representatives to facilitate floor consideration of a bill; when the House dissolves itself into the Committee of the Whole, it can suspend formal rules and consider a bill with a quorum of 100 rather than the usual 218

rule in 2020 to allow for remote voting for the first time in its history. Members staying away from the Capitol could name another member as a proxy to vote on their behalf.

9.4c   Floor Debate: The Senate

The Senate, being smaller, has a more flexible set of procedures. First, the Senate has only two calendars: an **Executive Calendar** for presidential nominations and treaties and a Calendar of General Orders for all other legislation. Second, there is no equivalent of the House Rules Committee. Thus the Senate imposes no time limits on general debate, no five-minute rule on amendments, and no restrictions on the number of amendments. In addition, amendments need not be germane to the bill under consideration.

Nongermane amendments, called **riders**, allow a proposal to bypass a hostile Senate committee that otherwise would have considered and probably killed it. The rider must then only survive the conference committee if the complete bill passes the Senate. Riders are also used to force the president to accept a program that would be vetoed were it to reach him as a separate piece of legislation. Attaching the rider to necessary legislation, such as a general appropriations bill that the president will feel compelled to sign, does this. One may wonder how, with such permissive rules, the Senate ever accomplishes anything. The answer is that through the mechanism of **unanimous consent agreements**, terms of Senate debates are limited. These agreements, usually secured by the majority leader in cooperation with the minority leader, are carefully negotiated to accommodate the desires of senators who wish to speak or offer amendments.

The best-known technique for forestalling the work of the Senate is the **filibuster**—a continuing debate designed to prevent passage of a bill. A single senator or a group of senators can conduct a filibuster. The filibuster is essentially a political device to stop a bill that the minority does not have the votes to defeat, to win concessions on a bill, or to arouse public opposition to it. Owing to the time constraints on a busy Senate (more committee meetings, more recorded votes, more bills considered), even the threat to delay business by a filibuster can force a concession on a bill. Defenders argue that the filibuster protects minority rights and requires the Senate to consider not only the extent of opposition but its depth and intensity as well. Critics claim that the filibuster thwarts majority will and allows a small minority to exercise disproportionate influence on a bill or even to defeat it altogether.

Until 1917 the Senate had no way of ending debate except through unanimous consent. At that time the Senate adopted Rule 22, a **cloture** (debate-ending) rule that allowed two-thirds of the senators present to end debate. In 1975 the rule was amended so that sixty members (or three-fifths of the membership) can shut off debate. Once cloture is invoked, the Senate can continue consideration of the bill for only thirty additional hours. Prior to the 1970s, a filibuster was a rare event, used primarily by southern Democrats to block civil rights legislation. Now it is almost commonplace and occurs on a wide range of issues. Cloture votes, which numbered six in the Ninetieth Congress (1967–1969), rose steadily beginning in the 1970s, and skyrocketed starting in the mid-2000s. In the recently completed 116th Congress, there were more than 240 cloture votes. In an effort to overcome their inability to invoke cloture for a large number of executive and non–Supreme Court judicial appointees, in 2013, Senate Democrats chose what is sometimes referred to as the "nuclear option." They changed the rules to allow for a simple majority to end a filibuster for these nominations. While this move created a temporary solution, some feared it would lead to more partisan extremism in the future. Indeed, it did so just a few years later, when Senate Republicans (in the majority after the 2014 elections) expanded the nuclear option to cover Supreme Court nominees.

Executive Calendar
One of two registers of business in the U.S. Senate that contains presidential nominations and treaties

riders
Provisions, usually attached to appropriation bills, which "ride" into law on the backs of necessary pieces of legislation, forcing the president to veto the entire bill in order to kill the amendment

unanimous consent agreement
A common mechanism used by the Senate leadership to limit Senate debate

filibuster
Continuing debate designed to prevent consideration of a particular bill; a technique used in the Senate

cloture
Rule 22 of the Senate in which discussion on a piece of legislation can be suspended after no more than thirty hours of debate by a vote of sixty members

9.4d   The Conference Committee: Resolving Senate-House Differences

Rarely do the Senate and House pass bills in identical form. If one house makes only minor changes in a bill passed by the other, the chamber that initially passed the bill will usually agree to the changes and send the bill on to the president for signature. But when there are major differences over a bill, a **House-Senate Conference Committee** must reconcile them. The House Speaker and the Senate presiding officers name the conferees on the recommendation of the chairperson of the committee that reported the bill. The majority from each delegation must be from the majority party in that chamber. Each chamber has one vote in the conference, which is determined by a vote of the majority of its delega-

Every year the United States Congress passes hundreds of laws.

Where do they end up?

In the United States Code, an extensive resource that is updated annually and accessible at this website:

http://www.bvtlab.com/4KCNp

tion. When the conference finishes its job, it sends the conference report or compromise bill back to the House and Senate for approval. Approval of the conference report by both houses constitutes final approval of the bill.

Numerous traps await a bill before it gets to the president's desk. Bills must pass the Senate and the House within the two-year period that makes up a particular Congress;

otherwise, the bill must start through the obstacle course anew with the next Congress. It can be buried in committee or by the House Rules Committee, stifled by a Senate filibuster, or caught in a conference committee deadlock. Sponsors of a bill must know congressional procedure, be sensitive to key personalities such as the Speaker or the important committee chairs, and must, at each crucial point, weave a majority coalition for the bill.

9.5   Congress and the Political System

The legislative process alone does not explain why some bills become law and others do not. Congress is also part of the broader political system. Everything it does affects citizens, as well as one or more interest groups and governmental agencies. These different constituencies labor mightily to influence congressional decisions.

9.5a   Lobbies

As the range of government programs, subsidies, and entitlements has grown, so has the number of interest groups with a stake in them. The result has been the proliferation of lobbies and lobbyists, as described in Chapter 7. Critics feel that lobbies distort the political process and give particular groups inordinate influence over legislation.

Lobbyists are most successful in affecting **distributive policies** (special interest subsidies such as water reclamation projects, farm price supports, and new post offices). These programs usually provoke little opposition because they are perceived as providing

House-Senate Conference Committee

A joint committee designed to reconcile differences between the House and Senate versions of a bill

distributive policies

Programs such as water reclamation projects that provide considerable benefits for a few people and relatively small costs for many, usually provoking little opposition

considerable benefits at little relative cost. As a result, the entire Congress rarely pays close attention to such questions. Lobbyists can then concentrate their efforts on a key subcommittee or committee, simplifying its task. Open committee sessions allow lobbyists to monitor congressional action quite carefully. Rather than waiting outside a closed door while a committee markup session is going on, a lobbyist may be right in the committee room suggesting precise legislative language or a compromise amendment.

Lobbies have the most difficulty affecting **redistributive policies**, those that produce benefits to some segments of society at substantive cost to others. These include broad budget decisions that place social programs against defense spending or proposals for tax reform. Such issues are frequently resolved on the floor of Congress, not in committee. Because they usually involve conflicts among interest groups, the result is often a compromise with no single lobby getting exactly what it wants.

Contemporary lobbying must go beyond working the halls of Congress; moving legislation often requires affecting public opinion. Therefore, lobbyists must employ the techniques of mass marketing: targeted mailings and emails, television advertising, and slick public relations campaigns. In twenty-four hours the National Rifle Association can generate millions of emails and faxes opposing a gun control measure; AARP—the retirees' lobby—swamped former Speaker Jim Wright in one day with over 15 million postcards and letters warning against tampering with the cost-of-living formula for Social Security.[23] Much of the increase in lobbying is a result of the weakened power of the committee chairs and the decentralization of power in Congress. Now that there are more committee members and staffers to be persuaded, more lobbyists are required to do the job.

9.5b   The Bureaucracy

Interest groups are not the only lobbying forces in Congress. The bureaucracy itself exercises considerable influence on the congressional process. Together with interest groups and congressional committees, bureaucratic agencies often develop informal partnerships called subgovernments or **iron triangles**. Each group scratches the back of the other. The agency gets its budget from the committee and political support from the interest group. The interest group gets favorable legislation from the committee and sympathetic treatment from the agency. The congressional committee members get campaign reelection support from the interest group and conscientious constituency service from the bureaucracy. These subgovernments have special influence over distributive policy.

The veterans programs provide an example of such interplay. In this case, the subgovernment includes the veterans groups, the veterans committees of Congress, and the Department of Veterans Affairs (see Figure 9.2). Together these pieces of the subgovernment conspire to protect veterans programs from the budget-cutter's scalpel. Veterans' benefits are usually not matters at the top of the president's agenda, nor are they issues that excite broad congressional interest. They are, in fact, typical of the type of distributive policies that are shaped by subgovernments.

To function effectively, an iron triangle requires that the participants be shielded from the glare of publicity. Over the past two decades the environment has changed, and the effectiveness of these subgovernments has declined. The media are more aggressive in covering Congress, the number of lobbies with competing interests in legislation has increased, and new public interest lobbies watch for special interest favoritism; no committee has exclusive control over such broad issues as energy, foreign trade, and the environment. In a period of tight budgets, fewer issues can be classified as distributive, providing benefits to a few without significant and visible costs to the many.[24]

redistributive policies
Programs such as tariffs or tax reforms that produce considerable benefits to some segments of society but high costs to others

iron triangle
The combination of interest group representatives, legislators, and government administrators seen as extremely influential in determining the outcome of political decisions

Figure 9.2   The "Iron Triangle" and Veterans Policy

The triangular relationship among congressional committees, bureaucratic agencies, and interest groups indicates how relatively few people can determine public policy on some questions. The relationship does not mean that the groups are always in agreement, but it does mean that the dominant opinion represented will usually have the largest say in setting veterans policy. Sometimes the components in the triangle are more numerous. A proposed change in educational benefits, for example, would involve higher-education lobbies and other committees and agencies. A change in job-training policy for veterans would involve the Labor Department as well as the labor committees in Congress.

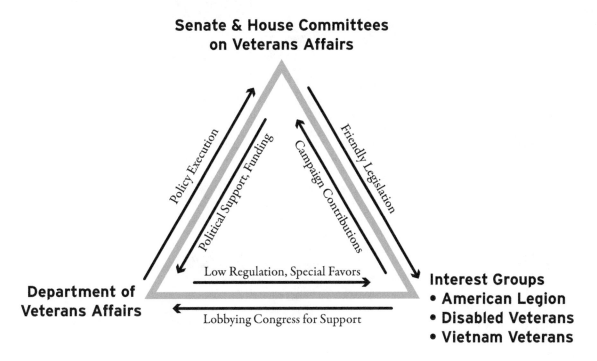

9.6   What Role for a Changing Congress?

Largely through its own efforts, Congress democratized its rules and opened up its procedures. The seniority system is no longer sacred. Committee chairs do not control their committees. Committee sessions are now accessible to the public. Junior members can make an immediate impact, often serving as subcommittee chairs; and the creation of the Congressional Budget Office, plus the addition of more professional staffers, has put Congress in the position to challenge the expertise of the executive branch.

Many people welcome the resurgence of congressional will as a necessary corrective to the presidential excesses that produced the Vietnam War and the Watergate scandal. They argue that the openness of Congress is essential to a democratic society, but other observers question whether Congress has gone too far in its reassertion of power and independence. Congress cannot control inflation, negotiate arms agreements, or solve

our trade deficit. Congressional leaders feel that the American government functions best under the leadership of the president. Only the president, they argue, can define national objectives that can arouse a majority of citizens. The historic statements of national policy, so the argument goes, were presidential not congressional: the Monroe Doctrine, the Emancipation Proclamation, and the War on Poverty. Although Congress cannot lead, it does have an important role to play. It provides more citizen access to policy making and offsets the impersonality of the bureaucracy. In a larger sense, Congress brings the parochialism of Main Street, the suburban kaffeeklatsch, and the union hall to Washington's corridors of power. The many and often-confusing voices with which Congress speaks are the clatter of the democratic process.

CHAPTER REVIEW

1. Since 1819 the Supreme Court has granted Congress great leeway in legislating on social and economic matters. Both houses have equal weight in writing laws; but the Senate—owing to its longer member terms, its special responsibilities (ratifying treaties and confirming presidential appointments), and its smaller size—seems to command somewhat greater prestige.

2. The task of members of Congress has many dimensions: mastering fields of legislation, bringing back a share of federal benefits for their state or district, meeting the needs of individual constituents, learning the norms and rules of their respective chambers, and voting on a wide variety of legislative questions. It is a demanding, complex, full-time job.

3. Power in the contemporary Congress is no longer the exclusive prerogative of a few senior members. In the House, much of the power has flowed to the subcommittees. Individual senators have become increasingly assertive. Junior members feel little obligation to serve a period of apprenticeship. Congress, as a result, is both more democratic and more unwieldy.

4. Leadership in Congress is based largely on persuasion and ability. Autocratic leaders are increasingly rare. The influence of the caucus requires that most congressional leaders be sensitive to the concerns of the rank-and-file members.

5. Before a bill can become a law, it must pass through a complete obstacle course. At each crucial point, successful sponsors must weave a majority coalition for their bill.

6. Congress, although influenced by presidential leadership, is not the president's rubber stamp and initiates much legislation on its own.

KEY TERMS

administrative assistant (AA) 292

bill of attainder 277

casework 282

checks and balances 277

closed rule 295

cloture 296

Committee of the Whole 295

Conference 286

congressional seniority 287

delegate role 281

distributive policies 297

Executive Calendar 296

ex post facto law 277

filibuster 296

franking privilege 282

House Calendar 294

House-Senate Conference Committee 297

iron triangle 298

joint committees 287

legislative assistant (LA) 292

legislative norms 283

majority leader (House) 285

majority leader (Senate) 286

mark-up 293

minority leader (House) 285

minority leader (Senate) 286

modified rule 295

necessary and proper clause 276

ombudsman 282

open rule 295

party whip 285

politico style 281

pork barrel politics 282

president of the Senate 286

president pro tempore 286

Private Calendar 294

reciprocity (or logrolling) 283

redistributive policies 298

riders 296

Rules Committee 285

Seventeenth Amendment 278

Speaker of the House 284

special or select committees 287

standing committees 287

trustee role 281

unanimous consent agreement 296

Union Calendar 294

READINGS FOR FURTHER STUDY

For a comprehensive overview of Congress, consult Roger H. Davidson, Walter J. Oleszek, Frances E. Lee, and Eric Schickler, *Congress and Its Members*, 17th ed. (Washington, DC: CQ Press, 2019), and Morris P. Fiorina, *Congress: Keystone of the Washington Establishment*, 2nd ed. (New Haven, CT: Yale University Press, 1989).

The most complete review of the rules and processes of Congress is Walter J. Oleszek, Elizabeth Rybicki, and Bill Heniff Jr., *Congressional Procedures and the Policy Process,* 11th ed. (Washington, DC: CQ Press, 2019). Another good examination of process is Barbara Sinclair, *Unorthodox Lawmaking: New Legislative Processes in the U.S. Congress,* 5th ed. (Washington, DC: CQ Press, 2016).

An excellent history of development and change in Congress is Nelson W. Polsby, *How Congress Evolves: Social Bases of Institutional Change* (New York: Oxford, 2005).

A collection of highly readable essays on the problems of the contemporary Congress can be found in Lawrence C. Dodd and Bruce I. Oppenheimer, eds., *Congress Reconsidered*, 11th ed. (Washington, DC: CQ Press, 2016).

Up-to-date information and lively accounts of individual senators and representatives are available in Michael Barone's and Grant Ujifusa's, *Almanac of American Politics* (Washington, DC: National Journal), published every two years.

A valuable collection of historical data appears in the Brookings Center report *Vital Statistics on Congress,* which is updated annually at https://www.brookings.edu/multi-chapter-report/vital-statistics-on-congress/.

NOTES

1. *McCulloch v. Maryland,* 17 U.S. (4 Wheaton) 316 (1819).

2. For example, *United States v. Lopez,* 514 U.S. 549 (1995) and *United States v. Morrison,* 529 U.S. 598 (2000).

3. *Wesberry v. Sanders,* 376 U.S. 1 (1964).

4. Quoted in Roger J. Davidson and Walter J. Oleszek, *Congress and Its Members,* 3rd ed. (Washington, DC: Congressional Quarterly, 1990), p. 23.

5. Chantal Da Silva, "With Krysten Sinema's Election, LGBT Representation in Congress Hits Double Digits," *Newsweek,* November 13, 2018, https://www.newsweek.com/kyrsten-sinemas -election-lgbt-representation-congress-hits-double -digits-1212716 (August 2, 2020).

6. David J. Vogler, *The Politics of Congress,* 4th ed. (Boston: Allyn & Bacon, 1983), p. 76.

7. The Gallup Organization, *"Congress and the Public,"* 2016.

8. The Gallup Organization, "Congress and the Public," 2020.

9. Hedrick Smith, *The Power Game: How Washington Works* (New York: Ballantine Books, 1989), p. 108; Davidson and Oleszek, *"Congress and Its Members,"* pp. 124–227.

10. Congressional Research Service, "Congressional Franked Mail: Overview," February 7, 2019, https://crsreports.congress.gov/product/pdf/IF /IF10489/3 (August 2, 2020).

11. Davidson and Oleszek, *"Congress and Its Members,"* pp. 130–131.

12. R. Kent Weaver, "The Politics of Blame Avoidance," *The Brookings Review 5* (Spring 1987): 43–47.

13. Barbara Sinclair, *The Transformation of the U.S. Senate* (Baltimore, MD: Johns Hopkins University Press, 1989), pp. 98–100.

14. Andy Plattner, "The Lure of the Senate: Influence and Prestige," *Congressional Quarterly Weekly Report* (May 25, 1985): 991–998.

15. Roger H. Davidson, "The New Centralization on Capitol Hill," *Review of Politics 50* (1988): 358–359.

16. "House Majority Leader's Shocking Defeat," *This Week* (June 20, 2014).

17. Quoted in Samuel C. Patterson, "Party Leadership in the U.S. Senate," *Legislative Studies Quarterly 14* (1989): 409.

18. *Congressional Quarterly Weekly Report* (December 8, 1990): 406.

19. Lawrence Dodd and Bruce Oppenheimer, "The House in Transition: Change and Consolidation," in *Congress Reconsidered,* 2nd ed. (Washington, DC: Congressional Quarterly, 1981), p. 42; Davidson and Oleszek, "Congress and Its Members," p. 230.

20. "Congressional Staffers: Who Are the People Behind the Scenes in Washington?" The Huffington Post, June 17, 2011, http://www.huffingtonpost. com/2011/06/17/congressional-staffers- infographic_n_879000.html (August 17, 2012).

21. Michael L. Mezey, "The Legislature, the Executive, and Public Policy: The Futile Quest for Congressional Power," in James A. Thurber, ed., *Divided Democracy* (Washington, DC: Congressional Quarterly, 1991), p. 107.

22. Daniella Diaz and Diedre Walsh, "Pelosi Sets Record with 8-Hour Marathon Speech on DACA," *CNN,* February 7, 2018, https://www.cnn. com/2018/02/07/politics/nancy-pelosi-house- democrats-spending-deal-congress-shutdown/index. html (October 2, 2018).

23. Smith, *The Power Game,* p. 383.

24. Morris P. Fiorina, *Congress: Keystone of the Washington Establishment,* 2nd ed. (New Haven, CT: Yale University Press, 1989), pp. 122–123.

POP QUIZ

1. Members of Congress who primarily vote according to their constituents' desires follow the _____ role of representation.

2. The _____ Committee clears all major legislation going to the floor of the House.

3. Congressional _____ can affect committee assignments, office space, and even deference shown a member on the floor.

4. The agency that reports to Congress on the efficiency and performance of federal programs is called the _____ .

5. The informal partnerships between interest groups, congressional committees, and bureaucratic agencies are called _____ .

6. By 2007 the percentage of African Americans in Congress finally came to equal the percentage of African Americans in the population as a whole.   T   F

7. Party whips in the House act as the heart of the party communication system.   T   F

8. A member who switches committees is able to transfer his seniority from the old committee to the new.   T   F

9. Committee staffers are responsible for developing the legislation that comes from the committees.   T   F

10. Once an effective and often-used strategy, the filibuster has been rarely used since the Senate adopted Rule 22 on cloture.   T   F

11. Most members of Congress see themselves as following the _____ role.
    A) trustee
    B) delegate
    C) politico
    D) party

12. Legislative norms include _____ .
    A) reciprocity
    B) personal courtesy
    C) subject specialization
    D) All of the above

13. Why are members of Congress motivated to choose a particular committee?
    A) To enhance their reelection prospects
    B) To shape national policy
    C) To gain influence within Congress
    D) All of the above

14. What does it mean when a bill is marked up?
    A) The bill's language and amendments have been decided upon.
    B) The bill is being delayed by a filibuster.
    C) The bill is being called up to bypass the Rules Committee.
    D) The bill is bottled up in the Rules Committee.

15. Which of the following is true of the Conference Committee?
    A) It reconciles differences between the two parties in the House.
    B) It has become primarily a formality.
    C) It is often the scene of very hard bargaining and compromise.
    D) It is closed to the public.

Answers:
1. delegate   2. Rules   3. seniority
4. Government Accountability Office
5. iron triangles or subgovernments   6. F
7. T   8. F   9. T   10. F   11. C
12. D   13. D   14. A   15. C

Chapter

10

Chapter 10

THE PRESIDENCY

In This Chapter

10.1 The President and Symbolic Leadership

10.2 The President and the Constitution

10.3 The President and the Executive Branch

10.4 The President and Congress: Foreign Policy

10.5 The President and Congress: The War Power

10.6 The President and Congress: Domestic Policy

10.7 The President and the Media

Chapter Objectives

The American presidency is an awe-inspiring and complex office. Its demands are numerous and often contradictory. The president is expected to be honest and trustworthy, yet tough if not ruthless; to be a moral leader who is above politics, as well as a political operator who can achieve results; to control government spending and taxes and yet provide extensive governmental services; and to preserve American honor against international threats and yet keep the peace. When presidents extend their power, they are chastised for being imperial; when they fail to offer decisive leadership, they are considered weak and ineffective.

Even the most powerful American presidents have rarely been able to dictate the political agenda. They have had to lead; and leadership in a democratic society requires an ability to persuade without being tiresome, a capacity to administer without getting lost in details, and a sense of when to compromise and when to stand one's ground. The office is a complex mixture of authority and constraints, too subtle to capture in any one theoretical model. Some presidents have mastered the office; some have been mastered by it.

Commentators on the presidency in the 1950s and 1960s stressed its great powers and the capacity of its occupant to accomplish great things. Franklin D. Roosevelt (1933–1945) was the model—a president who dominated Congress, shepherded through an ambitious reform agenda, centralized decision-making in his own hands, fully exercised his powers as commander in chief, and inspired the nation with his speeches. Roosevelt's presidency influenced many to regard the office in heroic terms.

The fall from political grace of Lyndon Johnson (1963–1969) over Vietnam and Richard Nixon (1969–1974) over Watergate led later scholars of the office to warn against the dangers of an imperial presidency. Responding to the mood of the general public, Congress in the mid-1970s passed a series of laws constraining the president's power. The two presidents of that period, Gerald Ford (1974–1977) and Jimmy Carter (1977–1981), thus besieged, appeared to be weak. Although weakened by the Iran-contra affair toward the end of his term, President Ronald Reagan (1981–1989) restored some personal power to the office, but not its institutional authority. George H. W. Bush (1989–1993), who was unable to exert the mastery over domestic and economic policy that he had shown in the Desert Storm operation, was defeated for reelection. Bill Clinton (1993–2001), although elected twice, tarnished the image of the presidency when his difficulties with marital fidelity and misleading testimony led him to become only the second president to be impeached by the House of Representatives. New directions in American foreign policy, particularly in regard to terrorism and war, largely shaped the presidency of George W. Bush (2001–2009). President Barack Obama's (2009–2017) challenges ranged from handling a massive recession to winding down two wars. It remains to be seen how history will judge his efforts. President Donald Trump (2017–2021) faced the difficulty of a very polarized electorate and tackling the presidency with no prior political experience. These challenges led to his impeachment for asking a foreign power to aid his reelection effort, a second impeachment for inciting insurrection in January of 2021, and his inability to reassure the nation and lead during a crisis. President Joe Biden (2021–) has inherited a challenging pandemic, and it remains to be seen what other challenges he will encounter.

10.1 The President and Symbolic Leadership

chief of state

The role the president plays as the ceremonial head of the nation that can also make the president a symbol of national unity during times of crisis

head of government

The chief executive officer of a government (The president is the head of government in the United States.)

America has no purely symbolic head of state. Unlike most Western democracies, America does not separate the ceremonial **chief of state** from the actual **head of government**. We have no constitutional monarch, as in Great Britain, the Netherlands, and Sweden, and no ribbon-cutting ceremonial president, as in Germany, Italy, and Israel. The American president is both monarch and prime minister, reigning as well as ruling.

As the head of state, the president in a single week may meet with the winners of the high school Voice of Democracy essay contest, honor the teacher of the year, and prepare a humorous speech for the Washington Gridiron Club. Although a president usually spends no more than one or two hours a week on such activities, they are not as trivial as they may sound. Such ceremonies are important to a nation's morale, its sense of unity, and its recognition of common values.

The ceremonial presidency also has a political dimension. Because the president is our only symbolic head of state, the office carries with it a considerable fund of public goodwill and support. Presidents, no matter how narrow their election victory, find that in the weeks and months after assuming office they are the objects of public adoration. According to opinion polls, their approval rating is rarely as high again.

During this honeymoon period some presidents have successfully translated public goodwill into notable political victories. Franklin Roosevelt, in his first hundred days, persuaded Congress to pass the bulk of his economic recovery program. Lyndon Johnson,

President Donald Trump speaks on November 4, 2020 at an event at the White House.

soon after succeeding John Kennedy (1961–1963), pushed through Congress the far-reaching Civil Rights Act of 1964 (see Chapter 3). Ronald Reagan, in the months following his first inauguration, won major victories on budget and tax issues.

In times of international crisis, the public will often rally to support the office. When the nation perceives itself to be threatened or to have been wronged, the president is the symbol of unity. After the Japanese attack on Pearl Harbor in 1941, Franklin Roosevelt's popularity rose 12 percent. After the Korean War broke out in 1950, Harry Truman's (1945–1953) rose 9 percent. Even after the ill-fated Bay of Pigs invasion in Cuba in 1961, John Kennedy's support increased 12 percent. After the hostages were seized in Iran in 1979, Jimmy Carter's popularity increased a dramatic 31 percent. Immediately after hostilities commenced in the Gulf War in 1991, George H. W. Bush's approval rating soared to 89 percent. His son's turnaround was even more dramatic. George W. Bush saw his approval rating move from 51 percent just before September 11, 2001, to 90 percent just after. Yet, when the United States became bogged down in a seemingly interminable war in Iraq, Bush's approval rating dipped to an abysmal 28 percent.

The fusion of symbolic and political authority in this office can result, however, in a distorted public image of what its occupant can achieve. Just as the public will rally to the president in a time of crisis, so will people frequently blame the president when events sour. Presidential popularity is often directly related to whether the news is good or bad. In other words, given the symbolic nature of the office, the public may both credit and blame a president for events over which he or she has little control.

Since the presidency has both symbolic and substantive power, a paradox is built into the office. The president is expected to be both the symbol of national unity and the intensely political leader of the executive branch. Inevitably, the president must promote solutions to problems that will alienate some faction of the public, and symbolic leadership will be sacrificed by the need for substantive leadership. The result is that presidential popularity frequently will decline from the beginning of a president's term to the end of it.

Dwight Eisenhower (1953–1961), Ronald Reagan (1981–1989), and Bill Clinton (1993–2001) were exceptions to the rule; they seemed to be able to reconcile the two roles. All three completed two full terms and left office as popular as they entered (see Table 10.1). Eisenhower avoided taking on issues that he knew would cost him support, such as civil rights, and jealously protected his political goodwill. Reagan took controversial positions, but his reassuring personality and rhetorical skills generated much public trust. Bill Clinton was often mired in personal scandal, but the public was largely able to separate

their disapproval of the president's personal life from their enthusiasm for his leadership skills and success in guiding the economy. All three were fortunate in avoiding protracted and unresolved military conflicts and in presiding over a period of general prosperity. The latter, above all, may be the key to presidential popularity.

Table 10.1 Public Approval Ratings of Presidents Roosevelt to Trump

Public approval ratings usually vary widely during a president's time in office. Sometimes they reflect the president's handling of events. At other times, they reflect public frustration over events largely out of a president's control.

	Beginning of Term	End of Term	High	Low	Average
Franklin Roosevelt*	—	—	84	54	75
Harry Truman	87	31	87	23	43
Dwight Eisenhower	68	59	79	49	65
John Kennedy	72	58	83	56	71
Lyndon Johnson	79	49	80	35	55
Richard Nixon	59	24	68	24	49
Gerald Ford	71	53	71	37	47
Jimmy Carter	66	34	75	21	47
Ronald Reagan	51	63	68	35	52
George H. W. Bush	51	49	89	32	61
Bill Clinton	58	65	73	37	55
George W. Bush	57	32	90	25	49
Barack Obama	67	59	67	40	48
Donald Trump	45	34	49	34	41

*Polls taken 1938–1943 only.

SOURCE: The Gallup Organization, 2021. Copyright © 2021 Gallup, Inc.

10.2   The President and the Constitution

To understand the presidency, one must start with the Constitution. As with members of Congress, discussed in Chapter 9, the Constitution is specific with regard to who may be president.

Only **natural-born citizens**, not **naturalized citizens**, qualify. Article II is the only place in which the Constitution distinguishes between one kind of citizenship and another. (A natural-born citizen is one who has American citizenship by birth, although it is unclear whether a person born abroad of American parents qualifies as natural-born within the meaning of the Constitution. A naturalized citizen is an alien who has become a citizen by virtue of a procedure established by Congress.) Moreover, a president must be thirty-five years of age or older and a resident of the United States for at least fourteen years.

Unlike representatives, who serve terms of two years, and senators, who serve terms of six, presidents have four-year terms. Although the Constitution in 1787 placed no limit on the number of terms a president could serve, George Washington's preference for a maximum of two terms set a tradition that remained unbroken until Franklin Roosevelt ran for his third term in 1940 and was then elected to a fourth term in 1944. Mainly in response to Roosevelt's multiple terms, the **Twenty-second Amendment** (1951) banned any future president from being elected president "more than twice." This amendment prohibits not only a third successive term but also an additional term even if a gap exists between the first two.

10.2a   Executive Power

The Constitution confers many powers on the Congress, but few substantive powers on the president. Indeed, Article I, which established Congress, is more than two times the length of Article II, which created the presidency. Section 1 of Article II begins with the **vesting clause**: "The executive Power shall be vested in a President of the United States." What do these words define? Does the phrase *executive power* give the president an inherent authority to meet emergencies in the absence of any specific constitutional or legislative mandate?

Presidents have interpreted this power differently throughout history. At one extreme, President William Howard Taft (1909–1913) construed his powers narrowly. Taft claimed, "The president can exercise no power which cannot be fairly and reasonably traced to some specific grant of constitutional or legislative power." By contrast, President Theodore Roosevelt (1901–1909), Taft's predecessor, argued that the president could "do anything that the needs of the nation demanded unless such action was forbidden by the Constitution or by the laws."[1] Roosevelt's broad interpretation of the office became known as the **stewardship theory**, and Taft's narrow interpretation as the **constitutional theory**.

Between these somewhat extreme views is the more balanced approach of Supreme Court Justice Robert H. Jackson, put forth in the steel seizure case: "When the President acts in absence of either a congressional grant or denial of authority ... there is a zone of twilight in which he and Congress may have concurrent authority." Jackson implied that the Court would decide such constitutional boundary disputes on the basis of "the imperatives of events and contemporary imponderables rather than on abstract theories of law."[2]

natural-born citizen
A person actually born in the United States

naturalized citizen
A person, born in another country, who becomes a citizen of the United States by a procedure set by Congress

Twenty-second Amendment
Ratified in 1951; it limits the president to two terms in office

vesting clause
The first clause of Article II; confers executive power in the president

stewardship theory
An expansive theory of presidential power, put forth by Theodore Roosevelt, that holds that the president can undertake any act as long as it is not prohibited by a specific provision of the Constitution or statutory law

constitutional theory
The concept, associated with President William Howard Taft, that the president cannot exercise any power unless it is based on a specific constitutional provision or legislative grant

Justice Jackson was close to the mark. Presidents since George Washington (1789–1797) have all possessed nearly identical formal constitutional powers, yet some have been far more influential than others. The reason comes from the *plasticity* of the presidency—the tendency of the office to be molded according to the energy and personality of its occupant in combination with the needs and challenges of the day.

POLITICAL CONTROVERSIES

Election 2020: A Presidential Election Breaks New Ground

On January 20, 2021, Joseph R. Biden Jr. was sworn in as the forty-sixth president of the United States. Having a new president is always an important event in and of itself, but the path to the presidency in 2020 was unprecedented in many ways.

In terms of demographics, the election marked only the third time a woman had been nominated as the vice presidential candidate by a major party. Both Democrat Geraldine Ferraro (1984) and Republican Sarah Palin (2008) were unsuccessful, but in 2020 Democrat Kamala Harris broke this glass ceiling—becoming both the first woman and first woman of color to be elected vice president. As for the presidency, Joe Biden became only the second Catholic to attain the office (John F. Kennedy having been the first) and, at 78, became the oldest person to assume the office.

The campaign also featured a degree of diversity rarely seen in a national political race. In the Democratic presidential primary season, no fewer than twenty-nine candidates vied for the party's nomination in a series of debates, caucuses, and primaries. The diverse field included multiple candidates of color, women,

and the first LGBTQ candidate—Pete Buttigieg—to garner delegates for a major party. Seven candidates earned at least some delegates and eventual winner Biden did not secure enough delegates for his party's nod until early June. Due to social distancing restrictions for COVID-19, many primary elections had to be postponed, and some states cancelled in-person voting entirely. The Democratic Convention was pushed back over a month and then held largely online.

On the Republican side, the contest was essentially over before it started. Having an incumbent eligible for reelection, the Republicans did what parties typically do in this situation and renominated Donald Trump with little serious opposition. This made pandemic-related changes to the primaries less significant, but the Republicans did make the unusual move of not writing a party platform, as they had done in presidential election years dating back to 1860, choosing instead to reaffirm the platform they had used in 2016.

The general election campaign featured unique elements as well—a planned series of three presidential debates had to be scaled back to two after President Trump contracted COVID-19, and the single vice presidential debate featured a wall of plexiglass between the two candidates for social distancing purposes. Many states chose to greatly expand options for mail balloting or early voting in order to decrease the risk of spreading disease.

Both candidates faced some degree of controversy as well. Joe Biden was accused by Trump of having a hand

in his son Hunter's business dealings in the Ukraine while serving as vice president. This topic itself had been the subject of President Trump's withholding of military aid to the Ukraine, which had led to his impeachment at the end of 2019. This scandal and others led a number of Republicans to avoid backing the first impeached president to run for reelection. Some of these Republicans formed a political action committee called the Lincoln Project to run advertisements endorsing Joe Biden.

An era of intense partisanship and these negative portraits of both nominees led many Americans to distrust and dislike the two candidates. In the weeks leading up to the election, just 49 percent of Americans had a favorable image of Joe Biden and only 45 percent had a favorable view of Donald Trump.[1]

The election itself—on November 3, 2020—was special in that it featured the largest number of voters in American history. Over 100 million voters cast their ballots early, and the total number of votes for president approached 160 million—about two-thirds of the voter-eligible population, a rate that had not been achieved in over 100 years. The popular vote was not particularly close, with Joe Biden collecting more than 5 million more votes than Donald Trump. Ultimately, the electoral vote was not particularly close either, with Biden's 306 to 232 edge equaling that of Trump's 2016 victory over Hillary Clinton.

What made the election so tense, and prevented a clear outcome for several days afterward, was that the

margin of victory was exceedingly small in several swing states, and the ballot counting procedures for mail-in ballots meant that some of these states took days to report their totals. Finally, four days after voting had ended, a clear picture took shape: Biden had emerged victorious by winning four different swing states by 1 percent or less of the vote.

But media outlets calling the election for Biden did not end the contest for some. As he had in 2016, throughout the 2020 race Trump refused to say that he would accept the results of the presidential election if he did not win, an action that some saw as undermining one of the core principles of American democracy— the peaceful transfer of power. True to form, Trump refused to accept defeat even weeks after the election, filing lawsuits to challenge the outcome in several close states, calling the election "rigged," leveling unfounded charges of widespread voter fraud, and encouraging his supporters to protest.

What do you remember most about the 2020 presidential election? What other important events can you recall, or have you read about, from previous presidential races? What changes do you think you will see in the 2024 race? If you were eligible to vote, did you? Why or why not?

1. The Gallup Organization, "Favorability: People in the News," October 27, 2020, https://news.gallup.com/poll/1618/Favorability-People-News.aspx.

10.2b The Power of Appointment

Section 2 of Article II states that the president "shall nominate, and by and with the Advice and Consent of the Senate, shall appoint Ambassadors, other public Ministers and Consuls, Judges of the Supreme Court, and all other Officers of the United States." For positions that require confirmation, the Senate generally allows presidents to select people with whom they feel comfortable personally and ideologically. The Senate restricts itself in most cases to the personal qualifications of the nominee and to any possible conflicts of interest.

The president's power to appoint also affects the judicial branch because the president appoints Supreme Court justices and all federal judges. These judges serve until they retire or, in rare circumstances, are impeached. Franklin Roosevelt's nine appointments to the Supreme Court changed its character for a generation, and Ronald Reagan's three appointments and George H. W. Bush's two gave the Court a decidedly conservative cast in the early 1990s. Although this was tempered somewhat by Clinton's two appointments, the balance of the Court remained an important issue through the 1996, 2000, and 2004 elections, an unusually lengthy period when no justices retired (see Chapter 12). This drought finally ended in 2005–2006 when George W. Bush appointed two new justices after Justice Sandra Day O'Connor retired and Chief Justice William Rehnquist passed away. The appointment power was again in the forefront in 2016 when the Senate's Republican majority refused to hold hearings or vote to confirm President Obama's Supreme Court nominee following the death of Justice Antonin Scalia (see "Politics and Ideas: The Politics of Judicial Vacancies" in Chapter 12). President Trump filled three Supreme Court seats during his single term in office, moving the balance of the Court in a conservative direction.

10.2c The Removal Power

The Supreme Court in *Myers v. United States*[3] declared that the president's power to remove non–civil service appointees was unrestricted and beyond the reach of Congress. Later the Court ruled in *Humphrey's Executor v. United States*[4] that President Roosevelt could not fire a member of the Federal Trade Commission (FTC), an independent regulatory commission, because of policy differences. The FTC Act specified that the president could remove a commissioner only for "inefficiency, neglect of duty, or malfeasance in

office." The Court ruled that the president's removal powers applied only to "purely executive offices." The FTC (and by inference all independent regulatory commissions) was a "quasi-legislative" and "quasi-judicial" agency, according to the Court; and the president's removal authority did not apply. (These commissions are discussed in greater detail in Chapter 11.) In 2020, the Court greatly weakened this precedent when it ruled in *Seila Law v. Consumer Fraud Protection Bureau* that President Trump could remove the director of the Consumer Fraud Protection Bureau (CFPB) despite Congress having created the position as a five-year term that could only be dismissed for "inefficiency, neglect of duty, or malfeasance."[5] The Roberts Court distinguished the FTC from the CFPB, finding that the latter was a much more purely executive office, placing its directorship within reach of the president's removal power.

Presidents cannot dismiss career civil servants except for cause (misconduct, inefficiency, incompetence, or criminal conduct). They can, however, transfer or demote them, subject to the procedures of the civil service laws. Presidents can also work through the budgetary process to reduce or eliminate funding for a particular agency, thus eliminating numerous jobs.

10.2d   The Power to Pardon

Article II, Section 2, gives the president the exclusive power to grant "Reprieves and Pardons for Offenses against the United States, except in Cases of Impeachment." The power includes the president's right to grant a full pardon, a conditional pardon, clemency for a class of people (amnesty), a commutation or reduction of a sentence, and the remission of fines. This power is limited to violations of federal laws and does not apply to state or local laws.

The use of this power rarely gains headlines, but it did in 1974, 1992, and 2020. On September 8, 1974, President Ford granted a complete pardon to former President Richard Nixon for any misdeeds that he might have committed during his presidency, which, of course, included the Watergate affair. Many criticized Ford's action as improper because formal charges had yet to be brought against Nixon. Without the benefit of trial, many argued, the full facts in Nixon's case and in the whole Watergate affair were unlikely to be uncovered. Others thought that Ford spared the country the unpleasant and disruptive sight of a former president placed on trial. On Christmas Eve 1992, President Bush pardoned former Secretary of Defense Caspar Weinberger and five others involved in the Iran-contra affair. The special prosecutor in the case, Lawrence E. Walsh, called the pardons a "cover-up" of misdeeds. Bush argued that Walsh's prosecutions did not represent legitimate law enforcement but were "the criminalization of policy differences." In 2020 President Trump commuted the forty-month sentence of his former adviser Roger Stone, who had been convicted of seven federal charges as part of Special Counsel Robert Mueller's investigation of Russian interference into the 2016 presidential election. Though Trump was within his constitutional authority to issue the commutation, some found it ethically dubious as Stone's crime was ostensibly committed to benefit then-candidate

President Richard Nixon's resignation, August 9, 1974

(White House photo, courtesy Richard Nixon Presidential Library via Wikimedia.)

Trump. Notwithstanding the merits of their decisions, Ford, Bush, and Trump were acting within their constitutional powers. The courts have established that a presidential pardon might be granted prior to a conviction or even an indictment.[6]

President Obama's pardons and grants of clemency were notable for their volume rather than the specific individuals involved. Over the course of his two terms in office, Obama granted clemency to or pardoned nearly two thousand individuals—more than his seven most recent predecessors combined.[7] Most of these pardons were for offenders who had already served lengthy sentences, and the actions were seen as a critique of harsh sentencing laws that the president wanted to see reformed. President Trump took a different tack—pardoning high-profile individuals like former vice presidential chief of staff Scooter Libby and former Arizona sheriff Joe Arpaio or flirting with the idea of pardoning people (including himself) who were swept up in the investigation of his own potential misdeeds, as described earlier in this section.

10.3 The President and the Executive Branch

In order to formulate and implement policy, presidents must appoint a considerable number of senior officials to whom they will turn for support and assistance. Who are these people? They include cabinet secretaries, undersecretaries, and the administrators and deputies of the various independent agencies—all of whom require Senate confirmation. These officials, plus about sixty senior White House aides whom the president can appoint without Senate confirmation, make up **the administration**—the people who direct government policy on the president's behalf.

10.3a The Cabinet

Despite its prestige, the president's cabinet (see Table 10.2) is not a collective high-level decision-making body. Because ours is not a parliamentary government, the president is not obligated to share responsibility with the cabinet. Its officers serve at the president's discretion, and the president is under no obligation to consult with them individually or collectively.

Individual officers can have great significance for the president. As will be discussed in Chapter 11, they serve as the president's arm in controlling the massive federal bureaucracy and in imposing his political priorities upon it. The cabinet also provides a mechanism for bringing into the administration people who represent different social, economic, and political constituencies. Often presidents will make appointments from constituent groups who did not support them but whose support they need.

After several years in office, presidents become more concerned with controlling the bureaucracy than with decorating their cabinet with people whose value is more symbolic than substantive. Thus, they look for cabinet officers who may be less well-known but will be more loyal.

The selection of the right cabinet is a difficult problem. Few cabinet officers, whatever their temperament or background, can serve simply as the president's loyal agent. They must also represent to the president the perspective of their department and the *constituent groups* it serves. For example, the secretary of labor should have a good working

the administration

The president plus senior officials such as cabinet officials, undersecretaries, and the administrators and deputies of the various independent agencies

Table 10.2   The Cabinet, 2021

The cabinet comprises the heads of the fifteen executive departments and certain other officials in the executive branch to whom the president has accorded cabinet rank. The vice president also participates in meetings of the cabinet, and from time to time the president may invite others to participate in the discussion of particular subjects.

Vice President	Secretary of Veterans Affairs
Secretary of State	Secretary of Homeland Security
Secretary of the Treasury	Administrator of the Environmental Protection Agency
Secretary of Defense	Director of the Office of Management and Budget
Attorney General	Director of National Intelligence
Secretary of the Interior	Director of the Central Intelligence Agency
Secretary of Agriculture	United States Trade Representative
Secretary of Commerce	United States Ambassador to the United Nations
Secretary of Labor	Chair of the Council of Economic Advisors
Secretary of Health and Human Services	Administrator of the Small Business Administration
Secretary of Housing and Urban Development	Presidential Science Advisor and Director of the
Secretary of Transportation	Office of Science and Technology Policy
Secretary of Energy	President's Chief of Staff
Secretary of Education	United States Special Presidential Envoy for Climate

SOURCE: https://www.whitehouse.gov/administration/cabinet/

---

relationship with organized labor; the secretary of the interior should have a solid relationship with the developers or the environmentalists, preferably both; and the secretary of agriculture must have a good rapport with farmers and the agribusiness community.

Not all cabinet officers are created equal. The cabinet is often divided into an **inner cabinet** and an **outer cabinet**.[8] The inner group consists of secretaries of state, defense, and the treasury, as well as the attorney general. These people handle issues of broad importance: national security, the economy, and the administration of justice. Of necessity, they have a direct and close working relationship with the president. The outer group is made up of the remaining members. These officers deal with sharply defined programs and are subject to considerable pressure from client groups. Only when a crucial issue arises will they gain frequent access to the president, and such instances are the exception. This lack of access by members of the outer cabinet often leads to a sense of isolation from the president, gravitation toward the constituent interests served by their departments, and a strained relationship with the White House staff.

To avoid such problems, President Reagan established the Economic Policy Council and the Domestic Policy Council, chaired, respectively, by the treasury secretary and the attorney general. The councils consisted of relevant cabinet officers and senior White House aides. They were designed to coordinate policy and to keep members of the outer cabinet in close contact with the president. When these councils met to make a crucial policy decision, the president would chair the meeting. Satisfied with this arrangement, subsequent presidents have maintained this system, though the Economic Policy Council was replaced by the National Economic Council in 1993.

From the president's perspective, the ideal cabinet member should be clearly in charge of his or her department, sensitive to the department's constituency, able to distinguish between the president's interest and those of that constituency, and able to work well with

inner cabinet

Cabinet officers whose departments handle issues of broad national importance, including the secretaries of state, defense, and the treasury, and the attorney general

outer cabinet

Cabinet officers whose departments deal with sharply defined programs and are subject to considerable pressure from client groups

Congress. Obviously, the job requires well-developed administrative and political skills. President Clinton was anxious to have a cabinet that "looked like America." Thus, out of sixteen cabinet-rank positions, Clinton appointed five women, four African Americans, and two Hispanics. However, his cabinet included a higher percentage of millionaires than did President Bush's cabinet. President George W. Bush indicated his priorities by affording cabinet-level status to the director of the Office of Management and Budget, the director of the National Drug Control Policy, and the U.S. Trade Representative. After the September 2001 terrorist attacks, Bush created the Office of Homeland Security. President Obama, whose lack of national experience had been a campaign issue for his opponents, named to his cabinet a number of former senators, governors, and other seasoned politicians, including Senator Hillary Rodham Clinton—his chief rival during the 2008 Democratic primaries—as secretary of state. One of Donald Trump's early actions after being elected president was to nominate Senator Jeff Sessions (R-AL) as attorney general. Trump later lamented this choice, criticizing Sessions for recusing himself from the Special Counsel investigation into Russia's role in the 2016 presidential election. Trump eventually fired Sessions in November 2018. Trump also made true on his campaign promise to "listen to the generals" by appointing retired general James Mattis as secretary of defense and retired general John Kelly as secretary of homeland security and later as Trump's chief of staff, though he eventually fired or accepted resignations from both men.

10.3b   The White House Staff

Prior to the presidency of Franklin Roosevelt, White House aides played no role in policy. They were clerks—managers of files, appointments, and correspondence. Cabinet officers were the president's primary source of advice and counsel. Today the president's closest confidants are rarely cabinet members, who spend much of their time managing their departments. Presidents now rely heavily on their White House staffs. They select for senior White House positions people with whom they are comfortable and with whom they share a common background and political perspective. The loyalty of these people is not to a political party, an ideology, or their own political careers but to the president, first and last.

Responsibilities of senior White House aides involve the following tasks:

- Giving the president broad-gauged advice not influenced by a departmental or interest group perspective

- Setting legislative strategy

- Keeping check on the bureaucracy

- Reviewing the performance of cabinet and subcabinet officials

- Planning the president's time

- Saying no for the president to people who want something that he or she cannot give

Presidents manage the White House to suit their own personalities. Eisenhower and Nixon preferred a formalistic system and a highly structured staff. Eisenhower, who had spent most of his adult life in the military, was comfortable with a clear chain of command. At the opposite end of the spectrum was the competitive style of Franklin Roosevelt. Roosevelt had no rigid chain of command and was, in fact, his own chief of staff. He insisted on surrounding himself with strong-minded generalists who had divergent points of view and who could work on a variety of problems.

POLITICS AND IDEAS

A Six-Year Term for Presidents?

In 1913, the Senate passed a resolution favoring a single six-year term for the president. Earlier presidents had advocated it as well. Although the idea has never been adopted, it continues to arouse interest. Is it a good idea? People who favor the proposal argue that it would free the president of reelection concerns and allow him or her to rise above partisan politics. A president could escape the lure of political expediency. Had not President Nixon been so concerned with reelection, some speculate, the Watergate affair might not have happened.

Should a president be above politics and unconcerned about reelection? Some commentators say no. The prospect of an election concentrates the mind of a political leader on issues of importance to the general public. In a democracy this should not be a fault. A concern for reelection would prevent presidents from becoming too isolated from the mood of the country. Besides, a single six-year term would make a president a "lame duck" from the very first day in the White House.

Another argument for the proposal maintains that presidents are rarely effective over two terms. Once reelected to a second term, particularly if by a wide margin, presidents can become intoxicated with their own power and overreach their authority. Four modern presidents made such miscalculations early in their second terms. Franklin Roosevelt introduced his court-packing scheme to Congress; Lyndon Johnson began escalating American involvement in Vietnam; Richard Nixon engaged in a cover-up of the Watergate affair; and Ronald Reagan became entangled in the Iran-contra affair.

Another argument against the idea came from Woodrow Wilson, who maintained that six years is too long for an ineffective president and too short for an outstanding one. Would a single six-year term allow a president to act like a statesperson, or would it contribute to his or her isolation from the public? Do limits on presidential terms (including the Twenty-second Amendment limiting presidents to two terms) thwart democracy, or do they protect us from potential usurpers of power?

Although the elder President Bush appointed a chief of staff, John Sununu, Bush's style was closer to Roosevelt's than Nixon's. Bush relied upon a process known as **multiple advocacy**, which was designed to allow the president to hear all sides of an issue. White House aides would stage policy debates for the president's benefit. Dubbed "scheduled train wrecks," these debates would involve senior officials with sharply differing views on such issues as clean air proposals. President Bush, who relished these debates, would take notes, interrupt with questions, and afterward solicit the views of others in the administration or Congress. With his passion for secrecy and surprise, Bush would often conceal his final decision from everyone until he was ready for a public announcement.

multiple advocacy

A system of advising the president in which all sides of an issue are presented

10.3c The Executive Office of the President

Executive Office of the President (EOP)

Created in 1939 to serve as the managerial arm of the presidency; includes such agencies as the National Security Council, the Office of Management and Budget, and the Council of Economic Advisers

Across a small side street from the White House is an imposing Victorian building that houses part of the **Executive Office of the President (EOP)**. The EOP was created in 1939 as the managerial arm of the modern presidency when a presidential commission uttered its famous recommendation: "The president needs help." In its early years, the EOP consisted of six administrative assistants and three advisory bodies—the National Resources Planning Board, the Liaison Office for Personnel Management, and the Office of Government Reports—all of which are now defunct.

The structure of the EOP reflects the dominant issues of the time. In the 1940s its agencies, such as the Office of Defense Mobilization, mirrored concerns with war and defense planning. In the 1960s and 1970s, the EOP agencies (Cost of Living Council,

Council on Environmental Quality, Energy Resources Council) paralleled the national concern with the problems of energy, the environment, and inflation.

During the Reagan years the EOP was pared back. One of its permanent agencies, the **Office of Management and Budget (OMB)**, became one of its most important. Created in 1921 as the Bureau of the Budget and renamed the Office of Management and Budget in 1970, the OMB has three major responsibilities:

1. Helping the president to develop the annual budget that gets submitted to Congress

2. Serving as a clearinghouse for legislative proposals submitted to the president by the various departments and ensuring that all such proposals are consistent with presidential objectives

3. Monitoring the implementation of the president's programs and making sure they are administered efficiently

Presidents usually employ the OMB to suit their own needs. Because the Nixon administration was interested in controlling the bureaucracy and in mobilizing the executive branch to support its programs, the OMB had the primary responsibility of supervising administration programs in some detail. Under Ford and Carter, the OMB played a relatively minor role.

During the Reagan and elder Bush administrations, OMB enjoyed a significant comeback. Richard Darman, Bush's OMB director, was a powerful member of Bush's administration, shaping the contours of the budget and negotiating budget and tax policy with Congress. Mick Mulvaney served as President Trump's OMB director and played a significant role in shaping policy before moving on to serve as acting chief of staff. As long as budgetary politics dominate a president's agenda, the OMB will remain a vital arm of the presidency.

The **National Security Council (NSC)**, established by the National Security Act of 1947, is an essential part of the EOP. It is designed to provide the president with advice and policy coordination on questions of national security. Its members are the president, the vice president, the secretary of state, the secretary of defense, and other officials the president may wish to add. As with the OMB, presidents use the NSC to suit their own styles.

Truman and Eisenhower employed the NSC to coordinate policy, but not to formulate it. Both relied on strong secretaries of state for policy advice. Under President Kennedy the council fell into disuse and was rarely convened. Instead, Kennedy relied on the NSC staff headed by the national security adviser to provide him with information and expertise.

When President Nixon appointed Dr. Henry Kissinger to be his national security adviser in 1969, the role of the NSC grew substantially. With Nixon's encouragement, Kissinger and his staff not only dominated policy making but also became deeply involved in the actual conduct of foreign policy, shutting out the State Department of Nixon's major diplomatic initiatives. Kissinger conducted the negotiations that led to Nixon's historic visit to China, the Vietnam armistice, and the SALT I treaty.

The NSC's involvement in foreign policy operations reached its height during the Iran-contra affair. Congressional restrictions had barred direct aid to the Nicaraguan contras, who were fighting to overturn the pro-Soviet Sandinista government. Frustrated

Office of Management and Budget

An agency in the Executive Office of the President that provides the president with budgetary information and advice and is responsible for compiling the president's annual budget proposal to Congress

National Security Council (NSC)

Designed to provide the president with advice and policy coordination on questions of national security; members include the president, the vice president, the secretaries of state and defense, and any other officials the president may add

by the restrictions, President Reagan authorized the NSC staff to seek contra assistance from friendly governments such as Israel and Saudi Arabia. Marine Lieutenant Colonel Oliver North, a senior NSC staffer, supervised this effort as well as those of private domestic groups seeking to provide funds for the contras. The president also authorized the NSC to oversee the secret sale of arms to Iran to encourage the release of our hostages. Without the president's apparent knowledge, part of the profits of that sale were diverted to contras. The affair seriously diminished Reagan's public support and resulted in extensive congressional investigations and lengthy criminal trials.

A presidential commission to examine the Iran-contra affair was appointed by Reagan and headed by former Texas senator John Tower. The Tower Commission recommended that the NSC "focus on advice and management, not implementation and execution." The first President Bush's NSC adviser, Brent Scowcroft, a member of the Tower Commission, appeared to follow this advice and kept the NSC out of covert operations. Under Scowcroft, the NSC functioned as an honest broker, coordinating advice from the bureaucracy and providing the president with policy options. When George W. Bush appointed Condoleezza Rice to be his national security adviser, she became both the first woman and first African American to hold this post. Donald Trump nominated retired Army Lieutenant General Michael Flynn to be his national security advisor, but Flynn held the post only a few weeks before resigning after it became known that he had misled the vice president and lied to the FBI regarding conversations he had with Russian diplomats prior to Trump's inauguration. Retired general H. R. McMaster held the post next, until he was replaced by former diplomat John Bolton in 2018. Bolton, in turn, was replaced by Robert O'Brien in 2019.

Swearing-in ceremony of Henry Kissinger as the secretary of state, September 22, 1973.

(National Archives via Wikimedia)

Find out about presidential history and current executive policy agendas at the official White House website.

http://www.bvtlab.com/Ma878

The **Council of Economic Advisers (CEA)**, established by the Employment Act of 1946, is another permanent part of the EOP. Consisting of three members and a small staff, its chairperson, usually a prominent academic economist, is the predominant figure. The CEA's primary task is to analyze economic issues, make economic forecasts, and prepare the president's annual economic report to Congress. The CEA can be an important source of economic advice for the president; however, it must share economic policy making with the OMB, the Treasury Department, and the Federal Reserve Board.

Council of Economic Advisers (CEA)

Established by the Employment Act of 1946 as a part of the Executive Office of the President; consists of a chairperson, usually a prominent academic economist, and two other members who have the primary task of analyzing economic issues for the president

The effectiveness of the CEA depends largely on the ability of the chair to gain the president's confidence and to translate obscure economic jargon into language the president can readily understand. President Reagan had little interest in the intricacies of economic policy; he let the CEA wither on the vine and even considered its abolition. George H. W. Bush, who had a fascination with details, frequently consulted with the CEA and let its chair become a major player in his administration.[9] Bill Clinton, who had promised in his campaign to focus on economic issues "like a laser," established a new National Economic Council to coordinate overall economic policy. It would have a status similar to the National Security Council. The chair of the CEA would now

POLITICAL CONTROVERSIES

Donald Trump: An Unconventional President

When Americans went to the polls and elected Donald J. Trump as president of the United States in 2016, they knew they were getting a different kind of president. His four years in office revealed both some anticipated and some unexpected features of his unique approach.

First, for good or ill, President Trump maintained many of the informal and antagonistic characteristics that defined candidate Trump. He maintained family members in his close inner circle—with his daughter Ivanka Trump serving as an adviser to the president and son-in-law Jared Kushner serving as a senior adviser to the president, both of which are positions within the Executive Office of the President. He continued his hostility to immigration in many forms—issuing a travel ban from many parts of the Muslim world, sending federal troops to the Mexican border to stop a reported caravan of immigrants, threatening to end birthright citizenship (a right guaranteed by the Fourteenth Amendment) via executive order, repeatedly taking steps to curtail the Deferred Action for Childhood Arrivals (DACA) program, and issuing a proclamation to limit immigration from countries with significant COVID-19 outbreaks. He also maintained an active and often bombastic Twitter account, often issuing tweets to his nearly 85 million followers in the early hours of the morning or using the platform to insult his adversaries as well as to make official announcements and set presidential policy. His

singular approach to the truth and his battles with the press continued as well. *The Washington Post* concluded that Trump made more than 20,000 false or misleading statements during his first three and one-half years in office, and Trump usually labeled negative stories about his administration as "fake news."[1]

Second, President Trump surprised many Washington insiders by "thinking outside the box"—or at least outside the Beltway. His approach to a number of important issues was unexpected. Sometimes Trump's fresh approach succeeded in attaining his objectives, such as his efforts to renegotiate the North American Free Trade Agreement (NAFTA). This tack led to drafting a new United States–Mexico–Canada Agreement (USMCA), which Trump argued would reduce America's trade deficit with the other partner nations. Other times, though, his efforts to cast off formal diplomacy in favor of strong-arm business tactics led him to bite off more than he could chew. This was the case in the trade war with the People's Republic of China. Trump launched the first salvo by instituting $34 billion worth of tariffs in mid-2018, citing intellectual property violations and a mounting trade imbalance.[2] China fired back almost immediately, and the two nations quickly escalated tariff threats that would affect hundreds of billions of dollars' worth of goods being imported into each nation by the other. Although the two sides eventually negotiated a trade deal that Trump touted, some experts warned that it "significantly hurt the American economy without solving the underlying economic concerns that the trade war was meant to resolve."[3] Still other unconventional actions will have longer-term consequences that remain to be seen—such as the president's ignoring of history and protocol in his efforts to dampen the nuclear threat posed by North Korea's

Kim Jong Un by meeting with the authoritarian dictator directly or his withdrawal from (rather than attempt to renegotiate) the Intermediate-Range Nuclear Forces (INF) Treaty because he believed Russia had "been violating it for many years."[4] Domestically, Trump's last full year in office was marked by a health pandemic and widespread protests for racial justice. In both cases the president's efforts to downplay serious issues had long-term consequences. Trump often disagreed with the government's health experts, for example, on issues like the benefits of wearing a face mask to help prevent the spread of COVID-19, a disease he contracted himself in October 2020.

Finally, and perhaps most significantly, President Trump spent nearly the entirety of his term in office under the specter of investigation—first by special counsel Robert Mueller and subsequently by Congress. While the FBI had been investigating potential Russian interference in the 2016 presidential election campaign since before the election itself, the investigation took a more serious turn in the spring of 2017, when Trump fired FBI Director James Comey and the Department of Justice responded by assigning Mueller to investigate, among other things, potential obstruction of justice and potential collusion between Russia and the Trump presidential campaign. Mueller's team indicted thirty-four individuals for federal crimes, eight of whom pled guilty or were convicted. Among the guilty were Trump's former campaign chairman, Paul Manafort, and his former National Security Advisor, Michael Flynn.[5] Although Mueller's final report did not draw a conclusion on whether or not the president had committed a crime, most Americans believed the investigation was warranted, and not a mere witch hunt, as the president himself had often claimed. According to opinion polls, 75 percent of Americans believed

Russia interfered in the 2016 presidential election, and 56 percent believed Trump himself acted either illegally or unethically in this matter.[6]

Congressional investigations of Donald Trump covered a variety of topics, but eventually zeroed in on a possible *quid pro quo* with Ukraine (see "The Trump Impeachment" in this chapter). Though a majority of Americans did not believe Trump should be removed from office, 54 percent thought it was definitely or probably true that President Trump "withheld U.S. aid to Ukraine until the Ukraine government agreed to investigate Joe Biden and his family."[7]

Whether you agreed or disagreed with his policy goals, President Trump undeniably provided a take

on the office of chief executive that was uniquely his own. What did you view most positively about the Trump administration? Why? What did you view most negatively? Why? What do you think will be the long-term legacy of this unconventional presidency?

1. "President Trump Has Made More Than 20,000 False or Misleading Claims," *The Washington Post,* July 13, 2020, https://www.washingtonpost.com /politics/2020/07/13/president-trump -has-made-more-than-20000-false-or -misleading-claims/ (August 10, 2020).

2. Ana Swanson, "Trump's Trade War with China Is Officially Underway," *The New York Times,* July 5, 2018, https://www.nytimes.com/2018/07/05 /business/china-us-trade-war-trump -tariffs.html (November 21, 2018).

3. Ryan Hass and Abraham Denmark, "More pain than gain: How the US-China trade war hurt America," The Brookings Institute, August 7, 2020, https://www.brookings.edu/blog/order -from-chaos/2020/08/07/more-pain-than -gain-how-the-us-china-trade-war-hurt -america/ (August 10, 2020).

4. "President Trump to Pull U.S. from Russia Missile Treaty," *BBC,* October 21, 2018, https://www.bbc.com/news/world-us -canada-45930206 (November 21, 2018).

5. Andrew Prokop, "All of Robert Mueller's Indictments and Plea Deals in the Russia Investigation So Far," *Vox,* October 10, 2018, https://www.vox.com/policy-and-politics /2018/2/20/17031772/mueller-indictments -grand-jury (November 21, 2018).

6. The Gallup Organization, "Russia," August 12, 2018, https://news.gallup.com /poll/1642/Russia.aspx (November 21, 2018); The Gallup Organization, "Three in 10 Say Trump Acted Illegally During 2016 Campaign," September 6, 2018, https://news.gallup.com/poll/241970 /three-say-trump-acted-illegally-during -2016-campaign.aspx (November 21, 2018).

7. The Gallup Organization, "The Presidency," November 14, 2019, https://news.gallup.com /poll/4729/Presidency.aspx (August 10, 2020).

Vice president-elect Kamala Harris, on December 4, 2020.

(vasilis asvestas / Shutterstock)

have to compete with yet another source of economic policy making. George W. Bush and Barack Obama relied on the CEA and many other economic experts as they led the country through the storms of recession.

10.3d The Vice President

Until 1941, when Franklin Roosevelt gave Henry Wallace a sizable policy role, vice presidents merely served in the ceremonial role as president and chief presiding officer of the Senate and had little influence on decisions in the White House. The office was a frequent target of ridicule and disdain, even by its occupants. The first vice president, John Adams, called it "the most insignificant office that ever the invention of man contrived or his imagination conceived."

Later vice presidents continued to find the job deeply frustrating. Harry Truman was not even aware of the existence of the secret atomic bomb project when he succeeded to the presidency upon Roosevelt's death. Richard Nixon, Eisenhower's vice president for two terms, served as partisan "hit man," making attacks on the Democrats that Eisenhower felt were beneath the dignity of the president to do himself. This same demeaning task Nixon later assigned to his own vice president, Spiro Agnew. Lyndon Johnson, who had been the powerful Senate majority leader, was given largely ceremonial responsibilities as John Kennedy's vice president. Johnson, a proud and sensitive man, felt humiliated in the job and considered himself merely a spectator in the Kennedy administration.

The experience of Walter Mondale as Jimmy Carter's vice president gave fresh hope that the office could become a vital part of the executive branch. Mondale served as President Carter's intimate adviser. He had an office in the White House West Wing, close to the president, and was given access to all important meetings and policy papers. Mondale had a private lunch every Monday with Carter so that he could give the president confidential and candid advice. By all accounts, Mondale was involved in all major policy decisions. The Carter–Mondale arrangement converted the vice presidency from an office without a role into that of a senior policy adviser to the president. The importance of the office was again revived when Dick Cheney stepped into the role in 2001. Publicly stating that he had no further political ambitions of his own, he became a key adviser to the president. Since George W. Bush had been elected with little foreign policy experience, Cheney's previous experience in Congress and as secretary of defense added weight to the administration in this important area. Joe Biden combined some of these previous roles as Barack Obama's vice president. A former senator with no future political ambitions, he added gravitas and experience to the administration. Well known for his verbal blunders, Biden was also able to be outspoken on issues in a manner that the president himself could (or should) not. As a former member of Congress and governor, Vice President Pence offered something that President Trump could not—political experience. His role included working with the legislature to find support for Trump administration policies. Vice President Kamala Harris brings a new perspective, as the first woman and first woman of color to hold the office.

(Cecil W. Stoughton, White House Photographer, via Wikimedia)

Lyndon B. Johnson takes the oath of office aboard Air Force One at Love Field Airport two hours and eight minutes after the assassination of John F. Kennedy. Jackie Kennedy (right), still in her blood-soaked clothes, looks on.

10.3e   Presidential Succession

Should a president be impeached and convicted, resign, or die in office, the vice president automatically becomes president and fills the remainder of the term. Should a president become disabled and unable to fulfill presidential duties, the **Twenty-fifth Amendment**, ratified in 1967, provided a mechanism whereby the vice president could serve as an acting president. Presidents can declare themselves disabled and can authorize the vice president to assume the presidency. Alternatively, the vice president and a majority of the cabinet can declare that the president is disabled, in which case the vice president also assumes the job. The president may claim at any time, however, that the disability is over and resume the office. Should the vice president and a majority of the cabinet disagree, the issue goes to Congress. If both houses decide by a two-thirds vote that the president is unfit to resume duties, the vice president continues as acting president.

The Twenty-fifth Amendment also established a mechanism to fill a vacancy in the vice presidency. During our nation's history, six vice presidents have died in office, two have resigned, and nine have succeeded to the presidency—in each case leaving the office vacant. The amendment now eliminates the possibility that the vacancy will stand for long. The president is authorized in the event of a vacancy to nominate a vice president,

Twenty-fifth Amendment
Ratified in 1967; provides the mechanism for the vice president to assume the presidency in the event of a presidential disability and the selection of a replacement for the vice president should that office become vacant

subject to confirmation by both houses of Congress. This procedure was first used in October 1973, when Spiro Agnew resigned because of allegations of misconduct. President Nixon selected Gerald Ford as vice president.

In the unlikely event of a simultaneous double vacancy in the presidency and the vice presidency, the **Presidential Succession Act of 1947** applies. It establishes the following line of succession: (1) the Speaker of the House; (2) the president pro tempore of the Senate; and (3) the cabinet secretaries in the chronological order of the establishment of their departments, beginning with the secretary of state and ending with the secretary of homeland security.

10.4 The President and Congress: Foreign Policy

In foreign policy the Constitution divides formal power between the president and Congress, but the president does maintain the initiative. The president negotiates treaties, mediates disputes, and proclaims friendship with new governments or works covertly to undermine them. Congress may reject these initiatives by refusing to ratify treaties, discouraging foreign arms sales, or outlawing covert activities. However, when presidents put their prestige on the line, as the elder President Bush did in securing support for his Gulf War policy, they generally prevail. Why is that? Congress fears eroding presidential influence in international negotiations, a fear that presidents use to their own advantage. Congress also lacks access to classified information and often defers to executive expertise. The reality is that Congress can influence foreign relations, but only the president can conduct them; thus the extent of Congress's influence is subject to the ebb and flow of history.

(White House photo by Paul Morse via Wikimedia)

President George Bush introduces the Joint Resolution to Authorize the Use of United States Armed Forces Against Iraq, October 2, 2002. The resolution was passed by both houses of Congress and signed into law two weeks later.

During the period from Pearl Harbor (1941) to the end of the Vietnam War (1973), the president dominated foreign policy, and congressional rebukes were rare and ineffective. The unpopularity of the Vietnam War, however, produced a subsequent public disdain for future military involvements and with it an end to the era of presidential domination. The president still had the leading role in foreign policy but no longer controlled the play.

Over President Nixon's veto in 1973, Congress passed the War Powers Resolution, requiring congressional approval after sixty days of any presidential decision to send troops into combat. In 1974 Congress passed the Hughes-Ryan Amendment, requiring congressional notification of covert operations conducted by the CIA. Emboldened by its newfound authority, Congress actually banned covert action in Angola from 1978 to 1983 and during the 1980s limited covert aid to the Nicaraguan contras. Presidential leadership in foreign policy now requires considerable skill and subtlety. Congress can be

Presidential Succession Act of 1947

Established the line of presidential succession after the vice president as follows: the Speaker of the House, the president pro tempore of the Senate, and the Cabinet secretaries in the order of the establishment of their departments

very independent unless a president carefully consults it and develops strong public support for his or her policies. That being said, threats to American national security are never taken lightly. When these risks are perceived, as in the early 2000s, Congress typically reacts by giving the president broad authority to act. Thus, George W. Bush received overwhelming Congressional support for his plan to invade Iraq. As with Vietnam, however, when the perceived threat recedes and public support for military actions begins to erode, presidents are often left on their own to defend their actions. Presidents since Nixon have uniformly disfavored the War Powers Resolution, questioning its authority. President Obama ignored it entirely in 2011 when he did not seek congressional approval after sixty days for troops he sent to Libya and in 2014 when he announced airstrikes and extended military action against the Islamic State of Iraq and Syria (ISIS).[10] President Trump, following his predecessors, only notified Congress after the fact when he authorized a drone strike to assassinate an Iranian general in 2020.

10.4a   Negotiating Treaties

By the terms of Article II of the Constitution, the president negotiates and signs treaties, subject to a vote of approval by two-thirds of the Senate. During the course of our history, the Senate has approved the vast majority of treaties. The most notable defeat came in 1919, when the Senate refused to ratify the Treaty of Versailles, which formally ended World War I and would have brought the United States into the League of Nations. This defeat provided a profound object lesson for future presidents.

President Woodrow Wilson (1913–1921), who negotiated the Treaty of Versailles, did not include a single senator from either party in the negotiating delegation, nor did he provide the Senate with information on the progress of the negotiations. In shutting the Senate out of the negotiating process, Wilson failed to build broad bipartisan support for the treaty.

Presidents Franklin Roosevelt and Harry Truman were careful to avoid Wilson's mistake and included both Democratic and Republican members of the Senate Foreign Relations Committee in the negotiations for the United Nations Treaty (1945) and the North Atlantic Treaty Organization (1949). During the decade that followed World War II, the Senate ratified without reservations or significant opposition mutual security treaties with over forty nations. Since then the Senate has become more jealous of its prerogatives; approval of important treaties is now rarely routine and often requires presidential concessions.

10.4b   Executive Agreements

Presidents can avoid the political brambles of Senate ratification by entering into executive agreements with foreign governments. These agreements do not require Senate approval. Theoretically, a treaty involves a legal relationship between nations, whereas an **executive agreement** is merely an understanding between heads of state. In practice, however, no distinction can be observed, and the Supreme Court has provided no clear guidelines.

In the early years of the Republic, executive agreements involved relatively minor matters, such as the settlement of claims American citizens had against foreign governments. Beginning with Franklin Roosevelt, however, executive agreements became a serious tool of foreign policy. In September 1940, Roosevelt agreed to trade fifty US destroyers to Great Britain in exchange for leases of naval bases on British territory in Newfoundland and the Caribbean. Toward the end of World War II, Roosevelt concluded

executive agreements
Agreements between heads of state that, unlike treaties, do not require approval by the Senate—there are no clear legal distinctions between the substance of a treaty and that of an executive agreement

a secret executive agreement with Joseph Stalin granting the Soviet Union territory and rights in the western Pacific previously belonging to China and Japan. In exchange Stalin agreed to enter the war against Japan.

Such secret agreements, unusual even in wartime, have now become almost commonplace. Of the 4,359 agreements in force in 1972, almost four hundred were classified and kept from Congress. Many involved commitments and informal alliances with other nations such as Spain, Laos, and Ethiopia.

To remedy what Congress considered an abuse of executive power, it passed the **Case Act** (1972), which placed some restrictions on the use of executive agreements, particularly secret ones. The Case Act requires that the secretary of state submit to the Senate the final text of any executive agreement. Should the agreement concern sensitive national security matters, it can be submitted in private to the Senate Foreign Relations Committee and the House Foreign Affairs Committee. The Case Act is largely symbolic and does not give Congress the power to alter or reject executive agreements. Moreover, compliance with the act is not easy to obtain. A 1976 Senate study disclosed that the executive branch had delayed submitting a number of executive agreements by almost a year and avoided submitting others by renaming them "arrangements."[11]

10.5   The President and Congress: The War Power

The war power is also divided in the Constitution. The formal power to declare war was given to Congress (Article I, Section 8: "The Congress shall have the power ... To declare war"), and thus the power to initiate war rests with it alone. The framers of the Constitution were careful, however, to leave the president with some independent war-making authority. At the urging of James Madison and Elbridge Gerry, the Constitutional Convention changed the original phrase from "make war" to "declare war." In changing this language, the framers intended to leave the president with the power *to repel sudden attacks on the United States, its territories, its possessions, or its armed forces.* The **commander-in-chief clause** (Article II, Section 2) was not designed to alter this relationship nor to grant the president additional war-making powers. The clause simply established the principle of civilian control over the military. The president was to be, in Alexander Hamilton's words, "the first general and admiral."

10.5a   The Mexican and Civil Wars

Presidents have used the power to control the armed forces in order to manipulate Congress and preempt the war power itself. In 1846, for example, President James Polk (1845–1849) ordered troops into the territory disputed by the United States and Mexico and set the stage for the Mexican War. The troops occupied high ground overlooking a Mexican village and aimed their artillery on the town square. The Mexican government, feeling threatened by the maneuver, responded militarily. Congress, at Polk's request, passed a declaration of war. Several years later the House of Representatives, feeling deceived by Polk's maneuver, passed a resolution that condemned him for a war "unnecessarily and unconstitutionally begun."

Case Act

Requires the secretary of state to submit to the Senate the final text of any executive agreement and allows agreements concerning sensitive national security matters to be submitted privately to the Senate Foreign Relations and House Foreign Affairs committees

commander-in-chief clause

Article II, Section 2 of the U.S. Constitution names the president as the civilian head of U.S. military forces

When Abraham Lincoln became president (1861–1865), he used the war power in a manner more consistent with the original understanding of the framers. After the attack on Fort Sumter (1861), which began the Civil War, Lincoln announced a blockade of the southern ports, increased the size of the army and navy, instructed the Treasury Department to spend $2 million to purchase military supplies, and in certain areas suspended the writ of habeas corpus (a judicial safeguard against unlawful imprisonment). Congress, which was not in session, had authorized none of these steps. On July 4, 1861, Congress, back in session, ratified all of Lincoln's actions except the suspension of the writ of habeas corpus and the naval blockade. The Supreme Court in the Prize Cases[12] declared that Lincoln was within his constitutional powers "in suppressing an insurrection."

10.5b   The Two World Wars

Twice in the twentieth century (1917 and 1941) Congress formally declared war and delegated vast discretionary powers to the president. During World War I Congress granted President Wilson almost dictatorial control over the economy. This included the power to seize mines and factories, fix prices, license the distribution of foodstuffs, and take over railroads and telephone lines. Although Wilson did not exercise all this authority, he did assume unprecedented control over prices, consumption, and industrial production.

Congress granted Franklin Roosevelt similar authority during World War II; but Roosevelt, who had a broad and expansive view of the office, asserted wartime powers independent of Congress. The most dramatic and controversial of Roosevelt's actions came early in World War II. On February 19, 1942, Roosevelt decreed that 112,000 persons of Japanese descent living in the Pacific Coast region (70,000 of whom were American citizens) be removed from their homes, stripped of their jobs and property, and sent to detention camps. Concern about sabotage was the justification, although there was no evidence of its likelihood; yet many of these people remained in the camps for the duration of the war. Congress later passed a law embodying the president's order and, in effect, ratifying it. In *Korematsu v. United States*[13] the Supreme Court upheld the exclusion program as within the combined war powers of Congress and the president. The entire case, repudiated by a government commission years later and the subject of renewed litigation in the 1980s, serves as a reminder of how difficult it is in time of war to maintain democratic standards and values. In a separate 2018 case, the Court referred to its decision in *Korematsu* as "gravely wrong."[14]

During World War II, President Franklin Roosevelt decreed that people of Japanese descent living in the Pacific Coast region of the United States were to be rounded up and sent to detention camps.

(Image courtesy of the War Relocation Authority, U.S. Department of the Interior, via Wikimedia.)

10.5c   The Cold War

Only when America became a global power after World War II did presidents assert independent war-making powers, in the context of the Cold War with the Soviet Union. The most dramatic example came in June 1950, when President Truman, on his own independent authority, ordered US ground, air, and naval forces to aid the government of South

Korea against an invasion of North Korean forces. Truman declined to ask Congress for a resolution authorizing this decision and simply cited his powers as commander in chief. Because the Korean invasion did not involve a sudden attack on American troops, citizens, or territory, Truman's unilateral action fell outside the framers' original understanding of the war power. Although Congress later implicitly ratified the decision by voting military appropriations for the war, Truman had nevertheless initiated America's involvement in a war that lasted three years and cost thirty thousand American lives.

During the next two decades, presidential war-making authority grew, nurtured by a new political consensus. Unlike the Americans of the eighteenth and nineteenth centuries who believed in having no permanent military alliances, limited international interests, and a small standing army, Americans of the mid-twentieth century concluded that only through collective security and armed strength could war be prevented. Given this political climate, presidents felt emboldened to establish overseas bases, station troops abroad, and even send them into combat—all on the president's own authority. Congress did little to object.

In 1955, President Eisenhower requested from Congress a joint resolution authorizing him to use military force to protect Taiwan from a possible invasion by the People's Republic of China. The resolution stated that the president had the authority "to employ the Armed Forces as he deems necessary" to defend Taiwan. This undated check to the president to make war on his own terms passed Congress overwhelmingly. The comments of House Speaker Sam Rayburn (D-TX) reflected the measure of congressional acquiescence to presidential authority in those Cold War years. "If the President had done what is proposed here without consulting Congress," Rayburn acknowledged, "he would have had no criticism from me."[15]

10.5d   The Vietnam Trauma

As hundreds of thousands of American troops entered the Vietnam War in the mid-1960s, presidential control of the war-making authority continued to go unchallenged. An alleged attack on two American destroyers by North Vietnamese patrol boats off their coastal waters triggered action from President Lyndon Johnson, who sought broad authority from Congress. At Johnson's request, Congress passed the **Gulf of Tonkin Resolution** (1964), which stated:

> The United States is, therefore, prepared, as the president determines, to take all necessary steps including the use of armed forces to assist any member or protocol state of the Southeast Asia Collective Defense Treaty requesting assistance in defense of its freedom.

The resolution passed unanimously in the House and with only two dissenting votes in the Senate, recognizing the president's claim to unilateral war-making authority.

As the Vietnam War lost public support, Congress sought to regain its constitutional authority largely through its control of spending power; but the task was arduous and the results were ambiguous. In 1970, Congress, fearing an extension of the war, barred the use of funds to "finance the introduction of the ground troops into Laos or Thailand." President Nixon circumvented the law, however, by ordering continued aerial bombing and paramilitary activities in Laos. After he authorized an invasion of Cambodia that year, Congress responded by prohibiting the use of funds for ground combat troops in that beleaguered country. Although Nixon eventually withdrew the ground troops from Cambodia, he continued the bombing.

Gulf of Tonkin Resolution

A congressional resolution passed in 1964 granting President Johnson the authority to undertake military activities in Southeast Asia

The Paris Peace Accords (1973) ended direct American combat involvement in Vietnam but not the bombing of Cambodia and Laos. Thus, the war continued—but with very little congressional support. Finally, in June 1973, Congress was able to use its power of the purse to control the power of the sword. President Nixon, weakened and distracted by the Watergate scandal, signed an appropriation bill that prohibited the further use of funds for all combat activities in Indochina as of August 15, 1973. However, the bill was signed only after American combat activities against the North Vietnamese had ended—and nine years after Congress had passed the Gulf of Tonkin Resolution.

10.5e The War Powers Resolution

Chastened by the Vietnam experience and anxious to recapture its war-making authority, Congress passed the War Powers Resolution in the fall of 1973 over President Nixon's veto. The resolution specified that the president could not commit troops to combat beyond sixty days unless authorized by Congress. It also stipulated that before introducing troops into combat, the president had to consult with Congress in every possible instance.

Both hawks and doves criticized the War Powers Resolution. Senator Barry Goldwater (R-AZ) argued that the sixty-day cutoff provision was an unconstitutional interference with the president's powers as commander in chief. Senator Thomas Eagleton (D-MO) claimed that the resolution placed no defined limits on when a president could take the country to war without prior congressional approval. So far the resolution has had little effect on presidential behavior, confirming neither the fears of its critics nor the hopes of its sponsors.

For years supporters of the resolution were concerned about the failure of presidents to abide fully by its provisions were the Congress to challenge the president. The effectiveness of the resolution depends on how seriously Congress takes its responsibilities. Congress was not tested until January 12, 1991, when it granted President George H. W. Bush the power, as authorized under the War Powers Resolution, to begin military operations to enforce the United Nations Security Council's resolutions demanding Saddam Hussein's military withdrawal from Kuwait. There was no way of knowing at the time that this military action would set the stage for another conflict with Iraq a decade later.

(U.S. Navy, 2003, via Wikimedia)

Engineering Aide First Class Scott Lyerla, assigned to Naval Mobile Construction Battalion One Five (NMCB-15), maintains security for his convoy with an M-60 machine gun while driving through Al Hillah, Iraq.

10.5f The Iraq War

After the 9/11 attacks the pendulum of war power quickly swung back in the direction of the president. George W. Bush acted decisively, and with congressional approval, by invading Afghanistan, a country that had harbored members of the al Qaeda terrorist network. In September 2002, he also issued a revised version of the National Security Strategy of the United States, a document that outlines the country's approach to defense. Among the new features of the Bush administration's plan was something called the Doctrine of Preemption. This stated that America's strategy would now be to attack potential enemies before they had the opportunity to attack the United States. The document also named

Iraq, Iran, and North Korea as part of an "axis of evil" that potentially threatened the United States.

George W. Bush argued that immediate action needed to be taken against Iraq because according to intelligence reports (later proved inaccurate), Iraq possessed and was continuing to develop weapons of mass destruction. Seeing no success from UN sanctions, Bush asked for and received broad authority from Congress to take action against Iraq. Although the American military swiftly defeated the armies of Saddam Hussein, maintaining the long-term stability of the region proved much more difficult. As costs and casualties continued to mount, however, there was little Congress could do. Once it had granted authority for military action, the only remaining congressional power was over spending; but with every proposed cut portrayed as risking American lives, it was clearly not feasible for Congress to exercise this authority either. Barack Obama announced plans to end the war shortly after taking office in 2009, and American troops completed their withdrawal on December 18, 2011, over eight years after the war began. Over 4,409 American troops were killed in Iraq and over 31,000 were wounded.[16] Information about Iraqi deaths has been more difficult to calculate, but the most thoroughly documented approach indicates that between 108,000 and 118,000 Iraqi civilians died in the conflict.[17]

As long as US foreign policy requires global political commitments and a powerful mobile military, any limits on the president's role as commander in chief will be difficult for Congress to impose. The era of US isolation and neutrality has long passed, and along with it a small standing army. Contemporary presidents shape a large defense budget, select major weapons systems, control access to classified information, and send large carrier task forces around the globe. Thus, congressional attempts to reassert authority meet with mixed results.

10.6 The President and Congress: Domestic Policy

In domestic policy, as well as foreign, the relationship between the president and Congress is rarely easy and never a predetermined fact. Presidents' capacities to push their legislative programs through Congress are strong indications of their powers and often determine their historical impact on the office. Few presidents have been able to dominate Congress; and those who have, have done so only for short periods. Presidents with an ambitious domestic agenda and aspirations beyond maintaining the status quo have a particular need for congressional support. Getting such support requires great skill, a sense of what the public will support, and a capacity to persuade 535 independent-minded senators and representatives. What are the political ingredients that enable presidents to be successful leaders of Congress? Recent experience suggests several.[18]

10.6a Legislative Skills

A president must know the legislative environment.   One of Franklin Roosevelt's advisers once explained that a president must understand who influences whom, who the key players are on an issue, and what a group wants that others can be persuaded either to accept or to tolerate. Lyndon Johnson made it his business to know as much as he could about the key members of Congress. By contrast, Jimmy Carter, whose legisla-

POLITICS AND IDEAS

A "New Kind of War"—The Ongoing War on Terrorism

When President George W. Bush (2001–2009) spoke to New York leaders in the wake of the September 11 attacks, he stated, "My resolve is steady and strong about winning this war that has been declared on America. It's a new kind of war. And I understand it's a new kind of war. And this government will adjust." These comments acknowledge the need for adaptation in light of a significant change. America has officially declared war five times and has been involved in numerous military conflicts, but the ongoing war on terrorism represents the first time that our nation has embarked on a war with a concept rather than a nation. What is a war on terrorism, and where does the authority to conduct such a war reside?

Article I, Section 8 of the U.S. Constitution states in part that "The Congress shall have Power ... To declare War ... and make Rules concerning Captures on Land and Water." On the other hand, Article II of the Constitution begins by vesting the executive power in the president. While it is widely agreed that the framers of the Constitution intended to provide the president with the authority to repel sudden attacks, but also intended to reserve for Congress the power to move the nation from a state of peace to a state of war, there is a large gray area in the middle of these two objectives. The distinction between presidential and congressional powers has proved difficult to maintain in practice.

Examples of congressional action in response to the terrorist attacks consist of a joint resolution authorizing the president to use military force; the Air Transportation Safety and System Stabilization Act, which, in part, provided economic subsidies for the struggling airline industry; the Patriot Act and its amendments, which authorized law enforcement agencies to develop a number of new tools for combating and preventing future terrorist attacks; and creation of the independent and bipartisan National Commission on Terrorist Attacks upon the United States (also known as the 9/11 Commission). In October 2006, a divided Congress passed the Military Commissions Act, which expanded the detention and interrogation powers (including the power to suspend the writ of habeas corpus) of military tribunals trying "alien unlawful enemy combatants engaged in hostilities against the United States."[1]

Presidential actions taken by President Bush included creating the new Department of Homeland Security; securing the diplomatic and military support of other world leaders; and, in coordination with his National Security Council, directing the military actions of Operation Enduring Freedom. Other actions have been taken by executive branch agencies that receive funding and authority from Congress and are, ultimately, under the direction of the president and his appointees. When the Federal Aviation Administration, for example, greatly expanded its Federal Air Marshal program, it did so with the approval of its parent agency, the Department of Transportation, and the funding of Congress. Opinion polls suggest that the American public wants Congress to become even more involved in making decisions about military action: 76 percent of Americans think the president should be required to seek congressional approval before using

military aircraft to bomb suspected terrorists, and 79 percent believe he should be required to have Congress's approval to send armed forces into action abroad.

In addition to granting powers, the Constitution also limits governmental power by placing many individual liberties off-limits from government control. Even though most Americans have welcomed increased security measures, it is unlikely that many Americans would willingly sacrifice all their freedoms just to decrease threats to their security. In fact, 65 percent of Americans believe that efforts to prevent terrorism should not violate civil liberties. Fortunately, the Constitution and its amendments—through such guarantees as free speech, free press, due process, and equal protection—assure us that we will not have to make such choices.

What else makes the war on terrorism a "new kind of war"? Is our Constitution equipped to handle such a war, or are changes necessary? When faced with a decision between maintaining fundamental freedoms for all Americans and increasing security to reduce the risk of future terrorist attacks, what criteria should we employ? Should our constitutional protections extend to noncitizens? Who in American government should make these decisions, and how do we know when they are making the right choices? Did the war on terrorism change under President Obama? Did it change under President Trump? If so, how? If not, why not?

1. Military Commissions Act of 2006.

SOURCES: George W. Bush, "President Pledges Assistance for New York in Phone Call with Pataki, Giuliani," September 13, 2001, http://www.whitehouse.gov/news/releases/2001/09/20010913-4.html (November 4, 2001); The Gallup Organization, "Public Wants Congress to Approve Military Action, Bombings," July 7, 2008; The Gallup Organization, "Americans Still Say Liberties Should Trump Anti-Terrorism," June 10, 2015.

tive performance was less than spectacular, was unfamiliar with the ways of Washington and held himself aloof from the congressional leadership.

A president needs a good sense of timing. Presidents must know when to lead and when to pause. For example, wars often deplete the national energy for reform, and Congress itself can reflect such a national mood. Postwar presidents Warren Harding (World War I), Truman (World War II), and Eisenhower (Korea) were unable to get much reform legislation from Congress. Harding and Eisenhower did not even try, but Truman did and found the going very difficult. Bill Clinton pushed for health-care reform before Americans had reached consensus on the type of change they wanted, but George W. Bush's plan for tax cuts was well received.

Presidents must establish their priorities and know where to concentrate their energies. Presidents will not get everything they ask from Congress; therefore, they must put forward programs that are not only important but that also have a chance of success. Early successes may build a reputation for political mastery that can be translated into future legislative victories. Ronald Reagan focused on the budget and taxes in his first year and achieved astonishing success.

Presidents must have a high-quality legislative liaison office. Presidents cannot personally keep in touch with all members of Congress. An effective liaison office gives members more access to the White House, if not to the president directly. It also provides the president with vital intelligence: How many votes are there for a particular bill? Which members need to be persuaded? What particular favors can be granted dissenters to sway their votes? The liaison office can build crucial loyalty and support for presidents and their policies.

Presidents must consult with party leaders in the opposition as well as in their own party when they are developing major policy initiatives. A president needs to have a strong working relationship with those who can report the mood of Congress. Jimmy Carter failed to consult with the appropriate congressional leaders when he unveiled his energy program in 1977. To the surprise of very few, Congress extensively revised and rewrote it.

Wise presidents remember Jefferson's advice: Great innovations should not and cannot be forced upon slender majorities. Major innovations require broad bipartisan support or else they will fail. Truman worked closely with leading senior Republicans in Congress in order to gain support for the United Nations treaty, the Marshall Plan (economic rehabilitation aid to Western Europe after World War II), and the North Atlantic Treaty Organization. Presidents Kennedy and Johnson, in building a consensus for their civil rights programs, cultivated relationships with Republican leaders in both houses. President Reagan's strong working relationship with conservative southern Democrats in the House (known as "Boll Weevils") was essential to his legislative success in 1981 and 1982. Bill Clinton failed to heed this advice early in his first term when he presented Congress and its slim Democratic majority with a sweeping plan for health-care reform. Rejection of this plan forced Clinton to be more cautious later in his administration. President Trump's desires to repeal the Affordable Care Act and build a wall between the United States and Mexico were repeatedly frustrated when the Republicans' slim majority in the Senate proved insufficient to carry out his plan.

10.6b   The Presidential Veto

The president has a number of constitutional and statutory powers available in dealing with Congress, but none is more important than the veto. According to Article I, Section 7, the president may veto a congressional bill within ten days after it reaches the president's desk. The president then returns the bill to the congressional chamber of origin with a message explaining the reasons and perhaps suggesting changes that could make the bill acceptable. Congress may override the veto by a two-thirds majority of each house of Congress. The bill then becomes a law without presidential approval. Should Congress announce its adjournment during the ten-day period, the president may employ a pocket veto by simply killing the bill without a formal message and without the need of returning it to Congress. Congress cannot override a pocket veto. Presidents cannot veto constitutional amendments, but they can veto joint resolutions that are formal expressions of congressional opinion and have the force of law. Table 10.3 summarizes presidential vetoes and overrides since Franklin Roosevelt.

Table 10.3   Presidential Vetoes and Overrides

The veto remains one of the president's most significant constitutional powers. Yet the president does not possess authority for an item veto—the power to reject part of a bill; the president must accept or reject the entire bill.

	Total Vetoes	Pocket Vetoes	Vetoes Overridden
Franklin Roosevelt (1933–1945)	635	263	9
Harry Truman (1945–1953)	250	70	12
Dwight Eisenhower (1953–1961)	181	108	2
John Kennedy (1961–1963)	21	9	0
Lyndon Johnson (1963–1969)	30	14	0
Richard Nixon (1969–1974)	43	17	7
Gerald Ford (1974–1977)	66	18	12
Jimmy Carter (1977–1981)	31	18	2
Ronald Reagan (1981–1989)	78	39	9
George H. W. Bush (1989–1993)	46	17	1
Bill Clinton (1993–2001)	37	1	2
George W. Bush (2001–2009)	12	0	4
Barack Obama (2009–2017)	12	0	1
Donald Trump (2017–2021)*	10	1	0

*Through January 2021

SOURCE: United States Senate, http://www.senate.gov/reference/Legislation/Vetoes/vetoCounts.htm (November 14, 2020).

The president, unlike a number of state governors, does not possess an item veto, which allows an executive to veto sections of a bill and sign the remaining portion. President Reagan, for one, was a vocal supporter of the item veto, the implementation of which would require a constitutional amendment. Under certain conditions, the president can refuse to spend part of an appropriations bill. Occasionally, a president may sign a bill and at the same time note that certain provisions are unconstitutional and cannot be enforced. The president's authority to do this has yet to be tested in court, however. As discussed in Chapter 9, a common congressional technique for avoiding a veto is to attach amendments (riders) to an appropriations bill. Frequently, the president cannot afford to veto such a bill without having the government run out of money. During the Vietnam War, Congress attached such riders to defense bills restricting the president's authority. President Nixon, in need of the appropriations to continue funding the war, was forced to accept these riders, which he otherwise surely would have vetoed.

In April 1996, Congress passed the Line Item Veto Act in an effort to allow the president the authority for item vetoes. After President Clinton first used this authority in early 1997, several members of Congress who had voted against the bill challenged the constitutionality of the law in court. In 1998, the Supreme Court held that the law violated the presentiment clause of Article I of the Constitution. Thus, the president's line item veto authority was short-lived.[19] In 2004, George W. Bush became the first president since John Quincy Adams to complete a full four-year term in office without vetoing a single piece of legislation. Although Bush eventually vetoed bills in his second term, starting with the rejection of a bill on stem cell research, he preferred the subtle—and more legally dubious—strategy of appending signing statements to bills with which he disagreed. Standing on his right to refuse to enforce legislation he deemed unconstitutional, Bush issued over 150 signing statements, challenging over 1,100 sections of legislation during his eight years in office, leading to an investigation by the American Bar Association, which approved a resolution condemning the practice.[20]

United States v. Nixon addressed only the president's right to withhold information from the courts. Since the Watergate scandal, Congress has become more assertive against such claims and suspicious that they were used to cover up maladministration.

(National Archives and Records Administration, via Wikimedia)

10.6c Executive Privilege

Control over policy requires control over information. Thus, since George Washington's time, presidents have claimed that personal communications with their advisers were immune from congressional or judicial scrutiny. Presidents have argued that they need the protection of confidentiality to ensure that they will receive frank and candid advice. The right of the president to refuse information requested by Congress and the courts is called executive privilege.

During the Watergate affair President Nixon attempted to enlarge the power of executive privilege. Nixon asserted that it included the authority to withhold from Congress and the courts information in the possession of any employee of the executive branch. In 1973, Nixon maintained that even the papers and tapes of conversations under subpoena by the Watergate special prosecutor were protected by executive privilege. Nixon's lawyer maintained that a president's claim of executive privilege was absolute and not subject to review by the courts or Congress. This

broad definition suffered a setback from the Supreme Court in *United States v. Nixon*[21] when it ruled that although the president did enjoy a right to executive privilege, the privilege was not absolute. The Court concluded that the need for the tapes and papers as evidence in the Watergate trial outweighed the president's claim of confidentiality and ordered Nixon to produce the tapes and papers.

In the criminal trial of Admiral John Poindexter, District Court Judge Harold H. Greene ordered President Reagan to turn over his personal diaries to the court. Judge Greene read the diaries *in camera* (in his private chambers), weighing the former president's claim of executive privilege against Poindexter's assertion that he could not get a fair trial without access to them. After reviewing one hundred diary entries, Judge Greene declared that the diaries furnished "no new insights" into the Iran-contra affair and concluded that Reagan's claim of executive privilege outweighed Poindexter's need for the material.[22]

United States v. Nixon and the Poindexter case addressed only the president's right to withhold information from the courts and not the right to withhold information from Congress. Since the Watergate scandal, Congress has become more assertive against such claims and suspicious that they were used to cover up maladministration, if not corruption. In 1982 there were, in fact, charges of collusion between top officials of the Environmental Protection Agency (EPA) and corporations cited for allegedly dumping toxic waste. When EPA director Anne Burford refused to hand over to a House subcommittee documents relating to the enforcement of the toxic-waste program, the House voted her in contempt of Congress.

POLITICS AND IDEAS

Immigration Reform: Laws and Executive Orders

President Obama announced an executive action on November 20, 2014. This order instructed the relevant federal agencies to take three sets of actions. First, it redirected the nation's deportation efforts to focus solely on criminals and threats to national security. Second, it expanded opportunities to stay in the United States for people born in the United States to undocumented immigrants. Third, the president developed a process for undocumented immigrants who have been in the country for at least five years and whose children are legal residents to remain in the country and receive work permits. While the plan does not grant amnesty or provide citizenship, it removes the threat of deportation for up to five million undocumented immigrants.

What is the difference between an executive order and a law? And why did the president issue the former, rather than call on Congress to pass the latter? Finally, were the president's actions constitutional? The answer to the first question is factual, but an answer to the second is more speculative. A law must be passed by both chambers of Congress and signed by the president. If the president vetoes the legislation, a congressional supermajority can override that action. Laws are meant to change public policy. Executive orders, on the other hand, are designed to give guidance to those in the government on how to carry out existing policies. In use since the presidency of George Washington, these orders are an important tool for enabling our chief executive to "execute" the laws.

One answer to the second question is partisan politics. Legislation passed by the Democrat-led Senate was not voted on by the Republican-led House of Representatives. While both Democrats and Republicans acknowledged that the current immigration system is flawed, they differed in their preferences for solving the problem. Many Democrats wanted a policy that would grant amnesty and a path to citizenship for those already in the country, but they were aware that too lenient a policy may encourage increases in undocumented immigration in the future. Furthermore, they

had to avoid policies that would strike voters as unfair. Many Republicans said that the focus should be on deportation and securing borders, but they also knew that this message could easily slide into racism and xenophobia. Republicans needed to focus on solutions rather than blame to avoid alienating the growing number of Hispanic voters, many of whom may otherwise be attracted to conservatism.

An answer to the third question was provided by the Supreme Court in 2016, when the justices let stand a lower court decision blocking the deferred action and work permit portions of Obama's plan.[1] The decision did not affect the president's orders to focus deportation efforts on criminals and national security threats. This outcome suggests that presidents are on firm constitutional ground when directing the enforcement priorities of executive agencies but are likely to overstep their authority when they seek to unilaterally create new policy.

Despite these differing approaches, and the questionable legality of the president's actions,

most Americans agree on the basic facts. We know that there are roughly 11.3 million undocumented immigrants in the United States. While many remain undetected, millions have been identified and are in various stages of the deportation process. During the first six years of the Obama administration, over 2.1 million undocumented immigrants were deported to their country of origin.[2] There is also bipartisan agreement that the eight million or so unauthorized workers in the United States aid the American economy because they "fill the growing gap between expanding low-skilled jobs and the shrinking pool of native-born Americans who are willing to take such jobs."[3] Simply removing all undocumented immigrants is not a viable economic solution. Finally, we know that our current laws are not effectively addressing the situation. Many people want to legally immigrate to the United States and many Americans want them to do so. But the State Department reports that 4.4 million potential immigrants have started the legal immigration process, and the wait for

a visa can take decades.[4] Clearly, this is a policy area ripe for reform.

Will the two parties—and two policy-making branches of government—work together to develop a comprehensive plan for immigration reform in 2021 or 2022? A majority of Americans say it is more important for political leaders in Washington to compromise to get things done rather than stick to their beliefs and risk doing little.[5] Only time will tell whether Congress and the president will listen to this preference. But until the two sides in this struggle acknowledge the need for compromise, America will limp along with a broken system—and immigrants will continue to cross our borders seeking opportunity.

1. "Obama Says Deportation Priorities Won't Change After Supreme Court Decision," *Huffington Post,* June 23, 2016.

2. *The Week,* September 26, 2014.

3. Maria Santana, "5 Immigration Myths Debunked," November 20, 2014, http://money.cnn.com/2014/11/20/news /economy/immigration-myths/ (November 26, 2014).

3. Ibid.

4. The Gallup Organization, 2018.

President Reagan, claiming executive privilege for Burford, had the Department of Justice challenge the contempt citation in federal court. The federal judge in the case, reluctant to enter into this unchartered area of law, urged both sides to settle their differences out of court. The judge stated, "When constitutional disputes arise concerning the respective powers of the legislative and executive branches, judicial intervention should be delayed until all possibilities for settlement have been exhausted."[23] As a result of the political controversies that developed around the toxic-waste program, Burford resigned; and President Reagan released all the documents to the relevant congressional committees. Presidents have to consider whether the assertion of a particular claim of executive privilege outweighs the political costs of withholding the information. In the matter of Anne Burford, President Reagan felt that the costs of asserting the privilege were too high.

In 2012, President Obama asserted executive privilege to avoid sharing with Congress documents related to Operation Fast and Furious—a bungled effort by the Bureau of Alcohol, Tobacco, and Firearms in which thousands of illegal firearms were sold in hopes of developing evidence against Mexican drug cartels. President Trump asserted executive privilege on multiple issues, most notably to keep his tax returns private when subpoenaed by Congress.

10.6d   Impeachment

In the struggle between the president and Congress, presidential impeachment and removal from office is the ultimate congressional weapon. Article II, Section 4, of the Constitution states: "The President, Vice President and all Civil Officers of the United States shall be removed from Office on Impeachment for, and Conviction of, Treason, Bribery, or other high Crimes and Misdemeanors."

The actual impeachment resembles a criminal indictment in which the House acts as the grand jury. The investigation is done by the House Judiciary Committee, which votes on whether to recommend impeachment to the full House. The House can vote to impeach by a simple majority. The question of guilt or innocence is then determined by a trial, conducted by the Senate. The chief justice of the United States serves as the presiding judge over the proceedings involving the president or the vice president, and a vote of two-thirds of the Senate is required for conviction and removal.

President Andrew Johnson (1865–1869) was impeached in 1868 by an overwhelming majority in the House, but escaped conviction in the Senate by one vote. More than a century later, in 1974, President Richard Nixon faced a serious threat of impeachment. After eight months of hearings, the House Judiciary Committee voted three articles of impeachment, charging Nixon with (1) obstruction of justice for encouraging perjury, destruction of evidence, and interfering with investigations by the FBI; (2) abuse of power for authorizing the FBI and IRS to harass his political opponents; and (3) contempt of Congress for refusal to comply with congressional subpoenas for tapes and papers relevant to the impeachment investigation. Before the House had an opportunity to vote on the Judiciary Committee report, Nixon resigned the presidency.

The Nixon experience helped to clarify the question of what is an impeachable offense. Treason and bribery are clear offenses, and Nixon was charged with neither. What, however, constitutes a "high crime and misdemeanor"? The framers, especially Alexander Hamilton and James Madison, believed that the phrase included the abuse of political power. By including the abuse of power in the articles of impeachment, the House Judiciary Committee accepted the view of Madison and Hamilton that high crimes and misdemeanors involve "the violation of some public trust." Nixon's attempt to use the FBI and the IRS against his political enemies was considered by the committee a threat to political order and therefore an impeachable offense.

10.6e   The Clinton Impeachment

The next case of presidential impeachment came in December 1998, when the House of Representatives passed two articles of impeachment against President Bill Clinton. The story of Clinton's impeachment begins in 1994, when an independent counsel was assigned the task of investigating a Clinton real estate investment known as Whitewater. Although the Whitewater investigation never led to charges against Clinton, Independent Counsel Kenneth Starr asked for and received authority to investigate additional leads on potential misdeeds that had turned up during the course of the Whitewater investigation. At the same time, Paula Jones, a former Arkansas state worker, was suing Clinton for sexual harassment. In January 1998, Clinton gave a deposition in that case in which he was asked questions about a number of possible improprieties, among them an affair with former White House intern Monica Lewinsky. At about the same time, Kenneth Starr, acting on a tip from Lewinsky's former friend Linda Tripp, sought authority to extend his investigation to cover possible wrongdoings (perjury, obstruction of justice) regarding the Lewinsky affair. In August 1998, President Clinton testified before a grand

(Courtesy of William J. Clinton Presidential Library, via Wikimedia)

Monica Lewinsky with former president Bill Cinton on February 28, 1997. Among other charges, Clinton was charged with lying about his relations with Lewinsky.

jury about his relationship with Lewinsky and allegations of his efforts to cover up that relationship. In his testimony, Clinton admitted that the relationship had been inappropriate. As a result, in September 1998, Starr issued to Congress a several-thousand-page report, which recommended impeachment based on inconsistencies between Clinton's January and August testimonies. In November and early December, the House wrestled with the gravity of the president's wrongdoing. Had he just been misleading and immoral, as the Democrats claimed; or did Clinton's actions constitute the kind of "high crimes and misdemeanors" that the Constitution outlined as impeachable offenses, as the Republicans claimed? Ultimately, a Republican-led House of Representatives that voted almost entirely along party lines voted to approve one article of impeachment that charged the president with lying under oath and another that charged him with obstruction of justice. In early 1999, this action created the need for an impeachment trial in the Senate, where two-thirds of the Senate could vote to convict and remove the president from office. By the time the final vote was taken on February 12, Congress, the president, and the American people were all weary of the issue. In the final tally, the Senate rejected both articles of impeachment. Ten different Republicans voted against either one or both of the articles, and not a single Democrat voted in favor of either.

10.6f   The Trump Impeachments

The most recent impeachment, of Donald Trump, raised similar questions of partisanship, as votes were largely along party lines. Though there were multiple efforts to begin impeachment proceedings against President Trump for obstructing congressional investigations during his first years in office, it was not until August 2019 that a clear-cut case of wrongdoing emerged. In that month, a government employee (whose identity was protected by whistleblower protection laws) raised a concern regarding inappropriate requests during President Trump's July 25th phone call with Ukrainian president Volodymyr Zelensky. The allegation was sent to the congressional intelligence committees and led to an investigation. Through subpoenaed documents and witness testimony, the House of Representatives concluded that Trump had asked Zelensky to announce he was opening corruption investigations into the Ukrainian gas company Burisma and into Ukraine's role in 2016 US election interference. The former was an issue because Hunter Biden had been a board member of Burisma and he was the son of Trump's likely opponent in the 2020 election, Joe Biden. The latter was an effort to pursue a discredited theory that Ukraine, and not Russia, had been the source of 2016 election meddling.

What made these actions impeachable offences, the House argued, was that Trump used the powers of the presidency in an effort to enlist a foreign power to support his personal reelection efforts. Furthermore, he attempted to pressure the Ukrainian president into these actions by withholding $400 million in military aid to Ukraine. In December 2019, the House voted to approve two articles of impeachment—one alleging that

President Trump had abused his power and a second stating he had obstructed Congress's investigation into the matter. The vote was 230–197 on the first article and 229–198 on the second, making Donald Trump the third impeached president in American history. Nearly all Democrats voted in favor of both measures and all Republicans voted against them. This dynamic set up a very predictable outcome for the impeachment trial in the Republican-led Senate. Ultimately, that body voted to acquit the president on both counts, with only Mitt Romney (R-UT) breaking party ranks. In doing so, he became the first Senator in the nation's history to vote to remove a president from his own party.

Then, just a week before leaving office, President Trump made history by becoming the first president to be impeached a second time. On January 13, 2021, the House voted 232–197 to impeach President Trump for "incitement of insurrection," arguing that the president's rhetoric had emboldened protestors to attempt a coup by breaking into the nation's capitol building. Though public opinion was evenly divided on whether Trump should be removed from office, opinions of Trump in general remained largely unchanged.[24] Were the Clinton and Trump impeachments the pursuit of justice against presidents who were acting above the law, or mere partisan attacks? The debate still goes on.

Listen to recorded speeches by every U.S. president since Benjamin Harrison, available at the Vincent Voice Library.

http://www.bvtlab.com/TY2X8

10.7   The President and the Media

Presidents and the media are usually involved in a love-hate relationship that resembles a bad marriage. They need each other, yet they have difficulty living together. Practically every president has complained about the press. George Washington charged that the unfavorable stories about his administration were "outrages of common decency." President Thomas Jefferson, a champion of a free press, stated, "Even the least informed of the people have learned that nothing in a newspaper is to be believed." Richard Nixon, who suffered serious criticism of his Vietnam policy, had a considerable number of Washington reporters on his "enemies list." During the Iran-contra affair, Ronald Reagan claimed that reporters were circling the White House like "sharks." George H. W. Bush championed this slogan during his unsuccessful 1992 reelection campaign: "Annoy the media. Reelect Bush/Quayle." The media found virtually nothing off-limits during the Bill Clinton administration, as discussion of his possible sexual improprieties became a frequent story in the national news. President Trump went so far as to declare the media "the enemy of the people" in multiple tweets during his presidency.

Such conflict is built into the relationship. Chief executives are advocates of their own administration and want to see it portrayed favorably. They also feel the responsibility of suppressing information that, in their eyes,

could damage national security. Presidents, therefore, are inclined to control the content and timing of information about their administrations. Reporters, in contrast, want to get their hands on as much interesting and relevant information as possible, regardless of its sensitivity. Many a president has had the day ruined by seeing material from a highly classified document cited in the morning papers.

Editors want stories that sell newspapers, increase web traffic, or improve television ratings. Trivial stories, such as Nancy Reagan's purchase of expensive china for the White House or the fashion choices of Melania Trump, often receive more attention than a complex and important issue.

As much as presidents may grouse about the media, they are not above using it for their own purposes. Michael Deaver, a senior aide to President Reagan, spent much of his time constructing effective visual backgrounds for presidential stories on the nightly news.

10.7a   Phases of the Relationship

The relationship between the president and the media can go through a series of phases. The first is cooperation and occurs in the early honeymoon stage of an administration. Presidents in this phase woo the media, grant numerous interviews, have nationally syndicated columnists for dinner, may visit influential reporters in their homes, and see to it that a reporter's calls to the White House are returned. During this time, stories frequently appear about what a breath of fresh air the administration has brought to Washington.

The second phase begins after the administration has settled in, begun to develop some internal conflicts, seen some sensitive information leak, suffered through its first crisis, and received its first series of negative stories. It is at this point that the relationship turns to one of conflict. Presidents will try more vigorously to control leaks, may deny critical reporters access to top officials, and favor those writers who support the administration. After enjoying a honeymoon with the press and beginning to see stories critical of his leadership, President Kennedy said he was "reading more and enjoying it less."

The third phase can be described as detachment. The president becomes less accessible to the press, holds fewer press conferences, and mainly appears before sympathetic audiences. In the final months of his administration, Lyndon Johnson, under constant attack for his Vietnam policy, spoke primarily at military installations. Besieged by negative stories during the Iran-contra affair, President Reagan went months without holding a news conference. Bill Clinton did the same in the wake of the Monica Lewinsky scandal. In this phase the media become more aggressive in seeking out stories. Their sources may be largely those outside the White House or from disgruntled former officials. Consequently, the stories may grow more negative. By the end of a presidential term, the relationship has exhausted itself.[25]

10.7b The Imperial President Versus the Imperial Media

Both the president and the media have powerful weapons at their disposal in dealing with each other. Presidents can decide what format to use in presenting their case to the public—a prime-time news conference, a fireside chat, or an off-the-record briefing. They can orchestrate their public appearances for the maximum visual effect. They can leak information to those reporters they favor and withhold it from those they disdain. President Trump developed an entirely new strategy for dealing with the press—employing his Twitter account as a weapon to attack the "fake news" media and speak directly to his 85 million followers.

The media, in turn, can do extensive investigative reporting and take advantage of leakers in the administration who want to undercut a particular presidential policy. Reporters can pressure presidents to release information through the Freedom of Information Act and barrage them with persistent questions at press conferences. They can portray presidential scandals as dramatic and initiate "who-done-its"—as was done in Watergate, Iran-contra, Whitewater, and the Mueller investigation—whetting the public appetite for more information and placing the administration on the defensive.

The contest is usually a standoff. No president has been able to manage the press, and although many debate the issue, the reality is that the media cannot actually make or break a president. The vast majority of American newspapers opposed Franklin Roosevelt and endorsed his opponents. Many Washington reporters had slight regard for Ronald Reagan's ability or wisdom. Yet such media opinions had little or no effect upon the ultimate judgment of the American people.

CHAPTER REVIEW

1. Because the president is the ceremonial head of state as well as the actual governmental leader, the office of the presidency has strong symbolic power. The president can use this power to rally the country in times of crisis, but the power and visibility of the office can also mean that the public will hold the president responsible for events over which the president may have no control.

2. The actual nature of the "executive power," which the Constitution grants to the president, is not clear, and presidents have given it different interpretations. The general contours of the specific powers of appointment, removal, and pardon, however, are quite clear and leave little room for ambiguity.

3. Although presidents have the complete power to appoint all their top advisers, they must be careful to appoint those who will both carry out their policies and run their department effectively.

4. In foreign policy, the Constitution divides power between the president and Congress. The president retains the initiative, but Congress can limit the president's options—and in the period since Vietnam, it has. To lead in foreign policy, presidents cannot simply impose their will; they must persuade both the public and Congress to accept their leadership.

5. In domestic policy, the task of presidential leadership is even more difficult. The president must be able to develop a close working relationship with Congress and have a clear sense of priorities and the public mood.

6. Conflict is inherent in the relationship between the president and the media. Presidents want the media to portray their administrations favorably, and the media are anxious for news that gains public attention regardless of how presidents and their administrations are characterized.

KEY TERMS

Case Act 326

chief of state 308

commander-in-chief clause 326

constitutional theory 311

Council of Economic Advisers (CEA) 320

executive agreements 325

Executive Office of the President (EOP) 318

Gulf of Tonkin Resolution 328

head of government 308

inner cabinet 316

multiple advocacy 318

National Security Council (NSC) 319

natural-born citizen 311

naturalized citizen 311

Office of Management and Budget 319

outer cabinet 316

Presidential Succession Act of 1947 324

stewardship theory 311

the administration 315

Twenty-fifth Amendment 323

Twenty-second Amendment 311

vesting clause 311

READINGS FOR FURTHER STUDY

For a broad overview of the presidency consult Joseph A. Pika, John Anthony Maltese, and Andrew Rudalevige, *The Politics of the Presidency*, 10th ed. (Washington, DC: CQ Press, 2020), and George C. Edwards III, Kenneth R. Mayer, and Stephen J. Wayne, *Presidential Leadership: Politics and Policy Making*, 11th ed. (Lanham, MD: Rowman & Littlefield, 2020).

Two excellent examinations of the role of personality in the presidency are Fred I. Greenstein's *The Presidential Difference*, 3rd ed. (Princeton, NJ: Princeton University Press, 2009) and James David Barber's *The Presidential Character,* 5th ed. (New York: Routledge, 2019).

A highly readable collection of essays on the contemporary presidency can be found in Michael Nelson, ed., *The Presidency and the Political System,* 12th ed. (Washington, DC: CQ Press, 2020). The best source for an understanding of the constitutional origin and development of the presidential office is Joseph M. Bessette and Jeffrey K. Tulis, *The Constitutional Presidency* (Baltimore: The Johns Hopkins University Press, 2009).

A useful general reference is Michael Genovese, ed., *Encyclopedia of the American Presidency,* 3rd ed. (New York: Facts On File, 2017).

The complex relationship among the president, Congress, and the people is explored in Samuel Kernell's *Going Public*, 4th ed. (Washington, DC: CQ Press, 2014).

An insiders' look at the Trump administration is provided by Bob Woodward's *Fear* (New York: Simon & Schuster, 2018); another perspective is offered by John Bolton's *The Room Where It Happened* (New York: Simon & Schuster, 2020).

NOTES

1. Quoted in Christopher H. Pyle and Richard M. Pious, *The President, Congress, and the Constitution* (New York: Free Press, 1984), pp. 68, 70.

2. Ibid., p. 130.

3. *Myers v. United States,* 272 U.S. 52 (1926).

4. *Humphrey's Executor v. United States,* 295 U.S. 602 (1935).

5. 591 U.S. ____ (2020).

6. Louis Fisher, *The Politics of Shared Power: Congress and the Executive,* 2nd ed. (Washington, DC: Congressional Quarterly, 1987), p. 11.

7. "President Obama Has Now Commuted the Sentences of 348 Individuals," June 3, 2016, https://www.whitehouse.gov (July 11, 2016).

8. Thomas E. Cronin, *The State of the Presidency,* 2nd ed. (Boston: Little, Brown, 1980), pp. 253–296.

9. Paul Strobin, "In the Loop," *National Journal* (March 24, 1990): 715–718.

10. Rich Lowry, "Obama Kills the War Powers Act," *National Review Online,* June 7, 2011.

11. Thomas M. Franck and Edward Weisband, *Foreign Policy by Congress* (New York: Oxford University Press, 1979), p. 142.

12. 67 U.S. (2 Black) 635 (1863).

13. 323 U.S. 214 (1944).

14. *Trump v. Hawaii,* 585 U.S. ____ (2018).

15. *Congressional Record* (January 25, 1955): 672.

16. U.S. Department of Defense, "Operation Iraqi Freedom U.S. Casualty Status," http://www.defense.gov/news/casualty.pdf (August 22, 2012).

17. Iraq Body Count, http://www.iraqbodycount.org/ (August 22, 2012).

18. The following discussion derives from Reo M. Christenson, "Presidential Leadership of Congress," in *Rethinking the Presidency,* ed. Thomas E. Cronin (Boston: Little, Brown, 1982), pp. 255–271.

19. *Clinton v. City of New York,* 524 U.S. 417 (1998).

20. *Boston Globe,* "Bar Group Will Review Bush's Legal Challenges," June 4, 2006, http://www.boston.com/news/nation/articles/2006/06/04/bar_group_will_review_bushs_legal_challenges/ (June 5, 2006); CNN.com, "Signing Statements Add Presidential Spin to New Laws," June 19, 2007; Signing Statements: George W. Bush, http://www.coherentbabble.com/signingstatements/signstateann.htm (August 16, 2008).

21. *United States v. Nixon,* 418 U.S. 683 (1974).

22. *The New York Times,* March 22, 1990, p. Al.

23. *Congressional Quarterly Weekly Report,* February 12, 1983, p. 334.

24. NBC News, "NBC/WSJ poll: Country remains divided over Trump's impeachment trial," February 2, 2020, https://www.nbcnews.com/politics/meet-the-press/nbc-wsj-poll-country-remains-divided-over-trump-s-impeachment-n1128326 (August 10, 2020).

25. Michael Baruch Grossman and Martha Joynt Kumar, *Portraying the President: The White House and the News Media* (Baltimore, MD: Johns Hopkins University Press, 1981), ch. 11.

POP QUIZ

1. A third presidential term is forbidden by the _____ Amendment.

2. The group of cabinet members who handle issues of broad importance such as national security, economy, and justice is called the _____.

3. Presidents can avoid the need for Senate ratification of treaties by entering into _____ with foreign governments.

4. The president does not possess a/an _____ veto, allowing him to veto sections of a bill.

5. The third and last phase of the relationship between the president and the media is characterized by _____ .

6. The Senate has the right to refuse a presidential appointment even if only on the grounds of opposition to a particular policy.   T   F

7. The primary responsibility of the Council of Economic Advisers is to help the president develop the annual federal budget.   T   F

8. During World War I, Congress granted President Wilson almost dictatorial control over the economy.   T   F

9. The president of the United States, unlike many governors, does not possess a line item veto.   T   F

10. A president's endorsement of a candidate has little influence on voters.   T   F

11. Which of the following is true of presidential pardon power?
    A) It applies equally to federal and state and local laws.
    B) It does not include clemency for a class of people.
    C) It rarely gains headlines.
    D) It may not be granted prior to a conviction or indictment.

12. The executive office responsible for the formulation, coordination, and implementation of economic and domestic policy is the _____ .
    A) Office of Management and Budget
    B) National Security Council
    C) Council of Economic Advisers
    D) Office of Policy Development

13. The constitutional power to declare war belongs to the _____ .
    A) courts
    B) Congress
    C) president
    D) military

14. Which of the following is true of the Gulf of Tonkin Resolution?
    A) It gave President Johnson broad authority to use military force in Southeast Asia.
    B) It was passed unanimously in the House, but was defeated in the Senate.
    C) It was revoked by Congress only three months after being passed.
    D) It requires the president to consult with Congress before introducing troops into combat.

15. The gap between what the public expects and what the president can do is greatest when it comes to _____ .
    A) economic policy
    B) foreign policy
    C) environmental policy
    D) military policy

Answers:
1. Twenty-second   2. inner cabinet
3. executive agreements   4. line item
5. detachment   6. T   7. F   8. T   9. T
10. T   11. C   12. D   13. B   14. A   15. A

Chapter

11

BUREAUCRACIES

In This Chapter

11.1   Bureaucracies as the Fourth Branch of Government

11.2   Executive Branch Organization: Types of Bureaucracies

11.3   The Search for Competence in the Civil Service

11.4   The Search for Bureaucratic Responsiveness:
        The Political Environment of Bureaucracies

11.5   Bureaucrats and Government Regulation

11.6   Bureaucracies: Targets and Mirrors of Conflict

Chapter Objectives

This chapter examines the work of the federal bureaucracy and its employees, who are called bureaucrats. Although bureaucrats have been favorite targets of criticism over the past several decades, the bureaucracy occupies an important place in American government. Congress and the president may attract more media attention; however, without bureaucrats, ideas might be discussed, speeches might be delivered, elections might be held, Congress might debate, presidents might sign bills—but nothing would actually happen. Ultimately, space stations are built, oil spills are cleaned up, and Social Security checks are delivered to the elderly because of the work of bureaucrats.

This chapter describes who bureaucrats are and what they do, the major organizational types of bureaucracies, and the means the nation has adopted to ensure competence in the bureaucracy. The chapter also examines the problem of bureaucratic responsibility. As reflected in conflicts among interest groups, Congress, and the president, Americans do not always agree on what bureaucrats should do.

Consequently, deciding to whom bureaucrats should be answerable is central to understanding bureaucrats and their place in the political system. Finally, the chapter explores how government regulations, as issued by bureaucratic agencies, illustrate the changing policy agenda and conflict over the appropriate role of government.

11.1 Bureaucracies as the Fourth Branch of Government

The Constitution contains specific articles on the legislature, the executive, and the judiciary; yet the document only alludes to bureaucracy in several short phrases. Compared to 1789, Congress is now larger, the president has much greater staff help, and the number of courts and judges has increased. The truly explosive growth in government, however, has occurred in the development and evolution of bureaucracies. The result has been a US government that employs about 2.7 million civilians and spends over $3 trillion annually—and much more than that when dealing with a crisis like COVID-19.

11.1a Bureaucracies: Translating Ideas into Action

Once an idea becomes public policy—that is, once Congress and the president agree to an idea and it becomes law—somebody must carry that idea into action. Bureaucracies exist because translating ideas into action always requires an organization of people and resources devoted to that task. For example, debate over the Social Security program is really a dispute over ideas and their attendant costs. Congress and the president decide whether the payroll tax should be cut or increased and whether benefit checks should be linked to increases in the cost of living, but they cannot translate those decisions into action. Implementation is left to bureaucrats—in the cases just mentioned, to employees of the Internal Revenue Service and the Social Security Administration.

Most Americans do not really ponder the intricacies of administering a huge Social Security program. Someone must determine who is eligible for Social Security and the exact amount of money each person will receive every month. The logistical demands inherent in the idea of a Social Security system inevitably require a group of people to administer the program on a day-to-day basis. Without bureaucrats, grandmothers and elderly uncles would simply not get their Social Security checks.

A **bureaucracy** is an organization that exists to accomplish certain goals. It consists of a group of people, hired because of specific duties they can perform and arranged in a hierarchy—an order based on rank in which each member is responsible to a person at the next higher level. The goals or objectives of a bureaucracy are called **public purposes**. Max Weber, the great German sociologist, identified bureaucracy as a unique form of decision-making authority. For Weber, a division of labor, hierarchy, expertise, and impersonal rules characterize an "ideal-type" bureaucracy.[1] These ideal characteristics distinguish bureaucracy as a unique form of social organization designed to make decisions and get things done.

bureaucracy
An organization that exists to accomplish certain goals or objectives called public purposes and that consists of a group of people hired and arranged in a hierarchy because of specific duties they can perform

public purpose
A goal or objective of a bureaucracy

11.1b Who Are the Bureaucrats?

The term **bureaucrat** in American government generally refers to any individual who works in the executive branch of government. The Social Security Administration, for example, comprises some sixty thousand employees who translate the idea of Social Security into action. Among these individuals are computer programmers and technicians, information officers, clerks, policy researchers, receptionists, and hearing officers—all of whom in some way contribute to the execution of the Social Security idea.

Table 11.1 shows a schematic organization of the United States government. It does not display actual patterns of authority or the real size (in numbers of people or dollars spent) of various units, but it does provide a general outline of the branches of government. In terms of numbers of people employed and dollars spent, the executive branch is the largest. It includes the president and the Executive Office staff, as well as bureaucracies such as executive departments (Department of Defense), independent establishments (National Aeronautics and Space Administration), and government corporations (U.S. Postal Service). Because the president and his or her staff are politically separate in many ways from executive departments, independent agencies, and government corporations, these latter units are sometimes called a **fourth branch** of government.[2]

Executive departments, independent agencies, and government corporations are sometimes called the fourth branch of government.

(Jonathan Weiss / Shutterstock)

Aerial view of the Pentagon in Washington, D.C.

("The Pentagon, January 2008" by David B. Gleason, available under a CC BY-SA 2.0 license)

11.1c Distinguishing Characteristics of Bureaucracies

The most distinguishing characteristic of bureaucracies is that only they are responsible for executing public policies. The bureaucratic units in the fourth branch are also fundamentally different from the other three branches in size, diversity of purpose, physical dispersion, and relative anonymity. Approximately 64,000 people work in the legislative and judicial branches, a number that is dwarfed by the nearly 2.7 million civilian employees in the executive branch.

Bureaucracies are as diverse as the public purposes of government. Getting satellites into orbit (National Aeronautics and Space Administration), protecting consumers from deceptive advertising (Federal Trade Commission), and collecting taxes (Internal Revenue Service in the Department of the Treasury) are public services executed by individual bureaucracies. The degree of diversity among bureaucratic units in the fourth branch is so vast that it makes the other three branches appear almost monolithic in comparison.

bureaucrats

Individuals working in the executive branch of government who have received their positions on the basis of some type of appointment

fourth branch

Viewed as separate from the presidency, the collection of executive departments, independent establishments, and government corporations

Table 11.1   The Government of the United States

The fourth branch comprises executive departments, independent establishments, and government corporations. Although the president appears to be in command of the executive departments and other agencies, his or her actual control is measured by the degree of influence he or she is able to have on their decisions and programs. Most bureaucrats have civil service status and cannot be dismissed at the president's discretion. Only a relatively few administrative heads serve "at the pleasure of the president."

The Constitution

Legislative Branch	Executive Branch	Judicial Branch
Congress (Senate & House)	**President**	**U.S. Supreme Court**
Architect of the Capitol	**Vice President**	Administrative Office of the U.S. Courts
Congressional Budget Office	**Executive Office of the President**	Federal Judicial Center
Government Accountability Office	Council of Economic Advisers	Territorial Courts
Government Publishing Office	Council on Environmental Quality	U.S. Courts of Appeals
Library of Congress	National Security Council	U.S. Court of Appeals for Armed Forces
U.S. Botanic Garden	Office of Administration	U.S. Court of Appeals for Veterans Claims
	Office of Management and Budget	U.S. District Courts
	Office of National Drug Control Policy	U.S. Court of Federal Claims
	Office of Science and Technology Policy	U.S. Court of International Trade
	Office of U.S. Trade Representative	U.S. Sentencing Commission
	Office of the Vice President	U.S. Tax Court
	White House Office	

Fourth Branch

Executive Departments	Independent Establishments and Government Corporations
Department of Agriculture	Administrative Conference of the United States
Department of Commerce	African Development Foundation
Department of Defense	Broadcasting Board of Governors
Department of Education	Central Intelligence Agency
Department of Energy	Commodity Futures Trading Commission
Department of Health and Human Services	Consumer Product Safety Commission
Department of Homeland Security	Corporation for National and Community Service
Department of Housing and Urban Development	Defense Nuclear Facilities Safety Board
Department of the Interior	Environmental Protection Agency
Department of Justice	Equal Employment Opportunity Commission
Department of Labor	Export-Import Bank of the United States
Department of State	Farm Credit Administration
Department of Transportation	Federal Communications Commission
Department of the Treasury	Federal Deposit Insurance Corporation
Department of Veterans Affairs	Federal Election Commission
	Federal Housing Finance Agency
	Federal Labor Relations Authority
	Federal Maritime Commission
	Federal Mediation and Conciliation Service
	Federal Mine Safety and Health Review Commission
	Federal Reserve System
	Federal Retirement Thrift Investment Board
	Federal Trade Commission
	General Services Administration
	Inter-American Foundation
	Merit Systems Protection Board

Fourth Branch (Cont.)

Independent Establishments and Government Corporations (Cont.)

National Aeronautics and Space Administration

National Archives and Records Administration

National Capital Planning Commission

National Credit Union Administration

National Foundation on the Arts and the Humanities

National Labor Relations Board

National Mediation Board

National Railroad Passenger Corporation (Amtrak)

National Science Foundation

National Transportation Safety Board

Nuclear Regulatory Commission

Occupational Safety and Health Review Commission

Office of the Director of National Intelligence

Office of Government Ethics

Office of Personnel Management

Office of Special Counsel

Overseas Private Investment Corporation

Peace Corps

Pension Benefit Guaranty Corporation

Postal Regulatory Commission

Railroad Retirement Board

Securities and Exchange Commission

Selective Service System

Small Business Administration

Social Security Administration

Tennessee Valley Authority

Trade and Development Agency

U.S. Agency for International Development

U.S. Commission on Civil Rights

U.S. International Trade Commission

U.S. Postal Service

SOURCE: U.S. Government Manual, 2020.

The Capitol, the White House, and the Supreme Court Building are familiar Washington landmarks. However, the bureaucracy has no such single physical symbol. Rather, individual bureaucracies are dispersed throughout the Washington area. Some are housed in highly visible and well-known places, such as the Pentagon or the J. Edgar Hoover FBI Building. Discovering where most bureaucracies are located, however, requires initiative and enterprise. Indeed, 86 percent of bureaucrats work outside Washington in thousands of regional and field offices throughout the nation.

Most bureaucracies usually carry on their work with little sustained public awareness. The president performs his tasks in what seems like a fishbowl. Congress receives enormous media attention, and major Supreme Court decisions are given extensive news coverage as well. Except for some highly visible cabinet secretaries, however, most bureaucrats work with relative anonymity. Their names and exactly what they do are unknown to most citizens.

In the early decades of the nineteenth century, only several thousand people worked for the executive branch. That number grew to about a quarter of a million by the beginning of the twentieth century. Executive branch employment expanded rapidly during the New Deal decade of the 1930s and reached its highest point ever, at almost 4 million, by the end of World War II. For several decades, the number of civilians working in the executive branch remained fairly stable, at about 3 million people. Over the past several years, it has declined slightly to about 2.7 million.

Many government employees, as clerks and office workers, do not fit into the stereotypical view of bureaucrats. Someone working for the federal government performs practically every occupation. Executive branch employees include engineers, accountants, investigators, biologists, mathematicians, librarians, and veterinarians. Many blue-collar occupations are represented as well. The range of jobs in the federal service suggests the wide variety of public purposes. Generalizations about bureaucrats and bureaucracy, therefore, almost always refer in fact to *some* bureaucrats, *some* bureaucracies, or a *portion* of the federal service.

11.2 Executive Branch Organization: Types of Bureaucracies

Individual bureaucracies are generally created in response to specific political pressures in a particular area of public policy. A mix of diverse demands and expectations in the political struggle to define the public purposes government ought to pursue produces an array of organizational types of bureaucracies.[3] In terms of size and visibility, five types are particularly important: the Executive Office of the President, executive departments, independent agencies, independent regulatory commissions, and government corporations.

11.2a The Executive Office of the President

The president has a variety of personal and institutional staff advisers, working in organizations such as the Office of Management and Budget, the National Security Council, and the Council of Economic Advisers. Beyond the economic and foreign policy advice they offer, executive office units are resources the president can use in his attempts to influence other bureaucracies in the executive branch.

11.2b Executive Departments

As a group, the executive departments are generally the largest and most visible bureaucracies in the national government. The heads of these departments make up the **president's cabinet**, a source of collective advice that the president may or may not seek as he sees fit. Cabinet status is naturally conferred on organizations whose governmental purposes, such as national defense, are crucial by any standard. Beyond the groups that carry out these crucial activities, just what organizations deserve cabinet status is a political question.

For example, following President Reagan's endorsement of the idea, Congress in 1988 gave cabinet status to the Veterans Administration. Creation of the Department of Veterans Affairs reflected the considerable political clout of veterans groups in their demand for

president's cabinet

Political institution comprised mainly of executive department heads that collectively serve as a source of advice for the president

representation in the cabinet. In recognition of the high place that environmental issues hold in the nation's policy agenda, newly elected President Bill Clinton pushed for legislation to elevate the Environmental Protection Agency to cabinet status. The absence of departments of science and consumer affairs suggests the crucial role that political support plays in awarding public purposes a place in the cabinet. President George W. Bush's early effort to create five Centers for Faith-Based and Community Initiatives within existing cabinet departments was a signal of his priorities for the nation.

The headquarters of the United States Environmental Protection Agency in Washington, D.C.

Table 11.2 shows that executive departments differ in their dates of creation, number of employees, and amounts of money they spend. Each department has a unique organizational history, and the dates of creation listed in the table mark either the beginning of cabinet status or significant organizational change. For example, the Department of Defense was created in 1949 following the consolidation of the departments of the Army, Navy, and Air Force into the National Military Establishment in 1947, even though the nation had a Department of War (the army) beginning in 1789.

In terms of number of employees (as Table 11.2 shows), the Department of Defense exceeds all the others. With about 700,000 civilian employees (the additional 2.4 million active and reserve military personnel are not included in the table), the Defense Department alone accounts for almost one-fourth of the total number of civilians working for the national government. Health and Human Services, largely because of the huge Social Security program and health-care expenditures, typically accounts for the largest single chunk of money that the government spends.

Executive departments have presidentially appointed secretaries and assistant secretaries who provide direction, but these departments are really organizational "umbrellas" or "holding companies" within which a variety of smaller bureaucratic units are located. For example, the Federal Bureau of Investigation (FBI) is a unit within the Department of Justice. The Federal Aviation Agency (FAA), which is responsible for the safety of airports and airliners, is located within the Department of Transportation. The National Institutes of Health (NIH), overseeing what is probably the largest life sciences research program in the world, is an agency within the Department of Health and Human Services. The NIH has as its public purpose the satisfaction of one of the most persistent public expectations of the twenty-first century, namely, that government discover the causes and cures of disease. Although it is only part of a cabinet department, the NIH itself spends more money than the Department of State and employs more people than the Department of Education. Along with the Centers for Disease Control and Prevention—another subunit of the Department of Health and Human Services—the NIH has more frequently been in the news as the government's voice of scientific expertise on the COVID-19 pandemic.

11.2c Independent Agencies

A third major type of bureaucratic unit is the **independent agency**. Among the best examples of such agencies are the National Aeronautics and Space Administration (NASA) and the Peace Corps. These units are called independent because they are located

independent agency

A type of bureaucratic unit organizationally located outside of an executive department and generally headed by a single individual

Table 11.2 The Executive Departments

Executive departments vary widely in terms of employees and budgets. Expenditures are not always related to size of staff, as the numbers for the departments of Defense and Health and Human Services show.

	Date of Creation	Employees	Budget (in billions)
Defense	1949*	700,000**	$530
Veterans Affairs	1988	235,000	$90
Homeland Security	2003	216,000	$41
Justice	1870	113,000	$25
Treasury	1789	100,000	$13
Agriculture	1862	100,000	$95
Energy	1977	100,000***	$23
Interior	1849	70,000	$16
Health and Human Services	1979	65,000	$700
Transportation	1966	55,000	$70
Commerce****	1913	38,000	$6.5
State	1789	30,000	$35
Labor	1913	15,000	$50
Housing and Urban Development	1965	9,000	$40
Education	1979	4,200	$68.6

* The War Department, predecessor of the Defense Department, was created in 1789.

** Number includes civilian employees only.

*** Number includes contract employees.

**** A Department of Commerce and Labor existed between 1903 and 1913.

SOURCES: Statistical Abstract of the United States, 2012; https://www.whitehouse.gov/about-the-white-house/the-executive-branch/, 2020.

(iStock / Getty Images Plus)

Another type of bureaucracy is an independent agency, such as the National Aeronautics and Space Administration (NASA).

outside executive departments. The president can hire and fire their heads, and the amount of money these agencies spend must go through the regular appropriations process whereby the president and Congress make final expenditure decisions.

The determination of whether an agency shall be placed inside or outside an executive department is strongly influenced by political considerations. Some groups may want an agency serving its purposes to be more highly visible, be unfettered by cabinet control, or have more direct access to the president. Agencies can also be granted independent status because of the judgment that no executive department would be an appropriate home for the agency. For example, NASA was established as an independent unit to avoid the inter-military service rivalry that marred the early space program and to give the nation's space program a nonmilitary cast.

11.2d Independent Regulatory Commissions

A fourth type of unit is the **independent regulatory commission**. As the title suggests, commissions composed of usually five to eleven people, rather than single individuals, head such units. The commission device was justified on the grounds that a group of experts in a particular field of economic activity, relatively insulated from partisan political considerations, could make reasonable and fair judgments on the basis of their technical knowledge.[4] The Interstate Commerce Commission, created in 1887 and terminated in 1996, served as an organizational model for subsequent regulatory efforts. The Consumer Product Safety Commission, established in 1972, is an example of a contemporary IRC.

Like independent agencies, independent regulatory commissions lie outside executive departments. However, the independence of the commissions has greater significance, for they have a special status that insulates them to some degree from control by the president. The terms of the commissioners are fixed, so the president may appoint new commissioners only when vacancies occur. Often their terms are longer than the president's. In addition, the Supreme Court has ruled that the president can remove commissioners only for causes specified in statutory law governing the commission. Because the commissions are not purely "executive" agencies, the president's controls over them are more limited.[5] The Court, however, reopened this question in 2020, when it determined that at least some independent agency heads are within the reach of presidential dismissal.[6]

11.2e Government Corporations

A fifth type of bureaucratic unit is the **government corporation**. Examples of government corporations include the National Railroad Passenger Corporation (Amtrak), the Federal Deposit Insurance Corporation, and the National Park Foundation. Government corporations provide services—such as rail transportation, offering insurance, or producing electric power—that are also provided by private corporations. In the provision of these services, government corporations generally produce much of their own revenue. For example, people must pay a specific fee to enter a national park.

Historically, certain types of essentially commercial enterprises have been judged to be of sufficient public importance to merit substantial government involvement. A system of insuring bank deposits is such an enterprise. Compared to other public bureaucracies, such corporations have been granted a degree of financial and operational flexibility because of the essentially commercial character of their work. Because they generally rely on user fees, they are not tied to the regular appropriations process as are other types of bureaucracies.[7]

11.3 The Search for Competence in the Civil Service

In assessing bureaucrats and their role, two questions are particularly important. First, how can the nation ensure that bureaucrats are competent? Second, to whom are bureaucrats responsive in the political system? The issue of responsiveness has become particularly important as government has grown over the last half-century, but concern over competence is as old as the republic itself.

---

independent regulatory commission

A type of bureaucratic unit organizationally located outside of an executive department, headed by a group of individuals called a commission, and charged with regulating a specific industry or economic practice

government corporation

A type of bureaucratic unit that offers some service for which the benefiting individual or institution must pay directly

President Andrew Jackson

President James Garfield's assassination led to the passage of the single most significant piece of legislation affecting public service, the Pendleton Act of 1883.

President Washington stressed the importance of "fitness of character" in appointments to high office. His ideal appointees tended to be educated members of the upper classes who looked on government as a high calling. When the Jeffersonians took control from the Federalists after the election of 1800, many moderate Federalists remained on the job. This era has been called one of "government by gentlemen" because the "business of governing was prestigious, and it was anointed with high moral imperatives of integrity and honor."[8]

11.3a   The Spoils System

The early period of integrity and honor is not nearly as widely known as the famous, or infamous, **spoils system**, the practice of making appointments to government jobs on the basis of party loyalty and support in election campaigns. The term *spoils system* comes from a statement made by Senator William L. Marcy of New York during a Senate debate over a presidential appointment in 1832: "They see nothing wrong in the rule that to the victor belong the spoils of the enemy."[9]

The beginning of the spoils system is traditionally associated with the presidency of Andrew Jackson (1829–1837), which began a period of "government by the common man," a reaction against the elitism of government service in earlier decades.[10] The spoils system led to wholesale changes in government personnel after presidential elections. Government posts were openly bargained for and traded. Presidents spent much of their time, not pondering great affairs of state, but dealing with people whose needs were much simpler—they wanted government jobs. The result was a view of government as an employment agency and a perception, continuing even today, of government and politics as a corrupt and dirty business.

In an irony of history, the single most important contributor to the demise of the spoils system was an individual who sorely wished to take advantage of it. Charles Guiteau asked President James Garfield (1881) for an appointment as consul to Paris. When he did not receive a government job, Guiteau shot the president, who died several months later. In galvanizing public opinion, an assassin's bullet accomplished what for so long had eluded reasoned debate.

spoils system

The practice of making appointments to government jobs on the basis of party loyalty and support in election campaigns

11.3b   The Pendleton Act and the Merit Principle

President Garfield's assassination, combined with public reaction against scandals and corruption in the preceding Grant and Hayes administrations, led to the passage of the single most significant piece of legislation affecting public service.

The **Pendleton Act** of 1883 established a Civil Service Commission whose task was to introduce the concept of merit as a condition of government employment. Merit was to be determined by competitive examinations that tested an individual's ability to perform the job in question. Expertise replaced partisan political connections as the criterion for selection. In the beginning, the Pendleton Act covered only about 10 percent of all government positions. However, as a result of a variety of executive and legislative actions over the past century, the vast majority of government jobs are now filled on the basis of merit. This emphasis on merit has been so strong that in 1939 Congress enacted the **Hatch Act**, which banned civil servants from participation in partisan political activity.

People become government employees through a variety of avenues. The military services have their own system of recruitment. Similarly, other agencies—such as the Postal Service, the FBI, and the State Department's Foreign Service—each have their own separate systems of hiring and merit. Most government jobs, however, are covered by the civil service system administered by the Office of Personnel Management. This agency has assumed most of the functions of the Civil Service Commission, which was abolished in 1978. For many positions, particularly at lower levels, competitive examinations are required. For others, individuals are rated on the basis of their experience and qualifications.

Clerical and administrative personnel within the competitive service are classified in a "general schedule" (GS) that is divided into fifteen "grades," with stages within each grade. Specific grades are based on the experience and qualifications of individuals, as well as the job responsibilities they are assigned. Lower grades are assigned to individuals who perform clerical, secretarial, or administrative support tasks. College graduates generally begin at grade five or above, whereas grades thirteen, fourteen, and fifteen are "midlevel management positions."[11] Individuals with higher-level positions beyond GS-15 are generally in the Senior Executive Service discussed below. Presidential appointments are in a separate Executive Schedule.

11.3c   The Civil Service Reform Act of 1978

As a candidate for the presidency, Jimmy Carter made reform of the federal bureaucracy one of his campaign themes. Among the most significant pieces of legislation enacted during his term was the **Civil Service Reform Act** of 1978, the most far-reaching attempt to change the civil service since the Pendleton Act. The act was intended to defend the merit principle and to provide incentives for high-quality work. It established a system of merit pay for midlevel managers and provided protections for whistle-blowers, individuals in the bureaucracy who report waste or fraud. The act also created the **Senior Executive Service (SES)**, a group of about eight thousand high-level civil servants who might be given bonuses, transferred among agencies, or demoted—all depending on their performance.[12]

President Carter established the **Office of Personnel Management (OPM)** as the government's principal personnel agency with ultimate responsibility for hiring and maintaining the highest-quality workforce. He also redesignated the Civil Service Commission as the **Merit Systems Protection Board**, charged with protecting individual employees against violations of the merit principle or actions taken against whistleblowers.

The 1978 reform has not lived up to its promise, however. In the decade following passage of the act, the merit pay system was hobbled by a lack of adequate funds and perceptions of inequity in merit pay awards.[13] Hopes that the SES would become a prestigious and respected group of senior civil servants were not fulfilled. SES members

Pendleton Act

Legislation passed in 1883 that created a Civil Service Commission charged with the task of using merit, rather than partisan political connections, as a condition of government employment

Hatch Act

Legislation that prohibits civil servants from participating in partisan political activity

Civil Service Reform Act

Legislation designed to improve the level of performance of civil servants by creating incentives for high-quality work, protecting whistle-blowers, and making it easier to fire inadequate employees

Senior Executive Service (SES)

Created by the Civil Service Reform Act of 1978, a class of civil servants drawn from the highest grades and who might be given bonuses, transferred among agencies, or demoted—all depending on the quality of their work

Office of Personnel Management (OPM)

Created in 1981 as part of the Executive Office of the President, focuses on the formulation, coordination, and implementation of domestic and economic policy, and provides staff support for the Economic and Domestic Policy Councils

Merit Systems Protection Board

An agency charged with protecting individual employees against violations of the merit principle or actions taken against whistle-blowers

expressed dissatisfaction with their political superiors, their compensation, and the generally unfavorable public perceptions of the federal civil service.[14] Some changes in these attitudes started to occur by the 1990s. For example, senior civil servants generally expressed satisfaction with their salaries after a generous pay raise in 1991.[15] The history of the 1978 act, nonetheless, shows that efforts to reform the civil service system are at once difficult and durable.

11.4 The Search for Bureaucratic Responsiveness: The Political Environment of Bureaucracies

Who determines what bureaucrats do is a matter of critical importance in any discussion of bureaucracy. Because the political system is one of dispersed power, the work of bureaucrats is shaped by a variety of individuals and institutions, including the president, Congress, the courts, and interest groups. Both the president and Congress can point to specific clauses in the Constitution that give each a claim to control over the bureaucracy. Conflict about who ought to control the bureaucracy is, therefore, inevitable.

11.4a The President

As the title "chief executive" suggests, the individual most responsible for the performance and actions of bureaucrats in the executive branch is the president of the United States. The Constitution charges the president with the responsibility to "take care that the Laws be faithfully executed." In addition, the Constitution authorizes the president to make appointments of department heads and allows the president to "require the opinion, in writing, of the principal officer in each of the executive Departments, upon any subject relating to the Duties of their respective Offices."

Despite such constitutional authority, incoming presidents have discovered that they have to work hard to achieve bureaucratic responsiveness to their demands and requests.[16] The relationship sometimes resembles more of a struggle among contestants than the easy downward flow of power suggested by neat organization charts.

Presidential control of bureaucracy is difficult for a variety of reasons. First, the sheer size and diversity of the executive branch means that close presidential control and direction of every bureaucrat is a literal impossibility.[17] Much of the work of government has a dynamic of its own; and each day, without direct presidential attention, the assigned tasks must be accomplished.

Second, as specialists in some area of public policy, bureaucrats tend to be committed to their own work rather than to the person of the president. Such commitment is strengthened by the fact that they usually hold relatively permanent positions, whereas presidents are in office for a much shorter period of time. Perhaps most important, bureaucrats, taking advantage of the dispersion of power in the political system, can make alliances with other groups and institutions. Congress, its committees, and political interest groups are among the main sources of power bureaucrats can tap in their struggles with the president.

Bureaucrats can delay action, take no action, or offer alternatives in response to a presidential request; but presidents determined to get action have at their disposal a variety

of tools to make bureaucrats responsive. First, the president has the power to make some three thousand appointments to the departments and agencies. These individuals, who include cabinet secretaries, assistant secretaries, and the heads of independent agencies, are the people the president depends on to carry forward his programs in the executive branch. President Reagan, for example, skillfully used his appointments to help shape his public policy goals. President Donald Trump won the presidency with the promise of new public policies to "Make America Great Again." Meeting that promise depended, in some measure, on the people Trump chose to fill important executive branch posts in his administration.

Second, presidents can use the budget process to propose cuts or increases in the financing of specific bureaucracies. Although the president cannot independently determine expenditures, his proposals can significantly affect the size of bureaucratic budgets. For example, in his budget proposals, President George W. Bush was the single most important individual shaping Defense Department spending and proposals to shift resources to new civilian technologies. Finally, subject to congressional approval, presidents can reorganize agencies to make them more compliant to their wishes. Using this power, presidents can abolish agencies, create new ones, and rearrange lines of responsibility among existing agencies.

11.4b Congress

The president's most powerful competitor in the effort to ensure bureaucratic responsiveness is Congress. According to the Constitution, presidential appointments shall be made "by and with the Advice and Consent of the Senate." The document also grants to Congress taxing powers to provide for "the general welfare of the United States." The Constitution grants what is probably the most potent power of Congress over bureaucracy by stating "no money shall be drawn from the Treasury, but in Consequence of Appropriations made by Law." Like the president and the president's staff, Congress cannot hope to oversee consistently and in any detailed fashion the daily operations of every bureaucratic unit. However, a Congress determined to make a difference can substantially shape bureaucratic behavior.

First, Congress has the ultimate responsibility for the creation and abolition of agencies. Second, the Senate must confirm presidential appointments, particularly those at the highest bureaucratic levels. Although presidents generally get approval for their appointees, the Senate occasionally exercises its constitutional right to reject nominees. The possibility of Senate rejection no doubt

(Lawrence Jackson, Whitehouse.com, 2009 via Wikimedia)

The president's most powerful competitor in the effort to ensure bureaucratic responsiveness is Congress. Here President Barack Obama speaks to a joint session of Congress regarding health-care reform.

(Getty Images)

One of the most potent powers of Congress over bureaucracy is its power to ensure "that no money shall be drawn from the United States Treasury, but in consequence of appropriations made by law."

eliminates some candidates from consideration at the outset. Third, congressional power to enact a budget means that Congress may substantially shape both the amount and the purpose of money bureaucrats spend. Finally, pursuant to its constitutional authority to enact laws, Congress can use its power to investigate bureaucratic behavior. In hearings before its committees, Congress can question bureaucrats about allegations of abuse of the purpose of specific legislation.

Congress engages in efforts to control bureaucracies partly because of self-interest. Reelection of its members frequently depends on what bureaucrats do and how they do it. Indeed, one observer argues that the growth of big government and the expansion of bureaucratic involvement in the lives of citizens are, in no small measure, the responsibility of Congress itself. According to this view, members of Congress find electoral profit in *pork-barreling* and *casework* activities.[18] Pork-barreling refers to the attempt by members of Congress to get as many federal dollars and projects to flow into their districts as possible. Casework refers to services to individual constituents who are having difficulties with government agencies, ranging from a lost Social Security check to getting a passport.

11.4c The Case of the Veto

As society has become increasingly technological and interdependent, Congress has delegated more generous discretionary authority to the president and executive agencies to grapple with the technical and complicated issues confronting government. To temper executive discretion, Congress also provided for a **legislative veto**. Under this provision, a vote by one or both houses of Congress—or even by a congressional committee in some instances—can halt an executive initiative, bypassing the president in the process. In this way, rather than initially specifying what could be done, Congress reserved for itself the right to react to what had been done. Congress has written legislative veto power into many laws, among which are statutes governing the rule-making powers of regulatory agencies. In one of its best-known exercises of legislative veto power, Congress invalidated a proposed agency regulation that would have required used-car dealers to give potential buyers more extensive information about the cars. Critics of legislative veto power charged that the provision allowed Congress to interfere with executive prerogatives. In 1983, in *Immigration and Naturalization Service v. Chadha*,[19] the Supreme Court declared the legislative veto unconstitutional because it violated the separation of powers mandated by the Constitution.

However, the Court's ruling did not settle the matter, for "the decision has been eroded by open defiance and subtle evasion."[20] The legislative veto power continues to be written into some statutes. In addition, informal arrangements provide that agencies will not take certain actions without consulting Congress. For example, NASA and the House Appropriations Committee have agreed that they will not exceed spending ceilings on NASA programs without informal committee approval. The legislative veto continues because bureaucrats need to exercise some discretion as they administer federal programs,

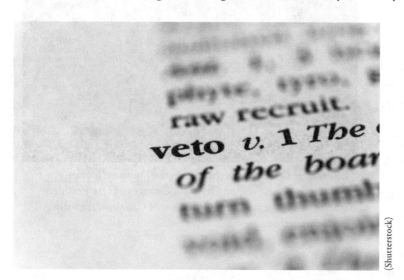

(Shutterstock)

legislative veto

Congressional power, which the Supreme Court ruled unconstitutional in 1983, to halt an executive initiative by a vote of one or both houses or by a congressional committee

but Congress needs to place limits on that discretion without always resorting to the cumbersome process of enacting laws. The continuing use of the legislative veto is the practical result of these realities.

11.4d   Interest Groups

Bureaucracies are engaged in day-to-day execution of public purposes; thus, political interest groups understandably try to shape what bureaucrats do. Practically every bureaucratic unit has the strong support of some group. In some cases, groups have what amounts to a proprietary interest in specific departments and agencies. Veterans groups consider the Department of Veterans Affairs "theirs," and farmers view the Department of Agriculture in much the same way. In other cases, groups compete as they press their claims on the same agency. The Environmental Protection Agency (EPA) is consistently in the middle of a cross fire of conflicting demands from environmental groups, which charge that the EPA is not enforcing environmental laws vigorously enough, and industrial groups, which argue that the EPA is enforcing such laws too vigorously. Debate over public purposes naturally extends to the work of bureaucracies.

Groups can make direct appeals to the bureaucrats themselves, for example, by commenting on proposed regulations; and groups can also make claims on bureaucracies through other institutions, such as the mass media, the courts, and Congress. Groups can use press conferences or advertising campaigns to influence bureaucratic decisions, or they can ask the courts to order bureaucracies to halt "unfavorable" actions or begin "favorable" actions. Most important, groups can try to influence Congress to use its substantial powers to bring about the kind of bureaucratic activity that groups see as favorable to their own interests.

One of the most familiar models of decision-making in American government is the **iron triangle**, composed of interest groups, relevant congressional committees, and one or more executive branch agencies (see Chapter 9, Figure 9.2, for an example of the iron triangle and veterans policy). Iron triangles characterize the decision-making process for many areas of public policy. One triangle, for example, consists of the Defense Department, congressional armed services committees, and corporate contractors who manufacture weapons systems.

Each of the sides of these triangles depends on, and can support, the other two because the triangles are held together by large doses of mutual self-interest. The development of a new aircraft or the continued production of an older one, for example, is a decision heavy with political and economic significance. Congressional appropriations for production not only satisfy units in the Department of Defense but also please aircraft companies, their suppliers and contractors, unions, and local communities—all of which benefit when government money is spent. Defense cuts strain these relationships. Attempts to cancel development of a new plane or to shift the contract for production to another company (and perhaps a different section of the country) are sure to provoke resistance from those who have the most to lose.

11.4e   The Courts

The courts play a more passive role in the political environment of bureaucracies and can significantly shape, in a variety of ways, what bureaucrats do. First, the courts can determine the constitutionality of some congressional or presidential action and can affect, therefore, the work of bureaucrats. More than a half-century ago, the Supreme Court ruled that Congress had unconstitutionally delegated its own powers to the National

iron triangle

The combination of interest group representatives, legislators, and government administrators seen as extremely influential in determining the outcome of political decisions

Recovery Administration, a New Deal agency created to help relieve the economic crisis in the Great Depression.[21] Although the Court since the New Deal has generally allowed Congress to determine the matter of delegation, controversial subjects, such as the legislative veto and claims of executive privilege, have been tested in the courts in recent years.

Second, the courts attempt to ensure procedural fairness in the efforts of bureaucratic units to promulgate rules and regulations. If the courts determine that a group has not been given adequate notice or the right to comment, the rule may be struck down. Third, in discerning congressional intent behind legislation that is either vague or ambiguous, the courts can decide what bureaucracies can or cannot do. For example, if Congress in statutory law bans the use of public funds in "programs where abortion is a method of family planning," can the Department of Health and Human Services (HHS) issue rules that forbid medical personnel in federally funded clinics from even *discussing* with patients abortion as an option? Although President Bill Clinton later lifted the ban, in 1991 the Supreme Court in *Rust v. Sullivan* upheld the HHS regulations banning such discussion as a plausible interpretation of the congressional statute.[22] When Congress is not precise in what a bureaucracy should or could do in a specific instance, the courts ultimately decide the legitimacy of bureaucratic action.

Want to work for a federal agency?

Find out how at the Office of Personnel Management's website.

http://www.bvtlab.com/a8P8m

Finally, as another example of judicial power over bureaucracies, the courts can determine whether rules issued by regulatory agencies are reasonable in light of available evidence. The courts must wait for cases to come to them, but judges can powerfully shape the work of bureaucrats.

11.5 | Bureaucrats and Government Regulation

Because of the great diversity among public purposes, bureaucrats engage in a wide range of activities, from doing research on AIDS to collecting taxes to building space stations. Issuing rules and regulations that affect a large number of individuals and companies throughout the nation has been the most controversial activity of bureaucrats over the past several decades. Regulations have produced sharp debate because of the costs and behavior changes they impose on the people affected. A review of regulatory policy illustrates the role of bureaucrats in public policy and the intensely political environment that shapes their work.

11.5a Regulation in Perspective

The Environmental Protection Agency has the Herculean task of producing regulations required by the Clean Air Act amendments that Congress enacted in 1990. For example, in the effort to limit the release of ozone-depleting chlorofluorocarbons (CFCs) into the atmosphere, Congress required the EPA to produce regulations on the servicing of motor vehicle air conditioners. The EPA rules are highly detailed and technical and provide an

illustration of the role of bureaucrats in translating ideas into action—in this instance producing specific requirements that will change behavior to protect the ozone layer.[23]

Evidence of regulations in a wide range of policy areas is all around us. Electricity used in millions of homes may be produced by nuclear power plants regulated by the Nuclear Regulatory Commission. Radio and television stations are regulated by the Federal Communications Commission. The Food and Drug Administration certifies the safety of prescription drugs. The EPA sets detailed standards for safe drinking water. The physical safety of workplaces is regulated by the Occupational Safety and Health Administration. Baby cribs and toys are subject to regulation by the Consumer Product Safety Commission. Although these are all examples of national agencies, the federal nature of American government means that many of these regulatory bodies have state-level counterparts as well. Most states, for example, control and regulate the sale of alcoholic beverages through a state agency.

(Shutterstock)

Ingredients of foods sold in America must pass federal inspection by meeting specific nutritional requirements. For example, hamburger meat is shaped by nearly 41,000 federal and state regulations.

Government regulations touch people's lives at the most basic levels. For example, it was once noted that more than three hundred federal regulations shape what goes into a pizza and how it may be sold.[24] Ingredients must meet specified nutritional requirements to pass federal inspection. Regulations similarly affect other common foods. The hamburger, a staple in the US, is shaped by forty-one thousand federal and state regulations.[25] Few people who eat pizza or hamburgers are aware of or give much thought to the dense network of rules that surrounds their meals. For those who produce and market pizza and hamburgers, however, these regulations are a constant reminder of the pervasiveness of government in even the ordinary activities of life. Such rules are intended to protect consumers from unsafe products and to try to ensure nutritional, high-quality meals.

One of the continuing issues in regulatory policy debate is whether regulatory agencies go beyond congressional intent in their creation of rules. Congress has delegated much authority to these agencies due to the fact that members of Congress have neither the time nor the expertise to draft such rules. How to place limits on experts without crippling their expertise is an ongoing issue in the relationship between legislators and policy makers.

11.5b Regulatory Agencies and Types of Regulations

Regulations are rules devised by government to shape the actions of individuals and groups to achieve purposes mandated by law.[26] With the increase in public expectations and the general expansion of government activity, rules and regulations cover practically every commercial activity and achieve a variety of policy goals. More than one hundred agencies have regulatory powers.

The distinction between economic regulation and social regulation is useful in understanding the regulatory goals of government. In **economic regulation**, a government agency issues rules that shape the structure of some industry or ban or encourage certain business practices. For example, the Federal Trade Commission is charged with limiting

regulations

Rules devised by government agencies that shape the actions of individuals and groups in order to achieve purposes mandated by law

economic regulation

Type of regulation in which a government agency issues rules that shape the structure of some industry, such as limiting entrance into the broadcast industry, or banning or encouraging certain business practices

Table 11.3 Selected Regulatory Agencies

Establishment of regulatory agencies has come in waves or groups, as Congress has responded to persistent political demands.

Agency	Date of Creation	Purpose
Interstate Commerce Commission (ICC)	1887	To regulate interstate surface transportation, including trains, trucks, buses, and water carriers (eliminated in 1996)
Federal Trade Commission (FTC)	1914	To protect economic competition against monopoly or restraints on trade, and to protect against unfair or deceptive trade practice
Food and Drug Administration (FDA)	1930*	To protect the health of citizens against impure and unsafe foods, drugs, cosmetics, and other potential hazards
Federal Communications Commission (FCC)	1934	To regulate interstate and foreign communications by radio, television, wire, satellite, and cable
Securities and Exchange Commission (SEC)	1934	To provide protection for investors and to ensure that securities markets are fair and honest and, when necessary, to provide the means to enforce securities laws through sanctions
National Labor Relations Board (NLRB)	1935	To safeguard employees' rights to organize, to determine through elections whether workers want unions as their bargaining representatives, and to prevent and remedy unfair labor practices
Equal Employment Opportunity Commission (EEOC)	1964	To eliminate discrimination in employment on the basis of race, color, religion, sex, national origin, disability, or age
Occupational Safety and Health Administration (OSHA)	1970	To develop, promulgate, and enforce occupational safety and health standards
Environmental Protection Agency (EPA)	1970	To control and abate pollution in the areas of air, water, solid waste, pesticides, radiation, and toxic substances
Consumer Product Safety Commission (CPSC)	1972	To protect the public against unreasonable risks of injury from consumer products, to develop consumer product safety standards, and to promote product safety and research
Nuclear Regulatory Commission (NRC)	1974**	To license and regulate the civilian use of nuclear energy to protect public health and safety and the environment
Federal Energy Regulatory Commission (FERC)	1977***	To set rates and charges for the transportation and sale of natural gas and oil by pipeline and for the transmission and sale of electricity and the licensing of hydroelectric power projects

* Assumed functions placed in the Department of Agriculture in 1906.

** Assumed many of the functions given to the Atomic Energy Commission in 1946.

*** Assumed many of the functions of the Federal Power Commission created in 1920.

SOURCE: Some statements of purpose were taken, with some modifications, from U.S. Government Manual, 2007–2008.

monopolistic practices. In **social regulation**, agencies issue rules that are designed to achieve social goals, such as fair treatment in employment, clean air, or safe workplaces.[27] For example, the Equal Employment Opportunity Commission is charged with limiting employment discrimination. The result is the enhancement of the political and social status of some groups, such as women and African Americans.

Regulatory agencies perform both **quasi-legislative** and **quasi-judicial** functions. In their quasi-legislative roles, agencies issue rules that, like legislation, apply to whole classes of people. For example, rules of the Securities and Exchange Commission (SEC) against stock market trading on the basis of insider information apply to all individuals and firms in the securities industry. As quasi-judicial bodies, agencies, like courts, can make decisions in individual cases. Because of action by the SEC, for instance, the mayor and city treasurer of Detroit were indicted in 2012 for securities law violations that included accepting gifts from a corporation that was attempting to influence investment of the city's pension funds.[28]

As another example, consumers or competitors can complain to the Federal Trade Commission that a company is engaged in deceptive advertising. The commission can investigate the charge with an **administrative law judge**, who hears the case in what amounts to a trial proceeding. Administrative law judges were mandated by the Administrative Procedure Act of 1946 as part of a general effort to provide procedural protections for individuals and groups in agency proceedings. Administrative law judges hold an insulated status in agencies to protect their judicial function, and their findings in particular cases can be appealed to the commission and, if necessary, to the federal courts.

Table 11.3 lists selected regulatory agencies, their dates of creation, and their purposes. Major government initiatives to regulate the economy first occurred in the decades around the beginning of the twentieth century. As industrialization proceeded in the late nineteenth century, the relationships between the buyers and sellers of goods and services became increasingly national in scope. The growth of corporations and nationalization of the economy brought a variety of unsavory practices, such as price gouging, and structures, such as monopolies, to the marketplace. Such iniquities led to demands that government remedy the imbalance between producers and purchasers. These problems frequently crossed state lines; and in many instances, redress involved the national government.

Establishment of regulatory agencies has come in waves or groups as Congress has responded to persistent political demands. The first wave occurred around the turn of the twentieth century and dealt with the unprecedented size and impact of major industrial corporations and with the problems encountered by the buyers and sellers of goods and services. The second, in the 1930s, sprang from the economic dislocation caused by the Great Depression. The third, in the 1960s and 1970s, came in response to demands to remedy inequalities and to protect the environment and the workplace.

In 1887, Congress created the Interstate Commerce Commission to regulate the railroads. The commission device was justified on the grounds that a group of technical experts in a particular field of economic activity, who were relatively insulated from partisan political considerations, could make reasonable and fair judgments. New industries and new demands for regulation came in the twentieth century, and the Interstate Commerce Commission served as a model for subsequent regulatory efforts. Other enactments followed, such as the Sherman Antitrust Act (1890) and the Federal Trade Commission Act (1914), which tried to limit the growing economic power of trusts and large corporations. The goal of regulation was to establish government as a counterweight to the concentration of economic power in a small number of businesses.

Another kind of regulation tried to protect consumers of specific products. In the ideal free market, companies compete with each other to sell products at the lowest price to consumers who make their purchase choices based on full information about the

social regulation

Type of regulation in which a government agency issues rules designed to achieve noneconomic policy goals, such as fair treatment in employment, clean air, or safe workplaces

quasi-legislative

A function of regulatory agencies in which they can make rules that, like legislation, apply to whole classes of people

quasi-judicial

A function of regulatory agencies in which, like a court, they can make decisions in individual cases

administrative law judge

An officer with relatively independent status in a regulatory agency who presides over and makes findings in judicial proceedings in which the agency's actions in individual cases are at issue

relative merits of the products. However, in the real world consumers either do not have access to such information or do not take the trouble to get it. Regulation of consumer products means that government action compensates for such market failures. Largely in response to publicity about unsavory practices in particular industries, Congress enacted the Pure Food and Drug Act (1906) and the Meat Inspection Act (1907) to protect unwary consumers. Such regulation continues, as contemporary rules on pizza and hamburgers suggest.

The next period of new regulatory activity occurred during the explosion of government initiatives during the New Deal of the 1930s. Regulation increased as part of the general response of government to the Great Depression. The drive for active government brought entire industries under federal regulation. Among the regulatory agencies created were the Securities and Exchange Commission for financial exchange markets, the Federal Communications Commission for electronic communications, and the Civil Aeronautics Board for the airline industry.[29] In the effort to combat unfair labor practices, the National Labor Relations Board was established to regulate employer-employee relationships in businesses in interstate commerce.

Until recent generations, most government regulations had predominantly economic goals. The objects of regulation were relationships among businesses—rates, business practices, and entry into an industry. However, in the 1960s and 1970s, new regulatory efforts went beyond economic concerns to encompass such social goals as affirmative action, worker safety, environmental protection, and consumer product safety. Among the regulatory agencies established were the Equal Employment Opportunity Commission to fight discrimination in the workplace, the Environmental Protection Agency to limit environmental pollution, the Occupational Safety and Health Administration to promote worker safety, and the Consumer Product Safety Commission to protect consumers from unsafe products. Social regulation has been the lightning rod drawing most of the conflict over regulation since the 1960s.

11.5c   The Regulatory Process

Regulatory agencies make rules that can have real consequences easily discernible to most people. For example, almost everyone has had the experience of struggling to open a "childproof" aspirin bottle, yet almost no one thinks about the circuitous route such regulations travel before they touch us. Figure 11.1 shows where regulations come from. All regulations ultimately have their roots in the Constitution, which grants Congress the power to pass laws and to establish agencies to accomplish specific purposes. Each act of Congress is published in the form of a **slip law**, which is the written text of the legislation. Depending on the subject matter, slip laws can range from a single page to several hundred pages in length. The slip laws passed by each session of Congress are bound together to form a volume of *U.S. Statutes-at-Large*. Laws currently in effect are classified by subject matter, such as transportation, labor, or public health and welfare, in the *U.S. Code*, a collection of dozens of volumes periodically revised to reflect changes in legislation.

Once established, agencies must abide by stringent procedural requirements in their promulgation of rules and regulations. To provide adequate notice and opportunity for hearing under the provisions of the Administrative Procedure Act of 1946, agencies must publish proposed rules to allow anyone affected to comment on them. Such rules appear in the *Federal Register* a daily government publication (now easily accessible on the internet) that also contains presidential proclamations and executive orders. On any given day the *Federal Register* may be several hundred pages in length, a fact that suggests the complexity and scope of the federal regulatory effort. All rules and regulations currently in effect

slip law

The written text of an act of Congress

U.S. Statutes-at-Large

Chronological compilation, by year, of slip laws passed in each session of Congress

U.S. Code

Compilation of laws currently in effect, classified by subject matter, such as transportation or labor

Federal Register

A daily government publication that contains proposed and final regulations, presidential proclamations, and executive orders

Figure 11.1   Where Regulations Come From

Regulatory authority lies in the Constitution, which authorizes Congress to enact and the president to approve the creation of departments and programs. A new piece of legislation appears first as a slip law and then in *U.S. Statutes-at-Large* and the *U.S. Code*. Established by such legislation, agencies issue and enforce regulations. These in turn appear in the *Federal Register* and later in the *Code of Federal Regulations*. Regulations may be contested in the courts.

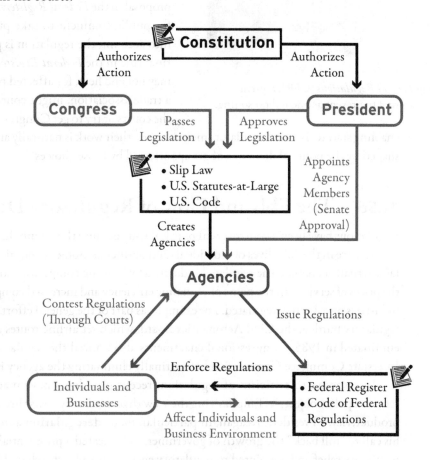

are compiled by agency and subject matter in the ***Code of Federal Regulations (CFR)***, a collection divided into fifty titles and consisting of over two hundred volumes, revised annually on a staggered basis. The regulations are arranged topically in the *CFR* just as statutes are arranged topically in the *U.S. Code*.

Regulations setting acceptable contaminant levels in drinking water traversed this process, as did those requiring childproof aspirin bottles to prevent accidental poisoning. In 1972 Congress enacted the Consumer Product Safety Act, which gave wide-ranging powers on consumer safety to the Consumer Product Safety Commission (CPSC). The act entered the *U.S. Statutes-at-Large* and the *U.S. Code*.[30] By publishing proposed rules in the *Federal Register*, receiving comment, and then issuing final rules, the commission establishes safety standards that a large number of consumer products must meet. The standards are compiled in the *Code of Federal Regulations*. The congressional act that established the CPSC is only twenty-seven pages in length; yet an entire volume of the *Code of Federal Regulations*, which is more than six hundred pages long, is devoted to the commission and its rules. Among the detailed safety standards in the *CFR* are twenty-one pages on poison prevention packaging requirements, including rules on aspirin bottles.

Code of Federal Regulations (CFR)

Compilation of U.S. administrative rules currently in effect, classified by agency and subject matter

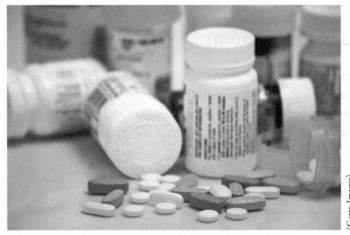

According to the *Code of Federal Regulations* (CFR), aspirin bottles must be made childproof to prevent accidental poisoning.

(Getty Images)

Agencies themselves may go through a complicated internal sequence of steps before they issue a rule.[31] A variety of groups and individuals within the agency, including lawyers, technicians, scientists, and economists, shape the proposed regulation. The proposed rule is then reviewed by the Office of Management and Budget, after which it appears as a proposal in the *Federal Register*. After a period for public comment to take public reaction into account, the regulation is published as a final rule in the *Federal Register*. The process may not end here; for affected parties, such as a trade association, might contest the rule in the courts or try to get Congress to change the enabling statute. Because regulators make choices, their work is naturally and continually shaped by the political demands of groups affected by those choices.

11.5d The Ebb and Flow of Regulatory Debate

Regulations have been a controversial political issue because they symbolize government interference in the daily lives of individuals and businesses. Some economic regulation, in fact, actually benefited the regulated industries by limiting competition and supporting the prices of services. In the name of economic efficiency and increased competition, some industries have been deregulated. For example, as part of the general effort to lighten the regulatory burden, the Civil Aeronautics Board, which set airline routes and rates, was eliminated in 1985. Congressional enactments also limited the regulatory role of the Interstate Commerce Commission before finally eliminating the agency in 1996.

In response to criticism of regulation, recent presidents have made regulatory reform a policy objective. Emphasizing the view that regulatory costs threaten economic productivity,[32] President Reagan, in particular, made **deregulation** a major theme in his call to "roll back" the growth of government. He created a presidential task force on regulatory relief and appointed to regulatory agencies people who shared his interest in reducing the impact of regulations. The budgets of regulatory agencies were cut, and many new proposed regulations were suspended. The Office of Management and Budget assumed an active role in assessing the costs and benefits of new rules; however, as "Politics and Economics: Regulations and Cost-Benefit Analysis" suggests, OMB review of regulations has been controversial.

As the 1980s wore on, critics saw deregulatory efforts as attempts to strip government of its power to pursue worthy economic and social goals.[33] A turning point came early in the decade in the battle between Congress and President Reagan over the EPA. In 1980, Congress gave to the EPA the task of cleaning up toxic waste dumps with money drawn from a "superfund" financed by a tax on chemicals. Within a short time critics charged that the EPA was being too responsive to the interests of the chemical companies and was not

Feeling overregulated? Did you know that the government invites comments from the public on *newly proposed regulations*?

Use this website to search new rules and participate in the federal rule-making process.

http://www.bvtlab.com/6w887

deregulation

Process of reducing the number and scope of government regulations

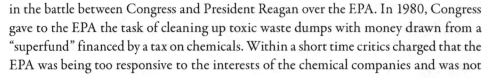

POLITICS AND ECONOMICS

Regulation and Cost-Benefit Analysis

Regulations obviously cost money. Regulatory agencies require buildings, people, and sometimes sophisticated equipment and research capabilities—all of which must be funded by tax dollars. Agency rules can also require that other people spend money. The protection of workers may require that companies make expensive physical alterations in the workplace. Environmental quality standards may require that manufacturing plants install special equipment to reduce air emissions. Companies may be forced to spend scarce research and development dollars to meet mandated consumer product safety standards. One of the most durable and volatile issues in regulatory policy debate is whether these costs are worth the effort.

Cost-benefit analysis is one of the techniques used to assess the impact of regulations. In theory, cost-benefit analysis should enable government officials to determine whether regulations are worth their costs. The technique can take complicated mathematical forms. In general, the costs of a regulation are tallied and then compared with the benefits the regulation is designed to gain. For example, are the benefits of the lives saved from cleaner air worth the costs of EPA enforcement activities and air scrubbers used in manufacturing plants? The matter is complicated by the fact that progressively higher standards may require geometrically higher costs. For example, cleaning the air of 90 percent of its particulate matter may be equal to or less than the cost of cleaning the next 5 percent.

Efforts to make cost-benefit analyses an integral part of rule-making have been controversial. In 1981 President Reagan issued an executive order requiring that agencies assessing proposed or existing regulations be guided by an analysis of costs and benefits. According to the order, agencies can make rules only if "the potential benefits to society for the regulation outweigh the potential costs to society." Agencies proposing major rules—rules having an impact of $100 million or more on the economy—must submit to the Office of Management and Budget (OMB) a regulatory impact analysis before the rule goes into effect. Critics in Congress charged that the OMB used its powers of reviewing regulatory costs and benefits to delay or weaken proposed rules designed to enhance worker or consumer safety or to meet environmental goals. In the George H. W. Bush administration, the White House Council on Competitiveness, headed by Vice President Dan Quayle, assumed the role of regulatory watchdog as it diluted rules it judged to be too costly. The OMB and the Competitiveness Council were strongly supported by those who wanted to keep in check what they saw as unreasonably costly regulations; but the sharp criticism of the limits these agencies placed on regulations illustrates the political debate that can swirl around cost-benefit analysis.

The existence of the debate indicates that cost-benefit analysis does not offer easy answers for public officials. Efforts to tally costs and benefits can become mired in questions such as how much a life is worth or how the benefit of a smogless day can be calculated. Political interests are highly resistant to conclusions that do not support their positions, regardless of how mathematically sound they appear. Acknowledging the limitations of cost-benefit analysis, what questions can be asked about any proposed rule to assess its worth?

vigorously enforcing the toxic waste law. The House of Representatives cited the head of the EPA (a Reagan appointee) for contempt of Congress for refusing to make available agency documents. Six congressional committees began investigations amid intense criticism that the agency reflected the Reagan administration's neglect of environmental concerns. To contain the political damage, the White House made sweeping changes in the agency's leadership and released the requested documents. The struggle uncovered the deep political support for strong governmental action in environmental protection.

By the mid-1980s, regulation as a volatile political issue temporarily receded, and renewed receptivity to government regulation became more evident. In 1986, Congress broadened environmental regulations on drinking water and toxic wastes.[34] Later in the decade some critics argued that the financial disaster of the collapse of savings and

loan institutions could have been avoided had the regulatory atmosphere not been so lax.[35] As a lagging economy dogged his presidency, President Bush, in his 1992 State of the Union address, called for a "moratorium on any new federal regulations that could hinder growth." Predictably, the moratorium drew fire from consumer and environmental groups and support from those charging that regulations pose a costly burden. The scope of regulatory activity was an issue in the 1992 presidential campaign; and Bill Clinton's victory promised, as a contrast to the Bush moratorium, greater receptivity in the White House to consumer and environmental regulations. However, a knotty task that the Bill Clinton administration confronted was making regulation more vigorous to protect the environment, workers, and consumers without limiting job growth and economic productivity.[36] By adopting many tenets of a market-driven approach to public management, known as "reinventing government," the Bill Clinton administration was largely able to succeed in its objectives.[37] Regulation continues to be a topic of scorn for some. President Trump proudly claimed to have cut more regulations than any president in US history.

(iStock / Getty Images Plus)

Regulatory bureaucrats caught in the middle of the crossfire of conflict surrounding regulations are really at the center of a debate over the appropriate role of government. Environmentalists want to protect wildlife and wilderness areas, but loggers fear a loss of jobs.

Regulatory bureaucrats caught in the middle of the crossfire of conflict surrounding regulation are really at the center of a debate over the appropriate role of government. The attempt to ban unsafe toys may be hailed by consumer groups, but criticized by manufacturers. Environmentalists want to protect endangered species and wilderness areas, but loggers fear a loss of jobs. Citizens with disabilities promote efforts to make buildings more accessible, but corporations and universities have worried about the high financial costs of providing such accessibility. Health groups vigorously support efforts to regulate cigarette advertising, but the tobacco industry views such regulation as a threat. Businesses cite the high financial burden of some worker safety requirements, but labor unions see efforts to limit such rules as increasing physical risks to workers. The contests over changes in regulatory efforts are more than differences over financial costs. The intensity of the debate may ebb and flow; however, conflict over regulations springs from disagreement over what government should do, who should benefit from government action, and whether compromises among competing goals can be achieved.

11.6 Bureaucracies: Targets and Mirrors of Conflict

For much of the past generation, bureaucrats have been the target of biting criticism from elected officials, candidates for public office, and private citizens. Like lightning rods, bureaucrats have drawn criticism aimed at government in general.

Four charges summarize the criticism. First, bureaucrats waste or defraud precious public resources. Second, they wrap much of their work in what appears to be endless amounts of **red tape**, which can be defined as "unnecessary" procedural requirements that impede needed action. Third, bureaucrats do work that either duplicates or conflicts with the work of other bureaucrats. Fourth, and perhaps most important, they play an independent and "political" role in public policy—that is, through their use of discretion, unelected bureaucrats make choices that either directly counter or go beyond the wishes of elected politicians.

Every large organization has individuals who work diligently and conscientiously and others whose work is either haphazard or detrimental to the goals of the organization. Given the size of the national government, it is inevitable that waste and fraud exist, but there is no agreement on their extent. The national government spends huge amounts of time and money trying to limit waste and ensure integrity of work. The battle is always being fought.[38]

The criticism of red tape can be more accurately leveled at groups in the political system generally, rather than at individual bureaucrats. One observer has argued, "One person's red tape may be another's treasured safeguard."[39] That is, what appears to be red tape is really the result of conflicting expectations on the parts of different groups in the political system. For example, advocates of nuclear power may decry the long bureaucratic process of hearings, certifications, and licensing procedures that accompanies the construction of a nuclear power plant. Environmentalists and some local residents may see such procedures as absolutely essential to public health and safety. Perhaps red tape is more a reflection of the attempt to satisfy political values in our society, such as consideration of different points of view, than it is an effort by bureaucrats to paralyze action.[40]

Similarly, charges that bureaucrats engage in work that duplicates or conflicts with the work of other bureaucrats can be explained in large measure by outside expectations. For example, in granting college funds to veterans, the Department of Veterans Affairs (DVA) may be duplicating the educational programs of the Department of Education; yet the political expectation that the DVA serve veterans encourages that agency to assume educational functions of its own. Similarly, the Agriculture Department represents the economic demands of tobacco farmers, while Health and Human Services represents the demands of health groups. The conflicting demands of different groups in society are largely reflected in conflict among different groups of bureaucrats.

The most serious criticism of bureaucrats, however, is that even though they are unelected, they independently make choices affecting public policy and play an unintended political role in the process. However, three qualifications need to be made about their political role. First, in executing policy purposes, bureaucrats obviously strive to achieve their institution's goals. For example, an administrator at the NIH may stress the importance of additional funding for cancer research or defense analysts may call for the construction of a new weapons system. Executing policy is bureaucrats' work; bureaucrats, not surprisingly, want the most favorable environment possible in which that work can proceed.

Second, bureaucrats cannot always exercise discretion in translating ideas into action. The Internal Revenue Service, for example, cannot decide to tax certain income groups at rates higher or lower than those prescribed by law. The greater the specificity of the idea written into law, the lower the degree of discretion bureaucrats have in translating that idea into action.

Third, if the law is vague or ambiguous, bureaucratic discretion is inevitable. In much legislation, Congress cannot possibly provide for every contingency or circumstance. Such detailed decisions fall to bureaucrats. For example, the Social Security Administration (SSA), in administering benefits to disabled Americans, must determine just what

red tape
Bureaucratic rules and procedures that seem to complicate and delay needed action unnecessarily

constitutes disability in individual cases. Depending on how rigorous that determination is, the SSA, in effect, can make public policy toward citizens with disabilities.[41]

In many areas of public policy, different groups and institutions have conflicting ideas on what government ought to do; they are interested in bureaucracy because they want to get their ideas translated into action. In large measure, the issue of bureaucratic responsiveness centers on the determination of whose ideas ought to be translated into action. In an enlightening and provocative statement, a civil servant in the EPA declared during a controversy over environmental policy: "I signed an oath of office, and it was not to the president. It was to the American people."[42] The statement implies that control over the bureaucracy comes to those who can successfully claim to determine what "the American people" want. The search for that determination, like the struggle to control bureaucracy, lies at the heart of political conflict.

CHAPTER REVIEW

1. The principal task of bureaucracy is the translation of policy ideas into action. Bureaucrats are people appointed to positions in the executive branch. Individuals responsible for executing public policies work relatively anonymously in bureaucracies. Compared to the other branches of government, bureaucracies are much larger, more diverse in purpose, and physically dispersed. The 2.7 million government employees work in a great variety of occupations.

2. Executive Office units advise and serve the president. The executive departments generally contain a large number of smaller bureaucratic units. Independent agencies are placed outside the executive departments, generally in response to political demands for greater visibility. More insulated from presidential control than other bureaucracies, independent regulatory agencies monitor various sectors of the economy. Government corporations are public bodies engaged in essentially commercial enterprises.

3. Government service was seen as a high calling in the early decades of the Republic. In the spoils system, government jobs were rewards for political service. The Pendleton Act of 1883 established the merit principle as the basis for government employment. The Civil Service Reform Act of 1978 attempted to protect the merit system and rid the system of abuses, but its success has been questioned.

4. The president can shape bureaucracies by exercising his appointment, budget proposal, and reorganization powers. Congress can contest the president in the struggle to control bureaucracy through its statutory, budget, confirmation, and investigative powers. In iron triangles, interest groups can work with members of Congress to make claims on bureaucracies. The courts can shape the work of bureaucracies by declaring laws unconstitutional, ensuring procedural fairness, interpreting statutes, and judging the reasonableness of agency actions.

5. Regulation is a major policy of government that affects practically everyone in some way. Economic regulation centers on specific industries, and social regulation tries to achieve a variety of social goals. Major regulatory initiatives were made in the late nineteenth and early twentieth centuries, during the New Deal, and in the 1960s and 1970s. Regulatory agencies issue rules pursuant to powers they receive from congressional enactments. Debates over the regulatory roles of government ebb and flow with the debates over the appropriate roles of government and who should bear the costs of government action.

6. Bureaucracies have been targets of sharp criticism over the past generation. Depending on the amount of discretion Congress allows in law, bureaucrats can potentially make policy. The issue of bureaucratic responsiveness centers principally on determining whose policy ideas should be implemented.

KEY TERMS

administrative law judge.................... 365

bureaucracy 348

bureaucrats................................349

Civil Service Reform Act 357

Code of Federal Regulations (CFR).......... 367

deregulation..............................368

economic regulation 363

Federal Register 366

fourth branch 349

government corporation................... 355

Hatch Act.................................357

independent agency.......................353

independent regulatory commission......... 355

iron triangle..............................361

legislative veto 360

Merit Systems Protection Board............357

Office of Personnel Management (OPM) 357

Pendleton Act 357

president's cabinet 352

public purpose.............................348

quasi-judicial 365

quasi-legislative 365

red tape 371

regulations 363

Senior Executive Service (SES) 357

slip law....................................366

social regulation 365

spoils system 356

U.S. Code 366

U.S. Statutes-at-Large 366

READINGS FOR FURTHER STUDY

The United States Government Manual (Washington, DC: Government Printing Office) is a basic reference work that contains a history, relevant congressional enactments, and an organization chart for each bureaucratic unit.

Donald F. Kettl's *The Politics of the Administrative Process*, 8th ed. (Washington, DC: CQ Press, 2020) is a comprehensive and erudite review of bureaucracies in the policy process.

A classic work on the obstacles to the implementation of policies is Jeffrey L. Pressman and Aaron B. Wildavsky's *Implementation*, 3rd ed. (Berkeley: University of California Press, 1984).

A look at change over time and the role of today's bureaucracy is found in Donald F. Kettl's *The Transformation of Governance: Public Administration for Twenty-first Century America,* 2nd ed. (Baltimore, MD: The Johns Hopkins University Press, 2015).

William T. Gormley Jr. and Steven J. Balla's *Bureaucracy and Democracy*, 4th ed. (Washington, DC: CQ Press, 2017) reviews and analyzes efforts to control bureaucracy in a democratic society.

Richard A. Harris and Sidney Milkis's *The Politics of Regulatory Change: A Tale of Two Agencies*, 2nd ed. (New York: Oxford University Press, 1996), examines the Federal Trade Commission and the Environmental Protection Agency within the context of regulatory politics.

A. Lee Fritschler and Catherine E. Rudder's *Smoking and Politics: Policymaking and the Federal Bureaucracy*, 6th ed. (Englewood Cliffs, NJ: Prentice-Hall, 2006) is an illuminating analysis of the Federal Trade Commission's attempt to regulate cigarette advertising.

John A. Rohr's *Civil Servants and Their Constitutions*, (Lawrence: University Press of Kansas, 2002) explores the relationship between the bureaucracy and the public.

NOTES

1. A more extended discussion can be found in H. H. Gerth and C. Wright Mills, eds., *From Max Weber: Essays in Sociology* (New York: Oxford University Press, 1958), pp. 196–198.

2. For an example of use of the phrase, see Kenneth J. Meier's *Politics and the Bureaucracy: Policymaking in the Fourth Branch of Government*, 3rd ed. (Pacific Grove, CA: Brooks/Cole, 1993).

3. Harold Seidman, *Politics, Position, and Power: The Dynamics of Federal Organization*, 3rd ed. (New York: Oxford University Press, 1980), p. 321.

4. For a more detailed assessment of the commission form, see Marver H. Bernstein's *Regulating Business by Independent Commission* (Princeton, NJ: Princeton University Press, 1966), pp. 23–30.

5. *Humphrey's Executor v. United States*, 295 U.S. 602 (1934).

6. *Seila Law v. Consumer Financial Protection Bureau*, 591 U.S. ___ (2020).

7. See Seidman, *Politics, Position, and Power*, pp. 265–276.

8. Frederick C. Mosher, *Democracy and the Public Service*, 2nd ed. (New York: Oxford University Press, 1982), pp. 58, 60.

9. U.S. Civil Service Commission, *Biography of an Ideal: A History of the Federal Civil Service* (Washington, DC: Government Printing Office, 1973), pp. 16–17.

10. Mosher, *Democracy and the Public Service*, pp. 64–66.

11. Many individuals who were formerly in grades sixteen, seventeen, and eighteen (which have been abolished) are now members of the Senior Executive Service. See Meier, *Politics and the Bureaucracy*, pp. 34–36.

12. Patricia W. Ingraham and David H. Rosenbloom, "Symposium on the Civil Service Reform Act of 1978: An Evaluation," *Policy Studies Journal 17* (1988–1989): 311–312, provide a more complete list of the act's goals. The symposium contains a series of articles assessing the act from various perspectives (pp. 311–447).

13. U.S. General Accounting Office, *Pay for Performance* (Washington, DC: Government Printing Office, 1989), p. 12.

14. U.S. General Accounting Office, *The Public Services: Issues Affecting Its Quality, Effectiveness, Integrity, and Stewardship* (Washington, DC: Government Printing Office, 1989), p. 34.

15. U.S. General Accounting Office, *Senior Executive Service: Opinions About the Federal Work Environment* (Washington, DC: Government Printing Office, 1992), p. 4.

16. For a concise history of presidential efforts to get control of bureaucracy, see Francis E. Rourke, "Responsiveness and Neutral Competence in American Bureaucracy," *Public Administration Review 52* (November–December 1992): 539–546.

17. Herbert Kaufman, "Fear of Bureaucracy: A Raging Pandemic," *Public Administration Review 41* (January–February 1980): 3–4.

18. Morris P. Fiorina, *Congress: Keystone of the Washington Establishment*, 2nd ed. (New Haven, CT: Yale University Press, 1989), pp. 40–47 and 85–94.

19. *INS v. Chadha*, 462 U.S. 919 (1983).

20. Louis Fisher, *Constitutional Dialogues: Interpretation as a Political Process* (Princeton, NJ: Princeton University Press, 1988), p. 225. This discussion of the persistence of the legislative veto draws on Fisher's analysis, pp. 226–228. See also Fisher's *Constitutional Conflicts Between Congress and the President* (Lawrence: University Press of Kansas, 1991), pp. 146–152.

21. *Schecter Poultry Corp. v. United States*, 295 U.S. 495 (1935).

22. *Rust v. Sullivan*, 59 U.S.L.W. 4451.

23. 57 *Federal Register* 31242 (July 14, 1992).

24. "A Pizza with the Works—Including 310 Regulations," *U.S. News & World Report* (May 31, 1982): 25, 55.

25. "Your Hamburger: 41,000 Regulations," *U.S. News & World Report* (February 11, 1980): 64.

26. This definition draws on Kenneth J. Meier's *Regulation: Politics, Bureaucracy, and Economics* (New York: St. Martin's Press, 1985), pp. 1–2.

27. See *Federal Regulatory Directory*, 6th ed. (Washington, DC: Congressional Quarterly, 1990), pp. 2, 5–13.

28. U.S. Securities and Exchange Commission, https://www.sec.gov/litigation/litreleases/2012/lr22362.htm (October 12, 2018).

29. To deregulate and allow the operation of market incentives in the airline industry, the Civil Aeronautics Board has since been abolished.

30. The act transferred responsibility for poison prevention packaging from the EPA and the Department of Health, Education, and Welfare to the new commission.

31. For example, see Gary C. Bryner's *Bureaucratic Discretion: Law and Policy in Federal Regulatory Agencies* (New York: Pergamon, 1987), pp. 98–105.

32. For a critique of regulation, see Murray L. Weidenbaum's *The Future of Business Regulation: Private Action and Public Demand* (New York: AMACOM, 1979).

33. See Susan J. Tolchin and Martin Tolchin's *Dismantling America: The Rush to Deregulate* (Boston: Houghton Mifflin, 1983).

34. Michael E. Kraft, "Environmental Gridlock: Searching for Consensus in Congress," in Norman J. Vig and Michael E. Kraft, eds., *Environmental Policy in the 1990s* (Washington, DC: Congressional Quarterly, 1990), pp. 110–111.

35. Jeff Gerth, "Regulators Say '80s Budget Cuts May Cost U.S. Billions in 1990," *The New York Times*, December 19, 1989, pp. Al, B10.

36. For a discussion of the debate over regulations in the campaign, see Gerald F. Seib and Bob Davis, "Bush and Clinton Joust Over How to Regulate U.S. Business Activity," *The Wall Street Journal*, September 23, 1992, pp. Al, A6.

37. David Osborne and Ted Gaebler, *Reinventing Government* (Reading, MA: Addison-Wesley, 1992).

38. See the discussion in Herbert Kaufman's *Red Tape: Its Origins, Uses, and Abuses* (Washington, DC: Brookings Institution, 1977), pp. 50–54.

39. Ibid., p. 4.

40. Ibid.

41. See, for example, Susan Gluck Mezey's *No Longer Disabled: The Federal Courts and the Politics of Social Security Disability* (Westport, CT: Greenwood, 1988).

42. Hugh B. Kaufman, quoted in Cass Peterson, "A Nagging Voice from E.P.A. Depths Now Singing from the Catbird Seat," *The Washington Post*, February 14, 1983, p. A9.

POP QUIZ

1. The most distinguishing characteristic of bureaucracies is that only they are responsible for _____ public policies.

2. One of the most important determinants of what purposes deserve Cabinet status is _____ _____.

3. The practice of making appointments to government jobs on the basis of party loyalty is called the _____ .

4. _____ has the ultimate responsibility for the creation and abolition of agencies.

5. Often justified as a safeguard against abuse, bureaucracies have been criticized for wrapping their work in endless amounts of _____ _____.

6. In American government the term *bureaucrat* generally refers to any individual who works in the executive branch of government.   T   F

7. Independent agencies are outside executive departments and their heads cannot be fired by the president.   T   F

8. According to the Hatch Act, civil servants are banned from participation in partisan political activity.   T   F

9. Salaries for public officials are usually equal or above the compensation rates for equivalent positions in the private sector.   T   F

10. When laws are vague or ambiguous, bureaucratic discretion is inevitable.   T   F

11. According to Max Weber, an ideal bureaucracy consists of _____ .
    A) expertise
    B) impersonal rules
    C) a hierarchical division of labor
    D) All of the above

12. Which of the following makes independent agencies independent?
    A) They are outside the regular appropriations process.
    B) The president cannot hire or fire their heads.
    C) They are located outside of the executive departments.
    D) They are not influenced by interest groups.

13. Government employment during the administration of George Washington was characterized by _____ .
    A) corruption
    B) political spoils
    C) integrity and honor
    D) lack of respect and prestige

14. Which of the following is one of the tools that the president has to make bureaucrats more responsive?
    A) Propose cuts or increases in the budgets of bureaucracies.
    B) Create or abolish agencies.
    C) Investigate bureaucratic power.
    D) All of the above

15. Which of the following is the most serious criticism of bureaucrats?
    A) They waste and defraud public resources.
    B) They affect public policies and play an unintended political role.
    C) They wrap their work in unnecessary amounts of red tape.
    D) They do work that duplicates or conflicts with other bureaucrats' work.

Answers:
1. executing   2. political support
3. spoils system   4. Congress   5. red tape
6. T   7. F   8. T   9. F   10. T   11. D
12. C   13. C   14. A   15. B

Chapter 12

(Shutterstock)

THE SUPREME COURT & AMERICAN JUDICIARY

In This Chapter

12.1   The National Court System

12.2   What Courts Do

12.3   The Supreme Court at Work

12.4   The Supreme Court and American Government: An Assessment

Chapter Objectives

One of the distinguishing characteristics of American government is the major role the Supreme Court and other courts play in governing the nation. Because of the importance of the issues that confront American judges, their decisions weigh heavily in shaping the liberties, fortunes, and quality of life of many citizens. Chief among courts is the United States Supreme Court, the third branch of government.

The Supreme Court enjoys prominence because of the Constitution and because Americans have been reluctant to place their fate entirely in the hands of elected officials and popular majorities. The Court, therefore, sits as an institution primarily responsible for interpreting the law of the land. Yet because the Court appears anti-democratic in a government that strives to be democratic, Americans have also been wary of giving judges too much power.

Explaining what judges do, discerning the Supreme Court's place in American government, and exploring how the Court decides cases are the objectives of this chapter.

12.1 The National Court System

A look at almost any recent term of the Supreme Court turns up decisions on subjects as varied as presidential powers, crime, taxation, religious freedom, and racial and sexual equality. The fact that the Supreme Court confronts important issues makes the Court similar to other major political institutions in Washington; however, three factors distinguish the Supreme Court and other courts from the rest of the national government:

1.   The judiciary operates only in the context of cases.

2.   The cases develop in a strictly prescribed fashion.

3.   Judges rely heavily on reason in justifying what they do.

The judiciary is distinctive because it is the part of government that speaks the language of the fundamental values of the political system.

12.1a   Cases: Raw Material for the Judiciary

case

A controversy to be decided by a court

criminal case

Judicial proceedings that the government begins against an individual following commission of a crime

crime

A public wrong; an offense, such as murder, against society at large—even though it may have been committed against only a single individual

civil case

Noncriminal legal action, such as divorces or attempts to recover damages following an automobile accident

state courts

Courts of the fifty states, as opposed to the federal, or national, courts

federal courts

The courts of the United States, as distinguished from the courts of the fifty states

The judiciary acts by deciding **cases**. A case is a dispute handled by a court. Like most disputes, there are at least two opposing parties. A case may pit one individual against another, a government agency against an individual, a corporation against the government, and so forth. Cases are criminal or civil.

Criminal cases result when the government begins legal action against someone following commission of a crime. A **crime** is a public wrong. That is, it is an offense, such as murder, against society at large—even though it may have been committed against only a single individual. **Civil cases** encompass all noncriminal legal actions and commonly include attempts to redress a private wrong or to settle a private dispute. Divorces and recovery of damages following an automobile accident, for example, present civil law questions. They involve efforts by one party to enforce a right or to be compensated for harm caused by another.

By deciding cases, courts, like other governmental institutions, attempt to resolve conflicts peacefully. It is only a slight exaggeration to say that disputes that bring a regiment of soldiers into the streets of some countries summon a battalion of lawyers into the courtrooms in the US.

12.1b   Fifty-one Judicial Systems

Topped by the Supreme Court, the national court system contains both state courts and federal courts. The latter, in turn, consist of district courts, courts of appeals, and a few special courts.

References to **state courts** and **federal courts** can be confusing to anyone not familiar with the political features of American federalism (see Chapter 2). Concisely put, each state has its own system of courts, and the national government has its own system of courts (see Figure 12.1 and Figure 12.2). The national courts are usually referred to, somewhat misleadingly, as "federal courts."

The two types of courts hear different kinds of cases. Almost all divorce and personal injury cases, for example, are heard in state courts, as are violations of state criminal laws. Antitrust actions and violations of federal criminal laws, by contrast, are adjudicated in federal courts. Someone charged with robbing a corner grocery will be tried in state

The role of the Supreme Court is to have the final say on interpreting the Constitution.
Associate Justice Ruth Bader Ginsburg (seated, second from right), passed away in
September 2020, and was replaced with Amy Coney Barrett.

(Courtesy of Fred Schilling, Collection of the Supreme Court of the United States, via Wikimedia)

Figure 12.1 The United States Court System

Almost all cases the Supreme Court decides each year are part of its appellate jurisdiction. These cases begin
in the state and federal courts.

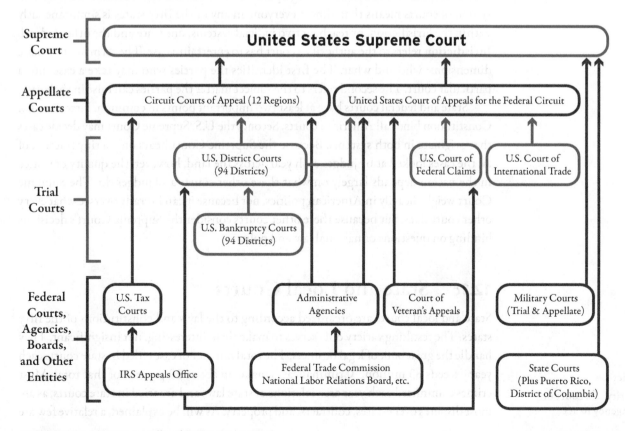

DATA SOURCE: Administrative Office of the United States Courts.

Figure 12.2 Typical Organization of State Courts

Each state has its own system of state courts. No system is exactly like another, but all are organized in a hierarchy similar to that pictured here. All states have courts of limited jurisdiction, courts of general jurisdiction, and a court of last resort. In Texas and Oklahoma, there are two separate courts of last resort—one for criminal appeals and one for all other types of cases. Most, but not all, states have at least one intermediate appellate court. In the twelve states that have no intermediate court, cases move on appeal from courts of general jurisdiction to the court of last resort.

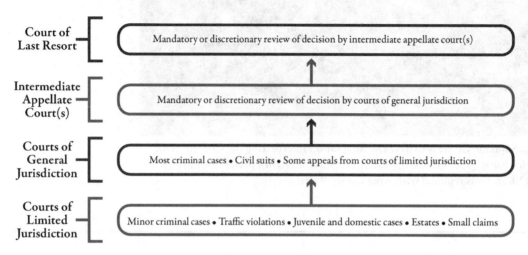

Court of Last Resort — Mandatory or discretionary review of decision by intermediate appellate court(s)

Intermediate Appellate Court(s) — Mandatory or discretionary review of decision by courts of general jurisdiction

Courts of General Jurisdiction — Most criminal cases • Civil suits • Some appeals from courts of limited jurisdiction

Courts of Limited Jurisdiction — Minor criminal cases • Traffic violations • Juvenile and domestic cases • Estates • Small claims

DATA SOURCE: National Center for State Courts.

court; someone charged with robbing a post office will be tried in federal court. The dual system of courts means that almost everyone in any of the fifty states is simultaneously within the jurisdiction, or reach, of two judicial systems, one state and the other federal. **Jurisdiction** refers to the authority a court has to entertain a case. The term has two basic dimensions: who and what. The first identifies the parties who may take a case into a particular court. The second refers to the subject matter the parties can raise in their case.

State and federal courts have at least two important points in common. First, the U.S. Constitution binds all American courts. Second, the U.S. Supreme Court may decide cases that originate in both systems. Because the Supreme Court hears only a tiny fraction of all the cases looked at by judges each year across the land, however, the quality of justice in the nation depends largely on what these other courts and judges do. The Supreme Court weighs heavily in American politics, not because it can literally oversee what every other court does, but because these other courts consider the Supreme Court's decisions binding on questions of national law and policy.

12.1c State and Local Courts

State and local courts are organized according to the laws and constitutions of the fifty states. The resulting variety only serves to make them interesting, not insignificant. They handle the great bulk of legal business. The total number of cases filed in state courts each year exceeds 83 million.[1] Criminal cases make up about 20 percent of that total. Most crimes committed each year are violations of state laws and are tried in state courts, as are most disputes over estates, contracts, and property. As will be explained, a relative few are

jurisdiction
Authority of a court or other agency to act

ever candidates for review by the U.S. Supreme Court. Most people in the US who go to court, then, go to state courts and only state courts.

The judicial systems of most states are divided into four levels (see Figure 12.2). At the bottom are **courts of limited jurisdiction**, which hear cases in villages, towns, and cities involving small claims, traffic violations, domestic matters, juvenile affairs, and minor criminal offenses. Such courts are variously labeled municipal court, county court, magistrate's court, traffic court, or recorder's court. Usually a judge sitting without a jury decides such cases. On the next tier are **courts of general jurisdiction**; usually one such court is located in each county. These courts receive appeals from the bottom tier and serve as trial courts for serious criminal offenses and civil suits involving substantial amounts of money. Again, the names vary from state to state: superior court, county court, or court of common pleas. Above these courts in many states, especially the more populous, are one or more **intermediate appellate courts**, which are labeled superior court or court of appeals; they accept appeals from the courts of general jurisdiction. At the top of the state system of courts is a **court of last resort**, usually called the supreme court. Most states have only one "supreme court," but Texas and Oklahoma have two, with one specifically designated to hear appeals in criminal cases. (In New York the highest court is called the Court of Appeals, and a supreme court is a court of general jurisdiction.)

Unlike federal judges, who are appointed for life and removable only by impeachment, most state judges are elected. In some states, judges run in nonpartisan elections or in partisan elections just as legislative candidates do. In other states the governor appoints judges from a list of nominees provided by a panel of lawyers and other citizens. The latter method is called the **Missouri Plan**, after the state that pioneered its use. Following initial election or appointment, judges may then be subject to retention votes every five or ten years. That is, instead of running for reelection like other officeholders, judges have their names placed on a ballot alongside the question, "Shall Judge X be continued in office for another term?" A negative vote creates a vacancy, and a new election is held or a new appointment is made. At present, nineteen states use a single method for selecting judges; in the remaining states judges are selected by one of two (or even three) methods, depending on the court involved.

Whether a judge is chosen by election or the Missouri Plan, the people can unseat state judges at the polls. Critics say that this possibility undercuts judicial independence, making judges too dependent on the voters and perhaps afraid to render unpopular decisions. Others reply that the people should retain control over all public officials, even judges. Experience shows that judges elected on partisan ballots are more likely than those chosen on nonpartisan ballots or under an appointment/retention plan to be turned out of office by the voters.

The vast majority of court cases take place in our nation's state court system. Find out about your state's court system through the National Center for State Courts.

http://www.bvtlab.com/GJ8nb

courts of limited jurisdiction

The lowest-level court in a state's judicial system that hears particular kinds of cases involving small claims, traffic violations, and minor criminal infractions

courts of general jurisdiction

The basic unit of a court system, receiving appeals from courts of limited jurisdiction and serving as trial courts for serious criminal offenses and civil suits involving substantial amounts of money

intermediate appellate courts

Courts between courts of general jurisdiction and the court of last resort; in the federal court system, the courts of appeals

court of last resort

The highest court within a particular judicial system, such as a state supreme court, to which a litigant may appeal a case

Missouri Plan

Method of selecting state judges, involving appointment from a list of recommended nominees and a later retention vote by the electorate

12.1d   United States District Courts

Of all federal courts, the Constitution only provides for the Supreme Court. Article III left the creation of other ("inferior") courts to the discretion of Congress. Plausibly, Congress could have permitted the existing state courts to handle national business but chose instead, in the Judiciary Act of 1789, to organize a separate court system for the nation as a whole.

United States district courts

Trial courts in the federal court system in which almost all federal cases begin; courts of general jurisdiction

Almost all federal cases (over 376,000 annually, excluding bankruptcy filings) begin in the ninety-four **United States district courts**, staffed by 673 judges. There are eighty-nine district courts in the fifty states, plus one each in the District of Columbia, Guam, Puerto Rico, the Virgin Islands, and the Northern Mariana Islands. Each state has at least one district court, and no district crosses a state line. Some states have two or three districts; and the populous states of California, New York, and Texas have four each (see Figure 12.3).

The jurisdiction of district courts extends to cases that arise under the Constitution, laws, and treaties of the United States, as well as admiralty and maritime cases. Questions of state law (such as liability in an automobile accident) may get into district court through diversity jurisdiction. This occurs when the parties to a case are citizens of different states and when the amount at issue is greater than $50,000. As a way of reducing the volume of cases in the district courts, Congress has considered repealing diversity jurisdiction altogether. Should this happen, cases now qualifying for diversity jurisdiction would be decided by state courts, entirely outside the federal court system.

Figure 12.3   Geographic Boundaries of U.S. Courts of Appeals and U.S. District Courts

The map shows how the ninety-four U.S. district courts and thirteen U.S. courts of appeals exist with the court systems of the fifty states and the District of Columbia.

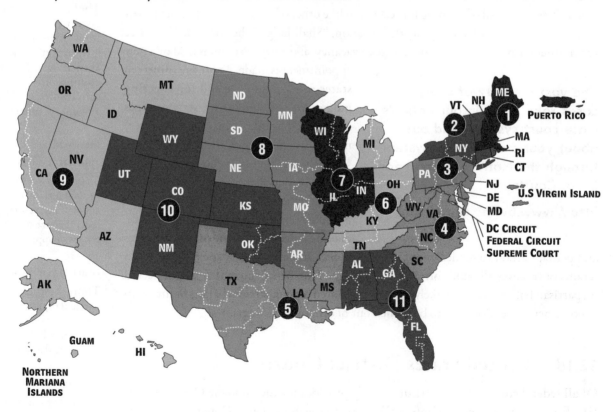

DATA SOURCE: Adapted from Administrative Office of the United States Courts, https://www.uscourts.gov/sites/default/files/u.s._federal_courts_circuit_map_1.pdf.

12.1e United States Courts of Appeals

Thirteen **United States courts of appeals**, staffed by 179 judges, occupy a middle position in the hierarchy of the federal judiciary. Twelve of these courts have a regional jurisdiction or circuit, as Figure 12.3 shows.

Although district judges sit individually in most cases, appeals judges normally sit in panels of three. In special situations, cases are heard *en banc*, with most of a circuit's bench sitting at once. Cases in the courts of appeals number more than 58,000 annually. Most are appeals from disappointed parties in the district courts and the U.S. Tax Court (see Figure 12.1). Under exceptional circumstances, cases may go from district courts directly to the Supreme Court, bypassing a court of appeals. Another large source of work for the appeals courts comes in the form of reviewing rulings of various administrative and regulatory agencies of the national government, such as the Federal Communications Commission, the Federal Trade Commission, and the National Labor Relations Board. The Court of Appeals for the District of Columbia Circuit hears more of these agency cases than any of the other appeals courts, making this court one of the most influential in the land.

(Wikimedia / Public Domain)

The thirteenth appeals court is the newest; and unlike the other twelve, it has a different—and a national—jurisdiction. The Court of Appeals for the Federal Circuit accepts appeals in patent cases from any district court, as well as all appeals from the Claims Court, the Court of International Trade, and the Court of Veterans Appeals. For most litigants, the courts of appeals are the courts of last resort in the federal judicial system, due to the fact that the Supreme Court accepts relatively few cases.

12.1f Special Courts

Congress has created other tribunals to hear particular kinds of cases in which considerable specialization and expertise are desirable. Into this category fall the following:

1. The *Court of Federal Claims* hears suits involving monetary damages against the US government.

2. The *Court of International Trade* adjudicates controversies concerning the classification and valuation of imported merchandise.

3. The U.S. *Tax Court* decides disputes between taxpayers and the Internal Revenue Service.

4. The *Court of Appeals for Veterans Claims* reviews decisions on benefits and entitlements from the Board of Veterans Appeals in the Department of Veterans Affairs. The newest special court, it heard its first case in 1990.

5. The *Court of Appeals for the Armed Forces* reviews judgments handed down by courts-martial in the several branches of the armed forces.

These courts rarely make the headlines, but they are quite important. In the first four, millions of dollars may ride on the outcome of decisions. The lives and liberties of hundreds of thousands of members of the US military are in the care of the fifth.

United States courts of appeals

Intermediate appellate courts in the federal court system, just below the Supreme Court

12.1g The Supreme Court of the United States

It is from these courts, state and federal, that the nine justices of the Supreme Court receive almost all the cases they decide each term. At present, some seven thousand to eight thousand new cases appear annually on their docket, joining about one thousand carried over from the previous term. All but a handful invoke the Court's **appellate jurisdiction**. Defined by Congress, this is the authority that the Court has to review decisions of the federal courts, as well as decisions of the highest state courts that raise **federal questions** (matters involving the interpretation of the Constitution, a statute, or a treaty of the United States). Today, almost all cases reach the Supreme Court on a *writ of certiorari* (Latin for "to be informed"). Except for a few cases involving the Voting Rights Act, review by the Supreme Court is plainly discretionary, not obligatory. It takes a minimum of four justices (one short of a majority) to agree to accept a case for review. This **rule of four** allows the Court not only to limit the number of cases it decides but also to engage or avoid particular issues.

A very few cases each term are candidates for the Court's **original jurisdiction**, meaning that the case begins or originates with the Court. Indeed, the number of "original" cases the Court decided between 1789 and 2020 totaled only about two hundred. The Supreme Court's original jurisdiction is spelled out in Article III of the Constitution and includes four kinds of disputes:

1. **Cases between one of the states and the US government** For example, in *United States v. Maine*,[2] the justices ruled that the national government—not the states—had control of oil deposits more than three miles offshore.

2. **Cases between two or more states** In 1967, Michigan and Ohio each claimed the same piece of mineral-rich territory in Lake Erie; and in a series of cases, Arizona and California have battled each other over water resources.[3]

3. **Cases involving foreign ambassadors, ministers, or consuls** The framers wanted cases that could involve the nation's relations with other countries to be heard initially by the highest court.

4. **Cases begun by a state against a citizen of another state or against another country** The **Eleventh Amendment**, however, requires suits initiated against a state by a citizen of another state or of a foreign country to begin in the courts of that state. The Eleventh Amendment came about because of a 1793 decision by the Supreme Court that a citizen of South Carolina could sue the state of Georgia in the federal courts.[4]

Only controversies between states qualify today exclusively as original cases in the Supreme Court. The justices have been content for Congress to grant concurrent original jurisdiction to the U.S. district courts for cases in the other three categories. As such, although one of these cases *could* begin in the Supreme Court, in almost every instance the case will begin in a district court—unless it involves a dispute between two states of the Union.

The Supreme Court is headed administratively by the chief justice of the United States (the position has been filled since September 2005 by John G. Roberts). Through the years, the Court has usually been known by the name of the chief justice (the Marshall Court, for example); however, the chief's vote in cases counts no more than the vote of any of the eight associate justices. The chief justice also presides over the judicial Conference of the United States, which is composed of representatives of the lower federal courts and makes recommendations to those courts, as well as to Congress, with regard to staffing needs and operating efficiency.

12.1h   Federal Judicial Selection

The Constitution gives the president power to appoint federal judges, subject to confirmation by a majority vote of the Senate. In practice, presidents rarely know, personally, any of the district or appeals judges they appoint. Judges on the district, appeals, and Supreme Court benches serve "during good behavior," a provision of the Constitution that effectively ensures lifetime tenure with removal only by impeachment. In contrast to presidents and members of Congress, the Constitution spells out no qualifications, such as age or citizenship, for any federal judge. Federal judges do not even have to be lawyers, although since 1789 each has had legal training of some kind. Today, it would be unthinkable for the Senate to approve a nominee who is not a law school graduate and a member of the bar.

Presidents overwhelmingly appoint members of their own political party to the federal bench (since 1900, only in the Taft, Hoover, and Ford administrations has the figure dropped below 90 percent). The choices for the district courts are usually made by officials in the Justice Department working with political leaders from the state in which the appointment is to be made. A state's US senators (one or both)—particularly if they are of the same party as the president—traditionally play a prominent role in the selection. There is some truth in the wisecrack that a federal judge is a lawyer who knows a senator. In contrast, appointment of appeals judges reflects more national and less local influence, with the attorney general and other officials in the Justice Department having a large say in the selection. District judges are obvious choices for appeals posts because they have observable judicial track records.

You can read the latest Supreme Court opinions, find biographical sketches of the current justices, and even see the Court's upcoming calendar at the Supreme Court website.

http://www.bvtlab.com/79868

Under present policy of the Senate Judiciary Committee, a "blue slip" (indicating disapproval) from a home-state senator is sufficient to block a judicial nominee outright if the administration fails to consult with home-state senators before naming a candidate. This is an example of **senatorial courtesy**, the practice that allows home-state senators considerable control over the fate of presidential nominees. If a senator submits a blue slip after having been consulted, the committee considers the senator's objections but does not always reject the nominee.

An additional screening role is played by the Standing Committee on the Federal Judiciary of the American Bar Association (ABA), the largest organization of lawyers in the country. Before the president sends a nominee's name to the Senate, the attorney general submits the name to the ABA committee for review. This committee then finds the candidate "well-qualified," "qualified," or "not qualified." Only occasionally will presidents nominate someone the committee considers not qualified; and some nominees are, nonetheless, confirmed by the Senate when they do. The ABA's participation in the review process is significant because it means that a private organization, in effect, shares the confirmation role the Constitution assigns to the Senate. The committee's screening attracts the most attention when the president nominates an individual to the Supreme Court.

In contrast to the other federal courts, vacancies on the Supreme Court occur relatively infrequently. Including the six original seats George Washington (1789–1797) filled, 115 persons have served on the Court through 2020. Supreme Court nominations are far more likely to personally occupy a president's time and attention. Such focus is not simply because the Supreme Court decides important questions but also because, once appointed,

senatorial courtesy

Custom in the Senate to reject, for federal office, a nominee who is unacceptable to a senator from the nominee's state when the senator and president are of the same party

justices tend to stay on the Court a long time—usually far longer than the president who named them remains in the White House. The following five considerations most often are at work as presidents make up their minds about whom to appoint:

1. **Professional qualifications**   How respected is the nominee?

2. **Acceptability to the Senate**   Will he or she be confirmed?

3. **Ideological fit**   Will the nominee support the president's program?

4. **Personal friendship**   Does the president want an old friend on the Court?

5. **Region, race, religion, gender, and other background factors**   Does a particular group need "representation" on the Court?

Since Washington's time, presidents have wanted a Court supportive of their administrations; yet they are not always successful in picking "right-thinking" justices. President Dwight Eisenhower (1953–1961) once remarked that appointing Earl Warren (1953–1969) as chief justice was "the biggest damnfool mistake I ever made" after Warren turned out to be more liberal than Ike had supposed. President Richard Nixon (1969–1974) hardly approved of Justice Harry A. Blackmun's (1970–1994) authorship of the 1973 abortion decision,[5] and presidents Ronald Reagan and George H. W. Bush were disappointed when three of their appointees (Justices Sandra O'Connor [1981–2006], Anthony Kennedy [1988–2018], and David Souter [1990–2009]) voted against administration positions on school prayer.[6]

Particular background factors have frequently been important in aiding or hurting one's chances to become a Supreme Court justice. Most presidents have taken geographical region into account. Moreover, religion, race, and gender have sometimes been important considerations as well. Even so, Supreme Court justices have hardly been representative of US society. Of the 115 justices who sat through 2020, all but twenty-four were Protestant males of Anglo-Saxon origin. Justice Antonin Scalia (1986–2016) was the Court's first Italian American member. Justice Thurgood Marshall (1967–1991) was the first African American member of the Court, and Justice O'Connor was its first female member. Clarence Thomas became the second African American to serve in 1991, and Ruth Bader Ginsburg (1993–2020) became the second woman in 1993. Barack Obama became the first president to appoint two women to the Court when he nominated Sonia Sotomayor (also the Court's first Hispanic justice) in 2009 and Elena Kagan in 2010. Most of the 115 have come from economically comfortable and civic-minded families. For example, Neil Gorsuch (2017–   ) is the son of Anne Burford, former director of the Environmental Protection Agency. All have been lawyers or have held law degrees. About one-third graduated from the most prestigious colleges and universities in the United States. Most have been active in public affairs or have held political office; but some, including Justice Byron White (1962–1993), had no prior judicial experience. Only three chief justices (out of a total of seventeen since 1789) have been elevated directly from associate justice. All other chief justices were nominated from outside the Court.

Whatever a president's motivations, the Senate must still vote to confirm the nominee. Such approval has been forthcoming most of the time, but on twenty-six occasions the Senate has not given it. Over the past hundred years, five presidents—Herbert Hoover (1929–1933), Lyndon Johnson (1963–1969), Richard Nixon (1969–1974), Ronald Reagan (1981–1989), and Barack Obama (2009–2017)—have had their choices blocked by the Senate. Nixon, in fact, struck out twice in succession before the Senate handily confirmed Judge Harry Blackmun, his third nominee for the same vacancy. When Reagan picked Judge Robert Bork to succeed retiring justice Lewis Powell (1972–1987), the Senate said no. Reagan's second choice, Judge Douglas Ginsburg, withdrew his name from consideration

after acknowledging disclosures that he had smoked marijuana as a student in the 1960s and as a member of the Harvard law faculty in the 1970s. Powell's seat remained vacant until early 1988 when the Senate confirmed Reagan's third choice, Judge Anthony M. Kennedy. The Senate employed a different strategy after the death of longtime conservative justice Antonin Scalia created a vacancy in 2016. Election-year politics led the Republican-majority Senate to refuse to schedule hearings for the Democratic president's nominee; the nomination expired at the end of the 2016 session of Congress (see "Politics and Ideas: The Politics of Judicial Vacancies"). Senate Republicans whistled a different tune, though, in 2020 when Justice Ruth Bader Ginsburg died just seven weeks before the presidential election. This time the Republican majority quickly confirmed the Republican president's nominee, Amy Coney Barrett (2020–).

President Donald J. Trump looks on as Anthony M. Kennedy, retired Associate Justice of the Supreme Court of the United States, swears in Judge Brett M. Kavanaugh to be the Supreme Court's 114th justice Monday, Oct. 8, 2018.

(Official White House Photo by Joyce N. Boghosian, via Wikimedia)

Although most presidents can expect to fill a vacancy or two, especially if they serve two terms, the period from 1994 to 2005 marked the longest drought in new appointees since 1823. In 2005, President George W. Bush finally had an opportunity to make appointments. Justice O'Connor announced her retirement in the summer of that year, and Chief Justice William Rehnquist died after a long battle with cancer on September 3, 2005. Bush nominated John R. Roberts, an appellate court judge who was raised Catholic in Buffalo, New York, and graduated from Harvard Law School, to be the next chief justice. The Senate confirmed him in a 78–22 vote. Bush then nominated White House Counsel Harriet Miers to the post of associate justice. Concerns about her abilities and qualifications from across the political spectrum led Bush to withdraw her nomination before it could be voted on. He then nominated appellate court judge Samuel Anthony Alito Jr. to the post. A native of New Jersey, Alito received his law degree from Yale University. His 58–42 confirmation vote by the Senate made him the second Italian American justice and created a Catholic majority on the Court for the first time. When Catholic justice Anthony Kennedy retired in 2018, he was replaced by Brett Kavanaugh, maintaining this Catholic majority. This majority grew to six of the nine justices when Amy Coney Barrett joined the Court in 2020.

12.2 What Courts Do

In the process of deciding cases, the Supreme Court and other courts perform several functions—including constitutional interpretation, statutory interpretation, fact determination, clarification of the boundaries of political authority, education and value application, and legitimization. Not all courts perform each function in every case, and some courts do more of one than another. As will be noted, fact determination is largely, though not exclusively, the province of trial courts. Appellate courts are heavily engaged in constitutional and statutory interpretation.

POLITICS AND IDEAS

The Politics of Judicial Vacancies

The U.S. Constitution designed the judicial branch of government to be removed from the politics of popular will by making judges at the federal level appointed to life terms, rather than elected to fixed terms. When it comes to the actual practice of judging, this structure is arguably quite effective—judges can decide cases without fear of being voted out of office for issuing an unpopular opinion. The appointment process, however, is controlled by two elected institutions—the presidency and the Senate—and the dynamics of those institutions are rarely apolitical. The three most recent appointments to the Supreme Court illustrate the political nature of judicial vacancies.

On February 13, 2016, Supreme Court Justice Antonin Scalia passed away while on a hunting trip in Texas. The seventy-nine-year-old jurist had been the longest-serving member of the Court at the time of his death, having served on the nation's highest court since his appointment by President Ronald Reagan in 1986. Justice Scalia's death left the Supreme Court without one of its most ardent conservative voices and created a vacancy that would not be filled for a very long time—a matter that quickly became a political issue of its own.

Justice Scalia's positions had been reliably conservative, which meant that his potential replacement by a Democratic president would likely alter the Court's ideological balance. Thus, the timing of Justice Scalia's passing created not only difficulties for the Court but also a political

conundrum for the other two branches of government. As a matter of Court procedure, Scalia's death meant that the remainder of the Court's 2015 term (which ran from October 2015 to October 2016) would be handled with an even number of justices rather than the full complement of nine. This unfortunate situation—which occurs whenever a justice retires or dies in the middle of a Court term—resulted in four cases being decided as 4–4 ties.

Beyond the disappointing conclusions to the handful of cases, the larger political issue became deciding upon Scalia's successor in an era of divided government. In March 2016, Democratic president Barack Obama, in his eighth and final year in office, nominated the chief judge of the U.S. Court of Appeals for the D.C. Circuit, Merrick Garland, to fill the vacancy left by Justice Scalia. Although presidents nominate potential justices, the U.S. Senate must confirm them. In 2016, Republicans made up a majority in the Senate, and majority leader Mitch McConnell (R-KY) declared that the Senate would not hold hearings or vote on whether to confirm Garland in 2016. McConnell noted that President Obama was essentially a "lame duck president" and that waiting until after the 2016 election to consider the new president's nominee would be the best way to "let the American people decide" the Court's future direction.[1]

This decision by the Senate majority led to one of the longest-lasting Supreme Court vacancies in U.S. history, as well as the longest period a Court nominee has ever had to wait for action by the Senate. The Senate refused to act on Garland's nomination, letting it expire with the end of the congressional session. At least one senator—Ted Cruz (R-TX)—indicated that Republicans might continue this strategy of delay indefinitely if faced with another

Democratic president beginning in 2017.

This threat was avoided when Republican Donald Trump won the presidency. Soon after taking office, Trump nominated Neil Gorsuch, a conservative judge from the Tenth Circuit Court of Appeals. Although Republicans still held a slim majority in the Senate, majority leader McConnell abandoned one hundred years of tradition and used the "nuclear option" of allowing a simple majority to end debate and hold a vote on the Gorsuch nomination rather than requiring a supermajority of sixty votes (see the discussion of "cloture" in Chapter 9). In the end, Gorsuch was confirmed by a vote of 54–45.

Tensions flared even higher in the summer of 2018 when Associate Justice Anthony Kennedy announced his retirement from the Court. Although appointed by Republican president Ronald Reagan, Kennedy had often been a "swing" justice during his three decades on the bench. His potential replacement by Trump's nominee—the consistently conservative appellate court judge Brett Kavanaugh—threatened to create a solidly conservative majority for years to come. Democratic senators' efforts to remind majority leader McConnell of his wariness to confirm a justice during an election year proved fruitless, and Kavanaugh seemed poised to coast to a quick confirmation.

Then, unexpectedly, ideology took a backseat to ethics. On September 16, 2018, psychology professor Dr. Christine Blasey Ford stated that Kavanaugh had sexually assaulted her while both had been teenagers—a charge that Kavanaugh denied.[2] This serious allegation led to testimony from both Blasey Ford and Kavanaugh before the Senate Judiciary Committee, as well as an FBI investigation. While national polls showed that

45 percent of people in the US believed Blasey Ford and only 33 percent believed Kavanaugh,[3] Senate leadership pushed ahead with the vote, confirming Kavanaugh by a vote of 50 to 48.

The third of these unusual situations took place in late 2020, when long-serving liberal justice Ruth Bader Ginsburg (1993–2020) died around seven weeks before the 2020 presidential election. This time, with majority leader McConnell still at the helm, the Senate decided to abandon its 2016 approach of letting "the American people decide" and began holding hearings to confirm President Trump's pick of conservative appellate court judge Amy Coney Barrett in just a matter of weeks. Ultimately, the Senate confirmed Barrett by a vote of 52–48 just one week prior to the presidential election.

Should the Senate be required to consider and vote on presidential appointments in a reasonable amount of time? Does the presence of an upcoming election change the Senate's role? Does the approach taken by Senate Republicans to dispense with the supermajority requirement to end debate make the Senate more democratic? Was the Senate designed to be democratic? What about the judiciary? How should the Senate handle charges of unethical, illegal, or untruthful behavior by a judicial nominee? What precedent will these recent Supreme Court nominations set for the future?

1. Mitch McConnell, quoted in Amita Kelly, "McConnell: Blocking Supreme Court Nomination 'About a Principle, Not a Person,'" NPR, March 16, 2016, http://www.npr.org/2016/03/16/470664561/mcconnell-blocking-supreme-court-nomination-about-a-principle-not-a-person (March 16, 2016).

2. Emma Brown, "California Professor, Writer of Confidential Brett Kavanaugh Letter, Speaks Out about Her Allegation of Sexual Assault," *The Washington Post,* September 16, 2018, https://www.washingtonpost.com/investigations/california-professor-writer-of-confidential-brett-kavanaugh-letter-speaks-out-about-her-allegation-of-sexual-assault/2018/09/16/46982194-b846-11e8-94eb-3bd52dfe917b_story.html?noredirect=on&utm_term=f7b518e20a1e (October 24, 2018).

3. Daniel Bush, "More Americans Believe Ford than Kavanaugh, According to New Poll," *PBS News Hour,* October 3, 2018, https://www.pbs.org/newshour/nation/more-americans-believe-ford-than-kavanaugh-according-to-new-poll (October 24, 2018).

12.2a   Constitutional Interpretation

American government is constitutional government—government according to basic institutions, procedures, and values inscribed in a written document. The Constitution of the United States is not without ambiguity, however. Because some of its provisions are not clear and because the framers could not possibly have anticipated all contemporary issues, the document invites interpretation. This need for interpretation, in turn, guarantees disagreement over what the correct interpretation should be.

Interpretation involves the power of **judicial review**, first formally declared by the United States Supreme Court in the 1803 case of *Marbury v. Madison*[7] (see Chapter 1). Judicial review provides a court with the authority to set aside decisions made by elected representatives of the people if the court concludes that a law violates the Constitution. Judicial review allows contending political groups to continue their political skirmishes in the context of cases built around opposing interpretations of particular clauses of the Constitution. Groups whose issues have not prevailed in executive offices or legislative chambers often resort to the courts. Whether the question involves education, immigration, or criminal justice, one side seeks to persuade the constitutional umpire that the other has broken the rules.

IT IS EMPHATICALLY THE PROVINCE AND DUTY OF THE JUDICIAL DEPARTMENT TO SAY WHAT THE LAW IS.

MARBURY v. MADISON

1803

(Wikimedia / Public Domain)

Inscription on the wall of the Supreme Court Building from *Marbury v. Madison,* in which Chief Justice John Marshall outlined the concept of judicial review.

judicial review

The authority of courts to set aside a legislative act as being in violation of the Constitution

12.2b   Statutory Interpretation

Many cases require courts to interpret statutes passed by Congress or state legislatures. In a typical term, about half the cases the Supreme Court decides involve the meaning the justices give to words the legislators have written. At first glance this task seems avoidable. Why are legislators not able to say exactly what they mean? Sometimes legislators expect judges to fill in the blanks, so to speak. Legislators will write laws that set up certain standards for judges to apply, or as a way of avoiding controversy legislators will deliberately choose language that is vague. In addition, ambiguities can arise that the people who wrote the law simply did not anticipate. Judges will often try to discover the **legislative intent** of a law by trying to figure out what the legislators who wrote the law would have wanted.

One of the first pages in this book refers to a copyright. The holder of the copyright has exclusive use and control of the work for a specified period of time. Over the past century, copyrights have been extended to motion pictures and television programs. When Congress last rewrote the Copyright Act in 1976, provision was made for "fair use." Fair use allows one to legally make copies of protected material "for purposes such as criticism, comment, news reporting, teaching, ... scholarship, or research"—all without violating the copyright or paying a fee to the holder of the copyright. Is in-home recording of television programs an example of fair use, or an infringement of copyright? Congress decreed only that certain factors are to be taken into account in deciding whether something amounts to fair use, leaving the task of adding precision to judges. With fuzzy guidance, different courts arrived at different conclusions. In the end, the Supreme Court announced that in-home video recording of copyrighted materials was fair use within the meaning of the statute.[8]

12.2c   Fact Determination

Often the meaning of statutes and constitutional passages may be clear, and cases turn on the facts instead. Through fact determination, judges select from competing testimony and evidence which facts they accept as true and which they reject as false. This task is inescapable because the judicial process in the United States is adversarial. That is, cases pit one side against the other. Each side attempts to build the stronger argument to persuade the judge or jury to accept its version of the truth. Fact discretion is perhaps most visible in a **trial court**, the arena in which the issues and merits of a case are heard for the first time. In the federal court system, trial courts are the district courts. In state court systems, trials occur in both the courts of limited and general jurisdiction (see Figure 12.1 and Figure 12.2).

12.2d   Clarification of the Boundaries of Political Authority

As explained in Chapter 1, the Constitution mandates separation of powers—the division of political functions among the three branches of government. It is not obvious, however, where the legitimate power of one branch stops and another's begins. Courts sometimes try to resolve this built-in tension. In 1952, for example, President Harry Truman (1945–1953) directed the secretary of commerce to seize and operate the nation's steel mills. Labor disputes in the steel industry threatened the supply of war materials needed for US troops in the Korean conflict. Truman based his actions not on any statutory authority but on the president's responsibility for national security as commander in chief of the armed forces.

legislative intent

A legislature's understanding of the meaning of a law and what it is designed to accomplish

trial court

A court of limited or general jurisdiction in which the disputed facts of a case are heard and decided

Voting 6–3, the Supreme Court held that Truman had exceeded his powers under the Constitution. Although Congress might provide for such a takeover of industries by statute, Congress had not done so. Furthermore, the Court found nothing in the Constitution authorizing the president to act on his own.[9]

President Harry Truman

12.2e Education and Value Application

In deciding cases, judges teach and apply values. Even an ordinary criminal trial involves a judgment on what kinds of behaviors are acceptable or unacceptable, on the part of both the suspect and the police. One of the hallmarks of constitutional government, after all, is that limits apply not just to the governed but to the governors as well. The constitutions and statutes of the state and national governments all represent value choices that define the kind of nation its citizens expect to enjoy. Judicial opinions give judges an opportunity to articulate those values. Of course, no one pretends that judicial opinions are widely read by the general public. They are, however, read and studied by journalists, scholars, and other opinion leaders, who in turn inform the public and help shape the attitudes people in the US have about the courts and the issues judges confront.

12.2f Legitimization

Because of the powers of judicial review, courts are expected to make sure that actions of public officials conform to the Constitution and statutes. In the great majority of cases, judges uphold the challenged laws or policies, thus placing a "seal of approval" on what others have done. Securing legitimacy may be crucial when a policy emerges from a long and loud national debate. Winners look to the judiciary for support; losers look to the judiciary for redress. Both typically see the courts as offering "the final word." During the civil rights movement of the 1960s, for example (see Chapter 3), Congress took the bold and controversial step of banning racial discrimination in restaurants, hotels, theaters, and other privately owned places of public accommodation. During debate on the bill in 1963 and 1964, opponents argued that the ban would be an unjustified intrusion into the right of owners of businesses to run their enterprises as they wished. The Supreme Court's decision upholding the constitutionality of the law virtually ended the controversy. Within a matter of months, most public agitation over the legitimacy of the new policy simply ceased.[10] A ruling can, however, inflame an issue, not soothe it. On occasion it may appear that the judges have thrust a broom handle into a hornet's nest, as the abortion controversy illustrates.

Congressman Peter Olson (R-TX) and young pro-life activists at the March for Life in 2015.

12.3 The Supreme Court at Work

Cases decided by the Supreme Court move through five distinct stages: petition for review, briefs on the merits, oral argument, conference and decision, and assignment and writing of opinions.

12.3a Petition for Review

Litigants who lose in lower courts begin climbing the steep slope toward the Supreme Court when their lawyers file documents called **briefs** with the Court's clerk. In these petitions for review, the opposing parties attempt to convince the justices that the issues the case raises are so important (or unimportant) that they deserve (or do not deserve) the Court's attention. As discussed previously, the Court will not accept a case unless a minimum of four justices agrees that the case warrants review.

From the thousands of cases on its docket each term, the justices will typically decide no more than 150 with full opinion (and only sixty to eighty in recent years), in accordance with the procedure laid out below. Other cases may be decided "summarily," without opinion by a directive affirming or reversing the lower court. Except for cases carried over into the following year's term, the justices deny review in all other cases. The result is that the lower court's decision stands (see Figure 12.4).

What factors seem to guide the Court in selecting cases for decision? Although the justices rarely explain their reasons for rejecting cases, chances for review by the nation's highest court are significantly increased if one or more of the following is present:

- The United States is a party to the case and requests Supreme Court review.

- The case presents a question that has been decided differently by different courts of appeals.

- The case involves an issue some of the justices are eager to resolve.

- A lower court has made a decision clearly at odds with established Supreme Court interpretation of a law or constitutional provision.

- The Court's workload permits accepting another case for decision.

- The case presents an issue of overriding importance to the nation.

Even if a case fits into one of the categories listed, the Supreme Court will not necessarily grant review. Because the Court's docket contains thousands of cases each term, a litigant's chances of having a case heard by the justices are usually very slim. Claims that someone will "take this all the way to the Supreme Court" are, therefore, more threat than promise.

12.3b Briefs on the Merits

Once the Court has placed a case on its "decision calendar," attorneys for the opposing sides file a second round of briefs. This time the arguments focus on the decision the justices should make, not on whether they should accept the case. *Amicus curiae* briefs supplement briefs of opposing counsel. Submitted by "friends of the court," these documents come from interest groups and others who are not parties to the case, but who have a stake in its outcome.

briefs
Documents filed with a court containing the arguments of the parties in a case

amicus curiae
Latin for "friend of the court," referring to persons, government agencies, or groups that are not parties to a case but nonetheless have an interest in its outcome and that make their views known by filing an *amicus curiae* brief with the court hearing the case

Figure 12.4 Caseload in the U.S. Supreme Court, 1950-2020

This figure shows the number of cases appealed to the Supreme Court in each of eight years and the number of cases decided with full opinion. The justices decide other cases summarily each term. The number of summary decisions each term sometimes equals the number of cases decided with full opinion. The volume of cases has grown almost eightfold since 1950, while the number of cases decided has varied only modestly. Indeed, since 1988 when 171 decisions were issued, the Court has been deciding fewer cases, a trend aided by the virtual elimination of the Court's obligatory appellate jurisdiction in 1988. Almost all of each year's cases come from the lower federal courts and the state supreme courts. Only a handful, at most, of original cases appears each term. A minimum of four justices must agree to hear a case.

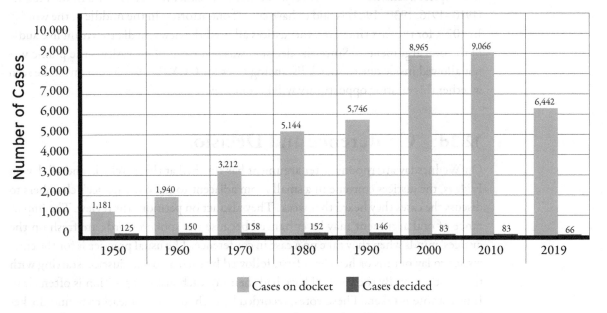

DATA SOURCES: Administrative Office of the United States Courts; 2019 Year-End Report on the Federal Judiciary.

One lawyer whose briefs the justices routinely read with extra care is the **solicitor general of the United States**—the third-ranking official in the Justice Department and the government's lawyer before the Supreme Court. In cases in which the government has lost in a lower court, the "S.G." decides whether the United States will petition the Supreme Court for review. If so, the solicitor general is responsible for both written briefs and oral argument supporting the government's position. The job is important because the United States is a party in about half the cases that confront the justices. Five solicitors general have gone on to serve as Supreme Court justices, most recently Elena Kagan (2010–).

solicitor general of the United States

In the Supreme Court, the lawyer for the United States who decides which cases the government will appeal to the Supreme Court

12.3c Oral Argument

The most public part of the Court's work is **oral argument**. On about forty days (always Mondays, Tuesdays, and Wednesdays), starting in October and concluding in late April, opposing lawyers face the justices. Cases are routinely allotted one hour with each side receiving thirty minutes. Oral argument, a spontaneous event, gives each justice an opportunity to ask questions about the case. Although not every justice asks a question in every case, Justice Clarence Thomas (1991–) has been noted to be unusually reticent. During a seven-year period between 2006 and 2013, he did not utter a single word during oral

oral argument

Event in which opposing counsel verbally presents their views to the court during the decision-making process of a court

argument.[11] Sometimes, questioning from the bench is lively and intense; at other times, the justices may barely seem interested. At all times, they rock back and forth in their leather swivel chairs, occasionally pass notes and whisper among themselves, and send pages on errands to fetch documents and law books. The justices attach great importance to the oral argument step of the decision-making procedure. Whether such arguments change many minds, however, is a question only the justices can answer.

An appearance before the Supreme Court can be intimidating even for the most seasoned advocates. Standing at the small lectern before the raised bench, an attorney can feel very lonely. Heightening the tension are the time limits, which the Court rigidly enforces. When five minutes remain, the marshal flicks a switch that turns on a white light at the lectern. A red light signals that time is up. The chief justice may allow counsel to complete a sentence or to answer a question, but Chief Justice Charles Evans Hughes (1910–1916, 1930–1941) is said to have cut off one attorney in the middle of the word *if*. In 2020, for the first time ever, the justices allowed the news media to stream live audio of the oral arguments.[12] Since the decision was made out of necessity—the public was not allowed inside due to social distancing rules for COVID-19—it remains to be seen whether this exciting opportunity will become a permanent feature.

12.3d Conference and Decision

On Wednesday afternoons, after argument has finished at three o'clock, and all day on Fridays, the justices convene in a small room adjacent to the chief justice's chambers to discuss the cases they heard that week. They also act on petitions for review. The importance of oral argument may be enhanced because the spoken words are fresh on the justices' minds when they take up a case in conference. The usual practice is for the chief justice to lay out his or her views first, followed by each associate justice, starting with the most senior. By the time all have had their say, each justice's position is often clear. If not, a vote is taken. These votes, recorded by each justice in a leather-bound docket book, are tentative. The decision does not become final until it is announced in court, weeks or even months later.

In contrast to the openness of oral argument, the conferences are closed. No pages or law clerks are present in the room, only the justices. If something is needed, the most junior justice acts as messenger and goes to the door. What happens inside the room is very secret. In fact, the Court has the best secrecy record in Washington. Leaks, as prevalent in the nation's capital as the summer humidity, are so rare at the Court that they make headlines when they occur. Confidentiality is crucial—not just because it gives the justices freedom to talk and maneuver amid the most controversial issues of the day, but also because political and economic fortunes often hang in the balance.

12.3e Assignment and Writing of Opinions

On Saturday or early in the week after the standard two-week session of oral argument, the chief justice circulates an assignment list to the justices. If part of the majority, the chief justice makes the opinion assignment in a particular case. If not, the task falls to the senior associate justice in the majority. The goal is an **opinion of the Court**, which is an explanation and justification of the decision agreed to by at least a bare majority of the justices. Between assignment of the opinion and announcement of the decision in open court, vigorous give-and-take routinely goes on among the justices. The justice writing an opinion has a draft printed in the Court's own print shop and done in strictest secrecy. Copies circulate among the other justices. Those in the majority will insist on

opinion of the Court
Statement representing the views of a majority of the judges of the Court

changes. It is not unusual for an opinion to go through a dozen or more rewrites. Each opinion of the Court, therefore, represents the consensus of the majority, not merely the views of its author. Justices in the majority may write one or more **concurring opinions** when they reject the majority's reasoning, while accepting its result; or they simply may have other thoughts to add.

In only about a third of the cases each term do all nine justices agree on the result. For the rest, justices in the minority typically write one or more **dissenting opinions**. These help to explain what divides the Court and are written for the express purpose of undercutting the logic and/or exposing the folly that dissenting justices find in the majority viewpoint.

Majority, concurring, and dissenting opinions are later collected and published as the *United States Reports*. This is the official record of the Court's work; it currently comprises almost six hundred volumes.

concurring opinion
A statement issued separately by a judge voting with the majority

dissenting opinion
A statement issued by a judge explaining his or her disagreement with the majority position

United States Reports
The official, published decisions of the United States Supreme Court

POLITICS AND ECONOMICS

The Supreme Court and Economic Policy

Although Supreme Court decisions today may affect the economy, just as they affect life in the US in other ways, between the years 1890 and 1937 the justices (and lower court judges too) played a far more active role in economic affairs. Then judges routinely reviewed the constitutionality of many kinds of social and economic laws that are now accepted without question.

In the decades after the Civil War, Congress and state legislatures passed hundreds of laws regulating working conditions, prices, wages and hours, and health standards in an effort to cope with the harmful effects of growth and industrialization. Opponents of such legislation advanced the arguments of laissez-faire economics, claiming that government regulation of business and economy should be kept to a minimum. Soon justices of the Supreme Court decided that freedom from economic regulation was a constitutionally protected liberty. This did

not mean that the Court turned aside all legislative attempts to improve the life of working people, but it did mean that the justices had what amounted to the last word on which regulatory policies were acceptable and which were not. For example, *Lochner v. New York* struck down a law that set a maximum number of working hours for bakery employees, and *Hammer v. Dagenhart* invalidated a congressional act banning interstate shipment of goods manufactured with child labor.

The Court's role as economic censor came under sharp attack when laissez-faire economics faced the realities of the Great Depression in the 1930s. As states and the national government responded with policies to deal with economic dislocation, the Court proved to be a stumbling block. In 1935 and 1936, the justices invalidated ten acts of Congress, cutting the heart out of President Franklin Roosevelt's New Deal program of economic recovery.

After his landslide reelection in 1936, Roosevelt proposed legislation (dubbed by its enemies the "court-packing plan") that would permit him to appoint one additional justice for every sitting justice over the age of seventy, up to a total bench size

of fifteen. Under the guise of aiding the justices with their work, the plan was actually a ploy to create seats for new justices who would support the president's programs. The plan never became law, but one or more justices quickly changed their positions in economic regulation cases to give the president the majority he needed. Tagged "the switch in time that saved nine," in *National Labor Relations Board v. Jones & Laughlin Steel Corporation* the Court upheld by a vote of 5–4 the far-reaching Wagner Labor Act of 1935, which created the National Labor Relations Board and guaranteed to unions the right of collective bargaining. The law remains the foundation of American labor policy. Thanks to changed views and a series of retirements and new justices, the Court soon made it clear that it was retreating from its old role as economic censor. Since that time, the Court has by and large left economic policy making to the president, Congress, and the states.

Recently, however, the Court has hinted that limits may still exist to a state's regulatory powers over property owners. Does the Constitution require the Court to keep its hands off economic policy?

12.3f Law Clerks

Assisting the justices are law clerks, recent law school graduates who typically serve a justice for a year. The justices use their clerks in a variety of ways: to do research, summarize *certiorari* petitions, and write and critique drafts of opinions. Justice Blackmun confessed that his clerks managed to entice him to an Orioles baseball game at least once a term! Diversions aside, a clerk's day is long and includes evenings and weekends. Nonetheless, the opportunities for close association with the justices can be rewarding. Of the justices on the Court in 2021, six (John Roberts, Elena Kagan, Neil Gorsuch, Brett Kavanaugh, Stephen Breyer, and Amy Coney Barrett) are former clerks.

12.4 The Supreme Court and American Government: An Assessment

Early in our nation's history, the justices assumed a prominent role in governing the nation. However, this role has never been free from controversy. For most of its history, the Court has seen itself as the guardian of preferred values. Years ago, for instance, the justices routinely censored social and economic legislation that they thought interfered unduly with property rights. In the years since President Franklin Roosevelt (1933–1945) confronted the justices in the "court-packing" fight of 1937 (see "Politics and Economics: The Supreme Court and Economic Policy"), the Court's decisions have emphasized civil liberties and civil rights instead. Now about half the cases each term involve a provision of the Bill of Rights or the Fourteenth Amendment.

12.4a Judicial Review and Democracy

As explained in Chapter 1 and as noted earlier in this chapter, the authority to interpret the Constitution carries with it the power of judicial review. Some critics assert that judicial review is antidemocratic because judges invalidate decisions made by elected representatives of the people. Moreover, they say that judicial review encourages citizens to rely on judges and not the political process to protect their rights. Without judicial review, elected officials would have to give more thought to the constitutionality of their actions. Besides, critics maintain, individual rights survive in nations like Great Britain, where judges exercise no judicial review at all.

Others reply that the very idea of a written constitution means that a majority is not always supposed to get what it wants. Democracy American-style stresses not just majority rule but also minority rights. Judicial review is but one of several constitutional features designed to control government power. Although citizens' control over their leaders through election is the primary check on government, judicial review can be an additional safeguard. Whatever the experience in other countries, enforcement of limits on government in this country seems to require the existence of institutions—like the federal courts—that are not directly accountable to the people.

12.4b Influences on Supreme Court Decision-Making

What are some of the major factors that shape the Supreme Court's decisions? In the face of Chief Justice Marshall's broad self-denial that "courts are the mere instruments of the law, and can will nothing,"[13] political leaders have long recognized that justices do not make decisions in a vacuum. Surely, "judicial decisions are not babies brought by constitutional storks."[14] Individual and institutional forces, as well as legal and extralegal factors, affect what the Court does.[15]

Foremost perhaps are the justices' own *political ideas*. A jurist adamantly opposed to capital punishment, for example, will be more inclined than one who is not to regard the death penalty as one of the "cruel and unusual punishments" prohibited by the Eighth Amendment. A justice who does not place high value on the free exchange of views will probably not be a strong defender of the First Amendment's guarantee of free speech. Indeed, research indicates that judicial decisions of most justices reflect a generally consistent ideological position.[16]

Role perception,[17] akin to but different from political ideas, is another factor that affects decision-making. What does being a justice mean to an individual named to the Supreme Court? Some justices have been result oriented—that is, they see their task as one of writing certain political ideas into their decisions. Other justices are process oriented; they are hesitant to interfere with majority rule. Although they are prepared to apply the constitutional brakes to runaway legislatures, they are less inclined to do so than their result-oriented colleagues. Instead, they believe that judges should allow maximum discretion to the people's elected representatives.

Jurists most eager to apply judicial review are **judicial activists**. Those most reluctant to do so are **judicial restraintists**. Yet even by practicing judicial restraint, the Court makes policy. Judicial restraint results in upholding the judgment made by some other part of the political system. By affirming someone else's judgment, the Court is legitimating it and making the original judgment the Court's own. When the Court upholds the validity of a search of someone's home by police, for example, it is accepting the police officer's understanding of the Fourth Amendment (see Chapter 3).

Whether an activist or restraintist, no justice today writes on a blank slate. Although a new case is rarely identical to one the Court has decided in years gone by, prior decisions in similar cases, called **precedents**, may point the way to the decision the Court should render. When courts adhere to legal principles established in prior cases, they are following the doctrine of *stare decisis* (Latin for "let the decision stand"). *Stare decisis* does not mean that the Supreme Court must rule as it ruled one hundred years ago, or even ten years ago; it does result, however, in the reluctance of justices to overrule decisions that are already "on the books." They do so only when a legal principle seems plainly wrong or when public necessity dictates a change.

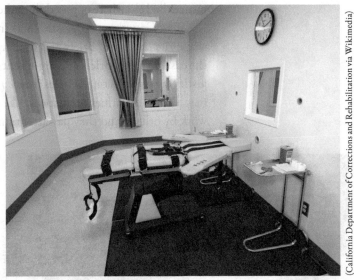

(California Department of Corrections and Rehabilitation via Wikimedia)

A justice's own personal political ideas may help determine his or her decisions. A justice who is against capital punishment is more inclined to regard the death penalty as cruel and unusual punishment than one who is for capital punishment.

judicial activists

Judges who are least hesitant to invoke judicial review to strike down an act of Congress or of a state legislature

judicial restraintists

Judges who are reluctant to invoke judicial review to strike down an act of Congress or of a state legislature

precedents

Prior decisions of courts that are cited as authority by other courts

stare decisis

A legal doctrine that suggests courts should follow precedent as a general rule, breaking with previous legal principles only on rare occasions

The power of precedent was an acknowledged factor in 1992 when five justices rejected the first Bush administration's request to overrule the 1973 landmark decision *Roe v. Wade*,[18] which created a constitutionally protected right to abortion. Three of the five (O'Connor, Kennedy, and Souter) indicated that they would not have sided with the majority position in *Roe* had they been on the Court in 1973. Nineteen years later, however, they believed that the Court should not turn back the clock.[19] In 2000, the Court upheld the judicially created requirement of *Miranda* warnings, even though several of the justices had elsewhere opposed the judicial activist stance taken in the *Miranda* decision.[20]

The Court's own decision-making process, described earlier in this chapter, also shapes its decisions. Briefs and oral argument inform the justices and define the issues the case presents. Briefs and arguments may even supply the reasoning the Court uses in justifying its decision. Articles in *law reviews*, the scholarly journals law schools publish, may also be of influence. Justices, like everyone else, are sensitive to evaluations of their work by others, and they pay attention to suggestions for evolution in the law that find their way into print. Moreover, because all justices participate in each case, *collegial interaction* becomes a factor. Discussion in conference and persuasive comment by one justice on an opinion drafted by another contribute to the form a decision eventually takes and sometimes cause a justice to change positions in a case.[21]

(Courtesy of Gerald Nino, CBP, U.S. Department of Homeland Security via Wikimedia)

Border patrol agent reads the *Miranda* rights to a suspected criminal.

Finally, justices are aware of *public opinion*. Although Justice John Paul Stevens (1975–2010) may have been correct in asserting that "it is the business of judges to be indifferent to unpopularity,"[22] public attitudes count, nevertheless, in judicial decisions in at least two ways. First, public attitudes may influence the meaning justices give certain provisions in the Constitution. In the case of capital punishment, for example, most states reenacted death penalty laws after the Supreme Court set rigorous new standards for capital punishment in 1972 (see Chapter 3).[23] State legislatures, in effect, were telling the Court that they did not think capital punishment was "cruel and unusual" but instead was a form of punishment the American people accepted. These new laws probably made it easier for some justices to decide, in 1976, that capital punishment is not cruel and unusual.[24] Second, courts matter in US government ultimately because their decisions are accepted and applied, if grudgingly, by the rest of the political system. Thus, public reaction to judicial decisions may affect compliance with them.

12.4c Checks on Judicial Power

Supreme Court justices and other federal judges enjoy substantial independence from outside political control. Thanks to the Constitution, they never face the voters in an election and may not have their salaries decreased by Congress. Although the Court is a potent institution in US government, it does not enjoy unlimited power. Through *constitutional amendment*, Congress and the states may correct the Supreme Court's interpretation of the Constitution. Admittedly, amending the Constitution is not easy, but the justices have been reversed by amendment four times.

The Eleventh Amendment (restricting federal court jurisdiction over the states) overturned *Chisholm v. Georgia*. The Fourteenth Amendment (granting both national and state citizenship to all persons born or naturalized in the United States) countered the infamous *Dred Scott* decision, which had held that the Constitution did not intend for African Americans to be citizens. The Sixteenth Amendment (allowing for a national tax on incomes) reversed *Pollock v. Farmers' Loan and Trust Co.,* and the Twenty-sixth Amendment (establishing a nationwide voting age of eighteen) set aside *Oregon v. Mitchell*.[25]

Similarly, *statutory amendment* allows Congress to correct the Court's interpretation of a statute. Although passing a law is easier than amending the Constitution, it still is not an easy task, as Chapter 9 made clear.

Congress may attack the Court by *withdrawing jurisdiction* to hear certain types of cases. Because Article III grants appellate jurisdiction to the Supreme Court "with such exceptions, and under such regulations as the Congress shall make," opponents of particular judicial doctrines can try to prevent certain types of cases from reaching the Court altogether. Such extreme measures are frequently threatened, but only very rarely carried out.

Congress may also *change the size* of the Court, which was the heart of President Franklin Roosevelt's "court-packing" proposal in 1937. Although the plan failed, the Court changed its interpretation of the Constitution to uphold the president's New Deal program (see "Politics and Economics: The Supreme Court and Economic Policy").

Appointment of new justices by the president can place new ideas as well as new personalities on the bench. *Senate confirmation*, however, may limit the range of a president's choices; however, judicial vacancies occur irregularly as well as infrequently. For example, President Nixon was able to name four justices between 1969 and 1971, whereas President Carter (1977–1981) was able to name none.

To be effective, Supreme Court decisions require *compliance*. Judges possess very little power to actually coerce obedience. Therefore, courts depend on others to obey and to carry out their decisions. An absence of widespread compliance with the Supreme Court's school integration decision of 1954[26] (see Chapter 3) meant that for nearly a decade the decision went largely unenforced. Reaction to this decision was a reminder that the Supreme Court needs the support of both state and federal courts, as well as other agencies of government, to carry out its judgments. Hostile reaction to the 1954 school decision highlighted an additional check: *litigation*. African American families were sometimes afraid to initiate legal action against local officials who continued to disregard the Supreme Court's decision. Without a case, no court could act. Unlike legislators, who may introduce bills, judges do not initiate the cases they decide.

As cases bring issues old and new to the Court each term, the justices play a part in American government. For more than two hundred years the Supreme Court has conducted a dialogue with the people that reflects the public's historic attraction to, and suspicion of, majority rule. "The people have seemed to feel that the Supreme Court," wrote Justice Robert H. Jackson (1941–1954), "whatever its defects, is still the most detached, dispassionate, and trustworthy custodian that our system affords for the translation of abstract into concrete constitutional commands."[27] The justices are the keepers of American constitutional morality. That truth is both a source of and limit on their power.

POLITICAL CONTROVERSIES

The Supreme Court and "Obamacare"

When, after years of negotiation and compromise, Congress finally passed and President Obama signed into law the Patient Protection and Affordable Care Act in 2010, the exhaustive *legislative* battle for health-care reform was finally over. Yet the battle in the *judiciary* was just beginning. Opponents, who rejected a larger government role in health care, derisively referred to the new law as "Obamacare" and filed suit in federal court as soon as the law was passed.

The act, which went into effect in 2014, requires states to coordinate health insurance exchanges, requires insurers to accept dependents up to age twenty-six, and prevents insurance companies from denying applicants with preexisting conditions. It also contains a provision known as the "individual mandate." This was the most controversial aspect of the new law, in that it requires all Americans (except those with income or religion exemptions) to either have at least a minimal amount of health insurance or pay a penalty to the Internal Revenue Service. Less-wealthy Americans are eligible for tax credits to purchase insurance plans. (In 2017, the Tax Cuts and Jobs Act reduced the amount of the penalty to zero dollars.)

The Supreme Court accepted the case on *writ of certiorari* from the Eleventh Circuit Court of Appeals. Over the course of three days in March 2012, the justices heard oral testimony in the case of *National Federation of Independent Business v. Sebelius*.[1] Americans, in a 2012 poll, were somewhat evenly split in their views of the law, with 45 percent viewing it favorably and 44 percent unfavorably.[2] Despite a majority of Americans believing that the federal government has a responsibility to make sure all Americans have health-care coverage, only 20 percent believed the individual mandate would pass constitutional muster.[3]

On June 28, 2012, Chief Justice Roberts announced the historic decision. By a vote of 5–4, the Court upheld nearly all of the law, including the individual mandate. (The portion of the law struck down removes the federal government's ability to reduce state Medicaid funding to states that refuse to expand coverage.) Writing for the majority in a complex opinion, Roberts reasoned that the individual mandate was a constitutional use of Congress's *taxing* power. This outcome was a surprise to many, who assumed the Court would strike down the mandate and base its decision on the commerce clause or the necessary and proper clause. However, a majority of justices did not find that route acceptable; and the typically conservative Roberts found himself siding, for the first time, with the four more liberal justices (Ginsburg, Breyer, Sotomayor, and Kagan) in a 5–4 decision.

Did the Court reach the correct conclusion? If you were a Supreme Court justice, how would you have decided this case? On what parts of the Constitution would you base your decision? Does health care seem more like a basic human right that everyone should have, or more like an option for those who can afford it? How would you design a health-care system? What outcomes would result from your answers?

1. 567 U.S. 519 (2012).

2. "Americans, Views on the Healthcare Law," June 22, 2012, The Gallup Organization, http://www.gallup.com/poll/155300/ Gallup-Editors-Americans-Views-Healthcare-Law.aspx (June 25, 2012).

3. Ibid.

CHAPTER REVIEW

1. As the highest court in the land, the Supreme Court of the United States annually confronts a variety of important political issues that appear in the form of cases. The system of courts in the United States consists of the federal courts and the courts of the fifty states. Major federal courts include the district courts and the courts of appeals, in addition to the United States Supreme Court. Supreme Court justices and all federal judges are appointed by the president and confirmed by a majority of the Senate.

2. In deciding cases, the Supreme Court and other US courts engage in constitutional and statutory interpretation, fact determination, clarification of the boundaries of political authority, education and value application, and legitimization.

3. Cases decided by the Supreme Court proceed through five major stages: petition for review, briefs on the merits, oral argument, conference and decision, and assignment and writing of the opinion of the Court.

4. The decisions of the Supreme Court are the products of several factors and have been a source of controversy during most of US history. Although the Court enjoys considerable political independence from Congress and the president, external checks on judicial power do exist.

KEY TERMS

amicus curiae 394

appellate jurisdiction 386

briefs 394

case 380

civil case 380

concurring opinion 397

court of last resort 383

courts of general jurisdiction 383

courts of limited jurisdiction 383

crime 380

criminal case 380

dissenting opinion 397

Eleventh Amendment 386

federal courts 380

federal question 386

intermediate appellate courts 383

judicial activists 399

judicial restraintists 399

judicial review 391

jurisdiction 382

legislative intent 392

Missouri Plan 383

opinion of the Court 396

oral argument 395

original jurisdiction 386

precedents 399

rule of four 386

senatorial courtesy 387

solicitor general of the United States 395

stare decisis 399

state courts 380

trial court 392

United States courts of appeals 385

United States district courts 384

United States Reports 397

writ of certiorari 386

READINGS FOR FURTHER STUDY

A helpful survey of the role of the Court during much of the nation's history is Robert G. McCloskey's *The American Supreme Court*, 6th ed. (Chicago: University of Chicago Press, 2016).

Henry J. Abraham's *Justices, Presidents, and Senators*, 5th ed. (Lanham, MD: Rowman & Littlefield, 2007), is the standard work on appointment of Supreme Court justices.

Behind Bakke: Affirmative Action and the Supreme Court, by Bernard Schwartz (New York: New York University Press, 1988), takes a close look at how the Court reached its decision in a single case.

David M. O'Brien's *Storm Center: The Supreme Court in American Politics*, 12th ed. (New York: Norton, 2020), explores the broader political environment in which the Supreme Court operates.

Important decisions of the Supreme Court interpreting the Constitution are readily found in edited form in casebooks such as *Constitutional Law in Contemporary America* (New York: West Publishing, 2017) by David Schultz, John R. Vile, and Michelle D. Deardorff, or *Constitutional Law for a Changing America*, 10th ed. (Washington, DC: CQ Press, 2019) by Lee Epstein and Thomas G. Walker.

The Supreme Court Compendium, 6th ed. (Washington, DC: CQ Press, 2015) by Lee Epstein, Jeffrey A. Segal, Harold J. Spaeth, and Thomas G. Walker contains information on almost all aspects of the Court's work.

NOTES

1. Court Statistics Project, *State Court Caseload Digest: 2018 Data* (National Center for State Courts, 2020).

2. *United States v. Maine,* 420 U.S. 515 (1975).

3. *Michigan v. Ohio*, 386 U.S. 1029 (1967); *Arizona v. California*, 460 U.S. 605 (1983).

4. *Chisholm v. Georgia*, 2 U.S. (2 Dallas) 419 (1793).

5. *Roe v. Wade*, 410 U.S. 113 (1973).

6. *Lee v. Weisman*, 60 U.S.L.W. 4723 (1992); Marcia Coyle, "The Court Confounds Observers," *National Law Journal*, July 13, 1992, p. 1.

7. 7The *Marbury* case and the concept of judicial review are discussed in Chapter 1.

8. *Sony Corporation v. Universal City Studios*, 464 U.S. 417 (1984).

9. *Youngstown v. Sawyer*, 343 U.S. 579 (1952).

10. *Heart of Atlanta Motel v. United States*, 379 U.S. 274 (1964).

11. Adam Liptak, "Justice Clarence Thomas Breaks His Silence," *The New York Times*, January 14, 2013.

12. Ted Johnson, "Supreme Court Set to Grant C-SPAN, Other Media Outlets A Long-Desired Wish: Live Audio Of Oral Arguments," *Deadline*, April 30, 2020, https://deadline.com/2020/04/supreme-court-c-span-live-audio-1202922580/ (August 13, 2020).

13. *Osborn v. Bank of the United States*, 22 U.S. (9 Wheaton) 738, 866 (1824).

14. Max Lerner, quoted in Henry J. Abraham's, *The Judicial Process*, 5th ed. (New York: Oxford University Press, 1986), p. 348.

15. Tracey E. George and Lee Epstein, "On the Nature of Supreme Court Decision Making," *American Political Science Review 86* (1992): 323.

16. David W. Rhode and Harold J. Spaeth, "Ideology, Strategy, and Supreme Court Decisions: William Rehnquist as Chief Justice," *Judicature 72* (1989): 247; Harold J. Spaeth and Stuart H. Teger, "Activism and Restraint: A Cloak for the Justices' Policy Preferences," in Stephen C. Halpern and Charles M. Lamb, eds., *Supreme Court Activism and Restraint* (Lexington, MA: Lexington Books, 1982), pp. 277–301.

17. Harold J. Spaeth, *Supreme Court Policy Making* (San Francisco: Freeman, 1979), pp. 109–139; Mark W. Cannon and David M. O'Brien, eds., *Views from the Bench* (Chatham, NJ: Chatham House, 1985), pp. 253–302.

18. 410 U.S. 113 (1973).

19. *Planned Parenthood of Southeastern Pennsylvania v. Casey*, 60 U.S.L.W. 4795 (1992).

20. *Dickerson v. United States*, 530 U.S. 428 (2000), *Miranda v. Arizona*, 384 U.S. 436 (1966).

21. Walter F. Murphy, *Elements of Judicial Strategy* (Chicago: University of Chicago Press, 1964), ch. 3.

22. "Reflections on the Removal of Sitting Judges," *Stetson Law Review 13* (1984): 215, 217.

23. *Furman v. Georgia*, 408 U.S. 238 (1972).

24. *Gregg v. Georgia*, 428 U.S. 153 (1976).

25. 2 U.S. (2 Dallas) 419 (1793); 60 U.S. (19 Howard) 393 (1857); 158 U.S. 601 (1895); 400 U.S. 112 (1970).

26. *Brown v. Board of Education*, 347 U.S. 483 (1954).

27. *The Supreme Court in the American System of Government* (Cambridge, MA: Harvard University Press, 1955), p. 23.

POP QUIZ

1. Almost all divorce and personal injury cases are heard in _____ courts.

2. The _____ Court hears suits involving monetary damages against the United States government.

3. Today, almost all cases reach the Supreme Court on a *writ of* _____.

4. Petitions for review filed by lawyers with the Supreme Court's clerk are called _____.

5. Congress and the states may correct the Supreme Court's interpretation of the Constitution through a _____.

6. The judiciary operates only in the context of cases.   T   F

7. Most federal and state judges are appointed for life and can be removed only by impeachment.   T   F

8. About half the cases the Supreme Court decides involve the meaning the justices give to words legislators have written.   T   F

9. Supreme Court conferences and deliberations are open to the public.   T   F

10. The most often used check on judicial power has been impeachment.   T   F

11. Which of the following applies to state courts that serve as trial courts for serious criminal offenses?
    A) They are courts of limited jurisdiction.
    B) They are courts of general jurisdiction.
    C) They are intermediate appellate courts.
    D) They are courts of last resort.

12. The Supreme Court's original jurisdiction includes which of the following types of cases?
    A) Cases between one of the states and the United States government
    B) Cases between two or more states
    C) Cases involving foreign ambassadors, ministers, or consuls
    D) All of the above

13. Fact discretion is most visible in _____.
    A) the Supreme Court
    B) legislative courts
    C) trial courts
    D) intermediate appellate courts

14. Documents submitted to the Court from interest groups and others who are not parties to the case but have a stake in its outcome are called _____.
    A) *amicus curiae* briefs
    B) *writs of certiorari*
    C) arraignments
    D) dissenting opinions

15. Checks on judicial power include which of the following?
    A) constitutional amendment
    B) impeachment
    C) withdrawing jurisdiction
    D) All of the above

Answers:
1. state   2. Claims   3. *certiorari*   4. briefs
5. constitutional amendment   6. T   7. F
8. T   9. F   10. F   11. B   12. D
13. C   14. A   15. D

Chapter

13

(Shutterstock)

GOVERNMENT & PUBLIC POLICY

In This Chapter

13.1   Public Policy in the Political Process
13.2   The Purposes and Presence of the National Government
13.3   Politics and Economic Self-Interest

Chapter Objectives

Public policy is collectively what governments do. This chapter begins by addressing what public policy is and how it relates to the political process. We will then learn to think about public policies so that what appears to be a chaotic mass of procedures, institutions, and personalities is more understandable. Finally, given the fact that government does so many different things, this chapter will attempt to differentiate among different kinds of public policies.

13.1

Public Policy in the Political Process

Public policy can be defined in a variety of ways, but the simplest is that "public policy is whatever governments choose to do or not to do."[1] Financing cancer research, providing a Social Security system, cutting or raising taxes, initiating or halting development of a new weapons system, and attempting to minimize the impact of a global pandemic are all examples of public policies. This chapter will introduce the process of public policy; the following three chapters will address economic, domestic, and foreign policies, respectively.

public policy
Whatever governments choose to do or not to do

407

(Shutterstock)

An example of the public's conflicting demands on government is interest rates. Reducing interest rates can help first-time homebuyers but can hurt senior citizens, whose investment income is bolstered by higher interest rates.

13.1a Conflict Over the Ends of Government

Government is always subject to conflicting demands due to the great differences among citizens in economic status, occupations, and political ideas. Different groups will likely press for public policies in their own interests, regardless of the effect those policies might have on other groups. The use of rules, procedures, representatives, and institutions is important to such groups only toward the end of achieving public policies favorable to them.

The results of public policy mirror conflicts in demands. No governmental action can affect all citizens in exactly the same way. Whatever government does will have varying consequences for different groups. For example, placing limits on Medicare spending will provide some relief to taxpayers by reducing pressure for higher taxes, but those same limits will place economic strains on hospitals and other health-care providers. Increasing the money supply to reduce interest rates will help first-time homebuyers by making mortgages easier to afford, but doing so

Figure 13.1   The Systems Model of Policy Making

The systems model describes policy making in terms of the relationship between a political system and its environment. "Inputs" (demands and supports) are converted into "outputs" (policy decisions). By affecting the environment of the political system, these outputs may generate new inputs.

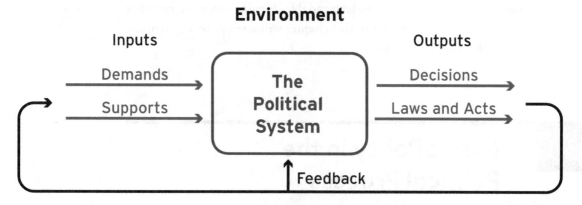

SOURCE: Adapted from James E. Anderson, Public Policymaking, 4th ed. (Boston: Houghton Mifflin, 2000), p. 18.

will hurt senior citizens who depend on higher interest rates to bolster their investment income. Differences in demands and in the consequences of government action create political conflict. At issue in the public policy debate is which groups shall win and which shall lose in the effort to shape government actions to their own interests.

13.1b Perspectives on Policy Making

The nature of politics and policy is such that a variety of models or explanations have been offered as accurate or desirable portrayals of public policy making. Among the most familiar is the **systems model**, which holds that policy is the product of an interlocking relationship between the political system and its social, cultural, and economic environment.[2] From its environment the political system receives "inputs" in the form of demands and supports. Through its decision-making process, the political system then converts demands into "outputs," which are authoritative or official decisions. These decisions may, in turn, affect the environment and shape new inputs into the system. For example, demands that government reduce the burden of regulations may result in government decisions to eliminate some regulations. These decisions may penalize people who benefited under the old regulations, and those people may then clamor for reinstatement. As another illustration, a court decision that weakens the constitutional claim to the right to have an abortion may shift much of the political battle over abortion to state legislatures.

Other models view policy making from different perspectives. The **bureaucratic model** posits the crucial role of bureaucracies and the commitment and expertise they can provide in making policy. Some models use ideological frameworks with an economic focus to explain how policies are or should be made. The **Marxism model** holds that public policy decisions in non-Marxist regimes reflect the interests of the ruling economic class at the expense of the workers. The **free-market capitalism model** sees a limited role for government, a role in which the natural forces of supply and demand are allowed to prevail in the marketplace. Other models might be discussed as well; the interplay of interests and passions that drives policy debate and the rich complexity of making public policy have produced numerous models of policy making.

Two of the most useful perspectives are elitism and pluralism. They are particularly helpful in understanding the maze of public policy because they address a fundamental question about which there has been much debate: *Who* makes public policy decisions?

Elitism holds that public policy decisions are made by a relatively small group of individuals acting in their own self-interest.[3] The theory takes a variety of forms, depending on who is included in the elite. Some elements of the mass media, big business, and the military have been variously portrayed as making up the elite. According to the model, members of the elite—on issues of importance to them—make public policy judgments in the interest of the elite rather than in the interest of the mass of citizens.

Pluralism holds that public policy decisions are the result of struggle among contesting groups rather than a single elite.[4] The groups represent various interests in society and press for decisions responsive to those interests. Policy is determined not by a single set of values as in elitism but by a contest of conflicting values held by various groups. Even though the number of participants in the making of public policy is small, they reflect and convey the broad range of positions held by the mass of citizens. Competing elites with different values ensure democratic responsiveness. In the pluralist view, government is a broker among groups, seeking to satisfy as many as possible. Conflicts among groups produce a balance so that no single group dominates. This is sometimes called the *countervailing theory of pressure politics*.

systems model
A model of policy making that holds that policy is the product of an interlocking relationship between institutions of government and their social, economic, and political environment

bureaucratic model
A model of policy making that holds that bureaucracies play a crucial role in making policy because of their commitment and the expertise they can provide

Marxism model
A model of policy making that holds that public policy decisions in non-Marxist regimes reflect the interests of the ruling economic class at the expense of workers

free-market capitalism model
A model of policy making that posits a limited role for government so that the natural forces of supply and demand are allowed to prevail in the marketplace

elitism
A model of policy making that holds that public policy decisions are made by a relatively small group of individuals acting in their own self-interest rather than in the interest of the mass of citizens

pluralism
A model of policy making that holds that public policy decisions are the result of struggles among contesting groups that reflect the various interests among citizens

A second issue is how decisions are made.[5] Two contrasting perspectives are the rational-comprehensive approach and incrementalism. The **rational-comprehensive model** involves a sequence of steps for "rational" decisions. Decision-makers identify problems, rank the values they wish to achieve, consider various policy alternatives that can attain these values, assess the costs and benefits of each alternative, and select and implement the policy strategy that can best achieve the stated values with the highest benefits and lowest costs. This model has been criticized for imposing unrealistic demands on people making policy decisions. Critics argue that information in the real world of policy making is limited and uncertain, and the clash of interests makes impossible any ranking of values.

Incrementalism is an alternative model that takes these criticisms into account. In the view of critics, the tie to past policies reduces the possibility of new policy approaches. Policy makers do not begin with a clean slate but rather focus on proposed marginal changes in existing policies. Deciding on budgets is an example. Rather than creating an entirely new budget each year, budget makers focus on proposed marginal changes from the previous year's budget. The same goes for policies like environmental regulation. A change to emissions standards for next year is likely to be greatly influenced by the existing standards. Imagine how difficult it would be to conduct business if future rules were often radically different from present rules.

By highlighting marginal changes in existing policies, incrementalism poses lower information demands. In addition, incrementalism holds that a capacity to achieve agreement among contesting interests defines good public policy. This definition of good policy is in sharp contrast to the rational-comprehensive emphasis on the search for costs and benefits of alternative policy approaches.[6]

Incrementalism has been criticized for being too conservative in its implications. In addition, the sensitivity to political power and the emphasis on agreement in the model risk the exclusion of interests without power. In the effort to be realistic and pragmatic, incrementalism neglects some interests in the search for the appropriate purposes of government.

Despite these criticisms, incrementalism does raise important questions in public policy. Under what circumstances is the political system capable of fundamental rather than incremental changes in policy? What does it take to make a substantial break with the past? Changes in the number of people insured by the Social Security system and increases in taxes to pay for the program have been incremental over the past eighty-five years, as Figure 13.2 shows; but the decision to establish the system in 1935 was a fundamental break with the past. Decisions to create new agencies (or abolish existing ones) or to initiate new programs (or terminate current ones) are fundamental rather than incremental. The circumstances allowing such decisions can be the threat of crisis or substantial changes in technology, in social or economic values, or in the alignment of political power. The model of incrementalism may be as important for the questions it raises about policy as it is for the explanations it offers.[7]

(iStock / Getty Images Plus)

According to the theory of elitism, relatively small groups of individuals, such as mass media, big business, and the military, act in their own self-interest to make public policy decisions that affect all Americans.

rational-comprehensive model

A model of decision-making that holds that policy makers should identify problems, consider various policy alternatives and their costs and benefits, and select and implement the policy strategy with the highest benefits and the lowest costs

incrementalism

A model of decision-making that holds that new policies should differ only marginally from existing policies

Table 13.1   Selected Perspectives on Policy Making

Given the complexity of making policy and the sharp conflicts that can drive policy debate, a variety of models, interpretations, and approaches have been offered as portraits of how policy is or should be made.

I. Models of the Policy-Making Process

Systems model	Policy is the product of an interlocking relationship between institutions of government and their surrounding social, economic, and political environments.
Bureaucratic model	Because of their commitment and the expertise they can provide, bureaucracies play a crucial role in making policy.
Marxism model	Public policy decisions reflect the interest of the ruling class at the expense of workers.
Free market capitalism model	The natural forces of supply and demand are allowed to work in the marketplace, and government plays only a limited role in shaping those forces.

II. Interpretations of Who Makes Public Policy

Elitism	Public policy decisions are made by a relatively small group of individuals acting in their own self-interest rather than the interest of all citizens.
Pluralism	Public policy decisions are the result of struggle among contesting groups, with the various interests among the masses reflected and represented in the policy process.

III. Approaches to How Public Policy Is Made

Rational comprehensive approach	Decision-makers should identify problems, rank the values they wish to achieve, consider various policy alternatives that can attain these values, assess the cost and benefits of each alternative, and select and implement the policy strategy that can best achieve the stated values with the highest benefits and lowest costs. Critics of the model argue that information in the real world of policy making is limited and uncertain and that the clash of interests in the policy process makes any ranking of values impossible.
Incrementalism	Since present decisions are only marginally different from past decisions, policy makers focus on proposed marginal changes in existing policies. A capacity to achieve agreement among contesting interests defines a good public policy. Critics of the model argue that the tie to past policies reduces the possibility of new policy approaches and that the sensitivity to political power and the emphasis on agreement risk the exclusion of interests without political power.

Figure 13.2   Incrementalism and Social Security Taxes

The creation of the Social Security program in 1935 was a fundamental change in government policy. Once Social Security was established, changes in the rates of taxes to pay for the program occurred in incremental steps over time. Short of an emergency of the magnitude of the Great Depression, it is unlikely that there will be any drastic and abrupt changes in the program. Rather, adjustments will come gradually.

The tax rates of 7.65 percent for employees and employers and 15.3 percent for the self-employed will remain in effect for future years unless Congress and the president decide to change Social Security tax rate policy.

DATA SOURCE: Social Security Bulletin, Annual Statistical Supplement, 2005, p. 87, and from Social Security Online, https://www.ssa.gov/OACT/ProgData/taxRates.html (August 13, 2020).

Whether looking at incrementalism or another policy-making model, it is good to remember that models are learning tools. By abstracting from reality, they try to explain why things happen as they do. The utility of a model lies in increasing our understanding of reality, yet no single model describes completely a complex political system. Thinking of events in terms of two or three models may be a better way to think about how policy is made and about who is influential in shaping policy.

13.1c   Stages in the Policy Process

In the real world of politics and conflict, the making of public policy frequently appears to be full of chaos. Groups demand or oppose, members of Congress respond or criticize, presidents agree or refuse, judges rule or defer, bureaucrats proceed or halt, and the mass media report or ignore. The making of public policy is not like a play where all the actors follow a predetermined script. Rather, in the making of policy, a group leader or a congressional representative may say and do things without knowing how others will respond or whether they will respond at all. In the efforts to shape policy, hope, uncertainty, and chance all play a role. Consequently, the policy process may seem to be a confusing clash of ideas, events, and personalities.

Public policy analysts try to break down the process of making policy into definable stages to order and make sense out of what appears to be chaotic.[8] Figure 13.3 portrays the stages in the evolution of public policies. In the real world, policies do not evolve in such neatly defined and apparently simple stages. Participants in the process make demands, offer responses, and make decisions without consciously following some analytical framework. Nonetheless, identification of these stages helps to make the evolution of public policies and the role of government procedures and institutions in the process more understandable.

Figure 13.3 Stages in the Policy Process

Although policies do not always develop in the neatly defined stages outlined below, an awareness of what happens in each stage helps us understand the process that occurs as government attempts to solve problems and accomplish goals. Any number and combination of persons and events can bring concerns to the attention of political leaders (stage 1). Policy makers in the executive and legislative branches then study the range of choices open to them to meet those concerns (stage 2). A variety of public officials may be involved in selecting a course of action or in deciding to do nothing at all (stage 3). The policy then becomes the responsibility of bureaucrats to administer (stage 4). Finally, evaluation occurs. Does the plan work? Is it worth its costs (stage 5)? The evaluation may become a factor in encouraging further policy making by government.

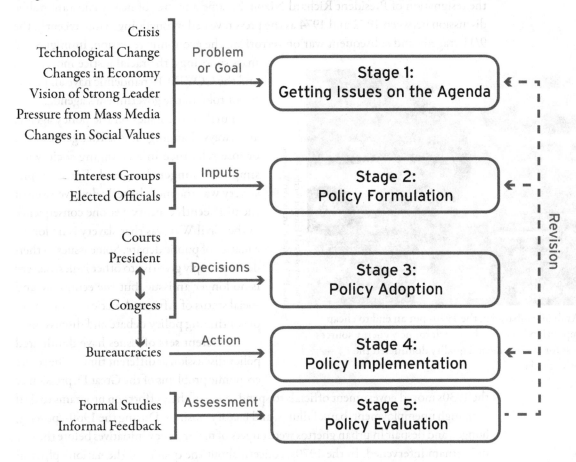

As Figure 13.3 shows, there are five stages in the evolution of policies:

1. A problem or issue must somehow get on the agenda of government.

2. Specific proposals to do something about the problem are discussed.

3. Government officials adopt a policy by choosing some specific strategy for action from among the proposals discussed.

4. Bureaucrats implement or translate into action the adopted proposal.

5. The policy is evaluated to determine whether or not it succeeded in solving or ameliorating the originally defined problem.

Stage 1: Getting Issues on the Agenda of Government

The **policy agenda** of government comprises the list of issues that engage the attention of elected officials. Obviously, governments cannot simultaneously deal with every conceivable problem. Like individuals, governments must make choices on which matters will get their attention at particular times. Issues get on the policy agenda in a variety of ways. No single explanation can capture the rich complexity of the process.[9]

Factors that contribute to moving some particular issue onto the government agenda include technological change, the demands of politically emerging groups, the evolution of social values, the threats of crisis or war, changing economic conditions, and the political will of a strong leader. Sometimes the mass media can create issues by focusing attention on particular concerns. For example, the Watergate affair, which resulted in the resignation of President Richard Nixon, became a matter of nearly constant public discussion between 1972 and 1974 as the press revealed wrongdoing. More recently, the 9/11 tragedy and subsequent war on terrorism, the economic recession, immigration, mass shootings, the racial justice movement, and the COVID-19 pandemic have all played major roles in the government's agenda.

Further, the issues on the policy agenda are always changing. Those that get resolved or lose relevance in a changing society are simply no longer discussed. For example, slavery was the most bitterly divisive issue of the nineteenth century, yet one consequence of the Civil War was that slavery is no longer a matter of public debate. Some issues in their demise simply give rise to other issues. Slavery is no longer an issue, but the economic and social status of African Americans is a matter of continuing policy debate and discussion.

(Courtesy of David Falconer for the EPA, circa 1973, National Archives via Wikimedia)

After the Arab oil embargo in the 1970s put an end to cheap energy, competition between the search for new energy sources and the quest for environmental quality dominated the government's agenda.

Different sets of issues have dominated policy discussion at different times. The severe economic problems of the Great Depression of the 1930s moved government officials to spend much of their efforts on programs to deal with high unemployment, bank failures, and factory closings. During the 1960s, poverty, hunger, and despair in urban ghettos were targets of major policy initiatives before the war in Vietnam intervened. In the 1970s, concern about the quality of the nation's physical environment emerged as a major policy issue. The Arab oil embargo of that decade also put a sudden end to cheap energy; consequently, the competition between the search for new energy sources and the quest for environmental quality dominated the agenda of those years.

Thus far in the twenty-first century, two issues seem to be overwhelming and affecting practically all others on the policy agenda: the use of money as a public resource and the role of the United States in the international arena. Domestically, how much the government should spend (and on what), how much and whom government should tax, the impact of budget deficits and surpluses on the economy, and how far the reach of the federal government (as opposed to that of states and private parties) should extend in such areas as Social Security, welfare, health care, and global climate change are the questions that drive most policy debate. In foreign affairs, how to respond to terrorism, whether and how to take unilateral military action in a world of increasing multinational organization, and the ethical responsibilities of superpower status are the

policy agenda

The public issues that engage the attention of elected officials

concerns driving policy. When new, large-scale concerns like the COVID-19 pandemic emerge they can create questions for both the money and international arenas. The policy agenda of government is like a kaleidoscope: The turn of decades results in constantly shifting patterns of issue concerns.

Stage 2: Policy Formulation

Once an issue gets on the agenda of government, public debate centers on specific proposals on what government ought to do and how to do it.[10] To say that government ought to "do something" about budget deficits, the needs of children in poverty, climate change, or drug addiction is only a beginning. To achieve results requires a specific **policy strategy**, some specific course of action designed to deal with the originally defined problem.

If the budget deficit is a problem, should we increase taxes, decrease spending, or press for a balanced budget amendment? If the needs of children in poverty are a problem, should we increase family assistance payments, track down absent fathers, or build orphanages? If climate change is a problem, should we ban the use of certain fuels, or should we tax their use to pay for research on alternative energies? If drug addiction is a problem, should we open more treatment centers, eradicate drug-producing crops around the world, or legalize the use of drugs? Of course, several policy strategies to deal with a problem might be pursued simultaneously, but the relative emphasis on one or another strategy can provoke intense controversy.

Questions of what government should do, who should benefit, and who should bear the costs of such action make up the raw material of policy debate. Groups with different ideological beliefs are likely to propose different solutions to policy problems. To reduce budget deficits, for example, conservatives are likely to propose cuts in social welfare spending, and liberals are likely to propose cuts in defense spending or the closing of tax loopholes for the wealthy. The groups that benefit from one proposal will suffer under the other. The demands of interest groups, debates in Congress, requests by bureaucracies, conflicts between political parties and candidates, presidential speeches, and reporting in the mass media all focus on the question of what government ought to do in some specific policy area.

Stage 3: Policy Adoption

Although an issue can get on the policy agenda and various policy strategies can be debated and discussed, nothing happens until institutions of government **adopt a policy** that started as a proposal. At some point a formal, authoritative decision must be made on the action government will take to address a particular concern. Ultimately, the institutions of government exist to make such formal, authoritative decisions.

Formal adoption occurs in several ways. A bill passed by both houses of Congress and duly signed by the president

---

Confused by the contradictory claims politicians sometimes make about public policy?

FactCheck.org, a project of the Annenberg Public Policy Center, is a nonpartisan and nonprofit effort to investigate the factual accuracy of claims made by political leaders. Check out the website and check up on the politicians.

http://www.bvtlab.com/nb76h

Interested in an internship or career in public policy?

The National Association of Schools of Public Affairs and Administration offers suggestions and starting points.

http://www.bvtlab.com/N8k8r

---

policy strategy
A specific course of action designed to deal with a public problem

policy adoption
A formal, authoritative decision, such as the enactment of legislation, made by institutions of government to address an issue on the policy agenda

is an example of formal adoption. For example, if growing budget deficits are deemed an important issue on the policy agenda, one specific strategy to deal with the problem might be a tax bill designed to raise revenue. If both houses can agree on a bill and if the president concurs on the wisdom and necessity of the measure, the resulting law is the formal adoption of a strategy for action. Similarly, decisions by the Supreme Court and the declaration of regulations by bureaucracies are also illustrations of adoption in the making of policy. If the Court requires busing to eliminate racially segregated schools, it is—by making an authoritative, formal decision—in effect adopting a strategy for action. If a regulatory agency requires the installation of air bags in automobiles, it too is adopting a strategy for action.

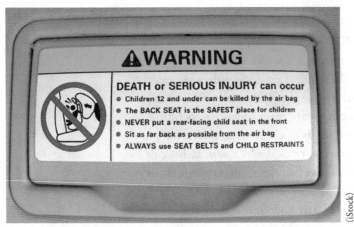

(iStock)

The warning label found in all cars with airbags resulted from the government's formal adoption of policy.

Adopting some policy strategy does not end the debate, however. The losers (both inside and outside the government) in the adoption process may retreat to other units in the political system and seek to have the decision changed or revised. A tax law may become an issue in a subsequent electoral campaign, or a regulatory decision on air bags may end up in the courts. Alternatively, those who have lost may simply wait for another day, when events or changing times or different officials will allow their position another hearing. In the short run, few issues are resolved by the adoption of some particular strategy for action. Rather, the discussion usually continues as revisions are proposed or as the consequences of the adopted strategy become matters of debate. The wheel of policy making turns endlessly. Moreover, failure to adopt a policy proposal is, in itself, policy making. It represents a formal, authoritative decision to leave policy where it was before the debate began, with the effect that taxes do not go up or air bags are not required.

Stage 4: Policy Implementation

Policy debate is really debate over *ideas*. For example, Congress and the president may decide that sending retired persons monthly checks funded by people currently employed is a good idea and formally adopt a strategy. However, that idea or strategy for action must be *implemented* before anything happens. A bureaucracy must be charged with the task of actually getting the right checks to the right people. Bureaucracies play the central role in this stage in the policy process, for they are ultimately responsible for **policy implementation**, or translating policy ideas into action. The difficulties and obstacles that frequently accompany the implementation process are suggested by the expressive (if lengthy) subtitle of a classic book: *How Great Expectations in Washington Are Dashed in Oakland; Or, Why It's Amazing That Federal Programs Work at All, This Being a Saga of the Economic Development Administration as Told by Two Sympathetic Observers Who Seek to Build Morals on a Foundation of Ruined Hopes.*[11] Clearly, implementation is neither automatic nor predictable.[12]

Continuing debate frequently accompanies the implementation process. In the judgment of the opponents of some particular policy strategy, a bureaucracy may outrun, or even contradict, the intent of Congress. For example, efforts in Congress to invalidate regulations of the Federal Trade Commission by legislative veto were attempts to put controls on the agency. Alternatively, a bureaucracy may not be vigorous enough in discharging its task. For example, in 2001, some members of Congress charged the

policy implementation
The translation of policy ideas into action

Environmental Protection Agency with being too vigorous in enforcement of prohibitions in rural areas, but far too lax in enforcing violations in places with greater political clout, like the metro Washington, DC, area.[13] A bureaucracy can be caught in the same cross fire of conflicting demands that were present in the debate before a strategy was formally adopted. On pollution control policy, for example, the EPA can be in the middle of conflict between environmentalists and business interests fearful of the costs of environmental regulations. In any case, the implementation stage in policy is frequently a continuation of the political struggle that surrounds an issue from the time it first gets on the policy agenda.

Stage 5: Policy Evaluation

The final analytical stage in the evolution of policies is evaluation.[14] This stage logically follows from the others because of the reasonable expectation that we ought to know whether a particular policy strategy "worked." Determining whether the formally adopted, implemented strategy in fact ameliorated or solved the originally defined problem is the goal of **policy evaluation**. However, the expectation that policy strategies ought to be evaluated definitively is more easily stated than actually met.

Formal evaluation of policies has received increased attention since the late 1960s. As the national government attempted to do more policy making, criticism surfaced that government did not deliver on its promises. Consequently, demands for policy evaluation intensified. The techniques of such formal evaluation range from simple before-and-after studies to more sophisticated controlled experiments. Do innovative education programs (new curricular efforts, charter schools, the expenditure of additional funds, etc.), in fact, improve learning skills among disadvantaged children? Do rehabilitation programs (employment, training, special counseling, etc.), in fact, reduce the likelihood that individuals released from prison will commit crimes again? In a controlled experiment, do individuals who receive a guaranteed income behave any differently from another group of individuals who do not?

Such questions are legitimate, but formal evaluation efforts almost never give unequivocal answers that end debate over the policy. In fact, debate frequently swirls about evaluation results, especially if the answers do not coincide with the expectations of the people who want the policy to work. Unfavorable results can almost always be explained away

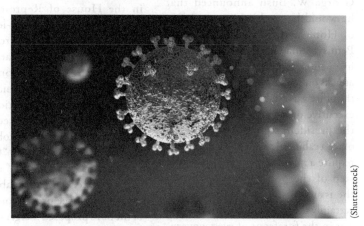

Coronavirus COVID-19 under the microscope. 3-D illustration.

by citing inadequate research instruments, insufficient time to assess the policy, or inaccurate interpretations of the findings.[15] For example, people who want school vouchers to work might criticize negative findings on vouchers because the study was based on too short a time span. Evaluation results are more likely to continue, rather than end, policy debate.

Not every government policy goes through a formal evaluation procedure. There may be insufficient time and money as well as analytical difficulties. For example, are nuclear weapons policies preventing nuclear war? The answer may be that they are for now; but if such a war should occur, the assertion would obviously be proved wrong, with dire consequences few wish to even contemplate. In this instance, the policy relies on hope rather than on unattainable evaluation results. In the absence of a cure for cancer or COVID-19, is the nation's medical research policy working? No reasonable person would

policy evaluation

The act of determining whether a formally adopted and implemented policy ameliorated or solved a public problem

suggest that cancer or COVID-19 research should be halted because individuals continue to die of the disease. Again, hope for success sustains the policy, yet the very existence of some policies constitutes almost a definition of success. The Social Security program, for example, is working as long as the checks are regularly sent out.

POLITICS AND ECONOMICS

The Road to a New Cabinet Department

America's response to the 9/11 terrorist attacks illustrated both the speed with which public policy can be enacted and the hurdles that must be overcome in the public policy process. On September 20, 2001—just nine days after the tragedy—President George W. Bush announced that he would be establishing an Office of Homeland Security, headed by Pennsylvania Governor Tom Ridge, in an effort to prevent future terrorist attacks on the United States. Although the office was established quickly via an executive order on October 8, 2001, the president's goal of making the office a cabinet-level department would require a much longer route. The first step of the policy process, getting the issue on the policy agenda, was certainly the easiest. Domestic security was in the forefront of every government official's mind in the autumn of 2001.

President Bush delivered the second stage, developing a policy strategy, during his address. He proposed a course of action to address the problem of terrorism. Specifically, he suggested a cabinet-level office designed to prevent future terrorist attacks, reduce American vulnerability, and help in recovery efforts for attacks that do occur.[1] In this case, strategy development occurred very quickly; this speed was a result of the gravity of the problem the policy addressed.

Policy adoption became a sticking point for homeland security. Although President Bush was able to swiftly establish an executive office without the need of additional approval, creation of a full-blown cabinet department requires a congressional act. Thus, on June 24, 2002, Representative Dick Armey (R-TX) introduced the Homeland Security Act of 2002 in the House of Representatives. Although the Republican-led House of Representatives voted to approve the bill just one month later (quick adoption by congressional standards), the Democratic majority in the Senate voiced reservations about the extent of the proposed department's powers. Senator Robert Byrd (D-WV) cautioned that "Congress must never act recklessly," as he and others voiced concerns about civil service employee protections in light of the bill's proposed merger of twenty-two federal agencies into a single department.[2] Eventual adoption would depend on the ability of Congress and the president to reach a compromise. This compromise was finally reached when the Senate passed a revised bill on November 19, 2002, and President Bush signed it into law.

Policy implementation involved a large-scale restructuring of existing offices and agencies, affecting over 170,000 federal employees. Even though an executive office was already in place, coordinating and organizing such a large number of workers into four newly created divisions took a considerable amount of time. Initial stages of policy implementation tend to be measured in months, but completion of large-scale policy changes can sometimes take years.

The final stage of the process, policy evaluation, started to take place as soon as President Bush announced his intentions. From the moment his speech ended, journalists, politicians, and policy analysts began assessing success and failure. In addition to formal evaluation, such as the annual appropriations process in Congress, informal evaluation of Homeland Security continues to occur every time security in the US is threatened. Although policies are tested constantly, only time can tell whether they will ultimately succeed or fail.

The speed of the public policy process varies. What aspects seem too fast? Too slow? Which perspective on policy making, discussed earlier in this chapter, provides the best description of efforts to create a Department of Homeland Security?

1. The Department of Homeland Security, http://www.whitehouse.gov/deptofhomeland (September 23, 2002).

2. "Democrats Urged to Act on Homeland Security Bill," September 18, 2002, http://www.cnn.com/2002/ALLPOLITICS /09/18/homeland.security.ap/index.html (September 23, 2002).

Although most policies are not evaluated formally, they are often appraised *informally* during the process of implementation. Some informal assessments of government programs include congressional budget and authorization hearings, the sharp policy conflicts between opposing candidates in electoral campaigns, presidential speeches to set the nation's policy priorities, and the eternal demands of interest groups. Ultimately, most evaluation of government policies is the product of the endless interplay of political passions at the root of all political conflict.

13.2 The Purposes and Presence of the National Government

Readers of newspapers and viewers of television newscasts are told almost daily of a bewildering array of national government actions. The Air Force presses to keep a new bomber program alive. NASA announces plans for a mission to Mars. The Nuclear Regulatory Commission publishes a new set of rules on certification procedures for the operation of nuclear power plants. The Supreme Court hands down a decision on the constitutionality of a campaign finance law. Congress continues to wrestle with budget deficits. The

president's budget director defends a plan to eliminate the inheritance tax. This blizzard of activity reflects the pervasiveness of the national government as well as the complexity and scope of its work.

(junrong / Shutterstock)

13.2a Views of Public Policy

No single set of categories can adequately capture everything government does. However, some divisions among policies can help make the scope of government activity more comprehensible. The identification of policy categories defines patterns of government action to clarify what government does and how it goes about its work.

Foreign policies, such as an international trade policy with China, can have important domestic consequences, such as affecting the price of international goods sold in the United States.

Perhaps the most common sets of policy categories are **foreign policy**, decisions about relations with other nations, and **domestic policy**, decisions about matters affecting citizens within the United States. Some foreign policies can have important domestic consequences. For example, international trade policy with China can affect the prices of goods in the United States. In general, however, public officials make foreign policy decisions in ways different from those used in social welfare policies. The president is less constrained by other officials and groups in the international arena than he is in seeking changes in the Social Security system. Interest groups tend to be less concerned about foreign policies than about domestic policies, which affect them more immediately and directly.[16] Domestic policy can be further subdivided into functional areas, such as education, health, transportation, energy, and environment.

foreign policy

A nation's collective decisions about relations with other nations

domestic policy

A category of public policy that is composed of policy decisions about matters affecting individuals within a political system

13.3 Politics and Economic Self-Interest

The presence or absence of *economic self-interest* can also be a useful criterion for differentiating policies. Economic self-interest plays little or no role in the disposition of issues such as abortion, the legal drinking age, same-sex marriage, and the draft. In each of these cases, money would not resolve the conflict. Some people, for example, vehemently believe that abortion is an undeniable evil while others see abortion as an inalienable right of women. Proponents of abortion argue that women should be able to decide not to have children for economic as well as personal reasons. However, money concerns are not paramount in this debate.

Another category includes government actions on matters in which money plays a central role. For example, debates over taxes and budget deficits are essentially economic questions. Who shall pay for government, and who shall receive how much out of it? Which states shall receive more than others in federal grants? Which groups shall bear the brunt of cuts in social welfare spending? Does inflation merit more government action and attention than unemployment?

Finally, in some policy debates economic self-interest and assertions of principle are mixed. Money plays an important but not exclusive role in these issues. Policies on civilian nuclear power, civil rights, and pornography are examples. Electric power companies have an economic interest in favorable governmental policies on nuclear plant construction. Similarly, groups like women, African Americans, and Americans with disabilities see active civil rights policies on hiring and promotion as favorable to their economic self-interest; but assertions of principle also play an important role in the debates. The opponents of civilian nuclear power see nuclear power plants as a threat to public health and the quality of the environment. Civil rights advocates see the enhanced status of certain groups as a matter of right and justice. Finally, while the producers and sellers of pornography assert the principle of freedom of speech, their opponents see the defense of pornography (from which money is made) as a defense of economic self-interest.

13.3a Categories of National Government Policies

No single set of categories can adequately capture everything government does. However, even though overlaps occur, some divisions among policies can help make the scope of government activity more comprehensible. Over time the national government has taken on new functions and responsibilities in response to crises, changing technologies, citizen demands, and political pressures. Six substantive categories can help to bring some order to the scope of national government policies.

Foreign and Defense Policies

The oldest functions of the national government are to conduct relationships with foreign nations, such as trade negotiations with Mexico and Canada, and to maintain national security against threats from other nations, using physical force if necessary, such as the use of troops in the 1991 Persian Gulf War or the Iraq War (2003–2011).

POLITICS AND ECONOMICS

The President and Economic Policy Making

Nowhere is the gap greater between what the public expects and what the president can do than in economic policy. Accustomed to general prosperity, the American public demands full employment, stable prices, and an increased standard of living. Presidents who fail to provide all of these things usually do not get reelected. Herbert Hoover, Gerald Ford, Jimmy Carter, and George H. W. Bush—all defeated incumbents—stand as examples. Hoover presided over the Great Depression; Ford served during a period of high unemployment; Carter contended with double-digit inflation; and Bush served during a recession and a slow recovery.

How much blame presidents should share for such conditions is unclear. They act under severe constraints, and it may seem unfair that they must take responsibility for things they cannot control. What are some of these constraints? First, the president can propose a budget and tax plan, but the Congress must approve them. The president must deal with a complex congressional budgeting process and the powerful special interests that influence Congress. Often the budget

the president does finally get from Congress does not resemble the one requested (see Chapter 14). Second, the president's budget must be prepared sixteen months before its enactment; during that period the economy can change dramatically. Third, the president must share power with the Federal Reserve Board, which sets interest rates and controls the supply of money in the economy. Fourth, much of the budget (approximately 75 percent) is controlled by legislation that is supported by powerful interests and hard to change—Social Security payments, Medicare, Medicaid, military pensions, and farm support subsidies, to name a few. The interest on the national debt, another legal obligation, now consumes more than 9 percent of the budget.

In addition to the problems of budget making, the president must contend with the economy itself, which is complex and unpredictable. The cycles of inflation and recession frequently elude economists' crystal balls. In addition, the US is part of the international economic system and is affected by events beyond the president's reach. The sharp increase in oil prices by the Organization of Petroleum Exporting Countries (OPEC) contributed to the high inflation of the 1970s.

Over the past four decades, Japan, the European Union, China, and South Korea have emerged as major economic powers, providing steep competition for key US industries such as steel,

automobiles, textiles, and electronics. In the 1980s, the US became dependent on Japanese purchases of government bonds to assist in financing its deficits, and upon Japanese investments in the private sector to help in sustaining its economic growth. Changes in the behavior and economic fortunes of countries such as Japan, and more recently China, can have a significant impact on our economy. The downturn in several Asian economies in the late 1990s, for example, created significant fluctuations in the American stock market.

Over the past four decades, presidents have devoted increased time and energy to economic policy. Their economic advisers have become major players in their administrations. The role of the OMB director in providing the president with budgetary advice and negotiating the budget with Congress has grown. The treasury secretary, who must advise the president on international economic policy and the supervision of the savings and loan industry, is usually a close confidant of the president. The president must also develop a good working relationship with the chair of the Federal Reserve Board. Whether or not the economic conditions that prevail during an administration are the results of the president's policy, the public will hold the president accountable.

Is affording the president praise and blame for the economy reasonable? How can the American public best hold politicians accountable?

Social Welfare

In terms of the amount of money spent by the national government, the growth of social welfare activities was the most significant policy change in the role of government in the twentieth century. Like a huge check processor, the national government takes money from taxpayers or borrows it and disburses cash or in-kind benefits, such as the Supplemental Nutrition Assistance Program, to millions of people who qualify because of old age, disability, unemployment, or poverty.

(Courtesy of the George Bush Library, National Archives, July, 1990, via Wikimedia)

The protection of legal and constitutional rights, through such measures as the Americans with Disabilities Act, has been a principal focus of national government activities in recent years.

Protection of Legal and Constitutional Rights

The protection of legal and constitutional rights has been one of the principal sets of national government activities over the past generation. Supreme Court justices, presidents, and members of Congress have all brought to bear, to varying degrees, the power and influence of the national government to protect the rights of a variety of groups, such as political, religious, and ethnic minorities; the LGBT community; Americans with disabilities; and people accused of crimes.

Promotion of Science and Technology

Basic research, new technologies, and changing public expectations have drawn the national government into efforts to achieve certain public policy goals with the help of science and technology. Examples of such policies include the civilian space program, continuing research efforts on diseases such as HIV/AIDS and cancer, the use of stem cells in research, therapeutic cloning, and the development of new civilian technologies to help the nation be more competitive in the world economy of the twenty-first century.

Regulation

Regulations are among the tools government uses to shape sectors of the economy. However, because their purposes go beyond economic goals, regulations can be considered a specific category of policy. As the chapter on bureaucracies indicated, government regulations are designed to structure relationships in specific industries, such as broadcasting and the marketing of securities, or to ensure social objectives, such as clean air and worker safety.[17]

Economic Policies

Given a national budget that now exceeds $4 trillion, what the national government does (or does not do) in its spending, taxing, and borrowing policies has enormous consequences for the economy. Spending on education and on transportation and communication networks will shape the kind of economy the nation has in coming decades. Tax laws that eliminate or create tax deductions and tax credits influence investment decisions made by individuals and corporations. Large deficits can encourage higher interest rates, just as higher government spending can reduce unemployment rates. Through its control of the money supply, the Federal Reserve can also affect interest and unemployment rates and private investment decisions. Government efforts to shape the economy through its spending, taxing, borrowing, and money supply decisions make up a major part of the policy agenda.

CHAPTER REVIEW

1. Public policy is whatever government chooses to do or not to do. Ultimately, political activity springs from conflict within society over what government ought to do and for whom or to whom it ought to do it. The elitism and pluralism models offer different explanations of who should make public policy decisions. The rational-comprehensive approach and incrementalism raise fundamental questions about how decisions are made.

2. Definable stages of policy making include: getting issues onto the agenda of government, formulating policy proposals, formally adopting policy, implementing policy, and evaluating policy.

3. Public policies can be distinguished from one another in a variety of ways. Economic self-interest is a useful criterion in distinguishing among policies. Six substantive categories differentiate national government policies: foreign and defense policies, social welfare, protection of legal and constitutional rights, promotion of science and technology, regulation, and economic policies.

KEY TERMS

bureaucratic model........................409

domestic policy...........................419

elitism...................................409

foreign policy............................419

free-market capitalism model..............409

incrementalism............................410

Marxism model.............................409

pluralism.................................409

policy adoption...........................415

policy agenda.............................414

policy evaluation.........................417

policy implementation.....................416

policy strategy...........................415

public policy.............................407

rational-comprehensive model..............410

systems model.............................409

READINGS FOR FURTHER STUDY

A good overview of public policy analysis and the stages of the public policy process can be found in James E. Anderson's *Public Policymaking*, 8th ed. (Boston: Cengage, 2015).

John Kingdon's *Agendas, Alternatives, and Public Policies*, 2nd ed. (New York: Longman, 2011) is an interesting discussion of the changing shape of the public policy agenda.

An excellent account of policy making, and an attempt to explain the apparent contradictions involved in the process, is Deborah A. Stone's *Policy Paradox: The Art of Political Decision Making*, 3rd ed. (New York: Norton, 2012).

The theories behind public policy are addressed in Paul A. Sabatier and Christopher M. Weible, eds., *Theories of the Policy Process: Theoretical Lenses on Public Policy*, 4th ed. (New York: Routledge, 2017), and in Thomas A. Birkland, *An Introduction to the Policy Process*, 5th ed. (New York: Routledge, 2019).

The causes for the rise and fall of public policies over time are explored in Frank R. Baumgartner and Bryan D. Jones, *Agendas and Instability in American Politics*, 2nd ed. (Chicago: University of Chicago Press, 2009).

Two quarterly journals of the Policy Studies Organization, the *Policy Studies Journal* and the *Review of Policy Research*, are sources of current scholarship on the field of policy analysis and on specific policy areas.

NOTES

1. Thomas R. Dye, *Understanding Public Policy*, 10th ed. (Englewood Cliffs, NJ: Prentice-Hall, 2001), p. 2.

2. For a comprehensive statement of the systems model, see David Easton, *A Systems Analysis of Political Life* (Chicago: University of Chicago Press, 1979).

3. For a classic statement on elitism, see C. Wright Mills, *The Power Elite*, 2nd ed. (New York: Oxford University Press, 2000).

4. An analysis of pluralism that helped set the terms of the debate with elitism is Robert Dahl's *Who Governs? Democracy and Power in an American City* (New Haven, CT: Yale University Press, 1961).

5. For a review of different analytical approaches to decision-making, see James W. Fesler and Donald F. Kettl, *The Politics of the Administrative Process* (Chatham, NJ: Chatham House, 1996).

6. The classic argument for incrementalism and its comparison to the rational-comprehensive approach is Charles Lindblom's "The Science of 'Muddling Through,'" *Public Administration Review 19* (1959): 79–88.

7. For a review of the criticisms of the rational-comprehensive approach and incrementalism, see Amitai Etzioni, "Mixed-Scanning: A 'Third' Approach to Decision-Making," *Public Administration Review 27* (1967): 385–392.

8. James E. Anderson, *Public Policymaking*, 5th ed. (Boston: Houghton Mifflin, 203), pp. 30–31.

9. See John W. Kingdon, *Agendas, Alternatives, and Public Policies*, 2nd ed. (New York: Addison-Wesley, 1995).

10. For a discussion of the contributions and limits of knowledge in efforts to resolve policy problems, see Peter deLeon's *Advice and Consent: The Development of the Policy Sciences* (New York: Russell Sage, 1988).

11. Jeffrey L. Pressman and Aaron B. Wildavsky, *Implementation*, 3rd ed. (Berkeley: University of California Press, 1984).

12. On the heightened attention that policy analysts have given to implementation over the last two decades, see Dennis Palumbo's *Public Policy in America: Government in Action*, 2nd ed. (Stamford, CT: Thomson, 1997).

13. "EPA Criticized for Selective Enforcement," *Environment and Climate News*, September 2001.

14. See Pressman and Wildavsky's *Implementation* for a discussion of the relationship between evaluation and implementation, pp. 181–205.

15. See, for example, Dye's *Understanding Public Policy*.

16. See, for example, Aaron Wildavsky, "The Two Presidencies," *Trans-Action* (December 1966): 7–14.

17. For a discussion of the purposes of regulation, see *Federal Regulatory Directory*, 10th ed. (Washington, DC: CQ Press, 2001).

POP QUIZ

1. Debates over procedures and rules are really debates over _____ .

2. A specific course of action designed to deal with the originally defined problem is called a policy _____ .

3. The _____ model of policy making holds that policy is the product of an interlocking relationship between institutions of government and their surrounding social, economic, and political environments.

4. One approach to policy making is that of _____, in which policy decisions vary only marginally from previous policy.

5. The goal of _____ is to determine whether the formally adopted, implemented strategy did in fact solve the original problem.

6. Policies that are designed to protect some common good always affect everyone in the same way.   T   F

7. The political will of a strong leader may help move some particular issue onto the government agenda.   T   F

8. When a policy is formally and legally implemented, debate over the issue usually ends.   T   F

9. It is required by law that every government policy go through a formal evaluation procedure.   T   F

10. Which of the following is true of public policy making?
    A) It is nonconflictual in a democratic system.
    B) It involves debate over rules but not procedures.
    C) It has varying consequences for different groups.
    D) It is designed to protect the common good.

11. The decision to deal with the drug abuse problem by opening more treatment centers would be an example of a policy _____ .
    A) agenda
    B) strategy
    C) adoption
    D) implementation

12. The idea that policy decisions reflect the interest of the ruling class at the expense of the workers is a tenet of the _____ model.
    A) elitism
    B) pluralism
    C) Marxism
    D) free-market capitalism

13. Bureaucracies play a central role in the policy process during the _____ stage.
    A) agenda building
    B) policy proposal
    C) policy adoption
    D) implementation

14. The final analytical stage in the evolution of policies is _____ .
    A) evaluation
    B) agenda building
    C) implementation
    D) adoption

15. Which of the following is true of policy evaluation?
    A) It is required by law.
    B) It formally ends the policy debate.
    C) It usually occurs informally during the implementation process.
    D) It has become increasingly accurate with precise measures.

Answers:
1. policy   2. strategy   3. systems
4. incrementalism   5. policy evaluation   6. F
7. T   8. F   9. F   10. C   11. B   12. C
13. D   14. A   15. C

Chapter

14

(Shutterstock)

PUBLIC POLICY & ECONOMICS

In This Chapter

14.1   Government and Economic Policy
14.2   The Deficit and the National Budget
14.3   The President and Congress in the Budgeting Process
14.4   The Search for Better Budget Procedures

Chapter Objectives

Economic issues are typically high on the political agenda because they affect so many people and often lead to sharp conflicts that the political process must resolve. This chapter defines fiscal and monetary policy, describes elements of economic policy, and outlines the tenets of three major schools of thought about economic policy: Keynesian economics, monetarist economics, and supply-side economics.

Given the importance of national budget policy in the twenty-first century, the chapter then pays special attention to spending choices in fiscal policy by surveying major categories of spending and addressing the issue of the deficit and why government expenditures are so hard to control. The chapter concludes with a review of how budget decisions are made and a discussion of the eternal search, driven by the persistence of high deficits, for better procedures in deciding how money will be spent.

14.1 Government and Economic Policy

Some of the sharpest conflicts in a society are economic—who gains and who loses, who gives and who receives, who has and who has not. These issues affect the lives and well-being of millions of people in the US. Further, with the development of an increasingly interdependent world economy, these issues affect billions of people around the world as well.

In its broadest sense, **economic policy** refers to the decisions a government makes that affect the production, distribution, and consumption of goods; the provision of services; the flow of income; and the accumulation of wealth. In a complex and interdependent modern economy, such as that of the United States, virtually everything the government does has economic consequences. For example, President Kennedy's 1961 declaration to put a man on the moon by 1970 set off an explosion of research in metallurgy, electronics, and computers during the 1960s. This research, in turn, sparked the growth of new high-tech industries and the introduction of consumer goods such as the personal computer.

The United States has the world's largest national economy. Its nominal gross domestic product was estimated to be over $20 trillion in 2018.

Nevertheless, the term *economic policy* is usually confined to decisions government makes with the explicit intention of influencing the economy. These decisions inevitably address fundamental questions about the role that government should play in the economy and society and about the kind of economy and society the United States should have.

14.1a Basic Issues of Economic Policy

Economic questions have been part of US politics since the earliest days of the Republic. As Chapter 1 explained, unpopular British tax policies helped to spark the drive for independence before 1776. Barriers to trade and threats to creditors contributed to the call for a new and stronger national government in 1787. Political conflicts today over taxes, deficits, surpluses, the national debt, trade, and alternative strategies for ensuring prosperity demonstrate the durability of economic issues on the nation's policy agenda. Current controversies illustrate five important economic issues that have recurred as themes throughout US history, from the beginning to the present.

First, *should government involve itself in economic affairs at all*? As discussed in Chapter 4, one long-standing philosophical view is that the government should stay out of economics and business. Known as **laissez-faire** (French for "leave things alone"), this idea maintains that completely free economic competition among individuals, each pursuing his or her own self-interest, will work naturally to the benefit of all.[1] Under laissez-faire, most economic regulations, such as regulation of the securities business, simply would not exist. This view contrasts starkly with **socialism**, which holds that people will be

economic policy

Decisions a government makes that affect the production, distribution, and consumption of goods; the provision of services; the flow of income; and the accumulation of wealth

laissez-faire

French for "leave things alone" and the view, in economics, that government should not interfere in the workings of the economy

socialism

The view in economics that economic decision-making should be completely under the control of political authority

best off if economic decision-making is completely under the control of the government and if government owns and operates most of the major industries. Although Americans have always favored laissez-faire much more than socialism, they divide over just where to strike the balance between the two.

Second, even if government does involve itself in economic affairs, *should it try to stabilize the economy, or should it remain neutral*? Over the course of American history, the economy has gone through periodic booms and busts. When the economy goes into a slump—a **recession** when the slump is relatively minor and short-lived, or a **depression** when it is serious and sustained—or when it accelerates too quickly, some people argue that the government should not interfere but should rather allow the economy to correct itself in time. Others want the government to moderate the trends. Before the arrival of the New Deal during the Great Depression of the 1930s, the view that government should remain neutral prevailed. Since then the judgment that government should take an active role in stabilizing the economy has been dominant. Today, the increasingly global nature of the US economy means that foreign, as well as domestic, policies are a part of this active governmental role.

Third, if government is to maintain economic stability, *which policies will achieve that goal*? Some economists believe that government should adjust its spending and taxing decisions when the economy needs to accelerate or to slow down. Others think the government should try to shape general economic activity by adjusting the money supply and interest rates to influence the willingness of individuals and companies to borrow money.

Fourth, aside from policies that affect the general health of the economy, *should government promote or discourage particular types of economic activity*? Some people believe that government should subsidize heavy industry, such as steel mills and shipyards, because they are vital in times of war. A variation on this theme, often favored by the neoliberals discussed in Chapter 4, is the idea of developing a national "industrial policy" that plots out cooperation between government and industry in identifying and supporting particularly promising new products and industries. Others believe that certain industries, such as textile plants, need government help to protect them from foreign competition because these industries provide employment to many people in the US. If necessary, government should engage in **protectionism** by restricting the flow of foreign goods into the United States. This is the approach President Trump took beginning in 2018, when he placed a global 25 percent tariff on the import of steel and a 10 percent tariff on the import of aluminum, as well as tariffs on hundreds of billions of dollars' worth of imports from the People's Republic of China.

Advocates of **free trade**, by contrast, argue that a nation's economy will be better off in the long run if local producers who cannot compete with more efficient foreign producers are allowed to die a natural economic death. A recent twist—called **outsourcing**—has seen American corporations establishing factories in foreign countries in order to take advantage of cheaper labor markets. While such practices often create inexpensive products for US consumers, many worry about the negative effect exporting jobs has on employment rates in the US. Debate surrounding trade agreements like the revision to the North American Free Trade Agreement has often focused on the effect such agreements have on US jobs and businesses.

The possibilities of success and failure suggest a fifth concern: *Should government foster economic equality among its citizens*? There is little support in this country for the idea that the government should ensure complete economic equality among all citizens. However, it is a principal tenet of contemporary liberalism that no citizen should be allowed to fall below a certain economic minimum. This view accounts for social welfare programs such as nutrition assistance and medical care for the poor. A more conservative position is that government should see that every citizen has equal opportunity and then

recession

A minor and relatively short period of economic decline

depression

A period of serious and sustained economic decline

protectionism

Opposite of *free trade;* belief that government should protect American business and industry by restricting the flow of foreign goods into the United States

free trade

Belief that America's economic interests are best served by allowing foreign producers to sell their goods without restriction in the United States

outsourcing

Establishment, by American corporations, of factories and offices in foreign countries to take advantage of cheaper labor markets

(Courtesy of Leif Skoogfors, FEMA Photo Library, via Wikimedia)

Free trade advocates believe that local producers who can't compete with foreign producers should be allowed to go out of business.

let economic forces work in their natural way. Extreme conservatives may find even this an unjustified intrusion into the economy.

Each of these five questions asks whether government should play an active or passive role. How each is answered has profound consequences for the kind of society in which people in the US live. Should taxes be raised or lowered? Should the supply of money be expanded or contracted? Should social welfare spending be increased or cut? Should the national government embark on a major program of capital investment or not? Such questions dominate most policy debate in the 2000s. This debate was on the front burner of American politics in both the 2008 and 2012 election cycles, when economic crises in the lending and financial sectors led politicians to scramble for solutions. It remained a key issue in 2016 and 2020, when the presidential campaign pitted a perceived laissez-faire Republican from the business world against Democrats with vast political experience who favored more government-oriented solutions.

POLITICS AND ECONOMICS

The Ideology of Economic Policy

In recent US history, several philosophies of economic policy have vied for acceptance as official government doctrine. The dominant perspective among Democrats since the New Deal has been Keynesian economics. For many years the primary challenge has come from advocates of monetarism, usually traditional conservative Republicans. Beginning in the Reagan years, some less orthodox Republican conservatives embraced the new (or at least newly packaged) doctrine of supply-side economics.

Keynesian Economics

The brilliant British economist John Maynard Keynes saw the health of an economy as dependent on the relationship between overall supply and demand in the economy. Supply is the total amount of goods and services produced in the economy; demand is the total amount of goods and services consumed. Economic problems arose, he argued, when supply and demand were not in balance. If supply exceeded demand, businesses would build up a backlog of unsold goods, cut back production, and lay off workers. Thus, supply exceeding demand would lead to unemployment. If demand exceeded supply, buyers would bid up the prices of goods; inflation would result. Only if supply and demand were in balance would the economy

experience maximum employment and minimum inflation.

Keynes argued that in complex modern economics, supply and demand would not automatically balance and that the imbalance would lead to economic problems. Keynes's solution was to have the government use its fiscal policy to bring the two into balance. If supply exceeded demand and unemployment threatened, the government could spend more than it received in taxes—that is, it could engage in deficit spending and bring total demand, and hence employment, up to the optimum level. If demand exceeded supply and inflation loomed, the government could collect more in taxes than it spent—that is, it could run a surplus—and bring total demand, and hence inflation, down. In other words, Keynesians emphasize using government fiscal policy to adjust the

level of demand to the point of balance with supply that will yield a low-inflation, high-employment economy.

Monetarism

Monetarists focus, as the name implies, on monetary policy. They see monetary policy, rather than fiscal policy, as the best way to control the level of demand for goods and services. If the Federal Reserve lets the amount of money grow too large and the cost of money (i.e., the interest rate) fall too low, consumers and business managers will borrow and spend so much money that demand will exceed supply and inflation will result. If money is in short supply and interest rates are high, consumer and business spending and borrowing will decline, supply will exceed demand, and unemployment will result.

One widely recognized monetarist prescription, advanced by the prominent economist Milton Friedman, is that growth in the money supply should be steady and gradual, roughly in pace with the growth in the amount of goods and services the economy produces. Anything more will lead to inflation, anything less to unemployment. Further, many monetarists, being conservative and suspicious of active governmental involvement in the economy, prefer adherence to this general rule rather than "politically" exercised discretion about monetary policy.

Supply-Side Economics

As one might expect, supply-side economics focuses on how much is produced in the economy rather than on how much is demanded, as in the Keynesian and monetarist perspectives. According to supply-side economics' leading theoretician, Arthur Laffer, government can affect the balance of supply and demand in the economy better by adjusting supply than by adjusting demand. In fact, government is seen as having created the imbalance by setting taxes so high (particularly for the highest income groups) that people have little incentive to work or to invest and thereby produce. Only if government reduces taxes sufficiently to restore incentives and make money available will people begin to work harder, invest more, and produce more. The stimulus to economic activity created by lower tax rates will, according to the supply-siders, be so great that tax revenues will actually increase as a result of higher employment and consumption.

Supply-side concerns have played an important role in recent debates over whether to reduce the deficit by taxing the rich. Rejecting liberal concerns about increasing inequality in income distribution, supply-siders have argued that income tax rates on the rich and rates for capital gains taxes on everyone should be kept low. Their argument is that the rich especially are more likely than the poor to invest their money (rather than spend it), thereby stimulating greater production and prosperity.

Compare these economic theories to the plans being offered by the president and congressional leaders. What similarities and differences do you see? What examples of successes and failures of these policies can you point to? Which approach seems most likely to achieve positive results in today's economy? Why?

14.1b Fiscal and Monetary Policy

Economic policies are of two major types: fiscal and monetary. The two are conceptually and practically distinct, although political decision-makers certainly must take the relationship between them into account. Some regulatory policy also involves economic issues, as discussed in the chapter on bureaucracies.

Determinations of how much and whom to tax, and how much and on what to spend, constitute the **fiscal policy** of the United States. The president makes tax and spending proposals and signs or vetoes legislation the Congress passes. The Constitution gives Congress the power "to lay and collect taxes, duties, imposts, and excises, to pay the debts and provide for the common defense and general welfare of the United States," and "to borrow money on the credit of the United States." Taken individually, decisions on these questions constitute much of the routine business of government. Should the savings from military spending cuts be put into constructing new bridges and highways? Should government raise the personal income tax or the corporate income tax to pay for new programs? Taken as a whole, these decisions by the president and Congress exert a powerful influence on the economic life of the nation. One of the more significant achievements of the Trump administration was passage of the Tax Cuts and Jobs Act in 2017. This wide-ranging law changed allowable tax deductions and temporarily reduced many individual income tax rates; it also permanently reduced the corporate tax rate from 35 percent to 21 percent. This law is an example of using fiscal policy to promote economic changes.

fiscal policy

Governmental decisions about taxing and spending that affect the economic life of a nation

Monetary policy, the second major type of economic policy, is the determination of how much money should circulate in the economy and what the cost of borrowing money, or the interest rate, should be. The Constitution gives Congress the power "to coin money, regulate the value thereof, and of foreign coin." In the landmark case of *McCulloch v. Maryland*,[2] the Supreme Court recognized Congress's "implied power" to determine monetary policy when it held that the Congress could charter a national bank, even though the Constitution did not explicitly give it that power (see Chapter 2). In other words, Congress possesses the power to set monetary policy for the United States. Pursuant to this power, Congress created the Federal Reserve System and delegated to it the power to make these decisions on the supply of money and the cost of borrowing.

The making of economic policy illustrates the classic interplay between institutions and ideas. In fiscal policy, the president and the **Office of Management and Budget (OMB)**, an Executive Office agency that puts together the president's annual budget proposal, interact with Congress and its committees to produce a national budget. In monetary policy, the Federal Reserve shapes the economy by manipulating the money supply and interest rates. As the box "Politics and Economics: The Ideology of Economic Policy" shows, officials in these government institutions choose from among competing economic doctrines in the proposals and decisions they make. Conflicting ideas are the roots of economic policy debate.

monetary policy

Government decisions about how much money should circulate in the economy and what the cost of borrowing money, the interest rate, should be

Office of Management and Budget (OMB)

An agency in the Executive Office of the President that provides the president with budgetary information and advice and is responsible for compiling the president's annual budget proposal to Congress

deficit

An excess of government expenditures over revenues

debt

The total amount of money that the national government owes to lenders, such as banks, individual and foreign investors, insurance companies, and the variety of financial institutions that purchase government securities

14.2 The Deficit and the National Budget

Grappling with fiscal policy choices—that is, what taxes to raise or lower, what spending to increase or cut—has dominated the policy agenda in recent decades. Taxing and spending issues touch the president at almost every turn in efforts to initiate and shape policy. Congress spends much of its time wrestling with the size and shape of the national budget. Sometimes elected officials find it easier to approve spending increases than tax increases, and the resulting budget deficits loom as a serious policy issue—Americans bristle at the prospect of making larger and larger payments for the interest on the national debt. Other times elected officials respond to budget difficulties and the economy by cutting spending programs and lowering taxes, pleasing some citizens but creating economic crises for others. This chapter will analyze the former problem—deficit spending.

14.2a The Deficit as a Political Issue

College students can readily understand the concepts of deficit and debt. A **deficit** occurs when expenditures (tuition, room, meals, and so forth) exceed revenues (income from a part-time job and money from parents, for example). A student makes up the difference by borrowing money. **Debt** is the sum of the deficits of prior years. A student who borrows $2,000 each year for four years graduates with a debt of $8,000 (plus interest). This debt will not be erased until the student earns enough money to meet both current expenses and payments on those college loans.

The federal government today is in a similar position because the government's expenses routinely exceed revenues. Demands on government a century ago were not nearly so great as they are now. The national government in the nineteenth century had

an almost embarrassing **surplus** (an excess of revenue over expenses) of funds. Difficult as it may be to believe, the national government had a budget surplus in seventy-one of the one hundred years between 1800 and 1900. In 1834, the total public debt was about $37,000, a sum translating to less than a penny per citizen.[3] Even though the national government regularly ran surpluses in the nineteenth century, the existence of government deficits and debt today is really not a new phenomenon. What is new is the size and persistence of the debt. Deficits have now become the norm in budget policy. Although a strong economy allowed the national government to run a surplus in the late 1990s, there was a budget deficit every year between 1970 and 1997, and again every year beginning in 2002.

Annual deficits and the federal debt increased substantially from the 1970s through the 1990s. In 1965, the annual deficit was a relatively modest $1.4 billion, but by 1975 the deficit began to exceed $50 billion annually. By 1985 the deficit was more than $200 billion. Over the relatively short period of ten years, annual budget deficits quadrupled.[4] Inflation accounts for some of this increase, but a tax cut pressed by President Reagan in 1981 and higher defense spending in the 1980s contributed substantially to the growth in deficits. Although there was a brief respite during the economic boom of the late 1990s, by 2002 deficit numbers again began to swell. The deficit for fiscal year 2020 is estimated at over $1 trillion.[5]

(Shutterstock)

College students can readily understand the concepts of deficit and debt. A deficit occurs when expenditures exceed revenues, such as income from a part-time job.

Even a budget surplus, however, does not mean the government is debt free. The accumulated federal debt—the total amount of money government owes to lenders, such as government trust funds, banks, insurance companies, and the various financial institutions that purchase government securities—has also increased sharply over the past four decades. Federal debt rose from $322 billion in 1965 to almost $1 trillion in 1980. The debt was $3 trillion in 1990 and grew to over $23.9 trillion by the end of 2020—more than $72,000 for every person in the country.[6]

Some of the debate over the deficit is colored by the belief that government ought to be guided by traditional values in the matter of money—"living within one's own means." However, as in other matters, economists disagree over the extent to which the deficit poses a problem. Some argue that government deficits are essential to stimulate consumer demand in a failing or even sluggish economy. That is, by cutting taxes or increasing spending, government pumps money into the private economy to allow the kind of consumer spending that counters a depressed economy. Some maintain that the nation has had large deficits in the past, particularly in wartime, and those deficits actually spurred the economy.

Many other economists argue, however, that large deficits that are the product of a fundamental imbalance between revenues and expenditures can have the effect of slowing down consumer spending and economic growth. Government borrowing to cover deficits results in government competition with all other potential borrowers in the economy, such as corporations that want to build plants or individuals who want to buy houses or cars. The deficit raises the cost of capital and the cost of doing business.

Most politicians and economists believe that persistent large deficits can lead to severe economic consequences. The long-term health of a society depends on its ability

surplus

An excess of government revenues over government expenditures

(Joseph Sohm / Shutterstock)

A tax cut and higher defense spending during the administration of fortieth U.S. president Ronald Reagan contributed to the deficit of the 1980s.

and willingness to save and invest for future growth. Resources must be invested in basic research, new products, new technologies, and education. If present consumption limits the amount of saving possible for such investment, the society risks a decline in the standard of living. The Congressional Budget Office reports that among the world's most developed countries the United States has had the greatest decline in national saving as a percentage of gross domestic product."[7] People in the US saved about 7.5 percent of their disposable income in 2020.[8] Federal budget deficits and the national debt are major contributors to a low national saving rate.

Persistent deficits figured prominently as a political issue in the 1992 presidential campaign. Third-party candidate Ross Perot skillfully used television to criticize both major parties for inaction on the deficit and the resulting public debt. Perot clearly struck a chord with voters. He received 19 percent of the popular vote in the election, the best showing for a third-party candidate in eighty years.[9] Although he received less than half that vote when he ran again in 1996, the Reform Party that he and his followers created indicated the importance of economic reform to many Americans.

Perot's electoral strength placed pressure on elected officials to grapple seriously with the deficit. That task is not easy. A booming economy, like the one the United States enjoyed in the mid- and late 1990s, can replace deficits with surpluses for a time, allowing

Think it's easy to balance the budget?

Try it yourself by playing the budget simulation game at this website.

http://www.bvtlab.com/h8RS8

politicians to delay making difficult economic decisions. Eventually, though, the dynamic nature of a macroeconomy ensures that challenges will return. At the beginning of the 2000s, economic downturns signaled the return of deficits and the tough policy choices that accompany them. By 2010, another political movement—the Tea Party—had emerged to challenge incumbent politicians to take the dangers of debt and deficit seriously. Candidates who were elected to Congress with the help of the Tea Party movement were instrumental in opposing increases to the government's debt ceiling—an upper limit to the amount of money the government can borrow—first established by Congress a hundred years ago. Although Congress continues to adjust the debt ceiling as necessary, opposition from economic conservatives makes clear that this is not a simple matter and that some legislators would rather shut down parts of the government by letting them run out of money than agree to compromises that would increase the national debt. In recent years these "deficit hawks" have lost traction and Congress has raised the debt ceiling multiple times—suspending it entirely until after the presidential election in 2020 so that spending during the COVID-19 crisis would not become a political issue.

Reducing the deficit is difficult because of the sharp conflict over the alternative ways of doing it—and the pain that lower deficits leave in their wake. Choosing among cutting expenditures, increasing taxes, or some combination of the two is really the essence of politics. For example, elimination of the revenue-sharing program through which the national government granted funds to local governments lowered the deficit somewhat.

However, elimination of the program also forced local governments to decide whether to increase their own taxes or cut services for local residents. As another example, building an orbiting space station or the superconducting super collider would be of great economic benefit to some contractors and some states, but at the same time it would cost the government tax dollars. Political leaders also face trade-off decisions regarding Social Security and Medicare. As the baby boom generation has begun retiring, these programs are paying out money to more individuals than the number they are collecting from, which may create a need to either increase the tax burden on working-age Americans or decrease benefits to those of retirement age. Neither option is likely to be popular because

A depiction of the space shuttle docked at the international space station orbiting Earth. (Elements of this image furnished by NASA.)

these decisions also mean that either the deficit or taxes will be higher. Raising taxes will cut the deficit, but higher taxes also mean less money in the pockets of consumers. Researchers want more government money to do their work. Social welfare advocates want more spending on poverty programs. The beneficiaries of government spending—such as military contractors, researchers, and state and local governments—obviously press to maintain and even increase their benefits. At the same time, taxpayers do not welcome proposals to raise federal revenues by increasing taxes.

These ongoing battles took a back burner in 2008 and 2009, as a national economic downturn reached crisis stage. Years of deregulation and poor decision-making in the lending industry finally took their toll, as banks and other financial institutions teetered on the brink of collapse. The resulting tightening of credit markets threatened to shut down the US economy on a large scale. Concerns over banking and credit instability sent the US stock markets into free fall, losing one-third of their value in a matter of days. By early October 2008, Congress passed a law allowing Treasury Secretary Henry Paulson to spend $700 billion to purchase shares in private banks. The move was intended to restore confidence and loosen up credit availability, but not to make this partial nationalization permanent. The government began selling its shares after a few years, after banks had an opportunity to recover and stabilize.[10]

14.2b   Major Components of the National Budget

Money's rise to the top of the policy agenda has deep roots in the past. Since the Great Depression of the 1930s, government has treated the economic and social needs of groups such as the elderly, the disabled, and the poor as public problems. Meeting these welfare demands has meant the expenditure of huge amounts of public money. War and the threat of war have also made their own heavy demands on public funds. Paying interest on borrowed money has itself become a major category of spending.

Figure 14.1 offers a graphic and useful summary of major budgetary trends over the past several decades. The figure divides the budget into five proportional categories: national defense, human resources, physical resources, net interest payments, and all other expenditures—which include programs such as cancer research, space exploration, highway construction, and environmental protection.

Figure 14.1 Federal Government Expenditures

Payments for individuals (identified here as human resources) and national defense are the largest categories of federal expenditures. National defense will consume just under 16 percent of the budget in 2022.

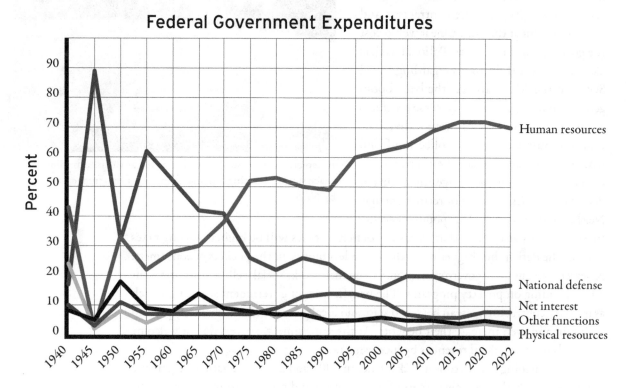

Federal Government Expenditures

DATA SOURCE: U.S. Office of Management and Budget, Historical Tables, Budget of the United States Government, Fiscal Year 2021 (Washington, DC: Government Printing Office, 2020).

National Defense

The national government has a constitutional responsibility to provide for the nation's security. Consequently, spending on defense has always consumed a significant portion of the budget. For example, of the $10.8 million that the national government spent in 1800, more than 55 percent went to the War Department (army) and the navy.[11] Figure 14.1 shows that at the height of World War II in 1945 almost 90 percent of the budget went to defense. After a postwar drop and then an increase in the early 1950s during the Korean conflict, the proportion of federal dollars going to defense began a general decline from almost 70 percent in 1954 to less than 23 percent in 1980. In absolute dollars, the amount spent on national defense increased over this period; yet defense expenditures consumed an increasingly smaller proportion of the total budget. Other expenditure items in the budget were growing at a faster rate, and the proportional decline in defense spending became a major political issue.

President George W. Bush

(White House photo by Eric Draper, 2001, via Wikimedia)

One of Ronald Reagan's (1981–1989) priorities was strengthening defense; and, as Figure 14.1 shows, the proportional amount of federal spending going to national defense increased in the 1980s. However, the breakup of the Soviet Union and the end of the Cold War weakened the military's claim on the budget beginning in the early 1990s, and the proportion of the budget spent on defense went down accordingly. In 2000, the national government spent just 16 percent of its budget on national defense, but this percentage rose to over 20 percent as President George W. Bush retooled the nation's military and intelligence sectors to address the threat of terrorism. In recent years, national defense has been 15–16 percent of the budget.

Payments for Individuals

Payments for individuals, the second major spending category in the budget, includes social support programs that are primarily a legacy of the New Deal of the 1930s and the Great Society of the 1960s. Sometimes called human resources, such programs include Social Security, Medicare, unemployment compensation, the Supplemental Nutrition Assistance Program (SNAP), Medicaid, and supplemental security income. Retired and disabled citizens receive monthly checks through the Social Security program. Medicare provides medical care for the elderly and the disabled. The short-term unemployed receive weekly checks through the unemployment compensation program. Individuals in need receive food, medical care, or cash through programs such as SNAP, Medicaid, or supplemental security income. In administering these programs, the national government takes money from some groups in the form of retirement contributions or taxes and transfers it to other groups either in the form of cash, such as Social Security checks, or in the form of in-kind payments, such as SNAP benefits.

This category of spending, compared to national defense, is a relatively new one for the national government. Only within the past half-century has the national government administered social support programs on such a comprehensive scale. This category has grown proportionally faster than any other since the 1940s, as Figure 14.1 graphically illustrates. In 1942, payments for individuals made up less than 20 percent of all federal spending, a proportion that increased to 38 percent in 1970. This category of spending consumed over 70 percent of the budget in 2021. Such growth has prompted reformers to suggest privatizing some of these programs. One study, for example, argues that transforming the government-run Social Security program into individually controlled private retirement accounts can reduce government spending while providing an efficient and solvent method for individual financial security during old age.[12]

Interest Costs

The third major category of spending, **net interest**, represents the cost that government must pay the public for the use of borrowed money to cover budget deficits. Most individuals have, at one time or another, encountered the inevitability of making interest payments on goods they purchase. For example, most people who wish to buy a new home simply do not have enough cash to cover the full purchase price. If they want to buy a $100,000 home, they may have to borrow $80,000 from a bank or mortgage company to add to the resources they have to make the purchase. College students often take out student loans to pay for college; even if their payments are deferred until they graduate, they will eventually have to pay the money back—with interest. Borrowing money is really nothing more than using money that belongs to others. Of course, the right to use this money comes at a price, which is the payment of interest.

Money is among the most expensive items individuals can buy; and how much it costs depends on interest rates, which are in constant flux. If a home purchaser borrows $80,000

net interest

Charges that the government must pay to the public for the use of money borrowed to cover budget deficits and added to the interest paid to government trust funds to create total interest costs

(Shutterstock)

There is a high cost to using other people's money. Just as homeowners must pay interest on loans to banks, so must the U.S. government pay interest to the investors and financial institutions that help cover the growing deficit.

at 5 percent interest to be repaid over thirty years, the total repayment at the end of that period will amount to more than $154,000, or almost two times the original $80,000 borrowed! The amount of interest paid will vary with interest rates and the time period of the loan, but this simple example illustrates the high cost of using other people's money.

Individuals borrow money because they want things that cost more than the cash they have on hand. Governments borrow money for much the same reason. Because the money demands on government exceed the amount of money government receives in taxes, borrowing money from individual investors and financial institutions that buy government securities must cover the resulting deficit. As the deficits rise, so too must the cost of borrowing money. In 1965, the government paid $8.6 billion in net interest, about 7 percent of total federal expenditures in that year. At about 7.8 percent of expenditures, interest payments alone were about $378 billion in 2021.

14.2c Mandatory Programs in the Budget

When the president and Congress begin to work on budget proposals every year, they do not begin with a clean budgetary slate. Present and future budgets build on past budgets in increments. This theory of **incrementalism** holds that "the largest determining factor of the size and content of this year's budget is last year's budget."[13] Expenditures are difficult to control largely because present decisions are shaped by past decisions. Budget makers cannot decide to reduce total spending from $3.9 trillion to, say, $500 billion in a single year. Just as a rapidly moving freight train cannot be stopped quickly (and without much screeching of brakes), so too budget expenditures cannot be massively and rapidly reduced from one year to the next.

Much of the budget comprises **mandatory programs** in which spending automatically increases from one year to the next without specific annual appropriations action by Congress. **Social entitlements**, programs in which eligible citizens receive benefits to which they are entitled by law, are a main source of mandatory programs and include Social Security, Medicare, Medicaid, public assistance programs, unemployment compensation, and retirement programs for federal employees. The largest of the mandatory programs is Social Security, which alone accounts for over 23 percent of the total budget. According to the Congressional Budget Office, "managing the growth of federal spending … will be largely a matter of controlling the growth of mandatory outlays."[14] In a creative attempt at reducing these costs to the government, George W. Bush recommended allowing individuals to retain control over a portion of their payroll taxes in personal retirement accounts.[15] Though the plan was not approved, it brought the issue of mandatory spending to the forefront of American politics.

Social Security provides a good illustration of the concept of mandatory spending. Congress and the president do not decide every year whether or not the nation should have a Social Security program. Once the program was established, it became a solid rock on the political landscape, and it continues to give eligible individuals benefits year

incrementalism

A model of decision-making that holds that new policies differ only marginally from existing policies

mandatory programs

Government programs, such as Social Security expenditures, in which spending automatically increases from one year to the next without specific annual appropriations action by Congress

social entitlements

Programs, such as Social Security and Medicaid, whereby eligible individuals receive benefits according to law

after year. A person who has made contributions to the Social Security system via payroll taxes becomes automatically eligible for full Social Security benefits upon retirement at age sixty-seven (or as low as age sixty-five for those born before 1960). Social Security expenditures are determined by the demographic movement of individuals into retire-

ment age and by increases in payments because of inflation. Congress and the president could substantially reduce those benefits, but only at very high political and social costs.

A related program that illustrates the difficulty of cutting the budget from one year to the next is net interest. By law, interest on the debt must be paid. Failure to make such interest payments would destroy investor confidence in government securities and result in economic consequences too grave to contemplate. Thus, Congress and the president do not have much choice in the matter of paying interest. The amount paid in a given

Social Security is the nation's largest social entitlement program, accounting for more than 23 percent of the total U.S. budget.

year will depend on interest rates and the size of deficits. Because of the necessity to pay interest and the existence of mandatory programs, budget makers cannot easily make proportionally large spending cuts from one year to the next.

In 2020, President Donald Trump's Office of Management and Budget estimated that over 61 percent of the 2021 budget would be earmarked for mandatory programs. Net interest payments and mandatory programs together would account for about 70 percent of the total budget in 2021. Some changes can be made in social entitlements, but the programs cannot be cut drastically; and interest must be paid. The concept of mandatory spending illustrates the obstacles Congress and the president face in their attempts to cut deficits.

14.3 The President and Congress in the Budgeting Process

Most people know very little about the details of the national budget or how various governmental institutions work together to arrive at specific taxing and spending policies. However, taxpayers are acutely aware of the degree to which their withholding taxes reduce their salaries, and beneficiaries of public programs notice even small changes in their benefits. From the perspective of individuals or specific groups, the politics of money is about maintaining or increasing the benefits of government spending while shifting the tax costs to someone else. If politics is the process of making choices among conflicting perceptions of national purpose, with different consequences for different people, then choices on the collection and use of public money are intensely political decisions.[16]

Budgets are essential because human wants must be tamed by the scarcity of resources. If human wants were limited, or if resources were unlimited, budgets would be unnecessary. However, because neither condition exists, the president and Congress are inevitably forced to wrestle with the necessity of coming up with a **budget**, or a planned statement of revenues and expenditures. One scholar has cited "the twin functions of a budget

budget
A planned statement of expenditure that includes specific categories of spending

process as an opportunity for claiming resources and as a procedure for rationing limited resources among claimants."[17] Budgeting lies at the intersection of the inevitability of demands and the necessity to impose constraints on those demands. Continuing budget deficits are simply a reflection of the political fact that satisfying demands is more appealing than the distasteful business of imposing constraints.

Because the money pie cannot be expanded infinitely, making budget policy is a battle over the shares of the pie that different programs should receive. In addition to the inevitability of disagreement, putting together a budget is a complicated process for several reasons. First, determining how much government will collect in taxes and how much it will spend in a given year is largely a matter of estimation. Budget makers cannot accurately predict the flow of dollars into and out of the federal treasury in a particular year. Such dollar flows are greatly influenced by the performance of the nation's economy, a matter over which the president and Congress have little short-term control. Second, budgeting is complicated and difficult because constructing a budget is a highly decentralized process. That is, a large number of individuals and groups, both inside and outside government, help to shape the budget. The president and his Office of Management and Budget, the executive agencies, Congress and a variety of its committees and their staffs, interest groups, and sometimes even the courts—all contribute to the making of budget decisions. At the center of political conflict, the budget process reflects the decentralization inherent in the political system itself. The process would certainly be more tidy and efficient if only one individual or committee could make all budget determinations, but the framers of the Constitution did not intend such a system. Especially in the budget process, ambition counters ambition, resulting in inevitable disorder and complexity.[18]

> **The U.S. Treasury Department's Bureau of the Public Debt continually updates the national debt down to the last penny.**
>
> **http://www.bvtlab.com/E8B97**

14.3a   The Stages of Budgeting

The most important governmental actors in the budgetary process are the president and his staff, Congress and its committees, and the executive agencies. Budgeting can be divided into three separate stages, with each of these three groups playing a primary role in one of them.[19]

1. **Presidential proposal**   The president and his staff compile agency requests for funds, shape those requests to fit presidential priorities, and then submit to Congress a proposed Budget of the United States Government.

2. **Congressional response**   Congress and its various committees review the presidential budget proposals and mold them to meet congressional priorities. If the president agrees with those congressional actions, they then become law.

3. **Agency expenditure of funds**   The executive agencies spend the money pursuant to budget laws enacted by Congress and signed by the president.

Each stage occurs every year. Actual expenditures take place during a **fiscal year**, which for US government budget and accounting purposes is a twelve-month period beginning each year on October 1 and ending on September 30 of the following calendar year. The calendar year designation given to the fiscal year is the calendar year in which the fiscal year ends. For example, fiscal year 2022 begins on October 1, 2021, and ends on September 30, 2022. Starting the fiscal year on October 1, rather than January 1, is based on the assumption that Congress will make budget decisions in the nine-month

fiscal year

For budget and accounting purposes in the national government, the twelve-month period beginning on October 1 and ending on September 30 of the following calendar year

period between the beginning of its session in January and October 1, the beginning of the fiscal year. That Congress does not always meet this deadline exemplifies the problems Congress has in making difficult budget choices.

As Figure 14.2 shows, the three stages of the budgeting process take a total of more than two years to complete. For example, the president and his staff began to formulate proposals for fiscal year 2022 in spring 2020, about eighteen months before the beginning of the fiscal year in October 2021. Given uncertainties in estimating receipts and expenditures, planning for a fiscal year so long in advance is obviously no easy task. The second stage of congressional action begins in February 2021, eight months before the start of fiscal year 2022. Agencies actually spend the money in the fiscal year itself, October 1, 2021, through September 30, 2022.

Not all budgetary action by all three sets of budgetary actors concentrates on a single fiscal year at a time. At a single point in a given calendar year, each of the three stages may be in progress for three different fiscal years. In spring 2021, for example, agencies were actually spending money in fiscal year 2021, Congress was reviewing presidential proposals for year fiscal 2022, and the president and his staff were beginning to plan for 2023. The need for planning and executing money decisions seems to be eternal, and so does the process of putting together a budget.

Figure 14.2   Major Steps in the Budgeting Process

The steps in the budgeting process for each fiscal year take two and a half years to complete. If appropriation action is not completed by September 30, Congress enacts temporary appropriations (i.e., a continuing resolution).

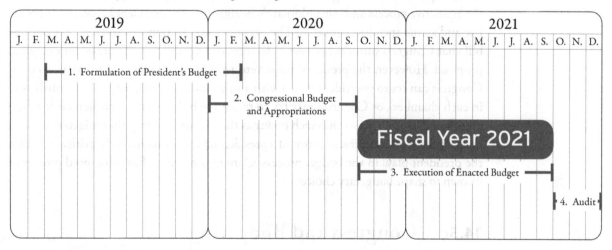

DATA SOURCES: Adapted from U.S. Office of Management and Budget, Analytical Perspectives, Budget of the United States Government, Fiscal Year 2021 (Washington, DC: Government Printing Office, 2020); and information contained in U.S. Office of Management and Budget, Budget System and Concepts, Fiscal Year 2009 (Washington, DC: Government Printing Office, 2008).

14.3b   The President in the Budget Process

The president is the single most important individual in the process of constructing a budget for the national government. The president's central role in the budgetary process springs from his unique position in the political system. More than the words and actions of any other person, what presidents say about the budget and the priorities their words and actions establish are especially important in shaping subsequent debate about the budget.

The president is guaranteed a central role in the budgetary process because of two important powers. First, with the help of the Office of Management and Budget, the president proposes a budget to Congress. Proposal power does not mean that presidents will necessarily get what they want. Congress can and does work its own will on the budget. The power to propose is a significant one because the president's budget proposal sets the tone of debate and becomes the standard against which congressional changes are measured.

The president's budget proposals are really political statements because, if enacted, they inevitably have different consequences for different groups. Depending on their budget priorities, presidents can propose more (or less) spending on defense or housing or education. They can propose changes in eligibility standards for entitlement programs with the hope of saving money in future years. They can propose tax cuts or increases with consequences for the general health of the economy, the size of the deficit, and the economic status of different income groups. Presidents can do all of these things with the great flair of publicity—natural to the office of the presidency—that brings guaranteed and immediate attention to their proposals. President Donald Trump announced his economic plan for fiscal year 2021 in his State of the Union address in February 2020. The plan contained a range of initiatives to stimulate economic growth and new jobs, strengthen national security, and enhance health care. Members of Congress can oppose presidential initiatives, but the president's proposals define the budget policy debate.

In addition to the authority to make budget proposals, the president has the constitutional power to *veto budget bills passed by Congress*. Appropriations bills go through the legislative process and must ultimately be signed by the president before they become law and actual spending proceeds. The president may be opposed to an appropriations bill that Congress submits because it diverges too much from the president's original proposal. However, the president must veto the entire bill rather than portions of it. Congress can try to override the veto with an extraordinary majority (a two-thirds vote in each chamber), or Congress may try to recast the bill in terms more agreeable to the president. No other person has such power as the president to stop the budgetary process in its tracks. The ever-present threat of a presidential veto dramatizes the critical role that the president plays in the budget process. Congress, however, has substantial powers of its own to shape budgetary choices.[20]

14.3c   Congress and Budgeting

Congressional power to make decisions on the budget is firm and clear. The Constitution states, "No money shall be drawn from the Treasury, but in Consequence of Appropriations made by Law." Presidential proposals cannot become law in the absence of congressional action. The first budgetary stage of presidential proposal is a triumph of simplicity compared to the second stage of congressional action.

Congress is a much more complicated institution than the presidency. By definition, the president is one individual to whom responsibility for budget proposals can be easily assigned. Congress is a fragmented institution with 535 individuals representing different

POLITICS AND ECONOMICS

Corporations and the Economy

Throughout American political history government regulation of the private economic sector (or lack thereof) has been a source of conflict and occasional corruption. One of the most famous incidents of economic misconduct, the Teapot Dome scandal of the 1920s, resulted in a prison sentence for a cabinet official. Secretary of the Interior Albert Fall leased federal oil reserves to his friends in the oil industry without seeking competitive bids and received kickbacks in return.

More recent examples of economic fraud are the corporate accounting debacles of the early 2000s. Created in 1934 as a response to the uncontrolled market forces that led to worldwide depression, the Securities and Exchange Commission (SEC) was designed to enforce laws requiring accurate and public disclosures of financial health by companies offering publicly traded securities, or stocks. One such rule requires companies to register with the SEC, a process that involves "a description of the company's properties and business; a description of the security to be offered for sale; information about the management of the company; and financial statements certified by independent accountants."[1] During late 2001 and early 2002, several corporations, including giants Enron and WorldCom, were found to have violated this rule by providing false financial reports. In other words, false accounting claims vastly overstated the projected earnings of the corporations, leading to artificially inflated stock prices. When the companies could no longer hide their insolvency, the false claims became public, the corporations filed for bankruptcy, many stockholders lost their investments, and many employees lost their jobs.

One of the most troubling aspects of this situation was that highly respected accounting firms, such as Arthur Andersen, played a big role in the fraudulent action. Accountants are supposed to provide independent audits of corporate financial claims; in these cases, however, the accounting firms shared in the guilt. In response to these corrupt practices, Congress passed—and the president signed—the Public Company Accounting Reform and Investor Protection Act in 2002, a measure designed to provide increased supervision over corporate accounting and stiffer penalties for misconduct—including twenty-year prison sentences for chief financial officers certifying false reports. In signing the new law, President Bush warned: "No boardroom in America is above or beyond the law."[2]

Can the government prevent corporate corruption through tougher regulation? Does the government have a duty to protect citizens from fraud? What role should the government play in the economic sphere?

1. Securities and Exchange Commission, "The Investor's Advocate: How the SEC Protects Investors and Maintains Market Integrity," December 1999, http://www.sec.gov/about/whatwedo.shtml (September 27, 2002).

2. Suzanne Malveaux, "Bush Signs Bill to Stop 'Book Cooking,'" CNN.com, July 30, 2002.

---

parts of the nation and inevitably reflecting conflicting views; through voting, however, each of these individuals can help to shape the budget that emerges from Congress.

Most of the important work of budget review and decision in Congress is done in committee. In addition to the authorizing committees (such as Agriculture and Armed Services), each chamber also has "money" committees, such as those on the budget, appropriations, and revenue (called Ways and Means in the House and Finance in the Senate committees). Each one of these committees can affect the budget in some way. Under the best of circumstances, the process of making budget decisions is never easy because the demand for government services always outruns the supply of money to fund those services. This fundamental difficulty is heightened in Congress by the large number of individuals and committees, each moved by diverse and conflicting interests, with the capacity to shape the budget.

For most government programs, Congress must take two separate steps before money can actually be spent. The first step is program **authorization**, or the congressional decision to create (or continue) a program and the agency administering it. Such authorizations begin in substantive legislative committees, such as the Agriculture, Armed

authorization

Congressional enactment that creates or continues a policy program and the agency administering it

Services, and Energy and Commerce committees. Authorizing legislation ordinarily contains statements of program and agency goals, as well as enabling powers to carry the program forward. Authorizations may be for one year, for several years, or open-ended.

(Shutterstock)

Attorney General William Barr Testifies before the US House Committee on the Judiciary on Oversight of the Department of Justice, (Washington, District of Columbia, USA).

The legislation also contains a statement of money authorized to be spent on the program. For example, an authorization measure may state that an expenditure not exceeding $700 million is authorized for the following fiscal year for, say, certain pollution abatement activities carried out by the Environmental Protection Agency. No money can be legally spent, however, as the result of such an authorization measure. Agencies do not have the legal right to actually spend money unless Congress takes the second step of appropriating funds pursuant to the authorization.

This second step is program **appropriations**, the congressional decision to fund an authorized program with a specific sum of money. Such appropriations decisions are shaped by recommendations from the Appropriations Committee in each chamber. The actual amount appropriated need not be the same as the amount authorized. For example, although $700 million may be authorized for pollution abatement, only $600 million may be actually appropriated.

The authorization-appropriations sequence does not apply to all government programs. For example, the authorization (creation and subsequent amendment) of most entitlement programs includes, in effect, a permanent appropriation to fund the program. By establishing the Social Security program, Congress has pledged that individuals reaching a certain age and meeting eligibility requirements will receive monthly checks. Congress can change the rules, but the amount of money spent in a given fiscal year is not dependent on specific congressional action for that year.

14.4 The Search for Better Budget Procedures

appropriation
Congressional enactment that funds an authorized program with a specific sum of money

line-item veto
Most state governors have this power, through which a chief executive, reacting to a bill passed by the legislature, may accept some items in the bill while also rejecting other items in the same bill. The president does not have this power.

The deficit is proof of the extraordinary difficulty Congress and the president have in coming to grips with decisions on cutting expenditures and raising taxes. The substantive issues are so difficult that policy makers have naturally considered whether different budget procedures might make their task easier. Would tough budget decisions be made more readily if procedures for arriving at them were different?

Proposed budget changes come in a variety of forms. The most controversial budget reforms are proposals to give the president **line-item veto** power and to add an amendment to the Constitution requiring a balanced budget. Under current rules, the president must sign or veto an entire bill sent by Congress. An appropriations bill may contain many specific programs, and the president must either accept or reject all of them in the bill. The line-item veto would give the president the power to reject some items in

the bill and to allow others to become law. Governors in forty-three states have line-item veto power, which proponents argue increases the managerial capability chief executives should have. With this power, its supporters say, presidents would not be forced to accept wasteful spending projects that members of Congress pack into a bill. Riding a wave of reform, Republicans in the 104th Congress passed the Line Item Veto Act in 1996 in order to provide the president with this power. President Clinton's first exercise of this power, however, was met with a legal challenge; and in 1998, the Supreme Court ruled the act invalid for its circumvention of the lawmaking procedure set forth in the Constitution. Although the law was struck down, the idea remains alive. Amendments have been introduced in recent years to change the Constitution in order to allow for a presidential line-item veto. Such a reform is not without its congressional detractors, though. Many members fear that the line-item veto would result in a discernible shift in budgetary power from Congress to the president. Given the much larger number of options the power would afford, presidential flexibility in determining the shape of the budget would greatly increase. Congressional ability to mold the budget would correspondingly diminish.

President Barack Obama meets with the National Commission on Fiscal Responsibility and Reform, a bipartisan panel tasked with finding ways to reduce federal deficits.

The size of deficits and a growing public debt have also sparked interest in a constitutional amendment that would require a balanced budget. Proponents of a **balanced budget amendment** argue that only a constitutional mandate will force Congress and the president to produce balanced budgets. Opponents hold that the amendment risks tax increases and major reductions in a wide range of politically popular programs. Several times over the past few decades, balanced budget amendment proposals have failed to get the constitutionally required two-thirds vote of the House and Senate before being sent on to the states for ratification. In 1992, Congress considered an amendment proposal that would have mandated a three-fifths majority, except in a military emergency, in the House and Senate to allow deficit spending. The amendment did not receive the necessary two-thirds vote in either chamber; however, the amendment had substantial support, a sign that the political frustration of dealing with persistent deficits has led to a serious search for extraordinary constitutional remedies. Such efforts, although still pursued in every Congress, have lost some momentum in the past few years.

Although the line-item veto power and the balanced budget amendment remain proposals, Congress and the president have passed three laws resulting in fundamental changes in the process of deciding on budget expenditures while wrestling with the pain of reducing deficits.

The Congressional Budget and Impoundment Control Act of 1974

Before 1974, Congress reviewed the president's budget in a highly decentralized, piecemeal fashion. Budget totals resulted from a process of summing up the work of separate committees rather than any conscious effort to consider the budget comprehensively. Nor was there institutionalized consideration of the relationship between spending and expected revenue, a violation of sound budget practice.

balanced budget amendment

A proposal for a constitutional amendment that would require the federal government to operate with a budget in which revenues equaled or exceeded expenditures

continuing resolution

Legislative action taken by Congress to allow spending to proceed at the previous year's level when Congress has not met the deadline for reaching agreement on appropriations for the next fiscal year

Congressional Budget and Impoundment Control Act of 1974

Legislation that significantly changed congressional budget procedures by creating budget committees, establishing a budget decision timetable, changing the fiscal year, placing limits on presidential impoundments, and establishing the Congressional Budget Office

Congressional Budget Office (CBO)

A congressional staff unit that provides Congress with budgetary expertise, independent of the president's budget staff, to help Congress clarify budgetary choices

sequestration

The process through which the president makes budget cuts in government programs to meet the mandates in law requiring ceilings on specific categories of spending

With increasing frequency, appropriations bills were not enacted by the beginning of the fiscal year. In the absence of appropriations laws, some agencies were forced to operate under a **continuing resolution**, a temporary funding measure passed by Congress. In addition, the relentless growth of the budget produced demands for more budgetary information, and the regularity of annual deficits sparked heated battles within Congress and between Congress and the president over who was to blame for the budgetary "red ink." In fact, in an unprecedented use of presidential impoundment powers, President Nixon refused to spend billions of dollars already appropriated. He did so on the grounds that he was forced to take action to limit spending because Congress had not done so.

As a response to these problems, the **Congressional Budget and Impoundment Control Act of 1974** changed the fiscal year from a July 1–June 30 sequence to an October 1–September 30 sequence in order to give Congress more time to review the president's budget. The act also created the **Congressional Budget Office (CBO)**, a congressional staff unit with the responsibility of providing Congress with needed information about the budget and the analytical expertise to sharpen budgetary choices for Congress; placed limits on the president's impoundment powers; created budget committees in both the House and Senate to provide a mechanism for comprehensive budget review by Congress; and established a timetable (revised by subsequent legislation) for the congressional budget review process.

The president submits his proposed budget to Congress early in the calendar year. Congressional committees review the programs within their jurisdictions and offer budget estimates to the budget committees by mid-March. With the help of the CBO, the budget committees pursue a more comprehensive budget review and report to the House and Senate a budget resolution containing targets for total revenues, total expenditures, and money to be spent in functional categories across the budget for the next fiscal year. The resolution is to be adopted by the full House and Senate by April 15. Legislation on appropriations and revenue is then to proceed in light of the budget targets set in the resolution. Congressional money decisions and budget targets are to be reconciled in time for spending to begin at the start of the fiscal year on October 1; however, in some years Congress has not been able to meet these procedural deadlines required by law. For example, in the fall of 1990 not a single one of the appropriations measures was enacted by the time the new fiscal year had begun.

Gramm-Rudman-Hollings

In response to the problem of deficits, Congress enacted the Balanced Budget and Emergency Deficit Control Act of 1985, more popularly known as Gramm-Rudman-Hollings after the senators who sponsored the legislation. The act, as later amended, mandated progressive annual cuts in the deficit and set into motion a process of automatic across-the-board spending cuts to achieve a balanced budget by 1993. The president ordered the cuts through the process of **sequestration**. Some programs—such as Social Security, Medicaid, and interest payments on the debt—were exempted from the cuts.

Gramm-Rudman-Hollings was enacted in the hopes of forcing Congress and the president to reduce the deficit. One problem with the deficit targets is that they encouraged the use of budget-reducing "gimmicks," which made it appear that cuts were made when in fact they were not. An example of a gimmick is pushing back a government payday several days from the fiscal year in question (say October 1) to the prior fiscal year (say September 29) so that the payroll will not be counted as expenditure in the fiscal year under review. However, since the money was spent anyway, if only at a different time, the cut was not real. The deficits continued, so Congress and the president tried a new law in 1990.

Budget Enforcement Act of 1990

Congress made fundamental changes in Gramm-Rudman-Hollings and tried a new approach to the deficit in the **Budget Enforcement Act of 1990**. The 1990 act shifts the emphasis of congressional action from deficit reduction to the control of spending.[21] Rather than being driven by overall deficit targets, Congress is limited by caps on discretionary spending and by constraints on changes in mandatory spending.

For fiscal years 1991 through 1993, the law placed caps on spending in each of the three categories of defense, international, and domestic discretionary— that is, nonmandatory—spending. The budget for the Federal Bureau of Investigation is an example of domestic discretionary spending because Congress can change FBI budget amounts from one year to the next. Medicare payments to hospitals to fund health care for the elderly is an example of mandatory spending because eligible individuals automatically and regularly receive benefits without specific congressional authorizing action from one year to the next. If discretionary spending exceeded the ceilings, then sequestration cuts were to be made within the category in which excess spending occurred. Under the law, all discretionary

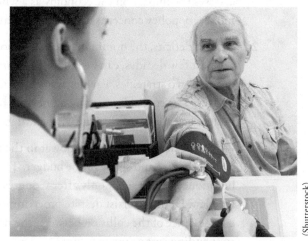

(Shutterstock)

Medicare payments to hospitals, which fund health care for the elderly, constitute mandatory spending. Eligible individuals automatically receive regular benefits without specific authorization from Congress.

spending was combined into a single category in fiscal years 1994 and 1995. In addition, mandatory program increases had to be balanced by cuts in nonexempt programs or by revenue increases. Cuts were not required during war or a downturn in economic growth.[22] These complex budgeting limits felt less restrictive during the economic upturn of the mid- and late 1990s. The return to deficit spending in 2002, however, reminded the government that it is crucial to have these rules in place for handling the less rosy economic forecasts that are often lurking just around the corner.

The rules of the Budget Enforcement Act were extended several times and then eventually replaced by a concept in the 2000s called PAYGO, or "pay as you go." This means that items added to a budget that result in additional spending must be accompanied by corresponding cuts or increases in revenue to offset their effects. This approach to handling the difficulties and temptations of deficit spending was codified as the **Statutory Pay-As-You-Go Act** in 2010. It maintains a similar—though more extensive—series of exemptions as previous laws. Despite these statutory efforts at limiting deficit spending, the practice continues.

Almost no one is satisfied with the procedures for considering and passing a budget. Elected officials and their staffs spend inordinate amounts of time dealing with budget issues. Congress has missed budget deadlines, government agencies have sometimes closed down temporarily for lack of spending authority, and deficits continue. Critics wonder, "Is this any way to run a government?" Efforts to tinker with existing procedures will continue, and proposals for new ones are inevitable;[23] however, tinkering with procedures is a symptom of a deeper political problem. Continuing entitlement programs at current levels, reducing the debt, and avoiding both tax increases and deep cuts in general government spending cannot all be achieved simultaneously. Such budgetary pressures have placed obvious strains on procedures for deciding budget policy. Ultimately, those pressures and strains emerge from the intense political resistance to spending cuts or tax increases. As recent budget proposals illustrate, harnessing wants with available resources remains the quintessential challenge to government in the 2000s.

Budget Enforcement Act of 1990

Legislation that fundamentally changed budget deficit reduction efforts from the focus on deficit targets contained in Gramm-Rudman-Hollings to a focus on ceilings or caps on specific categories of spending

Statutory Pay-As-You-Go Act

Law passed in 2010 that requires budget increases to be offset by either reductions elsewhere or increased revenues

CHAPTER REVIEW

1. Conflict over economic policy has been at or near the top of the political agenda throughout US history. Government makes two major types of economic policy: fiscal and monetary. Fiscal policy assesses the impact on the economy as a whole of governmental decisions to tax, spend, and borrow; monetary policy concerns the availability and cost of money and credit in the economy.

2. Budget deficits, the dominant economic policy issue Congress and the president faced for much of the past few decades, can be reduced by cutting expenditures, increasing taxes, or some combination of these two strategies. Payments for individuals make up the largest category in the national budget. The cost of borrowing money has become a significant national expenditure. Much of the budget is made up of mandatory spending.

3. Given the decentralization of power in the political system, no single individual or group alone can decide the size and shape of the budget. The president has the power to make budget proposals, but money can be spent only after Congress reviews and revises those proposals and enacts them into law. Deficits persist despite procedural changes. Continuing calls to revise procedures are a consequence of the collision between the necessity to impose constraints and the political resistance to spending cuts or tax increases.

KEY TERMS

appropriation............................446

authorization............................445

balanced budget amendment..............447

budget....................................441

Budget Enforcement Act of 1990...........449

Congressional Budget and Impoundment Control Act of 1974......................448

Congressional Budget Office (CBO).......448

continuing resolution 448

debt 434

deficit...................................434

depression...............................431

economic policy 430

fiscal policy 433

fiscal year 442

free trade................................431

incrementalism 440

laissez-faire..............................430

line-item veto............................446

mandatory programs......................440

monetary policy 434

net interest...............................439

Office of Management and Budget (OMB) ..434

outsourcing 431

protectionism 431

recession 431

sequestration 448

social entitlements 440

socialism.................................430

Statutory Pay-As-You-Go Act.............449

surplus..................................435

READINGS FOR FURTHER STUDY

For a thorough understanding of economic policy making, there is no better starting point than a good text on economics, such as Paul A. Samuelson and William D. Nordhaus's *Economics*, 19th ed. (New York: McGraw Hill, 2010), or *Macroeconomics,* 5th ed. by Paul Krugman and Robin Wells (New York: Worth, 2017).

Analyses of current economic problems, along with an excellent compendium of useful economic data, are found in the *Economic Report of the President*, written annually by the president's Council of Economic Advisers, and available online at https://www.whitehouse.gov/briefings-statements/growing-american-economy-economic
-report-president/.

Comprehensive information on the budget can be found in a document the Office of Management and Budget produces each year as the president submits a budget to Congress. The Budget of the United States Government contains extensive analysis of budgetary issues, detailed personnel and budgetary data for each agency in the government, and a variety of historical tables. The Congressional Budget Office also issues periodic reports that analyze the president's proposals, assess the state of the economy, and offer Congress spending and revenue options to reduce the deficit. See http://www.whitehouse.gov/omb/budget.

The New Politics of the Budgetary Process, 5th ed. (New York: Longman, 2004), by Aaron Wildavsky and Naomi Caiden, is a superb analysis of the political environment of budgeting and the enormous changes that have taken place since Wildavsky first wrote on the topic in 1964.

Irene S. Rubin takes up the topic of balanced budgets in *Balancing the Federal Budget* (New York: Chatham House, 2003).

An updated look at budgetary rules and politics is *The Federal Budget: Politics, Policy, and Process*, 3rd ed. (Washington, DC: Brookings, 2007), by Allen Schick with Felix LoStracco.

Two good recent texts focusing on economic policy are James J. Gosling's *Budgetary Politics in American Governments* 6th ed. (New York: Routledge, 2015) and Jeffrey E. Cohen's *Politics and Economic Policy in the United States*, 2nd ed. (Boston: Houghton Mifflin, 2000).

Finally, George C. Wilson's *This War Really Matters* (Washington, DC: CQ Press, 2000) is an inside look at the budget battles over defense spending.

NOTES

1. Eighteenth-century English economist Adam Smith called this idea the "invisible hand" in his classic *Wealth of Nations*.

2. 17 U.S. (4 Wheaton) 316 (1819).

3. Citizens for Budget Reform, "National Debt," http://www.budget.org/NationalDebt/Debt/ (September 25, 2002).

4. U.S. Office of Management and Budget, *Budget Baselines, Historical Data, and Alternatives for the Future* (Washington, DC: Government Printing Office, 1993), pp. 278–279.

5. U.S. Office of Management and Budget, *Historical Tables*, http://www.whitehouse.gov/omb/budget/ Historicals (August 14, 2020).

6. Ibid.

7. Congressional Budget Office, *Assessing the Decline in the National Saving Rate* (Washington, DC: Government Printing Office, 1993), pp. 2–3. National savings rates were compared for the period 1960 to 1989. This downward trend continued throughout the 1990s. See Bureau of Economic Analysis, "Note on the Personal Saving Rate," *Survey of Current Business* (February 1999): 8–9.

8. Bureau of Economic Analysis, "Personal Income and Outlays, June 2020 and Annual Update," July 31, 2020, http://www.bea.gov/ (August 15, 2020).

9. In 1912, after a split in the Republican Party, Theodore Roosevelt, a former president, received 27 percent of the popular vote as the candidate of the Progressive Party.

10. *Sacramento Bee*, "U.S. Public to Acquire Stake in Banks," 2008, http://www.sacbee.com (October 15, 2008).

11. U.S. Bureau of the Census, *Historical Statistics of the United States: Colonial Times to 1970*, pt. 2 (Washington, DC: Government Printing Office, 1975), pp. 1114–1115.

12. See, for example, June O'Neill, "The Trust Fund, the Surplus, and the Real Social Security Problem," *The Cato Project on Social Security Privatization 26* (April 9, 2002).

13. Aaron Wildavsky and Naomi Caiden, *The New Politics of the Budgetary Process*, 4th ed. (New York: Addison Wesley, 2000).

14. Congressional Budget Office, *Reducing the Deficit: Spending and Revenue Options* (Washington, DC: Government Printing Office, 1993), p. 225.

15. *A Blueprint for New Beginnings* (Washington, DC: Government Printing Office, 2001), pp. 45–48.

16. For the argument that "budgeting is at its very core political," see Donald F. Kettl, *Deficit Politics: Public Budgeting in Its Institutional and Historical Context* (New York: Macmillan, 1992), pp. 156–157.

17. Allen Schick, *Congress and Money: Budgeting, Spending, and Taxing* (Washington, DC: Urban Institute, 1980), p. 570.

18. See "Madisonian Budgeting, or Why the Process Is So Complicated," in Joseph White and Aaron Wildavsky, *The Deficit and the Public Interest: The Search for Responsible Budgeting in the 1980s* (Berkeley: University of California Press, 1989), pp. 1–17.

19. An excellent brief review of the budget process can be found in *The Budget System and Concepts, Budget of the United States Government, Fiscal Year 2005* (Washington, DC: Government Printing Office, 2004).

20. For a good review of relationships between the branches in the budgetary process, see *The Federal Budget: Politics, Policy, and Process*, 3rd ed. (Washington, DC: Brookings, 2007), by Allen Schick.

21. Congressional Budget Office, "The 1990 Budget Package: An Interim Assessment," December 1990, p. 2 (mimeo).

22. U.S. House of Representatives, Committee on Ways and Means, *Background Material on the Federal Budget and the President's Proposals for Fiscal Year 1994* (Washington, DC: Government Printing Office, 1993), pp. 71, 82

23. For a summary discussion of budget process reforms, see *Broken Purse Strings: Congressional Budgeting 1974 to 1988* (Washington, DC: Urban Institute, 1988), pp. 109–129, by Rudolph G. Penner and Alan J. Abramson.

POP QUIZ

1. _____ is French for "leave things alone." It is the belief that government should not interfere in the workings of the economy.

2. The _____ is the Executive Office agency that provides the president with budgetary information.

3. _____ is the sum of the deficits of prior years.

4. The president has the power to _____ budget bills passed by the Congress.

5. The _____ amendment is a proposed amendment to the Constitution that would require the federal government to operate with a budget in which revenues equaled or exceeded expenditures.

6. Free trade is the belief that US interests are better served by allowing foreign producers to sell their goods without restriction.   T   F

7. Monetary policy involves government decisions about how much money should circulate and what the interest rate should be.   T   F

8. Social Security, Medicare, and the Supplemental Nutrition Assistance Program are all examples of payments for individuals.   T   F

9. Line-item veto would give the president the power to accept some items in a bill and reject other items in the same bill.   T   F

10. Gramm-Rudman-Hollings mandated sequestration to achieve a balanced budget by 1991.   T   F

11. Government involvement in the economy has increased dramatically since which of the following occurred?
    A) The line-item veto was first utilized by President Clinton
    B) Establishment of the Congressional Budget Office (CBO)
    C) Ratification of the Gramm-Rudman-Hollings Act
    D) The New Deal and Great Depression

12. The fiscal policy of the government entails which of the following?
    A) The submission of governmental budgets on a twelve-month time frame starting with October 1 and ending with September 30 of every year
    B) Manipulating the money supply and interest rate
    C) Decisions about taxing and spending that affect the economic life of a nation
    D) Excesses in government revenues over government expenditures

13. Deficit is an excess of government's _____.
    A) revenues over expenditures
    B) expenditures on national defense
    C) expenditures on Social Security
    D) expenditures over revenues

14. Mandatory programs are government programs where which of the following occurs?
    A) Individual state participation is mandated by federal law.
    B) Spending is restricted to only programs mandated by federal law.
    C) Spending automatically increases without any action by the Congress.
    D) Spending is restricted to congressionally mandated programs.

15. The following are all examples of attempts to control the national debt except _____.
    A) balanced budget amendment
    B) socialism
    C) line-item veto
    D) PAYGO

Chapter

15

(iStock / Getty Images Plus)

DOMESTIC POLICY

In This Chapter

15.1   Debates Over Public Purposes
15.2   The Development of Federal Social Welfare Policy
15.3   The National Government as Social Insurer
15.4   Public Policy and Economic Inequality
15.5   Environmental Policy

Chapter Objectives

Americans typically divide the substance of public policy into two categories—foreign and domestic. While foreign policy will be the focus of the next chapter, in this chapter we explore a few of the thousands of **domestic policies** the US government enacts each year. In the 2021 fiscal year, domestic programs accounted for about $4 trillion in government spending. As explained in the previous chapter, much of this money (over two-thirds) is committed to nondiscretionary programs, such as Social Security, that have grown and changed incrementally over a long period of time.

However, some of the financial commitment—such as recent job creation efforts—is dedicated to new and developing programs. Thus, on an annual basis, Americans must face tough decisions about which programs to expand and which to abandon, when to continue with an existing approach and when to change course, and when to embark on something entirely new.

Since we cannot address the entire gamut of domestic policies in the space of a single chapter, we focus on two significant policy areas and explore them in detail. First, we look at social welfare programs, which range from mandatory entitlements that benefit everyone directly (e.g., Social Security) to needs-based efforts targeted at specific segments of society (e.g., welfare). These programs aim to ameliorate economic inequality.

domestic policy

A category of public policy that comprises policy decisions on matters affecting individuals within a political system

453

Second, this chapter addresses environmental policy. As the human population continues to grow and consume resources, Americans will be faced with more and more challenges in our efforts to devise a sustainable environmental policy that provides for the needs of human, plant, and animal ecosystems.

15.1 Debates Over Public Purposes

Differences over what government should do beyond protection of the nation against external threat and protection of individual citizens from each other are at the core of political conflict. Should the government fund programs for farmers, for the elderly, for the poor? Should the government subsidize the work of defense contractors, universities, and medical researchers? Should the government give aid to the middle class in the form of favorable tax policies and pensions?

Over the past century, enormous changes in the role of government have produced new relationships between the government and citizens. How these changes occur is an important issue in the analysis of policies. What government should do, who should gain the benefits of government action, and who should pay the costs are common questions in policy debate.

As explained in the policy process chapter (Chapter 13), new demands and new issues get on the policy agenda in a variety of ways. Changes in the social and economic

Government wrestles with satisfying the demands of myriad interest groups, which often use mass media to highlight their plights. Here, on February 3, 2017, President Donald Trump signs a financial regulation executive order.

(Courtesy of The Office of the President of the United States, 2017, via Wikimedia)

environment produce new groups and new problems and, consequently, new issues. Industrialization, the rise of corporations, and the emergence of a national economy shaped the post–Civil War period. The resulting stresses and strains changed relationships among groups, which then resorted to asking the government for help. Crises can also indelibly change the policy agenda. The Great Depression in the 1930s so threatened the nation's political and social institutions that the government enacted welfare and regulatory policies radically different from those of the past.

Debate over the appropriate role of the government frequently begins with the perceptions of the *self-interests* of various groups and individuals. Farmers want help in their battles against falling agricultural prices. Consumers want help in their battles against shoddy or dangerous products. The elderly want help in the economic uncertainties of retirement. Corporations want help in their battles against competitors.

Through political parties, the mass media, and interest groups, demands for help are made on government institutions. In the process, self-interest is frequently cloaked in the mantle of the *national interest*. That is, groups often claim that what is good for them is really good for the nation. Determining whether groups are right in such claims is the substance of much political debate. Since most politicians desire reelection, they do their best to satisfy (or even create) demands that the government provide help. These

demands are frequently in intractable conflict. Somebody must pay for farm programs, retirement pensions, and food and nutrition programs. Conflicts between the houses of Congress or between Congress and the president reflect these struggles.

Yet policies are not always the precise result of a collision of differing perceptions of self-interest. Some groups in and out of government favor certain policies because they are "right" and "fair." For example, the poor and the destitute lack the resources to exercise their economic claims on government. The idea that the government should provide needy citizens with life's basic necessities has a powerful appeal and political support that goes beyond self-interest.

15.1a   Social Welfare Policies

The expression **social welfare** has no precise definition. It is burdened by the unfavorable connotations frequently attached to the word *welfare*. To some, welfare simply means public money given to people whose desire to live off the public dole is greater than their desire to work for a living. However, within the category of social welfare policy are a large number of public programs serving heterogeneous groups of people. The Census Bureau defines the concept of social welfare as "all governmental programs directed specifically toward promoting the well-being of individuals and families."[1] This definition catches within its net a large number of programs. The breadth of the concept signals the wide-ranging presence of government in the lives of citizens.

(Shutterstock)

For families going through hard times, welfare payments may be the only way to feed or clothe their children. Some people, however, regard welfare recipients as simply unwilling to work, preferring to live off the public dole.

The data in Table 15.1 illustrate the growth of government social welfare spending since the start of the Great Depression. In 1929, government at all levels spent less than 4 percent of the gross national product (GNP) on social welfare programs. By 2020, this proportion had nearly quadrupled, increasing to more than 15 percent.

At 5 percent, social insurance programs constitute the second largest category of total social welfare spending. Medical programs, now the largest category, include Medicare and have been the fastest growing part of the social welfare budget in recent years. Public aid, comprising programs intended for the poor, such as the Supplemental Nutrition Assistance Program (SNAP) and Supplemental Security Income (SSI), is the third largest category. These are means-tested programs and are discussed later in this chapter. Recipients qualify for support only if their incomes are below a certain level. Social insurance and public aid are **social entitlements**, which are programs in which individuals receive benefits they are entitled to by law.

Social insurance alone accounts for about one-third of all social welfare expenditures. Social insurance, medical and health, and public aid combined account for about 90 percent of total social welfare spending, while veterans' affairs, education, and other programs make up the rest. A review of how the national government became so heavily committed to providing social welfare offers insights on how issues move onto the policy agenda.

social welfare

Governmental programs, such as social insurance and poverty programs, directed specifically toward promoting the well-being of individuals and families

social entitlements

Programs, such as Social Security and Medicaid, whereby eligible individuals receive benefits according to law

Table 15.1 Gross Domestic Product and Social Welfare Expenditures, 1929-2020

In 1929, government at all levels spent less than 4 percent of the gross national product (GNP) on social welfare programs. By the mid-1960s, government social welfare spending accounted for more than 10 percent of the gross domestic product (GDP). The largest category of social welfare spending comprises health and medical programs, followed by federal social insurance programs. Social welfare spending as a percentage of GDP gives an indication of how much society's total output of goods and services is devoted to these programs.

	1929		1940		1950		1960	
GNP	$101,000	(100.0)	$95,100	(100.0)	$266,800	(100.0)	$506,700	(100.0)
Total welfare	$3,921	(3.9)	$8,795	(9.2)	$23,508	(8.8)	$52,293	(10.3)
Social insurance	$342	(0.3)	$1,272	(1.3)	$4,947	(1.7)	$19,307	(3.8)
Education	$2,434	(2.4)	$2,561	(2.7)	$6,674	(2.5)	$17,626	(3.5)
Public aid	$60	(0.1)	$3,597	(3.8)	$2,496	(0.9)	$4,101	(0.8)
Health and medical programs	$351	(0.3)	$616	(0.6)	$2,064	(0.8)	$4,464	(0.9)
Veterans programs	$658	(0.6)	$629	(0.7)	$6,866	(2.6)	$5,479	(1.1)
Housing	—	—	$4	*	$15	*	$177	*
Other social welfare	$76	(0.1)	$116	(0.1)	$448	(0.2)	$1,139	(0.2)

	1970		1980		1990		2000	
GDP	$1,023,100	(100.0)	$2,718,900	(100.0)	$5,800,500	(100.0)	$9,951,500	(100.0)
Total welfare	$145,979	(14.3)	$492,213	(18.1)	$566,100	(9.8)	$1,027,827	(10.3)
Social insurance	$54,691	(5.3)	$229,754	(8.5)	$282,096	(4.8)	$445,450	(4.5)
Education	$50,846	(5.0)	$121,050	(4.5)	$12,286	(0.2)	$21,851	(0.2)
Public aid	$16,488	(1.6)	$72,703	(2.7)	$63,481	(1.1)	$106,285	(1.1)
Health and medical programs	$10,030	(1.0)	$26,762	(1.0)	$188,808	(3.3)	$427,194	(4.3)
Veterans programs	$9,078	(0.9)	$21,466	(0.8)	$17,687	(0.3)	$25,004	(0.3)
Other social welfare	$4,145	(0.4)	$13,599	(0.5)	$1,742	*	$2,043	*

	2010		2020**	
GDP	$14,798,500	(100.0)	$22,163,473	(100.0)
Total welfare	$2,386,633	(16.1)	$3,368,848	(15.2)
Social insurance	$706,737	(4.8)	$1,097,184	(5.0)
Education	$128,598	(0.9)	$195,526	(0.9)
Public aid	$622,210	(4.2)	$529,335	(2.4)
Health and medical programs	$820,704	(5.5)	$1,340,159	(6.0)
Veterans programs	$108,384	(0.7)	$215,077	(1.0)

Note: All monetary amounts are in millions. Percentage of GNP/GDP appears in parentheses. Figures prior to 1970 measure GNP rather than GDP.

*Less than 0.05 percent   **Some data for 2020 are estimates

DATA SOURCES: Data for 1929 and 1940 are taken from Social Security Administration. Data for 1950 and 1960 are taken from Social Security Administration, Social Security Bulletin: Annual Statistical Supplement, 1990 (Washington, DC: Government Printing Office, 1990), p. 100. All other data are from U.S. Census Bureau, Statistical Abstract of the United States (Washington, DC: Government Printing Office) and from the Office of Management and Budget, http://www.omb.gov.

15.2 The Development of Federal Social Welfare Policy

At the beginning of the Republic in the late eighteenth century, the national government was miniscule. The pervasive presence of the national government in the twenty-first century symbolizes the drastic changes in the relationship between government and individuals over the past two hundred years. Such changes did not come gradually. Rather, the national government's presence grew in relatively short bursts of activity, resulting in an ever-larger government that maintained its size in succeeding decades.

The domestic activities of the national government before the twentieth century were relatively limited. There were no Social Security programs, no health programs such as Medicare and Medicaid, no unemployment compensation programs, no food stamp/SNAP programs, no poverty programs, and no programs to meet the special needs of the elderly or individuals with disabilities. There were no public programs to help nineteenth-century factory workers who lost their jobs or were disabled or to help families who lost a breadwinner. The national government taxed relatively little, spent relatively little, and did relatively little. It was, consequently, a shadow rather than an omnipresent force in the daily lives of most citizens. Today a widely held expectation is that the national government should assume major responsibilities for social welfare. However, this contemporary expectation contrasts sharply with the political attitudes that were dominant a century ago.

15.2a The Philosophy of Social Darwinism

The dominant philosophy that shaped attitudes on the role of government in the late nineteenth century was **social Darwinism**, a set of ideas that applied Charles Darwin's theory of biological evolution to society. Darwin's theory held that physical changes in living organisms evolved as responses to the demands of survival and that organisms that adapted most successfully to their environments were most likely to survive. The theory of social Darwinism held that social relationships took place within a "struggle for survival" and that in this struggle only the "most fit" survive. Just as living organisms evolved to higher states, so too does society as a whole progress to a higher state as natural selection proceeds.

The theory seemed to offer intellectual justification for limited government and the unfettered growth and expansion of big industry and business in the late nineteenth century.[2] Since society could best progress to higher forms through its natural processes of competition and survival with no outside interference, government should not act on behalf of those too weak to survive on their own. Herbert Spencer, a British philosopher whose name is closely associated with social Darwinism, argued that government should limit itself to protecting the rights of individuals to pursue their own ends. In this view,

Herbert Spencer was a British philosopher who argued that government should only serve to protect the right of individuals to pursue their own ends.

(Smithsonian Institution Libraries, circa 1903, via Wikimedia)

social Darwinism

A set of ideas applying Charles Darwin's theory of biological evolution to society and holding that social relationships occur within a struggle for survival in which only the fittest survive

government should not assume the role of providing for social welfare because such action would interfere with natural forces acting to improve society as a whole.[3]

15.2b The Progressive Era

Social Darwinism, as a set of ideas about society and the role of government, was dominant in the generation after the Civil War. Rapid urbanization, nationalization of the economy, and bigness in industry meant an end to the relative self-sufficiency individuals enjoyed in a less complicated agricultural society. The concentration of large numbers of people in urban areas strained the ability of local governments to provide essential services and bred a variety of social problems such as poverty and inadequate housing. Increasingly large and faceless companies provided goods and services to consumers who had little power to influence corporate decisions. Similarly, the availability of jobs and the quality of the work environment were matters over which workers had little control.

Such conditions gave rise to questions about the consequences of unfettered free enterprise. The limited role that government played at all levels increasingly became a matter of policy debate. It was in this environment of rapid social and economic change that reform movements began. This period of reform, named the **Progressive Era** by historians, generally spanned the last decade of the nineteenth century and the years of the twentieth century before World War I.

Progressive public policy goals included the replacement of corrupt politics by civil service systems, the regulation of monopolies, and the protection of consumers against unsafe products. Progressives also pressed for a more substantive role for government in aiding specific groups who suffered due to rapid industrialism.[4] Most of the initiatives for such social welfare legislation came at the state, rather than the national, level. Laws on minimum wages, workers' compensation, and pensions all directly countered the social Darwinist view that government ought to play a minimal role in social and economic relationships. Progressive efforts at the state level to redress the economic and social imbalances created by rapid industrialization and urbanization laid the groundwork for the revolutionary change in the national government role that was to come.

Opinions vary on whether too many or too few people qualify for public assistance. The actual number of those receiving welfare (via TANF) is available from the Department of Health and Human Services.

http://www.bvtlab.com/367f7

Progressive Era

An urban reform movement of the late nineteenth and early twentieth centuries that called for direct primaries, restrictions on corporations, and improved public services that was influential in the administrations of Theodore Roosevelt and Woodrow Wilson

New Deal

The first two terms of President Franklin D. Roosevelt (1933–1945), whose revolutionary policy initiatives established a pervasive and active role for the national government

15.2c The New Deal Policy Revolution

The **New Deal** spanned the first two terms of President Franklin D. Roosevelt (1933–1945). His revolutionary initiatives established the pervasive and active national government role taken for granted today.

The easy tranquility of the national government during the 1920s was exploded by the Great Depression, a period of massive and severe economic hardship that rivaled the Civil War in its cataclysmic impact on the nation's political institutions. Banks failed, companies went bankrupt, home and farm mortgages were foreclosed, industrial production plummeted, and unemployment soared. Millions of people lost jobs, homes, and bank accounts, with the attendant social misery such losses inevitably bring.[5] Few government programs existed to cushion the shock of this economic disaster. Whatever government programs existed (almost entirely at the state and local level) were simply overwhelmed

by the sharp and sweeping economic decline. In responding to the economic crisis of the Great Depression, the national government for the first time assumed the active and extensive role now expected.

The Depression's impact on the public policy agenda was clear and unmistakable. Roosevelt was determined to take immediate and forceful action to bolster the nation's confidence in the government's ability to deal with the crisis. On the day after his inauguration as president, Roosevelt called Congress into special session, "convened in an atmosphere of wartime crisis." Congress gave every indication of wanting to be led, and the president accommodated this desire by sending to Capitol Hill a flurry of proposals for action. By the end of the special session, the famous "100 days," Congress passed every one of Roosevelt's fifteen proposals.[6]

Enacted during the New Deal was the insurance of bank deposits by the Federal Deposit Insurance Corporation, Social Security for the aged, unemployment compensation, and minimum wage and maximum-hours requirements. Designed to relieve the suffering of practically every social group touched by the Depression, these programs are all now embedded in the policy role of government. *Public expectations* that government "do something" about social and economic problems flowered during the Roosevelt presidency. An interlocking relationship between heightened public demands and government efforts to meet those demands developed. Government in Washington would no longer be distant, relaxed, and indifferent.

15.2d Expansion of the National Role in the Great Society

The New Deal firmly established the national government as the most important participant in ensuring the social and economic welfare of individuals. During subsequent decades, major New Deal programs such as Social Security, federal insurance for bank deposits, and unemployment compensation have been changed in incremental steps; but the existence of such programs is no longer seriously debated.

The next period of major change in the role of the national government occurred during the **Great Society** of Lyndon Johnson's presidency (1963–1969). Johnson assumed office after the assassination of President John F. Kennedy in November 1963, an event that seared the nation nearly as much as the attack on Pearl Harbor in 1941. National grief turned into popular support for proposals that Johnson pressed as unfinished business of the slain president. This support combined with Johnson's landslide victory over conservative Barry Goldwater and huge gains by the Democratic Party in Congress in 1964 to produce fertile ground for further growth of the national government's role.

The Civil Rights Act of 1964 and the Voting Rights Act of 1965 finally provided by law rights long denied to African Americans. The Equal Opportunity Act and the Food Stamp Act of 1964 explicitly dealt with the plight of poor Americans. The Elementary and Secondary Education Act of 1964 provided federal aid for the disadvantaged in the

(Courtesy of Arnold Newman, White House Press Office, 1964, via Wikimedia)

President Lyndon B. Johnson, who succeeded to the presidency after the assassination of John F. Kennedy in 1963, expanded the role of the national government with the Great Society.

Great Society
President Lyndon Johnson's term for an egalitarian society that aggressive governmental action to help the poor and disadvantaged would attempt to create in the 1960s

POLITICS AND IDEAS

Gun Violence: The Search for Solutions

By almost any measure, the US has a problem with gun violence. The rate of homicides by firearms in the United States is more than four times greater than in any other developed nation, and there were more than 39,000 gun deaths in the United States in 2018.[1] Although certainly not all violence in the United States is associated with guns, there are more guns than people in our country—and twice as many guns per capita as there are in any other country in the world.[2] Although the majority of gun owners are hunters, collectors, or otherwise safe and responsible owners, a concerning number are not. In 2019, 417 mass shootings occurred.[3] Unfortunately, many of these occur in or near schools.[4] Indeed, today's generation of students and young adults are familiar with something virtually unheard of in previous generations—school lockdowns due to the presence of (or feared presence of) an armed shooter.

Given that such a visible aspect of America's gun violence problem is associated with schools, it is perhaps not surprising that younger people in the US are leading the call for policy change. After a school shooting in Parkland, Florida, killed seventeen people in February 2018, students took charge, organizing a national school walkout and protests around the country. The tragedy led to the rise of youth leaders like Emma González, who declared: "Politicians who sit in their gilded House and Senate seats funded by the NRA telling us nothing could have been done to prevent this: we call BS!"[5] Nationally, polling showed that 70 percent of young likely voters age eighteen to twenty-nine favor stricter gun control laws.[6] This sentiment is not limited to youth. Among Americans of all ages, 64 percent believe laws governing the sale of firearms should be stricter than they are now.[7]

Just knowing that Americans want change does not necessarily make a policy solution any easier, however. When it comes to guns, policy change is complicated by the Second Amendment: "A well regulated militia, being necessary to the security of a free state, the right of the people to keep and bear arms, shall not be infringed." While legal scholars and laypeople alike bicker over the precise meaning of these words, nearly all acknowledge that the Second Amendment affords some protection for gun ownership in the United States. Those wishing to repeal the amendment entirely would face a difficult task. It is unlikely that a right with such ardent adherents could be dispensed with given the challenging nature of the amendment process (described in Chapter 1). Consider that such seemingly innocuous amendments as guaranteeing equal rights for women, reforming the Electoral College, and requiring a balanced budget have failed to attain the supermajority support needed to amend the constitution. The 29 percent of Americans who would like to ban all handguns—or even the 47 percent who would like to ban assault rifles—would fall well short of victory.[8]

Given this limitation, what changes could reasonably be proposed to reduce gun violence? Measures that have enjoyed high levels of support in public opinion polls include: required background checks (96 percent support), a thirty-day waiting period to purchase a gun (75 percent), and mandatory registration of firearms with the local police (70 percent).[9] School-specific measures with broad support include increased training for first responders on how to deal with active shooters (95 percent), increased security to enter school grounds (87 percent), programs to address students who may pose a threat (86 percent), and raising the legal age to purchase guns from eighteen to twenty-one (68 percent).[10] Frustratingly for many, this supermajority support has not translated into significant federal legislation, with some pointing to the influence of one of the country's most powerful lobby groups—the National Rifle Association—as a major impediment to change. Other evidence suggests that although strong majorities favor specific changes, a more general support for "the abstract idea of the right to own guns" prevents many from fully embracing laws they feel would limit such a right.[11]

So, if a constitutional amendment is out of the question, and if even more limited measures raise the hackles of gun advocates, what is to be done to reduce gun violence? One anti-violence advocate has suggested a novel approach: limiting ownership of guns to two per person. Noting that the Second Amendment does not mention how many guns one is entitled to bear, Doug Pennington argues, in an article for *Slate,* that mass shootings could be limited by protecting gun ownership but preventing people from stockpiling guns. Pointing out that most mass shooters employ many guns in the perpetration of their crime, and that "just 3 percent of Americans own half of America's guns," Pennington argues that relatively few Americans would be inconvenienced by this approach.[12] While such an unusual approach may not come to pass, Pennington's idea illustrates the type of outside-the-box thinking that is sometimes needed to fix seemingly intractable problems.

What do you see as the causes of gun violence in the United States? How can youth and young adults be part of the solution to this serious

problem? What would be your preferred solution? If your solution does not seem politically feasible, what approach would you recommend instead? Feel free to be creative.

1. German Lopez, "America's Gun Problem, Explained," *Vox,* November 8, 2018, https://www.vox.com/2015/10/3/9444417/gun-violence-united-states-america (November 21, 2018); Gun Violence Archive, 2020, https://www.gunviolencearchive.org/ (August 15, 2020).

2. Ibid.

3. Ibid.

4. Cortland Jeffrey, "School Shootings in U.S.: When, Where Each Shooting Has Occurred in 2018," *ABC15,* October 4, 2018, https://www.abc15.com/news/data/school-shootings-in-u-s-when-where-each-shooting-has-occurred-in-2018 (November 21, 2018).

5. Sebastian Murdock, "The Teens Are Coming for the NRA, and They Can't Be Stopped," *HuffPost,* February 24, 2018, https://www.huffingtonpost.com/entry/the-teens-are-coming-for-the-nra-and-they-cant-be-stopped_us_5a919197e4b03b55731ca1ba (November 21, 2018).

6. Harvard Institute of Politics, "Spring 2018 Youth Poll," April 18, 2018, http://iop.harvard.edu/spring-2018-poll (August 30, 2018).

7. The Gallup Organization, "Guns," 2020, https://news.gallup.com/poll/1645/Guns.aspx (August 15, 2020).

8. Ibid.

9. The Gallup Organization, "Direction from the American Public on Gun Policy," October 30, 2017, https://news.gallup.com/opinion/polling-matters/221117/direction-american-public-gun-policy.aspx (November 22, 2018).

10. The Gallup Organization, "Broad Agreement on Most Ideas to Curb School Shootings," March 15, 2018, https://news.gallup.com/poll/229805/broad-agreement-most-ideas-curb-school-shootings.aspx (November 22, 2018).

11. German Lopez, "America's Gun Problem, Explained"; "Worldwide Gun Deaths Reach 250,000 Yearly; US Ranks High."

12. Doug Pennington, "Two Guns per Person," *Slate,* October 13, 2017, https://slate.com/news-and-politics/2017/10/a-two-guns-per-person-limit-would-protect-americans-lives-and-liberty.html (November 22, 2018).

nation's schools. Perhaps the most significant change in the social welfare role of the national government was the amendment of the Social Security Act in 1965 to provide health care for the aged (Medicare) and the poor (Medicaid).

The Great Society was the last major period in which the national government embarked on new social welfare initiatives. Growing budget deficits and foreign policy concerns, coupled with the election of conservative leaders such as Nixon, Reagan, and the two Bushes, made continued expansion of social welfare programs both unpopular and unlikely. By the mid-1990s, in fact, efforts to reduce the scope of the federal role emerged. Most notably, attempts to reduce federal domestic spending focused on a restructuring of social insurance programs, which are described in the next section.

15.3   The National Government as Social Insurer

The principal consequence of the New Deal policy revolution is that the national government has assumed a major responsibility for the social welfare of individuals who are old, disabled, or unemployed. Rather than relying on private charities or state and local programs, people are *insured*, in effect, by the national government against the potentially harsh social and economic consequences that old age, disability, and unemployment can bring.

A significant feature of **social insurance programs** is that they serve all eligible people, regardless of income levels. To be sure, millions of individuals would fall into officially defined poverty in the absence of these programs, but the receipt of social insurance benefits is not dependent on income. An elderly person need not be poor to receive Social Security benefits, and people who have lost relatively high-paying jobs can be eligible for unemployment compensation. The beneficiaries of social insurance programs are individuals from practically all income levels, a fact that helps to explain the staunch political support on which these programs rest.

social insurance programs
Welfare programs that provide cash or services to the aged, the disabled, and the unemployed, regardless of income level

President Franklin Roosevelt signs the Social Security Act on August 14, 1935.

15.3a   Social Security

The **Social Security Act of 1935** was probably the most significant piece of domestic legislation ever enacted. Passed in the New Deal, the act provided for a system of old age insurance financed by taxes on workers and employers and a variety of categorical grants to the states to provide programs for cash assistance to the unemployed, dependent children, and the blind, disabled, and aged. The 1935 act has been amended many times, but it is significant because it firmly established for the first time a social welfare role for the national government.

Administered by the Social Security Administration in the Department of Health and Human Services, "Social Security" is really a bundle of separate programs rather than a single one. Within the Social Security umbrella are insurance programs for retired workers and their spouses (old age insurance), survivors of retired workers (survivors' insurance), and individuals with disabilities and their dependents (disability insurance). The total package is generally known by the acronym OASDI (old age, survivors', and disability insurance). The evolution of these programs is a classic example of **incrementalism**, a process through which policies once established are changed piecemeal over time. The number of workers covered, the amount of benefits, and the level of payroll taxes to pay for these Social Security programs have all increased incrementally over the past half-century.

In terms of expenditures—number of people receiving benefits, number of workers covered, and intensity of political support—the Social Security umbrella of programs is the national government's largest and single most important domestic policy. The OASDI consumed about 23 percent of all federal expenditures in fiscal year 2021. More than 64 million people are OASDI beneficiaries. Benefits vary for different groups and are indexed to increase each year; in 2020, retired workers received an average monthly benefit of about $2,081.[7] Figure 15.1 offers clues on the economic importance of Social Security to older Americans. Social Security benefits, as a proportion of income, rise as people get older and are the largest source of income for Americans over the age of sixty-five—facts that help explain the potent political support for the program.

In the original 1935 act, only workers in commerce and industry were insured; but in classic incremental fashion, other occupational groups—including self-employed farmers, military personnel, self-employed professionals, and even the president and vice president of the United States and members of Congress—have been progressively brought into the system. Coverage is now practically compulsory. Virtually every worker and employer in the United States must pay a payroll tax to fund the program.

These statistics suggest the potentially volatile political consequences that any change in Social Security can have. Practically no one can avoid being touched by the program in some tangible and specific way, either by receiving welcome benefit checks or by paying unwelcome taxes. The potential for intergenerational conflict in such a system is obvious. Younger workers may resent what they consider an increasingly rapacious payroll tax bite for a program that, they fear, may not even still be in existence when they retire. Retired workers may view the program differently. Since they paid taxes into the system during their working years, they feel they are simply getting back in benefits what they rightly

Social Security Act of 1935
Landmark legislation that firmly established for the first time a social welfare role for the national government by providing old age insurance and grants to the states to provide programs for cash assistance to the unemployed, dependent children, and the blind, disabled, and aged

incrementalism
A model of decision-making that holds that new policies differ only marginally from existing policies

Figure 15.1 Shares of Income for the Older Population

Older Americans rely heavily on Social Security income. Social Security benefits are the principal source of income for Americans over the age of sixty-five.

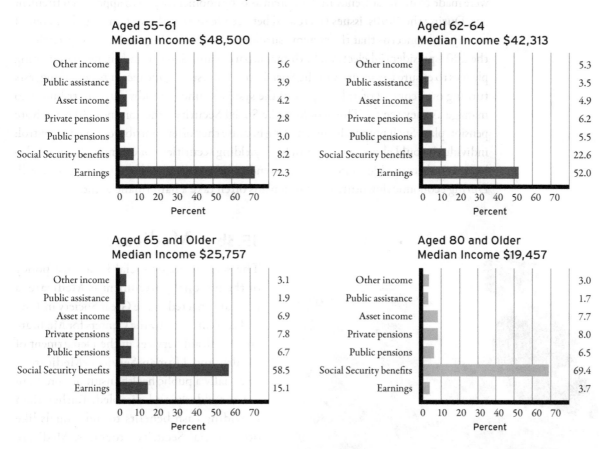

Aged 55–61
Median Income $48,500

	Percent
Other income	5.6
Public assistance	3.9
Asset income	4.2
Private pensions	2.8
Public pensions	3.0
Social Security benefits	8.2
Earnings	72.3

Aged 62–64
Median Income $42,313

	Percent
Other income	5.3
Public assistance	3.5
Asset income	4.9
Private pensions	6.2
Public pensions	5.5
Social Security benefits	22.6
Earnings	52.0

Aged 65 and Older
Median Income $25,757

	Percent
Other income	3.1
Public assistance	1.9
Asset income	6.9
Private pensions	7.8
Public pensions	6.7
Social Security benefits	58.5
Earnings	15.1

Aged 80 and Older
Median Income $19,457

	Percent
Other income	3.0
Public assistance	1.7
Asset income	7.7
Private pensions	8.0
Public pensions	6.5
Social Security benefits	69.4
Earnings	3.7

DATA SOURCES: Social Security Administration, Income of the Population 55 and Older, 2014 (Washington, DC: Social Security Administration, 2016).

deserve. Given the very scope of the program, its crucial importance to so many people, and the potential for group conflicts, presidents and members of Congress pondering program changes are in a political minefield.

By the late 1970s and early 1980s, it had become clear that major changes were essential if the program was to survive. Projections showed that expenditures (benefits) would soon exceed revenues (payroll taxes). A declining birthrate and a longer life expectancy meant that the number of retirees (beneficiaries) was growing faster than the number of workers paying taxes to fund the program. In addition, increases in benefit levels caused by inflation outpaced revenues.

The political consequences of the Social Security system "going broke" were too horrendous to contemplate. Unlike means-tested programs (to be discussed shortly) for which only lower-income people qualify, almost everyone expects to benefit directly from Social Security. This fact

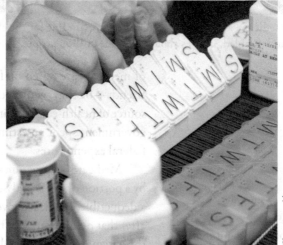

(Shutterstock)

Because of a declining birthrate and a longer life expectancy, the number of retirees (beneficiaries) is growing faster than the number of workers paying taxes to fund the Social Security program.

gives Social Security a political base far broader than that enjoyed by any means-tested welfare policy.

As a result of such concerns, the future of Social Security has been an almost constant topic on the American political scene for the past three decades. In the 1980s, adjustments—such as raising the payroll tax rate and gradually increasing the retirement age—were made to insure solvency in the system as baby boomers began to approach retirement age. During the 1990s, issues fluctuated between fears that the system would run out of money and concerns that the system's surplus funds were being used inappropriately. By the 2004 presidential election, both major-party candidates found themselves making pledges to ensure the security of the Social Security system. One recent proposal suggests turning over control of at least part of the system's funds to individual contributors to manage as they see fit. This would make Social Security function more like a private pension plan. Such proposals are tempting because they offer contributors greater control; individuals could choose to invest in high-yielding securities, for example. They are also hazardous because high rates of return tend to be accompanied by higher risks as well. During economic downturns, pension plans often take a hard financial hit.

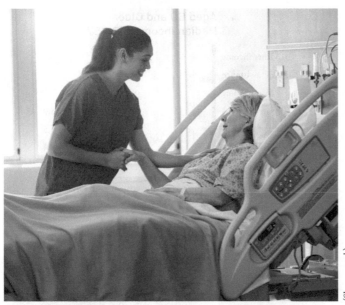

(Shutterstock)

Medicare, a major source of health-care funding for the elderly and disabled, insures about fifty-nine million people.

15.3b   Medicare

The second major social insurance policy of the national government is **Medicare**, a program enacted in the Great Society in 1965 and administered by the Centers for Medicare and Medicaid Services in the Department of Health and Human Services. Medicare is essentially a public health insurance program for the elderly and disabled. Rather than providing cash benefits to individuals like other Social Security programs, Medicare pays the providers of health care (hospitals, physicians, and other health professionals) for services given to patients who are aged, disabled, or afflicted with terminal illness. The program now insures about fifty-nine million people. In the past, the elderly and Americans with disabilities who were in need of medical care relied on families, private insurance plans, or the help of charities or friends—or they went without medical care. However, Medicare has become a major source of health-care funding for the elderly and disabled. In fiscal year 2021, the national government spent an estimated $728 billion on Medicare, or about 15 percent of total federal expenditures.

Medicare is a program with multiple parts. Part A is Hospital Insurance (HI), funded by a portion of the Social Security tax paid into a hospital trust fund. After a patient pays a deductible, Medicare covers hospital costs for two months, with patients sharing costs after that period. Part B of the program is Supplementary Medical Insurance (SMI): After the patient pays a deductible amount, SMI funds physician and outpatient services. SMI, which is voluntary, is funded by premiums paid by enrollees and general revenues from the federal treasury.[8]

Medicare was enacted after a bitter political struggle in which opponents of the measure argued that health insurance was "socialized medicine" and unwarranted

Medicare

A public health insurance program in which government pays the providers of health care for medical services given to patients who are aged or disabled

interference in the relationship between patients and physicians. Providing health care for the elderly and people with disabilities has proved, however, to be a highly popular program. Still, assumption of a major medical insurance role by the national government has inevitably created policy debates over costs—how high they should be and who should pay them. Efforts to ensure the financial soundness of Medicare are complicated by rising medical costs. Congress has attempted to control expenditures by placing ceilings on some of the medical costs the program will pay and by offering financial incentives to hospitals to keep costs low.

The original Medicare plan has been supplemented with additional coverage areas over the past few decades. One area in which many Americans wanted to see the program expand was prescription drug coverage for the elderly. The rising costs of prescription drugs place a particularly large burden on the elderly, many of whom have modest incomes and require multiple long-term prescriptions. To address these concerns, Medicare Part D went into effect in 2006 in order to provide prescription drug benefits for Medicare recipients. The most recent changes to Medicare—an expansion of this prescription drug coverage and adjustments to the Medicare tax, among other items—made up a portion of the 2010 Patient Protection and Affordable Care Act.

15.3c Unemployment Compensation

A third major social insurance policy is **unemployment compensation**, a program of temporary financial assistance for the unemployed first enacted in the original Social Security Act of 1935 and administered by the states and the Office of Workforce Security in the Department of Labor. Massive unemployment was one of the severe economic and social problems that sparked the assumption of a much greater social welfare role by government in the Great Depression. The problem obviously continues, for changes in the economy and the decline of some industries mean that official unemployment rates exceeding 5 percent are not unusual. During times of recession, the rate can go much higher. It went over 10 percent in 2009 and remained over 8 percent through 2012 before finally falling back under 6 percent by late 2014. It hovered just under 4 percent in the early months of 2020, but then skyrocketed to 14.7 percent in April—the highest level since the Great Depression—as a result of the COVID-19 pandemic and associated social distancing needs.

One of the most significant public policy changes in the past half-century is that unemployed workers now receive cash benefits for a short period of time while they seek other employment. For example, as foreign competition and changes in the international economy have racked their industries, unemployed steel and autoworkers have been beneficiaries of the program. Unemployment compensation is designed not for the chronically unemployed but for those who need financial assistance to keep afloat between jobs. Both the national and state governments tax employers to pay for the benefits and the administrative costs of the program. Eligibility requirements and benefit levels vary among the states. In general, an unemployed person receives weekly checks for up to twenty-six weeks and up to thirteen additional weeks in states where unemployment rates are particularly high. An example of such a time was the COVID-19 crisis. Though the extreme unemployment levels of mid-2020 decreased some in subsequent months, the massive increase in jobless claims led to legislation and presidential action to enhance and extend benefits for those in need.

unemployment compensation

A social insurance policy that grants temporary financial assistance to the unemployed

15.4 Public Policy and Economic Inequality

In addition to social insurance, the second major category of social welfare policy at the national level comprises programs explicitly designed to aid the poor. Table 15.2 offers a summary portrait of both types of programs. Each of these two categories of programs serves different groups of people and is shaped by different kinds of political pressures. In general, social insurance programs tend to be the larger of the two types in terms of the number of beneficiaries and the amount of money spent. Given their broader constituencies, these programs also tend to receive much stronger political support.

Programs specifically intended for the poor—and only the poor—are known as **means-tested programs** because the receipt of benefits is completely dependent on income level. Under these programs, individuals receive benefits only if they qualify by having little or no income. Unlike social insurance, beneficiaries of means-tested programs do not pay money into the programs before they receive benefits. Children whose parents have little or no income and the chronically unemployed are among the beneficiaries of such programs.

15.4a Measures of Economic Inequality

Political equality amid sharp economic inequality remains one of the great ironies of the American experience. Economic inequality is a fact of life supported by even casual observation. Differences in the clothes people wear, the food they eat, the entertainment they pursue, the cars they buy, and the houses they live in—all suggest great differences in economic status. One familiar measure of income disparity is a division of families into five groups (or quintiles) according to the proportion of total money income each group receives.

Perfect income equality would mean that each fifth of the population of families receives 20 percent of all money income—that is, each quintile of families receives an equal slice of the money pie. However, great income inequality persists. Table 15.3 shows that the lowest fifth of families received just 3.1 percent of aggregate income in 2019, while the highest fifth received 51.9 percent in the same year. The table also shows that the lowest three-fifths of families have lost ground, from a combined 32.0 percent of aggregate income in 1971 to 25.5 percent in 2019. In the same period the highest fifth increased aggregate income from 43.5 to 51.9 percent. A domestic policy question is the degree to which such growing income inequality will develop into a trenchant political issue in the twenty-first century. The Occupy movement, which started in 2011 with its emphasis on the stark contrast between incomes of the top 1 percent of the population and those of the bottom 99 percent, was an example of how dissatisfaction with income inequality can manifest into a political agenda. However, the movement failed to translate the anger into lasting political change.

Another measure of economic inequality is the proportion of the total population classified as poor in the United States. The term *poverty* is a human construct that does not have the same meaning in all societies. People are poor according to some economic standard against which they are judged, and those standards may vary greatly across the planet. A poor family in the US may have a consistent diet of rice and potatoes, but those in nations who have little or no food at all may consider such a diet a rich one.

means-tested programs

Type of social welfare program in which government provides cash or in-kind benefits to individuals who qualify by having little or no income

Table 15.2   Major Social Welfare Programs

Social insurance and means-tested programs are major categories of social welfare programs. Social insurance programs are generally funded by specific taxes and have the retired, the aged, individuals with disabilities, and the unemployed as their beneficiaries. Means-tested programs are designed for needy individuals, are funded by general revenues, and usually involve the states in their administration.

Social Insurance

Program	Date Enacted	Benefits	Funding Sources	Estimated Federal Cost in Billions, 2021
Social Security (old age, survivors', and disability insurance)	1935	Monthly checks for retired and disabled workers, their dependents, and survivors of retired workers	Social Security tax, paid by workers and employers	$1,150
Medicare	1965	Medical care for aged and disabled	Social Security tax, premiums paid by beneficiaries, general revenues	$722
Unemployment compensation	1935	Weekly checks for short-term unemployed workers	State and national taxes on employers	$33

Means-Tested Programs

Program	Date Enacted	Benefits	Funding Sources	Estimated Federal Cost in Billions, 2021
Temporary Assistance for Needy Families (TANF)	1935	Monthly checks for needy children and parents	National and state general revenues	$23
Supplemental Security Income	1972	Monthly cash payments for needy aged, blind, and disabled	National general revenues and state supplements	$54
Medicaid	1965	Medical care for needy individuals and families	National and state general revenues	$448
Food stamps/SNAP	1964	Monthly food cards for needy individuals and families	National general revenues and some state funds	$80

DATA SOURCE: All data are from Office of Management and Budget, Historical Tables, https://www.whitehouse.gov/omb/historical-tables/ (August 15, 2020).

Table 15.3   Aggregate Family Income by Quintiles

In the years between 1971 and 2017, the bottom four quintiles of families received a declining share of aggregate income, while the top quintile increased their share of aggregate income.

	1971	1981	1991	2001	2011	2019
Lowest fifth	4.1%	4.1%	3.8%	3.5%	3.2%	3.1%
Second fifth	10.6%	10.1%	9.6%	8.7%	8.4%	8.3%
Third fifth	17.3%	16.7%	15.9%	14.6%	14.3%	14.1%
Fourth fifth	24.5%	24.8%	24.4%	23.0%	23.0%	22.7%
Highest fifth	43.5%	44.3%	46.5%	50.1%	51.1%	51.9%

DATA SOURCE: U.S. Census Bureau, Income and Poverty in the United States: 2019.

The concept of **relative deprivation** indicates how variable definitions of poverty can be.[9] According to this concept, individuals with less money will feel poor or deprived relative to those who have more. Of course, the greater the material wealth in a particular society, the more likely individuals will feel poor if they do not possess material goods in the same degree as others in the society. The substantial political and economic obstacles to fundamental changes in the distribution of income suggest the persistence of poverty defined relatively.

Another approach consists of some absolute standard below which individuals can be defined as poor. The United States government has constructed a standard to measure the extent of poverty and its changes over time. Based on a Department of Agriculture finding on how much families spend on food, the Social Security Administration in 1964 established a **poverty threshold**—an income level below which individuals are defined as poor. That income level is different for families of different sizes and changes each year with changes in the consumer price index (CPI). By 2019, the average poverty threshold for a family of four was $25,924. Families with money income below this level are defined as poor.

Figure 15.2 shows the number of poor people in the United States between 1960 and 2019 on the basis of this poverty threshold. In 1960, almost 40 million people, or 22.2 percent of the total population, were defined as poor. Both the absolute number and the proportion of poor people declined until the early 1970s, before rising again beginning in the 1980s. In 2019, there were 34 million poor people in the US. At 10.5 percent, the proportion of Americans who were poor in 2019 was the lowest it has been since the government began using this measure in 1959.

Like almost all other social measures, the official definition of poverty has been subject to criticism. In particular, critics have charged that the income standard used by the government overestimates the number of poor people. First, only money income (such as wages and cash benefits from government) is included in the standard. Not included are noncash benefits, such as SNAP (food stamps), Medicare and Medicaid health benefits, and subsidized housing benefits, which many of the poor receive from the government. Counting such noncash benefits as income, critics argue, would greatly reduce the number of people officially defined as poor. On the other hand, when the Census Bureau makes adjustments for out-of-pocket costs, like those for medical care, the percentage of poor people shows an increase over the official measure, even when noncash benefits are included as income.[10]

relative deprivation

A definition of poverty that holds that individuals with less, regardless of their absolute income level, will feel poor or deprived relative to those who have more

poverty threshold

Income level differentiated by family size and annually adjusted for inflation, below which government defines individuals as being poor

Figure 15.2   Number and Proportion of Poor People in the United States, Selected Years, 1960–2019

Although the absolute number of poor people remains high, the percentage of poor in the population has been below 15 percent in recent years.

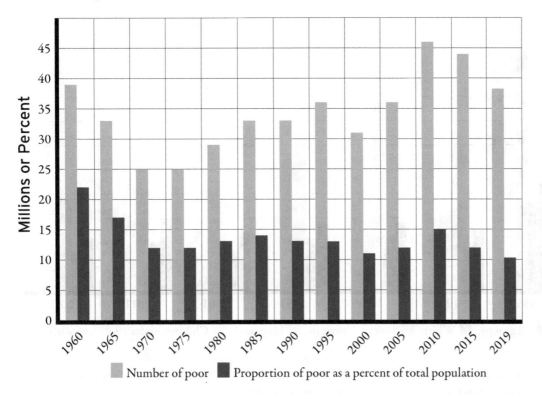

Number of poor ■ Proportion of poor as a percent of total population

DATA SOURCE: U.S. Census Bureau, Income and Poverty in the United States: 2019 (Washington, DC: Government Printing Office, 2020).

While aggregate numbers on poverty are open to criticism, no one questions the fact that poverty occurs disproportionately among different groups. Figure 15.3 displays poverty rates for selected groups in selected years since 1959. The graph shows that the poverty rate for whites tends to fall below the overall poverty rate, while the proportion of African Americans in poverty is consistently higher than the rate for the total population. The *absolute number* of whites in poverty exceeds the number of poor African Americans, but a higher *proportion* of the African American population is poor. In 1959, less than 20 percent of whites but more than 50 percent of African Americans were defined as poor. By 2019, 7.3 percent of non-Hispanic whites but 18.7 percent of African Americans still fell below the poverty threshold. Persons identifying themselves as Hispanic or Latinx have poverty rates higher than whites but slightly lower than African Americans. Poverty among children has fluctuated but is consistently at a higher rate than among the population as a whole. The group that has experienced the most consistent positive gains over the past several decades is the elderly. Although this group has historically experienced poverty at above average rates, recently that trend has begun to reverse itself. Today, whites and the elderly are among the groups least likely to be poor.

Figure 15.3 Poverty Rates for Selected Groups, Selected Years, 1959–2019

Although poverty rates are lower than they were in 1959, substantial differences among groups remain.

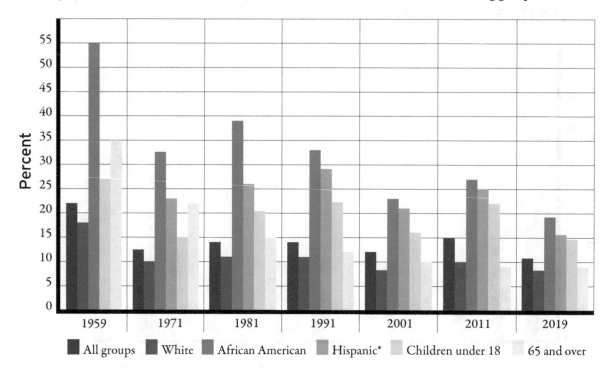

All groups ■ White ■ African American ■ Hispanic* ■ Children under 18 ■ 65 and over

DATA SOURCE: U.S. Census Bureau, Income and Poverty in the United States: 2019 (Washington, DC: Government Printing Office, 2020).

* Hispanic data were not available for 1959. The Hispanic data for the 1971 column are from 1972.

As Figure 15.3 indicates, poverty among children continues to exceed the overall poverty rate. The figure does not show that poverty rates differ among children of different races. The Census Bureau reports the startling fact that in 2019, more than 26 percent of African American children and nearly 21 percent of Hispanic children under the age of eighteen were poor.

15.4b Poverty as a Political and Social Problem

Widespread poverty in a land of affluence has been a vexing political and social problem, especially since the national government assumed a massive social welfare role over a half-century ago. Economic inequality persists despite the huge sums of money spent by the national government over the past half-century to ameliorate economic distress among citizens in need. Why people are poor is an issue that has bitterly divided citizens, politicians, policy analysts, and academics. No single reason can adequately explain the existence of poverty among such a large number of people.

Social scientists have generally offered two sets of explanations for why people are poor. The first holds that people are poor because they lack *personal qualities*, such as ambition or intelligence, which make successful competition in the economic market-place possible. A second explanation centers on the kind of social, economic, and cultural environment that is likely to be fertile ground for poverty. In this view, poverty is the

result of, for example, the absence of a good education, a weak or crumbling family structure, disability, or the lack of job opportunities. Sorting out these distinctions is no easy task. As an example, continuing failure to find a job can weaken ambition to go on.

The population of poor people in the United States is a constantly changing kaleidoscope, for individuals are falling into and climbing out of officially defined poverty from one year to the next. Personal crises, like the death of the family income-earner or loss of a job, can at least temporarily make some individuals poor. A rising unemployment rate increases the level of poverty, while falling unemployment has the opposite effect. Indeed, employment is no guarantee against poverty. In 2018, about 4.5 percent of the labor force, or 7 million people in the US, were classified as the **working poor**. These people worked or looked for work for at least half the year and yet were still officially defined as poor because their low earnings were not enough to pull their families above the poverty line.[11]

A range of government policies seeks to deal with poverty.

(FashionStock.com / Shutterstock)

Some proportion of the poor are in what some poverty analysts call an **underclass**, comprising individuals isolated from the rest of society and for whom poverty is a continuing way of life. Chronic unemployment, unstable family environments, welfare dependency, and a high incidence of crime are all characteristics of underclass poverty. Whether the growth of the underclass can be attributed to systemic economic changes that have resulted in fewer blue-collar jobs and more unemployment, self-destructive behavior patterns among the underclass poor, or some combination of economic and behavioral factors is an issue that reflects the general debate over the causes of poverty.[12]

Grappling with poverty in some way is the object of a range of government policies, including income transfer programs such as Social Security; but two categories of policy strategies illuminate government approaches. The first are **curative strategies** designed to get at the "root" causes of the problem, so that individuals can get out of poverty and lead productive, self-sufficient lives.[13] Expenditures on education, particularly targeted to the disadvantaged, are an example. In addition, employment training seeks to give individuals the skills necessary for a measure of economic success. Perhaps the most controversial example was the community action program of Lyndon Johnson's War on Poverty in the mid-1960s. That effort sought to involve the poor in initiating and coordinating local community efforts to combat poverty. The program began with the high hopes and optimism so characteristic of the Great Society; however, political support evaporated when some local community action groups, in their efforts to exert political power, criticized what they saw as the insensitivity of elected officials.[14]

The second category of antipoverty strategies is **alleviative** in approach;[15] that is, these strategies do not seek to cure poverty but simply to make it more bearable. Rather than trying to lift people out of poverty, such programs give cash or *in-kind* (noncash) *benefits* to poor individuals or families to help keep them afloat financially. Various forms of housing assistance, the school lunch program, and emergency fuel assistance fall into this category. In terms of expenditures, these programs as a group make up the national government's principal policy strategy for dealing with poverty. Illustrations of major means-tested programs whose principal aim is the alleviation of poverty are discussed in the following sections.

working poor

Individuals who, despite being employed or seeking employment, are still defined as poor because their low earnings are not enough to put them above the poverty threshold

underclass

A proportion of the poor comprising individuals isolated from the rest of society and for whom poverty is a continuing way of life

curative strategies

Policy strategies designed to reach the fundamental causes of poverty and to enable individuals to get out of poverty and lead productive, self-sufficient lives

alleviative strategies

Policy strategies designed to make poverty more bearable for individuals rather than designed to attack poverty by reaching its fundamental causes

15.4c Temporary Assistance for Needy Families

One of the oldest alleviative poverty programs at the national level is **Temporary Assistance for Needy Families (TANF)**, first enacted (under the name Aid to Families with Dependent Children [AFDC]) as part of the landmark Social Security Act of 1935. The program originally provided cash benefits for needy children under the age of sixteen, but subsequent amendments have raised the age limit and extended benefits to one adult relative or to both parents in needy families. TANF is a program administered by the states under the Office of Family Assistance in the Department of Health and Human Services and jointly funded about equally by state and federal revenues. The states determine eligibility standards and payment levels within guidelines established by the national government. Monthly benefits vary widely among the states. For example, the maximum monthly payment for a family of three in 2018 was $170 in Mississippi, $185 in Tennessee, $714 in California, and $923 in Alaska.[16]

The number of TANF recipients grew tremendously from its beginnings until the reform efforts of the 1990s. Just over half a million individuals received benefits in the first year of the program in 1936, but that number increased to almost 8.5 million in 1970. In fact, the number grew by 3.5 million between 1969 and 1971. The rate of growth declined in the early 1970s, and even the absolute number of beneficiaries declined in some later years. In 1994 the program hit its peak with 14.4 million individuals receiving cash benefits. Due to the reform described below, the caseload figures declined in the early 2000s and were about 2.9 million in 2019.[17]

Welfare was among the most controversial poverty programs because of the widely held perception that it creates a "welfare dependency" that is passed on from one generation of families to the next, with little hope of breaking out of what seems like a vicious cycle. Conservatives saw welfare as subsidizing the undeserving, while liberals decried the insensitivity of bureaucrats administering the program and the insufficiency of resources devoted to it.

Concerns from both ends of the political spectrum and the goal of making welfare less of an alleviative and more of a curative antipoverty strategy led Congress to pass the Personal Responsibility and Work Opportunity Reconciliation Act of 1996. Known more commonly as the **Welfare Reform Act**, this piece of legislation fundamentally altered welfare. First, in changing the acronym from AFDC to TANF, the law stressed the temporary nature of the cash payment program. In an effort to break the cycle of poverty, the act placed a two consecutive-year limit on receipt of benefits and a five-year lifetime limit. As recipients reached these limits, the states removed them from the rolls. The reform also required recipients to work at least part-time while receiving benefits, providing some exemptions for education and job training. While the reform effort has been undeniably successful at reducing welfare caseloads and expenditures (at least partially as a result of its strict time limitations), it remains to be seen whether this harsh approach to poverty will be successful at reducing poverty in the US over the long run.

15.4d Supplemental Security Income

President Nixon's proposal to guarantee incomes for poor families seemed to violate a widely held public expectation that incomes should be earned rather than simply granted. In this view, both economic efficiency and simple fairness demand that incomes be rewards for contributions to society rather than guarantees unrelated to any such contributions. However, in 1972 Congress enacted what amounts to a guaranteed income program for certain groups. Under the **Supplemental Security Income (SSI)** program, administered

Temporary Assistance for Needy Families (TANF)

Social welfare program, administered by the states and jointly funded by state and national revenues, that provides cash assistance, in participating states, to needy children and one adult relative or an unemployed parent

Welfare Reform Act

A 1996 law that fundamentally altered the AFDC welfare program by renaming it TANF and placing work and training requirements, as well as time limits, on its use

Supplemental Security Income (SSI)

Social welfare program administered by the Social Security Administration whereby the national government guarantees a certain level of income for the needy, aged, blind, and disabled

by the Social Security Administration, the national government guarantees a certain level of income for the needy among the aged, blind, and disabled. In 2020, the program spent more than $53 billion to serve over 8 million needy people.[18] The national government's successful enactment of SSI shortly after the bitter battle over a proposal to guarantee incomes for poor families suggests the warm political support enjoyed by certain categories of individuals. In effect, SSI represents a national commitment to support aged, blind, and disabled poor people who are clearly unable to support themselves.

POLITICS AND IDEAS

Political Ideologies and the Welfare State

Policy debate is fundamentally a collision of ideas on what the appropriate role of government should be. Nowhere has the collision of ideas been more evident than in debate over social welfare. The scope of government expenditures, the number of people directly touched, and the shape of political discourse throughout this and most of the previous century all attest to the central place of the issue in our politics.

The contemporary welfare state is primarily the handiwork of political liberals, of whom most have been in the Democratic Party. Viewing government as helper, provider, and protector of the disadvantaged, liberals successfully initiated and extended the programs that collectively make up the welfare state. In the liberal view, a significant government presence is right, just, and necessary to help redress the economic imbalances in a capitalist system.

Conservatives have generally opposed the creation and extension of social welfare programs, from the original Social Security Act in the New Deal to the Medicare program in the Great Society. They believe that such programs entrust government with decisions that should be left to individuals and groups in the private marketplace. Government intervention smothers initiative, risks values like independence, and threatens to overwhelm citizens in mindless bureaucracy and red tape.

Liberals and conservatives have been the major contestants in this battle of ideas, but other ideologies have contributed their own perspectives to the debate over government's social welfare role. Neoliberals see some welfare policies as too generous to middle-class recipients. Neoconservatives accept the necessity of a modest welfare state, but they argue that government's capacity to solve social problems has often been overestimated and that public programs frequently do not make good on their promises. Ideologies on the margins of political debate raise even more fundamental concerns. Democratic socialists press for much greater government control of the economy and a comprehensive welfare system. At the opposite end of the spectrum, libertarians argue that government should be limited to protecting the nation from external attack and preserving the individual rights of citizens. They question the very existence of a contemporary welfare state.

Today, few people seriously contest a fundamental social welfare role for government. Liberals and conservatives battle over whether more or less money should be spent on social welfare programs. However, social welfare policy debate has taken some new twists and turns. To maintain political support for welfare and to limit long-term dependency, liberals accepted a work requirement and time limit for welfare recipients in the 1996 Welfare Reform Act. Conservatives, for example, by supporting voucher programs to allow the poor to purchase their own housing, have tried to blend their traditional support for market incentives with acceptance of social welfare policies.

The shape of social welfare lies at the center of battles over budget deficits now common in American politics. Budget makers wrestle with the question of whether deficits can be eliminated without some reductions in social welfare spending. Conflicting ideas over what is appropriate government action complicate this debate over deficits. On what criteria should judgments on cuts or increases in social welfare programs be made? What solutions do you see to the enduring problem of poverty in the US?

15.4e Medicaid

Medicaid is a means-tested program, enacted in the Great Society, designed to provide medical care for the needy. Unlike TANF and SSI, **Medicaid** provides the poor with **in-kind benefits** rather than cash. That is, the needy receive a service (medical care) rather than cash, and money from the program goes directly to the providers (hospitals, physicians, etc.) of that service. The program, which consists of both Medicaid and the Children's Health Insurance Program (CHIP), funded medical care for more than 72 million needy people in 2020.[19] Like TANF, Medicaid is funded jointly by state and federal revenues and administered by individual states within guidelines established by the national government. The Centers for Medicare and Medicaid Services is the unit in the national government responsible for the program. While specific rules of eligibility are highly complex, individuals who receive TANF and SSI benefits are generally eligible for Medicaid services; children who fall through cracks in these programs are covered by CHIP. The rapid growth in Medicaid costs has become a political issue. In 2020, the program cost about $447 billion, a hefty sum in a year of fiscal strains. The Affordable Care Act created an option for states to begin expanding Medicaid coverage to cover all residents up to 133 percent of the poverty line in 2014. Though, as of late 2020, twelve states have chosen to participate, this option has proven very popular among voters and has increased the number of recipients by several million; it will bring continued change to the Medicaid program in the coming years.

15.4f The Supplemental Nutrition Assistance Program

Like Medicaid, the **Supplemental Nutrition Assistance Program (SNAP)** (formerly known as the *food stamp program*), was enacted in the 1960s to provide in-kind benefits to the needy rather than cash. The Food and Nutrition Service in the Department of Agriculture administers this program through state and local welfare offices. In this case, beneficiaries receive coupons (now typically in the form of debit cards) that they trade for food items at grocery stores or supermarkets. The coupons represent money, but they can be used only to purchase food. The national government pays for the cost of the cards but shares the administrative costs of the program with the states. Individuals and families who meet an income test qualify for SNAP. Like TANF beneficiaries, the number of food stamp recipients grew tremendously over time, from fewer than a half million people in the mid-1960s to more than 22 million in 1981.[20] In response to charges of waste and fraud in the program, eligibility rules were tightened in the early 1980s and the number of beneficiaries declined. However, rules were made more liberal later in the decade. The program is highly sensitive to changes in the economy. With higher unemployment rates, more people depend on the program for help. In 2008, what had originally been called the food stamp program was renamed SNAP. In 2020, national and state governments spent over $60 billion for about 43 million SNAP beneficiaries.[21]

15.4g Social Welfare Policy and Future Challenges

Since the late 1960s, social welfare debate has generally revolved not around new program initiatives but around the ways in which the nation can pay for existing programs, which consume ever-greater resources. If presidents Roosevelt and Johnson attempted to expand

Medicaid

A means-tested medical care program providing in-kind medical benefits for the poor

in-kind benefits

Noncash benefits, such as medical care services, that the needy receive from some social welfare programs

Supplemental Nutrition Assistance Program (SNAP)

A means-tested program (formerly known as the food stamp program) that provides the eligible needy with cards that can be used only to purchase food

the national government role in social welfare, presidents Reagan and Clinton tried to find economically possible and politically acceptable limits to that role. Changing economic conditions and how policy makers like President Joe Biden decide to deal with budget deficits and demands for federal spending in other sectors, such as military and defense policy, will determine the shape of social welfare policies in the twenty-first century. How much should social welfare cuts contribute to deficit reduction and other spending needs, or should social welfare programs be immune to cuts? If cuts are made, which groups—the elderly, or the working poor, or children, for example—should bear the brunt of the social and economic costs of the changes? The future shape of social welfare policies depends on how elected officials, interest groups, and individual voters respond to such questions.

15.5   Environmental Policy

While the previous section focused on the service-providing aspects of domestic policy via social welfare, this section addresses the regulatory aspects of the government's role in domestic policy via the environment. Over the past several decades, environmental protection has emerged as a highly visible political issue. Limiting pollution of the land, air, and water about us, as well as addressing global climate change, has become a major policy objective at all levels of government. Public policies to protect the environment try to cope with the by-products of technological change, such as air pollution in a nation so dependent on the automobile. At the same time, environmental policy relies on scientific research and technological advances to limit pollution, such as the installation of catalytic converters in cars to reduce auto exhaust emissions, or the promotion of hybrid vehicles and solar panels. Science and technology can also help to identify environmental problems, but the uncertainty of risk complicates regulatory efforts to reduce pollution and address climate change.

15.5a   Environmentalism on the Policy Agenda

The imposing catalog of threats to the environment helps to explain the deep well of political support for environmental protection efforts. Toxic waste dumps throughout the country contain used chemicals and other waste products of industrial production that can pose serious health threats. Burning fossil fuels to produce electricity emits into the atmosphere particles that are encircled by water droplets and carried by winds for hundreds of miles. They fall in the form of acid rain and kill forests and water life. Burning fossil fuels and the massive burning of tropical forestland for development dumps carbon dioxide into the atmosphere that traps the sun's heat and risks causing global warming with potentially dire consequences for the earth's climate. Scientists have also detected deterioration in the layer of ozone in the stratosphere high above the earth's surface. Ozone protects the planet from the damaging effects of the sun's ultraviolet radiation. Depletion of the protective ozone layer risks ultraviolet radiation damage to crops and an increase in the incidence of

The Endangered Species Act created federal protections for species at risk of extinction. The U.S. Fish and Wildlife Service maintains a searchable database of these threatened and endangered animals and plants at this website:

http://www.bvtlab.com/7DSBt

(Shutterstock)

Air pollution can make breathing hazardous for more than 110 million Americans living in certain regions of the country.

skin cancer. Taken as a whole, these increasingly erratic conditions make up a key problem for governments to confront in the twenty-first century: global climate change.

Radon, a colorless, odorless gas, seeps into millions of homes from decaying uranium in the earth and threatens occupants with higher risks of lung cancer. The mountains of solid waste the nation produces pose a national problem touching every community. Great strides have been made in limiting air pollution; but the Environmental Protection Agency reported in 2020 that even though air quality has improved over the past twenty years, more than 81 million people live in counties where the air is unhealthy at times due to high levels of pollutants—a consequence of the eighty million tons of pollution released into the air annually.[22]

One reason this catalog of dangers seems so imposing is that we now have a more refined capacity to detect environmental changes and minute quantities of potentially harmful substances. Sophisticated instruments and procedures allow environmental scientists to detect radon, pesticide residues, and tears in the ozone layer. In part, environmental issues get on the policy agenda because new knowledge pushes them there.

Protecting the environment has potent political support in the first decades of the twenty-first century. Campaigning politicians from across the political spectrum seek to align themselves with the environmentalist cause. The 2000 presidential campaign featured both a major-party candidate, Al Gore, who had made environmentalism a key feature of his political career, and the emergence of a formidable third party, the Green Party, which placed environmental policy at the core of its political agenda. Significant majorities of people in the US judge that high environmental standards are necessary to deal with a deteriorating environment, even if that means setting higher emissions and pollution standards for business and spending more money on the development of renewable energy resources.[23] This intense concern for environmental issues—focusing on topics such as logging in the national forests, the safety risks of offshore oil drilling, renewable energy sources, climate change, and cleaner fuel technology—continued through the early 2000s, with 74 percent of the US public in 2019 saying that they worry either a great deal or a fair amount about the quality of the environment and 65 percent saying that environmental protection should be given priority even at the risk of curbing economic growth.[24] The executive agency that has the task of meeting these public demands may have the toughest job in Washington.

15.5b The Environmental Protection Agency and Government Regulation

Environmental Protection Agency (EPA)

An independent agency that controls and abates air and water pollution and protects the environment from pollution by solid wastes, pesticides, radiation, and toxic substances

The political environment of the **Environmental Protection Agency (EPA)** contains a mix of pressures and constraints that severely tax efforts to meet the policy goal of environmental protection. The agency must deal with a staggering array of potential threats to the environment, including thousands of sources of pollution throughout the nation. Public and environmental interest group expectations for agency action are high, but so are the anxieties of businesses and industries that see environmental regulation as an economic cost that someone must pay.

POLITICAL CONTROVERSIES

Nuclear Power and the Environment

The high promise and menacing threat of nuclear energy have posed stark policy questions over the past seventy years. Flowing from basic research in particle physics, the ability to create nuclear fission reactions with enormous releases of energy led to development of weapons capable of almost incomprehensible destruction at the end of World War II. Nuclear technology also seemed to hold promise as a boundless source of energy to meet the nation's growing need for electrical power; the bubble broke in 1979, however, when an accident at the Three Mile Island nuclear power plant in Pennsylvania led to a partial meltdown of the reactor. The accident so shook public confidence in nuclear reactor safety that the industry has not yet recovered. No new nuclear power plants have been ordered since. Anxieties about nuclear power were exacerbated by the more serious accident in 1986 at the Chernobyl nuclear plant in the Ukraine, which was then part of the Soviet Union.

In a classic illustration of the promise and threat that science and technology pose for public policy, nuclear power is at the same time pressed as a solution to some environmental problems but feared to be a creator of others. For example, many climatologists argue that extensive use of fossil fuels like coal and oil releases into the atmosphere carbon dioxide that, along with other gases such as methane and nitrous oxides, acts like a shield that traps heat from the sun. This global warming creates the risk of dramatic climate changes that can turn fertile farmland into desert and that can put coastal regions under water by melting polar ice and raising ocean levels. A greater reliance on nuclear power plants to produce electricity would reduce fossil fuel damage to the atmosphere, but public anxiety about the safety of nuclear plants makes greater reliance on nuclear energy a controversial option. In fact, at the same time that fears about global warming emerged, New York State negotiated with the Long Island Lighting Company to close down the Shoreham nuclear power plant. Long Island residents and state and local elected officials opposed the plant because of fears that evacuation of the surrounding densely populated areas could not be quickly and reasonably accomplished in the event of a nuclear accident. Thus, a newly constructed, $5.5 billion plant never became operational. The decision not to use a facility that would reduce dependence on fossil fuels and that might help limit global warming illustrates the tough policy choices posed by nuclear energy. To many Long Islanders the decision was a wise move greeted by relief. To nuclear power advocates, closing down a perfectly good nuclear plant was folly.

Another tough environmental policy issue concerns the management of nuclear waste. Spent nuclear fuel remains highly radioactive, and potentially quite dangerous, for several hundred thousand years. Since no one wants this dangerous by-product near them, finding locations for safe storage of nuclear waste has been a troubling domestic policy problem. In 2002, after a decades-long, $4 billion scientific study, President Bush signed legislation establishing a new waste facility at Yucca Mountain, Nevada. The plan was for the waste depository to be maintained by the Department of Energy's Office of Civilian Radioactive Waste Management, making it the nation's "first long-term geologic repository for spent nuclear fuel and high-level radioactive waste."[1] Supporters of the project claim that a central location at a remote and secure site provides the safest solution for the problem of radioactive waste. Critics argue that an accident could endanger millions of lives (Yucca Mountain is just one hundred miles from Las Vegas) and that transporting radioactive waste from all over the country exacerbates the risks of radioactive contamination. Despite years of planning and development, the site remains years away from opening; and in 2009, after years of budget reductions for the project, the Obama administration announced it would look for a new site for a repository. In 2016, the owners of California's Diablo Canyon plant announced they would be closing the facility—California's last remaining nuclear power plant—by 2025.

In light of the promise and problems of nuclear energy, should more nuclear power plants be built, should more be closed down, or should we use less energy?

1. Office of Civilian Radioactive Waste Management, "The Yucca Mountain Project," http://www.ymp.gov/ (October 13, 2002).

(USDA photo by Charles O'Rear via Wikimedia)

The EPA administers laws that try to protect air, water, and land by regulating emission standards, toxic wastes, pesticides, radiation standards, and potentially dangerous substances.

The Environmental Protection Agency was established in 1970 by pulling together into a single unit the antipollution programs then spread among several agencies. More than four decades after its creation, the EPA is one of the biggest, and probably the most visible, regulatory agencies, employing over 15,000 people and (in fiscal year 2021) spending about $7.5 billion annually. The agency must administer laws that try to protect air, water, and land—a daunting task that encompasses regulation of auto emission standards, toxic wastes, pesticides, radiation standards, and potentially dangerous substances such as asbestos, mercury, lead, and radon. The demands on the EPA are a recipe of political passions, economic considerations, and scientific findings, a mix that makes the EPA's task at once fascinating and frustrating.

Since much of the EPA's work is based on research and technological innovation, science and technology help to structure its decisions, but party politics also play a role. For example, for fiscal year 2017, the EPA requested from Congress about $235 million for efforts to address climate change, but by fiscal year 2021 the budget request had eliminated climate change research entirely and focused more on reducing regulatory barriers.[25] The former request was made under a Democratic president and the latter under a Republican one; the priorities of political parties have an effect on the direction of environmental policy.

Science and technology inevitably play a role in EPA decisions. Substances posing health and environmental threats are frequently invisible, their consequences long-term, and their structures and incidence discoverable only by highly trained investigators in fields such as chemistry and the life sciences. Does the runoff of pesticides into rivers ultimately damage human health? What will global climate change do to climate patterns and ecosystems? How much of a carcinogen must an individual ingest before serious health effects occur? Ultimately, much of the EPA's work entails **risk assessment**, or estimating the degree of environmental risk a pollutant or ecosystem change poses, and **risk management**, or making decisions that try to reduce or contain the identified risk.[26] Even with the trappings of scientific research, however, risk assessment retains a large measure of uncertainty. Different models and different data sets can produce different answers to the question of whether a contaminant in minute amounts causes cancer.

Scientific research can help the EPA ask the appropriate questions and frame the debate; but if action is to be taken and environmental goals are to be reached, the agency must issue specific regulations that limit pollution by trying to change the behavior of individuals, companies, and governments. Regulatory agencies such as the EPA ultimately receive all their power from Congress, which adopts policies through the statutes it enacts. As the policy process chapter explained, the implementation of policies or the translation of policy ideas into action is left to bureaucrats. Congress identifies problems and establishes policy goals but delegates to regulatory agencies the power to write rules that specify in greater detail the definitions, criteria, and standards of behavior necessary to meet congressional intent. For example, bringing to bear its highly technical expertise, the Nuclear Regulatory Commission issues detailed rules guiding the operation of nuclear power plants. As another illustration, the Environmental Protection Agency

risk assessment

The process of estimating the potentially dangerous consequences of damage that might be caused by a particular practice, such as smoking, or by the use of a particular product, such as the impact of the burning of fossil fuels on global warming

risk management

The process of making decisions that try to reduce or contain identified risks

specifies maximum contaminant levels in drinking water. Congress may be very vague or very explicit in its statutes directing the work of regulatory agencies. Individuals in regulatory agencies with scientific and technical expertise are ultimately given the tasks of specifying, detailing, and defining in matters such as safe nuclear reactor procedures and acceptable drinking water contaminant levels.

Environmental regulations at once promise environmental benefits and impose monetary costs. Clean air and clean water are not free, and much debate ensues over who ought to pay how much. Heightened by media attention to toxic waste dumps, contaminated water, and carcinogens in the air, the EPA faces passionate demands from environmental groups to take aggressive action. At the same time, the agency is required by law or by presidential executive order to take into account economic considerations to ensure that the presumed benefits of environmental rules outweigh their costs. The EPA is, therefore, frequently in the middle of the political struggle over the appropriate role for government in environmental regulation, an issue that reverberates in other areas of government regulation as well. For example, President Trump took climate change and other environmental concerns less seriously than many of his predecessors, and his EPA administrators, Scott Pruitt and then Andrew Wheeler, echoed those sentiments with smaller budget requests and a scaling back of regulations. President Biden is likely to reverse this course because he campaigned on promises to take climate change and other environmental issues seriously by listening to experts and investing in technologies like wind power.

(Sheila Fitzgerald / Shutterstock)

As of June 30, 2018, Tesla Motors had sold more than 360,000 electric cars worldwide since delivery of its first Tesla Roadster in 2008.

15.5c The Future of Environmental Policy

As the US looks forward, environmental policy challenges abound. Our government's difficult task of balancing interests is, perhaps, highlighted best in this arena. The EPA and other federal agencies will continue to negotiate the conflicts between those seeking to preserve natural habitats and those wishing to pursue economic development of resources. Should we preserve the pristine environment of the Alaskan Arctic wilderness, or should we utilize this resource by drilling for oil there? Should we increase regulations and raise environmental standards for industries, even if this means economic hardship for some businesses and more expensive products for consumers? Should we join international efforts like the Paris Agreement to help slow the advance of global climate change, or should we study the issue further before taking any action? These are among the difficult questions American environmental policy must confront in the coming decades.

CHAPTER REVIEW

1. Government policies provide benefits to every income group. Social insurance and means-tested programs designed for the poor are the principal social welfare policies of the national government.

2. The philosophy of social Darwinism held that only a limited government role would allow society to progress, but substantial change in the activities of government began to occur in the Progressive Era. The real revolution in the social welfare role of the national government took place in the New Deal presidency of Franklin D. Roosevelt, who initiated a variety of new policies designed to cushion the economic hardship of the Great Depression. President Johnson's Great Society was the latest period of major new social welfare initiatives.

3. Social insurance programs, including Social Security and Medicare, tend to be the largest social welfare programs. The size of social insurance programs and the fact that their beneficiaries come from across the income spectrum mean that such programs can draw on widespread political support.

4. Poverty can be measured either relatively or according to some absolute standard. The causes and extent of poverty are continuing matters of debate, but official estimates based on an absolute income standard indicate that 10.5 percent of the US population in 2019 was poor. Programs designed to ameliorate poverty include Temporary Assistance for Needy Families, Medicaid, food stamps/SNAP, and Supplemental Security Income. In these "means-tested" programs, the national government, in most cases in cooperation with the states, grants cash or in-kind benefits to individuals who qualify on the basis of income.

5. Spending on some social welfare programs has been the target of budget cuts over the past two decades, but resistance to further cuts indicates the well of public support for a substantial social welfare policy role for the government. Many social welfare problems persist, but the future shape of social welfare programs depends on Americans' willingness to continue to support them in the face of other perceived fiscal needs.

6. Environmental protection efforts draw on a deep well of political support to deal with the varied threats to environmental quality. The Environmental Protection Agency, with the challenging task of administering the nation's environmental laws, confronts in its regulatory work a mix of political passions, economic considerations, and scientific data.

KEY TERMS

alleviative strategies 471

curative strategies 471

domestic policy 453

Environmental Protection Agency (EPA) 476

Great Society 459

incrementalism 462

in-kind benefits 474

means-tested programs 466

Medicaid 474

Medicare 464

New Deal 458

poverty threshold 468

Progressive Era 458

relative deprivation 468

risk assessment 478

risk management 478

social Darwinism 457

social entitlements 455

social insurance programs 461

social insurance programs 462

Social Security Act of 1935 462

social welfare 455

Supplemental Nutrition Assistance
Program (SNAP) 474

Supplemental Security Income (SSI) 472

Temporary Assistance for Needy
Families (TANF) 472

underclass 471

unemployment compensation 465

Welfare Reform Act 472

working poor 471

READINGS FOR FURTHER STUDY

Michael Harrington's *The Other America: Poverty in the United States*, reprint ed. (New York: Touchstone Books, 1997) was influential in moving poverty onto the policy agenda when it was first published in the early 1960s. This study is updated by *Rediscovering the Other America: The Continuing Crisis of Poverty and Inequality in the United States,* edited by Keith M. Kilty and Elizabeth A. Segal (New York: Routledge, 2003).

William Julius Wilson's *When Work Disappears: The World of the New Urban Poor* (New York: Vintage Books, 1997); Herbert J. Gans's *The War Against the Poor: The Underclass and Antipoverty Policy* (New York: Basic Books, 1996); and David K. Shipler's *The Working Poor: Invisible in America* (New York: Vintage, 2005) are good discussions of poverty and public policy.

An effort to understand issues of the contemporary working poor is *Nickel and Dimed: On (Not) Getting by in America* by Barbara Ehrenreich (New York: Picador, 2011).

The history of social welfare policy is described in Walter I. Trattner's *From Poor Law to Welfare State: A History of Social Welfare in America*, 6th ed. (New York: Free Press, 1999).

A good textbook approach to social welfare policy is *Social Welfare: Politics and Public Policy,* 8th ed., by Diana M. Dinitto and David H. Johnson (New York: Pearson, 2015).

An analysis of recent efforts to reform the welfare system is found in *Work Over Welfare: The Inside Story of the 1996 Welfare Reform Law* by Ron Haskins (Washington, DC: Brookings Institution Press, 2007) and in *Stretched Thin: Poor Families, Welfare Work, and Welfare Reform* by Sandra Morgen, Joan Acker, and Jill Weigt (Ithaca, NY: Cornell University Press, 2009).

Environmental policy is explored from a historical perspective in Samuel P. Hays's *A History of Environmental Politics Since 1945* (Pittsburgh, PA: University of Pittsburgh Press, 2000).

One of the most influential books in the development of an environmental movement in America when it was first released in 1962 was Rachel Carson's *Silent Spring* (Boston: Houghton Mifflin, 2002).

The process of environmental policy making is explored in Daniel J. Fiorino's *Making Environmental Policy* (Berkeley: University of California Press, 1995) and in Steven Cohen's *Understanding Environmental Policy*, 2nd ed. (New York: Columbia University Press, 2014).

A good text that explores the future of environmental policy is *Environmental Policy: New Directions for the Twenty-First Century*, 10th ed., by Norman J. Vig and Michael E. Kraft, eds (Washington, DC: CQ Press, 2018).

Finally, the relationship between technical experts and environmental policy advocates is examined in Frank Fischer's *Citizens, Experts, and the Environment: The Politics of Local Knowledge* (Durham, NC: Duke University Press, 2000).

NOTES

1. U.S. Bureau of the Census, *Historical Statistics of the United States: Colonial Times to 1970,* vol. 1 (Washington, DC: Government Printing Office, 1975), p. 332.

2. Richard Hofstadter, *Social Darwinism in American Thought,* rev. ed. (Boston: Beacon Press, 1955), p. 44.

3. Herbert Spencer, *Social Statics* (London: 1851; New York: Augustus M. Kelley, 1969), p. 323. For a review of the criticisms of social Darwinism, see Hofstadter, *Social Darwinism,* especially pp. 200–204.

4. Richard Hofstadter, *The Age of Reform* (New York: Knopf, 1955), p. 240.

5. See William E. Leuchtenburg, *The Perils of Prosperity, 1914–32,* 2nd ed. (Chicago: University of Chicago Press, 1993).

6. William F. Leuchtenburg, *Franklin D. Roosevelt and the New Deal* (New York: Harper & Row, 1963), pp. 43, 61.

7. Social Security Administration, *Annual Statistical Supplement to the Social Security Bulletin, 2020* https://www.ssa.gov/policy/docs/statcomps/supplement/2020/index.html (August 15, 2020).

8. For details on the program, see the Medicare website, located at http://www.medicare.gov/.

9. See Edward C. Banfield, *The Unheavenly City Revisited* (Prospect Heights, IL: Waveland Press, reissue 1990), pp. 129–130.

10. U.S. Census Bureau, *Income, Poverty, and Health Insurance Coverage in the United States: 2008* (Washington, DC: Government Printing Office, 2012).

11. For more detail on the working poor, see U.S. Bureau of Labor Statistics, *A Profile of the Working Poor, 2018* (Washington, DC: Government Printing Office, 2020).

12. See William Julius Wilson, *When Work Disappears: The World of the New Urban Poor* (New York: Vintage Books, 1997) and Herbert J. Gans, *The War Against the Poor: The Underclass and Antipoverty Policy* (New York: Basic Books, 1996).

13. For a discussion of curative strategies, see Thomas R. Dye, *Understanding Public Policy,* 10th ed. (Englewood Cliffs, NJ: Prentice-Hall, 2002).

14. For an interesting account of the community action program, see Daniel P. Moynihan, *Maximum Feasible Misunderstanding: Community Action in the War on Poverty* (New York: Free Press, 1970).

15. See Dye, *Understanding Public Policy.*

16. Congressional Research Service, "The Temporary Assistance for Needy Families (TANF) Block Grant: Responses to Frequently Asked Questions," July 16, 2020.

17. Ibid.

18. "SSI Monthly Statistics, June 2020," https://www.ssa.gov/policy/docs/statcomps/ssi_monthly/index.html (August 16, 2020).

19. Medicaid.gov, "April 2020 Medicaid and CHIP Enrollment Data Highlights," https://www.medicaid.gov/medicaid/program-information/medicaid-and-chip-enrollment-data/report-highlights/index.html (August 16, 2020).

20. Social Security Bulletin, *Annual Statistical Supplement, 1989,* p. 343.

21. Food and Nutrition Service, "SNAP Data Tables," https://www.fns.usda.gov/pd/supplemental-nutrition-assistance-program-snap (August 16, 2020).

22. Environmental Protection Agency, *Air-Trends,* http://www.epa.gov/air-trends/ (August 16, 2020).

23. The Gallup Organization, "Environment-Unfriendly Policies Have Yet to Damage Bush's Ratings," April 17, 2001, http://www.gallup.com (October 12, 2002).

24. The Gallup Organization, "Environment," March 10, 2019, http://www.gallup.com/poll/1615/Environment.aspx (August 16, 2020).

25. Environmental Protection Agency, "FY 2017 Proposed Budget Fact Sheet," https://www.epa.gov/planandbudget/fy-2017-proposed-budget-fact-sheet (July 25, 2016); United States Environmental Protection Agency Fiscal Year 2021 Justification of Appropriation Estimates for the Committee on Appropriations, February 2020, https://www.epa.gov/sites/production/files/2020-02/documents/fy-2021-congressional-justification-all-tabs.pdf (August 16, 2020).

26. These definitions are adapted from Science Advisory Board, *Reducing Risk: Setting Priorities and Strategies for Environmental Protection* (Washington, DC: Environmental Protection Agency, 1990), p. 2.

POP QUIZ

1. _____ are governmental programs directed specifically toward promoting the well-being of individuals and families (for example, social insurance).

2. The set of ideas that applied the theory of biological evolution to society and held that societal relationships occur within a struggle for survival in which only the fittest survive is known as _____.

3. _____ is a public health insurance program in which government pays the providers of health care for medical services given to patients who are aged or disabled.

4. _____ _____ are policy strategies designed to make poverty more bearable for individuals rather than designed to attack poverty by reaching its fundamental causes.

5. The independent agency that controls and abates air and water pollution and protects the environment from pollution from solid wastes, pesticides, radiation, and toxic substances is the _____.

6. The Progressive Era was a time when people applied Charles Darwin's theory of biological evolution to society and held that societal relationships occur within a struggle for survival in which only the fittest survive. T F

7. The Great Society was the policy initiatives enacted during the first two terms of President Franklin D. Roosevelt in an effort to relieve the suffering of those touched by the Depression. T F

8. Medicare is a public health insurance program in which government pays the providers of health care for medical services given to patients who are aged or disabled.   T   F

9. The Welfare Reform Act abolished the requirement that welfare recipients work at least part time in order to receive benefits.   T   F

10. Risk assessment is the process of making decisions that try to reduce or contain identified risks.   T   F

11. All of the following are programs initiated during the Great Society except the _____.
    A) Civil Rights Act
    B) Elementary and Secondary Act
    C) Social Security Act
    D) Food Stamp Act

12. The public health insurance program in which government pays the providers of health care for medical services given to patients who are aged or disabled is known as _____.
    A) Medicaid
    B) Supplemental Medical Insurance
    C) Social Security
    D) Medicare

13. Means-tested programs are a type of social welfare program in which government provides cash or in-kind benefits to individuals who qualify with which of the following?
    A) Having little or no income
    B) Having worked a minimum of ten years
    C) Having invested a set amount
    D) Having lived long lives

14. All *except* which of the following are attempts at welfare reform?
    A) Putting two-year limits on receiving benefits
    B) Providing unemployment compensation
    C) Changing the title from AFDC to TANF
    D) Requiring recipients to work at least part time

15. The process of making decisions that try to reduce or contain identified risks is called _____.
    A) risk assessment
    B) curative strategies
    C) alleviative strategies
    D) risk management

Answers:
1. Social welfare   2. social Darwinism
3. Medicare   4. Alleviative strategies
5. Environmental Protection Agency   6. F
7. F   8. T   9. F   10. F   11. C   12. D
13. A   14. B   15. D

Chapter 16

FOREIGN POLICY

In This Chapter

16.1   America's Role in the World
16.2   The Policy Machinery
16.3   Domestic Policy and National Security
16.4   Current Issues in Foreign and Defense Policy

Chapter Objectives

Foreign and defense policy are central concerns of the American government. The president spends well over half his time on these issues. Defense and security spending consumes about 15 percent of the total budget, representing about 53 percent of the discretionary part of the federal budget; and American military expenditures account for about 37 percent of all such expenditures worldwide, as much as the next seven countries combined.[1] The advent of nuclear, biological, and chemical weapons of mass destruction has raised the stakes of policy to enormous levels. Whereas a mistake in domestic policy can be serious, one in foreign and defense policy can be fatal.

During this period of endless crisis, personalities and events have influenced American policies and political institutions. Of particular importance are the roles of the president, Congress, and various agencies. This chapter also explores the effects of special economic and ethnic interests on defense and diplomacy as well as the major problems facing America as the world's twenty-first century superpower fighting a war on terrorism.

Foreign and defense policies are central concerns of the US government.

(Shutterstock)

isolationism

A belief that America should not involve itself in the quarrels of Europe and Asia and should pursue a policy of military nonintervention

foreign policy

Efforts to pursue national objectives beyond the geographic boundaries of the nation by engaging either diplomatically or militarily with one or more foreign nations or multinational organizations

internationalism

A foreign policy perspective that concludes that America's interests in peace abroad and liberty at home require its permanent involvement in world affairs

Cold War

An era of intense ideological tension between the Soviet Union and its allies and the United States and its allies lasting from roughly the end of World War II to the collapse of the Soviet Union in 1991

16.1 America's Role in the World

Prior to World War II, US involvement in world affairs had been sporadic. US participation in World War I was followed by our rejection of the League of Nations treaty and a withdrawal from active leadership in world affairs. Until the Japanese attack on Pearl Harbor on December 7, 1941, George Washington's advice, given in his farewell address, to "steer clear of permanent alliances with any portion of the foreign world" made good sense to most Americans. Especially in the 1920s and 1930s, **isolationism** was the American credo in **foreign policy**. This was the belief in noninvolvement in the affairs of other countries, especially staying aloof from armed conflict elsewhere in the world.

America emerged from World War II as the predominant industrial and military power. In the post–World War II era a new American credo was born: **internationalism**. This was the belief in the necessity of involvement in the affairs of other countries in order to protect the nation's political and economic security. Most Americans became convinced that peace abroad and liberty at home required our permanent involvement in global affairs. Accepting this new role, America took the lead in 1945 to form the United Nations. However, the breakdown of Soviet-American relations in 1946 and 1947 illustrated that the new era of internationalism meant not only responsibility but conflict and tension as well. After surviving the tense **Cold War**, which lasted for more than four decades, America emerged as the seeming victor of the struggle at the end of the 1980s. The collapse of the Soviet empire, however, did not mean smooth sailing ahead for American foreign policy. The post–Cold War era has seen America's role in the world change and expand in unanticipated directions. Some have welcomed America's leadership in global policy, which has included foreign aid contributions intended to stimulate developing economies. Others have found America's new internationalism domineering, paternalistic, and unwanted. A few have even taken extreme and unjust measures to express their anger at America—such as the terrorist attacks on the World Trade Center and Pentagon and the ongoing, smaller-scale killings. Today, the challenge of US foreign

policy is to provide political and economic leadership while ensuring national security. A solid majority of Americans (69 percent) favors the United States taking a major or leading role, but the percentage of Americans favoring a more limited role has risen from 19 percent to 30 percent over the past seventeen years.[2]

16.1a   The Cold War and the Post–Cold War Era

Although the United States and the Soviet Union had been allies during World War II, the rupture of relations between them had numerous causes that were steeped in mistrust and ideological division. Given the historic record, each nation had ample reasons to suspect the other.

Along with Britain and France, America had intervened militarily in Russia soon after the communist revolution of 1917 to obstruct that revolution and aid the Russian anticommunist forces. Although this intervention was brief and unsuccessful, it symbolized America's hostility toward this new revolutionary state. Finally, in 1933, America formally recognized the Soviet Union on the unrealized expectation of expanded trade; and during World War II, the countries became allies. That alliance was never easy. America delayed opening a second front in Western Europe, leaving the Soviets alone on the continent to face the German army. While the United States worked closely with Great Britain on the atomic bomb project, it refused even to inform the Soviets about the project until the bomb was used against Japan. Immediately after the war ended in Europe, President Harry Truman (1945–1953) abruptly curtailed providing military supplies, through a program known as lend-lease, to the Soviet Union. Thus the Soviets contended that they were never treated as a genuine ally by the United States.

Ideological differences added to the lack of trust. From the outset of their revolution, the Soviets believed that the Western capitalist states were hostile and would give them grudging acceptance, at best. From the American perspective, Soviet communism presented a profound challenge to our institutions and values. The Soviets emphasized economic development above all and saw no function for representative democracy, freedom of speech and religion, free enterprise, or independent trade unions.

Through this prism of mutual distrust the United States and the Soviet Union found it difficult to resolve the complex issues created by the defeats of Germany and Japan. As the Soviet army pushed German forces out of Poland, Romania, and Bulgaria in 1945, the Soviets imposed communist regimes on those countries. American suspicion of Soviet motives and hostility to the communist social system made it impossible to accept with tranquility Soviet control of Eastern Europe, now described as being sealed from the West by an "iron curtain." Most American leaders were convinced by 1946 that Soviet domination of Eastern Europe was a first step toward the control of all Europe.

The Soviets resented American insistence on free elections in Eastern Europe, arguing that they had a legitimate claim to dominant political influence in bordering countries vital to their security. The failure of the two superpowers to agree on the Eastern European

The failure of the United States and the Soviet Union to agree on the disposition of Germany resulted in the creation of two German states. The German capital was divided in half—into East Berlin and West Berlin—and separated by the Berlin Wall.

(iStock / Getty Images Plus)

POLITICS AND IDEAS

Contrasting Approaches to Foreign Policy: Idealism, Realism, and Isolationism

American foreign policy is a complex mixture of domestic pressures, geopolitical interests, and ideas. Over the course of the past 120 years, several fundamental ideas about foreign policy have emerged and have found articulate spokespersons and advocates.

One of those ideas is the concept of realism, which accepts conflict as a permanent part of international politics. Realists believe that foreign policy can, at best, limit conflict, not eliminate it. Peace and national self-interest, from the realist view, are best assured by constructing a stable balance of power. Since not all conflicts threaten the balance of power, realists support a policy of limits: A nation should only commit itself to those struggles where vital interests are at stake and when it has the means to prevail. President Theodore Roosevelt (1901–1909) was one of the earliest exponents of realism.

Roosevelt asserted America's primary interest in the Caribbean, where he could exclude the European powers without dragging the country into a major war. In 1903, he promoted Panama's rebellion from Colombia and then acquired the Canal Zone from Panama. In 1905, he placed the finances of Santo Domingo under American control to prevent any European country from asserting authority over that beleaguered country. Critics argued that such realism had only short-term benefits, brought America few friends, and encouraged the belief that military threats could solve all problems.

The idealist approach to foreign policy begins with the assumption that human nature is basically good and that war and other forms of conflict are not the normal condition of humankind. Political idealism holds that the goal of American foreign policy should be to promote the principles of universal peace, human rights, and democracy. President Woodrow Wilson (1913–1921) is the American statesperson most closely identified with this school of thought. In the years 1914–1916, Wilson sent American troops to Mexico, Haiti, and the Dominican Republic—not, as had Roosevelt, to stave off European intervention, but to establish democratic governments.

After war broke out in Europe in 1914, Roosevelt, then a private citizen, urged American intervention to prevent Germany from dominating Europe and thus upsetting the balance of power on that continent. Wilson was reluctant to intervene until Germany began unrestricted submarine warfare against American merchant ships. Then he justified involvement upon the most lofty of ideals. In asking Congress for a declaration of war, Wilson claimed that America would fight for "the ultimate peace of the world and for the liberation of its peoples ... the world must be made safe for democracy." When World War I ended, Wilson insisted upon a peace settlement, known as the Fourteen Points, that would require a global peacekeeping entity (the League of Nations), arms limitations, open diplomacy, and the self-determination of nations. The eventual treaty, signed in Versailles in 1919, embodied few of these principles except for the creation of the League of Nations and was rejected by the United States Senate.

In twenty years Europe was embroiled in another war. Critics argued that Wilson's efforts at peacemaking did not end European habits of power politics, hostile alliances, and imperialist politics. Such moralistic policies, critics contended, only lead to futile crusades and endless wars.

The doctrine of isolationism has deep roots in American history, going back to George Washington's admonition in his farewell address. According to the isolationist credo, America should be a beacon light of liberty for all humanity, but not attempt to impose its way of life on other societies. America would only be contaminated by its involvement in the power struggles of the world. One of the leading spokespersons for isolationism prior to World War II was President Herbert Hoover (1929–1933). Hoover saw no clear moral choice between imperialist Britain and communist Russia on one side and Nazi Germany and fascist Italy on the other. Hoover feared that permanent involvement in the affairs of the world would so enlarge the role of the government and the military in the life of the nation as to constitute a threat to our liberty. Most Americans spurned Hoover's advice, believing that America must play a continual role in the international community.

Do you see the influences of realism, idealism, or isolationism in contemporary foreign policy? What is the best approach for America to take in the future? President Trump drew a distinction between nationalism and globalism and identified himself as a nationalist. Which of the three approaches does that attitude most resemble?

issue also meant failure to agree on the disposition of Germany. As a result, the occupation zones in Germany evolved into separate German states—one allied with the West (the Federal Republic of Germany) and the other controlled by the Soviet Union (the German Democratic Republic). By 1947, Europe appeared to be permanently divided into an American sphere in Western Europe and a Soviet sphere in Eastern Europe. The Cold War would produce several tense moments in the decades to follow. President Truman's approach to the situation was to send economic aid to countries at risk of being influenced or destabilized by the Soviet Union. His plan of opposing Soviet aggression came to be known as the **Truman Doctrine** and was a guiding principle of American foreign policy during the Cold War. The Truman administration was also responsible for the **Marshall Plan** (named for Secretary of State George C. Marshall), a multiyear, multibillion-dollar program designed to help strengthen European economies, most of which had been devastated by World War II. The Marshall Plan became an American–Western European endeavor. After American aid of $12 billion over five years, European economies began to stabilize, forming the basis for a generation of Western European prosperity and democracy and further solidifying bonds to the United States.

The Soviets responded to the Truman Doctrine and the Marshall Plan by tightening their control over Eastern Europe, making both diplomatic and personal relationships between the two sides of Europe difficult. Such actions led America to develop a new foreign policy tack. Containment of the Soviet Union—holding communist political power within existing borders—became the hallmark of American foreign policy.

In April 1949, a total of twelve nations (the United States, Britain, France, Italy, the Netherlands, Belgium, Canada, Iceland, Luxembourg, Denmark, Norway, and Portugal) formed the **North Atlantic Treaty Organization (NATO)** and declared that an attack on one member would be considered an attack on all. NATO, the first mutual defense treaty signed by the United States since 1800, provided an American guarantee for the defense of Western Europe against a Soviet attack. The Soviet empire provided a counterbalance to NATO with the Warsaw Pact, established in 1955, and providing Eastern Europe with the same sort of alliance that NATO provided for the West. Interestingly, NATO never had to be used for the purposes of an all-out war during this era. Since the collapse of the Soviet empire, NATO has been expanded. It now contains twenty-nine member states, including some from the former Soviet Union's sphere of influence.

Although it was called the Cold War, this period also saw real military conflict, most notably in Korea and Vietnam. The Korean conflict (1950–1953) saw the American military deployed to the Korean peninsula when communist forces from North Korea crossed into South Korea. President Truman, following his containment policy, withdrew troops after the border between the two Koreas was resecured. The Vietnam conflict (1961–1973) also involved discord between communist and noncommunist factions in an Asian nation. This time the strategy was not as simple, and the result not as pleasing, for the American military. After nearly a decade of heavy fighting, and the loss of more than 50,000 American lives, the Nixon administration reached a cease-fire agreement and began to withdraw the American military in 1973, leaving the war-ravaged country to continue the conflict on its own. South Vietnamese forces eventually fell to the communist North Vietnamese in 1975.

The Vietnam War profoundly altered the public's patience with the costs of containment policy. If America's leaders were to maintain some semblance of this policy, a new strategy had to be developed. President Nixon and his National Security Adviser Henry Kissinger attempted to shape a policy that would accommodate itself to these new realities. Known as **détente** (a French word meaning "relaxation" or "calm"), this approach was designed to ease tensions between the United States and the Soviet Union. Rather than containing Soviet influence by elaborate and costly means, Nixon and Kissinger

Truman Doctrine

A policy, proclaimed by President Harry Truman in 1947, in which the United States would oppose the expansion of communism anywhere in the world

Marshall Plan

A multibillion-dollar American program begun after World War II for the economic rehabilitation of Western Europe

North Atlantic Treaty Organization (NATO)

Multinational organization formed in 1949 to provide for mutual defense against foreign attacks

détente

A French word meaning "relaxation" that was applied to Soviet-American relations in the early 1970s

Antiwar demonstrators march to support the end of the ongoing war in Vietnam.

("Student Vietnam War protesters" by University of Wisconsin Digital Collections, 1965, available under a CC 2.0 license via Wikimedia)

hoped that diplomacy could persuade the Soviets to limit their own behavior. Although détente did not live up to the expectations of either side, it did result in some important outcomes. It established a precedent for arms limitations negotiations; and it reduced American global commitments by advocating the **Nixon Doctrine**—a claim that America would no longer be responsible for providing, as it did in Korea and Vietnam, the military personnel to protect its allies.

While American efforts such as détente had some effect at easing Cold War tensions, the end of the war itself was largely a result of changes in Soviet policy. When Mikhail Gorbachev assumed power in the Soviet Union in 1985, Soviet-American relations began a period of profound alteration. With the Soviet economy in shambles, Gorbachev realized that his country required fundamental reform and could no longer afford the military and economic costs of competition with the West. In 1987, both countries signed the Intermediate-Range Nuclear Forces (INF) Treaty, which banned an entire category of nuclear weapons (missiles with ranges between 300 and 3,400 miles) and provided for intrusive on-site inspection procedures. Gorbachev had made virtually all the concessions. Even President Ronald Reagan, who early in his administration had dubbed the Soviet Union an "evil empire," concluded, as he left office, that a fundamental shift had occurred in Soviet policy. In 2018, President Trump, citing a distrust of Russia's adherence to the treaty, withdrew the United States from this historic treaty by 2019 and Russia soon followed suit.

It was, however, a series of cataclysmic events in the first two years of the George H. W. Bush administration that altered the political map of Europe and brought the Cold War to an end. In April 1989, the noncommunist Polish Solidarity movement was legalized, with Gorbachev's consent, and swept to an election victory that June. Throughout the autumn and winter of 1989, Hungary, Czechoslovakia, and Romania followed suit. By the end of 1989, the governments of all the Soviet Union's East European allies had collapsed. New regimes asked the Soviet Union to withdraw its military forces. The Warsaw Pact was in shambles and ceased to exist, for all intents and purposes.

Underscoring this was an agreement signed in the summer of 1990 between President Bush and West German Chancellor Helmut Kohl for a united Germany within the NATO alliance. The division of Europe into two armed camps

Nixon Doctrine

Proclaimed by President Nixon in 1969, a policy stipulating that the United States will support its allies with economic and military aid but that the allies should provide the bulk of the personnel for their own defense

Where does foreign policy come from?

One of the most influential bodies in the development of US foreign policy strategy is the National Security Council, which consists of the president and key advisers and is headed by the National Security Adviser. See what this organization is up to at this site:

http://www.bvtlab.com/8n886

marked the ending of the Cold War, but that did not mean the end of international conflict. The Iraqi invasion of Kuwait in August 1990 and the Gulf War that followed reminded the world of that grim fact. Without two rival superpowers, however, a major burden of responding to international politics seemingly fell to the United States alone—a reminder that American leadership in world affairs would not end with the Cold War.

POLITICAL CONTROVERSIES

The US vs. ISIS: A New Direction in the War on Terror?

In June 2013, President Barack Obama announced a shift in the ongoing war on terrorism. He stated that the extensive powers granted to the executive branch, the expanding use of drones to target enemies abroad, and the seemingly permanent detention of suspected terrorists put the United States at risk of living in a state of perpetual war. He intended to reduce or eliminate all of these approaches. Unfortunately, new threats and growing instability in the Middle East prevented a lasting shift away from war.

President Obama was awarded the Nobel Peace Prize in 2009 largely based on the perception that he would take the United States in a more peaceful direction than had his predecessor, George W. Bush. While the Iraq War that started in 2003 did eventually wind down at the end of 2011, new developments in international aggression made it challenging for the president to avoid military conflict. Notably,

in June 2014 an organization known as ISIS—the Islamic State of Iraq and Syria—announced its existence as a state.[1] Although earlier versions of this extremist rebel group had been around for over a decade, 2014 marked a turn in its strategy. Calling itself simply the Islamic State, the group of violent, fundamentalist Sunni Muslims announced a caliphate—a single religious state that would place the world under Islamic religious control— and began a series of well-publicized kidnappings and subsequent beheadings of Western civilians. These actions captured media attention around the world and called out for a response from the United States—a frequent target of ISIS attacks and messages.

In 2014, President Obama responded to these terrorist acts and the territorial gains made by ISIS with Operation Inherent Resolve—a plan for a multiyear military action designed to contain and weaken ISIS. Though the president was adamant about avoiding the use of American ground troops, the actions—which included airstrikes, military advisers, and support for groups opposing ISIS—cost billions of dollars and led to many lost lives. President Trump continued this line of attack, with the American military pursuing ISIS leader Abu Bakr al-Baghdadi, leading to his death in 2019. ISIS has the explicit goal of waging war against Western democracies like the United States and

has recruited an army to help carry out that goal. The threat is clear; the most effective response is less so.

Despite American military efforts, individuals claiming allegiance to ISIS have carried out numerous terrorist attacks in America and around the world—killing 130 in Paris, France, in November 2015; 14 in San Bernardino, California, in December 2015; 35 in Brussels, Belgium, in March 2016; 49 in Orlando, Florida, in June 2016; 84 in Nice, France, in July 2016; 4 significant attacks in 2017; a bombing in Pakistan in 2018; and attacks killing hundreds in Sri Lanka, Afghanistan, and Niger in 2019 and 2020, to list only a few of the largest attacks on international targets.

Was President Obama's approach to ISIS successful? What about President Trump's? How do we measure success in such circumstances? Was it the *right* choice to make? Neither George W. Bush nor Barack Obama entered office with plans of conducting multiple wars in the Middle East, yet both did. How much flexibility do presidents have to pursue their own path in foreign policy and how much are they limited by the circumstances in which they find themselves?

1. ISIS is also known as the Islamic State and as ISIL—the Islamic State of Iraq and the Levant. The latter term refers to a geographic region that covers parts of Syria as well as several other eastern Mediterranean countries.

SOURCES: "Redefining the War on Terrorism," The Week, June 7, 2013 2013; "A Worldwide State of Terror," DailyMail.com, July 12, 2018.

During the 1990s and the early decades of the twenty-first century, America has been in the process of redefining its role to accommodate the changing international sphere. Presidents Bush, Clinton, the second Bush, and Obama established a large role for American diplomacy and military presence around the world. In addition to the Gulf War, the first President Bush involved America in military actions in Panama and Somalia. President Clinton continued American efforts in Somalia and sent troops to Haiti and Bosnia, in addition to continuing bombings of Iraq. President George W. Bush campaigned for office as something of an isolationist; but when confronted with the

tragedy of international terrorism, he responded by using the US military in Afghanistan and Iraq. President Obama entered office promising a new tenor to American foreign policy—moving to shut down the military prison at Guantanamo Bay and to bring an end to the wars in Afghanistan and Iraq. Although implementing such changes proved difficult, the world recognized Obama's efforts for change; and, in 2009, he became the fourth US president to receive the Nobel Peace Prize. To be sure, some recent efforts were humanitarian in nature, and many were multinational efforts. Their sheer quantity, though, underscores the growing burden of American foreign policy in the post–Cold War world of the twenty-first century. Recently, even the idea that the Cold War is over has been cast into doubt. With aggressive military moves in the Crimea by Vladimir Putin—a Russian leader who has been in power as either president or prime minister for more than two decades—91 percent of Americans say they see the military power of Russia as a critical or important threat to the United States.[3] Despite the concerns of a vast majority of Americans, President Trump spoke highly of Putin and signaled, at times, a desire for more positive relations between the two countries.

16.2   The Policy Machinery

Since the Vietnam War, there has been no clear public consensus on foreign policy. Global containment was discredited by Vietnam, and the end of the Cold War has left policy makers without a clear political strategy. Consequently, every major foreign and defense policy initiative is subject to searching examination. President Carter was barely able to get the Panama Canal treaty, which returned control of the canal to Panama, through the Senate; he also had great difficulty in gaining Senate support for SALT (Strategic Arms Limitation Treaty) II. Despite his impressive election victories, President Reagan had no easy victories in Congress. His defense buildup was reduced, aid to the Nicaraguan contras was seriously circumscribed, and the MX missile program was severely limited. The vote to authorize the first President Bush to use military force against Iraq was marked by strong partisan cleavages. Even the second President Bush, who received incredible public support in the wake of the 9/11 attacks, faced significant opposition when he sought approval for large-scale military actions against Iraq.

Nonetheless, foreign policy in today's world still carries a large presidential stamp. Since 1945, the major policy initiatives (the Truman Doctrine, the Marshall Plan, NATO, the Korean intervention, the Vietnam War, détente, the Gulf War, the war on terrorism, and efforts to normalize relations with North Korea) have come from the White House. Gaining support for policy initiatives is increasingly difficult, however. Not only is Congress more independent, but the bureaucracy itself is also not easily corralled. Each agency frequently has its own perspective, with a cabinet secretary who may be its vigorous advocate.

The president, frequently operating through the National Security Council (NSC), attempts to control the play. The following sections explore and analyze the elaborate machinery of agencies and departments that the president seeks to dominate. They are responsible for the day-to-day operations of policy.

16.2a Department of State

Although the conduct of crisis diplomacy and the overall direction of foreign policy come from the White House, the **Department of State** has the primary responsibility for the routine daily functions of foreign policy. The department's activities include maintaining diplomatic relations with over 180 countries; operating over 250 embassies, consulates, and other posts around the world; representing the United States in scores of international organizations; being involved in the negotiations of treaties and other agreements with foreign nations; monitoring human rights policies of both our allies and our adversaries; supervising foreign aid programs; promoting cultural and educational exchanges; and making policy recommendations to the president and being responsible for their implementation.

("Budapest U.S. embassy" by Daniel Csörföly available under a CC BY-SA 3.0 license via Wikimedia)

The Department of State maintains diplomatic relations with over 180 countries and operates more than 250 embassies, consulates, and other posts around the world, including the U.S. Embassy in Budapest, Hungary.

Heading the department is the secretary of state, who reports directly to the president. In the Trump administration, this position was held by former CIA director Mike Pompeo, who replaced former oil executive Rex Tillerson in April 2018. Beneath the secretary are the deputy secretary of state, six undersecretaries, and a counselor. Below that level, the department is a mix of geographic and functional bureaus (see Figure 16.1). The *geographic* bureaus (such as African, European and Eurasian, Near Eastern, Western Hemisphere, East Asian, and South and Central Asian) have within them scores of country desks that are responsible for monitoring events around the world. The *functional* bureaus—which include Intelligence and Research, Public Diplomacy and Public Affairs, and Civilian Security, Democracy, and Human Rights—are responsible for specialized areas of policy. They inevitably involve other departments. For example, the Political-Military Affairs Bureau frequently interacts with the Pentagon and is crucial to Department of State (also known as State Department) participation in the development of military policy.

Attached to the State Department are the US permanent representative to the United Nations and the **United States Agency for International Development (USAID)**. In 1999 the United States Information Agency, which became the **Bureau of International Information Programs (IIP)**, was integrated into the department. USAID coordinates economic assistance programs, and IIP directs communications programs that provide information about the United States worldwide.

An elite corps of employees, known as foreign service officers (FSOs), staffs the State Department. They are selected through a rigorous series of written and oral exams. Few people would dispute the talent and ability of the FSOs, but they have been criticized for their caution, conformity, and elitism. These tendencies may be reinforced by the "up or out" promotion system in which a senior officer must advance beyond his or her present rank or be discharged.

Over the years the State Department has had difficulty leading foreign policy within the executive branch. In the modern age of diplomacy, the State Department must share its own field of foreign policy making with the Defense Department, the Central Intelligence Agency, and the NSC.

Department of State

Responsible for the routine daily functions of foreign policy; the department that represents the United States abroad; involved in international negotiations, supervising foreign aid and programs promoting cultural and educational exchange, and making policy recommendations to the president

United States Agency for International Development (USAID)

Agency of the State Department that coordinates economic assistance programs

Bureau of International Information Programs (IIP)

An agency of the State Department that directs overseas information programs

Figure 16.1 United States Department of State

In addition to its headquarters in Washington, known as Foggy Bottom, the State Department has over 140 embassies abroad, more than 100 consulates, and eight special missions to international organizations. Yet as measured by its budget and personnel, it is among the smaller executive departments. Of particular importance are functional bureaus and geographic bureaus.

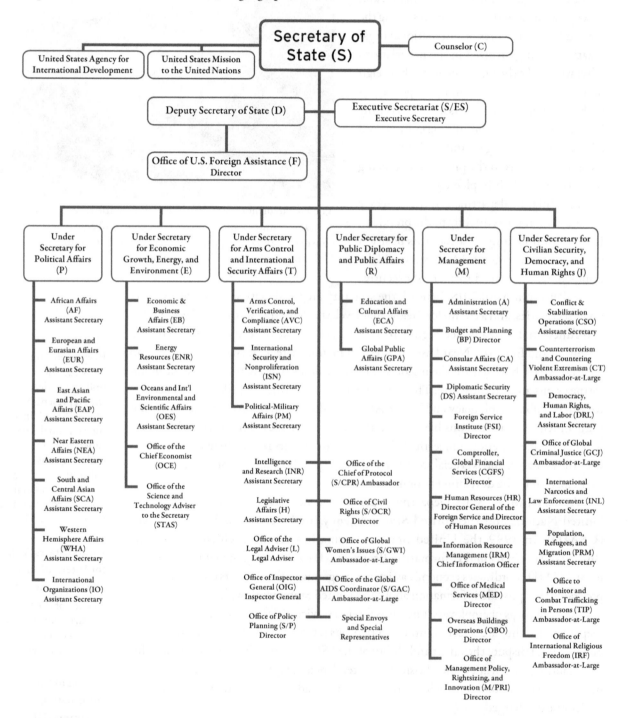

*The head of this organization reports directly to the Secretary of State (S) for certain purposes

SOURCE: Adapted from U.S. Department of State, Department Organization Chart, https://www.state.gov/r/pa/ei/rls/dos/99484.htm (August 16, 2020).

16.2b   Central Intelligence Agency

Established in 1947, the **Central Intelligence Agency (CIA)** was originally charged with gathering information and coordinating all intelligence operations in the federal government. As tensions increased during the Cold War, the CIA shifted its primary task from the collection of intelligence information to the conduct of secret political activities. Its early operations involved aiding in the installation of pro-American governments in Iran (1953) and Guatemala (1954). Covert activities became such an important part of the CIA between 1962 and 1970 that they consumed 52 percent of the agency's total budget and 55 percent of its personnel.[4]

Gina Haspel as she appeared before the Senate Intelligence Committee on May 9, 2018.

(Courtesy C-SPAN via Wikimedia)

In the early 1970s, public disclosure of CIA abuses put the agency on the defensive, thus weakening its political support. The abuses involved unsuccessful efforts to assassinate Fidel Castro in the early 1960s and an attempt to prevent Marxist-leaning Salvador Allende from taking office as president of Chile in 1970 after he had been legally elected. Congress then took steps to limit such activities. The Hughes-Ryan Amendment of 1974 required that the president notify Congress when a covert action was undertaken and certify its importance "to the national interests of the United States."

Presidents Ford and Carter set firm limits on CIA operations by placing covert activities under close presidential control. They prohibited such extreme measures as assassination and forbade any CIA operations within the United States. President Reagan, however, felt that the CIA had been unduly restricted. In 1981, he appointed William J. Casey as director of the CIA with the explicit mandate to revitalize the agency. Reagan amended the Ford and Carter orders and allowed some domestic CIA operations as long as their focus was on gathering significant foreign intelligence data.

The Reagan administration was far less reluctant than its predecessors to approve covert operations. The CIA increased its flow of small arms and other military equipment to the Afghan rebels combating the Soviet invaders. It provided millions of dollars in arms to Iranian paramilitary groups opposing the Khomeini government in Tehran. It also trained the personal security forces of Liberian dictator Samuel K. Doe. The CIA's most ambitious operation, however, involved the support of Nicaraguan exile groups, known as *contras*, seeking to overthrow the Marxist Sandinista government. Congress raised serious objections to this operation and barred funds, in 1982, "for the purpose of overthrowing the government of Nicaragua." In 1986, Congress, under considerable pressure from President Reagan, however, appropriated $100 million in contra aid. Only later did it come to light that some of the funds received from arms sales to Iran may have been diverted to the contras.

Although the current functions of the CIA are difficult to identify due to the classified nature of much of the intelligence-gathering work, the agency does make some of its activities public. For example, one recent effort has been the collection of intelligence on foreign terrorist groups. Although the budget of the CIA and its number of employees is not made public, documents leaked by former CIA and National Security Agency (NSA) employee Edward Snowden revealed that the 2013 CIA budget was $14.7 billion.[5]

The dilemma that CIA covert operations pose for our democratic society is severe. Can the American government conduct a secret foreign policy without subverting the

Central Intelligence Agency (CIA)

Agency, established by the National Security Act of 1947, that is responsible for gathering information and coordinating foreign intelligence operations in the federal government

principles of democratic control? Should it stand by helpless if international terrorists operate without constraints? There are no simple answers.

16.2c   Department of Defense

The **Department of Defense (DoD)**, housed in the famous Pentagon building, is a mammoth organization. It was created in 1947 and reorganized in 1949 to reduce interservice rivalry and to provide more coherence for national security policy. DoD comprises three basic organizations: the Office of the Secretary of Defense (OSD), the **Joint Chiefs of Staff (JCS)**, and the separate armed services, which are headed by a civilian service secretary and a uniformed service chief.

Overseeing this organization, the secretary of defense is one of the most powerful cabinet secretaries. The defense secretary has the challenging task of advising the president on crucial military decisions, serving as the link between the military leadership and the president, and building a policy consensus within the department. Frequently this task brings the secretary of defense into conflict with the secretary of state, who may emphasize diplomacy over force, arms control over military buildups, or alliance solidarity over unilateral US military action.

Such conflict was apparent from time to time in the second Bush administration. Secretary of Defense Donald Rumsfeld demonstrated a preference for an aggressive military response in the war on terrorism, even when this meant the United States must act unilaterally. This approach was sometimes at odds with the more cautious, diplomatic route preferred by former Secretary of State Colin Powell, himself a retired Army general and former chairperson of the Joint Chiefs of Staff; yet the approach seemed to work well for Secretary of State Condoleezza Rice. Nevertheless, when Republicans suffered setbacks in the 2006 midterm elections and voters expressed dissatisfaction with the Iraq War as a reason for the change, President Bush replaced Rumsfeld with former CIA director Robert Gates. Gates proved so successful in this office that he achieved the rare feat of retaining it despite a partisan change in the presidency with the election of Barack Obama. When Gates retired in 2011, Obama appointed another former CIA director—Leon Panetta—to fill the post. Former senator Chuck Hagel succeeded Panetta in 2013, and Ash Carter succeeded Hagel in 2015. In the Trump administration, James Mattis held the position from January 2017 until the end of 2018. He was succeeded by Patrick Shanahan as acting Defense Secretary until Mark Esper was confirmed in July 2019. Esper was succeeded by acting secretary Christopher C. Miller in November 2020.

The Joint Chiefs of Staff (JCS) consist of a chairperson, the chiefs of staff of the Army and the Air Force, the chief of naval operations, and the commandant of the Marine Corps. Until recently, the JCS advised the president and the secretary of defense on important military questions and also served as heads of their various services. A former chairperson of the JCS, General David Jones, argued that the service chiefs were unable to separate themselves from the interests of their individual service and to give objective advice on matters involving the defense budget. Another defense critic argued that the requirements of satisfying each individual service have weakened our capacity to prosecute

Lloyd J. Austin, secretary of defense, sworn in January 22, 2021.

(Department of Defense photo by Lisa Ferinando)

Department of Defense (DoD)

Established by the National Security Act of 1947 and responsible for formulating military policy and maintaining the armed forces

Joint Chiefs of Staff (JCS)

Heads of the various armed services and their chair who advise the president and the secretary of defense on important military questions

war successfully.[6] Thus, giving every service a mission assignment often took precedence over designing strategy. The failure of President Carter's Desert One Operation to rescue American hostages in Tehran in 1980 was attributed to the fact that every service had to be given a piece of the action.

Figure 16.2 Department of Defense

The Defense Department is practically an empire unto itself. The massive Pentagon office building covers 34 acres and contains a workforce of over 25,000 people. Approximately 2.8 million people are employed by Defense, over two-thirds of them in the armed forces. The Defense Department is divided mainly into the Office of the Secretary of Defense, the Joint Chiefs of Staff, and the three service departments.

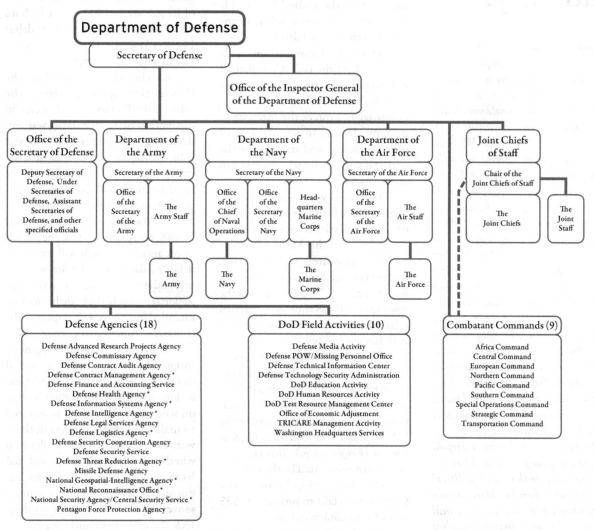

* Identified as a Combat Support Agency (CSA). Prepared by: Directorate for Organizational and Management Planning/ Office of the Director of Administration and Management/Office of the Secretary of Defence, December, 2013

SOURCE: Department of Defense, Organization Chart, http://odam.defense.gov/Portals/43/Documents/Functions/Organizational %20Portfolios/Organizations%20and%20Functions%20Guidebook/DoD_Organization_March_2012.pdf (December 29, 2014).

POLITICS AND IDEAS

Can Presidents Take the Country to War on Their Own Authority?

The Gulf War was no minor military operation, certainly as compared to the American interventions in Grenada (1983) and Panama (1989). It involved over 500,000 troops, several carrier battle groups, and an extensive air armada. Could President George H. W. Bush have committed such forces to battle, as did President Truman in Korea, without prior congressional approval? The issue was never politically joined, as Congress did authorize President Bush to use military force against Iraq on January 12, 1991. Nonetheless, President Bush had maintained that he had ample constitutional authority to initiate such action without a congressional mandate. Was he correct? This question remains a vital one for American foreign policy. The second President Bush faced a similar question—ironically enough, also with Iraq. Like his father, George W. Bush took the constitutionally assured route, receiving permission from Congress to invade Iraq on October 10, 2002.

In the following selections, excerpted from the 1991 congressional debate on this question, author and political commentator Robert W. Merry argues that constitutional history and political necessity both require that the president receive authorization from the Congress before taking the country to war. On the other hand, Senator Jesse Helms (R-NC)

in his speech to the Senate during the January 12 debate argues that the president had ample authority to make war without prior congressional consent.

Congressional Record—Senate
Jesse Helms

On August 27, 1787, the Constitutional Convention meeting in Philadelphia adopted without debate the words of Article II, section 2, clause 1, that the President is "Commander in Chief of the Army and Navy of the United States." He is also the head of the militia of the several States, if federalized.

Thus, the Constitution made the President the only Commander in Chief of the Armed Forces of this Nation. The President is, therefore, obligated to protect the interests of the United States, to defend the rights of its citizenry, and to preserve the national security by whatever means are necessary.

Thirteen years later, at the beginning of the second decade of the Constitutional Republic, Congressman John Marshall, before he was appointed Chief Justice, declared on the floor of the House of Representatives, "the President is the sole organ of the Nation in its external relations, and its sole representative with foreign nations."

There is no historical evidence that Chief Justice Marshall ever changed his mind. The phrase "sole organ of the Nation in its external relations" was emphatically restated by the U.S. Supreme Court in 1936 (*U.S. v. Curtiss Wright Corp.*). This view has never been repudiated by the Court.

On the other hand, the Constitution fails to provide for 535 other Commanders in Chief.

Article III, section 8, clauses 11–16, specifically enumerate the war powers of the Congress in the Constitution. Congress is given the

power: First, to declare war; second, to raise and support armies; third, to provide and maintain a navy; fourth, to make laws regulating the Armed Forces; and fifth, to support the militia of the Federal States. These specific powers encompass the sole authority of the U.S. Congress with regard to war.

Thus, Congress can in no way limit or authorize the President's constitutional authority as Commander in Chief. Congress has attempted to do that in the War Powers Act, an act which I strongly opposed at the time of its passage in 1973, and which no Chief Executive has ever accepted; but I believe that the War Powers Act is plainly unconstitutional.

In the short time that the Convention spent debating the subject, the Founders made a careful distinction between making war and declaring war. James Madison and Elbridge Gerry were responsible for enlarging the Presidential prerogative to enable the Chief Executive to meet the demands of national security.

As Madison warned in *Federalist No. 48*, encroachments by one branch upon another branch will upset the delicate balance of the tripartite constitutional system. Thus, it is exceedingly important to hold the branches to their intended functions with respect to the conduct of American foreign relations.

What the Framers originally intended ... was to make a careful distinction between declaring war and making war. The Constitution is silent on whether the President is required to make war after Congress declares war; at the same time, it is silent on whether the President is prohibited from making war if Congress has not declared war. Clearly, common sense requires that the President seek the agreement and cooperation of Congress in any endeavor that commits the lives and fortunes of the American people.

The powers to declare and make war are inherent powers of national sovereignty. The President has welcomed the cooperation of the United Nations and our allies in the United Nations who have supported us with diplomacy and by conducting troops. But the U.S. Constitution is superior to any obligations that we may or may not have undertaken by assenting to the U.N. Charter. No treaty can compel us, either in fact or in intention, to set aside any provision of the U.S. Constitution. The power to declare and make war therefore remains with the United States, and has not been delegated to the United Nations.

The U.S. Constitution was carefully crafted to allow much room for judgment. And in matters of war, the power to declare war does indeed lie with Congress ... nobody disputes that. But Congress has used that power only five times. On the other hand, the power to make war clearly belongs to the Commander in Chief, and we do not have but one Commander in Chief at a time.

From the Congressional Record, January 12, 1991, p. S387

President, Congress, and War Powers
Robert W. Merry

When presidents commit the country to military campaigns of such force, should they seek from Congress a declaration of war?

There are two elements to the question: the constitutional and the political.

Though the president is the country's commander in chief, the Constitution vests with Congress the power to "declare war." This division was a bold innovation when the Founding Fathers wrote it; at the time, all other governments vested the warmaking power solely in the executive.

But the Founders considered that approach dangerous. As James Madison wrote, "The Constitution supposes ... the executive is the branch of power most interested in war and most prone to it. It has accordingly, with studied care, vested the question of war in the legislature."

Through the country's 200-year saga, Congress has declared war five times: the War of 1812, the Mexican War (1846), the Spanish-American War (1898), World War I (1917), and World War II (1941). And yet the forces of history have fostered a constant growth in presidential prerogative in this crucial area.

"With few exceptions, the power to initiate and wage war has shifted to the executive branch," historian Louis Fisher wrote in 1972. This was particularly true after 1945, when the cold war and the advent of nuclear weapons and intercontinental missiles raised questions about the ability of Congress to act with sufficient speed in a modern global crisis.

Thus, we had the Korean and Vietnam conflicts, two major wars waged without any formal congressional approval. Congress provided financial support, of course, and passed vague expressions of assent such as the 1964 Tonkin Gulf Resolution.

But at the base of all this was the question of whether the government had simply decided to ignore the Constitution. What precisely did the congressional power to declare war mean? Did it confer any obligation on the executive branch to seek formal congressional assent before going to war? Did it impose obligations on Congress to assert its prerogative in such momentous matters?

In light of the past 45 years, these might seem like mere academic discussion points. ... But the political dimension renders them far more serious than that. In the 1950s and '60s, with World

War II fresh in the nation's consciousness, the American people were inclined to delegate to the executive broad discretion in the use of military force. And Congress pretty much went along. Thus, when President Dwight D. Eisenhower sent 14,300 marines to Lebanon in 1958, it caused hardly a political ripple in the United States. Johnson's Dominican Republic action generated far more domestic criticism, but the operation's success staved off any lasting political harm.

All that changed in the post-Vietnam era. Congress is more protective of its foreign policy prerogatives these days, more inclined to assert itself on operational matters and to criticize the president on delicate matters of state. In recent years, we have seen a House Speaker from the congressional majority party, Texas Democrat Jim Wright, virtually take control of the country's Central American policy.

All this underscores the political danger inherent in foreign military operations. When the stark realities become evident with the first signs of difficulty, the president becomes vulnerable to congressional second-guessing and naysaying. One could argue that the military challenge is daunting enough, without adding this political component.

And getting Congress aboard in the early days of national resolve is one way to lessen the political danger later on. It has been said that the postwar era was too dangerous and unstable to allow for consistent fealty to constitutional niceties such as the right of Congress to declare war. But that era is history now, and so perhaps it would be proper—and politically prudent—to return to the Constitution.

From Congressional Quarterly Weekly Report, August 25, 1990.

To improve the situation, Congress passed the Goldwater-Nichols Department of Defense Reorganization Act in 1986. It made the chair of the Joint Chiefs the principal military adviser to the secretary of defense and the president. Since the chair headed no specific service, he or she was expected to provide objective military advice and to avoid the bland consensus that could come from the Joint Chiefs. To reduce service rivalry further, the actual command of combat forces rests with nine unified commanders. The 2002 Unified Command Plan, which revised the previous structure, divided responsibility between five geographic and four structural unified commands.[7]

How much does America spend on National Defense?

Find the answer and historical analysis by consulting this page from the Congressional Budget Office:

http://www.bvtlab.com/8Tb7c

16.2d   The Role of Congress

Given the different philosophies, interests, and objectives of the 535 representatives and senators, there are practical limits on congressional power in this field. Congress cannot forge a coherent foreign policy, it cannot negotiate with foreign powers, it cannot respond quickly to international crises, and it cannot conduct the day-to-day business of foreign relations. Congress can, however, tell the president what the executive branch cannot do. In the 1970s, it limited the president's authority to conduct arms sales, to intervene in Angola, to continue the bombing of Cambodia and Laos during the Vietnam War, and to send troops into combat for longer than sixty days without congressional approval. Congress serves as a check or constraining force in foreign policy—and to its critics, it plays largely a negative role. As one former senator pointed out, foreign policy is a geopolitical chess game, and chess is not a team sport.[8]

Congress is poorly equipped to conduct foreign policy for three reasons: *parochialism*, *organizational weakness*, and *lack of information*. Parochialism is found in the constituency focus of the members. As a result, their attention to foreign policy can be only brief and determined by the newsworthy nature of the issue. Organizational weakness is found in the fragmented and diffuse centers of congressional decision-making. Over half of the standing committees in the House and Senate have jurisdiction over some area of foreign policy. No individual, set of individuals, or particular committee can speak for the entire Congress. Congress does not have the same resources as the executive branch for obtaining information and often must rely, therefore, upon the other branch.[9] It is, in part, because of these institutional weaknesses that Congress often abdicates the authority that it does have, turning over the reins of foreign policy almost entirely to the president. On October 10, 2002, Congress passed a joint resolution authorizing the president to deploy US armed forces in order to conduct military actions against Iraq with very little congressional oversight. The fact that the House and Senate only asked the president to report his actions to them from time to time after the United States started a military campaign, and that they authorized a broad use of force, indicates how difficult Congress finds it to limit the president in foreign and defense policy. After such authority is granted, the congressional role is largely limited to funding and oversight. In the Iraq War, for example, Congress continued to demonstrate its support for the conflict by passing supplemental spending bills. It also demonstrated its concern over the Abu Ghraib prison abuses and inadequate prewar intelligence estimates by holding committee hearings, issuing committee reports, and introducing resolutions on the chamber floors. When President Trump decided to bomb a Syrian airstrip in 2017 in retaliation for the

Syrian government's use of chemical weapons, he did not seek congressional approval for his action. Though a few individual legislators voiced objections, the branch as a whole did not take any action to impede the president's action.[10] But in 2020, when President Trump authorized the assassination of Iranian general Qasem Soleimani, Congress responded by passing a bipartisan Iran War Powers Resolution. The resolution, which restricted the president from engaging in hostilities with Iran without explicit authorization from Congress, was quickly vetoed by the president, demonstrating the ongoing nature of interbranch conflict regarding the war powers.[11]

16.3   Domestic Policy and National Security

In general, the public is more concerned with domestic questions than foreign and defense issues, but leaders cannot conduct national security policy in a political vacuum. Public opinion sets the outer limits of what is politically possible. Moreover, ethnic and economic interests exercise considerable influence on specific policies. The 9/11 attacks brought foreign policy and national security to the forefront of national attention for the first time in a decade or more, but even this severe attack eventually began taking a backseat to domestic politics.

16.3a   Public Moods and Foreign Policy

Public opinion surveys generally show the American people to be uninformed about the complexities and details of foreign policy. As a general matter, Americans today tend to think the government is doing enough to defend the nation, with only 17 percent of Americans indicating the government spends too little on defense, while 81 percent believe the government spends the right amount or too much on defense.[12] On specific issues, public opinion changes frequently, is affected by current events, and—in the short term—accepts dramatic decisions made by the president. Does public opinion, then, have any influence on foreign policy?

Public moods or general attitudes, rather than opinions on specific questions, are what really influence policy. Such moods set limits within which foreign policy decisions are made. After the Japanese attacked Pearl Harbor in 1941, the public mood shifted from isolationism to internationalism. This internationalist mood became the broad consensus that provided the basis of public support for the United Nations, the Marshall Plan, NATO, and other initiatives of that period.[13]

The Vietnam War created a split in the consensus between liberal and conservative internationalists. Opposed to America's participation in that war and disillusioned with military power, liberal internationalists supported such cooperative goals as increasing assistance to the developing nations, reaching accommodation with the Soviet Union, negotiating arms control, and combating world hunger. Conservative internationalists stressed competition, opposed détente with the Soviet Union, and emphasized military defense and the use of force to protect our allies and interests abroad.[14]

In the years that have followed the Vietnam War, the public mood has vacillated. In the mid-1970s, less than 50 percent of the public approved of the use of American troops to support even such allies as Western Europe and Japan from a Soviet attack. The seizure

(U.S. Army Photo by Sgt. Brandon Aird, via Wikimedia)

A first lieutenant looks at possible enemy positions during Operation Saray Has, near Forward Operating Base Naray, Afghanistan.

of American hostages in Iran and the Soviet invasion of Afghanistan in 1979, however, created a shift toward conservative internationalism; by 1980 a majority of Americans supported the use of troops to defend Western Europe and Japan.

The invasions of Grenada (1983) and Panama (1989), designed to oust dictatorships and install friendly democratic governments, found broad public support. These actions, however, were brief, involved relatively few troops, and resulted in minor casualties. Although the Gulf War in 1991 involved an enormous commitment of land, air, and naval forces, victory was so swift and decisive that public support never wavered. On the other hand, the Korean and Vietnam experiences revealed that Americans soon become impatient with protracted and unresolved land wars. American support for the war on terrorism, in all of its evolving phases, has been mixed. Support for the initial strikes against the Taliban government in Afghanistan in late 2001 was very high. In November 2001, 62 percent of Americans believed the United States should "mount a long-term war to defeat global terrorist networks."[15] As the scope of conflict broadened in the months that followed, however, support for military action decreased. By October 2002, only a slim majority (53 percent) supported an invasion of Iraq, and that majority disappeared entirely when qualifiers were added to the question. For example, only 37 percent of Americans would support such an invasion if the United Nations opposed the action, and only one-third would support the invasion if they knew there would be five thousand US casualties.[16] By October 2006, with American casualties continuing to rise, no weapons of mass destruction found, and military skirmishes continuing to destabilize Iraq, 58 percent of Americans believed that sending troops to Iraq had been a mistake. Furthermore, 64 percent of Americans believed the war was going very or somewhat badly for the United States, and more Americans thought the Iraqi insurgents were winning the war. Over half of Americans surveyed (54 percent) believed the United States should withdraw either immediately or within one year, despite President Bush's plan to remain through at least 2011. Finally, 52 percent of Americans believed the war with Iraq actually made the United States *less* safe from terrorism.[17] These opinions likely made an important difference in the 2006 midterm elections, where exit polls indicated voter dissatisfaction with the Bush administration's Iraq policy and voters made Democrats the majority party in both the House and Senate. Immediately following the election, Secretary of State Donald Rumsfeld resigned and key senators from both parties indicated an unwillingness to confirm President Bush's nominee John Bolton as the American ambassador to the United Nations.

By the summer of 2010, nearly nine years after the 9/11 attacks, there were 5,545 US military fatalities in the combined Iraq and Afghanistan operations. A consistent majority of Americans indicated a preference to see the Iraq War come to a close, with 62 percent indicating opposition to the war and 58 percent concluding that the war had been a mistake.[18] When President Obama moved to officially end the Iraq War by removing all US troops by December 2011, 75 percent of Americans approved of this decision.[19] By the time the Afghanistan War drew to a close at the end of 2014, it had become the longest military conflict in American history and had cost a total of nearly $1 trillion.[20] And despite one phase of the war ending, war in Afghanistan continued through the end

of the Obama administration and into the Trump administration and included several thousand American military personnel. Only in 2020 did the United States finally sign a peace agreement with Taliban leaders in Afghanistan, laying out plans to draw down the conflict and remove all American troops in 2021.[21] With the continued threat posed by the Islamic State, however, it seems that US military intervention in the Middle East will continue for the foreseeable future.

How do such moods affect foreign policy? They can place limits on the choices available to policy makers. The American public is clearer about what they do not want than about what should be done. During the late 1960s and early 1970s, public opinion opposed continued American involvement in the Vietnam War; but it gave no clear indication, however, as to how the Nixon administration should end that involvement. The government faces a similar situation today: Most Americans want a change in America's involvement in the Middle East, but they remain somewhat divided on exactly what that change should be.

16.3b Multinational Corporations and Banks

Multinational corporations are large corporations based in one country that have considerable assets and numerous subsidiaries in others. Some of the leading American giants are Walmart, ExxonMobil, Amazon.com, Berkshire Hathaway, and Apple.[22] These corporations command greater resources than many of the countries in the United Nations. Their sales today outrank all but the richest nations of the world. Walmart, for example, had over $523 billion in revenues in 2020, or approximately 2.4 percent of the US gross domestic product.

In 1975, the United States, through the CIA, actively opposed the Soviet- and Cuban-backed faction in Angola, known as the MPLA. The Gulf Oil Company, with extensive oil investments in Angola, however, made its royalty payments to the MPLA in amounts that far exceeded the budget of the CIA operation. When the State Department protested, Gulf temporarily suspended its payments. They were eventually resumed after the MPLA had triumphed over the pro-Western faction, and Gulf Oil continued to develop a cooperative relationship with the Marxist MPLA government.[23] In 2000, multinational corporations successfully lobbied for the passage of a bill providing permanent normalized trade relations (PNTR) with China. America had held the giant Asian country at arm's length in the past, due to a poor human rights record; but corporations lobbied diligently for America to reduce trade barriers. These efforts, in addition to $58 million in campaign contributions, may have played an important role in the policy change. The new trade status resulted in $123.9 billion in trade between the two nations in 2000, a 22 percent jump over the previous year.[24] By 2019, that figure topped the $550 billion mark.[25] However, the trade was imbalanced, in that the United States imported from China about four times what it exported, which irritated trade protectionists like President Trump. In 2018, the Trump administration began imposing tariffs on hundreds of billions of

("SZ Tour Wal-Mart interior Display on sale Aisle and visitors" by Hwangxiheng, available under a CC BY-SA 3.0 license via Wikmedia)

Walmart is a multinational corporation that is based in the United States and has considerable assets and numerous subsidiaries in other countries, such as this store in China.

multinational corporations
Large companies that carry on business in two or more countries simultaneously

ExxonMobil Research and Development Headquarters in Shanghai, China.

dollars' worth of goods from China and other nations, resulting in a trade war. While this had the effect of decreasing the overall amount of trade between the two nations, it did not immediately alter the balance of trade.

American banks have also become heavily involved in overseas activities. In 1980 American banks had made $280 billion in overseas loans, a large portion of which went to developing nations and Eastern Europe. By the end of 2005, American banks claimed over $1.29 trillion in international investment, with some of the recent growth coming in the form of loans to Western Europe and the Caribbean.[26] Today, US banks make up more than two-thirds of investment banking world-wide.[27] Are loans of this nature and magnitude in the interests of the American people? Critics of the banks contend that loans to unstable developing governments unnecessarily risk important investment capital. Supporters argue they can help development schemes and add to stability in these parts of the world.

The volume of these debts underscores the growing interdependence of the world economy. For example, what would happen if a major debtor nation defaulted on its loans? Clearly it could throw many of the major banks, and perhaps the entire international economy, into turmoil. Indeed this was just the risk the world economy faced in the late 1990s when several East Asian countries became mired in economic turmoil. It was only the proffering of over $200 billion in aid packages from the International Monetary Fund that prevented a much deeper and more widespread crisis.

While foreign loans and investments gave American banks and corporations a stake in the economies of these countries, the leverage of the multinational corporations can work both ways—opening the door to foreign influence over the American economy as well. Japanese companies, for example, made large investments in the United States, buying Columbia Records and the Rockefeller Center. The Japanese automobile and electronics industries depend heavily upon their American customers. Japanese companies contribute to state political campaigns, and the Japanese government spends millions each year lobbying Congress against legislation that would limit the market for Japanese goods. Over the past decade, as Japan's economy has stumbled, other nations, notably China, have followed this lead by investing in America, adding to the complexity of American foreign policy.

16.3c The Military-Industrial Complex

military-industrial complex

The Pentagon, defense contractors, unions in the defense industry, members of Congress whose states or districts receive considerable military funds, and academic strategists whose work is funded by the military

In his farewell address, President Eisenhower warned the American people "against the acquisition of unwarranted influence, whether sought or unsought, by the military-industrial complex. The potential for disastrous use of misplaced power exists and will persist." What is the military-industrial complex? Does its influence distort our national security policy?

Few observers deny the existence or importance of the **military-industrial complex**. It includes the Pentagon, major corporations whose profits depend on large defense contracts, members of Congress whose states and districts include these contractors or

military installations, unions whose members depend on defense work, and the numerous defense scientists and academic strategists whose work is funded by the military.

Critics find that the influence of the military-industrial complex distorts defense policy and weakens our economy. They charge that by absorbing so much of the country's scientific and engineering talent, it erodes our ability to compete with other industrialized countries in the application of advanced technology to consumer products.

Second, critics argue that the military-industrial complex favors the production of weapons that are too expensive and often obsolete. Much of the blame for this centers on Congress, which frequently funds weapons systems regardless of their military value, simply because they are produced in the districts of influential members.

Several of the nation's largest corporations—Boeing, General Dynamics, Lockheed Martin, Northrop Grumman, and Raytheon Technologies, for example—each have revenues in excess of $30 billion and gain a large percentage of their sales from the federal government, most of it related to defense.[28] These companies also operate some of the largest PACs in America and channel their contributions to members of Congress on the Appropriation and Armed Forces committees. In the 2020 election cycle, defense corporations spent over $10 million in campaign and soft money contributions by the end of June, with about 44 percent going to Democrats and 56 percent to Republicans.[29] Although it may be unfair to claim defense industry lobbying is the sole cause of defense spending, it is notable that America spends an average of $1 million per minute on defense.[30]

Although many Americans anticipated a decreased need for military spending after the end of the Cold War, such a windfall has not occurred. Throughout the 1990s, Defense Department officials and defense industry lobbyists insisted that America's economic well-being depended on a smoothly functioning international system, which could require the use of military power. The 9/11 attacks convinced many of this need. In fiscal year 2021, America devoted $60 billion exclusively to **homeland security**.[31]

Learning to live with the military-industrial complex is a formidable challenge to the American political system. In the era of the founders, large standing armies, entangling alliances, and centralized governments were evils to be avoided, not accommodated.

16.4   Current Issues in Foreign and Defense Policy

Faced with the limits of power and yet still burdened with the obligations of a superpower, America confronts issues that defy any easy or quick solutions. Policy makers face painful choices. They must recognize the demands of Congress and the public, the concerns of our allies, the unpredictable social forces in the developing world, and the ever-present dangers of nuclear arms and other weapons of mass destruction.

Shaping the defense budget in an era of fiscal austerity involves annual struggles with Congress. Dealing with the Western European allies who have grown prosperous and independent since the days of the Marshall Plan requires greater patience and tact. Confronting threats to the peace, such as international terrorist attacks, and the proliferation of nuclear weapons may take a measured balance of military force and shrewd diplomacy. Those problems will occupy our policy makers for some time to come.

homeland security
The effort of protecting United States soil, particularly from foreign or terrorist attack

16.4a 9/11 and the Ongoing War on Terrorism

When terrorists hijacked four airplanes to use as weapons against America on September 11, 2001, they did much more than kill thousands of innocent human beings. They prompted a new era of American foreign and defense policy, known generally as the war on terrorism. In the months following the attack, the Bush administration used military force to drive the Taliban government (which had been harboring the al Qaeda terrorist network responsible for the attack) from power in Afghanistan, identified several other potentially threatening countries as an "axis of evil," and prepared for a military invasion of Iraq, which it accused of amassing chemical and biological weapons. Although an independent commission appointed by President Bush later determined that Iraq had not possessed weapons of mass destruction, the administration continued to defend the invasion on the basis of Iraq posing an imminent terrorist threat.

In addition to these highly visible actions, the Bush administration also developed a broad strategy for approaching world affairs. Unveiled in September 2002, President Bush's *National Security Strategy of the United States of America* called for "a distinctly American internationalism that reflects the union of our values and our national interests."[32] The document, which was further revised in 2006, 2010, 2015, and 2017, set forth three goals: political and economic freedom, peaceful interstate relations, and respect for human dignity. The Bush administration hoped to attain these goals through a strong, worldwide military presence, encouraging free trade and economic development, and transforming national security institutions.

Photo by Mike Rieger / FEMA News Photo via Wikimedia

A firefighter surveys the remaining shell and tons of debris of the World Trade Center in New York City on September 25, 2001. Clearing the rubble from the collapsed twin towers and other surrounding buildings was a daunting task for the hundreds of workers at the site of the terrorist attack.

An example of this last point is the creation of a Department of Homeland Security. Although President Bush was able to create an Office of Homeland Security within the executive branch, he needed congressional approval to make this office a permanent, cabinet-level department. The struggles he encountered in this effort are illustrative of the difficulty in changing America's formal institutions. Congressional Democrats opposed Bush's proposal, in part, because by reclassifying 170,000 federal employees, the proposal removed the workers' job security. President Bush argued that national security should not be hamstrung by labor disputes, but Democrats were concerned that the Republican administration would use the reduced job protection clause to unfairly weed out employees for political reasons. As late Senator Arthur Vandenberg (R-MI) famously noted in regard to American foreign policy, "Politics ends at the water's edge." While this claim may have held true in an earlier era, the shape and direction of American defense policy in the twenty-first century continue to be a matter of domestic political difference.

16.4b International Organization and the Developing World

Another challenge of twenty-first century foreign policy is the great economic disparity between wealthy countries and poor countries. The latter group of countries, commonly referred to as **developing nations**, find themselves in the difficult position of attempting to gain an economic foothold and maintain political stability in a world where many other countries already have established themselves in the global market. Recognition of this difficult situation by the international community has resulted in two organizations whose mission is to help alleviate this problem. The two agencies, both part of the United Nations, are the **International Monetary Fund (IMF)** and the **World Bank**.

The IMF was created in 1945 to help U.N. member nations overcome problems in their balance of payments and to help avoid another worldwide depression like the one that dominated the 1930s. Starting with just 45 member nations, the IMF today consists of 189 countries and has resources (which it calls quotas) of $1 trillion. The IMF seeks to achieve its economic objectives through increased international trade, monetary stability, and cooperation, as well as by making funds available to nations experiencing debt crises.[33] Although its objectives are noble, some have criticized the organization and tactics of the IMF. For example, critics note that the members representing the wealthier, industrialized nations of the IMF executive board often control the decisions responsible for conducting the organization's day-to-day business. Some have argued that the United States, for example, takes a carrot-and-stick approach to funding decisions, rewarding nations that fall in line with American policy interests and punishing those that do not, regardless of the economic results on which the agency is supposed to focus.[34]

("Kristalina Georgieva Headshot," by World Bank Group/Grant Ellis, available under a CC by SA 4.0 International license via Wikimedia)

Kristalina Georgieva, chair and managing director of the International Monetary Fund since 2019.

Closely related to the IMF, the World Bank was created in 1944 to provide loans to poor countries, with a goal of promoting worldwide economic growth and reducing poverty. In 2020, the World Bank had over $150 billion in outstanding loans to developing nations. As signs of its success, the organization points to increases in life expectancy and literacy rates and decreases in infant mortality around the globe.[35] Like the IMF, however, this body has its critics. One charge is that the bank's narrow focus on economic development sometimes causes it to make decisions that are at odds with other important concerns, such as environmental protection.

So how does all of this affect American foreign policy? To start with, in an increasingly interconnected world, decisions that affect one nation, or group of nations, are likely to have an impact on every other country as well. If the problems of overpopulation, malnutrition, and underemployment go unattended in the developing world, the chances of civil wars, regional conflicts, and revolutions in those areas will increase. It is likely that such regional instability will adversely affect the political stability of the industrialized world as well. Second, as the world's largest economy—with China in second place and gaining—the United States plays a particularly crucial role in shaping the global economy. With such power comes responsibility. One of the challenges for American foreign policy in the twenty-first century is deciding which values should drive our economic relations with the rest of the world.

developing nations

Nations whose standard of living lags far behind that of the industrialized countries

International Monetary Fund (IMF)

A specialized agency of the United Nations designed to promote international monetary cooperation

World Bank

A specialized agency of the United Nations that makes loans to poorer nations for economic development

CHAPTER REVIEW

1. The foreign policy consensus after World War II represented a shift from isolationism to internationalism. During the Cold War years, this internationalism was characterized by the doctrine of containment. After the Cold War ended in 1989–1990, the United States had to develop a new approach to foreign policy, this time as the world's primary superpower.

2. Although the president no longer monopolizes foreign and defense policy making, he is the major actor and the primary initiator. Congress, though it cannot direct policy, can place important constraints on policy. Neither can the State Department dominate the foreign policy bureaucracy. As military action and covert activities have become an integral part of policy implementation, the Defense Department and the CIA have staked a permanent claim to much of the foreign policy turf.

3. A number of domestic constituencies, largely economic, have developed a strong interest in particular aspects of foreign and defense policy. Although their influence is considerable, it is difficult for them to overcome the determined will of the president.

4. Contemporary concerns, such as the war on terrorism and the economies of developing nations, defy solutions that can be reduced to simple formulas or doctrines. Every choice a policy maker makes may involve antagonizing an ally, a domestic constituency, members of Congress, or even part of the executive bureaucracy itself.

KEY TERMS

Bureau of International Information Programs (IIP) 493

Central Intelligence Agency (CIA) 495

Cold War 486

Department of Defense (DoD) 496

Department of State 493

détente 489

developing nations 507

foreign policy 486

homeland security 505

internationalism 486

International Monetary Fund (IMF) 507

isolationism 486

Joint Chiefs of Staff (JCS) 496

Marshall Plan 489

military-industrial complex 504

multinational corporations 503

Nixon Doctrine 490

North Atlantic Treaty Organization (NATO) 489

Truman Doctrine 489

United States Agency for International Development (USAID) 493

World Bank 507

READINGS FOR FURTHER STUDY

For a comprehensive overview of American foreign policy since 1945 see *American Foreign Policy Since World War II*, 21st ed. (Washington, DC: CQ Press, 2018), by Steven W. Hook and John W. Spanier, and *The Wise Men: Six Friends and the World They Made* (New York: Simon & Schuster, 2012), by Walter Isaacson and Evan Thomas.

Joseph S. Nye's *The Paradox of American Power: Why the World's Only Superpower Can't Go It Alone* (New York: Oxford University Press, 2003) explores the difficulties of the emerging role of the United States as the world's sole superpower.

An excellent account of presidents' actions in foreign and defense policy throughout American history is Louis Fisher's *Presidential War Power*, 3rd ed. (Lawrence: University Press of Kansas, 2013).

The process of defense budgeting is described insightfully in George C. Wilson's *This War Really Matters: Inside the Fight for Defense Dollars* (Washington, DC: CQ Press, 2000).

Emerging problems of a global economy are explored in Joseph E. Stiglitz's *Globalization and Its Discontents Revisited: Anti-Globalization in the Era of Trump* (New York: W.W. Norton, 2017).

American policy toward developing nations is explored by Robert Chase, ed., *The Pivotal States: A New Framework for U.S. Policy in the Developing World* (New York: W.W. Norton, 2000).

NOTES

1. Office of Management and Budget, *Fiscal Year 2021 Historical Tables,* https://www.whitehouse.gov/omb/historical-tables/ (August 16, 2020); National Priorities Project, "U.S. Military Spending vs. the World," https://www.nationalpriorities.org/campaigns/us-military-spending-vs-world/ (August 16, 2020).

2. The Gallup Organization, "U.S. Position in the World," https://news.gallup.com/poll/116350/Position-World.aspx (August 16, 2020).

3. The Gallup Organization, "Russia," February 10, 2019.

4. Charles W. Kegley and Eugene R. Wittkopf, *American Foreign Policy: Pattern and Process*, 4th ed. (New York: St. Martin's Press, 1991), p. 342; Foreign Policy Association, "International Defense Industry," http://www.fpa.org/newsletter_info2584 (November 1, 2004).

5. *The Washington Post*, "CIA Is Largest U.S. Spy Agency, According to Black Budget Leaked by Edward Snowden," August 30, 2013, http://www.washingtonpost.com/world/national-security/cia-is-largest-us-spy-agency-according-to-black-budget-leaked-by-edward-snowden/2013/08/29/d8d6d5de-10ec-11e3-bdf6-e4fc677d94a1_story.html (December 29, 2014).

6. David C. Jones, "Why the Joint Chiefs of Staff Must Change," in *Understanding U.S. Strategy: A Reader*, ed. Terry L. Heyns (Washington, DC: National Defense University Press, 1983), pp. 304–325; Edward Luttwak, *The Pentagon and the Art of War* (New York: Simon and Schuster, 1985).

7. Department of Defense, "Unified Command Plan," http://www.defense.gov/specials/unifiedcommand/ (October 16, 2002).

8. John G. Tower, "Congress Versus the President," *Foreign Affairs 60* (1981–1982): 18.

9. Martin E. Goldstein, *America's Foreign Policy: Drift or Decision* (Wilmington, DE: Scholarly Resources, 1984), p. 367.

10. Dara Lind, "Does Trump Need Congressional Approval to Strike Syria? The Debate, Explained." *Vox,* April 7, 2017, https://www.vox.com/policy-and-politics/2017/4/7/15217832/aumf-trump-syria-congress (November 17, 2018).

11. Nikki Carvajal, "Trump Vetoes Iran War Powers Resolution," CNN, May 6, 2020, https://www.cnn.com/2020/05/06/politics/trump-veto-iran-war-powers/index.html (August 17, 2020).

12. The Gallup Organization, "Military and National Defense," February 16, 2020, https://news.gallup.com/poll/1666/Military-National-Defense.aspx (August 17, 2020).

13. Gabriel A. Almond, *The American People and Foreign Policy* (New York: Praeger, 1962), p. 53.

14. William Schneider, "Conservatism, Not Internationalism: Trends in Foreign Policy Opinion, 1974–1982," in *Eagle Defiant: United States Foreign Policy in the 1980s*, eds. Kenneth Oye, Robert J. Lieber, and Donald Rothchild (Boston: Little, Brown, 1983), p. 45.

15. The Gallup Organization, "Americans on Iraq: Military Action or Diplomacy?" October 8, 2002, http://www.gallup.com/poll/tb/goverPubli /20021008.asp (October 17, 2002).

16. The Gallup Organization, "Top Ten Findings About Public Opinion and Iraq," October 8, 2002, http://www.gallup.com/poll/releases/pr021008.asp (October 17, 2002).

17. The Gallup Organization, "Iraq," http://www.gallup .com/poll/1633/iraq.aspx.

18. CNN/Opinion Research Corporation Poll, May 21–23, 2010; Gallup Poll, July 10–12, 2009.

19. The Gallup Organization, "Iraq," http://www.gallup .com/poll/1633/Iraq.aspx (September 17, 2012).

20. *Financial Times*, "$1tn Cost of Longest U.S. War Hastens Retreat from Military Intervention," December 14, 2014, http://www.ft.com/intl/cms /s/2/14be0e0c-8255-11e4-ace7-00144feabdc0 .html#slide0 (December 29, 2014).

21. David Welna and Colin Dwyer, "U.S. Signs Peace Deal With Taliban After Nearly 2 Decades of War in Afghanistan," NPR, February 29, 2020, https://www.witf.org/2020/02/29/u-s-signs-peace -deal-with-taliban-after-nearly-2-decades-of-war-in -afghanistan/ (August 17, 2020).

22. Fortune 500 2020, https://fortune.com/fortune500/ (August 17, 2020).

23. Richard J. Barnet, *Real Security: Restoring American Power in a Dangerous Decade* (New York: Simon & Schuster, 1981), p. 69.

24. The Center for Responsive Politics, "A Passage to China Update: House Approves PNTR," May 24, 2000, http://www.opensecrets.org (October 17, 2002); "Anxious Eyes on Beijing—and Washington," *Business Week*, April 30, 2001.

25. U.S. Census Bureau, https://www.census.gov/foreign -trade/balance/c5700.html (August 17, 2020).

26. Financial Markets Center, *Capital Flows Monitor*, (April 27, 2006).

27. "US Investment Banks Strengthen Global Lead Over Europe," Reuters, March 27, 2017, https://www.cnbc. com/2017/03/22/us-investment-banks-strengthen- global-lead-over-europe.html (November 17, 2018).

28. Fortune 500 2020, https://fortune.com/fortune500/ (August 17, 2020).

29. The Center for Responsive Politics, http://www .opensecrets.org/pacs/sector.php?cycle=2020&txt=D (August 17, 2020).

30. Friends Committee on National Legislation, https://www.fcnl.org/about/policy/issues/wars -militarism/pentagon-spending#:~:text=Congress %20and%20the%20Trump,than%20%241%20 million%20every%20minute. (August 17, 2020).

31. Office of Management and Budget, *Historical Tables*, https://www.whitehouse.gov/omb/historical -tables/ (August 17, 2020).

32. George W. Bush, *The National Security Strategy of the United States of America* (Washington, DC: Government Printing Office, 2002), p. 1.

33. International Monetary Fund, "The IMF at a Glance," https://www.imf.org/en/About (August 17, 2020).

34. Gustavo Gonzalez, "Aid to Brazil, Uruguay Fails to Dampen Criticism of IMF," *Third World Network Online*, http://www.twnside.org.sg/title/twr143g .htm (October 20, 2002).

35. The World Bank, "Annual Report 2019," https://www.worldbank.org/en/about/annual -report#anchor-annual (August 17, 2020).

POP QUIZ

1. The _____ is a specialized agency of the United Nations that makes loans to poorer nations for economic development.

2. General moods are important because they can place limits on the choices available to _____.

3. Public support never wavered during the _____ in 1991.

4. Congress can limit the president's authority to conduct _____.

5. The Department of _____ was established by the National Security Act in 1947.

6. Internationalism dominated American thought in the 1920s and 1930s.   T   F

7. America took a lead role and formed the United Nations in 1945.   T   F

8. One of the causes of the Cold War was that America insisted on free elections in Eastern Europe.   T   F

9. The Marshall Plan was an American program begun after World War II for the economic rehabilitation of Western Europe.   T   F

10. The Soviet Union responded to the Truman Doctrine and the Marshall Plan by tightening its control over Western Europe.   T   F

11. A French word meaning "relaxation" that was applied to American-Soviet relations is _____.
    A) détente
    B) louver
    C) frettage
    D) révolue

12. One of the events that ended the Cold War was the unification of _____ .
    A) Poland
    B) Germany
    C) Russia
    D) Spain

13. Right below the secretary of state is/are the _____.
    A) undersecretary
    B) coordinator
    C) bureaus
    D) deputy secretary of state

14. This organization coordinates economic assistance programs:
    A) Office of International Programs
    B) Agency for International Development
    C) World Bank
    D) Secretary of Economics

15. The CIA aided in the installment of a pro-American government in _____ .
    A) Iraq
    B) Hungary
    C) Turkey
    D) Iran

Answers:
1. World Bank   2. policy makers   3. Gulf War
4. arms sales   5. Defense   6. F   7. T   8. T
9. T   10. F   11. A   12. B   13. D   14. B
15. D

Appendix
01

(Shutterstock)

THE DECLARATION OF INDEPENDENCE

When in the Course of human events, it becomes necessary for one people to dissolve the political bands which have connected them with another, and to assume among the powers of the earth, the separate and equal station to which the Laws of Nature and of Nature's God entitle them, a decent respect to the opinions of mankind requires that they should declare the causes which impel them to the separation.

We hold these truths to be self-evident, that all men are created equal, that they are endowed by their Creator with certain unalienable Rights, that among these are Life, Liberty and the pursuit of Happiness.—That to secure these rights, Governments are instituted among Men, deriving their just powers from the consent of the governed, that whenever any Form of Government becomes destructive of these ends, it is the Right of the People to alter or to abolish it, and to institute new Government, laying its foundation on such principles and organizing its powers in such form, as to them shall seem most likely to effect their Safety and Happiness. Prudence, indeed, will dictate that Governments long established should not be changed for light and transient causes; and accordingly all experience hath shewn, that mankind are more disposed to suffer, while evils are sufferable, than to right themselves by abolishing the forms to which they are accustomed. But when a long train of abuses and usurpations, pursuing invariably the same Object evinces a design to reduce them under absolute Despotism, it is their right, it is their duty, to throw off such Government, and to provide new Guards for their future security.—Such has been the patient sufferance of these Colonies; and such is now the necessity which constrains them to alter their former Systems of Government. The history of the present King of Great Britain is a history of repeated injuries and usurpations, all having in direct object the establishment of an absolute Tyranny over these States. To prove this, let Facts be submitted to a candid world.

He has refused his Assent to Laws, the most wholesome and necessary for the public good.

He has forbidden his Governors to pass Laws of immediate and pressing importance, unless suspended in their operation till his Assent should be obtained; and when so suspended, he has utterly neglected to attend to them.

513

He has refused to pass other Laws for the accommodation of large districts of people, unless those people would relinquish the right of Representation in the Legislature, a right inestimable to them and formidable to tyrants only.

He has called together legislative bodies at places unusual, uncomfortable, and distant from the depository of their public Records, for the sole purpose of fatiguing them into compliance with his measures.

He has dissolved Representative Houses repeatedly, for opposing with manly firmness his invasions on the rights of the people.

He has refused for a long time, after such dissolutions, to cause others to be elected; whereby the Legislative powers, incapable of Annihilation, have returned to the People at large for their exercise; the State remaining in the mean time exposed to all the dangers of invasion from without, and convulsions within.

He has endeavoured to prevent the population of these States; for that purpose obstructing the Laws for Naturalization of Foreigners; refusing to pass others to encourage their migrations hither, and raising the conditions of new Appropriations of Lands.

He has obstructed the Administration of Justice, by refusing his Assent to Laws for establishing Judiciary powers.

He has made Judges dependent on his Will alone, for the tenure of their offices, and the amount and payment of their salaries.

He has erected a multitude of New Offices, and sent hither swarms of Officers to harrass our people, and eat out their substance.

He has kept among us, in times of peace, Standing Armies, without the Consent of our legislatures.

He has affected to render the Military independent of and superior to the Civil power.

He has combined with others to subject us to a jurisdiction foreign to our constitution, and unacknowledged by our laws; giving his Assent to their Acts of pretended Legislation:

For Quartering large bodies of armed troops among us:

For protecting them, by a mock Trial, from punishment for any Murders which they should commit on the Inhabitants of these States:

For cutting off our Trade with all parts of the world:

For imposing Taxes on us without our Consent:

For depriving us in many cases, of the benefits of Trial by Jury:

For transporting us beyond Seas to be tried for pretended offences:

For abolishing the free System of English Laws in a neighbouring Province, establishing therein an Arbitrary government, and enlarging its Boundaries so as to render it at once an example and fit instrument for introducing the same absolute rule into these Colonies:

For taking away our Charters, abolishing our most valuable Laws, and altering fundamentally the Forms of our Governments:

For suspending our own Legislatures, and declaring themselves invested with power to legislate for us in all cases whatsoever.

He has abdicated Government here, by declaring us out of his Protection, and waging War against us.

He has plundered our seas, ravaged our Coasts, burnt our towns, and destroyed the lives of our people.

He is at this time transporting large Armies of foreign Mercenaries to compleat the works of death, desolation and tyranny, already begun with circumstances of Cruelty & perfidy, scarcely paralleled in the most barbarous ages, and totally unworthy the Head of a civilized nation.

He has constrained our fellow Citizens taken Captive on the high Seas to bear Arms against their Country, to become the executioners of their friends and Brethren, or to fall themselves by their Hands.

He has excited domestic insurrections amongst us, and has endeavoured to bring on the inhabitants of our frontiers, the merciless Indian Savages, whose known rule of warfare, is an undistinguished destruction of all ages, sexes and conditions.

In every stage of these Oppressions We have Petitioned for Redress in the most humble terms: Our repeated Petitions have been answered only by repeated injury. A Prince whose character is thus marked by every act which may define a Tyrant, is unfit to be the ruler of a free people.

Nor have We been wanting in attentions to our Brittish brethren. We have warned them from time to time of attempts by their legislature to extend an unwarrantable jurisdiction over us. We have reminded them of the circumstances of our emigration and settlement here. We have appealed to their native justice and magnanimity, and we have conjured them by the ties of our common kindred to disavow these usurpations, which, would inevitably interrupt our connections and correspondence. They too have been deaf to the voice of justice and of consanguinity. We must, therefore, acquiesce in the necessity, which denounces our Separation, and hold them, as we hold the rest of mankind, Enemies in War, in Peace Friends.

We, therefore, the Representatives of the United States of America, in General Congress, Assembled, appealing to the Supreme Judge of the world for the rectitude of our intentions, do, in the Name, and by Authority of the good People of these Colonies, solemnly publish and declare, That these United Colonies are, and of Right ought to be Free and Independent States; that they are Absolved from all Allegiance to the British Crown, and that all political connection between them and the State of Great Britain, is and ought to be totally dissolved; and that, as Free and Independent States, they have full Power to levy War, conclude Peace, contract Alliances, establish Commerce, and to do all other Acts and Things which Independent States may of right do. And for the support of this Declaration, with a firm reliance on the protection of divine Providence, we mutually pledge to each other our Lives, our Fortunes and our sacred Honor.

John Hancock, Josiah Bartlett, Wm Whipple, Saml Adams, John Adams, Robt Treat Paine, Elbridge Gerry, Steph. Hopkins, William Ellery, Roger Sherman, Samel Huntington, Wm Williams, Oliver Wolcott, Matthew Thornton, Wm Floyd, Phil Livingston, Frans Lewis, Lewis Morris, Richd Stockton, Jno Witherspoon, Fras Hopkinson, John Hart, Abra Clark, Robt Morris, Benjamin Rush, Benja Franklin, John Morton, Geo Clymer, Jas Smith, Geo. Taylor, James Wilson, Geo. Ross, Caesar Rodney, Geo Read, Thos McKean, Samuel Chase, Wm Paca, Thos Stone, Charles Carroll of Carrollton, George Wythe, Richard Henry Lee, Th. Jefferson, Benja Harrison, Thos Nelson, Jr., Francis Lightfoot Lee, Carter Braxton, Wm Hooper, Joseph Hewes, John Penn, Edward Rutledge, Thos Heyward, Junr., Thomas Lynch, Junior, Arthur Middleton, Button Gwinnett, Lyman Hall, Geo Walton

Appendix

02

(Shutterstock)

THE CONSTITUTION OF THE UNITED STATES

We the People of the United States, in Order to form a more perfect Union, establish Justice, insure domestic Tranquility, provide for the common defence, promote the general Welfare, and secure the Blessings of Liberty to ourselves and our Posterity, do ordain and establish this Constitution for the United States of America.

Article I

Section 1

All legislative Powers herein granted shall be vested in a Congress of the United States, which shall consist of a Senate and House of Representatives.

Section 2

The House of Representatives shall be composed of Members chosen every second Year by the People of the several States, and the Electors in each State shall have the Qualifications requisite for Electors of the most numerous Branch of the State Legislature.

No person shall be a Representative who shall not have attained to the Age of twenty five Years, and been seven Years a Citizen of the United States, and who shall not, when elected, be an Inhabitant of that State in which he shall be chosen.

Representatives and direct Taxes shall be apportioned among the several States which may be included within this Union, according to their respective Numbers, which shall be determined by adding to the whole Number of free Persons, including those bound to Service for a Term of Years, and excluding Indians not taxed, three fifths of all other Persons. The actual Enumeration shall be made within three Years after the first Meeting of the Congress of the United States, and within every subsequent Term of ten Years, in such Manner as they shall by Law direct. The Number of Representatives shall not exceed one for every thirty Thousand, but each State shall have at Least one Representative; and until such enumeration shall be made, the State of New Hampshire shall be entitled

517

to chuse three, Massachusetts eight, Rhode-Island and Providence Plantations one, Connecticut five, New-York six, New Jersey four, Pennsylvania eight, Delaware one, Maryland six, Virginia ten, North Carolina five, South Carolina five, and Georgia three.

When vacancies happen in the Representation from any State, the Executive Authority thereof shall issue Writs of Election to fill such Vacancies. The House of Representatives shall chuse their Speaker and other Officers; and shall have the sole Power of Impeachment.

Section 3

The Senate of the United States shall be composed of two Senators from each State, chosen by the Legislature thereof, for six Years; and each Senator shall have one Vote.

Immediately after they shall be assembled in Consequence of the first Election, they shall be divided as equally as may be into three Classes. The Seats of the Senators of the first Class shall be vacated at the Expiration of the second Year, of the second Class at the Expiration of the fourth Year, and of the third Class at the Expiration of the sixth Year, so that one-third may be chosen every second Year; and if Vacancies happen by Resignation, or otherwise, during the Recess of the Legislature of any State, the Executive thereof may make temporary Appointments until the next Meeting of the Legislature, which shall then fill such Vacancies.

No Person shall be a Senator who shall not have attained to the Age of thirty Years, and been nine Years a Citizen of the United States, and who shall not, when elected, be an Inhabitant of that State for which he shall be chosen.

The Vice President of the United States shall be President of the Senate, but shall have no Vote, unless they be equally divided.

The Senate shall chuse their other Officers, and also a President pro tempore, in the Absence of the Vice President, or when he shall exercise the Office of President of the United States.

The Senate shall have the sole Power to try all Impeachments. When sitting for that Purpose, they shall be on Oath or Affirmation. When the President of the United States is tried, the Chief Justice shall preside: And no Person shall be convicted without the Concurrence of two thirds of the Members present.

Judgment in Cases of Impeachment shall not extend further than to removal from Office, and disqualification to hold and enjoy any Office of honor, Trust or Profit under the United States: but the Party convicted shall nevertheless be liable and subject to Indictment, Trial, Judgment and Punishment, according to Law.

Section 4

The Times, Places and Manner of holding Elections for Senators and Representatives, shall be prescribed in each State by the Legislature thereof; but the Congress may at any time by Law make or alter such Regulations, except as to the Places of chusing Senators.

The Congress shall assemble at least once in every Year, and such Meeting shall be on the first Monday in December, unless they shall by Law appoint a different Day.

Section 5

Each House shall be the Judge of the Elections, Returns and Qualifications of its own Members, and a Majority of each shall constitute a Quorum to do Business; but a smaller Number may adjourn from day to day, and may be authorized to compel the Attendance of absent Members, in such Manner, and under such Penalties, as each House may provide.

Each House may determine the Rules of its Proceedings, punish its Members for disorderly Behaviour, and, with the Concurrence of two thirds, expel a Member.

Each House shall keep a Journal of its Proceedings, and from time to time publish the same, excepting such Parts as may in their Judgment require Secrecy; and the Yeas and Nays of the Members of either House on any question shall, at the Desire of one fifth of those Present, be entered on the Journal.

Neither House, during the Session of Congress, shall, without the Consent of the other, adjourn for more than three days, nor to any other Place than that in which the two Houses shall be sitting.

Section 6

The Senators and Representatives shall receive a Compensation for their Services, to be ascertained by Law, and paid out of the Treasury of the United States. They shall in all Cases, except Treason, Felony and Breach of the Peace, be privileged from Arrest during their Attendance at the Session of their respective Houses, and in going to and returning from the same; and for any Speech or Debate in either House, they shall not be questioned in any other Place.

No Senator or Representative shall, during the Time for which he was elected, be appointed to any civil Office under the Authority of the United States, which shall have been created, or the Emoluments whereof shall have been encreased, during such time; and no Person holding any Office under the United States shall be a Member of either House during his Continuance in Office.

Section 7

All Bills for raising Revenue shall originate in the House of Representatives; but the Senate may propose or concur with Amendments as on other Bills.

Every Bill which shall have passed the House of Representatives and the Senate, shall, before it become a Law, be presented to the President of the United States; If he approve he shall sign it, but if not he shall return it, with his Objections to that House in which it shall have originated, who shall enter the Objections at large on their Journal, and proceed to reconsider it. If after such Reconsideration two thirds of that House shall agree to pass the Bill, it shall be sent, together with the Objections, to the other House, by which it shall likewise be reconsidered, and if approved by two thirds of that House, it shall become a Law. But in all such Cases the Votes of both Houses shall be determined by yeas and Nays, and the Names of the Persons voting for and against the Bill shall be entered on the Journal of each House respectively. If any Bill shall not be returned by the President within ten Days (Sundays excepted) after it shall have been presented to him, the Same shall be a Law, in like Manner as if he had signed it, unless the Congress by their Adjournment prevent its Return, in which Case it shall not be a Law.

Every Order, Resolution, or Vote to which the Concurrence of the Senate and House of Representatives may be necessary (except on a question of Adjournment) shall be presented to the President of the United States; and before the Same shall take Effect, shall be approved by him, or being disapproved by him, shall be repassed by two thirds of the Senate and House of Representatives, according to the Rules and Limitations prescribed in the Case of a Bill.

Section 8

The Congress shall have Power To lay and collect Taxes, Duties, Imposts and Excises, to pay the Debts and provide for the common Defence and general Welfare of the United States; but all Duties, Imposts and Excises shall be uniform throughout the United States;

To borrow Money on the credit of the United States;

To regulate Commerce with foreign Nations, and among the several States, and with the Indian Tribes;

To establish an uniform Rule of Naturalization, and uniform Laws on the subject of Bankruptcies throughout the United States;

To coin Money, regulate the Value thereof, and of foreign Coin, and fix the Standard of Weights and Measures;

To provide for the Punishment of counterfeiting the Securities and current Coin of the United States;

To establish Post Offices and post Roads;

To promote the Progress of Science and useful Arts, by securing for limited Times to Authors and Inventors the exclusive Right to their respective Writings and Discoveries;

To constitute Tribunals inferior to the supreme Court;

To define and punish Piracies and Felonies committed on the high Seas, and Offences against the Law of Nations;

To declare War, grant Letters of Marque and Reprisal, and make Rules concerning Captures on Land and Water;

To raise and support Armies, but no Appropriation of Money to that Use shall be for a longer Term than two Years;

To provide and maintain a Navy;

To make Rules for the Government and Regulation of the land and naval Forces;

To provide for calling forth the Militia to execute the Laws of the Union, suppress Insurrections and repel Invasions;

To provide for organizing, arming, and disciplining the Militia, and for governing such Part of them as may be employed in the Service of the United States, reserving to the States respectively, the Appointment of the Officers, and the Authority of training the Militia according to the discipline prescribed by Congress;

To exercise exclusive Legislation in all Cases whatsoever, over such District (not exceeding ten Miles square) as may, by Cession of particular States, and the Acceptance of Congress, become the Seat of the Government of the United States, and to exercise like Authority over all Places purchased by the Consent of the Legislature of the State in which the Same shall be, for the Erection of Forts, Magazines, Arsenals, dock-Yards, and other needful Buildings; And

To make all Laws which shall be necessary and proper for carrying into Execution the foregoing Powers, and all other Powers vested by this Constitution in the Government of the United States, or in any Department or Officer thereof.

Section 9

The Migration or Importation of such Persons as any of the States now existing shall think proper to admit, shall not be prohibited by the Congress prior to the Year one thousand eight hundred and eight, but a Tax or duty may be imposed on such Importation, not exceeding ten dollars for each Person.

The Privilege of the Writ of Habeas Corpus shall not be suspended, unless when in Cases of Rebellion or Invasion the public Safety may require it.

No Bill of Attainder or ex post facto Law shall be passed.

No Capitation, or other direct, Tax shall be laid unless, in Proportion to the Census or enumeration herein before directed to be taken.

No Tax or Duty shall be laid on Articles exported from any State.

No Preference shall be given by any Regulation of Commerce or Revenue to the Ports of one State over those of another: nor shall Vessels bound to, or from, one State, be obliged to enter, clear, or pay Duties in another.

No Money shall be drawn from the Treasury, but in Consequence of Appropriations made by Law; and a regular Statement and Account of the Receipts and Expenditures of all public Money shall be published from time to time.

No Title of Nobility shall be granted by the United States: And no Person holding any Office of Profit or Trust under them, shall, without the Consent of the Congress, accept of any present, Emolument, Office, or Title, of any kind whatever, from any King, Prince, or foreign State.

Section 10

No State shall enter into any Treaty, Alliance, or Confederation; grant Letters of Marque and Reprisal; coin Money; emit Bills of Credit; make any Thing but gold and silver Coin a Tender in Payment of Debts; pass any Bill of Attainder, ex post facto Law, or Law impairing the Obligation of Contracts, or grant any Title of Nobility.

No State shall, without the Consent of the Congress, lay any Imposts or Duties on Imports or Exports, except what may be absolutely necessary for executing its inspection Laws: and the net Produce of all Duties and Imposts, laid by any State on Imports or Exports, shall be for the Use of the Treasury of the United States; and all such Laws shall be subject to the Revision and Controul of the Congress.

No State shall, without the Consent of Congress, lay any Duty of Tonnage, keep Troops, or Ships of War in time of Peace, enter into any Agreement or Compact with another State, or with a foreign Power, or engage in War, unless actually invaded, or in such imminent Danger as will not admit of delay.

Article II

Section 1

The executive Power shall be vested in a President of the United States of America. He shall hold his Office during the Term of four Years, and, together with the Vice President, chosen for the same Term, be elected, as follows:

Each State shall appoint, in such Manner as the Legislature thereof may direct, a Number of Electors, equal to the whole Number of Senators and Representatives to which the State may be entitled in the Congress; but no Senator or Representative, or Person holding an Office of Trust or Profit under the United States, shall be appointed an Elector.

The Electors shall meet in their respective States, and vote by Ballot for two Persons, of whom one at least shall not be an Inhabitant of the same State with themselves. And they shall make a List of all the Persons voted for, and of the Number of Votes for each; which List they shall sign and certify, and transmit sealed to the Seat of the Government of the United States, directed to the President of the Senate. The President of the Senate shall, in the Presence of the Senate and House of Representatives, open all the Certificates, and the Votes shall then be counted. The Person having the greatest Number of Votes shall be the President, if such Number be a Majority of the whole Number of Electors appointed; and if there be more than one who have such Majority, and have an equal Number of Votes, then the House of Representatives shall immediately chuse by Ballot one of them for President; and if no Person have a Majority, then from the five highest on the List the said House shall in like Manner chuse the President. But in chusing the President, the Votes shall be taken by States, the Representation from each State having one Vote; a quorum for this Purpose shall consist of a Member or Members from two-thirds of

the States, and a Majority of all the States shall be necessary to a Choice. In every Case, after the Choice of the President, the Person having the greatest Number of Votes of the Electors shall be the Vice President. But if there should remain two or more who have equal Votes, the Senate shall chuse from them by Ballot the Vice President.

The Congress may determine the Time of chusing the Electors, and the Day on which they shall give their Votes; which Day shall be the same throughout the United States.

No Person except a natural born Citizen, or a Citizen of the United States, at the time of the Adoption of this Constitution, shall be eligible to the Office of President; neither shall any Person be eligible to that Office who shall not have attained to the Age of thirty-five Years, and been fourteen Years a Resident within the United States.

In Case of the Removal of the President from Office, or of his Death, Resignation, or Inability to discharge the Powers and Duties of the said Office, the Same shall devolve on the Vice President, and the Congress may by Law provide for the Case of Removal, Death, Resignation, or Inability, both of the President and Vice President, declaring what Officer shall then act as President, and such Officer shall act accordingly, until the Disability be removed, or a President shall be elected.

The President shall, at stated Times, receive for his Services a Compensation, which shall neither be encreased nor diminished during the Period for which he shall have been elected, and he shall not receive within that Period any other Emolument from the United States, or any of them.

Before he enter on the Execution of his Office, he shall take the following Oath or Affirmation:—"I do solemnly swear (or affirm) that I will faithfully execute the Office of President of the United States, and will to the best of my Ability, preserve, protect and defend the Constitution of the United States."

Section 2

The President shall be Commander in Chief of the Army and Navy of the United States, and of the Militia of the several States, when called into the actual Service of the United States; he may require the Opinion, in writing, of the principal Officer in each of the executive Departments, upon any Subject relating to the Duties of their respective Offices, and he shall have Power to grant Reprieves and Pardons for Offences against the United States, except in Cases of Impeachment.

He shall have Power, by and with the Advice and Consent of the Senate, to make Treaties, provided two thirds of the Senators present concur; and he shall nominate, and by and with the Advice and Consent of the Senate, shall appoint Ambassadors, other public Ministers and Consuls, Judges of the supreme Court, and all other Officers of the United States, whose Appointments are not herein otherwise provided for, and which shall be established by Law: but the Congress may by Law vest the Appointment of such inferior Officers, as they think proper, in the President alone, in the Courts of Law, or in the Heads of Departments.

The President shall have Power to fill up all Vacancies that may happen during the Recess of the Senate, by granting Commissions which shall expire at the End of their next Session.

Section 3

He shall from time to time give to the Congress Information of the State of the Union, and recommend to their Consideration such Measures as he shall judge necessary and expedient; he may, on extraordinary Occasions, convene both Houses, or either of them, and in Case of Disagreement between them, with Respect to the Time of Adjournment,

he may adjourn them to such Time as he shall think proper; he shall receive Ambassadors and other public Ministers; he shall take Care that the Laws be faithfully executed, and shall Commission all the Officers of the United States.

Section 4

The President, Vice President and all civil Officers of the United States, shall be removed from Office on Impeachment for, and Conviction of, Treason, Bribery, or other high Crimes and Misdemeanors.

Article III

Section 1

The judicial Power of the United States shall be vested in one supreme Court, and in such inferior Courts as the Congress may from time to time ordain and establish. The Judges, both of the supreme and inferior Courts, shall hold their Offices during good Behaviour, and shall, at stated Times, receive for their Services, a Compensation, which shall not be diminished during their Continuance in Office.

Section 2

The judicial Power shall extend to all Cases, in Law and Equity, arising under this Constitution, the Laws of the United States, and Treaties made, or which shall be made, under their Authority;—to all Cases affecting Ambassadors, other public Ministers and Consuls;—to all Cases of admiralty and maritime Jurisdiction;—to Controversies to which the United States shall be a Party;—to Controversies between two or more States;—between a State and Citizens of another State—between Citizens of different States,—between Citizens of the same State claiming Lands under Grants of different States, and between a State, or the Citizens thereof, and foreign States, Citizens or Subjects.

In all Cases affecting Ambassadors, other public Ministers and Consuls, and those in which a State shall be Party, the supreme Court shall have original Jurisdiction. In all the other Cases before mentioned, the supreme Court shall have appellate Jurisdiction, both as to Law and Fact, with such Exceptions, and under such Regulations as the Congress shall make.

The Trial of all Crimes, except in Cases of Impeachment, shall be by Jury; and such Trial shall be held in the State where the said Crimes shall have been committed; but when not committed within any State, the Trial shall be at such Place or Places as the Congress may by Law have directed.

Section 3

Treason against the United States, shall consist only in levying War against them, or in adhering to their Enemies, giving them Aid and Comfort. No Person shall be convicted of Treason unless on the testimony of two Witnesses to the same overt Act, or on Confession in open Court.

The Congress shall have Power to declare the Punishment of Treason, but no Attainder of Treason shall work Corruption of Blood, or Forfeiture except during the Life of the Person attainted.

Article IV

Section 1

Full Faith and Credit shall be given in each State to the public Acts, Records, and judicial Proceedings of every other State. And the Congress may by general Laws prescribe the Manner in which such Acts, Records and Proceedings shall be proved, and the Effect thereof.

Section 2

The Citizens of each State shall be entitled to all Privileges and Immunities of Citizens in the several States.

A Person charged in any State with Treason, Felony, or other Crime, who shall flee from Justice, and be found in another State, shall on Demand of the executive Authority of the State from which he fled, be delivered up, to be removed to the State having Jurisdiction of the Crime.

No Person held to Service or Labour in one State, under the Laws thereof, escaping into another, shall, in Consequence of any Law or Regulation therein, be discharged from such Service or Labour, but shall be delivered up on Claim of the Party to whom such Service or Labour may be due.

Section 3

New States may be admitted by the Congress into this Union; but no new State shall be formed or erected within the Jurisdiction of any other State, nor any State be formed by the Junction of two or more States, or Parts of States, without the Consent of the Legislatures of the States concerned as well as of the Congress.

The Congress shall have Power to dispose of and make all needful Rules and Regulations respecting the Territory or other Property belonging to the United States; and nothing in this Constitution shall be so construed as to Prejudice any Claims of the United States, or of any particular State.

Section 4

The United States shall guarantee to every State in this Union a Republican Form of Government, and shall protect each of them against Invasion; and on Application of the Legislature, or of the Executive (when the Legislature cannot be convened) against domestic Violence.

Article V

The Congress, whenever two-thirds of both Houses shall deem it necessary, shall propose Amendments to this Constitution, or, on the Application of the Legislatures of two-thirds of the several States, shall call a Convention for proposing Amendments, which, in either Case, shall be valid to all Intents and Purposes, as Part of this Constitution, when ratified by the Legislatures of three-fourths of the several States, or by Conventions in three-fourths thereof, as the one or the other Mode of Ratification may be proposed by the Congress; Provided that no Amendment which may be made prior to the Year One

thousand eight hundred and eight shall in any Manner affect the first and fourth Clauses in the Ninth Section of the first Article; and that no State, without its Consent, shall be deprived of its equal Suffrage in the Senate.

Article VI

All Debts contracted and Engagements entered into, before the Adoption of this Constitution, shall be as valid against the United States under this Constitution, as under the Confederation.

This Constitution, and the Laws of the United States which shall be made in Pursuance thereof; and all Treaties made, or which shall be made, under the Authority of the United States, shall be the supreme Law of the Land; and the Judges in every State shall be bound thereby, any Thing in the Constitution or Laws of any State to the Contrary notwithstanding.

The Senators and Representatives before mentioned, and the Members of the several State Legislatures and all executive and judicial Officers, both of the United States and of the several States, shall be bound by Oath or Affirmation, to support this Constitution; but no religious Test shall ever be required as a Qualification to any Office or public Trust under the United States.

Article VII

The Ratification of the Conventions of nine States, shall be sufficient for the Establishment of this Constitution between the States so ratifying the Same.

Done in Convention by the Unanimous Consent of the States present the Seventeenth Day of September in the Year of our Lord one thousand seven hundred and Eighty seven and of the Independance of the United States of America the Twelfth. In Witness whereof We have hereunto subscribed our Names.

Geo. Washington, President and deputy from Virginia; Delaware: Geo. Read, Gunning Bedford, Jr., John Dickinson, Richard Bassett, Jaco. Broom; Maryland: James McHenry, Daniel of St. Thomas' Jenifer, Danl. Carroll; Virginia: John Blair, James Madison, Jr.; North Carolina: Wm. Blount, Richd. Dobbs Spaight, Hu Williamson; South Carolina: J. Rutledge, Charles Cotesworth Pinckney, Charles Pinckney, Pierce Butler; Georgia: William Few, Abr. Baldwin; New Hampshire: John Langdon, Nicholas Gilman; Massachusetts: Nathaniel Gorham, Rufus King; Connecticut: Wm. Saml. Johnson, Roger Sherman; New York: Alexander Hamilton; New Jersey: Wil. Livingston, David Brearley, Wm. Paterson, Jona. Dayton; Pennsylvania: B. Franklin, Thomas Mifflin, Robt. Morris, Geo. Clymer, Thos. FitzSimons, Jared Ingersoll, James Wilson, Gouv. Morris

Articles in Addition to, and Amendment of, the Constitution of the United States of America, Proposed by Congress, and Ratified by the Legislatures of the Several States, Pursuant to the Fifth Article of the Original Constitution.

Amendment I   [1791]

Congress shall make no law respecting an establishment of religion, or prohibiting the free exercise thereof; or abridging the freedom of speech, or of the press; or the right of the people peaceably to assemble, and to petition the Government for a redress of grievances.

Amendment II   [1791]

A well regulated Militia, being necessary to the security of a free State, the right of the people to keep and bear Arms, shall not be infringed.

Amendment III   [1791]

No Soldier shall, in time of peace be quartered in any house, without the consent of the Owner, nor in time of war, but in a manner to be prescribed by law.

Amendment IV   [1791]

The right of the people to be secure in their persons, houses, papers, and effects, against unreasonable searches and seizures, shall not be violated, and no Warrants shall issue, but upon probable cause, supported by Oath or affirmation, and particularly describing the place to be searched, and the persons or things to be seized.

Amendment V   [1791]

No person shall be held to answer for a capital or otherwise infamous crime, unless on a presentment or indictment of a Grand Jury, except in cases arising in the land or naval forces, or in the Militia, when in actual service in time of War or public danger; nor shall any person be subject for the same offence to be twice put in jeopardy of life or limb; nor shall be compelled in any criminal case to be a witness against himself, nor be deprived of life, liberty, or property, without due process of law; nor shall private property be taken for public use, without just compensation.

Amendment VI   [1791]

In all criminal prosecutions, the accused shall enjoy the right to a speedy and public trial, by an impartial jury of the State and district wherein the crime shall have been committed, which district shall have been previously ascertained by law, and to be informed of the nature and cause of the accusation; to be confronted with the witnesses against him; to have compulsory process for obtaining witnesses in his favor, and to have the Assistance of Counsel for his defence.

Amendment VII   [1791]

In Suits at common law, where the value in controversy shall exceed twenty dollars, the right of trial by jury shall be preserved, and no fact tried by a jury, shall be otherwise reexamined in any Court of the United States, than according to the rules of the common law.

Amendment VIII   [1791]

Excessive bail shall not be required, nor excessive fines imposed, nor cruel and unusual punishments inflicted.

Amendment IX   [1791]

The enumeration in the Constitution, of certain rights, shall not be construed to deny or disparage others retained by the people.

Amendment X   [1791]

The powers not delegated to the United States by the Constitution, nor prohibited by it to the States, are reserved to the States respectively, or to the people.

Amendment XI   [1795]

The Judicial power of the United States shall not be construed to extend to any suit in law or equity, commenced or prosecuted against one of the United States by Citizens of another State, or by Citizens or Subjects of any Foreign State.

Amendment XII   [1804]

The Electors shall meet in their respective states and vote by ballot for President and Vice-President, one of whom, at least, shall not be an inhabitant of the same state with themselves; they shall name in their ballots the person voted for as President, and in distinct ballots the person voted for as Vice-President, and they shall make distinct lists of all persons voted for as President, and of all persons voted for as Vice-President, and of the number of votes for each, which lists they shall sign and certify, and transmit sealed to the seat of the government of the United States, directed to the President of the Senate;—The President of the Senate shall, in the presence of the Senate and House of Representatives, open all the certificates and the votes shall then be counted;—The person having the greatest number of votes for President, shall be the President, if such number be a majority of the whole number of Electors appointed; and if no person have such majority, then from the persons having the highest numbers not exceeding three on the list of those voted for as President, the House of Representatives shall choose immediately, by ballot, the President. But in choosing the President, the votes shall be taken by states, the representation from each state having one vote; a quorum for this purpose shall consist of a member or members from two thirds of the states, and a majority of all the states shall be necessary to a choice. And if the House of Representatives shall not choose a President whenever the right of choice shall devolve upon them, before the fourth day of March next following, then the Vice-President shall act as President, as in the case of the death or other constitutional disability of the President.—The person having the greatest number of votes as Vice-President, shall be the Vice-President, if such number be a majority of the whole number of Electors appointed, and if no person have a majority, then from the two highest numbers on the list, the Senate shall choose the Vice-President; a quorum for the purpose shall consist of two-thirds of the whole number of Senators, and a majority of the whole number shall be necessary to a choice. But no person constitutionally ineligible to the office of President shall be eligible to that of Vice-President of the United States.

Amendment XIII   [1865]

Section 1

Neither slavery nor involuntary servitude, except as a punishment for crime whereof the party shall have been duly convicted, shall exist within the United States, or any place subject to their jurisdiction.

Section 2

Congress shall have power to enforce this article by appropriate legislation.

Amendment XIV   [1868]

Section 1

All persons born or naturalized in the United States, and subject to the jurisdiction thereof, are citizens of the United States and of the State wherein they reside. No State shall make or enforce any law which shall abridge the privileges or immunities of citizens of the United States; nor shall any State deprive any person of life, liberty, or property, without due process of law; nor deny to any person within its jurisdiction the equal protection of the laws.

Section 2

Representatives shall be apportioned among the several States according to their respective numbers, counting the whole number of persons in each State, excluding Indians not taxed. But when the right to vote at any election for the choice of electors for President and Vice-President of the United States, Representatives in Congress, the Executive and Judicial officers of a State, or the members of the Legislature thereof, is denied to any of the male inhabitants of such State, being twenty-one years of age, and citizens of the United States, or in any way abridged, except for participation in rebellion, or other crime, the basis of representation therein shall be reduced in the proportion which the number of such male citizens shall bear to the whole number of male citizens twenty-one years of age in such State.

Section 3

No Person shall be a Senator or Representative in Congress, or elector of President and Vice-President, or hold any office, civil or military, under the United States, or under any State, who, having previously taken an oath, as a member of Congress, or as an officer of the United States, or as a member of any State legislature, or as an executive or judicial officer of any State, to support the Constitution of the United States, shall have engaged in insurrection or rebellion against the same, or given aid or comfort to the enemies thereof. But Congress may by a vote of two-thirds of each House, remove such disability.

Section 4

The validity of the public debt of the United States, authorized by law, including debts incurred for payment of pensions and bounties for services in suppressing insurrection or rebellion, shall not be questioned. But neither the United States nor any State shall assume or pay any debt or obligation incurred in aid of insurrection or rebellion against the United States, or any claim for the loss or emancipation of any slave; but all such debts, obligations, and claims shall be held illegal and void.

Section 5

The Congress shall have the power to enforce, by appropriate legislation, the provisions of this article.

Amendment XV   [1870]

Section 1

The right of citizens of the United States to vote shall not be denied or abridged by the United States or by any State on account of race, color, or previous condition of servitude—

Section 2

The Congress shall have power to enforce this article by appropriate legislation.

Amendment XVI   [1913]

The Congress shall have power to lay and collect taxes on incomes, from whatever source derived, without apportionment among the several States, and without regard to any census or enumeration.

Amendment XVII   [1913]

The Senate of the United States shall be composed of two Senators from each State, elected by the people thereof, for six years; and each Senator shall have one vote. The electors in each State shall have the qualifications requisite for electors of the most numerous branch of the State legislatures.

When vacancies happen in the representation of any State in the Senate, the executive authority of such State shall issue writs of election to fill such vacancies: Provided, That the legislature of any State may empower the executive thereof to make temporary appointments until the people fill the vacancies by election as the legislature may direct.

This amendment shall not be so construed as to affect the election or term of any Senator chosen before it becomes valid as part of the Constitution.

Amendment XVIII   [1919]

Section 1

After one year from the ratification of this article the manufacture, sale, or transportation of intoxicating liquors within, the importation thereof into, or the exportation thereof from the United States and all territory subject to the jurisdiction thereof for beverage purposes is hereby prohibited.

Section 2

The Congress and the several States shall have concurrent power to enforce this article by appropriate legislation.

Section 3

This article shall be inoperative unless it shall have been ratified as an amendment to the Constitution by the legislatures of the several States, as provided in the Constitution, within seven years from the date of the submission hereof to the States by the Congress.

Amendment XIX [1920]

The right of citizens of the United States to vote shall not be denied or abridged by the United States or by any State on account of sex.

Congress shall have power to enforce this article by appropriate legislation.

Amendment XX [1933]

Section 1

The terms of the President and Vice President shall end at noon on the 20th day of January, and the terms of Senators and Representatives at noon on the 3d day of January, of the years in which such terms would have ended if this article had not been ratified; and the terms of their successors shall then begin.

Section 2

The Congress shall assemble at least once in every year, and such meeting shall begin at noon on the 3d day of January, unless they shall by law appoint a different day.

Section 3

If, at the time fixed for the beginning of the term of the President, the President elect shall have died, the Vice President elect shall become President. If a President shall not have been chosen before the time fixed for the beginning of his term, or if the President elect shall have failed to qualify, then the Vice President elect shall act as President until a President shall have qualified; and the Congress may by law provide for the case wherein neither a President elect nor a Vice President elect shall have qualified, declaring who shall then act as President, or the manner in which one who is to act shall be selected, and such person shall act accordingly until a President or Vice President shall have qualified.

Section 4

The Congress may by law provide for the case of the death of any of the persons from whom the House of Representatives may choose a President whenever the right of choice shall have devolved upon them, and for the case of the death of any of the persons from whom the Senate may choose a Vice President whenever the right of choice shall have devolved upon them.

Section 5

Sections 1 and 2 shall take effect on the 15th day of October following the ratification of this article.

Section 6

This article shall be inoperative unless it shall have been ratified as an amendment to the Constitution by the legislatures of three-fourths of the several States within seven years from the date of its submission.

Amendment XXI [1933]

Section 1

The eighteenth article of amendment to the Constitution of the United States is hereby repealed.

Section 2

The transportation or importation into any State, Territory, or Possession of the United States for delivery or use therein of intoxicating liquors, in violation of the laws thereof, is hereby prohibited.

Section 3

This article shall be inoperative unless it shall have been ratified as an amendment to the Constitution by conventions in the several States, as provided in the Constitution, within seven years from the date of the submission hereof to the States by the Congress.

Amendment XXII [1951]

Section 1

No person shall be elected to the office of the President more than twice, and no person who has held the office of President, or acted as President, for more than two years of a term to which some other person was elected President shall be elected to the office of the President more than once. But this Article shall not apply to any person holding the office of President when this Article was proposed by the Congress, and shall not prevent any person who may be holding the office of President, or acting as President, during the term within which this Article becomes operative from holding the office of President or acting as President during the remainder of such term.

Section 2

This article shall be inoperative unless it shall have been ratified as an amendment to the Constitution by the legislatures of three-fourths of the several states within seven years from the date of its submission to the states by Congress.

Amendment XXIII [1961]

Section 1

The District constituting the seat of Government of the United States shall appoint in such manner as the Congress may direct:

A number of electors of President and Vice President equal to the whole number of Senators and Representatives in Congress to which the District would be entitled if it were a State, but in no event more than the least populous State; they shall be in addition to those appointed by the States, but they shall be considered, for the purposes of the election of President and Vice President, to be electors appointed by a State; and they shall meet in the District and perform such duties as provided by the twelfth article of amendment.

Section 2

The Congress shall have power to enforce this article by appropriate legislation.

Amendment XXIV [1964]

Section 1

The right of citizens of the United States to vote in any primary or other election for President or Vice President, for electors for President or Vice President, or for Senator or Representative in Congress, shall not be denied or abridged by the United States or any State by reason of failure to pay any poll tax or other tax.

Section 2

The Congress shall have the power to enforce this article by appropriate legislation.

Amendment XXV   [1967]

Section 1

In case of the removal of the President from office or of his death or resignation, the Vice President shall become President.

Section 2

Whenever there is a vacancy in the office of the Vice President, the President shall nominate a Vice President who shall take office upon confirmation by a majority vote of both Houses of Congress.

Section 3

Whenever the President transmits to the President pro tempore of the Senate and the Speaker of the House of Representatives his written declaration that he is unable to discharge the powers and duties of his office, and until he transmits to them a written declaration to the contrary, such powers and duties shall be discharged by the Vice President as Acting President.

Section 4

Whenever the Vice President and a majority of either the principal officers of the executive departments, or of such other body as Congress may by law provide, transmit to the President pro tempore of the Senate and the Speaker of the House of Representatives their written declaration that the President is unable to discharge the powers and duties of his office, the Vice President shall immediately assume the powers and duties of the office as Acting President.

Thereafter, when the President transmits to the President pro tempore of the Senate and the Speaker of the House of Representatives his written declaration that no inability exists, he shall resume the powers and duties of his office unless the Vice President and a majority of either the principal officers of the executive department, or of such other body as Congress may by law provide, transmit within four days to the President pro tempore of the Senate and the Speaker of the House of Representatives their written declaration that the President is unable to discharge the powers and duties of his office. There-upon Congress shall decide the issue, assembling within forty-eight hours for that purpose if not in session. If the Congress, within twenty-one days after receipt of the latter written declaration, or, if Congress is not in session, within twenty-one days after Congress is required to assemble, determines by two-thirds vote of both Houses that the President is unable to discharge the powers and duties of his office, the Vice President shall continue to discharge the same as Acting President; otherwise, the President shall resume the powers and duties of his office.

Amendment XXVI   [1971]

Section 1

The right of citizens of the United States, who are eighteen years of age or older, to vote shall not be denied or abridged by the United States or by any State on account of age.

Section 2

The Congress shall have power to enforce this article by appropriate legislation.

Amendment XXVII   [1992]

No law, varying the compensation for the services of the Senators and Representatives, shall take effect, until an election of Representatives shall have intervened.

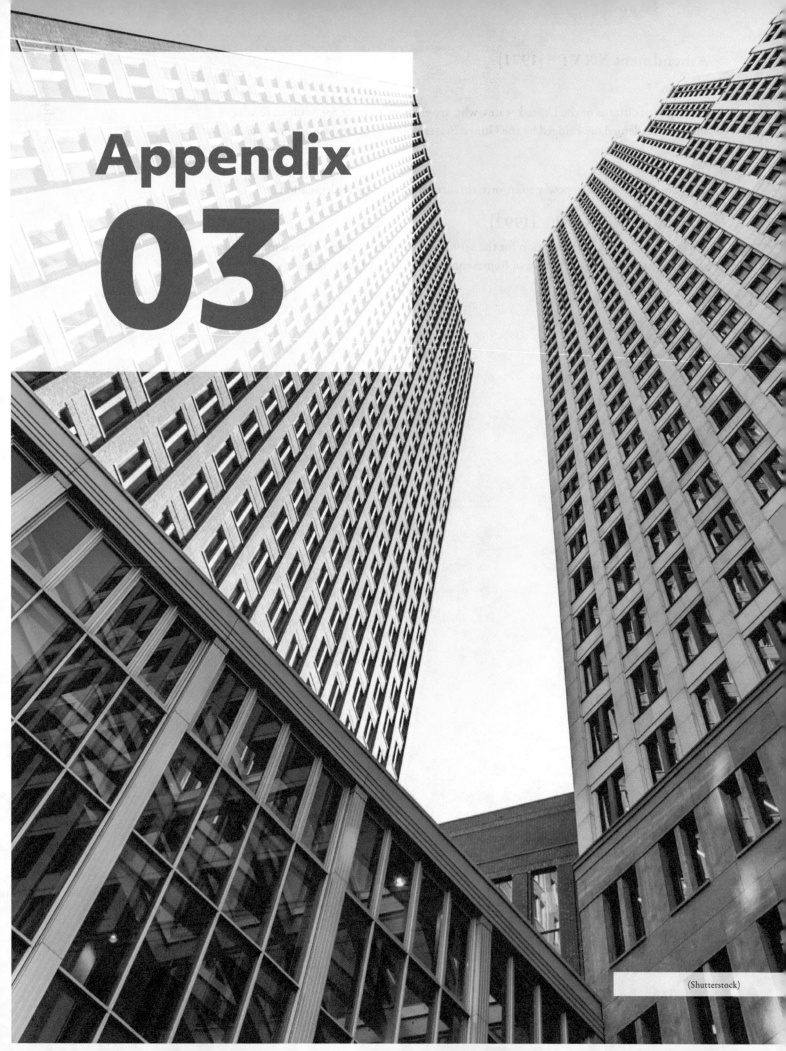

Appendix 03

GLOSSARY

A

administrative law judge

An officer with relatively independent status in a regulatory agency who presides over and makes findings in judicial proceedings in which the agency's actions in individual cases are at issue

administrative assistant (AA)

Top aide to a member of Congress who frequently acts on behalf of the legislator in dealing with staff, colleagues, constituents, and lobbyists

Americans for Democratic Action

The best-known pressure group for contemporary liberalism

affirmative action

Positive steps taken by public or private institutions to overcome the remaining effects of racial or sexual bias (Affirmative action programs attempt to achieve equality of result.)

agenda setting

The process by which the news media select and focus on a small number of stories from a large number of possibilities—shaping, in part, Americans' opinions about what is important

agents of socialization

A "teacher" in the process of political socialization, for example, the family, the school, a peer group, or the mass media

alleviative strategies

Policy strategies designed to make poverty more bearable for individuals rather than designed to attack poverty by reaching its fundamental causes

amicus curiae

Latin for "friend of the court," referring to persons, government agencies, or groups that are not parties to a case but nonetheless have an interest in its outcome and that make their views known by filing an *amicus curiae* brief with the court hearing the case

***amicus curiae* brief**

Latin for "friend of the court"—persons, government agencies, or groups that are not parties to a case but nonetheless have an interest in its outcome can make their views known by filing this brief with the court

Antifederalists

In the first years of government under the Constitution, Antifederalists in Congress were persons who opposed ratification of the Constitution in 1787 and 1788 and opposed policies associated with a strong central government such as a national bank

Annapolis Convention

The meeting of delegates from five states, held in Annapolis, Maryland, in 1786, to consider a common policy for trade among the American states; it resulted in a recommendation for a constitutional convention the following year

appellate jurisdiction

Includes cases a court receives from lower courts—
Congress defines the appellate jurisdiction of the
U.S. Supreme Court

appropriation

Congressional enactment that funds an authorized
program with a specific sum of money

B

backgrounders

News briefings in which reporters may not reveal the
identity of the source of their information

balanced budget amendment

A proposal for a constitutional amendment that would
require the federal government to operate with a budget in
which revenues equaled or exceeded expenditures

balance the ticket

A political party's effort to appeal to a wider cross-section
of voters by providing regional or ideological balance in its
nominations for president and vice president

bill of attainder

A law, prohibited by the Constitution, that punishes an
individual and bypasses the procedural safeguards of the
legal process

block grant

Transfers of cash from the national to state and local
governments in which state and local officials are allowed
discretion in spending the money within some broad policy
area, such as community development or social services

briefs

Documents filed with a court containing the arguments of
the parties in a case

Brown v. Board of Education of Topeka

Landmark Supreme Court decision [347 U.S. 483 (1954)]
that overturned the separate-but-equal standard of *Plessy v.
Ferguson* [163 U.S. 537 (1896)] and began an end to racial
segregation in public schools

C

capital case

A criminal proceeding in which the defendant is on trial
for his or her life

capitalism

An economic system based on private ownership of
property and free economic competition among individuals
and businesses

Articles of Confederation

This first plan of a national government for the thirteen
American states was replaced by the Constitution; under
the Articles, the states retained most political power

authorization

Congressional enactment that creates or continues a policy
program and the agency administering it

budget

A planned statement of expenditure that includes specific
categories of spending

Budget Enforcement Act of 1990

Legislation that fundamentally changed budget deficit
reduction efforts from the focus on deficit targets
contained in Gramm-Rudman-Hollings to a focus on
ceilings or caps on specific categories of spending

bureaucracy

An organization that exists to accomplish certain goals
or objectives called public purposes and that consists of a
group of people hired and arranged in a hierarchy because
of specific duties they can perform

bureaucratic model

A model of policy making that holds that bureaucracies
play a crucial role in making policy because of their
commitment and the expertise they can provide

bureaucrats

Individuals working in the executive branch of government
who have received their positions on the basis of some type
of appointment

Bureau of International Information Programs (IIP)

An agency of the State Department that directs overseas
information programs

case

A controversy to be decided by a court

Case Act

Requires the secretary of state to submit to the Senate the
final text of any executive agreement and allows agreements
concerning sensitive national security matters to be
submitted privately to the Senate Foreign Relations and
House Foreign Affairs committees

casework

The congressional task of handling requests by constituents for information or assistance with the federal bureaucracy

categorical grant-in-aid

Transfers of cash from the national to state and/or local governments for some specific purpose, usually with the accompanying requirement that state and local governments match the national money with some funds of their own

caucus

A meeting of members of a political party (the members of a party in a legislature are also referred to as a party caucus), used in some states to select delegates to the national conventions, which nominate presidential candidates

Central Intelligence Agency (CIA)

Agency, established by the National Security Act of 1947, that is responsible for gathering information and coordinating foreign intelligence operations in the federal government

checks and balances

The system of separate institutions sharing some powers that the Constitution mandates for the national government, the purpose of which is to keep power divided among the three branches: legislative, executive, and judicial

chief of state

The role the president plays as the ceremonial head of the nation that can also make the president a symbol of national unity during times of crisis

Christian Right

Conservative, religion-based groups that involve themselves in the political process

civil case

Noncriminal legal action, such as divorces or attempts to recover damages following an automobile accident

civil disobedience

A form of political protest in which advocates of a cause deliberately break a law as a means of asserting its illegitimacy or drawing attention to their cause

Civil Rights Act of 1964

Comprehensive legislation to end racial segregation in access to public accommodations and in employment in the public and private sectors

Civil Service Reform Act

Legislation designed to improve the level of performance of civil servants by creating incentives for high-quality work, protecting whistle-blowers, and making it easier to fire inadequate employees

clear and present danger test

Guideline devised by the Supreme Court in *Schenck v. United States* [249 U.S. 47 (1919)] to determine when speech could be suppressed under the First Amendment

class action suit

Legal action initiated on behalf of a large number of individuals without any common interest other than their grievance against the person or institution being sued

classical liberalism

A view, dating from the nineteenth century, that government should play a minimal role in society and should permit maximum economic freedom for the individual

closed primary

A primary election in which only the members of the party holding the election are allowed to participate

closed rule

An order from the House Rules Committee that prohibits amendments to a bill under consideration on the House floor

cloture

Rule 22 of the Senate in which discussion on a piece of legislation can be suspended after no more than thirty hours of debate by a vote of sixty members

coalition

A subgroup of a party, based on common social, economic, and religious characteristics

Code of Federal Regulations (CFR)

Compilation of US administrative rules currently in effect, classified by agency and subject matter

Cold War

An era of intense ideological tension between the Soviet Union and its allies and the United States and its allies lasting from roughly the end of World War II to the collapse of the Soviet Union in 1991

collective goods

Something of value that, by its nature, can be made available only to everybody or not to anyone at all

colony

A territory under the direct control of a parent state

commander-in-chief clause

Article II, Section 2 of the U.S. Constitution names the president as the civilian head of U.S. military forces

commerce clause

Found in Article I, Section 8, of the Constitution, this clause gives Congress the authority to regulate the country's economic environment

Committee of the Whole

A parliamentary device used by the House of Representatives to facilitate floor consideration of a bill; when the House dissolves itself into the Committee of the Whole, it can suspend formal rules and consider a bill with a quorum of 100 rather than the usual 218

comparable worth

An employment policy designed to overcome the economic inequities of sexual discrimination, mandating that persons holding jobs of equal responsibility and skill be paid the same

concurring opinion

A statement issued separately by a judge voting with the majority

confederation

A loose association of states in which dominant political power lies with the member states and not with the central government

Conference

The Republican leadership committee in the House

Congressional Budget and Impoundment Control Act of 1974

Legislation that significantly changed congressional budget procedures by creating budget committees, establishing a budget decision timetable, changing the fiscal year, placing limits on presidential impoundments, and establishing the Congressional Budget Office

Congressional Budget Office (CBO)

A congressional staff unit that provides Congress with budgetary expertise, independent of the president's budget staff, to help Congress clarify budgetary choices

congressional seniority

Based on a member's length of continuous service in the Congress, it can affect committee assignments, the amount of office space granted, and even the deference shown a member during floor debate

conservatism

A defense of the political and economic status quo against forces of change, holding that established customs, laws, and traditions should guide society

constitutionalism

The belief in limiting governmental power by a written charter

constitutional theory

The concept, associated with President William Howard Taft, that the president cannot exercise any power unless it is based on a specific constitutional provision or legislative grant

continuing resolution

Legislative action taken by Congress to allow spending to proceed at the previous year's level when Congress has not met the deadline for reaching agreement on appropriations for the next fiscal year

contract theory

Theory holding that the state gains its legitimacy from the consent of the governed and is formed primarily to protect the rights of individuals to life, liberty, and property

cooperative federalism

A model of federalism that features intertwining relationships and shared areas of responsibility between the national and state and local governments

council-manager

A form of government at the local level where an elected council exercises legislative powers and hires a city manager to perform executive and administrative duties

Council of Economic Advisers (CEA)

Established by the Employment Act of 1946 as a part of the Executive Office of the President; consists of a chairperson, usually a prominent academic economist, and two other members who have the primary task of analyzing economic issues for the president

court of last resort

The highest court within a particular judicial system, such as a state supreme court, to which a litigant may appeal a case

courts of general jurisdiction

The basic unit of a court system, receiving appeals from courts of limited jurisdiction and serving as trial courts for serious criminal offenses and civil suits involving substantial amounts of money

courts of limited jurisdiction

The lowest-level court in a state's judicial system that hears particular kinds of cases involving small claims, traffic violations, and minor criminal infractions

crime

A public wrong; an offense, such as murder, against society at large—even though it may have been committed against only a single individual

criminal case

Judicial proceedings that the government begins against an individual following commission of a crime

cross-cutting cleavage

The overlapping of interest group membership from individual to individual, with the result that society rarely finds the same people lined up on opposite sides on all the issues and is thus protected against political polarization

cruel and unusual punishment

Prohibited by the Eighth Amendment—at issue in capital cases

curative strategies

Policy strategies designed to reach the fundamental causes of poverty and to enable individuals to get out of poverty and lead productive, self-sufficient lives

D

de facto segregation

Programs or facilities that are racially segregated by private choice or private discrimination, not because of law or public policy

de jure segregation

Programs or facilities that are racially segregated because of law or public policy

dealignment

Period during which the partisan ties of the public diminish and the party system breaks down

debt

The total amount of money that the national government owes to lenders, such as banks, individual and foreign investors, insurance companies, and the variety of financial institutions that purchase government securities

decline

The idea that the American political parties are collapsing and may, perhaps, eventually disappear

deficit

An excess of government expenditures over revenues

delegated powers

Legal authority that the people in the states granted to the national government for certain purposes by ratifying the Constitution; can be either express or implied

delegate role

A concept of legislative work as simply voting the desires of one's constituents, regardless of one's own personal views

democracy

A system of government based on majority rule, protection of minority and individual rights, and the equality of all citizens before the law

democratic socialism

An economic system in which the major industries are owned by a democratically elected government responsible for planning and directing the economy

Department of Defense (DoD)

Established by the National Security Act of 1947 and responsible for formulating military policy and maintaining the armed forces

Department of State

Responsible for the routine daily functions of foreign policy; the department that represents the United States abroad; involved in international negotiations, supervising foreign aid and programs promoting cultural and educational exchange, and making policy recommendations to the president

depression

A period of serious and sustained economic decline

deregulation

Process of reducing the number and scope of government regulations

détente

A French word meaning "relaxation" that was applied to Soviet-American relations in the early 1970s

developing nations

Nations whose standard of living lags far behind that of the industrialized countries

direct mail

Method of contacting citizens by mail, rather than through personal contact or the mass media

direct popular election

Selection of officials on the basis of those receiving the largest number of votes cast, sometimes referring to a proposal to choose the president and vice president on this basis rather than through the Electoral College

dissenting opinion

A statement issued by a judge explaining his or her disagreement with the majority position

distributive policies

Programs such as water reclamation projects that provide considerable benefits for a few people and relatively small costs for many, usually provoking little opposition

domestic policy

A category of public policy that is composed of policy decisions about matters affecting individuals within a political system

dual federalism

A model of federalism in which national and state governments are separate and independent from each other, with each level exercising its own powers in its own jurisdiction

E

economic policy

Decisions a government makes that affect the production, distribution, and consumption of goods; the provision of services; the flow of income; and the accumulation of wealth

economic regulation

Type of regulation in which a government agency issues rules that shape the structure of some industry, such as limiting entrance into the broadcast industry, or banning or encouraging certain business practices

Eighth Amendment

The part of the Bill of Rights that prohibits "cruel and unusual punishment," which is often at issue in death penalty cases

Electoral College

Institution established by the Constitution for electing the president and vice president and whose members—electors chosen by the voters—actually elect the president and vice president

electoral functions

With reference to political parties, the ways in which parties, by seeking to win elections, help to bring order to campaigns and elections

Eleventh Amendment

The first reversal of a Supreme Court decision [*Chisholm v. Georgia*, 2 U.S. (2 Dallas) 419 (1793)] by constitutional amendment, denying federal courts jurisdiction in suits against a state brought by citizens of another state or a foreign country

elitism

A model of policy making that holds that public policy decisions are made by a relatively small group of individuals acting in their own self-interest rather than in the interest of the mass of citizens

Environmental Protection Agency (EPA)

An independent agency that controls and abates air and water pollution and protects the environment from pollution by solid wastes, pesticides, radiation, and toxic substances

equality of condition

A standard, beyond equality of opportunity, that requires policies (such as redistribution of income and other resources) that seek to reduce or eliminate the effects of past discrimination

equality of opportunity

A standard that calls for government to remove barriers of discrimination, such as segregation laws or racially exclusive hiring practices, that have existed in the past

equality of result

A standard, beyond equality of condition, that requires policies such as affirmative action or comparable worth that place some people on an equal footing with others

equal protection clause

Part of the Fourteenth Amendment that is the source of many civil rights and declares that no state shall deny to any person "the equal protection of the laws"

equal-time rule

A provision of the Communications Act of 1934 that requires radio and television stations to give or sell equivalent time to one political candidate if the station has given or sold time to another candidate for that office

establishment clause

Provision of the First Amendment barring government support of religion

exclusionary rule

Rule developed in *Mapp v. Ohio* [367 U.S. 643 (1961)] that prevents the state from bringing evidence against a defendant when that evidence was obtained illegally

exclusive

An interview that an official or other individual grants to one or more journalists that provides information not generally made available to all media

executive agreements

Agreements between heads of state that, unlike treaties, do not require approval by the Senate—there are no clear legal distinctions between the substance of a treaty and that of an executive agreement

Executive Calendar

One of two registers of business in the U.S. Senate that contains presidential nominations and treaties

Executive Office of the President (EOP)

Created in 1939 to serve as the managerial arm of the presidency; includes such agencies as the National Security Council, the Office of Management and Budget, and the Council of Economic Advisers

exit poll

A poll of voters taken as they leave a polling place and usually conducted by the media to get an advance indication of voting trends and facilitate analysis of the reasons behind the outcome of the election

ex post facto laws

Laws that make an act a crime after it was committed or increase the punishment for a crime already committed—prohibited by the Constitution

express powers

Powers specifically enumerated in the Constitution as belonging to the national government

F

fairness doctrine

A regulation of the Federal Communications Commission that required radio and television stations to devote some airtime to a balanced discussion of public issues; abolished in 1987

faithless elector

A person who is chosen to vote for particular presidential and vice-presidential candidates in the Electoral College but who, nevertheless, votes for different presidential and vice-presidential candidates

Federal Communications Commission (FCC)

An agency of the national government that regulates the telecommunications industry in the United States, including the licensing and operation of all radio and television stations

federal courts

The courts of the United States, as distinguished from the courts of the fifty states

Federal Election Campaign Act

Law passed in 1971 and amended several times that regulates campaign financing and requires full disclosure of sources and uses of campaign funds and limits contributions to political candidates

federal question

An issue that involves the interpretation of the Constitution or a statute or a treaty of the United States

federalism

A system of government in which both the national and state governments share power within the same political system

Federalists

A term for persons who advocated ratification of the Constitution in 1787 and 1788 and generally favored a strong central government; it was also the name of the dominant political party during the administrations of Presidents George Washington and John Adams

Federal Register

A daily government publication that contains proposed and final regulations, presidential proclamations, and executive orders

felony

A serious criminal offense, usually punishable by more than one year in prison

female suffrage

The right of women to vote, which was bestowed nationally by the Nineteenth Amendment in 1920

Fifteenth Amendment

Outlawed race-based restrictions on voting

fifth branch

Refers to the press in its role as a check on public officials, after the other four branches (Congress, the president, the Supreme Court, and the bureaucracy)

filibuster

Continuing debate designed to prevent consideration of a particular bill; a technique used in the Senate

First Amendment

The part of the Bill of Rights containing protections for political and religious expression

fiscal policy

Governmental decisions about taxing and spending that affect the economic life of a nation

fiscal year

For budget and accounting purposes in the national government, the twelve-month period beginning on October 1 and ending on September 30 of the following calendar year

foreign policy

Efforts to pursue national objectives beyond the geographic boundaries of the nation by engaging either diplomatically or militarily with one or more foreign nations or multinational organizations

formal party organization

One of the three components or distinguishable sectors of a political party; the official structure of a political party and includes people who officially belong to it, elected and appointed officers, and committees

Fourteenth Amendment

Ratified in 1868, the amendment altered the nature of the Union by placing significant restraints on state governments

Fourth Amendment

Part of the Bill of Rights that prohibits unreasonable searches and seizures of persons and their property

fourth branch

Viewed as separate from the presidency, the collection of executive departments, independent establishments, and government corporations

framing

The way that the media present a story, consisting of angle, tone, and point of view

franking privilege

A congressional benefit that permits members to send out official mail using their signature rather than postage

free exercise clause

Provision of the First Amendment guaranteeing religious freedom

free-market capitalism model

A model of policy making that posits a limited role for government so that the natural forces of supply and demand are allowed to prevail in the marketplace

free trade

Belief that America's economic interests are best served by allowing foreign producers to sell their goods without restriction in the United States

G

general election

Election, which occurs in November, to choose the candidates who will hold public office, following primary elections held during the spring and summer

government

The political and administrative organization of a state, nation, or locality

governmental functions

With reference to political parties, the ways in which parties, by seeking to win elections, help to organize the government, give coherence to public policy, and make government responsible to the people

government corporation

A type of bureaucratic unit that offers some service for which the benefiting individual or institution must pay directly

grass roots lobbying

Attempting to influence members of Congress by encouraging citizens in the home district or state to contact their legislators

Great Compromise

An agreement at the Constitutional Convention in 1787, arranged by the delegation from Connecticut, proposing to accept representation by population in the House and by states in the Senate; sometimes called the Connecticut Compromise

Great Society

President Lyndon Johnson's term for an egalitarian society that aggressive governmental action to help the poor and disadvantaged would attempt to create in the 1960s

Gulf of Tonkin Resolution

A congressional resolution passed in 1964 granting President Johnson the authority to undertake military activities in Southeast Asia

H

Hatch Act

Legislation that prohibits civil servants from participating in partisan political activity

head of government

The chief executive officer of a government (The president is the head of government in the United States.)

high-stimulus election

Election that the public finds interesting and important

homeland security

The effort of protecting United States soil, particularly from foreign or terrorist attack

home rule

A legal status in which local governments, especially large cities, can determine for themselves within broad parameters their own powers and functions without interference from the state government

House Calendar

The legislative schedule in the House of Representatives for non-money bills

House-Senate Conference Committee

A joint committee designed to reconcile differences between the House and Senate versions of a bill

I

ideology

A set of ideas concerning the proper political and economic system in which people should live

implied powers

Powers of national government that are not specifically cited in the Constitution but that are implicit in powers expressly granted by the Constitution

incitement test

The Court's current test for First Amendment restrictions that asks whether a speech act attempts or is likely to incite lawless action

incrementalism

A model of decision-making that holds that new policies differ only marginally from existing policies

independent agency

A type of bureaucratic unit organizationally located outside of an executive department and generally headed by a single individual

independent regulatory commission

A type of bureaucratic unit organizationally located outside of an executive department, headed by a group of individuals called a commission, and charged with regulating a specific industry or economic practice

industrial policy

Proposals for partnership in economic decision-making among government officials, corporate leaders, union officials, and public interest groups

in-kind benefits

Noncash benefits, such as medical care services, that the needy receive from some social welfare programs

inner cabinet

Cabinet officers whose departments handle issues of broad national importance, including the secretaries of state, defense, and the treasury, and the attorney general

interest group elitism

The idea that the leaders of interest groups may act in ways that promote their own interests rather than the interests of the broader membership of the group

interest groups

Associations of people who hold common views and who work together to influence what government does

intermediate appellate courts

Courts between courts of general jurisdiction and the court of last resort; in the federal court system, the courts of appeals

internationalism

A foreign policy perspective that concludes that America's interests in peace abroad and liberty at home require its permanent involvement in world affairs

International Monetary Fund (IMF)

A specialized agency of the United Nations designed to promote international monetary cooperation

interstate compact

A formal agreement between states designed to solve a problem faced by more than one state when such an agreement is necessary because political problems are not limited by geographic boundaries

iron triangle

The combination of interest group representatives, legislators, and government administrators seen as extremely influential in determining the outcome of political decisions

isolationism

A belief that America should not involve itself in the quarrels of Europe and Asia and should pursue a policy of military nonintervention

J

John Locke

English political philosopher whose ideas about political legitimacy influenced the American founders

Joint Chiefs of Staff (JCS)

Heads of the various armed services and their chair who advise the president and the secretary of defense on important military questions

joint committees

Permanent committees of Congress made up of members from both houses

journalists

People who gather, write, and report the news for newspapers, magazines, radio, television, and the internet

judicial activists

Judges who are least hesitant to invoke judicial review to strike down an act of Congress or of a state legislature

judicial restraintists

Judges who are reluctant to invoke judicial review to strike down an act of Congress or of a state legislature

judicial review

The authority of courts to set aside a legislative act as being in violation of the Constitution

jurisdiction

Authority of a court or other agency to act

K

Kentucky and Virginia Resolutions

A challenge to national supremacy, these state documents declared states to be the final authority on the meaning of the Constitution

L

laissez-faire

French for "leave things alone" and the view, in economics, that government should not interfere in the workings of the economy

laissez-faire economics

French for "leave things alone"; the view in economics that government should not interfere in the workings of the economy

leak

The deliberate release of information by an official to a journalist for a specific purpose

legal guilt

The concept that a defendant's factual guilt be established in accordance with the laws and the Constitution before criminal penalties can be applied

legislative assistant (LA)

A congressional aide who analyzes bills, drafts laws, writes speeches, and prepares position papers

legislative intent

A legislature's understanding of the meaning of a law and what it is designed to accomplish

legislative norms

The unwritten rules of acceptable behavior in Congress

legislative veto

Congressional power, which the Supreme Court ruled unconstitutional in 1983, to halt an executive initiative by a vote of one or both houses or by a congressional committee

***Lemon* test**

A standard announced in *Lemon v. Kurtzman* [403 U.S. 602 (1971)] to determine when a statute violates the establishment clause (The law in question must have a secular purpose and a neutral effect and must avoid an excessive entanglement between church and state.)

libel

Defamation of a person's character or reputation, not protected by the First Amendment (*New York Times Co. v. Sullivan* [376 U.S. 254 (1964)] makes it difficult for public figures and officials to bring successful libel suits against their critics.)

liberalism

An ideology that regards the individual as a rational being capable of overcoming obstacles to a better world and supporting changes in the political and economic status quo

libertarianism

A belief that the state should regulate neither the economic nor the moral life of its citizens

line-item veto

Most state governors have this power, through which a chief executive, reacting to a bill passed by the legislature, may accept some items in the bill while also rejecting other items in the same bill. The president does not have this power.

lobbying

Attempting to influence legislation under consideration, particularly through personal contact by group representatives

low-stimulus election

Election that the public finds uninteresting or unimportant

M

majority election

Election in which a candidate wins by getting more than one-half of the votes cast

majority leader (House)

Leader and chief spokesperson for the majority party in the House

majority leader (Senate)

Leader and chief spokesperson for the majority party in the Senate

mandatory programs

Government programs, such as Social Security expenditures, in which spending automatically increases from one year to the next without specific annual appropriations action by Congress

Marbury v. Madison

Landmark decision [5 U.S. (1 Cranch) 137 (1803)] by the Supreme Court in 1803 establishing the Supreme Court's power of judicial review

mark-up

The process in which a legislative committee sets the precise language and amendments of a bill

Marshall Plan

A multibillion-dollar American program begun after World War II for the economic rehabilitation of Western Europe

Marxism model

A model of policy making that holds that public policy decisions in non-Marxist regimes reflect the interests of the ruling economic class at the expense of workers

mass media

Instruments such as newspapers, magazines, radio, television, and the internet that provide the means for communicating with large numbers of people in a short period of time

mayor-council

A form of government at the local level that mirrors the executive-legislative structure at the state and national levels where the mayor has executive powers and the council has legislative powers

McCulloch v. Maryland

Supreme Court case in 1819 that established the constitutionality of a national bank and solidified national power by confirming that the federal government can exercise implied powers to carry out legitimate and otherwise constitutional ends

means-tested programs

Type of social welfare program in which government provides cash or in-kind benefits to individuals who qualify by having little or no income

media consultant

An expert hired by a political candidate to give advice on the use of the mass media, particularly television and direct mail, in a campaign for public office

Medicaid

A means-tested medical care program providing in-kind medical benefits for the poor

Medicare

A public health insurance program in which government pays the providers of health care for medical services given to patients who are aged or disabled

melting pot

Characterization of America as the coming together of a wide variety of racial, ethnic, and religious groups

Merit Systems Protection Board

An agency charged with protecting individual employees against violations of the merit principle or actions taken against whistle-blowers

military-industrial complex

The Pentagon, defense contractors, unions in the defense industry, members of Congress whose states or districts receive considerable military funds, and academic strategists whose work is funded by the military

minimalist state

A government that restricts its activities to providing only goods that the free market cannot produce

minority leader (House)

Leader and chief spokesperson for the minority party in the House

minority leader (Senate)

Leader and chief spokesperson for the minority party in the Senate

Miranda rights

Requirements announced in *Miranda v. Arizona* [384 U.S. 436 (1966)] to protect a suspect during a police interrogation

misdemeanor

Less serious criminal offense, usually punishable by not more than one year in jail

Missouri Plan

Method of selecting state judges, involving appointment from a list of recommended nominees and a later retention vote by the electorate

modified rule

An order from the House Rules Committee allowing a limited number of amendments to a bill during floor consideration

monetary policy

Government decisions about how much money should circulate in the economy and what the cost of borrowing money, the interest rate, should be

movement

An effort to attain an end through an organized set of actions and individuals

multinational corporations

Large companies that carry on business in two or more countries simultaneously

multiple advocacy

A system of advising the president in which all sides of an issue are presented

N

NAACP

National Association for the Advancement of Colored People; an organization founded to improve the social, economic, and political condition of African Americans

national committee

The body responsible for guiding political party organization on an ongoing basis

national convention

The quadrennial meeting of an American political party that focuses on the upcoming presidential election

National Security Council (NSC)

Designed to provide the president with advice and policy coordination on questions of national security; members include the president, the vice president, the secretaries of state and defense, and any other officials the president may add

natural-born citizen

A person actually born in the United States

naturalized citizen

A person, born in another country, who becomes a citizen of the United States by a procedure set by Congress

necessary and proper clause

Also called the "elastic clause," Article I, Section 8, of the Constitution, is the source of "implied powers" for the national government, as explained in *McCulloch v. Maryland* [17 U.S. (4 Wheaton) 316 (1819)]

neoconservatism

A belief associated with many former liberal intellectuals that contemporary liberalism has transformed the modest New Deal welfare state into an intrusive, paternalistic state

neoliberalism

A pragmatic form of liberalism that emphasizes such beliefs as the promotion of wealth rather than its redistribution and the reform of military practices rather than the simple reduction of military spending

net interest

Charges that the government must pay to the public for the use of money borrowed to cover budget deficits and added to the interest paid to government trust funds to create total interest costs

New Deal

The first two terms of President Franklin D. Roosevelt (1933–1945), whose revolutionary policy initiatives established a pervasive and active role for the national government

New Federalism

A view of federalism that posits an expanded role for state and local governments and holds that state and local governments should be entrusted with greater responsibilities

New Jersey Plan

Introduced in the Constitutional Convention in opposition to the Virginia Plan, it emphasized the dominance of the states

news briefing

An announcement or explanation of policy by an official

news release

A story written by a press agent for distribution to the media

Nielsen ratings

Surveys conducted by the A.C. Nielsen Company to measure the size of television audiences

Nineteenth Amendment

Constitutional amendment of 1920 giving women the right to vote

Ninth Amendment

Part of the Bill of Rights that cautions that the people possess rights not specified in the Constitution

Nixon Doctrine

Proclaimed by President Nixon in 1969, a policy stipulating that the United States will support its allies with economic and military aid but that the allies should provide the bulk of the personnel for their own defense

North Atlantic Treaty Organization (NATO)

Multinational organization formed in 1949 to provide for mutual defense against foreign attacks

Northwest Ordinance

This major statute, enacted by Congress in 1787 under the Articles of Confederation, provided for the development and government of lands west of Pennsylvania

O

obscenity

As applied by the Supreme Court, certain pornographic portrayals of sexual acts not protected by the First Amendment (The Supreme Court's current definition of the legally obscene appeared in *Miller v. California* [413 U.S. 5 (1973)].)

Office of Management and Budget (OMB)

An agency in the Executive Office of the President that provides the president with budgetary information and advice and is responsible for compiling the president's annual budget proposal to Congress

Office of Personnel Management (OPM)

Created in 1981 as part of the Executive Office of the President, focuses on the formulation, coordination, and implementation of domestic and economic policy, and provides staff support for the Economic and Domestic Policy Councils

ombudsman

A person who intervenes with the bureaucracy on behalf of individual citizens

open primary

A primary election in which any voter, regardless of party affiliation, can participate

open rule

An order from the House Rules Committee whereby amendments to a bill are permitted on the floor

opinion of the Court

Statement representing the views of a majority of the judges of the Court

oral argument

Event in which opposing counsel verbally presents their views to the court during the decision-making process of a court

original jurisdiction

Authority of a court over cases that begin in that court, such as courts of general jurisdiction having original jurisdiction over most criminal offenses—the original jurisdiction of the U.S. Supreme Court is very small

outer cabinet

Cabinet officers whose departments deal with sharply defined programs and are subject to considerable pressure from client groups

outsourcing

Establishment, by American corporations, of factories and offices in foreign countries to take advantage of cheaper labor markets

P

party convention

Regularly scheduled general meeting of a political party that is held for the purpose of ratifying party policies and deciding on party candidates

party identification

Psychological attachment that a citizen may feel toward a particular political party

party in the electorate

The individual citizens throughout the country who identify with a political party

party in the government

One of the three components or sectors of a political party: the party as embodied in those of its members who have been elected or appointed to public office, the organizations they establish, and the leaders they choose to help them carry out their work

party system

Period during which the pattern of support for political parties based on a particular set of important political issues remains reasonably stable

party whip

Member of each party's leadership responsible for party discipline and attendance for key votes

passive resistance

A form of civil disobedience in which protesters do not actively oppose government's attempts to control them, but rather refuse to cooperate by doing nothing—for example, by going limp when police try to pick them up or insisting on being carried to a police van rather than walking

Pendleton Act

Legislation passed in 1883 that created a Civil Service Commission charged with the task of using merit, rather than partisan political connections, as a condition of government employment

photo opportunity

An event scheduled to give newspaper reporters and television crews a chance to photograph someone

platform

A broad statement of the philosophy and program under which a party's candidates run for election

plea bargain

A deal with the prosecutor to obtain fewer or lesser charges or a lighter sentence

pluralism

A model of policy making that holds that public policy decisions are the result of struggles among contesting groups that reflect the various interests among citizens

pluralist democracy

A system in which the people rule and have their interests protected through the interaction of many different social, political, and economic groups, and in which the principal task of government is to manage group conflict and cooperation

plurality election

Election in which a candidate wins simply by getting more votes than any other candidate, even if it is less than a majority of the votes

policy adoption

A formal, authoritative decision, such as the enactment of legislation, made by institutions of government to address an issue on the policy agenda

policy agenda

The public issues that engage the attention of elected officials

policy evaluation

The act of determining whether a formally adopted and implemented policy ameliorated or solved a public problem

policy implementation

The translation of policy ideas into action

policy strategy

A specific course of action designed to deal with a public problem

political action committee (PAC)

Political organization set up to channel campaign money from a group to political candidates sympathetic to the group's political views

political efficacy

A person's sense of being able to accomplish something politically, an important determinant of political participation

political machine

Political organization that recruits and controls its membership through the use of its governmental authority to give benefits (jobs, contracts, etc.) to its supporters and deny them to its opponents

political party

A group that seeks to influence public policy by placing its own members in positions of governmental authority

political socialization

The process by which citizens acquire politically relevant knowledge, beliefs, attitudes, and patterns of behavior

politico style

A manner of representation in which members of Congress attempt to strike a balance between the interests of their constituents and the dictates of their own judgment and conscience

politics

The process of peacefully reconciling social and economic differences

polling

The process of using social science methods to get an accurate sense of the public's view about an issue or set of issues

poll tax

A tax on voting, applied discriminatorily to African Americans under "Jim Crow" in the post–Civil War South

populism

A political movement that sets the interests of the masses or common people against those of the political elite or the wealthy

pork barrel politics

The effort to enact legislation favoring a legislator's home district, often in the form of costly government spending that may not be advantageous to the country as a whole

positive state

A government that helps provide the goods, services, and conditions for a prosperous, equitable society

poverty threshold

Income level differentiated by family size and annually adjusted for inflation, below which government defines individuals as being poor

precedents

Prior decisions of courts that are cited as authority by other courts

Presidential Election Campaign Fund

Pool of money available that is collected from a $3 check-off on the federal income tax form and is available to presidential candidates for campaign expenses

Presidential Succession Act of 1947

Established the line of presidential succession after the vice president as follows: the Speaker of the House, the president pro tempore of the Senate, and the Cabinet secretaries in the order of the establishment of their departments

president of the Senate

A largely ceremonial role held by the vice president of the United States

president pro tempore

The presiding officer of the Senate in the absence of the vice president—largely honorific post and usually given to the senior majority party member

president's cabinet

Political institution comprised mainly of executive department heads that collectively serve as a source of advice for the president

press conference

A meeting of journalists and an official or other person at which the latter answers the questions posed by the former

presumption of innocence

A concept in criminal procedure that places the burden of proof in establishing guilt on the government

primary election

Preliminary election in which a party picks delegates to a party convention or its candidates for public office

priming

Occurs when the news media, especially television, set the terms by which the public judges its leaders

prior restraint

Official censorship before something is said or published, or censorship that halts publication already under way; is usually judged unconstitutional today under the First Amendment

Private Calendar

The schedule for House bills that concerns personal rather than general legislative matters

probable cause

A standard used in determining when police can conduct arrests and searches

progressivism

An urban reform movement of the late nineteenth and early twentieth centuries that called for direct primaries, restrictions on corporations, and improved public services and that was influential in the administrations of Theodore Roosevelt and Woodrow Wilson

proportional representation

A system for allocating seats in a legislative body in which the number of seats a party gets out of the total is based on the percentage of votes that the party receives in an election

protectionism

Opposite of *free trade;* belief that government should protect American business and industry by restricting the flow of foreign goods into the United States

public opinion

The array of beliefs and attitudes that people hold about political and related affairs

public policy

Whatever governments choose to do or not to do

public purpose

A goal or objective of a bureaucracy

Q

quasi-judicial

A function of regulatory agencies in which, like a court, they can make decisions in individual cases

quasi-legislative

A function of regulatory agencies in which they can make rules that, like legislation, apply to whole classes of people

R

rational actor model

A perspective that looks at politics as a system in which individuals and organizations pursue their self-interests, defined in terms of costs and benefits, and choose to do those things that give them the greatest benefit at the least cost

rational-comprehensive model

A model of decision-making that holds that policy makers should identify problems, consider various policy alternatives and their costs and benefits, and select and implement the policy strategy with the highest benefits and the lowest costs

realignment

A major change in the pattern of support for political parties and the important issues on which that pattern of support is based

recession

A minor and relatively short period of economic decline

reciprocity (or logrolling)

A practice whereby two or more members of Congress exchange support for legislation important to each other

redistributive policies

Programs such as tariffs or tax reforms that produce considerable benefits to some segments of society but high costs to others

red tape

Bureaucratic rules and procedures that seem to complicate and delay needed action unnecessarily

regional primary

A primary election held across an entire geographic area (for example, the South or the West) rather than within a single state

register

To place one's name on the list of citizens eligible to vote

regulations

Rules devised by government agencies that shape the actions of individuals and groups in order to achieve purposes mandated by law

relative deprivation

A definition of poverty that holds that individuals with less, regardless of their absolute income level, will feel poor or deprived relative to those who have more

republican (or representative) government

A style of government in which people elect representatives to make decisions in their place

reserved powers

Powers not specifically prohibited to the states and not delegated to the national government by the Constitution

residence requirements

State laws designed to limit the eligible electorate by requiring citizens to have been a resident of the voting district for a fixed period of time prior to an election

resurgence

The idea that American political parties, following a period of decline from the 1960s to the early 1980s, are now making a comeback, gaining in organizational, electoral, and governmental strength

riders

Provisions, usually attached to appropriation bills, which "ride" into law on the backs of necessary pieces of legislation, forcing the president to veto the entire bill in order to kill the amendment

risk assessment

The process of estimating the potentially dangerous consequences of damage that might be caused by a particular practice, such as smoking, or by the use of a particular product, such as the impact of the burning of fossil fuels on global warming

risk management

The process of making decisions that try to reduce or contain identified risks

Roe v. Wade

Supreme Court decision [410 U.S. 113 (1973)] establishing a constitutional right to abortion

rule of four

Procedure of the U.S. Supreme Court by which the affirmative votes of four justices are needed to accept a case for decision

Rules Committee

Powerful House committee that clears most important bills for floor consideration and decides the rule under which bills should be considered; also, the committee of a party convention that recommends changes in the way a party conducts its affairs

run-off election

An election pitting the leading candidates of a previous election against each other when the previous election has not produced a clear-cut winner

S

safe seats

Congressional districts in which the division of voters between the parties is so lopsided as to virtually ensure one party of victory

senatorial courtesy

Custom in the Senate to reject, for federal office, a nominee who is unacceptable to a senator from the nominee's state when the senator and president are of the same party

Senior Executive Service (SES)

Created by the Civil Service Reform Act of 1978, a class of civil servants drawn from the highest grades and who might be given bonuses, transferred among agencies, or demoted—all depending on the quality of their work

sense of duty

A motivating factor, felt by some citizens, to get involved in politics

separate-but-equal doctrine

The standard announced by the Supreme Court in *Plessy v. Ferguson* in 1896 that allowed racially separate facilities on trains (and by implication in public services such as education), as long as the separate facilities were equal (overturned by *Brown v. Board of Education of Topeka* in 1954)

sequestration

The process through which the president makes budget cuts in government programs to meet the mandates in law requiring ceilings on specific categories of spending

Seventeenth Amendment

Ratified in 1913, provides for the direct popular election of United States senators

Shays' Rebellion

A revolt by farmers from Massachusetts in 1786–1787 over the lack of economic relief, which led many to believe that a stronger central government was necessary

shield laws

Statutes that protect the identity of journalists' news sources or their knowledge of criminal acts

Sixteenth Amendment

Amendment to the Constitution, ratified in 1913, that gave Congress the power to tax incomes and thereby massively increase the potential revenue available to the national government

Sixth Amendment

Provision of the Bill of Rights assuring, among other things, the right to counsel

slip law

The written text of an act of Congress

social Darwinism

A set of ideas applying Charles Darwin's theory of biological evolution to society and holding that social relationships occur within a struggle for survival in which only the fittest survive

social entitlements

Programs, such as Social Security and Medicaid, whereby eligible individuals receive benefits according to law

social insurance programs

Welfare programs that provide cash or services to the aged, the disabled, and the unemployed, regardless of income level

socialism

The view in economics that economic decision-making should be completely under the control of political authority

socialization functions

With reference to political parties, the ways in which parties, by seeking to win elections, help to socialize voters into politics and form public opinion

social regulation

Type of regulation in which a government agency issues rules designed to achieve noneconomic policy goals, such as fair treatment in employment, clean air, or safe workplaces

Social Security Act of 1935

Landmark legislation that firmly established for the first time a social welfare role for the national government by providing old age insurance and grants to the states to provide programs for cash assistance to the unemployed, dependent children, and the blind, disabled, and aged

social welfare

Governmental programs, such as social insurance and poverty programs, directed specifically toward promoting the well-being of individuals and families

soft money

A category of campaign money that was created by an amendment to the campaign finance laws in 1979, allowing the national parties to raise and spend money, essentially without restriction, for state and local parties, routine operating expenses, and party-building activities, as long as the expenditures are not directly related to any federal campaign

solicitor general of the United States

In the Supreme Court, the lawyer for the United States who decides which cases the government will appeal to the Supreme Court

Speaker of the House

The presiding officer of the House of Representatives, who is selected by the majority party

special or select committees

Committees of Congress created periodically to study particular problems or new areas of legislation

spoils system

The practice of making appointments to government jobs on the basis of party loyalty and support in election campaigns

standing committees

The permanent committees of Congress that alone can approve legislation and send it to the floor of the House or Senate

stare decisis

A legal doctrine that suggests courts should follow precedent as a general rule, breaking with previous legal principles only on rare occasions

state committee

The body responsible for guiding a state political party organization on an ongoing basis

state courts

Courts of the fifty states, as opposed to the federal, or national, courts

Statutory Pay-As-You-Go Act

Law passed in 2010 that requires budget increases to be offset by either reductions elsewhere or increased revenues

stewardship theory

An expansive theory of presidential power, put forth by Theodore Roosevelt, that holds that the president can undertake any act as long as it is not prohibited by a specific provision of the Constitution or statutory law

Supplemental Nutrition Assistance Program (SNAP)

A means-tested program (formerly known as the food stamp program) that provides the eligible needy with cards that can be used only to purchase food

Supplemental Security Income (SSI)

Social welfare program administered by the Social Security Administration whereby the national government guarantees a certain level of income for the needy, aged, blind, and disabled

surplus

An excess of government revenues over government expenditures

symbolic speech

A speech act that centers on action or performance to communicate a point rather than on words

systems model

A model of policy making that holds that policy is the product of an interlocking relationship between institutions of government and their social, economic, and political environment

T

Temporary Assistance for Needy Families (TANF)

Social welfare program, administered by the states and jointly funded by state and national revenues, that provides cash assistance, in participating states, to needy children and one adult relative or an unemployed parent

Tenth Amendment

Amendment ratified in 1791 that reserves to the states powers not prohibited to them and not delegated to the national government by the Constitution

term limits

Laws restricting the number of terms an elected representative may serve—the Court has struck down state efforts to limit terms for federal offices, but has allowed state laws that limit terms for elected officials at the state level

the administration

The president plus senior officials such as cabinet officials, undersecretaries, and the administrators and deputies of the various independent agencies

The Federalist

A series of eighty-five essays written by Alexander Hamilton, John Jay, and James Madison and published in New York newspapers in 1787 and 1788, urging ratification of the Constitution

third party

In the American political context, a minor party that attracts only a small share of the electorate's vote and is a party other than the two major parties that have dominated politics through most of American history

Thirteenth Amendment

The first of the Civil War amendments to the Constitution; adopted in 1865, it banned slavery throughout the United States

Thomas Hobbes

Seventeenth-century English political philosopher who wrote about the basis of sovereignty residing in a social contract

three-fifths compromise

A temporary resolution to the controversy over slavery, this agreement allowed slaveholding states to count each slave as three-fifths of a person for purposes of congressional representation

trial court

A court of limited or general jurisdiction in which the disputed facts of a case are heard and decided

Truman Doctrine

A policy, proclaimed by President Harry Truman in 1947, in which the United States would oppose the expansion of communism anywhere in the world

trustee role

The concept that legislators should vote on the basis of their consciences and the broad interests of the nation, not simply on the views of their constituents

Twenty-fifth Amendment

Ratified in 1967; provides the mechanism for the vice president to assume the presidency in the event of a presidential disability and the selection of a replacement for the vice president should that office become vacant

Twenty-fourth Amendment

Adopted in 1964, forbids the use of poll taxes in federal elections (Since 1966, the Court has applied this proscription to state elections as well.)

U

unanimous consent agreement

A common mechanism used by the Senate leadership to limit Senate debate

underclass

A proportion of the poor comprising individuals isolated from the rest of society and for whom poverty is a continuing way of life

unemployment compensation

A social insurance policy that grants temporary financial assistance to the unemployed

Union Calendar

The House schedule for the consideration of tax and appropriation bills

unitary system

A system of government in which principal power lies at the level of a national or central government rather than at the level of some smaller unit (a state or a province) within the political system

United States Agency for International

V

vesting clause

The first clause of Article II; confers executive power in the president

Virginia Plan

The first plan of union proposed at the Constitutional Convention in 1787; it called for a strong central government

visual

An image or series of images representing news in action; a visual depiction of a political act, such as campaigning, which may carry more impact than words alone

Twenty-second Amendment

Ratified in 1951, this amendment restricts the president to two terms in office

Twenty-sixth Amendment

Constitutional amendment adopted in 1971 that fixed the minimum voting age at eighteen years

Twenty-third Amendment

Constitutional amendment adopted in 1961 granting the District of Columbia three electors in the Electoral College

Development (USAID)

Agency of the State Department that coordinates economic assistance programs

United States courts of appeals

Intermediate appellate courts in the federal court system, just below the Supreme Court

United States district courts

Trial courts in the federal court system in which almost all federal cases begin; courts of general jurisdiction

United States Reports

The official, published decisions of the United States Supreme Court

U.S. Code

Compilation of laws currently in effect, classified by subject matter, such as transportation or labor

U.S. Statutes-at-Large

Chronological compilation, by year, of slip laws passed in each session of Congress

Voting Rights Act of 1965

Major legislation designed to overcome racial barriers to voting, primarily in the Southern States; it was extended again in 2006 for twenty-five years

Voting Rights Act of 1970

The law that limited residence requirements to thirty days for presidential elections, further ensuring voting rights

W

warrant

Official authorization for government action

Welfare Reform Act

A 1996 law that fundamentally altered the AFDC welfare program by renaming it TANF and placing work and training requirements, as well as time limits, on its use

working poor

Individuals who, despite being employed or seeking employment, are still defined as poor because their low earnings are not enough to put them above the poverty threshold

World Bank

A specialized agency of the United Nations that makes loans to poorer nations for economic development

writ of certiorari

A petition for review by a higher court; the most common route for an appeal to reach the Supreme Court

writ of mandamus

Order by a court to a public official to perform a nondiscretionary or ministerial act

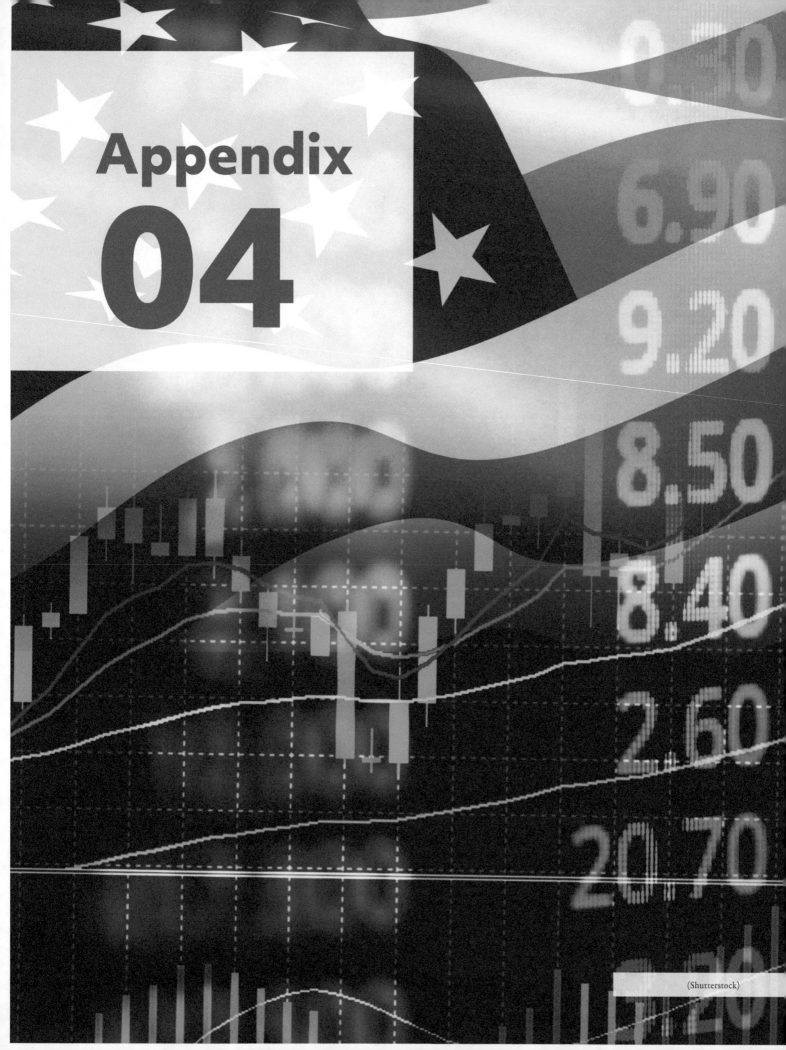

Appendix
04

INDEX

A

Adams, John 115
administration (presidential) 315
administrative assistant (AA) 292
administrative law judge 365
affirmative action 80, 88, 90
Affordable Care Act. *See* Patient
   Protection and Affordable Care Act
agenda setting 187–189
agents of socialization 144–145
alleviative strategies 471
Amendments, Constitutional
   First. (*see* First Amendment)
   Second 526
   Third 526
   Fourth 75, 526
   Fifth 526
   Sixth 76, 526
   Seventh 527
   Eighth 77–79, 527
   Ninth 79, 527
   Tenth 44, 527
   Eleventh 386, 401, 527
   Twelfth 527
   Thirteenth 83, 528
   Fourteenth. (*see* Fourteenth
      Amendment)
   Fifteenth 238, 529
   Sixteenth 53, 529
   Seventeenth 278, 529
   Eighteenth 529
   Nineteenth 92, 239, 243, 530
   Twentieth 25, 530
   Twenty-first 530–531
   Twenty-second 249, 311, 531
   Twenty-third 261, 531
   Twenty-fourth 239, 531–532
   Twenty-fifth 323, 532
   Twenty-sixth 239, 533
   Twenty-seventh 23, 533
   by subject 15–16

Americans for Democratic
   Action (ADA) 112
amicus curiae brief 206, 394
Annapolis Convention 10
Antifederalists 13
appellate jurisdiction 27, 386
appropriation 444
Articles of Confederation 7–9
authorization (congressional) 443

B

backgrounders 182
balance the ticket 258–259
balanced budget amendment 445
Biden, Joe
   election 229–230, 245, 261, 312–313
   electoral votes 260
   environmental policy 479
   likeability 246
   and the media 177, 189
   political experience 246
   vice presidency 323
bill of attainder 74, 277
Bill of Rights 64–66, 97
Bipartisan Campaign Reform
   Act (BCRA) 204
block grant 53
brief (legal) 394
briefing (news) 182
*Brown v. Board of Education of
   Topeka* 26, 51, 86, 97
Bryan, William Jennings 109
Budget Enforcement Act of 1990 447
budget (national)
   components 435–438
   Congress role in 439–440, 442–444
   deficit 432–435
   defined 439
   improving 444–447

budget (national), *continued*
   mandatory programs 438–439
   overview 448
   president's role in 319, 439–440, 442
   process stages 440–441
Bureau of International Information
   Programs (IIP) 493
bureaucracy
   characteristics 349, 351–352
   civil service 355–358
   and Congress 359–360, 373
   and the courts 361–362, 373
   criticism of 370–372, 373
   defined 348
   as fourth branch of
      government 348–352
   function 373
   and interest groups 361
   iron triangles 298–299, 361, 373
   and the presidency 358–359, 373
   regulation. (*see* regulation)
   types of 352–355, 373
bureaucrat 349, 373
bureaucratic model of
   policy making 409
Burke, Edmund 114
Burwell v. Hobby Lobby 73
Bush, George H. W.
   approval ratings 309, 310
   economic policy 319, 320
   election 252
   foreign policy 490–491, 492
   leadership 246
   midterm elections 268
   multiple advocacy 318
   pardons 314
   Supreme Court appointments
      313, 388
   vetoes 333
   war power 329
Bush, George W.
   approval ratings 146, 178, 309, 310

Bush, George W., *continued*
    cabinet 317
    economic policy 322, 437, 438
    election 211, 250, 252, 261
    foreign policy 325, 492, 502
    Iraq War 329–330
    leadership 246
    and the media 177, 191
    midterm elections 265, 268
    and neoconservatism 121
    and New Federalism 42
    public policy 418
    Supreme Court appointments
        313, 389
    vetoes 333, 334
    war on terrorism 331, 506

C

cabinet (presidential)
    changes after September 11
        attacks 418
    defined 352
    executive departments
        352–353, 354, 373
    importance of appointments 342
    in 2021 316
    overview 315–317
campaign finance 244, 254–
    256, 264–266, 269
capital case 76
capitalism xxx, 136–137
Carter, Jimmy
    approval ratings 309, 310
    bureaucracy reform 357–358
    economic policy 110
    foreign policy 492, 495, 497
    leadership 246
    and the media 189
    relationship with Congress 330, 332
    Supreme Court appointments 401
    vetoes 333
    vice presidency changes 323
Case Act 326
case (court) 380
casework 282
categorical grant-in-aid 53
caucus 227, 257
Central Intelligence Agency
    (CIA) 495–496, 508
checks and balances 17–19, 277
chief of state 308
Christian Right 210–211
Citizens United v. FEC 204
civil case 380
civil disobedience 152–153
civil liberties 63, 65–66, 97
civil rights 63–64, 84, 97. *See*
    also Bill of Rights
Civil Rights Act of 1964 87, 459
civil service 355–358
Civil Service Reform Act 357, 373
Civil War 327
class action suit 206
classical liberalism 107–109
clear and present danger test 67

Clinton, Bill
    approval ratings 178, 309–310
    cabinet 317, 353
    economic policy 320, 475
    election 252, 264
    environmental policy 353, 370
    foreign policy 491
    impeachment 308, 337–338
    likeability 246
    and the media 177, 186, 189, 339
    Supreme Court appointments 313
    vetoes 333, 334, 445
closed primary 257
closed rule 295
cloture 296
coalition 223
Code of Federal Regulations (CFR) 367
Cold War 327–328, 486–487,
    489–490, 508
collective goods xxxiii
colonies 5
commander-in-chief clause 326
commerce clause 22
Committee of the Whole 295
comparable worth 93
concurring opinions 397
confederation 34
Conference, the 286
Congress
    agencies 293
    budget process role 439–
        440, 442–444
    and bureaucracy 298–299,
        359–361, 373
    campaign process 264–268
    changes in 299–300, 301
    committee system 287–292, 299
    Constitutional powers 276–278
    domestic policy role 330
    ethical issues 283
    foreign policy role 324–326,
        500–501, 508
    House of Representatives.
        (*see* House of Representatives)
    impeachment power 337–339
    lawmaking 293–297, 301
    legislative norms 283–284
    and lobbies 297–298
    member functions 281–282, 301
    member profile 278–281
    midterm elections 241, 265, 268, 275
    overview 275–276
    and presidential powers 333–334
    Senate. (*see* Senate)
    staff 292–293
    war power 324, 326–330
Congressional Budget and
    Impoundment Control
    Act of 1974 446
Congressional Budget Office
    (CBO) 293, 446
Congressional Research
    Service (CRS) 293
congressional seniority 287
conservatism 108, 114–118,
    120–121, 126
Constitution, U.S. *See also* constitutions
    1787 form 15

Constitution, U.S., *continued*
    articles 517–525
    and bureaucracy 348
    changes to 22–31. *See*
        also Amendments, Constitutional
    features 16–19, 21–24
    necessary and proper clause 276
    need for 9
    overview 29
    and the presidency 311–315
    ratification 13–15
    and religion 70–73
    Supreme Court interpretation
        of 25–28
constitutional theory 311
constitutionalism xxxv, 4
constitutions 4–5, 52
continuing resolution 446
contract theory 107
cooperative federalism 49
coronavirus. *See* COVID-19 pandemic
council-manager 47
Council of Economic
    Advisers (CEA) 320
court of last resort 383
courts of general jurisdiction 383
courts of limited jurisdiction 383
COVID-19 pandemic
    America response to 20–21
    effect on bureaucracy 21, 348, 353
    effect on Congress 20, 281, 295–296
    effect on news consumption 178
    effect on presidential
        election 192, 240, 312
    effect on primary elections
        20, 257, 312
    effect on public policy 414, 417–418
    effect on the Supreme Court 396
    effect on unemployment 21, 138, 465
    and federalism 34, 42, 49
    and the media 20
    and the national deficit 434
    and public opinion 20, 119, 136, 155
    and Trump, Donald.
        (*see* Trump, Donald)
crime 380
criminal case 380
cross-cutting cleavage 213
cruel and unusual punishment 77–79
curative strategies 471

D

de facto segregation 87
de jure segregation 87
dealignment 225
debt 432
Declaration of Independence
    5–7, 29, 513–515
decline (political party) 226
deficit 432–435, 448
delegate role 281
delegated powers 43
democracy xxxiv–xxxvi,
    xxxvii, 200, 212–213

democratic socialism 108,
121–124, 126
Department of Defense (DoD)
496–497, 500, 508
Department of State 493–494
depression (economic) 429
deregulation 368
détente 489
developing nations 507, 508
direct mail 203
direct popular election 262
disaster relief 46–47, 49
dissenting opinions 397
distributive policies 297
domestic policy
Congress role in 330, 342
debates over purposes 454–455
defined 419, 453
environmental policy 475–479, 480
and gun violence 460–461
and national security 501–505
Office of Personnel Management
(OPM) 357
and poverty. (see poverty)
president's role in 330, 342
social welfare. (see social welfare)
Domestic Policy Council 316
dual federalism 49

E

economic policy
basic issues 428–430
and corporations 443
defined 428
fiscal policy 431–432
importance in policy agenda 422
national budget 435–439
overview 448
philosophies 430–431
president's role in 319, 421
and the Supreme Court 397
Economic Policy Council 316
economic regulation 363
economics xxix–xxx
Eighteenth Amendment 529
Eighth Amendment 77–79, 527
Eisenhower, Dwight 309, 310, 328, 333
elections
campaign finance 244,
254–256, 264–266, 269
campaign reform 244
campaign strategies 263–272
congressional 264–268, 269
COVID-19 effect on presidential
192, 240, 312
COVID-19 effect on
primary 20, 257, 312
direct popular 262
general 257
high-stimulus 241
incumbency 266–267, 269
low-stimulus 241
majority 217
media campaigns 251–253
midterm 241, 265, 268, 275
nomination process 256–259

elections, continued
plurality 217, 231
presidential 249–250, 269
primary 257
proportional representation 217
regional primary 258
run-off 217
Electoral College 39, 259–263, 527
electoral functions 215
Eleventh Amendment 386, 401, 527
elitism 202, 409
environmental policy 475–479, 480
Environmental Protection Agency
(EPA) 476, 478–479
equal protection clause 81, 83
equal-time rule 174
equality of condition 83
equality of opportunity 83
equality of result 83
Era of Good Feelings 223
establishment clause 71
ex post facto laws 74, 277
exclusionary rule 76
exclusive (media) 182
executive agreements 325–326
Executive Calendar 296
Executive Office of the President
(EOP) 318–320, 352
executive privilege 334–336
exit polls 252
express powers 43

F

fairness doctrine 174–175
faithless elector 261
Federal Communications
Commission (FCC) 174–175
federal courts 380
Federal Election Campaign
Act 204, 255
federal question 386
Federal Register 366
federalism
defined 34, 58
and disaster relief 46–47, 49
fiscal relationships in 53–54
governmental units in 48
in other countries 37–38
legal relationships in 50–52
models of 49–50, 58
modern 56–57
New Federalism 42
overview 34–38
political relationships in 54–56
Federalist No. 10 200, 207
Federalist, The 13, 164
Federalists 13
felony 76
female suffrage 239
Fifteenth Amendment 238, 529
Fifth Amendment 526
fifth branch 164
filibuster 296

First Amendment
contents 526
defined 66
freedom of assembly 69–70
freedom of the press 176, 193
importance 66–67
and political action committees
(PACs) 203
religious freedom 70–73
restrictions on 67–69
symbolic speech 69–70
fiscal policy 431–432
fiscal year 440
Floyd, George 89–90
Ford, Gerald 189, 310, 314, 333
foreign policy
approaches to 488
Central Intelligence Agency
(CIA) role in 495–496
Cold War era 487, 489–490, 508
Congress role in 324–326,
342, 500–501, 508
current issues in 505–507, 508
defined 419, 486
Department of Defense (DoD)
role in 496–497, 500
and the military-industrial
complex 504–505
and multinational
corporations 503–504
post–Cold War 492
president's role in 324–326,
342, 492, 508
pre–World War II 486–487
and public opinion 501–503
State Department role in 493–494
formal party organization 221
Fourteenth Amendment
birthright citizenship 321
contents 528–529
defined 64
equal protection clause 81, 83
limitations on government
powers 50–52
Fourth Amendment 75, 526
fourth branch of government
349, 350–351
framing (news) 189–190
franking privilege 282
free exercise clause 70
free-market capitalism model
of policy making 409
free trade 429

G

*Garcia v. San Antonio Metropolitan
Transit Authority* 51
general election 257
government
branches 350–351
defined xxxi
democratic xxxiv–xxxvi
and disaster relief 46–47, 49
federal system. (see federalism)
forms of 34–36
local 47–48
national 41–42, 58

government, *continued*
    overview xxxi–xxxiii, xxxvii
    powers 42–46
    republican (or representative) 16
    and the states 38–40, 44–46, 58
Government Accountability
    Office (GAO) 293
government corporations 350–351, 355
governmental functions (of
    political parties) 215
grants 53
grass roots lobbying 207
Great Compromise 13
Great Society 110, 459, 461, 480
Gulf of Tonkin Resolution 328
Gulf War 309, 502
gun violence 460–461

H

Hamilton, Alexander 13
Hammer v. Dagenhart 49, 397
Harper v. Virginia State Board
    of Elections 239
Harris, Kamala
    effect on vice presidency 323
    and political history 91,
        209, 259, 312
    role in the Senate 286
Hatch Act 357
head of government 308
high-stimulus elections 241
Hobbes, Thomas xxxii
home rule 47
homeland security 505
Hoover, Herbert 488
House Calendar 294
House of Representatives
    bill process 294–296
    roles of power in 284–286, 301
    Senate differences 279, 297
House-Senate Conference
    Committee 297

I

ideology. *See* political ideology
immigration 95–96, 335–336
impeachment 308, 337–339
implied powers 43
in-kind benefits 474
incitement test 67
incrementalism 410, 438, 462
incumbency 266–267, 269
independent agency 353–354
independent regulatory
    commission 355
industrial policy 111
inner cabinet 316
interest group elitism 213
interest groups
    and bureaucracy 361
    characteristics 201–203
    defined 200
    and democracy 212–213

interest groups, *continued*
    economic 207–208
    functions of 203–206, 231
    gridlock 214
    ideological 207, 211
    lobbies 297–298
    overview 206, 231
    public interest 207, 212, 213–214
    religious 207, 210–211
    single-issue 207, 211–212, 247
    social 207, 208–210
    type overview 207, 231
intermediate appellate courts 383
International Monetary
    Fund (IMF) 507
internationalism 486, 501, 508
internet regulation 175
interstate compact 39
Iran-contra affair 319–320, 339
Iraq War
    Congress role in 329, 500
    and presidential war power 329–330
    and public opinion 155,
        309, 502–503
iron triangle 206, 298–299, 361, 373
isolationism 486, 508

J

Jackson, Andrew 107, 356
Jay, John 13
Jefferson, Thomas 107
Jim Crow laws 238–239
Johnson, Andrew 337
Johnson, Lyndon
    approval ratings 310
    Civil Rights Act of 1964 309
    effect on the presidency 308
    Great Society 110, 459, 461, 480
    relationship with Congress 330
    vetoes 333
    vice presidency 322
    Vietnam War 328
    War on Poverty 471
Joint Chiefs of Staff (JCS) 496
joint committees 287
journalists 164
judicial activists 399
judicial restraintists 399
judicial review 25–28, 391, 398, 402
jurisdiction
    appellate 27, 386
    defined 382
    general 383
    government 34, 51
    limited 383
    original 27, 386

K

Kelo v. City of New London 56
Kennedy, John F. 191, 309, 310, 333
Kentucky and Virginia Resolutions 27
Keynesian economics 430–431
Korean War 328, 489
Korematsu v. United States 327

L

laissez-faire economics 108, 116, 428
leak (news) 181
legal guilt 74
legislative assistant (LA) 292
legislative intent 392
legislative norms 283
legislative veto 360
Lemon test 71, 72–73
LGBT rights 81–83, 97, 210
libel 69
liberalism
    classical 107–109
    contemporary 108, 109–112
    defined 107
    forms of 108
    milestones in 111–112
    neoliberalism 112–114
    populism 107–109, 126
    progressivism 107–109, 126
libertarianism 108, 124–125, 126
Lincoln, Abraham 327
line-item veto 444
lobbying 204–206, 207, 297–298
Lochner v. New York 397
Locke, John 6
logrolling 283
low-stimulus elections 241

M

Madison, James 13, 200, 207
majority election 217
majority leader 285, 286
mandatory programs 438
Marbury v. Madison 29
marijuana legalization 37, 125
mark-up 294
Marshall, Chief Justice John 43
Marshall Plan 489
Marxism model of policy making 409
Marbury v. Madison 25–28
mass media
    believability 180
    bias in 184, 186–192, 193
    campaign coverage 174,
        179–180, 189, 191
    Constitutional basis for 168–170
    defined 164
    and election campaigns 251–253
    equal-time rule 17
    fairness doctrine 174–175
    gatekeeping role 177–178
    media types 164–168
    milestones in 170–171
    monopolies 172–173, 193
    news consumption 169
    news source confidentiality 176
    overview 193
    as political vehicles 177, 181–184
    and the presidency 251–253,
        339–341, 342
    public policy influence 414
    regulation 170, 174–175
    spotlighting role 178–179

mayor-council 47
McCain-Feingold Act 204
McCulloch v. Maryland 43, 276, 432
means-tested programs 466,
    467, 472–475, 480
media consultant 251
media, the. *See* mass media
Medicaid
    defined 474
    and the Great Society 110
    and the national budget 437, 438
    state government role in 38
Medicare
    defined 464
    and the Great Society 110
    and the national budget 437, 438
    overview 464–465
    political support for 480
melting pot 200
Merit Systems Protection Board 357
Mexican War 326
midterm elections 241, 265, 268, 275
military-industrial complex 504–505
minimalist state xxxiii
minority leader 285, 286
Miranda rights 76, 400
misdemeanor 76
Missouri Plan 383
modified rule 295
monetary policy 432
movement, social 201
multinational corporations 503–504
multiple advocacy 318

N

NAACP 86
national committee 221
national convention 221
National Labor Relations Board v. Jones
    & Laughlin Steel Corporation 397
National Security Council (NSC) 319
natural-born citizen 311
naturalized citizen 311
necessary and proper clause 22, 276
neoconservatism 108, 120–121
neoliberalism 112–114
net interest 437
net neutrality 171, 175
New Deal
    and socialism 122
    and capitalism xxx
    creation 458–459, 480
    and liberalism 109–110
    Supreme Court response to 397, 401
New Federalism 42
New Jersey Plan 12
news briefing 182
news consumption 169
news release 182
Nielsen ratings 190
Nineteenth Amendment
    92, 239, 243, 530
Ninth Amendment 79, 527
Nixon Doctrine 490

Nixon, Richard
    approval ratings 310
    effect on the presidency 308
    election 218
    executive privilege 334
    foreign policy 319, 489
    impeachment 337
    and the media 186, 191, 339
    and New Federalism 42
    pardon 314
    Supreme Court appointments
        388, 401
    vetoes 333
    vice presidency 322
    Vietnam War 328–329
North Atlantic Treaty
    Organization (NATO) 489
Northwest Ordinance 10

O

Obama, Barack
    approval ratings 138, 310
    cabinet 317
    campaign finance 255
    economic policy 322
    election 91, 245, 261
    executive privilege 336
    foreign policy 325, 491, 492, 496
    immigration reform 95–96, 335–336
    likeability 246
    midterm elections 265, 268
    pardons 315
    Patient Protection and
        Affordable Care Act 402
    Supreme Court appointments
        91, 313, 388, 390
    vetoes 333
Obamacare. *See* Patient Protection
    and Affordable Care Act
obscenity 68
Occupy movement 123–124
Office of Management and
    Budget (OMB) 319, 432
Office of Personnel Management
    (OPM) 357
ombudsman 282
open primary 257
open rule 295
opinion of the Court 396
oral argument 395–396
original jurisdiction 27, 386
outer cabinet 316
outsourcing 429

P

party convention 258
party identification 149, 216
party in the electorate 222
party in the government 223
party system 223
party whip 285, 287
passive resistance 152

Patient Protection and
    Affordable Care Act
    and congressional staff 292
    and liberalism 111, 112
    and Medicaid 474
    and Medicare 465
    Supreme Court rulings
        on 50, 73, 402
    Trump desire to repeal, Donald 332
Pendleton Act 357, 373
Philadelphia Convention 10–13, 29
photo opportunity 183
platform 221
plea bargain 76
Plessy v. Ferguson 85
pluralism 202, 409
pluralist democracy 200
plurality election 217
policy adoption 415–416
policy agenda 414
policy evaluation 417–419
policy implementation 416–417
policy strategy 415
political action committees (PACs)
    and campaign finance 255–256
    and congressional elections 266, 269
    defined 203
    effect on party strength 227, 231
    and the military-industrial
        complex 505
    overview 203–205
political efficacy 149
political ideology
    contemporary 113
    debate over welfare 473
    defined xxxi
    differences in 138–141
    and economic status 142, 216
    generational 119
    overview 105, 106
    shared 133–138
political machine 221
political participation
    differences in 153–154
    forms of 150–153
    impact 154–155
    motives 149
    overview 157
    rationality of 155–156
political parties
    current 225–228
    dealignment 225
    decline of 226
    defined 214
    functions 214–215, 231
    future of 228–230
    influence on voting decisions 245
    past 223–225
    realignment 224
    resurgence 227
    structure 220–223
    two-party system 217–220, 231
political socialization
    agents of 144–145
    defined 143, 157
    development 145, 147
    diversity in 148
    functions 214–215

political socialization, *continued*
  influences on 135
  processes 143–144
politico style 281
politics xxviii–xxxi, xxxvi, xxxvii, 135
poll tax 238
polling 133
populism 107–109, 126
pork barrel politics 282
positive state xxxiii
poverty
  means-tested programs 466,
    467, 472–475, 480
  measuring 466–470, 480
  problem of 470–471
poverty threshold 468
precedent 399
presidency, the
  and bureaucracy 358–359, 373
  cabinet. (*see* cabinet (presidential))
  candidacy 249–250, 269
  and the Constitution 311–315, 342
  and domestic policy 330, 342
  and economic policy 421
  Executive Office of the President
    (EOP) 318–320
  and foreign policy 324–326,
    342, 492, 508
  impeachment 308, 337–339
  leadership 308–310, 342
  and the media 339–341, 342
  overview 307–308
  powers. (*see* presidential powers)
  role in the budgeting process
    439–440, 442
  succession 323–324, 530
  and the Supreme Court 387–389
  term limits 318
  White House staff 317–318
president of the Senate 286
president pro tempore 286
Presidential Election
  Campaign Fund 255
presidential powers
  appointment 313, 387–389
  executive 311–312, 342
  pardoning 314–315
  removal power 313–314
  veto 333–334, 360–361
  war 324, 326–330, 498–499
Presidential Succession Act of 1947 324
press conference 182
press release 182
press, the. *See* mass media
presumption of innocence 74
primary election 257
priming 179
prior restraint 68
Private Calendar 295
probable cause 75
Progressive Era 458
progressivism 107–109, 126
proportional representation 217
protectionism 429
Protestant ethic 136
protests 151–153

public opinion. *See also* political
  socialization
  defined 132–133
  differences in 138–141
  and foreign policy 501–503
  overview 157
  polling 133
  shared 133–138
  terrorism effects on 146–147
public policy
  categories 419, 420, 422, 423
  debates over 473
  defined 407
  domestic. (*see* domestic policy)
  economic. (*see* economic policy)
  and economic self-interest 420
  evaluation 417–419
  foreign. (*see* foreign policy)
  formulation 415
  implementation 416–417
  media effect on 414
  models 408–412
  overview 423
  policy adoption 415–416
  policy agenda 414–415
  stages 412–413, 423
public purpose 348

Q

quasi-judicial functions 365
quasi-legislative functions 365

R

rational actor model 155
rational-comprehensive model
  of policy making 410
Reagan, Ronald
  approval ratings 309–310
  cabinet 316, 352
  CIA revitalization 495
  and conservatism 118, 121
  and deregulation 368
  economic policy 320, 437, 475
  effect on the presidency 308
  election 225
  executive privilege 335–336
  foreign policy limitations 492
  Iran-Contra affair 320, 339
  likeability 246
  and the media 174, 177, 339
  midterm elections 268
  and the national deficit 433
  and New Federalism 42
  Supreme Court appointments
    313, 388–389, 390
  vetoes 333, 334
realignment 224
recession 429
reciprocity 283
red tape 371
redistributive policies 298
*Regents of the University of
  California v. Bakke* 88
regional primary 258
registration (voting) 239

regulation
  agencies 363–366, 373
  debate concerning 368–370, 373
  defined 363
  overview 362–363, 373
  process 366–368
  types of 363–366, 373
relative deprivation 468
religion 70–73
republican (representative)
  government 16
reserved powers 44
residence requirements (voting) 239
resurgence (political party) 227
riders 296, 334
risk assessment 478
risk management 478
Roe v. Wade 26, 79–81, 400
Roosevelt, Franklin D.
  approval ratings 309, 310
  effect on the presidency 308
  election 224
  and the media 167, 171
  New Deal program. (*see* New Deal)
  Social Security Act of 1935 462
  and the Supreme Court 313, 397, 401
  vetoes 333
  war power 327
Roosevelt, Theodore 109, 488
rule of four 386
Rules Committee 285
run-off election 217

S

safe seats 266
searches and seizures 65–66, 75–76
Second Amendment 526
Senate
  bill process 296–297
  Constitution outline 529
  House of Representatives
    differences 279, 301
  roles of power in 286–287
senatorial courtesy 387
Senior Executive Service (SES) 357
sense of duty 149
separate-but-equal doctrine 85
September 11 attacks
  effect on foreign policy 501, 505
  and the media 176, 177, 178
  and public opinion 146–147
  public policy response 418
  and the war on terrorism
    331, 502–503, 506
sequestration 446
Seventeenth Amendment 278, 529
Seventh Amendment 527
Shays' Rebellion 10
shield laws 176
Sixteenth Amendment 53, 529
Sixth Amendment 76, 526
slip law 366
Smith, Adam 107
Smith v. Allwright 238

social Darwinism 108,
    116, 457–458, 480
social entitlements 438, 455
social insurance programs 461, 480
social movement 201
social regulation 365
Social Security 437, 438, 462–464, 480
Social Security Act of 1935 462
social welfare
    budget cuts 475, 480
    debate over 473, 474
    defined 455
    history 457–459
    overview 455
    programs 461–465, 467
socialism 428. *See
    also* democratic socialism
socialization functions (of
    political parties) 214
soft money 256
solicitor general of the
    United States 395
South Carolina v. Baker 51
Speaker of the House 284
special or select committees 287
Spencer, Herbert 116
spoils system 356
standing committees 287
stare decisis 399
state committee 222
state courts 380, 382–383
State Department 493–494, 508
Statutory Pay-As-You-Go Act 447
stewardship theory 311
Sumner, William Graham 116
Supplemental Nutrition Assistance
    Program (SNAP) 38, 437, 455, 474
Supplemental Security Income
    (SSI) 455, 472–473
Supreme Court
    appointments to 313, 387–389, 403
    decision influences 399–400
    and economic policy 397
    judicial review 25–28, 391, 398, 402
    overview 386, 403
    power 400–401
    role in governmental conflicts 50–52
surplus 433
symbolic speech 69–70
systems model of policy
    making 408, 409

T

Temporary Assistance for Needy
    Families (TANF) 38, 472
Tenth Amendment 44, 527
term limits 267
Third Amendment 526
third party 218–220
Thirteenth Amendment 83, 528
three-fifths compromise 13
trial court 392

Truman Doctrine 489
Truman, Harry
    approval ratings 309, 310
    foreign policy 487, 489
    vetoes 333
    vice presidency 322
    war power 327–328, 392–393
Trump, Donald
    approval ratings 138, 310, 312
    cabinet 317
    campaign finance 256
    COVID-19 contraction 192, 312, 321
    COVID-19 response 20, 95, 229, 264
    and deregulation 370
    economic policy 429, 431,
        439, 503–504
    election 191, 229, 245
    electoral votes 260, 261
    environmental policy 479
    executive privilege 336
    foreign policy 21, 488, 490, 492
    immigration policy 95–96, 321
    impeachments 308, 338–339
    leadership 246
    likeability 246
    and the media 180, 189, 251, 339
    midterm elections 265, 268
    and neoconservatism 121
    pardons 314–315
    Supreme Court appointments
        313, 389, 390, 391
    and Twitter 177, 321
    unconventionality 321–322
    vetoes 333
    and the war on terror 491
    war power use 325, 500–501
trustee role 281
Twelfth Amendment 527
Twentieth Amendment 25, 530
Twenty-fifth Amendment 323, 532
Twenty-first Amendment 530–531
Twenty-fourth Amendment 239, 531
Twenty-second Amendment
    249, 311, 531
Twenty-seventh Amendment 23, 533
Twenty-sixth Amendment 239, 533
Twenty-third Amendment 261, 531

U

unanimous consent agreement 296
underclass 471
unemployment compensation 465
Union Calendar 294
unitary system 34
United States Agency for International
    Development (USAID) 493
United States courts of appeals 384–385
United States district courts 383–384
United States Reports 397
U.S. Code 366
U.S. Statutes-at-Large 366

V

vesting clause 311
veto 333–334, 360–361, 444–445
vice presidency 259, 322–323
Vietnam War 328–329, 489, 501
Virginia Plan 12
visual (media) 182, 190–192
voting
    decision influences 245–248, 269
    economic status influence 241–242
    exit polls 252
    requirements 238–240, 269
    turnout 240–244, 253–254, 269
Voting Rights Act of 1965
    90–91, 239, 459
Voting Rights Act of 1970 239

W

war on terrorism
    authority for 331
    effect on public opinion 502–503
    and foreign policy 506, 508
    and ISIS 491
War Powers Resolution 324, 329
warrant 75
Wealth of Nations 107
Welfare Reform Act 472
welfare state 473. *See also* social welfare
Wesberry v. Sanders 278
whip. *See* party whip
White House staff 317–318
Wilson, Woodrow 109, 325
working poor 471
World Bank 507
World War I 327
World War II 327
writ of certiorari 386
writ of mandamus 25

Appendix
05

UNDERSTANDING AMERICAN POLITICS:

Supplementary Materials: Pages: 565–724

Contents of Supplementary Materials

Some Useful Links for Students, p566

The Origin and Character of the American Revolutionary Consciousness, p567

    Early American Political Culture and the Importance of Religion: A Lesson by Contrast, p568

    The Ideological and Emotive Origins Versus Rational Political Arguments of Statesmen, p570

On the Interpretation of the Founders' Motives and the Character of Their Product, the Constitution of the United States, p575

Articles of Confederation, p580

"The Federalist Papers," No. 10 and No. 51 (1787–1788), p587

    The Federalist Paper No. 10 (by James Madison), p588

    • "The Same Subject Continued (from No. 9): The Union as a Safeguard Against Domestic Faction and Insurrection," or also known as "The Size and Variety of the Union as a Check on Faction."

    The Federalist Paper No. 51 (by James Madison), p592

    • "The Structure of the Government Must Furnish the Proper Checks and Balances Between the Different Departments."

Transcript of *Marbury v. Madison* (1803), p595

Transcript of *McCulloch v. Maryland* (1819), p600

Transcript of Monroe Doctrine (1823), p607

Transcript of Emancipation Proclamation (1863), p609

Transcript of *Brown v. Board of Education* (1954), p611

Transcript of Civil Rights Act (1964), p615

Transcript of Voting Rights Act (1965), p638

Instances of Use of United States Armed Forces Abroad, 1798–2004, p646

    Summary, p646

    Instances of Use of United States Armed Forces Abroad, 1798–2004, p647

Bill Summary & Status 93rd Congress (1973–1974), p672

Full Text of "War Powers Resolution," November 7, 1973, p674

Senate Resolution 85, from the Library of Congress, "Thomas" (March 1, 2011), p679

Full Text of "UN Resolution No. 1970", p681

Full Text of "UN Resolution No. 1973", p692

President Obama's Letter to Congress (March 21, 2011), p703

House Resolution 188 IH, from the Library of Congress, "Thomas" (March 30, 2011), p705

List of U.S. Presidents, p707

Images of U.S. Presidents, p709

Some Useful Links for Students

Librivox Audio of Thomas Paine's Common Sense (open, then choose "whole item," click on "zip file," then download and open it):
http://www.archive.org/details/commonsense_gg_librivox

Thomas.gov, a great website for searching materials regarding United States government and politics:
http://www.thomas.gov/

Federalist Papers:
http://thomas.loc.gov/home/histdox/fedpapers.html

Federalist Papers:
http://oll.libertyfund.org/?option=com_staticxt&staticfile=show.php%3Ftitle=788

Federalist Papers in Audio at Librivox:
http://www.archive.org/details/federalist_papers_librivox

Our Documents.gov:
http://ourdocuments.gov/doc.php?flash=true&doc=10

"A Concise Guide To The Federalist Papers As A Source Of The Original Meaning Of The United States Constitution," by Gregory E. Maggs.
http://www.bu.edu/law/central/jd/organizations/journals/bulr/documents/MAGGS.pdf

Publishing the Declaration:
http://www.loc.gov/today/cyberlc/feature_wdesc.php?rec=3709

Librivox Audio of the Bill of Rights (open, then select a reader, then download and open it):
http://www.archive.org/details/billofrights_madison_0801_librivox

On Ideology: Audio recording of Marx's Communist Manifesto,
http://www.archive.org/details/communistmanifesto_librivox

Text and principles of Great Britain's "Magna Carta" of 1215: Does anything look familiar?
http://www.bl.uk/treasures/magnacarta/translation/mc_trans.html

http://www.whitehouse.gov/

http://www.senate.gov/

http://www.house.gov/

http://www.congress.org/congressorg/home/

http://www.publicagenda.org/ For interesting public policy issues & info, "issue guides."

http://www.debates.org and http://www.debates.org/pages/deb2008.html

The Origin and Character of the American Revolutionary Consciousness

It is the purpose of this paper to present an understanding of (or one view of) the origin and character of the American 'revolutionary consciousness'. The sources of this consciousness are complex and arguable, depending upon one's perception and assumptions. The time of and nature of crystallization of these 'sources' of American revolutionary consciousness may, therefore, depend on those same individualistic assumptions. As we attempt to ascertain how, why, and when the colonists took on a new 'American' identity which differed from that of an Englishman's identity, it is worthwhile to query whether the change was slow and gradual, or sudden and discrete.

Were such changes based on rational versus irrational argumentation? Were they changes based on external actions or influences? I argue that the colonists were in the midst of fairly slowly changing and very contiguous identities. Any inquiry into why the sources of the 'American revolutionary consciousness', or new American identity, crystallized when they did, and why they led to revolution, must seek answers derived from one's interpretations and assumptions regarding those 'sources'! True objectivity and accuracy is difficulty to achieve. I propose that Bernard Bailyn is correct in his assertion, using a quote from John Adams, that the real "Revolution was in the minds and hearts of the people; a change in their religious sentiments, of their duties and obligations...*This radical change in the principles, opinions, sentiments, and affections of the people was the real American revolution* (Bailyn quoting John Adams, p160)."

The sources and origins of an American Revolutionary consciousness may be traced back to English political culture at *least* as far as the Magna Carta of 1215. According to full text translation of this document by G.R.C. Davis, the Section 1 states: "FIRST THAT WE HAVE *GRANTED TO GOD*, and by his present charter have *confirmed for us* and our heirs in perpetuity, that the English church shall be free, and shall have its rights undiminished, and its liberties unimpaired (Magna Carta, p1)." It is most noteworthy that such humans perceived it possible to 'Grant' anything to God, and that the charter of the Magna Carta confirms this 'for us'. Yet, emphasis in this section is on the liberty of the Church of England. Liberty for 'free' men follows in a secondary fashion, mentioned in Section 2, essentially defining what it means to be, or should mean to be, a free man. At the end of the first section, it is stated clearly: TO ALL FREE MEN OF OUR KINGDOM we have also granted, for us and our heirs for ever, all the *liberties* written out below, to have and to keep them... (the rest of the Magna Carta enumerates such liberties, paying much attention to property and what might be understood as due process) (Magna Carta, p1)." At this point in time being discussed, 1215, we may identify concerns for liberty that would undergo some changes and refinements over the following period of just under 600 years up to the era of the American Revolution (in ideas or as an actual event). Is this to be interpreted as an early commitment to some sense of individual rights and duties? Is it rational? Is it emotive, or irrational?

It is my understanding and assertion that the centuries that passed allowed for gradual changes and developments of political culture in England, Europe, and colonial America. With respect to English and subsequent American revolutionary political culture, or 'consciousness', the sense of individualism grew to a point of rejection of perceived unjust (and actual) restraints on liberty. For the colonists in America, this meant a rejection of perceived unjust (and actual) restraints on liberty as imposed by the English Parliament. The actions and arguments that took place in the 1760s and 1770s were of particular importance in facilitating further exacerbation of tension between England and the colonies, and influencing the acceleration of a more coherent and crystallized American revolutionary consciousness.

A few cautions are warranted. Identity may be understood from the internal point of view of the self, or the subject(s) of concern. Alternatively, an external assignment of identity may stem from the observer's point of view, which often does not precisely coincide with the view of the subject about his or her self. Hence, in determining how Englishmen came to shed an English identity in favor of a new 'American' identity in the colonies, we must look to their own assessments. The historical context of political, philosophical, and religious thought may assist any effort to interpret identities of colonists. Yet, it may be erroneous to assume that all colonists, particularly at later points

in time nearer to the revolution, are of one 'same', or homogenous identity. This anticipated variance casts doubt, as it complicates our efforts to conclusively pinpoint an exact moment in time at which the 'momentous step' toward revolution occurred, as perspectives and interpretations are expected to offer some disagreement.

In our efforts to determine and describe the sources or origins, we should hesitate to call them 'causes'. We must be careful to avoid overly simplified, linear and deterministic assumptions of causality, and no universal generalizations are herein made in regard to causality. Yet, as we understand the lexicon of causality to include 'remote' causes and 'proximate' causes, perhaps it is worthwhile to discuss the sources or factors of influence which were eventually consolidated into some amalgamation we may call an 'American revolutionary consciousness', or self-perceived American identity. Remote causes are more removed in time and direct relevance from an effect, or event concerned. As the causes become more influential and direct, or closer chronologically to the event, we may describe them as more 'proximate', and less remote. The proximate cause, if only one can be identified for a given circumstance or event, is generally the one that is largely credited with bringing about the effect. Whether such a proximate cause is *sufficient* to bring about the effect, or perhaps just necessary (among other causes), is another question.

For the purposes of this paper, I regard the historically distant and far removed 'sources' or origins of American revolutionary consciousness to be of interest and importance, but also as more 'remote sources' or 'remote origins'. The more 'proximate' sources or origins, (often perceived as the actual 'causes') are perhaps more identifiable in terms of dates, places, people, ideas and events, and are often assumed to be of primary importance. I do not assume that 'proximate sources' (causes, contributing factors) of the revolution are of supreme or paramount importance in comparison to that of the remote origins. However, such analysis should help to give credence to the sought-after 'point of crystallization' of sources and the perceived 'momentous step' toward revolution in the third quarter of the eighteenth century. If not for the foundations laid by remote origins or sources, perhaps the subsequent events would have occurred differently, if at all. Perhaps remote origins ought to be described as political culture, or at least described within the scope of political culture.

Early American Political Culture and the Importance of Religion: A Lesson by Contrast

How can one summarize the significance of religion to the various colonists without oversimplification of the subject? Without assuming that it can be done within the relatively limited scope and length of this paper, I argue that the Protestant varieties of Christianity had developed and moved to the new world, and justify caution against universalist generalizations of an absolutely homogenous political culture. Comparison and contrast of religious origin and its impact on colonial Latin America may help in drawing out the different characteristics of the North American colonists. In broad terms, the rigid hierarchy and strong 'centralist' tendencies of Catholicism in Latin America were contrary to that found in the Protestant versions of Christianity (see Claudio Véliz, The Centralist Tradition in Latin America, 1977). Central and South America had been colonized by both Spain and Portugal beginning in the early 1500s, and with them came Catholicism. For these societies of Iberian influence, St. Thomas Aquinas had provided the fundamental understanding of society as being organic, or monastic in nature. Emphasis was on the 'community', or the whole, rather than on the individuals, or the parts.

Thus, In Latin America, 'rights' of the individuals were not conceived of just as they had been by the Protestant colonists of North America. Instead, rights were often discussed as 'fueros', a Spanish term which translates as 'group rights'. This Latin American conceptualization of social and political institutions as being organized into hierarchical, organic, and with a strong centralist tradition of power stressed unity rather than individuality. By coincidence, or accident, this Catholic-based form of society and colonization was nicely over-laid on top of the previously existing social and power structures of the indigenous peoples such as the Aztecs, the Mayans, and a bit further south, the Incas of Peru. It has been argued that the colonization in Latin America was made possible (at least partially) by such coincidental marriage of pre-existing rigid hierarchy within organic, monastic societies in indigenous societies and that of the conquering Spanish and Portuguese versions of authority.

On the contrary, top down power structures within organic, monastic societies of this Iberian tradition were not so acceptable (if even relevant) to the colonial immigrants in North America. While the Catholics of Latin America were more likely to be found accepting divine authority as unquestionable and inseparable from their governments and their lives, the immigrants to Northern American colonies were of a much different cultural origin, and were colonizing the land in a different fashion. In North American colonies, values of personal achievement and of individual rights and liberty were at forefront of their concerns. Questioning the purpose, virtue, manner and scope of government authority over religious institutions was not uncommon within the political culture of North American colonists, at least more so than had been evidenced within Latin American countries.

This sort of individualist and highly critical political thought can be seen regularly as we peruse the literature from early periods up to the persuasive fire of the 'propagandists' just at the eve of the American Revolution. With frequent focus on liberty, given that perspectives and conclusions may vary somewhat, speakers and writers such as John Winthrop have disseminated their opinions and arguments, arguments which have helped to raise the political consciousness.

In his "Little Speech on Liberty" (1645), Winthrop proposed that "The great questions that have troubled the country are about the authority of the magistrates and the liberty of the people (Winthrop, 1645)." In his comments regarding the choice of magistrates, he explained that covenants exist between the leaders of government and those who are ruled. God's law and 'our own' (law) serve as the guidelines by which people will be judged by magistrates... even if only to the best of the magistrates 'skill'. Note Winthrop's expectation of error and infallibility on the part of those with authority. I find it quite interesting that he prefaces the commentary on liberty with the following encouragement: "I entreat you to consider that when you choose magistrates, you take them from among yourselves, men subject to like passions as you are. Therefore, when you see infirmities in us, you should reflect upon your own... (Winthrop, 1645)." Those in positions of authority are fallible humans. While his purpose for such a statement may have been to make for more reasonable expectations of leaders, I believe that Winthrop's comments make clear that the colonists 'should' perceive their government and authority figures as imperfect humans, people who are from and part of their own society. This represents a bit of a *transition* from feudal-England's political culture.

However, one might argue that with the decline of feudalism in England, with increasing acceptance of the Magna Carta, and with more significant authority of the English Parliament after 1641, the English political culture was a 'moving target'. As it may be perceived as more dynamic than static, American political culture ought not be too hastily measured against an English political culture that also shifts and grows within its own context. It was becoming more individualist-oriented insofar as what had been regarded as intolerable or unjust rule. Of course, the social-economic structure in England was undergoing significant change; it had been undergoing some degree of reform along economic affairs such as shifts in the means of production to the more familiar 'capitalism'. As *serfs* gained freedom, becoming *peasants* with the increased capacity to posses, trade, and benefit from their surpluses in production, these peasants enjoyed newly formed individual rights in England!

It is not absolutely clear (in any conclusive sense) at what precise point or to what degree such a shift in English political culture influenced the American colonial culture. This difficulty arises from the aforementioned suggestion that many generations in England are likely to have evolved their political ideas, attitudes and values that might be labeled 'political thought' in a very gradual and contiguous fashion. Thus, it seems arguable that while we attempt to ascertain how and when, in the American colonies, the liberalizing (or individual-rights oriented, perhaps liberty-obsessed) colonists shed their English identity, we must notice that the English too had been liberalizing from the vantage point of political thought. Political culture in England may not have changed as rapidly or in the same exact fashion as the political culture of the colonies (not to assume perfect homogeneity here either). Nonetheless, it had been undergoing change. So, great caution must be exercised when asserting that colonial 'political consciousness' had moved farther from its English roots, for the roots at any given period may have grown (even if slightly) into another form or even in a similar direction. As a result, the American passion for liberty, which I assert to be of key importance to this consciousness, or political culture, is not so clearly distinct from its English roots of inspiration.

Contrast such developments of liberal individualism in colonial North America and England against the Thomistic political culture of the Iberian Peninsula and its colonies in Latin America. Does the fundamental contrast lie in individual rights or liberty against the 'fueros' (group rights) which seem very sensible and appropriate under

such extreme organic conceptualizations of society? If yes, then perhaps the sources and origins of the American revolutionary consciousness are more similar to the political consciousness of progressive (small 'p') English thinkers than may be frequently understood! Perhaps our ever-increasing emphasis on individualism and liberty may be perceived as loosely corresponding, to some degree, with Englishmen such as John Locke (recall his <u>Second Treatise on Government</u>). Yet, perhaps more 'remote' origins from centuries past are responsible.

But, in 1645, Winthrop made it clear that *natural liberty* "is incompatible and inconsistent with authority, and cannot endure the least restraint of the most just authority (Winthrop)." Man, with such liberty, has the ability to do evil as well as good. Natural liberty is "common to man, (as) with beasts and other creatures (Winthrop, 1645)." *Civil or federal liberty*, on the other hand, he calls "moral," "in reference to the covenant between God and man in the moral law, and the *politic covenants and constitutions amongst the men themselves. This liberty is the proper end and object of authority* and cannot subsist without it; and it is a liberty to that only that is good, honest and just (Winthrop, 1645)." Such distinction in the purpose of government authority, I argue, has pervaded much American political thought since Winthrop's time. This is rather obviously supported by evidence throughout writings of Lovejoy's analysis of the Glorious Revolution, Bailyn's analysis of the ideological origins of the American Revolution, and Webking's well-focused contributions which detail political argument closer to the period of the revolution.

Questions of how to properly govern within their distinct churches resulted in varied responses. While Episcopalians endorsed a more top-down hierarchy involving Bishops, Presbyterians entertained a more bottom up approach, more pluralist in character. Conregregationists exhibited a belief in greater autonomy for each congregation, which was perceived to be independent as a self-governing body. Each congregation was free to pursue its particular sense of theology. Hence, diversity among the attitudes toward religious organization(s) within the colonies of North America represented a far greater sense of individuality and independence from state authority that had been the witnessed in colonized areas of Latin America.

Religious thought impacted political thought in both of these European-colonized regions of the world, resulting in contrary political cultures in North America and Latin America. Such a heterogeneity of religious and political thought in the North American British colonies included intellectual debate on the philosophic issues of individuality, natural rights, property, liberty, secularism, monarchy and divine right, Parliamentary representation, and even economic interests were often rooted in English writers, and influenced by English history. Great geographic distance came between these colonists and their homeland's monarchy and parliament of 'nobles'. Colonists also were socially distant from rigid class structure of England based on noble lords and monarchic authority. Very significantly, American-born colonists were without direct experience of feudalism as an actual social, political, and productive (economic) relation. As such, perhaps such disanalogies of experiences between colonial and English social relations no doubt made for inroads for new and innovative political thought, or political philosophy in the American colonies.

However, it must be recognized again that historical experiences of England were subject to changing social and political relations during the 1600s. In England, dissatisfaction with the English social and political structures during years past may be sited as responsible for generating new political discussions and issues for the homeland. No doubt, these issues resonated with people across the Atlantic, as citations of John Locke and the Magna Carta abound for years ahead (even today). Political turmoil in England, challenges to monarchical authority, and concerns evidenced by the Magna Carta gave cause for political debate not only in England but also in the colonies for quite some time. Creating and shaping just, fair, and good or virtuous government was a challenge underway *long* before the constitutional debates of 1787.

The Ideological and Emotive Origins Versus Rational Political Arguments of Statesmen

Robert H. Webking differentiates his work <u>The American Revolution and the Politics of Liberty</u> from that of Bernard Bailyn's <u>The Ideological Origins of the American Revolution</u>. Webking presents an interesting and knowledgeable analysis of six colonial thinkers who helped to form and develop 'rational' political arguments which may be

understood as contributing, in a catalytic sense, to the 'grounding' of the revolution. Hence, this political scientist understands that politics does matter, and that rational, reasonable argumentation is very relevant to comprehending how the revolution came about. Webking best explains his main point in his last chapter, and is worth quoting in the full text:

> "The leaders of the Americans argued for and participated in resistance and finally revolution because they understood three things. First, they knew of the importance of liberty for human beings. Second, they understood that actions undertaken by the British government abridged American liberties and threatened to impose upon America an absolute and arbitrary government. Finally, they understood that despotism must be attacked in its design stage because it is difficult to defeat once it has become well established. Well informed and well educated reason led them to act as they did (Webking, 173)."

Webking's differentiation of his own work from Bailyn's represents too hasty a dismissal of Bailyn's analysis as one that simply pertains to the 'irrational' beliefs of colonists.

It may be true that Bailyn pursued and presented ideological, or irrational, origins. It may also be true that Bailyn offered that a great deal of evidence for the existence of emotive arguments and rhetoric, or irrational beliefs, as contained in colonists' pamphlets and discussions of conspiracy, for example. These irrational beliefs and arguments were argued by Bailyn to have been influential in bringing about the revolution. Webking's argument that Bailyn represented to us *merely* an irrational basis for the revolution seems a bit too hasty and simplistic. If we accept that rational argument had its place in the annals of revolutionary thought and persuasion, perhaps it might be consistent to suppose that the irrational and emotive rhetoric may have served as a very reasonable means to goal-oriented ends of minimizing arbitrary government (hence rational). Even a 'rat-choicer' could conceivably explain away such an apparent and illusory contradiction... irrationality of emotive arguments, utilized as a means to rational ends.

Fallacies of the straw man, the false dilemma, and suppression of evidence are demonstrated by Webking early in his book. To illustrate such a claim, Bailyn's position is well worth some explanation and defense. Bailyn's suggestion for an 'irrational' basis, or origin of the American Revolution, was evident in his presentation of conspiracy as being of great importance. Colonists were arguably suspicious of the English as conspirators against them, and the English perceived the colonists as conspirators. However, Bailyn's book goes much farther into political and economic history to be characterized as illustrating purely irrational colonial thoughts, beliefs and rhetoric. Many may agree that the implications and connotations of ideology are negative, as having to do with irrational and biased normative beliefs about how the world should be. The colonists' increasing perceptions of conspiracy may have been somewhat erroneous in their agreement with a reality of British conspiracy, according to Bailyn. Yet, such perceptions of conspiracy, having been emotively (hence irrationally) charged and perhaps also grossly mistaken, as Bailyn argues, were nonetheless important as a factor in bringing about the revolution. It seems reasonable to accept that this perception of conspiracy was, at least, *one of* the more 'proximate' factors in the 1760s and 1770s that helped to further catalyze and consolidate 'American consciousness' and, ultimately, action.

Yes, Webking is correct in his assumption that Bailyn has promoted irrationality as important, but Webking is only partially correct about the overall message of Bailyn's book. Much of Bailyn's masterful piece discusses in depth a tremendous amount of what could be called 'rational origins', or sources of the revolution...even if only implicitly. The segments of his book that treat the economic history of commerce, trade, and trade-related laws such as the Stamp Act or Navigation Acts of the British Parliament have provided analysis of what might conceivably be described as discussions of rational economic and political thought. Bailyn's later segment, on the 'Contagion of Liberty', involved much discussion of what might be termed here rational argumentation and political reaction. For example, the disputes of religious liberty and taxation (in Ashfield, Massachusetts) that pitted the Baptists against the less tolerant Congragationists and their aggressive land grabs demonstrated that arguments for liberty (religious liberty in this case) may be interpreted as quite rational and reasonable.

Much similar evidence for rational colonial political thought is available within Bailyn's book, but is ignored by Webking. Webking seems to assume a false dichotomy of the rational versus irrational accounts of the origins of the revolution, contending that Bailyn is wrong for promoting the irrational, while Webking asserts the 'rational' as important and effectual to 'thought' of the times. However, Bailyn illustrates repeatedly that irrational beliefs may

be intertwined with argumentative and rational reasoning. In fact, even the most emotively charged rhetoric can employ sound reasoning to bolster conclusions. Thus, the rational and irrational may often be inseparable within any given argument or example of rhetoric.

Hence, Webking's fallacious 'suppression' of known relevant evidence within Bailyn's book, leads him to commit the fallacies of, first, the 'straw man argument' (the purposeful or even unintentional misrepresentation of his opponent's position), and second, the fallacy of the 'false dilemma' (an erroneous belief in a limited number of alternatives). The straw man is evident, as Bailyn's work is rich in examples of how the rational qualities of argumentation and belief formation supplant the irrational. The false dilemma is rooted in Webking's erroneous assumption that the rational and irrational beliefs which formed the basis of colonial thought can simply be separated in into discrete categories, according to a clear and false dichotomy of either 'this or that' (rational versus irrational thought). Yet, Bailyn shows, even if only implicitly, that rationality and irrationality may be understood as being more or less rational in degree. Perhaps a perception of a *continuum of rationality/irrationality,* varying in degrees of rationality, allows us to see how rational and irrational aspects (or qualities) may be present in any rhetoric or argument or belief, such as those positions taken by the North American colonists on so many diverse issues, and over so many years.

Bailyn is convincing in his arguments for when and how the crystalization of the sources of the American Revolutionary consciousness came about. He assures us that the Enlightenment and English libertarianism were influential: "Words and concepts had been reshaped in the colonists' minds in the course of a decade (circa 1776) of pounding controversy—strangely reshaped, turned in unfamiliar directions, toward conclusions that they could not themselves clearly perceive (Bailyn, p161)." He claims that a "critical probing of traditional concepts—part of the colonists effort to express reality as they knew it and to shape it to ideal ends—became the basis for all further discussions of enlightened reform, in Europe as well as in America (Bailyn, p161)." Interestingly, the newly pronounced American political culture is identified as a source of influence upon Europe after having grown from European (primarily English) roots! Three main issues became central to the American political thought; first, representation and consent of constituents; second, formations of constitutions and guarantees of individual 'rights'; and third, sovereignty.

The issue of representation and consent was of terrific importance to the colonists, and Bailyn argues it to be the "first serious intellectual problem to come between England and the colonies (Bailyn, p161)." Bailyn's perspective is critical to the purposes of this work, and deserves full text citation:

> "This shift in conception (of representation, consents, etc) took place rapidly; it began and for all practical purposes concluded in the two years of the Stamp Act controversy. But the intellectual position worked out by the Americans in that brief span of time had deep historical roots; it *crystallized,* in effect three generations of political experience. The ideas colonists put forward, rather than creating a new condition of fact, expressed one that had long existed; they articulated and in doing so generalized, systematized, gave moral sanction to what had emerged haphazardly, incompletely and insensibly (hence 'irrationally'), from the chaotic factionalism of colonial politics (Bailyn, p162)."

Virtual representation was ridiculed and found inappropriate to American concerns.

Constitutional matters were significant, and the American quest for guarantees of rights led to a process of "disengaging principles from institutions (Bailyn, p181)." He explains this *turning point* in our history: "The transition to more advanced ground was forced forward by the continuing need, after 1764, to distinguish fundamentals from the actions of government so that they might serve as limits and controls (Bailyn, p181)." Thus, it may well be argued that rationality was evident is such colonial pursuits. Hence, Bailyn implicitly argues by demonstration that 'rational' thought was extremely important, a point which is contrary to Webking's analysis of Bailyn's work. This sense of colonial 'rationality' is supported by further evidence on the seriousness of forming civil constitutions and also of their impacts. Note references made to *'painting for eternity'* (see Bailyn, pages 182-185).

Bailyn argues, and I agree entirely, that the colonial thinkers' interest in creating written guarantees within a constitution so as to protect so-called natural and universal rights, was truly *'momentous':* "These closely related changes—in the view of what a constitution was and of the proper emphasis in the understanding of rights—were momentous; they would shape the entire future development of American constitutional thought and practice. Yet,

they did not seem momentous at the time (Bailyn, p189)." It is important to note that this wonderful quote requires us to consider that such a shift, or change, is 'momentous'. Yet, insofar as we are aware, that those of us now able to look back through time perceive the paramount importance and implications of such political beliefs, values, and attitudes. Hence, the concept of self-identity of colonists may allow us to draw a distinction of perspective, between subjectivity of observers looking back, versus subjectivity of actors in the 1700s, the real participants.

'Sovereignty' was an issue that was passionately discussed in England in the 1640s, so was not 'new' in this sense. Where is the locus of supreme authority? Where should it be held? In the Monarch? In the Parliament? Should the sovereign state have unrestricted or unrestrained power and authority? Bailyn points out that Britain's Glorious Revolution resulted, for the English, in a Parliament with greater powers. It was:

> "a body absolute and arbitrary in its sovereignty; the creator and interpreter, not the subject, of law; the superior and master of all other rights and powers within the state… and it was this conceptualization, justified in the end by the theory of an ultimate supremacy of the people—a supremacy normally dormant and exercised at only moments of rebellion against tyrannical government—that was carried into the eighteenth century and into the debates that preceded the American Revolution… It had been a gradual development, and it had ended in a significant inversion (Bailyn, p201)."

Otis accepted the need for a supreme authority, but he claimed that it must be held within the people: "a supreme legislative and a supreme executive power must be placed somewhere in every commonwealth. Where there is no other positive provision or compact to the contrary, those powers remain in the whole body of the people (Otis, in Bailyn, p205)." Though Otis' arguments were criticized at the time for overall self-contradictions involving advice of submission, the idea of delineating new powers so as to restrain a governing body took hold in the colonies. Discussions of internal versus external powers of England became of great significance. The Declaratory Act, claiming supremacy of England's Parliament over the colonies in all matters and concerns, was an affirmation which was of terrific impact on colonial attitudes of resistance and commitment. By Parliament's determination to maintain supreme authority, with its promulgation of Acts including the Stamp Act, the Navigation Acts, and the Declaratory Act, I argue that the political culture of North American colonies became more fully crystallized, more passionate, and more prone to result in action on behalf of the colonies.

Individualism had, by this period of the 1770s, evolved from its early and more remote intellectual roots in England, and Europe more generally. Values, beliefs, and attitudes such as reflected in concepts of individual rights and liberties, 'civil' liberties, representation that is effective rather than merely 'virtual', consent, accountability, written constitutions (e.g. derived from charters) as guarantees of individual rights, sovereign authority held within the 'body of the people', are all elements of what became an important *American Revolutionary consciousness*, a 'new' political culture. The crystallization of a new political culture was the result of the real revolution of ideas, which arguably took an American character during the chaotic decades of the 1760s to 1770s. The rapidity of change in intellectual thought was due to the combination of both rational and irrational argumentation and beliefs. Events and acts from Parliament were largely interpreted as acts of control and restraint of liberty in the colonies. These were the more proximate causes or origins of the American Revolution (with special regard to the revolution of American colonists' ideas) and the subsequent rebellious violence. The achievement of the American Constitution shortly thereafter evidenced the embodiment of such a 'consciousness' of the fundamental principles, values, and beliefs, and it helped to institutionalize them for many generations to come.

References:

Bailyn, Bernard. <u>The Ideological Origins of the American Revolution.</u> Cambridge, MA: The Belknap Press of Harvard University Press. 1992

Lovejoy, David S. <u>The Glorious Revolution in America</u>. Hanover, N.H. : Wesleyan University Press. 1972

Webking, Robert H. <u>The American Revolution and the Politics of Liberty</u>. Baton Rouge: Louisiana State University Press. 1988

Winthrop, John. "A Little Speech on Liberty," 1645. Available in numerous printed sources, and also available online at: Electronic Text Center, University of Virginia Library. 2009. URL: http://etext.lib.virginia.edu/etcbin /toccer-new2?id=WinLibe.xml&images=images/modeng&data=/texts/english/modeng/parsed&tag =public&part=1&division=div1

Véliz, Claudio. <u>The Centralist Tradition in Latin America</u>. Princeton, N.J. : Princeton University Press. 1980

<u>Magna Carta</u>. 1215. Translated by G. R. C. Davis. London, United Kingdom: The British Library. 1982

On the Interpretation of the Founders' Motives and the Character of Their Product, the Constitution of the United States

"Wherever the real power in government lies, there is the danger of oppression. In our governments the real power lies in the majority of the Community, and the invasion of private rights is chiefly to be apprehended, not from acts of government contrary to the sense of its constituents, but from acts from which the government is the mere instrument of the major number of the constituents. This is a truth of great importance, but not sufficiently attended to, and is probably more strongly impressed upon my mind by facts, and reflections suggested by them, than on yours which has contemplated abuses of power issuing from a very different quarter. Wherever there is an interest and power to do wrong, wrong will generally be done, and not less readily by a powerful and interested party than by a powerful and interested prince."

James Madison in a letter to Jefferson, 1788

It is the purpose of this essay to first, 'attempt' to clarify the motives of the founders in their move to create the United Sates Constitution and leave the Articles of Confederation behind, on the ash heap of history. Second, I will link my understanding of the founder's motives to the 'character' of their product, the U.S. Constitution. It is assumed that the character of the Constitution, however it is to be interpreted by any discussant, must have been a product of the influence and purposes of the founders. Thus, as interpretations of motives have varied, so must interpretations of the meaning, or purposive character of the Constitution. An often assumed or implied dichotomy of motivation, between motives of economic interests and what I refer to as 'moral-based' motives (with a non-economic focus), will be shown to be a false dichotomy.

One point is essential to my interpretations of these matters, particularly of the founder's supposed 'motives'. Motives are difficult to know with absolute certainty. To understand a Constitution, one might analyze it in a littoral sense, breaking it down into its explicit component parts, followed by a synthesis and critique of the document as it appears. But, if the purpose of the document and the manner in which it had been shaped may extend beyond the narrow boundaries of the written word of the document itself, perhaps it is worth considering the origins of a *perceived* need for change. Why and how did the founders perceive a need to shift from the Articles of Confederation to the new Constitution? What purposes and motivations effected such a shift? Does the above quote from Madison to Jefferson suggest that founders' individual perspectives and motives may vary? Yes! How can we 'know' these motives? I do not assume that motives of an 'other' person may be easily and accurately understood by an observer, particularly when the onlooker is removed from the period and culture by two hundred years.

In fact, it is impossible to know with certainty what the true motives of another person may be, even when the 'other' person is present and available for inclusion in discussion. The 'other' person may directly state and affirm a given motive, as expressed verbally or in writing. Behavior and circumstances of an individual may also be of use in attempting to determine an individual's motive. The consideration of the founding period's broad context of social, political, and economic environments of the late 18th century should allow for greater understanding. We may hopefully be able to gain insight into first, what is important to an individual (such as each founder), and second, what is possible for him to achieve among his perceived alternatives. But, how are we able to be sure that any evidence offers a true, accurate, and complete understanding of the values, beliefs, priorities, and perceived alternatives of *another* person?

We cannot know with certainty the thoughts and feelings of others, such as the founders. Written and verbal testimony *seems* to offer direct evidence of an individual's intent, or motives. Also, evidence of circumstance may offer cogent reasons for the acceptance of our imputed conclusions. However, we are not entitled to assume or draw the conclusion that all information relevant to establishing 'motive' has been considered (or that no evidence has

been suppressed or omitted). We are simply unable to conclude that one's self-made assertions of purpose and intent, or motive, are true representations of his mindfulness. Often, ulterior motives are to blame for misleading of false indications (declarations) of motives.

The problem of perception, which involves subjectivity, may be the chief problem of interpretation of the founders' true motives. Even given written commentary and supposedly informative first-hand argumentation and assertions of their purposes, it remains implausible that their motives may be known in any comprehensive sense, and with absolute certainty. Nonetheless, our analysis and interpretation may allow us to debate and posit the motives of the founders, so that we may know the motives with some degree of probability, dependent upon what else may be the case, and cautioned under the limits of inductive reasoning.

Several authors have written in an effort to interpret the political thought behind the founders' positions during the creation of the Constitution each offer insight into some aspect or consideration of the founders' diverse priorities and concerns. The authors may agree on points of fact, while disagree of underlying reasons for taking any particular position on a Constitutional issue. Surely divisions among founders' grew apparent, most perceptible along the lines of Federalist versus Anti-federalist contenders, as was pointed out with great contrast by Herbert Storing in <u>What the Anti-federalists were for</u>. But what were the motives behind such positions? I believe that the matter distills down to two basic types of intent, or motivation of our individual founders. First, we may speak of the motivation to satisfy or protect economic interests (whether state, federal, or more directly private self-interest), and second, the more 'moral-based' motivation to create a virtuous, just, and stable government (however to be defined). These are both motivations of paramount importance to any inquiry of the political thought behind the Constitution.

One interpretation is the position that the founders, an elitist group, were influenced by motives of self-interest... an economic self-interest. The famous analysis by Charles Beard (or infamous, depending on one's 'perspective'!) holds that economic interests had a significant influence on the purposes expressed by the founding economic elite. Criticism of Beard's work can be expected to resonate with accusations that Beard ignores other motives such as the quest for virtue. Thus, I argue that a dichotomy is apparent between seekers and interpreters of the economic interest, and others seeking and interpreting motives as moral and virtue-based. Perception is crucial. As I credit Beard with pre-eminence among those in the economic interest 'camp', I will emphasize his work in order to present an illuminating interpretation of the founders' motivations relevant to 'economic interest'. Against this understanding of those such as Beard, I will continue to discuss the possible moral-based motives which I believe an economic interpretation *excessively downplays* or entirely *ignores* in attempt to discredit.

However, Beard never stated in <u>An Economic Interpretation of the United States</u> that the intents and purposes of the founders were certainly and exclusively based on economic considerations. Instead of claiming that such economic motives determined their decision-making and actions of the founders regarding the creation of the Constitution, he explicitly offered that economic interests must not be ignored in deference to advocates of abstract political theory, or motives of political virtue and justice. Note Beard's text:

> "And to my surprise I found that many fathers of the Republic regarded the conflict over the Constitution as springing essentially out of conflicts of economic interest, which had a certain geographical or sectional distribution...No attempt was made (in Beard's analysis) to take him (the reader) off his guard by some plausible formula of completeness and comprehensiveness. I simply sought to bring back into the mental picture of the Constitution those realistic features of economic interest, stress, and strain, which my masters had, for some reason, left out of it, or thrust far into the background as incidental rather than fundamental (Beard, pg xix–xx)."

This concern with economic interest, Beard contended, was simply a matter of emphasis that was missing from earlier analyses. Yet, the overall boldness of his argument, which we will discuss, seems to imply that perhaps Beard's 'modesty' (as expressed in such a claim) was merely designed to remove ammunition from the weapons of any anticipated objections of his likely critics.

Beard claimed that he was <u>*not*</u> proposing that members of the Constitutional convention were "working merely for their own pockets (Beard, pg xxviii)," as his 'superficial' critics charged. Instead, he held that the main inquiry of his book is this:

"Did they (the members) represent distinct groups whose economic interests they understood and felt in concrete, definite form through their own personal experience with identical property rights, or were they working merely under the guidance of abstract principles of political science? (Beard, pg xxviii)."

Of course, believing Beard's self-proclaimed sense of modesty in his assertion of the importance of economic interests is as problematic as any 'interpretation' of the motives of the founders.

We may find that Beard answered his own question of inquiry, as expressed above, on pages 152–188 of <u>An Economic Interpretation</u>, in a section entitled "The Constitution as an Economic Document." Specifically, on page 156 under subheading 'The Underlying Political Science of the Constitution', Beard argued that James Madison's position in *The Federalist #10* was of paramount importance. Of Madison, Beard offered: "Here he lays down, in no uncertain language, the principle that the first and elemental concern of every government is economic (Beard, pg156)."

Selectively quoting Madison, Beard suggested five elements that I propose to be of high importance for the case that the Constitution may be viewed as an economic document. Recalling Madison, he stated:

" *'The first object of government'*, he declares, is the protection of *'the diversity of the faculties of men, from which, the rights of property originate.'* **The chief business of government, from which, perforce, its essential nature must be derived, consists in the control and adjustment of conflicting economic interests...** *'The regulation of these various and interfering interests forms the principle task of modern legislation, and involves the spirit of the party and faction in the ordinary operations of the government* (Beard quoting Madison, Madison—in italics—, pg156)."

Here, Beard's claim that it is the 'essential nature' of government to control and adjust economic interests is in boldface for my emphasis, and I believe serves to complement Madison's expression rather well.

Second, Beard beautifully explained the causes for such 'conflicting political forces' using Madison: "...the most common and durable source of factions has been the various and unequal distribution of property. Those who hold and those who are without property have ever formed distinct interests in society (Beard, quoting Madison, pg 156)." Beard's third point is one which invites more contention, I suspect. He stated that "The theories of government which men entertain are *emotional reactions* to their propertied interests (Beard, pg 157)." Unfortunately, Beard's basis for this claim of 'emotional reactions' is not supported by his subsequent references to Madison, nor by Beard's own offerings. If Beard had been able to make a stronger argument for this point, he may have been able to show the creation of the Constitution to be somewhat based on emotional, irrational motivations! In addition, he may have been able to argue that *conflict* over economic interests is irrational-based, which would have made for an interesting academic dispute by challenging contemporary conceptions of 'man' as the self-interested 'rational actor'. Nonetheless, I argue that such a failure moderately diminishes his argument, or at least detracts from its potential.

His fourth point is that "unequal distribution of property is inevitable," and from it contending factions will arise in the state (Beard, pg157). It is here that Beard refers to Madison for concern for the 'minority', and the ensuing problem for government: "...the *supreme danger* will arise from the fusion of certain interests into an overbearing majority (a land-less proletariat), which will make its 'rights' paramount, and sacrifice the 'rights' of the majority (Beard, pg157)." Again, directly quoting Madison in order to bolster his argument, Beard noted the following: " *'To secure the public good'*, he declares, *'and private rights against the danger of such a faction and at the same time preserve the spirit and form of the popular government is the great object to which our inquiries are directed'* (Beard, quoting Madison, Madison—in italics—, pg157–158)." The utility of such a passage is terrific for the purposes of this paper. For, it is here that we may connect the 'motives' of the founders, which have been held to originate in concerns for economic interests by the founders, to the character of the Constitution. But, must all rights be economic-based?

In order to satisfy the 'motives' of the founders, they were faced with the challenge of operationalizing concepts of government structure which would effectively solve for the 'supreme danger' of the fusion of an overbearing majority, as Beard stated. The remedy was initiated in his fifth point, that a governmental system of checks and balances will prevent the contending interests from fusing into an unmanageable and oppressive majority. Again, calling on Madison, Beard alluded to the purpose and function of the new Constitution as one in which "public views are to be refined and enlarged *'by passing them through the medium of a chosen body of citizens'* (Beard, quoting Madison,

Madison—in italics—, p158)." This is the step-off point for Beard's argument, where he shifts from motivations and essential purposes of the founders to the actual construction of the government structure or system, with focus on the balance of power, on checks and balances.

So what might such an 'economic interpretation' of motives be missing? Beard has created a very persuasive position, which seems fairly sensible. He acknowledged that he was not capable of gathering all evidence, or data. Yet, he makes a reasonable appeal to readers that understand the longstanding high priority of concerns and values of individual's property (both real and personal). Unfortunately, the pure economic interpretation fails to satisfy those critics who tend to believe, in their world-views, that the *purpose* of good governance and specific forms of government is derived from a philosophic quest. This quest is one for wisdom. Such a quest involves matters of justice and virtue, issues reflective of what was believed to correspond with a human soul. What type of government is most just, and most virtuous? Specifically, what type is appropriate for the culture (with subset political culture) in the former colonies? Or appropriate among the states under the Articles of Confederation? Is such early-American political culture either homogenous or diverse? Does political culture require aspects of economic interests, or 'economic-culture' in order to be comprehensible? To what extent were colonial and early-American political cultures shaped by religion rather than economic 'interests' per se?

These questions present the founders' difficulty of creating a Constitution with moral origin. For contrast, terrific variance in moral values, views, and strongly opposed political opinions can be seen between present day Jews and Arabs in the Middle-East, or between Muslim fundamentalists and Christians in an array of countries. In such countries, 'politics' is rooted in far more than mere economic motivations. When one group fights for some sort of 'democracy', and another group views its own group's religion as the only legitimate authority, disputes are not at the level of economic interest. Political disputes are, at times, moral dilemmas.

For such societies, concepts of justice and virtue are in great variance, as are the often irreconcilable thoughts on what a so-called 'moral' government should entail. I argue that the Philadelphia Convention, while certainly *more* homogenous in its political culture than those evidenced by politically opposed factions in the Middle-East, must also have been *genuinely* involved in political deliberations with a moral-oriented, non-economic motivation. Perhaps such an element of moral or philosophic motivation was less noticeable (to some interpreters of history), less visible in the forest of economic concerns...but seems, none-the-less, to have been arguably real.

While some individuals may have tended to focus more on economic interests as sources of motivation, I believe that a quest for a *moral government* may be evidenced by the political discussions that had a strong philosophical bent. Even if only *some* such as Madison took the trouble to thoroughly delve into the annals of political philosophy in order to promote the most enlightened deliberations of the Constitution possible at that time, from what would such motivations have been derived? It seems reasonable to assume that, while admitting that Madison was involved in an economic motivation as shown by Beard, he was *also* attempting to create the just, fair, 'moral' government... however that might be defined.

Perhaps the difference in motivations might be described as the aim for the idealistic and the realistic as goals. Perhaps, in the founders' ambitions to seek an ideal society, a society that is just and virtuous, their ambitions may be understood as *idealistic ends*. Perhaps, we might understand the economic interest as a source of motivation that facilitated their deliberations in order to create, to design, and to implement the best possible 'workable', durable governmental structure... a 'republican' structure composed of its three branches and 'checks and balances' against tyranny. Perhaps the motivation of economic interests was, for the founders, necessary to further their moral ideals; it may be that economic-based motivations served as a means to further the greater, more evasive ends of an ideal society. It is recognized that some might argue that the economic interests were simply the ends-in-themselves, and the governmental structure was *only* seen by founders as a means to protecting those ends.

The essence, or nature, of the U.S. Constitution, as it is the blueprint for our structure and system of government and foundation for society, necessarily reflects the search for moral, just, and virtuous societal/governmental ideals *and* the more realist-based protection of the economic interests. It reflects both moral and the economic motives. In this work, we examined and considered an apparent dichotomy of motives. It has been argued in this article that, while understandable as distinguishable and separable concepts, the moral and economic motives were intertwined and often indistinguishable in the course of the founders' deliberation of the Constitution's design

(and its debated necessity!). These motives need not be conceptually severed from each other in a way that causes us, the interpreters of the motives, to entertain a false dichotomy. For the founders (at least for some such as James Madison), these were not mutually exclusive motives, but complimentary. To assume otherwise suggests the fallacy of the false dilemma. While perfection is not assumed for the Constitution of the United States, the character of the Constitution necessarily reflects motives aimed at both *idealist-oriented* ends and the *realist-oriented means* of building that 'city on the hill'.

References:

Madison, James. The Federalist #10, in the series of essays known as <u>The Federalist Papers</u>, by "Publius" (Alexander Hamilton, James Madison, and John Jay). Numerous versions abound. One version: Edited by Benjamin F. Wright, <u>The Federalist.</u> New York: Metro Books. 2002

Beard, Charles. With an Introduction by Louis Filler. <u>An Economic Interpretation of the Constitution of the United States</u>. New Brunswick, New Jersey: Transaction Publishers. 1998. Originally published by Beard and The Micmillan Company in 1913.

Storing, Herbert J. <u>What the Anti-Federalists Were FOR: The Political Thought of the Opponents of the Constitution</u>. Chicago: The University of Chicago Press. 1981

ARTICLES

OF

Confederation

AND

Perpetual Union

BETWEEN THE

STATES

OF

New Hampshire, Massachusetts Bay, Rhode Island, and Providence Plantations, Connecticut, New York, New Jersey, Pennsylvania, Delaware, Maryland, Virginia, North Carolina, South Carolina, and Georgia.

WILLIAMSBURG:

Printed by ALEXANDER PURDIE.

Articles of Confederation

To all to whom these presents shall come,
We, the undersigned, Delegates of the States affixed to our names, send greeting: 'Whereas the Delegates of the United States of America in Congress assembled, did on the fifteenth day of November, in the year of our Lord one thousand seven hundred and seventy and in the second year of the Independence of America, agree to certain Articles of Confederation and Perpetual Union between the states of New Hampshire Massachusetts Bay, Rhode Island and Providence Plantations, Connecticut, New York, New Jersey, Pennsylvania, Delaware, Maryland, Virginia, North Carolina, South Carolina, and Georgia, in the words following, viz.

ARTICLES OF CONFEDERATION AND PERPETUAL UNION,

between the States of New Hampshire Massachusetts Bay, Rhode Island and Providence Plantations, Connecticut, New York, New Jersey, Pennsylvania, Delaware, Maryland, Virginia, North Carolina, South Carolina, and Georgia.

ARTICLE 1

The style of this confederacy shall be, "THE UNITED STATES OF AMERICA."

ARTICLE 2

Each State retains its sovereignty, freedom, and independence, and every power, jurisdiction, and right, which is not by this confederation, expressly delegated to the United States, in Congress assembled.

ARTICLE 3

The said States hereby severally enter into a firm league of friendship with each other, for their common defence, the security of their liberties, and their mutual and general welfare, binding themselves to assist each other against all force offered to, or attacks made upon them, or any of them, on account of religion, sovereignty, trade, or any other pretence whatever.

ARTICLE 4

Section 1. The better to secure and perpetuate mutual friendship and intercourse among the people of the different States in this Union, the free inhabitants of each of these States, paupers, vagabonds, and fugitives from justice excepted, shall be entitled to all privileges and immunities of free citizens in the several States; and the people of each State shall have free ingress and regress to and from any other State, and shall enjoy therein all the privileges of trade and commerce, subject to the same duties, impositions, and restrictions, as the inhabitants thereof respectively; provided that such restrictions shall not extend so far as to prevent the removal of property imported into any State, to any other State, of which the owner is an inhabitant; provided also, that no imposition, duties, or restriction, shall be laid by any State on the property of the United States, or either of them.
Section 2. If any person guilty of, or charged with, treason, felony, or other high misdemeanor in any State, shall flee from justice, and be found in any of the United States, he shall, upon demand of the governor or executive power of the State from which he fled, be delivered up, and removed to the State having jurisdiction of his offence.

Section 3. Full faith and credit shall be given, in each of these States, to the records, acts, and judicial proceedings of the courts and magistrates of every other State.

ARTICLE 5

Section 1. For the more convenient management of the general interests of the United States, delegates shall be annually appointed in such manner as the legislature of each State shall direct, to meet in Congress on the first Monday in November, in every year, with a power reserved to each State to recall its delegates, or any of them, at any time within the year, and to send others in their stead, for the remainder of the year.

Section 2. No State shall be represented in Congress by less than two, nor by more than seven members; and no person shall be capable of being a delegate for more than three years, in any term of six years; nor shall any person, being a delegate, be capable of holding any office under the United States, for which he, or another for his benefit, receives any salary, fees, or emolument of any kind.

Section 3. Each State shall maintain its own delegates in a meeting of the States, and while they act as members of the committee of these States.

Section 4. In determining questions in the United States in Congress assembled, each State shall have one vote.

Section 5. Freedom of speech and debate in Congress shall not be impeached or questioned in any court or place out of Congress; and the members of Congress shall be protected in their persons from arrests and imprisonments during the time of their going to and from, and attendance on, Congress, except for treason, felony or breach of the peace.

ARTICLE 6

Section 1. No State, without the consent of the United States, in Congress assembled, shall send any embassy to, or receive any embassy from, or enter into any conference, agreement, alliance, or treaty, with any king, prince or State; nor shall any person holding any office of profit or trust under the United States, or any of them, accept of any present, emolument, office, or title of any kind whatever, from any king, prince, or foreign State; nor shall the United States, in Congress assembled, or any of them, grant any title of nobility.

Section 2. No two or more States shall enter into any treaty, confederation, or alliance whatever, between them, without the consent of the United States, in Congress assembled, specifying accurately the purposes for which the same is to be entered into, and how long it shall continue.

Section 3. No State shall lay any imposts or duties which may interfere with any stipulations in treaties, entered into by the United States, in Congress assembled, with any king, prince, or State, in pursuance of any treaties already proposed by Congress to the courts of France and Spain.

Section 4. No vessels of war shall be kept up in time of peace, by any State, except such number only as shall be deemed necessary by the United States, in Congress assembled, for the defence of such State, or its trade; nor shall anybody of forces be kept up, by any State, in time of peace, except such number only as, in the judgment of the United States, in Congress assembled, shall be deemed requisite to garrison the forts necessary for the defence of such State; but every State shall always keep up a well-regulated and disciplined militia, sufficiently armed and accoutred (equipped), and shall provide and constantly have ready for use, in public stores, a due number of field-pieces and tents, and a proper quantity of arms, ammunition, and camp equipage.

Section 5. No State shall engage in any war without the consent of the United States, in Congress assembled, unless such State be actually invaded by enemies, or shall have received certain advice of a resolution being formed by some nation of Indians to invade such State, and the danger is so imminent as not to admit of a delay till the United States, in Congress assembled, can be consulted; nor shall any State grant commissions to any ships or vessels of war, nor letters of marque or reprisal, except it be after a declaration of war by the United States, in Congress assembled, and then only against the kingdom or State, and the subjects thereof, against which war has been so declared, and under such regulations as shall be established by the United States, in Congress assembled, unless such State be

infested by pirates, in which case vessels of war may be fitted out for that occasion, and kept so long as the danger shall continue, or until the United States, in Congress assembled, shall determine otherwise.

ARTICLE 7

When land forces are raised by any State, for the common defence, all officers of, or under the rank of colonel, shall be appointed by the legislature of each State respectively by whom such forces shall be raised, or in such manner as such State shall direct, and all vacancies shall be filled up by the State which first made appointment.

ARTICLE 8

All charges of war, and all other expenses that shall be incurred for the common defence or general welfare, and allowed by the United States, in Congress assembled, shall be defrayed out of a common treasury, which-shall be supplied by the several States, in proportion to the value of all land within each State, granted to, or surveyed for, any person, as such land and the buildings and improvements thereon shall be estimated, according to such mode as the United States, in Congress assembled, shall, from time to time, direct and appoint. The taxes for paying that proportion shall be laid and levied by the authority and direction of the legislatures of the several States, within the time agreed upon by the United States, in Congress assembled.

ARTICLE 9

Section 1. The United States, in Congress assembled, shall have the sole and exclusive right and power of determining on peace and war, except in the cases mentioned in the sixth Article, of sending and receiving ambassadors; entering into treaties and alliances, provided that no treaty of commerce shall be made, whereby the legislative power of the respective States shall be restrained from imposing such imposts and duties on foreigners, as their own people are subjected to, or from prohibiting the exportation or importation of any species of goods or commodities whatsoever; of establishing rules for deciding, in all cases, what captures on land or water shall be legal, and in what manner prizes taken by land or naval forces in the service of the United States, shall be divided or appropriated; of granting letters of marque and reprisal in times of peace; appointing courts for the trial of piracies and felonies committed on the high seas; and establishing courts; for receiving and determining finally appeals in all cases of captures; provided that no member of Congress shall be appointed a judge of any of the said courts.

Section 2. The United States, in Congress assembled, shall also be the last resort on appeal, in all disputes and differences now subsisting, or that hereafter may arise between two or more States concerning boundary, jurisdiction, or any other cause whatever; which authority shall always be exercised in the manner following: Whenever the legislative or executive authority, or lawful agent of any State in controversy with another, shall present a petition to Congress, stating the matter in question, and praying for a hearing, notice thereof hall be given, by order of Congress, to the legislative or executive authority of the other State as controversy, and a day assigned for the appearance of the parties by their lawful agents, who shall then be directed to appoint, by joint con sent, commissioners or judges to constitute a court for hearing and determining the matter in question; but if they cannot agree, Congress shall name three persons out of each of the United States, and from the list of such persons each party shall alternately strike out one, the petitioners beginning, until the number shall be-reduced to thirteen; and from that number not less than seven, nor more than nine names, as Congress shall direct, shall, in the presence of Congress, be drawn out by lot; and the persons whose names shall be so drawn, or any five of them, shall be commissioners or judges, to hear and finally determine the controversy, so always as a major part of the judges, who shall hear the cause, shall agree in the determination; and if either party shall neglect to attend at the day appointed, without showing reasons which Congress shall judge sufficient, or being present, shall refuse to strike, the Congress shall proceed to nominate three persons out of each State, and the secretary of Congress shall strike in behalf of such party absent or refusing; and the judgment and sentence of the court, to be appointed in the manner before prescribed, shall be final and conclusive; and if any of the parties shall refuse to submit to the authority of such court, or to appear or defend their claim or cause, the court shall nevertheless proceed to pronounce sentence, or judgment, which shall in like manner be final and decisive; the judgment or sentence and other proceedings being in either case transmitted

to Congress, and lodged among the acts of Congress, for the security of the parties concerned; provided, that every commissioner, before he sits in judgment, shall take an oath, to be administered by one of the judges of the supreme or superior court of the State where the cause shall be tried, "well and truly to hear and determine the matter in question, according to the best of his judgment, without favour, affection, or hope of reward." Provided, also, that no State shall be deprived of territory for the benefit of the United States.

Section 3. All controversies concerning the private right of soil claimed under different grants of two or more States, whose jurisdictions, as they may respect such lands, and the States which passed such grants are adjusted, the said grants or either of them being at the same time claimed to have originated antecedent to such settlement of jurisdiction, shall, on the petition of either party to the Congress of the United States, be finally determined, as near as may be, in the same manner as is before prescribed for deciding disputes respecting territorial jurisdiction between different States.

Section 4. The United States, in Congress assembled, shall also have the sole and exclusive right and power of regulating the alloy and value of coin struck by their own authority, or by that of the respective States fixing the standard of weights and measures throughout the United States; regulating the trade and managing all affairs with the Indians, not members of any of the States; provided that the legislative right of any State, within its own limits, be not infringed or violated; establishing and regulating post offices from one State to another, throughout all the United States, and exacting such postage on the papers passing through the same, as may be requisite to defray the expenses of the said office; appointing all officers of the land forces in the service of the United States, excepting regimental officers; appointing all the officers of the naval forces, and commissioning all officers whatever in the service of the United States; making rules for the government and regulation of the said land and naval forces, and directing their operations.

Section 5. The United States, in Congress assembled, shall have authority to appoint a committee, to sit in the recess of Congress, to be denominated, "A Committee of the States," and to consist of one delegate from each State; and to appoint such other committees and civil officers as may be necessary for managing the general affairs of the United States under their direction; to appoint one of their number to preside; provided that no person be allowed to serve in the office of president more than one year in any term of three years; to ascertain the necessary sums of money to be raised for the service of the United States, and to appropriate and apply the same for defraying the public expenses; to borrow money or emit bills on the credit of the United States, transmitting every half year to the respective States an account of the sums of money so borrowed or emitted; to build and equip a navy; to agree upon the number of land forces, and to make requisitions from each State for its quota, in proportion to the number of white inhabitants in such State, which requisition shall be binding; and thereupon the Legislature of each State shall appoint the regimental officers, raise the men, and clothe, arm, and equip them, in a soldier-like manner, at the expense of the United States; and the officers and men so clothed, armed, and equipped, shall march to the place appointed, and within the time agreed on by the United States, in Congress assembled; but if the United States, in Congress assembled, shall, on consideration of circumstances, judge proper that any State should not raise men, or should raise a smaller number than its quota, and that any other State should raise a greater number of men than the quota thereof, such extra number shall be raised, officered, clothed, armed, and equipped in the same manner as the quota of such State, unless the Legislature of such State shall judge that such extra number cannot be safely spared out of the same, in which case they shall raise, officer, clothe, arm, and equip, as many of such extra number as they judge can be safely spared, and the officers and men so clothed, armed, and equipped, shall march to the place appointed, and within the time agreed on by the United States in Congress assembled.

Section 6. The United States, in Congress assembled, shall never engage in a war, nor grant letters of marque and reprisal in time of peace, nor enter into any treaties or alliances, nor coin money, nor regulate the value thereof nor ascertain the sums and expenses necessary for the defence and welfare of the United States, or any of them, nor emit bills, nor borrow money on the credit of the United States, nor appropriate money, nor agree upon the number of

vessels of war to be built or purchased, or the number of land or sea forces to be raised, nor appoint a commander-in-chief of the army or navy, unless nine States assent to the same, nor shall a question on any other point, except for adjourning from day to day, be determined, unless by the votes of a majority of the United States in Congress assembled.

Section 7. The Congress of the United States shall have power to adjourn to any time within the year, and to any place within the United States, so that no period of adjournment be for a longer duration than the space of six months, and shall publish the journal of their proceedings monthly, except such parts thereof relating to treaties, alliances, or military operations, as in their judgment require secrecy; and the yeas and nays of the delegates of each State, on any question, shall be entered on the journal, when it is desired by any delegate; and the delegates of a State, or any of them, at his or their request, shall be furnished with a transcript of the said journal, except such parts as are above excepted, to lay before the legislatures of the several States.

ARTICLE 10

The committee of the States, or any nine of them, shall be authorized to execute, in the recess of Congress, such of the powers of Congress as the United States, in Congress assembled, by the consent of nine States, shall, from time to time, think expedient to vest them with; provided that no power be delegated to the said committee, for the exercise of which, by the articles of confederation, the voice of nine States, in the Congress of the United States assembled, is requisite.

ARTICLE 11

Canada acceding to this confederation, and joining in the measures of the United States, shall be admitted into, and entitled to all the advantages of this Union: but no other colony shall be admitted into the same, unless such admission be agreed to by nine States.

ARTICLE 12

All bills of credit emitted, moneys borrowed, and debts contracted by or under the authority of Congress, before the assembling of the United States, in pursuance of the present confederation, shall be deemed and considered as a charge against the United States, for payment and satisfaction whereof the said United States and the public faith are hereby solemnly pledged.

ARTICLE 13

Every State shall abide by the determinations of the United States, in Congress assembled, on all questions which by this confederation are submitted to them. And the articles of this confederation shall be inviolably observed by every State, and the Union shall be perpetual; nor shall any alteration at any time hereafter be made in any of them, unless such alteration be agreed to in a Congress of the United States, and be afterwards confirmed by the legislatures of every State.

And whereas it hath pleased the great Governor of the world to incline the hearts of the legislatures we respectively represent in Congress, to approve of, and to authorize us to ratify the said articles of confederation and perpetual union, Know ye, that we, the undersigned delegates, by virtue of the power and authority to us given for that purpose, do, by these presents, in the name and in behalf of our respective constituents, fully and entirely ratify and confirm each and every of the said articles of confederation and perpetual union, and all and singular the matters and things therein contained. And we do further solemnly plight and engage the faith of our respective constituents, that they shall abide by the de terminations of the United States, in Congress assembled, on all questions which by the said confederation are submitted to them; and that the articles thereof shall be inviolably observed by the States we respectively represent, and that the Union shall be perpetual. In witness whereof, we have hereunto set our hands, in Congress.

Done at Philadelphia, in the State of Pennsylvania, the 9th day of July, in the year of our Lord 1778, and in the third year of the Independence of America.

On the part and behalf of the State of New Hampshire.—Josiah Bartlett, John Wentworth, Jun. (August 8, 1778.)

On the part and behalf of the State of Massachusetts Bay.—John Hancock, Samuel Adams, Elbridge Gerry, Francis Dana, James Lovell, Samuel Holten.

On the part and behalf of the State of Rhode Island and Providence Plantations.—William Ellery, Henry Marchant, John Collins.

On the part and behalf of the State of Connecticut.—Roger Sherman, Samuel Huntington, Oliver Wolcott, Titus Hosmer, Andrew Adams.

On the part and behalf of the State of New York.—.James Duane, Francis Lewis, William Duer, Gouv. Morris.

On the part and in behalf of the State of New Jersey.—Jno. Wither spoon, Nath. Scudder, (November 26, 1778.)

On the part and behalf of the State of Pennsylvania.—Robert Morris, Daniel Roberdeau, Jona. Bayard Smith, William Clingan, Joseph Reed (July 22, 1778.)

On the part and behalf of the State of Delaware.—Thomas M'Kean, (February 12, 1779,) John Dickinson, (May 5, 1779,) Nicholas Van Dyke.

On the part and behalf of the State of Maryland.—John Hanson, (March 1, 1781,) Daniel Carroll, (March 1,1781.)

On the part and behalf of the State of Virginia.—Richard Henry Lee, John Banister, Thomas Adams, Jno. Harvie, Francis Lightfoot Lee.

On the part and behalf of the State of North Carolina.—John Penn, (July 21, 1778,) Corns. Harnett, Jno. Williams.

On the part and behalf of the State of South Carolina.—Henry Laurens, William Henry Drayton, Jno. Mathews, Richard Hutson, Thos. Heyward, Jun.

On the part and behalf of the State of Georgia.—Jno. Walton, (July 24, 1778,) Edwd. Telfair, Edward Langworthy.

THE
FEDERALIST:
A COLLECTION OF
ESSAYS,

WRITTEN IN FAVOUR OF THE

NEW CONSTITUTION,

AS AGREED UPON BY THE

FEDERAL CONVENTION,

SEPTEMBER 17, 1787.

IN TWO VOLUMES.
VOL. I.

NEW-YORK :
PRINTED AND SOLD BY JOHN TIEBOUT,
No. 358 PEARL-STREET.
1799.

Transcripts of "The Federalist Papers," No. 10 and No. 51 (1787–1788)

The Federalist Paper No. 10 (by James Madison)

"The Same Subject Continued (from #9): The Union as a Safeguard Against Domestic Faction and Insurrection," or "The Size and Variety of the Union as a Check on Faction"

The Federalist No. X

To the People of the State of New York:

AMONG the numerous advantages promised by a well constructed Union, none deserves to be more accurately developed than its tendency to break and control the violence of faction. The friend of popular governments never finds himself so much alarmed for their character and fate, as when he contemplates their propensity to this dangerous vice. He will not fail, therefore, to set a due value on any plan which, without violating the principles to which he is attached, provides a proper cure for it. The instability, injustice, and confusion introduced into the public councils, have, in truth, been the mortal diseases under which popular governments have everywhere perished; as they continue to be the favorite and fruitful topics from which the adversaries to liberty derive their most specious declamations. The valuable improvements made by the American constitutions on the popular models, both ancient and modern, cannot certainly be too much admired; but it would be an unwarrantable partiality, to contend that they have as effectually obviated the danger on this side, as was wished and expected. Complaints are everywhere heard from our most considerate and virtuous citizens, equally the friends of public and private faith, and of public and personal liberty, that our governments are too unstable, that the public good is disregarded in the conflicts of rival parties, and that measures are too often decided, not according to the rules of justice and the rights of the minor party, but by the superior force of an interested and overbearing majority. However anxiously we may wish that these complaints had no foundation, the evidence, of known facts will not permit us to deny that they are in some degree true. It will be found, indeed, on a candid review of our situation, that some of the distresses under which we labor have been erroneously charged on the operation of our governments; but it will be found, at the same time, that other causes will not alone account for many of our heaviest misfortunes; and, particularly, for that prevailing and increasing distrust of public engagements, and alarm for private rights, which are echoed from one end of the continent to the other. These must be chiefly, if not wholly, effects of the unsteadiness and injustice with which a factious spirit has tainted our public administrations.

By a faction, I understand a number of citizens, whether amounting to a majority or a minority of the whole, who are united and actuated by some common impulse of passion, or of interest, adversed to the rights of other citizens, or to the permanent and aggregate interests of the community.

There are two methods of curing the mischiefs of faction: the one, by removing its causes; the other, by controlling its effects.

There are again two methods of removing the causes of faction: the one, by destroying the liberty which is essential to its existence; the other, by giving to every citizen the same opinions, the same passions, and the same interests.

It could never be more truly said than of the first remedy, that it was worse than the disease. Liberty is to faction what air is to fire, an aliment without which it instantly expires. But it could not be less folly to abolish liberty, which is essential to political life, because it nourishes faction, than it would be to wish the annihilation of air, which is essential to animal life, because it imparts to fire its destructive agency.

The second expedient is as impracticable as the first would be unwise. As long as the reason of man continues fallible, and he is at liberty to exercise it, different opinions will be formed. As long as the connection subsists between his reason and his self-love, his opinions and his passions will have a reciprocal influence on each other; and the former will be objects to which the latter will attach themselves. The diversity in the faculties of men, from which the rights of property originate, is not less an insuperable obstacle to a uniformity of interests. The protection of these faculties is the first object of government. From the protection of different and unequal faculties of acquiring property, the possession of different degrees and kinds of property immediately results; and from the influence of these on the sentiments and views of the respective proprietors, ensues a division of the society into different interests and parties.

The latent causes of faction are thus sown in the nature of man; and we see them everywhere brought into different degrees of activity, according to the different circumstances of civil society. A zeal for different opinions concerning religion, concerning government, and many other points, as well of speculation as of practice; an attachment to different leaders ambitiously contending for pre-eminence and power; or to persons of other descriptions whose fortunes have been interesting to the human passions, have, in turn, divided mankind into parties, inflamed them with mutual animosity, and rendered them much more disposed to vex and oppress each other than to co-operate for their common good. So strong is this propensity of mankind to fall into mutual animosities, that where no substantial occasion presents itself, the most frivolous and fanciful distinctions have been sufficient to kindle their unfriendly passions and excite their most violent conflicts. But the most common and durable source of factions has been the various and unequal distribution of property. Those who hold and those who are without property have ever formed distinct interests in society. Those who are creditors, and those who are debtors, fall under a like discrimination. A landed interest, a manufacturing interest, a mercantile interest, a moneyed interest, with many lesser interests, grow up of necessity in civilized nations, and divide them into different classes, actuated by different sentiments and views. The regulation of these various and interfering interests forms the principal task of modern legislation, and involves the spirit of party and faction in the necessary and ordinary operations of the government.

No man is allowed to be a judge in his own cause, because his interest would certainly bias his judgment, and, not improbably, corrupt his integrity. With equal, nay with greater reason, a body of men are unfit to be both judges and parties at the same time; yet what are many of the most important acts of legislation, but so many judicial determinations, not indeed concerning the rights of single persons, but concerning the rights of large bodies of citizens? And what are the different classes of legislators but advocates and parties to the causes which they determine? Is a law proposed concerning private debts? It is a question to which the creditors are parties on one side and the debtors on the other. Justice ought to hold the balance between them. Yet the parties are, and must be, themselves the judges; and the most numerous party, or, in other words, the most powerful faction must be expected to prevail. Shall domestic manufactures be encouraged, and in what degree, by restrictions on foreign manufactures? are questions which would be differently decided by the landed and the manufacturing classes, and probably by neither with a sole regard to justice and the public good. The apportionment of taxes on the various descriptions of property is an act which seems to require the most exact impartiality; yet there is, perhaps, no legislative act in which greater opportunity and temptation are given to a predominant party to trample on the rules of justice. Every shilling with which they overburden the inferior number, is a shilling saved to their own pockets.

It is in vain to say that enlightened statesmen will be able to adjust these clashing interests, and render them all subservient to the public good. Enlightened statesmen will not always be at the helm. Nor, in many cases, can such an adjustment be made at all without taking into view indirect and remote considerations, which will rarely prevail over the immediate interest which one party may find in disregarding the rights of another or the good of the whole.

The inference to which we are brought is, that the CAUSES of faction cannot be removed, and that relief is only to be sought in the means of controlling its EFFECTS.

If a faction consists of less than a majority, relief is supplied by the republican principle, which enables the majority to defeat its sinister views by regular vote. It may clog the administration, it may convulse the society; but it will be unable to execute and mask its violence under the forms of the Constitution. When a majority is included in a faction, the form of popular government, on the other hand, enables it to sacrifice to its ruling passion or interest

both the public good and the rights of other citizens. To secure the public good and private rights against the danger of such a faction, and at the same time to preserve the spirit and the form of popular government, is then the great object to which our inquiries are directed. Let me add that it is the great desideratum by which this form of government can be rescued from the opprobrium under which it has so long labored, and be recommended to the esteem and adoption of mankind.

By what means is this object attainable? Evidently by one of two only. Either the existence of the same passion or interest in a majority at the same time must be prevented, or the majority, having such coexistent passion or interest, must be rendered, by their number and local situation, unable to concert and carry into effect schemes of oppression. If the impulse and the opportunity be suffered to coincide, we well know that neither moral nor religious motives can be relied on as an adequate control. They are not found to be such on the injustice and violence of individuals, and lose their efficacy in proportion to the number combined together, that is, in proportion as their efficacy becomes needful.

From this view of the subject it may be concluded that a pure democracy, by which I mean a society consisting of a small number of citizens, who assemble and administer the government in person, can admit of no cure for the mischiefs of faction. A common passion or interest will, in almost every case, be felt by a majority of the whole; a communication and concert result from the form of government itself; and there is nothing to check the inducements to sacrifice the weaker party or an obnoxious individual. Hence it is that such democracies have ever been spectacles of turbulence and contention; have ever been found incompatible with personal security or the rights of property; and have in general been as short in their lives as they have been violent in their deaths. Theoretic politicians, who have patronized this species of government, have erroneously supposed that by reducing mankind to a perfect equality in their political rights, they would, at the same time, be perfectly equalized and assimilated in their possessions, their opinions, and their passions.

A republic, by which I mean a government in which the scheme of representation takes place, opens a different prospect, and promises the cure for which we are seeking. Let us examine the points in which it varies from pure democracy, and we shall comprehend both the nature of the cure and the efficacy which it must derive from the Union.

The two great points of difference between a democracy and a republic are: first, the delegation of the government, in the latter, to a small number of citizens elected by the rest; secondly, the greater number of citizens, and greater sphere of country, over which the latter may be extended.

The effect of the first difference is, on the one hand, to refine and enlarge the public views, by passing them through the medium of a chosen body of citizens, whose wisdom may best discern the true interest of their country, and whose patriotism and love of justice will be least likely to sacrifice it to temporary or partial considerations. Under such a regulation, it may well happen that the public voice, pronounced by the representatives of the people, will be more consonant to the public good than if pronounced by the people themselves, convened for the purpose. On the other hand, the effect may be inverted. Men of factious tempers, of local prejudices, or of sinister designs, may, by intrigue, by corruption, or by other means, first obtain the suffrages, and then betray the interests, of the people. The question resulting is, whether small or extensive republics are more favorable to the election of proper guardians of the public weal; and it is clearly decided in favor of the latter by two obvious considerations:

In the first place, it is to be remarked that, however small the republic may be, the representatives must be raised to a certain number, in order to guard against the cabals of a few; and that, however large it may be, they must be limited to a certain number, in order to guard against the confusion of a multitude. Hence, the number of representatives in the two cases not being in proportion to that of the two constituents, and being proportionally greater in the small republic, it follows that, if the proportion of fit characters be not less in the large than in the small republic, the former will present a greater option, and consequently a greater probability of a fit choice.

In the next place, as each representative will be chosen by a greater number of citizens in the large than in the small republic, it will be more difficult for unworthy candidates to practice with success the vicious arts by which

elections are too often carried; and the suffrages of the people being more free, will be more likely to centre in men who possess the most attractive merit and the most diffusive and established characters.

It must be confessed that in this, as in most other cases, there is a mean, on both sides of which inconveniences will be found to lie. By enlarging too much the number of electors, you render the representatives too little acquainted with all their local circumstances and lesser interests; as by reducing it too much, you render him unduly attached to these, and too little fit to comprehend and pursue great and national objects. The federal Constitution forms a happy combination in this respect; the great and aggregate interests being referred to the national, the local and particular to the State legislatures.

The other point of difference is, the greater number of citizens and extent of territory which may be brought within the compass of republican than of democratic government; and it is this circumstance principally which renders factious combinations less to be dreaded in the former than in the latter. The smaller the society, the fewer probably will be the distinct parties and interests composing it; the fewer the distinct parties and interests, the more frequently will a majority be found of the same party; and the smaller the number of individuals composing a majority, and the smaller the compass within which they are placed, the more easily will they concert and execute their plans of oppression. Extend the sphere, and you take in a greater variety of parties and interests; you make it less probable that a majority of the whole will have a common motive to invade the rights of other citizens; or if such a common motive exists, it will be more difficult for all who feel it to discover their own strength, and to act in unison with each other. Besides other impediments, it may be remarked that, where there is a consciousness of unjust or dishonorable purposes, communication is always checked by distrust in proportion to the number whose concurrence is necessary.

Hence, it clearly appears, that the same advantage which a republic has over a democracy, in controlling the effects of faction, is enjoyed by a large over a small republic,—is enjoyed by the Union over the States composing it. Does the advantage consist in the substitution of representatives whose enlightened views and virtuous sentiments render them superior to local prejudices and schemes of injustice? It will not be denied that the representation of the Union will be most likely to possess these requisite endowments. Does it consist in the greater security afforded by a greater variety of parties, against the event of any one party being able to outnumber and oppress the rest? In an equal degree does the increased variety of parties comprised within the Union, increase this security. Does it, in fine, consist in the greater obstacles opposed to the concert and accomplishment of the secret wishes of an unjust and interested majority? Here, again, the extent of the Union gives it the most palpable advantage.

The influence of factious leaders may kindle a flame within their particular States, but will be unable to spread a general conflagration through the other States. A religious sect may degenerate into a political faction in a part of the Confederacy; but the variety of sects dispersed over the entire face of it must secure the national councils against any danger from that source. A rage for paper money, for an abolition of debts, for an equal division of property, or for any other improper or wicked project, will be less apt to pervade the whole body of the Union than a particular member of it; in the same proportion as such a malady is more likely to taint a particular county or district, than an entire State.

In the extent and proper structure of the Union, therefore, we behold a republican remedy for the diseases most incident to republican government. And according to the degree of pleasure and pride we feel in being republicans, ought to be our zeal in cherishing the spirit and supporting the character of Federalists.

PUBLIUS.

The "Federalist," or the "Federalist Papers" are widely available through many publishers and with many variants of introduction.

One good source for Federalist Papers:
U.S. National Archives & Records Administration, 700 Pennsylvania Avenue NW, Washington, DC 20408

Available online at many locations, including:
http://www.ourdocuments.gov/doc.php?doc=10&page=transcript

The Federalist Paper No. 51 (by James Madison)

"The Structure of the Government Must Furnish the Proper Checks and Balances Between the Different Departments"

The Federalist No. 51

To the People of the State of New York:

TO WHAT expedient, then, shall we finally resort, for maintaining in practice the necessary partition of power among the several departments, as laid down in the Constitution? The only answer that can be given is, that as all these exterior provisions are found to be inadequate, the defect must be supplied, by so contriving the interior structure of the government as that its several constituent parts may, by their mutual relations, be the means of keeping each other in their proper places. Without presuming to undertake a full development of this important idea, I will hazard a few general observations, which may perhaps place it in a clearer light, and enable us to form a more correct judgment of the principles and structure of the government planned by the convention.

In order to lay a due foundation for that separate and distinct exercise of the different powers of government, which to a certain extent is admitted on all hands to be essential to the preservation of liberty, it is evident that each department should have a will of its own; and consequently should be so constituted that the members of each should have as little agency as possible in the appointment of the members of the others. Were this principle rigorously adhered to, it would require that all the appointments for the supreme executive, legislative, and judiciary magistracies should be drawn from the same fountain of authority, the people, through channels having no communication whatever with one another. Perhaps such a plan of constructing the several departments would be less difficult in practice than it may in contemplation appear. Some difficulties, however, and some additional expense would attend the execution of it. Some deviations, therefore, from the principle must be admitted. In the constitution of the judiciary department in particular, it might be inexpedient to insist rigorously on the principle: first, because peculiar qualifications being essential in the members, the primary consideration ought to be to select that mode of choice which best secures these qualifications; secondly, because the permanent tenure by which the appointments are held in that department, must soon destroy all sense of dependence on the authority conferring them.

It is equally evident, that the members of each department should be as little dependent as possible on those of the others, for the emoluments annexed to their offices. Were the executive magistrate, or the judges, not independent of the legislature in this particular, their independence in every other would be merely nominal. But the great security against a gradual concentration of the several powers in the same department, consists in giving to those who administer each department the necessary constitutional means and personal motives to resist encroachments of the others. The provision for defense must in this, as in all other cases, be made commensurate to the danger of attack. Ambition must be made to counteract ambition. The interest of the man must be connected with the constitutional rights of the place. It may be a reflection on human nature, that such devices should be necessary to control the abuses of government. But what is government itself, but the greatest of all reflections on human nature? If men were angels, no government would be necessary. If angels were to govern men, neither external nor internal controls on government would be necessary. In framing a government which is to be administered by men over men, the great difficulty lies in this: you must first enable the government to control the governed; and in the next place oblige it to control itself.

A dependence on the people is, no doubt, the primary control on the government; but experience has taught mankind the necessity of auxiliary precautions. This policy of supplying, by opposite and rival interests, the defect of better motives, might be traced through the whole system of human affairs, private as well as public. We see it particularly displayed in all the subordinate distributions of power, where the constant aim is to divide and arrange the several offices in such a manner as that each may be a check on the other that the private interest of every individual may be a sentinel over the public rights. These inventions of prudence cannot be less requisite in the distribution of the supreme powers of the State. But it is not possible to give to each department an equal power of self-defense. In

republican government, the legislative authority necessarily predominates. The remedy for this inconveniency is to divide the legislature into different branches; and to render them, by different modes of election and different principles of action, as little connected with each other as the nature of their common functions and their common dependence on the society will admit. It may even be necessary to guard against dangerous encroachments by still further precautions. As the weight of the legislative authority requires that it should be thus divided, the weakness of the executive may require, on the other hand, that it should be fortified.

An absolute negative on the legislature appears, at first view, to be the natural defense with which the executive magistrate should be armed. But perhaps it would be neither altogether safe nor alone sufficient. On ordinary occasions it might not be exerted with the requisite firmness, and on extraordinary occasions it might be perfidiously abused. May not this defect of an absolute negative be supplied by some qualified connection between this weaker department and the weaker branch of the stronger department, by which the latter may be led to support the constitutional rights of the former, without being too much detached from the rights of its own department? If the principles on which these observations are founded be just, as I persuade myself they are, and they be applied as a criterion to the several State constitutions, and to the federal Constitution it will be found that if the latter does not perfectly correspond with them, the former are infinitely less able to bear such a test.

There are, moreover, two considerations particularly applicable to the federal system of America, which place that system in a very interesting point of view. First. In a single republic, all the power surrendered by the people is submitted to the administration of a single government; and the usurpations are guarded against by a division of the government into distinct and separate departments. In the compound republic of America, the power surrendered by the people is first divided between two distinct governments, and then the portion allotted to each subdivided among distinct and separate departments. Hence a double security arises to the rights of the people. The different governments will control each other, at the same time that each will be controlled by itself. Second. It is of great importance in a republic not only to guard the society against the oppression of its rulers, but to guard one part of the society against the injustice of the other part. Different interests necessarily exist in different classes of citizens. If a majority be united by a common interest, the rights of the minority will be insecure.

There are but two methods of providing against this evil: the one by creating a will in the community independent of the majority that is, of the society itself; the other, by comprehending in the society so many separate descriptions of citizens as will render an unjust combination of a majority of the whole very improbable, if not impracticable. The first method prevails in all governments possessing an hereditary or self-appointed authority. This, at best, is but a precarious security; because a power independent of the society may as well espouse the unjust views of the major, as the rightful interests of the minor party, and may possibly be turned against both parties. The second method will be exemplified in the federal republic of the United States. Whilst all authority in it will be derived from and dependent on the society, the society itself will be broken into so many parts, interests, and classes of citizens, that the rights of individuals, or of the minority, will be in little danger from interested combinations of the majority.

In a free government the security for civil rights must be the same as that for religious rights. It consists in the one case in the multiplicity of interests, and in the other in the multiplicity of sects. The degree of security in both cases will depend on the number of interests and sects; and this may be presumed to depend on the extent of country and number of people comprehended under the same government. This view of the subject must particularly recommend a proper federal system to all the sincere and considerate friends of republican government, since it shows that in exact proportion as the territory of the Union may be formed into more circumscribed Confederacies, or States oppressive combinations of a majority will be facilitated: the best security, under the republican forms, for the rights of every class of citizens, will be diminished: and consequently the stability and independence of some member of the government, the only other security, must be proportionately increased. Justice is the end of government. It is the end of civil society. It ever has been and ever will be pursued until it be obtained, or until liberty be lost in the pursuit. In a society under the forms of which the stronger faction can readily unite and oppress the weaker, anarchy may as truly be said to reign as in a state of nature, where the weaker individual is not secured against the violence of the stronger; and as, in the latter state, even the stronger individuals are prompted, by the uncertainty of their

condition, to submit to a government which may protect the weak as well as themselves; so, in the former state, will the more powerful factions or parties be gradually induced, by a like motive, to wish for a government which will protect all parties, the weaker as well as the more powerful.

It can be little doubted that if the State of Rhode Island was separated from the Confederacy and left to itself, the insecurity of rights under the popular form of government within such narrow limits would be displayed by such reiterated oppressions of factious majorities that some power altogether independent of the people would soon be called for by the voice of the very factions whose misrule had proved the necessity of it. In the extended republic of the United States, and among the great variety of interests, parties, and sects which it embraces, a coalition of a majority of the whole society could seldom take place on any other principles than those of justice and the general good; whilst there being thus less danger to a minor from the will of a major party, there must be less pretext, also, to provide for the security of the former, by introducing into the government a will not dependent on the latter, or, in other words, a will independent of the society itself. It is no less certain than it is important, notwithstanding the contrary opinions which have been entertained, that the larger the society, provided it lie within a practical sphere, the more duly capable it will be of self-government. And happily for the REPUBLICAN CAUSE, the practicable sphere may be carried to a very great extent, by a judicious modification and mixture of the FEDERAL PRINCIPLE.

PUBLIUS.

The "Federalist," or the "Federalist Papers" are widely available through many publishers and with many variants of introduction.

One good source for Federalist Papers:
U.S. National Archives & Records Administration, 700 Pennsylvania Avenue NW, Washington, DC 20408
Available online at many locations, including: http://www.ourdocuments.gov/doc.php?doc=10&page=transcript

Transcript of *Marbury v. Madison* (1803)

Chief Justice Marshall delivered the opinion of the Court.

At the last term on the affidavits then read and filed with the clerk, a rule was granted in this case, requiring the Secretary of State to show cause why a mandamus should not issue, directing him to deliver to William Marbury his commission as a justice of the peace for the county of Washington, in the district of Columbia.

No cause has been shown, and the present motion is for a mandamus. The peculiar delicacy of this case, the novelty of some of its circumstances, and the real difficulty attending the points which occur in it, require a complete exposition of the principles on which the opinion to be given by the court is founded....

In the order in which the court has viewed this subject, the following questions have been considered and decided:

1st. Has the applicant a right to the commission he demands?

2d. If he has a right, and that right has been violated, do the laws of his country afford him a remedy?

3d. If they do afford him a remedy, is it a mandamus issuing from this court?

The first object of inquiry is — 1st. Has the applicant a right to the commission he demands? . . .

It [is] decidedly the opinion of the court, that when a commission has been signed by the president, the appointment is made; and that the commission is complete, when the seal of the United States has been affixed to it by the secretary of state....

To withhold his commission, therefore, is an act deemed by the court not warranted by law, but violative of a vested legal right.

This brings us to the second inquiry; which is 2dly. If he has a right, and that right has been violated, do the laws of his country afford him a remedy?

The very essence of civil liberty certainly consists in the right of every individual to claim the protection of the laws, whenever he receives an injury. One of the first duties of government is to afford that protection. [The] government of the United States has been emphatically termed a government of laws, and not of men. It will certainly cease to deserve this high appellation, if the laws furnish no remedy for the violation of a vested legal right....

By the constitution of the United States, the President is invested with certain important

political powers, in the exercise of which he is to use his own discretion, and is accountable only to his country in his political character, and to his own conscience. To aid him in the performance of these duties, he is authorized to appoint certain officers, who act by his authority and in conformity with his orders.

In such cases, their acts are his acts; and whatever opinion may be entertained of the manner in which executive discretion may be used, still there exists, and can exist, no power to control that discretion. The subjects are political. They respect the nation, not individual rights, and being entrusted to the executive, the decision of the executive is conclusive....

But when the legislature proceeds to impose on that officer other duties; when he is directed peremptorily to perform certain acts; when the rights of individuals are dependent on the performance of those acts; he is so far the officer of the law; is amenable to the laws for his conduct; and cannot at his discretion sport away the vested rights of others.

The conclusion from this reasoning is, that where the heads of departments are the political or confidential agents of the executive, merely to execute the will of the President, or rather to act in cases in which the executive possesses a constitutional or legal discretion, nothing can be more perfectly clear than that their acts are only politically

examinable. But where a specific duty is assigned by law, and individual rights depend upon the performance of that duty, it seems equally clear, that the individual who considers himself injured, has a right to resort to the laws of his country for a remedy....

It is, then, the opinion of the Court [that Marbury has a] right to the commission; a refusal to deliver which is a plain violation of that right, for which the laws of his country afford him a remedy.

It remains to be enquired whether,

3dly. He is entitled to the remedy for which he applies. This depends on — 1st. The nature of the writ applied for, and,

2dly. The power of this court.

1st. The nature of the writ....

This, then, is a plain case for a mandamus, either to deliver the commission, or a copy of it from the record; and it only remains to be enquired,

Whether it can issue from this court.

The act to establish the judicial courts of the United States authorizes the Supreme Court "to issue writs of mandamus in cases warranted by the principles and usages of law, to any courts appointed, or persons holding office, under the authority of the United States."

The Secretary of State, being a person holding an office under the authority of the United States, is precisely within the letter of the description; and if this court is not authorized to issue a writ of mandamus to such an officer, it must be because the law is unconstitutional, and therefore incapable of conferring the authority, and assigning the duties which its words purport to confer and assign.

The constitution vests the whole judicial power of the United States in one Supreme Court, and such inferior courts as congress shall, from time to time, ordain and establish. This power is expressly extended to all cases arising under the laws of the United States; and, consequently, in some form, may be exercised over the present case; because the right claimed is given by a law of the United States.

In the distribution of this power it is declared that "the Supreme Court shall have original jurisdiction in all cases affecting ambassadors, other public ministers and consuls, and those in which a state shall be a party. In all other cases, the Supreme Court shall have appellate jurisdiction."

It has been insisted, at the bar, that as the original grant of jurisdiction, to the supreme and inferior courts, is general, and the clause, assigning original jurisdiction to the Supreme Court, contains no negative or restrictive words, the power remains to the legislature, to assign original jurisdiction to that court in other cases than those specified in the article which has been recited; provided those cases belong to the judicial power of the United States.

If it had been intended to leave it in the discretion of the legislature to apportion the judicial power between the supreme and inferior courts according to the will of that body, it would certainly have been useless to have proceeded further than to have defined the judicial power, and the tribunals in which it should be vested. The subsequent part of the section is mere surplusage, is entirely without meaning, if such is to be the construction. If congress remains at liberty to give this court appellate jurisdiction, where the constitution has declared their jurisdiction shall be original; and original jurisdiction where the constitution has declared it shall be appellate; the distribution of jurisdiction, made in the constitution, is form without substance.

Affirmative words are often, in their operation, negative of other objects than those affirmed; and in this case, a negative or exclusive sense must be given to them or they have no operation at all.

It cannot be presumed that any clause in the constitution is intended to be without effect; and, therefore, such a construction is inadmissible, unless the words require it.

If the solicitude of the convention, respecting our peace with foreign powers, induced a provision that the supreme court should take original jurisdiction in cases which might be supposed to affect them; yet the clause would have proceeded no further than to provide for such cases, if no further restriction on the powers of congress had been intended. That they should have appellate jurisdiction in all other cases, with such exceptions as congress might make, is no restriction; unless the words be deemed exclusive of original jurisdiction.

When an instrument organizing fundamentally a judicial system, divides it into one supreme, and so many inferior courts as the legislature may ordain and establish; then enumerates its powers, and proceeds so far to distribute them, as to define the jurisdiction of the supreme court by declaring the cases in which it shall take original jurisdiction, and that in others it shall take appellate jurisdiction; the plain import of the words seems to be, that in one class of cases its jurisdiction is original, and not appellate; in the other it is appellate, and not original. If any other construction would render the clause inoperative, that is an additional reason for rejecting such other construction, and for adhering to their obvious meaning.

To enable this court, then, to issue a mandamus, it must be shown to be an exercise of appellate jurisdiction, or to be necessary to enable them to exercise appellate jurisdiction.

It has been stated at the bar that the appellate jurisdiction may be exercised in a variety of forms, and that if it be the will of the legislature that a mandamus should be used for that purpose, that will must be obeyed. This is true, yet the jurisdiction must be appellate, not original.

It is the essential criterion of appellate jurisdiction, that it revises and corrects the proceedings in a cause already instituted, and does not create that cause. Although, therefore, a mandamus may be directed to courts, yet to issue such a writ to an officer for the delivery of a paper, is in effect the same as to sustain an original action for that paper, and, therefore, seems not to belong to appellate, but to original jurisdiction. Neither is it necessary in such a case as this, to enable the court to exercise its appellate jurisdiction.

The authority, therefore, given to the Supreme Court, by the act establishing the judicial courts of the United States, to issue writs of mandamus to public officers, appears not to be warranted by the constitution; and it becomes necessary to enquire whether a jurisdiction, so conferred, can be exercised.

The question, whether an act, repugnant to the constitution, can become the law of the land, is a question deeply interesting to the United States; but happily, not of an intricacy proportioned to its interest. It seems only necessary to recognize certain principles, supposed to have been long and well established, to decide it.

That the people have an original right to establish, for their future government, such principles as, in their opinion, shall most conduce to their own happiness, is the basis on which the whole American fabric has been erected. The exercise of this original right is a very great exertion; nor can it, nor ought it, to be frequently repeated. The principles, therefore, so established, are deemed fundamental. And as the authority from which they proceed is supreme, and can seldom act, they are designed to be permanent.

This original and supreme will organizes the government, and assigns to different departments their respective powers. It may either stop here, or establish certain limits not to be transcended by those departments.

The government of the United States is of the latter description. The powers of the legislature are defined and limited; and that those limits may not be mistaken, or forgotten, the constitution is written. To what purpose are powers limited, and to what purpose is that limitation committed to writing, if these limits may, at any time, be passed by those intended to be restrained? The distinction between a government with limited and unlimited powers is abolished, if those limits do not confine the persons on whom they are imposed, and if acts prohibited and acts allowed, are of equal obligation. It is a proposition too plain to be contested, that the constitution controls any legislative act repugnant to it; or, that the legislature may alter the constitution by an ordinary act.

Between these alternatives there is no middle ground. The constitution is either a superior, paramount law, unchangeable by ordinary means, or it is on a level with ordinary legislative acts, and, like other acts, is alterable when the legislature shall please to alter it.

If the former part of the alternative be true, then a legislative act contrary to the constitution is not law: if the latter part be true, then written constitutions are absurd attempts, on the part of the people, to limit a power in its own nature illimitable.

Certainly all those who have framed written constitutions contemplate them as forming the fundamental and paramount law of the nation, and consequently, the theory of every such government must be, that an act of the legislature, repugnant to the constitution, is void.

This theory is essentially attached to a written constitution, and is, consequently, to be considered, by this court, as one of the fundamental principles of our society. It is not therefore to be lost sight of in the further consideration of this subject.

If an act of the legislature, repugnant to the constitution, is void, does it, notwithstanding its invalidity, bind the courts, and oblige them to give it effect? Or, in other words, though it be not law, does it constitute a rule as operative as if it was a law? This would be to overthrow in fact what was established in theory; and would seem, at first view, an absurdity too gross to be insisted on. It shall, however, receive a more attentive consideration.

It is emphatically the province and duty of the judicial department to say what the law is. Those who apply the rule to particular cases, must of necessity expound and interpret that rule. If two laws conflict with each other, the courts must decide on the operation of each.

So if a law be in opposition to the constitution; if both the law and the constitution apply to a particular case, so that the court must either decide that case conformably to the law, disregarding the constitution; or conformably to the constitution, disregarding the law; the court must determine which of these conflicting rules governs the case. This is of the very essence of judicial duty.

If, then, the courts are to regard the constitution, and the constitution is superior to any ordinary act of the legislature, the constitution, and not such ordinary act, must govern the case to which they both apply.

Those then who controvert the principle that the constitution is to be considered, in court, as a paramount law, are reduced to the necessity of maintaining that the courts must close their eyes on the constitution, and see only the law.

This doctrine would subvert the very foundation of all written constitutions. It would declare that an act which, according to the principles and theory of our government, is entirely void, is yet, in practice, completely obligatory. It would declare that if the legislature shall do what is expressly forbidden, such act, notwithstanding the express prohibition, is in reality effectual. It would be giving to the legislature a practical and real omnipotence, with the same breath which professes to restrict their powers within narrow limits. It is prescribing limits, and declaring that those limits may be passed at pleasure.

That it thus reduces to nothing what we have deemed the greatest improvement on political institutions — a written constitution — would of itself be sufficient, in America, where written constitutions have been viewed with so much reverence, for rejecting the construction. But the peculiar expressions of the constitution of the United States furnish additional arguments in favour of its rejection.

The judicial power of the United States is extended to all cases arising under the constitution.

Could it be the intention of those who gave this power, to say that in using it the constitution should not be looked into? That a case arising under the constitution should be decided without examining the instrument under which it arises?

This is too extravagant to be maintained.

In some cases, then, the constitution must be looked into by the judges. And if they can open it at all, what part of it are they forbidden to read or to obey?

There are many other parts of the constitution which serve to illustrate this subject.

It is declared that "no tax or duty shall be laid on articles exported from any state." Suppose a duty on the export of cotton, of tobacco, or of flour; and a suit instituted to recover it. Ought judgment to be rendered in such a case? Ought the judges to close their eyes on the constitution, and only see the law?

The constitution declares that "no bill of attainder or ex post facto law shall be passed." If, however, such a bill should be passed, and a person should be prosecuted under it; must the court condemn to death those victims whom the constitution endeavors to preserve?

"No person," says the constitution, "shall be convicted of treason unless on the testimony of two witnesses to the same overt act, or on confession in open court."

Here the language of the constitution is addressed especially to the courts. It prescribes, directly for them, a rule of evidence not to be departed from. If the legislature should change that rule, and declare one witness, or a confession out of court, sufficient for conviction, must the constitutional principle yield to the legislative act?

From these, and many other selections which might be made, it is apparent, that the framers of the constitution contemplated that instrument as a rule for the government of courts, as well as of the legislature. Why otherwise does it direct the judges to take an oath to support it? This oath certainly applies, in an especial manner, to their conduct in their official character. How immoral to impose it on them, if they were to be used as the instruments, and the knowing instruments, for violating what they swear to support!

The oath of office, too, imposed by the legislature, is completely demonstrative of the legislative opinion on this subject. It is in these words: "I do solemnly swear that I will administer justice without respect to persons, and do equal right to the poor and to the rich; and that I will faithfully and impartially discharge all the duties incumbent on me as _____, according to the best of my abilities and understanding, agreeably to the constitution, and laws of the United States." Why does a Judge swear to discharge his duties agreeably the constitution of the United States, if that constitution forms no rule for his government? If it is closed upon him, and cannot be inspected by him?

If such be the real state of things, this is worse than solemn mockery. To prescribe, or to take this oath, becomes equally a crime.

It is also not entirely unworthy of observation that in declaring what shall be the supreme law of the land, the constitution itself is first mentioned; and not the laws of the United States generally, but those only which shall be made in pursuance of the constitution, have that rank.

Thus, the particular phraseology of the constitution of the United States confirms and strengthens the principle, supposed to be essential to all written constitutions, that a law repugnant to the constitution is void; and that courts, as well as other departments, are bound by that instrument.

The rule must be discharged.

Source:

U.S. National Archives & Records Administration, 700 Pennsylvania Avenue NW, Washington, DC 20408
Available at: http://www.ourdocuments.gov/doc.php?doc=19&page=transcript

Transcript of *McCulloch v. Maryland* (1819)

Chief Justice Marshall delivered the opinion of the Court.

In the case now to be determined, the defendant, a sovereign State, denies the obligation of a law enacted by the legislature of the Union, and the plaintiff, on his part, contests the validity of an act which has been passed by the legislature of that State. The constitution of our country, in its most interesting and vital parts, is to be considered; the conflicting powers of the government of the Union and of its members, as marked in that constitution, are to be discussed; and an opinion given, which may essentially influence the great operations of the government. No tribunal can approach such a question without a deep sense of its importance, and of the awful responsibility involved in its decision. But it must be decided peacefully, or remain a source of hostile legislation, perhaps of hostility of a still more serious nature; and if it is to be so decided, by this tribunal alone can the decision be made. On the Supreme Court of the United States has the constitution of our country devolved this important duty.

The first question made in the cause is, has Congress power to incorporate a bank?

It has been truly said that this can scarcely be considered as an open question, entirely unprejudiced by the former proceedings of the nation respecting it. The principle now contested was introduced at a very early period of our history, has been recognized by many successive legislatures, and has been acted upon by the judicial department, in cases of peculiar delicacy, as a law of undoubted obligation....

The power now contested was exercised by the first Congress elected under the present constitution. The bill for incorporating the bank of the United States did not steal upon an unsuspecting legislature, and pass unobserved. Its principle was completely understood, and was opposed with equal zeal and ability. After being resisted, first in the fair and open field of debate, and afterwards in the executive cabinet, with as much persevering talent as any measure has ever experienced, and being supported by arguments which convinced minds as pure and as intelligent as this country can boast, it became a law. The original act was permitted to expire; but a short experience of the embarrassments to which the refusal to revive it exposed the government, convinced those who were most prejudiced against the measure of its necessity, and induced the passage of the present law. It would require no ordinary share of intrepidity to assert that a measure adopted under these circumstances was a bold and plain usurpation, to which the constitution gave no countenance.

These observations belong to the cause; but they are not made under the impression that, were the question entirely new, the law would be found irreconcilable with the constitution.

In discussing this question, the counsel for the State of Maryland have deemed it of some importance, in the construction of the constitution, to consider that instrument not as emanating from the people, but as the act of sovereign and independent States. The powers of the general government, it has been said, are delegated by the States, who alone are truly sovereign; and must be exercised in subordination to the States, who alone possess supreme dominion.

It would be difficult to sustain this proposition. The Convention which framed the constitution was indeed elected by the State legislatures. But the instrument, when it came from their hands, was a mere proposal, without obligation, or pretensions to it. It was reported to the then existing Congress of the United States, with a request that it might "be submitted to a convention of delegates, chosen in each State by the people thereof, under the recommendation of its legislature, for their assent and ratification." This mode of proceeding was adopted; and by the convention, by Congress, and by the State legislatures, the instrument was submitted to the people. They acted upon it in the only manner in which they can act safely, effectively, and wisely, on such a subject, by assembling in convention. It is true, they assembled in their several States — and where else should they have assembled? No political dreamer was ever wild enough to think of breaking down the lines which separate the States, and of compounding the American people into one common mass. Of consequence, when they act, they act in their States. But the measures

they adopt do not, on that account, cease to be the measures of the people themselves, or become the measures of the State governments.

From these conventions the constitution derives its whole authority. The government proceeds directly from the people; is "ordained and established" in the name of the people; and is declared to be ordained, "in order to form a more perfect union, establish justice, ensure domestic tranquility, and secure the blessings of liberty to themselves and to their posterity." The assent of the States, in their sovereign capacity, is implied in calling a convention, and thus submitting that instrument to the people. But the people were at perfect liberty to accept or reject it; and their act was final. It required not the affirmance, and could not be negatived, by the State governments. The constitution, when thus adopted, was of complete obligation, and bound the State sovereignties....

of this fact on the case), is, emphatically, and truly, a government of the people. In form and in substance it emanates from them. Its powers are granted by them, and are to be exercised directly on them, and for their benefit.

This government is acknowledged by all to be one of enumerated powers. The principle, that it can exercise only the powers granted to it, [is] now universally admitted. But the question respecting the extent of the powers actually granted, is perpetually arising, and will probably continue to arise, as long as our system shall exist....

Among the enumerated powers, we do not find that of establishing a bank or creating a corporation. But there is no phrase in the instrument which, like the articles of confederation, excludes incidental or implied powers; and which requires that everything granted shall be expressly and minutely described. Even the 10th amendment, which was framed for the purpose of quieting the excessive jealousies which had been excited, omits the word "expressly," and declares only that the powers "not delegated to the United States, nor prohibited to the States, are reserved to the States or to the people"; thus leaving the question, whether the particular power which may become the subject of contest has been delegated to the one government, or prohibited to the other, to depend on a fair construction of the whole instrument. The men who drew and adopted this amendment had experienced the embarrassments resulting from the insertion of this word in the articles of confederation, and probably omitted it to avoid those embarrassments. A constitution, to contain an accurate detail of all the subdivisions of which its great powers will admit, and of all the means by which they may be carried into execution, would partake of the prolixity of a legal code, and could scarcely be embraced by the human mind. It would probably never be understood by the public. Its nature, therefore, requires, that only its great outlines should be marked, its important objects designated, and the minor ingredients which compose those objects be deduced from the nature of the objects themselves. That this idea was entertained by the framers of the American constitution, is not only to be inferred from the nature of the instrument, but from the language. Why else were some of the limitations, found in the ninth section of the 1st article, introduced? It is also, in some degree, warranted by their having omitted to use any restrictive term which might prevent its receiving a fair and just interpretation. In considering this question, then, we must never forget that it is a constitution we are expounding.

Although, among the enumerated powers of government, we do not find the word "bank," or "incorporation," we find the great powers to lay and collect taxes; to borrow money; to regulate commerce; to declare and conduct a war; and to raise and support armies and navies. The sword and the purse, all the external relations, and no inconsiderable portion of the industry of the nation, are entrusted to its government. It can never be pretended that these vast powers draw after them others of inferior importance, merely because they are inferior. Such an idea can never be advanced. But it may with great reason be contended, that a government, entrusted with such ample powers, on the due execution of which the happiness and prosperity of the nation so vitally depends, must also be entrusted with ample means for their execution. The power being given, it is the interest of the nation to facilitate its execution. It can never be their interest, and cannot be presumed to have been their intention, to clog and embarrass its execution by withholding the most appropriate means. . . require it) which would impute to the framers of that instrument, when granting these powers for the public good, the intention of impeding their exercise by withholding a choice of means? If, indeed, such be the mandate of the constitution, we have only to obey; but that instrument does not profess to enumerate the means by which the powers it confers may be executed; nor does it prohibit the creation of

a corporation, if the existence of such a being be essential to the beneficial exercise of those powers. It is, then, the subject of fair inquiry, how far such means may be employed.

It is not denied, that the powers given to the government imply the ordinary means of execution. That, for example, of raising revenue, and applying it to national purposes, is admitted to imply the power of conveying money from place to place, as the exigencies of the nation may require, and of employing the usual means of conveyance. But it is denied that the government has its choice of means; or, that it may employ the most convenient means, if, to employ them, it be necessary to erect a corporation....

The government which has a right to do an act, and has imposed on it the duty of performing that act, must, according to the dictates of reason, be allowed to select the means; and those who contend that it may not select any appropriate means, that one particular mode of effecting the object is excepted, take upon themselves the burden of establishing that exception.... The power of creating a corporation, though appertaining to sovereignty, is not like the power of making war, or levying taxes, or of regulating commerce, a great substantive and independent power, which cannot be implied as incidental to other powers, or used as a means of executing them. It is never the end for which other powers are exercised, but a means by which other objects are accomplished.... The power of creating a corporation is never used for its own sake, but for the purpose of effecting something else. No sufficient reason is, therefore, perceived, why it may not pass as incidental to those powers which are expressly given, if it be a direct mode of executing them.

But the constitution of the United States has not left the right of Congress to employ the necessary means, for the execution of the powers conferred on the government, to general reasoning. To its enumeration of powers is added that of making "all laws which shall be necessary and proper for carrying into execution the foregoing powers, and all other powers vested by this constitution, in the government of the United States, or in any department thereof."

The counsel for the State of Maryland have urged various arguments, to prove that this clause, though in terms a grant of power, is not so in effect; but is really restrictive of the general right, which might otherwise be implied, of selecting means for executing the enumerated powers....

Almost all compositions contain words, which, taken in their rigorous sense, would convey a meaning different from that which is obviously intended. It is essential to just construction, that many words which import something excessive should be understood in a more mitigated sense — in that sense which common usage justifies. The word "necessary" is of this description. It has not a fixed character peculiar to itself. It admits of all degrees of comparison; and is often connected with other words, which increase or diminish the impression the mind receives of the urgency it imports. A thing may be necessary, very necessary, absolutely or indispensably necessary. To no mind would the same idea be conveyed by these several phrases. This comment on the word is well illustrated by the passage cited at the bar, from the 20th section of the 1st article of the constitution. It is, we think, impossible to compare the sentence which prohibits a State from laying "imposts, or duties on imports or exports, except what may be absolutely necessary for executing its inspection laws," with that which authorizes Congress "to make all laws which shall be necessary and proper for carrying into execution" the powers of the general government, without feeling a conviction that the convention understood itself to change materially the meaning of the word "necessary," by prefixing the word "absolutely." This word, then, like others, is used in various senses; and, in its construction, the subject, the context, the intention of the person using them, are all to be taken into view.

Let this be done in the case under consideration. The subject is the execution of those great powers on which the welfare of a nation essentially depends. It must have been the intention of those who gave these powers, to insure, as far as human prudence could insure, their beneficial execution. This could not be done by confiding the choice of means to such narrow limits as not to leave it in the power of Congress to adopt any which might be appropriate, and which were conducive to the end. This provision is made in a constitution intended to endure for ages to come, and, consequently, to be adapted to the various crises of human affairs. To have prescribed the means by which government should, in all future time, execute its powers, would have been to change, entirely, the character of the instrument, and give it the properties of a legal code. It would have been an unwise attempt to provide, by immutable

rules, for exigencies which, if foreseen at all, must have been seen dimly, and which can be best provided for as they occur. To have declared that the best means shall not be used, but those alone without which the power given would be nugatory, would have been to deprive the legislature of the capacity to avail itself of experience, to exercise its reason, and to accommodate its legislation to circumstances. If we apply this principle of construction to any of the powers of the government, we shall find it so pernicious in its operation that we shall be compelled to discard it....

The result of the most careful and attentive consideration bestowed upon this clause is, that if it does not enlarge, it cannot be construed to restrain the powers of Congress, or to impair the rights of the legislature to exercise its best judgment in the selection of measures to carry into execution the constitutional powers of the government. If no other motive for its insertion can be suggested, a sufficient one is found in the desire to remove all doubts respecting the right to legislate on that vast mass of incidental powers which must be involved in the constitution, if that instrument be not a splendid bauble.

We admit, as all must admit, that the powers of the government are limited, and that its limits are not to be transcended. But we think the sound construction of the constitution must allow to the national legislature that discretion, with respect to the means by which the powers it confers are to be carried into execution, which will enable that body to perform the high duties assigned to it, in the manner most beneficial to the people. Let the end be legitimate, let it be within the scope of the constitution, and all means which are appropriate, which are plainly adapted to that end, which are not prohibited, but consist with the letter and spirit of the constitution, are constitutional....

Should Congress, in the execution of its powers, adopt measures which are prohibited by the constitution; or should Congress, under the pretext of executing its powers, pass laws for the accomplishment of objects not entrusted to the government; it would become the painful duty of this tribunal, should a case requiring such a decision come before it, to say that such an act was not the law of the land. But where the law is not prohibited, and is really calculated to effect any of the objects entrusted to the government, to undertake here to inquire into the degree of its necessity, would be to pass the line which circumscribes the judicial department, and to tread on legislative ground. This court disclaims all pretensions to such a power.

After this declaration, it can scarcely be necessary to say that the existence of State banks can have no possible influence on the question. No trace is to be found in the constitution of an intention to create a dependence of the government of the Union on those of the States, for the execution of the great powers assigned to it. Its means are adequate to its ends; and on those means alone was it expected to rely for the accomplishment of its ends. To impose on it the necessity of resorting to means which it cannot control, which another government may furnish or withhold, would render its course precarious, the result of its measures uncertain, and create a dependence on other governments, which might disappoint its most important designs, and is incompatible with the language of the constitution. But were it otherwise, the choice of means implies a right to choose a national bank in preference to State banks, and Congress alone can make the election.

After the most deliberate consideration, it is the unanimous and decided opinion of this Court, that the act to incorporate the Bank of the United States is a law made in pursuance of the constitution, and is a part of the supreme law of the land....

It being the opinion of the Court, that the act incorporating the bank is constitutional; and that the power of establishing a branch in the State of Maryland might be properly exercised by the bank itself, we proceed to inquire —

2. Whether the State of Maryland may, without violating the constitution, tax that branch?

That the power of taxation is one of vital importance; that it is retained by the States; that it is not abridged by the grant of a similar power to the government of the Union; that it is to be concurrently exercised by the two governments: are truths which have never been denied. But, such is the paramount character of the constitution, that its capacity to withdraw any subject from the action of even this power, is admitted. The States are expressly forbidden to lay any duties on imports or exports, except what may be absolutely necessary for executing their inspection laws. If the obligation of this prohibition must be conceded, the same paramount character would seem to restrain, as

it certainly may restrain, a State from such other exercise of this power; as is in its nature incompatible with, and repugnant to, the constitutional laws of the Union....

On this ground the counsel for the bank place its claim to be exempted from the power of a State to tax its operations. There is no express provision for the case, but the claim has been sustained on a principle which so entirely pervades the constitution, is so intermixed with the materials which compose it, so interwoven with its web, so blended with its texture, as to be incapable of being separated from it, without rending it into shreds.

This great principle is, that the constitution and the laws made in pursuance thereof are supreme; that they control the constitution and laws of the respective States, and cannot be controlled by them. From this, which may be almost termed an axiom, other propositions are deduced as corollaries, on the truth or error of which, and on their application to this case, the cause has been supposed to depend. These are, 1st. that a power to create implies a power to preserve. 2nd. That a power to destroy, if wielded by a different hand, is hostile to, and incompatible with these powers to create and to preserve. 3d. That where this repugnancy exists, that authority which is supreme must control, not yield to that over which it is supreme....

That the power of taxing by the States may be exercised so as to destroy it, is too obvious to be denied. But taxation is said to be an absolute power, which acknowledges no other limits than those expressly prescribed in the constitution, and like sovereign power of every other description, is trusted to the discretion of those who use it. But the very terms of this argument admit that the sovereignty of the State, in the article of taxation itself, is subordinate to, and may be controlled by, the constitution of the United States. How far it has been controlled by that instrument must be a question of construction. In making this construction, no principle not declared, can be admissible, which would defeat the legitimate operations of a supreme government. It is of the very essence of supremacy to remove all obstacles to its action within its own sphere, and so to modify every power vested in subordinate governments, as to exempt its own operations from their own influence. This effect need not be stated in terms. It is so involved in the declaration of supremacy, so necessarily implied in it, that the expression of it could not make it more certain. We must, therefore, keep it in view while construing the constitution.

The argument on the part of the State of Maryland is, not that the States may directly resist a law of Congress, but that they may exercise their acknowledged powers upon it, and that the constitution leaves them this right in the confidence that they will not abuse it.

Before we proceed to examine this argument, and to subject it to the test of the constitution, we must be permitted to bestow a few considerations on the nature and extent of this original right of taxation, which is acknowledged to remain with the States. It is admitted that the power of taxing the people and their property is essential to the very existence of government, and may be legitimately exercised on the objects to which it is applicable, to the utmost extent to which the government may choose to carry it. The only security against the abuse of this power, is found in the structure of the government itself. In imposing a tax the legislature acts upon its constituents....

The sovereignty of a State extends to everything which exists by its own authority, or is so introduced by its permission; but does it extend to those means which are employed by Congress to carry into execution powers conferred on that body by the people of the United States? We think it demonstrable that it does not. Those powers are not given by the people of a single State. They are given by the people of the United States, to a government whose laws, made in pursuance of the constitution, are declared to be supreme. Consequently, the people of a single State cannot confer a sovereignty which will extend over them.

If we measure the power of taxation residing in a State, by the extent of sovereignty which the people of a single State possess, and can confer on its government, we have an intelligible standard, applicable to every case to which the power may be applied. We have a principle which leaves the power of taxing the people and property of a State unimpaired; which leaves to a State the command of all its resources, and which places beyond its reach, all those powers which are conferred by the people of the United States on the government of the Union, and all those means which are given for the purpose of carrying those powers into execution. We have a principle which is safe for the States, and safe for the Union. We are relieved, as we ought to be, from clashing sovereignty; from interfering

powers; from a repugnancy between a right in one government to pull down what there is an acknowledged right in another to build up; from the incompatibility of a right in one government to destroy what there is a right in another to preserve. We are not driven to the perplexing inquiry, so unfit for the judicial department, what degree of taxation is the legitimate use, and what degree may amount to the abuse of the power. The attempt to use it on the means employed by the government of the Union, in pursuance of the constitution, is itself an abuse, because it is the usurpation of a power which the people of a single State cannot give.

We find, then, on just theory, a total failure of this original right to tax the means employed by the government of the Union, for the execution of its powers. The right never existed, and the question whether it has been surrendered, cannot arise.

But, waiving this theory for the present, let us resume the inquiry, whether this power can be exercised by the respective States, consistently with a fair construction of the constitution?

That the power to tax involves the power to destroy; that the power to destroy may defeat and render useless the power to create; that there is a plain repugnance, in conferring on one government a power to control the constitutional measures of another, which other, with respect to those very measures, is declared to be supreme over that which exerts the control, are propositions not to be denied. But all inconsistencies are to be reconciled by the magic of the word CONFIDENCE. Taxation, it is said, does not necessarily and unavoidably destroy. To carry it to the excess of destruction would be an abuse, to presume which, would banish that confidence which is essential to all government.

But is this a case of confidence? Would the people of any one State trust those of another with a power to control the most insignificant operations of their State government? We know they would not. Why, then, should we suppose that the people of any one State should be willing to trust those of another with a power to control the operations of a government to which they have confided their most important and most valuable interests? In the legislature of the Union alone, are all represented. The legislature of the Union alone, therefore, can be trusted by the people with the power of controlling measures which concern all, in the confidence that it will not be abused. This, then, is not a case of confidence, and we must consider it as it really is.

If we apply the principle for which the State of Maryland contends, to the constitution generally, we shall find it capable of changing totally the character of that instrument. We shall find it capable of arresting all the measures of the government, and of prostrating it at the foot of the States. The American people have declared their constitution, and the laws made in pursuance thereof, to be supreme; but this principle would transfer the supremacy, in fact, to the States.

If the States may tax one instrument, employed by the government in the execution of its powers, they may tax any and every other instrument. They may tax the mail; they may tax the mint; they may tax patent rights; they may tax the papers of the custom-house; they may tax judicial process; they may tax all the means employed by the government, to an excess which would defeat all the ends of government. This was not intended by the American people. They did not design to make their government dependent on the States....

The Court has bestowed on this subject its most deliberate consideration. The result is a conviction that the States have no power, by taxation or otherwise, to retard, impede, burden, or in any manner control, the operations of the constitutional laws enacted by Congress to carry into execution the powers vested in the general government. This is, we think, the unavoidable consequence of that supremacy which the constitution has declared.

We are unanimously of opinion, that the law passed by the legislature of Maryland, imposing a tax on the Bank of the United States, is unconstitutional and void.

This opinion does not deprive the States of any resources which they originally possessed. It does not extend to a tax paid by the real property of the bank, in common with the other real property within the State, nor to a tax imposed on the interest which the citizens of Maryland may hold in this institution, in common with other property of the same description throughout the State. But this is a tax on the operations of the bank, and is, consequently, a tax

on the operation of an instrument employed by the government of the Union to carry its powers into execution. Such a tax must be unconstitutional.

Source:

U.S. National Archives & Records Administration
700 Pennsylvania Avenue NW, Washington, DC 20408
Available at: http://www.ourdocuments.gov/doc.php?doc=21&page=transcript

Transcript of Monroe Doctrine (1823)

(Part of the speech that was delivered to U.S. Congress, December 2, 1823)

...At the proposal of the Russian Imperial Government, made through the minister of the Emperor residing here, a full power and instructions have been transmitted to the minister of the United States at St. Petersburg to arrange by amicable negotiation the respective rights and interests of the two nations on the northwest coast of this continent. A similar proposal has been made by His Imperial Majesty to the Government of Great Britain, which has likewise been acceded to. The Government of the United States has been desirous by this friendly proceeding of manifesting the great value which they have invariably attached to the friendship of the Emperor and their solicitude to cultivate the best understanding with his Government. In the discussions to which this interest has given rise and in the arrangements by which they may terminate the occasion has been judged proper for asserting, as a principle in which the rights and interests of the United States are involved, that the American continents, by the free and independent condition which they have assumed and maintain, are henceforth not to be considered as subjects for future colonization by any European powers ...

It was stated at the commencement of the last session that a great effort was then making in Spain and Portugal to improve the condition of the people of those countries, and that it appeared to be conducted with extraordinary moderation. It need scarcely be remarked that the results have been so far very different from what was then anticipated. Of events in that quarter of the globe, with which we have so much intercourse and from which we derive our origin, we have always been anxious and interested spectators. The citizens of the United States cherish sentiments the most friendly in favor of the liberty and happiness of their fellow-men on that side of the Atlantic. In the wars of the European powers in matters relating to themselves we have never taken any part, nor does it comport with our policy to do so. It is only when our rights are invaded or seriously menaced that we resent injuries or make preparation for our defense. With the movements in this hemisphere we are of necessity more immediately connected, and by causes which must be obvious to all enlightened and impartial observers. The political system of the allied powers is essentially different in this respect from that of America. This difference proceeds from that which exists in their respective Governments; and to the defense of our own, which has been achieved by the loss of so much blood and treasure, and matured by the wisdom of their most enlightened citizens, and under which we have enjoyed unexampled felicity, this whole nation is devoted. We owe it, therefore, to candor and to the amicable relations existing between the United States and those powers to declare that we should consider any attempt on their part to extend their system to any portion of this hemisphere as dangerous to our peace and safety. With the existing colonies or dependencies of any European power we have not interfered and shall not interfere. But with the Governments who have declared their independence and maintain it, and whose independence we have, on great consideration and on just principles, acknowledged, we could not view any interposition for the purpose of oppressing them, or controlling in any other manner their destiny, by any European power in any other light than as the manifestation of an unfriendly disposition toward the United States. In the war between those new Governments and Spain we declared our neutrality at the time of their recognition, and to this we have adhered, and shall continue to adhere, provided no change shall occur which, in the judgement of the competent authorities of this Government, shall make a corresponding change on the part of the United States indispensable to their security.

The late events in Spain and Portugal shew that Europe is still unsettled. Of this important fact no stronger proof can be adduced than that the allied powers should have thought it proper, on any principle satisfactory to themselves, to have interposed by force in the internal concerns of Spain. To what extent such interposition may be carried, on the same principle, is a question in which all independent powers whose governments differ from theirs are interested, even those most remote, and surely none of them more so than the United States. Our policy in regard to Europe, which was adopted at an early stage of the wars which have so long agitated that quarter of the globe, nevertheless remains the same, which is, not to interfere in the internal concerns of any of its powers; to consider the government de facto as the legitimate government for us; to cultivate friendly relations with it, and to preserve those relations by

a frank, firm, and manly policy, meeting in all instances the just claims of every power, submitting to injuries from none. But in regard to those continents circumstances are eminently and conspicuously different.

It is impossible that the allied powers should extend their political system to any portion of either continent without endangering our peace and happiness; nor can anyone believe that our southern brethren, if left to themselves, would adopt it of their own accord. It is equally impossible, therefore, that we should behold such interposition in any form with indifference. If we look to the comparative strength and resources of Spain and those new Governments, and their distance from each other, it must be obvious that she can never subdue them. It is still the true policy of the United States to leave the parties to themselves, in hope that other powers will pursue the same course....

Source:

U.S. National Archives & Records Administration, 700 Pennsylvania Avenue NW, Washington, DC 20408
Available at: http://www.ourdocuments.gov/doc.php?doc=23&page=transcript

Transcript of Emancipation Proclamation (1863)

By the President of the United States of America:

A Proclamation.

Whereas, on the twenty-second day of September, in the year of our Lord one thousand eight hundred and sixty-two, a proclamation was issued by the President of the United States, containing, among other things, the following, to wit:

"That on the first day of January, in the year of our Lord one thousand eight hundred and sixty-three, all persons held as slaves within any State or designated part of a State, the people whereof shall then be in rebellion against the United States, shall be then, thenceforward, and forever free; and the Executive Government of the United States, including the military and naval authority thereof, will recognize and maintain the freedom of such persons, and will do no act or acts to repress such persons, or any of them, in any efforts they may make for their actual freedom.

"That the Executive will, on the first day of January aforesaid, by proclamation, designate the States and parts of States, if any, in which the people thereof, respectively, shall then be in rebellion against the United States; and the fact that any State, or the people thereof, shall on that day be, in good faith, represented in the Congress of the United States by members chosen thereto at elections wherein a majority of the qualified voters of such State shall have participated, shall, in the absence of strong countervailing testimony, be deemed conclusive evidence that such State, and the people thereof, are not then in rebellion against the United States."

Now, therefore I, Abraham Lincoln, President of the United States, by virtue of the power in me vested as Commander-in-Chief, of the Army and Navy of the United States in time of actual armed rebellion against the authority and government of the United States, and as a fit and necessary war measure for suppressing said rebellion, do, on this first day of January, in the year of our Lord one thousand eight hundred and sixty-three, and in accordance with my purpose so to do publicly proclaimed for the full period of one hundred days, from the day first above mentioned, order and designate as the States and parts of States wherein the people thereof respectively, are this day in rebellion against the United States, the following, to wit:

Arkansas, Texas, Louisiana, (except the Parishes of St. Bernard, Plaquemines, Jefferson, St. John, St. Charles, St. James Ascension, Assumption, Terrebonne, Lafourche, St. Mary, St. Martin, and Orleans, including the City of New Orleans) Mississippi, Alabama, Florida, Georgia, South Carolina, North Carolina, and Virginia, (except the forty-eight counties designated as West Virginia, and also the counties of Berkley, Accomac, Northampton, Elizabeth City, York, Princess Ann, and Norfolk, including the cities of Norfolk and Portsmouth[)], and which excepted parts, are for the present, left precisely as if this proclamation were not issued.

And by virtue of the power, and for the purpose aforesaid, I do order and declare that all persons held as slaves within said designated States, and parts of States, are, and henceforward shall be free; and that the Executive government of the United States, including the military and naval authorities thereof, will recognize and maintain the freedom of said persons.

And I hereby enjoin upon the people so declared to be free to abstain from all violence, unless in necessary self-defence; and I recommend to them that, in all cases when allowed, they labor faithfully for reasonable wages.

And I further declare and make known, that such persons of suitable condition, will be received into the armed service of the United States to garrison forts, positions, stations, and other places, and to man vessels of all sorts in said service.

And upon this act, sincerely believed to be an act of justice, warranted by the Constitution, upon military necessity, I invoke the considerate judgment of mankind, and the gracious favor of Almighty God.

In witness whereof, I have hereunto set my hand and caused the seal of the United States to be affixed.

Done at the City of Washington, this first day of January, in the year of our Lord one thousand eight hundred and sixty three, and of the Independence of the United States of America the eighty-seventh.

By the President: ABRAHAM LINCOLN

WILLIAM H. SEWARD, Secretary of State.

Source:

U.S. National Archives & Records Administration, 700 Pennsylvania Avenue NW, Washington, DC 20408
Available at: http://www.ourdocuments.gov/doc.php?doc=34&page=transcript

Transcript of *Brown v. Board of Education* (1954)

SUPREME COURT OF THE UNITED STATES

Brown v. Board of Education, 347 U.S. 483 (1954) (USSC+)

Argued December 9, 1952

Reargued December 8, 1953

Decided May 17, 1954

APPEAL FROM THE UNITED STATES DISTRICT COURT FOR THE DISTRICT OF KANSAS*

Syllabus

Segregation of white and Negro children in the public schools of a State solely on the basis of race, pursuant to state laws permitting or requiring such segregation, denies to Negro children the equal protection of the laws guaranteed by the Fourteenth Amendment — even though the physical facilities and other "tangible" factors of white and Negro schools may be equal.

(a) The history of the Fourteenth Amendment is inconclusive as to its intended effect on public education.

(b) The question presented in these cases must be determined not on the basis of conditions existing when the Fourteenth Amendment was adopted, but in the light of the full development of public education and its present place in American life throughout the Nation.

(c) Where a State has undertaken to provide an opportunity for an education in its public schools, such an opportunity is a right which must be made available to all on equal terms.

(d) Segregation of children in public schools solely on the basis of race deprives children of the minority group of equal educational opportunities, even though the physical facilities and other "tangible" factors may be equal.

(e) The "separate but equal" doctrine adopted in *Plessy v. Ferguson*, 163 U.S. 537, has no place in the field of public education.

(f) The cases are restored to the docket for further argument on specified questions relating to the forms of the decrees.

Opinion

MR. CHIEF JUSTICE WARREN delivered the opinion of the Court.

These cases come to us from the States of Kansas, South Carolina, Virginia, and Delaware. They are premised on different facts and different local conditions, but a common legal question justifies their consideration together in this consolidated opinion.

In each of the cases, minors of the Negro race, through their legal representatives, seek the aid of the courts in obtaining admission to the public schools of their community on a nonsegregated basis. In each instance, they had been denied admission to schools attended by white children under laws requiring or permitting segregation according to race. This segregation was alleged to deprive the plaintiffs of the equal protection of the laws under the Fourteenth Amendment. In each of the cases other than the Delaware case, a three-judge federal district court denied relief to the plaintiffs on the so-called "separate but equal" doctrine announced by this Court in *Plessy v. Ferguson*, 163 U.S. 537. Under that doctrine, equality of treatment is accorded when the races are provided substantially equal facilities, even though these facilities be separate. In the Delaware case, the Supreme Court of Delaware

adhered to that doctrine, but ordered that the plaintiffs be admitted to the white schools because of their superiority to the Negro schools.

The plaintiffs contend that segregated public schools are not "equal" and cannot be made "equal," and that hence they are deprived of the equal protection of the laws. Because of the obvious importance of the question presented, the Court took jurisdiction. Argument was heard in the 1952 Term, and reargument was heard this Term on certain questions propounded by the Court.

Reargument was largely devoted to the circumstances surrounding the adoption of the Fourteenth Amendment in 1868. It covered exhaustively consideration of the Amendment in Congress, ratification by the states, then-existing practices in racial segregation, and the views of proponents and opponents of the Amendment. This discussion and our own investigation convince us that, although these sources cast some light, it is not enough to resolve the problem with which we are faced. At best, they are inconclusive. The most avid proponents of the post-War Amendments undoubtedly intended them to remove all legal distinctions among "all persons born or naturalized in the United States." Their opponents, just as certainly, were antagonistic to both the letter and the spirit of the Amendments and wished them to have the most limited effect. What others in Congress and the state legislatures had in mind cannot be determined with any degree of certainty.

An additional reason for the inconclusive nature of the Amendment's history with respect to segregated schools is the status of public education at that time. In the South, the movement toward free common schools, supported by general taxation, had not yet taken hold. Education of white children was largely in the hands of private groups. Education of Negroes was almost nonexistent, and practically all of the race were illiterate. In fact, any education of Negroes was forbidden by law in some states. Today, in contrast, many Negroes have achieved outstanding success in the arts and sciences, as well as in the business and professional world. It is true that public school education at the time of the Amendment had advanced further in the North, but the effect of the Amendment on Northern States was generally ignored in the congressional debates.

Even in the North, the conditions of public education did not approximate those existing today. The curriculum was usually rudimentary; ungraded schools were common in rural areas; the school term was but three months a year in many states, and compulsory school attendance was virtually unknown. As a consequence, it is not surprising that there should be so little in the history of the Fourteenth Amendment relating to its intended effect on public education.

In the first cases in this Court construing the Fourteenth Amendment, decided shortly after its adoption, the Court interpreted it as proscribing all state-imposed discriminations against the Negro race. The doctrine of "separate but equal" did not make its appearance in this Court until 1896 in the case of *Plessy v. Ferguson*, supra, involving not education but transportation. American courts have since labored with the doctrine for over half a century. In this Court, there have been six cases involving the "separate but equal" doctrine in the field of public education. In *Cumming v. County Board of Education*, 175 U.S. 528, and *Gong Lum v. Rice*, 275 U.S. 78, the validity of the doctrine itself was not challenged. In more recent cases, all on the graduate school level, inequality was found in that specific benefits enjoyed by white students were denied to Negro students of the same educational qualifications. Missouri ex rel. *Gaines v. Canada*, 305 U.S. 337; *Sipuel v. Oklahoma*, 332 U.S. 631; *Sweatt v. Painter*, 339 U.S. 629; *McLaurin v. Oklahoma State Regents*, 339 U.S. 637. In none of these cases was it necessary to reexamine the doctrine to grant relief to the Negro plaintiff. And in *Sweatt v. Painter*, supra, the Court expressly reserved decision on the question whether *Plessy v. Ferguson* should be held inapplicable to public education.

In the instant cases, that question is directly presented. Here, unlike *Sweatt v. Painter*, there are findings below that the Negro and white schools involved have been equalized, or are being equalized, with respect to buildings, curricula, qualifications and salaries of teachers, and other "tangible" factors. Our decision, therefore, cannot turn on merely a comparison of these tangible factors in the Negro and white schools involved in each of the cases. We must look instead to the effect of segregation itself on public education.

In approaching this problem, we cannot turn the clock back to 1868, when the Amendment was adopted, or even to 1896, when *Plessy v. Ferguson* was written. We must consider public education in the light of its full development and its present place in American life throughout the Nation. Only in this way can it be determined if segregation in public schools deprives these plaintiffs of the equal protection of the laws.

Today, education is perhaps the most important function of state and local governments. Compulsory school attendance laws and the great expenditures for education both demonstrate our recognition of the importance of education to our democratic society. It is required in the performance of our most basic public responsibilities, even service in the armed forces. It is the very foundation of good citizenship. Today it is a principal instrument in awakening the child to cultural values, in preparing him for later professional training, and in helping him to adjust normally to his environment. In these days, it is doubtful that any child may reasonably be expected to succeed in life if he is denied the opportunity of an education. Such an opportunity, where the state has undertaken to provide it, is a right which must be made available to all on equal terms.

We come then to the question presented: Does segregation of children in public schools solely on the basis of race, even though the physical facilities and other "tangible" factors may be equal, deprive the children of the minority group of equal educational opportunities? We believe that it does.

In *Sweatt v. Painter*, supra, in finding that a segregated law school for Negroes could not provide them equal educational opportunities, this Court relied in large part on "those qualities which are incapable of objective measurement but which make for greatness in a law school." In *McLaurin v. Oklahoma State Regents*, supra, the Court, in requiring that a Negro admitted to a white graduate school be treated like all other students, again resorted to intangible considerations: ." . . his ability to study, to engage in discussions and exchange views with other students, and, in general, to learn his profession." Such considerations apply with added force to children in grade and high schools. To separate them from others of similar age and qualifications solely because of their race generates a feeling of inferiority as to their status in the community that may affect their hearts and minds in a way unlikely ever to be undone. The effect of this separation on their educational opportunities was well stated by a finding in the Kansas case by a court which nevertheless felt compelled to rule against the Negro plaintiffs:

Segregation of white and colored children in public schools has a detrimental effect upon the colored children. The impact is greater when it has the sanction of the law, for the policy of separating the races is usually interpreted as denoting the inferiority of the negro group. A sense of inferiority affects the motivation of a child to learn. Segregation with the sanction of law, therefore, has a tendency to [retard] the educational and mental development of negro children and to deprive them of some of the benefits they would receive in a racial[ly] integrated school system.

Whatever may have been the extent of psychological knowledge at the time of *Plessy v. Ferguson*, this finding is amply supported by modern authority. Any language in *Plessy v. Ferguson* contrary to this finding is rejected.

We conclude that, in the field of public education, the doctrine of "separate but equal" has no place. Separate educational facilities are inherently unequal. Therefore, we hold that the plaintiffs and others similarly situated for whom the actions have been brought are, by reason of the segregation complained of, deprived of the equal protection of the laws guaranteed by the Fourteenth Amendment. This disposition makes unnecessary any discussion whether such segregation also violates the Due Process Clause of the Fourteenth Amendment.

Because these are class actions, because of the wide applicability of this decision, and because of the great variety of local conditions, the formulation of decrees in these cases presents problems of considerable complexity. On reargument, the consideration of appropriate relief was necessarily subordinated to the primary question — the constitutionality of segregation in public education. We have now announced that such segregation is a denial of the equal protection of the laws. In order that we may have the full assistance of the parties in formulating decrees, the cases will be restored to the docket, and the parties are requested to present further argument on Questions 4 and 5 previously propounded by the Court for the reargument this Term The Attorney General of the United States is again invited to participate. The Attorneys General of the states requiring or permitting segregation in

public education will also be permitted to appear as amici curiae upon request to do so by September 15, 1954, and submission of briefs by October 1, 1954.

It is so ordered.

* Together with No. 2, *Briggs et al. v. Elliott et al.*, on appeal from the United States District Court for the Eastern District of South Carolina, argued December 9-10, 1952, reargued December 7-8, 1953; No. 4, *Davis et al. v. County School Board of Prince Edward County, Virginia, et al.*, on appeal from the United States District Court for the Eastern District of Virginia, argued December 10, 1952, reargued December 7-8, 1953, and No. 10, *Gebhart et al. v. Belton et al.*, on certiorari to the Supreme Court of Delaware, argued December 11, 1952, reargued December 9, 1953.

Source:

U.S. National Archives & Records Administration, 700 Pennsylvania Avenue NW, Washington, DC 20408 Available at: http://www.ourdocuments.gov/doc.php?doc=87&page=transcript

Transcript of Civil Rights Act (1964)

An Act

To enforce the constitutional right to vote, to confer jurisdiction upon the district courts of the United States to provide injunctive relief against discrimination in public accommodations, to authorize the Attorney General to institute suits to protect constitutional rights in public facilities and public education, to extend the Commission on Civil Rights, to prevent discrimination in federally assisted programs, to establish a Commission on Equal Employment Opportunity, and for other purposes.

Be it enacted by the Senate and House of Representatives of the United States of America in Congress assembled, That this Act may be cited as the "Civil Rights Act of 1964."

TITLE I—VOTING RIGHTS

SEC. 101. Section 2004 of the Revised Statutes (42 U.S.C. 1971), as amended by section 131 of the Civil Rights Act of 1957 (71 Stat. 637), and as further amended by section 601 of the Civil Rights Act of 1960 (74 Stat. 90), is further amended as follows:

(a) Insert "1" after "(a)" in subsection (a) and add at the end of subsection (a) the following new paragraphs:

"(2) No person acting under color of law shall—

"(A) in determining whether any individual is qualified under State law or laws to vote in any Federal election, apply any standard, practice, or procedure different from the standards, practices, or procedures applied under such law or laws to other individuals within the same county, parish, or similar political subdivision who have been found by State officials to be qualified to vote;

"(B) deny the right of any individual to vote in any Federal election because of an error or omission on any record or paper relating to any application, registration, or other act requisite to voting, if such error or omission is not material in determining whether such individual is qualified under State law to vote in such election; or

"(C) employ any literacy test as a qualification for voting in any Federal election unless (i) such test is administered to each individual and is conducted wholly in writing, and (ii) a certified copy of the test and of the answers given by the individual is furnished to him within twenty-five days of the submission of his request made within the period of time during which records and papers are required to be retained and preserved pursuant to title III of the Civil Rights Act of 1960 (42 U.S.C. 1974—74e; 74 Stat. 88): Provided, however, That the Attorney General may enter into agreements with appropriate State or local authorities that preparation, conduct, and maintenance of such tests in accordance with the provisions of applicable State or local law, including such special provisions as are necessary in the preparation, conduct, and maintenance of such tests for persons who are blind or otherwise physically handicapped, meet the purposes of this subparagraph and constitute compliance therewith.

"(3) For purposes of this subsection—

"(A) the term 'vote' shall have the same meaning as in subsection (e) of this section;

"(B) the phrase 'literacy test' includes any test of the ability to read, write, understand, or interpret any matter."

(b) Insert immediately following the period at the end of the first sentence of subsection (c) the following new sentence: "If in any such proceeding literacy is a relevant fact there shall be a rebuttable presumption that any person who has not been adjudged an incompetent and who has completed the sixth grade in a public school in, or a private school accredited by, any State or territory, the District of Columbia, or the Commonwealth of Puerto Rico where

instruction is carried on predominantly in the English language, possesses sufficient literacy, comprehension, and intelligence to vote in any Federal election."

(c) Add the following subsection "(f)" and designate the present subsection "(f)" as subsection "(g)": "(f) When used in subsection (a) or (c) of this section, the words 'Federal election' shall mean any general, special, or primary election held solely or in part for the purpose of electing or selecting any candidate for the office of President, Vice President, presidential elector, Member of the Senate, or Member of the House of Representatives."

(d) Add the following subsection "(h)":

"(h) In any proceeding instituted by the United States in any district court of the United States under this section in which the Attorney General requests a finding of a pattern or practice of discrimination pursuant to subsection (e) of this section the Attorney General, at the time he files the complaint, or any defendant in the proceeding, within twenty days after service upon him of the complaint, may file with the clerk of such court a request that a court of three judges be convened to hear and determine the entire case. A copy of the request for a three-judge court shall be immediately furnished by such clerk to the chief judge of the circuit (or in his absence, the presiding circuit judge of the circuit) in which the case is pending. Upon receipt of the copy of such request it shall be the duty of the chief justice of the circuit or the presiding circuit judge, as the case may be, to designate immediately three judges in such circuit, of whom at least one shall be a circuit judge and another of whom shall be a district judge of the court in which the proceeding was instituted, to hear and determine such case, and it shall be the duty of the judges so designated to assign the case for hearing at the earliest practicable date, to participate in the hearing and determination thereof, and to cause the case to be in every way expedited.

An appeal from the final judgment of such court will lie to the Supreme Court.

"In any proceeding brought under subsection (c) of this section to enforce subsection (b) of this section, or in the event neither the Attorney General nor any defendant files a request for a three-judge court in any proceeding authorized by this subsection, it shall be the duty of the chief judge of the district (or in his absence, the acting chief judge) in which the case is pending immediately to designate a judge in such district to hear and determine the case. In the event that no judge in the district is available to hear and determine the case, the chief judge of the district, or the acting chief judge, as the case may be, shall certify this fact to the chief judge of the circuit (or, in his absence, the acting chief judge) who shall then designate a district or circuit judge of the circuit to hear and determine the case.

"It shall be the duty of the judge designated pursuant to this section to assign the case for hearing at the earliest practicable date and to cause the case to be in every way expedited."

TITLE II—INJUNCTIVE RELIEF AGAINST DISCRIMINATION IN PLACES OF PUBLIC ACCOMMODATION

SEC. 201. (a) All persons shall be entitled to the full and equal enjoyment of the goods, services, facilities, and privileges, advantages, and accommodations of any place of public accommodation, as defined in this section, without discrimination or segregation on the ground of race, color, religion, or national origin.

(b) Each of the following establishments which serves the public is a place of public accommodation within the meaning of this title if its operations affect commerce, or if discrimination or segregation by it is supported by State action:

(1) any inn, hotel, motel, or other establishment which provides lodging to transient guests, other than an establishment located within a building which contains not more than five rooms for rent or hire and which is actually occupied by the proprietor of such establishment as his residence;

(2) any restaurant, cafeteria, lunchroom, lunch counter, soda fountain, or other facility principally engaged in selling food for consumption on the premises, including, but not limited to, any such facility located on the premises of any retail establishment; or any gasoline station;

(3) any motion picture house, theater, concert hall, sports arena, stadium or other place of exhibition or entertainment; and

(4) any establishment (A)(i) which is physically located within the premises of any establishment otherwise covered by this subsection, or (ii) within the premises of which is physically located any such covered establishment, and (B) which holds itself out as serving patrons of such covered establishment.

(c) The operations of an establishment affect commerce within the meaning of this title if (1) it is one of the establishments described in paragraph (1) of subsection (b); (2) in the case of an establishment described in paragraph (2) of subsection (b), it serves or offers to serve interstate travelers or a substantial portion of the food which it serves, or gasoline or other products which it sells, has moved in commerce; (3) in the case of an establishment described in paragraph (3) of subsection (b), it customarily presents films, performances, athletic teams, exhibitions, or other sources of entertainment which move in commerce; and (4) in the case of an establishment described in paragraph (4) of subsection (b), it is physically located within the premises of, or there is physically located within its premises, an establishment the operations of which affect commerce within the meaning of this subsection. For purposes of this section, "commerce" means travel, trade, traffic, commerce, transportation, or communication among the several States, or between the District of Columbia and any State, or between any foreign country or any territory or possession and any State or the District of Columbia, or between points in the same State but through any other State or the District of Columbia or a foreign country.

(d) Discrimination or segregation by an establishment is supported by State action within the meaning of this title if such discrimination or segregation (1) is carried on under color of any law, statute, ordinance, or regulation; or (2) is carried on under color of any custom or usage required or enforced by officials of the State or political subdivision thereof; or (3) is required by action of the State or political subdivision thereof.

(e) The provisions of this title shall not apply to a private club or other establishment not in fact open to the public, except to the extent that the facilities of such establishment are made available to the customers or patrons of an establishment within the scope of subsection (b).

SEC. 202. All persons shall be entitled to be free, at any establishment or place, from discrimination or segregation of any kind on the ground of race, color, religion, or national origin, if such discrimination or segregation is or purports to be required by any law, statute, ordinance, regulation, rule, or order of a State or any agency or political subdivision thereof.

SEC. 203. No person shall (a) withhold, deny, or attempt to withhold or deny, or deprive or attempt to deprive, any person of any right or privilege secured by section 201 or 202, or (b) intimidate, threaten, or coerce, or attempt to intimidate, threaten, or coerce any person with the purpose of interfering with any right or privilege secured by section 201 or 202, or (c) punish or attempt to punish any person for exercising or attempting to exercise any right or privilege secured by section 201 or 202.

SEC. 204. (a) Whenever any person has engaged or there are reasonable grounds to believe that any person is about to engage in any act or practice prohibited by section 203, a civil action for preventive relief, including an application for a permanent or temporary injunction, restraining order, or other order, may be instituted by the person aggrieved and, upon timely application, the court may, in its discretion, permit the Attorney General to intervene in such civil action if he certifies that the case is of general public importance. Upon application by the complainant and in such circumstances as the court may deem just, the court may appoint an attorney for such complainant and may authorize the commencement of the civil action without the payment of fees, costs, or security.

(b) In any action commenced pursuant to this title, the court, in its discretion, may allow the prevailing party, other than the United States, a reasonable attorney's fee as part of the costs, and the United States shall be liable for costs the same as a private person.

(c) In the case of an alleged act or practice prohibited by this title which occurs in a State, or political subdivision of a State, which has a State or local law prohibiting such act or practice and establishing or authorizing a State or

local authority to grant or seek relief from such practice or to institute criminal proceedings with respect thereto upon receiving notice thereof, no civil action may be brought under subsection (a) before the expiration of thirty days after written notice of such alleged act or practice has been given to the appropriate State or local authority by registered mail or in person, provided that the court may stay proceedings in such civil action pending the termination of State or local enforcement proceedings.

(d) In the case of an alleged act or practice prohibited by this title which occurs in a State, or political subdivision of a State, which has no State or local law prohibiting such act or practice, a civil action may be brought under subsection (a): Provided, That the court may refer the matter to the Community Relations Service established by title X of this Act for as long as the court believes there is a reasonable possibility of obtaining voluntary compliance, but for not more than sixty days: Provided further, That upon expiration of such sixty-day period, the court may extend such period for an additional period, not to exceed a cumulative total of one hundred and twenty days, if it believes there then exists a reasonable possibility of securing voluntary compliance.

SEC. 205. The Service is authorized to make a full investigation of any complaint referred to it by the court under section 204(d) and may hold such hearings with respect thereto as may be necessary. The Service shall conduct any hearings with respect to any such complaint in executive session, and shall not release any testimony given therein except by agreement of all parties involved in the complaint with the permission of the court, and the Service shall endeavor to bring about a voluntary settlement between the parties.

SEC. 206. (a) Whenever the Attorney General has reasonable cause to believe that any person or group of persons is engaged in a pattern or practice of resistance to the full enjoyment of any of the rights secured by this title, and that the pattern or practice is of such a nature and is intended to deny the full exercise of the rights herein described, the Attorney General may bring a civil action in the appropriate district court of the United States by filing with it a complaint (1) signed by him (or in his absence the Acting Attorney General), (2) setting forth facts pertaining to such pattern or practice, and (3) requesting such preventive relief, including an application for a permanent or temporary injunction, restraining order or other order against the person or persons responsible for such pattern or practice, as he deems necessary to insure the full enjoyment of the rights herein described.

(b) In any such proceeding the Attorney General may file with the clerk of such court a request that a court of three judges be convened to hear and determine the case. Such request by the Attorney General shall be accompanied by a certificate that, in his opinion, the case is of general public importance. A copy of the certificate and request for a three-judge court shall be immediately furnished by such clerk to the chief judge of the circuit (or in his absence, the presiding circuit judge of the circuit) in which the case is pending. Upon receipt of the copy of such request it shall be the duty of the chief judge of the circuit or the presiding circuit judge, as the case may be, to designate immediately three judges in such circuit, of whom at least one shall be a circuit judge and another of whom shall be a district judge of the court in which the proceeding was instituted, to hear and determine such case, and it shall be the duty of the judges so designated to assign the case for hearing at the earliest practicable date, to participate in the hearing and determination thereof, and to cause the case to be in every way expedited. An appeal from the final judgment of such court will lie to the Supreme Court.

In the event the Attorney General fails to file such a request in any such proceeding, it shall be the duty of the chief judge of the district (or in his absence, the acting chief judge) in which the case is pending immediately to designate a judge in such district to hear and determine the case. In the event that no judge in the district is available to hear and determine the case, the chief judge of the district, or the acting chief judge, as the case may be, shall certify this fact to the chief judge of the circuit (or in his absence, the acting chief judge) who shall then designate a district or circuit judge of the circuit to hear and determine the case.

It shall be the duty of the judge designated pursuant to this section to assign the case for hearing at the earliest practicable date and to cause the case to be in every way expedited.

SEC. 207. (a) The district courts of the United States shall have jurisdiction of proceedings instituted pursuant to this title and shall exercise the same without regard to whether the aggrieved party shall have exhausted any administrative or other remedies that may be provided by law.

(b) The remedies provided in this title shall be the exclusive means of enforcing the rights based on this title, but nothing in this title shall preclude any individual or any State or local agency from asserting any right based on any other Federal or State law not inconsistent with this title, including any statute or ordinance requiring nondiscrimination in public establishments or accommodations, or from pursuing any remedy, civil or criminal, which may be available for the vindication or enforcement of such right.

TITLE III—DESEGREGATION OF PUBLIC FACILITIES

SEC. 301. (a) Whenever the Attorney General receives a complaint in writing signed by an individual to the effect that he is being deprived of or threatened with the loss of his right to the equal protection of the laws, on account of his race, color, religion, or national origin, by being denied equal utilization of any public facility which is owned, operated, or managed by or on behalf of any State or subdivision thereof, other than a public school or public college as defined in section 401 of title IV hereof, and the Attorney General believes the complaint is meritorious and certifies that the signer or signers of such complaint are unable, in his judgment, to initiate and maintain appropriate legal proceedings for relief and that the institution of an action will materially further the orderly progress of desegregation in public facilities, the Attorney General is authorized to institute for or in the name of the United States a civil action in any appropriate district court of the United States against such parties and for such relief as may be appropriate, and such court shall have and shall exercise jurisdiction of proceedings instituted pursuant to this section. The Attorney General may implead as defendants such additional parties as are or become necessary to the grant of effective relief hereunder.

(b) The Attorney General may deem a person or persons unable to initiate and maintain appropriate legal proceedings within the meaning of subsection

(a) of this section when such person or persons are unable, either directly or through other interested persons or organizations, to bear the expense of the litigation or to obtain effective legal representation; or whenever he is satisfied that the institution of such litigation would jeopardize the personal safety, employment, or economic standing of such person or persons, their families, or their property.

SEC. 302. In any action or proceeding under this title the United States shall be liable for costs, including a reasonable attorney's fee, the same as a private person.

SEC. 303. Nothing in this title shall affect adversely the right of any person to sue for or obtain relief in any court against discrimination in any facility covered by this title.

SEC. 304. A complaint as used in this title is a writing or document within the meaning of section 1001, title 18, United States Code.

TITLE IV—DESEGREGATION OF PUBLIC EDUCATION

DEFINITIONS

SEC. 401. As used in this title—

(a) "Commissioner" means the Commissioner of Education.

(b) "Desegregation" means the assignment of students to public schools and within such schools without regard to their race, color, religion, or national origin, but "desegregation" shall not mean the assignment of students to public schools in order to overcome racial imbalance.

(c) "Public school" means any elementary or secondary educational institution, and "public college" means any institution of higher education or any technical or vocational school above the secondary school level, provided that such public school or public college is operated by a State, subdivision of a State, or governmental agency within a State, or operated wholly or predominantly from or through the use of governmental funds or property, or funds or property derived from a governmental source.

(d) "School board" means any agency or agencies which administer a system of one or more public schools and any other agency which is responsible for the assignment of students to or within such system.

SURVEY AND REPORT OF EDUCATIONAL OPPORTUNITIES

SEC. 402. The Commissioner shall conduct a survey and make a report to the President and the Congress, within two years of the enactment of this title, concerning the lack of availability of equal educational opportunities for individuals by reason of race, color, religion, or national origin in public educational institutions at all levels in the United States, its territories and possessions, and the District of Columbia.

TECHNICAL ASSISTANCE

SEC. 403. The Commissioner is authorized, upon the application of any school board, State, municipality, school district, or other governmental unit legally responsible for operating a public school or schools, to render technical assistance to such applicant in the preparation, adoption, and implementation of plans for the desegregation of public schools. Such technical assistance may, among other activities, include making available to such agencies information regarding effective methods of coping with special educational problems occasioned by desegregation, and making available to such agencies personnel of the Office of Education or other persons specially equipped to advise and assist them in coping with such problems.

TRAINING INSTITUTES

SEC. 404. The Commissioner is authorized to arrange, through grants or contracts, with institutions of higher education for the operation of short-term or regular session institutes for special training designed to improve the ability of teachers, supervisors, counselors, and other elementary or secondary school personnel to deal effectively with special educational problems occasioned by desegregation. Individuals who attend such an institute on a full-time basis may be paid stipends for the period of their attendance at such institute in amounts specified by the Commissioner in regulations, including allowances for travel to attend such institute.

GRANTS

SEC. 405. (a) The Commissioner is authorized, upon application of a school board, to make grants to such board to pay, in whole or in part, the cost of—

(1) giving to teachers and other school personnel inservice training in dealing with problems incident to desegregation, and

(2) employing specialists to advise in problems incident to desegregation.

(b) In determining whether to make a grant, and in fixing the amount thereof and the terms and conditions on which it will be made, the Commissioner shall take into consideration the amount available for grants under this section and the other applications which are pending before him; the financial condition of the applicant and the other resources available to it; the nature, extent, and gravity of its problems incident to desegregation; and such other factors as he finds relevant.

PAYMENTS

SEC. 406. Payments pursuant to a grant or contract under this title may be made (after necessary adjustments on account of previously made overpayments or underpayments) in advance or by way of reimbursement, and in such installments, as the Commissioner may determine.

SUITS BY THE ATTORNEY GENERAL

SEC. 407. (a) Whenever the Attorney General receives a complaint in writing—

(1) signed by a parent or group of parents to the effect that his or their minor children, as members of a class of persons similarly situated, are being deprived by a school board of the equal protection of the laws, or

(2) signed by an individual, or his parent, to the effect that he has been denied admission to or not permitted to continue in attendance at a public college by reason of race, color, religion, or national origin, and the Attorney General believes the complaint is meritorious and certifies that the signer or signers of such complaint are unable, in his judgment, to initiate and maintain appropriate legal proceedings for relief and that the institution of an action will materially further the orderly achievement of desegregation in public education, the Attorney General is authorized, after giving notice of such complaint to the appropriate school board or college authority and after certifying that he is satisfied that such board or authority has had a reasonable time to adjust the conditions alleged in such complaint, to institute for or in the name of the United States a civil action in any appropriate district court of the United States against such parties and for such relief as may be appropriate, and such court shall have and shall exercise jurisdiction of proceedings instituted pursuant to this section, provided that nothing herein shall empower any official or court of the United States to issue any order seeking to achieve a racial balance in any school by requiring the transportation of pupils or students from one school to another or one school district to another in order to achieve such racial balance, or otherwise enlarge the existing power of the court to insure compliance with constitutional standards. The Attorney General may implead as defendants such additional parties as are or become necessary to the grant of effective relief hereunder.

(b) The Attorney General may deem a person or persons unable to initiate and maintain appropriate legal proceedings within the meaning of subsection

(a) of this section when such person or persons are unable, either directly or through other interested persons or organizations, to bear the expense of the litigation or to obtain effective legal representation; or whenever he is satisfied that the institution of such litigation would jeopardize the personal safety, employment, or economic standing of such person or persons, their families, or their property.

(c) The term "parent" as used in this section includes any person standing in loco parentis. A "complaint" as used in this section is a writing or document within the meaning of section 1001, title 18, United States Code.

SEC. 408. In any action or proceeding under this title the United States shall be liable for costs the same as a private person.

SEC. 409. Nothing in this title shall affect adversely the right of any person to sue for or obtain relief in any court against discrimination in public education.

SEC. 410. Nothing in this title shall prohibit classification and assignment for reasons other than race, color, religion, or national origin.

TITLE V—COMMISSION ON CIVIL RIGHTS

SEC. 501. Section 102 of the Civil Rights Act of 1957 (42 U.S.C. 1975a; 71

Stat. 634) is amended to read as follows:

"RULES OF PROCEDURE OF THE COMMISSION HEARINGS

"SEC. 102. (a) At least thirty days prior to the commencement of any hearing, the Commission shall cause to be published in the Federal Register notice of the date on which such hearing is to commence, the place at which it is to be held and the subject of the hearing. The Chairman, or one designated by him to act as Chairman at a hearing of the Commission, shall announce in an opening statement the subject of the hearing.

"(b) A copy of the Commission's rules shall be made available to any witness before the Commission, and a witness compelled to appear before the Commission or required to produce written or other matter shall be served with a copy of the Commission's rules at the time of service of the subpoena.

"(c) Any person compelled to appear in person before the Commission shall be accorded the right to be accompanied and advised by counsel, who shall have the right to subject his client to reasonable examination, and to make objections on the record and to argue briefly the basis for such objections. The Commission shall proceed with reasonable dispatch to conclude any hearing in which it is engaged. Due regard shall be had for the convenience and necessity of witnesses.

"(d) The Chairman or Acting Chairman may punish breaches of order and decorum by censure and exclusion from the hearings.

"(e) If the Commission determines that evidence or testimony at any hearing may tend to defame, degrade, or incriminate any person, it shall receive such evidence or testimony or summary of such evidence o testimony in executive session. The Commission shall afford any person defamed, degraded, or incriminated by such evidence or testimony an opportunity to appear and be heard in executive session, with a reasonable number of additional witnesses requested by him, before deciding to use such evidence or testimony. In the event the Commission determines to release or use such evidence or testimony in such manner as to reveal publicly the identity of the person defamed, degraded, or incriminated, such evidence or testimony, prior to such public release or use, shall be given at a public session, and the Commission shall afford such person an opportunity to appear as a voluntary witness or to file a sworn statement in his behalf and to submit brief and pertinent sworn statements of others. The Commission shall receive and dispose of requests from such person to subpoena additional witnesses.

"(f) Except as provided in sections 102 and 105 (f) of this Act, the Chairman shall receive and the Commission shall dispose of requests to subpoena additional witnesses.

"(g) No evidence or testimony or summary of evidence or testimony taken in executive session may be released or used in public sessions without the consent of the Commission. Whoever releases or uses in public without the consent of the Commission such evidence or testimony taken in executive session shall be fined not more than $1,000, or imprisoned for not more than one year.

"(h) In the discretion of the Commission, witnesses may submit brief and pertinent sworn statements in writing for inclusion in the record. The Commission shall determine the pertinency of testimony and evidence adduced at its hearings.

"(i) Every person who submits data or evidence shall be entitled to retain or, on payment of lawfully prescribed costs, procure a copy or transcript thereof, except that a witness in a hearing held in executive session may for good cause be limited to inspection of the official transcript of his testimony. Transcript copies of public sessions may be obtained by the public upon the payment of the cost thereof. An accurate transcript shall be made of the testimony of all witnesses at all hearings, either public or executive sessions, of the Commission or of any subcommittee thereof.

"(j) A witness attending any session of the Commission shall receive $6 for each day's attendance and for the time necessarily occupied in going to and returning from the same, and 10 cents per mile for going from and returning to his place of residence. Witnesses who attend at points so far removed from their respective residences as to prohibit return thereto from day to day shall be entitled to an additional allowance of $10 per day for expenses of subsistence including the time necessarily occupied in going to and returning from the place of attendance. Mileage payments shall be tendered to the witness upon service of a subpoena issued on behalf of the Commission or any subcommittee thereof.

"(k) The Commission shall not issue any subpoena for the attendance and testimony of witnesses or for the production of written or other matter which would require the presence of the party subpoenaed at a hearing to be held outside of the State wherein the witness is found or resides or is domiciled or transacts business, or has appointed an agent for receipt of service of process except that, in any event, the Commission may issue subpoenas for the

attendance and testimony of witnesses and the production of written or other matter at a hearing held within fifty miles of the place where the witness is found or resides or is domiciled or transacts business or has appointed an agent for receipt of service of process.

"(l) The Commission shall separately state and currently publish in the Federal Register (1) descriptions of its central and field organization including the established places at which, and methods whereby, the public may secure information or make requests; (2) statements of the general course and method by which its functions are channeled and determined, and (3) rules adopted as authorized by law. No person shall in any manner be subject to or required to resort to rules, organization, or procedure not so published."

SEC. 502. Section 103(a) of the Civil Rights Act of 1957 (42 U.S.C.

1975b(a); 71 Stat. 634) is amended to read as follows:

"SEC. 103. (a) Each member of the Commission who is not otherwise in the service of the Government of the United States shall receive the sum of $75 per day for each day spent in the work of the Commission, shall be paid actual travel expenses, and per diem in lieu of subsistence expenses when away from his usual place of residence, in accordance with section 5 of the Administrative Expenses Act of 1946, as amended (5 U.S.C 73b-2; 60 Stat. 808)."

SEC. 503. Section 103(b) of the Civil Rights Act of 1957 (42 U.S.C.

1975(b); 71 Stat. 634) is amended to read as follows:

"(b) Each member of the Commission who is otherwise in the service of the Government of the United States shall serve without compensation in addition to that received for such other service, but while engaged in the work of the Commission shall be paid actual travel expenses, and per diem in lieu of subsistence expenses when away from his usual place of residence, in accordance with the provisions of the Travel Expenses Act of 1949, as amended

(5 U.S.C. 835—42; 63 Stat. 166)."

SEC. 504. (a) Section 104(a) of the Civil Rights Act of 1957 (42 U.S.C. 1975c(a); 71 Stat. 635), as amended, is further amended to read as follows:

"DUTIES OF THE COMMISSION

"SEC. 104. (a) The Commission shall—

"(1) investigate allegations in writing under oath or affirmation that certain citizens of the United States are being deprived of their right to vote and have that vote counted by reason of their color, race, religion, or national origin; which writing, under oath or affirmation, shall set forth the facts upon which such belief or beliefs are based;

"(2) study and collect information concerning legal developments constituting a denial of equal protection of the laws under the Constitution because of race, color, religion or national origin or in the administration of justice;

"(3) appraise the laws and policies of the Federal Government with respect to denials of equal protection of the laws under the Constitution because of race, color, religion or national origin or in the administration of justice;

"(4) serve as a national clearinghouse for information in respect to denials of equal protection of the laws because of race, color, religion or national origin, including but not limited to the fields of voting, education, housing, employment, the use of public facilities, and transportation, or in the administration of justice;

"(5) investigate allegations, made in writing and under oath or affirmation, that citizens of the United States are unlawfully being accorded or denied the right to vote, or to have their votes properly counted, in any election of presidential electors, Members of the United States Senate, or of the House of Representatives, as a result of any patterns or practice of fraud or discrimination in the conduct of such election; and

"(6) Nothing in this or any other Act shall be construed as authorizing the Commission, its Advisory Committees, or any person under its supervision or control to inquire into or investigate any membership practices or internal

operations of any fraternal organization, any college or university fraternity or sorority, any private club or any religious organization."

(b) Section 104(b) of the Civil Rights Act of 1957 (42 U.S.C. 1975c(b); 71 Stat. 635), as amended, is further amended by striking out the present subsection "(b)" and by substituting therefor:

"(b) The Commission shall submit interim reports to the President and to the Congress at such times as the Commission, the Congress or the President shall deem desirable, and shall submit to the President and to the Congress a final report of its activities, findings, and recommendations not later than January 31, 1968."

SEC. 505. Section 105(a) of the Civil Rights Act of 1957 (42 U.S.C. 1975d(a); 71 Stat. 636) is amended by striking out in the last sentence thereof "$50 per diem" and inserting in lieu thereof "$75 per diem."

SEC. 506. Section 105(f) and section 105(g) of the Civil Rights Act of 1957 (42 U.S.C. 1975d (f) and (g); 71 Stat. 636) are amended to read as follows:

"(f) The Commission, or on the authorization of the Commission any subcommittee of two or more members, at least one of whom shall be of each major political party, may, for the purpose of carrying out the provisions of this Act, hold such hearings and act at such times and places as the Commission or such authorized subcommittee may deem advisable. Subpoenas for the attendance and testimony of witnesses or the production of written or other matter may be issued in accordance with the rules of the Commission as contained in section 102 (j) and (k) of this Act, over the signature of the Chairman of the Commission or of such subcommittee, and may be served by any person designated by such Chairman. The holding of hearings by the Commission, or the appointment of a subcommittee to hold hearings pursuant to this subparagraph, must be approved by a majority of the Commission, or by a majority of the members present at a meeting at which at least a quorum of four members is present.

"(g) In case of contumacy or refusal to obey a subpoena, any district court of the United States or the United States court of any territory or possession, or the District Court of the United States for the District of Columbia, within the jurisdiction of which the inquiry is carried on or within the jurisdiction of which said person guilty of contumacy or refusal to obey is found or resides or is domiciled or transacts business, or has appointed an agent for receipt of service of process, upon application by the Attorney General of the United States shall have jurisdiction to issue to such person an order requiring such person to appear before the Commission or a subcommittee thereof, there to produce pertinent, relevant and nonprivileged evidence if so ordered, or there to give testimony touching the matter under investigation; and any failure to obey such order of the court may be punished by said court as a contempt thereof."

SEC. 507. Section 105 of the Civil Rights Act of 1957 (42 U.S.C. 1975d; 71 Stat. 636), as amended by section 401 of the Civil Rights Act of 1960 (42 U.S.C. 1975d(h); 74 Stat. 89), is further amended by adding a new subsection at the end to read as follows:

"(i) The Commission shall have the power to make such rules and regulations as are necessary to carry out the purposes of this Act."

TITLE VI—NONDISCRIMINATION IN FEDERALLY ASSISTED PROGRAMS

SEC. 601. No person in the United States shall, on the ground of race, color, or national origin, be excluded from participation in, be denied the benefits of, or be subjected to discrimination under any program or activity receiving Federal financial assistance.

SEC. 602. Each Federal department and agency which is empowered to extend Federal financial assistance to any program or activity, by way of grant, loan, or contract other than a contract of insurance or guaranty, is authorized and directed to effectuate the provisions of section 601 with respect to such program or activity by issuing rules, regulations, or orders of general applicability which shall be consistent with achievement of the objectives of the statute authorizing the financial assistance in connection with which the action is taken. No such rule, regulation, or order shall become effective unless and until approved by the President. Compliance with any requirement

adopted pursuant to this section may be effected (1) by the termination of or refusal to grant or to continue assistance under such program or activity to any recipient as to whom there has been an express finding on the record, after opportunity for hearing, of a failure to comply with such requirement, but such termination or refusal shall be limited to the particular political entity, or part thereof, or other recipient as to whom such a finding has been made and, shall be limited in its effect to the particular program, or part thereof, in which such non-compliance has been so found, or (2) by any other means authorized by law: Provided, however, That no such action shall be taken until the department or agency concerned has advised the appropriate person or persons of the failure to comply with the requirement and has determined that compliance cannot be secured by voluntary means. In the case of any action terminating, or refusing to grant or continue, assistance because of failure to comply with a requirement imposed pursuant to this section, the head of the federal department or agency shall file with the committees of the House and Senate having legislative jurisdiction over the program or activity involved a full written report of the circumstances and the grounds for such action. No such action shall become effective until thirty days have elapsed after the filing of such report.

SEC. 603. Any department or agency action taken pursuant to section 602 shall be subject to such judicial review as may otherwise be provided by law for similar action taken by such department or agency on other grounds. In the case of action, not otherwise subject to judicial review, terminating or refusing to grant or to continue financial assistance upon a finding of failure to comply with any requirement imposed pursuant to section 602, any person aggrieved (including any State or political subdivision thereof and any agency of either) may obtain judicial review of such action in accordance with section 10 of the Administrative Procedure Act, and such action shall not be deemed committed to unreviewable agency discretion within the meaning of that section.

SEC. 604. Nothing contained in this title shall be construed to authorize action under this title by any department or agency with respect to any employment practice of any employer, employment agency, or labor organization except where a primary objective of the Federal financial assistance is to provide employment.

SEC. 605. Nothing in this title shall add to or detract from any existing authority with respect to any program or activity under which Federal financial assistance is extended by way of a contract of insurance or guaranty.

TITLE VII—EQUAL EMPLOYMENT OPPORTUNITY DEFINITIONS

SEC. 701. For the purposes of this title—

(a) The term "person" includes one or more individuals, labor unions, partnerships, associations, corporations, legal representatives, mutual companies, joint-stock companies, trusts, unincorporated organizations, trustees, trustees in bankruptcy, or receivers.

(b) The term "employer" means a person engaged in an industry affecting commerce who has twenty-five or more employees for each working day in each of twenty or more calendar weeks in the current or preceding calendar year, and any agent of such a person, but such term does not include (1) the United States, a corporation wholly owned by the Government of the United States, an Indian tribe, or a State or political subdivision thereof, (2) a bona fide private membership club (other than a labor organization) which is exempt from taxation under section 501(c) of the Internal Revenue Code of 1954: Provided, That during the first year after the effective date prescribed in subsection (a) of section 716, persons having fewer than one hundred employees (and their agents) shall not be considered employers, and, during the second year after such date, persons having fewer than seventy-five employees (and their agents) shall not be considered employers, and, during the third year after such date, persons having fewer than fifty employees (and their agents) shall not be considered employers: Provided further, That it shall be the policy of the United States to insure equal employment opportunities for Federal employees without discrimination because of race, color, religion, sex or national origin and the President shall utilize his existing authority to effectuate this policy.

(c) The term "employment agency" means any person regularly undertaking with or without compensation to procure employees for an employer or to procure for employees opportunities to work for an employer and includes an agent of such a person; but shall not include an agency of the United States, or an agency of a State or political

subdivision of a State, except that such term shall include the United States Employment Service and the system of State and local employment services receiving Federal assistance.

(d) The term "labor organization" means a labor organization engaged in an industry affecting commerce, and any agent of such an organization, and includes any organization of any kind, any agency, or employee representation committee, group, association, or plan so engaged in which employees participate and which exists for the purpose, in whole or in part, of dealing with employers concerning grievances, labor disputes, wages, rates of pay, hours, or other terms or conditions of employment, and any conference, general committee, joint or system board, or joint council so engaged which is subordinate to a national or international labor organization.

(e) A labor organization shall be deemed to be engaged in an industry affecting commerce if (1) it maintains or operates a hiring hall or hiring office which procures employees for an employer or procures for employees opportunities to work for an employer, or (2) the number of its members (or, where it is a labor organization composed of other labor organizations or their representatives, if the aggregate number of the members of such other labor organization) is (A) one hundred or more during the first year after the effective date prescribed in subsection (a) of section 716, (B) seventy-five or more during the second year after such date or fifty or more during the third year, or (C) twenty-five or more thereafter, and such labor organization—

(1) is the certified representative of employees under the provisions of the National Labor Relations Act, as amended, or the Railway Labor Act, as amended;

(2) although not certified, is a national or international labor organization or a local labor organization recognized or acting as the representative of employees of an employer or employers engaged in an industry affecting commerce; or

(3) has chartered a local labor organization or subsidiary body which is representing or actively seeking to represent employees of employers within the meaning of paragraph (1) or (2); or

(4) has been chartered by a labor organization representing or actively seeking to represent employees within the meaning of paragraph (1) or (2) as the local or subordinate body through which such employees may enjoy membership or become affiliated with such labor organization; or

(5) is a conference, general committee, joint or system board, or joint council subordinate to a national or international labor organization, which includes a labor organization engaged in an industry affecting commerce within the meaning of any of the preceding paragraphs of this subsection.

(f) The term "employee" means an individual employed by an employer.

(g) The term "commerce" means trade, traffic, commerce, transportation, transmission, or communication among the several States; or between a State and any place outside thereof; or within the District of Columbia, or a possession of the United States; or between points in the same State but through a point outside thereof.

(h) The term "industry affecting commerce" means any activity, business, or industry in commerce or in which a labor dispute would hinder or obstruct commerce or the free flow of commerce and includes any activity or industry "affecting commerce" within the meaning of the Labor-Management Reporting and Disclosure Act of 1959.

(i) The term "State" includes a State of the United States, the District of Columbia, Puerto Rico, the Virgin Islands, American Samoa, Guam, Wake Island, The Canal Zone, and Outer Continental Shelf lands defined in the Outer Continental Shelf Lands Act.

EXEMPTION

SEC. 702. This title shall not apply to an employer with respect to the employment of aliens outside any State, or to a religious corporation, association, or society with respect to the employment of individuals of a particular religion to perform work connected with the carrying on by such corporation, association, or society of its religious activities or to an educational institution with respect to the employment of individuals to perform work connected with the educational activities of such institution.

DISCRIMINATION BECAUSE OF RACE, COLOR, RELIGION, SEX, OR NATIONAL ORIGIN

SEC. 703. (a) It shall be an unlawful employment practice for an employer—

(1) to fail or refuse to hire or to discharge any individual, or otherwise to discriminate against any individual with respect to his compensation, terms, conditions, or privileges of employment, because of such individual's race, color, religion, sex, or national origin; or

(2) to limit, segregate, or classify his employees in any way which would deprive or tend to deprive any individual of employment opportunities or otherwise adversely affect his status as an employee, because of such individual's race, color, religion, sex, or national origin.

(b) It shall be an unlawful employment practice for an employment agency to fail or refuse to refer for employment, or otherwise to discriminate against, any individual because of his race, color, religion, sex, or national origin, or to classify or refer for employment any individual on the basis of his race, color, religion, sex, or national origin.

(c) It shall be an unlawful employment practice for a labor organization—

(1) to exclude or to expel from its membership, or otherwise to discriminate against, any individual because of his race, color, religion, sex, or national origin;

(2) to limit, segregate, or classify its membership, or to classify or fail or refuse to refer for employment any individual, in any way which would deprive or tend to deprive any individual of employment opportunities, or would limit such employment opportunities or otherwise adversely affect his status as an employee or as an applicant for employment, because of such individual's race, color, religion, sex, or national origin; or

(3) to cause or attempt to cause an employer to discriminate against an individual in violation of this section.

(d) It shall be an unlawful employment practice for any employer, labor organization, or joint labor-management committee controlling apprenticeship or other training or retraining, including on-the-job training programs to discriminate against any individual because of his race, color, religion, sex, or national origin in admission to, or employment in, any program established to provide apprenticeship or other training.

(e) Notwithstanding any other provision of this title, (1) it shall not be an unlawful employment practice for an employer to hire and employ employees, for an employment agency to classify, or refer for employment any individual, for a labor organization to classify its membership or to classify or refer for employment any individual, or for an employer, labor organization, or joint labor-management committee controlling apprenticeship or other training or retraining programs to admit or employ any individual in any such program, on the basis of his religion, sex, or national origin in those certain instances where religion, sex, or national origin is a bona fide occupational qualification reasonably necessary to the normal operation of that particular business or enterprise, and (2) it shall not be an unlawful employment practice for a school, college, university, or other educational institution or institution of learning to hire and employ employees of a particular religion if such school, college, university, or other educational institution or institution of learning is, in whole or in substantial part, owned, supported, controlled, or managed by a particular religion or by a particular religious corporation, association, or society, or if the curriculum of such school, college, university, or other educational institution or institution of learning is directed toward the propagation of a particular religion.

(f) As used in this title, the phrase "unlawful employment practice" shall not be deemed to include any action or measure taken by an employer, labor organization, joint labor-management committee, or employment agency with respect to an individual who is a member of the Communist Party of the United States or of any other organization required to register as a Communist-action or Communist-front organization by final order of the Subversive Activities Control Board pursuant to the Subversive Activities Control Act of 1950.

(g) Notwithstanding any other provision of this title, it shall not be an unlawful employment practice for an employer to fail or refuse to hire and employ any individual for any position, for an employer to discharge any individual from

any position, or for an employment agency to fail or refuse to refer any individual for employment in any position, or for a labor organization to fail or refuse to refer any individual for employment in any position, if—

(1) the occupancy of such position, or access to the premises in or upon which any part of the duties of such position is performed or is to be performed, is subject to any requirement imposed in the interest of the national security of the United States under any security program in effect pursuant to or administered under any statute of the United States or any Executive order of the President; and

(2) such individual has not fulfilled or has ceased to fulfill that requirement.

(h) Notwithstanding any other provision of this title, it shall not be an unlawful employment practice for an employer to apply different standards of compensation, or different terms, conditions, or privileges of employment pursuant to a bona fide seniority or merit system, or a system which measures earnings by quantity or quality of production or to employees who work in different locations, provided that such differences are not the result of an intention to discriminate because of race, color, religion, sex, or national origin, nor shall it be an unlawful employment practice for an employer to give and to act upon the results of any professionally developed ability test provided that such test, its administration or action upon the results is not designed, intended or used to discriminate because of race, color, religion, sex or national origin. It shall not be an unlawful employment practice under this title for any employer to differentiate upon the basis of sex in determining the amount of the wages or compensation paid or to be paid to employees of such employer if such differentiation is authorized by the provisions of section 6(d) of the Fair Labor Standards Act of 1938, as amended (29 U.S.C. 206(d)).

(i) Nothing contained in this title shall apply to any business or enterprise on or near an Indian reservation with respect to any publicly announced employment practice of such business or enterprise under which a preferential treatment is given to any individual because he is an Indian living on or near a reservation.

(j) Nothing contained in this title shall be interpreted to require any employer, employment agency, labor organization, or joint labor-management committee subject to this title to grant preferential treatment to any individual or to any group because of the race, color, religion, sex, or national origin of such individual or group on account of an imbalance which may exist with respect to the total number or percentage of persons of any race, color, religion, sex, or national origin employed by any employer, referred or classified for employment by any employment agency or labor organization, admitted to membership or classified by any labor organization, or admitted to, or employed in, any apprenticeship or other training program, in comparison with the total number or percentage of persons of such race, color, religion, sex, or national origin in any community, State, section, or other area, or in the available work force in any community, State, section, or other area.

OTHER UNLAWFUL EMPLOYMENT PRACTICES

SEC. 704. (a) It shall be an unlawful employment practice for an employer to discriminate against any of his employees or applicants for employment, for an employment agency to discriminate against any individual, or for a labor organization to discriminate against any member thereof or applicant for membership, because he has opposed, any practice made an unlawful employment practice by this title, or because he has made a charge, testified, assisted, or participated in any manner in an investigation, proceeding, or hearing under this title.

(b) It shall be an unlawful employment practice for an employer, labor organization, or employment agency to print or publish or cause to be printed or published any notice or advertisement relating to employment by such an employer or membership in or any classification or referral for employment by such a labor organization, or relating to any classification or referral for employment by such an employment agency, indicating any preference, limitation, specification, or discrimination, based on race, color, religion, sex, or national origin, except that such a notice or advertisement may indicate a preference, limitation, specification, or discrimination based on religion, sex, or national origin when religion, sex, or national origin is a bona fide occupational qualification for employment.

EQUAL EMPLOYMENT OPPORTUNITY COMMISSION

SEC. 705. (a) There is hereby created a Commission to be known as the Equal Employment Opportunity Commission, which shall be composed of five members, not more than three of whom shall be members of the same political party, who shall be appointed by the President by and with the advice and consent of the Senate. One of the original members shall be appointed for a term of one year, one for a term of two years, one for a term of three years, one for a term of four years, and one for a term of five years, beginning from the date of enactment of this title, but their successors shall be appointed for terms of five years each, except that any individual chosen to fill a vacancy shall be appointed only for the unexpired term of the member whom he shall succeed. The President shall designate one member to serve as Chairman of the Commission, and one member to serve as Vice Chairman. The Chairman shall be responsible on behalf of the Commission for the administrative operations of the Commission, and shall appoint, in accordance with the civil service laws, such officers, agents, attorneys, and employees as it deems necessary to assist it in the performance of its functions and to fix their compensation in accordance with the Classification Act of 1949, as amended. The Vice Chairman shall act as Chairman in the absence or disability of the Chairman or in the event of a vacancy in that office.

(b) A vacancy in the Commission shall not impair the right of the remaining members to exercise all the powers of the Commission and three members thereof shall constitute a quorum.

(c) The Commission shall have an official seal which shall be judicially noticed.

(d) The Commission shall at the close of each fiscal year report to the Congress and to the President concerning the action it has taken; the names, salaries, and duties of all individuals in its employ and the moneys it has disbursed; and shall make such further reports on the cause of and means of eliminating discrimination and such recommendations for further legislation as may appear desirable.

(e) The Federal Executive Pay Act of 1956, as amended (5 U.S.C. 2201-2209), is further amended—

(1) by adding to section 105 thereof (5 U.S.C. 2204) the following clause:

"(32) Chairman, Equal Employment Opportunity Commission"; and

(2) by adding to clause (45) of section 106(a) thereof (5 U.S.C. 2205(a)) the following: "Equal Employment Opportunity Commission (4)."

(f) The principal office of the Commission shall be in or near the District of Columbia, but it may meet or exercise any or all its powers at any other place. The Commission may establish such regional or State offices as it deems necessary to accomplish the purpose of this title.

(g) The Commission shall have power—

(1) to cooperate with and, with their consent, utilize regional, State, local, and other agencies, both public and private, and individuals;

(2) to pay to witnesses whose depositions are taken or who are summoned before the Commission or any of its agents the same witness and mileage fees as are paid to witnesses in the courts of the United States;

(3) to furnish to persons subject to this title such technical assistance as they may request to further their compliance with this title or an order issued thereunder;

(4) upon the request of (i) any employer, whose employees or some of them, or (ii) any labor organization, whose members or some of them, refuse or threaten to refuse to cooperate in effectuating the provisions of this title, to assist in such effectuation by conciliation or such other remedial action as is provided by this title;

(5) to make such technical studies as are appropriate to effectuate the purposes and policies of this title and to make the results of such studies available to the public;

(6) to refer matters to the Attorney General with recommendations for intervention in a civil action brought by an aggrieved party under section 706, or for the institution of a civil action by the Attorney General under section 707, and to advise, consult, and assist the Attorney General on such matters.

(h) Attorneys appointed under this section may, at the direction of the Commission, appear for and represent the Commission in any case in court.

(i) The Commission shall, in any of its educational or promotional activities, cooperate with other departments and agencies in the performance of such educational and promotional activities.

(j) All officers, agents, attorneys, and employees of the Commission shall be subject to the provisions of section 9 of the Act of August 2, 1939, as amended (the Hatch Act), notwithstanding any exemption contained in such section.

PREVENTION OF UNLAWFUL EMPLOYMENT PRACTICES

SEC. 706. (a) Whenever it is charged in writing under oath by a person claiming to be aggrieved, or a written charge has been filed by a member of the Commission where he has reasonable cause to believe a violation of this title has occurred (and such charge sets forth the facts upon which it is based) that an employer, employment agency, or labor organization has engaged in an unlawful employment practice, the Commission shall furnish such employer, employment agency, or labor organization (hereinafter referred to as the "respondent") with a copy of such charge and shall make an investigation of such charge, provided that such charge shall not be made public by the Commission. If the Commission shall determine, after such investigation, that there is reasonable cause to believe that the charge is true, the Commission shall endeavor to eliminate any such alleged unlawful employment practice by informal methods of conference, conciliation, and persuasion. Nothing said or done during and as a part of such endeavors may be made public by the Commission without the written consent of the parties, or used as evidence in a subsequent proceeding. Any officer or employee of the Commission, who shall make public in any manner whatever any information in violation of this subsection shall be deemed guilty of a misdemeanor and upon conviction thereof shall be fined not more than $1,000 or imprisoned not more than one year.

(b) In the case of an alleged unlawful employment practice occurring in a State, or political subdivision of a State, which has a State or local law prohibiting the unlawful employment practice alleged and establishing or authorizing a State or local authority to grant or seek relief from such practice or to institute criminal proceedings with respect thereto upon receiving notice thereof, no charge may be filed under subsection (a) by the person aggrieved before the expiration of sixty days after proceedings have been commenced under the State or local law, unless such proceedings have been earlier terminated, provided that such sixty-day period shall be extended to one hundred and twenty days during the first year after the effective date of such State or local law. If any requirement for the commencement of such proceedings is imposed by a State or local authority other than a requirement of the filing of a written and signed statement of the facts upon which the proceeding is based, the proceeding shall be deemed to have been commenced for the purposes of this subsection at the time such statement is sent by registered mail to the appropriate State or local authority.

(c) In the case of any charge filed by a member of the Commission alleging an unlawful employment practice occurring in a State or political subdivision of a State, which has a State or local law prohibiting the practice alleged and establishing or authorizing a State or local authority to grant or seek relief from such practice or to institute criminal proceedings with respect thereto upon receiving notice thereof, the Commission shall, before taking any action with respect to such charge, notify the appropriate State or local officials and, upon request, afford them a reasonable time, but not less than sixty days (provided that such sixty-day period shall be extended to one hundred and twenty days during the first year after the effective day of such State or local law), unless a shorter period is requested, to act under such State or local law to remedy the practice alleged.

(d) A charge under subsection (a) shall be filed within ninety days after the alleged unlawful employment practice occurred, except that in the case of an unlawful employment practice with respect to which the person aggrieved has followed the procedure set out in subsection (b), such charge shall be filed by the person aggrieved within two

hundred and ten days after the alleged unlawful employment practice occurred, or within thirty days after receiving notice that the State or local agency has terminated the proceedings under the State or local, law, whichever is earlier, and a copy of such charge shall be filed by the Commission with the State or local agency.

(e) If within thirty days after a charge is filed with the Commission or within thirty days after expiration of any period of reference under subsection (c) (except that in either case such period may be extended to not more than sixty days upon a determination by the Commission that further efforts to secure voluntary compliance are warranted), the Commission has been unable to obtain voluntary compliance with this title, the Commission shall so notify the person aggrieved and a civil action may, within thirty days thereafter, be brought against the respondent named in the charge (1) by the person claiming to be aggrieved, or (2) if such charge was filed by a member of the Commission, by any person whom the charge alleges was aggrieved by the alleged unlawful employment practice. Upon application by the complainant and in such circumstances as the court may deem just, the court may appoint an attorney for such complainant and may authorize the commencement of the action without the payment of fees, costs, or security. Upon timely application, the court may, in its discretion, permit the Attorney General to intervene in such civil action if he certifies that the case is of general public importance. Upon request, the court may, in its discretion, stay further proceedings for not more than sixty days pending the termination of State or local proceedings described in subsection (b) or the efforts of the Commission to obtain voluntary compliance.

(f) Each United States district court and each United States court of a place subject to the jurisdiction of the United States shall have jurisdiction of actions brought under this title. Such an action may be brought in any judicial district in the State in which the unlawful employment practice is alleged to have been committed, in the judicial district in which the employment records relevant to such practice are maintained and administered, or in the judicial district in which the plaintiff would have worked but for the alleged unlawful employment practice, but if the respondent is not found within any such district, such an action may be brought within the judicial district in which the respondent has his principal office. For purposes of sections 1404 and 1406 of title 28 of the United States Code, the judicial district in which the respondent has his principal office shall in all cases be considered a district in which the action might have been brought.

(g) If the court finds that the respondent has intentionally engaged in or is intentionally engaging in an unlawful employment practice charged in the complaint, the court may enjoin the respondent from engaging in such unlawful employment practice, and order such affirmative action as may be appropriate, which may include reinstatement or hiring of employees, with or without back pay (payable by the employer, employment agency, or labor organization, as the case may be, responsible for the unlawful employment practice). Interim earnings or amounts earnable with reasonable diligence by the person or persons discriminated against shall operate to reduce the back pay otherwise allowable. No order of the court shall require the admission or reinstatement of an individual as a member of a union or the hiring, reinstatement, or promotion of an individual as an employee, or the payment to him of any back pay, if such individual was refused admission, suspended, or expelled or was refused employment or advancement or was suspended or discharged for any reason other than discrimination on account of race, color, religion, sex or national origin or in violation of section 704(a).

(h) The provisions of the Act entitled "An Act to amend the Judicial Code and to define and limit the jurisdiction of courts sitting in equity, and for other purposes," approved March 23, 1932 (29 U.S.C. 101-115), shall not apply with respect to civil actions brought under this section.

(i) In any case in which an employer, employment agency, or labor organization fails to comply with an order of a court issued in a civil action brought under subsection (e), the Commission may commence proceedings to compel compliance with such order.

(j) Any civil action brought under subsection (e) and any proceedings brought under subsection (i) shall be subject to appeal as provided in sections 1291 and 1292, title 28, United States Code.

(k) In any action or proceeding under this title the court, in its discretion, may allow the prevailing party, other than the Commission or the United States, a reasonable attorney's fee as part of the costs, and the Commission and the United States shall be liable for costs the same as a private person.

SEC. 707. (a) Whenever the Attorney General has reasonable cause to believe that any person or group of persons is engaged in a pattern or practice of resistance to the full enjoyment of any of the rights secured by this title, and that the pattern or practice is of such a nature and is intended to deny the full exercise of the rights herein described, the Attorney General may bring a civil action in the appropriate district court of the United States by filing with it a complaint (1) signed by him (or in his absence the Acting Attorney General), (2) setting forth facts pertaining to such pattern or practice, and (3) requesting such relief, including an application for a permanent or temporary injunction, restraining order or other order against the person or persons responsible for such pattern or practice, as he deems necessary to insure the full enjoyment of the rights herein described.

(b) The district courts of the United States shall have and shall exercise jurisdiction of proceedings instituted pursuant to this section, and in any such proceeding the Attorney General may file with the clerk of such court a request that a court of three judges be convened to hear and determine the case. Such request by the Attorney General shall be accompanied by a certificate that, in his opinion, the case is of general public importance. A copy of the certificate and request for a three-judge court shall be immediately furnished by such clerk to the chief judge of the circuit (or in his absence, the presiding circuit judge of the circuit) in which the case is pending. Upon receipt of such request it shall be the duty of the chief judge of the circuit or the presiding circuit judge, as the case may be, to designate immediately three judges in such circuit, of whom at least one shall be a circuit judge and another of whom shall be a district judge of the court in which the proceeding was instituted, to hear and determine such case, and it shall be the duty of the judges so designated to assign the case for hearing at the earliest practicable date, to participate in the hearing and determination thereof, and to cause the case to be in every way expedited. An appeal from the final judgment of such court will lie to the Supreme Court.

In the event the Attorney General fails to file such a request in any such proceeding, it shall be the duty of the chief judge of the district (or in his absence, the acting chief judge) in which the case is pending immediately to designate a judge in such district to hear and determine the case. In the event that no judge in the district is available to hear and determine the case, the chief judge of the district, or the acting chief judge, as the case may be, shall certify this fact to the chief judge of the circuit (or in his absence, the acting chief judge) who shall then designate a district or circuit judge of the circuit to hear and determine the case.

It shall be the duty of the judge designated pursuant to this section to assign the case for hearing at the earliest practicable date and to cause the case to be in every way expedited.

EFFECT ON STATE LAWS

SEC. 708. Nothing in this title shall be deemed to exempt or relieve any person from any liability, duty, penalty, or punishment provided by any present or future law of any State or political subdivision of a State, other than any such law which purports to require or permit the doing of any act which would be an unlawful employment practice under this title.

INVESTIGATIONS, INSPECTIONS, RECORDS, STATE AGENCIES

SEC. 709. (a) In connection with any investigation of a charge filed under section 706, the Commission or its designated representative shall at all reasonable times have access to, for the purposes of examination, and the right to copy any evidence of any person being investigated or proceeded against that relates to unlawful employment practices covered by this title and is relevant to the charge under investigation.

(b) The Commission may cooperate with State and local agencies charged with the administration of State fair employment practices laws and, with the consent of such agencies, may for the purpose of carrying out its functions and duties under this title and within the limitation of funds appropriated specifically for such purpose, utilize the

services of such agencies and their employees and, notwithstanding any other provision of law, may reimburse such agencies and their employees for services rendered to assist the Commission in carrying out this title. In furtherance of such cooperative efforts, the Commission may enter into written agreements with such State or local agencies and such agreements may include provisions under which the Commission shall refrain from processing a charge in any cases or class of cases specified in such agreements and under which no person may bring a civil action under section 706 in any cases or class of cases so specified, or under which the Commission shall relieve any person or class of persons in such State or locality from requirements imposed under this section. The Commission shall rescind any such agreement whenever it determines that the agreement no longer serves the interest of effective enforcement of this title.

(c) Except as provided in subsection (d), every employer, employment agency, and labor organization subject to this title shall (1) make and keep such records relevant to the determinations of whether unlawful employment practices have been or are being committed, (2) preserve such records for such periods, and (3) make such reports therefrom, as the Commission shall prescribe by regulation or order, after public hearing, as reasonable, necessary, or appropriate for the enforcement of this title or the regulations or orders thereunder. The Commission shall, by regulation, require each employer, labor organization, and joint labor-management committee subject to this title which controls an apprenticeship or other training program to maintain such records as are reasonably necessary to carry out the purpose of this title, including, but not limited to, a list of applicants who wish to participate in such program, including the chronological order in which such applications were received, and shall furnish to the Commission, upon request, a detailed description of the manner in which persons are selected to participate in the apprenticeship or other training program. Any employer, employment agency, labor organization, or joint labor-management committee which believes that the application to it of any regulation or order issued under this section would result in undue hardship may (1) apply to the Commission for an exemption from the application of such regulation or order, or (2) bring a civil action in the United States district court for the district where such records are kept. If the Commission or the court, as the case may be, finds that the application of the regulation or order to the employer, employment agency, or labor organization in question would impose an undue hardship, the Commission or the court, as the case may be, may grant appropriate relief.

(d) The provisions of subsection (c) shall not apply to any employer, employment agency, labor organization, or joint labor-management committee with respect to matters occurring in any State or political subdivision thereof which has a fair employment practice law during any period in which such employer, employment agency, labor organization, or joint labor-management committee is subject to such law, except that the Commission may require such notations on records which such employer, employment agency, labor organization, or joint labor-management committee keeps or is required to keep as are necessary because of differences in coverage or methods of enforcement between the State or local law and the provisions of this title. Where an employer is required by Executive Order 10925, issued March 6, 1961, or by any other Executive order prescribing fair employment practices for Government contractors and subcontractors, or by rules or regulations issued thereunder, to file reports relating to his employment practices with any Federal agency or committee, and he is substantially in compliance with such requirements, the Commission shall not require him to file additional reports pursuant to subsection (c) of this section.

(e) It shall be unlawful for any officer or employee of the Commission to make public in any manner whatever any information obtained by the Commission pursuant to its authority under this section prior to the institution of any proceeding under this title involving such information. Any officer or employee of the Commission who shall make public in any manner whatever any information in violation of this subsection shall be guilty of a misdemeanor and upon conviction thereof, shall be fined not more than $1,000, or imprisoned not more than one year.

INVESTIGATORY POWERS

SEC. 710. (a) For the purposes of any investigation of a charge filed under the authority contained in section 706, the Commission shall have authority to examine witnesses under oath and to require the production of documentary evidence relevant or material to the charge under investigation.

(b) If the respondent named in a charge filed under section 706 fails or refuses to comply with a demand of the Commission for permission to examine or to copy evidence in conformity with the provisions of section 709(a), or if any person required to comply with the provisions of section 709 (c) or (d) fails or refuses to do so, or if any person fails or refuses to comply with a demand by the Commission to give testimony under oath, the United States district court for the district in which such person is found, resides, or transacts business, shall, upon application of the Commission, have jurisdiction to issue to such person an order requiring him to comply with the provisions of section 709 (c) or (d) or to comply with the demand of the Commission, but the attendance of a witness may not be required outside the State where he is found, resides, or transacts business and the production of evidence may not be required outside the State where such evidence is kept.

(c) Within twenty days after the service upon any person charged under section 706 of a demand by the Commission for the production of documentary evidence or for permission to examine or to copy evidence in conformity with the provisions of section 709(a), such person may file in the district court of the United States for the judicial district in which he resides, is found, or transacts business, and serve upon the Commission a petition for an order of such court modifying or setting aside such demand. The time allowed for compliance with the demand in whole or in part as deemed proper and ordered by the court shall not run during the pendency of such petition in the court. Such petition shall specify each ground upon which the petitioner relies in seeking such relief, and may be based upon any failure of such demand to comply with the provisions of this title or with the limitations generally applicable to compulsory process or upon any constitutional or other legal right or privilege of such person. No objection which is not raised by such a petition may be urged in the defense to a proceeding initiated by the Commission under subsection (b) for enforcement of such a demand unless such proceeding is commenced by the Commission prior to the expiration of the twenty-day period, or unless the court determines that the defendant could not reasonably have been aware of the availability of such ground of objection.

(d) In any proceeding brought by the Commission under subsection (b), except as provided in subsection (c) of this section, the defendant may petition the court for an order modifying or setting aside the demand of the Commission.

SEC. 711. (a) Every employer, employment agency, and labor organization, as the case may be, shall post and keep posted in conspicuous places upon its premises where notices to employees, applicants for employment, and members are customarily posted a notice to be prepared or approved by the Commission setting forth excerpts from or, summaries of, the pertinent provisions of this title and information pertinent to the filing of a complaint.

(b) A willful violation of this section shall be punishable by a fine of not more than $100 for each separate offense.

VETERANS' PREFERENCE

SEC. 712. Nothing contained in this title shall be construed to repeal or modify any Federal, State, territorial, or local law creating special rights or preference for veterans.

RULES AND REGULATIONS

SEC. 713. (a) The Commission shall have authority from time to time to issue, amend, or rescind suitable procedural regulations to carry out the provisions of this title. Regulations issued under this section shall be in conformity with the standards and limitations of the Administrative Procedure Act.

(b) In any action or proceeding based on any alleged unlawful employment practice, no person shall be subject to any liability or punishment for or on account of (1) the commission by such person of an unlawful employment practice if he pleads and proves that the act or omission complained of was in good faith, in conformity with, and in reliance on any written interpretation or opinion of the Commission, or (2) the failure of such person to publish and file any information required by any provision of this title if he pleads and proves that he failed to publish and file such information in good faith, in conformity with the instructions of the Commission issued under this title regarding the filing of such information. Such a defense, if established, shall be a bar to the action or proceeding, notwithstanding that (A) after such act or omission, such interpretation or opinion is modified or rescinded or is

determined by judicial authority to be invalid or of no legal effect, or (B) after publishing or filing the description and annual reports, such publication or filing is determined by judicial authority not to be in conformity with the requirements of this title.

FORCIBLY RESISTING THE COMMISSION OR ITS REPRESENTATIVES

SEC. 714. The provisions of section 111, title 18, United States Code, shall apply to officers, agents, and employees of the Commission in the performance of their official duties.

SPECIAL STUDY BY SECRETARY OF LABOR

SEC. 715. The Secretary of Labor shall make a full and complete study of the factors which might tend to result in discrimination in employment because of age and of the consequences of such discrimination on the economy and individuals affected. The Secretary of Labor shall make a report to the Congress not later than June 30, 1965, containing the results of such study and shall include in such report such recommendations for legislation to prevent arbitrary discrimination in employment because of age as he determines advisable.

EFFECTIVE DATE

SEC. 716. (a) This title shall become effective one year after the date of its enactment.

(b) Notwithstanding subsection (a), sections of this title other than sections 703, 704, 706, and 707 shall become effective immediately.

(c) The President shall, as soon as feasible after the enactment of this title, convene one or more conferences for the purpose of enabling the leaders of groups whose members will be affected by this title to become familiar with the rights afforded and obligations imposed by its provisions, and for the purpose of making plans which will result in the fair and effective administration of this title when all of its provisions become effective. The President shall invite the participation in such conference or conferences of (1) the members of the President's Committee on Equal Employment Opportunity, (2) the members of the Commission on Civil Rights, (3) representatives of State and local agencies engaged in furthering equal employment opportunity, (4) representatives of private agencies engaged in furthering equal employment opportunity, and (5) representatives of employers, labor organizations, and employment agencies who will be subject to this title.

TITLE VIII—REGISTRATION AND VOTING STATISTICS

SEC. 801. The Secretary of Commerce shall promptly conduct a survey to compile registration and voting statistics in such geographic areas as may be recommended by the Commission on Civil Rights. Such a survey and compilation shall, to the extent recommended by the Commission on Civil Rights, only include a count of persons of voting age by race, color, and national origin, and determination of the extent to which such persons are registered to vote, and have voted in any statewide primary or general election in which the Members of the United States House of Representatives are nominated or elected, since January 1, 1960. Such information shall also be collected and compiled in connection with the Nineteenth Decennial Census, and at such other times as the Congress may prescribe. The provisions of section 9 and chapter 7 of title 13, United States Code, shall apply to any survey, collection, or compilation of registration and voting statistics carried out under this title: Provided, however, That no person shall be compelled to disclose his race, color, national origin, or questioned about his political party affiliation, how he voted, or the reasons therefore, nor shall any penalty be imposed for his failure or refusal to make such disclosure. Every person interrogated orally, by written survey or questionnaire or by any other means with respect to such information shall be fully advised with respect to his right to fail or refuse to furnish such information.

TITLE IX—INTERVENTION AND PROCEDURE AFTER REMOVAL IN CIVIL RIGHTS CASES

SEC. 901. Title 28 of the United States Code, section 1447(d), is amended to read as follows:

"An order remanding a case to the State court from which it was removed is not reviewable on appeal or otherwise, except that an order remanding a case to the State court from which it was removed pursuant to section 1443 of this title shall be reviewable by appeal or otherwise."

SEC. 902. Whenever an action has been commenced in any court of the United States seeking relief from the denial of equal protection of the laws under the fourteenth amendment to the Constitution on account of race, color, religion, or national origin, the Attorney General for or in the name of the United States may intervene in such action upon timely application if the Attorney General certifies that the case is of general public importance. In such action the United States shall be entitled to the same relief as if it had instituted the action.

TITLE X—ESTABLISHMENT OF COMMUNITY RELATIONS SERVICE

SEC. 1001. (a) There is hereby established in and as a part of the Department of Commerce a Community Relations Service (hereinafter referred to as the "Service"), which shall be headed by a Director who shall be appointed by the President with the advice and consent of the Senate for a term of four years. The Director is authorized to appoint, subject to the civil service laws and regulations, such other personnel as may be necessary to enable the Service to carry out its functions and duties, and to fix their compensation in accordance with the Classification Act of 1949, as amended. The Director is further authorized to procure services as authorized by section 15 of the Act of August 2, 1946 (60 Stat. 810; 5 U.S.C. 55(a)), but at rates for individuals not in excess of $75 per diem.

(b) Section 106(a) of the Federal Executive Pay Act of 1956, as amended (5 U.S.C. 2205(a)), is further amended by adding the following clause thereto:

"(52) Director, Community Relations Service."

SEC. 1002. It shall be the function of the Service to provide assistance to communities and persons therein in resolving disputes, disagreements, or difficulties relating to discriminatory practices based on race, color, or national origin which impair the rights of persons in such communities under the Constitution or laws of the United States or which affect or may affect interstate commerce. The Service may offer its services in cases of such disputes, disagreements, or difficulties whenever, in its judgment, peaceful relations among the citizens of the community involved are threatened thereby, and it may offer its services either upon its own motion or upon the request of an appropriate State or local official or other interested person.

SEC. 1003. (a) The Service shall, whenever possible, in performing its functions, seek and utilize the cooperation of appropriate State or local, public, or private agencies.

(b) The activities of all officers and employees of the Service in providing conciliation assistance shall be conducted in confidence and without publicity, and the Service shall hold confidential any information acquired in the regular performance of its duties upon the understanding that it would be so held. No officer or employee of the Service shall engage in the performance of investigative or prosecuting functions of any department or agency in any litigation arising out of a dispute in which he acted on behalf of the Service. Any officer or other employee of the Service, who shall make public in any manner whatever any information in violation of this subsection, shall be deemed guilty of a misdemeanor and, upon conviction thereof, shall be fined not more than $1,000 or imprisoned not more than one year.

SEC. 1004. Subject to the provisions of sections 205 and 1003(b), the Director shall, on or before January 31 of each year, submit to the Congress a report of the activities of the Service during the preceding fiscal year.

TITLE XI—MISCELLANEOUS

SEC. 1101. In any proceeding for criminal contempt arising under title II, III, IV, V, VI, or VII of this Act, the accused, upon demand therefor, shall be entitled to a trial by jury, which shall conform as near as may be to the practice in criminal cases. Upon conviction, the accused shall not be fined more than $1,000 or imprisoned for more than six months.

This section shall not apply to contempts committed in the presence of the court, or so near thereto as to obstruct the administration of justice, nor to the misbehavior, misconduct, or disobedience of any officer of the court in respect to writs, orders, or process of the court. No person shall be convicted of criminal contempt hereunder unless the act or omission constituting such contempt shall have been intentional, as required in other cases of criminal contempt.

Nor shall anything herein be construed to deprive courts of their power, by civil contempt proceedings, without a jury, to secure compliance with or to prevent obstruction of, as distinguished from punishment for violations of, any lawful writ, process, order, rule, decree, or command of the court in accordance with the prevailing usages of law and equity, including the power of detention.

SEC. 1102. No person should be put twice in jeopardy under the laws of the United States for the same act or omission. For this reason, an acquittal or conviction in a prosecution for a specific crime under the laws of the United States shall bar a proceeding for criminal contempt, which is based upon the same act or omission and which arises under the provisions of this Act; and an acquittal or conviction in a proceeding for criminal contempt, which arises under the provisions of this Act, shall bar a prosecution for a specific crime under the laws of the United States based upon the same act or omission.

SEC. 1103. Nothing in this Act shall be construed to deny, impair, or otherwise affect any right or authority of the Attorney General or of the United States or any agency or officer thereof under existing law to institute or intervene in any action or proceeding.

SEC. 1104. Nothing contained in any title of this Act shall be construed as indicating an intent on the part of Congress to occupy the field in which any such title operates to the exclusion of State laws on the same subject matter, nor shall any provision of this Act be construed as invalidating any provision of State law unless such provision is inconsistent with any of the purposes of this Act, or any provision thereof.

SEC. 1105. There are hereby authorized to be appropriated such sums as are necessary to carry out the provisions of this Act.

SEC. 1106. If any provision of this Act or the application thereof to any person or circumstances is held invalid, the remainder of the Act and the application of the provision to other persons not similarly situated or to other circumstances shall not be affected thereby.

Approved July 2, 1964.

Source:

U.S. National Archives & Records Administration, 700 Pennsylvania Avenue NW, Washington, DC 20408
Available at: http://www.ourdocuments.gov/doc.php?doc=97&page=transcript

Transcript of Voting Rights Act (1965)

AN ACT To enforce the fifteenth amendment to the Constitution of the United States, and for other purposes.

Be it enacted by the Senate and House of Representatives of the United States of America in Congress assembled, That this Act shall be known as the "Voting Rights Act of 1965."

SEC. 2. No voting qualification or prerequisite to voting, or standard, practice, or procedure shall be imposed or applied by any State or political subdivision to deny or abridge the right of any citizen of the United States to vote on account of race or color.

SEC. 3. (a) Whenever the Attorney General institutes a proceeding under any statute to enforce the guarantees of the fifteenth amendment in any State or political subdivision the court shall authorize the appointment of Federal examiners by the United States Civil Service Commission in accordance with section 6 to serve for such period of time and for such political subdivisions as the court shall determine is appropriate to enforce the guarantees of the fifteenth amendment (1) as part of any interlocutory order if the court determines that the appointment of such examiners is necessary to enforce such guarantees or (2) as part of any final judgment if the court finds that violations of the fifteenth amendment justifying equitable relief have occurred in such State or subdivision: Provided, That the court need not authorize the appointment of examiners if any incidents of denial or abridgement of the right to vote on account of race or color (1) have been few in number and have been promptly and effectively corrected by State or local action, (2) the continuing effect of such incidents has been eliminated, and (3) there is no reasonable probability of their recurrence in the future.

(b) If in a proceeding instituted by the Attorney General under any statute to enforce the guarantees of the fifteenth amendment in any State or political subdivision the court finds that a test or device has been used for the purpose or with the effect of denying or abridging the right of any citizen of the United States to vote on account of race or color, it shall suspend the use of tests and devices in such State or political subdivisions as the court shall determine is appropriate and for such period as it deems necessary.

(c) If in any proceeding instituted by the Attorney General under any statute to enforce the guarantees of the fifteenth amendment in any State or political subdivision the court finds that violations of the fifteenth amendment justifying equitable relief have occurred within the territory of such State or political subdivision, the court, in addition to such relief as it may grant, shall retain jurisdiction for such period as it may deem appropriate and during such period no voting qualification or prerequisite to voting, or standard, practice, or procedure with respect to voting different from that in force or effect at the time the proceeding was commenced shall be enforced unless and until the court finds that such qualification, prerequisite, standard, practice, or procedure does not have the purpose and will not have the effect of denying or abridging the right to vote on account of race or color: Provided, That such qualification, prerequisite, standard, practice, or procedure may be enforced if the qualification, prerequisite, standard, practice, or procedure has been submitted by the chief legal officer or other appropriate official of such State or subdivision to the Attorney General and the Attorney General has not interposed an objection within sixty days after such submission, except that neither the court's finding nor the Attorney General's failure to object shall bar a subsequent action to enjoin enforcement of such qualification, prerequisite, standard, practice, or procedure.

SEC. 4. (a) To assure that the right of citizens of the United States to vote is not denied or abridged on account of race or color, no citizen shall be denied the right to vote in any Federal, State, or local election because of his failure to comply with any test or device in any State with respect to which the determinations have been made under subsection (b) or in any political subdivision with respect to which such determinations have been made as a separate unit, unless the United States District Court for the District of Columbia in an action for a declaratory judgment brought by such State or subdivision against the United States has determined that no such test or device has been used during the five years preceding the filing of the action for the purpose or with the effect of denying or abridging

the right to vote on account of race or color: *Provided,* That no such declaratory judgment shall issue with respect to any plaintiff for a period of five years after the entry of a final judgment of any court of the United States, other than the denial of a declaratory judgment under this section, whether entered prior to or after the enactment of this Act, determining that denials or abridgments of the right to vote on account of race or color through the use of such tests or devices have occurred anywhere in the territory of such plaintiff. An action pursuant to this subsection shall be heard and determined by a court of three judges in accordance with the provisions of section 2284 of title 28 of the United States Code and any appeal shall lie to the Supreme Court. The court shall retain jurisdiction of any action pursuant to this subsection for five years after judgment and shall reopen the action upon motion of the Attorney General alleging that a test or device has been used for the purpose or with the effect of denying or abridging the right to vote on account of race or color.

If the Attorney General determines that he has no reason to believe that any such test or device has been used during the five years preceding the filing of the action for the purpose or with the effect of denying or abridging the right to vote on account of race or color, he shall consent to the entry of such judgment

(b) The provisions of subsection (a) shall apply in any State or in any political subdivision of a state which (1) the Attorney General determines maintained on November 1, 1964, any test or device, and with respect to which (2) the Director of the Census determines that less than 50 percentum of the persons of voting age residing therein were registered on November 1, 1964, or that less than 50 percentum of such persons voted in the presidential election of November 1964.

A determination or certification of the Attorney General or of the Director of the Census under this section or under section 6 or section 13 shall not be reviewable in any court and shall be effective upon publication in the Federal Register.

(c) The phrase "test or device" shall mean any requirement that a person as a prerequisite for voting or registration for voting (1) demonstrate the ability to read, write, understand, or interpret any matter, (2) demonstrate any educational achievement or his knowledge of any particular subject, (3) possess good moral character, or (4) prove his qualifications by the voucher of registered voters or members of any other class.

(d) For purposes of this section no State or political subdivision shall be determined to have engaged in the use of tests or devices for the purpose or with the effect of denying or abridging the right to vote on account of race or color if (1) incidents of such use have been few in number and have been promptly and effectively corrected by State or local action, (2) the continuing effect of such incidents has been eliminated, and (3) there is no reasonable probability of their recurrence in the future.

(e)

(1) Congress hereby declares that to secure the rights under the fourteenth amendment of persons educated in American-flag schools in which the predominant classroom language was other than English, it is necessary to prohibit the States from conditioning the right to vote of such persons on ability to read, write, understand, or interpret any matter in the English language.

(2) No person who demonstrates that he has successfully completed the sixth primary grade in a public school in, or a private school accredited by, any State or territory, the District of Columbia, or the Commonwealth of Puerto Rico in which the predominant classroom language was other than English, shall be denied the right to vote in any Federal, State, or local election because of his inability to read, write, understand, or interpret any matter in the English language, except that, in States in which State law provides that a different level of education is presumptive of literacy, he shall demonstrate that he has successfully completed an equivalent level of education in a public school in, or a private school accredited by, any State or territory, the District of Columbia, or the Commonwealth of Puerto Rico in which the predominant classroom language was other than English.

SEC. 5. Whenever a State or political subdivision with respect to which the prohibitions set forth in section 4(a) are in effect shall enact or seek to administer any voting qualification or prerequisite to voting, or standard, practice, or

procedure with respect to voting different from that in force or effect on November 1, 1964, such State or subdivision may institute an action in the United States District Court for the District of Columbia for a declaratory judgment that such qualification, prerequisite, standard, practice, or procedure does not have the purpose and will not have the effect of denying or abridging the right to vote on account of race or color, and unless and until the court enters such judgment no person shall be denied the right to vote for failure to comply with such qualification, prerequisite, standard, practice, or procedure: Provided, That such qualification, prerequisite, standard, practice, or procedure may be enforced without such proceeding if the qualification, prerequisite, standard, practice, or procedure has been submitted by the chief legal officer or other appropriate official of such State or subdivision to the Attorney General and the Attorney General has not interposed an objection within sixty days after such submission, except that neither the Attorney General's failure to object nor a declaratory judgment entered under this section shall bar a subsequent action to enjoin enforcement of such qualification, prerequisite, standard, practice, or procedure. Any action under this section shall be heard and determined by a court of three judges in accordance with the provisions of section 2284 of title 28 of the United States Code and any appeal shall lie to the Supreme Court.

SEC. 6. Whenever (a) a court has authorized the appointment of examiners pursuant to the provisions of section 3(a), or (b) unless a declaratory judgment has been rendered under section 4(a), the Attorney General certifies with respect to any political subdivision named in, or included within the scope of, determinations made under section 4(b) that (1) he has received complaints in writing from twenty or more residents of such political subdivision alleging that they have been denied the right to vote under color of law on account of race or color, and that he believes such complaints to be meritorious, or (2) that, in his judgment (considering, among other factors, whether the ratio of nonwhite persons to white persons registered to vote within such subdivision appears to him to be reasonably attributable to violations of the fifteenth amendment or whether substantial evidence exists that bona fide efforts are being made within such subdivision to comply with the fifteenth amendment), the appointment of examiners is otherwise necessary to enforce the guarantees of the fifteenth amendment, the Civil Service Commission shall appoint as many examiners for such subdivision as it may deem appropriate to prepare and maintain lists of persons eligible to vote in Federal, State, and local elections. Such examiners, hearing officers provided for in section 9(a), and other persons deemed necessary by the Commission to carry out the provisions and purposes of this Act shall be appointed, compensated, and separated without regard to the provisions of any statute administered by the Civil Service Commission, and service under this Act shall not be considered employment for the purposes of any statute administered by the Civil Service Commission, except the provisions of section 9 of the Act of August 2, 1939, as amended (5 U.S.C. 118i), prohibiting partisan political activity: Provided, That the Commission is authorized, after consulting the head of the appropriate department or agency, to designate suitable persons in the official service of the United States, with their consent, to serve in these positions. Examiners and hearing officers shall have the power to administer oaths.

SEC. 7. (a) The examiners for each political subdivision shall, at such places as the Civil Service Commission shall by regulation designate, examine applicants concerning their qualifications for voting. An application to an examiner shall be in such form as the Commission may require and shall contain allegations that the applicant is not otherwise registered to vote.

(b) Any person whom the examiner finds, in accordance with instructions received under section 9(b), to have the qualifications prescribed by State law not inconsistent with the Constitution and laws of the United States shall promptly be placed on a list of eligible voters. A challenge to such listing may be made in accordance with section 9(a) and shall not be the basis for a prosecution under section 12 of this Act. The examiner shall certify and transmit such list, and any supplements as appropriate, at least once a month, to the offices of the appropriate election officials, with copies to the Attorney General and the attorney general of the State, and any such lists and supplements thereto transmitted during the month shall be available for public inspection on the last business day of the month and, in any event, not later than the forty-fifth day prior to any election. The appropriate State or local election official shall place such names on the official voting list. Any person whose name appears on the examiner's list shall be entitled and allowed to vote in the election district of his residence unless and until the appropriate election officials shall have been notified that such person has been removed from such list in accordance with subsection

(d): Provided, That no person shall be entitled to vote in any election by virtue of this Act unless his name shall have been certified and transmitted on such a list to the offices of the appropriate election officials at least forty-five days prior to such election.

(c) The examiner shall issue to each person whose name appears on such a list a certificate evidencing his eligibility to vote.

(d) A person whose name appears on such a list shall be removed therefrom by an examiner if (1) such person has been successfully challenged in accordance with the procedure prescribed in section 9, or (2) he has been determined by an examiner to have lost his eligibility to vote under State law not inconsistent with the Constitution and the laws of the United States.

SEC. 8. Whenever an examiner is serving under this Act in any political subdivision, the Civil Service Commission may assign, at the request of the Attorney General, one or more persons, who may be officers of the United States, (1) to enter and attend at any place for holding an election in such subdivision for the purpose of observing whether persons who are entitled to vote are being permitted to vote, and (2) to enter and attend at any place for tabulating the votes cast at any election held in such subdivision for the purpose of observing whether votes cast by persons entitled to vote are being properly tabulated. Such persons so assigned shall report to an examiner appointed for such political subdivision, to the Attorney General, and if the appointment of examiners has been authorized pursuant to section 3(a), to the court.

SEC. 9. (a) Any challenge to a listing on an eligibility list prepared by an examiner shall be heard and determined by a hearing officer appointed by and responsible to the Civil Service Commission and under such rules as the Commission shall by regulation prescribe. Such challenge shall be entertained only if filed at such office within the State as the Civil Service Commission shall by regulation designate, and within ten days after the listing of the challenged person is made available for public inspection, and if supported by (1) the affidavits of at least two persons having personal knowledge of the facts constituting grounds for the challenge, and (2) a certification that a copy of the challenge and affidavits have been served by mail or in person upon the person challenged at his place of residence set out in the application. Such challenge shall be determined within fifteen days after it has been filed. A petition for review of the decision of the hearing officer may be filed in the United States court of appeals for the circuit in which the person challenged resides within fifteen days after service of such decision by mail on the person petitioning for review but no decision of a hearing officer shall be reversed unless clearly erroneous. Any person listed shall be entitled and allowed to vote pending final determination by the hearing officer and by the court.

(b) The times, places, procedures, and form for application and listing pursuant to this Act and removals from the eligibility lists shall be prescribed by regulations promulgated by the Civil Service Commission and the Commission shall, after consultation with the Attorney General, instruct examiners concerning applicable State law not inconsistent with the Constitution and laws of the United States with respect to (1) the qualifications required for listing, and (2) loss of eligibility to vote.

(c) Upon the request of the applicant or the challenger or on its own motion the Civil Service Commission shall have the power to require by subpoena the attendance and testimony of witnesses and the production of documentary evidence relating to any matter pending before it under the authority of this section. In case of contumacy or refusal to obey a subpoena, any district court of the United States or the United States court of any territory or possession, or the District Court of the United States for the District of Columbia, within the jurisdiction of which said person guilty of contumacy or refusal to obey is found or resides or is domiciled or transacts business, or has appointed an agent for receipt of service of process, upon application by the Attorney General of the United States shall have jurisdiction to issue to such person an order requiring such person to appear before the Commission or a hearing officer, there to produce pertinent, relevant, and nonprivileged documentary evidence if so ordered, or there to give testimony touching the matter under investigation, and any failure to obey such order of the court may be punished by said court as a contempt thereof.

SEC. 10. (a) The Congress finds that the requirement of the payment of a poll tax as a precondition to voting (i) precludes persons of limited means from voting or imposes unreasonable financial hardship upon such persons as a precondition to their exercise of the franchise, (ii) does not bear a reasonable relationship to any legitimate State interest in the conduct of elections, and (iii) in some areas has the purpose or effect of denying persons the right to vote because of race or color. Upon the basis of these findings, Congress declares that the constitutional right of citizens to vote is denied or abridged in some areas by the requirement of the payment of a poll tax as a precondition to voting.

(b) In the exercise of the powers of Congress under section 5 of the fourteenth amendment and section 2 of the fifteenth amendment, the Attorney General is authorized and directed to institute forthwith in the name of the United States such actions, including actions against States or political subdivisions, for declaratory judgment or injunctive relief against the enforcement of any requirement of the payment of a poll tax as a precondition to voting, or substitute therefor enacted after November 1, 1964, as will be necessary to implement the declaration of subsection (a) and the purposes of this section.

(c) The district courts of the United States shall have jurisdiction of such actions which shall be heard and determined by a court of three judges in accordance with the provisions of section 2284 of title 28 of the United States Code and any appeal shall lie to the Supreme Court. It shall be the duty of the judges designated to hear the case to assign the case for hearing at the earliest practicable date, to participate in the hearing and determination thereof, and to cause the case to be in every way expedited.

(d) During the pendency of such actions, and thereafter if the courts, notwithstanding this action by the Congress, should declare the requirement of the payment of a poll tax to be constitutional, no citizen of the United States who is a resident of a State or political subdivision with respect to which determinations have been made under subsection 4(b) and a declaratory judgment has not been entered under subsection 4(a), during the first year he becomes otherwise entitled to vote by reason of registration by State or local officials or listing by an examiner, shall be denied the right to vote for failure to pay a poll tax if he tenders payment of such tax for the current year to an examiner or to the appropriate State or local official at least forty-five days prior to election, whether or not such tender would be timely or adequate under State law. An examiner shall have authority to accept such payment from any person authorized by this Act to make an application for listing, and shall issue a receipt for such payment. The examiner shall transmit promptly any such poll tax payment to the office of the State or local official authorized to receive such payment under State law, together with the name and address of the applicant.

SEC. 11. (a) No person acting under color of law shall fail or refuse to permit any person to vote who is entitled to vote under any provision of this Act or is otherwise qualified to vote, or willfully fail or refuse to tabulate, count, and report such person's vote.

(b) No person, whether acting under color of law or otherwise, shall intimidate, threaten, or coerce, or attempt to intimidate, threaten, or coerce any person for voting or attempting to vote, or intimidate, threaten, or coerce, or attempt to intimidate, threaten, or coerce any person for urging or aiding any person to vote or attempt to vote, or intimidate, threaten, or coerce any person for exercising any powers or duties under section 3(a), 6, 8, 9, 10, or 12(e).

(c) Whoever knowingly or willfully gives false information as to his name, address, or period of residence in the voting district for the purpose of establishing his eligibility to register or vote, or conspires with another individual for the purpose of encouraging his false registration to vote or illegal voting, or pays or offers to pay or accepts payment either for registration to vote or for voting shall be fined not more than $10,000 or imprisoned not more than five years, or both: Provided, however, That this provision shall be applicable only to general, special, or primary elections held solely or in part for the purpose of selecting or electing any candidate for the office of President, Vice President, presidential elector, Member of the United States Senate, Member of the United States House of Representatives, or Delegates or Commissioners from the territories or possessions, or Resident Commissioner of the Commonwealth of Puerto Rico.

(d) Whoever, in any matter within the jurisdiction of an examiner or hearing officer knowingly and willfully falsifies or conceals a material fact, or makes any false, fictitious, or fraudulent statements or representations, or makes or uses any false writing or document knowing the same to contain any false, fictitious, or fraudulent statement or entry, shall be fined not more than $10,000 or imprisoned not more than five years, or both.

SEC. 12. (a) Whoever shall deprive or attempt to deprive any person of any right secured by section 2, 3, 4, 5, 7, or 10 or shall violate section 11(a) or (b), shall be fined not more than $5,000, or imprisoned not more than five years, or both.

(b) Whoever, within a year following an election in a political subdivision in which an examiner has been appointed (1) destroys, defaces, mutilates, or otherwise alters the marking of a paper ballot which has been cast in such election, or (2) alters any official record of voting in such election tabulated from a voting machine or otherwise, shall be fined not more than $5,000, or imprisoned not more than five years, or both

(c) Whoever conspires to violate the provisions of subsection (a) or (b) of this section, or interferes with any right secured by section 2, 3 4, 5, 7, 10, or 11(a) or (b) shall be fined not more than $5,000, or imprisoned not more than five years, or both.

(d) Whenever any person has engaged or there are reasonable grounds to believe that any person is about to engage in any act or practice prohibited by section 2, 3, 4, 5, 7, 10, 11, or subsection (b) of this section, the Attorney General may institute for the United States, or in the name of the United States, an action for preventive relief, including an application for a temporary or permanent injunction, restraining order, or other order, and including an order directed to the State and State or local election officials to require them (1) to permit persons listed under this Act to vote and (2) to count such votes.

(e) Whenever in any political subdivision in which there are examiners appointed pursuant to this Act any persons allege to such an examiner within forty-eight hours after the closing of the polls that notwithstanding (1) their listing under this Act or registration by an appropriate election official and (2) their eligibility to vote, they have not been permitted to vote in such election, the examiner shall forthwith notify the Attorney General if such allegations in his opinion appear to be well founded. Upon receipt of such notification, the Attorney General may forthwith file with the district court an application for an order providing for the marking, casting, and counting of the ballots of such persons and requiring the inclusion of their votes in the total vote before the results of such election shall be deemed final and any force or effect given thereto. The district court shall hear and determine such matters immediately after the filing of such application. The remedy provided in this subsection shall not preclude any remedy available under State or Federal law.

(f) The district courts of the United States shall have jurisdiction of proceedings instituted pursuant to this section and shall exercise the same without regard to whether a person asserting rights under the provisions of this Act shall have exhausted any administrative or other remedies that may be provided by law

SEC. 13. Listing procedures shall be terminated in any political subdivision of any State (a) with respect to examiners appointed pursuant to clause (b) of section 6 whenever the Attorney General notifies the Civil Service Commission, or whenever the District Court for the District of Columbia determines in an action for declaratory judgment brought by any political subdivision with respect to which the Director of the Census has determined that more than 50 percentum of the nonwhite persons of voting age residing therein are registered to vote, (1) that all persons listed by an examiner for such subdivision have been placed on the appropriate voting registration roll, and (2) that there is no longer reasonable cause to believe that persons will be deprived of or denied the right to vote on account of race or color in such subdivision, and (b), with respect to examiners appointed pursuant to section 3(a), upon order of the authorizing court. A political subdivision may petition the Attorney General for the termination of listing procedures under clause (a) of this section, and may petition the Attorney General to request the Director of the Census to take such survey or census as may be appropriate for the making of the determination provided for in this section. The District Court for the District of Columbia shall have jurisdiction to require such survey or

census to be made by the Director of the Census and it shall require him to do so if it deems the Attorney General's refusal to request such survey or census to be arbitrary or unreasonable.

SEC. 14. (a) All cases of criminal contempt arising under the provisions of this Act shall be governed by section 151 of the Civil Rights Act of 1957 (42 U.S.C.1995).

(b) No court other than the District Court for the District of Columbia or a court of appeals in any proceeding under section 9 shall have jurisdiction to issue any declaratory judgment pursuant to section 4 or section 5 or any restraining order or temporary or permanent injunction against the execution or enforcement of any provision of this Act or any action of any Federal officer or employee pursuant hereto.

(c)

(1) The terms "vote" or "voting" shall include all action necessary to make a vote effective in any primary, special, or general election, including, but not limited to, registration, listing pursuant to this Act, or other action required by law prerequisite to voting, casting a ballot, and having such ballot counted properly and included in the appropriate totals of votes cast with respect to candidates for public or party office and propositions for which votes are received in an election.

(2) The term "political subdivision" shall mean any county or parish, except that, where registration for voting is not conducted under the supervision of a county or parish, the term shall include any other subdivision of a State which conducts registration for voting.

(d) In any action for a declaratory judgment brought pursuant to section 4 or section 5 of this Act, subpoenas for witnesses who are required to attend the District Court for the District of Columbia may be served in any judicial district of the United States: Provided, That no writ of subpoena shall issue for witnesses without the District of Columbia at a greater distance than one hundred miles from the place of holding court without the permission of the District Court for the District of Columbia being first had upon proper application and cause shown.

SEC. 15. Section 2004 of the Revised Statutes (42 U.S.C.1971), as amended by section 131 of the Civil Rights Act of 1957 (71 Stat. 637), and amended by section 601 of the Civil Rights Act of 1960 (74 Stat. 90), and as further amended by section 101 of the Civil Rights Act of 1964 (78 Stat. 241), is further amended as follows:

(a) Delete the word "Federal" wherever it appears in subsections (a) and (c);

(b) Repeal subsection (f) and designate the present subsections (g) and (h) as (f) and (g), respectively.

SEC. 16. The Attorney General and the Secretary of Defense, jointly, shall make a full and complete study to determine whether, under the laws or practices of any State or States, there are preconditions to voting, which might tend to result in discrimination against citizens serving in the Armed Forces of the United States seeking to vote. Such officials shall, jointly, make a report to the Congress not later than June 30, 1966, containing the results of such study, together with a list of any States in which such preconditions exist, and shall include in such report such recommendations for legislation as they deem advisable to prevent discrimination in voting against citizens serving in the Armed Forces of the United States.

SEC. 17. Nothing in this Act shall be construed to deny, impair, or otherwise adversely affect the right to vote of any person registered to vote under the law of any State or political subdivision.

SEC. 18. There are hereby authorized to be appropriated such sums as are necessary to carry out the provisions of this Act

SEC 19. If any provision of this Act or the application thereof to any person or circumstances is held invalid, the remainder of the Act and the application of the provision to other persons not similarly situated or to other circumstances shall not be affected thereby.

Approved August 6, 1965.

Instances of Use of United States Armed Forces Abroad, 1798–2004

by Richard F. Grimmett, Specialist in National Defense

DEPARTMENT OF THE NAVY—NAVAL HISTORICAL CENTER
805 KIDDER BREESE SE—WASHINGTON NAVY YARD, WASHINGTON DC 20374-5060

Foreign Affairs, Defense, and Trade Division
Washington DC: Congressional Research Service
Library of Congress, October 5, 2004

Summary

This report lists hundreds of instances in which the United States has used its armed forces abroad in situations of military conflict or potential conflict or for other than normal peacetime purposes. It was compiled in part from various older lists and is intended primarily to provide a rough survey of past US military ventures abroad, without reference to the magnitude of the given instance noted. The listing often contains references, especially from 1980 forward, to continuing military deployments especially US military participation in multinational operations associated with NATO or the United Nations. Most of these post-1980 instances are summaries based on Presidential reports to Congress related to the War Powers Resolution. A comprehensive commentary regarding any of the instances listed is not undertaken here.

The instances differ greatly in number of forces, purpose, extent of hostilities, and legal authorization. Eleven times in its history the US has formally declared war against foreign nations. These eleven US war declarations encompassed five separate wars: the war with Great Britain declared in 1812, the war with Mexico declared in 1846, the War with Spain declared in 1898, the First World War, during which the US declared war with Germany and with Austria-Hungary during 1917, World War II, during which the US declared war against Japan, Germany, and Italy in 1941, and against Bulgaria, Hungary, and Rumania in 1942. Some of the instances were extended military engagements that might be considered undeclared wars. These include the Undeclared Naval War with France from 1798 to 1800; the First Barbary War from 1801 to 1805; the Second Barbary War of 1815; the Korean War of 1950–53; the Vietnam War from 1964 to 1973; the Persian Gulf War of 1991, global actions against foreign terrorists after the September 11, 2001 attacks on the United States, and the War with Iraq in 2003. With the exception of the Korean War, all of these conflicts received Congressional authorization in some form short of a formal declaration of war. Other, more recent instances often involve deployment of US military forces as part of a multinational operation associated with NATO or the United Nations. Current legislation, H.R. 10 and S. 2845, contains provisions that could strengthen the intelligence capabilities of the United States to combat international terrorism and to support current and future American military operations overseas in a more effective manner.

The majority of the instances listed prior to World War II were brief Marine or Navy actions to protect US citizens or promote US interests. A number were actions against pirates or bandits. Covert actions, disaster relief, and routine alliance stationing and training exercises are not included here, nor are the Civil and Revolutionary Wars and the continual use of US military units in the exploration, settlement, and pacification of the Western part of the United States. This report will be updated as warranted.

Instances of Use of United States Armed Forces Abroad, 1798–2004

The following list reviews hundreds of instances in which the United States has utilized military forces abroad in situations of military conflict or potential conflict to protect US citizens or promote US interests. The list does not include covert actions or numerous instances in which US forces have been stationed abroad since World War II in occupation forces or for participation in mutual security organizations, base agreements, or routine military assistance or training operations. Because of differing judgments over the actions to be included, other lists may include more or fewer instances.2

The instances vary greatly in size of operation, legal authorization, and significance. The number of troops involved range from a few sailors or Marines landed to protect American lives and property to hundreds of thousands in Korea and Vietnam and millions in World War II. Some actions were of short duration and some lasted a number of years. In some instances a military officer acted without authorization; some actions were conducted solely under the President's powers as Chief Executive or Commander in Chief; other instances were authorized by Congress in some fashion. In eleven separate cases [in five wars] (listed in **bold-face type**) the United States formally declared war against foreign nations. For most of the instances listed, however, the status of the action under domestic or international law has not been addressed. Most instances listed since 1980, are summaries of US military deployments reported to Congress by the President as a result of the War Powers Resolution. Several of these Presidential reports are summaries of activities related to an on-going operation previously reported. It is important to note that inclusion in this list does not connote either legality or level of significance of the instance described. This report covers uses of US military force abroad from 1798 through the end of September 2004. It will be revised as circumstances warrant.

1798–1800—*Undeclared Naval War with France*. This contest included land actions, such as that in the Dominican Republic, city of Puerto Plata, where marines captured a French privateer under the guns of the forts. Congress authorized military action through a series of statutes.

1801–05—*Tripoli*. The First Barbary War included the USS *George Washington* and USS *Philadelphia* affairs and the Eaton expedition, during which a few marines landed with United States Agent William Eaton to raise a force against Tripoli in an effort to free the crew of the *Philadelphia*. Tripoli declared war but not the United States, although Congress authorized US military action by statute.

1806—*Mexico (Spanish territory)*. Capt. Z. M. Pike, with a platoon of troops, invaded Spanish territory at the headwaters of the Rio Grande on orders from Gen. James Wilkinson. He was made prisoner without resistance at a fort he constructed in present day Colorado, taken to Mexico, and later released after seizure of his papers.

1806–10—*Gulf of Mexico*. American gunboats operated from New Orleans against Spanish and French privateers off the Mississippi Delta, chiefly under Capt. John Shaw and Master Commandant David Porter.

1810—*West Florida (Spanish territory)*. Gov. Claiborne of Louisiana, on orders of the President, occupied with troops territory in dispute east of the Mississippi as far as the Pearl River, later the eastern boundary of Louisiana. He was authorized to seize as far east as the Perdido River.

1812—*Amelia Island and other parts of east Florida, then under Spain*. Temporary possession was authorized by President Madison and by Congress, to prevent occupation by any other power; but possession was obtained by Gen. George Matthews in so irregular a manner that his measures were disavowed by the President.

1812–15—War of 1812. On June 18, 1812, the United States declared war between the United States and the United Kingdom of Great Britain and Ireland. Among the issues leading to the war were British interception of neutral ships and blockades of the United States during British hostilities with France.

1813—*West Florida (Spanish territory)*. On authority given by Congress, General Wilkinson seized Mobile Bay in April with 600 soldiers. A small Spanish garrison gave way. Thus US advanced into disputed territory to the Perdido River, as projected in 1810. No fighting.

1813–14—*Marguesas Islands*. US forces built a fort on the island of Nukahiva to protect three prize ships which had been captured from the British.

1814—*Spanish Florida*. Gen. Andrew Jackson took Pensacola and drove out the British with whom the United States was at war.

1814–25—*Caribbean*. Engagements between pirates and American ships or squadrons took place repeatedly especially ashore and offshore about Cuba, Puerto Rico, Santo Domingo, and Yucatan. Three thousand pirate attacks on merchantmen were reported between 1815 and 1823. In 1822 Commodore James Biddle employed a squadron of two frigates, four sloops of war, two brigs, four schooners, and two gunboats in the West Indies.

1815—*Algiers*. The second Barbary War was declared against the United States by the Dey of Algiers of the Barbary states, an act not reciprocated by the United States. Congress did authorize a military expedition by statutes. A large fleet under Decatur attacked Algiers and obtained indemnities.

1815—*Tripoli*. After securing an agreement from Algiers, Decatur demonstrated with his squadron at Tunis and Tripoli, where he secured indemnities for offenses during the War of 1812.

1816—*Spanish Florida*. United States forces destroyed Nicholls Fort, called also Negro Fort, which harbored raiders making forays into United States territory.

1816–18—*Spanish Florida—First Seminole War*. The Seminole Indians, whose area was a haven for escaped slaves and border ruffians, were attacked by troops under Generals Jackson and Gaines and pursued into northern Florida. Spanish posts were attacked and occupied, British citizens executed. In 1819 the Floridas were ceded to the United States.

1817—*Amelia Island (Spanish territory off Florida)*. Under orders of President Monroe, United States forces landed and expelled a group of smugglers, adventurers, and freebooters.

1818—*Oregon*. The USS Ontario dispatched from Washington, landed at the Columbia River and in August took possession of Oregon territory. Britain had conceded sovereignty but Russia and Spain asserted claims to the area.

1820–23—*Africa*. Naval units raided the slave traffic pursuant to the 1819 act of Congress.

1822—*Cuba*. United States naval forces suppressing piracy landed on the northwest coast of Cuba and burned a pirate station.

1823—*Cuba*. Brief landings in pursuit of pirates occurred April 8 near Escondido; April 16 near Cayo Blanco; July 11 at Siquapa Bay; July 21 at Cape Cruz; and October 23 at Camrioca.

1824—*Cuba*. In October the USS Porpoise landed bluejackets near Matanzas in pursuit of pirates. This was during the cruise authorized in 1822.

1824—*Puerto Rico (Spanish territory)*. Commodore David Porter with a landing party attacked the town of Fajardo which had sheltered pirates and insulted American naval officers. He landed with 200 men in November and forced an apology. Commodore Porter was later court-martialed for overstepping his powers.

1825—*Cuba*. In March cooperating American and British forces landed at Sagua La Grande to capture pirates.

1827—*Greece*. In October and November landing parties hunted pirates on the islands of Argenteire, Miconi, and Androse.

1831–32—*Falkland Islands*. Captain Duncan of the USS *Lexington* investigated the capture of three American sealing vessels and sought to protect American interests.

1832—*Sumatra.*—February 6 to 9. A naval force landed and stormed a fort to punish natives of the town of Quallah Battoo for plundering the American ship *Friendship.*

1833—*Argentina.*—October 31 to November 15. A force was sent ashore at Buenos Aires to protect the interests of the United States and other countries during an insurrection.

1835–36—*Peru.*—December 10, 1835, to January 24, 1836, and August 31 to December 7, 1836. Marines protected American interests in Callao and Lima during an attempted revolution.

1836—*Mexico.* General Gaines occupied Nacogdoches (Tex.), disputed territory, from July to December during the Texan war for independence, under orders to cross the "imaginary boundary line" if an Indian outbreak threatened.

1838–39—*Sumatra.*—December 24, 1838, to January 4, 1839. A naval force landed to punish natives of the towns of Quallah Battoo and Muckie (Mukki) for depredations on American shipping.

1840—*Fiji Islands.*—July. Naval forces landed to punish natives for attacking American exploring and surveying parties.

1841—*Drummond Island, Kingsmill Group.* A naval party landed to avenge the murder of a seaman by the natives.

1841—*Samoa.*—February 24. A naval party landed and burned towns after the murder of an American seaman on Upolu Island.

1842—*Mexico.* Commodore T.A.C. Jones, in command of a squadron long cruising off California, occupied Monterey, Calif., on October 19, believing war had come. He discovered peace, withdrew, and saluted. A similar incident occurred a week later at San Diego.

1843—*China.* Sailors and marines from the St. Louis were landed after a clash between Americans and Chinese at the trading post in Canton.

1843—*Africa.*—November 29 to December 16. Four United States vessels demonstrated and landed various parties (one of 200 marines and sailors) to discourage piracy and the slave trade along the Ivory coast, and to punish attacks by the natives on American seamen and shipping.

1844—*Mexico.* President Tyler deployed US forces to protect Texas against Mexico, pending Senate approval of a treaty of annexation. (Later rejected.) He defended his action against a Senate resolution of inquiry.

1846–48—Mexican War. On May 13, 1846, the United States recognized the existence of a state of war with Mexico. After the annexation of Texas in 1845, the United States and Mexico failed to resolve a boundary dispute and President Polk said that it was necessary to deploy forces in Mexico to meet a threatened invasion.

1849—*Smyrna.* In July a naval force gained release of an American seized by Austrian officials.

1851—*Turkey.* After a massacre of foreigners (including Americans) at Jaffa in January, a demonstration by the Mediterranean Squadron was ordered along the Turkish (Levant) coast.

1851—*Johanns Island (east of Africa).*—August. Forces from the US sloop of war *Dale* exacted redress for the unlawful imprisonment of the captain of an American whaling brig.

1852–53—*Argentina.*—February 3 to 12, 1852; September 17, 1852 to April 1853. Marines were landed and maintained in Buenos Aires to protect American interests during a revolution.

1853—*Nicaragua.*—March 11 to 13. US forces landed to protect American lives and interests during political disturbances.

1853–54—*Japan.* Commodore Perry and his expedition made a display of force leading to the "opening of Japan."

1853–54—*Ryukyu and Bonin Islands.* Commodore Perry on three visits before going to Japan and while waiting for a reply from Japan made a naval demonstration, landing marines twice, and secured a coaling concession from

the ruler of Naha on Okinawa; he also demonstrated in the Bonin Islands with the purpose of securing facilities for commerce.

1854—*China.*—April 4 to June 15 to 17. American and English ships landed forces to protect American interests in and near Shanghai during Chinese civil strife.

1854—*Nicaragua.*—July 9 to 15. Naval forces bombarded and burned San Juan del Norte (Greytown) to avenge an insult to the American Minister to Nicaragua.

1855—*China.*—May 19 to 21. US forces protected American interests in Shanghai and, from August 3 to 5 fought pirates near Hong Kong.

1855—*Fiji Islands.*—September 12 to November 4. An American naval force landed to seek reparations for depredations on American residents and seamen.

1855—*Uruguay.*—November 25 to 29. United States and European naval forces landed to protect American interests during an attempted revolution in Montevideo.

1856—*Panama, Republic of New Grenada.*—September 19 to 22. US forces landed to protect American interests during an insurrection.

1856—*China.*—October 22 to December 6. US forces landed to protect American interests at Canton during hostilities between the British and the Chinese, and to avenge an assault upon an unarmed boat displaying the United States flag.

1857—*Nicaragua.*—April to May, November to December. In May Commander C.H. Davis of the United States Navy, with some marines, received the surrender of William Walker, who had been attempting to get control of the country, and protected his men from the retaliation of native allies who had been fighting Walker. In November and December of the same year United States vessels Saratoga, Wabash, and Fulton opposed another attempt of William Walker on Nicaragua. Commodore Hiram Paulding's act of landing marines and compelling the removal of Walker to the United States, was tacitly disavowed by Secretary of State Lewis Cass, and Paulding was forced into retirement.

1858—*Uruguay.*—January 2 to 27. Forces from two United States warships landed to protect American property during a revolution in Montevideo.

1858—*Fiji Islands.*—October 6 to 16. A marine expedition chastised natives for the murder of two American citizens at Waya.

1858–59—*Turkey.* The Secretary of State requested a display of naval force along the Levant after a massacre of Americans at Jaffa and mistreatment elsewhere "to remind the authorities (of Turkey) of the power of the United States."

1859—*Paraguay.* Congress authorized a naval squadron to seek redress for an attack on a naval vessel in the Parana River during 1855. Apologies were made after a large display of force.

1859—*Mexico.* Two hundred United States soldiers crossed the Rio Grande in pursuit of the Mexican bandit Cortina.

1859—*China.*—July 31 to August 2. A naval force landed to protect American interests in Shanghai.

1860—*Angola, Portuguese West Africa.*—March 1. American residents at Kissembo called upon American and British ships to protect lives and property during problems with natives.

1860—*Colombia, Bay of Panama.*—September 27 to October 8. Naval forces landed to protect American interests during a revolution.

1863—*Japan.*—July 16. The USS *Wyoming* retaliated against a firing on the American vessel *Pembroke* at Shimonoseki.

1864—*Japan.*—July 14 to August 3. Naval forces protected the United States Minister to Japan when he visited Yedo to negotiate concerning some American claims against Japan, and to make his negotiations easier by impressing the Japanese with American power.

1864—*Japan.*—September 4 to 14. Naval forces of the United States, Great Britain, France, and the Netherlands compelled Japan and the Prince of Nagato in particular to permit the Straits of Shimonoseki to be used by foreign shipping in accordance with treaties already signed.

1865—*Panama.*—March 9 and 10. US forces protected the lives and property of American residents during a revolution.

1866—*Mexico.* To protect American residents, General Sedgwick and 100 men in November obtained surrender of Matamoras. After three days he was ordered by US Government to withdraw. His act was repudiated by the President.

1866—*China.* From June 20 to July 7, US forces punished an assault on the American consul at Newchwang.

1867—*Nicaragua.* Marines occupied Managua and Leon.

1867—*Formosa.*—June 13. A naval force landed and burned a number of huts to punish the murder of the crew of a wrecked American vessel.

1868—*Japan (Osaka, Hiolo, Nagasaki, Yokohama, and Negata).*—February 4 to 8, April 4 to May 12, June 12 and 13. US forces were landed to protect American interests during the civil war in Japan.

1868—*Uruguay.*—February 7 and 8, 19 to 26. US forces protected foreign residents and the customhouse during an insurrection at Montevideo.

1868—*Colombia.*—April. US forces protected passengers and treasure in transit at Aspinwall during the absence of local police or troops on the occasion of the death of the President of Colombia.

1870—*Mexico.*—June 17 and 18. US forces destroyed the pirate ship Forward, which had been run aground about 40 miles up the Rio Tecapan.

1870—*Hawaiian Islands.*—September 21. US forces placed the American flag at half mast upon the death of Queen Kalama, when the American consul at Honolulu would not assume responsibility for so doing.

1871—*Korea.*—June 10 to 12. A US naval force attacked and captured five forts to punish natives for depredations on Americans, particularly for murdering the crew of the *General Sherman* and burning the schooner, and for later firing on other American small boats taking soundings up the Salee River.

1873—*Colombia (Bay of Panama).*—May 7 to 22, September 23 to October 9. U.S. forces protected American interests during hostilities between local groups over control of the government of the State of Panama.

1873–96—*Mexico.* United States troops crossed the Mexican border repeatedly in pursuit of cattle and other thieves and other brigands. There were some reciprocal pursuits by Mexican troops into border territory. Mexico protested frequently. Notable cases were at Remolina in May 1873 and at Las Cuevas in 1875. Washington orders often supported these excursions. Agreements between Mexico and the United States, the first in 1882, finally legitimized such raids. They continued intermittently, with minor disputes, until 1896.

1874—*Hawaiian Islands.*—February 12 to 20. Detachments from American vessels were landed to preserve order and protect American lives and interests during the coronation of a new king.

1876—*Mexico.*—May 18. An American force was landed to police the town of Matamoras temporarily while it was without other government.

1882—*Egypt.*—July 14 to 18. American forces landed to protect American interests during warfare between British and Egyptians and looting of the city of Alexandria by Arabs.

1885—*Panama (Colon).*—January 18 and 19. US forces were used to guard the valuables in transit over the Panama Railroad, and the safes and vaults of the company during revolutionary activity. In March, April, and May in the cities of Colon and Panama, the forces helped reestablish freedom of transit during revolutionary activity.

1888—*Korea.*—June. A naval force was sent ashore to protect American residents in Seoul during unsettled political conditions, when an outbreak of the populace was expected.

1888—*Haiti.*—December 20. A display of force persuaded the Haitian Government to give up an American steamer which had been seized on the charge of breach of blockade.

1888–89—*Samoa.*—November 14, 1888, to March 20, 1889. US forces were landed to protect American citizens and the consulate during a native civil war.

1889—*Hawaiian Islands.*—July 30 and 31. US forces protected American interests at Honolulu during a revolution.

1890—*Argentina.* A naval party landed to protect US consulate and legation in Buenos Aires.

1891—*Haiti.* US forces sought to protect American lives and property on Navassa Island.

1891—*Bering Strait.*—July 2 to October 5. Naval forces sought to stop seal poaching.

1891—*Chile.*—August 28 to 30. US forces protected the American consulate and the women and children who had taken refuge in it during a revolution in Valparaiso.

1893—*Hawaii.*—January 16 to April 1. Marines were landed ostensibly to protect American lives and property, but many believed actually to promote a provisional government under Sanford B. Dole. This action was disavowed by the United States.

1894—*Brazil.*—January. A display of naval force sought to protect American commerce and shipping at Rio de Janeiro during a Brazilian civil war.

1894—*Nicaragua.*—July 6 to August 7. US forces sought to protect American interests at Bluefields following a revolution.

1894-95—*China.* Marines were stationed at Tientsin and penetrated to Peking for protection purposes during the Sino-Japanese War.

1894–95—*China.* A naval vessel was beached and used as a fort at Newchwang for protection of American nationals.

1894–96—*Korea.*—July 24, 1894 to April 3, 1896. A guard of marines was sent to protect the American legation and American lives and interests at Seoul during and following the Sino-Japanese War.

1895—*Colombia.*—March 8 to 9. US forces protected American interests during an attack on the town of Bocas del Toro by a bandit chieftain.

1896—*Nicaragua.*—May 2 to 4. US forces protected American interests in Corinto during political unrest.

1898—*Nicaragua.*—February 7 and 8. US forces protected American lives and property at San Juan del Sur.

1898—The Spanish-American War. On April 25, 1898, the United States declared war with Spain. The war followed a Cuban insurrection against Spanish rule and the sinking of the USS Maine in the harbor at Havana.

1898–99—*China.*—November 5, 1898 to March 15, 1899. US forces provided a guard for the legation at Peking and the consulate at Tientsin during contest between the Dowager Empress and her son.

1899—*Nicaragua.* American and British naval forces were landed to protect national interests at San Juan del Norte, February 22 to March 5, and at Bluefields a few weeks later in connection with the insurrection of Gen. Juan P. Reyes.

1899—*Samoa.*—February-May 15. American and British naval forces were landed to protect national interests and to take part in a bloody contention over the succession to the throne.

1899–1901—*Philippine Islands.* US forces protected American interests following the war with Spain and conquered the islands by defeating the Filipinos in their war for independence.

1900—*China.*—May 24 to September 28. American troops participated in operations to protect foreign lives during the Boxer rising, particularly at Peking. For many years after this experience a permanent legation guard was maintained in Peking, and was strengthened at times as trouble threatened.

1901—*Colombia (State of Panama).*—November 20 to December 4. US forces protected American property on the Isthmus and kept transit lines open during serious revolutionary disturbances.

1902—*Colombia.*—April 16 to 23. US forces protected American lives and property at Bocas del Toro during a civil war.

1902—*Colombia (State of Panama).*—September 17 to November 18. The United States placed armed guards on all trains crossing the Isthmus to keep the railroad line open, and stationed ships on both sides of Panama to prevent the landing of Colombian troops.

1903—*Honduras.*—March 23 to 30 or 31. US forces protected the American consulate and the steamship wharf at Puerto Cortez during a period of revolutionary activity.

1903—*Dominican Republic.*—March 30 to April 21. A detachment of marines was landed to protect American interests in the city of Santo Domingo during a revolutionary outbreak.

1903—*Syria.*—September 7 to 12. US forces protected the American consulate in Beirut when a local Moslem uprising was feared.

1903–04—*Abyssinia.* Twenty-five marines were sent to Abyssinia to protect the US Consul General while he negotiated a treaty.

1903–14—*Panama.* US forces sought to protect American interests and lives during and following the revolution for independence from Colombia over construction of the Isthmian Canal. With brief intermissions, United States Marines were stationed on the Isthmus from November 4, 1903, to January 21, 1914 to guard American interests.

1904—*Dominican Republic.*—January 2 to February 11. American and British naval forces established an area in which no fighting would be allowed and protected American interests in Puerto Plata and Sosua and Santo Domingo City during revolutionary fighting.

1904—*Tangier, Morocco.* "We want either Perdicaris alive or Raisula dead." A squadron demonstrated to force release of a kidnapped American. Marines were landed to protect the consul general.

1904—*Panama.*—November 17 to 24. US forces protected American lives and property at Ancon at the time of a threatened insurrection.

1904–05—*Korea.*—January 5, 1904, to November 11, 1905. A guard of Marines was sent to protect the American legation in Seoul during the Russo-Japanese War.

1906–09—*Cuba.*—September 1906 to January 23, 1909. US forces sought to restore order, protect foreigners, and establish a stable government after serious revolutionary activity.

1907—*Honduras.*—March 18 to June 8. To protect American interests during a war between Honduras and Nicaragua, troops were stationed in Trujillo, Ceiba, Puerto Cortez, San Pedro, Laguna and Choloma.

1910—*Nicaragua.*—May 19 to September 4. US forces protected American interests at Bluefields.

1911—*Honduras.*—January 26. American naval detachments were landed to protect American lives and interests during a civil war in Honduras.

1911—*China.* As the nationalist revolution approached, in October an ensign and 10 men tried to enter Wuchang to rescue missionaries but retired on being warned away, and a small landing force guarded American private property

and consulate at Hankow. Marines were deployed in November to guard the cable stations at Shanghai; landing forces were sent for protection in Nanking, Chinkiang, Taku and elsewhere.

1912—*Honduras.* A small force landed to prevent seizure by the government of an American-owned railroad at Puerto Cortez. The forces were withdrawn after the United States disapproved the action.

1912—*Panama.* Troops, on request of both political parties, supervised elections outside the Canal Zone.

1912—*Cuba.*—June 5 to August 5. US forces protected American interests on the Province of Oriente, and in Havana.

1912—*China.*—August 24 to 26, on Kentucky Island, and August 26 to 30 at Camp Nicholson. US forces protected Americans and American interests during revolutionary activity.

1912—*Turkey.*—November 18 to December 3. US forces guarded the American legation at Constantinople during a Balkan War.

1912–25—*Nicaragua.*—August to November 1912. US forces protected American interests during an attempted revolution. A small force, serving as a legation guard and seeking to promote peace and stability, remained until August 5, 1925.

1912–41—*China.* The disorders which began with the overthrow of the dynasty during Kuomintang rebellion in 1912, which were redirected by the invasion of China by Japan, led to demonstrations and landing parties for the protection of US interests in China continuously and at many points from 1912 on to 1941. The guard at Peking and along the route to the sea was maintained until 1941. In 1927, the United States had 5,670 troops ashore in China and 44 naval vessels in its waters. In 1933 the United States had 3,027 armed men ashore. The protective action was generally based on treaties with China concluded from 1858 to 1901.

1913—*Mexico.*—September 5 to 7. A few marines landed at Ciaris Estero to aid in evacuating American citizens and others from the Yaqui Valley, made dangerous for foreigners by civil strife.

1914—*Haiti.*—January 29 to February 9, February 20 to 21, October 19. Intermittently US naval forces protected American nationals in a time of rioting and revolution.

1914—*Dominican Republic.*—June and July. During a revolutionary movement, United States naval forces by gunfire stopped the bombardment of Puerto Plata, and by threat of force maintained Santo Domingo City as a neutral zone.

1914–17—*Mexico.* Undeclared Mexican—American hostilities followed the Dolphin affair and Villa's raids and included capture of Vera Cruz and later Pershing's expedition into northern Mexico.

1915–34—*Haiti.*—July 28, 1915, to August 15, 1934. US forces maintained order during a period of chronic political instability.

1916—*China.* American forces landed to quell a riot taking place on American property in Nanking.

1916–24—*Dominican Republic.*—May 1916 to September 1924. American naval forces maintained order during a period of chronic and threatened insurrection.

1917—*China.* American troops were landed at Chungking to protect American lives during a political crisis.

1917–18—World War I. On April 6, 1917, the United States declared war with Germany and on December 7, 1917, with Austria-Hungary. Entrance of the United States into the war was precipitated by Germany's submarine warfare against neutral shipping.

1917–22—*Cuba.* US forces protected American interests during insurrection and subsequent unsettled conditions. Most of the United States armed forces left Cuba by August 1919, but two companies remained at Camaguey until February 1922.

1918–19—*Mexico.* After withdrawal of the Pershing expedition, US troops entered Mexico in pursuit of bandits at least three times in 1918 and six times in 1919. In August 1918 American and Mexican troops fought at Nogales.

1918–20—*Panama.* US forces were used for police duty according to treaty stipulations, at Chiriqui, during election disturbances and subsequent unrest.

1918–20—*Soviet Russia.* Marines were landed at and near Vladivostok in June and July to protect the American consulate and other points in the fighting between the Bolshevik troops and the Czech Army which had traversed Siberia from the western front. A joint proclamation of emergency government and neutrality was issued by the American, Japanese, British, French, and Czech commanders in July. In August 7,000 men were landed in Vladivostok and remained until January 1920, as part of an allied occupation force. In September 1918, 5,000 American troops joined the allied intervention force at Archangel and remained until June 1919. These operations were in response to the Bolshevik revolution in Russia and were partly supported by Czarist or Kerensky elements.

1919—*Dalmatia.* US forces were landed at Trau at the request of Italian authorities to police order between the Italians and Serbs.

1919—*Turkey.* Marines from the USS Arizona were landed to guard the US Consulate during the Greek occupation of Constantinople.

1919—*Honduras.*—September 8 to 12. A landing force was sent ashore to maintain order in a neutral zone during an attempted revolution.

1920—*China.*—March 14. A landing force was sent ashore for a few hours to protect lives during a disturbance at Kiukiang.

1920—*Guatemala.*—April 9 to 27. US forces protected the American Legation and other American interests, such as the cable station, during a period of fighting between Unionists and the Government of Guatemala.

1920–22—*Russia (Siberia).*—February 16, 1920, to November 19, 1922. A Marine guard was sent to protect the United States radio station and property on Russian Island, Bay of Vladivostok.

1921—*Panama—Costa Rica.* American naval squadrons demonstrated in April on both sides of the Isthmus to prevent war between the two countries over a boundary dispute.

1922—*Turkey.*—September and October. A landing force was sent ashore with consent of both Greek and Turkish authorities, to protect American lives and property when the Turkish Nationalists entered Smyrna.

1922-23—*China.* Between April 1922 and November 1923 marines were landed five times to protect Americans during periods of unrest.

1924—*Honduras.*—February 28 to March 31, September 10 to 15. US forces protected American lives and interests during election hostilities.

1924—*China.*—September. Marines were landed to protect Americans and other foreigners in Shanghai during Chinese factional hostilities.

1925—*China.*—January 15 to August 29. Fighting of Chinese factions accompanied by riots and demonstrations in Shanghai brought the landing of American forces to protect lives and property in the International Settlement.

1925—*Honduras.*—April 19 to 21. US forces protected foreigners at La Ceiba during a political upheaval.

1925—*Panama.*—October 12 to 23. Strikes and rent riots led to the landing of about 600 American troops to keep order and protect American interests.

1926-33—*Nicaragua.*—May 7 to June 5, 1926; August 27, 1926, to January 3, 1933. The coup d'etat of General Chamorro aroused revolutionary activities leading to the landing of American marines to protect the interests of the United States. United States forces came and went intermittently until January 3, 1933.

1926—*China.*—August and September. The Nationalist attack on Hankow brought the landing of American naval forces to protect American citizens. A small guard was maintained at the consulate general even after September 16, when the rest of the forces were withdrawn. Likewise, when Nationalist forces captured Kiukiang, naval forces were landed for the protection of foreigners November 4 to 6.

1927—*China.*—February. Fighting at Shanghai caused American naval forces and marines to be increased. In March a naval guard was stationed at American consulate at Nanking after Nationalist forces captured the city. American and British destroyers later used shell fire to protect Americans and other foreigners. Subsequently additional forces of marines and naval forces were stationed in the vicinity of Shanghai and Tientsin.

1932—*China.* American forces were landed to protect American interests during the Japanese occupation of Shanghai.

1933—*Cuba.* During a revolution against President Gerardo Machado naval forces demonstrated but no landing was made.

1934—*China.* Marines landed at Foochow to protect the American Consulate.

1940—*Newfoundland, Bermuda, St. Lucia,—Bahamas, Jamaica, Antigua, Trinidad, and British Guiana.* Troops were sent to guard air and naval bases obtained by negotiation with Great Britain. These were sometimes called lend-lease bases.

1941—*Greenland.* Greenland was taken under protection of the United States in April.

1941—*Netherlands (Dutch Guiana).* In November the President ordered American troops to occupy Dutch Guiana, but by agreement with the Netherlands government in exile, Brazil cooperated to protect aluminum ore supply from the bauxite mines in Surinam.

1941—*Iceland.* Iceland was taken under the protection of the United States, with consent of its government, for strategic reasons.

1941—*Germany.* Sometime in the spring the President ordered the Navy to patrol ship lanes to Europe. By July US warships were convoying and by September were attacking German submarines. In November, the Neutrality Act was partly repealed to protect US military aid to Britain.

1941–45—World War II. On December 8, 1941, the United States declared war with Japan, on December 11 with Germany and Italy, and on June 5, 1942, with Bulgaria, Hungary and Romania. The United States declared war against Japan after the surprise bombing of Pearl Harbor, and against Germany and Italy after those nations, under the dictators Hitler and Mussolini, declared war against the United States. The US declared war against Bulgaria, Hungary and Rumania in response to the declarations of war by those nations against the United States.

1945—*China.* In October 50,000 US Marines were sent to North China to assist Chinese Nationalist authorities in disarming and repatriating the Japanese in China and in controlling ports, railroads, and airfields. This was in addition to approximately 60,000 US forces remaining in China at the end of World War II.

1946—*Trieste.* President Truman ordered the augmentation of US troops along the zonal occupation line and the reinforcement of air forces in northern Italy after Yugoslav forces shot down an unarmed US Army transport plane flying over Venezia Giulia. Earlier US naval units had been dispatched to the scene.

1948—*Palestine.* A marine consular guard was sent to Jerusalem to protect the US Consul General.

1948—*Berlin.* After the Soviet Union established a land blockade of the US, British, and French sectors of Berlin on June 24, 1948, the United States and its allies airlifted supplies to Berlin until after the blockade was lifted in May 1949.

1948–49—*China.* Marines were dispatched to Nanking to protect the American Embassy when the city fell to Communist troops, and to Shanghai to aid in the protection and evacuation of Americans.

1950–53—*Korean War.* The United States responded to North Korean invasion of South Korea by going to its assistance, pursuant to United Nations Security Council resolutions. US forces deployed in Korea exceeded 300,000 during the last year of the conflict. Over 36,600 US military were killed in action.

1950–55—*Formosa (Taiwan).* In June 1950 at the beginning of the Korean War, President Truman ordered the US Seventh Fleet to prevent Chinese Communist attacks upon Formosa and Chinese Nationalist operations against mainland China.

1954–55—*China.* Naval units evacuated US civilians and military personnel from the Tachen Islands.

1956—*Egypt.* A marine battalion evacuated US nationals and other persons from Alexandria during the Suez crisis.

1958—*Lebanon.* Marines were landed in Lebanon at the invitation of its government to help protect against threatened insurrection supported from the outside. The President's action was supported by a Congressional resolution passed in 1957 that authorized such actions in that area of the world.

1959–60—*The Caribbean.* 2d Marine Ground Task Force was deployed to protect US nationals during the Cuban crisis.

1962—*Thailand.* The 3d Marine Expeditionary Unit landed on May 17, 1962 to support that country during the threat of Communist pressure from outside; by July 30 the 5,000 marines had been withdrawn.

1962—*Cuba.* On October 22, President Kennedy instituted a "quarantine" on the shipment of offensive missiles to Cuba from the Soviet Union. He also warned Soviet Union that the launching of any missile from Cuba against nations in the Western Hemisphere would bring about US nuclear retaliation on the Soviet Union. A negotiated settlement was achieved in a few days.

1962–75—*Laos.* From October 1962 until 1975, the United States played an important role in military support of anti-Communist forces in Laos.

1964—*Congo.* The United States sent four transport planes to provide airlift for Congolese troops during a rebellion and to transport Belgian paratroopers to rescue foreigners.

1964–73—*Vietnam War.* US military advisers had been in South Vietnam for a decade, and their numbers had been increased as the military position of the Saigon government became weaker. After citing what he termed were attacks on US destroyers in the Tonkin Gulf, President Johnson asked in August 1964 for a resolution expressing US determination to support freedom and protect peace in Southeast Asia. Congress responded with the Tonkin Gulf Resolution, expressing support for "all necessary measures" the President might take to repel armed attacks against US forces and prevent further aggression. Following this resolution, and following a Communist attack on a US installation in central Vietnam, the United States escalated its participation in the war to a peak of 543,000 military personnel by April 1969.

1965—*Dominican Republic.* The United States intervened to protect lives and property during a Dominican revolt and sent more troops as fears grew that the revolutionary forces were coming increasingly under Communist control.

1967—*Congo.* The United States sent three military transport aircraft with crews to provide the Congo central government with logistical support during a revolt.

1970—*Cambodia.* US troops were ordered into Cambodia to clean out Communist sanctuaries from which Viet Cong and North Vietnamese attacked US and South Vietnamese forces in Vietnam. The object of this attack, which lasted from April 30 to June 30, was to ensure the continuing safe withdrawal of American forces from South Vietnam and to assist the program of Vietnamization.

1974—*Evacuation from Cyprus.* United States naval forces evacuated US civilians during hostilities between Turkish and Greek Cypriot forces.

1975—*Evacuation from Vietnam.* On April 3, 1975, President Ford reported US naval vessels, helicopters, and Marines had been sent to assist in evacuation of refugees and US nationals from Vietnam.3

1975—*Evacuation from Cambodia.* On April 12, 1975, President Ford reported that he had ordered US military forces to proceed with the planned evacuation of US citizens from Cambodia.

1975—*South Vietnam.* On April 30 1975, President Ford reported that a force of 70 evacuation helicopters and 865 Marines had evacuated about 1,400 US citizens and 5,500 third country nationals and South Vietnamese from landing zones near the US Embassy in Saigon and the Tan Son Nhut Airfield.

1975—*Mayaguez incident.* On May 15, 1975, President Ford reported he had ordered military forces to retake the SS *Mayaguez*, a merchant vessel en route from Hong Kong to Thailand with U.S. citizen crew which was seized from Cambodian naval patrol boats in international waters and forced to proceed to a nearby island.

1976—*Lebanon.* On July 22 and 23, 1974, helicopters from five US naval vessels evacuated approximately 250 Americans and Europeans from Lebanon during fighting between Lebanese factions after an overland convoy evacuation had been blocked by hostilities.

1976—*Korea.* Additional forces were sent to Korea after two American soldiers were killed by North Korean soldiers in the demilitarized zone between North and South Korea while cutting down a tree.

1978—*Zaire.* From May 19 through June 1978, the United States utilized military transport aircraft to provide logistical support to Belgian and French rescue operations in Zaire.

1980—*Iran.* On April 26, 1980, President Carter reported the use of six US transport planes and eight helicopters in an unsuccessful attempt to rescue American hostages being held in Iran.

1981—*El Salvador.* After a guerilla offensive against the government of El Salvador, additional US military advisers were sent to El Salvador, bringing the total to approximately 55, to assist in training government forces in counterinsurgency.

1981—*Libya.* On August 19, 1981, US planes based on the carrier *USS Nimitz* shot down two Libyan jets over the Gulf of Sidra after one of the Libyan jets had fired a heat-seeking missile. The United States periodically held freedom of navigation exercises in the Gulf of Sidra, claimed by Libya as territorial waters but considered international waters by the United States.

1982—*Sinai.* On March 19, 1982, President Reagan reported the deployment of military personnel and equipment to participate in the Multinational Force and Observers in the Sinai. Participation had been authorized by the Multinational Force and Observers Resolution, Public Law 97-132.

1982—*Lebanon.* On August 21, 1982, President Reagan reported the dispatch of 80 marines to serve in the multi-national force to assist in the withdrawal of members of the Palestine Liberation force from Beirut. The Marines left September 20, 1982.

1982–1983—*Lebanon.* On September 29, 1982, President Reagan reported the deployment of 1200 marines to serve in a temporary multinational force to facilitate the restoration of Lebanese government sovereignty. On Sept. 29, 1983, Congress passed the Multinational Force in Lebanon Resolution (P.L. 98-119) authorizing the continued participation for eighteen months.

1983—*Egypt.* After a Libyan plane bombed a city in Sudan on March 18, 1983, and Sudan and Egypt appealed for assistance, the United States dispatched an AWACS electronic surveillance plane to Egypt.

1983–89—*Honduras.* In July 1983 the United States undertook a series of exercises in Honduras that some believed might lead to conflict with Nicaragua. On March 25, 1986, unarmed US military helicopters and crewmen ferried Honduran troops to the Nicaraguan border to repel Nicaraguan troops.

1983—*Chad*. On August 8, 1983, President Reagan reported the deployment of two AWACS electronic surveillance planes and eight F-15 fighter planes and ground logistical support forces to assist Chad against Libyan and rebel forces.

1983—*Grenada*. On October 25, 1983, President Reagan reported a landing on Grenada by Marines and Army airborne troops to protect lives and assist in the restoration of law and order and at the request of five members of the Organization of Eastern Caribbean States.

1984—*Persian Gulf*. On June 5, 1984, Saudi Arabian jet fighter planes, aided by intelligence from a US AWACS electronic surveillance aircraft and fueled by a U.S. KC-10 tanker, shot down two Iranian fighter planes over an area of the Persian Gulf proclaimed as a protected zone for shipping.

1985—*Italy*. On October 10, 1985, US Navy pilots intercepted an Egyptian airliner and forced it to land in Sicily. The airliner was carrying the hijackers of the Italian cruise ship Achille Lauro who had killed an American citizen during the hijacking.

1986—*Libya*. On March 26, 1986, President Reagan reported to Congress that, on March 24 and 25, US forces, while engaged in freedom of navigation exercises around the Gulf of Sidra, had been attacked by Libyan missiles and the United States had responded with missiles.

1986—*Libya*. On April 16, 1986, President Reagan reported that US air and naval forces had conducted bombing strikes on terrorist facilities and military installations in Libya.

1986—*Bolivia*. US Army personnel and aircraft assisted Bolivia in anti-drug operations.

1987–88—*Persian Gulf*. After the Iran-Iraq War resulted in several military incidents in the Persian Gulf, the United States increased US joint military forces operations in the Persian Gulf and adopted a policy of reflagging and escorting Kuwaiti oil tankers through the Gulf. President Reagan reported that US ships had been fired upon or struck mines or taken other military action on September 23, October 10, and October 20, 1987 and April 19, July 4, and July 14, 1988. The United States gradually reduced its forces after a cease-fire between Iran and Iraq on August 20, 1988.

1988—*Panama*. In mid-March and April 1988, during a period of instability in Panama and as pressure grew for Panamanian military leader General Manuel Noriega to resign, the United States sent 1,000 troops to Panama, to "further safeguard the canal, US lives, property and interests in the area." The forces supplemented 10,000 US military personnel already in Panama.

1989—*Libya*. On January 4, 1989, two US Navy F-14 aircraft based on the USS John F. Kennedy shot down two Libyan jet fighters over the Mediterranean Sea about 70 miles north of Libya. The US pilots said the Libyan planes had demonstrated hostile intentions.

1989—*Panama*. On May 11, 1989, in response to General Noriega's disregard of the results of the Panamanian election, President Bush ordered a brigade-sized force of approximately 1,900 troops to augment the estimated 11,000 US forces already in the area.

1989—*Andean Initiative in War on Drugs*. On September 15, 1989, President Bush announced that military and law enforcement assistance would be sent to help the Andean nations of Colombia, Bolivia, and Peru combat illicit drug producers and traffickers. By mid-September there were 50–100 US military advisers in Colombia in connection with transport and training in the use of military equipment, plus seven Special Forces teams of 2–12 persons to train troops in the three countries.

1989—*Philippines*. On December 2, 1989, President Bush reported that on December 1 US fighter planes from Clark Air Base in the Philippines had assisted the Aquino government to repel a coup attempt. In addition, 100 marines were sent from the US Navy base at Subic Bay to protect the US Embassy in Manila.

1989–90—*Panama*. On December 21, 1989, President Bush reported that he had ordered US military forces to Panama to protect the lives of American citizens and bring General Noriega to justice. By February 13, 1990, all the invasion forces had been withdrawn.

1990—*Liberia*. On August 6, 1990, President Bush reported that a reinforced rifle company had been sent to provide additional security to the US Embassy in Monrovia, and that helicopter teams had evacuated US citizens from Liberia.

1990—*Saudi Arabia*. On August 9, 1990, President Bush reported that he had ordered the forward deployment of substantial elements of the US armed forces into the Persian Gulf region to help defend Saudi Arabia after the August 2 invasion of Kuwait by Iraq. On November 16, 1990, he reported the continued buildup of the forces to ensure an adequate offensive military option.

1991—*Iraq*. On January 18, 1991, President Bush reported that he had directed US armed forces to commence combat operations on January 16 against Iraqi forces and military targets in Iraq and Kuwait, in conjunction with a coalition of allies and UN Security Council resolutions. On January 12 Congress had passed the Authorization for Use of Military Force against Iraq Resolution (P.L. 102-1). Combat operations were suspended on February 28, 1991.

1991—*Iraq*. On May 17, 1991, President Bush stated in a status report to Congress that the Iraqi repression of the Kurdish people had necessitated a limited introduction of US forces into northern Iraq for emergency relief purposes.

1991—*Zaire*. On September 25–27, 1991, after widespread looting and rioting broke out in Kinshasa, US Air Force C-141s transported 100 Belgian troops and equipment into Kinshasa. US planes also carried 300 French troops into the Central African Republic and hauled back American citizens and third country nationals from locations outside Zaire.

1992—*Sierra Leone*. On May 3, 1992, US military planes evacuated Americans from Sierra Leone, where military leaders had overthrown the government.

1992—*Kuwait*. On August 3, 1992, the United States began a series of military exercises in Kuwait, following Iraqi refusal to recognize a new border drawn up by the United Nations and refusal to cooperate with UN inspection teams.

1992—*Iraq*. On September 16, 1992 President Bush stated in a status report to Congress that he had ordered US participation in the enforcement of a prohibition against Iraqi flights in a specified zone in southern Iraq, and aerial reconnaissance to monitor Iraqi compliance with the cease-fire resolution.

1992—*Somalia*. On December 10, 1992, President Bush reported that he had deployed US armed forces to Somalia in response to a humanitarian crisis and a UN Security Council Resolution determining that the situation constituted a threat to international peace. This operation, called Operation Restore Hope, was part of a US-led United Nations Unified Task Force (UNITAF) and came to an end on May 4, 1993. US forces continued to participate in the successor United Nations Operation in Somalia (UNOSOM II), which the UN Security Council authorized to assist Somalia in political reconciliation and restoration of peace.

1993—*Iraq*. On January 19, 1993, President Bush said in a status report that on December 27, 1992, US aircraft shot down an Iraqi aircraft in the prohibited zone; on January 13 aircraft from the United States and coalition partners had attacked missile bases in southern Iraq; and further military actions had occurred on January 17 and 18. Administration officials said the United States was deploying a battalion task force to Kuwait to underline the continuing US commitment to Kuwaiti independence.

1993—*Iraq*. On January 21, 1993, shortly after his inauguration, President Clinton said the United States would continue the Bush policy on Iraq, and US aircraft fired at targets in Iraq after pilots sensed Iraqi radar or anti-aircraft fire directed at them.

1993—*Bosnia*. On February 28, 1993, the United States began an airdrop of relief supplies aimed at Muslims surrounded by Serbian forces in Bosnia.

1993—*Bosnia*. On April 13, 1993, President Clinton reported US forces were participating in a NATO air action to enforce a UN ban on all unauthorized military flights over Bosnia-Hercegovina.

1993—*Iraq*. In a status report on Iraq of May 24, President Clinton said that on April 9 and April 18 US warplanes had bombed or fired missiles at Iraqi anti-aircraft sites which had tracked US aircraft.

1993—*Somalia*. On June 10, 1993, President Clinton reported that in response to attacks against UN forces in Somalia by a factional leader, the US Quick Reaction Force in the area had participated in military action to quell the violence. On July 1, President Clinton reported further air and ground military operations on June 12 and June 17 aimed at neutralizing military capabilities that had impeded UN efforts to deliver humanitarian relief and promote national reconstruction, and additional instances occurred in the following months.

1993—*Iraq*. On June 28, 1993, President Clinton reported that on June 26 US naval forces had launched missiles against the Iraqi Intelligence Service's headquarters in Baghdad in response to an unsuccessful attempt to assassinate former President Bush in Kuwait in April 1993.

1993—*Iraq*. In a status report of July 22, 1993, President Clinton said on June 19 a US aircraft had fired a missile at an Iraqi anti-aircraft site displaying hostile intent. US planes also bombed an Iraqi missile battery on August 19, 1993.

1993—*Macedonia*. On July 9, 1993, President Clinton reported the deployment of 350 US soldiers to the former Yugoslav Republic of Macedonia to participate in the UN Protection Force to help maintain stability in the area of former Yugoslavia.

1993—*Haiti*. On October 20, 1993, President Clinton reported that US ships had begun to enforce a UN embargo against Haiti.

1994—*Bosnia*. On February 17, 1994, President Clinton reported that the United States had expanded its participation in United Nations and NATO efforts to reach a peaceful solution to the conflict in former Yugoslavia and that 60 US aircraft were available for participation in the authorized NATO missions.

1994—*Bosnia*. On March 1, 1994, President Clinton reported that on February 28 US planes patrolling the "no-fly zone" in former Yugoslavia under the North Atlantic Treaty Organization (NATO) shot down 4 Serbian Galeb planes.

1994—*Bosnia*. On April 12, 1994, President Clinton reported that on April 10 and 11, US warplanes under NATO command had fired against Bosnian Serb forces shelling the "safe" city of Gorazde.

1994—*Rwanda*. On April 12, 1994, President Clinton reported that combat-equipped US military forces had been deployed to Burundi to conduct possible non-combatant evacuation operations of US citizens and other third-country nationals from Rwanda, where widespread fighting had broken out. By September 30, 1994, all US troops had departed from Rwanda and surrounding nations. In the Defense Appropriations Act for FY1995 (P.L. 103-335, signed September 30, 1994), Congress barred use of funds for US military participation in or around Rwanda after October 7, 1994, except for any action necessary to protect US citizens.

1994—*Macedonia*. On April 19, 1994, President Clinton reported that the US contingent in the former Yugoslav Republic of Macedonia had been augmented by a reinforced company of 200 personnel.

1994—*Haiti*. On April 20, 1994, President Clinton reported that US naval forces had continued enforcement of the UN embargo in the waters around Haiti and that 712 vessels had been boarded since October 20, 1993.

1994—*Bosnia*. On August 22, 1994, President Clinton reported the use on August 5 of US aircraft under NATO to attack Bosnian Serb heavy weapons in the Sarajevo heavy weapons exclusion zone upon request of the UN Protection Forces.

1994—*Haiti*. On September 21, 1994, President Clinton reported the deployment of 1,500 troops to Haiti to restore democracy in Haiti. The troop level was subsequently increased to 20,000.

1994—*Bosnia*. On November 22, 1994, President Clinton reported the use of US combat aircraft on November 21, 1994, under NATO, to attack bases used by Serbs to attack the town of Bihac in Bosnia.

1994—*Macedonia*. On December 22, 1994, President Clinton reported that the US Army contingent in the former Yugoslav Republic of Macedonia continued its peacekeeping mission and that the current contingent would soon be replaced by about 500 soldiers from the 3rd Battalion, 5th Cavalry Regiment, 1st Armored Division from Kirchgons, Germany.

1995—*Somalia*. On March 1, 1995, President Clinton reported that on February 27, 1995, 1,800 combat-equipped US armed forces personnel began deployment into Mogadishu, Somalia, to assist in the withdrawal of UN forces assigned there to the United Nations Operation in Somalia (UNOSOM II). This mission was completed on March 3, 1995.

1995—*Haiti*. On March 21, 1995, President Clinton reported that US military forces in Haiti as part of a UN Multinational Force had been reduced to just under 5,300 personnel. He noted that as of March 31, 1995, approximately 2,500 US personnel would remain in Haiti as part of the UN Mission in Haiti (UNMIH).

1995—*Bosnia*. On May 24, 1995, President Clinton reported that US combat-equipped fighter aircraft and other aircraft continued to contribute to NATO's enforcement of the no-fly zone in airspace over Bosnia-Herzegovina. US aircraft, he noted, were also available for close air support of UN forces in Croatia. Roughly 500 US soldiers continued to be deployed in the former Yugoslav Republic of Macedonia as part of the UN Preventive Deployment Force (UNPREDEP). US forces continued to support UN refugee and embargo operations in this region.

1995—*Bosnia*. On September 1, 1995, President Clinton reported that "US combat and support aircraft" had been used beginning on August 29, 1995, in a series of NATO air strikes against Bosnian Serb Army (BSA) forces in Bosnia-Herzegovina that were threatening the UN-declared safe areas of Sarajevo, Tuzla, and Gorazde. He noted that during the first day of operations, "some 300 sorties were flown against 23 targets in the vicinity of Sarajevo, Tuzla, Gorazde and Mostar."

1995—*Haiti*. On September 21, 1995, President Clinton reported that currently the United States had 2,400 military personnel in Haiti as participants in the UN Mission in Haiti (UNMIH). In addition, 260 US military personnel were assigned to the US Support Group Haiti.

1995—*Bosnia*. On December 6, 1995, President Clinton reported to Congress, that he had "ordered the deployment of approximately 1,500 US military personnel" to Bosnia-Herzegovina and Croatia as part of a NATO "enabling force" to lay the groundwork for the prompt and safe deployment of the NATO-led Implementation Force (IFOR)," which would be used to implement the Bosnian peace agreement after its signing. The President also noted that he had authorized deployment of roughly 3,000 other US military personnel to Hungary, Italy, and Croatia to establish infrastructure for the enabling force and the IFOR.

1995—*Bosnia*. On December 21, 1995, President Clinton reported to Congress that he had ordered the deployment of approximately 20,000 US military personnel to participate in the NATO-led Implementation Force (IFOR) in the Republic of Bosnia-Herzegovina, and approximately 5,000 US military personnel would be deployed in other former Yugoslav states, primarily in Croatia. In addition, about 7,000 US support forces would be deployed to Hungary, Italy and Croatia and other regional states in support of IFOR's mission.

1996—*Haiti*. On March 21, 1996, President Clinton reported to Congress that beginning in January 1996 there had been a "phased reduction" in the number of United States personnel assigned to the United Nations Mission in Haiti (UNMIH). As of March 21, 309 US personnel remained a part of UNMIH. These US forces were "equipped for combat."

1996—*Liberia*. On April 11, 1996, President Clinton reported to Congress that on April 9, 1996 due to the "deterioration of the security situation and the resulting threat to American citizens" in Liberia he had ordered US military forces to evacuate from that country "private US citizens and certain third-country nationals who had taken refuge in the US Embassy compound...."

1996—*Liberia.* On May 20, 1996, President Clinton reported to Congress the continued deployment of US military forces in Liberia to evacuate both American citizens and other foreign personnel, and to respond to various isolated "attacks on the American Embassy complex" in Liberia. The President noted that the deployment of US forces would continue until there was no longer any need for enhanced security at the Embassy and a requirement to maintain an evacuation capability in the country.

1996—*Central African Republic.* On May 23, 1996, President Clinton reported to Congress the deployment of US military personnel to Bangui, Central African Republic, to conduct the evacuation from that country of "private US citizens and certain U.S. Government employees," and to provide "enhanced security for the American Embassy in Bangui."

1996—*Bosnia.* On June 21, 1996, President Clinton reported to Congress that United States forces totaling about 17,000 remain deployed in Bosnia "under NATO operational command and control" as part of the NATO Implementation Force (IFOR). In addition, about 5,500 US military personnel were deployed in Hungary, Italy and Croatia, and other regional states to provide "logistical and other support to IFOR." The President noted that it was the intention that IFOR would complete the withdrawal of all troops in the weeks after December 20, 1996, on a schedule "set by NATO commanders consistent with the safety of troops and the logistical requirements for an orderly withdrawal." He also noted that a US Army contingent (of about 500 US soldiers) remained in the Former Yugoslav Republic of Macedonia as part of the United Nations Preventive Deployment Force (UNPREDEP).

1996—*Rwanda and Zaire.* On December 2, 1996, President Clinton reported to Congress that to support the humanitarian efforts of the United Nations regarding refugees in Rwanda and the Great Lakes Region of Eastern Zaire, he had authorized the use of US personnel and aircraft, including AC-130U planes to help in surveying the region in support of humanitarian operations, although fighting still was occurring in the area, and US aircraft had been subject to fire when on flight duty.

1996—*Bosnia.* On December 20, 1996, President Clinton reported to Congress that he had authorized US participation in an IFOR follow-on force in Bosnia, known as SFOR (Stabilization Force), under NATO command. The President said the US forces contribution to SFOR was to be "about 8,500" personnel whose primary mission is to deter or prevent a resumption of hostilities or new threats to peace in Bosnia. SFOR's duration in Bosnia is expected to be 18 months, with progressive reductions and eventual withdrawal.

1997—*Albania.* On March 15, 1997, President Clinton reported to Congress that on March 13, 1997, he had utilized US military forces to evacuate certain U.S. Government employees and private US citizens from Tirana, Albania, and to enhance security for the US Embassy in that city.

1997—*Congo and Gabon.* On March 27, 1997, President Clinton reported to Congress that, on March 25, 1997, a standby evacuation force of US military personnel had been deployed to Congo and Gabon to provide enhanced security for American private citizens, government employees, and selected third country nationals in Zaire, and to be available for any necessary evacuation operation.

1997—*Sierra Leone.* On May 30, 1997, President Clinton reported to Congress that on May 29 and May 30, 1997, US military personnel were deployed to Freetown, Sierra Leone, to prepare for and undertake the evacuation of certain US government employees and private US citizens.

1997—*Bosnia.* On June 20, 1997, President Clinton reported to Congress that US Armed Forces continued to support peacekeeping operations in Bosnia and other states in the region in support of the NATO-led Stabilization Force (SFOR). He reported that currently most US military personnel involved in SFOR were in Bosnia, near Tuzla, and about 2,800 US troops were deployed in Hungary, Croatia, Italy, and other regional states to provide logistics and other support to SFOR. A US Army continent of about 500 also remained in the Former Yugoslav Republic of Macedonia as part of the UN Preventive Deployment Force (UNPREDEP).

1997—*Cambodia.* On July 11, 1997, President Clinton reported to Congress that in an effort to ensure the security of American citizens in Cambodia during a period of domestic conflict there, he had deployed a Task Force of

about 550 US military personnel to Utapao Air Base in Thailand. These personnel were to be available for possible emergency evacuation operations in Cambodia as deemed necessary.

1997—*Bosnia.* On December 19, 1997, President Clinton reported to Congress that he intended "in principle" to have the United States participate in a security presence in Bosnia when the NATO SFOR contingent withdrew in the summer of 1998.

1998—*Guinea-Bissau.* On June 12, 1998, President Clinton reported to Congress that, on June 10, 1998, in response to an army mutiny in Guinea-Bissau endangering the US Embassy, US government employees and citizens in that country, he had deployed a standby evacuation force of US military personnel to Dakar, Senegal, to remove such individuals, as well as selected third country nationals, from the city of Bissau. The deployment continued until the necessary evacuations were completed.

1998—*Bosnia.* On June 19, 1998, President Clinton reported to Congress regarding activities in the last six months of combat-equipped US forces in support of NATO's SFOR in Bosnia and surrounding areas of former Yugoslavia.

1998—*Kenya and Tanzania.* On August 10, 1998, President Clinton reported to Congress that he had deployed, on August 7, 1998, a Joint Task Force of US military personnel to Nairobi, Kenya, to coordinate the medical and disaster assistance related to the bombings of the U.S. Embassies in Kenya and Tanzania. He also reported that teams of 50–100 security personnel had arrived in Nairobi, Kenya, and Dar es Salaam, Tanzania, to enhance the security of the US Embassies and citizens there.

1998—*Albania.* On August 18, 1998, President Clinton reported to Congress that he had, on August 16, 1998, deployed 200 US Marines and 10 Navy SEALS to the US Embassy compound in Tirana, Albania, to enhance security against reported threats against US personnel.

1998—*Afghanistan and Sudan.* On August 21, 1998, by letter, President Clinton reported to Congress that he had authorized airstrikes on August 20th against camps and installations in Afghanistan and Sudan used by the Osama bin Laden terrorist organization. The President did so based on what he viewed as convincing information that the bin Laden organization was responsible for the bombings, on August 7, 1998, of the US Embassies in Kenya and Tanzania.

1998—*Liberia.* On September 29, 1998, President Clinton reported to Congress that on September 27, 1998 he had, due to political instability and civil disorder in Liberia, deployed a stand-by response and evacuation force of 30 US military personnel to augment the security force at the US Embassy in Monrovia, and to provide for a rapid evacuation capability, as needed, to remove US citizens and government personnel from the country.

1998—*Iraq.* During the period from December 16–23, 1998, the United States, together with the United Kingdom, conducted a bombing campaign, termed Operation Desert Fox, against Iraqi industrial facilities deemed capable of producing weapons of mass destruction, and against other Iraqi military and security targets.

1998–1999 *Iraq.* Beginning in late December 1998, and continuing during 1999, the United States, together with forces of the coalition enforcing the "no-fly" zones over Iraq, conducted military operations against the Iraqi air defense system on numerous occasions in response to actual or potential threats against aircraft enforcing the "no-fly" zones in northern and southern Iraq.

1999—*Bosnia.* On January 19, 1999, President Clinton reported to Congress that he was continuing to authorize the use of combat-equipped US Armed Forces in Bosnia and other states in the region as participants in and supporters of the NATO-led Stabilization Force (SFOR). He noted that the US SFOR military personnel totaled about 6,900, with about 2,300 US military personnel deployed to Hungary, Croatia, Italy and other regional states. Also some 350 US military personnel remain deployed in the Former Yugoslav Republic of Macedonia (FYROM) as part of the UN Preventive Deployment Force (UNPREDEP).

1999—*Kenya.* On February 25, 1999, President Clinton reported to Congress that he was continuing to deploy US military personnel in that country to assist in providing security for the US embassy and American citizens

in Nairobi, pending completion of renovations of the American embassy facility in Nairobi, subject of a terrorist bombing in August 1998.

1999—*Yugoslavia*. On March 26, 1999, President Clinton reported to Congress that, on March 24, 1999, US military forces, at his direction, and in coalition with NATO allies, had commenced air strikes against Yugoslavia in response to the Yugoslav government's campaign of violence and repression against the ethnic Albanian population in Kosovo.

1999—*Yugoslavia/Albania*. On April 7, 1999, President Clinton reported to Congress, that he had ordered additional US military forces to Albania, including rotary wing aircraft, artillery, and tactical missiles systems to enhance NATO's ability to conduct effective air operations in Yugoslavia. About 2,500 soldiers and aviators are to be deployed as part of this task force. The President also reported the deployment of US military forces to Albania and Macedonia to support humanitarian disaster relief operations for Kosovar refugees.

1999—*Yugoslavia/Albania*. On May 25, 1999, President Clinton reported to Congress, "consistent with the war Powers Resolution" that he had directed "deployment of additional aircraft and forces to support NATO's ongoing efforts [against Yugoslavia], including several thousand additional US Armed Forces personnel to Albania in support of the deep strike force located there." He also directed that additional US forces be deployed to the region to assist in "humanitarian operations."

1999—*Yugoslavia/Kosovo*. On June 12, 1999, President Clinton reported to Congress, "consistent with the War Powers Resolution" that he had directed the deployment of about "7,000 US military personnel as the US contribution to the approximately 50,000-member, NATO-led security force (KFOR)" currently being assembled in Kosovo. He also noted that about "1,500 US military personnel, under separate US command and control, will deploy to other countries in the region, as our national support element, in support of KFOR."

1999—*Bosnia*. On July 19, 1999, President Clinton reported to Congress "consistent with the War Powers Resolution" that about 6,200 US military personnel were continuing to participate in the NATO-led Stabilization Force (SFOR) in Bosnia, and that another 2,200 personnel were supporting SFOR operations from Hungary, Croatia, and Italy. He also noted that US military personnel remain in the Former Yugoslav Republic of Macedonia to support the international security presence in Kosovo (KFOR).

1999—*East Timor*. On October 8, 1999, President Clinton reported to Congress "consistent with the War Powers Resolution" that he had directed the deployment of a limited number of US military forces to East Timor to support the U.N. multinational force (INTERFET) aimed at restoring peace to East Timor. US support has been limited initially to "communications, logistics, planning assistance and transportation." The President further noted that he had authorized deployment of the amphibious ship USS Belleau Wood, together with its helicopters and her complement of personnel from the 31st Marine Expeditionary Unit (Special Operations Capable) (MEU SOC) to the East Timor region, to provide helicopter airlift and search and rescue support to the multinational operation. US participation was anticipated to continue until the transition to a UN peacekeeping operation was complete.

1999—*Yugoslavia/Kosovo*. On December 15, 1999, President Clinton reported to Congress "consistent with the War Powers Resolution" that U.S. combat-equipped military personnel continued to serve as part of the NATO-led security force in Kosovo (KFOR). He noted that the American contribution to KFOR in Kosovo was "approximately 8,500 US military personnel." US forces were deployed in a sector centered around "Urosevac in the eastern portion of Kosovo." For US KFOR forces, "maintaining public security is a key task." Other US military personnel are deployed to other countries in the region to serve in administrative and logistics support roles for US forces in KFOR. Of these forces, about 1,500 US military personnel are in Macedonia and Greece, and occasionally in Albania.

1999–2000—*Iraq*. At various times during 1999, and continuing throughout 2000 the United States, together with forces of the coalition enforcing the "no-fly" zones over Iraq, conducted military operations against the Iraqi air defense system on numerous occasions in response to actual or potential threats against aircraft enforcing the "no-fly" zones in northern and southern Iraq.

2000—*Bosnia*. On January 25, 2000, President Clinton reported to Congress "consistent with the War Powers Resolution" that the US continued to provide combat-equipped US Armed Forces to Bosnia-Herzegovina and other states in the region as part of the NATO led Stabilization Force (SFOR). The President noted that the US force contribution was being reduced from "approximately 6,200 to 4,600 personnel," with the US forces assigned to Multinational Division, North, centered around the city of Tuzla. He added that approximately 1,500 US military personnel were deployed to Hungary, Croatia, and Italy to provide "logistical and other support to SFOR," and that US forces continue to support SFOR in "efforts to apprehend persons indicted for war crimes."

2000—*East Timor*. On February 25, 2000, President Clinton reported to Congress "consistent with the War Powers Resolution" that he had authorized the participation of a small number of US military personnel in support of the United Nations Transitional Administration in East Timor (UNTAET), which has a mandate to maintain law and order throughout East Timor, and to facilitate establishment of an effective administration there, delivery of humanitarian assistance and support the building of self-government. The President reported that the US contingent was small: three military observers, and one judge advocate. To facilitate and coordinate US military activities in East Timor, the President also authorized the deployment of a support group (USGET), consisting of 30 US personnel. US personnel would be temporarily deployed to East Timor, on a rotational basis, and through periodic ship visits, during which US forces would conduct "humanitarian and assistance activities throughout East Timor." Rotational activities should continue through the summer of 2000.

2000—*Sierra Leone*. On May 12, 2000, President Clinton, "consistent with the War Powers Resolution" reported to Congress that he had ordered a US Navy patrol craft to deploy to Sierra Leone to be ready to support evacuation operations from that country if needed. He also authorized a US C-17 aircraft to deliver "ammunition, and other supplies and equipment" to Sierra Leone in support of United Nations peacekeeping operations there.

2000—*Yugoslavia/Kosovo*. On June 16, 2000, President Clinton reported to Congress, "consistent with the War Powers Resolution," that the US was continuing to provide military personnel to the NATO-led KFOR security force in Kosovo. US forces were numbered at 7,500, but were scheduled to be reduced to 6,000 when ongoing troop rotations were completed. US forces in Kosovo are assigned to a sector centered near Gnjilane in eastern Kosovo. Other US military personnel are deployed to other countries serving in administrative and logistics support roles, with approximately 1,000 US personnel in Macedonia, Albania and Greece.

2000—*Bosnia*. On July 25, 2000, President Clinton reported to Congress, "consistent with the War Powers Resolution," that combat-equipped US military personnel continued to participate in the NATO-led Stabilization Force (SFOR) in Bosnia-Herzegovina, being deployed to Bosnia, and other states in the region in support of peacekeeping efforts in former Yugoslavia. US military personnel levels have been reduced from 6,200 to 4,600. Apart from the forces in Bosnia, approximately 1,000 US personnel continue to be deployed in support roles in Hungary, Croatia, and Italy.

2000—*East Timor*. On August 25, 2000, President Clinton reported to Congress, "consistent with the War Powers Resolution," that the United States was currently contributing three military observers to the United Nations Transitional Administration in East Timor (UNTAET) that is charged by the UN with restoring and maintaining peace and security there. He also noted that the US was maintaining a military presence in East Timor separate from UNTAET, comprised of about 30 US personnel who facilitate and coordinate US military activities in East Timor and rotational operations of US forces there. US forces currently conduct humanitarian and civic assistance activities for East Timor's citizens. US rotational presence operations in East Timor are presently expected, the President said, to continue through December 2000.

2000—*Yemen*. On October 14, 2000, President Clinton reported to Congress, "consistent with the War Powers Resolution," that on October 12, 2000, in the wake of an attack on the USS Cole in the port of Aden, Yemen, he had authorized deployment of about 45 military personnel from US Naval Forces Central Command to Aden to provide "medical, security, and disaster response assistance." The President further reported that on October 13, 2000 about 50 US military security personnel arrived in Aden, and that additional "security elements" may

be deployed to the area, to enhance the ability of the US to ensure the security of the USS Cole and the personnel responding to the incident. In addition, two US Navy surface combatant vessels are operating in or near Yemeni territorial waters to provide communications and other support, as required.

2000—*Yugoslavia/Kosovo.* On December 18, 2000, President Clinton reported to Congress, "consistent with the War Powers Resolution," that the United States was continuing to provide approximately 5,600 US military personnel in support of peacekeeping efforts in Kosovo as part of the NATO-led international security force in Kosovo (KFOR). An additional 500 US military personnel are deployed as the National Support Element in Macedonia, with an occasional presence in Albania and Greece. US forces are assigned to a sector centered around Gnjilane in the eastern portion of Kosovo. The President noted that the mission for these US military forces is maintaining a safe and secure environment through conducting "security patrols in urban areas and in the countryside throughout their sector."

2001—*East Timor.* On March 2, 2001, President George W. Bush reported to Congress, "consistent with the War Powers Resolution," that US armed forces were continuing to support the United Nations peacekeeping effort in East Timor aimed at providing security and maintaining law and order in East Timor, coordinating delivery of humanitarian assistance, and helping establish the basis for self-government in East Timor. The US currently has three military observers attached to the United Nations Transitional Administration in East Timor (UNTAET). The United States also has a separate military presence, the US Support Group East Timor (USGET), of approximately 12 US personnel, including a security detachment, which "facilitates and coordinates" US military activities in East Timor.

2001—*Yugoslavia/Kosovo.* On May 18, 2001, President George W. Bush reported to Congress, "consistent with the War Powers Resolution," that the United States was continuing to provide approximately 6,000 US military personnel in support of peacekeeping efforts in Kosovo as part of the NATO-led international security force in Kosovo (KFOR). An additional 500 US military personnel are deployed as the National Support Element in Macedonia, with an occasional presence in Greece and Albania. US forces in Kosovo are assigned to a sector centered around Gnjilane in the eastern portion. President Bush noted that the mission for these US military forces is maintaining a safe and secure environment through conducting security patrols in urban areas and in the countryside through their sector.

2001—*Bosnia.* On July 25, 2001, President George W. Bush reported to Congress, "consistent with the War Powers Resolution, about 3,800 combat-equipped US Armed Forces continued to be deployed in Bosnia-Herzegovina, and other regional states as part of the NATO-led Stabilization Force (SFOR). Most were based at Tuzla in Bosnia. About 500 others were based in Hungary, Croatia, and Italy, providing logistical and other support.

2001—*Iraq.* At various times throughout 2001, the United States, together with forces of the coalition enforcing the "no-fly" zones over Iraq, conducted military operations against the Iraqi air defense system on numerous occasions in response to actual or potential threats against aircraft enforcing the "no-fly" zones in northern and southern Iraq.

2001—*East Timor.* On August 31, 2001, President George W. Bush reported to Congress, "consistent with the War Powers Resolution," that US armed forces were continuing to support the United Nations peacekeeping effort in East Timor aimed at providing security and maintaining law and order in East Timor, coordinating delivery of humanitarian assistance, and helping establish the basis for self-government in East Timor. The US currently has three military observers attached to the United Nations Transitional Administration in East Timor (UNTAET). The United States also has a separate military presence, the US Support Group East Timor (USGET), of approximately 20 US personnel, including a security detachment, which "facilitates and coordinates" US military activities in East Timor, as well as a rotational presence of US forces through temporary deployments to East Timor. The President stated that US forces would continue a presence through December 2001, while options for a US presence in 2002 are being reviewed, with the President's objective being redeployment of USGET personnel, as circumstances permit.

2001—*Terrorism threat.* On September 24, 2001, President George W. Bush reported to Congress, "consistent with the War Powers Resolution," and "Senate Joint Resolution 23" that in response to terrorist attacks on the World Trade Center and the Pentagon he had ordered the "deployment of various combat-equipped and combat support forces to a number of foreign nations in the Central and Pacific Command areas of operations." The President noted

in efforts to "prevent and deter terrorism" he might find it necessary to order additional forces into these and other areas of the world...." He stated that he could not now predict "the scope and duration of these deployments," or the "actions necessary to counter the terrorist threat to the United States."

2001—*Afghanistan*. On October 9, 2001, President George W. Bush reported to Congress, "consistent with the War Powers Resolution," and "Senate Joint Resolution 23" that on October 7, 2001, US Armed Forces "began combat action in Afghanistan against Al Qaida terrorists and their Taliban supporters." The President stated that he had directed this military action in response to the September 11, 2001 attacks on US "territory, our citizens, and our way of life, and to the continuing threat of terrorist acts against the United States and our friends and allies." This military action was "part of our campaign against terrorism" and was "designed to disrupt the use of Afghanistan as a terrorist base of operations."

2001—*Yugoslavia/Kosovo*. On November 19, 2001, President George W. Bush reported to Congress, "consistent with the War Powers Resolution," that the United States was continuing to provide approximately 5,500 US military personnel in support of peacekeeping efforts in Kosovo as part of the NATO-led international security force in Kosovo (KFOR). An additional 500 US military personnel are deployed as the National Support Element in Macedonia, with an occasional presence in Greece and Albania. US forces in Kosovo are assigned to a sector centered around Gnjilane in the eastern portion. President Bush noted that the mission for these US military forces is maintaining a safe and secure environment through conducting security patrols in urban areas and in the countryside through their sector.

2002—*Bosnia*. On January 21, 2002, President George W. Bush reported to Congress, "consistent with the War Powers Resolution," that about 3,100 combat-equipped US Armed Forces continued to be deployed in Bosnia-Herzegovina, and other regional states as part of the NATO-led Stabilization Force (SFOR). Most American forces were based at Tuzla in Bosnia. About 500 others were based in Hungary, Croatia, and Italy, providing logistical and other support.

2002—*East Timor*. On February 28, 2002, President George W. Bush reported to Congress, "consistent with the War Powers Resolution," that US Armed Forces were continuing to support the United Nations peacekeeping effort in East Timor aimed at providing security and maintaining law and order in East Timor, coordinating delivery of humanitarian assistance, and helping establish the basis for self-government in East Timor. The United States currently has three military observers attached to the United Nations Transitional Administration in East Timor (UNTAET). The United States also has a separate military presence, the US Support Group East Timor (USGET), comprised of approximately 10 US personnel, including a security detachment, which "facilitates and coordinates" US military activities in East Timor, as well as a rotational presence of US forces through temporary deployments to East Timor. The President stated that US forces would continue a presence through 2002. The President noted his objective was to gradually reduce the "rotational presence operations," and to redeploy USGET personnel, as circumstances permitted.

2002—*Terrorism threat*. On March 20, 2002, President George W. Bush reported to Congress, "consistent with the War Powers Resolution," on US efforts in the "global war on Terrorism." He noted that the "heart of the al-Qaeda training capability" had been "seriously degraded," and that the remainder of the Taliban and the al-Qaeda fighters were being "actively pursued and engaged by the US, coalition and Afghan forces." The US was also conducting "maritime interception operations...to locate and detain suspected al-Qaeda or Taliban leadership fleeing Afghanistan by sea." At the Philippine Government's invitation, the President had ordered deployed "combat-equipped and combat support forces to train with, advise, and assist" the Philippines' Armed Forces in enhancing their "existing counterterrorist capabilities." The strength of US military forces working with the Philippines was projected to be 600 personnel. The President noted that he was "assessing options" for assisting other nations, including Georgia and Yemen, in enhancing their "counterterrorism capabilities, including training and equipping their armed forces." He stated that US combat-equipped and combat support forces would be necessary for these efforts, if undertaken.

2002—*Yugoslavia/Kosovo*. On May 17, 2002, President George W. Bush reported to Congress, "consistent with the War Powers Resolution," that the US military was continuing to support peacekeeping efforts of the NATO-led international security force in Kosovo (KFOR). He noted that the current US contribution was about 5,100 military personnel, and an additional 468 personnel in Macedonia; with an occasional presence in Albania and Greece.

2002—*Bosnia*. On July 22, 2002, President George W. Bush reported to Congress, "consistent with the War Powers Resolution," that the US military was continuing to support peacekeeping efforts of the NATO-led Stabilization Force (SFOR) in Bosnia-Herzegovina and other regional states. He noted that the current US contribution was "approximately 2,400 personnel." Most US forces in Bosnia-Herzegovina are assigned to the Multinational Division, North headquartered in Tuzla. An additional 60 US military personnel are deployed to Hungary and Croatia to provide logistical and other support.

2002—*Terrorism threat*. On September 20, 2002, President Bush reported to Congress "consistent with the War Powers Resolution," that US "combat-equipped and combat support forces" have been deployed to the Philippines since January 2002 to train with, assist and advise the Philippines' Armed Forces in enhancing their "counterterrorist capabilities." He added that US forces were conducting maritime interception operations in the Central and European Command areas to combat movement, arming or financing of "international terrorists." He also noted that US combat personnel had been deployed to Georgia and Yemen to help enhance the "counterterrorist capabilities" of their armed forces.

2002—*Cote d'Ivoire*. On September 26, 2002, President Bush reported to Congress "consistent with the War Powers Resolution," that in response to a rebellion in Cote d'Ivoire that he had on September 25, 2002 sent US military personnel into Cote d'Ivoire to assist in the evacuation of American citizens and third country nationals from the city of Bouake; and otherwise assist in other evacuations as necessary.

2002—*Yugoslavia/Kosovo*. On November 15, 2002, the President reported to Congress "consistent with the War Powers Resolution" that the US was continuing to deploy combat equipped military personnel as part of the NATO-led international security force in Kosovo (KFOR). Currently there are approximately 4,350 US military personnel in Kosovo, with an additional 266 military personnel in Macedonia. The United States also has an occasional presence in Albania and Greece, associated with the KFOR mission.

2003—*Bosnia*. On January 21, 2003, President George W. Bush reported to Congress, "consistent with the War Powers Resolution," that about 1,800 US Armed Forces personnel continued to be deployed in Bosnia-Herzegovina, and other regional states as part of the NATO-led Stabilization Force (SFOR). Most were based at Tuzla in Bosnia. About 80 others were based in Hungary and Croatia, providing logistical and other support.

2003—*Terrorism threat*. On March 20, 2003, President Bush reported to Congress, "consistent with the War Powers Resolution," as well as P.L. 107-40, and "pursuant to" his authority as Commander-in-Chief, that he had continued a number of US military operations globally in the war against terrorism. These military operations included ongoing US actions against al-Qaeda fighters in Afghanistan; collaborative anti-terror operations with forces of Pakistan in the Pakistan/Afghanistan border area; "maritime interception operations on the high seas" in areas of responsibility of the Central and European Commands to prevent terrorist movement and other activities; and military support for the armed forces of Georgia and Yemen in counter-terrorism operations.

2003—*Iraq War*. On March 21, 2003, President Bush reported to Congress, "consistent with the War Powers Resolution," as well as P.L. 102-1 and P.L. 107-243, and "pursuant to" his authority as Commander-in-Chief, that he had "directed US Armed Forces, operating with other coalition forces, to commence operations on March 19, 2003, against Iraq." He further stated that it was not possible to know at present the duration of active combat operations or the scope necessary to accomplish the goals of the operation "to disarm Iraq in pursuit of peace, stability, and security both in the Gulf region and in the United States."

2003—*Yugoslavia/Kosovo*. On May 14, 2003, President Bush reported to Congress, "consistent with the War Powers Resolution," that combat-equipped US military personnel continued to be deployed as part of the NATO-led

international security force in Kosovo (KFOR). He noted that about 2,250 US military personnel were deployed in Kosovo, and additional military personnel operated, on occasion, from Macedonia, Albania, and Greece in support of KFOR operations.

2003—*Liberia*. On June 9, 2003, President Bush reported to Congress, "consistent with the War Powers Resolution," that on June 8 he had sent about 35 combat-equipped US military personnel into Monrovia, Liberia, to augment US Embassy security forces, to aid in the possible evacuation of US citizens if necessary. The President also noted that he had sent about 34 combat-equipped US military personnel to help secure the US Embassy in Nouakchott, Mauritania, and to assist in evacuation of American citizens if required. They were expected to arrive at the US embassy by June 10, 2003. Back-up and support personnel were sent to Dakar, Senegal, to aid in any necessary evacuation from either Liberia or Mauritania.

2003—*Bosnia*. On July 22, 2003, President Bush reported to Congress, "consistent with the War Powers Resolution," that the United States continued to provide about 1,800 combat-equipped military personnel in Bosnia-Herzegovina in support of NATO's Stabilization Force (SFOR) and its peacekeeping efforts in this country.

2003—*Liberia*. On August 13, 2003, President Bush reported to Congress, "consistent with the War Powers Resolution," that in response to conditions in Liberia, on August 11, 2003, he had authorized about 4,350 US combat-equipped military personnel to enter Liberian territorial waters in support of UN and West African States efforts to restore order and provide humanitarian assistance in Liberia.

2003—*Terrorism threat*. On September 19, 2003, President Bush reported to Congress "consistent with the War Powers Resolution," that US "combat-equipped and combat support forces" continue to be deployed at a number of locations around the world as part of US anti-terrorism efforts. American forces support anti-terrorism efforts in the Philippines, and maritime interception operations continue on the high seas in the Central, European, and Pacific Command areas of responsibility, to "prevent the movement, arming, or financing of international terrorists." He also noted that "US combat equipped and support forces" had been deployed to Georgia and Djibouti to help in enhancing their "counterterrorist capabilities."

2003—*Yugoslavia/Kosovo*. On November 14, 2003, the President reported to Congress "consistent with the War Powers Resolution" that the United States was continuing to deploy combat equipped military personnel as part of the NATO-led international security force in Kosovo (KFOR). Currently there are approximately 2,100 US military personnel in Kosovo, with additional American military personnel operating out of Macedonia, Albania and Greece, in support of KFOR operations.

2004—*Bosnia*. On January 22, 2004, the President reported to Congress "consistent with the War Powers Resolution" that the United States was continuing to deploy combat equipped military personnel to Bosnia and Herzegovina in support of NATO's Stabilization Force (SFOR) and its peacekeeping efforts in this country. About 1,800 US personnel are participating.

2004—*Haiti*. On February 25, 2004, the President reported to Congress "consistent with the War Powers Resolution" that, on February 23, he had sent a combat-equipped "security force" of about "55 US military personnel from the US Joint Forces Command" to Port-au-Prince, Haiti to augment the US Embassy security forces there and to protect American citizens and property in light of the instability created by the armed rebellion in Haiti.

2004—*Haiti*. On March 2, 2004, the President reported to Congress "consistent with the War Powers Resolution" that on February 29 he had sent about "200 additional US combat-equipped, military personnel from the US Joint Forces Command" to Port-au-Prince, Haiti for a variety of purposes, including preparing the way for a UN Multinational Interim Force, and otherwise supporting UN Security Council Resolution 1529 (2004).

2004—*Terrorism: Bosnia and Haiti*. On March 20, 2004, the President reported to Congress "consistent with the War Powers Resolution," a consolidated report giving details of multiple on-going United States military deployments and operations "in support of the global war on terrorism (including in Afghanistan)," as well as operations in Bosnia and Herzegovina, Kosovo, and Haiti. In this report, the President noted that US anti-terror related

activities were underway in Georgia, Djibouti, Kenya, Ethiopia, Yemen, and Eritrea. He further noted that US combat-equipped military personnel continued to be deployed in Kosovo as part of the NATO-led KFOR (1,900 personnel); in Bosnia and Herzegovina as part of the NATO-led SFOR (about 1,100 personnel); and approximately 1,800 military personnel were deployed in Haiti as part of the UN Multinational Interim Force.

(**Note 1.**) This list through 1975 is reprinted with few changes from: US Congress. House. Committee on International Relations [now Foreign Affairs]. Subcommittee on International Security and Scientific Affairs. Background Information on the Use of US Armed Forces in Foreign Countries, 1975 Revision. Committee print, 94th Congress, 1st session. Prepared by the Foreign Affairs Division, Congressional Research Service, Library of Congress. Washington, US Government Printing Office, 1975. 84 p.

(**Note 2.**) Other lists include Goldwater, Senator Barry. War Without Declaration. A Chronological List of 199 US Military Hostilities Abroad Without a Declaration of War. 1798-1972. Congressional Record, V. 119, July 20, 1973: S14174–14183; US Department of State. Armed Actions Taken by the United States Without a Declaration of War, 1789-1967. Research Project 806A. Historical Studies Division. Bureau of Public Affairs; Collins, John M. America's Small Wars. New York, Brassey's, 1990. For a discussion of the evolution of lists of military actions and legal authorization for various actions, see Wormuth, Francis D. and Edwin B. Firmage, *To Chain the Dog of War; the War Power of Congress in History and Law.* Dallas, Southern Methodist University Press, 1986. P. 133–149.

(**Note 3.**) This and subsequent mentions of Presidential reports refer to reports the President has submitted to Congress that might be considered pursuant to the War Powers Resolution (Public Law 91–148, November 7, 1973). For a discussion of the War Powers Resolution and various types of reports required under it, see The War Powers Resolution: Eighteen Years of Experience, CRS Report 92–133 F; or The War Powers Resolution: Presidential Compliance, CRS Issue Brief IB81050, updated regularly.

Reproduced from source: http://www.history.navy.mil/library/online/forces.htm, 14 March 2005

Bill Summary & Status 93rd Congress (1973–1974)

H.J.RES.542
War Powers Resolution

Sponsor: Rep Zablocki, Clement J. [WI-4] (introduced 5/3/1973) Cosponsors (14)
Latest Major Action: 11/7/1973 Public law 93-148.
Note: Public Law enacted over veto.

SUMMARY AS OF:
11/7/1973—Public Law.

(LATEST SUMMARY)

War Power Resolution—Declares that it is the purpose of this Act to fulfill the intent of the framers of the Constitution of the United States and insure that the collective judgment of both the Congress and the President will apply to the introduction of the Armed Forces of the United States in hostilities, or in situations where imminent involvement in hostilities is clearly indicated by the circumstances, and to the continued use of such forces in hostilities.

Requires that the President shall in every possible instance consult with Congress before introducing United States Armed Forces into hostilities or into situations where imminent involvement is clearly indicated by the circumstances.

Provides that in the absence of a declaration of **war** by the Congress, in any case in which the Armed Forces of the United States are introduced in hostilities, or in situations where imminent involvement in hostilities is clearly indicated by the circumstances, such use of the Armed Forces of the United States in hostilities pursuant to this Act shall be reported within 48 hours in writing by the President to the Speaker of the House of Representatives and the President pro tempore of the Senate, together with a full account of the circumstances under which such hostilities were initiated, the estimated scope and duration of such hostilities, and the constitutional and legislative authority under which the introduction of hostilities took place.

Provides that nothing in this Act is intended to alter the provisions of existing treaties.

Sets forth the criteria for Congressional consideration of joint resolutions and concurrent resolutions introduced pursuant to this Act.

Provides that this Act shall take effect on the date of its enactment.

MAJOR ACTIONS:

5/3/1973	Introduced in House
6/15/1973	Reported to House from the Committee on Foreign Affairs with amendment, H. Rept. 93–287.
7/18/1973	Passed/agreed to in House: Measure passed House, amended, roll call #352 (244–170).
7/20/1973	Passed/agreed to in Senate: Measure passed Senate, amended.
10/4/1973	Conference report filed in House, H. Rept. 93-547.
10/10/1973	Conference report agreed to in Senate: Senate agreed to conference report, roll call #465 (75–20).
10/12/1973	Conference report agreed to in House: House agreed to conference report, roll call #520 (238–123).
10/12/1973	Cleared for White House

10/12/1973	Measure presented to President.
10/24/1973	Vetoed by President, H. Doc. 93–171.
11/7/1973	Passed House over veto: Motion to override veto passed House, roll call #563 (284–135).
11/7/1973	Passed Senate over veto: Motion to override veto passed Senate, roll call #478 (75–18).
11/7/1973	Public law 93–148.

ALL ACTIONS: (Floor Actions/Congressional Record Page References)

5/3/1973	Referred to House Committee on Foreign Affairs.
6/15/1973	Reported to House from the Committee on Foreign Affairs with amendment, H. Rept. 93–287.
7/18/1973	Measure passed House, amended, roll call #352 (244–170).
7/20/1973	Measure passed Senate, amended.
7/31/1973	Conference scheduled in House.
7/31/1973	Conference scheduled in Senate.
10/4/1973	Conference report filed in House, H. Rept. 93–547.
10/10/1973	Senate agreed to conference report, roll call #465 (75–20).
10/12/1973	House agreed to conference report, roll call #520 (238–123).
10/12/1973	Cleared for White House
10/12/1973	Measure presented to President.
10/24/1973	Vetoed by President, H. Doc. 93–171.
11/7/1973	Motion to override veto passed House, roll call #563 (284–135).
11/7/1973	Motion to override veto passed Senate, roll call #478 (75–18).
11/7/1973	Public law 93–148.

Reproduced from source: Library of Congress, "Thomas" at http://thomas.loc.gov/cgi-bin/bdquery/D?d093:5:./temp/~bdT7Iu:@@@L&summ2=m&|/bss/d093query.html|
#amendments

Full Text of "War Powers Resolution," November 7, 1973

(Reproduced from source: the Avalon Project at
http://avalon.law.yale.edu/20th_century/warpower.asp.)
Also see Library of Congress: US Code 50, Chapter 33 with relevant resolutions/authorizations at http://uscode.
house.gov/download/pls/50C33.txt

War Powers Resolution

Joint Resolution
Concerning the War Powers of Congress and the President.

Resolved by the Senate and the House of Representatives of the United States of America in Congress assembled,

SHORT TITLE

SECTION 1. This joint resolution may be cited as the "War Powers Resolution".

PURPOSE AND POLICY

SEC. 2. (a) It is the purpose of this joint resolution to fulfill the intent of the framers of the Constitution of the United States and insure that the collective judgement of both the Congress and the President will apply to the introduction of United States Armed Forces into hostilities, or into situations where imminent involvement in hostilities is clearly indicated by the circumstances, and to the continued use of such forces in hostilities or in such situations.

(b) Under article I, section 8, of the Constitution, it is specifically provided that the Congress shall have the power to make all laws necessary and proper for carrying into execution, not only its own powers but also all other powers vested by the Constitution in the Government of the United States, or in any department or officer thereof.

(c) The constitutional powers of the President as Commander-in-Chief to introduce United States Armed Forces into hostilities, or into situations where imminent involvement in hostilities is clearly indicated by the circumstances, *are exercised only pursuant to*

> *(1) a declaration of war,*
>
> *(2) specific statutory authorization, or*
>
> *(3) a national emergency created by attack upon the United States, its territories or possessions, or its armed forces.*

CONSULTATION

SEC. 3. *The President in every <u>possible</u> instance shall consult with Congress before introducing United States Armed Forces into hostilities or into situation where imminent involvement in hostilities is clearly indicated by the circumstances, and* after *every* such introduction *shall consult regularly with the Congress until United States Armed Forces are no longer engaged in hostilities or have been removed from such situations.*

REPORTING

SEC. 4. *(a) In the absence of a declaration of war, in any case in which United States Armed Forces are introduced—*

(1) into hostilities or into situations where imminent involvement in hostilities is clearly indicated by the circumstances;

(2) into the territory, airspace or waters of a foreign nation, while equipped for combat, except for deployments which relate solely to supply, replacement, repair, or training of such forces; or

(3) in numbers which substantially enlarge United States Armed Forces equipped for combat already located in a foreign nation; *the president shall submit within 48 hours* to the Speaker of the House of Representatives and to the President pro tempore of the Senate a report, in writing, setting forth—

(A) the circumstances necessitating the introduction of United States Armed Forces;

(B) the constitutional and legislative authority under which such introduction took place; and

(C) the estimated scope and duration of the hostilities or involvement.

(b) The President shall provide such other information as the Congress may request in the fulfillment of its constitutional responsibilities with respect to committing the Nation to war and to the use of United States Armed Forces abroad

(c) Whenever United States Armed Forces are introduced into hostilities or into any situation described in subsection (a) of this section, the President shall, so long as such armed forces continue to be engaged in such hostilities or situation, report to the Congress periodically on the status of such hostilities or situation as well as on the scope and duration of such hostilities or situation, but *in no event shall he report to the Congress less often than once every six months.*

CONGRESSIONAL ACTION

SEC. 5. (a) Each report submitted pursuant to section 4(a)(1) shall be transmitted to the Speaker of the House of Representatives and to the President pro tempore of the Senate on the same calendar day. Each report so transmitted shall be referred to the Committee on Foreign Affairs of the House of Representatives and to the Committee on Foreign Relations of the Senate for appropriate action. If, when the report is transmitted, the Congress has adjourned sine die or has adjourned for any period in excess of three calendar days, the Speaker of the House of Representatives and the President pro tempore of the Senate, if they deem it advisable (or if petitioned by at least 30 percent of the membership of their respective Houses) shall jointly request the President to convene Congress in order that it may consider the report and take appropriate action pursuant to this section.

(b) *Within sixty calendar days* after a report is submitted or is required to be submitted pursuant to section 4(a)(1), whichever is earlier, the President shall terminate any use of United States Armed Forces with respect to which such report was submitted (or required to be submitted), unless the Congress (1) has declared war or has enacted a specific authorization for such use of United States Armed Forces, (2) has extended by law such sixty-day period, or (3) is physically unable to meet as a result of an armed attack upon the United States. Such sixty-day period shall be extended for not more than an additional thirty days if the President determines and certifies to the Congress in writing that unavoidable military necessity respecting the safety of United States Armed Forces requires the continued use of such armed forces in the course of bringing about a prompt removal of such forces.

(c) Notwithstanding subsection (b), at any time that United States Armed Forces are engaged in hostilities outside the territory of the United States, its possessions and territories without a declaration of war or specific statutory authorization, such forces shall be removed by the President if the Congress so directs by concurrent resolution.

CONGRESSIONAL PRIORITY PROCEDURES FOR JOINT RESOLUTION OR BILL

SEC. 6. (a) Any joint resolution or bill introduced pursuant to section 5(b) at least thirty calendar days before the expiration of the sixty-day period specified in such section shall be referred to the Committee on Foreign Affairs of the House of Representatives or the Committee on Foreign Relations of the Senate, as the case may be, and such committee shall report one such joint resolution or bill, together with its recommendations, not later than twenty-four calendar days before the expiration of the sixty-day period specified in such section, unless such House shall otherwise determine by the yeas and nays.

(b) Any joint resolution or bill so reported shall become the pending business of the House in question (in the case of the Senate the time for debate shall be equally divided between the proponents and the opponents), and shall be voted on within three calendar days thereafter, unless such House shall otherwise determine by yeas and nays.

(c) Such a joint resolution or bill passed by one House shall be referred to the committee of the other House named in subsection (a) and shall be reported out not later than fourteen calendar days before the expiration of the sixty-day period specified in section 5(b). The joint resolution or bill so reported shall become the pending business of the House in question and shall be voted on within three calendar days after it has been reported, unless such House shall otherwise determine by yeas and nays.

(d) In the case of any disagreement between the two Houses of Congress with respect to a joint resolution or bill passed by both Houses, conferees shall be promptly appointed and the committee of conference shall make and file a report with respect to such resolution or bill not later than four calendar days before the expiration of the sixty-day period specified in section 5(b). In the event the conferees are unable to agree within 48 hours, they shall report back to their respective Houses in disagreement. Notwithstanding any rule in either House concerning the printing of conference reports in the Record or concerning any delay in the consideration of such reports, such report shall be acted on by both Houses not later than the expiration of such sixty-day period.

CONGRESSIONAL PRIORITY PROCEDURES FOR CONCURRENT RESOLUTION

SEC. 7. (a) Any concurrent resolution introduced pursuant to section 5(b) at least thirty calendar days before the expiration of the sixty-day period specified in such section shall be referred to the Committee on Foreign Affairs of the House of Representatives or the Committee on Foreign Relations of the Senate, as the case may be, and one such concurrent resolution shall be reported out by such committee together with its recommendations within fifteen calendar days, unless such House shall otherwise determine by the yeas and nays.

(b) Any concurrent resolution so reported shall become the pending business of the House in question (in the case of the Senate the time for debate shall be equally divided between the proponents and the opponents), and shall be voted on within three calendar days thereafter, unless such House shall otherwise determine by yeas and nays.

(c) Such a concurrent resolution passed by one House shall be referred to the committee of the other House named in subsection (a) and shall be reported out by such committee together with its recommendations within fifteen calendar days and shall thereupon become the pending business of such House and shall be voted on within three calendar days after it has been reported, unless such House shall otherwise determine by yeas and nays.

(d) In the case of any disagreement between the two Houses of Congress with respect to a concurrent resolution passed by both Houses, conferees shall be promptly appointed and the committee of conference shall make and file a report with respect to such concurrent resolution within six calendar days after the legislation is referred to the committee of conference. Notwithstanding any rule in either House concerning the printing of conference reports in the Record or concerning any delay in the consideration of such reports, such report shall be acted on by both Houses not later than six calendar days after the conference report is filed. In the event the conferees are unable to agree within 48 hours, they shall report back to their respective Houses in disagreement.

INTERPRETATION OF JOINT RESOLUTION

SEC. 8. (a) Authority to introduce United States Armed Forces into hostilities or into situations wherein involvement in hostilities is clearly indicated by the circumstances shall not be inferred—

(1) from any provision of law (whether or not in effect before the date of the enactment of this joint resolution), including any provision contained in any appropriation Act, unless such provision specifically authorizes the introduction of United States Armed Forces into hostilities or into such situations and stating that it is intended to constitute specific statutory authorization within the meaning of this joint resolution; or

(2) from any treaty heretofore or hereafter ratified unless such treaty is implemented by legislation specifically authorizing the introduction of United States Armed Forces into hostilities or into such situations and stating that it is intended to constitute specific statutory authorization within the meaning of this joint resolution.

(b) Nothing in this joint resolution shall be construed to require any further specific statutory authorization to permit members of United States Armed Forces to participate jointly with members of the armed forces of one or more foreign countries in the headquarters operations of high-level military commands which were established prior to the date of enactment of this joint resolution and pursuant to the United Nations Charter or any treaty ratified by the United States prior to such date.

(c) For purposes of this joint resolution, the term "introduction of United States Armed Forces" includes the assignment of member of such armed forces to command, coordinate, participate in the movement of, or accompany the regular or irregular military forces of any foreign country or government when such military forces are engaged, or there exists an imminent threat that such forces will become engaged, in hostilities.

(d) Nothing in this joint resolution—

(1) is intended to alter the constitutional authority of the Congress or of the President, or the provision of existing treaties; or

(2) shall be construed as granting any authority to the President with respect to the introduction of United States Armed Forces into hostilities or into situations wherein involvement in hostilities is clearly indicated by the circumstances which authority he would not have had in the absence of this joint resolution.

SEPARABILITY CLAUSE

SEC. 9. If any provision of this joint resolution or the application thereof to any person or circumstance is held invalid, the remainder of the joint resolution and the application of such provision to any other person or circumstance shall not be affected thereby.

EFFECTIVE DATE

SEC. 10. This joint resolution shall take effect on the date of its enactment.

CARL ALBERT
Speaker of the House of Representatives.

JAMES O. EASTLAND
President of the Senate pro tempore.

IN THE HOUSE OF REPRESENTATIVES, U.S.,

November 7, 1973.

The House of Representatives having proceeded to reconsider the resolution (H. J. Res 542) entitled "Joint resolution concerning the war powers of Congress and the President", returned by the President of the United States with his objections, to the House of Representatives, in which it originated, it was

Resolved, That the said resolution pass, two-thirds of the House of Representatives agreeing to pass the same.

Attest:

W. PAT JENNINGS
Clerk.

I certify that this Joint Resolution originated in the House of Representatives.

W. PAT JENNINGS
Clerk.

IN THE SENATE OF THE UNITED STATES

November 7, 1973

The Senate having proceeded to reconsider the joint resolution (H. J. Res. 542) entitled "Joint resolution concerning the war powers of Congress and the President", returned by the President of the United States with his objections to the House of Representatives, in which it originated, it was

Resolved, That the said joint resolution pass, two-thirds of the Senators present having voted in the affirmative.

Attest:

FRANCIS R. VALEO
Secretary.

Reproduced from source: Yale Law School, the Avalon Project at
http://avalon.law.yale.edu/20th_century/warpower.asp.

Also see Library of Congress: US Code 50, Chapter 33 War Powers Resolution, with relevant resolutions/authorizations at
http://uscode.house.gov/download/pls/50C33.txt.

Senate Resolution 85, from the Library of Congress, "Thomas" (March 1, 2011)

112th CONGRESS
1st Session
S. RES. 85

Strongly condemning the gross and systematic violations of human rights in Libya, including violent attacks on protesters demanding democratic reforms, and for other purposes.

IN THE SENATE OF THE UNITED STATES
March 1, 2011

Mr. MENENDEZ (for himself, Mr. KIRK, Mr. LAUTENBERG, Mr. DURBIN, Mrs. GILLIBRAND, Mr. SANDERS, Mr. WHITEHOUSE, Mr. SCHUMER, Mr. CASEY, Mr. WYDEN, and Mr. CARDIN) submitted the following resolution; which was considered and agreed to

RESOLUTION

Strongly condemning the gross and systematic violations of human rights in Libya, including violent attacks on protesters demanding democratic reforms, and for other purposes.

Whereas Muammar Gadhafi and his regime have engaged in gross and systematic violations of human rights, including violent attacks on protesters demanding democratic reforms, that have killed thousands of people;

Whereas Muammar Gadhafi, his sons and supporters have instigated and authorized violent attacks on Libyan protesters using warplanes, helicopters, snipers and soldiers and continue to threaten the life and well-being of any person voicing opposition to the Gadhafi regime;

Whereas the United Nations Security Council and the international community have condemned the violence and use of force against civilians in Libya and on February 26, 2011, the United Nations Security Council unanimously agreed to refer the ongoing situation in Libya to the International Criminal Court, impose an arms embargo on the Libyan Arab Jamahiriya, including the provision of mercenary personnel, freeze the financial assets of Muammar Gadhafi and certain family members, and impose a travel ban on Gadhafi, certain family members and senior advisors;

Whereas Muammar Gadhafi has ruled Libya for more than 40 years by banning and brutally opposing any individual or group opposing the ideology of his 1969 revolution, criminalizing the peaceful exercise of expression and association, refusing to permit independent journalists' and lawyers' organizations, and engaging in torture and extrajudicial executions, including the 1,200 detainees killed in Abu Salim Prison in June 1996;

Whereas Libya took formal responsibility for the terrorist attack that brought down Pan Am Flight 103 over Lockerbie, Scotland, killing 270 people, 189 of whom were U.S. citizens and high-ranking Libyan officials have indicated that Muammar Gadhafi personally ordered the attack; and

Whereas Libya was elected to the United Nations Human Rights Council on May 13, 2010 for a period of 3 years, sending a demoralizing message of indifference to the families of the victims of Pan Am flight 103 and Libyan citizens that have endured repression, arbitrary arrest, enforced disappearance or physical assault in their struggle to obtain basic human and civil rights: Now, therefore, be it

Resolved, That the Senate—

(1) applauds the courage of the Libyan people in standing up against the brutal dictatorship of Muammar Gadhafi and for demanding democratic reforms, transparent governance, and respect for basic human and civil rights;

(2) strongly condemns the gross and systematic violations of human rights in Libya, including violent attacks on protesters demanding democratic reforms;

(3) calls on Muammar Gadhafi to desist from further violence, recognize the Libyan people's demand for democratic change, resign his position and permit a peaceful transition to democracy governed by respect for human and civil rights and the right of the people to choose their government in free and fair elections;

(4) calls on the Gadhafi regime to immediately release persons that have been arbitrarily detained, to cease the intimidation, harassment and detention of peaceful protestors, human rights defenders and journalists, to ensure civilian safety, and to guarantee access to human rights and humanitarian organizations;

(5) welcomes the unanimous vote of the United Nations Security Council on resolution 1970 referring the situation in Libya to the International Criminal Court, imposing an arms embargo on the Libyan Arab Jamahiriya, freezing the assets of Gadhafi and family members, and banning international travel by Gadhafi, members of his family, and senior advisors;

(6) urges the Gadhafi regime to abide by United Nations Security Council Resolution 1970 and ensure the safety of foreign nationals and their assets, and to facilitate the departure of those wishing to leave the country as well as the safe passage of humanitarian and medical supplies, humanitarian agencies and workers, into Libya in order to assist the Libyan people;

(7) urges the United Nations Security Council to take such further action as may be necessary to protect civilians in Libya from attack, including the possible imposition of a no-fly zone over Libyan territory;

(8) welcomes the African Union's condemnation of the 'disproportionate use of force in Libya' and urges the Union to take action to address the human rights crisis in Libya and to ensure that member states, particularly those bordering Libya, are in full compliance with the arms embargo imposed by United Nations Security Council Resolution 1970 against the Libyan Arab Jamahiriya, including the ban on the provision of armed mercenary personnel;

(9) welcomes the decision of the United Nations Human Rights Council to recommend Libya's suspension from the Council and urges the United Nations General Assembly to vote to suspend Libya's rights of membership in the Council;

(10) welcomes the attendance of Secretary of State Clinton at the United Nations Human Rights Council meeting in Geneva and 1) urges the Council's assumption of a country mandate for Libya that employs a Special Rapporteur on the human rights situation in Libya and 2) urges the U.S. Ambassador to the United Nations to advocate for improving United Nations Human Rights Council membership criteria at the next United Nations General Assembly in New York City to exclude gross and systematic violators of human rights; and

(11) welcomes the outreach that has begun by the United States Government to Libyan opposition figures and supports an orderly, irreversible transition to a legitimate democratic government in Libya.

Reproduced from source: Library of Congress, "Thomas" at http://thomas.loc.gov/cgi-bin/query/C?c112:./temp/~c112DUKPza

Full Text of "UN Resolution No. 1970"

26 February 2011

Security Council

SC/10187/Rev.1**

Department of Public Information • News and Media Division • New York

Security Council
6491st Meeting* (PM)

IN SWIFT, DECISIVE ACTION, SECURITY COUNCIL IMPOSES TOUGH MEASURES ON LIBYAN REGIME, ADOPTING RESOLUTION 1970 IN WAKE OF CRACKDOWN ON PROTESTERS
Situation Referred to International Criminal Court;
Secretary-General Expresses Hope Message 'Heard and Heeded' in Libya

Deploring what it called "the gross and systematic violation of human rights" in strife-torn Libya, the Security Council this evening demanded an end to the violence and decided to refer the situation to the International Criminal Court while imposing an arms embargo on the country and a travel ban and assets freeze on the family of Muammar Al-Qadhafi and certain Government officials.

Unanimously adopting resolution 1970 (2011) under Article 41 of the Charter's Chapter VII, the Council authorized all Member States to seize and dispose of military-related materiel banned by the text. It called on all Member States to facilitate and support the return of humanitarian agencies and make available humanitarian and related assistance in Libya and expressed its readiness to consider taking additional appropriate measures as necessary to achieve that.

Through the text, the Council also decided to establish a new committee to monitor sanctions, to liaison with Member States on compliance and to respond to violations and to designate the individuals subject to the targeted measures. Individuals and entities immediately subjected to the targeted sanctions were listed in an Annex to the resolution.

Regarding its referral of the situation in Libya since 15 February 2011 to the Prosecutor of the International Criminal Court, the Council recognized that States not party to the Rome Statute that established the Court had no obligations to it, but urged all States and concerned organizations to cooperate fully with the Court's Prosecutor.

The Council affirmed it would keep the actions of the Libyan authorities under continuous review and would be prepared to strengthen, modify, suspend or lift the prescribed measures in light of compliance or non-compliance with the resolution.

Following the adoption of the text, Secretary-General Ban Ki-moon welcomed the Council's "decisive" action. "While it cannot, by itself, end the violence and the repression, it is a vital step—a clear expression of the will of a united community of nations," he said.

He expressed hope that the message that "gross violations of basic human rights will not be tolerated and that those responsible for grave crimes will be held accountable" would be "heard and heeded" by the Libyan regime and that it would bring hope and relief to those still at risk. He looked for similar action from the General Assembly and the international community as a whole, and warned that even bolder steps might be necessary.

In their explanations of vote, Council members welcomed the unanimity of the action and expressed solidarity with the people of Libya, hoping that their "swift and decisive" intervention would help bring them relief. Many expressed hope that the resolution was a strong step in affirming the responsibility of States to protect their people as well as the legitimate role of the Council to step in when they failed to meet that responsibility.

With the referral of the situation to the International Criminal Court, France's representative hoped the vote would open a new era in commitment to the protection of populations. Further to that goal, Brazil's representative expressed strong reservations to the provision in the resolution allowing for exemptions from jurisdiction of nationals from non-States parties, saying those were not helpful to advance the cause of justice and accountability.

Noting that five Council members were not parties to the Rome Statute that set up the International Criminal Court, including India, that country's representative said he would have preferred a "calibrated approach" to the issue. However, he was convinced that the referral would help to bring about the end of violence and he heeded the call of the Secretary-General on the issue, while stressing the importance of the provisions in the resolution regarding non-States parties to the Statute.

Some speakers, such as the representatives of Lebanon and the Russian Federation, stressed the importance of affirming the sovereignty and territorial integrity of Libya. The Chinese representative said he had supported the resolution taking into account the special circumstances in Libya.

Speaking last, Libya's representative said that the Council's action represented moral support for his people and was a signal that an end must be put to the fascist regime in Tripoli. He launched an appeal to all the officers of the Libyan armed forces to support their own people, and welcomed the referral to the International Criminal Court, as well as the decision not to impose sanctions on those who might abandon Mr. Al-Qadhafi in the end.

Also speaking this evening were the representatives of the United Kingdom, South Africa, Nigeria, United States, Colombia, Portugal, Germany, and Bosnia and Herzegovina and Gabon.

The meeting was opened at 8:10 p.m. and closed at 8:55 p.m.

Resolution

The full text of resolution 1970 (2011) reads as follows:

"The Security Council,

"Expressing grave concern at the situation in the Libyan Arab Jamahiriya and condemning the violence and use of force against civilians,

"Deploring the gross and systematic violation of human rights, including the repression of peaceful demonstrators, expressing deep concern at the deaths of civilians, and rejecting unequivocally the incitement to hostility and violence against the civilian population made from the highest level of the Libyan government,

"Welcoming the condemnation by the Arab League, the African Union, and the Secretary General of the Organization of the Islamic Conference of the serious violations of human rights and international humanitarian law that are being committed in the Libyan Arab Jamahiriya,

"Taking note of the letter to the President of the Security Council from the Permanent Representative of the Libyan Arab Jamahiriya dated 26 February 2011,

"Welcoming the Human Rights Council resolution A/HRC/S-15/2 of 25 February 2011, including the decision to urgently dispatch an independent international commission of inquiry to investigate all alleged violations of international human rights law in the Libyan Arab Jamahiriya, to establish the facts and circumstances of such violations and of the crimes perpetrated, and where possible identify those responsible,

"Considering that the widespread and systematic attacks currently taking place in the Libyan Arab Jamahiriya against the civilian population may amount to crimes against humanity,

"*Expressing concern* at the plight of refugees forced to flee the violence in the Libyan Arab Jamahiriya,

"*Expressing concern* also at the reports of shortages of medical supplies to treat the wounded,

"*Recalling* the Libyan authorities' responsibility to protect its population,

"*Underlining* the need to respect the freedoms of peaceful assembly and of expression, including freedom of the media,

"*Stressing* the need to hold to account those responsible for attacks, including by forces under their control, on civilians,

"*Recalling* article 16 of the Rome Statute under which no investigation or prosecution may be commenced or proceeded with by the International Criminal Court for a period of 12 months after a Security Council request to that effect,

"*Expressing concern* for the safety of foreign nationals and their rights in the Libyan Arab Jamahiriya,

"*Reaffirming* its strong commitment to the sovereignty, independence, territorial integrity and national unity of the Libyan Arab Jamahiriya.

"*Mindful* of its primary responsibility for the maintenance of international peace and security under the Charter of the United Nations,

"*Acting* under Chapter VII of the Charter of the United Nations, and taking measures under its Article 41,

"1.   *Demands* an immediate end to the violence and calls for steps to fulfil the legitimate demands of the population;

"2.   *Urges* the Libyan authorities to:

(a)   Act with the utmost restraint, respect human rights and international humanitarian law, and allow immediate access for international human rights monitors;

(b)   Ensure the safety of all foreign nationals and their assets and facilitate the departure of those wishing to leave the country;

(c)   Ensure the safe passage of humanitarian and medical supplies, and humanitarian agencies and workers, into the country; and

(d)   Immediately lift restrictions on all forms of media;

"3.   *Requests* all Member States, to the extent possible, to cooperate in the evacuation of those foreign nationals wishing to leave the country;

ICC referral

"4.   *Decides* to refer the situation in the Libyan Arab Jamahiriya since 15 February 2011 to the Prosecutor of the International Criminal Court;

"5.   *Decides* that the Libyan authorities shall cooperate fully with and provide any necessary assistance to the Court and the Prosecutor pursuant to this resolution and, while recognizing that States not party to the Rome Statute have no obligation under the Statute, urges all States and concerned regional and other international organizations to cooperate fully with the Court and the Prosecutor;

"6.   *Decides* that nationals, current or former officials or personnel from a State outside the Libyan Arab Jamahiriya which is not a party to the Rome Statute of the International Criminal Court shall be subject to the exclusive jurisdiction of that State for all alleged acts or omissions arising out of or related to operations in the Libyan Arab Jamahiriya established or authorized by the Council, unless such exclusive jurisdiction has been expressly waived by the State;

"7.   *Invites* the Prosecutor to address the Security Council within two months of the adoption of this resolution and every six months thereafter on actions taken pursuant to this resolution;

"8. *Recognizes* that none of the expenses incurred in connection with the referral, including expenses related to investigations or prosecutions in connection with that referral, shall be borne by the United Nations and that such costs shall be borne by the parties to the Rome Statute and those States that wish to contribute voluntarily;

Arms embargo

"9. *Decides* that all Member States shall immediately take the necessary measures to prevent the direct or indirect supply, sale or transfer to the Libyan Arab Jamahiriya, from or through their territories or by their nationals, or using their flag vessels or aircraft, of arms and related materiel of all types, including weapons and ammunition, military vehicles and equipment, paramilitary equipment, and spare parts for the aforementioned, and technical assistance, training, financial or other assistance, related to military activities or the provision, maintenance or use of any arms and related materiel, including the provision of armed mercenary personnel whether or not originating in their territories, and decides further that this measure shall not apply to:

(a)   Supplies of non-lethal military equipment intended solely for humanitarian or protective use, and related technical assistance or training, as approved in advance by the Committee established pursuant to paragraph 24 below;

(b)   Protective clothing, including flak jackets and military helmets, temporarily exported to the Libyan Arab Jamahiriya by United Nations personnel, representatives of the media and humanitarian and development works and associated personnel, for their personal use only; or

(c)   Other sales or supply of arms and related materiel, or provision of assistance or personnel, as approved in advance by the Committee;

"10. *Decides* that the Libyan Arab Jamahiriya shall cease the export of all arms and related materiel and that all Member States shall prohibit the procurement of such items from the Libyan Arab Jamahiriya by their nationals, or using their flagged vessels or aircraft, and whether or not originating in the territory of the Libyan Arab Jamahiriya;

"11. *Calls upon* all States, in particular States neighbouring the Libyan Arab Jamahiriya, to inspect, in accordance with their national authorities and legislation and consistent with international law, in particular the law of the sea and relevant international civil aviation agreements, all cargo to and from the Libyan Arab Jamahiriya, in their territory, including seaports and airports, if the State concerned has information that provides reasonable grounds to believe the cargo contains items the supply, sale, transfer, or export of which is prohibited by paragraphs 9 or 10 of this resolution for the purpose of ensuring strict implementation of those provisions;

"12. *Decides* to authorize all Member States to, and that all Member States shall, upon discovery of items prohibited by paragraph 9 or 10 of this resolution, seize and dispose (such as through destruction, rendering inoperable, storage or transferring to a State other than the originating or destination States for disposal) items the supply, sale, transfer or export of which is prohibited by paragraph 9 or 10 of this resolution and decides further that all Member States shall cooperate in such efforts;

"13. *Requires* any Member State when it undertakes an inspection pursuant to paragraph 11 above, to submit promptly an initial written report to the Committee containing, in particular, explanation of the grounds for the inspections, the results of such inspections, and whether or not cooperation was provided, and, if prohibited items for transfer are found, further requires such Member States to submit to the Committee, at a later stage, a subsequent written report containing relevant details on the inspection, seizure, and disposal, and relevant details of the transfer, including a description of the items, their origin and intended destination, if this information is not in the initial report;

"14. *Encourages* Member States to take steps to strongly discourage their nationals from travelling to the Libyan Arab Jamahiriya to participate in activities on behalf of the Libyan authorities that could reasonably contribute to the violation of human rights;

Travel ban

"15. *Decides* that all Member States shall take the necessary measures to prevent the entry into or transit through their territories of individuals listed in Annex I of this resolution or designated by the Committee established pursuant to paragraph 24 below, provided that nothing in this paragraph shall oblige a State to refuse its own nationals entry into its territory;

"16. *Decides* that the measures imposed by paragraph 15 above shall not apply:

(a)   Where the Committee determines on a case-by-case basis that such travel is justified on the grounds of humanitarian need, including religious obligation;

(b)   Where entry or transit is necessary for the fulfilment of a judicial process;

(c)   Where the Committee determines on a case-by-case basis that an exemption would further the objectives of peace and national reconciliation in the Libyan Arab Jamahiriya and stability in the region; or

(d)   Where a State determines on a case-by-case basis that such entry or transit is required to advance peace and stability in the Libyan Arab Jamahiriya and the States subsequently notifies the Committee within forty-eight hours after making such a determination;

Asset freeze

"17. *Decides* that all Member States shall freeze without delay all funds, other financial assets and economic resources which are on their territories, which are owned or controlled, directly or indirectly, by the individuals or entities listed in Annex II of this resolution or designated by the Committee established pursuant to paragraph 24 below, or by individuals or entities acting on their behalf or at their direction, or by entities owned or controlled by them, and decides further that all Member States shall ensure that any funds, financial assets or economic resources are prevented from being made available by their nationals or by any individuals or entities within their territories, to or for the benefit of the individuals or entities listed in Annex II of this resolution or individuals designated by the Committee;

"18. *Expresses* its intention to ensure that assets frozen pursuant to paragraph 17 shall at a later stage be made available to and for the benefit of the people of the Libyan Arab Jamahiriya;

"19. *Decides* that the measures imposed by paragraph 17 above do not apply to funds, other financial assets or economic resources that have been determined by relevant Member States:

(a)   To be necessary for basic expenses, including payment for foodstuffs, rent or mortgage, medicines and medical treatment, taxes, insurance premiums, and public utility charges or exclusively for payment of reasonable professional fees and reimbursement of incurred expenses associated with the provision of legal services in accordance with national laws, or fees or service charges, in accordance with national laws, for routine holding or maintenance of frozen funds, other financial assets and economic resources, after notification by the relevant State to the Committee of the intention to authorize, where appropriate, access to such funds, other financial assets or economic resources and in the absence of a negative decision by the Committee within five working days of such notification;

(b)   To be necessary for extraordinary expenses, provided that such determination has been notified by the relevant State or Member States to the Committee and has been approved by the Committee; or

(c)   To be the subject of a judicial, administrative or arbitral lien or judgment, in which case the funds, other financial assets and economic resources may be used to satisfy that lien or judgment provided that the lien or judgment was entered into prior to the date of the present resolution, is not for the benefit of a person or entity designated pursuant to paragraph 17 above, and has been notified by the relevant State or Member States to the Committee;

"20. *Decides* that Member States may permit the addition to the accounts frozen pursuant to the provisions of paragraph 17 above of interests or other earnings due on those accounts or payments due under contracts, agreements or

obligations that arose prior to the date on which those accounts became subject to the provisions of this resolution, provided that any such interest, other earnings and payments continue to be subject to these provisions and are frozen;

"21. *Decides* that the measures in paragraph 17 above shall not prevent a designated person or entity from making payment due under a contract entered into prior to the listing of such a person or entity, provided that the relevant States have determined that the payment is not directly or indirectly received by a person or entity designated pursuant to paragraph 17 above, and after notification by the relevant States to the Committee of the intention to make or receive such payments or to authorize, where appropriate, the unfreezing of funds, other financial assets or economic resources for this purpose, 10 working days prior to such authorization;

Designation criteria

"22. *Decides* that the measures contained in paragraphs 15 and 17 shall apply to the individuals and entities designated by the Committee, pursuant to paragraph 24 (b) and (c), respectively;

(a)   Involved in or complicit in ordering, controlling, or otherwise directing, the commission of serious human rights abuses against persons in the Libyan Arab Jamahiriya, including by being involved in or complicit in planning, commanding, ordering or conducting attacks, in violation of international law, including aerial bombardments, on civilian populations and facilities; or

(b)   Acting for or on behalf of or at the direction of individuals or entities identified in subparagraph (a).

"23. *Strongly encourages* Member States to submit to the Committee names of individuals who meet the criteria set out in paragraph 22 above;

New Sanctions Committee

"24. *Decides* to establish, in accordance with rule 28 of its provisional rules of procedure, a Committee of the Security Council consisting of all the members of the Council (herein "the Committee"), to undertake to following tasks:

(a)   To monitor implementation of the measures imposed in paragraphs 9, 10, 15, and 17;

(b)   To designate those individuals subject to the measures imposed by paragraphs 15 and to consider requests for exemptions in accordance with paragraph 16 above;

(c)   To designate those individuals subject to the measures imposed by paragraph 17 above and to consider requests for exemptions in accordance with paragraphs 19 and 20 above;

(d)   To establish such guidelines as may be necessary to facilitate the implementation of the measures imposed above;

(e)   To report within thirty days to the Security Council on its work for the first report and thereafter to report as deemed necessary by the Committee;

(f)   To encourage a dialogue between the Committee and interested Member States, in particular those in the region, including by inviting representatives of such States to meet with the Committee to discuss implementation of the measures;

(g)   To seek from all States whatever information it may consider useful regarding the actions taken by them to implement effectively the measures imposed above;

(h)   To examine and take appropriate action on information regarding alleged violations or non-compliance with the measures contained in this resolution;

"25. *Calls upon* all Member States to report to the Committee within 120 days of the adoption of this resolution on the steps they have taken with a view to implementing effectively paragraphs 9, 10, 15 and 17 above;

Humanitarian assistance

"26. *Calls upon* all Member States, working together and acting in cooperation with the Secretary General, to facilitate and support the return of humanitarian agencies and make available humanitarian and related assistance in the Libyan Arab Jamahiriya, and requests the States concerned to keep the Security Council regularly informed on the progress of actions undertaken pursuant to this paragraph, and expresses its readiness to consider taking additional appropriate measures, as necessary, to achieve this;

Commitment to review

"27. *Affirms* that it shall keep the Libyan authorities' actions under continuous review and that it shall be prepared to review the appropriateness of the measures contained in this resolution, including the strengthening, modification, suspension or lifting of the measures, as may be needed at any time in light of the Libyan authorities' compliance with relevant provisions of this resolution;

"28. *Decides* to remain actively seized of the matter."

Annex I

Travel ban

1. Al-Baghdadi, Dr Abdulqader Mohammed
Passport number: B010574. Date of birth: 01/07/1950.
Head of the Liaison Office of the Revolutionary Committees. Revolutionary Committees involved in violence against demonstrators.

2. Dibri, Abdulqader Yusef
Date of birth: 1946. Place of birth: Houn, Libya.
Head of Muammar Qadhafi's personal security. Responsibility for regime security. History of directing violence against dissidents.

3. Dorda, Abu Zayd Umar
Director, External Security Organisation. Regime loyalist. Head of external intelligence agency.

4. Jabir, Major General Abu Bakr Yunis
Date of birth: 1952. Place of birth: Jalo, Libya.
Defence Minister. Overall responsibility for actions of armed forces.

5. Matuq, Matuq Mohammed
Date of birth: 1956. Place of birth: Khoms.
Secretary for Utilities. Senior member of regime. Involvement with Revolutionary Committees. Past history of involvement in suppression of dissent and violence.

6. Qadhaf Al-dam, Sayyid Mohammed
Date of birth: 1948. Place of birth: Sirte, Libya.
Cousin of Muammar Qadhafi. In the 1980s, Sayyid was involved in the dissident assassination campaign and allegedly responsible for several deaths in Europe. He is also thought to have been involved in arms procurement.

7. Qadhafi, Aisha Muammar
Date of birth: 1978. Place of birth: Tripoli, Libya.
Daughter of Muammar Qadhafi. Closeness of association with regime.

8. Qadhafi, Hannibal Muammar
Passport number: B/002210. Date of birth: 20/09/1975. Place of birth: Tripoli, Libya. Son of Muammar Qadhafi. Closeness of association with regime.

9. Qadhafi, Khamis Muammar
Date of birth: 1978. Place of birth: Tripoli, Libya.
Son of Muammar Qadhafi. Closeness of association with regime. Command of military units involved in repression of demonstrations

10. Qadhafi, Mohammed Muammar
Date of birth: 1970. Place of birth: Tripoli, Libya.
Son of Muammar Qadhafi. Closeness of association with regime.

11. Qadhafi, Muammar Mohammed Abu Minyar
Date of birth: 1942. Place of birth: Sirte, Libya.
Leader of the Revolution, Supreme Commander of Armed Forces. Responsibility for ordering repression of demonstrations, human rights abuses.

12. Qadhafi, Mutassim
Date of birth: 1976. Place of birth: Tripoli, Libya.
National Security Adviser. Son of Muammar Qadhafi. Closeness of association with regime.

13. Qadhafi, Saadi
Passport number: 014797. Date of birth: 25/05/1973. Place of birth: Tripoli, Libya.
Commander Special Forces. Son of Muammar Qadhafi. Closeness of association with regime. Command of military units involved in repression of demonstrations.

14. Qadhafi, Saif al-Arab
Date of birth: 1982. Place of birth: Tripoli, Libya.
Son of Muammar Qadhafi. Closeness of association with regime.

15. Qadhafi, Saif al-Islam
Passport number: B014995. Date of birth: 25/06/1972. Place of birth: Tripoli, Libya.
Director, Qadhafi Foundation. Son of Muammar Qadhafi. Closeness of association with regime. Inflammatory public statements encouraging violence against demonstrators.

16. Al-Senussi, Colonel Abdullah
Date of birth: 1949. Place of birth: Sudan.
Director Military Intelligence. Military Intelligence involvement in suppression of demonstrations. Past history includes suspicion of involvement in Abu Selim prison massacre. Convicted in absentia for bombing of UTA flight. Brother-in-law of Muammar Qadhafi.

Annex II

Asset freeze

1. Qadhafi, Aisha Muammar
Date of birth: 1978. Place of birth: Tripoli, Libya.
Daughter of Muammar Qadhafi. Closeness of association with regime.

2. Qadhafi, Hannibal Muammar
Passport number: B/002210. Date of birth: 20/09/1975. Place of birth: Tripoli, Libya. Son of Muammar Qadhafi. Closeness of association with regime.

3. Qadhafi, Khamis Muammar
Date of birth: 1978. Place of birth: Tripoli, Libya.
Son of Muammar Qadhafi. Closeness of association with regime. Command of military units involved in repression of demonstrations.

4. Qadhafi, Muammar Mohammed Abu Minyar
Date of birth: 1942. Place of birth: Sirte, Libya.
Leader of the Revolution, Supreme Commander of Armed Forces. Responsibility for ordering repression of demonstrations, human rights abuses.

5. Qadhafi, Mutassim
Date of birth: 1976. Place of birth: Tripoli, Libya.
National Security Adviser. Son of Muammar Qadhafi. Closeness of association with regime.

6. Qadhafi, Saif al-Islam
Passport number: B014995. Date of birth: 25/06/1972. Place of birth: Tripoli, Libya.
Director, Qadhafi Foundation. Son of Muammar Qadhafi. Closeness of association with regime. Inflammatory public statements encouraging violence against demonstrators.

Statements

MARK LYALL GRANT (United Kingdom) welcomed the adoption, noting that his country was gravely concerned over the violence and had condemned the actions of the Libyan leadership. The text, he said, was a powerful signal of the determination of the international community to stand with the Libyan people as they charted their future.

HARDEEP SINGH PURI (*India*) hoped that calm and stability were restored without further violence and called for measures to ensure the safety of the Indian population in Libya, as well as those attempting to leave. Noting that five Council members were not parties to the Rome Statute, including India, he said he would have preferred a "calibrated approach" to the issue. However, he was convinced that the referral of the situation to the International Criminal Court would help to bring about the end of violence, and he heeded the call of the Secretary-General on the issue. He, therefore, had voted in favour of the resolution, while stressing the importance of its provisions regarding non-States parties to the Rome Statute.

BASO SANGQU (South Africa) said his country was deeply concerned about the situation in Libya. The resolution adopted by the Security Council sent a clear and unambiguous message to Libya to stop the indiscriminate use of force in that country, and the measures it contained could contribute to the long-term objective of bringing peace and stability to the nation.

U. JOY OGWU (Nigeria) said that she was deeply concerned about the inflammatory rhetoric and loss of life occurring in Libya. As many had been calling for swift action, it was fitting that the Council had taken decisive action today. Nigeria supported the resolution and its "comprehensive" targeted sanctions. It was convinced that the text would deter individuals from supporting the regime and would provide for the protection of civilians and respect for international humanitarian and human rights law. The delegation believed that the resolution would swiftly address the ongoing violence.

SUSAN RICE (United States) welcomed the fact that the Council had spoken with one voice this evening, in a clear warning to the Libyan Government that it must stop the killing. Calling the text a strong resolution, she said that this was about people's ability to shape their own future. Their rights were not negotiable and could not be denied.

NAWAF SALAM (Lebanon), noting the denunciation by the League of Arab States of the crimes committed against Libyan civilians, said he concurred with its opinion, as well as its support for the right of Libyan citizens to express their opinion. That was why he had voted in favour of the resolution. He stressed the importance of reaffirming the territorial unity of Libya and expressed deep sorrow over the lives lost.

VITALY CHURKIN (Russian Federation) said he supported the resolution because of his country's deep concern over the situation, its sorrow over the lives lost and its condemnation of the Libyan Government's actions. He opposed counterproductive interventions, but he said that the purpose of the resolution was to end the violence and to preserve the united sovereign State of Libya with its territorial integrity. Security for foreign citizens, including Russian citizens, must be ensured.

LI BAODONG (China) said that China was very much concerned about the situation in Libya. The greatest urgency was to cease the violence, to end the bloodshed and civilian casualties, and to resolve the crisis through peaceful means, such as dialogue. The safety and interest of the foreign nationals in Libya must be assured. Taking into account the special circumstances in Libya, the Chinese delegation had voted in favour of the resolution.

NÉSTOR OSORIO (Colombia) said the Colombian Government was pleased with the resolution, which had emerged as a result of a "timely process of consultation", in tune with the sense of urgency demanded by the international community. The resolution sent the "direct and solid message" that the violence in Libya must cease and that those responsible for it must answer for their crimes. Moreover, the decision to refer the situation to the International Criminal Court was an appropriate one. Colombia clearly rejected the calls for violence from official sectors in Libya, and condemned the violation of basic rights and freedoms of that country's citizens, including the right to life and to peaceful assembly. Colombia had co-sponsored yesterday's Human Rights Council resolution on the situation. Libya must find a way to respond legitimately to its people's demands, and the international community must remain united to bring an end to the violence there.

JOSÉ FILIPE MORAES CABRAL (Portugal) welcomed the unanimous adoption of the resolution, which he said sent a clear, united message against the crimes being committed against civilians in Libya. He expressed deep concern over the plight of refugees and other humanitarian issues, including the safety of foreigners. Impunity would not be tolerated and serious crimes would be prosecuted.

GÉRARD ARAUD (France) welcomed the fact that the Council had unanimously answered yesterday's appeal by the Libyan representative. The referral of the matter to the International Criminal Court might ensure that those responsible for the crimes were brought to justice. The Court had once again showed the rationale for its existence. The resolution recalled the accountability of each State for the protection of its population and the role of the international community when that responsibility was not met. He hoped the vote would open a new era for the international community as a whole.

PETER WITTIG (Germany) welcomed what he called the Council's swift, decisive, united and strong message that the violation of the rights of the Libyan people would not be tolerated. The referral to the International Criminal Court demonstrated the determination not to allow impunity. It should be clear to all that the Council would continue to follow the situation closely.

IVAN BARBALIC (Bosnia and Herzegovina) said that in the current situation time was of the essence, and that the Security Council had to react "unanimously and urgently" to end the violence and prevent further escalation of the situation in Libya. His delegation had closely followed the popular movement in Libya, and was appalled at the "unacceptable level of violence" targeted at civilians there. Bosnia and Herzegovina condemned in the strongest possible terms the violence and loss of life, and therefore fully supported the decision to refer those responsible to the International Criminal Court. He called for an immediate stop to the violence. Worried about the outflow of refugees and the high number of internally displaced persons there, he called on international organizations to provide humanitarian aid and services to those affected by the violence.

ALFRED ALEXIS MOUNGARA MOUSSOTSI (Gabon) said that the situation existing in Libya over the last two weeks required an answer and a "strong, clear message" from the Security Council. Gabon had decided to add its voice to the resolution, not only to end the violence, but also to advise the Libyan regime of the consequences of its actions. Gabon was also ready to support other measures that the Council might adopt in support of the Libyan people and their right to life and free speech.

MARIA LUIZA RIBEIRO VIOTTI (Brazil) said that her delegation was deeply disturbed by the dramatic situation in Libya. The measures adopted today were meant to halt the violence, ensure the protection of civilians and promote respect for international law. The resolution was a "clear signal" of the Council's readiness to respond to the situation in a manner consistent with its responsibilities. Brazil was a long-standing supporter of the integrity and universalization of the Rome Statute, and opposed the exemption from jurisdiction of nationals of those countries not parties to it. Brazil, therefore, expressed its strong reservation to the resolution's operative paragraph 6, and

reiterated its firm conviction that initiatives aimed at establishing those exemptions were not helpful to advance the cause of justice and accountability.

IBRAHIM DABBASHI (Libya) expressed his condolences to the martyrs who had fallen under the repression of the Libyan regime, and thanked Council Members for their unanimous action, which represented moral support for his people, who were resisting the attacks. The resolution would be a signal that an end must be put to the fascist regime in Tripoli.

He launched an appeal to all the officers of the Libyan armed forces to support their own people and renounce their support for Muammar Al-Qadhafi, whom he called "criminal" and whom he said was prepared to go to extremes to keep up the repression. He appealed also to the Libyan people to keep up their struggle to restore the State to the people. He welcomed, in addition, the referral of the situation to the International Criminal Court and the fact that sanctions were not being imposed on those who might abandon Mr. Al-Qadhafi in the end.

BAN KI-MOON, United Nations Secretary-General, welcomed the resolution. "While it cannot, by itself, end the violence and the repression, it is a vital step—a clear expression of the will of a united community of nations," he said. Calling the events in Libya "clear-cut violations of all norms governing international behaviour and serious transgressions of international human rights and humanitarian law", he said it was of great importance that the Council was determined to reach consensus and uphold its responsibilities.

He hoped that the strong message that "gross violations of basic human rights will not be tolerated and that those responsible for grave crimes will be held accountable" would be heeded by the regime in Libya and that it would bring hope and relief to those still at risk. The sanctions were a necessary step to speed the transition to a new system of governance that had the people's consent and participation.

He pledged to monitor the situation closely and remain in touch with world and regional leaders to support swift and concrete action. Expressing solidarity with the Libyan people in coping with the humanitarian impacts, he hoped that the new future for which they yearned would soon be theirs. Commending the Council for its decisive action, he looked for similar determination from the General Assembly and the Human Rights Council.

"Today's measures are tough. In the coming days even bolder action may be necessary," he said.

----

* The 6490th Meeting was closed.

** Reissued to revise second paragraph.

Reproduced from source: The United Nations at http://www.un.org/News/Press/docs/2011/sc10187.doc.htm

Full Text of "UN Resolution No. 1973"

17 March 2011

Security Council

SC/10200

Department of Public Information • News and Media Division • New York

Security Council
6498th Meeting (Night)

SECURITY COUNCIL APPROVES 'NO-FLY ZONE' OVER LIBYA, AUTHORIZING 'ALL NECESSARY MEASURES' TO PROTECT CIVILIANS, BY VOTE OF 10 IN FAVOUR WITH 5 ABSTENTIONS

Demanding an immediate ceasefire in Libya, including an end to the current attacks against civilians, which it said might constitute "crimes against humanity", the Security Council this evening imposed a ban on all flights in the country's airspace—a no-fly zone—and tightened sanctions on the Qadhafi regime and its supporters.

Adopting resolution 1973 (2011) by a vote of 10 in favour to none against, with 5 abstentions (Brazil, China, Germany, India, Russian Federation), the Council authorized Member States, acting nationally or through regional organizations or arrangements, to take all necessary measures to protect civilians under threat of attack in the country, including Benghazi, while excluding a foreign occupation force of any form on any part of Libyan territory—requesting them to immediately inform the Secretary-General of such measures.

Recognizing the important role of the League of Arab States in the maintenance of international peace and security in the region, and bearing in mind the United Nations Charter's Chapter VIII, the Council asked the League's member States to cooperate with other Member States in implementing the no-fly zone.

The Council stressed the need to intensify efforts to find a solution to the crisis that responded to the legitimate demands of the Libyan people, noting actions being taken on the diplomatic front in that regard. It further demanded that Libyan authorities comply with their obligations under international law and take all measures to protect civilians and meet their basic needs and to ensure the rapid and unimpeded passage of humanitarian assistance.

In that connection, the Council specified that the flight ban would not apply to flights that had as their sole purpose humanitarian aid, the evacuation of foreign nationals, enforcing the ban or other purposes "deemed necessary for the benefit of the Libyan people."

It further decided that all States should deny permission to any Libyan commercial aircraft to land in or take off from their territory unless a particular flight had been approved in advance by the committee that was established to monitor sanctions imposed by resolution 1970 (2011).

In tightening the asset freeze and arms embargo established by that resolution, the Council this evening further detailed conditions for inspections of transport suspected to be violating the embargo, requesting States enforcing the embargo to coordinate closely with each other and the Secretary-General on the measures they were taking towards implementation.

It requested the Secretary-Secretary to create an eight-member panel of experts to assist the Security Council committee in monitoring the sanctions.

Introducing the resolution, the Foreign Minister of France, Alain Juppé, said "the situation on the ground is more alarming than ever, marked by the violent re-conquest of cities that have been released". The Security Council could not stand by and "let the warmongers flout international legality". The world was experiencing "a wave of great revolutions that would change the course of history", but the will of the Libyan people had been "trampled under the feet of the Qadhafi regime". Earlier Council measures had been ignored and violence against Libyan civilians had redoubled.

He said that the urgent need to protect the civilian population had led to the elaboration of the current resolution, which authorized the Arab League and those Member States wishing to do so to take all measures to protect areas that were being threatened by the Qadhafi regime. "We have very little time left—perhaps only a matter of hours," he said, adding that each hour and day that passed "increased the weight" on the international community's shoulders.

Speaking after the vote, representatives who had supported the text agreed that the strong action was made necessary because the Qadhafi regime had not heeded the first actions of the Council and was on the verge of even greater violence against civilians as it closed in on areas previously dominated by opposition in the east of the country. They stressed that the objective was solely to protect civilians from further harm.

Lebanon's speaker stressed that the text would not result in the occupation of "one inch" of Libyan territory by foreign forces. The representative of the United Kingdom pledged that partners in the North Atlantic Treaty Organization (NATO) and the Arab League were now ready to act to support the text.

The representative of the United States said that today, the Council had responded to the Libyan peoples' cry for help. The Council's purpose was clear: to protect Libyan civilians. The Security Council had authorized the use of force, including enforcement of a no-fly zone, to protect civilians and civilian areas targeted by Colonel Muammar Al-Qadhafi, his allied forces and mercenaries.

The representatives of China and the Russian Federation, explaining their abstentions, prioritized peaceful means of resolving the conflict and said that many questions had not been answered in regard to provisions of the resolution, including, as the Russian representative put it, how and by whom the measures would be enforced and what the limits of the engagement would be. He said the resolution included a sorely needed ceasefire, which he had called for earlier. China had not blocked the action with a negative vote in consideration of the wishes of the Arab League and the African Union, its representative said.

The delegations of India, Germany and Brazil, having also abstained, equally stressed the need for peaceful resolution of the conflict and warned against unintended consequences of armed intervention.

Statements were also made by the representatives of Bosnia and Herzegovina, Colombia, Portugal, Nigeria and South Africa.

The meeting was opened at 6:25 p.m. and closed at 7:20 p.m.

Action on Draft

Speaking before the vote, ALAIN JUPPÉ, Minister for Foreign Affairs of France, said the world was experiencing "a wave of great revolutions that would change the course of history", as people throughout North Africa and the Middle East were calling for "a breath of fresh air", for freedom of expression and democracy. Such calls for democratic transition had echoed through Tunisia, Egypt and Morocco. Everyone had witnessed the events with great hope and he believed "this new Arab springtime is good news for all". The changes required the international community not to "give lessons", but to help the people of those countries build a new future.

Yet, he said, while such transitions in other countries had not been met with extreme violence, the will of the Libyan people had been "trampled under the feet of the Qadhafi regime", as Colonel Muammar Al-Qadhafi mercilessly attacked his own people. In light of those actions, the international community had responded swiftly; the General Assembly had suspended the country from the Human Rights Council, determining that the systematic and widespread attacks could constitute crimes against humanity. In addition, the Security Council's earlier resolution had called for an immediate end to the violence and had referred the situation in Libya to the International Criminal Court.

Unfortunately, those measures had not been enough and violence against Libyan civilians had been redoubled, he said. Again, the international community had acted with unanimity, particularly through the League of Arab States' call on the Security Council to enact a no-fly zone and the African Union's strong call for an end to the violence. "Yet, the situation on the ground is more alarming than ever, marked by the violent re-conquest of cities that have been released," he said, stressing that the Security Council could not stand by and "let the warmongers flout international legality".

In light of that, France had been working assiduously with the United Kingdom, the United States and other members of the international community calling for means to protect the civilian population. Those efforts had led to the elaboration of the current resolution, which authorized the Arab League and those Member States wishing to do so to take all measures to protect areas that were being threatened by the Qadhafi regime. "We have very little time left—perhaps only a matter of hours," he said, adding that each hour and day that passed "increased the weight" on the international community's shoulders. The Security Council had acted to ensure that democracy prevailed.

The Council then adopted resolution 1973 (2011) by a vote of 10 in favour to none against, with 5 abstentions (Brazil, China, Germany, India, Russian Federation).

NAWAF SALAM (Lebanon) said that Libya was suffering heavily, with hundreds of victims dying and thousands displaced. Faced with those risks and the great danger of those crimes, the United Nations had acted earlier, but Colonel Qadhafi had not heeded those actions. Lebanon, agreeing with the League of Arab States, had then called on the Security Council to establish measures to protect civilians. The Libyan authorities had lost all their legitimacy and the resolution was aimed at protecting Libyan civilians.

He stressed that the resolution would not have as a consequence occupation of "even an inch" of Libyan territory. He hoped that the resolution would have a deterrent role and end the Libyan authorities' use of force. He reaffirmed full support for the county's sovereignty, the need for full cooperation between the United Nations and the League of Arab States, pursuant to Chapter VIII of the United Nations Charter, and the necessity of a peaceful solution to the situation. The resolution was fraught with hope for Libya and its people, he concluded.

MARK LYALL GRANT (United Kingdom), agreeing that the Libyan regime had lost legitimacy, had violated the Council's resolutions and was on the verge of assaulting Benghazi, said he had pressed for the early adoption of the current resolution. He pledged that partners in the North Atlantic Treaty Organization (NATO) and the Arab League were now ready to act to support the text. The resolution put the United Nations clearly behind the highest values of the Organization.

PETER WITTIG (Germany) said the Security Council's intention was to stop the violence in Libya and send a message to Colonel Qadhafi and his associates "that their time is over [and] they must relinquish power immediately". While the Council acted on Libya, North Africa was undergoing major political changes, meriting the international community's full support. The aim should be to promote political transition in Libya, stop the violence and begin a true political process. "The people of Libya who have so clearly expressed their aspirations for democracy should be supported," he said, adding that the Interim National Council was an important interlocutor in that regard.

He said his country was particularly concerned by the plight of the Libyan people and believed it was crucial to tighten existing sanctions to "cut [the Libyan regime] off" from the funds that had propped it up for so long. Decisions regarding the use of military force were always extremely difficult to take. Indeed, in the implementation of the resolution just adopted, Germany saw great risks, and the likelihood of large-scale loss of life should not be underestimated. Those that participated in its implementation could be drawn into a protracted military conflict that could draw in the wider region. If the resolution failed, it would be wrong to assume that any military intervention would be quickly and efficiently carried out. Germany had decided not to support the resolution and would not contribute its own forces to any military effort that arose from its implementation. Germany had abstained from the vote.

SUSAN RICE (United States) said that today, the Council had responded to the Libyan peoples' cry for help. The Council's purpose was clear: to protect Libyan civilians. The Council had adopted an earlier resolution that had sent a strong message, but Colonel Qadhafi and those that still stood by him had continued to grossly and systematically

violate the most fundamental rights of the Libyan people. The Arab League had subsequently called on the Council to take more stringent measures, and the current resolution was an answer to that call, as well as a strong response to the situation in the ground.

She said the Security Council had authorized the use of force, including enforcement of a no-fly zone, to protect civilians and civilian areas targeted by Colonel Qadhafi, his allied forces and mercenaries. The text also tightened measures already approved under resolution 1970 (2011). In addition, it established a panel of experts to monitor short- and long-term implementation of the sanctions. She stressed that the future of Libya should be decided by the Libyan people. The United States stood with the people of Libya in their struggle to exercise their fundamental rights.

MANJEEV SINGH PURI (India), explaining his abstention, expressed great concern over the welfare of the population of Libya and supported the appointment of the Secretary-General's Envoy. The report of that Envoy and that of others had not yet been received. As a consequence, today's resolution was based on very little clear information, including a lack of certainty regarding who was going to enforce the measures. There must be certainty that negative outcomes were not likely before such wide-ranging measures were adopted. Political efforts must be the priority in resolving the situation.

MARIA LUIZA RIBERIO VIOTTI (Brazil) said her delegation was deeply concerned about the situation in Libya and regretted that the "strong message" sent by resolution 1970 (2011) had note yet been heeded. The Brazilian Government had earlier condemned the violence being carried out by Libyan authorities and had called on them to uphold and protect the right of free expression of the protesters and to seek a solution to the crisis through meaningful dialogue. Her delegation's vote today should in no way be interpreted as condoning the behaviour of the Libyan authorities or as disregard for the need to protect civilians and respect for their rights.

She said that while Brazil stood in solidarity with all movements in the region expressing their legitimate demands for better governance, and had taken into account the Arab League's call for strong measures to stop the violence through a no-fly zone, it believed that the resolution contemplated measures that went beyond that call. "We are not convinced that the use of force as provided for in operative paragraph 4 of the present resolution will lead to the realization of our common objective—the immediate end of violence and the protection of civilians," she said, adding that Brazil was also concerned that the measures approved today might have the unintended effect of exacerbating the current tensions on the ground and "causing more harm than good to the very same civilians we are committed to protecting". No military action alone would succeed in ending the conflict. Protecting civilians, ensuring lasting settlement and addressing the legitimate demands of Libyan citizens demanded a political process.

IVAN BARBALIC (Bosnia and Herzegovina) reiterated his delegation's grave concern about the rapidly deteriorating situation in Libya. The Libyan people desperately needed humanitarian assistance, and the unimpeded access of that relief was an absolute necessity. He called on Libyan authorities to end their violence against the Libyan people and he believed the resolution was an answer to their legitimate call and to the call of regional organizations.

NÉSTOR OSORIO (Colombia) said his delegation was convinced that the purpose of the new resolution was essentially humanitarian and was conducive to bringing about conditions that would lead to the protection of civilians under attack from a regime that had lost all legitimacy. The Council had acted because the Government, through its actions, had shown that it was not up to protecting and promoting the rights of its people.

Colombia deplored the fact that the measures under resolution 1970 (2011) had not been heeded. It was also concerned that the current text had not been adopted unanimously. Colombia believed that the best way to ratchet up the pressure on the Qadhafi regime was to impose a no-fly zone, as called for by the League of Arab States. The grave situation on the ground made it clear that all conditions were present for the Council to enact further measures and tighten the sanctions approved under resolution 1970 (2011).

VITALY CHURKIN (Russian Federation) said he had abstained, although his country's position opposing violence against civilians in Libya was clear. Work on the resolution was not in keeping with Security Council practice, with many questions having remained unanswered, including how it would be enforced and by whom, and what the

limits of engagement would be. His country had not prevented the adoption of the resolution, but he was convinced that an immediate ceasefire was the best way to stop the loss of life. His country, in fact, had pressed earlier for a resolution calling for such a ceasefire, which could have saved many additional lives. Cautioning against unpredicted consequences, he stressed that there was a need to avoid further destabilization in the region.

JOSÉ FILIPE MORAES CABRAL (Portugal) said his country had voted in favour of the text because the attacks against civilians had continued after the passage of the last Council resolution, and conditions were deteriorating. He affirmed that today's resolution addressed his country's priorities, including protecting civilians, facilitation of unimpeded humanitarian aid, promotion of a national dialogue and guarantees for the territorial integrity and independence of Libya. He supported all diplomatic efforts to resolve the situation.

U. JOY OGWU (Nigeria) said the resolution had been necessitated by the persistently grave and dire situation in Libya. "The current State of affairs leaves an indelible imprint on the conscience and compels us to act," she said, adding that her delegation's persistent calls for peace were rooted in the need to ensure the protection of civilians and the delivery of humanitarian assistance to those most in need, many of whom were Nigerian nationals. The League of Arab States and the African Union had spoken with one voice in condemnation of the situation in Libya.

She said that while her delegation had supported the current text, it also believed that foreign occupation was not an option to ensure peace. Nigeria supported language in the current text that negated that possibility. Nigeria was also encouraged by the fact that the political path to a solution was endorsed in the text. "Today, we have sent an unequivocal message to the Libyan people that the dignity and safety of every man woman and child is paramount," she said, adding that when the fate of innocent civilians was in question, the international community, undaunted, must be ready to respond.

BASO SANGQU (South Africa) said his delegation was deeply concerned by what was fast becoming a civil war in Libya. He hoped it could be resolved in a peaceful manner, according to the will of the Libyan people. Any solution must also preserve the solidarity and integrity of Libya and, as such, South Africa supported the dispatch by the African Union of a special mission to the country. He encouraged that mission to work closely with the Secretary-General's newly appointed Special Envoy on finding a peaceful solution.

He said that South Africa regretted that the Council's previous resolution had not been heeded and believed that by adopting the current text, the Council had acted responsibly to answer the call of Libyan people. It would also speed humanitarian assistance to those that needed it most. He hoped the letter and spirit of the present resolution would be implemented in full.

Security Council President LI BAODONG (China), speaking in his national capacity, said that the continuing deterioration of the situation in Libya was of great concern to China. However, the United Nations Charter must be respected and the current crisis must be ended through peaceful means. China was always against the use of force when those means were not exhausted. His delegation had asked specific questions that failed to be answered and, therefore, it had serious difficulty with the resolution. It had not blocked the passage of the resolution, however, because it attached great importance to the requests of the Arab League and the African Union. At the same time, he supported the efforts of the Secretary-General's Envoy to resolve the situation by peaceful means.

Resolution

The full text of resolution 1973 (2011) reads as follows:

"The Security Council,

"Recalling its resolution 1970 (2011) of 26 February 2011,

"Deploring the failure of the Libyan authorities to comply with resolution 1970 (2011),

"Expressing grave concern at the deteriorating situation, the escalation of violence, and the heavy civilian casualties,

"*Reiterating* the responsibility of the Libyan authorities to protect the Libyan population and reaffirming that parties to armed conflicts bear the primary responsibility to take all feasible steps to ensure the protection of civilians,

"*Condemning* the gross and systematic violation of human rights, including arbitrary detentions, enforced disappearances, torture and summary executions,

"*Further condemning* acts of violence and intimidation committed by the Libyan authorities against journalists, media professionals and associated personnel and urging these authorities to comply with their obligations under international humanitarian law as outlined in resolution 1738 (2006),

"*Considering* that the widespread and systematic attacks currently taking place in the Libyan Arab Jamahiriya against the civilian population may amount to crimes against humanity,

"*Recalling* paragraph 26 of resolution 1970 (2011) in which the Council expressed its readiness to consider taking additional appropriate measures, as necessary, to facilitate and support the return of humanitarian agencies and make available humanitarian and related assistance in the Libyan Arab Jamahiriya,

"*Expressing its determination* to ensure the protection of civilians and civilian populated areas and the rapid and unimpeded passage of humanitarian assistance and the safety of humanitarian personnel,

"*Recalling* the condemnation by the League of Arab States, the African Union and the Secretary-General of the Organization of the Islamic Conference of the serious violations of human rights and international humanitarian law that have been and are being committed in the Libyan Arab Jamahiriya,

"*Taking note* of the final communiqué of the Organization of the Islamic Conference of 8 March 2011, and the communiqué of the Peace and Security Council of the African Union of 10 March 2011 which established an ad hoc High-Level Committee on Libya,

"*Taking note also* of the decision of the Council of the League of Arab States of 12 March 2011 to call for the imposition of a no-fly zone on Libyan military aviation, and to establish safe areas in places exposed to shelling as a precautionary measure that allows the protection of the Libyan people and foreign nationals residing in the Libyan Arab Jamahiriya,

"*Taking note further* of the Secretary-General's call on 16 March 2011 for an immediate ceasefire,

"*Recalling* its decision to refer the situation in the Libyan Arab Jamahiriya since 15 February 2011 to the Prosecutor of the International Criminal Court, and stressing that those responsible for or complicit in attacks targeting the civilian population, including aerial and naval attacks, must be held to account,

"*Reiterating its concern* at the plight of refugees and foreign workers forced to flee the violence in the Libyan Arab Jamahiriya, welcoming the response of neighbouring States, in particular Tunisia and Egypt, to address the needs of those refugees and foreign workers, and calling on the international community to support those efforts,

"*Deploring* the continuing use of mercenaries by the Libyan authorities,

"*Considering* that the establishment of a ban on all flights in the airspace of the Libyan Arab Jamahiriya constitutes an important element for the protection of civilians as well as the safety of the delivery of humanitarian assistance and a decisive step for the cessation of hostilities in Libya,

"*Expressing concern* also for the safety of foreign nationals and their rights in the Libyan Arab Jamahiriya,

"*Welcoming* the appointment by the Secretary General of his Special Envoy to Libya, Mr. Abdul Ilah Mohamed Al-Khatib and supporting his efforts to find a sustainable and peaceful solution to the crisis in the Libyan Arab Jamahiriya,

"*Reaffirming* its strong commitment to the sovereignty, independence, territorial integrity and national unity of the Libyan Arab Jamahiriya,

"*Determining* that the situation in the Libyan Arab Jamahiriya continues to constitute a threat to international peace and security,

"*Acting* under Chapter VII of the Charter of the United Nations,

"1.   *Demands* the immediate establishment of a ceasefire and a complete end to violence and all attacks against, and abuses of, civilians;

"2.   *Stresses* the need to intensify efforts to find a solution to the crisis which responds to the legitimate demands of the Libyan people and notes the decisions of the Secretary-General to send his Special Envoy to Libya and of the Peace and Security Council of the African Union to send its ad hoc High-Level Committee to Libya with the aim of facilitating dialogue to lead to the political reforms necessary to find a peaceful and sustainable solution;

"3.   *Demands* that the Libyan authorities comply with their obligations under international law, including international humanitarian law, human rights and refugee law and take all measures to protect civilians and meet their basic needs, and to ensure the rapid and unimpeded passage of humanitarian assistance;

"Protection of civilians

"4.   *Authorizes* Member States that have notified the Secretary-General, acting nationally or through regional organizations or arrangements, and acting in cooperation with the Secretary-General, to take all necessary measures, notwithstanding paragraph 9 of resolution 1970 (2011), to protect civilians and civilian populated areas under threat of attack in the Libyan Arab Jamahiriya, including Benghazi, while excluding a foreign occupation force of any form on any part of Libyan territory, and requests the Member States concerned to inform the Secretary-General immediately of the measures they take pursuant to the authorization conferred by this paragraph which shall be immediately reported to the Security Council;

"5.   *Recognizes* the important role of the League of Arab States in matters relating to the maintenance of international peace and security in the region, and bearing in mind Chapter VIII of the Charter of the United Nations, requests the Member States of the League of Arab States to cooperate with other Member States in the implementation of paragraph 4;

"No-fly zone

"6.   *Decides* to establish a ban on all flights in the airspace of the Libyan Arab Jamahiriya in order to help protect civilians;

"7.   *Decides further* that the ban imposed by paragraph 6 shall not apply to flights whose sole purpose is humanitarian, such as delivering or facilitating the delivery of assistance, including medical supplies, food, humanitarian workers and related assistance, or evacuating foreign nationals from the Libyan Arab Jamahiriya, nor shall it apply to flights authorised by paragraphs 4 or 8, nor other flights which are deemed necessary by States acting under the authorization conferred in paragraph 8 to be for the benefit of the Libyan people, and that these flights shall be coordinated with any mechanism established under paragraph 8;

"8.   *Authorizes* Member States that have notified the Secretary-General and the Secretary-General of the League of Arab States, acting nationally or through regional organizations or arrangements, to take all necessary measures to enforce compliance with the ban on flights imposed by paragraph 6 above, as necessary, and requests the States concerned in cooperation with the League of Arab States to coordinate closely with the Secretary General on the measures they are taking to implement this ban, including by establishing an appropriate mechanism for implementing the provisions of paragraphs 6 and 7 above,

"9.   *Calls upon* all Member States, acting nationally or through regional organizations or arrangements, to provide assistance, including any necessary overflight approvals, for the purposes of implementing paragraphs 4, 6, 7 and 8 above;

"10. *Requests* the Member States concerned to coordinate closely with each other and the Secretary-General on the measures they are taking to implement paragraphs 4, 6, 7 and 8 above, including practical measures for the monitoring and approval of authorised humanitarian or evacuation flights;

"11. *Decides* that the Member States concerned shall inform the Secretary-General and the Secretary-General of the League of Arab States immediately of measures taken in exercise of the authority conferred by paragraph 8 above, including to supply a concept of operations;

"12. *Requests* the Secretary-General to inform the Council immediately of any actions taken by the Member States concerned in exercise of the authority conferred by paragraph 8 above and to report to the Council within 7 days and every month thereafter on the implementation of this resolution, including information on any violations of the flight ban imposed by paragraph 6 above;

"Enforcement of the arms embargo

"13. *Decides that* paragraph 11 of resolution 1970 (2011) shall be replaced by the following paragraph: "Calls upon all Member States, in particular States of the region, acting nationally or through regional organisations or arrangements, in order to ensure strict implementation of the arms embargo established by paragraphs 9 and 10 of resolution 1970 (2011), to inspect in their territory, including seaports and airports, and on the high seas, vessels and aircraft bound to or from the Libyan Arab Jamahiriya, if the State concerned has information that provides reasonable grounds to believe that the cargo contains items the supply, sale, transfer or export of which is prohibited by paragraphs 9 or 10 of resolution 1970 (2011) as modified by this resolution, including the provision of armed mercenary personnel, calls upon all flag States of such vessels and aircraft to cooperate with such inspections and authorises Member States to use all measures commensurate to the specific circumstances to carry out such inspections";

"14. *Requests* Member States which are taking action under paragraph 13 above on the high seas to coordinate closely with each other and the Secretary-General and further requests the States concerned to inform the Secretary-General and the Committee established pursuant to paragraph 24 of resolution 1970 (2011) ("the Committee") immediately of measures taken in the exercise of the authority conferred by paragraph 13 above;

"15. *Requires* any Member State whether acting nationally or through regional organisations or arrangements, when it undertakes an inspection pursuant to paragraph 13 above, to submit promptly an initial written report to the Committee containing, in particular, explanation of the grounds for the inspection, the results of such inspection, and whether or not cooperation was provided, and, if prohibited items for transfer are found, further requires such Member States to submit to the Committee, at a later stage, a subsequent written report containing relevant details on the inspection, seizure, and disposal, and relevant details of the transfer, including a description of the items, their origin and intended destination, if this information is not in the initial report;

"16. *Deplores* the continuing flows of mercenaries into the Libyan Arab Jamahiriya and *calls upon* all Member States to comply strictly with their obligations under paragraph 9 of resolution 1970 (2011) to prevent the provision of armed mercenary personnel to the Libyan Arab Jamahiriya;

"Ban on flights

"17. Decides that all States shall deny permission to any aircraft registered in the Libyan Arab Jamahiriya or owned or operated by Libyan nationals or companies to take off from, land in or overfly their territory unless the particular flight has been approved in advance by the Committee, or in the case of an emergency landing;

"18. *Decides that* all States shall deny permission to any aircraft to take off from, land in or overfly their territory, if they have information that provides reasonable grounds to believe that the aircraft contains items the supply, sale, transfer, or export of which is prohibited by paragraphs 9 and 10 of resolution 1970 (2011) as modified by this resolution, including the provision of armed mercenary personnel, except in the case of an emergency landing;

"Asset freeze

"19. Decides that the asset freeze imposed by paragraph 17, 19, 20 and 21 of resolution 1970 (2011) shall apply to all funds, other financial assets and economic resources which are on their territories, which are owned or controlled, directly or indirectly, by the Libyan authorities, as designated by the Committee, or by individuals or entities acting on their behalf or at their direction, or by entities owned or controlled by them, as designated by the Committee, and decides further that all States shall ensure that any funds, financial assets or economic resources are prevented from being made available by their nationals or by any individuals or entities within their territories, to or for the benefit of the Libyan authorities, as designated by the Committee, or individuals or entities acting on their behalf or at their direction, or entities owned or controlled by them, as designated by the Committee, and directs the Committee to designate such Libyan authorities, individuals or entities within 30 days of the date of the adoption of this resolution and as appropriate thereafter;

"20. *Affirms* its determination to ensure that assets frozen pursuant to paragraph 17 of resolution 1970 (2011) shall, at a later stage, as soon as possible be made available to and for the benefit of the people of the Libyan Arab Jamahiriya;

"21. *Decides* that all States shall require their nationals, persons subject to their jurisdiction and firms incorporated in their territory or subject to their jurisdiction to exercise vigilance when doing business with entities incorporated in the Libyan Arab Jamahiriya or subject to its jurisdiction, and any individuals or entities acting on their behalf or at their direction, and entities owned or controlled by them, if the States have information that provides reasonable grounds to believe that such business could contribute to violence and use of force against civilians;

"Designations

"22. Decides that the individuals listed in Annex I shall be subject to the travel restrictions imposed in paragraphs 15 and 16 of resolution 1970 (2011), and decides further that the individuals and entities listed in Annex II shall be subject to the asset freeze imposed in paragraphs 17, 19, 20 and 21 of resolution 1970 (2011);

"23. **Decides** that the measures specified in paragraphs 15, 16, 17, 19, 20 and 21 of resolution 1970 (2011) shall apply also to individuals and entities determined by the Council or the Committee to have violated the provisions of resolution 1970 (2011), particularly paragraphs 9 and 10 thereof, or to have assisted others in doing so;

"Panel of Experts

"24. Requests the Secretary-General to create for an initial period of one year, in consultation with the Committee, a group of up to eight experts ("Panel of Experts"), under the direction of the Committee to carry out the following tasks:

(a)   Assist the Committee in carrying out its mandate as specified in paragraph 24 of resolution 1970 (2011) and this resolution;

(b)   Gather, examine and analyse information from States, relevant United Nations bodies, regional organisations and other interested parties regarding the implementation of the measures decided in resolution 1970 (2011) and this resolution, in particular incidents of non-compliance;

(c)   Make recommendations on actions the Council, or the Committee or State, may consider to improve implementation of the relevant measures;

(d)   Provide to the Council an interim report on its work no later than 90 days after the Panel's appointment, and a final report to the Council no later than 30 days prior to the termination of its mandate with its findings and recommendations;

"25. *Urges* all States, relevant United Nations bodies and other interested parties, to cooperate fully with the Committee and the Panel of Experts, in particular by supplying any information at their disposal on the implementation of the measures decided in resolution 1970 (2011) and this resolution, in particular incidents of non-compliance;

"26. *Decides* that the mandate of the Committee as set out in paragraph 24 of resolution 1970 (2011) shall also apply to the measures decided in this resolution;

"27. *Decides* that all States, including the Libyan Arab Jamahiriya, shall take the necessary measures to ensure that no claim shall lie at the instance of the Libyan authorities, or of any person or body in the Libyan Arab Jamahiriya, or of any person claiming through or for the benefit of any such person or body, in connection with any contract or other transaction where its performance was affected by reason of the measures taken by the Security Council in resolution 1970 (2011), this resolution and related resolutions;

"28. *Reaffirms* its intention to keep the actions of the Libyan authorities under continuous review and underlines its readiness to review at any time the measures imposed by this resolution and resolution 1970 (2011), including by strengthening, suspending or lifting those measures, as appropriate, based on compliance by the Libyan authorities with this resolution and resolution 1970 (2011);

"29. *Decides* to remain actively seized of the matter."

Libya: United Nations Security Council proposed designations

Number	Name	Justification	Identifier
Annex I: Travel Ban			
1	QUREN SALIH QUREN AL QADHAFI	Libyan Ambassador to Chad. Has left Chad for Sabha. Involved directly in recruiting and coordinating mercenaries for the regime.	
2	Colonel AMID HUSAIN AL KUNI	Governor of Ghat (South Libya). Directly involved in recruiting mercenaries.	

Number	Name	Justification	Identifier
Annex II: Asset Freeze			
1	Dorda, Abu Zayd Umar	Position: Director, External Security Organisation	
2	Jabir, Major General AbuBakr Yunis	Position: Defence Minister	Title: Major General DOB: --/--/1952. POB: Jalo, Libya
3	Matuq, Matuq Mohammed	Position: Secretary for Utilities	DOB: --/--/1956. POB: Kohms
4	Qadhafi, Mohammed Muammar	Son of Muammar Qadhafi. Closeness of association with regime	DOB: --/--/1970. POB: Tripoli, Libya
5	Qadhafi, Saadi	Commander Special Forces. Son of Muammar Qadhafi. Closeness of association with regime. Command of military units involved in repression of demonstrations	DOB: 25/05/1973. POB: Tripoli, Libya
6	Qadhafi, Saif al Arab	Son of Muammar Qadhafi. Closeness of association with regime	DOB: --/--/1982. POB: Tripoli, Libya
7	Al Senussi, Colonel Abdullah	Position: Director Military Intelligence	Title: Colonel DOB: --/--/1949. POB: Sudan

Entities			
1	Central Bank of Libya	Under control of Muammar Qadhafi and his family, and potential source of funding for his regime.	
2	Libyan Investment Authority	Under control of Muammar Qadhafi and his family, and potential source of funding for his regime.	a.k.a: Libyan Arab Foreign Investment Company (LAFICO) Address: 1 FatehTower Office, No 99 22nd Floor, Borgaida Street, Tripoli, Libya, 1103
3	Libyan Foreign Bank	Under control of Muammar Qadhafi and his family and a potential source of funding for his regime.	
4	Libyan Africa Investment Portfolio	Under control of Muammar Qadhafi and his family, and potential source of funding for his regime.	Address: Jamahiriya Street, LAP Building, PO Box 91330, Tripoli, Libya
5	Libyan National Oil Corporation	Under control of Muammar Qadhafi and his family, and potential source of funding for his regime.	Address: Bashir Saadwi Street, Tripoli, Tarabulus, Libya

Source: United Nations at http://www.un.org/News/Press/docs/2011/sc10200.doc.htm

President Obama's Letter to Congress (March 21, 2011)

The White House
Office of the Press Secretary
For Immediate Release
March 21, 2011

Letter from the President regarding the commencement of operations in Libya
TEXT OF A LETTER FROM THE PRESIDENT TO THE SPEAKER OF THE HOUSE OF
REPRESENTATIVES AND THE PRESIDENT PRO TEMPORE OF THE SENATE
March 21, 2011

Dear Mr. Speaker: (Dear Mr. President:)

At approximately 3:00 p.m. Eastern Daylight Time, on March 19, 2011, at my direction, U.S. military forces commenced operations to assist an international effort authorized by the United Nations (U.N.) Security Council and undertaken with the support of European allies and Arab partners, to prevent a humanitarian catastrophe and address the threat posed to international peace and security by the crisis in Libya. As part of the multilateral response authorized under U.N. Security Council Resolution 1973, U.S. military forces, under the command of Commander, U.S. Africa Command, began a series of strikes against air defense systems and military airfields for the purposes of preparing a no-fly zone. These strikes will be limited in their nature, duration, and scope. Their purpose is to support an international coalition as it takes all necessary measures to enforce the terms of U.N. Security Council Resolution 1973. These limited U.S. actions will set the stage for further action by other coalition partners.

United Nations Security Council Resolution 1973 authorized Member States, under Chapter VII of the U.N. Charter, to take all necessary measures to protect civilians and civilian populated areas under threat of attack in Libya, including the establishment and enforcement of a "no-fly zone" in the airspace of Libya. United States military efforts are discrete and focused on employing unique U.S. military capabilities to set the conditions for our European allies and Arab partners to carry out the measures authorized by the U.N. Security Council Resolution.

Muammar Qadhafi was provided a very clear message that a cease-fire must be implemented immediately. The international community made clear that all attacks against civilians had to stop; Qadhafi had to stop his forces from advancing on Benghazi; pull them back from Ajdabiya, Misrata, and Zawiya; and establish water, electricity, and gas supplies to all areas. Finally, humanitarian assistance had to be allowed to reach the people of Libya.

Although Qadhafi's Foreign Minister announced an immediate cease-fire, Qadhafi and his forces made no attempt to implement such a cease-fire, and instead continued attacks on Misrata and advanced on Benghazi. Qadhafi's continued attacks and threats against civilians and civilian populated areas are of grave concern to neighboring Arab nations and, as expressly stated in U.N. Security Council Resolution 1973, constitute a threat to the region and to international peace and security. His illegitimate use of force not only is causing the deaths of substantial numbers of civilians among his own people, but also is forcing many others to flee to neighboring countries, thereby destabilizing the peace and security of the region. Left unaddressed, the growing instability in Libya could ignite wider instability in the Middle East, with dangerous consequences to the national security interests of the United States. Qadhafi's defiance of the Arab League, as well as the broader international community moreover, represents a lawless challenge to the authority of the Security Council and its efforts to preserve stability in the region. Qadhafi has forfeited his responsibility to protect his own citizens and created a serious need for immediate humanitarian assistance and protection, with any delay only putting more civilians at risk.

The United States has not deployed ground forces into Libya. United States forces are conducting a limited and well-defined mission in support of international efforts to protect civilians and prevent a humanitarian disaster. Accordingly, U.S. forces have targeted the Qadhafi regime's air defense systems, command and control structures, and other capabilities of Qadhafi's armed forces used to attack civilians and civilian populated areas. We will seek a rapid, but responsible, transition of operations to coalition, regional, or international organizations that are postured to continue activities as may be necessary to realize the objectives of U.N. Security Council Resolutions 1970 and 1973.

For these purposes, I have directed these actions, which are in the national security and foreign policy interests of the United States, pursuant to my constitutional authority to conduct U.S. foreign relations and as Commander in Chief and Chief Executive.

I am providing this report as part of my efforts to keep the Congress fully informed, consistent with the War Powers Resolution. I appreciate the support of the Congress in this action.

BARACK OBAMA

Reproduced from source, Whitehouse.gov at http://www.whitehouse.gov/the-press-office/2011/03/21/letter-president-regarding-commencement-operations-libya

House Resolution 188 IH, from the Library of Congress, "Thomas" (March 30, 2011)

112th CONGRESS
1st Session
H. RES. 188

Expressing the sense of the House of Representatives regarding the regime of Mu'ammar al-Qadhaffi.

IN THE HOUSE OF REPRESENTATIVES

March 30, 2011

Mr. ROHRABACHER submitted the following resolution; which was referred to the Committee on Foreign Affairs

RESOLUTION

Expressing the sense of the House of Representatives regarding the regime of Mu'ammar al-Qadhaffi.

Whereas the people of Libya have risen up in rebellion against the tyrannical rule of Mu'ammar al-Qadhaffi, a man who seized power by force and has ruled by force ever since;

Whereas Qadhaffi has oppressed the people of Libya and squandered their wealth;

Whereas, on March 3, 2011, President Barack Obama said about the situation in Libya, 'The violence must stop; Mu'ammar Qadhaffi has lost the legitimacy to lead and he must leave', a position he reaffirmed on March 21, 2011;

Whereas, on March 17, 2011, Qadhaffi threatened a civilian massacre by claiming in a radio address, 'We are coming tonight ... We will have no mercy and no pity with them';

Whereas Qadhaffi has shown himself to be an enemy of the United States and a threat to international security, including—

(1) the April 5, 1986, bombing by Libyan agents of the La Belle discotheque in West Berlin, which killed 2 United States soldiers and wounded 50 others, among some 200 total victims of the blast;

(2) the December 21, 1988, destruction of Pan Am flight 103 over Lockerbie, Scotland, by a bomb planted by a Libyan agent, killing 190 United States citizens out of the total loss of 243 passengers, 16 crew members, and 11 civilians on the ground; and

(3) a clandestine nuclear weapons program, which was only ended after the seizure by the United States Navy of a shipment of uranium-enrichment components bound for Libya in October 2003; and

Whereas the Libyan people have not asked for United States ground troops to do their fighting for them, and President Barack Obama has pledged not to deploy ground troops: Now, therefore, be it

Resolved, That—-

(1) it is the sense of the House of Representatives that--

(A) the regime of Mu'ammar al-Qadhaffi is no longer the legitimate government of Libya;

(B) the Transitional National Council, based in eastern Libya at Benghazi and headed by Mustafa Abdul Jalil, consisting of those Libyans who have declared their intentions to establish a constitutional, multiparty democracy, should be considered the legitimate representatives of the Libyan people and nation;

(C) the United States should encourage the post-Qadhaffi government to repay the expenses incurred by the United States Armed Forces during military operations undertaken to protect the Libyan people; and

(D) as Speaker of the House of Representatives John Boehner wrote in his letter to President Obama on March 23, 2011, 'a UN Security Council resolution does not substitute for a U.S. political and military strategy', the United States course in Libya must be determined in accord with United States interests and values and in consultation with allies; and

(2) the House of Representatives--

(A) supports President Barack Obama's strategy of protecting the Libyan people in their struggle for freedom from the Qadhaffi tyranny without risking the direct intervention of United States ground forces in the Libyan civil war;

(B) supports the freezing of the assets of Qadhaffi and his regime wherever they can be found, with the understanding that these assets will be made available to the legitimate representatives of the Libyan people once they have been duly recognized by the United States Government; and

(C) calls for the United States in cooperation with its allies to provide the Libyan freedom fighters with the arms, supplies, and other materials needed to oust the Qadhaffi regime from power and liberate the entire country.

Reproduced from source, Thomas.gov at http://thomas.gov/cgi-bin/query /C?c112:./temp/~c1128vVuuw

List of U.S. Presidents

1. George Washington (1789–97), no party.

2. John Adams (1797–1801), Federalist.

3. Thomas Jefferson (1801–09), Democratic-Republican.

4. James Madison (1809–17), Democratic-Republican.

5. James Monroe (1817–25), Democratic-Republican.

6. John Quincy Adams (1825–29), Democratic-Republican.

7. Andrew Jackson (1829–37), Democratic.

8. Martin Van Buren (1837–41), Democratic.

9. William Henry Harrison (1841), Whig.

10. John Tyler (1841–45), Whig.

11. James K. Polk (1845–49), Democratic.

12. Zachary Taylor (1849–50), Whig.

13. Millard Fillmore (1850–53), Whig.

14. Franklin Pierce (1853–57), Democratic.

15. James Buchanan (1857–61), Democratic.

16. Abraham Lincoln (1861–65), Republican.

17. Andrew Johnson (1865–69), Republican.

18. Ulysses S. Grant (1869–77), Republican.

19. Rutherford B. Hayes (1877–1881), Republican.

20. James Garfield (1881), Republican.

21. Chester Arthur (1881–85), Republican.

22. Grover Cleveland (1885–89), Democrat.

23. Benjamin Harrison (1889–93), Republican.

24. Grover Cleveland (1893–97), Democrat.

25. William McKinley (1897–1901), Republican.

26. Theodore Roosevelt (1901–09), Republican.

27. William Howard Taft (1909–13), Republican.

28. Woodrow Wilson (1913–21), Democrat.

29. Warren Harding (1921–23), Republican.

30. Calvin Coolidge (1923–29), Republican.

31. Herbert Hoover (1929–33), Republican.

32. Franklin D. Roosevelt (1933–45), Democrat.

33. Harry S Truman (1945–53), Democrat.

34. Dwight D. Eisenhower (1953–61), Republican.

35. John F. Kennedy (1961–63), Democrat.

36. Lyndon B. Johnson (1963–69), Democrat.

37. Richard Nixon (1969–74), Republican.

38. Gerald Ford (1974–77), Republican.

39. James Carter (1977–81), Democrat.

40. Ronald Reagan (1981–89), Republican.

41. George H.W. Bush (1989–93), Republican.

42. William J. Clinton (1993–2001), Democrat.

43. George W. Bush (2001–09), Republican.

44. Barack Obama (2009–17), Democrat.

45. Donald Trump (2017–21), Republican.

46. Joseph R. Biden Jr. (2021–), Democrat.

Source: http://www.history.com/topics/the-us-presidents

For additional info, including images of presidents, visit the Library of Congress, Prints and Photographs Reading Room, at http://www.loc.gov/rr/print/list/057_chron.html

Websites of interest:

*See PBS's "American Experience" programming. Here, you may watch a variety of interesting videos on US Presidents:

http://www.pbs.org/wgbh/americanexperience/collections/presidents/

*See "The American Presidents Series", with info and interactive timeline:

http://www.americanpresidentsseries.com/authors.asp

Images of U.S. Presidents

(Art/Photo Gallery from Whitehouse.gov: https://www.whitehouse.gov/1600/Presidents)

1. George Washington 1789-1797

2. John Adams 1797-1801

3.
Thomas Jefferson 1801-1809

4.
James Madison 1809-1817

5.
James Monroe 1817-1825

6.
John Quincy Adams 1825-1829

7.
Andrew Jackson 1829-1837

8.
Martin Van Buren 1837-1841

9. William Henry Harrison 1841

10. John Tyler 1841-1845

11. James K. Polk 1845-1849

12.
Zachary Taylor 1849-1850

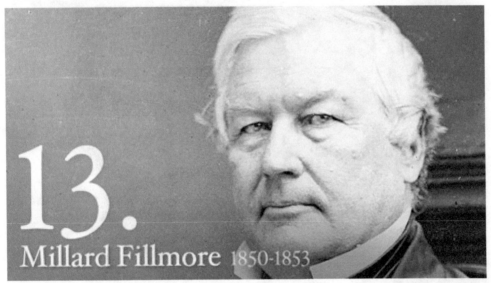

13.
Millard Fillmore 1850-1853

14.
Franklin Pierce 1853-1857

15.
James Buchanan 1857-1861

16.
Abraham Lincoln 1861-1865

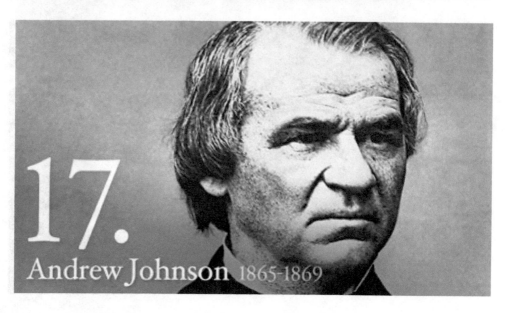

17.
Andrew Johnson 1865-1869

18.
Ulysses S. Grant 1869-1877

19.
Rutherford B. Hayes 1877-1881

20.
James A. Garfield 1881

21.
Chester Alan Arthur 1881-1885

22.
Grover Cleveland 1885-1889

23.
Benjamin Harrison 1889-1893

24.
Grover Cleveland 1893-1897

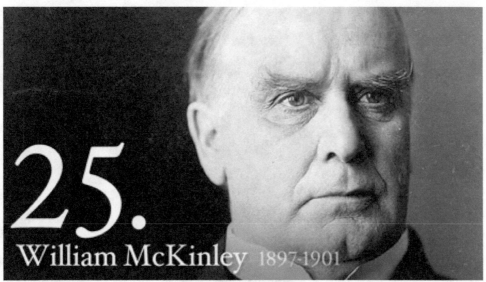

25.
William McKinley 1897-1901

26.
Theodore Roosevelt 1901-1909

27.
William H. Taft 1909-1913

28.
Woodrow Wilson 1913-1921

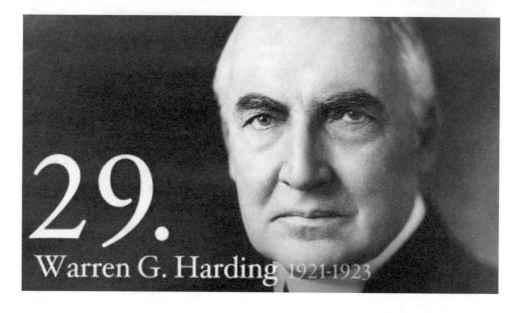

29.
Warren G. Harding 1921-1923

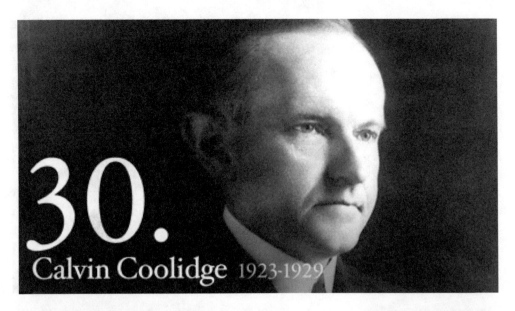

30.
Calvin Coolidge 1923-1929

31.
Herbert Hoover 1929-1933

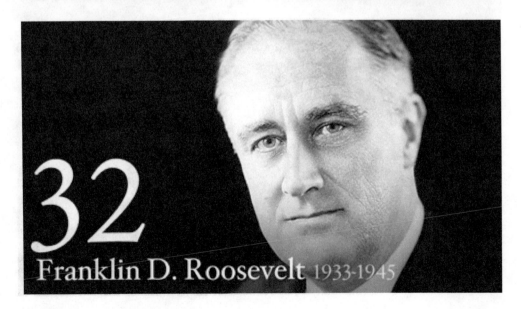

32
Franklin D. Roosevelt 1933-1945

33.
Harry S. Truman 1945-1953

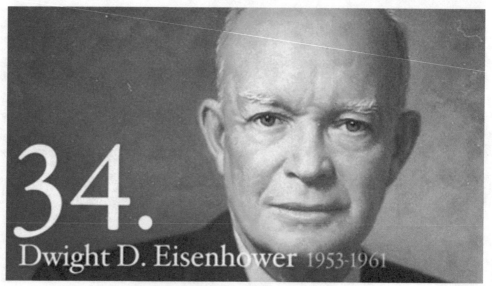

34.
Dwight D. Eisenhower 1953-1961

35.
John F. Kennedy 1961-1963

36. Lyndon B. Johnson 1963-1969

37. Richard M. Nixon 1969-1974

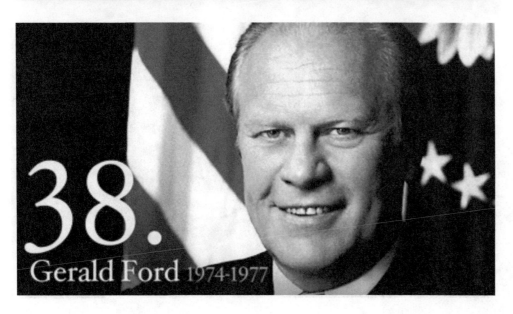

38. Gerald Ford 1974-1977

39.
Jimmy Carter 1977-1981

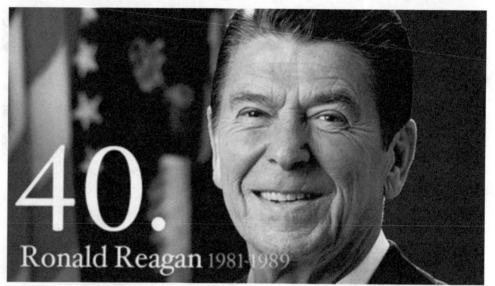

40.
Ronald Reagan 1981-1989

41.
George H. W. Bush 1989-1993

42.
Bill Clinton 1993-2001

43.
George W. Bush 2001-2009

44.
Barack Obama 2009-2017

45.

Donald Trump 2017-2021

46.

Joseph Biden 2021-